Fodor's

NEW ENGLAND

Contents

Welcome to New England

New England's distinctive sights and landscapes make it a classic American destination. Vermont's and New Hampshire's blazing fall foliage, Connecticut's Colonial towns, and Maine's rocky coast are just a few regional icons. Massachusetts, home to Boston's stirring Revolutionary-era sites, is one of many places where history comes alive. You can sample the good life too, with visits to Newport's Gilded Age mansions in Rhode Island or a stay in a sleek country inn. Enjoy nature's bounty, whether you're skiing, hiking, or simply taking in a magnificent view. This book was produced in the middle of the COVID-19 pandemic. As you plan your upcoming travels to New England, please confirm that places are still open and let us know when we need to make updates by writing to us at editors@fodors.com.

TOP REASONS TO GO

★ **Fall Foliage:** Scenic drives and walks reveal America's best festival of colors.

★ **History:** The Freedom Trail, Mystic Seaport, and more preserve a fascinating past.

★ **Small Towns:** A perfect day includes strolling a town green and locavore dining.

★ **The Coast:** Towering lighthouses and pristine beaches, plus whale-watching and sailing.

★ **Outdoor Fun:** Top draws are Acadia National Park, Cape Cod, and the Appalachian Trail.

★ **Regional Food:** Maine lobster and blueberries, Vermont maple syrup and cheese.

Fodor's Features

MAPS

EXPERIENCE
NEW ENGLAND

26 ULTIMATE EXPERIENCES

New England offers terrific experiences that should be on every traveler's list. Here are Fodor's top picks for a memorable trip.

PEMIGEWASSET RIVER
1886

1 Count Covered Bridges

There are 54 of these iconic American symbols still in use in New Hampshire. In fact, the Cornish-Windsor Bridge (1866), which spans the Connecticut River between Cornish, NH, and Windsor, VT, is New England's only covered bridge that connects two states, the country's longest wooden bridge, and the world's longest two-span covered bridge. *(Ch. 10)*

2 Drive Down to "P-town"

Lively, historical, colorful, busy, sometimes campy, Provincetown (on the tip of Cape Cod) is full of inns, restaurants, shops, galleries, and nightlife. It's also one of the world's foremost LGBTQ vacation destinations. *(Ch. 5)*

3 Boating on Lake Champlain

The 107-mile-long lake is hugely popular for recreation—especially boating. You can rent numerous types of vessels, take lessons, or, cruise aboard *Spirit of Ethan Allen*, the lake's only "floating restaurant." *(Ch. 9)*

4 Have a Maine Lobster

A trip to Maine isn't complete without a meal featuring the official state crustacean. Whether you choose a classic lobster dinner, a bowl of lobster stew, or a lobster roll, bring your appetite. *(Ch. 12)*

5 Visit the Ocean State

Known as "the Ocean State" for a reason, Rhode Island's south coast is replete with long strips of powdery white sand facing great swells of the Atlantic Ocean just beckoning you to dive in. *(Ch. 8)*

6 Hike Mt. Monadnock

At 3,165 feet, Mt. Monadnock looms over southwestern New Hampshire. The only way to reach the summit is by foot, and the miles of trails attract well over 120,000 hikers each year. *(Ch. 10)*

7 Climb Aboard a Whaler at Mystic Seaport

More than 60 buildings fill this re-created 19th-century village, and a number of historic vessels including the *Charles W. Morgan*, the last of the wooden whaling ships. *(Ch. 7)*

8 Explore Acadia National Park

At New England's only national park, drive or bike the 27-mile Park Loop Road, climb the 1,530-foot summit of Cadillac Mountain, or explore miles of trails and carriage roads. *(Ch. 12)*

9 Dinosaurs in Connecticut

Check out Yale Peabody Museum's "Great Hall of Dinosaurs" before heading north to Rocky Hill and Dinosaur State Park—one of North America's largest dinosaur track sites. *(Ch. 7)*

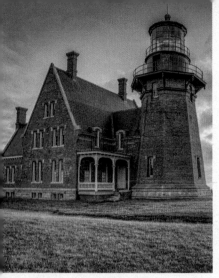

10 Ferry Over to Block Island

Just 12 miles off Rhode Island's south coast, this laid-back island has 17 miles of sandy beaches, the 200-foot-high Mohegan Bluffs, the tranquil Great Salt Pond, and the charming town of New Shoreham. *(Ch. 8)*

11 Boating on Lake Winnipesaukee

At 182 miles around, you won't run out of space or adventures at New Hampshire's largest lake. Boats rentals are available to explore more than 250 islands, and there are numerous waterfront restaurants. *(Ch. 10)*

12 Vintage Steam Trains

The 12-mile round-trip journey along the picturesque Connecticut River will delight the whole family—particularly because the train's 1920s-era coaches are pulled by a vintage steam locomotive. *(Ch. 7)*

13 The Beautiful Berkshires

The "far west" of Massachusetts is green, mountainous, and scattered with interesting towns and villages tucked into pretty valleys. There are outdoor activities, artist enclaves, and excellent leaf-peeping. *(Ch. 6)*

14 Visit a Working Farm

Several Vermont farmers welcome visitors for a day, overnight, or a few days. Guests can help with chores like collecting eggs, milking cows, feeding sheep, picking veggies, or baking bread. *(Ch. 9)*

15 Historic and Hip Portland

Old Port has eclectic restaurants, boutiques, and high-end apartments, while the Arts District has the Portland Museum of Art. The Eastern Promenade has a 2-mile paved trail at the water's edge. *(Ch. 12)*

16 Whaling (and Lizzie Borden)

New Bedford was the world's most important whaling port in the 1800s. Visit the town's whaling museum, then tour the Lizzie Borden Bed & Breakfast ... the "creep factor" is real. *(Ch. 4)*

17 Try Your Luck at a Mega-casino

Foxwoods and Mohegan Sun are 15 minutes apart in southeastern Connecticut. Both have slot machines, gaming tables, restaurants, shops, hotels, and a full schedule of events. *(Ch. 7)*

18 Ski Vermont

The Green Mountains form the spine of Vermont, and snuggled in and around all of the peaks are nearly two-dozen major ski resorts, including Sugarbush, Snow, Stratton, and Stowe. *(Ch. 9)*

19 Take a Walk Around Providence

Enjoy restaurants, beautifully restored Colonial homes, picturesque universities, the magnificent Museum of Art, RISD, and, if your timing is right, WaterFire. *(Ch. 8)*

20 See How "the Other Half" Lived in Newport

America's wealthiest families summered here in the 19th century. Many of the mansions have been beautifully preserved and are open to the public for tours. *(Ch. 8)*

21 Cruise on a Windjammer

Pretty Camden Harbor and nearby Rockland are home ports for a fleet of owner-operated schooners that take guests on voyages around Maine's rugged coast, peninsulas, and islands. *(Ch. 12)*

22 Go Back in Time

Plimoth Plantation is a living-history museum that replicates one of the country's original settlements. Old Sturbridge Village, another living-history museum, re-creates rural New England life. *(Ch. 4, 6)*

23 Walk Boston's Freedom Trail

Boston's Freedom Trail is a 2½-mile-long marked path that links 16 historical landmarks, starting at the Boston Common and ending at the Bunker Hill Monument and USS *Constitution*. *(Ch. 4)*

24 Vermont Sugar Shacks

There are about 1,500 sugarhouses in Vermont. In 2017 those shacks produced about 2 million gallons of syrup, or about half of all maple syrup consumed in the United States. *(Ch. 9)*

25 Wend Your Way Through the White Mountains

Mt. Washington (6,288 feet) is the highest peak in New Hampshire and the northeastern U.S. There are great views, but it's cold and windy even in midsummer. *(Ch. 10)*

26 Treat Yo'self at Ben & Jerry's

At the Ben & Jerry's Factory in Waterbury, take the half-hour guided factory tour to watch ice cream being made, then mosey over to the Scoop Shop for a treat. *(Ch. 9)*

WHAT'S WHERE

1 Boston. Massachusetts's capital city is also New England's hub, where soaring skyscrapers cast shadows on Colonial graveyards.

2 Cape Cod, Nantucket, and Martha's Vineyard. Great beaches, delicious seafood, and artsy shopping districts fill scenic Cape Cod, chic Martha's Vineyard, and old-monied Nantucket.

3 The Berkshires and Western Massachusetts. The mountainous Berkshires live up to the storybook image of rural New England while supporting a thriving arts scene. Farther east, the Pioneer Valley is home to a string of historic settlements.

4 Connecticut. The bustling southwest contrasts with the Quiet Corner in the northeast, known as an antiquing destination. Small villages line the southeastern coast, within reach of a pair of casinos. The Connecticut River Valley and Litchfield Hills boast grand old inns, rolling farmlands, and state parks.

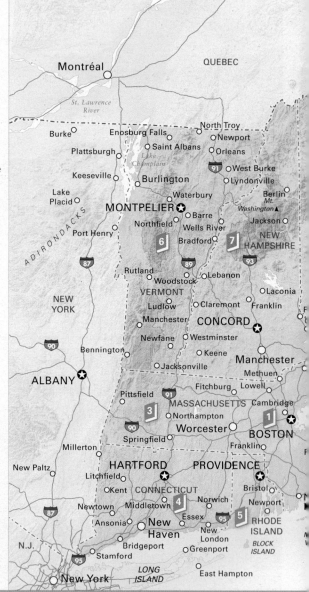

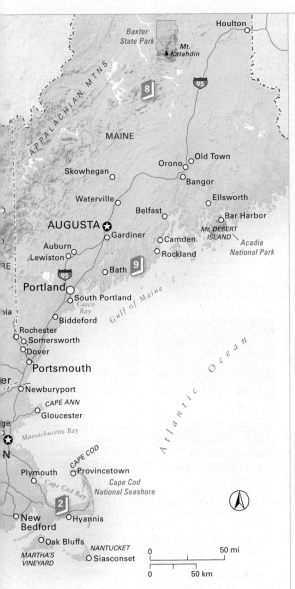

5 Rhode Island. New England's smallest state has great sailing and glitzy mansions in Newport. South County has sparsely populated beaches and fertile countryside; scenic Block Island is a short ferry ride away.

6 Vermont. Vermont has farms, freshly starched towns and small cities, quiet country lanes, and bustling ski resorts.

7 New Hampshire. Portsmouth is the star of the state's 18-mile coastline. The Lakes Region is a popular summertime escape, and the White Mountains' dramatic vistas attract photographers and adventurous hikers farther north.

8 Inland Maine. The largest New England state's rugged interior—including the Western Lakes and vast North Woods regions—attracts skiers, hikers, campers, anglers, and other outdoors enthusiasts.

9 The Maine Coast. Classic villages, rocky shorelines, and picturesque Main Streets abound. Portland is a foodie town; Acadia National Park is where majestic mountains meet the coast; Bar Harbor is the park's gateway town.

New England's Best Seafood Shacks

AUNT CARRIE'S, NARRAGANSETT, RI
Local lore states that this modest clam shack is where New Englanders first came up with the brilliant idea of frying fresh clams into cakes in the early 1920s. Since then, this joint has been serving up seafood, including traditional Rhode Island shore dinners—clam chowder, steamers, clam cakes, coleslaw, fried flounder, French fries, and sometimes a lobster for good measure.

BITE INTO MAINE, CAPE ELIZABETH, ME
Since 2008, this spot's been serving high-quality lobster rolls—locally sourced, never-frozen—no matter the season. The traditional lobster roll is one of the best, but the contemporary twists make the trip worth it, and the LBT (Lobster Bacon and Tomato) sandwich is sheer heaven.

TWO LIGHTS LOBSTER SHACK, CAPE ELIZA-BETH, ME
You'd be hard-pressed to find a more stunning view than the panorama that spreads out across the ocean from this classic Maine seafood shack. Flanked by the historic twin lighthouses for which it is named, this shack has been serving up seafood since the 1920s.

ABBOTT'S LOBSTER IN THE ROUGH, NOANK, CT
Nestled on the banks of the storied Mystic River, Abbott's Lobster in the Rough has been serving delicious seafood dishes since 1947. Plan enough time to appreciate the view while enjoying the stuffed clams and pitch-perfect lobster rolls. And remember, the shack is BYOB.

CAPTAIN SCOTT'S LOBSTER DOCK, NEW LONDON, CT
Often touted as New London's best kept secret, Captain Scott's is a little off the beaten path, but it's worth it for the tasty Rhode Island Clam Chowder and piping hot clam fritters, not to mention a thick lobster bisque that will leave you swooning.

FIVE ISLANDS LOBSTER, GEORGETOWN, ME
Located on a lively working wharf overlooking Sheepscot Bay, this seafood spot welcomes hungry folks with its delicious seafood and stunning views. The family-friendly atmosphere extends to the menu, which also has options for diners not entirely keen on seafood.

FLO'S CLAM SHACK AND DRIVE-IN, PORTSMOUTH, RI
The original Flo's Clam Shack got its start in 1936 when the owner set up shop in a chicken coop and began serving its signature fresh, juicy fried clams. Flo's has been wiped out by five massive hurricanes since then but somehow manages to keep on trucking, serving up the same heavenly seafood that keeps locals and visitors coming back time and time again.

ARNOLD'S LOBSTER AND CLAM BAR, EASTHAM, MA
This legendary spot serves up generous portions of traditional fried and fresh seafood dishes along with hearty baked potatoes, a raw bar, and fresh salads. There's a kid-friendly menu, on-site minigolf, and an ice-cream stand.

BOB LOBSTER, NEWBURYPORT, MA
A trip to Plum Island isn't complete unless you grab a bite to eat at this local favorite, which got its start as a local seafood market. The menu always includes homemade seafood pies, creamy seafood chowders loaded with fresh meat, and a to-die-for lobster mac-n-cheese.

CLAM BOX OF IPSWICH, IPSWICH, MA
Since 1938, this unmistakable saltbox shack—red-and-white-striped awnings and unique architectural shape—has been a go-to spot for locals and visitors alike. The fried clams are an institution, but you also can't go wrong with one of their seafood rolls or homemade coleslaw.

Buy Local: Best New England Souvenirs

ANTIQUES AND COLLECTIBLES
Collectibles and antiques abound from cities like Boston (Charles Street), Providence (Wickenden Street), and Portland (Old Port District) to towns like Woodbury and Middlebury, CT; Chester, VT; Essex, MA; Littleton, NH; and Wells, ME. In May, July, and September, there's Massachusetts's Brimfield Antiques & Collectibles Show.

JAMS AND PRESERVES
Pick up strawberry preserves, apple butter, cranberry sauce, or blueberry jam at farmers' markets or country stores like Old Wethersfield (CT), Brown & Hopkins (RI), Wayside (MA), Old Country Store & Museum (NH), East Boothbay (ME), or the Vermont Country Store.

MOCCASINS
Maine shoemakers craft some of the best moccasins, and Quoddy, known for its custom, made-to-order moccasins, deck shoes, and boots, is one of the best. Reach out when you're Down East or back home; the wait for shoes is worth it. Ditto with Wassookeag, another great Maine maker of bespoke footwear.

CANVAS BAGS
Nothing says durability like canvas; nothing says coastal New England like sailing. Portland-based Sea Bags has creative, rope-handled totes made from recycled sails. Port Canvas in Arundel, Maine, also hand-crafts sporty, customizable canvas totes and duffels—perfect for lugging your souvenirs home.

MAPLE SYRUP
Each spring, sugarhouses tap their maple trees and boil the resultant sap down into syrup. Although it takes about 40 gallons of sap to make 1 gallon of syrup, locally made varieties are readily available—Grades A and B and in light, medium, and dark (for baking only) shades of amber. The best known states are New Hampshire and Vermont, which, by the way, has its own strict grading system.

TOYS

Vermont Teddy Bears are guaranteed for life; there's even a hospital for Teddy emergencies! Vermont's Real Good Toys makes finely crafted dollhouses and miniature accessories. New Hampshire's Annalee Dolls are distinctive, cute, and collectible—especially the holiday ones.

YARN AND KNITWEAR

The wares of independent spinners and knitters can be found throughout the region. Noteworthy companies include Bartlett yarns, Inc., which has been in Maine since 1821; Rhode Island's North Light Fibers; New Hampshire's Harrisville Designs, and Maine's Swans Island Company.

FLANNEL WOOLENS

New England's textile industry declined in the 1920s and '30s, but Vermont's Johnson Woolen Mills is still going strong. The warm, soft, and often boldly checked flannel shirts, jackets, capes, wraps, scarves, and hats sold in its factory store and elsewhere are splurge-worthy classics.

CRAFT BEER AND CIDER

New England has a long brewing history, but it's the region's newer, trendier operations that are most interesting like New Hampshire's Schilling Beer Co. and Vermont's Hill Farmstead Brewery. There's a small brewery (or cidery) in almost every city and small town. Notable ciders include Maine's Urban Farm Fermentory and Vermont's family-friendly Cold Hollow.

LOBSTER

Seafood markets, lobster pounds, and even some independent lobstermen sell lobster to-go. As soon as you buy them, you have 48 hours (max) to cook them, and lobsters must be kept sedated (i.e., lightly chilled) but alive, with claws rubber-banded, until then. Another option: ask about shipping or look into online pack-and-ship retailers like Maine Lobster Now, The Lobster Guy, and Lobsters New England.

New England's Most Picturesque Towns

BRISTOL, RI
Tucked between Providence and Newport, this small New England town has a lot to offer in the way of history, but its charm lies chiefly in its breathtaking scenery and well-preserved, historic architecture, comprised of picture perfect Colonial, 19th-century, and Gilded Age buildings.

WOODSTOCK, VT
This quintessential Vermont town is ridiculously, wonderfully picturesque—classic covered bridges, local cheese makers, cider mills, working farms and orchards, sugar shacks, meandering brick streets, and a town center that is straight out of a Norman Rockwell painting.

KENT, CT
Located in the northwest corner of Connecticut, the historic town of Kent is a lively mix of art galleries, shops, and restaurants. There are also great outdoor destinations like Kent Falls State Park, home to the state's tallest waterfall, and the Appalachian Trail's longest river walk.

SIASCONSET, MA
This tiny Nantucket town gives visitors exactly what they want—sweeping panoramas of the Atlantic and Sankaty Head Light, rows of classic New England saltbox houses, delightfully overflowing gardens chock-full of beach peas and roses enclosed in white picket fences, and scenic coastal walks.

EASTPORT, ME
Most of Maine's visitors don't make it past the Mid-Coast, but Down East Maine is more than worth the hike, if only to pay a visit to Eastport, a picturesque seaside town with historic architecture situated on pristine Moose Island. A world apart, Eastport prides itself on its fishing and lobstering industries, excellent local arts scene, and vibrant indigenous community.

DAMARISCOTTA, ME

Just north of Wiscasset, this often overlooked village is surrounded by salt marsh preserves and oyster beds. The village's historic brick architecture and quaint but vibrant Main Street overlooks the harbor where the annual and delightfully oddball Pumpkinfest and Regatta takes place.

NEWBURYPORT, MA

First settled by Europeans in 1635, this seaside town has immaculate redbrick streets and a vibrant working harbor that delivers that quintessential, New England feel. Classic seafood shacks, charming taverns with old-world flair, and a bevy of upscale specialty boutiques add to the charm.

CAMDEN, ME

With its brick architecture and Victorian mansions, Maine doesn't get any more picturesque than this village. Situated in the heart of the Mid-Coast, the charming town with its restaurants, galleries, and boutiques is surrounded by a working harbor that's dotted with windjammers.

ESSEX, CT

On the southwestern bank of the beautiful Connecticut River lies Essex, a quaint New England town scattered with cozy inns and taverns and historical architecture that are best explored on foot. With a picture-perfect harbor, a historic working steam train, and a delightfully eclectic cluster of buildings, Essex has a lot to offer in the way of small town charm.

JACKSON, NH

With a village green reached via a covered bridge and a slew of charming country inns, farm-to-table eateries, and ruggedly scenic trails for hiking and cross-country skiing, this peaceful hamlet lies in the heart of the White Mountains.

New England's Best Beaches

FOOTBRIDGE BEACH, OGUNQUIT, ME
This spot offers excellent swimming, beach combing, and bodysurfing opportunities, as well as a boat launch for kayaks, small boats, and standup paddleboards. Typically less crowded than neighboring Ogunquit Beach, it's reached by crossing a foot bridge that runs over the Ogunquit River.

HAMMONASSET BEACH, MADISON, CT
At about 2 miles long, Connecticut's largest beach beckons day-trippers and campers to its shore for superb birding, swimming, and sandy strolls on the charming wooden boardwalk. There are also picnic spots, bike trails, great fishing, and the Meigs Point Nature Center.

EAST BEACH, MARTHA'S VINEYARD, MA
Between Cape Pogue Wildlife Refuge and Wasque Reservation on Chappaquiddick Island, East Beach—also known as Leland Beach—is popular for surf fishing. The half-mile beach is also excellent for birding, swimming, and peaceful sunset walks, but there's an entrance fee.

GOOSE ROCKS BEACH, KENNEBUNKPORT, ME
A wildly popular beach in warmer months and equally as beautiful in the off-season, Goose Rocks Beach is treasured for its long stretch of clean sand and close proximity to town. Parking can be tough in the high season and permits are required, but it's well worth the headache to get up early and snatch a spot for a glorious day in the sun at this picture-perfect beach.

WALLIS SANDS STATE BEACH, RYE, NH
This family-friendly swimmers' beach near Portsmouth has bright white sand, a picnic area, a store, and beautiful views of the Isles of Shoals.

EAST MATUNUCK STATE BEACH, SOUTH KINGS-TOWN, RI
With well over 100 acres of sandy shoreline, this popular beach on Block Island Sound has everything you need for a perfect seaside outing with the whole family, including a beach pavilion with changing rooms, a concession stand, and a lifeguard tower.

SAND BAR STATE PARK, MILTON, VT
Vermont is not known for its beaches, but its plethora of lakes means that there are actually quite a few beaches worth checking out. This 2,000-foot-long beach remains shallow well out from shore, making it a perfect spot for families with young kids.

Sand Beach, Acadia, ME

NAUSET LIGHT BEACH, EASTHAM, MA
Adjacent to Coast Guard Beach, this long, sandy beach is backed by tall dunes, frilly grass, and heathland. The trail to the Three Sisters lighthouses takes you through a pitch-pine forest. Parking can fill up quickly in the summer, so get here early or you may have to swim elsewhere.

PEMAQUID BEACH, NEW HARBOR, ME
Although not as long as the beach at nearby Reid State Park, Pemaquid Beach is a draw for families and couples looking for a quintessential beach day complete with an umbrella, sand bucket, and ice cream, all of which can be rented or purchased from the kiosk near the changing facilities and community center.

MT. SUNAPEE STATE PARK, NEWBURY, NH
One of the prettiest and most relaxing of New Hampshire's many noteworthy freshwater beaches, this family-welcoming stretch of sand in the shadows of one of the state's favorite ski mountains is lovely for swimming, or renting kayaks, canoes, and standup paddleboards.

NORTH BEACH, BURLINGTON, VT
Located on Lake Champlain, the area's largest beach is also the only one with lifeguards during the summer. There's a grassy picnic area, a snack bar, and a playground, as well as kayak, canoe, and stand-up paddle board rentals.

RACE POINT BEACH, PROVINCETOWN, MA
Designated by President Kennedy as part of Cape Cod National Seashore in 1961, this sandy beach is well known for its strong currents, which makes it great for surfers and serious swimmers. Its location on the Seashore's extreme northern side also makes it an excellent spot for sunbathing.

New England's Best Historical Sites

FREEDOM TRAIL, BOSTON, MA
The iconic, red-lined, 2½-mile trail features 16 historical sites, including the Old South Meeting House, where the Sons of Liberty organized their Tea Party, and Old North Church, where those two fateful lanterns were hung. Across the Charles River in Charlestown are the USS *Constitution* (aka Old Ironsides) and the Bunker Hill Monument.

PORTLAND HEAD LIGHT, CAPE ELIZABETH, ME
Built in 1791, this 80-foot lighthouse is one of New England's most picturesque in any season. The keeper's quarters (operational 1891–1989) house a seasonally open museum and gift shop; surrounding Fort William Park, site of an army fort between 1872 and 1964, is open year-round.

SHELBURNE MUSEUM, SHELBURNE, VT
Nothing says "Vermont" like a big red barn, and the museum has two really big, really red barns that house American fine, folk, and decorative art as well as vintage toys, hats, decoys, and firearms. There's a vintage carousel, miniature circus-parade figurines in the Circus Building, and more than 200 horse-drawn vehicles. There's even an old Lake Champlain steamship.

MAINE MARITIME MUSEUM, BATH, ME
The museum's permanent exhibits cover it all from Bath Iron Works' role in building the nation's navy to a collection of more than 100 small wooden water crafts. In warmer months, board the 1906 schooner, the *Mary E.*, for sails with docents.

STRAWBERY BANKE, PORTSMOUTH, NH
Located in colonial downtown Portsmouth, the seasonal, 10-acre living-history complex has docents in period garb portraying tavern keepers, merchants, artisans, and other every-day folk, and more than 35 structures dating from the 17th to 20th centuries.

MYSTIC SEAPORT MUSEUM, MYSTIC, CT

The year-round Seaport Village contains sloops, schooners, tugboats, and other historic vessels that are open for tours, sails, and hands-on maritime experiences. Exhibits have intriguing seafaring themes and there's a planetarium. Don't miss the *Charles W. Morgan*, an 1841 whaling ship.

CLIFF WALK, NEWPORT, RI

The 3½-mile trail is hair-raising in spots, and the amazing views along either side are distracting, so wander with care. There are 10 mansions open to the public for touring, including the Italian Palazzo–style The Breakers; Rosecliff, modeled on a Versailles garden retreat; and The Elms, a French Chateau–style confection.

MARK TWAIN HOUSE AND MUSEUM, HARTFORD, CT

Twain penned classics such as *The Adventures of Tom Sawyer* and *A Connecticut Yankee in King Arthur's Court* here, and exhibits showcase the writer's storied life. If you have the time, plan a visit to the neighboring Harriet Beecher Stowe Center (combination tickets are available).

LEXINGTON AND CONCORD, MA

These two towns embody the American spirit. Minute Man National Historic Park, site of the first official Revolutionary War battle, is bookended by visitor centers in Lincoln, just outside Lexington, and Concord. In Concord, visit the Ralph Waldo Emerson House, Thoreau Farm, Walden Pond, or Orchard House, where Louisa May Alcott wrote *Little Women*.

PLIMOTH PLANTATION, PLYMOUTH, MA

Role players—portraying actual 1620s Plymouth Colony settlers—attend to 17th-century life at this bayside village. There's a longhouse where Native Americans showcase early Wampanoag culture. *The Mayflower II* is a replica of the ship that carried the Pilgrims to the New World.

Best Outdoor Activities

SKI VERMONT AND NEW HAMPSHIRE

Not far from the U.S.-Canadian border, some of New England's best ski slopes (and top-notch resorts) can be found in Vermont's Green Mountains (Jay Peak and Stowe) and New Hampshire's White Mountains (Bretton Woods and Cannon Mountain).

GO SAILING IN NEWPORT

One of the world's prime sailing capitals, Rhode Island's most famous port city is filled to the brim with rigs, including the America's Cup fleet. Numerous boats can be chartered for day trips or longer journeys, or you can try your hand at sailing a boat yourself.

FLY-FISHING ON THE HOUSATONIC RIVER

This pristine river rich with trout and bass curves through northwestern Connecticut's verdant Litchfield Hills, delighting both ardent and novice fly-fishing enthusiasts. In the quaint town of Cornwall, Housatonic Anglers and Housatonic River Outfitters offer lessons and guided fishing adventures.

PADDLE LAKE CHAMPLAIN

Leaf peeping and Vermont are virtually synonymous, but most visitors don't think about taking in the Green Mountain State's stunning fall foliage from out on the water. Best accessed from Burlington, you can rent a standup paddleboard or kayak to explore the lake while surrounded by majestic mountains covered in thick forests that put on a colorful display. Far from the crowds, you'll feel like nature is putting on a show just for you.

HIT THE LINKS IN MAINE AND NEW HAMPSHIRE

Coastal Maine and New Hampshire's mountains have some stunning, beautifully maintained golf courses that reward players with great challenges and magnificent scenery. The course at Rockport's Samoset Resort ranks among the best in the coastal New England, while Crotched Mountain in the Monadnocks and Waukewan near Lake Winnipesaukee are top courses in New Hampshire.

HIKE THE APPALACHIAN TRAIL

This is a bucket list item for hardcore trekkers, but tackling the entire length of America's most notorious hiking trail is a commitment. You can always explore some of its most scenic stretches, however, many of them set along the 161-mile leg through New Hampshire. Featuring more miles above treeline than

Go on a leaf peeping cycle tour along the Stowe Bike Path, VT.

any other state, this is one of the route's most challenging and rewarding sections, with steep inclines leading to stunning alpine tundra and breathtaking views.

BOATING ON THE ALLAGASH WILDERNESS WATERWAY

The 92-mile-long series of rivers, streams, ponds, and lakes that comprises this northern Maine waterway ribbon their way through the delicate, tundralike landscape of the Northern Woods. The waterway remains fairly rustic with limited resources along the route, which seems to be one of the major reasons it attracts fans of canoeing and kayaking.

BIKING THE CAPE COD RAIL TRAIL

Passing through six Cape Cod towns, the Cape Cod Rail Trail covers 22 miles of paved trails. The reliably level terrain allows feasibly attainable long-distance excursions along the coastal landscape in a single day for all levels. During the winter months, exchange your wheels for skis to enjoy some of the Cape's best cross-country skiing.

TAKE A LEAF PEEPING CYCLE TOUR

With its many nature preserves, green spaces, and hiking trails, Vermont shines in every season, but autumn may be its finest. You'd be hard-pressed to find a lovelier stroll through an autumnal Vermont landscape than in the charming village of Stowe, which is home to the Stowe Recreational Path, a paved, 5½-mile greenway that leads you to picture-perfect village and mountain views.

EXPLORE ACADIA NATIONAL PARK

Boasting around 160 miles of pristine coastal hiking trails and meandering carriage roads peppered with charming stone bridges, America's oldest national park east of the Mississippi River offers bountiful opportunities to experience Maine's raw, natural beauty.

New England with Kids

Favorite family vacation spots in New England include Boston, Cape Cod, New Hampshire's White Mountains and Lakes Region, Mystic and southeastern Connecticut, and coastal Maine. You'll find reasonably priced, kid-friendly hotels and family-style restaurants throughout New England, as well as museums, beaches, parks, planetariums, and lighthouses.

CAR SEATS

Each New England state has specific requirements regarding age and weight requirements for children in car seats and for whether you can smoke in a car with children as passengers. If you will need a car seat, make sure your rental-car agency has one or bring your own. Many airlines won't charge if you check your car seat, or there are numerous travel options like the Mifold or BubbleBum.

LODGING

New England has many family-oriented resorts with lively children's programs. Farms that accept guests can be great fun for children. Rental houses and apartments abound, particularly around ski areas and beaches. In the off-season, these can be especially economical, because most have kitchens—reducing your dependency on restaurant dining.

Most hotels in New England allow children under a certain age to stay in their parents' room at no extra charge, but others charge for them as extra adults; be sure to find out the cutoff age. Bed-and-breakfasts and historic inns are not always suitable for kids, and many flat-out refuse to accommodate them. In Maine, only hotels and inns with five or fewer rooms can put age restrictions on children.

Most lodgings that welcome infants and small children will provide a crib or cot, but remember to provide notice so that one will be available for you. Many family resorts make special accommodations for small children during meals.

MASSACHUSETTS

Children's Museum, Boston. Make bubbles, climb through a maze, and while away the hours in this fun museum just for tykes in Downtown Boston. A special play area for those under three lets them run around in a safe environment. There are seasonal festivals throughout the year.

Magic Wings Butterfly Conservatory & Gardens, Deerfield. Almost 4,000 free-flying native and tropical butterflies are the star attraction here, contained within an 8,000-square-foot glassed enclosure that keeps the temperature upward of 80°F year-round. Relax around the Japanese koi pond on one of numerous benches and watch the kids chase the colorful creatures as they flit about. Or walk outside to the Iron Butterfly Outdoor Gardens, where flowers attract still more butterflies.

Massachusetts Audubon Wellfleet Bay Wildlife Sanctuary, South Wellfleet. With its numerous programs and its beautiful salt-marsh surroundings, this is a favorite stop for Cape vacationers year-round. Five miles of nature trails weave throughout the sanctuary's 1,100 acres of marsh, beach, and woods. If you're careful and quiet, you may be able to get close to sunbathing seals or birds like the great blue heron. Naturalists are on hand for guided walks and lectures.

Plimoth Plantation, Plymouth. Want to know what life was like in Colonial America? A visit to this living-history museum is like stepping into a time machine and zooming back to the year 1627. Guides dress in period costume and act like early-17th-century Pilgrims.

CONNECTICUT
Connecticut Science Center, Hartford. With unique, high-quality, and highly interactive exhibits, this science center is a must. It's geared toward older kids, but there is a kids space for the under-seven set. There's also a 3D theater.

Dinosaur State Park, Rocky Hill. Dinosaur lovers can explore a 200-million year-old fossil trackway, take in interactive exhibits, and even cast a dinosaur footprint to take home.

Mystic Aquarium and Seaport Museum, Mystic. This aquarium is one of only a few North American facilities to feature endangered Steller sea lions; it's also home to New England's only beluga whale. You'll also see African penguins, harbor seals, graceful sea horses, Pacific octopuses, and sand tiger sharks—kids can even touch a cownose ray. Nearby Mystic Seaport is another great attraction for families.

RHODE ISLAND
Block Island. Hop on the ferry at Port Judith and head to Block Island for an easy and scenic bike ride or just to spend the day at one of its many gorgeous, and often uncrowded, beaches.

Providence Children's Museum. Aimed at children ages 1–11, PCM explores arts, culture, history, and science. Exhibits are based on the developmental needs of children and embrace a wide range of learning styles.

Roger Williams Park and Zoo, Providence. Home to more than 100 species of animals from around the world, Roger Williams Park

has more than 40 acres to explore. One highlight is Marco Polo's Adventure Trek, with camels, moon bears, snow leopards, red crowned cranes, and red pandas. Look for interactive educational programs.

VERMONT
ECHO Leahy Center for Lake Champlain, Burlington. Lots of activities and hands-on exhibits make learning about the geology and ecology of Lake Champlain an engaging experience.

Montshire Museum of Science, Norwich. This interactive museum uses more than 60 hands-on exhibits to explore nature and technology. The building sits amid 110 acres of nature trails and woodlands, where live animals roam freely.

Shelburne Farms, Shelburne. This working dairy farm is also an educational and cultural resource center. Visitors can watch artisans make the farm's famous cheddar cheese from the milk of more than 100 purebred and registered Brown Swiss cows. A children's farmyard and walking trails round out the experience.

NEW HAMPSHIRE
Lost River Gorge and Whale's Tale Waterpark, Lincoln and North Woodstock. Kids can scramble through boulder caves in Lost River Gorge, and float on inner tubes and bodysurf in a giant wave pool at one of New England's biggest water parks. More family fun is nearby at Franconia Notch State Park.

Lake Winnipesaukee, Weirs Beach. The largest lake in the state, Lake Winnipesaukee provides plenty of family-friendly fun. Base yourself in the Laconia community of Weirs Beach, where kids can swim, play arcade games, cruise the lake, take a scenic railroad along the shoreline, and even see a drive-in movie.

SEE Science Center, Manchester. For kids who love LEGO, the models of old Manchester and the millyard are sure to impress. There are also rotating exhibits and science demonstrations.

MAINE
Acadia National Park, Mount Desert Island. Head out on a whale- and puffin-watching trip from Bar Harbor, drive up scenic Cadillac Mountain, swim at Echo Lake Beach, hike one of the many easy trails, and don't forget to sample some wild blueberry pie.

Coastal Maine Botanical Garden, Boothbay. The "children's garden" is a wonderland of stone sculptures, rope bridges, small teahouselike structures with grass roofs, and even a hedge maze. Children and adults alike adore the separate woodland fairy area.

Maine Narrow Gauge Railroad Museum, Portland. For train fans, check out the scenic rides on these narrow-gauge trains. In the winter, they have Polar Express theme trips.

New England Today

THE PEOPLE

The idea of the self-reliant, thrifty, and often stoic New England Yankee has taken on almost mythic proportions in American folklore, but in some parts of New England—especially in rural Maine, New Hampshire, and Vermont—there still is some truth to this image. It makes sense—you need to be independent if you farm an isolated field, live in the middle of a remote forest, or work a fishing boat miles off the coast. As in any part of the country, there are stark differences between the city mice and the country mice of New England. Both, however, are usually knowledgeable and fiercely proud of the region, its rugged beauty, and its contributions to the nation.

NEW ENGLAND AND COVID-19

In the spring of 2020, the United States (including New England) was gravely impacted by COVID-19. Restaurants, hotels, shops, bars, and even cultural institutions were forced to close. If you're currently planning a visit, remember to call ahead to verify open hours, and to make sure the property is open.

CONNECTICUT

Connecticut has long been a melting pot, attracting immigrants who landed in New York or Boston and then sought work outside the city or simply yearned for life in the "country." Longtime Connecticut Yankees, celebrated authors and artists, and successful businesspeople blend easily with continuing generations of immigrants. Their hard work has contributed to the state having the nation's highest per-capita income (as of 2014). The founders saw "the Constitution State" as the model for our national government. Today's Connecticut voters generally vote Democratic for national offices but fluctuate between the parties for state and municipal officeholders, albeit with a decided blue lean in the 2000s. Small manufacturers and defense contractors have been mainstays of Connecticut's economy since colonial days, supplying brass buttons for Revolutionary War and Civil War uniforms and Colt 45s to tame the Wild West. Today's workers build airplane engines, helicopters, and submarines. In between, bright minds came up with the cotton gin, the Erector Set, and the Frisbee.

MASSACHUSETTS

The Commonwealth of Massachusetts, New England's most populous state, is often just seen through the lens of its capital city, Boston. It's home to the majority of the state's population. As a whole, the majority blue state (though it has a Republican governor) is doing well. It's generally enjoyed the lowest unemployment rate in New England, and one that's better than the national average, since 2000, though the inflation rate, especially in Greater Boston, has been the highest in the nation in recent years. Boston-centric though it may be, the state does have its own very distinct regional identities, especially tourism-driven and ocean-minded Cape Cod and the islands and also the quieter, rural, and artsy western side of the state, which includes the Berkshires and the Pioneer Valley.

MAINE

In recent decades, Maine's Congressional delegation has often been around 50–50—half Democrat and Republican, and half male and female, which somewhat resembles the makeup of the state. Voters legalized recreational marijuana in 2016, but regulatory snags have delayed opening of retail pot shops (expected by fall 2020). Since 2000, Somali immigration has generated both tensions and welcome cultural diversity in Lewiston and Portland. As paper mills shutter, farming is on the upswing, while the billion-dollar tourism industry struggles to find enough workers yet fuels rising real estate prices and rents in popular destinations.

NEW HAMPSHIRE

With its state motto of "Live Free or Die" and a long-running political reputation as one of the nation's swingiest—albeit slightly left of center—states, New Hampshire marches to its own drummer. The fifth smallest—and 10th least populous—state in America maintains a fierce libertarian streak, collects neither sales tax nor income tax, and each presidential year holds the country's first primary. Like the rest of northern New England, ruggedly mountainous New Hampshire is characterized by a mostly rural, heavily wooded topography that gives way to more densely populated small cities and suburbs only in its southeastern corner. Relatively prosperous, with the eighth-highest median household income in the country, New Hampshire has also enjoyed slow but steady growth in recent years, lagging behind only Massachusetts in population growth since 2010 among New England's six states.

RHODE ISLAND

It may be the smallest state, but Rhode Island is actually the country's second most densely populated state. Providence, the capital city, is a college town with a young vibe. To the north, descendants of French Canadian, Italian, and Irish workers who arrived during the birth of the American Industrial Revolution populate the cities and towns. Democrats have held sway over Rhode Island politics since the 1930s with a few notable exceptions. The revered Senator Claiborne Pell and John Chafee were Republicans, for example, as was Mayor "Buddy" Cianci of Providence, who was convicted on RICO charges and served four years in prison. Rhode Island was the birthplace of the American Industrial Revolution, and manufacturing has always been the predominant influence on the state's economy. Jewelry, silverware, machinery, and textiles have always been important local products, and Galilee continues to be a busy commercial fishing port.

VERMONT

Few states are more proud of its rugged, independent, and liberal spirit than Vermont. From Ethan Allen to Bernie Sanders, Vermonters have never been afraid to follow a different drumbeat and be outspoken about it. This is perhaps never more on display than in the state's long-standing protection of the environment that borders on obsession. It's one of only four states than ban billboards (Maine is the only other in New England), and strict regulations on land use and development makes many towns and villages appear as if pulled from Norman Rockwell paintings. During fall, the peak tourist season, the landscape literally takes your breath away with an array of fiery reds, golds, oranges, and bronze bursting from the hills and valleys. Cities are few and far between, with Burlington topping out at just 43,000 people, but a robust cultural and arts scene thrives throughout the state, thanks to the abundance of colleges, collectives, and individual artists that continually draw inspiration from the Vermont spirit and beauty. Locals and tourists do the same on the ski slopes, hiking trails, bike paths, and swimming holes, and there's plenty for all.

What to Read and Watch

LOBSTERMAN BY DAHLOV IPCAR

Ipcar, a native New Englander, is best remembered as a writer and illustrator of children's books, many of which took place in her home state of Maine. One of her classics, *Lobsterman,* portrays the day in the life of a lobsterman and his son as they work along Maine's coast.

IT BY STEPHEN KING

You won't find Derry, Maine, on any map, but you can visit it via a number of chilling tales courtesy of horror writer Stephen King, including his 1986 novel *It,* which was adapted into a TV miniseries and a 2017 film, and follows a group of friends who try to kill a monster that terrorizes their town.

WE HAVE ALWAYS LIVED IN THE CASTLE BY SHIRLEY JACKSON

Merricat Blackwood lives in isolation on her family's estate with her sister Constance and their infirm Uncle Julian. When an estranged cousin arrives, the already uneasy state of the Blackwood home is thrown into disarray.

LITTLE WOMEN BY LOUISA MAY ALCOTT

Published in 1868, the book has remained a beloved coming of age story loosely based on the author's own life. The story follows four sisters—Meg, Jo, Beth, and Amy—and their mother after the family patriarch must leave their Massachusetts's home to act as a pastor during the Civil War.

THE SECRET HISTORY BY DONNA TARTT

Richard leaves his working class California home behind in order to attend a liberal arts college in Vermont. Once there he falls in with a privileged group of classics students. But beneath the group's veneer of charm and sophistication is a dark, violent secret.

JAWS

The movie (1975) that singlehandedly invented the summer blockbuster also happens to be the reason you jump out of your skin when a bit of seaweed brushes against your leg at the beach. In this all-time classic, the town of Amity Beach (filmed on Martha's Vineyard) is terrorized by an insatiable, man-eating, great white shark.

THE IRON GIANT

This charming 1999 animated film tells the story of Hogarth, a young boy who befriends a giant robot after it crashes in Maine. When a paranoid government agent tries to destroy the giant, Hogarth saves the gentle-hearted automaton.

THE DEPARTED

Martin Scorsese's 2006 remake is a twisty crime drama set against the backdrop of Boston's criminal underworld. When both the police and the mob discover they have a rat among them, the infiltrators have to race against the clock in order to uncover the other's identity.

GOOD WILL HUNTING

Will Hunting is a mathematical genius with a troubled past. An MIT professor offers to help him avoid jail time if he studies mathematics and starts seeing a therapist. Through his therapy sessions with Dr. Sean Maguire, Will comes to terms with the trauma of his past and learns how to keep himself from sabotaging his future.

WHITE CHRISTMAS

This 1954 holiday classic, brimming with good cheer and the iconic music of Irving Berlin, follows a song and dance team and a pair of performing sisters as they travel to a Vermont inn where they've been booked to perform over Christmas. The inn is on the verge of failure, so they stage a nationally televised yuletide extravaganza in order to save it.

TRAVEL SMART

2

Updated by
Andrew Collins

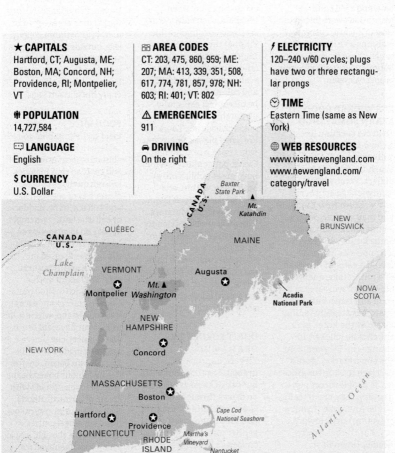

★ **CAPITALS**
Hartford, CT; Augusta, ME;
Boston, MA; Concord, NH;
Providence, RI; Montpelier,
VT

♛ **POPULATION**
14,727,584

💬 **LANGUAGE**
English

$ **CURRENCY**
U.S. Dollar

☎ **AREA CODES**
CT: 203, 475, 860, 959; ME:
207; MA: 413, 339, 351, 508,
617, 774, 781, 857, 978; NH:
603; RI: 401; VT: 802

⚠ **EMERGENCIES**
911

🚗 **DRIVING**
On the right

⚡ **ELECTRICITY**
120–240 v/60 cycles; plugs
have two or three rectangular prongs

🕑 **TIME**
Eastern Time (same as New
York)

🌐 **WEB RESOURCES**
www.visitnewengland.com
www.newengland.com/
category/travel

CANADA
U.S.

QUÉBEC

Baxter
State Park

Mt.
Katahdin

NEW
BRUNSWICK

MAINE

CANADA
U.S.

Lake
Champlain

VERMONT

Mt. ▲
Montpelier Washington

Augusta

Acadia
National Park

NOVA
SCOTIA

NEW
HAMPSHIRE

NEW YORK

Concord

MASSACHUSETTS

Boston

Hartford

Providence

CONNECTICUT

RHODE
ISLAND

Cape Cod
National Seashore

Martha's
Vineyard

Nantucket

Atlantic Ocean

N.J.

Know Before You Go

New England has its share of regional character, color, and flavor—not to mention a few geographical and seasonal challenges. Here are some tips that will enrich your trip and ease your travels.

COVID-19

Parts of New England were gravely impacted by COVID-19. Restaurants, hotels, shops, bars, and even cultural institutions were forced to closed. If you're currently planning a visit, remember to call ahead to verify open hours, and to make sure the property is open.

IT'S WICKED GOOD TO LEARN SOME LINGO

To avoid seeming like a chowdah-head (aka "chowder head" aka "idiot"), brush up on some basic dialect. Want a big, long sandwich? In southern and western New England, you may want to order a grinder instead of a sub. Some locals will order a frappe—or in Rhode Island a cabinet—instead of a milk shake, and a few old-timers still refer to a soda as a tonic, but this custom is steadily fading away. At the hotel, grab the clickah (clicker) to change the TV station. At the supermarket, grab a carriage to shop for groceries. If people direct you to a rotary, they mean traffic circle. And, even if you're traveling north toward, say, Bar Harbor, you're headed Down East.

YOU CAN'T ALWAYS GET THEAH FROM HEAH

As this famous regional saying implies, the shortest distance between two points isn't always a straight—or single—line. Finding the real New England means driving (and getting lost on) its scenic byways. And GPS and cell-phone service will be disrupted, especially up north, so pack road maps or an atlas. There are a few places where you won't need a car, though. Cities, particularly Boston, have great public transit options to, within, and around them. Block Island, Nantucket, and Martha's Vineyard are bike-friendly and have good taxi and/or shuttle services. In Acadia National Park, you'll have to trade your car for hiking boots, a bike, or a carriage (an actual horse and buggy, not a shopping cart).

DON'T FORGET THE DRAMAMINE

Elevations aren't as dramatic as those out west, but car sickness is possible on drives through the Green or White Mountains. Even south, amid the gentler terrain of Massachusetts's Berkshires or Connecticut's Litchfield Hills, roads ribbon up, down, and around—just as they do along rugged, often precipitous stretches of Atlantic coast.

EVEN THE CITIES ARE RELATIVELY SMALL

Boston, the region's largest city, has just less than 700,000 residents; the next biggest, Worcester, Massachusetts, has about 186,000, which is about 20,000 more than Providence. Still, most cities have thriving cultural scenes; several are major university towns (New Haven, Providence, Burlington) and/or are steeped in history (Portland). Regardless, outside the Interstate 95 corridor, you can allow less time for urban explorations and more time to enjoy bucolic settings.

FOOD 101

Field-or-fishing-boat-to-table is the norm, with abundant local produce and seafood that includes lobster; quahogs or other clams; bay or sea scallops; and pollack, hake, haddock, or cod (the latter two might appear on local menus as "scrod"). In Maine, lobster-roll meat is dressed in mayonnaise; in southern New England, it's often drizzled with melted butter. Chowder is creamy, except in Rhode Island, where it has a clear but flavorful broth, and Connecticut, where it might be made with milk and contain bacon. Boston has its famous baked beans and cream pies (made with cream or custard); Rhode Island has its johnnycakes (fried cornmeal patties). Everywhere, though, maple syrup adorns shaved ice (or snow!) and ice cream as well as pancakes; breakfast home fries are griddled and seasoned just so; and craft beer and cider pair well with boiled dinners and Yankee pot roast. Be sure to try a Moxie, an "energizing," regionally unique soft drink.

IN THE LAND OF THE COUNTRY INN, IT'S BEST TO BOOK AHEAD

Although there are abundant chain hotels and several large, notable Victorians—seaside and near the slopes—smaller inns, often historical and privately owned, are among the best lodgings. Although the growth of Airbnb has made it easier to find rooms in charming old homes, it's still prudent to book well ahead, especially during peak seasons, when there might also be a two- or three-night minimum. And "peak seasons" vary. Leaf-peeping season is roughly late September to mid-October in Maine, New Hampshire, and Vermont and mid- to late October in Connecticut, Massachusetts, and Rhode Island. In the southern ski areas, the season runs December through March; up north it might be November through April or even May.

THE ATLANTIC IS COLD UP HERE

Even in late August, ocean temperatures off Maine and New Hampshire only climb to the upper 50s or lower 60s—still limb-numbingly chilly. Wet suits (and water shoes for rockier shores) are musts. Temperatures are warmer near Boston

and points south, where the Atlantic's summer highs are in the mid-60s to mid- to upper 70s. Obviously, the farther north you go, the shorter the beach season, with some properties reducing their hours or shuttering entirely between Labor Day and Memorial Day or July 4.

WHEN IT COMES TO PARKS, THE STATES HAVE 'EM

Although much of New England is woodsy, the entire region has only one national park (Acadia) and two national forests (Green Mountain and White Mountain). That said, there are plenty of opportunities to hike, canoe, kayak, mountain bike, camp, and otherwise embrace the outdoors in the plethora of park or recreation and wilderness areas overseen by each state.

SOME OF THE BUGS BITE

First, it's the black flies, whose bites leave red, itchy welts. May is the prime season, and it's particularly notorious in the three northern states. Then, in July, it's the deer flies. Summer also sees greenhead flies (aka saltmarsh greenheads) in some coastal areas. On hikes, use insect repellent and wear clothing that covers your arms and legs. And don't forget to check for ticks. The disease they're known to carry was named after a New England town: Lyme, Connecticut.

THE PEOPLE ARE WARM AND WELCOMING

The idea of the self-reliant, thrifty, and often stoic New England Yankee has taken on almost mythic proportions in American folklore, but in some parts of New England— especially in rural Maine, New Hampshire, and Vermont— there still is some truth to this image, which shouldn't come as a surprise. You need to be independent if you farm an isolated field, live in the middle of a vast forest, or work a fishing boat miles off the coast. As in any part of the country, there are stark differences between the city mice and the country mice of New England. Both, however, are usually knowledgeable and fiercely proud of the region, its rugged beauty, and its contributions to the nation.

SPORTS IS A RELIGION

This is Sox and Pats country. New England fans—with the exception of those in southwestern Connecticut, who are just as likely to root for New York teams—follow Massachusetts's sports teams as if they were their own. Boston is home to three of the region's four major sports teams—Red Sox baseball, Bruins hockey, and Celtics basketball. The New England Patriots (football) play nearby in the small suburb of Foxboro. The city is also home to the Boston Marathon, New England's largest sporting event and the world's oldest annual marathon.

Getting Here and Around

Air

Most travelers visiting New England use a major gateway, such as Boston, Providence, Hartford/Springfield, Manchester, or even New York City or Albany, and then rent a car to explore the region. The New England states form a fairly compact region, with few important destinations more than six hours apart by car. It's costly and generally impractical to fly within New England, the exceptions being the island resort destinations of Martha's Vineyard and Nantucket in Massachusetts and Block Island in Rhode Island, which have regular air service from Boston and a few regional airports.

Boston's Logan Airport is one of the nation's most important domestic and international airports, with direct flights arriving from all over North America and abroad. New England's other major airports receive few international flights (mostly from Canada) but receive many direct domestic flights from East Coast and Midwest destinations and, to a lesser extent, from the western United States. Some sample flying times to Boston are: 2½ hours from Chicago, 6½ hours from London, and 6 hours from Los Angeles. Times from other U.S. cities are similar, if slightly shorter, to Albany and Hartford, assuming you can find direct flights.

AIRPORTS

The main gateway to New England is Boston's Logan International Airport (BOS). Bradley International Airport (BDL), in Windsor Locks, Connecticut (12 miles north of Hartford), is convenient to Western Massachusetts and much of Connecticut. T. F. Green International Airport (PVD), just outside Providence, Rhode Island, and Manchester-Boston Regional Airport (MHT), in New Hampshire, are other major airports—and

alternative approaches to Boston, which is a one-hour drive from each. Additional New England airports served by major carriers include Portland International Jetport (PWM) in Maine and Burlington International Airport (BTV) in Vermont.

Other convenient airports are Albany International Airport (ALB) in Albany, New York, near Western Massachusetts and Vermont; Westchester County Airport (HPN) in White Plains, New York, near Southern Connecticut; Bangor International Airport (BGR) in Bangor, Maine; and Barnstable Municipal Airport in Hyannis, Massachusetts. You can access Nantucket and Martha's Vineyard via ferries from Hyannis or fly directly to each island's airport.

FLIGHTS

The three major U.S. legacy airlines, along with Frontier, JetBlue, and Southwest, have scheduled flights to—with just some occasional exceptions—the airports in Albany, Boston, Hartford, Manchester, Portland, Providence, and Westchester County. Alaska, Boutique Air, Hawaiian, Spirit, and Sun Country fly into Boston. Cape Air, a regional carrier, serves various New England airports in Maine, New Hampshire, Vermont, and Massachusetts—including those on Cape Cod and the islands. New England Airlines serves Block Island with regularly scheduled flights to and from Westerly, Rhode Island.

Boat

Principal ferry routes in New England connect New Bedford on the mainland and Cape Cod with Martha's Vineyard and Nantucket, Boston with Provincetown, Providence with Newport, Newport and Point Judith with Block Island, and Connecticut with Block Island and New York's

Travel Times from Boston to:	By Air	By Car
Acadia National Park (ME)	1 hour	5 hours
Burlington, VT	No direct flight	3½ hours
Hartford, CT	No direct flight	1¾ hours
New York, NY	¾–1 hour	4 hours
Portland, ME	No direct flight	2 hours
Providence, RI	No direct flight	1 hour
Provincetown, MA	½ hour	2¼ hours

Long Island. Other ferry routes provide access to islands off the Maine coast and across Lake Champlain between Vermont and upstate New York. International service between Portland, Yarmouth, and Bar Harbor in Maine and Nova Scotia is also available. With the exception of the Lake Champlain ferries—which are first-come, first-served—reservations are advisable for cars.

Bus

With fares starting at just $1 if you reserve early enough, BoltBus buses equipped with Wi-Fi and electrical outlets connect Boston and New Haven with New York, Washington, D.C., and other Mid-Atlantic cities. Megabus also offers low fares, and its buses (also with Wi-Fi) serve New York City and many other points on the East Coast. Both Bolt-Bus and Megabus use Boston's South Station.

Once in New England, regional bus service is relatively extensive, especially in southern New England, but although it's often useful for getting between key points, it's generally impractical if you're exploring rural areas. That said, it can be a handy and affordable means of getting around, as buses travel many routes that trains do not, including to Logan and other key airports. Concord Coach buses connect Boston with several cities in New Hampshire and Maine; the company also operates a route between New York City and Portland. C&J buses (with Wi-Fi) serve Dover (near Durham) and Portsmouth, New Hampshire, Ogunquit, Maine, and Newburyport, Massachusetts; C&J also provides service to New York City. Both Concord and C&J leave from Boston's South Station, which is connected to the Amtrak rail station, and from Logan Airport.

Car

New England is best explored by car. Inland, especially in northwestern Connecticut, western Massachusetts, Vermont, New Hampshire, and Maine, public transportation options are limited; a car is essential. Coastal areas can get congested in summer, especially the roads to and from Cape Cod. Cars are a nuisance in Boston; street parking can be hard to find and hotel parking often costs a fortune. It can also be hard to find public parking in Providence and near the beach in many resort towns along the coast. Interstate 95 enters New England at the New York border, follows the Connecticut shoreline, and then heads north to Providence, Boston, and Portland before ending at the Canadian border in Calais, Maine. Interstate 90, the Massachusetts Turnpike, is a toll road that goes across the state from the

Getting Here and Around

New York border (near Albany) to Boston. If you rent a car at Logan International Airport, allow plenty of time to return it—as much as an hour to be on the safe side. Other major highways traverse the region, including Interstate 84 (across Connecticut and part of Massachusetts), Interstate 91 (north New Haven through Massachusetts and Vermont to Canada), Interstate 93 (north from Boston through New Hampshire to Canada), and Interstate 89 (north from Concord, New Hampshire through Vermont to Canada).

GASOLINE

Gas stations are easy to find along major highways and in most communities throughout the region, but beware that in rural parts of northern New England, it's possible even on numbered routes to go 30 miles or more between stations—it's best to keep your tank at least a quarter full at all times in these areas. Gas prices are relatively similar across New England, though a bit lower in the northern states, and often highest in city centers or remote small towns. Virtually all have self-serve pumps that accept credit or debit cards.

PARKING

In Boston and other large cities, finding a parking space on the street can be time-consuming and nerve-wracking. Your best bet is to park in a garage, but rates in Boston can top $40 and run $20 to $30 in other New England cities. In smaller cities, street parking is usually simpler, though parking garages are still convenient and, for the most part, reasonably priced. Pay attention to signs: some cities allow only residents to park on certain streets or limit street parking in winter to allow for snow removal. In most small towns, parking is not a problem—though some beach and lake parking areas are reserved for those with resident stickers.

CAR RENTAL

A car is the most practical way to get around New England. Major airports serving the region all have on-site car-rental agencies. A few train or bus stations have one or two car-rental agencies on-site, as well.

Rates at Boston's Logan Airport vary greatly according to supply and demand but generally begin at around $50 per day and $300 per week for an economy car with air-conditioning, automatic transmission, and unlimited mileage. The same car might go for around $40 per day and $220 per week at a smaller airport, such as Providence's or Hartford's. These rates do not include state tax on car rentals, which varies depending on the airport but generally runs 12%–15%. You can often save greatly, as much as $150 to $200 a week, by renting away from the airport, even factoring in the cost of an Uber or Lyft ride there and back.

Most agencies won't rent to drivers under the age of 21, and several major agencies won't rent to anyone under 25 or over the age of 75. When picking up a rental car, non-U.S. residents need a voucher for any prepaid reservation made in their home country, a passport, a driver's license, and a travel policy that covers each driver. Logan Airport is spread out and usually congested; if returning a rental vehicle there, allow plenty of time to do so before heading to your flight.

🚆 Train

Amtrak offers frequent daily service along its Northeast Corridor route from Washington, D.C., Philadelphia, and New York to Boston, with stops in Connecticut and Rhode Island. Amtrak's high-speed Acela trains link Boston and Washington, with stops at New York, Philadelphia, and other cities along the way. The *Downeaster* connects Boston and Brunswick, Maine, with stops in coastal New Hampshire and Portland.

Other Amtrak services include the *Vermonter* between Washington, D.C., and St. Albans, Vermont (via New York City); the *Ethan Allen Express* between New York and Rutland, Vermont (via Albany, NY); and the *Lake Shore Limited* between Boston and Chicago, which stops at Pittsfield, Springfield, Worcester, and Framingham in Massachusetts.

Several commuter services are handy for travelers. The Massachusetts Bay Transportation Authority (MBTA) operates within Boston and connects the city with outlying areas on the north and south shores of the state. Metro-North Railroad's New Haven Line offers service from New York City along the Connecticut coast up to New Haven, with spur lines north to New Canaan, Danbury, and Waterbury. Also in Connecticut, Shore Line East serves coastal towns between New Haven and New London.

⊞ When to Go

All six New England states are year-round destinations. Winter is popular with skiers, summer draws beach lovers, and fall delights those who love the bursts of autumnal color. Spring can also be a great time, with sugar shacks transforming maple sap into all sorts of tasty things. ■TIP→ **You'll probably want to avoid rural areas during mud season (April to early May) and black fly season (May to early June).**

Memorial Day sets off the great migration to the beaches and the mountains, and summer begins in earnest on July 4. Those who want to drive to Cape Cod in July or August, beware: on Friday and Sunday, weekenders clog the overburdened U.S. 6. The same applies to the Maine Coast and its feeder roads, Interstate 95 and U.S. 1.

In the fall, a rainbow of reds, oranges, yellows, purples, and other vibrant hues emerges. The first scarlet and gold colors appear in mid-September in northern areas; "peak" color occurs at different times from year to year. Generally, it's best to visit the northern reaches in late September and early October and move south as October progresses.

CLIMATE

In winter, coastal New England is cold and damp; inland temperatures may be lower, but generally drier conditions make them easier to bear. Snowfall is heaviest in the interior mountains and can range up to several hundred inches per year in northern Maine, New Hampshire, and Vermont. Spring is often windy and rainy; in some years it feels as if winter tumbles directly into summer. Coastal areas can be quite humid in summer, while inland, particularly at higher elevations, there's a prevalence of cool summer nights. Autumn temperatures can be mild even into October.

Essentials

🍴 Dining

Although certain ingredients and preparations are common to the region as a whole, New England's cuisine varies greatly from place to place. Urban centers like Boston, Providence, New Haven, and Portland—and upscale resort areas such as the Berkshires, Martha's Vineyard, and Nantucket—have stellar restaurants, many of them with culinary luminaries at the helm and a reputation for creative—and occasionally daring—menus.

Many small-town restaurants in quiet parts of New England now feature more international recipes as well as sourcing increasingly from local farms, fisheries, and other purveyors. Menus in upscale and tourism-driven communities often note which Vermont dairy or Berkshires farm a particular goat cheese or heirloom tomato came from. Options for ethnic food have also improved greatly in recent years, especially when it comes to Italian, French, Japanese, Indian, and Thai eateries. There are also plenty of old-school diners, cafés, and rustic taverns serving burgers and other comfort food—some serve breakfast all day.

RESERVATIONS AND DRESS

It's a good idea to make a reservation when you can. We specifically mention them only when reservations are essential—there's no other way you'll ever get a table—or when they are not accepted. For popular restaurants or during the high season, book as far ahead as you can and reconfirm as soon as you arrive. Large parties should always call ahead to check the reservations policy. We mention dress only when men are required to wear a jacket or a jacket and tie, which is rarely in New England.

WINE, BEER, AND SPIRITS

New England is no stranger to craft brewing. The granddaddy of New England's independent breweries is the Boston Beer Company, maker of Samuel Adams, but these days ardent beer lovers consider Sam Adams to be almost too mainstream to be interesting, especially given that virtually every New England town with at least a half-dozen restaurants now has a brewpub, and some of the best beer in the region is produced by tiny operations that sell their beer only on-site. Artisan cider has also become increasingly popular, with Middlebury, Vermont's Green Mountain Cidery—the maker of Woodchuck Hard Cider—one of the region's stars.

New England is beginning to earn some respect as a wine-producing region. Cabernet Franc, Vidal, Riesling, and other grape varieties capable of withstanding the region's harsher winters and relatively shorter growing season compared to California and other leading areas have been the basis of promising enterprises such as Rhode Island's Sakonnet Vineyards and Connecticut's Hopkins Vineyard (part of the Connecticut Wine Trail). Even Vermont and New Hampshire have gotten into the act with the Snow Farm Vineyard in the Lake Champlain Islands, Boyden Valley Winery in the Green Mountains, and Seven Birches in the White Mountains.

Although a patchwork of state and local regulations affect the hours and locations of places that sell alcoholic beverages (e.g., Massachusetts bans "happy hour"), New England licensing laws are fairly liberal. State-owned or-franchised stores sell hard liquor in New Hampshire, Maine, and Vermont. New Hampshire offers some the region's lowest prices due to the lack of a sales tax; look for state-run liquor "supermarkets" on interstates in the southern part of the state—it's technically illegal to take untaxed liquor across state lines, but this law is virtually never enforced except in cases of drivers transporting huge quantities.

⊕ Health and Safety

Lyme disease, so named for its having been first reported in the town of Lyme, Connecticut, is a potentially debilitating disease carried by deer ticks. They thrive in dry, brush-covered areas, particularly in coastal areas. Always use insect repellent: the potential for outbreaks of Lyme disease makes it imperative that you protect yourself from ticks from early spring through summer and into fall. To prevent bites, wear light-color clothing and tuck pant legs into socks. Look for black ticks about the size of a pinhead around hairlines and the warmest parts of the body. If you have been bitten, consult a physician—especially if you see the telltale bull's-eye bite pattern. Flulike symptoms often accompany a Lyme infection. Early treatment is imperative.

New England's most annoying insect pests are black flies and mosquitoes. The former are a phenomenon of late spring and early summer and are generally a problem only in densely wooded areas of the far north. Mosquitoes, however, are a nuisance just about everywhere. The best protection against both pests is repellent containing DEET; if you're camping in the woods during black fly season, you'll also want to use fine mesh screening in eating and sleeping areas and even wear mesh headgear. One pest particular to coastal areas, especially salt marshes, is the greenhead fly, which has a nasty bite and is hard to kill. It is best repelled by a liberal application of Avon Skin So Soft or a similar product.

Rural New England is one of the country's safest regions. In cities—Boston, in particular—observe the usual precautions: avoid out-of-the-way or poorly lighted areas at night; keep handbags close to your body and don't let them out of your sight; and be on your guard in subways and on buses, not only during the deserted wee hours but also during crowded rush hours, when pickpockets may be at work. Keep your valuables in the hotel or room safe. When using an ATM, choose busy, well-lighted places, such as bank lobbies.

If planning to leave a car overnight to make use of off-road trails or camping facilities, look for a supervised parking area and don't leave any valuable in sight; cars left at trailhead parking lots are sometimes a target for theft or vandalism.

🛏 Lodging

As is true for most of the country, in cities you'll find plenty of chain properties, a handful of grande dames, and a growing number of hip boutique hotels. Elsewhere, though, New England is very much the domain of distinctive, independently owned country inns and bed-and-breakfasts, as well as a number of restored or well-kept old-fashioned cottage compounds and motels. In addition to often having distinct charms and scenic locations, these one-of-a-kind properties also provide a glimpse of local life. In ski areas and some coastal resort towns, you'll also find condo resorts offering a full slate of dining and recreational amenities.

Hotel prices are the lowest cost of a standard double room in high season.

Essentials

APARTMENT AND HOUSE RENTALS

You are most likely to find a house, apartment, or condo rental in areas of New England where ownership of second homes is common, such as beach resorts and ski country. Both Airbnb and VRBO have a large presence throughout New England, and many resort communities also have local rental agencies.

BED-AND-BREAKFASTS AND INNS

In many less touristy areas, bed-and-breakfasts offer an affordable, homey experience and sometimes quite lavish breakfasts that will fill you up for the better part of the day. Inns are similar but usually bigger, with 10 or more rooms, and rates that may or may not include breakfast. Often but not always, inns are a bit fancier and pricier than a typical bed-and-breakfast and have more amenities, such as restaurants, bars, pools, and even spas or tennis courts.

HOTELS

Major hotel and motel chains are amply represented in New England, but don't overlook the many small, independent motels—these mom-and-pop operations often offer cheerful, convenient accommodations and great rates.

Reservations are always a good idea, and are essential, as far in advance as possible on weekends and during peak seasons in summer and winter resort areas, in college towns in September and at graduation time in spring, and in areas renowned for autumn foliage. Most hotels and motels will hold your reservation until 6 pm; call ahead if you plan to arrive late.

In Vermont, Boston, and some other regions, all hotels are no-smoking by law; elsewhere, smoking is allowed only in designated guest rooms. All lodgings listed have private baths unless otherwise noted.

Packing

The principal rule of weather in New England is that there are no rules. A cold, foggy spring morning often warms to a bright, 60°F afternoon. A summer breeze can suddenly turn chilly, and rain often appears with little warning. Thus, the best advice on how to dress is to layer your clothing, peeling off or adding garments as needed. Even in summer, you should bring long pants, a sweater or two, and a light jacket, for evenings are often chilly, and sea spray can make things cool. Showers are frequent, so pack a waterproof windbreaker or raincoat and umbrella.

Casual sportswear—walking shoes and jeans or khakis—will take you almost everywhere, but swimsuits and bare feet will not. Shirts and shoes are required attire at even the most casual venues. Dress in restaurants is generally casual, except at some of the distinguished restaurants in Boston, Newport, Maine coastal towns (such as Kennebunkport), a few inns in the Berkshires, and in Litchfield and Fairfield counties in Connecticut, where sportier attire is expected. Upscale resorts, at the very least, will require men to wear long pants and collared shirts at dinner, and jeans are often frowned upon.

In summer, bring a hat and sunscreen. You can bring or buy insect repellent. If you find yourself in walking in wooded areas, near brush, or around foliage from early spring through fall, be sure to check your body for ticks, which can cause Lyme disease if not removed.

Best Tours

BIKE TOURS

Backroads. This internationally respected company offers luxurious multiday cycling tours along the Maine Coast, in Vermont's mountains, and across Martha's Vineyard and Nantucket. ☎ 800/462–2848 ⊕ www.backroads.com ✉ From $2200.

Urban Adventours. This bike shop in downtown Boston conducts guided tours of the city, Cambridge, and surrounding towns. For example, the ambitious 26-mile Paul Revere tour traces the patriot's famous ride. ☎ 617/670–0637 ⊕ www.urbanadventours.com ✉ From $55.

FOOD TOURS

Maine Food for Thought. Guided tours take you to six of Portland's best restaurants for a sampling of their dishes and discussions about the importance of the farm-to-table movement in Maine. ☎ 207/619–2075 ⊕ www.mainefoodforthought.com.

Portsmouth Eats. On White Table, Best of Portsmouth, and Sweet and Savory walking tours—mostly on weekends—you get to taste the culinary delights of four or five establishments in New Hampshire's coastal city. ☎ 603/571–3287 ⊕ www.portsmouth-eats.com ✉ From $37.

GENERAL INTEREST TOURS

New England Vacation Tours. This versatile company conducts everything from packages that include flights and tours in luxury coaches to ones that involve cruises and sightseeing excursions on land. All transportation is covered, and every detail is attended to. You can also create a completely customized itinerary to take you wherever your heart desires—the people here are very easy to work with. ☎ 800/742–7669 ⊕ www.newenglandvacationtours.com ✉ Call for prices.

Northeast Unlimited Tours. As the name indicates, Northeast Unlimited's range of itineraries includes New England. The eight-day Taste of New England tour, for example, hits all the highlights from Boston to Maine. ☎ 800/759–6820 ⊕ www.newenglandtours.com ✉ From $1959.

Wolfe Adventures & Tours. Wolfe specializes in tours for groups, including families. New England tours include Boston, Newport, the White Mountains, Vermont farms, maritime adventures, Cape Cod, and more. ☎ 888/449–6533 ⊕ wolfetours.com ✉ Call for prices.

Great Itineraries

Cape Cod Beaches and Villages, 7 Days

Cape Cod can be all things to all visitors, with quiet villages and lively resorts, gentle bay-side wavelets and crashing surf. A car is the best way to meander along Massachusetts's beach-lined, arm-shape peninsula, but in busy town centers—such as Falmouth, Hyannis, Chatham, and Provincetown—you can get around quite easily on foot. Keep in mind that Cape-bound traffic is particularly bad on Friday late afternoon–evening and Saturday morning–afternoon (most house rentals are Saturday to Saturday), and traffic in the other direction is rough on Sunday, especially in the afternoon. Cross as early in the day as possible or wait until well after rush hour. For most visitors, time at the beach is key, but there is plenty to do and see once you've had enough sun and surf or if the weather doesn't cooperate. And about those beaches: be prepared to pay for day passes—most beach parking lots charge a sometimes-hefty fee.

Fly in: Logan International Airport (BOS), Boston

Fly out: Logan International Airport (BOS), Boston

DAY 1: HYANNIS

The crowded Mid Cape is a center of activity, and its heart is **Hyannis.** Here you can cruise around the harbor or go on a deep-sea fishing trip. There are shops and restaurants along Main Street and plenty of kid-friendly amusements. Fans of John F. Kennedy shouldn't miss the museum in his honor. End the day with a concert at the **Cape Cod Melody Tent** (open seasonally) or the Cotuit Center for the Arts.

Logistics: 72 miles; via I–90 W, I–93 S, Rte. 3 S, U.S. 6 E, and Rte. 132 S; 1½ hours from Logan airport.

DAY 2: FALMOUTH

For your first excursion, wander along Route 28 until you reach **Falmouth** in the Upper Cape. Here you can stroll around the village green, duck into some of the historic houses, and stop at the Waquoit Bay National Estuarine Research Reserve for a walk along the barrier beach. Take some time to check out the village of **Woods Hole,** a center for international marine research, and the year-round ferry port for Martha's Vineyard. A small aquarium has regional sea-life exhibits and touch tanks. If you have extra time, head north to the lovely old town of **Sandwich,** known for the **Sandwich Glass Museum,** and the beautiful grounds and collection of antique cars at **Heritage Museums and Gardens.**

Logistics: 21 miles; via Rte. 28 N; 48 minutes, starting in Hyannis.

DAY 3: BARNSTABLE, YARMOUTH PORT, DENNIS

Spend your day exploring the northern reaches of the Mid Cape with a drive along scenic Route 6A, which passes through the charming, slow-paced villages of **Barnstable, Yarmouth Port,** and **Dennis.** There are beaches and salt marshes, antiques shops and galleries, and old cemeteries along this route. Yarmouth Port's **Bass Hole Boardwalk** makes for a particularly beautiful stroll. In Dennis there are historic houses to tour, and the **Cape Cod Museum of Art** merits a stop. End the day by climbing 30-foot Scargo Tower to watch the sun set. At night you can catch a film at the Cape Cinema, on the grounds of the **Cape Playhouse.**

If you're traveling with kids, spend some time in the southern sections of Yarmouth and Dennis, where Route 28 passes by countless amusement centers and miniature-golf courses.

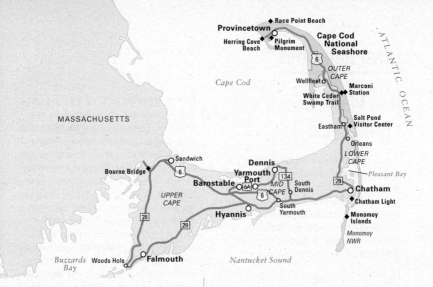

Logistics: 9 miles; via Rte. 6A E; 20 minutes, starting in Hyannis.

DAY 4: CHATHAM

Chatham, with its handsome Main Street, is a perfect destination for strolling, shopping, and dining. A trip to the nearby **Monomoy Islands** is a must for bird-watchers and nature lovers. Back in town, you can watch glassblowing at the **Chatham Glass Company,** visit the **Atwood House Museum,** and drive over to take in the view from **Chatham Light.**

Logistics: 19½ miles; via U.S. 6 E; 35 minutes, starting in Hyannis.

DAY 5: CAPE COD NATIONAL SEASHORE

On Day 5, leave your Hyannis hub and head for the farther reaches of Cape Cod. Take U.S. 6 east, before making a slight detour onto the less commercial end of Route 28. On the way north toward Orleans you'll drive past sailboat-speckled views of Pleasant Bay.

Stop in Eastham at the Cape Cod National Seashore's **Salt Pond Visitor Center.** Take time to stroll along one of the beaches—there are more than 40 miles of pristine sand from which to choose—or bike on the many picturesque trails. Head slightly farther north to historic **Marconi Station,** which was the landing point for the transatlantic telegraph early in the 20th century, or park your car in **Wellfleet's** historic downtown area, where you'll find a bounty of intriguing shops and galleries. It's also worth walking the short but stunning White Cedar Swamp Trail. Continue on to Provincetown to spend two nights at the tip of the Cape.

Logistics: 47 miles; via U.S. 6 E; 1¼ hours, starting in Hyannis.

DAYS 6 AND 7: PROVINCETOWN

Bustling **Provincetown** sits at the very end of the Cape, and there's a lot to see and do here. You can park the car and forget about it until you leave town, as everything is easily walkable. Catch a whale-watching boat and take a trolley tour through town, or bike through the **Cape Cod National Seashore** on its miles of trails. Climb the **Pilgrim Monument** for a spectacular view of the area—on an exceptionally clear day you can see the Boston skyline. Visit museums, shops, and art galleries, or spend the afternoon swimming and sunning on the beaches at **Herring Cove** or **Race Point.**

Logistics: 116 miles; via U.S. 6 W, Rte. 3 N and I–93 N; 2½ hours, starting in Provincetown and ending in Boston.

Great Itineraries

New Haven, Boston, and Providence, 5 Days

These three cities all have some of the best dining the Northeast has to offer, and each makes a case for having the finest Italian cuisine in the region, leaving you to judge whose cuisine reigns supreme. In addition, history buffs can get their fill while exploring New England's Colonial and maritime past.

Fly in: Bradley International Airport (BDA), Hartford

Fly out: Logan International Airport (BOS), Boston

DAY 1: NEW HAVEN

Start your journey in **New Haven,** Connecticut. The Constitution State's second-largest city is home to **Yale University,** named for British shipping merchant Elihu Yale. Take an hour-long walking tour with one of the university's guides and feast your eyes on the iconic Gothic-style structures that adorn the campus. After you've worked up an appetite, a stop for New Haven–style pizza is a must. Less than a mile from campus are two institutions known for thin-crust pies cooked in brick ovens: **Pepe's Pizzeria** and **Sally's Apizza.** For the burger enthusiast, there's **Louis' Lunch** on Crown Street. Don't ask for ketchup; it's been taboo here since they opened in 1895. Spend your first night in New Haven.

Logistics: 53 miles; via I–91 S; 1 hour staring at Bradley airport.

DAY 2: NEW HAVEN TO PROVIDENCE

On your second day, get an early start, and head north on Interstate 95 to make your way toward Providence, Rhode Island. There are plenty of small towns bursting with New England's maritime history along Connecticut's shoreline. Stop in Niantic, New London, or **Stonington** and explore the region's rich seafaring history. If you're planning on making one stop on the way to Rhode Island, the seaside village of **Mystic** is worth at least a half day to explore the seaport or to take a boat out on the water. **Mystic Seaport,** with its nearly 500 ships and more than 60 preserved historic buildings, will transport you back to 19th-century New England. For those looking to try their luck at a game of chance, take a slight detour north on Interstate 395 to either of Connecticut's two casinos, **Foxwoods Resort Casino** or **Mohegan Sun.** Overnight in Providence or in any of the seaside towns along the way.

Logistics: 103 miles; via I–95 N; 1 hour 45 minutes, starting in New Haven.

DAY 3: PROVIDENCE

Rhode Island's capital holds treasures like **Benefit Street,** with its Federal-era homes, and the **RISD Museum of Art** at the Rhode Island School of Design. Be sure to savor a knockout Italian meal on Atwells Avenue in **Federal Hill—Pane e Vino** is a popular choice. For dessert, it's hard to top the cannoli at **Scialo Bros. Bakery.** If you're visiting in early June, sample authentic eats from all over Italy, while live music fills the streets, during the Federal Hill Stroll. On summer nights, catch a Paw Sox baseball game at McCoy

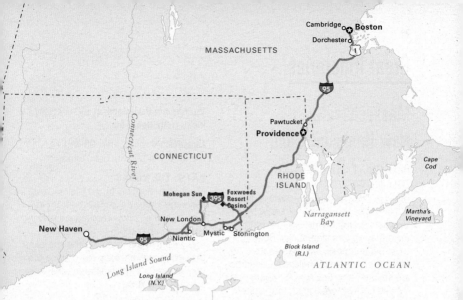

Stadium in the neighboring town of **Pawtucket,** home of the beloved Triple-A farm team for the Boston Red Sox. Also in the warmer months, typically late May–early November, Providence hosts **WaterFire,** a public celebration of art and performance. The festival's 100 bonfires on the rivers of downtown Providence attracts tens of thousands of viewers each year for the popular event. Spend the night in a downtown Providence hotel for easy access to sights and restaurants.

DAYS 4 AND 5: BOSTON

A short drive north on Interstate 95 will bring you to **Boston,** New England's cultural and commercial hub. To savor Boston's centuries-old ties to the sea, take a half-day stroll past **Faneuil Hall** and **Quincy Market** or a boat tour of the harbor (you can even head out on a whale-watching tour from here). In Boston, famous buildings such as Faneuil Hall are not merely civic landmarks, but national icons. From the **Boston Common,** the 2.5-mile **Freedom Trail** links treasures of America's struggle for independence, such as the **USS *Constitution*** (better known as "Old Ironsides") and **Old North Church** (of "one

if by land, two if by sea" fame). Be sure to walk the gas-lighted streets of **Beacon Hill,** too. Boston's **North End** is the oldest residential neighborhood in the city, and has great dining options like **Antico Forno,** which offers pizza baked in a wood-burning brick oven.

The following day, either explore the massive **Museum of Fine Arts** and the grand boulevards and shops of **Back Bay,** or visit colorful **Cambridge,** home of **Harvard University** and the **Massachusetts Institute of Technology (MIT).** Lively **Harvard Square** is a perfect place to do some people-watching or catch a street performance; the **All Star Sandwich Bar** is an excellent choice for lunch. For an experience unique to the Boston area, head a few miles south of the city along U.S. 1 to Dorchester's **Boston Bowl** to cap off your trip with candlepin bowling. Here, at all hours of the night, Bay Staters play a smaller version of 10-pin bowling that uses balls weighing less than 3 pounds and allows participants to bowl three balls per frame instead of two.

Logistics: 50 miles; via I–95 N and I–93 N; 1 hour, starting in Providence.

Great Itineraries

Massachusetts, New Hampshire, and Maine, 7 Days

Revel in the coast beauty of three New England states—Massachusetts, New Hampshire, and Maine—on the path from the region's largest city, Boston, to its highest peak, Mt. Washington. An assortment of New England's treasures are at your fingertips as you negotiate the ins and outs of the jagged northeastern coastline, before ascending the heights of the White Mountains.

Fly in: Logan International Airport (BOS), Boston

Fly out: Logan International Airport (BOS), Boston

DAY 1: THE NORTH SHORE AND NEW HAMPSHIRE COAST

After flying into Boston, pick up a rental car and head for the North Shore of Massachusetts. In **Salem**, the **Peabody Essex Museum** and the **Salem Maritime National Historic Site** chronicle the evolution of the country's early shipping fortunes. Spend some time exploring more of the North Shore, including the old fishing port of **Gloucester**, and **Rockport**, a great place to find that seascape rendered in oils. **Newburyport**, with its Federal-style ship-owners' homes, is home to the **Parker River National Wildlife Refuge**, beloved by birders and beach walkers.

New Hampshire fronts the Atlantic for a scant 18 miles, but its coastal landmarks range from honky-tonk **Hampton Beach** to quiet **Odiorne Point State Park** in Rye and urbane and historic Portsmouth, where pre-Revolutionary high society built Georgian- and Federal-style mansions—visit a few at the **Strawbery Banke Museum**. Stay the night in **Portsmouth** at the centrally located **Ale House Inn.**

Logistics: 64 miles; via I–95 N; 1 hour 10 minutes, starting at Logan airport.

DAY 2: THE YORKS

Much of the appeal of the Maine Coast lies in geographical contrast—from its long stretches of swimming and walking beaches in the south to the rugged, rocky cliffs in the north. As the shoreline physically evolves, each town along the way reveals a slightly different character, starting with **York.**

In **York Village** take a leisurely stroll through the buildings of the **Museums of Old York** getting a glimpse of 18th-century life in this gentrified town. Spend time wandering between shops or walking nature trails and beaches around York Harbor. There are several grand lodging options here, most with views of the harbor. If you prefer a livelier pace, continue on to **York Beach,** a haven for families with plenty of entertainment venues. Stop at Fox's Lobster House after visiting **Nubble Light** for a seaside lunch or dinner.

Logistics: 10 miles; via I–95 N; 15 minutes, starting in Portsmouth.

DAY 3: OGUNQUIT AND THE KENNEBUNKS

For well over a century, **Ogunquit** has been a favorite vacation spot for those looking to combine the natural beauty of the ocean with a sophisticated environment. Take a morning walk along the Marginal Way to see the waves crashing against the rocks. In **Perkins Cove,** have lunch, stroll the shopping areas, or sign on with a lobster-boat cruise to learn about Maine's most important fishery— the state's lobster industry satisfies more than 90% of the world's appetite.

Head north to the Kennebunks, allowing at least two hours to wander through the shops and historic homes of Dock Square in **Kennebunkport.** This is an ideal place to rent a bike and ramble around backstreets, head out Ocean Avenue past large mansions, or ride to one of several beaches to relax awhile. Spend your third night in Kennebunkport.

Logistics: 22 miles; via I–95 N and Rte. 9 E; 30 minutes, starting in York.

DAYS 4 AND 5: PORTLAND
If you have time, you can easily spend several days in **Portland,** Maine's largest city, exploring its historic neighborhoods, shopping and eating in the **Old Port,** or visiting one of several excellent museums. A brief side trip to **Cape Elizabeth** takes you to **Portland Head Light,** Maine's first lighthouse, which was commissioned by George Washington in 1787. The lighthouse is on the grounds of Fort Williams Park and is an excellent place for a picnic; be sure to spend some time wandering the ample grounds. There are also excellent walking trails (and views) at nearby Two Lights State Park. If you want to take a boat tour while in Portland, get a ticket for Casco Bay Lines and see some of the islands that dot the bay. Spend two nights in Portland.

Logistics: 28 miles; via I–95 N; 40 minutes, starting in Kennebunkport.

DAY 6: BRETTON WOODS
Wake up early and drive to **Bretton Woods,** New Hampshire, where you will spend nights six and seven. The driving time from Portland to Bretton Woods is approximately three hours, due to windy two-lane mountain roads. Drive northwest along U.S. 302 toward Sebago Lake, a popular water-sports area in the summer, and continue on toward the time-honored New England towns of Naples and Bridgton. Just 15 miles from the border of New Hampshire, and nearing Crawford Notch, U.S. 302 begins to thread through New Hampshire's **White Mountains,** passing

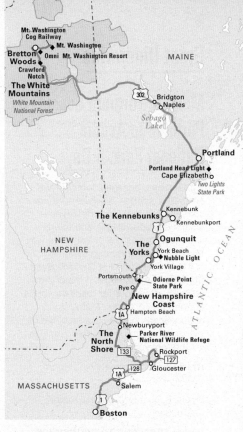

beneath brooding **Mt. Washington** before arriving in Bretton Woods.

Logistics: 98 miles; via Rte. 113 N and U.S. 302 W; 3 hours, starting from Portland.

DAY 7: THE WHITE MOUNTAINS
In Bretton Woods, the **Mount Washington Cog Railway** chugs to the summit, and the **Omni Mount Washington Resort** recalls the glory days of White Mountain resorts. Beloved winter activities here include snowshoeing and skiing on the grounds; you can even zipline. Afterward, defrost with a cup of steaming hot cider while checking out vintage photos of the International Monetary Conference (held here in 1944), or head to the Cave, a Prohibition-era speakeasy, for a drink.

Logistics: 159 miles; via I–93 S; 2½ hours, starting at the Omni Mount Washington Resort and ending in Boston.

Great Itineraries

Maine's Northern Coast: Portland to Acadia National Park, 6 Days

Lighthouses, beaches, lobster rolls, and water sports—Maine's northern coast has something for everyone. Quaint seaside villages and towns line the shore as U.S. 1 winds its way toward the easternmost swath of land in the United States at Quoddy Head State Park. Antiquing is a major draw, so keep an eye out for roadside shops crammed with gems. Maine's only national park, Acadia, is a highlight of the tour, drawing more than 2 million visitors per year.

Fly in: Portland International Jetport (PWM), Portland

Fly out: Bangor International Airport, (BGR), Bangor

DAY 1: PORTLAND TO BRUNSWICK
Use Maine's maritime capital as your jumping-off point to head farther up the Maine Coast, or, as Mainers call it, "Down East." Plan to spend half of your first day in Portland, then head to Brunswick for the night.

Portland shows off its restored waterfront at the **Old Port.** From there, before you depart, you can grab a bite at either of two classic Maine eateries: **Gilbert's Chowder House** or **Becky's Diner,** or check out what's new in the buzzy restaurant scene here. For a peek at the freshest catch of the day, wander over to the **Harbor Fish Market,** a Portland institution since 1968, and gaze upon Maine lobsters and other delectable seafood. Two lighthouses on nearby **Cape Elizabeth, Two Lights** and **Portland Head,** still stand vigil.

Following U.S. 1, travel northeast along the ragged, island-strewn coast of Down East Maine and make your first stop at the retail outlets of **Freeport,** home of **L.L. Bean.** Almost 3 million people visit the massive flagship store every year, where you can find everything from outerwear to camping equipment. Just 10 miles north of Freeport on U.S. 1, **Brunswick** is home to the campus of **Bowdoin College,** the superb **Bowdoin College Museum of Art,** and also features a superb coastline for kayaking. Plan for dinner and an overnight in Bath.

Logistics: 30 miles; via U.S. 1 N; 30 minutes from Portland airport.

DAY 2: BATH
In **Bath,** Maine's shipbuilding capital, tour the **Maine Maritime Museum,** stopping for lunch on the waterfront. Check out the boutiques and antiques shops, or take in the plenitude of beautiful homes. From here it's a 30-minute detour down Route 127 to Georgetown Island and Reid State Park, where you will find a quiet beach lining Sheepscot Bay—and maybe even a sand dollar or two to take home, if you arrive at low tide. For a stunning vista, make your way to Griffith Head.

Drive north and reconnect with U.S. 1. Continue through the towns of **Wiscasset** and **Damariscotta,** where you may find yourself pulling over to stop at the outdoor flea markets and intriguing antiques shops that line the road. Another hour from here is **Rockland,** where you'll spend your second night.

Logistics: 52 miles; via U.S. 1 N; 1 hour 15 minutes, starting in Brunswick.

DAY 3: ROCKLAND, CAMDEN, AND CASTINE
From Rockland, spend the day cruising on a majestic schooner or reserve a tee time at Somerset Resorts' 18-hole

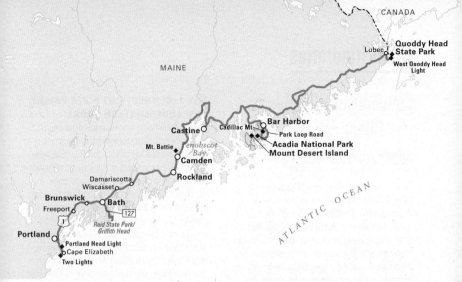

championship course that overlooks the Rockland Harbor. If you're an art lover, save some time for Rockland's **Farnsworth Art Museum,** the **Wyeth Center,** and the **Maine Center for Contemporary Art.**

In **Camden** and **Castine,** exquisite inns occupy homes built from inland Maine's gold and timber. Camden is an ideal place to stay overnight as you make your way closer to Acadia National Park; it is a beautiful seaside town with hundreds of boats bobbing in the harbor, immaculately kept antique homes, streets lined with boutiques and specialty stores, and restaurants serving lobster at every turn. The modest hills (by Maine standards, anyway) of nearby Mt. Battie offer good hiking and a great spot from which to picnic and view the surrounding area. It is also one of the hubs for the beloved and historic windjammer fleet—there is no better way to see the area than from the deck of one of these graceful beauties.

Logistics: 62 miles; via U.S. 1 N and Rte. 166 S; 1½ hours, starting in Rockland.

DAYS 4 AND 5: MOUNT DESERT ISLAND AND ACADIA NATIONAL PARK
On Day 4, head out early for **Bar Harbor** and plan to spend two nights here, using the bustling village as jumping-off point for the park—Bar Harbor is less than 5 miles from the entrance to **Mount Desert Island** 's 27-mile Park Loop Road. Spend at least a day exploring **Acadia National Park,** Maine's only national park and its most popular tourist destination. Enjoy the island's natural beauty by kayaking its coast, biking the 45-mile, historic, unpaved, carriage-road system, and driving to the summit of **Cadillac Mountain** for a stunning panorama.

Logistics: 52 miles; via Rte. 166 N, U.S. 1 N and Rte. 3 E; 1¼ hours, starting in Castine.

DAY 6: BAR HARBOR TO QUODDY HEAD STATE PARK
About 100 miles farther along U.S. 1 and "Way Down East" is Quoddy Head State Park in Lubec, Maine. Here, on the easternmost tip of land in the United States, sits the **West Quoddy Head Light,** one of 60 lighthouses that dot Maine's rugged coastline. Depending on the time of year (and your willingness to get up very early), you may be lucky enough to catch the East Coast's first sunrise here.

Logistics: 103 miles; via U.S. 1 N; 2½ hours, starting in Bar Harbor. From the park, it is 119 miles (2½ hours) to the Bangor airport via Rte. 9 W.

Great Itineraries

Connecticut Wineries and Rhode Island Mansions, 5 Days

Travel through the Lower Connecticut River Valley as you meander toward the eastern section of the state's Wine Trail. While you sample varietals from the area's best wineries, get a taste of New England's literary and maritime history along the way. Stay overnight in seaside Mystic, another highlight, and then finish your tour by gawking at Newport's grand mansions and strolling the gorgeous Cliff Walk.

Fly in: Bradley International Airport (BGR), Hartford

Fly out: T. F. Green Airport (PVD), Warwick

DAY 1: HARTFORD
Start your journey in **Hartford,** Connecticut. The **Mark Twain House and Museum,** which Samuel Clemens and his wife built in the city's Victorian neighborhood of Nook Farm, is adjacent to the **Harriet Beecher Stowe Center,** which is also worth a visit. Downtown, you can visit the Nutmeg State's ornate **State Capitol** and the **Wadsworth Atheneum Museum of Art,** which houses fine Impressionist and Hudson River School paintings. Sports fans, take note: the **Naismith Memorial Basketball Hall of Fame** is only a quick detour up Interstate 91, in **Springfield,** Massachusetts, where Dr. James Naismith invented basketball in 1891. Spend your first night in Hartford.

DAY 2: CONNECTICUT RIVER VALLEY AND SOUTHEASTERN SHORE
Just a half-hour southeast of Hartford along Route 2 is your first wine stop, Priam Vineyards, in Colchester. Sample any of the boutique wines before bearing south on Route 149 to explore the centuries-old river towns of **East Haddam,** Chester, and **Essex.** In East Haddam, stop at Gillette Castle State Park—with its medieval-style stone mansion built for actor William Gillette—before crossing the Connecticut River on the historic (since 1769), eight-car Hadlyme-Chester ferry (April–November). In Essex, take a ride on the **Essex Steam Train**—the 12-mile excursion showcases the area's well-preserved countryside. (You can also return to Essex via riverboat.)

Continue on to **Mystic,** where the days of wooden ships and whaling adventures live on at **Mystic Seaport.** This world-class museum offers a peek into the past with restored vessels, historic buildings, figureheads, ship carvings, and much more. Spend your second night in Mystic.

Logistics: 60 miles; via Rte. 2 E; 1 hour, starting in Hartford (not including stops).

DAY 3: CONNECTICUT WINE TRAIL
A patchwork of six wineries—the heart of the eastern section of the **Connecticut Wine Trail**—sits in the southeastern corner of the state. Taste through the portfolio at each of the picturesque vineyards until you find the perfect bottle to take home; many wineries offer self-guided walks through peaceful vineyards, allowing you to roam on your own. **Stonington Vineyards** has daily guided tours, and Jonathan Edwards Winery,

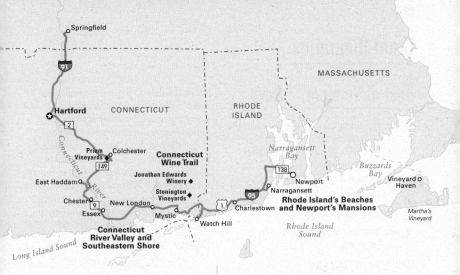

farther inland in North Stonington, is a serene setting for picnics. Cap off the day by crossing the state line into Rhode Island and spend the night in **Watch Hill.** You can wander the grounds of the **Watch Hill Lighthouse;** in its museum, open midweek afternoons in summer, you can see the original Fresnel lens, a binnacle, mariners' sea chests, and historical documents and photos about the lighthouse and the area.

Logistics: 13½ miles; via U.S. 1 N; 25 minutes, starting in Mystic (not including stops).

DAYS 4 AND 5: RHODE ISLAND'S BEACHES AND NEWPORT'S MANSIONS

En route to Newport along U.S. 1 from **Watch Hill,** sandy beaches dot the coast from Misquamicut and Weekapaug to **Charlestown** and **Narragansett.** If it's summer and the weather is fine, spend the afternoon at the beach before continuing on to Newport. Despite its Colonial downtown and seaside parks, to most people **Newport** means mansions—the most opulent enclave of private homes

ever built in the United States. Turn-of-the-20th-century "summer cottages" such as the **Breakers** and **Marble House** are must-sees. Embark on the scenic **Cliff Walk** for remarkable views of these great houses on one side and the Atlantic Ocean on the other. Newport's downtown is excellent for window-shopping, and there are plenty of places to enjoy fresh seafood.

Newport is known to many as the sailing capital of the East Coast, and you may get the best feel for it from the deck of a schooner cruising its famous harbor. Tours generally last around 90 minutes, and some offer beverages and snacks. Tennis enthusiasts can visit the **International Tennis Hall of Fame,** which, along with exhibits focusing on the legends of the game, has a unique interior designed by architect Stanford White. You can easily spend a few days exploring Newport.

Logistics: 39½ miles; via U.S. 1 N; 1 hour, starting in Watch Hill. From Newport, it is 26 miles (30 minutes) to T. F. Green Airport via RI 138 W and RI 4 N.

Great Itineraries

Best of Vermont, 7 Days

Following roads that weave through the Green Mountains and charming towns, this 200-mile journey is ideal at any time of year and covers Vermont from top to bottom.

Fly in: Bradley International Airport (BDL), Hartford

Fly out: Burlington International Airport (BTV), Burlington

DAY 1: BRATTLEBORO

Artsy **Brattleboro** is the perfect place to begin a tour of Vermont, and it's worth taking a day to do some shopping and exploring. Catch a movie at the art deco **Latchis Theatre,** browse in a bookstore, or simply grab a cup of joe and people-watch. For dinner, make a reservation well in advance at tiny **T.J. Buckley's,** one of the best restaurants in the state. Spend your first night in Brattleboro.

Logistics: 78 miles; via I–91 N; 1 hour and 15 minutes from Bradley airport.

DAYS 2-4: KILLINGTON

Depart Brattleboro heading west on Route 9 and link up with Route 100 in Wilmington. As you travel north along the eastern edge of **Green Mountain National Forest,** you'll pass a plethora of panoramic overlooks and delightful ski towns. Stop to snap a photo, or take a moment to peruse the selection at a funky general store, as you make your way toward gigantic Killington Peak. Spend the next three nights in **Killington,** the largest ski resort in Vermont, and an outdoor playground year-round. A tip for skiers: one of the closest places to the slopes to stay is **The Mountain Top Inn & Resort.**

Wake up early to carve the mountain's fresh powder in winter. Nonskiers can still enjoy the snow, whether at the tubing park, on a snowmobile adventure, or in snowshoes on one of several trails. In summer, long after the ground has thawed, those trails are opened to mountain bikers and hikers. For a more leisurely activity, try your hand at the 18-hole disc-golf course. The excellent Grand Spa is also a lovely way to spend the day.

Logistics: 94 miles; via Rte. 9 W, Rte. 100 N, 2½ hours, starting in Brattleboro.

DAY 5: KILLINGTON TO BURLINGTON

Continue on Route 100 north until you reach Hancock, then head west on Route 125. Welcome to the land of poet Robert Frost, who spent almost 40 years living in Vermont, summering in the nearby tiny mountain town of Ripton, where he wrote numerous poems. Plaques along the 1.2-mile **Robert Frost Interpretive Trail,** a quiet woodland walk that takes about 30 minutes, display commemorative quotes from his poems, including his classic, "The Road Not Taken." After your stroll, head north on U.S. 7 until you hit Burlington.

Burlington, Vermont's largest city and home to the **University of Vermont,** is located on the eastern shore of Lake Champlain. Bustling in the summer and fall, the **Burlington Farmers' Market** is filled with everything from organic meats and cheeses to freshly cut flowers and maple syrup. Spend the night in Burlington. In the evening, check out **Nectar's,** where the band Phish played their first bar gig, or wander into any of the many other pubs and cafés that attract local musicians.

Logistics: 84 miles; via Rte. 100 N, Rte. 125 W, and U.S. 7 N; 2½ hours, starting in Killington.

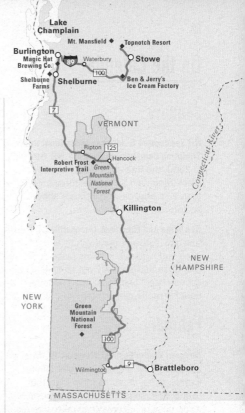

DAY 6: SHELBURNE AND LAKE CHAMPLAIN

On your second day in Burlington, you can take a day trip south to the **Magic Hat Brewing Company**; established in 1994, it was at the forefront of Vermont's micro-brewery explosion. Take a free half-hour guided or self-guided tour of the Artifactory (even dogs are welcome), and fill a growler from one of the 48 taps pumping out year-round, seasonal, and experimental brews. A stone's throw down U.S. 7, in **Shelburne,** is family-friendly **Shelburne Farms.** Watch the process of making cheese from start to finish, or wander the gorgeous 1,400-acre estate designed by Frederick Law Olmsted, co-designer of New York's Central Park. The grounds overlook beautiful **Lake Champlain** and make the perfect setting for a picnic. In winter Shelburne Farms offers sleigh rides and other themed activities; if you're visiting in late July, don't miss the **Vermont Cheesemakers Festival,** showcasing more than 200 varieties of cheese crafted by 40 local purveyors. If you can't get enough, you can opt to spend the night here.

Logistics: 3.6 miles, via U.S. 7 to Magic Hat; another 3.4 miles to Shelburne Farms; 40 minutes round-trip altogether.

DAY 7: STOWE

A 30-minute drive down Interstate 89 from Burlington reunites you with Route 100 in the town of Waterbury. Head north in the direction of Stowe, and in under 2 miles you can make the obligatory pit stop at **Ben & Jerry's Ice Cream Factory.** The factory tour offers a lively behind-the-scenes look at how their ice cream is made; at the end of the tour, you get to taste limited-release creations only available at the factory before voting on your favorites.

Next, set out for the village of **Stowe.** Its proximity to Mt. Mansfield (Vermont's highest peak at 4,395 feet) has made Stowe a popular ski destination since the 1930s. If there's snow on the ground, hit the slopes, hitch a ride on a one-horse open sleigh, or simply put your feet up by the fire and enjoy a Heady Topper (an unfiltered, hoppy, American Double IPA beloved by beer aficionados the world over). In warmer weather, pop into the cute shops and art galleries that line the town's main street and sample some of the finest cheddar cheese and maple syrup that Vermont has to offer. Rejuvenate yourself at **Topnotch Resort,** which offers more than 100 different treatments. Spend your final night here.

Logistics: 36 miles; via I–89 S and Rte. 100 N; 45 minutes, starting in Burlington. From Stowe to the Burlington airport: 33 miles; via Rte. 100 and I–89 N; 41 minutes.

On the Calendar

January

NH Sanctioned & Jackson Invitational Snow Sculpting Competition, Jackson, NH. Started in 2000, the free event takes places at Black Mountain Ski and features more than 12 teams carving intricate snow sculptures. ⊕ *jacksonnh.com*

Sun Wine and Food Fest, Uncasville, CT. This four-day festival, Connecticut's largest wine and food event, takes place at Mohegan Sun and features tastings, chef appearances, and cooking demonstrations. ⊕ *mohegansun.com*

February

Newport Winter Festival, Newport, RI. What's billed as "New England's Largest Winter Extravaganza" features more than 150 events that range from food and music to a chili cook-off. ⊕ *www.newportwinterfestival.com*

Winter Carnival, Dartmouth, NH. Started in 1911, Dartmouth's winter festival celebrates the season with races, polar bear plunges, and snow sculpture contests. ⊕ *students.dartmouth.edu/collis/events/winter-carnival*

March

Connecticut Spring Antiques Show, Hartford, CT. Started in 1973, this is the premier gathering for collectors of early American furniture and decorative arts. ⊕ *www.ctspringshow.com*

April

Vermont Maple Festival, St. Albans, VT. This weekend is all about syrup. There's a pancake breakfast, a carnival and parade, and, of course, plenty of yummy maple treats. ⊕ *www.facebook.com/VermontMapleFestival*

May

Brimfield Antique and Collectible Shows, Brimfield, MA. Since the 1950s, Brimfield has welcomed thousands of visitors for a weeklong antiques and flea market extravaganza every May, July, and September. ⊕ *www.brimfieldantiquefleamarket.com*

WaterFire, Providence, RI. Late May through early November, more than 80 bonfires are lit on the city's three rivers on select weekends. ⊕ *waterfire.org*

June

Elephant's Trunk Country Flea Market, New Milford, CT. Open Sunday from late March through mid-December, Elephant's Trunk features antiques, up-cyclers, farm stands, food stalls, and vendors of all kinds. ⊕ *www.etflea.com*

Festival of Historic Homes, Providence, RI. Hosted by the Providence Preservation Society, this series of home tours highlights the city's historic neighborhoods, architecture, and history. ⊕ *www.providencehousetour.com*

Jacob's Pillow Dance Festival, Beckett, MA. This acclaimed festival, held mid-June through August, features more than 350 free performances, talks, tours, exhibits, community events, and classes. ⊕ *www.jacobspillow.org*

Strolling of the Heifers, Brattleboro, VT. An annual local food-focused showcase includes a parade of about 100 cows dressed in their Sunday best. ⊕ *www.strollingoftheheifers.com*

July

Harborfest, Boston, MA. Boston's yearly festivities centered around Independence Day include the hugely popular Chowderfest cook-off as well as a parade and fireworks show. ⊕ *www.bostonharborfest.com*

Sailfest, New London, CT. A weekend of fireworks, music on multiple stages, more than 200 vendors lining the streets, and boat cruises draw visitors to Connecticut's southeastern shore. ⊕ *sailfest.org*

Vermont Cheesemakers Festival, Shelburne, VT. Artisanal cheeses and local beer and wine highlight this daylong festival that features samples of more than 200 cheese varieties from 40 artisan cheese makers. ⊕ *www.vtcheesefest.com*

August

League of New Hampshire Craftsmen's Fair, Newbury, NH. More than 350 talented artisans show their diverse wares at the nation's oldest juried crafts festival, held since 1940 over nine days at Mt. Sunapee Resort. ⊕ *www.wiltonbbf.com*

Maine Lobster Festival, Rockland, ME. Stuff your face with lobster tails and claws during this "lobstravaganza" that puts almost 20,000 pounds of delicious crustacean at your finger tips. ⊕ *www.mainelobsterfestival.com*

Wilton Blueberry Festival, Wilton, ME. You can pick your own wild blueberries and sample baked goods from pancakes to pies at the annual festival. ⊕ *www.wiltonbbf.com*

September

The Big E, West Springfield, MA. Also known as the Eastern States Exposition, this is the eastern seaboard's largest agricultural fair. ⊕ *www.thebige.com*

October

New Hampshire Pumpkin Festival, Laconia, NH. This family-friendly gathering near Lake Winnipesaukee tries to outdo itself each October by featuring the most lighted pumpkins. ⊕ *www.nhpumpkinfestival.com*

Salem Haunted Happenings, Salem, MA. This monthlong celebration's activities range from ghost tours and psychic readings to family-friendly events and art exhibits. ⊕ *www.hauntedhappenings.org*

Wellfleet OysterFest, Wellfleet, MA. This deliciously entertaining weekend celebrates the town's famous mollusk with food, art, and music. ⊕ *www.wellfleetoysterfest.org*

November

America's Hometown Thanksgiving Celebration, Plymouth, MA. Celebrated the weekend before Thanksgiving in the holiday's birthplace, this event focuses on history, Americana, Pilgrims, and Native Americans. ⊕ *usathanksgiving.com*

December

Winter Wassail Weekend, Woodstock, VT. The annual fete features a parade with holiday-costume clad horses and riders, live music, house tours, kids' activities, and a Wassail Feast. ⊕ *www.woodstockvt.com*

Contacts

✈ Air

AIRPORTS Albany International Airport. ☎ 518/242–2200 ⊕ www.albanyairport.com. **Bangor International Airport.** ☎ 207/992–4600 ⊕ www.flybangor.com. **Barnstable Municipal Airport.** ✉ 480 Barnstable Rd., Hyannis ☎ 508/775–2020 ⊕ www.town.barnstable.ma.us/airport. **Bradley International Airport.** ☎ 860/292–2000 ⊕ www.bradleyairport.com. **Burlington International Airport.** ☎ 802/863–2874 ⊕ www.btv.aero. **Logan International Airport.** ☎ 800/235–6426 ⊕ www.massport.com Ⓜ Blue, Silver. **Manchester-Boston Regional Airport.** ☎ 603/624–6539 ⊕ www.flymanchester.com. **Martha's Vineyard Airport.** ✉ 71 Airport Rd., West Tisbury ☎ 508/693–7022 ⊕ www.mvyairport.com. **Nantucket Memorial Airport.** ✉ 14 Airport Rd., Nantucket ☎ 508/325–5300 ⊕ www.nantucketairport.com. **Portland International Jetport.** ☎ 207/774–7301 ⊕ www.portlandjetport.org. **Provincetown Municipal Airport.** ☎ 508/487–0241 ⊕ www.provincetown-ma.gov. **T. F. Green International Airport.** ☎ 401/737–8222 ⊕ www.pvdairport.com. **Westchester County Airport.** ☎ 914/995–4860 ⊕ airport.westchestergov.com.

AIRLINE CONTACTS Cape Air. ☎ 800/227–3247 ⊕ www.capeair.com. **New England Airlines.** ☎ 800/243–2460 ⊕ www.blockislandsairline.com.

⛴ Boat

Bay State Cruise Company. ✉ Commonwealth Pier, 200 Seaport Blvd., Boston ☎ 617/748–1428, 877/783–3779 ⊕ baystatecruisecompany.com. **Boston Harbor Cruises.** ✉ Long Wharf, 1 Seaport La., Boston ☎ 877/733–9425, 617/227–4321, 877/733–9425 ⊕ www.bostonharborcruises.com. **Freedom Cruise Line.** ✉ Saquatucket Harbor, 702 Main St., Harwich Port ☎ 508/432–8999 ⊕ www.nantucketislandferry.com. **Hy-Line Cruises.** ✉ Hyannis Terminal, 220 Ocean St., Hyannis ☎ 800/492–8082 ⊕ www.hylinecruises.com. **Island Queen.** ✉ 75 Falmouth Heights Rd., Falmouth ☎ 508/548–4800 ⊕ www.islandqueen.com. **Seastreak.** ✉ 49 State Pier, New Bedford ☎ 800/262–8743 ⊕ www.seastreak.com. **Steamship Authority.** ✉ 1 Cowdry Rd., Woods Hole ☎ 508/477–8600 ⊕ www.steamshipauthority.com. **Vineyard Fast Ferry.** ✉ 1347 Quonset Rd., North Kingstown ☎ 401/295–4040 ⊕ www.vineyardfastferry.com.

🚆 Train

Amtrak. ☎ 800/872–7245 ⊕ www.amtrak.com. **Massachusetts Bay Transportation Authority.** (MBTA). ☎ 617/222–3200 ⊕ www.mbta.com. **Metro-North Railroad.** ☎ 511 within New York State, 877/690–5114 from Connecticut ⊕ www.mta.info/mnr. **Shore Line East.** ☎ 877/287–4337 ⊕ www.shorelineeast.com.

📍 Visitor Information

Connecticut Office of Tourism. ☎ 888/288–4748 ⊕ www.ctvisit.com. **Greater Boston Convention & Visitors Bureau.** ☎ 888/733–2678 ⊕ www.bostonusa.com. **Maine Office of Tourism.** ☎ 888/624–6345 ⊕ www.visitmaine.com. **Massachusetts Office of Travel and Tourism.** ☎ 800/227–6277, 617/973–8500 ⊕ www.visitma.com. **New Hampshire Division of Travel and Tourism Development.** ☎ 800/386–4664 ⊕ www.visitnh.gov. **New England Today.** ⊕ www.newengland.com. **Rhode Island Tourism Division.** ☎ 800/556–2484 ⊕ www.visitrhodeisland.com. **Vermont Department of Tourism and Marketing.** ☎ 800/837–6668 ⊕ www.vermontvacation.com. **Visit New England.** ⊕ www.visitnewengland.com.

BEST FALL FOLIAGE DRIVES AND ROAD TRIPS

3

A CELEBRATION

Picture this: one scarlet maple offset by the stark white spire of a country church, a whole hillside of brilliant foliage foregrounded by a vintage barn, or perhaps a covered bridge straddling a cobalt river. Such iconic scenes have launched a thousand Instagram posts and turned New England into the ultimate fall destination for leaf peepers.

OF COLOR

By Susan MacCallum-Whitcomb

Above, Vermont's Green Mountains are multicolored in the fall (and often white in winter).

Mother Nature, of course, puts on an annual autumn performance elsewhere, but this one is a showstopper. Like the landscape, the mix of deciduous (leaf-shedding) trees is remarkably varied here and creates a broader than usual palette. New England's abundant evergreens lend contrast, making the display even more vivid. Every September and October, leaf peepers arrive to cruise along country lanes, join outdoor adventures, or simply stroll on town greens.

Did you know the brilliant shades actually lurk in the leaves all year long? Leaves contain three pigments. The green chlorophyll, so dominant in summer that it obscures the red anthocyanins and orangey-yellow carotenoids, decreases in fall and reveals a crayon box of color.

PREDICTING THE PEAK

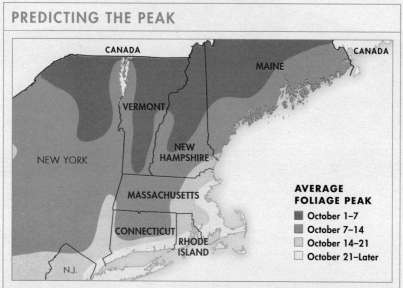

AVERAGE FOLIAGE PEAK
- October 1–7
- October 7–14
- October 14–21
- October 21–Later

LOCATION

Pinning down precisely when colors will appear remains an inexact science, although location plays a major role. Typically, the transformation begins in the highest and northernmost parts of New England in mid-September, then moves steadily into lower altitudes and southern sectors throughout October.

For trip planning, think in terms of regions rather than states. In Maine (a huge state that runs north–south) leaf color can peak anytime from the fourth week of September to the third week of October, depending on the locale.

WEATHER

Early September weather is another deciding factor. From the foliage aficionado's perspective, the ideal scenario is calm, temperate days capped by nights that are cool but still above freezing. If the weather is too warm, it delays the onset of the season. If it's too dry or windy, the leaves shrivel up or blow off.

COLOR CHECK RESOURCES

Curious about current conditions? In season, most states maintain websites reporting on foliage conditions. Weather Channel has peak viewing maps and Foliage Network uses a network of spotters to chart changes.

- **Connecticut:** ☎ 800/282–6863
  ⊕ www.ct.gov/dep
- **Foliage Network:**
  ⊕ www.foliagenetwork.com
- **Maine:** ☎ 888/624–6345
  ⊕ www.mainefoliage.com
- **Massachusetts:** ☎ 800/227–6277
  ⊕ www.massvacation.com

- **New Hampshire:** ☎ 800/258–3608
  ⊕ www.visitnh.gov
- **Rhode Island:** ☎ 800/556–2484
  ⊕ www.visitrhodeisland.com
- **Vermont:** ☎ 800/837–6668
  ⊕ www.vermontvacation.com
- **Weather Channel:** ⊕ www.weather.com

TOP TREES FOR COLOR

A **AMERICAN BEECH.** This tree's smooth, steel-gray trunk is crowned with gold, copper, and bronze-tinted leaves in autumn, giving it a metallic sheen. Though the elliptical leaves sometimes hang on all winter, its "fruit" goes fast because beechnuts are a popular snack for birds, squirrels, and even bears.

B **NORTHERN RED OAK.** The upside of oaks is that they retain their fall shading until late in the season—the downside is that, for most species, that color is a boring brown. Happily, the northern red isn't like other members of the oak family. Its elongated, flame-shaped leaves turn fiery crimson and incandescent orange.

C **QUAKING ASPEN.** Eyes and ears both prove useful when identifying this aspen. Look for small, ovate leaves that usually become almost flaxen. Or listen for the leaves' quake: a sound, audible in even a gentle breeze, which the U.S. Forest Service likens to that made by "thousands of fluttering butterfly wings."

D **SUGAR MAPLE.** The leaf of the largest North American maple species is so lovely that Canada put it on its national flag. Each generally has five multi-pointed lobes—plus enough anthocyanin to produce a deep red color. The tree itself produces plentiful sap and is the cornerstone of New England's syrup industry.

E **WHITE ASH.** This tall tree typically grows to between 65 to 100 feet. Baseball enthusiasts admire the wood (which is used to craft bats); while foliage fans admire the compound leaves, each consisting of five to nine slightly serrated, tapering leaflets. They range in hue from burgundy and purple to amber.

F **WHITE BIRCH.** A papery, light, bright bark makes this slender hardwood easily recognizable. Centuries ago, Native Americans used birch wood to make everything from canoes to medicinal teas. Today's photographers know the bark also makes great pictures since it provides a sharp contrast to the tree's vibrant yellow leaves.

FANTASTIC FALL ITINERARY

The Berkshires

Fall is the perfect time to visit New England—country roads wind through dense forests exploding into reds, oranges, yellows, and purples. For inspiration, here is an itinerary for the truly ambitious that links the most stunning foliage areas; choose a section to explore more closely. Like autumn itself, this route works its way south from northern Vermont into Connecticut, with one or two days in each area.

VERMONT

NORTHWEST VERMONT

In Burlington, the elms will be turning colors on the University of Vermont campus. You can ride the ferry across Lake Champlain for great views of Vermont's Green Mountains and New York's Adirondacks. After visiting the resort town of Stowe, detour off Route 100 beneath the cliffs of Smugglers' Notch. The north country's palette unfolds in Newport, where the blue waters of Lake Memphremagog reflect the foliage.

NORTHEAST KINGDOM

After a side trip along Lake Willoughby, explore St. Johnsbury, where the Fairbanks Museum and St. Johnsbury Athenaeum reveal Victorian tastes in art and natural-history collecting. In Peacham, stock up for a picnic at the Peacham Store.

NEW HAMPSHIRE

WHITE MOUNTAINS AND LAKES REGION

In New Hampshire, Interstate 93 narrows as it winds through craggy Franconia Notch. Get off the interstate for the sinuous Kancamagus Highway portion of Route 112 that passes through the mountains to Conway. In Center Harbor, in the Lakes Region, you can ride the *MS Mount Washington* for views of the Lake Winnipesaukee shoreline, or ascend to Moultonborough's Castle in the Clouds for a falcon's-eye look at the colors.

MT. MONADNOCK

In Concord, stop at the Museum of New Hampshire History and the State House. Several trails climb Mt. Monadnock, near Jaffrey Center, and colorful vistas extend as far as Boston.

⇨ **For local drives perfect for an afternoon, also see our Fall Foliage Drive Spotlights on Western Massachusetts, Connecticut, Rhode Island, Vermont, New Hampshire, and Inland Maine.**

THE MOOSE IS LOOSE!

Take "Moose Crossing" signs seriously because things won't end well if you hit an animal that stands six feet tall and weighs 1,200 pounds. Some 40,000 reside in northern New England. To search out these ungainly creatures in the wild, consider an organized moose safari in northern New Hampshire or Maine.

MASSACHUSETTS
THE MOHAWK TRAIL
In Shelburne Falls, Massachusetts, the Bridge of Flowers displays the last of autumn's blossoms. Follow the Mohawk Trail section of Route 2 as it ascends into the Berkshire Hills—and stop to take in the view at the hairpin turn just east of North Adams (or drive up Mt. Greylock, the tallest peak in New England, for more stunning vistas). In Williamstown, the Clark Art Institute houses a collection of impressionist works.

THE BERKSHIRES
The scenery around Lenox, Stockbridge, and Great Barrington has long attracted the talented and the wealthy. Near U.S. 7, you can visit the homes of novelist Edith Wharton (the Mount, in Lenox), sculptor Daniel Chester French (Chesterwood, in Stockbridge), and diplomat Joseph Choate (Naumkeag, in Stockbridge).

CONNECTICUT
THE LITCHFIELD HILLS
This area of Connecticut combines the feel of upcountry New England with exclusive urban polish. The wooded shores of Lake Waramaug are home to country inns and wineries in pretty towns. Litchfield has a perfect village green—an idealized New England town center.

FOLIAGE PHOTO HINT
Don't just snap the big panoramic views. Look for single, brilliantly colored trees with interesting elements nearby, like a weathered gray stone wall or a freshly painted white church. These images are often more evocative than big blobs of color or panoramic shots.

LEAF PEEPER PLANNER

Hot-air balloons and ski-lift rides give a different perspective on fall's color.

Enjoying fall doesn't necessarily require a multistate road trip. If you are short on time (or energy), a simple autumnal stroll might be just the ticket: many state parks even offer free short ranger-led rambles.

HIKE AND BIKE ON A TOUR

You can sign on for foliage-focused hiking holidays with **Country Walkers** (☎ 800/234–6900 ⊕ www.country-walkers.com) and **Boundless Journeys** (☎ 800/941–8010 ⊕ www.boundless-journeys.com); or cycling ones with **Discovery Bike Tours** (☎ 800/257–2226 ⊕ www.discoverybiketours.com) and **VBT Bicycling Vacations** (☎ 800/245–3868 ⊕ www.vbt.com). Individual state tourism boards list similar operators elsewhere.

SOAR ABOVE THE CROWDS

New Hampshire's Cannon Mountain (☎ 603/823–8800 ⊕ www.cannonmt.com) is only one of several New England ski resorts that provides gondola or aerial tram rides during foliage season. Area hot-air balloon operators, like **Balloons of Vermont, LLC** (☎ 802/369–0213 ⊕ www.balloonsofvermont.com), help you take it in from the top.

ROOM AT THE INN?

Accommodations fill quickly in autumn. Vermont's top lodgings sell out months in advance for the first two weeks in October. So book early and expect a two-night minimum stay requirement. If you can't find a quaint inn, try basing yourself at a B&B or off-season ski resort. Also, be prepared for some sticker shock; if you can travel midweek, you'll often save quite a bit.

RIDE THE RAILS OR THE CURRENT

Board the **Essex Steam Train** for a ride through the Connecticut countryside (☎ 800/377–3987 ⊕ www.essexsteam-train.com) or float through northern Rhode Island on the **Blackstone Valley Explorer** riverboat (☎ 401/724–2200 ⊕ www.rivertourblackstone.com).

MASSACHUSETTS FALL FOLIAGE DRIVE

When fall foliage season arrives, the Berkshires are the place to appreciate the autumnal grandeur. Winding roads lined with dramatic trees ablaze—notably maples, birches, and beeches—pass alongside meadows, pasture, farmland, mountains, rivers, and lakes.

Although this complete scenic loop is only about 35 miles, you could easily spend the day making your way leisurely along the circuit. Begin in North Adams, a city transformed by art, and spend some time at the Massachusetts Museum of Contemporary Art (MASS MoCA). Just west of downtown off Route 2, the Notch Road leads into the **Mt. Greylock State Reservation,** ambling upward to the summit. At 3,491 feet, it's the state's highest point and affords expansive views of the countryside. Hike any of the many trails throughout the park, picnic at the peak, or stay for a meal at the rustic **Bascom Lodge.** Continue your descent on the Notch Road to Rockwell Road to exit the park and join Route 7 South.

BEST TIME TO GO

Peak leaf viewing generally happens in mid-October. Trees growing near water tend to have more vibrant colors that peak a bit sooner. The state regularly updates fall foliage information by phone and online (☎ 800/632–8038 ⊕ www.massvacation.com).

PLANNING YOUR TIME

This scenic loop is only about 35 miles, but you could easily spend the day leisurely exploring the circuit.

Follow Route 7 South into the small town center of Lanesborough, where you'll turn left onto Summer Street. Horse farms and wide-open pastures make up the landscape, with distant mountain peaks hovering grandly in the background. If you want to pick your own apples, take a 1½-mile detour off Summer Street and stop at **Lakeview Orchard.**

Summer Street continues to tiny Berkshire Village, where you'll pick up Route 8 heading back toward North Adams. Running parallel to Route 8 from Lanesborough to Adams, is the paved **Ashuwillticook Rail Trail** for biking and walking. Right in the midst of two mountain ranges, the trail abuts wetlands, mixed woodland (including beech, birch, and maple trees), the Hoosac River, and the Cheshire Reservoir. In Cheshire, **Whitney's Farm Market** is busy on fall weekends with pony rides, pumpkin picking, a corn maze, and hayrides; plus it sells baked goods like the pumpkin whoopie pie.

Continuing on Route 8, you'll start to leave farm country as you make your way back to North Adams. Once a part of its much larger neighbor, the town of Adams still has active mills and the **Susan B. Anthony Birthplace Museum.** The 1817 Federal home of her birth has been fully restored.

NEED A BREAK?

Bascom Lodge. Built in the 1930s, this mountaintop lodge retains its rustic charm with comfortable, no-frills lodging and a restaurant in a stunning setting. ⊠ *Mt. Greylock State Reservation, Adams* ☎ *413/743–1591* ⊕ *www.bascomlodge.net* ⊘ *Closed Nov.–May.*

Lakeview Orchard. Here you can pick your own bushel of apples (and other fall fruit) and sip on freshly pressed cider. The friendly farmers also sell homemade pies and pastries, but make sure to sample their singular (and superb) cider doughnuts. ⊠ *94 Old Cheshire Rd., Lanesborough* ☎ *413/448–6009* ⊕ *www.lakevieworchard.com.*

Whitney's Farm Market. Whitney's Farm has a large market with baked goods and a deli; you can also pick your own seasonal fruit. The fun Pumpkin Fest takes place on weekends, mid-September–October. ⊠ *1775 S. State Rd., Cheshire* ☎ *413/442–4749* ⊕ *www.whitneysfarm.com.*

CONNECTICUT FALL FOLIAGE DRIVE

Tucked into the heart of Litchfield County, the crossroads village of New Preston perches above a 20-foot waterfall on the Aspetuck River. Just north of here, you'll find Lake Waramaug nestled in the rolling foothills and, to the east, Mt. Tom—both ablaze with rich color every fall.

Start in **New Milford** and stroll along historic Main Street. Here you'll find one of the longest town greens in the state, as well as many shops, galleries, and restaurants within a short walk. Hop in the car and drive south on Main Street, then turn left to head north on wooded Route 202. Continue north on Route 202 to the junction of Route 45, follow signs for Lake Waramaug. If you prefer to hike or bike, though, the **New Milford River Trail** extends about 5 miles along the Housatonic River, from Gaylordsville (northwest of the New Milford town green) north to the village of Kent. It's a beautiful walk or ride along a wide gravel trail, with short side routes down to the water, and especially lovely in autumn.

BEST TIME TO GO

Peak foliage occurs early October–early November. In season, the website (⊕ www.ct.gov/deep/foliage) includes daily updates on leaf color. Hope for a wet spring, warmer fall days, and cool (but not too cool) fall nights for the most dramatic display.

PLANNING YOUR TIME

It's less than 30 miles from New Milford to the center of Litchfield, but with stops at the New Milford River Trail, Lake Waramaug, and Mt. Tom you could easily spend most of the day enjoying the scenery.

Route 45 will bring you through the tiny village center of New Preston; stop here for a bit of shopping at **Dawn Hill Antiques.** Continue on 45 north to Lake Waramaug. The 8-mile drive around the lake is stunning in autumn with the fiery foliage of red maples, rusty brown oaks, and yellow birches reflected in the water. The beach area of **Lake Waramaug State Park,** about halfway around the lake, is a great place for a picnic, or even a quick dip on a warm fall day. **Hopkins Vineyard** is open daily for tastings; head to its Hayloft Wine Bar to enjoy a glass of wine and the spectacular lake views.

After completing a loop of Lake Waramaug, head back to Route 202 North toward Litchfield. Another excellent leaf-peeping locale is **Mt. Tom State Park,** about 4 miles or so from the junction of Routes 45 and 202. Here you can hike the mile-long trail to the summit and climb to the top of a stone tower that provides 360-degree views of the countryside's colors—the vibrant reds of the sugar maples are always among the most dazzling. After your hike, continue north on Route 202, ending your journey in the quintessential New England town of Litchfield. Peruse the shops and galleries in the town center and end the day with a dinner at the chic **West Street Grill.**

NEED A BREAK?

Dawn Hill Antiques. This shop is filled with mainly Swedish antiques selected by the owners on their regular trips to Europe. ✉ *11 Main St., New Preston* ☎ *860/868–0066* ⊕ *dawnhillantiques.com.*

Hopkins Vineyard. This winery produces more than 13 different wines, from sparkling to dessert. Tastings are available, and a wine bar in the hayloft with views of the lake serves a fine cheese-and-pâté board. ✉ *25 Hopkins Rd., off N. Shore Rd., New Preston* ☎ *860/868–7954* ⊕ *www.hopkinsvineyard.com* ⮕ *Tours $20.*

West Street Grill. This sophisticated dining room on the town green is the place to see and be seen. It's the perfect spot for a casual lunch or formal dinner. ✉ *43 West St., Litchfield* ☎ *860/567–3885* ⊕ *www.weststreetgrill.com.*

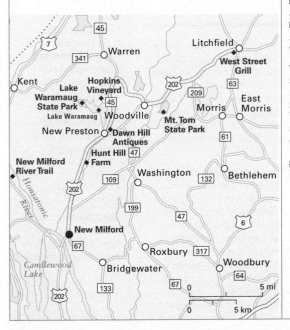

3 Best Fall Foliage Drives and Road Trips · CONNECTICUT FALL FOLIAGE DRIVE

RHODE ISLAND FALL FOLIAGE DRIVE

The Rhode Island state tree is the red maple, whose leaves turn to shades of gold, purple, and scarlet in fall.

This tiny state is also home to such diverse species as scarlet oak, white oak, northern red oak, yellow birch, gray birch, ash, and black cherry. Pine forests dominate the southern woodlands, so the most dramatic leaf peeping is in the northern and western regions. Along the way, you'll find dense forests, rolling meadows with centuries-old stone walls, an occasional orchard or pumpkin patch, and archetypal New England country stores.

This tour through the state's quieter corners begins in **Providence,** where you can stroll along **Benefit Street,** admiring its architectural treasures and trees that burst up through brick sidewalks. Drive north from Providence on Route 122 and then Route 114 North for about 9 miles to Cumberland, a small town with undulating woodland crowned by a canopy of sugar maple, scarlet oak, and birch trees. Stop at **Diamond Hill Vineyards,** whose grapevines and apple trees yield an intriguing selection of wines, including some sweet varieties made from fruits and berries grown on-site—perfect on a cool October day.

BEST TIME TO GO

Foliage peaks in the second and third weeks of October, beginning in the state's northwestern corner and moving south toward the coast. Color can last more than two weeks in years without big storms but with plenty of cool, crisp autumn nights.

PLANNING YOUR TIME

The drive totals about 80 miles and takes four to eight hours, depending on stops.

Drive west about 12 miles on Route 116 to Greenville, turning west on U.S. 44 for 7 miles to the hamlet of Chepachet, where Colonial and Victorian buildings contain antique shops and quirky stores. Don't miss **Brown & Hopkins Country Store,** one of the country's oldest continuously operating general stores—complete with a nostalgia-inducing candy counter—or the **Tavern on Main,** a restaurant in a rambling 18th-century building that some say is haunted.

Follow U.S. 44 West 5 miles to the burst of changing colors in **Pulaski Memorial Recreation Area.** Turn left onto Route 94 and follow this for about 13 miles to Route 102, then continue southeast another 20 miles to Exeter. This mostly undeveloped route from Chepachet to Exeter is lined with red maple, white oak, beech, elm, and poplar trees.

From Route 102, continue east to Wickford, a Colonial seaport whose pretty harbor opens to Narragansett Bay. The town's oak- and beech-shaded lanes are perfect for a late-afternoon stroll among the galleries and boutiques.

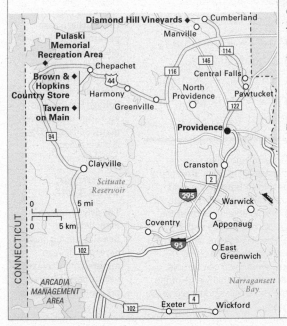

NEED A BREAK?

Brown & Hopkins Country Store. Opened in 1809, this store carries candles, reproduction antiques, penny candy, and handmade soaps. ⊠ *1179 Putnam Pike, Chepachet* ☎ *401/568–4830* ⊕ *www.brownandhopkins.com.*

Diamond Hill Vineyards. This winery produces Pinot Noir from grapes grown on-site, as well as wines made from local apples, blueberries, and other fruit. ⊠ *3145 Diamond Hill Rd., Cumberland* ☎ *401/333–2751* ⊕ *www.diamondhillvineyards.com* ⊠ *Free.*

Pulaski Memorial Recreation Area. The 100-acre recreation area has fishing, picnic spots, easy hiking trails, and the 13-acre Peck Pond. ⊠ *151 Pulaski Rd., Chepachet* ☎ *401/568–2085* ⊕ *www.riparks.com.*

Tavern on Main. Try Rylee's Seafood Bomb (shrimp and scallops over blue crab ravioli topped with lobster) or the Biggest Lobster Roll served on a grilled sub roll. ⊠ *1157 Putnam Pike, Chepachet* ☎ *401/710–9788* ⊕ *www.tavernonmainri.com.*

Best Fall Foliage Drives and Road Trips RHODE ISLAND FALL FOLIAGE DRIVE 3

VERMONT FALL FOLIAGE DRIVE

Nearly 80% of Vermont is forested, with cities few and far between. The state's interior is a rural playground for leaf peepers, and it's widely considered to exhibit the most intense range of colors anywhere on the continent. Its tiny towns and hamlets—the few distractions from the dark reds, yellows, oranges, and russets—are as pristine as nature itself.

Begin this drive in Manchester Village, along the old-fashioned, well-to-do homes lining Main Street, and continue south to Arlington, North Bennington, and Old Bennington. Stop just a mile south along Route 7A at **Hildene.** The 412 acres of explorable grounds at the estate of Abraham Lincoln's son are ablaze with color, and the views over the Battenkill Valley are as good as any you can find. Drive south another mile along 7A to the **Equinox Valley Nursery,** where you can sample delicious apple cider and doughnuts amid views of the arresting countryside. A few more miles south along 7A is the small town of Arlington.

BEST TIME TO GO

Late September and early October are the times to go, with the southern area peaking about a week later than the north. Remember to book hotels in advance. The state has a Fall Foliage Hotline and an online interactive map (☎ 802/828–3239 ⊕ www.foliage-vermont.com).

PLANNING YOUR TIME

The drive from Manchester to Bennington outlined here takes just 30 minutes, but a relaxed pace is best suited to taking in all the sights.

From Route 7A in Arlington you can take two adventurous and stunning detours. One is pure foliage: follow Route 313 west a few miles to the New York State border for more beautiful views. Or head east 1 mile to East Arlington, where there's a delightful chocolate emporium. (You can continue even farther east from this spot to Kelly Stand Road leading into the Green Mountains—a little-known route that can't be beat.) Back on 7A South in Arlington, stop at the delightful **Arlington Dairy Bar** for a Vermont creemee.

Farther south in Shaftsbury is **Clear Brook Farm,** a brilliant place for fresh produce and pumpkins. Robert Frost spent much of his life in South Shaftsbury, and you can learn about his life at his former home, the **Stone House.** From South Shaftsbury take Route 67 through North Bennington and continue on to Route 67A in Old Bennington. Ride the elevator up the 306-foot-high **Bennington Battle Monument** to survey the season's progress across four states. Back down from the clouds, walk a few serene blocks to the cemetery of the **Old First Church,** where Robert Frost is buried, and contemplate his autumnal poem, "Nothing Gold Can Stay."

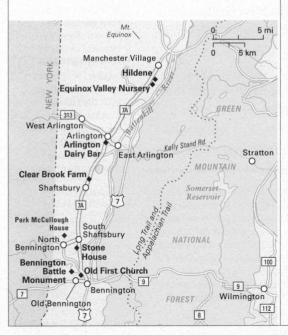

3

Best Fall Foliage Drives and Road Trips VERMONT FALL FOLIAGE DRIVE

NEED A BREAK?

Arlington Dairy Bar. Along 7A waits a big red dairy barn surrounded on all sides by Vermont's color-changing landscape. There are few greater ways to enjoy fall foliage than leaning on the hood of your car with a double scoop of local pumpkin and maple walnut ice cream, or a chocolate-dipped Vermont creemee. ✉ *3158 Rte. 7A, Arlington* ☎ *802/375–2546* ⊕ *www.facebook.com/ ArlingtonDairyBar.*

Clear Brook Farm. This 25-acre certified organic farm sells its own produce, in addition to plants, baked goods, and other seasonal treats. ✉ *47 Hidden Valley Rd., Manchester* ☎ *802/442–4273* ⊕ *www.clearbrook-farm.com.*

Equinox Valley Nursery. This nursery carries fresh produce, seasonal snacks, and cider doughnuts. There's family-friendly fall activities—a corn maze, hayrides, and pumpkin carving—as well as the property's 300-odd scarecrows. ✉ *1158 Main St., Manchester* ☎ *802/362–2610* ⊕ *www. equinoxvalleynursery. com* ✄ *Free.*

NEW HAMPSHIRE FALL FOLIAGE DRIVE

Quaint villages graced with green commons, white town halls, and covered bridges: southwestern New Hampshire is dominated by the imposing rocky summit of Mt. Monadnock and the brilliant colors of autumn. Kancamagus Highway is another classic foliage route, but for more solitude and less traffic, try this more accessible route that peaks a few weeks later than the state's far north.

The Granite State is the second-most-forested state in the nation; by mid-October the colors of the leaves of its maple, birch, elm, oak, beech, and ash trees range from green to gold, purple to red, and orange to auburn. Routes 12, 101, 124, and U.S. 202 form a loop around **Mt. Monadnock.** Start on the picturesque Main Street in Keene with a stop for coffee at Prime Roast Café; for New Hampshire–made products, take a walk on Main Street or detour west on Route 9 to reach **Stonewall Farm** for something more pastoral.

BEST TIME TO GO

The best time to view foliage in southern New Hampshire is generally early October, but it can vary by up to four weeks. For updates about leaf changes, visit the Foliage Tracker page on the website of **Visit New Hampshire** (☎ *800/386–4664* ⊕ *www.visitnh.gov*).

PLANNING YOUR TIME

Expect to travel about 55 miles. The journey can take up to a full day if you stop to explore along the way.

From Keene, travel east on Route 101 through Dublin. In **Peterborough,** browse the local stores like the Peterborough Basket Company—the country's oldest continuously operating basket manufacturer—whose attitudes and selections mirror the state's independent spirit. If you need a bite to eat before continuing on your journey or later for dinner, stop by **Harlow's Pub,** a convivial spot in Peterborough's scenic downtown.

Then turn south on U.S. 202 toward Jaffrey Village. Just west on Route 124, in historic Jaffrey Center, be sure to visit the **Meeting House Cemetery,** where author Willa Cather is buried. One side trip, 4 miles south on U.S. 202, leads to the majestic **Cathedral of the Pines** in Rindge, one of the best places in the region for foliage viewing because evergreens offset the brilliant shades of red.

Heading west on Route 124, you can take Dublin Road to the main entrance of **Monadnock State Park** or continue along to the Old Toll Road parking area for one of the most popular routes up the mountain, the **Old Halfway House Trail.** All the hiking trails have great views, including the area's many lakes. Continuing on U.S. 124, head southwest on Fitzwilliam Road to Fitzwilliam. If you have time, pop into **Bloomin' Antiques** to browse their selection of fine art and unusual antiques.

NEED A BREAK?

Bloomin' Antiques. Fine art and unusual antiques. ⊠ 3 Templeton Tpke., Fitzwilliam ☎ 800/386-4664 ⊕ www.bloominantiquesnh.com.

Harlow's Pub. Open for lunch, dinner, and Sunday brunch, this friendly tavern with a patio overlooking Peterborough's scenic village center serves creative comfort fare and local craft beer. ⊠ 3 School St., Peterborough ☎ 603/924-6365 ⊕ www.harlowspub.com.

Stonewall Farm. A working dairy farm with a dramatic setting amid fields and forests, Stonewall is open daily and presents an active schedule of events, including maple sugaring and seasonal horse-drawn hayrides. Walking and snowshoeing trails lace the property, and a farm shop sells organic produce, gourmet snacks, and the farm's own luscious Frisky Cow Gelato. Young children love the discovery room, and the interactive greenhouse is geared for all ages. ⊠ 242 Chesterfield Rd., Keene ☎ 603/357-7278 ⊕ www.stonewallfarm.org.

3

Best Fall Foliage Drives and Road Trips

NEW HAMPSHIRE FALL FOLIAGE DRIVE

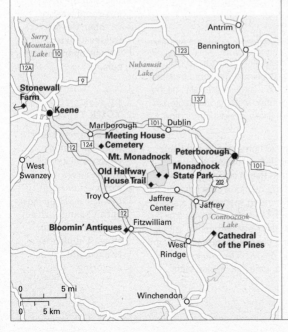

INLAND MAINE FALL FOLIAGE DRIVE

Swaths of pine, spruce, and fir trees offset the red, orange, and yellow of maples and birches along this popular foliage drive through western Maine's mountains.

Wending its way to the four-season resort town of Rangeley, near its northern terminus, the route passes stunning overlooks, forest-lined lakes, waterfalls, hiking trails, and a state park. Mountain vistas are reflected in the many (often connected) lakes, ponds, rivers, and streams.

Route 17 heads north past old homesteads and fields along the Swift River Valley before making a mountainous switchback ascent to **Height of Land,** the drive's literal pinnacle. The must-stop overlook here has off-road parking, interpretive panels, stone seating, and a short path to the **Appalachian Trail.** On a clear day, you can look west to mountains on the New Hampshire border. **Mooselookmeguntic Lake** and **Upper Richardson Lake** seem to float amid the forestland below. A few miles north of here is an overlook for Rangeley Lake, also with interpretive panels.

BEST TIME TO GO

Fall color usually peaks in the first or second week of October. Get fall foliage updates at ⊕ *www.mainefoliage. com.*

PLANNING YOUR TIME

The Rangeley Lakes National Scenic Byway and a state byway (⊕ *www. exploremaine.org/ byways*) make up most of this 58-mile drive (1½ hours without stops), but plan for a relaxed, full day of exploring.

In tiny, welcoming Oquossoc, where Routes 17 and 4 meet, stop at the **Gingerbread House Restaurant** for breakfast or lunch, or for just baked goods or an ice cream. The hamlet is also home to the **Outdoor Heritage Museum,** where you can learn why visitors have come here to fish, hunt, and enjoy the outdoors since the mid-1800s. The trailhead for **Bald Mountain,** a popular hike, is just outside the village.

Rangeley, 7 miles east on Route 4, has restaurants, inns, a waterfront park, and outdoorsy shops. The countryside sweeps into view along public hiking trails at the 175-acre **Wilhelm Reich Museum.** There's also hiking at Rangeley Lakes Trail Center on Saddleback Mountain.

The road to **Rangeley Lake State Park** is accessible from both Routes 4 and 17, as is the **Appalachian Trail.** Overhanging foliage frames waterfalls at the scenic rest areas at each end of the drive: at Coos Canyon on Route 17 en route to Height of Land, and at Smalls Falls on Route 4 near Madrid, the terminus. Both spots have swimming holes, several falls, and paths with views of their drops. Coos Canyon is along the Swift River, a destination for recreational gold panning. You can rent or buy panning equipment at **Coos Canyon Rock and Gift,** across from its namesake. It also sells sandwiches, ice cream, and snacks.

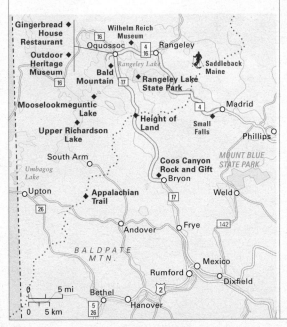

NEED A BREAK?

Coos Canyon Rock and Gift. The gift shop offers jewelry, souvenirs, T-shirts, prospecting equipment, books, and more. ⊠ 472 *Swift River Rd. (Rte. 17), Byron* ☎ 207/364–4900 ⊕ *www.cooscanyonrock-andgift.com.*

Rangeley Lakes Heritage. Trust The trust protects 14,000 acres of land in the Rangeley Lakes area. Both online and at its Rangeley office, the trust has maps and descriptions of its 35 miles of recreational trails and access roads, along with information about fishing, hunting, snowmobiling, picnicking, and other outdoor activities. ⊠ *2424 Main St., Rangeley* ☎ 207/864–7311 ⊕ *www.rlht.org.*

Wilhelm Reich Museum. This seasonal museum showcases the life and work of controversial physician-scientist Wilhelm Reich (1897–1957). There are magnificent views from the observatory and great trails throughout the 175-acre property, which is open year-round. ⊠ *19 Orgonon Circle, off Rte. 4, Rangeley* ☎ 207/864–3443 ⊕ *www. wilhelmreichmuseum. org* 🎟 *Museum $8, grounds free.*

Chapter 4

BOSTON AND ENVIRONS

Updated by
Cheryl Fenton, Leigh Harrington,
and Kim Foley MacKinnon

◉ Sights	🍴 Restaurants	🛏 Hotels	🛍 Shopping	🍸 Nightlife
★★★★★	★★★★★	★★★★★	★★★★★	★★★★★

WELCOME TO BOSTON AND ENVIRONS

TOP REASONS TO GO

★ **Freedom's Ring:** Walk through America's early history on the 2½-mile Freedom Trail that snakes through town.

★ **Ivy-Draped Campus:** Hang in Harvard Square like a collegian or hit the university's museums: the Sackler (ancient art), the Botanical Museum, the Peabody (archaeology), and the Natural History Museum.

★ **Posh Purchases:** Strap on some stilettos and join the quest for fashionable finds on Newbury Street, Boston's answer to Manhattan's 5th Avenue.

★ **Sacred Ground:** Root for (or boo) the Red Sox at baseball's most hallowed shrine, Fenway Park.

★ **Tea Time:** Interact with the city's history at the Boston Tea Party Ships & Museum: greet reenactors and explore replicas of the ships at the actual spot where the tea met the sea.

1 Beacon Hill and Boston Common. Many historic landmarks of old Boston.

2 The West End. The Museum of Science and TD Garden.

3 Government Center. Faneuil Hall and the trio of buildings that share its name.

4 The North End. Boston's Little Italy.

5 Charlestown. Bunker Hill Monument and the USS *Constitution.*

6 Downtown. Numerous Freedom Trail sights as well the Theater District, Chinatown, the residential Leather District, and the Financial District.

7 The Waterfront. Wharves, walking paths, and Boston Harbor views.

8 The Seaport. Across from the Waterfront with the Boston Convention and Exhibition Center, the Institute of Contemporary Art, and swanky restaurants and hotels.

9 The Back Bay. Iconic brownstones, ritzy Newbury Street shopping, and must-see destinations like the Boston Public Library and Trinity Church.

10 The South End. Locally owned boutiques, the country's largest extant Victorian row house district, and home to many of Boston's LGBTQ community.

11 Fenway and Kenmore Square. Fenway Park, the Museum of Fine Arts, and the Isabella Stewart Gardner Museum.

12 Cambridge. Harvard University plays a huge part in the personality of Harvard Square, while MIT asserts its tech and biotech leanings in Kendall and Central squares.

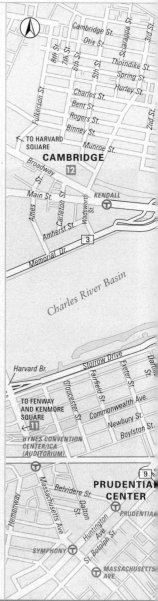

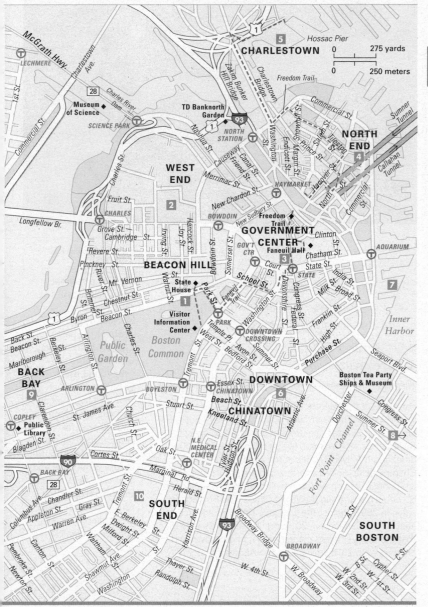

McGrath Hwy.

LECHMERE

Charlestown Ave.

Commercial St.

28

Charles River Dam

Museum of Science

SCIENCE PARK

Charles St.

Longfellow Br.

Cambridge St.

Grove St.

CHARLES

Revere St.

Pinckney St.

River St.

Mt. Vernon

Chestnut St.

Byron

Beacon St.

Back St.

Beacon St.

Marlborough

BACK BAY

9

COPLEY

Public Library

Blagden St.

Berkeley St.

Arlington St.

Clarendon St.

St. James Ave.

Church St.

ARLINGTON

BOYLSTON

Stuart St.

Boylston St.

CORTES ST.

90

BACK BAY

28

Columbus Ave.

Chandler St.

Appleton St.

Gray St.

Warren Ave.

Tremont St.

E. Berkeley St.

Dwight St.

Milford St.

10

SOUTH END

Canton St.

Shawmut Ave.

Pembroke St.

Newton St.

Washington

Thayer St.

Randolph St.

Charlestown Ave.

Zakim Bunker Hill Bridge

5

CHARLESTOWN

Hossac Pier

0   275 yards

0   250 meters

Freedom Trail

Charlestown Bridge

TD Banknorth Garden

93

Nashua St.

NORTH STATION

Washington St.

Causeway St.

Friend St.

Canal St.

Merrimac St.

WEST END

2

Fruit St.

Hancock St.

Joy St.

Irving St.

BEACON HILL

Bowdoin St.

Somerset St.

Cambridge St.

New Chardon St.

BOWDOIN

New Sudbury St.

Freedom Trail

GOVERNMENT CENTER

GOV'T CTR

Faneuil Hall

3

Commercial St.

Sumner Tunnel

St. Stephen St.

Margin St.

Prince St.

Tileston St.

Hanover St.

NORTH END

4

Callahan Tunnel

Endicott St.

HAYMARKET

North St.

Commercial St.

Clinton

Chatham St.

State St.

STATE

India St.

Broad St.

AQUARIUM

7

Inner Harbor

St. House

State House

Walnut St.

Park St.

1

Visitor Information Center

Temple Pl.

West St.

Fanueil Trail

School St.

Court St.

Devonshire St.

Congress St.

Federal St.

Washington St.

Milk St.

Franklin St.

High St.

PARK

DOWNTOWN CROSSING

Avon St.

Summer St.

Purchase St.

Seaport Blvd.

Boston Common

Public Garden

Boston Common

Tremont St.

Bedford St.

Essex St.

CHINATOWN

Beach St.

DOWNTOWN

6

Kneeland St.

CHINATOWN

Atlantic Ave.

Boston Tea Party Ships & Museum

Dorchester

Summer St.

Congress St.

8

Fort Point Channel

Oak St.

N.E. MEDICAL CENTER

Tyler St.

Hudson St.

Marginal Rd.

Herald St.

Harrison Ave.

93

Broadway Bridge

BROADWAY

SOUTH BOSTON

A St.

B St.

C St.

Cypher St.

W. 1st St.

W. 2nd St.

W. 3rd St.

W. 4th St.

W. Broadway

FENWAY PARK

Take yourself out to a ball game at legendary Fenway Park.

For baseball fans a trip to Fenway Park is a religious pilgrimage. The Boston Red Sox have played here since 1912. The oldest Major League Baseball ballpark is one of the last of its kind, a place where the scoreboard is hand-operated and fans endure uncomfortable seats.

For much of the ballpark's history Babe Ruth's specter loomed large. The team won five titles by 1918 but endured an 86-year title drought after trading away the Sultan of Swat. The Sox "reversed the curse" in 2004, defeating the rival Yankees in the American League Championship Series after being down 3–0 in the series (an unheard of comeback in baseball) and sweeping the St. Louis Cardinals in the World Series. The Red Sox won again in 2007, against the Colorado Rockies, and again against the Cardinals in 2013, the first time since 1918 that the team cinched the series in its hometown and once more in 2018 against the Los Angeles Dodgers. The curse is no more.

FENWAY PARK TOURS

If you can't see the Sox, you can still see the Green Monster up close by going on a tour of the park. The one-hour Fenway walking tours run year-round, and if you go on the day's last tour on a home-game day, you can watch batting practice. Tours run hourly from 9 am to 5 pm (or four hours before game time) and cost $21. Check the site for info on premium tours. ☎ 617/226–6666 ⊕ boston.redsox.mlb. com/bos/ballpark/ tour.jsp.

THE NATION
The Red Sox have the most rabid fans in baseball. Knowledgeable and dedicated, they follow the team with religious-like intensity.

THE GREEN MONSTER
Fenway's most dominant feature is the 37-foot-high wall that looms over left field. It's just over 300 feet from home plate and in the field of play, so deep fly balls that would have been outs in other parks sometimes become home runs. The Monster also stops line drives that would have been over the walls of other stadiums.

THE MUSIC
Fans sing "Take Me Out to the Ballgame" during the seventh-inning stretch in every ballpark, but at Fenway they also sing Neil Diamond's "Sweet Caroline" at the bottom of the eighth. If the Sox win, the Standells' "Dirty Water" blasts over the loudspeakers.

THE CURSE
In 1920 the Red Sox traded pitcher Babe Ruth to the Yankees, where he became a home-run-hitting baseball legend. Some fans—most famously *Boston Globe* columnist Dan Shaughnessy, who wrote a book called *The Curse of the Bambino*—blamed this move for the team's 86-year title drought, but others will claim that "The Curse" was just a media-driven storyline used to explain the team's past woes. Still, fans who watched a ground ball roll between Bill Buckner's legs in the 1986 World Series or saw Aaron Boone's winning home run in the 2003 A.L.D.S. swear the curse was real.

THE WEATHER
If you plan on catching a game at Fenway in the spring, bring warm clothes or a blanket. It can get chilly, especially in the stands. April lows are in the 40s and in May it can still get down to 50.

VISIT THE NATION

Not lucky enough to nab tickets ahead of time? Try your luck at Gate E two hours before the game, when a handful of tickets are sold. There's a one-ticket limit, so everyone in your party must be in line.

If that doesn't yield results, you can still experience the Nation. Head down to the park and hang out on Jersey Street, which borders the stadium. On game days it's closed to cars and filled with vendors, creating a street-fair atmosphere. Duck into a nearby sports bar and enjoy the game with other fans who weren't fortunate enough to secure seats. A favorite is the **Cask'n Flagon**, at Brookline Avenue and Lansdowne Street, across the street from Fenway.

The closest you can get to Fenway without buying a ticket is the **Bleacher Bar** (⊠ *82A Lansdowne St.*). There's a huge window in the center field wall overlooking the field. Get here early—it starts filling up a few hours before game time.

There's history and culture around every bend in Boston—skyscrapers nestle next to historic hotels, while modern marketplaces line the antique cobblestone streets. But to Bostonians, living in a city that blends yesterday and today is just another day in their beloved city.

It's difficult to fit Boston into a stereotype because of the city's many layers. The deepest is the historical one, the place where musket-bearing revolutionaries vowed to hang together or hang separately. The next tier, a dense spread of Brahmin fortune and fortitude, might be labeled the Hub. It was this elite caste of Boston society, descended from wealthy English Protestants who first settled the state, that funded and patronized the city's universities and cultural institutions, gaining Boston the label "the Athens of America" and felt only pride in the slogan "Banned in Boston." Over that layer lies Beantown, home to the Red Sox faithful and the raucous Bruins fans who crowded the old Boston "*Gah*-den"; this is the city whose ethnic loyalties account for its many distinct neighborhoods. Crowning these layers are the students who converge on the area's universities and colleges every fall.

Planning

If you have a couple of days, hit Boston's highlights—Beacon Hill, the Freedom Trail, and the Public Garden—the first day, and then check out the Museum of Fine Arts or the Isabella Stewart Gardner Museum the morning of the second day. Reserve day two's afternoon for an excursion to Harvard or shopping on Newbury Street.

Getting Here and Around

AIR
More than 40 airlines operate at Boston's major airport, Logan International Airport (BOS), offering nonstop flights to 120 cities. Flying times to Boston from New York average 1 hour; it's 1½ hours from Washington, D.C., 2¼ hours from Chicago, 3 hours from Miami, 3½ hours from Dallas, 5½ hours from Los Angeles, 6½ hours from London, 13 hours from Tokyo, and 20 hours from Sydney. Delta, American Airlines, and JetBlue run daily shuttle flights from New York and Washington, D.C.

Logan is across the harbor, barely 2 miles from Downtown, and can be easily reached by taxi, water taxi, or bus/subway via MBTA's Silver or Blue line. Logan's four passenger terminals are identified by the letters A, B, C, and E. Some airlines use different terminals for international and domestic flights; most international flights arrive at Terminal E. There's a visitor center in Terminal C.

T. F. Green Airport (PVD) in Providence, Rhode Island, and Manchester Boston Regional Airport (MHT) in New Hampshire are about an hour's drive from Boston.

CONTACTS Logan International Airport (Boston). ⊠ *I–90 East to Ted Williams Tunnel, Boston* ☎ *800/235–6426* ⊕ *www.*

massport.com/logan-airport Ⓜ *Airport.*
Manchester Boston Regional Airport. ✉ *Off I–293N/Rte. 101W, Exit 13, Manchester* ☎ *603/624–6539* ⊕ *www.flymanchester. com.* **T. F. Green Airport.** ✉ *2000 Post Rd., off I–95, Exit 13, Warwick* ☎ *401/691– 2000* ⊕ *www.pvdairport.com.*

BIKE

The city has a growing number of stands for locking your bike, and they can be hitched to racks on the front of most buses or carried onto subway cars (with the exception of the Green Line) during nonpeak hours ("peak" is 7–10 am and 4–7 pm. "Pedal and Park" bike cages are available to cyclists at major transit hubs like Alewife and Forest Hills stations.

■ TIP➔ **Helmets are required for anyone 16 or younger.**

Boston's short-term bike rental program is primarily commuter-oriented, but it can also be a handy and fun way for travelers to cover relatively short distances. Members are able to unlock a bike from a dock, ride it for up to two hours at a time (45 minutes a trip if you choose a monthly membership), and then return it to any other dock. There's no additional charge for any ride that lasts less than 30 minutes, and the docks are in dozens of metro area locations.

CONTACTS Bluebikes. ☎ *855/948–2929* ⊕ *www.bluebikes.com.* **MassBike.** *Massachusetts Bicycle Coalition* ✉ *50 Milk St., 16th fl., Downtown* ☎ *617/542–2453* ⊕ *massbike.org.*

BOAT

Several boat companies make runs between the airport and Downtown destinations. Take the free Shuttle Bus 66 from any terminal to the airport's ferry dock to catch Boston's water taxis: Rowes Wharf Water Taxi, Boston Harbor Cruises, and MBTA Harbor Express.

MBTA commuter boat service operates weekdays between several Downtown harbor destinations, Charlestown, and quite a few locations on the South Shore. One-way fares range from $3.70 to $9.75 depending on destination; seniors and students ride half-price, children under 11 are free. Schedules change seasonally, so call ahead.

CONTACTS Boston Harbor Cruises. ☎ *617/227–4321* ⊕ *www.bostonharborcruises.com.* **MBTA Harbor Express.** ☎ *617/222–6999, 617/222–3200* ⊕ *www. mbta.com/schedules/ferry.* **Rowes Wharf Water Taxi.** ☎ *617/406–8584 pick-up line, 617/261–6620 questions* ⊕ *www. roweswharfwatertaxi.com.*

CAR

In a place where roads often evolved from cow paths, driving is no simple task. A surfeit of one-way streets and inconsistent signage add to the confusion. Street parking is hard to come by, as much of it is resident-permit-only. Your own car is helpful if you're taking side trips, but for exploring the city it will only be a burden. Also, Bostonians give terrible directions, since few of them actually drive.

PEDICAB

Pedicabs, human-powered three-wheeled bicycle rickshaws that hold two adults easily and three with difficulty, are popular in spring and summer around Boston and Cambridge. You can hail one on the street, or phone ☎ *617/266–2005* for one, with an average wait of 15–20 minutes. They are usually used to get from point A to a not-too-distant point B; on Red Sox game days, pedicabs swarm towards Fenway Park, usually arriving ahead of auto traffic.

There are no fixed fares, since the bikers work for tips; pay your biker (cash only) what you think the ride was worth, though be ready for a sour look if you pay much less than $10 a mile or so. Try to agree on a fee ahead of time. Most pedicabs also offer tours, with minimum fixed fees.

CONTACT Boston Pedicab. ☎ *617/266– 2005* ⊕ *www.bostonpedicab.com.*

PUBLIC TRANSIT

The "T," as the subway system is affectionately nicknamed, is the cornerstone of a far-reaching public transit network that also includes aboveground trains, buses, and ferries. Its five color-coded lines will put you within a block of virtually anywhere. Subways operate from 5 am to 1 am (schedules vary by line). The same goes for buses, which crisscross the city and suburbia.

There are two stored-value options: a plastic CharlieCard or paper CharlieTicket, both of which are reusable and reloadable with cash, or credit or debit cards. Getting a CharlieCard makes it easier to transfer between the subway and the bus, because such transfers are free and you don't need to keep track of individual tickets. At a station, obtain a CharlieCard from an attendant or a CharlieTicket from a machine. CharlieCards can't yet be used on commuter rail, commuter boats, or Inner Harbor ferries. A standard adult subway fare is $2.40 with a CharlieCard or $2.90 with a ticket or cash (children ages 11 and under ride free, while senior citizens and students with proper ID are discounted). For buses it's $1.70 with a CharlieCard or $2 with a ticket or cash (more for an Inner or Outer Express bus). Commuter rail and ferry fares depend on the route. For details on schedules, routes, and rates, visit the MBTA (Massachusetts Bay Transportation Authority) website. For most visitors, the best deal will be the unlimited one-day ($12.75) or one-week ($22.50).

"Inbound" trains head into the city center (Park Street Station) and "outbound" trains head away from it. If you get on the Red Line at South Station, the train heading toward Alewife (Cambridge) is inbound. But once you reach Park Street, the train becomes outbound. Similarly, the Green Line to Fenway Park would be the Boston College or Cleveland Circle train. Large maps prominently posted at each station show

the line(s) that serve it, with each stop marked; small maps are overhead in each car. Free 24-hour shuttle buses connect Airport Blue Line Station with all airline terminals. Shuttle Bus 22 runs between the subway and Terminals A and B, and Shuttle Bus 33 runs between the subway and Terminals C and E.

The Red Line originates at Braintree and Quincy Center to the south; the routes join near South Boston at the JFK/UMass stop and continue to Alewife, the northwest corner of Cambridge by suburban Arlington. (The Mattapan high-speed line, or M-line, is considered part of the overall Red Line. Originating in Ashmont Station, it transports passengers via vintage yellow trolleys to Mattapan Square.)

The Green Line operates elevated trolleys that dip underground in the city center. The line originates at Cambridge's Lechmere, heads south, and divides into four westward routes: B ends at Boston College (Commonwealth Avenue); C ends at Cleveland Circle (Beacon Street, in Brighton); D ends at Riverside (Newton at Route 128); and E ends at Heath Street (Huntington Avenue in Jamaica Plain).

The Blue Line runs weekdays from Bowdoin Square (and weeknights and weekends from Government Center) to the Wonderland Racetrack in Revere, north of Boston. The Blue Line is best if you're heading to North Station, Faneuil Hall, the North End/Waterfront, or the Back Bay (the Hynes Convention Center, Prudential Center area). The Orange Line runs from Oak Grove in north suburban Malden southwesterly to Forest Hills near the Arnold Arboretum in Jamaica Plain.

The Silver Line (a bus line with its own dedicated lanes) has four routes. SL1 connects South Station to Logan Airport; SL2 runs between South Station and the Design Center; SL4 connects Dudley Square and South Station; and SL5 runs between Downtown Crossing and Dudley Square, also stopping in Boylston.

CONTACT MBTA. ☎ *800/392–6100, 617/222–3200, 617/222–5146 TTY* ⊕ *www.mbta.com.*

TAXI

Cabs are available 24/7. Rides within the city cost $2.60 for the first 1/7 mile and 40¢ for each 1/7 mile thereafter (tolls, where applicable, are extra).

TRAIN

Boston is served by Amtrak at North Station, South Station, and Back Bay Station. North Station is the terminus for Amtrak's *Downeaster* service from Boston to New Hampshire and Maine. South Station and Back Bay Station, nearby, accommodate frequent Northeast Corridor departures to and arrivals from New York, Philadelphia, and Washington, D.C. Amtrak's Acela train cuts the travel time between Boston and New York to 3½ hours. South Station and Back Bay Station are the two stops in Boston for Amtrak's *Lake Shore Limited,* which travels daily between Boston and Chicago by way of Albany, Buffalo, and Cleveland.

Activities

Everything you've heard about the zeal of Boston fans is true; you cheer, and you pray, and you root some more. "Red Sox Nation" witnessed a miracle in 2004, with the reverse of the curse and the team's first World Series victory since 1918.

Then in 2007, 2013, and 2018 they proved it wasn't just a fluke with three more Series wins. In 2008 the Celtics ended their 18-year NBA championship drought with a victory over longtime rivals the LA Lakers. And six-time champions the New England Patriots are still a force to be reckoned with.

Whether it's taking advantage of being by the water with harbor strolls, riverfront Frisbee games, or logging in picturesque miles of jogging, active Bostonians love their extensive parks, paths, and waterways. Winter winds redirect that energy to white slopes, frozen rinks, and, for those who don't want to don down coats, sheltered gyms and pools.

Dining

In a city synonymous with tradition, Boston chefs have spent recent years rewriting culinary history. The stuffy, wood-paneled formality is gone; the endless renditions of *chowdah,* lobster, and cod have retired; and the assumption that true foodies better hop the next Amtrak to New York is also—thankfully—a thing of the past. Small, upscale neighborhood spots that use local New England ingredients—fresh fish and shellfish, locally grown fruits and vegetables, handmade cheeses, and humanely raised heritage game and meats—to delicious effect have taken their place. Traditional eats can still be found (Beantown Pub remains the best place for baked beans), but many diners now gravitate toward innovative food in understated environs. Whether you're looking for casual French, down-home Southern cooking, some of the country's best sushi, or Vietnamese banh mi sandwiches, Boston restaurants are ready to deliver. *Restaurant reviews have been shortened. For full information, visit Fodors.com.*

WHAT IT COSTS in U.S. Dollars			
$	$$	$$$	$$$$
AT DINNER			
under $18	$18–$24	$25–$35	over $35

Lodging

Because of its status as a major college town, Boston students dictate the flow of hotel traffic. Commencement weekends in May and June book months in advance; prices can be triple the off-season rate, with minimum stays of two to four nights. Those returning students invade their city again for move-in months of August and September. Leaf-peepers arrive in early October, and fall conventions bring waves of business travelers, especially in the Seaport District. Events such as the Boston Marathon in April and the Head of the Charles in October are busy times for large hotels and small inns alike.

The hotel tax in Boston adds 14.95% to your bill; some hotels also tack on energy, service, or occupancy surcharges. Though it's not an absolute necessity, many visitors prefer to bring a car, but then parking is another expense to consider. Almost all lodgings have parking, and most charge for the privilege—anywhere from $15 per day for self-garaging to $35 for valet. When looking for a hotel, don't write off the pricier establishments immediately. Price categories are determined by "rack rates"—the list price of a hotel room, which is usually discounted. Specials abound, particularly in Downtown on weekends. With so many new rooms in Boston, pricing is very competitive, so always check out the hotel website in advance for current special offers. *Hotel reviews have been shortened. For full information, visit Fodors.com.*

WHAT IT COSTS in U.S. Dollars			
$	$$	$$$	$$$$
FOR TWO PEOPLE			
under $200	$200–$299	$300–$399	over $399

Nightlife

Whether it's cheering on local sports at a watering hole, rocking out at an underground club, applauding a symphonic performance, or chilling with cocktails in an elegant lounge, Boston has a nightlife vibe to suit all types and moods. Consider it a Cinderella city, set aglow with energy that for some ends all too soon. With the T (subway and bus) making its final runs between midnight and 1 am, most nightspots follow accordingly, closing their doors typically by 2 am. Though night owls may be disappointed by the meager late-night options, except in Chinatown, visitors find plenty of possibilities for stepping out on the early side. The martini set may stroll Newbury and Boylston streets in the Back Bay or Downtown, selecting from swank restaurants, lounges, and clubs. Coffee and tea drinkers can find numerous cafés in Cambridge and Somerville, particularly Harvard and Davis squares. Microbrew enthusiasts find viable options at sports bars, pop-up beer gardens, and craft breweries, especially on the Rose Kennedy Greenway, along the water, near campuses and sports arenas. The thriving "lounge" scene in Downtown's cooler hybrid bar-restaurant-clubs provides a mellower, more mature alternative to the collegiate indie spots, and DJs spin the late night dance parties into a frenzy with house music at crowded clubs like The Grand in the Seaport. Tourists crowd Faneuil Hall for its pubs, comedy spots, and dance scenes. The South and North Ends cater to the "dinner-and-drinks" set. Several casual indie rock and music clubs abound with plenty of local bands on stage and cold beer behind the bar in Allston, Somerville, and Cambridge.

Performing Arts

Boston's cultural attractions are a bracing mix of old-world aesthetics and new-world experimentation. At the classical end of the spectrum, revered institutions like the Museum of Fine Arts, the Boston Symphony Orchestra and Boston Pops, and the Isabella Stewart Gardner Museum offer refined experiences. For less reverential attitudes toward the arts, the Institute of Contemporary Art (ICA) features edgy electronic concerts, and graffiti and multimedia exhibitions. Museums like the MFA, the Gardner, and the ICA also host special shows and festivals in strikingly handsome performance spaces.

Shopping

Shopping in Boston in many ways mirrors the city itself: a mix of classic and cutting-edge, the high-end and the handmade, and international and local sensibilities. There is a strong network of idiosyncratic gift stores, handicrafts shops, galleries, and a growing number of savvy, independent fashion boutiques. Boston's shops and department stores lie concentrated in the area bounded by Quincy Market, the Back Bay, and Downtown, with plenty of bargains in the Downtown Crossing area. The South End's gentrification creates its own kind of consumerist milieus, from housewares shops to avant-garde art galleries. In Cambridge you can find many shops around Harvard and Central squares, with independent boutiques migrating west along Massachusetts Avenue ("Mass Ave.") toward Porter Square and beyond. There's no state sales tax on clothing. However, there's a 6.25% sales tax on clothes priced higher than $175 per item; the tax is levied on the amount in excess of $175.

Most major shopping neighborhoods are easily accessible on the T: Boston's Charles Street and Downtown Crossing and Cambridge's Harvard, Central, and Porter squares are on the Red Line; Copley Place, Faneuil Hall, and Newbury Street are on the Green Line; the South End is an easy trip on the Orange Line.

Visitor Information

Contact the city and state tourism offices for details about seasonal events, discount passes, trip planning, and attraction information. The National Park Service has a Boston office for Boston's historic sites that provides maps and directions. The Welcome Center and Boston Common Visitor Information Center offer general information. The Cambridge Tourism Office's information booth is in Harvard Square, near the main entrance to the Harvard T stop.

Boston.com, home of the *Boston Globe* online, has news and feature articles, ample travel information, and links to towns throughout Massachusetts. The Bostonian Society (⊕ *bostonhistory. org*) answers some frequently asked questions about Beantown history on its website. The iBoston (⊕ *www.iboston. org*) page has wonderful photographs of architecturally and historically important buildings. *The Improper Bostonian* (⊕ *www.improper.com*) and *WickedLocal* (⊕ *www.wickedlocal.com*) provide a more relaxed (and irreverent) take on Boston news and information.

CONTACTS Boston Common Visitor Information Center. ⊠ *Downtown* ☎ *617/536–4100* ⊕ *www.bostonusa.com/visit/planyourtrip/ resources/vic.* **Greater Boston Convention and Visitors Bureau.** ⊠ *2 Copley Pl. Suite 105, Back Bay* ☎ *888/733–2678, 617/536–4100* ⊕ *www.bostonusa.com.* **National Parks Service Visitor Center.** ⊠ *Faneuil Hall, Downtown* ☎ *617/242–5601* ⊕ *www.nps.gov/bost.*

When to Go

Summer brings reliable sunshine, sailboats to Boston Harbor, concerts to the Esplanade, and café tables to assorted sidewalks. If you're dreaming of a classic shore vacation, summer is prime.

Weather-wise, late spring and fall are the optimal times to visit Boston. Aside from mild temperatures, the former offers blooming gardens throughout the city and the latter sees the surrounding countryside ablaze with brilliantly colored foliage. At both times expect crowds.

Autumn attracts hordes of leaf peepers, and more than 250,000 students flood into the area each September, then pull out in May and June. Hotels and restaurants fill up quickly on move-in, move-out, and graduation weekends.

Winters are cold and windy.

Beacon Hill and Boston Common

Beacon Hill is Boston at its most Bostonian. Redbrick row houses dressed with black shutters and the occasional violet-hued windowpane filter into view, and narrow streets return you to the 19th century just as surely as if you had stumbled into a time machine. Across Beacon Street from Beacon Hill, the wide expanse of Boston Common has provided green space for locals since 1634.

◉ Sights

★ Acorn Street
BUILDING | Often called the city's most photographed passageway, Acorn Street offers its visitors an iconic image of "historic Boston." Short, steep, and narrow, the cobblestone street may be Boston's roughest ride, so leave your car behind. Brick row houses—once the homes of

19th-century artisans and tradespeople—line one side, and on the other, doors lead to Mt. Vernon's hidden gardens. Find American flags, creative door knockers, window boxes, and gas lights aplenty. ⊠ Between W. Cedar and Willow Sts., Beacon Hill Ⓜ Park.

★ Boston Common
CITY PARK | FAMILY | Nothing is more central to the city than Boston Common, the oldest public park in the United States. Dating from 1634, the Common started as 50 acres where freemen could graze their cattle. (Cows were banned in 1830.) Don't confuse the Common with its sister park, the Public Garden, where the Swan Boats glide. Around the park, visit-worthy sites include Brewer Fountain Plaza, the start of the Freedom Trail, Boston Common Visitor Information Center, the Soldiers and Sailors Monument, the Frog Pond, Central Burying Ground, and the Robert Gould Shaw 54th Regiment Memorial. ■ TIP→ This is Freedom Trail stop 1. ⊠ Bounded by Beacon, Charles, Tremont, and Park Sts., Beacon Hill ⊕ www.boston.gov/parks/boston-common Ⓜ Park, Boylston.

★ Charles Street
COMMERCIAL CENTER | You won't see any glaring neon, in keeping with the historic character of the area, but Charles Street more than makes up for the general lack of commercial development on Beacon Hill with a plethora of antiques shops, clothing boutiques, small restaurants, and cafés. Once the home of Oliver Wendell Holmes and the publisher James T. Fields (of the famed Bostonian firm of Ticknor and Fields), Charles Street sparkles at dusk from gas-fueled lamps, making it a romantic place for an evening stroll. ⊠ Between Beacon and Cambridge Sts., Beacon Hill Ⓜ Charles/MGH.

★ Massachusetts State House
BUILDING | FAMILY | On July 4, 1795, the surviving fathers of the Revolution were on hand to enshrine the ideals of their new Commonwealth in a graceful seat

of government designed by Charles Bulfinch. Governor Samuel Adams and Paul Revere laid the cornerstone; Revere would later roll the copper sheathing for the dome. Inside the building, visitors can check out Doric Hall, with its statuary and portraits; the Hall of Flags, where an exhibit shows the battle flags from all the wars in which Massachusetts regiments have participated; the Great Hall, an open space used for state functions that houses 351 flags from the cities and towns of Massachusetts; the governor's office; and the chambers of the House and Senate. Free guided tours; call for reservation. **■ TIP→ This is Freedom Trail stop 2.** ✉ *24 Beacon St., Beacon Hill* ☎ *617/727–3676* 🌐 *www.sec.state.ma.us/trs/trsidx.htm* 🎟 *Free* 🕒 *Closed weekends* [M] *Park.*

Museum of African American History

MUSEUM | FAMILY | The Museum of African American History was established in 1964 to recognize Boston's African American community, from slavery through the abolitionist movement. The Abiel Smith School, the first public school in the nation built specifically for black children, now serves as the museum's main building, filled with exhibits. The African Meeting House was built in 1806 entirely by black labor; in 1832, William Lloyd Garrison formed the New England Anti-Slavery Society here, and in 2011 the building completed a $9.5 million restoration. ✉ *46 Joy St., Beacon Hill* ☎ *617/725–0022* 🌐 *maah.org* 🎟 *$10* 🕒 *Closed Sun.* [M] *Park.*

🍴 Restaurants

Harvard Gardens

$ | AMERICAN | A Beacon Hill legend, this was the first bar in the city to get its liquor license after the repeal of Prohibition. It opened in 1930, and was owned by the same family until the 1990s. **Known for:** a killer, house-made Bloody Mary mixed with the bar's own peppercorn vodka; a Reuben sandwich stuffed with corned beef that's made in-house; casual, comfortable vibe that's a little bit different from a typical Beacon Hill experience. [$] *Average main: $17* ✉ *316 Cambridge St., Beacon Hill* ☎ *617/523–2727* 🌐 *www.harvardgardens.com* [M] *Charles/MGH.*

★ No. 9 Park

$$$$ | EUROPEAN | Welcome to the first and now flagship restaurant in acclaimed chef Barbara Lynch's empire. Even after 20 years, No. 9 Park continues to win rave reviews for Lynch's stellar, unique interpretation of fine French and Italian cuisine. **Known for:** a chef's six-course, wine-paired tasting menu, served for the whole table; polished service; Lynch's memorably rich, prune-stuffed gnocchi drizzled with bits of foie gras, which is always offered, even if you don't see it on the menu. [$] *Average main: $46* ✉ *9 Park St., Beacon Hill* ☎ *617/742–9991* 🌐 *www.no9park.com* [M] *Park.*

☕ Coffee and Quick Bites

★ The Paramount

$ | AMERICAN | FAMILY | Don't be surprised to see a queue at this neighborhood hot spot, no matter the time of day. Regulars happily line up for waffles topped with fresh fruit, caramel and banana french toast, huge salads, and hefty sandwiches, all made to order as you do from the counter. **Known for:** long, but quick-moving, lines; decadent, all-day breakfast

Did You Know? 👁

Beacon Hill's north slope played a key part in African American history. A community of free blacks lived here in the 1800s; many worshipped at the African Meeting House, established in 1805 and still standing. It came to be known as the "Black Faneuil Hall" for the fervent antislavery activism that started within its walls.

items; Old Bay-seasoned homefries. Ⓢ *Average main: $12* ✉ *44 Charles St., Beacon Hill* ☎ *617/720–1152* ⊕ *www. paramountboston.com* Ⓜ *Charles/MGH.*

★ Tatte Bakery & Café

$ | **ISRAELI** | Tzurit Or's upscale bakery and café takes pastries to the next level with items like kouign-amann, pistachio croissants, and Jerusalem bagels. While these items are staples, the majority of the menu changes frequently, but you can expect hearty plates all day, from breakfast sandwiches and tartines to salads, bowls, and shakshuka (an egg dish with tomatoes and peppers), all with a Middle Eastern spin. **Known for:** Or's take on traditional North African shakshuka, served with challah bread; signature nut tarts that are as pretty as they are tasty; convivial atmosphere. Ⓢ *Average main: $12* ✉ *70 Charles St., Beacon Hill* ☎ *617/723–5555* ⊕ *www.tattebakery. com* Ⓜ *Charles/MGH.*

 Hotels

★ XV Beacon

$$$$ | **HOTEL** | The 1903 Beaux Arts exterior of this intimate, luxury boutique hotel is a study in sophistication and elegance. **Pros:** rooftop deck with amazing city views; complimentary Lexus car service; dogs of any size welcome for no fee. **Cons:** some rooms are small; can be expensive on weekends during peak months; no view from classic rooms. Ⓢ *Rooms from: $575* ✉ *15 Beacon St., Beacon Hill* ☎ *617/670–1500, 877/982–3226* ⊕ *www.xvbeacon.com* ⌑ *63 rooms* ⭐ *No meals* Ⓜ *Park.*

The West End

A few decades ago this district—separated from Beacon Hill by Cambridge Street—resembled a typical medieval city: thoroughfares that twisted and turned, maddening one-way lanes, and streets that were a veritable hive of people. Today little remains of the *old* Old West End except for a few brick tenements and a handful of monuments, including the first house built for Harrison Gray Otis. The biggest surviving structures with any real history are two public institutions, Massachusetts General Hospital and the former Suffolk County Jail, which dates from 1849. The onetime prison is now part of the luxurious, and wryly named, Liberty Hotel. Here you'll also find TD Banknorth Garden, the home away from home for loyal Bruins and Celtics fans. In addition, the innovative Museum of Science is one of the neighborhood's more modern attractions. The newest addition to the skyline here is the Leonard P. Zakim Bunker Hill Bridge, which spans the Charles River just across from the TD Banknorth Garden.

⊙ Sights

★ Museum of Science

COLLEGE | **FAMILY** | From its perch above the Charles River, the Museum of Science sits half in Cambridge and half in Boston. This unique trait is the first of many at this 70-plus-year-old institution that's focused on science, technology, and hands-on learning. Diverse permanent exhibits explore dinosaurs, the electromagnetic spectrum, modern conservation, math, motion, nanotechnology, the natural world, space travel, and more. The Theater of Electricity hosts explosive daily lightening shows. Add-ons to admission include: the live Butterfly Garden; the multisensory 4-D Theater; Thrill Ride 360 dynamic simulator; and the Charles Hayden Planetarium. The Mugar Omni Theater with IMAX programming reopened in spring 2020 after a complete renovation. ✉ *Science Park, West End* ☎ *617/723–2500* ⊕ *www.mos.org* ⌑ *$29* Ⓜ *Science Park.*

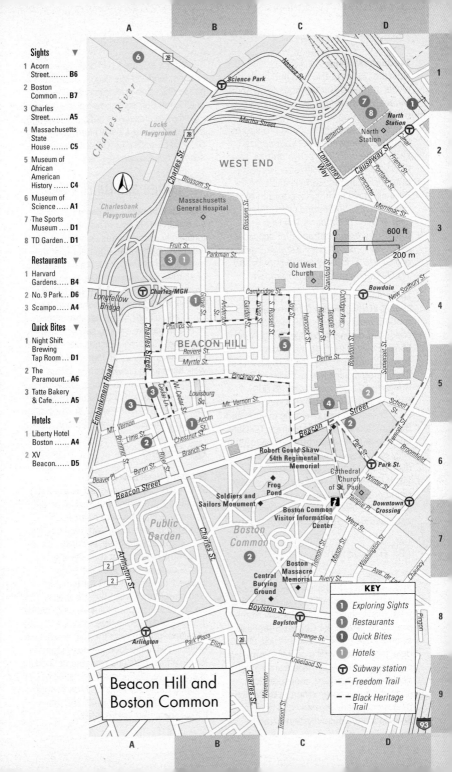

Sights ▼

1 Acorn Street....... **B6**
2 Boston Common **B7**
3 Charles Street....... **A5**
4 Massachusetts State House **C5**
5 Museum of African American History **C4**
6 Museum of Science **A1**
7 The Sports Museum **D1**
8 TD Garden .. **D1**

Restaurants ▼

1 Harvard Gardens..... **B4**
2 No. 9 Park.. **D6**
3 Scampo..... **A4**

Quick Bites ▼

1 Night Shift Brewing Tap Room ... **D1**
2 The Paramount.. **A6**
3 Tatte Bakery & Cafe....... **A5**

Hotels ▼

1 Liberty Hotel Boston **A4**
2 XV Beacon...... **D5**

KEY

1 Exploring Sights
1 Restaurants
1 Quick Bites
1 Hotels
Ⓣ Subway station
- - - Freedom Trail
- - Black Heritage Trail

Beacon Hill and Boston Common

The Sports Museum

MUSEUM | FAMILY | The fifth and sixth levels of the TD Garden house The Sports Museum, where displays of memorabilia and photographs showcase New England–based amateur and pro sports history and legends. Test your sports knowledge with interactive games, see how you stand up to life-size statues of heroes Carl Yastrzemski and Larry Bird, and take an hour-long tour of the museum. ⊠ *100 Legends Way, West End ✛ Use TD Garden's The Hub on Causeway grand entrance for access* ☎ *617/624–1234* ⊕ *www.sportsmuseum. org* ✍ *$15* ⊘ *Closed during games and TD Garden events* Ⓜ *North Station.*

TD Garden

SPORTS VENUE | FAMILY | This mammoth, modern facility opened in 1995 to the chagrin of diehard local sports fans who occasionally still grieve the crusty, old Boston Garden. Today, the home arena of the Boston Celtics (basketball) and Boston Bruins (hockey) seats nearly 20,000 patrons and also hosts headlining musical acts, Disney on Ice, wrestling events, and Boston's iconic Beanpot tourney. TD Garden Arena Tours depart from the ProShop daily during summer only; get tickets ($15) at ProShop. ⊠ *100 Legends Way, West End ✛ Use The Hub on Causeway grand entrance for access to TD Garden* ☎ *617/624–1050* ⊕ *www.tdgarden.com* ⊘ *Closed during events* Ⓜ *North Station.*

🍴 Restaurants

★ Scampo

$$$$ | ITALIAN | The Italian word "scampo" translates to "escape" in English, and that's what this restaurant at the Liberty Hotel—the former site of the Charles Street Jail—is: an escape into chef-owner Lydia Shire's delectable, buttery take on Italian-American cuisine. Everything is made from scratch, down to the bread and cheese options, and including a dozen different exceptional pastas and nearly as many crusty pizzas. **Known for:** the house-made-mozzarella

bar feature at least a half-dozen creamy options; Tandoori-oven cooked, crusty pizzas (the lamb is a classic) and breads; one hearty Sunday supper special, served weekly, like at Nonna's house. $ *Average main: $41* ⊠ *The Liberty Hotel, 215 Charles St., West End* ☎ *617/536–2100* ⊕ *www. scampoboston.com* Ⓜ *Charles/MGH.*

☕ Coffee and Quick Bites

Night Shift Brewing Tap Room

$ | AMERICAN | FAMILY | This place is hard to classify, and satisfies a variety of different needs, although beer is at the forefront. There's a small breakfast menu of sandwiches and pastries to go with great coffee options using Night Shift's own signature roasted beans, and the lunch and dinner menu has items made from scratch like salads, sandwiches, flatbreads, and main dishes, about half of which have beer as an ingredient in some way. **Known for:** brews its own beers; roasts its own coffee beans; tasty food. $ *Average main: $17* ⊠ *1 Lovejoy Wharf, West End* ☎ *617/294–4233* ⊕ *www.night-shiftbrewing.com* Ⓜ *North Station.*

🛏 Hotels

★ Liberty Hotel Boston

$$$ | HOTEL | Since it opened in late 2007, the buzz surrounding the chic Liberty—formerly Boston's Charles Street Jail—was at first deafening, with bankers, tech geeks, foreign playboys, and fashionistas all scrambling to call it their own; more than a decade later, the Liberty has evolved into what is part retreat, part nightclub. **Pros:** Lydia Shire's popular restaurant Scampo; exclusive daily events including art exhibits, live music, and yoga sessions; proximity to the Esplanade and Beacon Hill. **Cons:** loud in-house nightlife; long waits at bars and restaurants; parking is expensive. $ *Rooms from: $350* ⊠ *215 Charles St., West End* ☎ *617/224–4000* ⊕ *www.libertyhotel.com* ⇲ *298 rooms* 🍽 *No meals* Ⓜ *Charles/MGH.*

Government Center

This is a section of town Bostonians love to hate. While it's not Boston's prettiest locale (it's home to some of the city's bleakest architecture), it does have plenty of feathers in its tricorn cap, including City Hall Plaza (the site of feisty political rallies, summer concerts, and festivals), the country's oldest pushcart market (cobble-stoned Quincy Market), and the site where speeches were held encouraging independence from Great Britain (18th-century Faneuil Hall).

◉ Sights

★ Faneuil Hall Marketplace

HISTORIC SITE | FAMILY | Faneuil Hall has always sat in the middle of Boston's main marketplace and, to be clear, the single building facing Congress Street is the real Faneuil Hall, though locals often give that name to all five buildings in this shopping complex. Bostonians pronounce it *Fan-yoo'uhl* or *Fan-yuhl*. It was erected in 1742, the gift of wealthy merchant Peter Faneuil, who wanted the hall to serve as both a place for town meetings and a public market. It burned in 1761 and was immediately reconstructed according to the original plan of its designer, the Scottish portrait painter John Smibert (who lies in the Granary Burying Ground). In 1763 the political leader James Otis helped inaugurate the era that culminated in American independence when he dedicated the rebuilt hall to the cause of liberty.

In 1772 Samuel Adams stood here and first suggested that Massachusetts and the other colonies organize a Committee of Correspondence to maintain semi-clandestine lines of communication in the face of hardening British repression. In later years the hall again lived up to Otis's dedication when the abolitionists Wendell Phillips and Charles Sumner pleaded for support from its podium. The tradition continues to this day: in presidential-election years the hall is the site of debates between contenders in the Massachusetts primary.

Faneuil Hall was substantially enlarged and remodeled in 1805 according to a Greek Revival design of the noted architect Charles Bulfinch; this is the building you see today. Its purposes remain the same: the balconied Great Hall is available to citizens' groups on presentation of a request signed by a required number of responsible parties; it also plays host to regular concerts.

Inside Faneuil Hall are dozens of paintings of famous Americans, including the mural *Webster's Reply to Hayne* and Gilbert Stuart's portrait of Washington at Dorchester Heights. Park rangers give informational talks about the history and importance of Faneuil Hall every half hour. There are interactive displays about Boston sights and National Park Service rangers at the visitor center on the first floor can provide maps and other information.

On the building's top floors are the headquarters and museum and library of the **Ancient & Honorable Artillery Company of Massachusetts,** which is free to visit (but a $3 donation is welcome). Founded in 1638, it's the oldest militia in the Western Hemisphere, and the third oldest in the world, after the Swiss Guard and the Honorable Artillery Company of London. The museum is open weekdays 9 am to 3:30 pm.

When such men as Andrew Jackson and Daniel Webster debated the future of the Republic here, the fragrances of bacon and snuff—sold by merchants in **Quincy Market** across the road—greeted their noses. Today the aroma of coffee wafts through the hall from a snack bar. The shops at ground level sell New England bric-a-brac. ✉ *Faneuil Hall Sq., Government Center* ☏ *617/523–1300* ⊕ *www.nps.gov/bost/learn/historyculture/fh.htm* 🎟 *Free* Ⓜ *Government Center, Aquarium, State.*

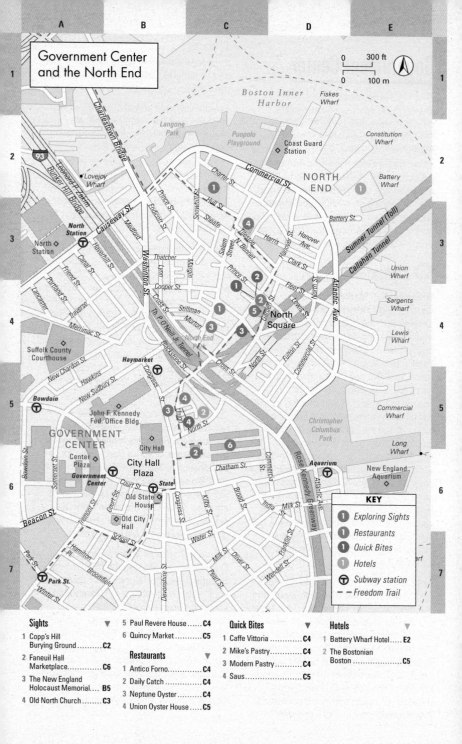

Government Center
and the North End

Boston Inner Harbor

Fiskes Wharf

NORTH END

Constitution Wharf

Battery Wharf

Langone Park

Puopolo Playground

Coast Guard Station

Commercial St.

Charter St.

Prince St.

Hull St.

Snowhill St.

Sheafe

Salem Street

Tileston

N. Bennet

Harris

Hanover Ave.

Clark St.

Battery St.

Sumner Tunnel (Toll)

Callahan Tunnel

Union Wharf

Sargents Wharf

Lewis Wharf

Charlestown Bridge

Leonard P. Zakim

Butler Hill Bridge

Lovejoy Wharf

North Station

North Station

Causeway St.

Medford

Endicott St.

Thatcher

Lyman

Cooper St.

Cross St.

Margin

Prince St.

Fleet St.

Lewis St.

Garden St.

North Square

Atlantic Ave.

Haverhill St.

Canal St.

Friend St.

Portland St.

Lancaster

Traverse

Merrimac St.

Washington St.

Th. P. O'Neill Jr. Tunnel

Stillman

Morton

North End Park

North St.

Fulton St.

Commercial St.

Suffolk County Courthouse

New Chardon St.

Hawkins

Haymarket

Blackstone St.

Cross St.

New Sudbury St.

Congress St.

Union St.

North St.

Commercial St.

Christopher Columbus Park

Commercial Wharf

Bowdoin

John F. Kennedy Fed. Office Bldg.

GOVERNMENT CENTER

Center Plaza

Government Center

City Hall

City Hall Plaza

Chatham St.

Commercial St.

Rose Kennedy Greenway

Long Wharf

Bowdoin St.

Somerset St.

Court St.

State

Old State House

Old City Hall

Congress St.

Kilby St.

Broad St.

India

Milk St.

Aquarium

Atlantic Ave.

New England Aquarium

Beacon St.

Tremont St.

Hamilton Pl.

Broomfield

School St.

Devonshire St.

Water St.

Milk St.

Oliver St.

Pearl St.

Wendell St.

Franklin St.

Park St.

Winter St.

Park St.

Sights ▼

1 Copp's Hill Burying Ground **C2**

2 Faneuil Hall Marketplace.............. **C6**

3 The New England Holocaust Memorial.... **B5**

4 Old North Church **C3**

5 Paul Revere House **C4**

6 Quincy Market **C5**

Restaurants ▼

1 Antico Forno.............. **C4**

2 Daily Catch **C4**

3 Neptune Oyster **C4**

4 Union Oyster House **C5**

Quick Bites ▼

1 Caffe Vittoria **C4**

2 Mike's Pastry.............. **C4**

3 Modern Pastry............ **C4**

4 Saus...................... **C5**

Hotels ▼

1 Battery Wharf Hotel **E2**

2 The Bostonian Boston **C5**

KEY

1 Exploring Sights

1 Restaurants

1 Quick Bites

1 Hotels

Ⓣ Subway station

- - - Freedom Trail

The New England Holocaust Memorial

MEMORIAL | Located at the north end of Union Park, the Holocaust Memorial is the work of Stanley Saitowitz, whose design was selected through an international competition; the finished memorial was dedicated in 1995. During the day the six 50-foot-high glass-and-steel towers seem at odds with the 18th-century streetscape of Blackstone Square behind it; at night, they glow like ghosts while manufactured steam from grates in the granite base makes for a particularly haunting scene. Recollections by Holocaust survivors are set into the glass-and-granite walls; the upper levels of the towers are etched with 6 million numbers in random sequence, symbolizing the Jewish victims of the Nazi horror. ⊠ *Union St. near Hanover St., Government Center* ☎ *617/457–8755* ⊕ *www. nehm.org* Ⓜ *Haymarket, Government Center, State.*

★ Quincy Market

MARKET | **FAMILY** | The market consists of three block-long annexes: **Quincy Market, North Market,** and **South Market.** The structures were designed in 1826 to alleviate the cramped conditions of Faneuil Hall and clean up the refuse that collected in Town Dock, the pond behind it. The central structure has kept its traditional market-stall layout, but the stalls now purvey international and specialty foods: sushi, frozen yogurt, bagels, calzones, sausage-on-a-stick, Chinese noodles, barbecue, and baklava, plus all the boutique chocolate-chip cookies your heart desires. Along the arcades on either side of the Central Market are vendors selling sweatshirts, photographs of Boston, and arts and crafts—some schlocky, some not—alongside a couple of patioed bars and restaurants. The North and South markets house a mixture of chain stores and specialty boutiques. ⊠ *Bordered by Clinton, Commercial, and Chatham Sts., Government Center* ☎ *617/523–1300* ⊕ *www.quincy-market.com* Ⓜ *Government Center, Aquarium, State.*

🍴 Restaurants

Union Oyster House

$$$ | **SEAFOOD** | Opening its doors in 1826 and earning a place on the National Historic Landmark list, Union Oyster House is Boston's oldest restaurant. Dine like Daniel Webster (alongside his nightly hangover-heavy tumbler of brandy and water) and order oysters on the half shell at the ground-floor raw bar in the oldest part of the restaurant. **Known for:** oldest Boston restaurant; long waits on weekends; oysters. Ⓢ *Average main: $28* ⊠ *41 Union St., Government Center* ☎ *617/227–2750* ⊕ *www.unionoyster-house.com* Ⓜ *Haymarket.*

☕ Coffee and Quick Bites

Saus

$ | **CAFÉ** | With 15 unique sauces on the menu, including homemade hot beer mustard, truffle ketchup, cheddar ale, smoky chipotle mayo, and gravy, Saus believes in the power of the condiment, which accompany its made-from-scratch sandwiches. The hand-cut fries are house-aged and twice fried, and they're known for their Friks, hand-rolled beef and pork sausages. **Known for:** Frik sausages; large variety of dipping sauces; tiny space. Ⓢ *Average main: $9* ⊠ *33 Union St., Government Center* ⊕ *www. sausboston.com* Ⓜ *Government Center.*

🛏 Hotels

The Bostonian

$$$ | **HOTEL** | **FAMILY** | Near historic Faneuil Hall, the Bostonian has guest rooms featuring Frette linens, pillowtop mattresses, and 40-inch TVs—many also have French doors with step-out balconies showcasing city views and the popular North End. Warmed up with red wall coverings, the lobby provides sofas and arm chairs, perfect for relaxing with a book chosen from one of the floor-to-ceiling bookshelves. **Pros:** updated fitness center; great location for sightseeing; free Wi-Fi. **Cons:** some rooms get street noise; Faneuil Hall can get clogged with tourists; parking is expensive. $ *Rooms from: $309* ✉ *Faneuil Hall Marketplace, 26 North St., Downtown* ☎ *617/523–3600, 866/866–8086* ⊕ *www.millennium-hotels.com* ⤵ *201 rooms* ⊙ *No meals* Ⓜ *Haymarket, Aquarium.*

Nightlife

Black Rose
BARS/PUBS | Hung with 20 bright county banners, decorated with pictures of Ireland and portraits of Samuel Beckett, Lady Gregory, and James Joyce, the Rose draws as many tourists as Irish-loving locals. Friendly Irish bartenders serve up pints, blarney, and far more Irish whiskies (42) than Scotches (14). Nightly shows by traditional Irish and contemporary musicians confirm its abiding Gaelic good cheer, or *craic*. Dine on Guinness beef stew and fish-and-chips—all served by staffers with authentic brogues. ✉ *160 State St., Government Center* ☎ *617/742–2286* ⊕ *www.blackroseboston.com* Ⓜ *Aquarium, State.*

🛍 Shopping

★ Boston Public Market
FOOD/CANDY | Open year-round, the indoor Boston Public Market offers a great place to grab a sandwich, sample local foods, and even pick up a tasty souvenir. The New England–centric marketplace has more than three-dozen vendors, selling everything from fresh herbs and fruit to meat and seafood, as well as plenty of food stalls. Everything sold at the market is produced or originated in New England including nonperishables like wool and carved wooden bowls. There's also a food demonstration kitchen, where visitors might be able to catch a live cooking class (with samples). Since it's all about staying with the season, the exciting about visiting the BPM is that no two days are the same. The Kids' Nook is a designated area for kids to gather and play, with activities throughout the week. ✉ *100 Hanover St., Government Center* ⊕ *bostonpublicmarket.org* Ⓜ *Haymarket/Government Center.*

The North End

The warren of small streets on the northeast side of Government Center is the North End, Boston's Little Italy. In the 17th century the North End *was* Boston, as much of the rest of the peninsula was still under water or had yet to be cleared. Here the town grew rich for a century and a half before the birth of American independence. The quarter's dwindling ethnic character lingers along Salem or Hanover Street, where you can still hear people speaking with Abruzzese accents.

👁 Sights

Copp's Hill Burying Ground
CEMETERY | An ancient and melancholy air hovers like a fine mist over this Colonial-era burial ground. The North End graveyard incorporates four cemeteries established between 1660 and 1819. Near the Charter Street gate is the tomb of the Mather family, the dynasty of church divines (Cotton and Increase were the most famous sons) who held sway in Boston during the heyday of the old theocracy. Also buried here is Robert Newman, who crept into the steeple of the Old North Church to hang the lanterns warning of the British attack the night of Paul Revere's ride. Look for the tombstone of Captain Daniel Malcolm; it's pockmarked with musket-ball fire from British soldiers, who used the stones for target practice. Across the street is 44 Hull (Boston's historic Skinny House), the city's **narrowest house,** measuring at just a mere 10 feet wide. ✉ *Intersection of Hull St. and Snowhill Rd., North End* ☎ *617/635–7361* ⊕ *www.cityofboston.gov/parks/hbgi/CoppsHill.asp* Ⓜ *North Station.*

★ Old North Church

BUILDING | At one end of the **Paul Revere Mall** is a church famous not only for being the oldest standing church building in Boston (built in 1723) but for housing the two lanterns that glimmered from its steeple on the night of April 18, 1775. This is Christ, or Old North, Church, where Paul Revere and the young sexton Robert Newman managed that night to signal the departure by water of the British regulars to Lexington and Concord. Newman, carrying the lanterns, ascended the steeple, while Revere began his clandestine trip by boat across the Charles.

Although William Price designed the structure after studying Christopher Wren's London churches, Old North—which still has an active Episcopal congregation (including descendants of the Reveres)—is an impressive building in its own right. Inside, note the gallery and the graceful arrangement of pews; the bust of George Washington, pronounced by the Marquis de Lafayette to be the truest likeness of the general he ever saw; the brass chandeliers, made in Amsterdam in 1700 and installed here in 1724; and the clock, the oldest still running in an American public building. Try to visit when changes are rung on the bells, after the 11 am Sunday service; they bear the inscription, "We are the first ring of bells cast for the British Empire in North America." The steeple itself is not the original—the tower was destroyed in a hurricane in 1804 and was replaced in 1954. On the Sunday closest to April 18, descendants of the patriots reenact the raising of the lanterns in the church belfry during a special ticketed evening service, which also includes readings of Longfellow's renowned poem, "Paul Revere's Ride" and Revere's first-person account of that fateful night. Visitors are welcome to drop in, but to see the bell-ringing chamber and the crypts, take the 30-minute behind-the-scenes tour.

Behind the church is the **Washington Memorial Garden,** where volunteers cultivate a plot devoted to plants and flowers favored in the 18th century. ✉ *193 Salem St., North End* ☎ *617/858–8231* ⊕ *www.oldnorth.com* ✉ *$3 suggested donation; $6 behind-the-scenes tour* Ⓜ *Haymarket, North Station.*

Paul Revere House

HOUSE | FAMILY | Originally on the site was the parsonage of the Second Church of Boston, home to the Rev. Increase Mather, the Second Church's minister. Mather's house burned in the great fire of 1676, and the house that Revere was to occupy was built on its location about four years later, nearly 100 years before Revere's 1775 midnight ride through Middlesex County. Revere owned it from 1770 until 1800, although he lived there for only 10 years and rented it out for the next two decades. Pre-1900 photographs show it as a shabby warren of storefronts and apartments. The clapboard sheathing is a replacement, but 90% of the framework is original; note the Elizabethan-style overhang and leaded windowpanes. A few Revere furnishings are on display here, and just gazing at his silverwork—much more of which is displayed at the Museum of Fine Arts—brings the man alive. Special events are scheduled throughout the year, many designed with children in mind, such as role play by characters dressed in period costume serving apple-cider cake and other colonial-era goodies, a silversmith practicing his trade, a dulcimer player entertaining a crowd, or a military-reenactment group in full period regalia.

The immediate neighborhood also has Revere associations. The little cobbled stoned park in North Square is named after Rachel Revere, his second wife, and the adjacent brick **Pierce-Hichborn House** once belonged to relatives of Revere and is open for $4 guided tours only. The garden connecting the Revere house and the Pierce-Hichborn House is planted

4

Boston and Environs THE NORTH END

with flowers and medicinal herbs favored in Revere's day. ✉ *19 North Sq., North End* ☎ *617/523–2338* ⊕ *www.paulreverehouse.org* 💲 *$5 (cash only)* 🕐 *Closed Mon. Jan.–Mar.* Ⓜ *Haymarket, Aquarium, Government Center.*

🍴 Restaurants

★ Antico Forno

$$ | ITALIAN | Many of the menu choices here come from the eponymous wood-burning brick oven, which turns out surprisingly delicate thin-crust pizzas simply topped with tomato and buffalo mozzarella or complicated combos like pistachio pesto, fresh mozzarella, and sausage. While the name, which translates to "old oven," gives the pizzas top billing, Antico excels at a variety of Italian country dishes that harken back to the Old Country, like veal parmigiana, osso buco with pork shanks, chicken saltimbocca, and handmade pastas; the specialty, gnocchi, is rich and creamy but light. **Known for:** wood-fired, brick-oven pizza; Italian country classics; casual, jovial atmosphere. 💲 *Average main: $22* ✉ *93 Salem St., North End* ☎ *617/723–6733* ⊕ *www.anticofornoboston.com* Ⓜ *Haymarket.*

★ Daily Catch

$$ | SEAFOOD | You've just got to love this shoebox-size place—for the noise, the intimacy, the complete absence of pretense, and, above all, the Sicilian-style seafood, which proved so popular, it spawned two other locations (one in Brookline and another in Boston's Seaport area). With garlic and olive oil forming the foundation for almost every dish, this cheerful, bustling spot specializes in calamari, black squid-ink pastas, and linguine with clam sauce, all served in the skillets in which they were cooked, hot from the stove. **Known for:** garlic-rich preparations; luscious seafood skillet pastas; intimate, elbow-to-elbow dining. 💲 *Average main: $24* ✉ *323 Hanover St., North End* ☎ *617/523–8567* ⊕ *thedailycatch.com* 🚫 *No credit cards* Ⓜ *Haymarket.*

★ Neptune Oyster

$$$ | SEAFOOD | This *piccolo* oyster bar, the first of its kind in the neighborhood, has only 22 chairs, but the long marble bar adorned with mirrors has extra seating for 15 more patrons, who can watch the oyster shuckers deftly undo handfuls of more than a dozen different kinds of bivalves to savor as an appetizer or on a *plateau di frutti di mare*, a gleaming tower of oysters and other raw-bar items piled over ice that you can order from the slip of paper they pass out listing each day's crustacean options. Daily specials run the gamut, from lobster spaghetti to scarlet prawns to sea urchin bucatini. **Known for:** casual setting; Italian-style seafood; generously packed lobster roll. 💲 *Average main: $34* ✉ *63 Salem St., North End* ☎ *617/742–3474* ⊕ *www.neptuneoyster.com* Ⓜ *Haymarket.*

☕ Coffee and Quick Bites

★ Caffe Vittoria

$ | ITALIAN | FAMILY | Established in 1929, Caffe Vittoria—Boston's oldest Italian café—is rightfully known as Boston's most traditional Italian café, which is one of the reason's why the place is packed with locals. With gleaming brass, marble tabletops, four levels of seating, three bars that serve aperitifs, one of the city's best selections of grappa, and one massive, ancient espresso maker, this old-fashioned café will make you want to lose yourself in these surroundings. **Known for:** specialty coffee drinks; grapa; gelato. 💲 *Average main: $10* ✉ *290–296 Hanover St., North End* ☎ *617/227–7606* ⊕ *www.caffevittoria.com* 🚫 *No credit cards.*

Mike's Pastry

$ | BAKERY | Every local knows the white box with the blue and white string as a to-go treasure chest of Italian delicacies. Known for their cannoli, Mike's has been bringing the best in pastries and cookies to the North End (and presidential patrons like Bill Clinton) since

1946. **Known for:** cannoli; long lines; cases of Italian cookies. $ *Average main: $9* ⊠ *300 Hanover St., North End* ☎ *617/742–3050* ⊕ *www.mikespastry. com.*

Modern Pastry

$ | ITALIAN | The North End's other favorite cannoli king, Modern is a hit with the locals. Using old world recipes that were relied on for more than 150 years, their crusts are flaky, their fillings rich, and they have a selection of torrone nougat confections, cookies, French horns, and Napoleons. **Known for:** dainty cannoli; deliciously moist cakes; handmade Italian candies. $ *Average main: $8* ⊠ *257 Hanover St., North End* ☎ *617/523–3783* ⊕ *www.modernpastry. com* ⊟ *No credit cards.*

🛏 Hotels

Battery Wharf Hotel

$$$$ | HOTEL | FAMILY | One of the growing number of lodgings clustered along Boston's ever-expanding Harborwalk—a pretty pedestrian path that runs from Charlestown to Dorchester—the Battery Wharf Hotel looks more like a gated community than a chain hotel. **Pros:** walking distance to more than 80 world-class restaurants; on-site Exhale Spa has discounted spa services and fitness classes for hotel guests; great North End location; water taxi stand on-site. **Cons:** far from Newbury Street and South End shopping; 15- to 20-minute walk to nearest T stations; hotel is in two separate buildings. $ *Rooms from: $400* ⊠ *3 Battery Wharf, North End* ☎ *617/657–1834* ⊕ *www.battery-wharfhotelboston.com* ⇥ *166 rooms* ❑ *No meals* Ⓜ *Haymarket, North Station.*

Mike's vs. Modern

Welcome to Boston's long-standing cannoli war. Mike's Pastry and Modern Pastry are widely considered the North End's two best cannoli spots, but locals can't seem to agree on which is better, splitting their strong allegiance right down the center. Modern's cannoli are smaller and more delicate than Mike's, while Mike's are crunchier, sweeter, and boast more flavors (18 to be exact). Which will you choose?

🛍 Shopping

★ **Shake the Tree**

SPECIALTY STORES | Irresistible defines this one-stop shop, brimming with an eclectic array of floral dresses and tops, wide-legged pants, letterpress greeting cards, small brand apothecary, craft cocktail supplies, global cookbooks, woven baskets, and mixed media jewelry that you never knew you needed. Owner Marian Klausner creates an inspiring award-winning selection from her global travels. ⊠ *67 Salem St., North End* ☎ *617/742–0484* ⊕ *www.shakethetreeboston.com* Ⓜ *Haymarket.*

Charlestown

Boston started here. Charlestown was a thriving settlement a year before Colonials headed across the Charles River at William Blaxton's invitation to found the city proper. Today the district's attractions include two of the most visible—and vertical—monuments in Boston: the Bunker Hill Monument, which commemorates the grisly battle that became a symbol of patriotic resistance against the British, and the USS *Constitution*, whose masts continue to tower over the waterfront where she was built more than 200 years ago.

◉ Sights

★ Bunker Hill Monument

MEMORIAL | Two misunderstandings surround this famous monument. First, the Battle of Bunker Hill was actually fought on Breed's Hill, which is where the monument sits today. (The real Bunker Hill is about ½ mile to the north of the monument.) In truth, Bunker was the originally planned locale for the battle, and for that reason its name stuck. Second, although the battle is generally considered a Colonial success, the Americans lost. It was a Pyrrhic victory for the British Redcoats, who sacrificed nearly half of their 2,200 men; American casualties numbered 400 to 600. One thing is true: the Battle of Bunker Hill put the British on notice that were up against a formidable opponent. According to history books, this is also the location of the famous war cry, "Don't fire until you see the whites of their eyes," uttered by American colonel William Prescott or General Israel Putnam (there's still debate on who gave the actual command). This was a shout out to an 18th-century Prussian warning to soldiers that lack of ammunition and notorious musket inaccuracy meant every shot needed to count. The Americans did employ a deadly delayed-action strategy on June 17, 1775, and conclusively proved themselves capable of defeating the forces of the British Empire.

Among the dead were the brilliant young American doctor and political activist Joseph Warren, recently commissioned as a major general but fighting as a private, and the British major John Pitcairn, who two months prior had led the Redcoats into Lexington. Pitcairn is believed to be buried in the crypt of Old North Church.

In 1823 the committee formed to construct a monument on the site of the battle chose the form of an Egyptian obelisk. Architect Solomon Willard designed a 221-foot-tall granite obelisk, a tremendous feat of engineering for its day. The Marquis de Lafayette laid the cornerstone of the monument in 1825, but because of a lack of funds, it wasn't dedicated until 1843. Daniel Webster's stirring words at the ceremony commemorating the laying of its cornerstone have gone down in history: "Let it rise! Let it rise, till it meets the sun in his coming. Let the earliest light of the morning gild it, and parting day linger and play upon its summit."

The monument's zenith is reached by a flight of 294 tightly spiraled steps. There's no elevator, but the views from the observatory are worth the effort of the arduous climb. From April through June, due to high numbers, all visitors who wish to climb must first obtain a pass from the Bunker Hill Museum at 43 Monument Square. Climbing passes are free, but limited in number and can be either reserved up to two weeks in advance or on a first-come, first-served basis. The museum's artifacts and exhibits tell the story of the battle, while a detailed diorama shows the action in miniature. ⊠ *Monument Sq., Charlestown* ☎ *617/242–5641* ⊕ *www.nps.gov/bost/historyculture/bhm.htm* ▣ *Free* Ⓜ *Community College.*

★ USS *Constitution*

MILITARY SITE | **FAMILY** | Affectionately known as "Old Ironsides," the USS *Constitution* rides proudly at anchor in her berth at the Charlestown Navy Yard. The oldest commissioned ship in the U.S. fleet is a battlewagon of the old school, of the days of "wooden ships and iron men"—when she and her crew of 200 succeeded at the perilous task of asserting the sovereignty of an improbable new nation. Every July 4, she's towed out for a celebratory turnabout in Boston Harbor, the very place her keel was laid in 1797.

The venerable craft has narrowly escaped the scrap heap several times in her long history. She was launched on October 21, 1797, as part of the nation's fledgling navy. Her hull was made of live oak, the toughest wood grown in North America; her bottom was sheathed in copper, provided by Paul Revere at a nominal cost. Her principal service was during Thomas Jefferson's campaign against the Barbary pirates, off the coast of North Africa, and in the War of 1812. In 42 engagements her record was 42–0.

The nickname "Old Ironsides" was acquired during the War of 1812, when shots from the British warship *Guerrière* appeared to bounce off her hull. Talk of scrapping the ship began as early as 1830, but she was saved by a public campaign sparked by Oliver Wendell Holmes's poem "Old Ironsides." She underwent a major restoration in the early 1990s. Today she continues, the oldest commissioned warship afloat in the world, to be a part of the U.S. Navy. In 2015, she was dry docked for a 26-month restoration that included replacement of select hull planks, the 1995 copper sheathing, and deck beams, returning to the water in 2017.

The navy personnel who look after the *Constitution* maintain a 24-hour watch. Instead of taking the T, you can get closer to the ship by taking MBTA Bus 93 to Chelsea Street from Haymarket. Or you can take the Boston Harbor Cruise water shuttle from Long Wharf to Pier 4. ⊠ *Charlestown Navy Yard, 55 Constitution Rd., Charlestown* ☎ *617/242–7511* ⊕ *ussconstitutionmuseum.org* ✉ *Free* Ⓜ *North Station.*

★ **USS** *Constitution* **Museum**
MUSEUM | FAMILY | With nearly 2,000 artifacts and more than 10,000 archival records pertaining to the USS *Constitution* on display, exhibits spark excitement about maritime culture and naval service. All ages enjoy "All Hands on Deck: A Sailor's Life in 1812," complete with

opportunities to scrub decks, scramble aloft to furl a sail, eat a meal of salted meat and ship's biscuit, and crawl into a hammock. History buffs get a stem-to-stern look at the ship's history, from its creation to battles. ⊠ *Charlestown* ⚓ *Adjacent to USS Constitution, Charlestown Navy Yard* ☎ *617/426–1812* ⊕ *www. ussconstitutionmuseum.org* ✉ *Suggested donation from $5* Ⓜ *North Station; MBTA Bus 92 to Charlestown City Sq. or Bus 93 to Chelsea St. from Haymarket; or Boston Harbor Cruise water shuttle from Long Wharf to Pier 4.*

🍴 Restaurants

Warren Tavern
$ | AMERICAN | Built in 1780 and reportedly one of the country's oldest taverns, this restored colonial neighborhood pub in the quaint and historic gaslight district was once frequented by George Washington and Paul Revere. After a blustery walk through the Navy Yard, grab a seat by the fireplace and warm yourself with a hearty chowder or short rib shepherd's pie and Sam Adams draft. **Known for:** historical atmosphere; beer selection; short rib shepherd's pie. Ⓢ *Average main: $14* ⊠ *2 Pleasant St., Charlestown* ☎ *617/241–8142* ⊕ *www.warrentavern. com* Ⓜ *Community College.*

Downtown

Boston's commercial and financial districts—the area commonly called Downtown—are in a maze of streets that seem to have been laid out with little logic; they are village lanes now lined with modern 40-story office towers. Just as the Great Fire of 1872 swept the old Financial District clear, the Downtown construction in more recent times has obliterated many of the buildings where 19th-century Boston businessmen sat in front of their rolltop desks. Yet historic sites remain tucked among the skyscrapers; a number of them have been linked together to make up a fascinating section of the Freedom Trail.

Reportedly, it's the third largest Chinatown in the United States, after those in San Francisco and Manhattan, although today's neighborhood runs the spectrum of many Far East cultures, from Thai to Taiwanese, Korean to Cambodian. Today, Beach Street serves as Chinatown's main street. Just west of Chinatown, the majority of Boston's historic stages reside in the Theater District, which means the area is a hot spot for ballet, opera, Broadway tours, stand-up comedy, and other performing arts productions. And, then, to the east of Chinatown, a very small enclave known as the Leather District features a few destination standouts, including the city's best sushi restaurant and South Station.

◉ Sights

Benjamin Franklin Statue/Boston Latin School

PUBLIC ART | FAMILY | This stop on the Freedom Trail, in front of Old City Hall, commemorates the noted revolutionary, statesman, and inventor. His likeness also marks the original location of Boston Latin School, the country's oldest public school (founded in 1635), which still molds young minds, albeit from the Fenway neighborhood today. Franklin attended Boston Latin with three other signers of the Declaration of Independence—Samuel Adams, John Hancock, and Robert Treat Paine—but he has the dubious distinction of being the only one of the four not to graduate. ■TIP→ This is Freedom Trail stop 6. ⊠ 45 School St., Downtown ☎ 617/635–3911 ⊕ www. thefreedomtrail.org Ⓜ Park.

Boston Massacre Site

MEMORIAL | FAMILY | A circle of cobblestones in front of the Old State House marks the site of the Boston Massacre. To recap: it was on the snowy evening of

March 5, 1770, that nine British soldiers fired in panic upon a taunting mob of more than 75 colonists who were upset over British occupation and taxation. Five townsmen died. In the legal action that followed, the defense of the accused soldiers was undertaken by John Adams and Josiah Quincy, both of whom vehemently opposed British oppression but were devoted to the principle of fair trial. All but two of the nine regulars charged were acquitted; the others were branded on the hand for the crime of manslaughter. Paul Revere lost little time in capturing the "massacre" in a dramatic engraving that soon became one of the Revolution's most potent images of propaganda. ■TIP→ This is Freedom Trail stop 10. ⊠ 206 Washington St., Downtown ⊕ www.thefreedomtrail.org Ⓜ State.

★ King's Chapel

RELIGIOUS SITE | FAMILY | Both somber and dramatic, King's Chapel looms over the corner of Tremont and School streets. Its distinctive shape wasn't achieved entirely by design; for lack of funds, it was never topped with a steeple. The first chapel on this site was erected in 1688 for the establishment of an Anglican place of worship, and it took five years to build the solid Quincy-granite structure seen today. The chapel's bell is Paul Revere's largest and, in his judgment, his sweetest sounding. For a behind-the-scenes look at the bell or crypt, take a guided tour. You won't be disappointed. ■TIP→ Freedom Trail stop 5. ⊠ 58 Tremont St., Downtown ☎ 617/523–1749 ⊕ www.kings-chapel. org ⊠ $4 suggested donation; $7 Bell & Bones tour; $5 Art & Architecture tour Ⓜ Park, State, Government Center.

★ Old South Meeting House

HISTORIC SITE | FAMILY | This is the second-oldest church building in Boston, and were it not for Longfellow's celebration of the Old North in "Paul Revere's Ride," it might well be the most famous. Today, visitors can learn about its history through exhibits and audio programs. Some of

The Old South Meeting House is Boston's second-oldest church building; it's also where the spark was lit for the infamous Boston Tea Party.

the fiercest of the town meetings that led to the Revolution were held here, culminating in the gathering of December 16, 1773, which was called by Samuel Adams to confront the crisis of three ships, laden with dutiable tea, anchored at Griffin's Wharf. The activists wanted the tea returned to England, but the governor would not permit it—and the rest is history. The Voices of Protest exhibit celebrates Old South as a forum for free speech from Revolutionary days to the present. ■ TIP→ This is Freedom Trail stop 8. ✉ 310 Washington St., Downtown 🕾 617/720–1713 ⊕ www.revolutionaryspaces.org 🎫 $6 Ⓜ State, Downtown Crossing.

★ Old State House

BUILDING | FAMILY | This colonial-era landmark has one of the most recognizable facades in Boston, with its gable adorned by a brightly gilded lion and silver unicorn, symbols of British imperial power. This was the seat of the colonial government from 1713 until the Revolution, and after the evacuation of the British from Boston in 1776 it served the independent Commonwealth until its replacement on Beacon Hill was completed in 1798. The Declaration of Independence was first read in public in Boston from its balcony. John Hancock was inaugurated here as the first governor under the new state constitution. Today, it's an interactive museum with exhibits, artifacts, and 18th-century artwork, and tells the stories of Revolutionary Bostonians through costumed guides. ■ TIP→ This is Freedom Trail stop 9.

✉ 206 Washington St., Downtown 🕾 617/720–1713 ⊕ www.revolutionaryspaces.org 🎫 $12 Ⓜ State, Government Center.

Rose Kennedy Greenway

CITY PARK | FAMILY | This one linear mile of winding parks marks the path the highway once took through the city (the Big Dig project is legendary for not the best of reasons, as the most expensive highway project in the United States), adds much-needed flora and fauna to the area and has turned into a delightful backyard playground that stretches from the North End to Chinatown. Lawn

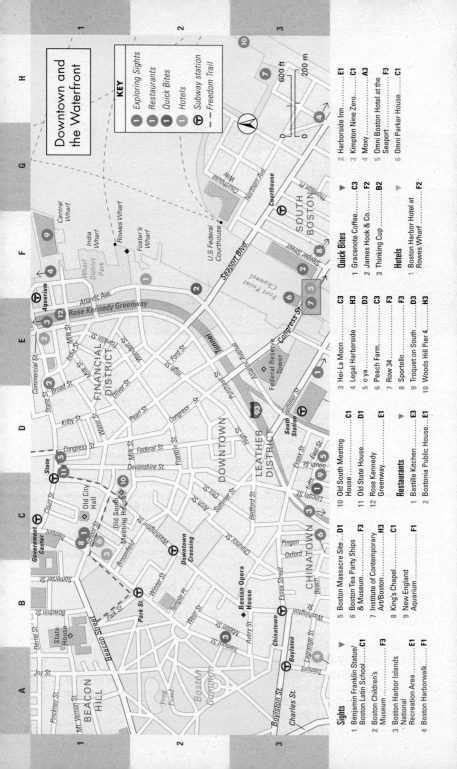

Downtown and the Waterfront

KEY

- ① Exploring Sights
- ① Restaurants
- ① Quick Bites
- ① Hotels
- Ⓣ Subway station
- - - Freedom Trail

0 — 600 ft
0 — 200 m

Sights ▶

1 Benjamin Franklin Statue/
  Boston Latin School C1
2 Boston Children's
  Museum F3
3 Boston Harbor Islands
  National
  Recreation Area E1
4 Boston Harborwalk F1

5 Boston Massacre Site D1
6 Boston Tea Party Ships
  & Museum F3
7 Institute of Contemporary
  Art/Boston H3
8 King's Chapel C1
9 New England
  Aquarium F1

10 Old South Meeting
   House C1
11 Old State House D1
12 Rose Kennedy
   Greenway E1

Restaurants ▶

1 Bastille Kitchen E3
2 Bostonia Public House ... E1

3 Hei-La Moon C3
4 Legal Harborside H3
5 oya D3
6 Peach Farm C3
7 Row 34 .... F3
8 Sportello F3
9 Troquet on South D3
10 Woods Hill Pier 4 .... H3

Quick Bites ▶

1 Gracenote Coffee C3
2 James Hook & Co. F2
3 Thinking Cup B2

Hotels ▶

1 Boston Harbor Hotel at
  Rowes Wharf F2

2 Harborside Inn E1
3 Kimpton Nine Zero C1
4 Moxy A3
5 Omni Boston Hotel at the
  Seaport F3
6 Omni Parker House. C1

furniture and games, seasonal farmers and artist markets, art installations, water features, live performances, free Wi-Fi, and more make it a lively spot, especially in warmer months. There's a one-of-a-kind, hand-carved carousel; and the food truck scene has grown into a bustling lunchtime destination (not to mention the seasonal Trillium Beer Garden hotspot). The park's website has a map of its 17 acres; a pleasant stroll through all of them will take you from the North End to Chinatown. ⊠ *Downtown* ⊹ *Between New Sudbury St. in North End and Beach St. in Chinatown; along Atlantic Ave.* ⊕ *www.rosekennedygreenway.org* Ⓜ *State, Haymarket, Chinatown, Aquarium.*

🍴 Restaurants

★ Bostonia Public House

$$$ | **AMERICAN** | **FAMILY** | Airy and classic in atmosphere, this modern restaurant focuses on two things: food and local history (it is, after all, situated in a historic 1902 building). The menu features elevated takes on comfort food; at lunch expect more sandwiches. **Known for:** weekend brunch set to live music; long bar with lots of seating; really, really good food. Ⓢ *Average main: $30* ⊠ *131 State St., Downtown* ☎ *617/948–9800* ⊕ *www.bostoniapublichouse.com* Ⓜ *Aquarium.*

★ Hei-La Moon

$ | **CHINESE** | **FAMILY** | Hei-La Moon is located on Beach Street, but don't get lost looking for it; you have to put Chinatown at your back and cross Surface Road, almost into the Leather District. But once you do locate this Cantonese dim sum palace, you will be glad for it—locals fill the large, ornately decorated dining room pretty early in the morning, drinking tea and noshing on small plates brought around by waitstaff on carts. **Known for:** endless dim sum; inexpensive prices; few English-speaking staff. Ⓢ *Average main: $10* ⊠ *88 Beach St., Chinatown* ☎ *617/338–8813* Ⓜ *South Station.*

★ o ya

$$$$ | **SUSHI** | If you want to experience the best sushi you've ever tasted— and you have the purse for it—eat at upscale Tim and Nancy Cushman's Leather District restaurant (this was the first, but there's also Manhattan and Mexico City locations). Despite o ya's tucked away location and hidden door, the place isn't exactly a secret: critics from the *New York Times, Bon Appetit,* and *Food & Wine* have all named this improvisational sushi spot among the best in the country. **Known for:** delicate, beautiful, sophisticated sushi; spectacular omakase tasting menu: 17 courses ($185) or 21 courses ($285); expensive prices. Ⓢ *Average main: $60* ⊠ *9 East St., Chinatown* ☎ *617/654–9900* ⊕ *o-ya.restaurant/o-ya-boston* ⊘ *Closed Sun. and Mon.* Ⓜ *South Station.*

★ Peach Farm

$ | **CANTONESE** | **FAMILY** | It may look a bit worse for wear, but this authentic Cantonese restaurant is a Chinatown landmark among locals and neighborhood visitors. What's really special is the live fish tank where diners can select the fish they want to eat—and it's cooked to order fresh—while the extensive menu offers perhaps too many options, but the waitstaff is happy to give recommendations. **Known for:** incredibly fresh seafood; house-fried rice with sweet Chinese sausage and scallops; late-night hours— until 3 am. Ⓢ *Average main: $12* ⊠ *4 Tyler St., Chinatown* ☎ *617/482–3332* ⊕ *www.peachfarmboston.com* Ⓜ *Chinatown, South Station.*

★ Troquet on South

$$$$ | **FRENCH FUSION** | Despite having what might well be Boston's longest wine list, with nearly 500 vintages (more than 50 of which are available by the glass), plus an interactive champagne cart, this French fusion spot flies somewhat under the radar. Still, locals know that Troquet offers all the ingredients for a lovely and delectable evening: a generous space for drinking and dining, a knowledgeable yet unpretentious staff, and decadent fare, beginning with chewy rolls and farm-churned butter scooped from a bucket, and dishes like seared Hudson Valley foie gras and decadent duck a l'Orange. **Known for:** exceptional wine selection; mouthwatering bistro fare; excellent cheese cart. $ *Average main: $45* ⊠ *107 South St., Theater District* ☎ *617/695–9463* ⊕ *troquetboston.com* ⊙ *No lunch Sat. Closed Sun.* Ⓜ *Boylston.*

☕ Coffee and Quick Bites

★ Gracenote Coffee
$ | **CAFÉ** | Gracenote roasts top-shelf coffee beans using its own unique process here in Massachusetts, and then serves it in a teeny Leather District storefront just across the border from Chinatown. The flavor is well worth the slightly out-of-the-way jaunt to this hipster haven for pour-overs and espresso drinks that are the focus of the menu. **Known for:** unmatched coffee; extensive variety of milk alternatives; really friendly baristas. $ *Average main: $5* ⊠ *108 Lincoln St., Chinatown* ⊕ *www.gracenotecoffee.com* Ⓜ *South Station.*

★ Thinking Cup
$ | **CAFÉ** | Across Tremont Street from Boston Common, Thinking Cup caters to a mixed crowd of area professionals and comm students from nearby Emerson College. Rarely is the coffeehouse not packed with caffeine addicts looking for their next fix of Stumptown coffee, whether it's in the form of a single origin pour over or a macchiato. **Known for:** signature lattes: the hazelnut is made with roasted hazelnut paste, and the honey-cinnamon with a house-made syrup; awesome sandwiches, especially the Jittery Hen, made with coffee-braised chicken; no Wi-Fi access. $ *Average main: $10* ⊠ *165 Tremont St., Downtown* ☎ *617/482–5555* ⊕ *www.thinkingcup. com* Ⓜ *Boylston, Park.*

🛏 Hotels

★ Kimpton Nine Zero
$$$ | **HOTEL** | **FAMILY** | This Kimpton boutique hotel is sleek, sleek, sleek—all smooth lines, neutral tones, wood, and leather, and then bam! sudden bursts of vibrant color and pop art. **Pros:** in-room spa therapy available; late-afternoon hosted lobby wine reception (daily, 5–6 pm); in-room yoga mats. **Cons:** smallish rooms; fee for Wi-Fi; no airport shuttle. $ *Rooms from: $350* ⊠ *90 Tremont St., Downtown* ☎ *617/772–5800, 866/906–9090* ⊕ *www. ninezero.com* ⊐ *190 rooms* ⦿Ⓞ *No meals* Ⓜ *Park, Government Center.*

Moxy
$$ | **HOTEL** | One of Boston's newest hotels—it opened in October 2019—Moxy is an Instagrammer's dream come true with its sleek exterior and artful flair (say, like custom murals by well-known street artists). **Pros:** 24th-floor rooftop lounge for guest-only use; floor-to-ceiling windows and viewfinders in every room; Bar Moxy work-fun space featuring board games, free Wi-Fi, coffee, cocktails, and food. **Cons:** not good for families; lots of street noise; small rooms. $ *Rooms from: $280* ⊠ *240 Tremont St., Theater District* ☎ *617/793–4200* ⊕ *www.marriott.com/hotels/travel/bosox-moxy-boston-downtown* ⊐ *340 rooms* ⦿Ⓞ *No meals* Ⓜ *Boylston, Chinatown.*

🎭 Performing Arts

Boch Center Wang Theatre and Shubert Theatre
CONCERTS | The historic Wang Theatre, which opened in 1925 and holds an audience of 3,500, and its 1910 little sister, the Shubert Theatre, partner up to create this performance-space complex dedicated to national and international productions, dance companies, concerts, and headlining comics. ■ **TIP➔ Check out the schedule online, and order your tickets before you come to town.**

265 and 270 Tremont St., Theater District ☎ *800/982–2787 Wang Theatre, 866/348–9738 Shubert Theatre* ⊕ *www. bochcenter.org* Ⓜ *Boylston.*

Charles Playhouse

THEATER | The Charles Playhouse celebrated its 175th anniversary in 2014 with a $2 million renovation. The vintage stage—also formerly serving as a church, Prohibition-era speakeasy, and jazz club—has been hosting two long-running local favorites: *Blue Man Group* since 1995, and the zany whodunit *Shear Madness* since 1980. Blue Man Group's uniquely exhilarating production features a trio of deadpan performance artists painted vivid cobalt as they pound drums, share eureka moments, spray sloppy good will, and freely dispense toilet paper. ■TIP➔ **First-timer alert: dress casual, especially if you're seated down front.** ✉ *74 Warrenton St., Theater District* ☎ *617/426–6912 general box office, 800/258–3626 Blue Man Group tickets, 617/426–5225 Shear Madness tickets* ⊕ *www.charlesplayhouse.com* Ⓜ *Boylston.*

★ **Citizens Bank Opera House**

DANCE | FAMILY | The 2,700-seat, meticulously restored, vaudville-era beaux arts building has been lavished with $35 million worth of gold leaf, lush carpeting, and rococo ornamentation, and it reopened to the public in 2004 after being dormant and neglected for about 12 years. Since then, it has been Boston's premiere destination for touring Broadway companies as well as the home theater for Boston Ballet and all its productions, including its famous *The Nutcracker.* ■TIP➔ **The Opera House offers really cool one-hour, guided historical tours, and 25-minute backstage tours, which must be reserved online in advance.** ✉ *539 Washington St., Theater District* ☎ *617/695–6955 Boston Ballet tickets, 800/982–2787 Broadway show tickets* ⊕ *www.bostonoperahouse.com* ✉ *$17 historical tour; $10 backstage tour* Ⓜ *Boylston, Chinatown, Downtown Crossing.*

🛍 **Shopping**

★ **Brattle Book Shop**

BOOKS/STATIONERY | Bibliophiles can't get enough of this old-timey book store that is, literally, chockablack with books—floor to ceiling and stuffed into corners. The store has been in operation since 1825, and today, owner Ken Gloss (a fixture on PBS' *Antiques Road Show*) fields queries from passionate book lovers about out-of-print, rare, antique and foreign language tomes, and also last year's used best-seller. If you're in need of a read for the ride home, browse the rolling carts in Brattle's adjacent outdoor lot, where books of all genres go for $5, $3, or just $1. ✉ *9 West St., Downtown* ☎ *617/542–0210* ⊕ *www.brattlebookshop.com* 🕐 *Closed Sun.* Ⓜ *Downtown Crossing.*

The Waterfront

Along the Waterfront, you'll encounter wharf after wharf of harbor activity: private vessels, luxury yachts, harbor cruises, ferries, and more. Long Wharf, Central Wharf with the New England Aquarium, and Rowes Wharf are the three most prominent. Other attractions in this neighborhood include Boston HarborWalk, the Rose Kennedy Greenway, and the lesser-known gem just offshore, the Boston Harbor Islands. Many upscale hotels and restaurants make the most of the expansive water views.

👁 **Sights**

★ **Boston Harbor Islands National Recreation Area**

BUILDING | FAMILY | Comprising 34 tiny islands and peninsulas, this is one of the city's best hidden gems—and it's literally out of sight. Stretching from South Boston (Castle Island) to the coastlines of South Shore towns Hingham and Hull, each island is different, but most feature abundant nature with miles of lightly traveled trails, shoreline, sea life and wild plants. The focal point of the national park is 39-acre Georges Island and its partially restored pre–Civil War Fort Warren that once held Confederate prisoners. Other islands worth visiting include Peddocks Island, which holds the remains of Ft. Andrews, and Spectacle Island, a popular destination for swimming (with lifeguards). Lovells, Peddocks, Grape, and Bumpkin islands all allow camping with a permit, from late June through Labor Day. Pets and alcohol are not allowed on the Harbor Islands.

■ TIP➔ **Ferries shuttle visitors from Boston to Georges and Spectacle islands daily during summer months. Plan to spend a whole day exploring!** ⊠ *Boston Harbor Islands National and State Park Welcome Center, 191 W. Atlantic Ave., Waterfront* ☎ *617/223–8666* ⊕ *www.bostonharborislands.org* ⊘ *Closed mid-Oct.–mid–May* Ⓜ *Aquarium.*

★ New England Aquarium

ZOO | FAMILY | As interesting and exciting as it is educational, this aquarium is a must for those who are curious about what lives in and around the sea. The building's glass-and-steel exterior is constructed to mimic fish scales, and seals bark and swim in the outdoor tank. Inside the main facility, more than 30,000 animals of 800 different species frolic in simulated habitats. Penguins, hands-on creature touch tanks, and sea lions, are a few star exhibits. The real showstopper, though, is the four-story, 200,000-gallon ocean-reef tank. Ramps winding around the tank lead to the top level and allow you to view the inhabitants from many vantage points. Don't miss the five-times-a-day feedings; each lasts nearly an hour and takes divers 24 feet into the tank. ⊠ *1 Central Wharf, Waterfront* ☎ *617/973–5200* ⊕ *www.neaq.org* ⊠ *$32; $10 IMAX; $55 whale watch* Ⓜ *Aquarium.*

☕ Coffee and Quick Bites

James Hook & Co.

$$$ | SEAFOOD | FAMILY | This Waterfront seafood shanty in the heart of Downtown leaves all its frills for its lobster-loaded rolls; they're served with mayo or with butter, in a bun, and wrapped with foil so you can sit for a minute or eat it on the go. Other specialties include lobster mac and cheese, whole boiled lobster, stuffed clams, and the shrimp and corn chowder. **Known for:** lobster rolls; whole-cooked lobsters; rustic vibe and no-frills seating. Ⓢ *Average main: $35* ⊠ *440 Atlantic Ave., Waterfront* ☎ *617/423–5501* ⊕ *www. jameshooklobster.com* Ⓜ *South Station.*

🏨 Hotels

Boston Harbor Hotel at Rowes Wharf

$$$$ | HOTEL | Boston has plenty of iconic landmarks, but none are as synonymous with uber-hospitality as the Boston Harbor Hotel. **Pros:** free Wi-Fi and in-room tablet; premier views of Boston Harbor or the city; water shuttle to Logan Airport. **Cons:** pricey; the spa books up early, so make an advance reservation; not convenient to the Back Bay, South End, and Fenway neighborhoods. Ⓢ *Rooms from: $700* ⊠ *70 Rowes Wharf, Waterfront* ☎ *617/439–7000, 800/752–7077* ⊕ *www. bhh.com* ⇴ *232 rooms* ⦿ *No meals* Ⓜ *Aquarium, South Station.*

Harborside Inn

$$ | HOTEL | With rates that are considerably lower than most Waterfront hotels, this hotel with an understated charm is an exceptional value. **Pros:** free Wi-Fi; close to key tourist sites; inexpensive. **Cons:** no on-site restaurant; no turndown service; no valet. Ⓢ *Rooms from: $260* ⊠ *185 State St., Waterfront* ☎ *617/723–7500, 888/723–7565* ⊕ *www.harborsideinnboston.com* ⇴ *116 rooms* ⦿ *No meals* Ⓜ *Aquarium.*

The Seaport

What's the appeal of the Seaport District? Bostonians have only been able to answer that question recently. As the neighborhood becomes developed and its former life as a parking lot wasteland fades from peoples' minds, locals have realized its gorgeous potential, something the Moakley Courthouse, the Institute of Contemporary Art/Boston, and restaurateur-chef Barbara Lynch recognized more than a decade back.

Of all of Boston's neighborhoods, the Seaport is the least "Bostonian" in appearance. In fact, with all its skyscrapers and shiny glass, the Seaport could have been plucked straight out of New York. It's new, it's fresh, it's young.

◉ Sights

★ Boston Children's Museum
MUSEUM | FAMILY | The country's second-oldest children's museum has always been ahead of the curve with creative hands-on exhibits, cultural diversity, and problem solving. Some of the most popular stops are also the simplest, like the bubble-making machinery and the two-story climbing maze. At the Japanese House you're invited to take off your shoes and step inside a Kyoto silk merchant's home. The "Boston Black" exhibit stimulates dialogue about ethnicity and community, and children can dig, climb, and build at the Construction Zone. In the toddler PlaySpace, children under three can run free in a safe environment. There's also a full schedule of special exhibits, festivals, and performances. ⌧ 308 Congress St., Fort Point Channel ☎ 617/426–6500 ⊕ www.bostonchildrensmuseum.org ⛴ $18 Ⓜ South Station.

Boston HarborWalk
TRAIL | For the last 30-plus years, a number of agencies and organizations have been collaborating to create a waterfront walking path along Boston's shoreline—currently, it stretches 43 miles. Boston's Seaport District boasts a hearty portion of the HarborWalk, which winds from Fort Point Channel, around Fan Pier, up Seaport Boulevard and out and around Black Falcon Cruise Terminal. Along the way, pedestrians can see art exhibits, stationary viewfinders, open green spaces, and incredible Boston Harbor views. Marked signs point the way, and maps can be found online. ⌧ Seaport ✛ Congress St. Bridge by Children's Museum ⊕ www.bostonharborwalk.org Ⓜ South Station.

★ Boston Tea Party Ships & Museum
LOCAL INTEREST | FAMILY | Situated at the Congress Street Bridge near the site of Griffin's Wharf, this lively museum offers an interactive look at the past in a place as close as possible to the actual spot where the Boston Tea Party took place on December 16, 1773. Actors in period costumes greet patrons, assign them real-life Colonial personas, and then ask a few people to heave boxes of tea into the water from aboard historical reproductions of the ships forcibly boarded and unloaded the night Boston Harbor became a teapot. There are 3D holograms, talking portraits, and even the Robinson Half Tea Chest, one of two original tea chests known to exist. ◼ TIP→ Abigail's Tea Room (you don't need a museum ticket for entry) features a tea tasting of five tea blends that would have been aboard the ships. ⌧ Congress St. Bridge, Fort Point Channel ⊕ www.bostonteapartyship.com ⛴ $30 Ⓜ South Station.

★ **Institute of Contemporary Art/Boston**
MUSEUM | The ICA mounts temporary exhibits by the contemporary art world's brightest talents, as well as curated pieces from its permanent collection, all of which are as cutting edge as the breathtaking, cantilevered edifice jutting out over Boston Harbor that houses them. The ICA's fourth floor is where most happens: incredible art and stunning water views. The Poss Family Mediatheque serves as a great resting spot for families. Live programming, from film festivals to outdoor live music concerts take place regularly. Don't miss the ICA Store on ground level, where you can pick up an inventive trinket of your own. ✉ *25 Harbor Shore Dr., Seaport* ☎ *617/478–3100* 🌐 *www.icaboston.org* 🎟 *$15* ⏲ *Closed Mon.* [M] *Courthouse.*

🍴 Restaurants

★ **Bastille Kitchen**
$$$ | **BRASSERIE** | Clubby, homey, grand: all describe the look and feel of this Fort Point–located, contemporary French restaurant that will provide one of the best meals you've ever eaten in Boston. At first glance, the ambience can feel a little sceney, but that all falls away when you taste the chef's take on brasserie staples like moules frites, garlic escargot, duck à l'orange, and salmon Provençal. **Known for:** excellent service; outstanding food; tucked away, in-the-know location. [$] *Average main: $30* ✉ *49 Melcher St., Fort Point Channel* ☎ *617/556–8000* 🌐 *www.bastillekitchen.net* ⏲ *Closed Sun.* [M] *South Station.*

★ **Legal Harborside**
$$$$ | **SEAFOOD** | Three huge floors, three different menus, and one spectacular view makes Legal Harborside a worthy flagship for Boston's iconic Legal Sea Foods brand. The first level pays tribute to Legal's 1950s fish market with a casual vibe and simple menu of seafood favorites; a raw bar shucks a dozen-plus varieties of fresh oysters, too. **Known for:** prime waterfront location; excellent seafood options; Legal Seafood's flagship restaurant. [$] *Average main: $40* ✉ *270 Northern Ave., Seaport* ☎ *617/477–2900* 🌐 *www.legalseafoods.com/restaurants/boston-legal-harborside* [M] *World Trade Center.*

★ **Row 34**
$$$ | **SEAFOOD** | This modern beer-bar-meets-oyster-bar vibes boisterous energy contained only by its soaring ceilings. A neighborhood crowd comes for the excellent menu devoted to raw oysters, fried seafood, a variety of "rolls," and fish-based entrées. **Known for:** local oysters fresh from restaurant's own oyster farm; seafood—carnivores and vegetarians should head elsewhere; excellent selection of American craft beer. [$] *Average main: $27* ✉ *383 Congress St., Seaport* ☎ *617/553–5900* 🌐 *www.row34.com* [M] *World Trade Center.*

★ **Sportello**
$$ | **ITALIAN** | One of the city's most widely awarded chefs, Barbara Lynch had the foresight to create a culinary statement in the Seaport, long before it was cool to do so. Her Italian trattoria, Sportello, serves rustic, market-fresh fare in a chic, white, upscale "diner"-like setting, where diners can order à la carte, try a two- or three-course prix-fixe (at lunch), or have the kitchen cook up a three-course family style meal of their choosing for the table. **Known for:** pasta made in-house daily, by hand; casual, modern vibe; top-quality ingredients. [$] *Average main: $22* ✉ *348 Congress St., Fort Point Channel* ☎ *617/737–1234* 🌐 *www.sportelloboston.com* [M] *South Station.*

★ **Woods Hill Pier 4**
$$$$ | **MODERN AMERICAN** | Kristin Canty's brand new restaurant features floor-to-ceiling windows and sweeping, 270-degree views of the Boston Harbor waterfront. Neutral tones and vertical ceiling panels that mimic ocean waves create a cozy environment and a place where you can hang out for a while, which is ideal since the well-curated menu features midsized

plates that are meant to be shared; plan to order two to three per person. **Known for:** incredible panoramic views of Boston Harbor; pasture-raised, sustainable and organic farm-to-table ingredients; a killer Sunday brunch. [$] *Average main: $40* ✉ *300 Pier 4 Blvd., Seaport* ☎ *617/981–4577* 🌐 *www.woodshillpier4.com* [M] *Courthouse.*

Hotels

★ Omni Boston Hotel at the Seaport

$$$$ | **HOTEL** | Opened in 2021, this brand new Omni hotel debuts a chic, modern counterpoint to its grand dame Downtown property, the Omni Parker House. **Pros:** year-round, outdoor, heated pool with bar area; multiple food and drink options on-site; brand new accommodations. **Cons:** far from Back Bay and Beacon Hill shopping; tight restrictions on pet policy. [$] *Rooms from: $399* ✉ *450 Summer St., Seaport* ☎ *888/444–6664, 617/476–6664* 🌐 *www.omnihotels.com* 🛏 *1055 rooms* 🍴 *No meals* [M] *World Trade Center, Silver Line Way.*

Nightlife

★ Drink

BARS/PUBS | Barbara Lynch handles this elegant den of iniquity as only a chef of world-wide acclaim would—like a restaurant. Behind the bar, tenders chip ice off a giant block and use herbs, infusions, and elixirs to custom create a top-shelf libation for your palate; that is, there is no drink list. Low, beamed ceilings and a wooden bar that snakes through the space maximizes room for a discerning cocktail crowd. A limited menu features snacks and things, including a burger made from Wagyu beef, of course. Drink is one of the best bars in Boston, and it's hugely popular, so you'll likely wait in line to get in, but once you do, there's room to breathe. ✉ *348 Congress St., Fort Point Channel* ☎ *617/695–1806* 🌐 *www.drinkfortpoint.com* [M] *South Station.*

The Back Bay

The Back Bay is a mix of the historic and the new, happily coexisting in one of the city's loveliest areas, with everything from landmarks, like Trinity Church, and green spaces, such as the Esplanade, to a multitude of hip bars and fine-dining restaurants.

Sights

★ Boston Public Garden

NATIONAL/STATE PARK | **FAMILY** | America's oldest botanical garden, the Public Garden is replete with gorgeous formal plantings. Keep in mind that the Boston Public Garden and Boston Common (not Commons!) are two separate entities with different histories and purposes and a distinct boundary between them at Charles Street. The central feature of the Public Garden is its irregularly shaped pond, intended to appear, from any vantage point along its banks, much larger than its nearly 4 acres. The pond has been famous since 1877 for its foot-pedal-powered (by a captain) **Swan Boats** (🌐 *swanboats.com*), which make leisurely cruises during warm months. The dominant work among the park's statuary is Thomas Ball's equestrian **George Washington** (1869), which faces the head of Commonwealth Avenue at the Arlington Street gate, but follow the children quack-quacking along the pathway between the pond and the park entrance at Charles and Beacon Streets to the *Make Way for Ducklings* bronzes sculpted by Nancy Schön, a tribute to the 1941 classic children's story by Robert McCloskey. ✉ *Bounded by Arlington, Boylston, Charles, and Beacon Sts., Back Bay* ☎ *617/522–1966 Swan Boats* 🌐 *friendsofthepublicgarden.org* 🎟 *Swan Boats $4* [M] *Arlington.*

The Swan Boats have been an iconic part of Boston Public Garden since 1877.

★ Boston Public Library

LIBRARY | FAMILY | This venerable institution is a handsome temple to literature and a valuable research library, but you don't need a library card to enjoy the magnificent art. The library offers free art and architecture tours daily. The corridor leading from the annex opens onto the Renaissance-style **courtyard**—an exact copy of the one in Rome's Palazzo della Cancelleria—around which the original library is built. A covered arcade furnished with chairs rings a fountain; you can bring books or lunch into the courtyard, which is open all the hours the library is open, and escape the bustle of the city. Beyond the courtyard is the main entrance hall of the 1895 building, with its immense stone lions by Louis St. Gaudens, vaulted ceiling, and marble staircase. The corridor at the top of the stairs leads to **Bates Hall,** one of Boston's most sumptuous interior spaces. This is the main reference reading room, 218 feet long with a barrel-arch ceiling 50 feet high. ✉ *700 Boylston St., at Copley Sq., Back Bay* ☎ *617/536–5400* ⊕ *www.bpl.org* Ⓜ *Copley.*

Mary Baker Eddy Library for the Betterment of Humanity

LIBRARY | FAMILY | One of the largest single collections by and about an American woman is housed at this library, located on the Christian Science Plaza. The library also includes two floors of exhibits, which celebrate the power of ideas and provide context to the life and achievements of Mary Baker Eddy (1821–1910).

The library is also home to the fascinating **Mapparium,** a huge stained-glass globe whose 30-foot interior can be traversed on a footbridge, where you can experience a unique sound-and-light show while viewing an accurate representation of the world from 1935. The Hall of Ideas showcases quotes from the world's greatest thinkers, which travel around the room and through a virtual fountain. In the Quest Gallery, explore how Mary Baker Eddy founded a church and a college, and at the age of 87, launched *The Christian Science Monitor* newspaper. ✉ *200 Massachusetts Ave., Back Bay*

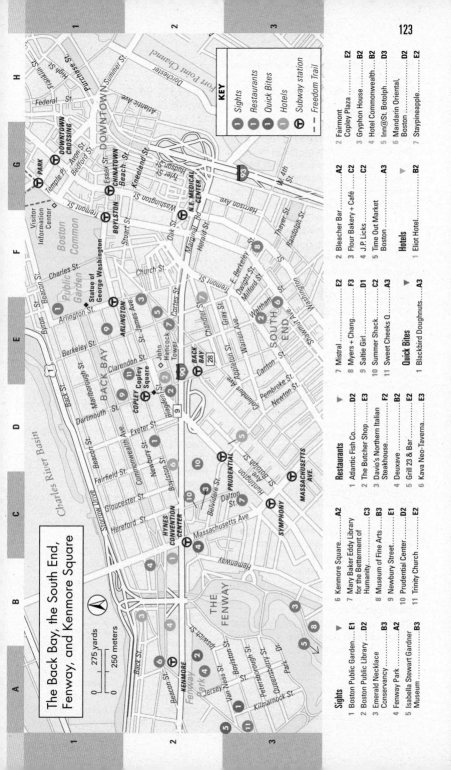

123

The Back Bay, the South End, Fenway, and Kenmore Square

0 275 yards
0 250 meters

Sights ▶

1 Boston Public Garden....**E1**
2 Boston Public Library....**D2**
3 Emerald Necklace
   Conservancy............**B3**
4 Fenway Park..............**A2**
5 Isabella Stewart Gardner
   Museum..................**B3**

6 Kenmore Square.........**A2**
7 Mary Baker Eddy Library
   for the Betterment of
   Humanity...............**C3**
8 Museum of Fine Arts....**B3**
9 Newbury Street..........**E1**
10 Prudential Center.......**D2**
11 Trinity Church...........**E2**

Restaurants ▶

1 Atlantic Fish Co..........**D2**
2 The Butcher Shop........**E3**
3 Davio's Northern Italian
   Steakhouse..............**F2**
4 Deuxave.................**B2**
5 Grill 23 & Bar............**E2**
6 Kava Neo-Taverna.......**E3**

7 Mistral...................**E2**
8 Myers + Chang..........**F3**
9 Saltie Girl...............**D1**
10 Summer Shack..........**C2**
11 Sweet Cheeks Q.........**A3**

Quick Bites ▶

1 Blackbird Doughnuts....**A3**

2 Bleacher Bar.............**A2**
3 Flour Bakery + Café.....**C2**
4 J.P. Licks................**C2**
5 Time Out Market
   Boston..................**A3**

Hotels ▶

1 Eliot Hotel...............**B2**

2 Fairmont
   Copley Plaza...........**E2**
3 Gryphon House..........**B2**
4 Hotel Commonwealth...**B2**
5 Inn@St. Botolph........**D3**
6 Mandarin Oriental,
   Boston..................**D2**
7 Staypineapple...........**E2**

☎ 617/450–7000 ⊕ www.marybakered-dylibrary.org ☞ Hall of Ideas and 3rd-fl. library free, exhibits $6 Ⓜ Prudential.

Newbury Street

NEIGHBORHOOD | Eight-block-long Newbury Street has been compared to New York's 5th Avenue, and certainly this is the city's poshest shopping area, with branches of Chanel, Diane von Furstenberg, Burberry, Barbour, Fred Perry, and other top names in fashion. But here the pricey boutiques are more intimate than grand, and people live above the trendy restaurants and ubiquitous hair salons, giving the place a neighborhood feel. Toward the Massachusetts Avenue end, cafés proliferate and the stores get funkier, ending with Newbury Comics and Urban Outfitters. ✉ From Arlington St. to Massachusetts Ave., Back Bay ⊕ www.newbury-st.com Ⓜ Hynes, Copley.

Prudential Center

STORE/MALL | FAMILY | The 52-story Prudential Tower, or the "Pru," dominates the acreage between Boylston Street and Huntington Avenue. Its enclosed shopping mall is connected by a glass bridge to the more upscale Copley Place. The popular food emporium, Eataly, located in the Pru, offers a great spot for a quick bite. As for the Prudential Tower itself, the architectural historian Bainbridge Bunting made an acute observation when he called it "an apparition so vast in size that it appears to float above the surrounding district without being related to it." Later modifications to the Boylston Street frontage of the Prudential Center effected a better union of the complex with the urban space around it, but the tower itself floats on, vast as ever. **Prudential Center Skywalk Observatory,** a 50th-floor observatory atop the Prudential Tower, offers panoramic vistas of Boston, Cambridge, and the suburbs to the west and south—on clear days, you can even see Cape Cod. Your ticket includes an audio tour, admission to the Dreams

of Freedom Museum, and the multimedia theater. ✉ 800 Boylston St., Back Bay ☎ 800/746–7778, 617/859–0648 for Skywalk ⊕ www.prudentialcenter.com ☞ Skywalk $21 Ⓜ Prudential Center, Copley Station.

★ Trinity Church

RELIGIOUS SITE | In his 1877 masterpiece, architect Henry Hobson Richardson brought his Romanesque Revival style to maturity; all the aesthetic elements for which he was famous come together magnificently—bold polychromatic masonry, careful arrangement of masses, sumptuously carved interior woodwork—in this crowning centerpiece of Copley Square. A full appreciation of its architecture requires an understanding of the logistical problems of building it here. The Back Bay is a reclaimed wetland with a high water table. Bedrock, or at least stable glacial till, lies far beneath wet clay. Like all older Back Bay buildings, Trinity Church sits on submerged wooden pilings. But its central tower weighs 9,500 tons, and most of the 4,500 pilings beneath the building are under that tremendous central mass. The pilings are checked regularly for sinkage by means of a hatch in the basement. For a nice respite, try to catch one of the Friday organ concerts beginning at 12:15. The 11:15 Sunday service is usually followed by a free guided tour. ✉ 206 Clarendon St., Back Bay ☎ 617/536–0944 ⊕ trinitychurchboston.org ☞ Entrance free, guided and self-guided tours Tues.–Fri., $10 ◷ Closed Mon. Ⓜ Copley.

🍴 Restaurants

★ Atlantic Fish Co

$$$ | SEAFOOD | Designed to look like an ocean vessel with gorgeous wood finishes and nautical artwork, this local seafood restaurant delivers first-class fish, so fresh that the extensive menus are printed daily to reflect the day's catch, served broiled, baked, blackened, fried, grilled, or pan-seared. Unsnap your

starched napkin and begin with a platter of chilled seafood (lobster, littlenecks, oysters, crab, and shrimp), followed by any one of the specialties ranging from whole-bellied fried Ipswich clams to pan-seared bass with lobster ravioli in an unctuous lobster cream sauce. **Known for:** elegant seafood; solicitous service in a lux atmosphere; great outdoor patio. [$] *Average main: $35* ✉ *761 Boylston St., Back Bay* ☎ *617/267–4000* 🌐 *www.atlanticfish.com* [M] *Copley.*

★ **Davio's Northern Italian Steakhouse**

$$$$ | ITALIAN | Comfy armchairs and a grand, high-ceilinged dining room give diners a heightened sense of self-importance, beginning with lunch when the city's power elite stop in for great pastas (half portions are available), prime NY-aged steaks, and oversize salads. For dinner, some patrons snag quick, pretheater bites at the bar while others opt for a more leisurely experience, lingering over sophisticated Italian dishes like tagliatelle Bolognese and succulent grilled veal chops with creamy potatoes and Port wine sauce. **Known for:** delectable Italian classics; generous portions; elegant setting and service. [$] *Average main: $39* ✉ *75 Arlington St., Back Bay* ☎ *617/357–4810* 🌐 *www.davios.com* 🕒 *No lunch weekends* [M] *Arlington.*

★ **Deuxave**

$$$ | MODERN AMERICAN | At the corner of two avenues (Commonwealth and Massachusetts), which is how this restaurant got its name (deux is French for "two"), you'll find this snazzy, dark-wood enclave serving sophisticated dishes like spice-crusted Ahi tuna and braised pork belly, pan-seared Atlantic halibut, and organic chicken with parsnip and foie gras agnolotti. Make sure to pair your meal with a bottle from the thoughtfully crafted and surprisingly affordable wine list and served by an attentive staff. **Known for:** modern French food; nine-hour French onion soup; reasonably priced wine list. [$] *Average main: $35* ✉ *371 Commonwealth Ave., Back Bay* ☎ *617/517–5915* 🌐 *www.deuxave.com* 💳 *No credit cards* [M] *Hynes.*

★ **Grill 23 & Bar**

$$$$ | STEAKHOUSE | Pinstripe suits, dark paneling, Persian rugs, and waiters in white jackets give this single-location steak house a posh tone, and the kitchen places a premium on seasonal, organic ingredients and sustainable and humanely raised meats; the divine coconut cake is worth saving room for dessert. Two bars, a big, buzzing one overlooking Berkeley Street and a quieter, smaller one on the second floor by the cozy fireplace, serve excellent drinks, specialty Scotches, and bar bites, along with the full menu. **Known for:** locally owned steak house; Brandt family beef; party-dress vibe. [$] *Average main: $40* ✉ *161 Berkeley St., Back Bay* ☎ *617/542–2255* 🌐 *grill23.com* 🕒 *No lunch* [M] *Back Bay/South End.*

★ **Saltie Girl**

$$$ | SEAFOOD | Step into this snug Back Bay raw bar specializing in snappy cocktails and luscious preparations of all things seafood and you'll fall hook, line, and sinker for everything on the menu, including platters of fresh-shucked oysters on crushed ice, torched salmon belly with charred avocado, smoked fish that would make a New York deli owner proud, seafood-topped toasts, and arguably the best warm lobster roll in the city, a butter-drenched affair overflowing with fresh lobster meat. Rounding out the menu and decorating the restaurant's walls are 80-plus tins of domestic and imported gourmet fish and shellfish (including caviar!) served in all their oily goodness with bread, butter, smoked salt, lemon, and sweet pepper jam. **Known for:** creative seafood dishes; large tinned seafood selection; hip crowd. [$] *Average main: $25* ✉ *281 Dartmouth St., Back Bay* ☎ *617/267–0691* 🌐 *saltiegirl.com.*

Summer Shack

$$ | **SEAFOOD** | **FAMILY** | Boston uberchef Jasper White's casual New England seafood restaurant is a boisterous, bright, fun eatery next to the Prudential Center (he also has one in Cambridge and at Mohegan Sun in Connecticut), where creamy clam chowder and fried Ipswich clams share menu space with golden crab cakes and cedar-planked, maple-lemon glazed salmon. In addition to a handful of chicken and meat dishes for those not into seafood, White features the most succulent lobsters in the city (he has a patented process for cooking them), all brought to you by an eager-to-please staff. **Known for:** fresh seafood; succulent lobster; fun, casual atmosphere. $ *Average main: $24* ⊠ *50 Dalton St., Back Bay* ☎ *617/867–9955* ⊕ *www.summershackrestaurant.com* Ⓜ *Hynes.*

🛏 Hotels

★ Eliot Hotel

$$ | **HOTEL** | One of the city's best small hotels, located on posh Commonwealth Avenue, expertly merges the old blue-blood Boston aesthetic with modern flair (like contemporary rugs mingling with crystal chandeliers); everyone from well-heeled Sox fans to traveling CEOs to tony college parents have noticed. **Pros:** great location near Fenway and Newbury Street; top-notch restaurant; pet-friendly; beautiful rooms. **Cons:** can be pricey; some complain of elevator noise; parking is expensive. $ *Rooms from: $285* ⊠ *370 Commonwealth Ave., Back Bay* ☎ *617/267–1607, 800/443–5468* ⊕ *www.eliothotel.com* ⇘ *95 rooms* ¶ *No meals* Ⓜ *Hynes.*

★ Fairmont Copley Plaza

$$$ | **HOTEL** | **FAMILY** | Since 1912, this decadent, unabashedly romantic hotel has welcomed guests in style, immediately impressing as they enter under the trademark red awning, flanked by golden lion statues, into the lobby decked out in Italian marble, stunning coffered ceilings, and gorgeous crystal chandeliers. **Pros:** prime Back Bay location, centrally located in Copley Square; luxurious gym; 24-hour daily in-room dining. **Cons:** small bathrooms; valet parking is expensive; due to the historical nature, room sizes vary greatly. $ *Rooms from: $350* ⊠ *138 St. James Ave., Back Bay* ☎ *617/267–5300, 866/540–4417* ⊕ *www.fairmont.com/copley-plaza-boston* ⇘ *383 rooms* ¶ *No meals* Ⓜ *Copley, Back Bay.*

★ Inn@St. Botolph

$$ | **B&B/INN** | **FAMILY** | The posh yet homey 16-room Inn@St. Botolph follows an edgy hotel model—no front desk, no restaurant, no keys, and no valet (there is, however, an office on-site that is staffed 24/7). **Pros:** guests get 25% off meals at Columbus Hospital Group restaurants; free Wi-Fi; self-service laundry on-site. **Cons:** DIY parking; no traditional front desk check-in services; may be too "off the beaten path" for some. $ *Rooms from: $279* ⊠ *99 St. Botolph St., Back Bay* ☎ *617/236–8099* ⊕ *www.innatstbotolph.com* ⇘ *16 rooms* ¶ *Free breakfast* Ⓜ *Prudential.*

Mandarin Oriental, Boston

$$$$ | **HOTEL** | The Mandarin Oriental, Boston manages to combine classic New England elegance with the luxurious touches the brand is known for around the world, including top-notch service, amenities galore, and public areas adorned with museum-quality art, while large guest rooms include contemporary Asian design and oversize bathrooms with soaking tubs and separate walk-in showers. **Pros:** amazing service; very quiet; good-size rooms. **Cons:** small fitness center; rates are exorbitant; valet parking is expensive. $ *Rooms from: $795* ⊠ *776 Boylston St., Back Bay* ☎ *617/535–8888* ⊕ *www.mandarinoriental.com/boston* ⇘ *150 rooms* ¶ *No meals* Ⓜ *Prudential, Copley, Back Bay.*

☕ Coffee and Quick Bites

J.P. Licks

$ | CAFÉ | Simple but sublime cones have made many addicted to the fun and funky likes of J.P. Licks, which serves a traditional stable of ice-cream flavors, like peanut butter cookies 'n' cream and mint chip, along with hard and soft frozen yogurt offerings, best smothered with the shop's superb hot fudge sauce and any of the wet (whipped cream, marshmallow sauce) and dry (M&M's, Heath Bar) toppings. **Known for:** Boston-based business; creative flavors; coffee beans roasted in-house. $ *Average main: $6* ⊠ *1106 Boylston St., Back Bay* ☎ *857/233–5805* ⊕ *www.jplicks.com.*

▼ Nightlife

Bukowski Tavern

BARS/PUBS | This narrow barroom has a literary flair and more than 100 brews for your sipping pleasure, served by a no-nonsense bar staff. You'll see many a beer nerd hanging out at the bar, but hungry folks also come to the funky joint for the creative burgers, hot dogs, and other comfort foods. Make sure to bring cash; no credit cards are accepted. ⊠ *50 Dalton St., Back Bay* ☎ *617/437–9999* ⊕ *www. bukowskitavern.com* Ⓜ *Hynes.*

★ Oak Long Bar + Kitchen

BARS/PUBS | This stunning flagship bar in the 1912 Fairmont Copley Plaza Hotel is a "see and be seen" hot spot, with the original sky-high coffered ceilings, catbird views over Copley Square, and top-notch bartenders. Inside, coveted barstools are filled with an upscale crowd, while outside in warm weather, patrons can sit at outdoor tables while perusing a menu of signature martinis, single malts, shareable platters, and desserts. People-watch and enjoy a panorama that encompasses the Boston Public Library and Trinity

Church in this historic spot. ⊠ *Fairmont Copley Plaza, 138 St. James Ave., Back Bay* ☎ *617/267–5300* ⊕ *www.fairmont. com/copleyplaza* Ⓜ *Copley.*

🎭 Performing Arts

★ Symphony Hall

CONCERTS | One of the world's best acoustical concert halls—some say *the* best—has been home since 1900 to the Boston Symphony Orchestra (BSO) and the Boston Pops. Led by conductor Keith Lockhart, the Pops concerts take place in May and June and around the winter holidays. The hall is also used by visiting orchestras, chamber groups, soloists, and local ensembles. Rehearsals and daytime concerts for students are open to the public, with discounted tickets. If you can't attend a concert, you can still see the magnificent hall on a free guided tour. Visit the venue's website for dates and times. ⊠ *301 Massachusetts Ave., Back Bay* ☎ *617/266–1492* ⊕ *www.bso. org* Ⓜ *Symphony.*

🛍 Shopping

This is the neighborhood of the elegant Mandarin Oriental Hotel—so need we say more about the shops you'll find here? Just in case: elegant, chic, modern, stylish. It's also home to Newbury Street, Boston's version of LA's Rodeo Drive. It's a shoppers' paradise, from high-end names such as Anne Fontaine to tiny specialty shops such as the Fish and Bone with up-to-the-minute art galleries and dazzling jewelers thrown into the mix.

Parallel to Newbury Street is Boylston Street, where you'll find a few standout shops such as Pompanoosuc Mills (hand-crafted furnishing) scattered among the other chains and restaurants.

★ Society of Arts & Crafts

CRAFTS | More than a century old, this is the country's oldest nonprofit crafts organization. In addition to selling a fine assortment of ceramics, jewelry, glass, woodwork, and furniture from a rotating roster of more than 400 of the country's finest artists, the soaring space sponsors free art exhibits, and a featured artist in residence, who you can see working in the studio. ⊠ *100 Pier 4, Suite 200, Back Bay* ✛ *Above Ocean Prime restaurant on 2nd fl.* ☎ *617/266–1810* ⊕ *www.society-ofcrafts.org* ☾ *Closed weekends* Ⓜ *Silver Line MBTA to Court St. station.*

The South End

Adjacent to the Back Bay, the South End nonetheless has its own identity, with stunning Victorian row houses, art galleries galore, Boston's largest gay community, and plenty of unique shops and restaurants of every type.

🍴 Restaurants

The Butcher Shop

$$$ | AMERICAN | Chef Barbara Lynch, one of the city's most acclaimed chefs, reenvisioned the classic meat market as a polished wine bar–cum–hangout, serving those who either want to stop in for a glass of wine and a casual, quick snack of homemade prosciutto and artisanal cheeses or relax longer over dinner specials like tagliatelle Bolognese, roasted bone marrow with grilled bread, and beef tenderloin with crispy potatoes. **Known for:** excellent cooked and cured meats; rustic atmosphere; friendly service. Ⓢ *Average main: $30* ⊠ *552 Tremont St., South End* ☎ *617/423–4800* ⊕ *www.thebutchershopboston.com* Ⓜ *Back Bay.*

★ Kava Neo-Taverna

$$$ | GREEK | This sweet little white-washed taverna serves authentic Greek cuisine, with many ingredients imported directly from the Mediterranean, such as the feta, fish, and octopus. Order some crisp white wine off the mainly Greek wine list to sip with a parade of home-style dishes, from tasty meze plates to entrées like grilled lamb chops. **Known for:** authentic Greek favorites; taverna feel; high-quality ingredients. Ⓢ *Average main: $27* ⊠ *315 Shawmut Ave., South End* ☎ *617/356–1100* ⊕ *www.kavaneotaverna. com* ☾ *No lunch weekdays.*

★ Mistral

$$$$ | FRENCH | Boston's fashionable set flocks to this long-popular South End restaurant with polished service and upscale yet unpretentious French-Mediterranean cuisine with fail-safe favorites like tuna tartare, duck with cherries, and French Dover sole. The seasonally tweaked menu rarely changes—but no one's complaining; a luxurious à la carte brunch is served on Sunday. **Known for:** sophisticated Mediterranean cuisine; superb service; white-cloth, country French decor. Ⓢ *Average main: $36* ⊠ *223 Columbus Ave., South End* ☎ *617/867–9300* ⊕ *mistralbistro.com* ☾ *No lunch* Ⓜ *Back Bay.*

★ Myers + Chang

$$ | CHINESE | Pink and orange dragon decals cover the windows of this all-day Chinese café, where Joanne Chang (of Flour bakery fame) taps her familial cooking roots to create shareable platters of creative dumplings, wok-charred udon noodles, and stir-fries brimming with fresh ingredients and plenty of hot chili peppers, garlic, fresh herbs, crushed peanuts, and lime. The staff is young and fun, and the crowd generally follows suit. **Known for:** Asian soul food; fabulous cocktails; great service. Ⓢ *Average main: $22* ⊠ *1145 Washington St., South End* ☎ *617/542–5200* ⊕ *www.myersand-chang.com* Ⓜ *Back Bay.*

Coffee and Quick Bites

★ Flour Bakery + Café

$ | **AMERICAN** | **FAMILY** | When folks need coffee, a great sandwich, or an irresistible sweet, like a pecan sticky bun, lemon tart, or double chocolate cookie—or just a place to sit and chat—they come to one of owner Joanne Chang's eight Flour bakeries, including this one in the South End. A communal table in the middle acts as a gathering spot, around which diners enjoy morning pastries, homemade soups, hearty bean and grain salads, and specialty sandwiches, which change with the seasons. **Known for:** scrumptious sweets; delicious salads and sandwiches; laid-back setting. [$] *Average main: $9* ✉ *1595 Washington St., South End* ☎ *617/267–4300* 🌐 *www.flourbakery.com* [M] *Massachusetts Ave.*

Hotels

Staypineapple

$$ | **B&B/INN** | This small property, part of small brand of hotels, has a fresh, contemporary style with lots and lots of yellow accents along with complimentary Wi-Fi, plush pillow top beds, and marble bathrooms with walk-in glass showers. **Pros:** can't beat the price; friendly staff; the South End is a prime location for foodies. **Cons:** area parking is brutally hard or expensive; rooms can be noisy; might be too quirky for some. [$] *Rooms from: $225* ✉ *26 Chandler St., South End* ☎ *857/444–6111, 800/842–3450* 🌐 *www.staypineapple.com/south-end-boston* 🛏 *56 rooms* 🍴 *No meals* [M] *Back Bay.*

Nightlife

★ Darryl's Corner Bar & Kitchen

CAFES—NIGHTLIFE | This longtime neighborhood soul-food and jazz hangout still looks spiffy, and features real Southern cooking and live bands nearly nightly at light cover charges. Come for favorites like mac and cheese or glorified chicken and waffles, and on Sunday there is an all-you-can-eat blues brunch starting at 10 am. Theatergoers receive dining discounts. ✉ *604 Columbus Ave., South End* ☎ *617/536–1100* 🌐 *www.dcbkboston.com* [M] *Massachusetts Ave.*

Franklin Café

BARS/PUBS | A neighborhood institution for more than 20 years, The Franklin's renowned for creative cocktails, local microbrews, fine wines, and modern American food. There's no sign: just look for the white martini logo (or folks waiting for a dinner table) to know you're there. A full menu is served until 1:30 am every single night of the week, and the bar is open until 2 am. ✉ *278 Shawmut Ave., South End* ☎ *617/350–0010* 🌐 *www.franklincafe.com* [M] *Back Bay.*

★ Wally's Café

MUSIC CLUBS | A rare gem for jazz and blues fans, Wally's Café, founded in 1947, is the oldest continuously operating family-owned jazz club in America. Patrons may see nostalgic stars like Branford Marsalis or Esperanza Spalding drop by, because the place is internationally renowned for its steady stream of heated performances by local bands and guests. Wally's diverse crowd attracts regulars from the South End and Roxbury, and music-hungry students, especially from Berklee College of Music. It's jammed every night of the year and there's never a cover. Monday it's blues and Thursday it's Latin jazz. Daily jam sessions run from 6 to 9 pm; bring your horn!

Arrive early if you want a seat, because the line can be brutal. ✉ *427 Massachusetts Ave., South End* ☎ *617/424–1408* ⊕ *www.wallyscafe.com* 🎟 *Free* Ⓜ *Massachusetts Ave., Symphony.*

Fenway and Kenmore Square

The Back Bay Fens marshland gave this neighborhood its name, but two iconic institutions give it its character: Fenway Park, which in 2004 saw the triumphant reversal of an 86-year drought for Boston's beloved Red Sox, and the Isabella Stewart Gardner Museum, the legacy of a high-living Brahmin who attended a concert at Symphony Hall in 1912 wearing a headband that read "Oh, You Red Sox." Not far from the Gardner is another major cultural magnet: the Museum of Fine Arts. Kenmore Square, a favorite haunt for Boston University students, adds a bit of youthful flavor to the mix.

👁 Sights

★ Emerald Necklace Conservancy

NATURE PRESERVE | FAMILY | The six large public parks known as Boston's Emerald Necklace stretch 7 miles from the Back Bay Fens to Franklin Park in Dorchester, and include Arnold Arboretum, Jamaica Pond, Olmsted Park, and the Riverway. The linear parks, designed by master landscape architect Frederick Law Olmsted more than 100 years ago, remain a well-groomed urban masterpiece. ✉ *125 The Fenway, The Fenway* ☎ *617/522–2700* ⊕ *www.emeraldnecklace.org.*

★ Fenway Park

SPORTS VENUE | FAMILY | Fenway Park is Major League Baseball's oldest ballpark and has seen some stuff since its 1912 opening. For one, it's the home field for the Boston Red Sox, which overcame the curse of the bambino to win World Series

championships in 2004, 2007, 2013, and 2018. Ticket-holding Sox fans can browse display cases mounted inside Fenway Park before and during a ballgame; these shed light on and show off memorabilia from particular players and eras of the club team's history. Fenway offers hour-long behind-the-scenes-style guided walking tours of the park; there are also specialized tour options. ✉ *4 Jersey St., Gate D, Kenmore Square* ☎ *617/226–6666 tours* ⊕ *www.mlb.com/redsox/ballpark/tours* 🎟 *$21* Ⓜ *Kenmore, Fenway.*

★ Isabella Stewart Gardner Museum

MUSEUM | A spirited society woman, Isabella Stewart came in 1860 from New York to marry John Lowell Gardner, one of Boston's leading citizens. She built a Venetian palazzo to hold her collected arts in one of Boston's newest neighborhoods. Her will stipulated that the building remain exactly as she left it—paintings, furniture, and the smallest object in a hall cabinet—and that is as it has remained. The palazzo includes such masterpieces as Titian's *Europa,* Giotto's *Presentation of Christ in the Temple,* Piero della Francesca's *Hercules,* and John Singer Sargent's *El Jaleo.* Spanish leather panels, Renaissance hooded fireplaces, and Gothic tapestries accent salons; eight balconies adorn the majestic Venetian courtyard. There's a Raphael Room, Spanish Cloister, Gothic Room, Chinese Loggia, and a magnificent Tapestry Room for concerts. On March 18, 1990, thieves disguised as police officers stole 12 works, including Vermeer's *The Concert.* None of the art has been recovered, and because Mrs. Gardner's will prohibited substituting other works for any stolen art, empty expanses of wall identify spots where the paintings once hung. ■TIP→ **A quirk of the museum's admission policy waives entrance fees to anyone named Isabella and on your birthday.** ✉ *25 Evans Way, The Fenway* ☎ *617/566–1401* ⊕ *www.gardnermuseum.org* 🎟 *$15* 🕒 *Closed Tues.* Ⓜ *Museum.*

Kenmore Square

NEIGHBORHOOD | Two blocks north of Fenway Park is Kenmore Square, where you'll find shops, restaurants, and the city's iconic sign advertising Citgo gasoline. The red, white, and blue neon sign from 1965 is so thoroughly identified with the area that historic preservationists fought, successfully, to save it. The old Kenmore Square punk clubs have given way to a block-long development of pricey stores and restaurants, as well as brick sidewalks, gaslight-style street lamps, and tree plantings. In the shadow of Fenway Park between Brookline and Ipswich is **Lansdowne Street,** a nightlife magnet for the trendy who have their pick of dance clubs and pregame bars. The urban campus of Boston University begins farther west on Commonwealth Avenue, in blocks thick with dorms, shops, and restaurants. ✉ *Convergence of Beacon St., Commonwealth Ave., and Brookline Ave., The Fenway* Ⓜ *Kenmore.*

★ Museum of Fine Arts

MUSEUM | **FAMILY** | The MFA's collection of approximately 450,000 objects was built from a core of paintings and sculpture from the Boston Athenæum, historical portraits from the city of Boston, and donations by area universities. The MFA has more than 70 works by John Singleton Copley; major paintings by Winslow Homer, John Singer Sargent, Fitz Henry Lane, and Edward Hopper; and a wealth of American works ranging from native New England folk art and Colonial portraiture to New York abstract expressionism of the 1950s and 1960s.

More than 30 galleries contain the MFA's European painting and sculpture collection, dating from the 11th century to the 20th. Contemporary art has a dynamic home in the MFA's dramatic I. M. Pei–designed building. ✉ *465 Huntington Ave., The Fenway* ☎ *617/267–9300* ⊕ *www.mfa.org* 🎟 *$25 (good for 2 days in a 10-day period)* Ⓜ *Museum.*

🍴 Restaurants

★ Island Creek Oyster Bar

$$$ | **SEAFOOD** | As the name indicates, this Hotel Commonwealth restaurant specializes in seafood, beginning with oysters that come fresh from the restaurant's own oyster farm in nearby Duxbury Bay, as well as Maine, Prince Edward Island, and Puget Sound (Washington). Beyond raw options, look for panfried crab cakes, steamed little neck clams, chowders, bisques, and daily fish selections ranging from cornmeal-crusted skate wing and herb-crusted cod to grilled Maine salmon and New Bedford monkfish with Maine yellow eye beans and chorizo. **Known for:** superb oysters; delish seafood dishes; loud, lively, fun feel. 💲 *Average main: $34* ✉ *500 Commonwealth Ave., Kenmore Square* ☎ *617/532–5300* ⊕ *www.islandcreekoysterbar.com* Ⓜ *Kenmore.*

★ Sweet Cheeks Q

$$ | **SOUTHERN** | Red Sox fans, foodies, and Fenway residents flock to this meat-lover's mecca, where Texas-style barbecue is the name of the game. Hefty slabs of dry-rubbed heritage pork, great northern beef brisket, and plump chickens cook low and slow in a jumbo black smoker then come to the table heaped on a tray lined with butcher paper, along with homemade sweet pickles, shaved onion, and your choice of "hot scoops" (collard greens, mac 'n' cheese) or "cold scoops" (coleslaw, potato salad). **Known for:** finger-licking barbecue; scrumptious sides; jeans and T-shirt atmosphere. 💲 *Average main: $22* ✉ *1381 Boylston St., The Fenway* ☎ *617/266–1300* ⊕ *www.sweetcheeksq.com* Ⓜ *Fenway.*

4

Boston and Environs FENWAY AND KENMORE SQUARE

Coffee and Quick Bites

Blackbird Doughnuts
$ | **AMERICAN** | Creative, delicious and irresistible, these sweet treats from Blackbird Doughnuts have a cult following—even rock star Adele praised them when in town for a concert. One of several outposts in the city, the Fenway location is tiny and it's a good idea to get there early before your fave flavor sells out. **Known for:** fan favorite Boston Cream; creative, unusual flavors; turn your doughnut into an ice-cream sandwich with soft serve. [$] *Average main: $3* ✉ *20 Kilmarnock St., The Fenway* ☎ *617/482–9000* 🌐 *www.blackbird-doughnuts.com/fenway* [M] *Fenway.*

Bleacher Bar
$ | **AMERICAN** | This Fenway restaurant is famous for its enormous garage window which looks into Fenway Park, but it's also a fun place to relax with friends, nosh on nachos or fries, and catch all sorts of sporting events on the TV. **Known for:** sneaky way to see a Red Sox game; beers and burgers; sports fans. [$] *Average main: $13* ✉ *82A Lansdowne St., The Fenway* ☎ *617/262–2424* 🌐 *www.bleacherbarboston.com* [M] *Kenmore.*

Time Out Market Boston
$ | **INTERNATIONAL** | A food hall curated by the media company known for its magazines and books, Time Out Market Boston features 15 dining outlets run by some of Boston's most acclaimed chefs, plus two bars, a demo cooking area, and communal seating. The 25,200-square-foot space is a fun place to sample everything from sweet treats at Union Square Donuts to meatballs at Chef Michael Schlow's, one of the city's most acclaimed chefs. **Known for:** variety of eateries; fun vibe; located in historic building. [$] *Average main: $15* ✉ *401 Park Dr., The Fenway* ☎ *978/393–8088* 🌐 *www.timeoutmarket.com/boston* [M] *Fenway.*

Hotels

★ **Gryphon House**
$$ | **B&B/INN** | The staff in this value-packed, four-story, 19th-century brownstone is helpful and friendly, and the suites are thematically decorated: one evokes rustic Italy; another is inspired by neo-Gothic art. **Pros:** elegant suites are lush and spacious; gas fireplaces in all rooms; free Wi-Fi. **Cons:** may be too fussy for some; no elevator; no wheelchair access. [$] *Rooms from: $265* ✉ *9 Bay State Rd., Kenmore Square* ☎ *617/375–9003, 877/375–9003* 🌐 *www.innboston.com* 🛏 *8 suites* 🍴 *Free breakfast* [M] *Kenmore.*

★ **Hotel Commonwealth**
$$$ | **HOTEL** | Luxury and service without pretense make this hip spot a solid choice. **Pros:** down bedding; perfect locale for Red Sox fans; happening bar scene at Eastern Standard; free Wi-Fi. **Cons:** area is absolutely mobbed during Sox games; small gym; pricey rates. [$] *Rooms from: $399* ✉ *500 Commonwealth Ave., Kenmore Square* ☎ *617/933–5000, 866/784–4000* 🌐 *www.hotelcommonwealth.com* 🛏 *245 rooms* 🍴 *No meals* [M] *Kenmore.*

Cambridge

Boston's Left Bank—an uber-liberal academic enclave—is a must-visit if you're spending more than a day or two in the Boston area. Cambridge is packed with world-class cultural institutions, quirky shops, restaurants galore, and tons of people-watching.

Sights

★ **Harvard Art Museums**
MUSEUM | This is Harvard University's oldest museum and, in late 2014, it became the combined collections of the Busch-Reisinger, Fogg, and Arthur M. Sackler museums. All three were united under one glorious, mostly glass roof,

Harvard University's Radcliffe Quad is surrounded by undergrad housing; it's about a 12-minute walk, or half a mile, from Harvard Square.

under the umbrella name Harvard Art Museums. Housed in a facility designed by award-winning architect Renzo Piano, the 204,000-square-foot museum is spread over seven levels, allowing more of Harvard's 250,000-piece art collection, featuring European and American art from the Middle Ages to the present day, to be seen in one place. Highlights include American and European paintings, sculptures, and decorative arts from the Fogg Museum; Asian art, Buddhist cave-temple sculptures, and Chinese bronzes in the Arthur M. Sackler; and works by German expressionists, materials related to the Bauhaus, and postwar contemporary art from German-speaking Europe from the Busch-Reisinger Museum. In addition to the gallery spaces, there's a 300-seat theater, Jenny's café, a museum shop, the Calderwood Courtyard, plus conservation and research labs. ⊠ *32 Quincy St., Harvard Square* ☎ *617/495–9400* ⊕ *www.harvardartmuseums.org* 🚇 *$20* Ⓜ *Harvard.*

★ **Harvard Museum of Natural History**
MUSEUM | FAMILY | The Harvard Museum of Natural History (which exhibits specimens from the Museum of Comparative Zoology, Harvard University Herbaria, and the Mineralogical and Geological Museum) reminds us nature is the original masterpiece. Cases are packed with zoological specimens, from tiny hummingbirds and deer mice to rare Indian rhinoceros and one of the largest Amazon pirarucu ever caught. View fossils and skeletons alongside marvelous minerals, including a 1,600-pound amethyst geode. Harvard's world-famous Blaschka "Glass Flowers" is a creative approach to flora, with more than 4,300 hand-blown glass plant models. The museum combines historic exhibits drawn from the university's vast collections with new and changing multimedia exhibitions such as *New England Forests and Mollusks: Shelled Masters of the Marine Realm,* and the renovated Earth & Planetary Sciences gallery. ⊠ *26 Oxford*

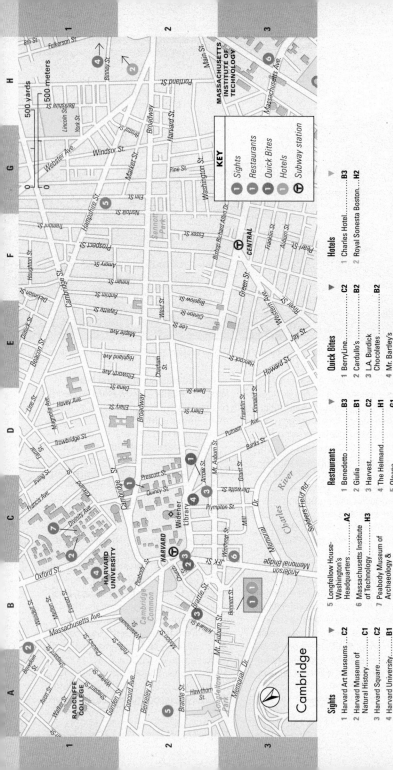

Cambridge

500 yards
500 meters

KEY

- ⓵ Sights
- ⓵ Restaurants
- ⓵ Quick Bites
- ⓵ Hotels
- Ⓣ Subway station

Sights
1 Harvard Art Museums ... **C2**
2 Harvard Museum of Natural History ... **C1**
3 Harvard Square ... **C2**
4 Harvard University ... **B1**
5 Longfellow House–Washington's Headquarters ... **A2**
6 Massachusetts Institute of Technology ... **H3**
7 Peabody Museum of Archaeology & Ethnology ... **C1**

Restaurants
1 Benedetto ... **B3**
2 Giulia ... **B1**
3 Harvest ... **C2**
4 The Helmand ... **H1**
5 Oleana ... **G1**
6 Orinoco ... **C3**

Quick Bites
1 BerryLine ... **C2**
2 Cardullo's ... **B2**
3 L.A. Burdick Chocolates ... **B2**
4 Mr. Bartley's Gourmet Burgers ... **C2**

Hotels
1 Charles Hotel ... **B3**
2 Royal Sonesta Boston ... **H2**

St., Harvard Square ☎ *617/495–3045*
⊕ *www.hmnh.harvard.edu* ⊿ *$15; ticket
includes admission to adjacent Peabody
Museum* Ⓜ *Harvard.*

★ Harvard Square

PLAZA | **FAMILY** | Tides of students, tourists, and politically charged proponents are all part of the nonstop pedestrian flow at this most celebrated of Cambridge crossroads. Harvard Square is where Massachusetts Avenue, coming from Boston, turns and widens into a triangle broad enough to accommodate a brick peninsula (above the T station). The restored 1928 kiosk in the center of the square once served as the entrance to the MBTA station, and is now home to lively street musicians and artists selling their paintings and photos on blankets. Harvard Yard, with its lecture halls, residential houses, libraries, and museums, is one long border of the square; the other three are composed of clusters of banks, retailers, and restaurants.

Time in the Square raises people-watching to a high art form. On an average afternoon you'll hear earnest conversations in dozens of foreign languages; see every kind of youthful uniform from slouchy sweats to impeccable prep; wander by street musicians playing guitars and flutes; and wonder at how students reading text books out in the sunshine can get any work done among the commotion.

The historic buildings are worth noting. It's a thrill to walk though the big brick-and-wrought-iron gates to Harvard Yard on up to Widener Library, the University's flagship library. More than 50 miles of bookshelves snake around this imposing neoclassical structure, designed by one of the nation's first major African American architects, Julian Abele. It holds more than 3.5 million volumes in 450 languages, but is unfortunately not open to the public.

Across Garden Street, through an ornamental arch, is **Cambridge Common,** decreed a public pasture in 1631. It's said that under a large tree that once stood in this meadow George Washington took command of the Continental Army on July 3, 1775. A stone memorial now marks the site of the "Washington Elm." Also on the Common is the Irish Famine Memorial by Derry artist Maurice Harron, unveiled in 1997 to coincide with the 150th anniversary of "Black '47," the deadliest year of the potato famine. At the center of the Common a large memorial commemorates the Union soldiers who lost their lives in the Civil War. On the far side of the Common is a fantastic park and newly renovated playground. ⊠ *Harvard Square* ⊕ *www.harvardsquare.com* Ⓜ *Harvard.*

Harvard University

COLLEGE | The tree-studded, shady, and redbrick expanse of **Harvard Yard**—the very center of Harvard University—has weathered the footsteps of Harvard students for hundreds of years. In 1636 the Great and General Court of the Massachusetts Bay Colony voted funds to establish the colony's first college, and a year later chose Cambridge as the site. Named in 1639 for John Harvard, a young Charlestown clergyman who died in 1638 and left the college his entire library and half his estate, Harvard remained the only college in the New World until 1693, by which time it was firmly established as a respected center of learning. Local wags refer to Harvard as WGU—World's Greatest University—and it's certainly the oldest and most famous American university.

Although the college dates from the 17th century, the oldest buildings in Harvard Yard are from the 18th century (though you'll sometimes see archaeologists digging here for evidence of older structures). Together the buildings chronicle American architecture from the Colonial era to the present. **Holden Chapel,** completed in 1744, is a Georgian gem. The graceful **University Hall** was designed in 1815 by Charles Bulfinch. An 1884 statue of John Harvard by Daniel Chester French stands outside; ironically for a school with the motto of "Veritas" ("Truth"), the model for the statue was a member of the class of 1882 and not Harvard himself. **Sever Hall,** completed in 1880 and designed by Henry Hobson Richardson, represents the Romanesque revival that was followed by the neoclassical (note the pillared facade of Widener Library) and the neo-Georgian, represented by the sumptuous brick houses along the Charles River, many of which are now undergraduate residences. **Memorial Church,** a graceful steepled edifice of modified Colonial Revival design, was dedicated in 1932. Just north of the Yard is **Memorial Hall,** completed in 1878 as a memorial to Harvard men who died in the Union cause; it's High Victorian both inside and out. It also contains the 1,166-seat Sanders Theatre, which serves as the university's largest lecture hall, site of year-round concerts by students and professionals, and the venue for the festive Christmas Revels.

Many of Harvard's cultural and scholarly facilities are important sights in themselves, but most campus buildings, other than museums and concert halls, are off-limits to the general public.

The **Harvard Information Center,** in the Smith Campus Centre, has a small exhibit space, distributes maps of the university area, and offers free student-led tours of Harvard Yard. The tour doesn't include visits to museums, and it doesn't take you into campus buildings, but it provides a fine orientation. The information center is open year-round (except during spring recess and other semester breaks). From the end of June through August, guides offer tours every half hour; however, it's best to call ahead to confirm times. You can also download a mobile tour on your smart phone.

✉ *Bounded by Massachusetts Ave. and Mt. Auburn, Holyoke, and Dunster Sts., 1350 Massachusetts Ave., Harvard Square* ☎ *617/495–1573 Information Center* ⊕ *www.harvard.edu* Ⓜ *Harvard.*

Longfellow House-Washington's Headquarters

HOUSE | Henry Wadsworth Longfellow, the poet whose stirring tales of the Village Blacksmith, Evangeline, Hiawatha, and Paul Revere's midnight ride thrilled 19th-century America, once lived in this elegant Georgian mansion. One of several original Tory Row homes on Brattle Street, the house was built in 1759 by John Vassall Jr., and George Washington lived (and slept!) here during the Siege of Boston from July 1775 to April 1776. Longfellow first boarded here in 1837 and later received the house as a gift from his father-in-law on his marriage to Frances Appleton, who burned to death here in an accident in 1861. For 45 years Longfellow wrote his famous verses here and filled the house with the exuberant spirit of his literary circle, which included Ralph Waldo Emerson, Nathaniel Hawthorne, and Charles Sumner, an abolitionist senator. Longfellow died in 1882, but his presence in the house lives on—from the Longfellow family furniture to the wallpaper to the books on the shelves (many the poet's own). The home is preserved and run by the National Park Service; guided tours are offered Memorial Day through October. The formal garden is the perfect place to relax; the grounds are open year-round. Longfellow Park, across the street, is the place to stand to take photos of the house. The park was created to preserve the view immortalized in the poet's "To the River Charles." ✉ *105 Brattle St., Tory Row* ☎ *617/876–4491* ⊕ *www.nps.gov/long* 🎟 *Free* 🕐 *Closed Mon. and Tues.* Ⓜ *Harvard.*

Massachusetts Institute of Technology

COLLEGE | Founded in 1861, MIT moved to Cambridge from Copley Square in the Back Bay in 1916. Once dissed as "the factory," particularly by its Ivy League neighbor, Harvard University, MIT mints graduates that are the sharp blades on the edge of the information revolution. It's perennially in the top five of *U.S. News and World Report's* college rankings. It has long since fulfilled the predictions of its founder, the geologist William Barton Rogers, that it would surpass "the universities of the land in the accuracy and the extent of its teachings in all branches of positive science." Its emphasis shifted in the 1930s from practical engineering and mechanics to the outer limits of scientific fields.

Architecture is important at MIT. Although the original buildings were obviously designed by and for scientists, many represent pioneering designs of their times. The **Kresge Auditorium,** designed by Eero Saarinen, with a curving roof and unusual thrust, rests on three, instead of four, points. The nondenominational **MIT Chapel,** a circular Saarinen design, is lighted primarily by a roof oculus that focuses natural light on the altar and by reflections from the water in a small surrounding moat; it's topped by an aluminum sculpture by Theodore Roszak. The serpentine **Baker House,** now a dormitory, was designed in 1947 by the Finnish architect Alvar Aalto in such a way as to provide every room with a view of the Charles River. Sculptures by Henry Moore and other notable artists dot the campus. The latest addition is the Green Center, punctuated by the splash of color that is Sol LeWitt's 5,500-square-foot mosaic floor.

The East Campus, which has grown around the university's original neoclassical buildings of 1916, also has outstanding modern architecture and sculpture, including the stark high-rise **Green Building** by I. M. Pei, housing the Earth Science Center. Just outside is Alexander Calder's giant stabile (a stationary mobile) *The Big Sail.* Another Pei work on the East Campus is the **Wiesner Building,** designed in 1985, which houses the **List Visual Arts Center.** Architect Frank Gehry made his mark on the campus with the cockeyed, improbable **Ray & Maria Stata Center,** a complex of buildings on Vassar Street. The center houses computer, artificial intelligence, and information systems laboratories, and is reputedly as confusing to navigate on the inside as it is to follow on the outside. East Campus's **Great Dome,** which looms over neoclassical Killian Court, has often been the target of student "hacks" and has at various times supported a telephone booth with a ringing phone, a life-size statue of a cow, and a campus police cruiser. Nearby, the domed **Rogers Building** has earned unusual notoriety as the center of a series of hallways and tunnels dubbed "the infinite corridor." Twice each winter the sun's path lines up perfectly with the corridor's axis, and at dusk students line the third-floor hallway to watch the sun set through the westernmost window. The phenomenon is known as "MIT-henge."

MIT maintains an information center in the Rogers Building, and offers free tours of the campus weekdays at 11 and 3. Check the schedule, as the tours are often suspended during school holidays. General hours for the information center are weekdays 9 to 5. ⊠ *77 Massachusetts Ave., Kendall Square* ☎ *617/253–4795* ⊕ *www.mit.edu* Ⓜ *Kendall/MIT.*

Peabody Museum of Archaeology & Ethnology

MUSEUM | With one of the world's outstanding anthropological collections, the Peabody Museum is among the oldest anthropology museums in the world. Its collections focus on Native American and Central and South American cultures and are comprised of more than 1.2 million objects. The Hall of the North American Indian is particularly outstanding, with art, textiles, and models of traditional dwellings from across the continent. The Mesoa-merican room juxtaposes ancient relief carvings and weavings with contemporary works from the Maya and other peoples. Of special note is the museum's only sur-viving collection of objects acquired from Native American people during the Lewis and Clark expedition. ⊠ *11 Divinity Ave., Harvard Square* ☎ *617/496–1027* ⊕ *www. peabody.harvard.edu* ⊴ *$15, includes admission to the adjacent Harvard Muse-um of Natural History* Ⓜ *Harvard.*

🍴 Restaurants

★ Benedetto

$$$ | ITALIAN | Chef Michael Pagliarini, whose devoted fan base will wait hours for his mouthwatering pastas and Italian food at Giulia up the street, is turning out an even more ambitious menu of seasonal Italian small bites, silky pastas, and mains. Start with a cocktail and some chicken liver mousse crostini and grilled octopus while you figure out whether to get the Ossabaw Island pork tortellini or the pappardelle with foraged mushrooms before your entrée of skate wing with brown butter or the Rohan duck over lentils. **Known for:** masterful Italian cooking; elegant airy setting; incredible pastas. Ⓢ *Average main: $33* ⊠ *The Charles Hotel, 1 Bennett St., Harvard Square* ☎ *617/661–5050* ⊕ *www. benedettocambridge.com* ☯ *No lunch.*

★ Giulia

$$$ | ITALIAN | With exposed brick walls and soft lighting, the heart and soul of this charming Italian restaurant is its communal pasta table at which Chef Michael Pagliarini spends hours hand-rolling superlative pastas for dishes like buckwheat pizzoccheri and pasta *alla bolognese*. Plates such as house-made lamb sausage, octopus and smoked squid, and Sardinian flatbread are original, generous, and, of course delicious. Known for its romantic nature, it's the perfect place for lovers to linger over a chocolate terrine and a cappuccino. **Known for:** excellent Italian food; silky

pastas; warm, softly lit space. Ⓢ *Average main: $30* ⊠ *1682 Massachusetts Ave., Harvard Square* ☎ *617/441–2800* ⊕ *www. giuliarestaurant.com* ☯ *Closed Sun.*

★ Harvest

$$$ | AMERICAN | Once a favorite of former Cambridge resident Julia Child, this sophisticated shrine to New England cuisine has been a perennial go-to spot for Harvard students when their parents are in town for more than 45 years. The seasonal menu could feature Cape scal-lop crudo, fresh pasta with braised veal and pesto, or fresh Cape lobster with lemon hollandaise. **Known for:** elegant New England cuisine; expansive wine list; pretty patio dining area. Ⓢ *Average main: $34* ⊠ *44 Brattle St., on walkway, Brattle Street* ☎ *617/868–2255* ⊕ *harvest-cambridge.com* Ⓜ *Harvard.*

★ The Helmand

$$$ | AFGHAN | The area's first Afghan restaurant, named after the country's most important river, welcomes you into its cozy Kendall Square confines with Afghan rugs, a wood-burning oven, and exotic, yet extremely approachable food that reflects the motherland's location halfway between the Middle East and India. Standouts, beyond the chewy warm bread, include magical names from a far-away land like *aushak* (leek-stuffed ravioli over yogurt with beef ragu and mint), *chapendaz* (marinated grilled beef tenderloin served with cum-in-spiced hot pepper–tomato puree), and a vegetarian baked pumpkin platter. **Known for:** excellent Afghan fare; enveloping atmosphere; incredible breads. Ⓢ *Average main: $25* ⊠ *143 1st St., Kendall Square* ☎ *617/492–4646* ⊕ *helmandrestaurant. com* ☯ *No lunch* Ⓜ *Lechmere.*

★ Oleana

$$$ | MEDITERRANEAN | With two restau-rants (including Sofra in Cambridge) and two cookbooks to her name, chef-owner Ana Sortun continues to bewitch area diners with her intricately spiced eastern Mediterranean meze (small plates) made with fresh-picked produce from her

husband's nearby Siena Farms. Oleana's menu changes often, but look for the hot, crispy-fried mussels starter and Sultan's Delight (tamarind-glazed beef with smoky eggplant puree) along with large plates of Turkish-spiced lamb and lemon chicken. **Known for:** eastern Mediterranean menu; mouthwatering small plates; deft use of spices. $ *Average main: $27* ⊠ *134 Hampshire St., Central Square* ☎ *617/661–0505* ⊕ *www.oleanarestaurant.com* ⊘ *No lunch* Ⓜ *Central.*

★ Orinoco

$$ | **LATIN AMERICAN** | Don't miss this red clapboard, Pan-Latin American restaurant located down an alleyway in Harvard Square. Owner Andres Banger's dream to bring bountiful plates of superfresh family fare from his home country of Venezuela to Cambridge (as well as Brookline Village and the South End) rewards diners with delectable, palm-sized *arepas,* or crispy, hot, corn-flour pockets stuffed with beans, cheese, chicken, or pork; *pabellon criollo,* moist shredded beef with stewed beans, rice, and plantains; and red chili adobo–marinated, charred *pollo* (chicken). **Known for:** Venezuelan specialties; generous portions; great value. $ *Average main: $18* ⊠ *56 JFK St., Harvard Square* ☎ *617/354–6900* ⊕ *www.orinocokitchen.com* ⊘ *Closed Mon.*

☕ Coffee and Quick Bites

BerryLine

$ | **CAFÉ** | Two postdoctoral-fellowship students founded this two-location tasty oasis that serves superlative soft frozen yogurt made from milk, cane sugar, fresh fruit, and other natural ingredients. The shop has featured well over 150 frozen yogurt flavors like rose, chocolate coconut, passion fruit, and green tea, and dedicated staff bakers create many of the homemade toppings including the cheesecake chunks, chewy mochi bits, brownie bites, and honey-nut granola. **Known for:** award-winning fro yo; homemade bakery toppings; fresh fruit add-ons. $ *Average main: $3* ⊠ *3 Arrow St., Harvard Square* ☎ *617/868–3500* ⊕ *www.berryline.com.*

Cardullo's

$ | **DELI** | This snug, nearly 70-year-old shop (family-owned-and-operated up until a few years ago) in Harvard Square purveys exotic imports, including cheeses, chocolates, biscuits, jams, olive oils, and mustards, along with sandwiches, cheeses and charcuterie to go. You'll also find a generous assortment of champagnes and domestic caviar, fine wines, and assorted beers. **Known for:** New England goods; made-to-order sandwiches and charcuterie; international gourmet sweet shop. $ *Average main:* ⊠ *6 Brattle St., Harvard Square* ☎ *617/491–8888, 800/491–8288* ⊕ *www.cardullos.com* ⊘ *No dinner* Ⓜ *Harvard.*

L.A. Burdick Chocolates

$ | **AMERICAN** | This charming artisanal chocolatier is a staple for locals and tourists alike, who come for its famously adorable signature chocolate mice, chocolate bonbons, and chocolate bars. The elegant, life-changing hot cocoa may be just the thing to restore flagging spirits or weary feet with variations on the classic milk chocolate, including dark, spicy, and white. **Known for:** dreamy drinking chocolate; chocolate milk and penguins; cozy atmosphere. $ *Average main: $10* ⊠ *52 Brattle St., Brattle Street* ☎ *617/491–4340* ⊕ *www.burdickchocolate.com* Ⓜ *Harvard.*

Mr. Bartley's Gourmet Burgers

$ | **AMERICAN** | **FAMILY** | It may be perfect cuisine for the student metabolism: a huge variety of variously garnished thick burgers with sassy names (many of them celebrities), deliciously crispy regular and sweet-potato fries, award-winning onion rings, and toppings like an egg or mac n' cheese. There's also a competent veggie burger, along with comforting dinner fare like baked meat loaf, fried chicken, and franks and beans. **Known for:** creative burgers; thick frappes; loud atmosphere.

$ *Average main: $15* ✉ *1246 Massachusetts Ave., Harvard Square* ☎ *617/354–6559* ⊕ *www.mrbartley.com* ⊘ *Closed Sun. and Mon.* Ⓜ *Harvard.*

🛏 Hotels

★ Charles Hotel
$$$ | **HOTEL** | **FAMILY** | It used to be that the Charles was *the* place to stay in Cambridge, and while other luxury hotels have since arrived to give it a little healthy competition, this Harvard Square staple is standing strong. **Pros:** two blocks from the T Red Line to Boston; on-site jazz club and hip Noir bar; on-site 4,000-square-foot Corbu Spa & Salon. **Cons:** luxury comes at a price; restricted pool hours for children; coffee pots and tea kettles are available by request only. $ *Rooms from: $399* ✉ *1 Bennett St., Harvard Square* ☎ *617/864–1200, 800/882–1818* ⊕ *www.charleshotel.com* 🛏 *295 rooms* ⦿| *No meals* Ⓜ *Harvard.*

★ Royal Sonesta Boston
$$$ | **HOTEL** | **FAMILY** | Right next to the Charles River, the certified-green Sonesta has one of the best city skylines and sunset views in Boston. **Pros:** walk to Museum of Science and T to Downtown Boston; complimentary shuttle to Cambridge-area attractions; nice pool. **Cons:** pay parking; river-view guest rooms have much better view than Cambridge-view rooms; no a/c in rooms. $ *Rooms from: $379* ✉ *40 Edwin Land Blvd., off Memorial Dr., Kendall Square* ☎ *617/806–4200, 800/766–3782* ⊕ *www.sonesta.com/boston* 🛏 *400 rooms* ⦿| *No meals* Ⓜ *Lechmere.*

▼ Nightlife

★ Toad
BARS/PUBS | This is where local hipsters make their home. Bands, beers, and burgers sum up this snug and amiable little Porter Square hideaway attached to Christopher's. The bar is maple, the toads ceramic, and microbrews on tap are a dozen-plus. Nightly music comes in many a stripe, and usually in double bills at 7 and 10 pm. Check out Sunday spins after 5 pm: bring your own vinyl. Twelve taps, Toad T-shirts, and never a cover charge: what's not to like? ✉ *1912 Massachusetts Ave., Porter Square* ☎ *617/497–4950 recording* ⊕ *www.toadcambridge.com* Ⓜ *Porter.*

🎭 Performing Arts

★ American Repertory Theater
THEATER | Founded by Robert Brustein and since 2009 under the helm of Tony Award–winning director Diane Paulus, the ART is one of America's most celebrated regional theaters, winning Tonys for Broadway originals *All the Way* and *Once* and revivals of *The Glass Menagerie, Pippin,* and *The Gershwins' Porgy and Bess.* The ART often premieres new works and seeks to expand the boundaries of theater through productions such as *Waitress, Finding Neverland,* and *Natasha, Pierre & The Great Comet of 1812* among others. The Loeb Drama Center, home of the ART, houses two theaters: the Mainstage and The Ex, a smaller black box often staging productions by the irreverent Harvard-Radcliffe Dramatic Club. OBERON, the ART's "club theater" with flexible stage design, engages young audiences in immersive theater (and has attracted national acclaim for its groundbreaking model) with gay, alternative, and cutting-edge programming. ✉ *64 Brattle St., Harvard Sq., Cambridge* ☎ *617/547–8300* ⊕ *americanrepertorytheater.org* Ⓜ *Harvard.*

★ Sanders Theatre
CONCERTS | This gilt-wood jewel box of a stage is the preferred venue for many of Boston's classical orchestras and the home of Harvard University's many ensembles. Located in the Memorial Hall, 180-degree stage design and superb acoustics afford intimacy and crystal projection. A favorite of folk, jazz, and world-music performers, the 1,000-seat Sanders hosts the holiday favorite, *Christmas Revels,* a traditional

participatory Yule celebration. Winston Churchill, Martin Luther King, Wynton Marsalis, Leonard Bernstein, and Oprah Winfrey have lectured at this famed seat of oratory and music. ⊠ *Harvard University, 45 Quincy St., Harvard Sq., Cambridge* ☎ *617/496–2222 box office* ⊕ *www.fas.harvard.edu/~memhall/ sanders.html* Ⓜ *Harvard.*

🏃 Activities

★ Head of the Charles Regatta

BOATING | In mid-October about 400,000 spectators turn out to cheer the more than 11,000 male and female athletes who come from all over the world to compete in the annual Head of the Charles Regatta, which in 2014 marked its 50th anniversary. Crowds line the banks of the Charles River with blankets and beer (although the police disapprove of the latter), cheering on their favorite teams and generally using the weekend as an excuse to party. Limited free parking is available, but the chances of finding an open space close to the race route are slim; take public transportation if you can. During the event, free shuttles run between the start and end point of the race route on both sides of the river. ⊠ *Banks of the Charles River, Harvard Square* ☎ *617/868–6200* ⊕ *www.hocr.org* Ⓜ *Harvard, Central.*

👜 Shopping

★ The Harvard Coop

BOOKS/STATIONERY | What began in 1882 as a nonprofit service for students and faculty is now managed by Barnes & Noble College, a separate entity that manages college campus bookstores. Housed in the same location since 1906 and affectionately called The Coop (pronounced "coop," not "co-op"), the store sells books and textbooks (many discounted), school supplies, clothes, and accessories plastered with the Harvard emblem, as well as

basic housewares geared toward dorm dwellers. If you need a public restroom, you'll find it here. And if you're looking for MIT swag, they have a location on that campus as well. ⊠ *1400 Massachusetts Ave., Harvard Square* ☎ *617/499– 2000* ⊕ *store.thecoop.com* Ⓜ *Harvard.*

★ Leavitt & Peirce

GIFTS/SOUVENIRS | A throwback to another era, this storied museum-like tobacco shop has been in the same location since 1883, when it served as a clubby gathering spot for young Harvard men, who puffed away while playing pool on the back billiard tables. While Harvard oars, hockey sticks, and photos still adorn the ivy-green walls, the store now caters to a broader clientele in search of quality smoking items, old-fashioned straight razors and shave brushes, chess and checker sets, and small gift items, such as beer steins. Don't miss the four chess tables on the second level, where you can rent pieces for $2 an hour (checkers and backgammon are available, too). ⊠ *1316 Massachusetts Ave., Harvard Square* ☎ *617/547–0576* ⊕ *www.leavitt-peirce. com* Ⓜ *Harvard.*

Side Trips from Boston

Lexington

16 miles northwest of Boston.

Incensed against the British, American colonials burst into action in Lexington in April 1775. On April 18, patriot leader Paul Revere alerted the town that British soldiers were approaching. The next day, as the British advance troops arrived in Lexington on their march toward Concord, the Minutemen were waiting to confront the redcoats in what became the first skirmish of the Revolutionary War.

These first military encounters of the American Revolution are very much a part of present-day Lexington, a modern suburban town that sprawls out from the historic sites near its center. Although the downtown area is generally lively, with ice-cream and coffee shops, boutiques, and a great little movie theater, the town becomes especially animated each Patriots' Day (April 19 but celebrated on the third Monday in April), when costume-clad groups re-create the Minutemen's battle maneuvers and Paul Revere rides again.

To learn more about the city and the 1775 clash, stop by the **Lexington Visitor Center.**

GETTING HERE AND AROUND

Massachusetts Bay Transportation Authority (MBTA) operates bus service in the greater Boston area and serves Lexington.

TOURS
CONTACTS Liberty Ride Trolley Tour.
✉ *1605 Massachusetts Ave.* ☎ *781/862–1450* ⊕ *www.tourlexington.us/liberty-ride-trolley-tours.*

VISITOR INFORMATION
CONTACTS Lexington Visitors Center.
✉ *1605 Massachusetts Ave.* ☎ *781/862–1450* ⊕ *www.lexingtonchamber.org.*

 ## Sights

Buckman Tavern
HISTORIC SITE | While waiting for the arrival of the British on the morning of April 19, 1775, the Minutemen gathered at this 1690 tavern. A half-hour tour takes in the tavern's seven rooms, which have been restored to the way they looked in the 1770s. Among the items on display is an old front door with a hole made by a British musket ball. ✉ *1 Bedford St.* ☎ *781/862–3763* ⊕ *www.lexingtonhistory.org* 🎫 *$10* 🕐 *Closed Oct. 31–Apr.*

Hancock-Clarke House
HISTORIC SITE | On April 18, 1775, Paul Revere came here to warn patriots John Hancock and Sam Adams (who were staying at the house while attending the Provincial Congress in nearby Concord) of the advance of British troops. Hancock and Adams, on whose heads the British king had put a price, fled to avoid capture. The house, a parsonage built in 1698, is a 10-minute walk from Lexington Common. Inside is the Treasures of the Revolution exhibit, and outside, a Colonial herb garden. ✉ *36 Hancock St.* ☎ *781/862–3763* ⊕ *www.lexingtonhistory.org* 🎫 *$10* 🕐 *Closed Oct. 31–Apr.*

Lexington Common National Historic Site
MILITARY SITE | It was on this 2-acre triangle of land, commonly referred to as simply the "Battle Green," on April 19, 1775, that the first confrontation between British soldiers, who were marching from Boston toward Concord, and the Colonial militia known as the Minutemen took place. The Minutemen—so called because they were able to prepare themselves at a moment's notice—were led by Captain John Parker, whose role in the American Revolution is commemorated in Henry Hudson Kitson's renowned 1900 *Minuteman* statue. Facing downtown Lexington at the tip of Battle Green, the statue's in a traffic island, and therefore makes for a difficult photo op. ✉ *Junction of Massachusetts Ave. and Bedford St.* ⊕ *www.lexingtonma.gov/battle-green* 🎫 *Free.*

Minute Man National Historical Park
NATIONAL/STATE PARK | FAMILY | West of Lexington's center stretches this 1,000-acre park that also extends into nearby Lincoln and Concord. Begin your park visit at the **Minute Man Visitor Center** in Lexington to see the free multimedia presentation, "The Road to Revolution," a captivating introduction to the events of April 1775. Staffed by costumed park

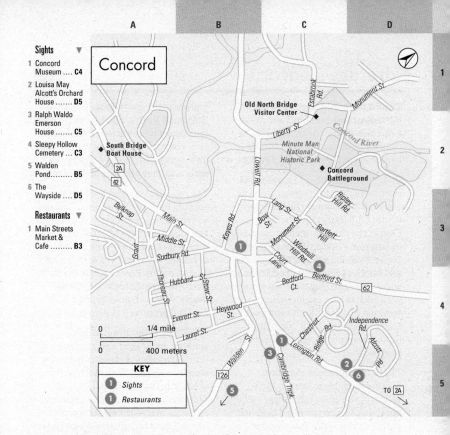

Concord

Sights ▼

1. Concord Museum **C4**
2. Louisa May Alcott's Orchard House **D5**
3. Ralph Waldo Emerson House **C5**
4. Sleepy Hollow Cemetery ... **C3**
5. Walden Pond......... **B5**
6. The Wayside **D5**

Restaurants ▼

1. Main Streets Market & Cafe **B3**

KEY
- ① Sights
- ① Restaurants

---

volunteers, the Whittemore House has a hands-on "Try on 1775!" exhibit where kids can wear Colonial clothing and gather ingredients for a meal. Continuing along Highway 2A toward Concord, you pass the point where Revere's midnight ride ended with his capture by the British; it's marked with a boulder and plaque, as well as an enclosure with wayside exhibits. You can also visit the 1732 **Hartwell Tavern,** a restored drover's (driver's) tavern staffed by park employees in period costume; they frequently demonstrate musket firing, militia drills, and talk about life in Colonial Massachusetts. ✉ *Rte. 2A, ¼ mile west of Rte. 128* ☎ *978/369–6993* ⊕ *www.nps.gov/mima.*

Concord

About 10 miles west of Lexington, 21 miles northwest of Boston.

The Concord of today is a modern suburb with a busy center filled with arty shops, places to eat, and (recalling the literary history made here) old bookstores. Autumn lovers, take note: Concord is a great place to start a fall foliage tour. From Boston, head west along Route 2 to Concord, and then continue on to find harvest stands and apple picking around Harvard and Stow.

GETTING HERE AND AROUND

The MBTA runs buses to Concord. On the MBTA Commuter Rail, Concord is a 40-minute ride on the Fitchburg Line, which departs from Boston's North Station.

Literary Concord

The first wholly American literary movement was born in Concord, the tiny town west of Boston that, quite coincidentally, also witnessed the beginning of the American Revolution.

Under the influence of essayist and poet Ralph Waldo Emerson, a group eventually known as the Transcendental Club (but called the Hedges Club at the time) assembled regularly in Emerson's Concord home. Henry David Thoreau, a fellow townsman and famous proponent of self-reliance, was an integral club member, along with such others as pioneering feminist Margaret Fuller and poet Ellery Channing, both drawn to Concord simply because of Emerson's presence.

These are the names that have become indelible bylines in high-school anthologies and college syllabi, but Concord also produced beloved authors outside the Transcendentalist movement. These writers include Louisa May Alcott of *Little Women* fame and children's book author Harriet Lothrop, pseudonymously known as Margaret Sydney. Even Nathaniel Hawthorne, whose various temporary homes around Massachusetts constitute a literary trail all their own, resided in Concord during the early and later portions of his career.

The cumulative inkwells of these authors have bestowed upon Concord a literary legacy unique in the United States, both for its influence on literature in general and for the quantity of related sights packed within such a small radius. From Alcott's Orchard House to Hawthorne's Old Manse, nearly all their houses remain standing, well preserved and open for tours.

The Thoreau Institute, within walking distance of a reconstruction of Thoreau's famous cabin in the woods at Walden Pond, is a repository of his papers and original editions. Emerson's study sits in the Concord Museum, across the street from his house. Even their final resting places are here, on Authors Ridge in Sleepy Hollow Cemetery, a few short blocks from the town common.

VISITOR INFORMATION

CONTACTS Concord Visitor Center. ⊠ *58 Main St.* ☎ *978/369–3120* ⊕ *concordma. gov/1920/Visitor-Center.*

 Sights

Concord Museum

MUSEUM | FAMILY | The original contents of Emerson's private study, as well as the world's largest collection of Thoreau artifacts, reside in this 1930 Colonial Revival building just east of the town center. The museum provides a good overview of the town's history, from its original Native American settlement to the present.

Highlights include Native American artifacts, furnishings from Thoreau's Walden Pond cabin (there's a replica of the cabin itself on the museum's lawn), and one of the two lanterns hung at Boston's Old North Church to signal that the British were coming by sea. If you've brought children, ask for a free family activity pack. ⊠ *200 Lexington Rd., GPS address is 53 Cambridge Tpke.* ☎ *978/369–9763* ⊕ *www.concordmuseum.org* ⤶ *$12.*

Louisa May Alcott's Orchard House

HOUSE | The dark brown exterior of Louisa May Alcott's family home sharply contrasts with the light, wit, and energy so much in evidence within. Named for the apple orchard that once surrounded it, Orchard House was the Alcott family home from 1857 to 1877. Here Louisa wrote *Little Women*, based in part on her life with her three sisters; and her father, Bronson, founded the Concord School of Philosophy—the building remains behind the house. Because Orchard House had just one owner after the Alcotts left, and because it became a museum in 1911, more than 80% of the original furnishings remain, including the semicircular shelf-desk where Louisa wrote *Little Women*. ✉ *399 Lexington Rd.* ☎ *978/369-4118* ⊕ *www.louisamayalcott.org* 💲 *$10.*

Ralph Waldo Emerson House

HOUSE | The 19th-century essayist and poet Ralph Waldo Emerson lived briefly in the Old Manse in 1834–35, then moved to this home, where he lived until his death in 1882. Here he wrote the *Essays*. Except for artifacts from Emerson's study, now at the nearby Concord Museum, the Emerson House furnishings have been preserved as the writer left them, down to his hat resting on the newel post. You must join one of the half-hour-long tours to see the interior. ✉ *28 Cambridge Tpke., at Lexington Rd.* ☎ *978/369-2236* ⊕ *www.nps.gov/places/ralph-waldo-emerson-house.htm* 💲 *$9* ⊗ *Closed Nov.–mid-Apr., and Mon.–Wed. mid-Apr.–Oct.* ☞ *Call ahead for tour-scheduling information.*

Sleepy Hollow Cemetery

CEMETERY | This garden cemetery on the National Registry of Historic Places served as a place of inspiration and a final resting place for American literary greats like Louisa May Alcott, Ralph Waldo Emerson, Henry David Thoreau, and Nathaniel Hawthorne. Each Memorial Day Alcott's grave is decorated in commemoration of her death. ✉ *Bedford St. (Rte. 62), 24 Court La. and Bedford St.* ✛ *1 block east of Monument Sq. in Concord* ☎ *978/318-3233* ⊕ *www.friendsofsleepyhollow.org.*

★ Walden Pond

NATIONAL/STATE PARK | For lovers of Early American literature, a trip to Concord isn't complete without a pilgrimage to Henry David Thoreau's most famous residence. Here, in 1845, at age 28, Thoreau moved into a one-room cabin—built for $28.12—on the shore of this 100-foot-deep kettle hole formed by the retreat of an ancient glacier. Living alone for the next two years, Thoreau discovered the benefits of solitude and the beauties of nature. *Walden*, published in 1854, is a mixture of philosophy, nature writing, and proto-ecology. The site of the original house is staked out in stone. A full-size, authentically furnished replica of the cabin stands about ½ mile from the original site, near the Walden Pond State Reservation parking lot. During the summer, don't be shocked if you aren't allowed entrance: Walden Pond has a visitor capacity. ✉ *915 Walden St. (Rte. 126)* ✛ *To get to Walden Pond State Reservation from center of Concord—a trip of only 1½ miles—take Concord's Main St. a block west from Monument Sq., turn left onto Walden St., and head for intersection of Rtes. 2 and 126. Cross over Rte. 2 onto Hwy. 126, heading south for ½ mile* ☎ *978/369-3254* ⊕ *www.mass.gov/locations/walden-pond-state-reservation* 💲 *Free, but parking is $8 for vehicles with Massachusetts plates, $15 for vehicles with non-Massachusetts plates* ☞ *No dogs allowed.*

The Wayside

HOUSE | Nathaniel Hawthorne lived at the Old Manse in 1842–45, working on stories and sketches; he then moved to Salem (where he wrote *The Scarlet Letter*) and later to Lenox (*The House of the Seven Gables*). In 1852 he returned to Concord, bought this rambling structure called The Wayside, and lived here until his death in 1864. The home certainly appealed to literary types: the subsequent owner of The Wayside, Margaret Sidney, wrote the children's book *Five Little Peppers and How They Grew* (1881), and before Hawthorne moved in, the Alcotts lived here, from 1845 to 1848. An exhibit center, in the former barn, provides information about the Wayside authors and links them to major events in American history. Hawthorne's tower-study, with his stand-up writing desk, is substantially as he left it. ✉ *455 Lexington Rd.* ☎ *978/318–7863* ⊕ *www. nps.gov/mima/learn/historyculture/the-wayside.htm* ✑ *$7* ⊘ *Closed in winter.*

🍴 Restaurants

Main Streets Market & Cafe

$$ | **AMERICAN** | Cyclists, families, and sightseers pack into this brick building, which was used to store munitions during the Revolutionary War. Wood floors and blackboard menus add a touch of nostalgia, but the extensive menu includes many modern hits, including ale mac and cheese, meat loaf, and a Yankee pot roast dinner. **Known for:** live music five nights a week; summertime ice-cream counter; open early for breakfast. Ⓢ *Average main: $18* ✉ *42 Main St.* ☎ *978/369–9948* ⊕ *www.main-streetsmarketandcafe.com.*

Gloucester

37 miles northeast of Boston, 8 miles northeast of Manchester-by-the-Sea.

On Gloucester's fine seaside promenade is a famous statue of a man steering a ship's wheel, his eyes searching the horizon. The statue, which honors those who go down to the sea in ships, was commissioned by the town citizens in celebration of Gloucester's 300th anniversary in 1923. The oldest seaport in the nation (with some of the North Shore's best beaches) is still a major fishing port. Sebastian Junger's 1997 book *A Perfect Storm* was an account of the fate of the *Andrea Gail*, a Gloucester fishing boat caught in the storm of the century in October 1991. In 2000 the book was made into a movie, filmed on location in Gloucester.

VISITOR INFORMATION

CONTACTS Cape Ann Chamber of Commerce. ✉ *33 Commercial St.* ☎ *978/283–1601* ⊕ *www.capeannchamber.com.*

👁 Sights

Cape Ann Museum

MUSEUM | The Cape Ann Museum celebrates the art, history, and culture of Cape Ann. The museum's collections include fine art from the 19th century to the present, artifacts from the fishing, maritime, and granite-quarrying industries, as well as textiles, furniture, a library-archives, and two historic houses. ✉ *27 Pleasant St.* ☎ *978/283–0455* ⊕ *www.capeannmuseum.org* ✑ *$12* ⊘ *Closed Mon.*

Hammond Castle Museum

MUSEUM | Inventor John Hays Hammond Jr., credited with more than 500 patents, including remote control via radio waves, built this structure in 1926 to resemble a "medieval" stone castle. The museum contains medieval-style furnishings and paintings, and the Great Hall houses an impressive 8,200-pipe organ. From the castle you can see Norman's Woe Rock, made famous by Longfellow in his poem "The Wreck of the Hesperus." In July and August, unique "Spiritualism Tours" are an additional option on Thursday nights (for an extra fee), with discussion of topics like the Ouija board, spirit photography, séances, and the science behind Spiritualism. ✉ *80 Hesperus Ave., south side of Gloucester off Rte. 127* ☎ *978/283–2080* ⊕ *www.hammondcastle.org* ✑ *$15* ⊘ *Closed Mon. and Jan.–early Apr.*

Rocky Neck

NEIGHBORHOOD | On a peninsula within Gloucester's working harbor, the town's creative side thrives in this neighborhood, one of the oldest continuously working artists' colonies in the United States. Its alumni include Winslow Homer, Maurice Prendergast, Jane Peter, and Cecilia Beaux. Call for winter hours. ✉ *6 Wonson St.* ☎ *978/515–7004* ⊕ *www.rockyneckartcolony.org.*

Beaches

Gloucester has some of the best beaches on the North Shore. From Memorial Day through mid-September, parking costs $25 on weekdays and $30 on weekends, when the lots often fill by 10 am.

Good Harbor Beach

BEACH—SIGHT | This beach has calm, waveless waters and soft sand, and is surrounded by grassy dunes, making it perfect any time of year. In summer (June, July, and August), it is lifeguard patrolled, handicap accessible, and there is a snack bar if you don't feel like packing in food. The restrooms and showers are wheelchair accessible, and you can pick up beach toys at the concessions. On weekdays parking is plentiful, but the lot fills by 10 am on weekends. In June, green flies can be bothersome. **Amenities:** food and drink; lifeguards; parking (fee); showers; toilets. **Best for:** swimming; walking. ✉ *Gloucester* ✥ *Clearly signposted from Rte. 127A* 🌐 *gloucester-ma.gov* 🎟 *Parking from $30 per car.*

Long Beach

BEACH—SIGHT | Just as its name implies, this soft-sand beach that is half in Rockport, half in Gloucester is long, and it's also broad. It draws crowds from the houses that border it, particularly on weekends. Pay attention to the tide schedule, or you may find there's no beach to sit on. Cape Ann Motor Inn is nearby. Parking is very limited. Don't even think of parking on neighborhood streets if you don't have a town parking sticker—you will be towed. However, there is a lot on the Gloucester side. **Amenities:** none. **Best for:** swimming; walking. ✉ *Off Rte. 127A on Gloucester-Rockport town line, Off Rockport Rd.*

★ Wingaersheek Beach

BEACH—SIGHT | With white sand and dunes, Wingaersheek Beach is a well-protected cove with both a beach side and a boat side. The white Annisquam lighthouse is in the bay. The beach is known for its miles of white sand and calm waters. On weekends arrive early. The parking lot generally fills up by midmorning. It's handicap accessible and beach wheelchairs are available on request. **Amenities:** food and drink; parking (fee); toilets. **Best for:** swimming; walking. ✉ *232 Atlantic St.* ✥ *Take Rte. 128 N to Exit 13* 🌐 *gloucester-ma.gov* 🎟 *Limited parking, from $30 per car.*

Restaurants

Passports

$$ | ECLECTIC | FAMILY | In the heart of Downtown Gloucester, Passports serves a modern take on classic New England seafood. The fried oysters and house haddock are favorites here, and there's always local art hanging on the walls for patrons to buy. **Known for:** lively atmosphere; warm, fresh popovers; great, central location. [$] *Average main: $22* ✉ *110 Main St.* ☎ *978/281–3680* 🌐 *www.facebook.com/PassportsRestaurant.*

Hotels

Cape Ann's Marina Resort & Spa

$$ | RESORT | FAMILY | This year-round hotel less than a mile from downtown Gloucester comes alive in summer with an on-site restaurant and deep-sea fishing excursions. **Pros:** free Wi-Fi; full marina; indoor pool and Jacuzzi with poolside bar. **Cons:** hotel surrounded by parking lots; price hike during summer; bar area can be loud in summer. [$] *Rooms from: $226* ✉ *75 Essex Ave.* ☎ *978/283–2116, 800/626–7660* 🌐 *www.capeannmarina.com* 🔑 *31 rooms* 🍴 *No meals.*

★ Castle Manor Inn

$ | B&B/INN | With original woodwork and cozy fireplaces, this restored 1900 Victorian inn perfectly captures the Cape Ann aesthetic. **Pros:** discount parking passes to the local beaches; historic; close to Gloucester's beaches. **Cons:** closes for the winter; roads in the area can be windy and confusing; may be too intimate for some travelers. $ *Rooms from: $150* ✉ *141 Essex Ave.* ☎ *978/515-7386* ⊕ *www.castlemanorinn.com* ⇥ *10 rooms* ⍩ *No meals.*

Salem

16 miles northeast of Boston, 4 miles west of Marblehead.

Known for years as the Witch City, Salem is redefining itself. Though numerous witch-related attractions and shops still draw tourists, there's much more to the city. First, a bit on its bewitched past....

The witchcraft hysteria emerged from the trials of 1692, when several Salem-area girls fell ill and accused some of the townspeople of casting spells on them. More than 150 men and women were charged with practicing witchcraft, a crime punishable by death. After the trials later that year, 19 people were hanged and one man was crushed to death.

Though the witch trials might have built Salem's infamy, it'd be a mistake to ignore the town's rich maritime and creative traditions, which played integral roles in the country's evolution. Frigates out of Salem opened the Far East trade routes and generated the wealth that created America's first millionaires. Among its native talents are writer Nathaniel Hawthorne, the intellectual Peabody sisters, navigator Nathaniel Bowditch, and architect Samuel McIntire. This creative spirit is today celebrated in Salem's internationally recognized museums, waterfront shops and restaurants, galleries, and wide common.

To learn more on the area, stop by the **Regional Visitor's Center.** Innovatively designed in the Old Salem Armory, the center has exhibits, a 27-minute film, maps, and a gift shop.

VISITOR INFORMATION

CONTACTS Destination Salem. ✉ *81 Washington St., Suite 204* ☎ *978/741-3252, 877/725-3662* ⊕ *www.salem.org.* **Salem Armory Visitor Center.** ✉ *2 New Liberty St.* ☎ *978/740-1650* ⊕ *www.nps.gov/ner/sama.*

◉ Sights

House of the Seven Gables

HOUSE | Immortalized in Nathaniel Hawthorne's classic novel, this site is itself a historic treasure. Built in 1668 and also known as the Turner-Ingersoll Mansion, the house includes the famous secret staircase, a re-creation of Hepzibah's cent shop from *The House of Seven Gables*, and some of the finest Georgian interiors in the country. Also on the property is the small house where Hawthorne was born in 1804; built in 1750, it was moved from its original location a few blocks away. ✉ *115 Derby St.* ☎ *978/744-0991* ⊕ *www.7gables.org* 🎟 *$17.*

★ Peabody Essex Museum

MUSEUM | Salem's world-class museum celebrates superlative works from around the globe and across time, including American art and architecture, Asian export art, photography, maritime art and history, as well as Native American, Oceanic, and African art. With a collection of 1.8 million works, housed in a contemplative blend of modern design, the museum represents a diverse range of styles; exhibits include pieces ranging from American decorative and seamen's art to an interactive Art & Nature Center and photography. While there be sure to tour the Yin Yu Tang house. This fabulous 200-year-old house dates to the Qing Dynasty (1644–1911) of China. The museum brought it over from China in sections and reassembled it here. ✉ *East India Sq.* ☎ *978/745-9500, 866/745-1876* ⊕ *www.pem.org* 🎟 *$20* ⊘ *Closed Mon.*

Landlubbers can go to sea at Salem's Peabody Essex Museum.

Salem Maritime National Historic Site

LIGHTHOUSE | Near Derby Wharf, this 9¼-acre site focuses on Salem's heritage as a major seaport with a thriving overseas trade. It includes the 1762 home of Elias Derby, America's first millionaire; the 1819 Custom House, made famous in Nathaniel Hawthorne's *The Scarlet Letter*; and a replica of the *Friendship,* a 171-foot, three-masted 1797 merchant vessel. There's also an active lighthouse dating from 1871, as well as the nation's last surviving 18th-century wharves. Newer to the site is the 1770 Pedrick Store House, moved from nearby Marblehead and reassembled right on Derby Wharf; the two-story structure once played a vital role in the lucrative merchant seaside trade. The grounds are open 24/7, but buildings open on a seasonal schedule. ⊠ *193 Derby St.* ☎ *978/740–1650 visitor center* ⊕ *www. nps.gov/sama/index.htm* ✉ *Free with exception of film "Witch Hunt: Exam the Evidence".*

Salem Witch Museum

MUSEUM | An informative and fascinating introduction to the 1692 witchcraft hysteria, this museum offers a look at 1692 with 13 life-size stage sets featuring narration of what life was like at that time, plus a 15-minute guided tour through the exhibit, "Witches: Evolving Perceptions," which describes witch hunts through the years. ⊠ *19½ Washington Sq. N* ☎ *978/744–1692* ⊕ *www.salemwitchmuseum.com* ✉ *$13.*

🍴 Restaurants

Finz Seafood & Grill

$$ | SEAFOOD | This contemporary seafood restaurant on Salem Harbor treats patrons to prime canal views. Seafood potpie and lobster rolls highlight the lunch menu, while sesame-crusted tuna or steamed lobster are dinner favorites, but burgers and steaks are available for meat eaters. **Known for:** outdoor seating; classic New England seafood; large sushi menu. $ *Average main: $24* ⊠ *76 Wharf St.* ☎ *978/744–8485* ⊕ *www.hipfinz.com.*

The First Witch Trial

It was in Danvers, not Salem, that the first witch trial was held, originating with the family of Samuel Parris, a minister who moved to the area in 1680 from Barbados, bringing with him two slaves, including one named Tituba. In 1691 Samuel's daughter, Betty, and niece, Abigail, began having "fits." Tituba, who had told Betty and Abigail stories of magic and witchcraft from her homeland, baked a "witch cake" to identify the witches who were harming the girls. The girls in turn accused Tituba of witchcraft.

After three days of "questioning," which included beatings from Samuel and a promise from him to free her if she cooperated, Tituba confessed to meeting the devil (in the form of a black hog or dog). She also claimed there were other witches in the village, confirming the girls' accusations against Sarah Good and Sarah Osborne, but she refused to name any others. Tituba's trial prompted the frenzy that led to the deaths of 20 accused "witches."

Hotels

★ Amelia Payson House

$$ | B&B/INN | Built in 1845, this Greek Revival house is a comfortable bed-and-breakfast near all the historic attractions. **Pros:** fireplaces in each room; outdoor lounge with a fire pit; on-site parking. **Cons:** no children under 12; hard to get reservations; might be too quaint for some. $ *Rooms from: $225* ✉ *16 Winter St.* ☎ *978/744–8304* ⊕ *www.amelia-paysonhouse.com* ➶ *3 rooms* ⦿ *Free breakfast.*

The Hawthorne Hotel

$ | HOTEL | Elegantly restored, this full-service historic hotel celebrates the town's most famous writer and is within walking distance from the town common, museums, and waterfront. **Pros:** lovely, historic lobby; free parking available behind hotel; free Wi-Fi. **Cons:** many rooms are small; two-night minimum June through October; pricey pet policy. $ *Rooms from: $189* ✉ *18 Washington Sq. W* ☎ *978/744–4080, 800/729–7829* ⊕ *www.hawthornehotel.com* ➶ *93 rooms* ⦿ *No meals* ➴ *$50 charge per room per night for pets.*

Performing Arts

Cry Innocent: The People versus Bridget Bishop

THEATER | This show, the longest continuously running play north of Boston, transports audience members to Bridget Bishop's witchcraft hearing of 1692. After hearing historical testimonies, the audience cross-examines the witnesses and decides whether to send Bridget to trial or not. Actors respond in character revealing much about the Puritan frame of mind. Each show is different and allows audience members to play their "part" in history. ✉ *Old Town Hall, 32 Derby Sq.* ☎ *978/810–2588* ⊕ *www.historyalivesalem.com* ➴ *$25.*

Rockport

41 miles northeast of Boston, 4 miles northeast of Gloucester on Rte. 127.

Rockport, at the very tip of Cape Ann, derives its name from the local granite formations. Many Boston-area structures are made of stone cut from its long-gone quarries. Today the town is a tourist center with a well-marked, centralized downtown that is easy to navigate and access on foot. Unlike typical tourist-trap landmarks, Rockport's shops sell quality arts, clothing, and gifts, and its restaurants serve seafood or home-baked cookies rather than fast food. Walk past shops and colorful clapboard houses to the end of Bearskin Neck for an impressive view of the Atlantic Ocean and the old, weather-beaten lobster shack known as Motif No. 1 because of its popularity as a subject for amateur painters and photographers.

VISITOR INFORMATION
CONTACTS Rockport Visitor Center. ✉ *Upper Main St. (Rte. 127)* ☎ *978/546–9372* 🌐 *www.rockportusa.com.*

🍴 Restaurants

Brackett's Ocean View
$$ | **SEAFOOD** | Enormous windows in this quiet, homey restaurant offer excellent views across Sandy Bay, along with plenty of chowder, fish cakes, lobster, and other seafood dishes. While the restaurant is only open seasonally, next door is their cafe, Brothers' Brew Coffee Shop, open year-round. **Known for:** local seafood; every table has a waterfront view; great downtown location. [$] *Average main: $18* ✉ *25 Main St.* ☎ *978/546–2797* 🌐 *www.bracketts.com* ⏲ *Closed Columbus Day–mid-Apr.*

🛏 Hotels

Bearskin Neck Motor Lodge
$$ | **HOTEL** | **FAMILY** | Near the end of Bearskin Neck, this small brick-and-shingle motel offers guests the best of both worlds: beautiful, oceanfront rooms, as well as easy access to shopping and restaurants. **Pros:** all rooms have balconies and unobstructed ocean views; central location; mini-refrigerators in rooms. **Cons:** lots of summertime tourists; heavy "classic motel" vibe; no pets allowed. [$] *Rooms from: $220* ✉ *64 Bearskin Neck* ☎ *978/546–6677, 877/507–6272* 🌐 *www.bearskinneckmotorlodge.com* ⏲ *Closed early Dec.–Mar.* 🔑 *8 rooms* 🍽 *No meals.*

Plymouth

40 miles south of Boston.

On December 26, 1620, 102 weary men, women, and children disembarked from the *Mayflower* to found the first permanent European settlement north of Virginia. Today Plymouth is characterized by narrow streets, clapboard mansions, shops, antiques stores, and a scenic waterfront. To mark Thanksgiving, the town holds a parade, historic-house tours, and other activities. Historic statues dot the town, including depictions of William Bradford, Pilgrim leader and governor of Plymouth Colony for more than 30 years, on Water Street; a Pilgrim maiden in Brewster Gardens; and Massasoit, the Wampanoag chief who helped the Pilgrims survive, on Carver Street.

VISITOR INFORMATION
CONTACTS Plymouth Visitor Information Center. ✉ *130 Water St., at Rte. 44* ☎ *508/747–7525* 🌐 *www.seeplymouth.com.*

👁 Sights

Mayflower II
LIGHTHOUSE | **FAMILY** | This seaworthy replica of the 1620 *Mayflower* was built in England through research and a bit of guesswork, then sailed across the Atlantic in 1957. As you explore the interior and exterior of the ship, which was extensively refurbished in time for Plymouth's 400th anniversary in 2020, sailors in modern dress answer your questions about both the reproduction and the original ship, while costumed guides provide a 17th-century perspective. Plymouth Rock is nearby. ✉ *State Pier* ☎ *508/746–1622* 🌐 *www.plimoth.org* 🎟 *From $9; heritage passes and combination tickets include Plimoth Plantation and Plimoth Grist Mill* ⏲ *Closed mid-Nov.–mid-Mar.*

National Monument to the Forefathers

MEMORIAL | Said to be the largest freestanding granite statue in the United States, this allegorical monument stands high on an 11-acre hilltop site. Designed by Hammet Billings of Boston in 1854 and dedicated in 1889, it depicts Faith, surrounded by Liberty, Morality, Justice, Law, and Education, and includes scenes from the Pilgrims' early days in Plymouth. ✉ *72 Allerton St.* 🌐 *www.seeplymouth.com/things-to-do/national-monument-forefathers.*

Pilgrim Hall Museum

MUSEUM | **FAMILY** | From the waterfront sights, it's a short walk to one of the country's oldest public museums. Established in 1824, Pilgrim Hall Museum transports you back to the time of the Pilgrims' landing with objects carried by those weary travelers to the New World. Historic items on display include a carved chest, a remarkably well-preserved wicker cradle, Myles Standish's sword, and John Alden's Bible. In addition, the museum presents the story of the Wampanoag, the native people who lived here 10,000 years before the arrival of the Pilgrims, and who are still live here today. ✉ *75 Court St. (Rte. 3A)* ☎ *508/746–1620* 🌐 *www.pilgrimhall.org* 🎟 *$12* 🕒 *Closed Jan.*

★ Plimoth Plantation

MUSEUM VILLAGE | **FAMILY** | Against the backdrop of the Atlantic Ocean, and 3 miles south of downtown Plymouth, this living museum shares the rich, interwoven story of the Plymouth Colony and the Wampanoag homeland through engaging daily programs and special events. A 1620s Pilgrim village has been carefully re-created, from the thatch roofs, cramped quarters, and open fireplaces to the long-horned livestock. Throw away your preconception of white collars and funny hats; through ongoing research, the Plimoth staff has developed a portrait of the Pilgrims that's more complex than the dour folk in school textbooks. Listen to the accents of the "residents," who never break out of character. Feel free to engage them in conversation about their life. Don't worry, 21st-century museum educators are on hand to help answer any questions you have as well. On the Wampanoag homesite meet native people speaking from a modern perspective of the traditions, lifeways, and culture of Eastern Woodlands Indigenous people. Note that there's not a lot of shade here in summer. ✉ *137 Warren Ave. (Rte. 3A)* ☎ *508/746–1622* 🌐 *www.plimoth.org* 🎟 *$32* 🕒 *Closed late-Nov.–mid-Mar.*

Plymouth Rock

MEMORIAL | **FAMILY** | This landmark rock, just a few dozen yards from the *Mayflower II,* is popularly believed to have been the Pilgrims' stepping-stone when they left the ship. Given the stone's unimpressive appearance—it's little more than a boulder—and dubious authenticity (as explained on a nearby plaque), the grand canopy overhead seems a trifle ostentatious. Still, more than a million people a year come to visit this world-famous symbol of courage and faith. ■ **TIP→ The views of Plymouth Harbor alone are worth the visit.** ✉ *Water St.* ☎ *508/747–5360* 🌐 *www.mass.gov/locations/pilgrim-memorial-state-park.*

🍴 Restaurants

Blue-Eyed Crab Grille & Raw Bar

$$$ | **CARIBBEAN** | **FAMILY** | Grab a seat on the outside deck overlooking the water at this friendly, somewhat funky (plastic fish dangling from the ceiling), Caribbean-inspired eatery. Enjoy fruity cocktails on the patio, or hang out in the colorful dining room. **Known for:** views of the water; funky decor; tropical cocktails. [$] *Average main: $25* ✉ *170 Water St.* ☎ *508/747–6776* 🌐 *www.blue-eyedcrab.com.*

Chapter 5

CAPE COD, MARTHA'S VINEYARD, AND NANTUCKET

Updated by
Kim MacKinnon

◉ Sights   🍴 Restaurants   🏨 Hotels   🛍 Shopping   🍸 Nightlife

★★★☆☆   ★★★★☆   ★★★★☆   ★★★★☆   ★★☆☆☆

WELCOME TO CAPE COD, MARTHA'S VINEYARD, AND NANTUCKET

TOP REASONS TO GO

★ **Beaches:** Cape Cod's picturesque beaches are the ultimate reason to go. The high sand dunes, gorgeous sunsets, and never-ending sea will get you every time.

★ **Visiting Lighthouses:** Lighthouses rise along Cape Cod's coast like architectural exclamation points. Highlights include Eastham's beautiful Nauset Light and Chatham and Nobska Lights for their spectacular views.

★ **Biking the Trails:** Martha's Vineyard and Nantucket each have dedicated bike paths, but the Cape Cod Rail Trail from South Dennis to south Wellfleet (with a spur out to Chatham) is the definitive route, with more than 25 miles of relatively flat terrain.

★ **Setting Sail:** Area tour operators offer everything from sunset schooner cruises to charter fishing expeditions. Whale-watching adventures are popular mid-April–October.

★ **Browsing the Galleries:** The Cape was a prominent art colony in the 19th century, and today it has a number of galleries.

1 Sandwich. Heritage and Sandwich Glass museums.

2 Falmouth. The family-friendly Old Silver Beach.

3 Hyannis. The Cape's unofficial capital.

4 Barnstable. West Barnstable, Cotuit, Marston Mills, Osterville, Centerville, and Hyannis.

5 Yarmouth. South and West Yarmouth, and Yarmouthport.

6 Dennis. Museums and B&Bs.

7 Brewster. Rich in conservation lands and state parks.

8 Harwich. Boats of all shapes and sizes anchor in the harbors.

9 Chatham. A quietly posh seaside resort.

10 Orleans. Beautiful homes and beaches.

11 Eastham. A town full of hidden treasures.

12 Wellfleet. World-renowned for its oysters.

13 Truro. High dunes, estuaries, and vineyards.

14 Provincetown. Fun-loving town at the Cape's tip.

15 Martha's Vineyard. 7 miles off the Cape's south-west tip.

16 Nantucket. 30 miles south of Hyannis.

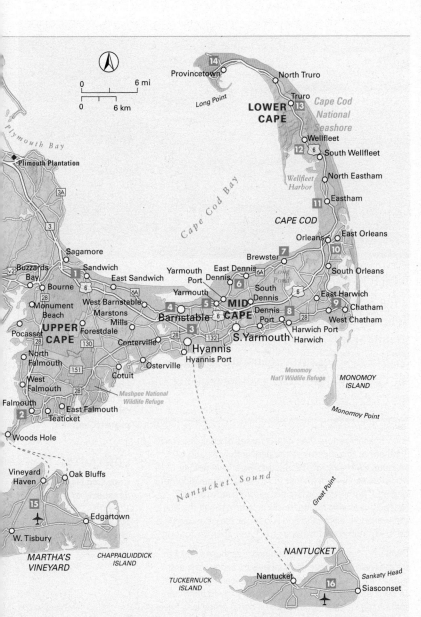

CAPE COD NATIONAL SEASHORE

John F. Kennedy certainly knew a good thing when he saw it. During his presidency, Kennedy marked off a magnificent 40-mile swath of the Massachusetts coast, protecting it for future generations. Today the Cape Cod National Seashore remains the Cape's signature site.

Encompassing more than 44,000 acres of coastline from Chatham to Provincetown, the park is truly a national treasure. Without protection, such expansive beauty would surely have been lost to rampant overdevelopment long ago. Within its borders are extraordinary ocean beaches, dramatic dunes, ancient swamps, salt marshes, and wetlands; pitch-pine and scrub-oak forest; much wildlife; and a number of historic structures open for touring.

There's no question that the National Seashore's beaches are the main attractions for sunbathers, swimmers, and surfers. It's not at all uncommon for the parking lots to fill up by 11 am on hot, sunny days. Arrive early to find your spot on the sand, or venture out on some of the less-traveled trails to find solitude in high season.

BEST TIME

Swimming is best in summer; the park becomes sublime in the fall, with golden salt-marsh grasses and ruby-red cranberry bogs. Winter and early spring nearly guarantee you'll have the place to yourself.

CONTACTS

Cape Cod National Seashore. ⊠ *Doane Rd., off U.S. 6* ☎ *508/255–3421* ⊕ *www.nps.gov/coco*

BEST WAYS TO EXPLORE

TAKE A WALK
Walking the marked trails, beaches, and wooded fire roads is an excellent way to truly experience the diverse natural splendor within the park. There are 11 self-guided trails that begin at various points, leading through shaded swamps, alongside marshes, and through meadows, forest, and dunes. Most of the terrain is flat and sometimes sandy.

RIDE A BIKE
Three well-maintained bicycle trails run through parts of the park. In Eastham, the short Nauset Trail heads from the Salt Pond Visitor Center through the woods and out to Coast Guard Beach. Truro's Head, off the Meadow Trail, edges a large salt meadow that's an ideal place for birding. The most physically demanding—and most dramatic—of the park's bike trails is the Province Lands Trail, more than 7 miles of steep hills and hairpin curves through forest and sand dunes. Mountain bikers can make their own trails on the miles of fire roads.

SEE THE SIGHTS
Several historic homes and sites are open for touring, and there are also a few notable overlooks easily accessible by car. Climb the steep steps of lighthouses in Eastham and Truro or see rescue reenactments at the Old Harbor Life-Saving Station in Provincetown. Scenic overlooks include Eastham's exquisite Ft. Hill area; Wellfleet's Marconi Station Site, where the first transatlantic wireless message was sent in 1903; Truro's Pilgrim Heights; and Provincetown's scenic 2-mile Race Point Road.

TOUR WITH A RANGER
There is a full schedule of mostly free ranger-guided activities mid-April–Thanksgiving. Combining history, folklore, science, and nature, rangers take visitors right to the source, whether for a full-moon hike in the dunes, a campfire on the beach, a paddling trip, or a photography workshop.

SHIFTING SANDS
Forged by massive moving glaciers more than 20,000 years ago, Cape Cod's landscape is still in perpetual motion, continually shaped by the powerful forces of sand, wind, and water. The Cape's land is slowly giving way to rising ocean levels and erosion, losing an average of nearly 4 feet of outer beach per year. Many a home or structure has succumbed to the unrelenting ocean over the years; some—like Truro's Highland Light and Eastham's Nauset Light—have been moved to safety. Eventually Cape Cod will likely be lost to the sea, but not for thousands of years.

You'll see many signs on beaches and trails asking walkers to keep off the dunes. Take heed, for much of the fragile landscape of the outer Cape is held together by its dune formations and the vegetation that grows within them.

Cape Cod, Martha's Vineyard, and Nantucket CAPE COD NATIONAL SEASHORE

THE CAPE'S BEST BEACHES

Blessed by a great variety of surrounding waters, Cape Cod, Martha's Vineyard, and Nantucket boast some of the world's best beaches. They face the wild, bracing surf of the Atlantic Ocean on one side, while the warmer and gentler waters of Cape Cod Bay or the Nantucket Sound sweep the opposite shores.

Cape Cod alone has more than 150 beaches—enough to keep the most inveterate beachcomber busy all year long. One can still capture that sense of adventure that enchanted Thoreau so long ago while walking the isolated stretches of towering dune-backed beaches from Eastham to Provincetown. Families love the easy access and more placid beaches of the bay and sound, which in turn tend to be more crowded. If saltwater isn't your thing, the Cape has dozens of freshwater kettle holes inland that were carved in the far-distant past by receding glaciers. Aside from warm, salt-free water, some—like Scargo Lake in Dennis—are also blessed with sandy beaches.

HISTORY LESSON

In this centuries-old area even a fun-in-the-sun day can double as a history lesson. In the Lower Cape, Eastham's popular **First Encounter Beach** has a bronze plaque that marks the spot where Myles Standish and his *Mayflower* buddies first encountered Native Americans in 1620.

UPPER CAPE

For Families: Parents love North Falmouth's **Old Silver**—a long crescent of soft white sand—for its relatively calm, warm water, and kids enjoy poking around the shallow tidal pools full of sea life.

MID CAPE

For Wanderers: Stretching 6 miles across a peninsula that ends at Sandy Neck Light, **Sandy Neck Beach** in West Barnstable offers a spectacular combination of sand, sea, and dunes perfect for strolling and bird-watching.

For Active Types: Encompassing 1½ miles of soft, white sand on Nantucket Sound, busy West Dennis Beach has plenty of space to try windsurfing, play a game of beach volleyball, or just sit back and enjoy the people-watching.

LOWER CAPE

For Traditionalists: Locals contend that Eastham's **Nauset Light Beach** and **Coast Guard Beach,** both set within the Cape Cod National Seashore, are the quintessential beaches. Combining serious surf, sweeping expanses of sand, magnificent dunes, and mesmerizing views, these spots deliver on the wow factor.

For Bird-Watchers: On the barrier beaches of the **Monomoy National Wildlife Refuge,** accessible by boat tours from

Chatham, you're bound to see more sandpipers and plovers than people. Summer through early fall, shorebirds and waterfowl flock here to nest, rest, and feast in tidal flats.

OUTER CAPE

For Views: After the winding drive amid the dunes and scrub in the National Seashore, **Race Point Beach** in Provincetown literally is the end of the road. Cape Cod Bay and the Atlantic meet here in a powerful tumbling of waves; views are vast and include extraordinary sunsets as well whale sightings.

For Night Owls: After-hours, it's tough to beat **Cahoon Hollow Beach** in Wellfleet. The water here is chilly but the music at the Beachcomber bar and restaurant is hot.

MARTHA'S VINEYARD

For Photographers: Perhaps no beach in this region is more photogenic than that below the **Aquinnah Cliffs.** The colorful clay cliffs face west, primed for gorgeous sunset photos.

NANTUCKET

For Sand Castle Connoisseurs: Jetties Beach has the finest sand castle–building material: hordes gather to prove it during Sandcastle & Sculpture Day, held annually in mid-August.

Even if you haven't visited Cape Cod and islands, you can likely—and accurately—imagine "sand dunes and salty air, quaint little villages here and there." As that 1950s Patti Page song promises, "you're sure to fall in love with old Cape Cod."

Cape Codders are fiercely protective of the environment. Despite some occasionally rampant development, planners have been careful to preserve nature and encourage responsible, eco-conscious building. Nearly 30% of the Cape's 412 square miles is protected from development, and another 35% has not yet been developed (on Nantucket and Martha's Vineyard, percentages of protected land are far higher). Opportunities for sports and recreation abound, as the region is rife with biking and hiking trails, serene beaches, and waterways for boating and fishing. One somewhat controversial potential development has been a large-scale "wind farm" in Nantucket Sound, comprising some 130 turbines, each about 260 feet tall and several miles offshore.

The area is also rich in history. Many don't realize that the Pilgrims landed here first: in November 1620, the lost and travel-weary sailors dropped anchor in what is now Provincetown Harbor and spent five weeks here, scouring the area for food and possible settlement. Were it not for the aid of the resident Native Americans, the strangers would barely have survived. Even so, they set sail again for fairer lands, ending up across Cape Cod Bay in Plymouth.

Virtually every period style of residential American architecture is well represented on Cape Cod, including—of course—that seminal form named for the region, the Cape Cod–style house. These low, 1½-story domiciles with clapboard or shingle siding—more traditionally the latter in these parts—and gable roofs have been a fixture throughout Cape Cod since the late 17th century. You'll also find grand Georgian and Federal mansions from the Colonial era, as well as handsome Greek Revival, Italianate, and Second Empire houses that date to Victorian times. Many of the most prominent residences were built for ship captains and sea merchants. In recent decades, the region has seen an influx of angular, glassy, contemporary homes, many with soaring windows and skylights, and massive wraparound porches that take advantage of their enviable sea views.

MAJOR REGIONS

The Cape is divided into four major areas and is shaped roughly like an arm bent at the elbow: the **Upper Cape** (the shoulder); the **Mid Cape** (the upper arm); the **Lower Cape** (the bicep and forearm); and the **Outer Cape** (the wrist and hand). Each of the Cape's 15 towns are further broken up into smaller villages.

The Upper Cape (closest to the bridges) has the oldest towns like **Sandwich** and **Falmouth,** plus fine beaches and fascinating little museums. The Mid Cape has sophisticated Colonial-era hamlets but also motels and miniature golf courses. There's **Barnstable, Dennis,** and **Yarmouth,** as well as **Hyannis,** the Cape's unofficial capital. The Lower Cape consists of **Brewster, Chatham, Harwich,** and **Orleans.** Here you'll find casual clam shacks, lovely lighthouses, funky art galleries, and stellar natural attractions. **Eastham, Wellfleet, Truro,** and **Provincetown** populate the narrow forearm of the Outer Cape, which is famous for sand dunes, crashing surf, and scrubby pines.

The islands, **Martha's Vineyard** and **Nantucket,** lie to the south. Martha's Vineyard is about 7 miles off the Cape's southwest tip, while Nantucket is some 30 miles south of Hyannis. Both are connected to the Cape by ferries, and both also have air service.

Planning

The region can be enjoyed for a few days or a few weeks, depending on the nature of your trip. As the towns are all quite distinct on Cape Cod, it's best to organize your trip based on your interests: an outdoors enthusiast would want to head to the National Seashore region, for example; those who prefer shopping and amusements would do better in the Mid Cape area. As one Fodors.com forum member noted, the Cape is generally "not something to see … instead, people go to spend a few days or weeks, relax, go to the beach … that sort of thing." A day trip to Nantucket to wander the historic downtown is manageable; several days is best to appreciate Martha's Vineyard's diversity.

Getting Here and Around

AIR
The major air gateways are Boston's Logan International Airport and Providence's T. F. Green International Airport. Most major airlines fly to Boston; several fly to Providence; even fewer fly directly to the Cape and islands, and many of those flights are seasonal. Smaller municipal airports are in Barnstable, Martha's Vineyard, Nantucket, and Provincetown.

CAR
Cape Cod is easily reached from Boston via Route 3 and from Providence via Interstate 195. Once you cross Cape Cod Canal, you can follow U.S. 6. Without any traffic, it takes about an hour to 90 minutes to reach the canal from either Boston or Providence. Allow an extra 30–60 minutes' travel time in peak periods.

Parking, in general, can be a challenge in summer, especially in congested downtowns and at popular beaches. If you can walk, bike, carpool, or cab it somewhere, do so. But unless you are planning to focus your attention on a single community, you'll probably need a car on the Cape. Authorities on both Nantucket and Martha's Vineyard strongly encourage visitors to leave their cars on the mainland: taking a vehicle onto the island ferries is expensive and requires reservations (another option is renting upon arrival), and there is ample and efficient transportation once you arrive.

FERRY
Martha's Vineyard and Nantucket are easily reached by passenger ferries (traditional and high-speed boats) from several Cape towns; farther afield you can get a seasonal ferry from Plymouth, MA; New Bedford, CT; Highlands, NJ; and Manhattan. Ferries to Provincetown embark from Boston and Plymouth. Some services run year-round, while others are seasonal. Even parking for the ferries must be reserved during the busy season, but passenger reservations are rarely necessary. Trip times vary from as little as 45 minutes to about two hours and run $8.50–$39 one-way; bicycles can be taken aboard many ferries for $4, while cars cost $43.50–$68 one-way (reservations required and very limited).

TRAIN

The seasonal *Cape Flyer* passenger train only runs on weekends (Friday–Sunday) from Boston's South Station, Memorial Day–Labor Day. The 2½-hour trip makes stops in Braintree, Brockton, Middleborough, Wareham Village, Buzzards Bay, Bourne, and Hyannis. Round-trip fare from Boston is $40; bring your bike for no extra fee. Kids 11 and under ride free with adult.

CONTACT Cape Flyer. ⊠ *Hyannis Transportation Center, 215 Iyannough Rd., Barnstable* ☎ *508/775–8504* ⊕ *www. capeflyer.com.*

Restaurants

Cape Cod kitchens have long been closely associated with seafood: the waters off the Cape and islands yield a bounty of lobsters, clams, oysters, scallops, and myriad fish that make their way onto local menus. In addition to the region's strong Portuguese influence, globally inspired and contemporary fare commonly turn up among restaurant offerings. Also gaining in popularity is the use of locally, and often organically, raised produce, meat, and dairy.

Note that ordering an expensive lobster dinner may push your meal into a higher price category than this guide's price range shows for the restaurant. You can indulge in fresh local seafood and clambakes at seat-yourself shanties for a lower price than at their fine-dining counterparts. *Restaurant reviews have been shortened. For full information, visit Fodors.com.*

Hotels

B&Bs are king in the Cape, so you can bed down in a former sea captain's home or even a converted church. However, there are also a few larger resorts and even a handful of chain hotels. You'll want to make reservations for inns well in advance during peak summer periods. Smoking is prohibited in all Massachusetts hotels. *Hotel reviews have been shortened. For full information, visit Fodors.com.*

CONDO AND HOUSE RENTALS

Many travelers to the Cape and the islands rent a house if they're going to stay for a week or longer. Many local real-estate agencies deal with rentals. Be sure to book a property well in advance of your trip: prime properties are often rented out to the same people year after year. Expect rentals on both Martha's Vineyard and Nantucket to be significantly higher than those on the Cape, simply because there are fewer options.

WHAT IT COSTS in U.S. Dollars			
$	$$	$$$	$$$$
RESTAURANTS			
under $18	$18–$24	$25–$35	over $35
HOTELS			
under $200	$200–$299	$300–$399	over $399

When to Go

The Cape and islands teem with activity during high season: roughly late June to Labor Day. If you're dreaming of a classic shore vacation, this is prime time. However, along with the dream come daunting crowds and high costs. Fall has begun to rival summer in popularity, at least on weekends through late October, when the weather is temperate and the scenery remarkable. Many restaurants, shops, and hotels remain open in winter, too, making the area desirable even during the coldest months. The region enjoys fairly moderate weather most of the year, with highs typically in the upper 70s and 80s in summer, and in the upper 30s and lower 40s in winter. Snow and rain are not uncommon during the cooler months, and it can be windy any time.

Visitor Information

Numerous towns on the Cape have weekly beach and lawn concerts, pancake breakfasts, art shows, and more. The Cape Week Section of the *Cape Cod Times* (⊕ *www. capecodonline.com*) is a great source for information to help plan your days, as is the Cape Cod Chamber of Commerce (⊕ *www.capecodchamber.org*).

Sandwich

3 miles east of Sagamore Bridge, 11 miles west of Barnstable.

The oldest town on Cape Cod, Sandwich was established in 1637 by some of the Plymouth Pilgrims and incorporated on March 6, 1638. Today, it is a well-preserved, quintessential New England village with a white-columned town hall and streets lined with 18th- and 19th-century houses.

VISITOR INFORMATION

CONTACTS Sandwich Chamber of Commerce. ⊠ *520 Rte. 130, Sandwich Center* ☎ *508/681–0918* ⊕ *www.sandwichchamber.com.*

◉ Sights

★ Heritage Museums and Gardens
MUSEUM | FAMILY | These 100 beautifully landscaped acres overlooking the upper end of Shawme Pond are one of the region's top draws. Paths crisscross the grounds, which include gardens planted with hostas, heather, herbs, and fruit trees. Rhododendrons are in full glory mid-May–mid-June, and daylilies reach their peak mid-July–early August. In 1967, pharmaceuticals magnate Josiah K. Lilly III purchased the estate and turned it into a nonprofit museum. One highlight is the reproduction Shaker Round Barn, which showcases classic and historic cars—including a 1919 Pierce-Arrow, a 1915 Milburn Light Electric, a 1911 Stanley Steamer, and a 1930

yellow-and-green Duesenberg built for movie star Gary Cooper. The art museum has an extraordinary collection of New England folk art, including paintings, weather vanes, Nantucket baskets, and scrimshaw. Both adults and children can enjoy riding on a Coney Island–style carousel dating to the early 20th century. Other features include Hidden Hollow, an outdoor activity center for families with children.

A shuttle bus, equipped with a wheelchair lift and space to stow baby strollers, transports visitors on certain days. In summer, concerts are held in the gardens, often on Wednesday or Saturday evening or on Sunday afternoon. The center of the complex is about ¾ mile on foot from the in-town end of Shawme Pond. ⊠ *67 Grove St., Sandwich Center* ☎ *508/888–3300* ⊕ *www.heritagemuseumsandgardens.org* ⊠ *$20.*

Sandwich Boardwalk
PROMENADE | FAMILY | The long sweep of Cape Cod Bay stretches out around the beach at the end of the Sandwich Boardwalk, where a platform provides fine views, especially at sunset. You can look out toward Sandy Neck, Wellfleet, and Provincetown or toward the white cliffs beyond Sagamore. Near this mostly rocky beach are dunes covered with rugosa roses, which have a delicious fragrance; this is a good place for birding. The creeks running through the salt marsh make for great canoeing. From the town center it's about a mile to the boardwalk; cross Route 6A on Jarves Street, and at its end turn left, then right, and continue to the boardwalk parking lot. ⊠ *Jarves St., Sandwich Center.*

Sandwich Glass Museum
MUSEUM | Shimmering glass was manufactured here nearly two centuries ago, and the Sandwich Glass Museum shows you what the factory looked like in its heyday. There's an "ingredient room" showcasing a wide spectrum of glass colors, along with the minerals added to the sand to obtain them,

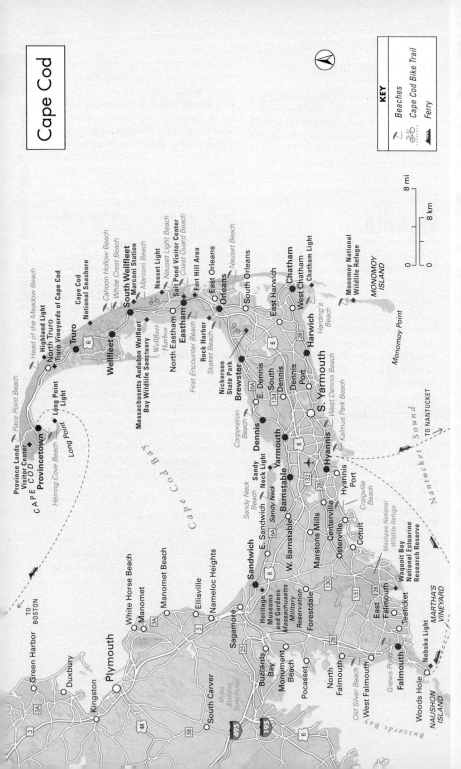

Cape Cod

KEY

- Beaches
- Cape Cod Bike Trail
- Ferry

8 mi

8 km

TO BOSTON

Green Harbor

Duxbury

Kingston

Plymouth

South Carver

Myles Standish State Forest

White Horse Beach

Manomet

Manomet Beach

Ellisville

Namelo Heights

Buzzards Bay

Monument Beach

Pocasset

North Falmouth

West Falmouth

Woods Hole

NAUSHON ISLAND

Falmouth

Teaticket

East Falmouth

Nobska Light

Grevs Pond

Old Silver Beach

MARTHA'S VINEYARD

Buzzards Bay

Sagamore

Heritage Museums and Gardens

Massachusetts Military Reservation

Forestdale

Sandwich

E. Sandwich

W. Barnstable

Marstons Mills

Centerville

Osterville

Cotuit

Mashpee National Wildlife Refuge

Waquoit Bay National Estuarine Research Reserve

Sandy Neck Beach

Sandy Neck

Sandy Neck Light

Barnstable

Hyannis Port

Hyannis

Craigville Beach

Kalmus Park Beach

S. Yarmouth

West Dennis Beach

Yarmouth

Yarmouth Port

Dennis

Dennis Port

S. Dennis

E. Dennis

Corporation Beach

Brewster

Nickerson State Park

Skaket Beach

Rock Harbor Beach

First Encounter Beach

Wellfleet Harbor

Massachusetts Audubon Wellfleet Bay Wildlife Sanctuary

Wellfleet

Truro

North Truro

Highland Light

Head of the Meadow Beach

Cahoon Hollow Beach

White Crest Beach

Marconi Beach

Marconi Station

South Wellfleet

Cape Cod National Seashore

Nauset Light

Nauset Light Beach

Salt Pond Visitor Center

Coast Guard Beach

Fort Hill Area

Eastham

North Eastham

Orleans

East Orleans

South Orleans

Nauset Beach

East Harwich

West Chatham

Chatham

Chatham Light

Harding's Beach

Harwich

Monomoy National Wildlife Refuge

MONOMOY ISLAND

Monomoy Point

Nantucket Sound

TO NANTUCKET

Cape Cod Bay

Herring Cove Beach

Long Point

Long Point Light

Province Lands Visitor Center

Provincetown

CAPE COD

Race Point Beach

Truro Vineyards of Cape Cod

and an outstanding collection of blown and pressed glass in many shapes and hues. Large lamps, vases, and pitchers are impressive, as are the hundreds of candlesticks on display. There are glass-blowing demonstrations daily on the hour from 10 to 3. The extensive gift shop sells some handsome reproductions, including many made by local and national artisans. Also home to the Sandwich Historical Society, the museum hosts historic walking tours on certain days June–October. ✉ 129 Main St., Sandwich Center ☎ 508/888–0251 ⊕ www.sand-wichglassmuseum.org 🎟 $12 ⏱ Closed Jan.; Mon. and Tues. Feb. and Mar.

🍴 Restaurants

British Beer Company
$ | BRITISH | FAMILY | This traditional British "public house" has an expansive menu that includes typical pub fare, such as fish-and-chips and burgers, as well as ribs, steak tips, and pizza. Entertainment options throughout the week include karaoke, trivia night, and a variety of bands that usually perform Thursday–Saturday. **Known for:** reasonable prices; fun vibe; great kids' menu. 💲 Average main: ✉ 46 Rte. 6A ☎ 508/833–9590 ⊕ www.britishbeer.com.

Pilot House
$$$ | SEAFOOD | Views of the bustling Cape Cod Canal abound from this casual spot's enviable waterside perch. Seafood is the main catch here, particularly pleasing eaten alfresco under an umbrella or by the fire pit. **Known for:** great views of the canal; daily live music; local seafood. 💲 Average main: $27 ✉ 14 Gallo Rd., Sandwich Center ☎ 508/888–8889 ⊕ www.pilothousecapecod.com ⏱ Closed Mon. and Tues. Nov.–Apr.

☕ Coffee and Quick Bites

Café Chew
$ | AMERICAN | Offering breakfast and lunch, Café Chew serves everything from espressos to-go to breakfast favorites like pancakes and omelets. At lunch, a variety of soups, salads, and sandwiches should please every palate. **Known for:** baked goods; fair trade coffee; reasonable lunch specials. 💲 Average main: $10 ✉ 4 Merchants Rd. ☎ 508/888–7717 ⊕ www.cafechew.com ⏱ No dinner.

Twin Acres Ice Cream Shoppe
$ | AMERICAN | FAMILY | Pop into this popular spot for an ice-cream cone, lobster roll, or a milk shake and enjoy it on the 2 acres of landscaped grounds dotted with gardens. **Known for:** 70-plus ice-cream flavors; hot dogs; vegan, dairy-free, and sugar-free options. 💲 Average main: $6 ✉ 21 Rte. 6A ☎ 508/888–0566 ⊕ www.twinacresicecreamshoppe.com.

🛏 Hotels

★ Belfry Inn & Bistro
$$ | B&B/INN | This sophisticated complex comprises a 1901 former church (the Abbey), an ornate wood-frame 1882 Victorian (the Painted Lady), and an 1827 Federal-style house (the Village House), and the theme in each is a nod to the buildings' respective histories—the Painted Lady's charmingly appointed guest rooms, for example, are named after former inhabitants. **Pros:** great in-town location; bright, beautiful, and spacious rooms; dramatic architecture. **Cons:** some steep stairs; not suited for families; some rooms can be on the smaller side. 💲 Rooms from: $214 ✉ 6 Jarves St., Sandwich Center ☎ 508/888–8550, 800/844–4542 ⊕ www.belfryinn.com ⤶ 22 rooms ◉ Free breakfast.

Isaiah Jones Homestead Bed & Breakfast

$$ | B&B/INN | Expect extraordinary service in an equally stellar setting—graceful lines and high ceilings, authentic period antiques and moody stained glass—at this venerable Victorian. **Pros:** easy walk to town center; beautiful grounds; elegant surroundings. **Cons:** some steep stairs; some bathrooms are small; close quarters might not be for everyone. $ *Rooms from: $229* ⊠ *165 Main St., Sandwich Center* ☎ *508/888–9115, 800/526–1625* ⊕ *www.isaiahjones.com* ⊐ *7 rooms* ◎ *Free breakfast.*

🛍 Shopping

Downtown Sandwich has quite a few specialty shops, as well as several good antiques co-ops, boutiques, and galleries. Along Route 6A, you'll find more of the same, just spread out along the miles.

★ **Titcomb's Bookshop**

BOOKS/STATIONERY | You'll find used, rare, and new books here, including a large collection of Americana. There's also an extensive selection of children's books. Look for frequent author events and book signings. ⊠ *432 Rte. 6A, East Sandwich* ☎ *508/888–2331* ⊕ *www.titcombsbook-shop.com.*

Falmouth

15 miles south of Bourne Bridge, 20 miles south of Sandwich.

Falmouth, the Cape's second-largest town, was settled in 1660. Today it is largely suburban, with a mix of old and new developments and a sizable year-round population. Many residents commute to other towns on the Cape, to southeastern Massachusetts, and even to Boston. The town has a quaint downtown area, with a typically old New England village green and a shop-lined Main Street. South of town center, Falmouth faces Nantucket Sound and has several often-crowded beaches popular with families. To the east, the Falmouth Heights neighborhood mixes inns, B&Bs, and private homes, nestled close together on residential streets leading to the sea. Bustling Grand Avenue, the main drag in Falmouth Heights, hugs the shore and the beach.

The village of Woods Hole, part of Falmouth, is home to several major scientific institutions—the National Marine Fisheries Service, the Marine Biological Laboratory (MBL), the Woods Hole Oceanographic Institution, and the U.S. Geological Survey's Branch of Marine Geology—and is a departure point for ferries to Martha's Vineyard.

GETTING HERE AND AROUND

Heading from the Bourne Bridge toward Falmouth, County Road and Route 28A are prettier alternatives to Route 28, and Sippewisset Road meanders near Buzzards Bay between West Falmouth and Woods Hole. If you're coming from Falmouth to Woods Hole, either ride your bicycle down the straight and flat Shining Sea Trail or take the Cape Cod Regional Transit Authority's WHOOSH trolley. In summer, the basically one-street village overflows with thousands of visiting scientists, students, and tourists heading to the islands. Parking, limited to a relatively small number of metered spots on the street, can be nearly impossible.

CONTACTS Cape Cod Regional Transit Authority. ☎ *800/352–7155* ⊕ *www.cape-codtransit.org.*

VISITOR INFORMATION

CONTACTS Falmouth Chamber of Commerce and Visitor Center. ⊠ *20 Academy La.* ☎ *508/548–8500, 800/526–8532* ⊕ *www. falmouthchamber.com.*

Sights

Nobska Light

LIGHTHOUSE | This imposing lighthouse has spectacular views from its base of the nearby Elizabeth Islands and of Martha's Vineyard, across Vineyard Sound. The 42-foot cast-iron tower, lined with brick, was built in 1876 with a stationary light. It shines red to indicate dangerous waters or white for safe passage. Friends of Nobska Light, a nonprofit group, has been carefully restoring the structure (the lighthouse keeper's house was turned into a museum in 2020). The grounds are open daily from dawn to dusk for sightseeing, though parking is very limited. Best to arrive by bike along the scenic bike path. ■ **TIP➜ Tours depend on both weather and volunteer availability. Call ahead to inquire.** ✉ 233 Nobska Rd., Woods Hole ⊕ www.friendsofnobska.org ⛱ Free.

Ocean Science Exhibit Center

LOCAL INTEREST | **FAMILY** | Here visitors can get a glimpse of the extraordinary scientific marine research that goes on within the Woods Hole Oceanographic Institute. Climb inside a replica of Alvin, the submersible that dove thousands of feet deep to explore the wreck of the Titanic. Other exhibits show footage of the rich life at vast depths of the ocean. Scientists give informative lectures on a regular basis in July and August. ✉ 15 School St., Woods Hole ☎ 508/289–2252 ⊕ www.whoi.edu/main/ocean-science-exhibit-center ⛱ $3 suggested donation ♥ Closed Jan.–mid-Apr.

Waquoit Bay National Estuarine Research Reserve

NATURE PRESERVE | **FAMILY** | Encompassing 3,000 acres of estuaries, woodlands, salt marshes, and barrier beaches, this research reserve is a good place for walking, kayaking, fishing, and birding. In July and August, there are nature programs for families, including an outdoor lecture series on Tuesday evening. **South Cape Beach** is part of the reserve; you can lie out on the sand or join one of the interpretive walks. **Flat Pond Trail** runs through several different habitats, including fresh- and saltwater marshes. You can reach **Washburn Island** on your own by boat, or by joining a Saturday-morning tour; it offers 330 acres of pine barrens and trails, swimming, and 10 wilderness campsites (you need your own boat to access the campsite, plus an advance reservation and permit are required). ✉ 149 Rte. 28, Waquoit Village ✛ 3 miles west of Mashpee rotary ☎ 508/457–0495 ⊕ www.waquoitbayreserve.org ⛱ Free; daily parking fee for beach and a fee to camp.

★ Woods Hole Science Aquarium

ZOO | **FAMILY** | This impressive facility displays numerous large tanks and many more smaller ones filled with regional fish and shellfish. Rooms are small, but they are crammed with stuff to see. Magnifying glasses and a dissecting scope help you examine marine life. Several hands-on pools hold banded lobsters, crabs, snails, starfish, and other creatures. The stars of the show are two harbor seals, on view in the outdoor pool near the entrance; watch their feedings, most days, at 11 and 4. ✉ 166 Water St., Woods Hole ☎ 508/495–2001 ⊕ www.fisheries.noaa.gov/new-england-mid-atlantic/outreach-and-education/woods-hole-science-aquarium ⛱ Free ♥ Closed weekends.

🏖 Beaches

Old Silver Beach

BEACH—SIGHT | **FAMILY** | This long, beautiful crescent of soft white sand is anchored by the Sea Crest Beach Resort at one end. It's especially good for small children because a sandbar keeps it shallow at the southern end and creates tidal pools full of crabs and minnows. Very popular, this beach has its share of crowds on nice, sunny days. **Amenities:** food and drink; lifeguards; parking (fee); showers; toilets. **Best for:** swimming; walking. ✉ 296 Quaker Rd., North Falmouth ⊕ www.falmouthmass.us ⛱ $20 daily parking.

🍴 Restaurants

★ C Salt Wine Bar & Grille

$$$ | **AMERICAN** | With an open kitchen that turns out some excellent and artful dishes, especially seafood, this tiny place keeps its tables full and its guests happy (reservations strongly recommended). Fine service by a friendly and knowledgeable staff adds greatly to the overall atmosphere. **Known for:** raw oyster selection; notable wine list; excellent service. [$] *Average main: $32* ✉ *75 Davis Straits (Rte. 28)* ☎ *774/763–2954* 🌐 *www.csaltfalmouth.com.*

Jim's Clam Shack

$ | **SEAFOOD** | Fried clams are crisp and fresh at this basic seafood joint right on Falmouth Harbor; the meaty lobster roll and the fish-and-chips platter are good choices, too. Place your order at the counter, and then take your tray to the picnic tables on the roof deck for the best views. **Known for:** clam strips; crowds; waterfront perch. [$] *Average main: $16* ✉ *227 Clinton Ave., Falmouth Harbor* ☎ *508/540–7758* 🕒 *Closed early Sept.–mid-May.*

★ La Cucina Sul Mare

$$$ | **ITALIAN** | Northern Italian and Mediterranean cooking distinguish this classy, popular place. Make sure to come hungry—portions of classic favorites here are huge—and expect a long wait during prime hours in season. **Known for:** zuppa de pesce; boisterous atmosphere; attentive service. [$] *Average main: $28* ✉ *237 Main St., Falmouth Center* ☎ *508/548–5600* 🌐 *www.lacucinasulmare.com* 🕒 *Closed Mon.*

☕ Coffee and Quick Bites

Pie in the Sky Bakery & Cafe

$ | **BAKERY** | Crowds line up for tasty treats at this beloved bakery, in business since 1982, which serves up a lot more than pie, though that is not to be missed. Sticky buns and scones fly out of the kitchen at breakfast, while daily soup specials, wraps, and salads are popular at lunch. **Known for:** made-from-scratch baked goods; delicious quiches; popovers. [$] *Average main: $8* ✉ *10 Water St., Woods Hole* ☎ *508/540–5475* 🌐 *www.piecoffee.com.*

🛏 Hotels

The Captain's Manor Inn

$$ | **B&B/INN** | With its expansive landscaped grounds ringed by a wrought-iron fence, this elegant 1849 Italianate inn with a wraparound porch and grand foyer resembles a private estate. **Pros:** easy walk to town center; elegant setting; ample grounds make you feel worlds away from the hustle and bustle. **Cons:** not for those with small children; long stairway to second-floor rooms; not for those traveling on a budget. [$] *Rooms from: $299* ✉ *27 W. Main St., Falmouth Center* ☎ *508/388–7336* 🌐 *www.captainsmanorinn.com* 🔑 *7 rooms* 🍴 *Free breakfast.*

Coonamessett Inn

$$$ | **B&B/INN** | At this delightful inn, a Lark Hotel property, five buildings of one- and two-bedroom suites ring a landscaped lawn that leads to a scenic wooded pond. **Pros:** lush grounds; high marks for restaurant's food; large rooms. **Cons:** constant weddings; some complain the continental breakfast is too small; no room service. [$] *Rooms from: $339* ✉ *311 Gifford St., at Jones Rd.* ☎ *508/548–2300* 🌐 *www.thecoonamessett.com* 🔑 *29 rooms* 🍴 *Free Breakfast.*

★ Inn on the Sound

$$ | **B&B/INN** | At this understated and serene but stylish inn, perched on a bluff overlooking Vineyard Sound, common areas include an art-laden living room with a boulder fireplace and water views, oversize windows, and modern white couches; a bistrolike breakfast room; and a porch with more stunning water views. **Pros:** grand water views; elegant

setting; easy walk to beach. **Cons:** not an in-town location; not for those with small children; no pets. $ *Rooms from: $299* ✉ *313 Grand Ave., Falmouth Heights* ☎ *508/457-9666* ⊕ *www.innonthesound. com* ➪ *12 rooms* ❏❘ *Free breakfast.*

Woods Hole Passage
$$ | **B&B/INN** | **FAMILY** | A century-old carriage house and barn have been converted into a romantic showcase with more than 2 acres that include beautiful gardens; when you want to explore outside the grounds, hop on the town trolley, which runs right by the inn. **Pros:** family-friendly; easy walk to beach; extremely helpful innkeepers; Martha's Vineyard ferry is five minutes away. **Cons:** not an in-town location; some steep stairs; two-night minimum stay on weekends year-round. $ *Rooms from: $239* ✉ *186 Woods Hole Rd., Woods Hole* ☎ *508/548-9575* ⊕ *www.woodsholepassage.com* ➪ *5 rooms* ❏❘ *Free breakfast.*

⚆ Activities

BASEBALL

The Cape Cod Baseball League, begun in 1885, is an invitational league of college players that counts Carlton Fisk, Ron Darling, Mo Vaughn, Nomar Garciaparra, and the late Thurman Munson as alumni. Considered the country's best summer league, it's scouted by every major-league team. The 10 teams of the Cape Cod Baseball League play a 44-game season mid-June–mid-August; games held at all 10 fields are free.

Falmouth Commodores
BASEBALL/SOFTBALL | **FAMILY** | The Falmouth Commodores of the collegiate Cape Cod Baseball League play their home games at Guv Fuller Field, mid-June–mid-August. Players and coaches lead youth baseball clinics in June and July. ✉ *790 Main St., Falmouth Center* ⊕ *www.falmouthcommodores.com* ✉ *Free.*

BIKING
★ **Shining Sea Bikeway**
BICYCLING | The wonderful Shining Sea Bikeway is almost 11 miles of paved bike path through four of Falmouth's villages, running from Woods Hole to North Falmouth. It follows the shore of Buzzards Bay, providing water views, and dips into oak and pine woods; a detour onto Church Street takes you to Nobska Light. A brochure is available at the trailheads. If you're taking your bike to Martha's Vineyard, park in one of Falmouth's Steamship Authority lots and ride to the ferry. Free shuttles from Falmouth to the Woods Hole ferry dock have bike carriers. There's also a parking area near Depot Avenue, on County Road at the other end. ✉ *Falmouth.*

FISHING
Eastman's Sport & Tackle
FISHING | Freshwater ponds are good for perch, pickerel, trout, and more; get the required license (along with rental gear) at Eastman's Sport & Tackle. It's a good resource if you are looking for local guides. ◼**TIP→ Anglers over the age of 16 will also need a saltwater fishing license.** ✉ *783 Main St., Falmouth Center* ☎ *508/548-6900* ⊕ *www.eastmanssporttackle.com.*

👜 Shopping

Falmouth Village has an easily walkable and attractive Main Street, lined with specialty shops—you won't find major chain stores here—and an assortment of good restaurants. The pretty Marine Park is home to many events, including an impressive Thursday afternoon Farmers' Market held mid-May–mid-October, noon to 6.

Bean & Cod
FOOD/CANDY | This specialty food shop sells cheeses, breads, great sandwiches, including lobster rolls, and picnic fixings, along with coffees and teas. They also pack and ship gift baskets. ✉ *145 Main St., Falmouth Center* ☎ *508/548-8840.*

Hyannis

23 miles east of the Bourne Bridge, 21 miles northeast of Falmouth.

Perhaps best known for its association with the Kennedy clan, the Hyannis area was also a vacation site for President Ulysses S. Grant in 1874 and later for President Grover Cleveland. A bustling year-round hub of activity, Hyannis has the Cape's largest concentration of businesses, shops, malls, hotels and motels, restaurants, and entertainment venues.

GETTING HERE AND AROUND

There's plenty of public parking around town, on both sides of Main Street as well as in several public parking lots. The island ferry companies have designated parking lots ($15–$20 daily fee in summer season) with free shuttles to the docks. Hyannis is the Cape's transit hub and is served by a number of bus routes.

CONTACTS Hyannis Transportation Center. ⊠ *215 Iyanough Rd., Barnstable* ☎ *800/352–7155* ⊕ *www.capecodtransit. org.*

VISITOR INFORMATION

CONTACTS Hyannis Chamber of Commerce. ☎ *508/775–2201* ⊕ *www.hyannis.com.*

👁 Sights

Cape Cod Maritime Museum
MUSEUM | FAMILY | This waterfront museum stands as testament and tribute to the bustle of the harbor that it overlooks. Changing maritime art exhibits, classes on boatbuilding and other nautical arts, and an active boatbuilding shop all highlight the importance of the sea, in past and present alike. Take a harbor sail on the historic replica Crosby Catboat *Sarah* , and learn "dead reckoning"—real navigation without the aid of modern technology. ⊠ *135 South St., Hyannis Harbor* ☎ *508/775–1723* ⊕ *www. capecodmaritimemuseum.org* 🎫 *$10* 🕐 *Limited hrs Jan.–May.*

John F. Kennedy Hyannis Museum
MUSEUM | In Main Street's Old Town Hall, this museum explores JFK's Cape years (1934–63) through enlarged and annotated photographs culled from the archives of the JFK Library near Boston, as well as a seven-minute video narrated by Walter Cronkite. Changing exhibits focus on various members of the family at different stages of their life and career. Events include lectures, book signings, and speaking engagements by those with close connections to the family, both past and present. Expansion is underway to incorporate an auditorium, community room, and media center to further educational and community activities. ⊠ *397 Main St.* ☎ *508/790–3077* ⊕ *www. jfkhyannismuseum.org* 🎫 *$13* 🕐 *Closed Sun.–Wed. Dec.–mid-Apr.*

🏖 Beaches

Kalmus Park Beach
BEACH—SIGHT | FAMILY | This wide, sandy beach has an area set aside for windsurfers and a sheltered area that's good for kids. It's a great spot for watching boats go in and out of the harbor. **Amenities:** food and drink; lifeguards; parking (fee); showers; toilets. **Best for:** swimming; walking; windsurfing. ⊠ *End of Ocean St., Hyannis Harbor* ⊕ *www.townofbarnstable.us* 🎫 *Parking $20.*

🍴 Restaurants

⭐ **Brazilian Grill**
$$$ | BRAZILIAN | At this all-you-can-eat churrascaria, waiters continually circulate through the dining room offering more than a dozen grilled meats—beef, pork, chicken, sausage, and the beloved Brazilian chicken hearts on large, swordlike skewers. The massive buffet is laden with soups, salads, and side dishes, including plantains, rice, and beans (vegetarians could happily eat from the buffet). **Known for:** grilled meats, Brazilian style; loud and festive

atmosphere; homemade flan. $ *Average main: $35 ⊠ 680 Main St., West End ☎ 508/771–0109 ⊕ www.brazilian-grill-capecod.com.*

★ **Naked Oyster Bistro & Raw Bar**

$$$ | ECLECTIC | More than 1,000 oysters are eaten here on an average summer weekend, a good deal of them procured near daily from the restaurant's own oyster farm in nearby Barnstable. You'll always find close to two dozen raw and "dressed" oyster dishes; there's also a nice range of nonoyster entrées, salads, and appetizers. **Known for:** oyster stew; locally sourced ingredients; lively atmosphere. $ *Average main: $32 ⊠ 410 Main St. ☎ 508/778–6500 ⊕ www.nakedoyster.com ⊗ Closed Sun. mid-Oct.–mid-Apr.*

☕ Coffee and Quick Bites

Katie's Ice Cream

$ | AMERICAN | Making small batch ice cream and pastries in-house daily, Katie's has a huge following for its delicious flavors, like the popular Cape Cod Mud, a concoction of coffee ice cream, chocolate, house-made fudge, roasted almonds, and chopped chocolate sandwich cookies. Try to figure out the secret recipe of the Cape Cod Sand ice cream, a hit since 2002, when it was developed by Katie's younger brother Gene, but don't expect anyone to give it away. **Known for:** creative flavors, like lavender honeycomb and ginger lemon cookie; friendly staff; offers both soft serve and hard-packed ice cream. $ *Average main: $5 ⊠ 568 Main St. ☎ 508/771–6889 ⊕ katiesicecreamcapecod.com.*

🛏 Hotels

★ **Anchor-In**

$$$ | HOTEL | Most rooms at this small-scale motel on the north end of Hyannis Harbor have harbor views and small balconies overlooking the water, and its simple street-side appearance belies its spacious and immaculate accommodations, extensive grounds, and warm, B&B-style personal service from Lisa and Skip Simpson. **Pros:** easy walk to downtown; great harbor views; well-appointed rooms. **Cons:** no elevator—second-floor rooms accessed via stairs; not for the budget-minded; crowded area. $ *Rooms from: $329 ⊠ 1 South St., Hyannis Harbor ☎ 508/775–0357 ⊕ www.anchorin. com ⌿ 42 rooms |☉| Free breakfast.*

SeaCoast Inn

$ | HOTEL | While the rooms at this hotel are basic, it's conveniently located between downtown and the harbor—look for the abundantly blooming window boxes. **Pros:** rooms are big and very clean; reasonable rates; walk to beaches, downtown, and ferries. **Cons:** not a scenic location; no great views; midway between town and harbor. $ *Rooms from: $169 ⊠ 33 Ocean St., Downtown ☎ 508/775–3828 ⊕ www. seacoastcapecod.com ⊗ Closed Nov.–mid-Apr. ⌿ 26 rooms |☉| No meals.*

🎭 Performing Arts

Cape Cod Melody Tent

CONCERTS | FAMILY | In 1950, actress Gertrude Lawrence and her husband, producer-manager Richard Aldrich, opened the Cape Cod Melody Tent to showcase Broadway musicals and concerts. Today, it's the region's top venue for pop concerts and comedy shows. Performers who have played here in the round include the Indigo Girls, Lyle Lovett, Tony Bennett, Diana Krall, and Crosby, Stills & Nash. The Tent also holds a children's theater series in July and August, Wednesday at 11 am. ✉ *21 W. Main St., West End* ☎ *508/775–5630* ⊕ *www.melodytent.org.*

🏃 Activities

BASEBALL

Hyannis Harbor Hawks

BASEBALL/SOFTBALL | FAMILY | The Hyannis Harbor Hawks of the collegiate Cape Cod Baseball League play home games at McKeon Park mid-June–mid-August. Interested 5- to 17-year-olds can sign up with the Youth Baseball Academy. ✉ *McKeon Park, High School Rd.* ☎ *508/420–0962* ⊕ *www.harborhawks. org.*

🛍 Shopping

Main Street in downtown Hyannis has gradually become gentrified in recent years and is now one of the top shopping destinations on the Cape, buzzing with several art galleries and antiques shops, numerous clothiers, and a slew of other, mostly independent, boutiques and gift emporia. You'll also find quite a few restaurants along this walkable stretch, including several cafés that are nice for a cup of coffee or a light snack. Heading through the villages of Barnstable along Route 6A, you'll find no shortage of intriguing art galleries and rustic antiques shops.

Christmas Tree Shops andThat!

SPECIALTY STORES | This Cape mainstay—the chain originated here—is a bargain shoppers' haven. Take home Cape souvenirs at a great discount along with just about anything you might need (or not need) to decorate your home. There are multiple locations throughout the Cape, from the Sagamore Bridge to Orleans. ✉ *655 Iyanough Rd.* ☎ *508/778–5521* ⊕ *www.christmastreeshops.com.*

HyArts Artist Shanties

ART GALLERIES | Located in two areas on Ocean Street (51 and 180), on a boardwalk that parallels the Hyannis Harbor and at Bismark Park, several artist shanties host a rotating slate of Cape Cod-based artists. Work ranges from photography and paintings to handmade jewelry, ceramics, and wood carving. Hours vary for artists, so check the website for details. ✉ *Hyannis Harbor, 51 Ocean St., Hyannis Harbor* ☎ *508/862–4990* ⊕ *arts-barnstable.com/hyarts-shanties.*

Barnstable

4 miles north of Hyannis.

With nearly 50,000 year-round residents, Barnstable is the largest town on the Cape. It's also the second oldest, founded in 1639. You can get a feeling for its age in Barnstable Village, on and near Main Street (Route 6A), a lovely area of large old homes.

GETTING HERE AND AROUND

Most people drive to Barnstable via Route 6 or Route 6A. The Cape Cod Regional Transit Authority operates the Barnstable Villager, a small bus that travels from Barnstable to Hyannis. Service is daily late June–Labor Day; buses run about every hour.

🏖 Beaches

Sandy Neck Beach

BEACH—SIGHT | FAMILY | Sandy Neck Beach stretches some 6 miles across a peninsula that ends at **Sandy Neck Light.** The beach is one of the Cape's most beautiful—dunes, sand, and bay spread endlessly east, west, and north. The marsh used to be harvested for salt hay; now it's a haven for birds, which are out and about in the greatest numbers in morning and evening. The lighthouse, standing a few feet from the eroding shoreline at the tip of the neck, has

been out of commission since 1952. It was built in 1857 to replace an 1827 light, and it used to run on acetylene gas. As you travel east along Route 6A from Sandwich, Sandy Neck Road is just before the Barnstable line, although the beach itself is in West Barnstable. **Amenities:** food and drink; lifeguards; parking (fee); showers; toilets. **Best for:** sunset; swimming; walking. ✉ *Sandy Neck Rd., West Barnstable* 🌐 *www.town.barnstable.ma.us/sandyneckpark/default.aspx* 🎫 *Parking $20.*

🍴 Restaurants

Barnstable Restaurant & Tavern

$$ | **AMERICAN** | This handsome old building right in the village center, across from the courthouse, holds both a formal restaurant and a more relaxed tavern; dine street-side on the brick patio in nice weather. Fresh seafood dishes and the chef's rich pasta dishes are local favorites. **Known for:** Tavern burger; Friday-night live music on the patio; pizzas. [$] *Average main: $19* ✉ *3176 Main St.* ☎ *508/362–2355* 🌐 *www.barnstablerestaurant.com* 🕒 *Closed Mon. and Tues.*

☕ Coffee and Quick Bites

Kalmus Beach Snack Bar

$ | **AMERICAN** | Seaside favorites like clam chowder, fried clams, lobster rolls, burgers, hot dogs, fries, and more, complete the menu. Enjoy your meal at the picnic tables with great views of Hyannis Harbor. **Known for:** lobster rolls; fried seafood; homemade chocolate chip ice-cream sandwiches. [$] *Average main: $12* ✉ *670 Ocean St., Hyannis* ☎ *508/778–0777* 🌐 *www.facebook.com/Kalmussnackbar* 🕒 *Closed Mon.*

🛏 Hotels

★ **Honeysuckle Hill**

$$ | **B&B/INN** | There are plenty of thoughtful touches at this 1810 Queen Anne–style cottage: fresh flowers in every room, lavish breakfasts, refrigerators stocked with beverages, and beach chairs with umbrellas (perfect for nearby Sandy Neck Beach); there's even an outdoor hot tub and shower. **Pros:** lush gardens on the grounds; tasteful, large rooms; very short drive to Sandy Neck Beach. **Cons:** most rooms are accessed via steep stairs; no water views; not an in-town location. [$] *Rooms from: $229* ✉ *591 Rte. 6A, West Barnstable* ☎ *508/362–8418, 866/444–5522* 🌐 *www.honeysucklehill.com* 🛏 *5 rooms* 🍽 *Free breakfast.*

Yarmouth

Yarmouth Port 3 miles east of Barnstable Village, West Yarmouth 2 miles east of Hyannis.

Once known as Mattacheese, or "the planting lands," Yarmouth was settled in 1639 by farmers from the Plymouth Bay Colony. By then the Cape had begun a thriving maritime industry, and men turned to the sea to make their fortunes. Many impressive sea captains' houses—some now B&Bs and museums—still line enchanting Route 6A and nearby side streets, and Yarmouth Port has some real old-time stores in town. West Yarmouth has a very different atmosphere, stretched on busy commercial Route 28 south of Yarmouth Port.

GETTING HERE AND AROUND

Route 6A is the main route to Yarmouth Port, and there are lovely streets heading north toward the water and through hidden residential areas filled with beautiful old homes. West Yarmouth lies in the midst of busy Route 28, between

Hyannis and South Yarmouth. If you want to avoid this road entirely, a sensible option is to take speedy U.S. 6 to the exit nearest what you want to visit and then cut south across the interior. If you must travel the Route 28 area, take Buck Island Road, which runs north of and parallel to much of the busy route in West and South Yarmouth. Like West Yarmouth, South Yarmouth has a stretch of blight and overdevelopment on Route 28, but it also has some nice beaches that are good for families. Avoid Route 28 if you aim to get anywhere quickly.

VISITOR INFORMATION

CONTACTS Yarmouth Chamber of Commerce. ☎ *508/778–1008, 800/732–1008* 🌐 *www.yarmouthcapecod.com.*

Sights

Bass Hole Boardwalk

PROMENADE | FAMILY | Taking in one of Yarmouth Port's most beautiful areas, Bass Hole Boardwalk extends over a swampy creek, crosses salt marshes, and winds around vegetated wetlands and upland woods. Gray's Beach is a little crescent of sand with still water that's good for kids inside the roped-in swimming area. At the end of the boardwalk, benches provide a place to relax and look out over abundant marsh life and, across the creek, the beautiful, sandy shores of Dennis's Chapin Beach. At low tide you can walk out on the flats for almost a mile. ✉ *Center St., near Gray's Beach parking lot, Yarmouth Port* 🌐 *www.yarmouth.ma.us/678/Bass-Hole-Grays-Beach.*

Edward Gorey House

MUSEUM | Explore the eccentric doodles and offbeat humor of the late acclaimed artist and illustrator. Regularly changing exhibitions, arranged in the downstairs rooms of Gorey's former home, include drawings of his oddball characters and reveal the mysterious psyche of the sometimes dark but always playful illustrator. ✉ *8 Strawberry La., Yarmouth Port* ☎ *508/362–3909* 🌐 *www.edwardgoreyhouse.org* 🎟 *$8* ⏲ *Closed Jan.–mid-Apr.*

Restaurants

★ Inaho

$$$ | JAPANESE | Yuji Watanabe, chef-owner of the Cape's best Japanese restaurant, makes early-morning journeys to Boston's fish markets to shop for the freshest local catch, and the resulting selection of sushi and sashimi is vast and artful. The serene and simple Japanese garden out back has a traditional koi pond. **Known for:** chef's tasting menu; moody lighting; seafood tempura. [$] *Average main: $31* ✉ *157 Main St., Yarmouth Port* ☎ *508/362–5522* ⏲ *Closed Sun. No lunch.*

The Optimist Café

$ | BRITISH | From the outside, this bold Gothic Victorian looks like something out of a Brothers Grimm tale, with its steeply pitched roof, fanciful turrets, frilly gingerbread trim, and deep rose-and-green paint job. There is a great selection for breakfast (served all day) and lunch, featuring traditional English fare like smoked fish dishes, curries, scones, and crumpets. **Known for:** hearty ploughman's lunch; proper afternoon tea; eclectic surroundings. [$] *Average main: $14* ✉ *134 Rte. 6A, Yarmouth Port* ☎ *508/362–1024* 🌐 *www.optimistcafe.com* ⏲ *No dinner.*

Coffee and Quick Bites

Jerry's Seafood & Dairy Freeze

$ | SEAFOOD | FAMILY | This simple shack serves fried clams and onion rings, a variety of sandwiches and subs, as well as thick frappes (milk shakes), frozen yogurt, and soft-serve ice cream, at good prices. Even better, it's open year-round. **Known for:** Greek-style pizza; superfriendly service; ice cream. [$] *Average main: $13* ✉ *654 Rte. 28, West Yarmouth* ☎ *508/775–9752* 🌐 *www.jerryscapecod.com.*

Hotels

Bayside Resort

$$ | **HOTEL** | **FAMILY** | A bit more upscale than most properties along Route 28, the Bayside overlooks pristine salt marshes and Lewis Bay, and although it's not right on the water, there's a small beach and a large outdoor pool with a café (there's also an indoor pool). **Pros:** ideal for families with children; close to attractions of busy Route 28; views of the water. **Cons:** no beach swimming; not for those seeking intimate surroundings; public areas can be noisy. [$] *Rooms from: $259* ✉ *225 Rte. 28, West Yarmouth* ☎ *508/775–5669, 800/243–1114* 🌐 *www.baysideresort.com* 🛏 *128 rooms* 🍴 *Free breakfast.*

★ Capt. Farris House

$$ | **B&B/INN** | A short hop off congested Route 28 sits this imposing 1845 Greek Revival home. **Pros:** beautiful grounds; ideal location for exploring Mid Cape area; close to area restaurants and attractions. **Cons:** no elevator; not close to the beach; not for those with small children. [$] *Rooms from: $210* ✉ *308 Old Main St., Bass River Village* ☎ *508/760–2818* 🌐 *www.captainfarris.com* 🛏 *10 rooms* 🍴 *Free breakfast.*

★ The Inn at Cape Cod

$$$ | **B&B/INN** | A stately 19th-century Greek Revival building with imposing columns, the inn has one of the most dramatic facades of any house on the Cape; it sits near the Botanical Trails and has its own fine gardens, patios, and tree-shaded lawns. **Pros:** elegant lodging; close to attractions; serene surroundings. **Cons:** no water views or direct beach access; some steep stairs; not for small children. [$] *Rooms from: $325* ✉ *4 Summer St., Yarmouth Port* ☎ *508/375–0590, 800/850–7301* 🌐 *www.innatcapecod.com* 🛏 *9 rooms* 🍴 *Free breakfast.*

★ Liberty Hill Inn

$$ | **B&B/INN** | Smartly and traditionally furnished common areas—including the high-ceiling parlor, the formal dining room, and the wraparound porch—are a major draw to this dignified 1825 Greek Revival house. **Pros:** tasteful surroundings; beautiful grounds; extravagant homemade breakfast. **Cons:** some steep stairs; some bathrooms have only small shower stalls; not a waterfront location. [$] *Rooms from: $200* ✉ *77 Rte. 6A, Yarmouth Port* ☎ *508/362–3976* 🌐 *www.libertyhillinn.com* 🕒 *Closed Feb.–mid-Mar.* 🛏 *9 rooms* 🍴 *Free breakfast.*

Nightlife

Oliver's & Planck's Tavern

BARS/PUBS | Fish tanks illuminate this friendly bar, which hosts live music on most summer nights. There's also a midweek trivia night. ✉ *960 Main St., off Rte. 6A, Yarmouth Port* ☎ *508/362–6062* 🌐 *oliversandplancks.com.*

Performing Arts

Cultural Center of Cape Cod

ART GALLERIES—ARTS | This lively center plays host to a full schedule of art openings and exhibits, workshops, readings, various performances, and great live music. ✉ *307 Old Main St., South Yarmouth* ☎ *508/394–7100* 🌐 *www.cultural-center.org.*

Shopping

If you're heading along Route 6A, expect to see a multitude of art galleries, craft and antiques stores, specialty shops, and boutiques that adhere to the modest and subdued aesthetics demanded by the Historic Commission. Over on Route 28, though, there are no building codes or rules on good taste; there you'll find larger stores that can advertise their wares with flashy signage, selling souvenirs, T-shirts, and other fun vacation goodies.

Just Picked
GIFTS/SOUVENIRS | This Cape Cod–focused shop features local artisans and crafters who fill its shelves with a wide variety of home, garden, food, and gift items. ✉ *13 Willow St., Yarmouth Port* ☎ *508/362–0207* ⊕ *justpickedgifts.com.*

🏃 Activities

BASEBALL
Yarmouth-Dennis Red Sox
BASEBALL/SOFTBALL | FAMILY | The Yarmouth-Dennis Red Sox of the collegiate Cape Cod Baseball League play home games at Dennis-Yarmouth High School's Red Wilson Field, mid-June–mid-August. Baseball clinics for girls and boys age five and up run throughout the season. ✉ *Dennis-Yarmouth High School, 210 Station Ave., South Yarmouth* ☎ *508/394–9387* ⊕ *ydredsox.pointstreaksites.com/view/ydredsox.*

Dennis

Dennis Village 4 miles east of Yarmouth Port, West Dennis 1 mile east of South Yarmouth.

The back streets of Dennis Village still retain the Colonial charm of their seafaring days. The town, which was incorporated in 1793, was named for the Reverend Josiah Dennis. There were 379 sea captains living here when fishing, salt making, and shipbuilding were the main industries, and the elegant houses they constructed—now museums and B&Bs—still line the streets.

GETTING HERE AND AROUND
Route 6A is also known as Main Street as it passes through Dennis Village. If you're driving between West Dennis and Harwich, Lower County Road is a more scenic alternative to overdeveloped Route 28: it gives you occasional glimpses of the sea between the cottages and beachfront hotels.

VISITOR INFORMATION
CONTACTS Dennis Chamber of Commerce. ☎ *508/398–3568, 508/398–3568* ⊕ *www.dennischamber.com.*

👁 Sights

★ Cape Cod Museum of Art
MUSEUM | This multiple-gallery museum on the grounds of the Cape Playhouse has a permanent collection of more than 850 works by important Cape-associated artists such as Hans Hoffman, William Paxton, and Charles Hawthorne; Hawthorne was the founder of America's first artists' colony in 1899 in Provincetown. Rich in cultural programming, changing exhibits, special events, workshops, and classes are held throughout the year. ✉ *60 Hope La.* ☎ *508/385–4477* ⊕ *www.ccmoa.org* 🎟 *$10* 🕐 *Closed Mon.–Wed.*

Scargo Tower
VIEWPOINT | On a clear day, you'll have unbeatable views of Scargo Lake, Dennis Village's scattered houses below, Cape Cod Bay, and distant Provincetown from the top of this tower. A wooden tower built on this site in 1874 was one of the Cape's first tourist attractions; visitors would pay a nickel to climb to the top for the views. That tower burned down, and the present all-stone 30-foot tower was built in 1901 to replace it. Winding stairs bring you to the top; don't forget to read the unsightly but amusing graffiti on the way up. Expect crowds at sunrise and sunset. ✉ *Scargo Hill Rd., off Rte. 6A or Old Bass River Rd., South Dennis* 🎟 *Free.*

🏖 Beaches

Parking at all Dennis beaches is $25 per day in season ($30 on weekends and holidays) for nonresidents.

Corporation Beach
BEACH—SIGHT | FAMILY | Once a privately owned packet landing, this is a beautiful crescent of white sand backed by low dunes on Cape Cod Bay. Between the

upper parking lot and the beach, the DPM Surfside Grill, operated by the same owners of local staple Dennis Public Market, serves great sandwiches, grill favorites, fried seafood, and other seafood classics as well as drinks, snacks, and ice cream allowing your beach day to last a little longer. **Amenities:** food and drink; lifeguards; parking (fee); showers; toilets. **Best for:** sunset; swimming; walking. ✉ *250 Corporation Rd.* 🚗 *Parking from $25.*

West Dennis Beach

BEACH—SIGHT | FAMILY | This is one of the best beaches on the south shore (Nantucket Sound), with the crowds to prove it. A breakwater was started here in 1837 in an effort to protect the mouth of Bass River, but that was abandoned when a sandbar formed on the shore side. It's a long, wide, and popular sandy beach, stretching for 1½ miles, with marshland and the Bass River across from it. **Amenities:** food and drink; lifeguards; parking (fee); toilets. **Best for:** swimming; walking; windsurfing. ✉ *Lighthouse Rd., off Lower County Rd., West Dennis* 🚗 *Parking from $25.*

🍴 Restaurants

Captain Frosty's

$ | SEAFOOD | FAMILY | A great stop after the beach, this modest joint has a regular menu of seafood classics like fried clams and fish-and-chips supplemented by specials posted on the board and a counter where you order and take a number written on a french-fries box. There's seating inside as well as outside on a shady brick patio. **Known for:** classic fried seafood platters; soft-serve ice cream and frappes; chaotic parking lot during high season. $ *Average main: $15* ✉ *219 Rte. 6A* ☎ *508/385–8548* ⊕ *www. captainfrosty.com* ⊗ *Closed Tues. Closed early Sept.–mid-Apr.*

FIN Cape Cod

$$$ | SEAFOOD | As the name suggests, seafood is the star here, from salmon to red snapper, halibut to tuna, and all very recently caught in Atlantic waters. Two floors of seating in an antique home make for an eclectic setting aglow with candlelight in the company of many satisfied diners. **Known for:** oyster chowder with smoked bacon; attentive and knowledgeable service; extensive wine list. $ *Average main: $34* ✉ *800 Main St., off Rt. 6A* ☎ *508/385–2096* ⊕ *fincapecod. com* ⊗ *Closed Mon.*

The Oyster Company

$$$ | SEAFOOD | Supplies pour in from the restaurant's own oyster farm in the bay, though oysters (and clams) from other towns are well represented and can be had a variety of ways—raw on the half shell is the best way to enjoy these superfresh bivalves. It's a fun place all around, with great food and a boisterous atmosphere. **Known for:** $1.50 oysters til 6:30; the "Red Sox" martini (among other fanciful martinis); locally sourced food. $ *Average main: $26* ✉ *202 Depot St., Dennis Port* ☎ *508/398–4600* ⊕ *www. theoystercompany.com.*

☕ Coffee and Quick Bites

Grumpy's

$ | AMERICAN | Open year-round, this friendly family-owned and operated restaurant serves up homey food for breakfast and lunch. Favorites from the extensive menu include traditional breakfast items like pancakes and eggs for breakfast, and fish-and-chips and a variety of sandwiches at lunch. **Known for:** daily blackboard specials; seafood platters; friendly vibe. $ *Average main: $12* ✉ *1408 Main St., East Dennis* ☎ *508/385–2911 for takeout* ⊕ *www. grumpyscapecod.com* ⊗ *No dinner.*

Hotels

★ Isaiah Hall B&B Inn
$ | **B&B/INN** | Lilacs and pink roses trail the white-picket fence outside this 1857 Greek Revival farmhouse on a quiet residential road near the bay, where innkeepers Jerry and Judy Neal set the scene for a romantic getaway with guest rooms that have country antiques, floral-print wallpapers, fluffy quilts, and Priscilla curtains. **Pros:** beautiful grounds; near beaches and attractions; generous breakfast and cookies in the afternoon. **Cons:** not for those with children under seven; some very steep steps; some rooms are on the small side. [$] *Rooms from: $175* ✉ *152 Whig St.* ☎ *508/385–9928* 🌐 *www.isaiahhallinn.com* 🛏 *12 rooms* 🍴 *Free breakfast.*

Nightlife

Harvest Gallery Wine Bar
WINE BARS—NIGHTLIFE | Near the Cape Playhouse, this friendly place has an extensive wine list, a good variety of hors d'oeuvres and other nibbles, eclectic artwork, and live music. ✉ *776 Main St.* ☎ *508/385–2444* 🌐 *www.harvestgallery-winebar.com* ☞ *Closed Wed.*

Performing Arts

★ Cape Playhouse
THEATER | **FAMILY** | For Broadway-style dramas, comedies, and musicals, attend a production at the Cape Playhouse, the country's oldest professional summer theater. In 1927 Raymond Moore, who had been working with a theatrical troupe in Provincetown, bought an 1838 Unitarian meetinghouse and converted it into a theater. The opening performance was *The Guardsman,* starring Basil Rathbone. Other stars who performed here in the early days—some in their professional stage debuts—include Bette Davis (who first worked here as an usher), Gregory Peck, Lana Turner, Ginger Rogers, Humphrey Bogart, Tallulah Bankhead, and Henry Fonda, who appeared with his then-unknown 20-year-old daughter, Jane. Behind-the-scenes tours are available. The playhouse offers children's theater on Friday morning in July and August. The 26-acre property includes a restaurant, the Cape Cod Museum of Art, and the Cape Cinema. ✉ *820 Rte. 6A* ☎ *508/385–3911, 877/385–3911* 🌐 *www.capeplayhouse.com.*

Activities

BIKING

You can pick up the Cape's premier bike path, the more than 25-mile **Cape Cod Rail Trail** (🌐 *www.mass.gov/dcr*), at several points; continuing expansion has now extended to South Yarmouth, with plans to reach farther west to Barnstable. Though it is possible, riding the entire trail in a single day doesn't do justice to its sights and side trips. Many cyclists, especially those with small kids, prefer the piecemeal method because they can relax and enjoy the sights—and not turn their legs to jelly in the process.

There is ample parking at the lot off Route 134 south of U.S. 6, near Theophilus Smith Road in South Dennis, and it ends at the post office in South Wellfleet. Access points in Brewster are Long Pond Road, Underpass Road, and Nickerson State Park. There's also a spur off the trail that goes to Chatham.

A guidebook published by the Dennis Chamber of Commerce includes bike tours and maps. You can rent bikes from a number of places along the Cape Cod Rail Trail.

Learn more about the Cape's marshlands, forests, and ponds at the Cape Cod Museum of Natural History in neighboring Brewster.

Brewster

7 miles northeast of Dennis, 20 miles east of Sandwich.

Brewster's location on Cape Cod Bay makes it a perfect place to learn about the region's ecology. The Cape Cod Museum of Natural History is here, and the area is rich in conservation lands, state parks, forests, freshwater ponds, and brackish marshes. When the tide is low in Cape Cod Bay, you can stroll the beaches and explore tidal pools up to 2 miles from the shore on the Brewster flats.

GETTING HERE AND AROUND

Brewster—6 miles north of Chatham and 5 miles west of Orleans—is spread along Route 6A. Take it slow through the town limits, not just in honor of the speed limit, but to appreciate the abundant display of grand old homes, fanciful rose arbors, antiques shops, and countless historic details that make this one of the region's prettiest towns.

VISITOR INFORMATION

CONTACTS Brewster Chamber of Commerce. ☎ 508/896–3500 ⊕ brewster-cape-cod.com.

◉ Sights

Brewster Store

STORE/MALL | Built in 1852 as a church, this local landmark has been a typical New England general store since 1866, with such essentials as daily newspapers, penny candy, groceries, and benches out front for conversation. It specializes in oil lamps and antique lanterns of all types. Out back, the Brewster Scoop serves ice cream mid-June–early September. Upstairs, memorabilia from antique toys to World War II bond posters is displayed. Downstairs there's a working antique nickelodeon; locals warm themselves by the old coal stove in colder months. ⊠ 1935 Rte. 6A ☎ 508/896–3744 ⊕ www.brewsterstore.com.

★ Cape Cod Museum of Natural History
MUSEUM | FAMILY | A short drive west from the heart of Brewster, this spacious museum and its pristine grounds include a shop, a natural-history library, and exhibits such as a working beehive and a pond- and sea-life room with live specimens. Walking trails wind through 80 acres of forest, marshland, and ponds, all rich in birds and other wildlife. The exhibit hall upstairs has a wall display of aerial photographs documenting the process by which the famous Chatham sandbar was split in two. In summer there are guided field walks, nature programs, and art classes for preschoolers through ninth graders. ✉ *869 Rte. 6A, West Brewster* ☎ *508/896–3867* 🌐 *www.ccmnh.org* 🎟 *$10.*

Nickerson State Park
NATIONAL/STATE PARK | FAMILY | These 1,961 acres were once part of a vast estate belonging to Roland C. Nickerson, son of Samuel Nickerson, a Chatham native who founded the First National Bank of Chicago. Roland and his wife, Addie, lavishly entertained such visitors as President Grover Cleveland at their private beach and hunting lodge in English country-house style, with coachmen dressed in tails and top hats and a bugler announcing carriages entering the front gates. In 1934 Addie donated the land for the state park in memory of Roland and their son, who died during the 1918 flu epidemic.

The park consists of acres of oak, pitch-pine, hemlock, and spruce forest speckled with seven freshwater kettle ponds formed by glaciers. Some ponds are stocked with trout for fishing. You can swim, canoe, sail, and kayak in the ponds, and bicycle along 8 miles of paved trails that have access to the Cape Cod Rail Trail. Bird-watchers seek out the thrushes, wrens, warblers, woodpeckers, finches, larks, cormorants, great blue herons, hawks, owls, and ospreys. Red foxes and white-tailed deer are occasionally spotted in the woods. The over 400 campsites are extremely popular: reservations are necessary. ✉ *3488 Rte. 6A, East Brewster* ☎ *508/896–3491* 🌐 *www.mass.gov/locations/nickerson-state-park* 🎟 *$8 parking (MA resident), $30 (nonresident) Memorial Day–Oct.*

🍴 Restaurants

Brewster Fish House
$$$ | SEAFOOD | There is nothing ordinary about the menu here: seafood selections range from just-off-the-boat scallops to tuna, local oysters, and octopus. It can be noisy and it's always crowded in summer, but it's worth the wait. **Known for:** artful seafood presentations; sophisticated atmosphere; locally sourced ingredients. [$] *Average main: $26* ✉ *2208 Rte. 6A* ☎ *508/896–7867* 🌐 *www.brewsterfishhousecapecod.com* 🕒 *Closed Mon. and Tues.*

★ Chillingsworth
$$$$ | FRENCH | One of the crown jewels of Cape restaurants, Chillingsworth combines formal presentation with an excellent French menu, with classics like escargots, roasted duck, and seared veal loin served with style and elegance. Less expensive à la carte options are served in the more casual, patio-style Chill's Bistro. **Known for:** one of the best restaurants on the Cape; excellent service; located at the historic 300-year-old estate. [$] *Average main: $70* ✉ *2449 Rte. 6A, East Brewster* ☎ *508/896–3640* 🌐 *www.chillingsworth.com* 🕒 *Closed Sun.–Tues. Closed Thanksgiving–mid-May.*

JT's Seafood
$$ | SEAFOOD | FAMILY | Fresh and ample portions of fried seafood take center stage at this casual joint, which is very popular with families. Place your order at the counter and sit inside or out: be sure to save room for ice cream. **Known for:** fried clams; hot lobster rolls; clam chowder. [$] *Average main: $21* ✉ *2689 Rte. 6A* ☎ *508/896–3355* 🌐 *www.jt-seafood.com* 🕒 *Closed mid-Oct.–mid-Apr.*

Hotels

★ Captain Freeman Inn

$$ | B&B/INN | Named for the sea captain who had the home built in 1866, this gracious inn retains its aged elegance with original ornate plaster ceiling medallions, marble fireplaces, and sturdy yet graceful construction. **Pros:** authentic historic lodging with modern amenities; it's a short walk to Breakwater Beach on the bay, even shorter to the ice-cream shop next to the Brewster General Store; extravagant breakfast and afternoon tea. **Cons:** not for those with children; not a waterfront location; most rooms upstairs. [$] *Rooms from: $259* ✉ *15 Breakwater Rd.* ☎ *508/896–7481* 🌐 *www.captainfreemaninn.com* 🛏 *10 rooms* 🍴 *Free breakfast.*

★ Ocean Edge Resort & Golf Club

$$$$ | RESORT | FAMILY | The expansive Ocean Edge Resort & Golf Club, set on 429 acres of prime Cape Cod real estate, offers a host of amenities and perks, from a Jack Nicklaus–designed golf course and a private beach to several pools, tennis courts, and a gorgeous spa. **Pros:** five pools, two inside; access to private beach; great kids' activities. **Cons:** expensive; busy with weddings in summer; Arbor and Britterige Villas at The Villages do not have access to the private beach. [$] *Rooms from: $500* ✉ *2907 Main St.* ☎ *508/896–9000* 🌐 *www.oceanedge.com* 🛏 *337 rooms* 🍴 *No meals.*

★ Old Sea Pines Inn

$ | B&B/INN | FAMILY | With its white-column portico and wraparound veranda overlooking a broad lawn, Old Sea Pines, which housed a "charm and personality" school in the early 1900s, resembles a vintage summer estate. **Pros:** welcomes families; beautiful grounds; reasonable rates. **Cons:** no TV in main building; steep stairway to upper floors; not for those looking for upscale design; family suites have shared baths. [$] *Rooms from: $170* ✉ *2553 Rte. 6A* ☎ *508/896–6114* 🌐 *www.oldseapinesinn.com* 🕒 *Limited room availability Nov.–Apr.* 🛏 *24 rooms* 🍴 *Free breakfast.*

Performing Arts

MUSIC

Brewster Town-band Concerts

CONCERTS | FAMILY | Sunday evenings by the bay are filled with the sounds of the town-band concerts, held in the gazebo on the grounds of Drummer Boy Park. Bring your beach chairs, blankets, and a picnic for a lovely evening outing. The park is about ½ mile west of the Cape Cod Museum of Natural History, on the western side of Brewster. ✉ *Drummer Boy Park, Rte. 6A, West Brewster* 🌐 *thebrewsterband.weebly.com* 🎟 *Free.*

THEATER

Cape Cod Repertory Theatre Co

THEATER | FAMILY | Several impressive productions, from original works to the classics, are staged every year in this indoor Arts and Crafts–style theater set way back in the woods. There are mesmerizing outdoor shows for kids offered on weekday mornings during the summer, as well as hour-long puppet shows. ✉ *3299 Rte. 6A, west of Nickerson State Park, East Brewster* ☎ *508/896–1888* 🌐 *www.caperep.org* 🕒 *Closed Dec.–Mar.*

Activities

BASEBALL

Brewster Whitecaps

BASEBALL/SOFTBALL | FAMILY | The Brewster Whitecaps of the collegiate Cape Cod Baseball League play home games mid-June–mid-August. Kids 6–13 can sign up for fun clinics led by the players. ✉ *Stony Brook Elementary School, 384 Underpass Rd.* ☎ *508/896–8500* 🌐 *www.brewsterwhitecaps.com.*

Shopping

With Brewster's abundant historic and natural appeal, it's no surprise that shoppers will benefit from the bounty of antiques shops, art galleries, and specialty shops here.

★ Brewster Book Store

BOOKS/STATIONERY | FAMILY | A special place, Brewster Book Store is filled to the rafters with all manner of books by local and international authors, with an extensive fiction selection and kids' section. Author signings and children's story times take place year-round. ⊠ 2648 Rte. 6A, East Brewster ☎ 508/896–6543 ⊕ www.brewsterbookstore.com.

Harwich

6 miles south of Brewster, 5 miles east of Dennis.

The Cape's famous cranberry industry took off in Harwich in 1844, when Alvin Cahoon was its principal grower. Today you'll still find working cranberry bogs throughout Harwich. Three naturally sheltered harbors on Nantucket Sound make the town, like its English namesake, popular with boaters. You'll find dozens of elegant sailboats and elaborate yachts in Harwich's harbors, plus plenty of charter fishing boats. Every August the town pays celebratory homage to its large boating population with a grand regatta, Sails Around the Cape.

GETTING HERE AND AROUND

The center of Harwich, 6 miles south of Brewster, is easily accessed off Exit 10 of U.S. 6. It sits right at the crossroads of several roads that branch off to various towns. Route 39, which becomes Main Street in town, leads to Orleans; Bank Street, next to the Brooks Free Library, is the most direct route to Harwich Port.

VISITOR INFORMATION

CONTACTS Harwich Chamber of Commerce. ⊠ Harwich Port ☎ 508/432–1600, 800/442–7942 ⊕ www.harwichcc.com.

Restaurants

★ Buca's Tuscan Roadhouse

$$$ | ITALIAN | This romantic roadhouse near the Chatham border, adorned with tiny white lights, wine bottles, and warm-hue walls, might just transport you to Italy—and if it doesn't, the fantastic food certainly will. There are always excellent specials added to the menu; in the fall and winter, look for value-priced entrées. **Known for:** authentic Italian food; atmosphere; crowds: make reservations. $ Average main: $34 ⊠ 4 Depot Rd. ☎ 508/432–6900 ⊕ www.bucas-tuscanroadhouse.com ⓧ No lunch.

★ Cape Sea Grille

$$$ | AMERICAN | This chef-owned gem with distant sea views uses what's locally available as the inspiration for an ever-changing and creative menu that's complemented by a vibrant, welcoming atmosphere. There are also generous wine, martini, and drink lists. **Known for:** inviting atmosphere; inventive seafood entrées; creative cocktails. $ Average main: $34 ⊠ 31 Sea St., Harwich Port ☎ 508/432–4745 ⊕ www.capeseagrille. com ⓧ Closed Mon. and Tues.

Coffee and Quick Bites

Sundae School

$ | AMERICAN | FAMILY | Churning out ice cream in small batches since 1976, this popular place usually has lines out the door. The shop uses only the freshest ingredients, so flavors like banana or blueberry are made with the real deal, but you can always count on the classics like vanilla and chocolate. **Known for:** amazing hot fudge sundaes; creative flavors; friendly service. $ Average main: $5 ⊠ 606 Main St., Harwich Port ☎ 508/430–2444 ⊕ www.sundaeschool. com ⓧ Closed Labor Day–Memorial Day.

🛏 Hotels

★ Wequassett Inn Resort and Golf Club

$$$$ | RESORT | FAMILY | On 22 acres of shaded landscape partially surrounded by Pleasant Bay, 20 Cape-style cottages and an attractive hotel make up this traditionally elegant resort by the sea. **Pros:** attentive service; activities and programs for all ages; babysitting services and full children's program. **Cons:** rates are steep; not an in-town location; isolated area. Ⓢ *Rooms from: $700* ✉ *2173 Orleans Rd. (Rte. 28)* ☎ *508/432–5400, 800/225–7125* ⊕ *www.wequassett.com* ⊗ *Closed Nov.– Mar.* ⤴ *120 rooms* ⦿ *No meals.*

Winstead Inn & Beach Resort

$$$$ | B&B/INN | With its graceful columns and welcoming front veranda, the regal Winstead Inn sits along a quiet street; many of the rooms have a view of the heated, outdoor saltwater pool, a real oasis with potted palms, fountains, and flowers. **Pros:** spacious, elegant rooms; pretty pool area; beach access. **Cons:** numerous stairs; not for those on a budget; beach guests can't use pool. Ⓢ *Rooms from: $400* ✉ *114 Parallel St.* ☎ *508/432–4444, 800/870–4405* ⊕ *www. winsteadinn.com* ⊗ *Closed Nov.–Easter* ⤴ *29 rooms* ⦿ *Free breakfast.*

🏃 Activities

BASEBALL

Harwich Mariners

BASEBALL/SOFTBALL | FAMILY | The Harwich Mariners of the collegiate Cape Cod Baseball League play home games at Whitehouse Field on Oak Street mid-June–mid-August. The team leads a youth clinic for boys and girls. ✉ *Whitehouse Field, 75 Oak St.* ☎ *508/432–2000* ⊕ *www.harwichmariners.org.*

👜 Shopping

Harwich Port has a busy little Main Street area lined with shops and restaurants, though the majority of Harwich is somewhat rural with little in the way of a dense shopping area. In East Harwich, on the way to Orleans, is a large commercial center with a large grocery store, drug stores, and a few other options.

Cape Cod Lavender Farm

LOCAL SPECIALTIES | Cape Cod Lavender Farm consists of some 14,000 lavender plants, making it one of the largest such farms on the East Coast. Harvest (best for visits) is usually around mid-June– July, when you'll see acres and acres of stunning purple waves. The farm sells soaps and bath salts, candles, potpourri, marmalade, lemonade, and many other lavender-infused goods. Keep your eyes peeled for its sign (on the right) as you're driving south on Route 124—it's easy to miss. ✉ *Corner of Rte. 124 and Weston Woods Rd., off U.S. 6, Exit 10* ☎ *508/432–8397* ⊕ *www.capecodlavenderfarm.com.*

Chatham

5 miles east of Harwich.

At the bent elbow of the Cape, with water nearly surrounding it, Chatham has all the charm of a quietly posh seaside resort, with plenty of shops but none of the crass commercialism that plagues some other towns on the Cape. The town has gray-shingle houses—many improbably large and grandiose—with tidy awnings and cheerful flower gardens, an attractive Main Street with crafts and antiques stores alongside dapper cafés, and a five-and-dime. Although it can get crowded in high season—and even on weekends during shoulder seasons—Chatham remains a true New England village.

VISITOR INFORMATION

CONTACTS Chatham Chamber of Commerce.
☎ *508/945–5199, 800/715–5567* ⊕ *www. chathaminfo.com.*

 ## Sights

Atwood House Museum

MUSEUM | Built by sea captain Joseph C. Atwood in 1752, this museum has a gambrel roof, hand-hewn floor planks, an old kitchen with a wide hearth and a beehive oven, and some antique dolls and toys. The New Gallery displays portraits of local sea captains. The Joseph C. Lincoln Room has the manuscripts, first editions, and mementos of the Chatham writer, and antique tools are displayed in a room in the basement. There's also a local commercial fishing gallery. The 1974 Durand Wing has collections of seashells from around the world, as well as threaded Sandwich glass, Parian-ware figures, unglazed porcelain vases, figurines, and busts. In a remodeled freight shed are the stunning and provocative murals (1932–45) by Alice Stallknecht Wight portraying religious scenes in Chatham settings. On the grounds are an herb garden, the old turret and lens from the Chatham Light, and a simple camp house rescued from eroding North Beach. ⊠ *347 Stage Harbor Rd., West Chatham* ☎ *508/945–2493* ⊕ *www.chathamhistoricalsociety.org* ☞ *$10* ⊗ *Closed Sun. and Mon. Closed Nov.–May (special events scheduled in off-season).*

Chatham Light

LIGHTHOUSE | The view from this lighthouse—of the harbor, the sandbars, and the ocean beyond—justifies the crowds. The lighthouse is especially dramatic on a foggy night, as the beacon's light pierces the mist. Coin-operated telescopes allow a close look at the famous "Chatham Break," the result of a fierce 1987 nor'easter that blasted a channel through a barrier beach just off the coast. The U.S. Coast Guard auxiliary, which supervises the lighthouse, offers free tours May–October on most Wednesdays; otherwise, the interior is off-limits. There is free parking in front of the lighthouse—the 30-minute limit is strictly monitored. ⊠ *Main St., near Bridge St., West Chatham* ☎ *508/945–3830* ☞ *Free.*

Fish Pier

MARINA | **FAMILY** | Smells and sights are abundant here; keep an eye out for the many lingering seals who are hoping for a free meal. The unloading of the boats is a big local event, drawing crowds who watch it all from an observation deck. From their fishing grounds 3–100 miles offshore, fishermen bring in haddock, cod, flounder, lobster, halibut, and pollack, which are packed in ice and shipped to New York and Boston or sold at the fish market here. Also here is *The Provider,* a monument to the town's fishing industry, showing a hand pulling a fish-filled net from the sea. ⊠ *54 Barcliff Rd. Ext., North Chatham* ⊕ *www.chatham-ma.gov/chatham-fish-pier* ☞ *Free.*

★ Monomoy National Wildlife Refuge

NATURE PRESERVE | This 2,500-acre preserve includes the Monomoy Islands, a fragile 9-mile-long barrier-beach area south of Chatham. A haven for bird-watchers, the refuge is an important stop along the North Atlantic Flyway for migratory waterfowl and shorebirds—peak migration times are May and late July. It also provides nesting and resting grounds for 285 species, including gulls—great black-backed, herring, and laughing—and several tern species. White-tailed deer wander the islands, and harbor and gray seals frequent the shores in winter. The only structure on the islands is the **South Monomoy Lighthouse,** built in 1849. The visitor center offers maps and some guided walks in the summer. ⊠ *Wikis Way, Morris Island* ☎ *508/945–0594* ⊕ *www.fws.gov/refuge/Monomoy* ☞ *Free.*

Beaches

Harding's Beach

BEACH—SIGHT | FAMILY | West of Chatham center, on the calmer and warmer waters of Nantucket Sound, Harding's Beach is very popular with families. It can get crowded, so plan to arrive earlier or later in the day. **Amenities:** food and drink; lifeguards; parking (fee); showers; toilets. **Best for:** swimming; walking; windsurfing. ⊠ *Harding's Beach Rd., off Barn Hill Rd., West Chatham* ⊕ *www.chathaminfo.com/beaches* ⊠ *Parking $20.*

Restaurants

Del Mar Bar and Bistro

$$$ | **ECLECTIC** | Fanciful cocktails, an intriguing menu, live music, and daily blackboard specials make this a popular Chatham spot. There's also a changing tapas menu for quick bites at the bar. **Known for:** wood-fired meals; live jazz; intriguing specials. Ⓢ *Average main: $26* ⊠ *907 Rte. 28* ☎ *508/945–9988* ⊕ *www. delmarbistro.com* ⊗ *No lunch.*

Impudent Oyster

$$$ | **SEAFOOD** | This cozy, festive tavern, a favorite for more than 40 years, is a great place for a romantic meal or dinner with the kids, and the menu offers light burgers and sandwiches, as well as more-substantial fare. It's always packed, and there's not a ton of seating, so reserve on weekends. **Known for:** spicy local mussels with chorizo; local favorite dining spot; oysters Rockefeller. Ⓢ *Average main: $31* ⊠ *15 Chatham Bars Ave.* ☎ *508/945–3545* ⊕ *www.theimpudentoyster.com* ⊗ *Closed Tues. and Wed.*

Nightlife

Chatham Squire

BARS/PUBS | Boasting four bars (including a raw bar), this is a rollicking year-round local hangout, drawing a young crowd to the bar side and a mixed crowd of locals to the restaurant. There's live entertainment on weekends. ⊠ *487 Main St.* ☎ *508/945–0942* ⊕ *www. thesquire.com.*

Chatham Town-Band Concerts

CONCERTS | FAMILY | Chatham's summer town-band concerts—a tradition that began in the 1940s—begin at 8 pm on Friday and draw thousands of onlookers. As many as 500 fox-trot on the roped-off dance floor, and there are special dances for children and sing-alongs for all. ⊠ *Kate Gould Park, Main St.* ☎ *508/945–5199* ⊕ *www.chathamband.com* ⊠ *Free.*

Activities

BASEBALL

Chatham Anglers

BASEBALL/SOFTBALL | FAMILY | Chatham Anglers baseball games are great free entertainment by the collegiate-level players in the Cape Cod Baseball League. Clinics for aspiring 6- to 17-year-olds are led by the team. ⊠ *Veterans' Field, 1 Veterans Field Rd., near rotary* ☎ *508/996–5004* ⊕ *www.chathamanglers.com.*

Shopping

Main Street is a busy shopping area with a diverse range of merchandise, from the pocketbook-friendly to the pricier and more upscale. Here you'll find galleries, crafts, clothing stores, bookstores, and a few good antiques shops.

Chatham Jam and Jelly Shop

FOOD/CANDY | This shop sells delicious concoctions like rose-petal jelly, apple-lavender chutney, and wild beach plum jelly, its most popular flavor, as well as all the old standbys. All preserves are made on-site in small batches. ⊠ *16 Seaquanset Rd., at Rte. 28, West Chatham* ☎ *508/945–3052* ⊕ *www.chathamjamandjellyshop.com* ⊗ *Closed Sun.*

★ **Yankee Ingenuity**

GIFTS/SOUVENIRS | Here you'll find a varied selection of unique jewelry and lamps and a wide assortment of unusual, beautiful trinkets at reasonable prices (especially for Chatham). ⊠ *525 Main St.* ☎ *508/945–1288* ⊕ *www.yankee-ingenuity.com.*

Orleans

8 miles north of Chatham, 35 miles east of Sagamore Bridge.

Orleans has a long heritage in fishing and seafaring, and many beautifully preserved homes from the Colonial era can still be seen in the small village of East Orleans, home of the town's Historical Society and Museum. In other areas of town, such as down by Rock Harbor, more modestly grand homes stand near the water's edge.

GETTING HERE AND AROUND

Downtown Orleans, 8 miles north of Chatham, is a kind of extended triangle made by Route 28, Route 6A, and Main Street. Main Street crosses Route 28 as it makes its way east toward the lovely enclave of East Orleans and Nauset Beach. Heading west, Main Street blends into Rock Harbor Road, which makes its journey all the way to Cape Cod Bay. A bus connecting Hyannis and Orleans serves the Lower Cape region. Year-round transport on the Flex service goes from Harwich to Provincetown, serving the towns of Brewster, Orleans, Eastham, Wellfleet, and Truro along the way.

VISITOR INFORMATION

CONTACTS **Orleans Chamber of Commerce.** ☎ *508/255–1386, 508/255–1386* ⊕ *orleanscapecod.org.*

◉ Sights

Rock Harbor

MARINA | FAMILY | This harbor was the site of a War of 1812 skirmish in which the Orleans militia kept a British warship from docking. In the 19th century Orleans had an active saltworks, and a flourishing packet service between Rock Harbor and Boston developed. Today it's the base of charter-fishing and party boats in season, as well as of a small commercial fishing fleet. Sunsets over the harbor are spectacular, and it's a great place to watch the boats float past. Parking is free. ⊠ *Rock Harbor Rd.*

⊕ Beaches

There is a daily parking fee for both beaches mid-June–Labor Day. Keep your parking ticket: it can be used at any Orleans beach for that calendar date, including the two freshwater ponds in town. The increased presence of great white sharks in the area (they dine on the massive seal population) seems to be both a tourist boon and a concern. It's not unusual to hear the blare of lifeguard whistles followed by orders to exit the water until the coast is clear. Best tip: don't swim with the seals.

Nauset Beach

BEACH—SIGHT | FAMILY | This town-managed beach—not to be confused with Nauset Light Beach on the National Seashore—is a 10-mile sweep of sandy ocean beach with low dunes and large waves good for bodysurfing or board surfing. Despite its size, the massive parking lot often fills up on sunny days; arrive quite early or in the late afternoon if you want to claim a spot. The beach gets extremely crowded in summer; unless you walk a ways, expect to feel very close to your neighbors on the sand. **Amenities:** food and drink; lifeguards; parking (fee); showers; toilets. **Best for:** sunrise; surfing; swimming; walking.

✉ *Beach Rd., Nauset Heights* ☎ *508/240–3780* 🌐 *orleanscapecod.org/beaches* 🎫 *Parking $20 Memorial Day–Labor Day.*

Skaket Beach

BEACH—SIGHT | **FAMILY** | On Cape Cod Bay, Skaket Beach is a sandy stretch with calm, warm water good for children. When the tide is out, you can walk seemingly endlessly on the sandy flats. The parking lot fills up fast on hot July and August days; try to arrive before 11 or after 2. The many tide pools make this a favorite spot for families. Sunsets here draw a good crowd. **Amenities:** food and drink; lifeguards; parking (fee); showers; toilets. **Best for:** sunset; swimming; walking. ✉ *Skaket Beach Rd.* ☎ *508/240–3775* 🌐 *orleanscapecod.org/beaches* 🎫 *Parking $20 Memorial Day–Labor Day.*

🍴 Restaurants

Land Ho!

$$ | **AMERICAN** | Tried-and-true tavern fare is the rule at Orleans's flagship local restaurant. The scene is usually fun and boisterous; dozens of homemade wooden signs heralding local businesses hang from the rafters above the red-checker tablecloths. **Known for:** daily blackboard specials; thriving local bar scene; sea clam pie. [$] *Average main: $18* ✉ *38 Cove Rd.* ☎ *508/255–5165* 🌐 *www.land-ho.com.*

Mahoney's Atlantic Bar and Grill

$$$ | **ECLECTIC** | This always-hopping downtown spot serves commendable dinner fare and draws big crowds for cocktails and appetizers. The bar is long and comfortable, and is a good spot to dine if there are no tables available. **Known for:** seafood bouillabaisse; specialty cocktails; lively local hangout. [$] *Average main: $30* ✉ *28 Main St.* ☎ *508/255–5505* 🌐 *www.mahoneysatlantic.com* ⏲ *No lunch.*

🛏 Hotels

★ A Little Inn on Pleasant Bay

$$$ | **B&B/INN** | This gorgeously decorated inn occupies a 1798 building on a bluff beside a cranberry bog, and many of the rooms look clear out to the bay for which it's named (others face the lush gardens)—there's even a small private beach with its own dock. **Pros:** great water views; abundant buffet breakfast; spacious baths. **Cons:** not an in-town location; not for those traveling with children under age 10; expensive. [$] *Rooms from: $375* ✉ *654 S. Orleans Rd., South Orleans* ☎ *508/255–0780, 888/332–3351* 🌐 *www.alittleinnonpleasantbay.com* ⏲ *Closed Oct.–mid-May* 🛏 *9 rooms* 🍴 *Free breakfast.*

Ship's Knees Inn

$$$ | **B&B/INN** | Giving a generous nod to its name and its 19th-century heritage, this inn is full of nautical and historic touches: seaside artwork and furnishings, steeply pitched roof lines, wide-plank floors, antiques, and a good deal of painted furniture. **Pros:** short walk to beach; beautifully maintained property; pool. **Cons:** two rooms share a bath; some steep stairs; not for those traveling with small children. [$] *Rooms from: $330* ✉ *186 Beach Rd.* ☎ *508/255–1312* 🌐 *www.shipskneesinn.com* 🛏 *17 rooms, 1 apartment* 🍴 *Free breakfast.*

🏃 Activities

BASEBALL

Orleans Firebirds

BASEBALL/SOFTBALL | **FAMILY** | The Orleans Firebirds of the collegiate Cape Cod Baseball League play home games at Eldredge Park mid-June–mid-August. Kids can sign up for daily clinics with the players. ✉ *Eldredge Park, Rte. 28 at Eldredge Pkwy.* ☎ *508/255–0793* 🌐 *www.orleansfirebirds.com* 🎫 *Free.*

BOATING AND FISHING

Many of Orleans's freshwater ponds offer good fishing for perch, pickerel, trout, and more. Anglers will need a license for both fresh and saltwater fishing. Pleasant Bay is ideal and popular for boating as well as kayaking.

Arey's Pond Boat Yard

BOATING | There's a sailing school here offering individual and group lessons. The company also rents sailboats, kayaks, row boats, and standup paddleboards. ⊠ 45 Arey's La., off Rte. 28, South Orleans ☎ 508/255–0994 ⊕ www. areyspondboatyard.com.

Goose Hummock Shop

FISHING | Fishing licenses and gear are available at the Goose Hummock Shop, which also rents powerboats, canoes, paddleboards, and kayaks. Lessons and tours are available. ⊠ 15 Rte. 6A ☎ 508/255–0455 ⊕ www.goose.com.

Eastham

3 miles north of Orleans, 6 miles south of Wellfleet.

Often overlooked on the speedy drive up toward Provincetown on Route 6, Eastham is a town full of hidden treasures. Unlike other towns on the Cape, it has no official town center or Main Street; the highway bisects it, and the town touches both Cape Cod Bay and the Atlantic. Amid the gas stations, convenience stores, restaurants, and large motel complexes, Eastham's wealth of natural beauty takes a little exploring to find.

GETTING HERE AND AROUND

Eastham's main drag is busy Route 6, which gives visitors no feel for the town's natural beauty. It's hard to get lost in Eastham, which is about 3 miles north of Orleans. You're never more than a few miles from the road ending at a beach. Take the time to meander about and see what's off the highway on both the bay and ocean sides.

VISITOR INFORMATION

CONTACTS Eastham Chamber of Commerce. ☎ 508/240–7211 ⊕ www.easthamchamber.com.

◉ Sights

★ Cape Cod National Seashore

NATIONAL/STATE PARK | FAMILY | The region's most expansive national treasure, Cape Cod National Seashore was established in 1961 by President John F. Kennedy, for whom Cape Cod was home and haven. The 27,000-acre park, extending from Chatham to Provincetown, protects 30 miles of superb beaches; great rolling dunes; swamps, marshes, and wetlands; and pitch-pine and scrub-oak forest. Self-guided nature trails, as well as biking and horse trails, lace through these landscapes. Hiking trails lead to a red-maple swamp, Nauset Marsh, and to Salt Pond; the Buttonbush Trail is a nature path for people with vision impairments. A hike or bike ride to Coast Guard Beach leads to a turnout looking out over marsh and sea. A section of the cliff here was washed away in 1990, revealing the remains of a prehistoric dwelling. The National Seashore has two visitor centers, one in Eastham and one in Provincetown.

Salt Pond Visitor Center, at the southern end of the Cape, offers guided walks, boat tours, demonstrations, and lectures mid-April–Thanksgiving, as well as evening beach walks, campfire talks, and other programs (many are free) in summer. The center includes a museum with displays on whaling and the old saltworks, as well as early Cape Cod artifacts including scrimshaw, the journal that Mrs. Penniman kept while on a whaling voyage with her husband, and some of the Pennimans' possessions, such as their tea service and the captain's top hat. An air-conditioned auditorium shows films on geology, sea rescues, whaling, Henry David Thoreau, and Guglielmo Marconi. ✉ *Salt Pond Visitor Center, 50 Doane Rd.* ☎ *508/255–3421 for Salt Pond Visitor Center* ⊕ *www.nps.gov/caco* ✉ *Free.*

★ Fort Hill Area

NATIONAL/STATE PARK | The road to the Cape Cod National Seashore's Ft. Hill area ends at a parking area with a lovely view of old farmland traced with stone fences that rolls gently down to Nauset Marsh. The marsh winds around brilliant green grasses and makes its way to the ocean beyond; it is one of the more dramatic views on the Cape. Appreciated by bird-watchers and nature photographers, trails pass through wetlands and to Skiff Hill, an overlook with benches and informative plaques that quote Samuel de Champlain's account of the area from when he moored off Nauset Marsh in 1605. Also on Skiff Hill is Indian Rock, a large boulder moved to the hill from the marsh below. Once used by the local Nauset tribe as a sharpening stone, the rock is cut with deep grooves and smoothed in circles where ax heads were whetted. Trails are open from dawn to dusk. ✉ *Fort Hill Rd., off U.S. 6* ⊕ *www.nps.gov/caco* ✉ *Free.*

Nauset Light

LIGHTHOUSE | Moved 350 feet back from its perch at cliff's edge in 1996, this much-photographed red-and-white lighthouse tops the bluff where the Three Sisters Lighthouses once stood. (The Sisters themselves can be seen in a little landlocked park surrounded by trees; they're reached by paved walkways off Nauset Light Beach's parking lot.) How the lighthouses got there is a long story. In 1838 three brick lighthouses were built 150 feet apart on the bluffs in Eastham overlooking a particularly dangerous area of shoals (shifting underwater sandbars). In 1892, after the eroding cliff dropped the towers into the ocean, they were replaced with three wooden towers. In 1918, two were moved away, as was the third in 1923. Eventually the National Park Service acquired the Three Sisters and brought them together in the inland park, where they would be safe. Lectures on and guided tours of the lighthouses (free, donations accepted) are conducted Sunday early May–October, as well as Tuesday and Wednesday in July and August. ✉ *Ocean View Dr. and Cable Rd.* ☎ *508/240–2612* ⊕ *www.nausetlight.org* ✉ *Free.*

⊕ Beaches

Coast Guard Beach

BEACH—SIGHT | FAMILY | Coast Guard Beach, part of the National Seashore, is a long beach backed by low grass and heathland. A handsome former Coast Guard station is also here, though it's not open to the public. The beach has a very small parking lot that fills up early, so park at the Salt Pond Visitor Center or at the lot up Doane Road from the center and take the free shuttle to the beach. At high tide the size of the beach shrinks considerably, so watch your blanket. ■ TIP→ **Daily parking is $25; the annual seashore pass grants access to all six national park beaches and costs the same as three days of parking. Amenities:** lifeguards; parking (fee); showers; toilets. **Best for:** sunrise; surfing; swimming; walking. ✉ *Off Ocean View Dr.* ⊕ *www.nps.gov/caco/planyourvisit/coast-guard-beach-eastham.htm* ✉ *Parking $25.*

First Encounter Beach

BEACH—SIGHT | FAMILY | A great spot for watching sunsets over Cape Cod Bay, First Encounter Beach is rich in history. Near the parking lot, a bronze marker commemorates the first encounter between local Native Americans and passengers from the *Mayflower,* led by Captain Myles Standish, who explored the entire area for five weeks in 1620 before moving on to Plymouth. The beach is popular with families who favor its warmer, calmer waters and tide pools. **Amenities:** parking (fee); showers; toilets. **Best for:** sunset; swimming; walking; windsurfing. ✉ *End of Samoset Rd., off Rte. 6* ✉ *Parking $20.*

★ Nauset Light Beach

BEACH—SIGHT | Adjacent to Coast Guard Beach, this long, sandy beach is backed by tall dunes, frilly grasses, and heathland. The trail to the Three Sisters lighthouses takes you through a pitch-pine forest. Parking here fills up very quickly in summer; plan to arrive early or you may have to go elsewhere. **■TIP➜ Daily parking is $25; the annual seashore pass grants access to all six national park beaches and costs the same as three days of parking.** **Amenities:** lifeguards; parking (fee); showers; toilets. **Best for:** sunrise; surfing; swimming; walking. ✉ *Off Ocean View Dr.* 🌐 *www.nps.gov/caco/planyourvisit/nauset-light-beach.htm* 🎟 *Parking $25.*

Restaurants

Arnold's Lobster & Clam Bar

$$ | **SEAFOOD** | **FAMILY** | You can't miss this hot spot on the side of Route 6: look for the riot of colorful flowers lining the road and the patient folks waiting in long lines for fried seafood and other fixings. Unusual for a clam shack like this is the full bar, offering beer, wine, mixed drinks, and the house specialty: margaritas. **Known for:** lobster rolls and fried clams; ice cream from Richardson's Dairy Farm; raw bar. [$] *Average main: $21* ✉ *3580 Rte. 6* ☎ *508/255–2575* 🌐 *www.arnoldsrestaurant.com* 💳 *No credit cards* 🕒 *Closed Tues. and Wed. Closed mid-Oct.–Apr.*

Fairway Restaurant and Pizzeria

$$ | **ITALIAN** | **FAMILY** | The friendly, family-run Fairway specializes in Italian comfort food but also has a very popular breakfast. Attached to the Hole in One Donut Shop—a favorite among locals for early-morning coffee and exceptional doughnuts and muffins—the Fairway puts a jar of crayons on every paper-covered table and sells its own brand of root beer. **Known for:** hearty pizza; homemade dessert; eggplant Parmesan. [$] *Average main: $24* ✉ *4295 Rte. 6, North Eastham* ☎ *508/255–3893* 🌐 *www.fairwaycapecod.com* 🕒 *No lunch.*

Hotels

★ Fort Hill Bed and Breakfast

$$$ | **B&B/INN** | This enchanting, adults-only B&B is in an 1864 Greek Revival farmhouse nestled in the tranquil Ft. Hill area—the only lodging within the National Seashore—which is minutes off busy U.S. 6, but steps away from quiet, secluded trails that wind through cedar forests, fields crisscrossed by old stone fences, and a red-maple swamp. **Pros:** pastoral setting; close to nature trails; private and elegant lodging. **Cons:** not for those traveling with children; need to make reservations far in advance; only three rooms. [$] *Rooms from: $375* ✉ *75 Fort Hill Rd.* ☎ *508/240–2870* 🌐 *www.forthillbedandbreakfast.com* 🕒 *Closed mid-Oct.–May* 🛏 *2 suites, 1 cottage* 🍴 *Free breakfast.*

★ Whalewalk Inn & Spa

$$$ | **B&B/INN** | Set amid 3 landscaped acres, this 1830 whaling master's home has wide-plank pine floors, fireplaces, and 19th-century country antiques that provide historical appeal. **Pros:** beautiful grounds; elegantly appointed rooms; decadent spa treatments. **Cons:** not for those traveling with small children; no water views; not an in-town location. [$] *Rooms from: $300* ✉ *220 Bridge Rd.* ☎ *508/255–0617, 800/440–1281* 🌐 *www.whalewalkinn.com* 🕒 *Closed Dec.–Mar.* 🛏 *16 rooms* 🍴 *Free breakfast.*

Wellfleet and South Wellfleet

6 miles north of Eastham, 13 miles southeast of Provincetown.

Still famous for its world-renowned and succulent namesake oysters, Wellfleet is today a tranquil community; many artists and writers call it home. Less than 2 miles wide, it's one of the most attractively developed Cape resort towns, with a number of fine restaurants, historic houses, and art galleries, and a good old Main Street in the village proper.

GETTING HERE AND AROUND

Like many Cape Cod towns, Wellfleet is spread out on either side of U.S. 6. Wellfleet Village is on the bay side, about 3 miles north of the entrance to Marconi Beach. Main Street makes its way past several businesses. A left turn will take you toward the harbor along Commercial Street, which is full of shops and galleries. The center of Wellfleet is quite compact, so it's best to leave your car in one of the public parking areas and take off on foot.

For a scenic loop through a classic Cape landscape near Wellfleet's Atlantic beaches—with scrub and pines on the left, heathland meeting cliffs and ocean below on the right—take LeCount Hollow Road just north of the Marconi Station turnoff. All the beaches on this strip rest at the bottom of a tall grass-covered dune, which lends dramatic character to this outermost shore. Winter storms continue to drastically alter the dunescape; don't be surprised to find a precipitous descent to area beaches.

Some beaches are restricted in the busy summer season to locals and long-term renters; the Beach Sticker Office issues permits so you can visit (you need a proof-of-stay form).

VISITOR INFORMATION

CONTACTS Wellfleet Beach Sticker Office. ☎ 508/349–9818 ⊕ www.wellfleet-ma. gov. **Wellfleet Chamber of Commerce.** ✉ South Wellfleet ☎ 508/349–2510 ⊕ www. wellfleetchamber.com.

Sights

Marconi Station

HISTORIC SITE | On the Atlantic side of the Cape is the site of the first transatlantic wireless station erected on the U.S. mainland. It was from here on January 18, 1903, that Italian radio and wireless-telegraphy pioneer Guglielmo

Marconi sent the first American wireless message to Europe: "most cordial greetings and good wishes" from President Theodore Roosevelt to King Edward VII of England. There's a lookout deck that offers a vantage point of both the Atlantic and Cape Cod Bay. Off the parking lot, a 1½-mile trail and boardwalk lead through the Atlantic White Cedar Swamp, one of the most beautiful trails on the seashore; free maps and guides are available at the trailhead. Marconi Beach, south of the Marconi Station on Marconi Beach Road, is one of the National Seashore's lovely ocean beaches. ✉ *Marconi Site Rd., South Wellfleet* ☎ *508/255–3421* ⊕ *www. nps.gov/caco* ✏ *Free.*

★ **Massachusetts Audubon Wellfleet Bay Wildlife Sanctuary**

NATURE PRESERVE | FAMILY | Encompassing nearly 1,000 acres, this reserve is home to more than 250 species of birds. The jewel of the Massachusetts Audubon Society, the sanctuary is a superb place for walking, birding, and watching the sun set over the salt marsh and bay. The **Esther Underwood Johnson Nature Center** contains two 700-gallon aquariums that offer an up-close look at marine life common to the region's tidal flats and marshlands. From the center you can hike five short nature trails, including a fascinating boardwalk trail that leads over a salt marsh to a small beach, or you can wander through the butterfly garden. ✉ *291 U.S. 6, South Wellfleet* ☎ *508/349–2615* ⊕ *www.massaudubon. org/wellfleetbay* ✏ *$8* ⊗ *Closed Mon.*

Beaches

Extensive storm-induced erosion has made the cliffs to most of Wellfleet's ocean beaches quite steep, so be prepared for a taxing trek up and down the dune slope. Only the Cape Cod National Seashore beach at Marconi has steps; some have handrails to aid in the descent.

Artists and birders flock to the Wellfleet Bay Wildlife Sanctuary, protected by the Massachusetts Audubon Society.

Though this does not apply to the beaches listed in this section, access to several Wellfleet beaches requires resident or temporary resident parking stickers (this includes saltwater and freshwater ponds) in season only, from the last week of June through Labor Day. For the rest of the year anyone can visit these beaches for free. ■TIP→ **Note that people arriving on foot or by bicycle, or after 5 pm, can visit the beaches at any time; the sticker is for parking only.**

Cahoon Hollow Beach

BEACH—SIGHT | The restaurant and music club on top of the dune are the main attractions at Cahoon Hollow Beach, which tends to draw younger and slightly rowdier crowds. It's a big Sunday-afternoon party place. The Beachcomber restaurant has paid parking, which is reimbursed when you buy something to eat or drink. Erosion has made getting to the beach a steep climb. **Amenities:** food and drink; lifeguards; parking (fee); toilets. **Best for:** partiers; surfing; swimming; walking. ✉ *Ocean View Dr., Greater Wellfleet* 🅿 *Parking $20.*

★ Marconi Beach

BEACH—SIGHT | Marconi Beach, part of the Cape Cod National Seashore, is accessed via a very long and steep series of stairs lead down to the beach. It's also popular with both surfers and surf casters looking for striped bass or bluefish. Erosion from fierce storms has compromised beach access. ■TIP→ **Daily parking is $25; the annual seashore pass grants access to all six national park beaches and costs the same as three days of parking.** **Amenities**: lifeguards; parking (fee); showers; toilets. **Best for:** sunrise; surfing; swimming; walking. ✉ *Marconi Beach Rd., off U.S. 6, South Wellfleet* ⊕ *www.nps.gov/caco* 🅿 *Parking $25.*

White Crest Beach

BEACH—SIGHT | White Crest Beach is a prime surfer hangout where the dudes often spend more time waiting for waves than actually riding them. If you're up to the challenge, join one of the spontaneous volleyball games. The other challenge will be working your way down (and then up) to the water: Mother Nature and her fury have made this a steep trek.

Amenities: lifeguards; parking (fee); toilets. **Best for:** sunrise; surfing; swimming; walking. ✉ *Ocean View Dr., Greater Wellfleet* 🎫 *Parking $30.*

🍴 Restaurants

Mac's on the Pier

$$ | **SEAFOOD** | **FAMILY** | Right at Wellfleet Harbor, this ambitious little spot serves some of the freshest seafood around. You can always sit along the pier and soak up the great water views while you chow down on a vast variety of local fish dishes, plus globe-trotting fare like sushi, grilled-scallop burritos, and linguiça sausage sandwiches. **Known for:** excellent sushi; lobster mac and cheese; local oysters. [$] *Average main: $20* ✉ *265 Commercial St., Wellfleet Harbor* ☎ *508/349–9611* 🌐 *www.macsseafood.com* 🕒 *Closed mid-Sept.–late May.*

Moby Dick's

$$ | **SEAFOOD** | **FAMILY** | A meal at this good-natured, rough-hewn fish shack with a hypernautical theme is an absolute Cape Cod tradition for some people. Bring your own libations, and if you need to kill time (the lines are sometimes daunting), stop inside Moby's Cargo, the bustling gift shop next door. **Known for:** the Nantucket Bucket—a pound of whole-belly Monomoy steamers, a pound of native mussels, and corn on the cob served in a bucket; lobster bisque; friendly international staff. [$] *Average main: $22* ✉ *3225 Rte. 6, Greater Wellfleet* ☎ *508/349–9795* 🌐 *www.mobydicksrestaurant.com* 🕒 *Closed Tues. Closed mid-Oct.–Apr.*

★ PB Boulangerie Bistro

$$$ | **FRENCH** | Once a clam shack, this bistro has found new life and caused a serious sensation in this seaside town selling just-baked breads and succulent pastries—by early morning (even in off-season) the line snakes down the ramp and into the parking lot. There's outdoor and indoor seating for breakfast, lunch, and dinner; the latter attracts a multitude of eager patrons in search of the finer flavors of this French kitchen. **Known for:** delectable French pastries; fresh bread; authentic French experience. [$] *Average main: $35* ✉ *15 LeCount Hollow Rd., South Wellfleet* ☎ *508/349–1600* 🌐 *www.pbboulangeriebistro.com* 🕒 *Closed Tues. and Jan.*

★ Wicked Oyster

$$$ | **AMERICAN** | For some of the most innovative fare in Wellfleet, secure a table in this 18th-century clapboard house, known for taking the local catch to flavorful new heights. Breakfast is a favorite here; there's also an outstanding wine list. **Known for:** clam chowder; shrimp spring rolls; local favorite for breakfast and dinner. [$] *Average main: $27* ✉ *50 Main St., Downtown Wellfleet* ☎ *508/349–3455* 🌐 *www.thewickedo.com* 🕒 *No lunch July and Aug.*

Winslow's Tavern

$$ | **SEAFOOD** | This 1805 Federal-style captain's house contains five dining rooms; try for a table on the patio overlooking the center of town. The kitchen specializes in bistro-inspired seafood, mostly with American and Mediterranean preparations. **Known for:** daily oyster happy hour; ideal perch on Main Street; Winslow Wagyu burger. [$] *Average main: $24* ✉ *316 Main St., Downtown Wellfleet* ☎ *508/349–6450* 🌐 *www.winslowstavern.com* 🕒 *Closed mid-Oct.–mid-May.*

🛏 Hotels

Even'tide

$ | **HOTEL** | **FAMILY** | Long a summer favorite, this peaceful motel is set back from the main road, surrounded by 5 acres of trees and lawns, which include a 60-foot indoor pool. **Pros:** short drive or bike ride to Wellfleet's beaches; suites are a bargain for families; direct access to Cape Cod Rail Trail. **Cons:** need a car to get downtown; motel-style rooms; no dining venues. [$] *Rooms from: $169*

What the Shark?   👁

In 2018, Massachusetts had it's first fatal shark attack since 1936—only the fourth recorded in the state's history—when a young man was killed in the waters off Wellfleet. Unfortunately, shark sightings have increased every year. One of the major factors is the increase in the protected seal population on the outer Cape—more seals, means more sharks coming to eat. People share the waters with these native inhabitants and our greatest defense is education and common sense.

Be Shark Smart
A good rule of thumb is, don't swim where there are seals. Avoid murky water and areas where there's evidence of fish feeding. Make sure you pay attention to all signs at the beaches and if the lifeguards say get out of the water, it's best to listen. And, keep an eye out for the purple flag, because if it's flying, white sharks are in the area. Visit the Atlantic White Shark Conservancy's website ⊕ *www.atlanticwhite-shark.org* for more information.

✉ *650 Rte. 6, South Wellfleet* ☎ *508/349-3410, 800/368-0007* ⊕ *www.eventide-motel.com* ◷ *Closed mid-Oct.–Apr.* ⇆ *31 rooms, 9 cottages* ❍ *No meals* ⌇ *1- or 2-wk minimum for cottages in summer.*

🎭 Performing Arts

FILM
★ **Wellfleet Drive-In Theater**
FILM | FAMILY | A classic Cape experience is the Wellfleet Drive-In Theater, located near the Eastham town line. Regulars spend the night in style: chairs, blankets, and picnic baskets. Films start at dusk nightly May–September, and there's also a standard indoor cinema with four screens, a miniature-golf course, and a bar and grill. It's also the home of the beloved Wellfleet Flea Market, held weekends late spring–mid-October. ✉ *51 U.S. 6, South Wellfleet* ☎ *508/349-7176* ⊕ *www.wellfleetcinemas.com.*

THEATER
Wellfleet Harbor Actors Theater
THEATER | The well-regarded Wellfleet Harbor Actors Theater continues its tradition, since 1985, of producing provocative, often edgy, world premieres of American plays, satires, farces, and black comedies

in its mid-May–late-September season. In July and August there are productions aimed for kids, held under a white tent. From October to April, opera lovers can watch performances from the Met, live in HD. ✉ *2357 U.S. 6, Greater Wellfleet* ☎ *508/349-9428* ⊕ *www.what.org.*

🏃 Activities

BOATING
Jack's Boat Rental
BOATING | Jack's rents canoes, kayaks, pedal boats, sailboats, surfboards, boogie boards, and sailboards. Delivery is available for three-plus-day rentals for a fee. ✉ *2616 Rte. 6, at Cahoon Hollow Rd., Greater Wellfleet* ☎ *508/349-9808, 508/349-7553* ⊕ *www.jacksboatrental.com.*

🛍 Shopping

Downtown Wellfleet is best approached on foot; along the way you'll find many art galleries and clothing boutiques. You'll pay a handsome premium for fresh fruits, vegetables, and flowers behind the Town Hall at Hatch's—but what a beautiful display. There's also the Wellfleet Marketplace for groceries, books, beer, and wine. In the height of summer, the price is worth not having to drive 15 miles to Orleans. The Wednesday-morning Wellfleet Farmers' Market, held behind the Congregational Church (200 Main Street), is a fine place to fill your basket with local food. The Wellfleet Flea Market draws people from all over the Cape who drive the distance to find bargains.

FLEA MARKET
Wellfleet Flea Market
OUTDOOR/FLEA/GREEN MARKETS | The giant Wellfleet Flea Market sets up shop in the parking lot of the Wellfleet Drive-In Theater mid-April–June, September, and October, weekends and holiday Mondays 8–3; July and August, Wednesday, Thursday, weekends, and holiday Mondays 8–3. You'll find antiques, cosmetics, kitchen supplies, socks, old advertising posters, books, plants, trinkets, and plenty more among the many vendors. A snack bar and playground keep fatigue at bay. ⊠ 51 Rte. 6, South Wellfleet ☎ 508/349–7176 ⊕ www. wellfleetcinemas.com/flea-market.

Truro

13 miles north of Eastham, 9½ miles southeast of Provincetown.

Today Truro is a town of high dunes, estuaries, and rivers fringed by grasses, rolling moors, and houses sheltered in tiny valleys. It's a popular retreat for artists, writers, politicos, and numerous vacationing psychoanalysts. Edward Hopper summered here from 1930 to 1967, finding the Cape light ideal for his austere brand of realism. One of the largest towns on the Cape in terms of land area—almost 43 square miles—it's also the smallest in population, with about 1,400 year-round residents. Truro is also the Cape's narrowest town, and from a high perch you can see the Atlantic Ocean on one side and Cape Cod Bay on the other.

If you thought neighboring Wellfleet's downtown area was small, wait till you see (or don't see) Truro's. It consists of

a post office, a town hall, and a shop or two—you'll know it by the sign that says "Downtown Truro" at a little plaza entrance. Truro also has a library, a firehouse, and a police station, but that's about all. The North Truro section contains most of the town's accommodations, either along U.S. 6 or fronting the bay along Route 6A, just south of the Provincetown border. Many people who live or vacation in Truro choose it for its easygoing, quiet personality and lack of development—and its proximity to the excitement and commerce of Provincetown.

Settled in 1697, Truro has had several names during its long history. It was originally called Pamet after the local Native Americans, but in 1705 the name was changed to Dangerfield in response to all the sailing mishaps off its shores. "Truroe" was the final choice, named for a Cornish town that homesick settlers thought it resembled; the final "e" was eventually dropped. The town relied on the sea for its income: whaling, shipbuilding, and cod fishing were the main industries.

GETTING HERE AND AROUND
Truro sits near the end of Cape Cod, just 2 miles north of Wellfleet. U.S. 6 is the way most people reach Truro, though the real beauty of the town lies farther afield on back roads that lead to either Cape Cod Bay or the Atlantic. The Cape is fairly narrow here, so you will never find yourself hopelessly lost.

The Provincetown/North Truro Shuttle, run by the Cape Cod Regional Transit Authority, provides a much-needed transportation boost. Traveling along Route 6A, it stops wherever a passenger requests; it runs every 30 minutes and can carry bicycles.

Sights

Highland House Museum

MUSEUM | Home to the Truro Historical Society, the 1907 Highland House was once a grand summer hotel in its time, boasting of many private rooms, meals, and even one shared indoor bathroom. Now a museum, each season a new exhibition heralds Truro's rich history; upstairs you can see how early settlers lived and the unique industries they created to survive. There is also a room dedicated to Edward and Jo Hopper and their art and lives in Truro. Throughout the summer, talks, live music events, and children's programs are offered. ⌧ *6 Highland Light Rd., North Truro* ☎ *508/487–3397* ⊕ *www.trurohistoricalsociety.org* ⊠ *$8* ⊗ *Closed Sun. and closed Oct.–May.*

Highland Light

LIGHTHOUSE | Truly a breathtaking sight, this is the Cape's oldest lighthouse. The first light on this site, powered by 24 whale-oil lamps, began warning ships of Truro's treacherous sandbars in 1797—the dreaded Peaked Hills Bars, to the north, had claimed hundreds of ships. The current light, a 66-foot tower built in 1857, is powered by two 1,000-watt bulbs reflected by a huge Fresnel lens; its beacon is visible for more than 20 miles.

One of four active lighthouses on the Outer Cape, Highland Light has the distinction of being listed in the National Register of Historic Places. Henry David Thoreau used it as a stopover in his travels across the Cape's backside (as the Atlantic side is called). Twenty-five-minute tours of the lighthouse are given daily in summer; especially grand are the special full-moon tours. Children must be 48 inches tall to enter. ⌧ *27 Highland Light Rd., North Truro* ☎ *508/487–1121* ⊕ *www.highlandlighthouse.org* ⊠ *$4* ⊗ *Closed mid-Oct.–mid-May.*

★ Truro Vineyards of Cape Cod

WINERY/DISTILLERY | Owned and operated by the Roberts family, this vineyard has greatly stepped up production, and has begun experimenting with some new varieties. The vineyard makes several notable blends, both red and white. It also makes a red table wine that's flavored with cranberries and known for its unusual bottle, shaped like a lighthouse. Free tours are given daily at 1 and 3, Memorial Day–Columbus Day; tastings are available throughout the day. There is also an aged rum and gin distillery on the property, South Hollow Spirits, which produces organic spirits; tours and tastings available. There are many excellent wine and food events scheduled throughout the summer. It's a great place to picnic, and there's a resident food truck on-site. ⌧ *Rte. 6A, North Truro* ☎ *508/487–6200* ⊕ *www.trurovineyardsofcapecod.com* ⊠ *Free.*

🎭 Performing Arts

Payomet Performing Arts Center of Truro

ARTS CENTERS | **FAMILY** | From mid-June through late September, the Payomet Performing Arts Center of Truro presents a wide range of concerts, plays, films, music, and classes inside a big tent at Cape Cod National Seashore. Past performers have included the Cape Cod Opera, Patty Larkin, and the Shakespeare on the Cape troupe. There's also a kids' summer stage, featuring children's entertainment. ⌧ *29 Old Dewline Rd., North Truro* ☎ *508/349–2929* ⊕ *www.payomet.org.*

Provincetown

9 miles northwest of Wellfleet, 62 miles from Sagamore Bridge.

Many people know that the Pilgrims stopped here at the curved tip of Cape Cod before proceeding to Plymouth. Historical records suggest that an earlier visitor, Thorvald, brother of Viking Leif

Erikson, came ashore here in AD 1004 to repair the keel of his boat and consequently named the area Kjalarness, or Cape of the Keel. In 1602, Bartholomew Gosnold came to Provincetown and named the area Cape Cod after the abundant codfish he found in the local waters.

Incorporated as a town in 1727, Provincetown was for many decades a bustling seaport, with fishing and whaling as its major industries. In the late 19th century, groups of Portuguese fishermen and whalers began to settle here, lending their expertise and culture to an already cosmopolitan town. Fishing is still an important source of income for many Provincetown locals, but today the town ranks among the world's leading whale-watching—rather than whale-hunting—outposts.

Artists began to arrive in the late 1890s to take advantage of the unusual Cape Cod light; in fact, Provincetown is the nation's oldest continuous art colony. By 1916, with five art schools flourishing here, painters' easels were nearly as common as shells on the beach. This bohemian community, along with the availability of inexpensive summer lodgings, attracted young rebels, as well as writers like John Reed (*Ten Days That Shook the World*) and Mary Heaton Vorse (*Footnote to Folly*), who in 1915 began the Cape's first significant theater group, the Provincetown Players. The young, then unknown Eugene O'Neill joined them in 1916, when his *Bound East for Cardiff* premiered in a tiny wharf-side East End fish house.

America's original gay resort, Provincetown today is as appealing to artists as it is to gay and lesbian—as well as straight—tourists. The awareness brought by the AIDS crisis and, more recently, Massachusetts's legalization of same-sex marriage, has turned the town into the most visibly gay vacation community in America.

GETTING HERE AND AROUND

You're at the end of the line here, which means driving to Provincetown in the height of summer often means slogging through slow traffic. Congestion is heaviest around Wellfleet and it can be slow going. Driving the 3 miles of Provincetown's main downtown thoroughfare, Commercial Street, in season could take forever. No matter, there are plenty of pretty vistas on the way along U.S. 6 and Route 6A. Parking is not one of Provincetown's better amenities (there are two large, paid central parking lots if you can find a space), so bike and foot are the best and most popular ways to explore the downtown area. But Provincetown can also be reached by air (year-round via Cape Air from Boston) or ferry (multiple options from Boston in season).

The Provincetown/North Truro Shuttle, run by the Cape Cod Regional Transit Authority, provides a much-needed seasonal transportation boost in season (mid-June–mid-September). Once in Provincetown, the shuttle heads up Bradford Street, with alternating trips to Herring Cove Beach, Race Point Beach, Pilgrim Park, and the Provincetown Airport. Bikes are accommodated.

BUS CONTACTS Cape Cod Regional Transit Authority. ☎ *800/352–7155* ⊕ *www.capecodtransit.org.*

VISITOR INFORMATION

CONTACTS Provincetown Business Guild. ✉ *Downtown Center* ☎ *508/487–2313, 800/637–8696* ⊕ *www.ptown.org.* **Provincetown Chamber of Commerce.** ✉ *Downtown Center* ☎ *508/487–3424* ⊕ *www.ptownchamber.com.*

◉ Sights

★ Commercial Street

NEIGHBORHOOD | Take a casual stroll by the many architectural styles—Greek Revival, Victorian, Second Empire, and Gothic, to name a few—used in the design of the impressive houses for wealthy sea captains and merchants. The center of town is where you'll find the crowds and the best people-watching, especially if you try to find an empty spot on the benches in front of the exquisitely renovated Town Hall. The East End has a number of nationally renowned galleries; the West End has a number of small inns with neat lawns and elaborate gardens. There is one-way vehicle traffic on this street, though pedestrians dominate the pavement, particularly in July and August. Commercial Street runs parallel to the water, so there is always a patch of sand close at hand, should you need a break. ✉ *Provincetown* ⊕ *ptowntourism.com.*

Pilgrim Monument

MEMORIAL | The first thing you'll see in Provincetown is this grandiose edifice, somewhat out of proportion to the rest of the low-rise town. The monument commemorates the Pilgrims' first landing in the New World and their signing of the Mayflower Compact (the first Colonial American rules of self-governance) before they set off to explore the mainland. Climb the 116 steps and 60 short ramps of the 252-foot-high tower for a panoramic view—dunes on one side, harbor on the other, and the entire bay side of Cape Cod beyond. At the tower's base is a museum of Lower Cape and Provincetown history, with exhibits on whaling, shipwrecks, and scrimshaw. There are also arrowheads, tools, and images of the local Native American Wampanoag tribe, the town's first fire engine, a recreation of a 19th century sea captain's parlor, a diorama of the Mayflower Compact being signed, and more. ✉ *1 High Pole Hill Rd., Downtown Center* ☎ *508/487–1310* ⊕ *www.pilgrim-monument.org* 💰 *$17.*

★ Province Lands Visitor Center

NATIONAL/STATE PARK | Part of the Cape Cod National Seashore, the Province Lands stretch from High Head in Truro to the tip of Provincetown and are scattered with ponds, cranberry bogs, and scrub. More than 7 miles of bike and walking trails lace through forests of stunted pines, beech, and oak and across desertlike expanses of rolling dunes. At the visitor center you'll find short films on local geology and exhibits on the life of the dunes and the shore. You can also pick up information on guided walks, birding trips, lectures, and other programs, as well as on the Province Lands' pristine beaches, Race Point and Herring Cove, and walking, biking, and horse trails. Don't miss the awe-inspiring panoramic view of the dunes and the surrounding ocean from the observation deck. This terrain provides optimal conditions for the deer tick, which can cause Lyme disease, so use extra caution. ✉ *171 Race Point Rd., east of U.S. 6, Greater Provincetown* ☎ *508/487–1256* ⊕ *www.nps.gov/caco* 💰 *Free* ⊘ *Visitor center closed Nov.–Apr.*

★ Provincetown Art Association and Museum

LOCAL INTEREST | Founded in 1914 to collect and exhibit the works of artists with Provincetown connections, this facility has a 1,650-piece permanent collection, displayed in changing exhibitions that mix up-and-comers with established 20th-century figures like Milton Avery, Philip Evergood, William Gropper, Charles Hawthorne, Robert Motherwell, Claes Oldenburg, Man Ray, John Singer Sargent, Andy Warhol, and Agnes Weinrich. A stunning contemporary wing has greatly expanded the exhibit space. The museum store carries books of local interest, including works by or about area artists and authors, as well as posters, crafts, cards, and gift items. Art classes (single day and longer) offer the opportunity to study under such talents as Hilda Neily, Selina Trieff, and Doug Ritter. ✉ *460 Commercial St., East End* ☎ *508/487–1750* ⊕ *www.paam.org* 💰 *$13* ⊘ *Closed Mon.–Wed. Oct.–May.*

Beaches

Herring Cove Beach

BEACH—SIGHT | FAMILY | Herring Cove Beach is relatively calm and warm for a National Seashore beach, but it's not as pretty as some because its parking lot isn't hidden behind dunes. It's close to town, so in warm weather it's always crowded. The lot to the right of the bathhouse is a great place to watch the sunset. ■ **TIP→ Daily parking is $25; the annual seashore pass grants access to all six national park beaches and costs $60.** **Amenities:** food and drink; lifeguards; parking (fee); toilets; showers. **Best for:** sunset; swimming; walking. ✉ *Provincetown* 🌐 *www.nps.gov/caco* 🎫 *From late June–early Sept. $25 per vehicle.*

★ Race Point Beach

BEACH—SIGHT | FAMILY | Race Point Beach, one of the Cape Cod National Seashore beaches in Provincetown, has a wide swath of sand stretching far off into the distance around the point and Coast Guard station. Because of its position facing north, the beach gets sun all day long. Keep an eye out for whales offshore; it's also a popular fishing spot. ■ **TIP→ Daily parking is $25; the annual seashore pass grants access to all six national park beaches is $60.** **Amenities:** lifeguards; parking (fee); showers; toilets. **Best for:** sunrise; sunset; surfing; swimming; walking. ✉ *Race Point Rd., east of U.S. 6* ☎ *508/487–1256* 🌐 *www.nps.gov/caco* 🎫 *From late June–early Sept. $25 per vehicle, $10 per person.*

Restaurants

★ The Canteen

$ | AMERICAN | Bustling from breakfast until 11 pm, this casual spot specializes in classics like grilled cheese sandwiches, hand-cut fries, and local seafood in a lively spot. Order at the counter, then grab a seat at one of the picnic tables street-side or in a little shady grove out back; there's also a large beer menu with New England offerings, a good selection of wines, and delicious house-made lemonade and iced tea. **Known for:** hot or cold lobster rolls; raw bar; great atmosphere out back. [$] *Average main: $13* ✉ *225 Commercial St., Downtown Center* ☎ *508/487–3800* 🌐 *www.thecanteenptown.com.*

Lobster Pot

$$$ | SEAFOOD | Provincetown's Lobster Pot, a mainstay for 40 years, is fit to do battle with all the lobster shanties anywhere (and everywhere) else on the Cape; although it's often jammed with tourists, the crowds reflect the generally high quality and the water views can't be beat. The hardworking kitchen turns out classic New England cooking: lobsters, generous and filling seafood platters, and some of the best chowder around. **Known for:** locally award-winning clam chowder; local icon; extensive menu. [$] *Average main: $27* ✉ *321 Commercial St., Downtown Center* ☎ *508/487–0842* 🌐 *www.ptownlobsterpot.com* 🕒 *Closed in winter.*

★ The Mews Restaurant & Cafe

$$$ | AMERICAN | This perennial favorite with magnificent harbor views focuses on seafood and grilled meats with a cross-cultural flair (there's also a lighter bistro menu for smaller appetites). The view of the bay from the bar is nearly perfect, and the gentle lighting makes this a romantic spot to have a drink. **Known for:** waterfront setting; ambience; two levels of dining. [$] *Average main: $27* ✉ *429 Commercial St., East End* ☎ *508/487–1500* 🌐 *mewsptown.com.*

Napi's

$$$ | ECLECTIC | The food and the interior share a penchant for unusual, striking juxtapositions—a classical sculpture in front of an abstract canvas, for instance, or cod amandine and Brazilian-style shrimp (sautéed with garlic, herbs, and lime). The local art collection on display here is worthy and significant; Napi has been collecting gems for many, many years. **Known for:**

international flavors; Early Bird specials a steal; ample vegetarian options. $ *Average main: $28* ✉ *7 Freeman St., Downtown Center* ☎ *508/487–1145* ⊕ *www.napisptown.com* ⊗ *No lunch May–Sept.*

★ The Pointe

$$$ | AMERICAN | Inside the snazzy Crowne Pointe Inn, this intimate, casually handsome restaurant occupies the parlor and sunroom of a grand sea captain's mansion and serves finely crafted, healthful, modern American food with daily specials focused on local ingredients. There's a substantial wine list, with more than a hundred selections to choose from, as well as a large martini menu. **Known for:** superb service; cocktails in the lounge; truffle popcorn. $ *Average main: $27* ✉ *Crowne Pointe Inn, 82 Bradford St., Downtown Center* ☎ *508/487–2365* ⊕ *www.provincetown-restaurant.com* ⊗ *Closed Mon.–Wed. No lunch.*

Red Inn

$$$ | AMERICAN | Inside the striking red house on P-town's West End (also an enchanting B&B with rooms starting at $305 in summer), the Red Inn is perhaps even better known as one of the Outer Cape's most romantic dining destinations—the views are simply stunning. The menu changes with the season, but always features the freshest local seafood and dishes like lamb chops seasoned with spices. **Known for:** exquisite location; raw bar happy hour; homemade desserts. $ *Average main: $34* ✉ *15 Commercial St., West End* ☎ *508/487–7334* ⊕ *www.theredinn. com* ⊗ *Closed Jan.–mid-Apr.*

 Hotels

★ Brass Key

$$$ | B&B/INN | One of the Cape's most luxurious small resorts, this meticulously kept year-round getaway comprises a beautifully restored main house—originally a sea captain's home built in 1828—and several other carefully groomed buildings and cottages all centered on a beautifully landscaped pool area. **Pros:** ultraposh rooms; beautiful and secluded grounds; pool on-site. **Cons:** among the highest rates in town; not for those with children; significant minimum-stay requirements in summer. $ *Rooms from: $375* ✉ *67 Bradford St., Downtown Center* ☎ *508/487–9005, 800/842–9858* ⊕ *www.brasskey.com* ⤴ *43 rooms* ❑| *Free breakfast* ☞ *Pets allowed in certain rooms.*

★ Crowne Pointe Historic Inn and Spa

$$$ | B&B/INN | Created meticulously from six different buildings, this inn hasn't a single detail left unattended—period furniture and antiques fill common areas and guest rooms; a queen-size bed is the smallest you'll find, dressed in 300-thread-count linens; treats are left on the pillow for nightly turndown service; and there's complimentary wine and cheese in the afternoon. **Pros:** great on-site amenities like the full-service Shui Spa; posh and luxurious room decor; professional and well-trained staff. **Cons:** among the highest rates in town; significant minimum-stay requirements in summer; no children allowed. $ *Rooms from: $340* ✉ *82 Bradford St., Downtown Center* ☎ *508/413–2213, 877/276–9631* ⊕ *www.crownepointe.com* ⤴ *40 rooms* ❑| *Free breakfast.*

Eben House

$$$ | B&B/INN | A rigorous interior renovation in 2015 on this 1776 property—among the oldest of the few remaining brick colonials in town—took it from sad to chic. **Pros:** simple, stunning interior design; exceptional service; saltwater pool. **Cons:** some rooms accessed via steep stairs; on busy road; no children under age 16. $ *Rooms from: $300* ✉ *90 Bradford St., Downtown Center* ☎ *508/487–0386* ⊕ *www.ebenhouse. com* ⊗ *Closed weekdays Nov.–Apr.* ⤴ *14 rooms* ❑| *Free breakfast.*

Harbor Hotel Provincetown

$$$ | HOTEL | Directly across the street from the bay on the eastern edge of town, this hip and sleek hotel has a lively vibe, with a poolside bar, outdoor fire pit, and Whaler's Lounge, which is home to movie nights, live music, cocktails, and food. **Pros:** hotel is on the shuttle stop to town; great views and easy access to bay beach; great amenities like free bicycles. **Cons:** very long walk to town center; bay-view rooms closed in winter; additional amenity fee charged. $ *Rooms from: $309* ⊠ *698 Commercial St., Greater Provincetown* ☎ *800/422–4224* ⊕ *www.harborhotelptown.com* ⇆ *129 rooms* ⦿ *No meals.*

Salt House Inn

$$ | B&B/INN | Though one side of this aged beauty sits right on busy Conwell Street, the interior is all serenity, bathed in white, an ideal backdrop for the brilliant wood floors, statement furniture, and art pieces—think Colonial farmhouse with a decidedly modern and hip edge. **Pros:** in-town location, walk to everything; on-site concierge service is extremely helpful without being intrusive; on-site complimentary parking. **Cons:** some rooms are quite small; some rooms extremely close to the road; some rooms with detached (but private) bathroom. $ *Rooms from: $275* ⊠ *6 Conwell St., Downtown Center* ☎ *508/487–1911* ⊕ *www.salthouseinn.com* ⊗ *Closed Nov.–Mar.* ⇆ *15 rooms* ⦿ *Free breakfast.*

★ White Porch Inn

$$ | B&B/INN | This sterling, light-filled B&B offers a soothing respite from the bustle of town; opt for one of the carriage-house rooms for even more seclusion. **Pros:** a selection of wines and small bites are set out each afternoon for guests; steps from East End shopping and dining; enthusiastic and friendly staff. **Cons:** somewhat long walk to West End shopping and businesses; not for those with children; limited parking. $ *Rooms from: $299* ⊠ *7 Johnson St., Downtown Center* ☎ *508/364–2549,* *508/487–0592* ⊕ *www.whiteporchinn.com* ⇆ *10 rooms* ⦿ *Free breakfast.*

ⓨ Nightlife

Provincetown is a party town. While the nightclub scene is decidedly gay, in most venues there is a clear "straight-friendly" welcome.

BARS

Paramount

DANCE CLUBS | Part of the Crown & Anchor complex of entertainment options, the Paramount is the hotel's main nightlife venue, offering poolside dancing to skilled DJs—including many names from the top international dance scene—on many nights. It's also host to cabaret performances and live theater. Next door is a video bar and a male-only leather bar, The Vault. Cover charges vary. ⊠ *247 Commercial St., Downtown Center* ☎ *508/487–1430* ⊕ *www.onlyatthecrown. com/paramount.*

ⓝ Performing Arts

During the busy summer season, hawkers in full-on drag or wearing very little at all compete with the din on Commercial Street to announce showtimes of the evening's performances. Pick your pleasure: dancing poolside at a few big nightclubs; watching talented drag performers strut their stuff; enjoying excellent live theater; strolling between art galleries; or sipping colorful cocktails at the water's edge. Much of the summer entertainment is first-class, drawing top Broadway and cabaret performers from New York City and beyond, offered at prices that would be a bargain back home.

THEATER

The Art House

CONCERTS | Every season showcases a powerhouse of performances. Hot tickets include the Broadway @ concert series, hosted by pianist Seth Rudestsky, with such previous guests as Neil

Patrick Harris and David Burtka, Matthew Broderick and Sarah Jessica Parker, Sam Harris, and Lea DeLaria. Other acts, like beloved drag queen Varla Jean Merman and the Well-Strung Quartet, light up the stage every summer. ✉ *214 Commercial St., Downtown Center* ☎ *508/487–9222* ⊕ *www.ptownarthouse.com.*

Post Office Cafe & Cabaret

MUSIC | Downstairs, it's a lively place for breakfast and lunch, with tables looking out onto Commercial Street. Upstairs, you can expect even jauntier—and often playfully raunchy—entertainment in the nightly cabaret offerings. ✉ *303 Commercial St., Downtown Center* ☎ *508/487–0006* ⊕ *www.postofficecabaret.com.*

The Provincetown Theater

DANCE | This year-round venue provides excellent theater, showcasing many new works, as well as more unusual fare. In addition, there are dance performances, readings by playwrights, and workshops. ✉ *238 Bradford St., East End* ☎ *508/487–7487* ⊕ *www.provincetowntheater.org.*

🏃 Activities

TOURS

★ **Art's Dune Tours**

TOUR—SPORTS | Art's Dune Tours has been taking eager passengers into the dunes of Province Lands since 1946. A bumpy but controlled ride (about one hour) transports you through sometimes surreal sandy vistas peppered with beach grass, along a shoreline patrolled by seagulls and sandpipers. Head out at sunset for a stunning ride, available with or without a clambake feast; on Sunday there is a special Race Point Lighthouse Tour. ✉ *4 Standish St., Downtown Center* ☎ *508/487–1950, 800/894–1951* ⊕ *www.artsdunetours.com* 🎫 *From $33* ☽ *Closed mid-Nov.–mid-Apr.*

WHALE-WATCHING

★ **Dolphin Fleet**

WHALE-WATCHING | FAMILY | Tours are led by scientists from the Center for Coastal Studies in Provincetown, who provide commentary while collecting data on the whales they've been monitoring for years. They know many of them by name and will tell you about their habits and histories. These trips are most often exciting and incredibly thrilling with close-up encounters. ■ TIP→ **Look for discount coupons in local free brochures and publications, as well as online.** ✉ *Chamber of Commerce Bldg., MacMillan Wharf, Downtown Center* ☎ *508/240–3636, 800/826–9300* ⊕ *www.whalewatch.com* 🎫 *From $55.*

🛍 Shopping

Provincetown shopping can be artistic, sophisticated, whimsical, and even downright tawdry—a perfect reflection of the town's very character. There is also a wide selection of touristy schlock. You'll find exquisite original art galleries primarily on the east end but also next to taffy and fudge shops, high-end home decor and designer clothing boutiques next to tattoo parlors and T-shirt shops, and even boutiques specializing in alternative interests (think leather and adult novelties). Most shopping is concentrated along Commercial Street.

ART GALLERIES

★ **Julie Heller Gallery**

ART GALLERIES | Julie Heller Gallery has contemporary artists as well as some Provincetown icons. The gallery has works from the Sol Wilson and Milton Avery estates, as well as from such greats as Robert Motherwell, Agnes Weinrich, and Blanche Lazzell. There's another location at 465 Commercial Street. ✉ *2 Gosnold St., Downtown Center* ☎ *508/487–9607* ⊕ *www.juliehellergallery.com.*

The Schoolhouse Gallery

ART GALLERIES | The Schoolhouse Gallery, in an 1844 former school, shows the works of more than 50 local and national artists (modern and contemporary), as well as that of printmakers and photographers. ⊠ *494 Commercial St., East End* ☎ *508/487–4800* ⊕ *www.galleryschoolhouse.com.*

SPECIALTY STORES

Marine Specialties

SPECIALTY STORES | Marine Specialties is full of treasures, knickknacks, and clothing. Here you can purchase some very reasonably priced casual- and military-style clothing, as well as seashells, marine supplies, stained-glass lamps, candles, rubber sharks (you get the idea), and prints of old advertisements. ⊠ *235 Commercial St., Downtown Center* ☎ *508/487–1730.*

Tim's Used Books

BOOKS/STATIONERY | Set back off the street at the end of a wooden walkway, Tim's Used Books is packed with volumes of volumes—rooms of used-but-in-good-shape books, including some rare and out-of-print texts. It's a great place to lose track of time. ⊠ *242 Commercial St., Downtown Center* ☎ *508/487–0005.*

Martha's Vineyard

Far less developed than Cape Cod—thanks to a few local conservation organizations—yet more cosmopolitan than neighboring Nantucket, Martha's Vineyard is an island with a double life. From Memorial Day through Labor Day, the quieter (some might say the real) Vineyard quickens into a vibrant, star-studded place.

The busy main port, Vineyard Haven, welcomes day-trippers fresh off ferries and private yachts to browse in its array of shops. Oak Bluffs, where pizza and ice-cream emporiums reign supreme, has the air of a Victorian boardwalk.

Edgartown is flooded with seekers of chic who wander tiny streets that hold boutiques, stately whaling captains' homes, and charming inns.

Summer regulars have included a host of celebrities over the years, among them Oprah Winfrey, Carly Simon, Ted Danson, Spike Lee, and Diane Sawyer; former president Barack Obama and his family vacationed here nearly every summer of his two terms in the Oval Office. If you're planning to stay overnight on a summer weekend, be sure to make reservations well in advance; spring is not too early. Things stay busy on September and October weekends, a favorite time for weddings, but begin to slow down soon after. In many ways the Vineyard's off-season persona is even more appealing than its summer self, with more time to linger over pastoral and ocean vistas, free from the throngs of cars, bicycles, and mopeds.

GETTING ORIENTED

The island is roughly triangular, measuring about 20 miles east to west and 10 miles north to south. The west end of the Vineyard, known as Up-Island—from the nautical expression of going "up" in degrees of longitude as you sail west—is more rural and wild than the eastern Down-Island end, comprising Vineyard Haven, Oak Bluffs, and Edgartown.

Vineyard Haven (Tisbury). One of the island's busiest towns, Vineyard Haven sees ferry traffic all year long. A fairly compact downtown area keeps most shopping and dining options within easy reach.

Oak Bluffs. Once a Methodist campground, Oak Bluffs is a little less refined than the other towns. It has a vibrant vacation vibe, with lots of nightlife, dining, and shopping.

Edgartown. Dominated by the impeccably kept homes of 19th-century sea captains, Edgartown has a sense of sophistication. There's great history here, and several museums tell the story.

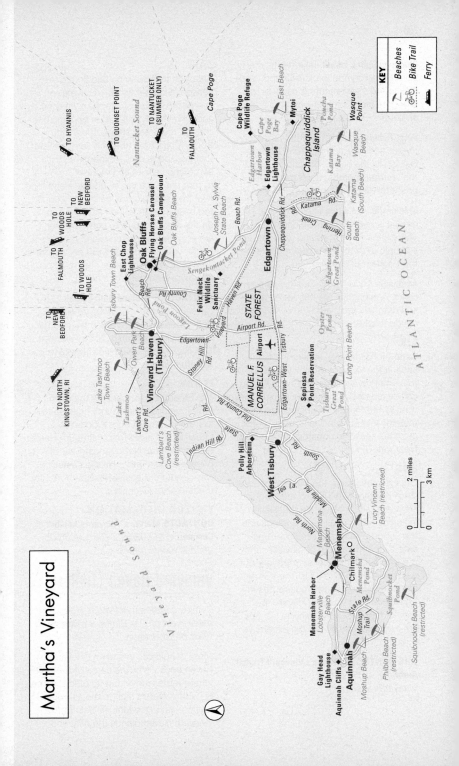

Martha's Vineyard

KEY

Beaches

Bike Trail

Ferry

TO HYANNIS

TO QUONSET POINT

TO NANTUCKET (SUMMER ONLY)

Nantucket Sound

TO NEW BEDFORD

TO WOODS HOLE

TO FALMOUTH

TO WOODS HOLE

TO NEW BEDFORD

TO FALMOUTH

TO NORTH KINGSTOWN, RI

Cape Poge

Cape Poge Wildlife Refuge

East Beach

Mytoi

Cape Poge Bay

Poucha Pond

Wasque Point

Edgartown Harbor

Edgartown Lighthouse

Chappaquiddick Island

Katama Bay

Wasque Beach

Oak Bluffs

East Chop Lighthouse

Flying Horses Carousel

Oak Bluffs Campground

Oak Bluffs Beach

Joseph A. Sylvia State Beach

Beach Rd.

Katama Rd.

Katama (South Beach)

South Beach

Herring Creek

Chappaquiddick Rd.

Tisbury Town Beach

Beach Rd.

County Rd.

Sengekontacket Pond

Felix Neck Wildlife Sanctuary

Edgartown

Edgartown Great Pond

ATLANTIC OCEAN

Lagoon Pond

Vineyard Haven Rd.

STATE FOREST

Oyster Pond

Long Point Beach

Owen Park Beach

Vineyard Haven (Tisbury)

Edgartown-Vineyard Haven Rd.

Airport Rd.

Airport

Tisbury Rd.

Lake Tashmoo Town Beach

Lake Tashmoo

Edgartown-West Tisbury Rd.

Sepiessa Point Reservation

Tisbury Great Pond

Lambert's Cove Rd.

Lambert's Cove Beach (restricted)

Stoney Hill Rd.

MANUEL F. CORRELLUS

Indian Hill Rd.

State Rd.

Polly Hill Arboretum

West Tisbury

South Rd.

Lucy Vincent Beach (restricted)

Tea La.

Middle Rd.

Menemsha Rd.

North Rd.

Menemsha Beach

Menemsha

Chilmark

Menemsha Pond

Squibnocket Pond

Menemsha Harbor

Lobsterville Beach

State Rd.

Moshup Trail

Squibnocket Beach (restricted)

Gay Head Lighthouse

Aquinnah Cliffs

Aquinnah

Moshup Beach

Philbin Beach (restricted)

Squibnocket Beach (restricted)

Vineyard Sound

2 miles

3 km

0

Chappaquiddick Island. Take the tiny ferry from Edgartown to explore Chappaquiddick Island's vast nature preserves. It's a favorite place for bird-watchers and anglers.

West Tisbury. There's beautiful farm country out this way, and the 1859 Grange Hall is still the center of action. During the warmer months, don't miss the bountiful West Tisbury Farmers' Market.

Menemsha. An active fishing harbor, Menemsha is known for its splendid sunsets. There are a few shops and galleries, and a couple of excellent take-out spots for the freshest of seafood.

Aquinnah. Known until recently as Gay Head, Aquinnah is famous for its grand and dramatic red clay cliffs, as well as the resident lighthouse.

AIR

Cape Air has regular, year-round flight service to the island from Hyannis, Boston, and Providence's T. F. Green Airport and seasonal service (starting mid-June) from White Plains, NY (including a bus transfer to and from Manhattan). JetBlue provides seasonal nonstop service from New York–JFK.

BUS

Once on the island, the Martha's Vineyard Transit Authority (VTA) provides regular service to all six towns on the island, including stops at all ferry landings and the airport. The buses can accommodate a limited number of bicycles, and the island has an excellent network of well-maintained bike trails. The VTA also has free in-town shuttle-bus routes in Edgartown and Vineyard Haven. You can also get around by bicycle (rentals are available) and by taxi (an expensive option).

BUS CONTACTS Martha's Vineyard Transit Authority. (*VTA*) ☎ *508/693–9940* ⊕ *www. vineyardtransit.com.*

CAR

Although traffic can be bad during the season, it can be handy to have a car in order to see all of Martha's Vineyard and travel freely. Instead of bringing one over on the Steamship Authority ferry from Woods Hole (the only ferry service that transports cars—expensively), it's sometimes easier and more economical to rent one once you're on the island for a few days of exploring, particularly during the busy season when car reservations on the ferry are hard to come by. Don't expect a bargain for on-island rentals either; you'll pay about $180 per day for a Jeep. The island does its best to discourage extra automobile traffic.

CONTACTS A-A Island Auto Rental. ⊠ *5 Corners, 4 Water St., Vineyard Haven* ☎ *508/696–5300* ⊕ *www.mvautorental. com.* **Sun 'n' Fun Rentals.** ⊠ *28 Lake Ave., Oak Bluffs* ☎ *508/693–5457* ⊕ *www. sunnfunrentals.com.*

FERRY

The Steamship Authority is the main ferry (operating year-round) heading to Martha's Vineyard from Woods Hole. Other ferries leave from Falmouth Harbor (Island Queen); North Kingstown, RI (Vineyard Fast Ferry); Hyannis (Hy-Line); New Bedford (Seastreak); New York City (Seastreak, seasonally).

VISITOR INFORMATION

CONTACTS Martha's Vineyard Chamber of Commerce. ☎ *508/693–7589, 800/505–4815* ⊕ *www.mvy.com.*

Vineyard Haven (Tisbury)

7 miles southeast of Woods Hole, 3½ miles west of Oak Bluffs, 8 miles northwest of Edgartown.

Most people call this town Vineyard Haven because of the name of the port where ferries arrive, but its official name is Tisbury. Not as high-toned as Edgartown or as honky-tonk as Oak Bluffs, Vineyard Haven blends the past and present with a touch of the bohemian. Visitors step off the ferry right into the bustle of the harbor, one block from the shops and restaurants of Main Street.

GETTING HERE AND AROUND

Vineyard Haven sees ferry traffic year-round, so this port town is always active. If you're traveling without a car, you can get around by taxi or the white buses run by Martha's Vineyard Transit Authority. Bike, scooter, and car rentals are also possibilities. Much of the downtown area is easily explored on foot, and a good number of the lodgings are within reach. Vineyard Haven is 3½ miles west of Oak Bluffs.

Beaches

Lake Tashmoo Town Beach

BEACH—SIGHT | FAMILY | Swimmers have access to the warm, relatively shallow, brackish Lake Tashmoo from this beach—or cooler, gentler Vineyard Sound. It's a favorite spot for surf casters. **Amenities:** lifeguards; parking (no fee); toilets. **Best for:** sunset; swimming. ⊠ *End of Herring Creek Rd.* ⊕ *www.mvy.com/beaches. html.*

Owen Park Beach

BEACH—SIGHT | FAMILY | This small, sandy harbor beach is just steps away from the ferry terminal in Vineyard Haven, making it a great spot to catch some last rays before heading home. **Amenities:** lifeguards; toilets. **Best for:** swimming. ⊠ *Off Main St.* ⊕ *www.mvy.com/beaches.html.*

Tisbury Town Beach

BEACH—SIGHT | This public beach is next to the Vineyard Haven Yacht Club. It is only accessed by foot or bike: no parking here. But it's a nice place for a picnic. **Amenities:** none. **Best for:** swimming. ⊠ *End of Owen Little Way, off Main St.* ⊕ *www.mvy.com/beaches.html.*

🍴 Restaurants

Beach Road

$$$ | SEAFOOD | With its ample windows looking out to the serene lagoon, lofted ceilings, and mellow globe lighting held aloft by sturdy ropes, the decor aptly reflects the kitchen's "sea-to-table" theme for its seasonally inspired and locally sourced offerings. The massive bar is a popular spot for dining and cocktails. **Known for:** $1 nightly oyster happy hour; intriguing small plates; elegant farm-house atmosphere. $ *Average main: $28* ⊠ *79 Beach Rd.* ☎ *508/693–8582* ⊕ *www.beachroadmv.com.*

Black Dog Tavern

$$$ | AMERICAN | FAMILY | This island landmark—more popular with tourists than locals—lies just steps from the ferry terminal in Vineyard Haven. The dining room—roaring fireplace, dark-wood walls, maritime memorabilia, and a grand view of the water—makes everyone feel so at home; there's additional seating on the patio when the weather allows. **Known for:** menu featuring local fish, chowders, and chops; hour-long wait for breakfast in July and August; welcoming atmosphere. $ *Average main: $25* ⊠ *20 Beach St. Ext.* ☎ *508/693–9223* ⊕ *www. theblackdog.com.*

🛏 Hotels

Crocker House Inn

$$$$ | B&B/INN | This casual 1890 farm-house-style inn is tucked into a quiet lane off Main Street, minutes from the ferries and Owen Park Beach. **Pros:** great owners; short walk from town; easygoing vibe. **Cons:** not for those with small children; books up quickly in summer; pricey. $ *Rooms from: $450* ⊠ *12 Crocker Ave.* ☎ *508/693–1151, 800/772–0206* ⊕ *www.crockerhouseinn. com* ↪ *8 rooms* ⟡| *Free breakfast.*

Mansion House

$$ | HOTEL | There has been a hostelry on this conveniently located Main Street site just above Vineyard Haven Harbor since 1794. **Pros:** on-site spa; steps from shopping and ferry; light-filled rooms. **Cons:** location can be a little noisy; pool and spa can be busy with nonhotel guests; limited parking. $ *Rooms from: $250* ⊠ *9 Main St.* ☎ *509/693–2200, 800/332–4112* ⊕ *www.mvmansionhouse.com* ⟿ *40 rooms* ⫯⊙⫯ *Free breakfast.*

🎭 Performing Arts

THEATER
Vineyard Playhouse

FILM | The Vineyard Playhouse has a year-round schedule of professional productions. From mid-June through early September, a troupe performs drama, classics, and comedies on the air-conditioned main stage. Summer Shakespeare and other productions take place at the natural amphitheater at Tashmoo Overlook on State Road in Vineyard Haven—bring insect repellent and a blanket or lawn chair. The theater is wheelchair accessible and provides hearing devices. ⊠ *24 Church St.* ☎ *508/696–6300* ⊕ *mvplayhouse.org/theater.*

🛍 Shopping

Vineyard Haven has a nice concentration of shopping along Main Street, which is intersected with several shorter streets that also hold shops of interest. Conveniently, since many people arrive by ferry without their vehicles, the majority of shopping is easily accessible right from the ferry docks. You won't find any large-scale chain stores here—rather, a good variety of upscale clothing shops, galleries, and other independently owned businesses selling everything from kitchenware to luxury bath products.

Oak Bluffs

3½ miles east of Vineyard Haven.

Circuit Avenue is the bustling center of the Oak Bluffs action, with most of the town's shops, bars, and restaurants. Colorful gingerbread-trimmed guesthouses and food and souvenir joints enliven Oak Bluffs Harbor, once the setting for several grand hotels. This small town is more high-spirited than haute, more fun than refined. ■ TIP→ **Look for the yellow tourist information booth at the bottom of Circuit Avenue. It's open June–mid-October and is staffed with helpful folks from the area.**

GETTING HERE AND AROUND
Oak Bluff is the terminal for seasonal ferries. If you have a car, it's best to find a space and leave it while you walk, bike, or take the white buses operated by Martha's Vineyard Transit Authority.

👁 Sights

East Chop Lighthouse
LIGHTHOUSE | This lighthouse was built out of cast iron in 1876 to replace an 1828 tower (used as part of a semaphore system) that burned down. The 40-foot structure stands high atop a 79-foot bluff with spectacular views of Nantucket Sound. Open Sunday evenings at sunset (from 6 pm) in summer. ⊠ *E. Chop Dr.* ☎ *508/627–4441* ⊕ *mvmuseum.org/visit/east-chop* ⟿ *$5.*

Flying Horses Carousel
CAROUSEL | FAMILY | A National Historic Landmark, this is the nation's oldest continuously operating merry-go-round. Handcrafted in 1876—the horses have real horsehair and glass eyes—and brought from Coney Island in 1884, the ride gives children a taste of entertainment from an era before smartphones. Kids delight in trying to grab the brass ring for a free ride. ⊠ *15 Lake Ave.* ☎ *508/693–9481* ⊕ *vineyardtrust.org/property/flying-horses-carousel* ⟿ *$3.*

★ Oak Bluffs Campground

NEIGHBORHOOD | This 34-acre warren of streets is tightly packed with more than 300 gaily painted Carpenter Gothic Victorian cottages with wedding-cake trim; they date mainly to the 1860s and '70s, when visitors coming for Methodist revivalist services began to lease lots and build houses for summer use. As you wander through this fairy-tale setting, imagine it on a balmy summer evening, lighted by the warm glow of paper lanterns hung from every cottage porch. This describes the scene on Illumination Night at the end of the Camp Meeting season, which is attended these days by some fourth- and fifth-generation cottagers—and newcomers: some houses do change hands, and some are rented. Attendees mark the occasion as they have for more than a century, with lights, song, and open houses for families and friends. Ninety-minute tours of the area are conducted at 11 am on Tuesday and Thursday in July and August; join Community Sings on Wednesday evening. ✉ *Off Circuit Ave.* ☎ *508/693–0525* 🌐 *www.mvcma.org* 🎫 *Tour $12.*

Beaches

Joseph A. Sylvia State Beach

BEACH—SIGHT | **FAMILY** | This 2-mile-long sandy beach has a view of Cape Cod across Nantucket Sound. Occasional food vendors and calm, warm waters make it a popular spot for families. Arrive early or late in high summer: the parking spots fill up quickly. It's best to bike, walk, or take the shuttle here. **Amenities:** parking (no fee). **Best for:** swimming. ✉ *Off Beach Rd., between Oak Bluffs and Edgartown* 🌐 *www.mvy.com/beaches.html.*

Restaurants

Linda Jean's

$ | **AMERICAN** | **FAMILY** | This is a classic local hangout, a diner that serves food the way a diner should: with hearty helpings and inexpensive prices. Want breakfast at 6 am? **Known for:** local favorite; blueberry pancakes; homemade onion rings. [$] *Average main: $12* ✉ *25 Circuit Ave.* ☎ *508/693–4093* 🌐 *www.lindajeansrestaurantmv.com.*

Offshore Ale Company

$$ | **AMERICAN** | The island's first microbrewery restaurant is quite popular with locals and visitors alike, especially since it is open year-round. There are private wooden booths, a dart board in the corner, and live music year-round. **Known for:** rotating beers on tap; friendly staff; fish-and-chips. [$] *Average main: $22* ✉ *30 Kennebec Ave.* ☎ *508/693–2626* 🌐 *www.offshoreale.com* 🕘 *No lunch weekdays.*

Red Cat Kitchen

$$$$ | **SEAFOOD** | Standing at nearly 6½ feet tall and covered with colorful tattoos, chef-owner Ben Deforest turns out an extraordinary array of dishes—chorizo-stuffed local calamari, crab and wild mushroom risotto, or truffle arancini—from a tiny kitchen visible from the dining room. Regulars love the funky artwork, thundering tunes, and the irreverent spirit of the place, but no question here: it's the food that keeps them coming back. **Known for:** frequently changing (sometimes daily) seasonal-based menu; crispy Brussels sprouts; ample portions. [$] *Average main: $42* ✉ *14 Kennebec Ave.* ☎ *508/696–6040* 🌐 *www.redcatkitchen.com* 🕘 *Closed Nov.–Mar.*

Sweet Life Café

$$$$ | **AMERICAN** | Housed in a charming Victorian house, this island favorite's warm hues, low lighting, and handsome antique furniture will make you feel like you've entered someone's home. The cooking is more sophisticated than home style, however: dishes are prepared in inventive ways and change often with the seasons. **Known for:** superb desserts; outdoor dining by candlelight in a shrub-enclosed garden; locally sourced food. [$] *Average main: $37* ✉ *63 Upper Circuit Ave.* ☎ *508/696–0200*

🌐 *www.sweetlifemv.com* ⏲ *Closed Mon. and Jan.–Mar. No lunch.*

Hotels

Madison Inn

$$ | **B&B/INN** | While this stylish little inn doesn't have the high prices of nearby hotels, it does have all the amenities you need including coffee and tea available all day and night, and complimentary snack basket in each room. **Pros:** extremely reasonable rates; location is right in town and everything is walkable; sophisticated lodging. **Cons:** no parking; some rooms on the small side; no dining venue on-site. [$] *Rooms from: $205* ✉ *18 Kennebec Ave.* ☎ *508/693–2760, 800/564–2760* 🌐 *www.madisoninnmv.com* ⏲ *Closed Nov.–mid-Apr.* 🛏 *16 rooms* 🍴 *No meals.*

Pequot Hotel

$$ | **B&B/INN** | In this casual cedar-shingle inn on a tree-lined street, the first floor has a wide porch with rocking chairs—perfect for enjoying coffee or tea with the cookies that are set out in the afternoon—and there's a small breakfast room where you can help yourself to bagels, muffins, and cereal in the morning. **Pros:** great location; reasonable rates; charmingly offbeat. **Cons:** some rooms are small; some rooms with no TV; no dining venue on-site. [$] *Rooms from: $225* ✉ *19 Pequot Ave.* ☎ *508/693–5087, 800/947–8704* 🌐 *www.pequothotel.com* ⏲ *Closed mid-Oct.–Apr.* 🛏 *31 rooms, 1 apartment* 🍴 *Free breakfast.*

Nightlife

Loft

BARS/PUBS | This adults-only venue makes its home in the vast space above the MV Chowder Co. and has long historic roots. Today it's home to an over-21 "playground" consisting of numerous pool tables, Ping-Pong, darts, shuffleboard, foosball, video games, a full bar, and frequent live music and DJ-led dance parties. A full menu is available in the restaurant below. ✉ *9 Oak Bluffs Ave.* ☎ *508/696–3000.*

Activities

FISHING

Dick's Bait & Tackle

FISHING | You can buy fishing accessories and bait, and check out a current copy of the fishing regulations here. ✉ *108 New York Ave.* ☎ *508/693–7669.*

Edgartown

6 miles southeast of Oak Bluffs.

Once a well-to-do whaling center, Edgartown remains the Vineyard's toniest town and has preserved parts of its elegant past. Sea captains' houses from the 18th and 19th centuries, with well-manicured gardens and lawns, line the streets.

A sparsely populated area with many nature preserves, where you can fish, Chappaquiddick Island, 1 mile southeast of Edgartown, makes for a pleasant day trip or bike ride on a sunny day. The "island" is actually connected to the Vineyard by a long sand spit that begins in South Beach in Katama. It's a spectacular 2¾-mile walk, or you can take the ferry, which departs about every five minutes.

GETTING HERE AND AROUND

Once you've reached Edgartown, a car isn't necessary. It's actually a hindrance, as parking can be very tight in summer. The Martha's Vineyard Transit Authority operates a fleet of buses that can get you almost anywhere you want to go. The town runs a helpful visitor center on Church Street.

The best way to get around Chappaquiddick Island is by bike; bring one over on the ferry ($6 round-trip for bike and rider) and ride the few miles to Cape Pogue Wildlife Refuge. Sign up for a tour with the Trustees of Reservations for an in-depth look at the island's wonders.

◉ Sights

Cape Poge Wildlife Refuge

NATURE PRESERVE | FAMILY | A conglomeration of habitats where you can swim, walk, fish, or just sit and enjoy the surroundings, the Cape Poge Wildlife Refuge, on the easternmost shore of Chappaquiddick Island, encompasses more than 6 square miles of wilderness. Its dunes, woods, cedar thickets, moors, salt marshes, ponds, tidal flats, and barrier beach serve as an important migration stopover and nesting area for numerous sea- and shorebirds. You'll need an oversand permit to drive your own vehicle or you can call to inquire about guided tours. ✉ *East end of Dike Rd., Chappaquiddick Island* ☎ *508/627–7689* ⊕ *www.thetrustees.org/places-to-visit/cape-cod-islands/cape-pogue.html.*

Edgartown Lighthouse

LIGHTHOUSE | FAMILY | Surrounded by a public beach, this cast-iron tower was floated by barge from Ipswich, Massachusetts, in 1938. It is still an active navigational aid. Renovations in 2007 included the installation of a staircase that visitors can ascend for great views. There's a touching memorial to children who have died, in the form of engraved granite cobblestones, surrounding the lighthouse. ✉ *121 N. Water St.* ☎ *508/627–4441* ⊕ *mvmuseum.org/visit/edgartown* 💲 *$5* 🕑 *Closed Labor Day–May.*

Felix Neck Wildlife Sanctuary

NATURE PRESERVE | FAMILY | The nearly 200-acre Massachusetts Audubon Society preserve, 3 miles outside Edgartown toward Oak Bluffs and Vineyard Haven, has 4 miles of hiking trails traversing marshland, fields, woods, seashore, and waterfowl and reptile ponds. Naturalist-led events include sunset hikes, stargazing, snake or bird walks, and kayaking tours. ✉ *100 Felix Neck Rd., off Edgartown–Vineyard Haven Rd.* ☎ *508/627–4850* ⊕ *www.massaudubon.org* 💲 *$4.*

Martha's Vineyard Museum

MUSEUM | Perched on 1 acre overlooking the Lagoon Pond and outer Vineyard Haven harbor, the museum is located in the formerly shuttered 1895 Marine Hospital, which the nonprofit organization purchased in 2011, renovated, and made its home in 2019. The expansive property includes 14 exhibition areas, a classroom, program room, research library, gift shop, and small café. Exhibits include "One Island, Many Stories," which explores the history of the island; "Challenges of the Sea," which gives an overview of island shipwrecks, navigation, and more; and "Flashes of Brilliance," with an 1854 Fresnel lens from the Gay Head Light. ✉ *151 Lagoon Pond Rd.* ☎ *508/627–4441* ⊕ *mvmuseum.org* 💲 *$12.*

★ Mytoi

NATURE PRESERVE | The Trustees of Reservations' 14-acre preserve is a serene, beautifully tended, Japanese-inspired garden with a creek-fed pool spanned by a bridge and rimmed with Japanese maples, azaleas, bamboo, and irises. A boardwalk runs through part of the grounds, where you're apt to see box turtles and hear the sounds of songbirds. There are few more enchanting spots on the island. Restrooms and fresh water are available. ✉ *56 Dike Bridge Rd., 2 miles from Chappaquiddick Rd., Chappaquiddick Island* ☎ *617/542–7696* ⊕ *www.thetrustees.org/places-to-visit/cape-cod-islands/mytoi.html* 💲 *$3.*

◎ Beaches

South Beach Katama Beach

BEACH—SIGHT | This very popular and accessible 3–4 mile stretch of Atlantic-facing beach is backed by high dunes. The protected salt pond cove is good for families on one side, while big waves on the other side draw surfers. Buses leave about every 30 minutes from town ($2 each way). **Amenities:** toilets; lifeguards; parking (no fee). **Best for:**

surfing; sunrise; walking. ✉ *Katama Rd.* ✣ *4 miles south of Edgartown* 🌐 *www.mvy.com/beaches.html.*

🍴 Restaurants

Alchemy Bistro and Bar

$$$$ | **EUROPEAN** | Alchemy aims for a European-chic bistro-style scene and menu, missing only the patina of age—and French working-folks' prices—but you can expect quality and imagination. On balmy evenings, the half-dozen outdoor tables on the candlelit brick patio are highly coveted. **Known for:** specialty cocktails; swanky candle-lit ambience; impressive wine list. $ *Average main: $38* ✉ *71 Main St.* ☎ *508/627–9999* 🌐 *www.alchemyedgartown.com* 🕒 *Closed Sun. No lunch.*

★ **Détente**

$$$$ | **AMERICAN** | A dark, intimate wine bar and restaurant with hardwood floors and richly colored banquette seating, Détente serves more than a dozen wines by the glass as well as numerous half bottles. Even if you're not much of an oenophile, it's worth a trip just for the innovative food, much of it from local farms and seafood purveyors. **Known for:** hip, sophisticated atmosphere; hand-rolled pasta; exquisite food preparations. $ *Average main: $38* ✉ *15 Winter St.* ☎ *508/627–8810* 🌐 *www.detentemv.com* 🕒 *Closed Sun. and Mon. and Nov.–late Apr. No lunch.*

The Dunes

$$$$ | **SEAFOOD** | **FAMILY** | The airy restaurant at Winnetu Oceanside Resort draws plenty of discerning diners to sample some of the island's most exquisite and creatively prepared seafood. It's the only dining room with a south-facing water view, and a stunning one at that—especially if you're lucky enough to sit outside on the large dining and drinking area. **Known for:** supervised separate dining area for families with children; water taxi from Edgartown; exceptional service. $ *Average main: $37* ✉ *Winnetu Oceanside Resort, 31 Dunes Rd.* ☎ *508/627–3663* 🌐 *www.winnetu.com* 🕒 *Closed mid-Oct.–mid-Apr. No lunch.*

l'étoile

$$$$ | **FRENCH** | Michael Brisson has been at the helm of this creative French kitchen since the mid-1980s, yet his dedication to fresh, exquisitely prepared local food remains as fervent as ever. Changing with what's seasonally available, his menu many include sautéed Menemsha fluke or perhaps roasted Long Island duck breast; for lighter fare or to indulge in a fancy martini, head to the stunning copper bar with its sleek leather-backed chairs or the lovely terrace for alfresco dining. **Known for:** elegant surroundings; foie gras; excellent service. $ *Average main: $45* ✉ *The Sydney Martha's Vineyard, 22 N. Water St.* ☎ *508/627–5187* 🌐 *www.letoile.net* 🕒 *Closed Mon. and Tues. and Dec.–late Apr.*

☕ Coffee and Quick Bites

Espresso Love

$ | **CAFÉ** | When you need a pick-me-up, pop into Espresso Love for a cappuccino and a homemade raspberry scone or blueberry muffin. If you prefer something cold, the staff also makes fruit smoothies. **Known for:** breakfast sandwiches; friendly staff; make-your-own salad bowls. $ *Average main: $8* ✉ *17 Church St.* ☎ *508/627–9211* 🌐 *www.espressolove.com.*

🛏 Hotels

Charlotte Inn

$$$$ | **B&B/INN** | From the moment you walk up to the dark-wood Scottish barrister's desk to check in at this regal 1864 inn, you'll be surrounded by the trappings and customs of a bygone era—beautiful antique furnishings, objets d'art, and paintings fill the property. **Pros:**

over-the-top lavish; quiet yet convenient location; beautifully landscaped. **Cons:** can feel overly formal; intimidating if you don't adore museum-quality antiques; not for those with children. $ *Rooms from: $700* ✉ *27 S. Summer St.* ☎ *508/627–4751, 800/735–2478* ⊕ *www.thecharlotteinn.com* �snⁿ *19 rooms* ¶◎¶ *No meals.*

Edgartown Inn

$$$ | **B&B/INN** | The inside of the former home of whaling captain Thomas Worth still evokes its late-18th-century origins—but with the boutique Lark Hotels group now in charge, the updated decor is best described as farmhouse chic, with airy spaces and vintage notes. **Pros:** great value; rich in history—Nathaniel Hawthorne wrote much of his Twice-Told Tales here; close to shopping and dining. **Cons:** many rooms are accessed by stairs only; not for those with small children; pricey parking. $ *Rooms from: $349* ✉ *56 N. Water St.* ☎ *508/939–4005* ⊕ *www.theedgartowninn.com* ⋩ *12 rooms* ¶◎¶ *Free breakfast.*

Harbor View Hotel and Resort

$$$$ | **RESORT** | **FAMILY** | A $15 million revamp in 2019 of this historic hotel, composed of a gray-shingled, 1891 Victorian building with wraparound veranda and a gazebo, plus two other historic buildings, and cottages, gave new life to a popular island mainstay. **Pros:** great harbor views; on-site restaurants; many special packages. **Cons:** a few blocks from commercial district; steep rates; lots of weddings. $ *Rooms from: $429* ✉ *131 N. Water St.* ☎ *844/248–1167* ⊕ *www.harborviewhotel.com* ⋩ *108 rooms* ¶◎¶ *No meals.*

★ Hob Knob

$$$$ | **B&B/INN** | This 19th-century Gothic Revival boutique hotel blends the amenities and service of a luxury property with the ambience and charm of a small B&B with art and antiques that help capture the island's rural, seaside charm. **Pros:** full breakfast—organic and

locally gathered—and lavish afternoon tea are included; on-site spa; a short walk from the harbor, it's on the main road into town—but far enough out to avoid crowds. **Cons:** steep rates; not overlooking harbor; not for those with small children. $ *Rooms from: $495* ✉ *128 Main St.* ☎ *508/627–9510, 800/696–2723* ⊕ *www.hobknob.com* ⋩ *17 rooms* ¶◎¶ *Free breakfast.*

★ Winnetu Oceanside Resort

$$$$ | **RESORT** | **FAMILY** | A departure from most properties on the island, the contemporary Winnetu—styled after the grand multistory resorts of the Gilded Age—has successfully struck a fine balance in that it both encourages families and provides a contemporary seaside-resort experience for couples. **Pros:** a full slate of excellent children's programs offered late June–early September; resort arranges bicycling and kayaking trips, lighthouse tours, boat excursions to Nantucket Island, and other island activities; fantastic restaurant. **Cons:** not an in-town location; lots of kids in summer; books up quickly. $ *Rooms from: $495* ✉ *31 Dunes Rd.* ☎ *866/335–1133, 508/310–1733* ⊕ *www.winnetu.com* ☉ *Closed late Oct.–mid-Apr.* ⋩ *58 suites, 80 homes* ¶◎¶ *No meals.*

🛍 Shopping

Edgartown Books

BOOKS/STATIONERY | This longtime island favorite carries a large selection of island-related titles and periodicals, and the staff will be happy to make a summer reading recommendation. A wonderful little café behind the bookshop, called Behind the Bookstore, serves fine coffee, breakfast, lunch, and dinner. ✉ *44 Main St.* ☎ *508/627–8463* ⊕ *www.edgartownbooks.com.*

West Tisbury

8 miles west of Edgartown, 6½ miles south of Vineyard Haven.

West Tisbury retains its rural appeal and maintains its agricultural tradition at several active horse and produce farms. The town center looks very much like a small New England village, complete with a white-steepled church.

Sights

Polly Hill Arboretum

GARDEN | **FAMILY** | The late horticulturist and part-time Vineyard resident Polly Hill tended some 2,000 species of plant and developed nearly 100 species herself on her old sheep farm in West Tisbury. On-site are azaleas, tree peonies, dogwoods, hollies, lilacs, magnolias, and more. Hill raised them from seeds without the use of a greenhouse, and her patience is the inspiration of the arboretum. Run as a nonprofit center, the arboretum also runs guided tours, a lecture series, and a visitor center and gift shop. It's a beautiful spot for a picnic. The grounds are open year-round. ✉ *809 State Rd.* ☎ *508/693–9426* 🌐 *www.pollyhillarboretum.org* 🎟 *$5* 🕓 *Visitor center closed mid-Oct.–late May.*

Sepiessa Point Reservation

NATURE PRESERVE | A paradise for bird-watchers, Sepiessa Point Reservation consists of 174 acres on splendid Tisbury Great Pond. There are expansive pond and ocean views, walking trails around coves and saltwater marshes, horse trails, swimming areas, and a boat launch. ✉ *Tiah's Cove Rd.* ☎ *508/627–7141* 🌐 *www.mvlandbank.com* 🎟 *Free.*

Restaurants

★ State Road Restaurant

$$$ | **AMERICAN** | **FAMILY** | High ceilings, exposed beams, and a beautiful stone fireplace make for a warm and light-filled meal. The menu takes advantage of delightfully prepared local and organic products, creating memorable dishes. **Known for:** creative and large selection of plates ample for sharing and sampling; wonderful ambience; Sunday brunch (no reservations accepted). [$] *Average main: $35* ✉ *688 State Rd.* ☎ *508/693–8582* 🌐 *www.stateroadrestaurant.com* 🕓 *Closed Mon.*

Hotels

★ Lambert's Cove Inn, Farm & Restaurant

$$$$ | **B&B/INN** | A narrow road winds through pine woods and beside creeper-covered stone walls to this posh, handsomely designed farmhouse inn (1790) surrounded by extraordinary gardens and old stone walls set on 8 acres. **Pros:** guests receive free passes (and transport) to beautiful and private Lambert's Cove beach (there's also a pool); fantastic restaurant; serene grounds. **Cons:** need a car to explore island; far from the action; pricey. [$] *Rooms from: $400* ✉ *90 Manaquayak Rd., off Lambert's Cove Rd.* ☎ *508/693–2298* 🌐 *www.lambertscoveinn.com* 🔑 *15 rooms* 🍴 *Free breakfast.*

Shopping

Alley's General Store

CONVENIENCE/GENERAL STORES | **FAMILY** | Step back in time with a visit to Alley's General Store, a local landmark since 1858, and the island's oldest retail business. Alley's sells a truly general variety of goods: everything from hammers to housewares and dill pickles to sweet muffins as well as great things you find only in a country store. There's even a post office inside. ✉ *299 State Rd.* ☎ *508/693–0088* 🌐 *vineyardtrust.org/property/alleys-general-store.*

Sacred to the Wampanoag Tribe, the red-hue Aquinnah Cliffs are a popular attraction on Martha's Vineyard.

Menemsha

1½ miles southwest of West Tisbury.

Unspoiled by the "progress" of the past few decades, this working port is a jumble of weathered fishing shacks, fishing and pleasure boats, drying nets, and lobster pots. The village is popular with cyclists who like to stop for ice cream or chowder. Menemsha is often busy with folks eager to see the sunset.

GETTING HERE AND AROUND

You can take a Martha's Vineyard Transit Authority bus here; there's frequent service in summer and more limited service the rest of the year. If you're exploring the area by bike, you can get between Menemsha and the Aquinnah Cliffs via the Menemsha Bike Ferry. It's a quick trip across the water ($8 round-trip), but it saves a lot of riding on the busy State Road.

◉ Sights

Menemsha Harbor

NEIGHBORHOOD | Where Menemsha Pond meets Vineyard Sound, this tiny seaside outpost has been an active fishing center for centuries. Well-weathered fishing boats, including some that have been in the same family for generations, tie up at the docks when not out to sea. Spectacular sunsets make this a very popular evening spot. Several fish markets offer the freshest catch of the day. There's also a beach here, with gentle waters that are welcoming to families. If the harbor looks familiar, it might be because several scenes from the movie *Jaws* were filmed here. ⊠ *Basin Rd.*

☕ Coffee and Quick Bites

★ Larsen's

$ | SEAFOOD | Basically a retail fish store, Larsen's has a raw take-out counter and will also boil lobsters for you. Dig into a plate of fresh littlenecks or cherrystones; oysters are not a bad alternative.

Known for: made-to-order lobster roll; freshest seafood; friendly service. [$] *Average main: $14* ✉ *Dutcher's Dock, 56 Basin Rd.* ☎ *508/645–2680* 🌐 *www.larsensfishmarket.com* 🕓 *Closed mid-Oct.–mid-May.*

Menemsha Galley

$ | **AMERICAN** | Line up at this charming family-owned spot, around for more than 70 years, for everything from chowder to fresh swordfish sandwiches to soft serve ice cream. Once you pick up your order, enjoy it sitting on the rocks at the harbor or head to the beach. **Known for:** Galley fries; reasonable prices; friendly staff. [$] *Average main: $10* ✉ *515 North Rd.* ☎ *508/645–9819* 🕓 *Closed in winter (generally Columbus Day–mid-May).*

Aquinnah

6½ miles west of Menemsha, 10 miles southwest of West Tisbury, 17 miles southwest of Vineyard Haven.

Aquinnah, called Gay Head until the town voted to change its name in 1997, is an official Native American township. The Wampanoag tribe is the guardian of the 420 acres that constitute the Aquinnah Native American Reservation. Aquinnah (pronounced a- *kwih*-nah) is Wampanoag for "land under the hill." You can get a good view of Menemsha and Nashaquitsa ponds, the woods, and the ocean beyond from Quitsa Pond Lookout on State Road. The town is best known for the red-hued Aquinnah Cliffs. This is the end of the world, or so it seems when you're standing on the edge of the cliff looking out over the ocean.

GETTING HERE AND AROUND

Aquinnah, 6½ miles west of Menemsha and 10 miles southwest of West Tisbury, gets lots of traffic, for good reason. You can drive here (and pray for a parking space) or ride the Martha's Vineyard Transit Authority buses, which have frequent service in summer.

Sights

★ **Aquinnah Cliffs**

VIEWPOINT | A National Historic Landmark, the spectacular Aquinnah Cliffs are part of the Wampanoag Reservation land. These dramatically striated walls of red clay are the island's major attraction, as evinced by the tour bus–filled parking lot. Native American crafts and food shops line the short approach to the overlook, from which you can see the Elizabeth Islands to the northeast across Vineyard Sound and Nomans Land Island, a wildlife preserve, 3 miles off the Vineyard's southern coast. ✉ *State Rd.*

Gay Head Lighthouse

LIGHTHOUSE | This brick lighthouse (also called the Aquinnah Lighthouse) was successfully moved back from its precarious perch atop the rapidly eroding cliffs in spring 2015. Bad weather may affect its hours. Parking can be limited here, but views are outstanding. ✉ *9 Aquinnah Circle* ☎ *508/645–2300* 🌐 *www.gayheadlight.org* 🎟 *$5.*

Hotels

Outermost Inn

$$$ | **B&B/INN** | This rambling, sun-filled inn by the Aquinnah Cliffs stands alone on acres of moorland, a 10-minute walk from the beach. **Pros:** spectacular setting; extremely popular restaurant, open to the public, serves a nightly prix-fixe dinner in summer; service. **Cons:** far from bigger towns on island; steep rates; not suitable for young kids. [$] *Rooms from: $360* ✉ *81 Lighthouse Rd.* ☎ *508/645–3511* 🌐 *www.outermostinn.com* 🕓 *Closed mid-Oct.–mid-May* 🛏 *7 rooms* 🍴 *Free breakfast.*

Nantucket

At the height of its prosperity in the early 19th century, the little island of Nantucket was the foremost whaling port in the world. Its harbor bustled with whaling ships and merchant vessels; chandleries, cooperages, and other shops crowded the wharves. Burly ship hands loaded barrels of whale oil onto wagons, which they wheeled along cobblestone streets to refineries and candle factories. Sea breezes carried the smoke and smells of booming industry through town as its inhabitants eagerly took care of business. Shipowners and sea captains built elegant mansions, which today remain remarkably unchanged, thanks to a very strict building code initiated in the 1950s. The entire town of Nantucket is now an official National Historic District encompassing more than 800 pre-1850 structures within 1 square mile.

Day-trippers usually take in the architecture and historical sites, dine at one of the many delightful restaurants, and browse in the pricey boutiques, most of which stay open mid-April–December. Signature items include Nantucket lightship baskets, originally crafted by sailors whiling away a long watch; artisans who continue the tradition now command prices of $700 and up, and antiques are exponentially more expensive.

GETTING ORIENTED

Nantucket is a boomerang-shape island 26 miles southeast of Hyannis on Cape Cod, and 107 miles southeast of Boston. Its nearest neighbor to the west is the somewhat larger island of Martha's Vineyard; eastward, the nearest landfall would be the Azores off Portugal. The island has only one town, which also goes by the name of Nantucket. The only other community of note is tiny Siasconset, a cluster of shingled seaside manses and lovingly restored fishing shacks 8 miles west of town. A 3-mile main road directly south of town leads to Surfside Beach, among the island's most popular. Nantucket's small but busy airport is located east of Surfside.

Nantucket Town. As the ferry terminal— from Hyannis and, seasonally, Martha's Vineyard—Nantucket Town is the hub of all activity and the starting point for most visits. At the height of summer, its narrow cobblestone streets are in a constant state of near-gridlock. The town itself is easily walkable, and bikes are available for exploring.

Siasconset and Wauwinet. An allee of green lawns leads to the exclusive summer community of Siasconset (or 'Sconset, as locals say). Tucked away on either side of the village center are warrens of tiny, rose-covered cottages, some of them centuries old. About 5 miles northwest is the even tinier community of Wauwinet, which boasts the country's second-oldest yacht club.

GETTING HERE AND AROUND

Year-round flight service to Nantucket from Boston and Hyannis is provided by Cape Air and Nantucket Airlines. American Airlines offers seasonal service to the island from Washington, D.C., Charlotte, NC, and New York's LaGuardia. Jet Blue, United, and Delta also offer seasonal flights from select cities.

Arriving by ferry puts you in the center of town, and several ferry companies offer service to Nantucket from two different ports, either year-round or seasonally. You can board in Hyannis (Hy-Line, Steamship Authority) or Harwich Port (Freedom Cruise Line). The only company that carries cars is Steamship Authority; car service is very expensive, and reservations must be made far in advance.

There is little need for a car here to explore; ample public transportation and smoothly paved bike paths can take you to the further reaches with ease. The Nantucket Regional Transit Authority (NRTA) runs shuttle buses from in town to most areas of the island. Service is generally available late May–mid-October. If you're still determined to rent a car while on Nantucket, book early—and expect to spend at least $95 a day during high season. If your car is low-slung, don't attempt the dirt roads. Some are deeply pocked with puddles, and

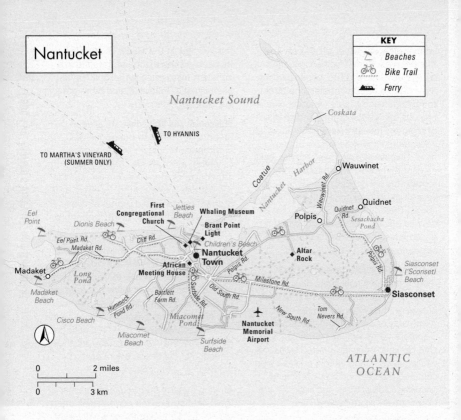

Nantucket

KEY
- Beaches
- Bike Trail
- Ferry

Nantucket Sound

Coskata

TO HYANNIS

TO MARTHA'S VINEYARD (SUMMER ONLY)

Wauwinet

Coatue

Nantucket Harbor

Wauwinet Rd.

Quidnet

Polpis

Sesachacha Pond

Eel Point

Dionis Beach

First Congregational Church

Jetties Beach

Whaling Museum

Brant Point Light

Children's Beach

Eel Point Rd.

Madaket Rd.

Cliff Rd.

Nantucket Town

Altar Rock

Polpis Rd.

Siasconset ('Sconset) Beach

Madaket

Long Pond

African Meeting House

Old South Rd.

Milestone Rd.

Siasconset

Madaket Beach

Bartlett Farm Rd.

Hummock Pond Rd.

Surfside Rd.

New South Rd.

Tom Nevers Rd.

Cisco Beach

Miacomet Pond

Nantucket Memorial Airport

Miacomet Beach

Surfside Beach

ATLANTIC OCEAN

0 — 2 miles

0 — 3 km

some are virtual sandpits, challenging even to four-wheel-drive vehicles.

VISITOR INFORMATION

CONTACTS Nantucket Chamber of Commerce. ☎ 508/228–1700 ⊕ www.nantucketchamber.org. **Nantucket Visitor Services and Information Bureau.** ☎ 508/228–0925 ⊕ www.nantucket-ma.gov.

Nantucket Town

30 miles southeast of Hyannis, 107 miles southeast of Boston.

After the Great Fire of 1846 leveled all its wooden buildings, Main Street was widened to prevent future flames from hopping across the street. The cobblestone thoroughfare has a harmonious symmetry: the Pacific Club anchors its foot, and the Pacific National Bank, another redbrick building, squares off the head. The cobblestones were brought to the island as ballast in returning ships and laid to prevent the wheels of carts heavily laden with whale oil from sinking into the dirt. At the center of Lower Main is an old horse trough, today overflowing with flowers. From here the street gently rises; at the bank it narrows to its prefire width and leaves the commercial district for an area of mansions that escaped the blaze.

TOURS

★ **Nantucket Historical Association** (*NHA*) **MUSEUM** | This association maintains an assortment of venerable properties in town. A $20 pass gets you into all of the association's sites, including the glorious Whaling Museum, the Oldest House, Old Mill, Old Gaol, Greater Light, and the Fire Hose Cart House. Reserve in advance for two very popular walking tours, which depart daily late May–early November: a 60-minute downtown tour and an 80-minute historic house tour. Both cost $10. ⊠ *15 Broad St., Nantucket* ☎ *508/228–1894* ⊕ *www.nha.org.*

Sights

African Meeting House

MUSEUM | When the island abolished slavery in 1773, Nantucket became a destination for free blacks and escaping slaves. The African Meeting House was built in the 1820s as a schoolhouse, and it functioned as such until 1846, when the island's schools were integrated. A complete restoration has returned the site to its authentic 19th-century appearance. Next door is the late-18th-century Florence Higginbotham house, originally purchased by Seneca Boston, a former slave and weaver. ⊠ *29 York St., Nantucket* ☎ *508/228–9833* ⊕ *maah.org* ⌂ *$10.*

Brant Point Light

LIGHTHOUSE | The promontory where this 26-foot-tall, white-painted beauty stands offers views of the harbor and town. The point was once the site of the second-oldest lighthouse in the country (1746); the present, much-photographed light was built in 1901. There are no tours inside the lighthouse, but the grounds are open to the public. ⊠ *End of Easton St., across footbridge, Nantucket* ⊕ *www.nps.gov/nr/travel/maritime/brn.htm.*

First Congregational Church

RELIGIOUS SITE | The tower of this church provides the best view of Nantucket—for those willing to climb its 94 steps. Rising 120 feet, the tower is capped by a weather vane depicting a whale catch. Peek in at the church's 1852 trompe-l'oeil ceiling. ⊠ *62 Centre St., Nantucket* ☎ *508/228–0950* ⊕ *www.nantucketfcc.org* ⌂ *Tower tour $5.*

★ Whaling Museum

MUSEUM | **FAMILY** | With exhibits that include a fully rigged whaleboat and a skeleton of a 46-foot sperm whale, this must-see museum—a complex that includes a restored 1846 spermaceti candle factory—offers a crash course in the island's colorful history. Items on display include harpoons and other whale-hunting implements; portraits of whaling captains and their wives (a few of whom went whaling as well); the South Seas curiosities they brought home; a large collection of sailors' crafts; a full-size tryworks once used to process whale oil; and the original 16-foot-high 1850 lens from Sankaty Head Lighthouse. The Children's Discovery Room provides interactive-learning opportunities. Be sure to climb—or take the elevator—up to the observation deck for a view of the harbor. ⊠ *13–15 Broad St., Nantucket* ☎ *508/228–1894* ⊕ *www.nha.org* ⌂ *$20, includes other historic sites* ☉ *Closed Sun. and Jan.–Mar.*

🏖 Beaches

Jetties Beach

BEACH—SIGHT | **FAMILY** | A short bike or shuttle-bus ride from town, Jetties Beach is popular with families because of its calm surf. It's also a good place to try out kayaks and sailboards. The shore is a lively scene, with a playground and volleyball nets on the beach and adjacent public tennis courts. There is a boardwalk to the beach (special wheelchairs are available). You'll have a good view of passing ferries—and an even better one if you clamber out on the jetty itself. (Careful, it's slippery.) **Amenities**: food and drink; lifeguards; parking (fee); showers; toilets; water sports. **Best for**: swimming; windsurfing. ⊠ *Bathing Beach Rd., 1½ miles northwest of Straight Wharf, Nantucket* ⊕ *www.nantucket-ma.gov/Facilities/Facility/Details/Jetties-Beach-34.*

Each beach on Nantucket has a unique approach—sometimes getting there is half the fun.

★ Surfside Beach

BEACH—SIGHT | Surfside Beach, accessible via the Surfside Bike Path (3 miles) or by shuttle bus, is the island's most popular surf beach. This wide strand of sand comes fully equipped with conveniences. It draws teens and young adults as well as families and is great for kite flying and, after 5 pm, surf casting. **Amenities**: food and drink; lifeguards; parking (fee); showers; toilets. **Best for**: surfing; swimming; walking. ✉ *Surfside Rd., South Shore* 🌐 *www.nantucket-ma.gov/facilities/facility/details/surfsidebeach-44.*

🍴 Restaurants

Brotherhood of Thieves

$$ | **AMERICAN** | **FAMILY** | No, it's not really an 1840s whaling bar—though the atmospheric basement, which dates all the way back to 1972, presents a more convincing front than the newer, spiffier upper floors, which attract families and friendly singles alike. A swanky lounge offers a tapas menu, along with a large and varied wine and craft beer selection; outside seating is a delight under the canopy of trailing vines and foliage. **Known for:** juicy burgers and signature curly fries; reasonably priced meals; appealing shared plates menu. [$] *Average main: $24* ✉ *23 Broad St., Nantucket* ☎ *508/228–2551* 🌐 *www.brotherhoodofthieves.com* 🕓 *Closed Tues.*

Keepers/Fog Island Café

$$ | **AMERICAN** | **FAMILY** | Cherished year-round for its exceptional breakfasts, Keepers/Fog Island is just as fine a spot for dinner, when fresh fish and classic steaks are popular menu items. Chef-owners Mark and Anne Dawson—both Culinary Institute of America grads—seem determined to provide the best possible service to visitors and locals alike. **Known for:** exceptional breakfasts like huevos rancheros; ample portions; reasonable prices. [$] *Average main: $24* ✉ *5 Amelia Dr., Nantucket* ☎ *508/228–0009* 🌐 *www.fogisland.com* 🕓 *No breakfast Mon.–Thurs. No dinner Wed.*

Lola 41 degrees

$$$$ | ECLECTIC | The menu at Lola features items from countries on the 41st parallel like Japan and Italy—believe us when we say everywhere this restaurant ventures is good. The place started out as (and remains) a superpopular watering hole for the chic set. **Known for:** sushi and sake; specialty cocktails; hopping scene for young sophisticates. $ *Average main: $38* ✉ *15 S. Beach St., Nantucket* ☎ *508/325–4001* ⊕ *www.lola41.com* ⊗ *No lunch mid-Apr.–mid-Oct.*

The Pearl

$$$$ | ASIAN | With its white onyx bar illuminated a Curaçao blue and its walls awash in flowing voile, this ultracool space would seem right at home in South Beach. Asian-theme selections focus on local shellfish and seafood with some very rewarding results. **Known for:** wok-fried lobster; specialty cocktails; sophisticated scene. $ *Average main: $39* ✉ *12 Federal St., Nantucket* ☎ *508/228–9701* ⊕ *www. thepearlnantucket.com* ⊗ *Closed Tues. and Jan.–Apr. No lunch.*

★ Straight Wharf

$$$$ | MODERN AMERICAN | This loftlike restaurant with a harborside deck has enjoyed legendary status since the mid-1970s; the couple now in command—Gabriel Frasca and Amanda Lydon—have lent this venerable institution a more barefoot air, appropriate to the place and season, and are intense champions of local crops and catches. Hurricane lamps lend a soft glow to well-spaced tables lined with butcher paper, and dish towels serve as napkins. **Known for:** menu changes daily; locally sourced ingredients; outdoor seating with water view. $ *Average main: $45* ✉ *6 Harbor Sq., Nantucket* ☎ *508/228–4499* ⊕ *www. straightwharfrestaurant.com* ⊗ *Closed Mon. and mid-Oct.–mid-May.*

🛏 Hotels

Jared Coffin House

$$$$ | B&B/INN | The largest house in town when it was built in 1845, this three-story brick manse is still plenty impressive, and the property is actually comprised of two buildings, the Main House (closed off season) and the Jared Coffin House. **Pros:** knowledgeable concierge; in-town location; historical setting. **Cons:** some tiny rooms; street noise in front; no pets. $ *Rooms from: $425* ✉ *29 Broad St., Nantucket* ☎ *800/248–2405* ⊕ *www.jaredcoffinhouse. com* ⤳ *54 rooms* ¶⊙¶ *Free breakfast.*

★ The Nantucket Hotel and Resort

$$$$ | RESORT | FAMILY | The original impressive 19th-century shell remains, though its interior is sleek, gleaming, and crisp, with a blend of calming neutrals and navy. **Pros:** immaculate and large rooms, many with kitchens; ideal for families; full-service restaurant. **Cons:** can be noisy in summer; expensive; many children in summer. $ *Rooms from: $700* ✉ *77 Easton St., Nantucket* ☎ *508/228–4747, 866/807–6011* ⊕ *www.thenantuckethotel.com* ⊗ *Closed Feb.* ⤳ *42 rooms, 2 cottages* ¶⊙¶ *Free breakfast.*

Ships Inn

$$$ | B&B/INN | This 1831 home exudes history: it was built for whaling captain Obed Starbuck on the site of the birthplace of abolitionist Lucretia Mott. **Pros:** large rooms; handsome decor; ideal in-town location. **Cons:** on busy street; not for those traveling with small children (under nine); no pets. $ *Rooms from: $300* ✉ *13 Fair St., Nantucket* ☎ *508/228–0040* ⊕ *www.shipsinnnantucket.com* ⊗ *Closed late Oct.–late May* ⤳ *10 rooms* ¶⊙¶ *Free breakfast.*

★ Union Street Inn

$$$$ | B&B/INN | Ken Withrow worked in the hotel business, Deborah Withrow in high-end retail display, and guests get the best of both worlds in this 1770 house, a stone's throw from the bustle of Main Street. **Pros:** pampering by pros; several

rooms have a wood-burning fireplace; impeccable design. **Cons:** bustle of town; some small rooms; not for those with children. $ *Rooms from: $589* ✉ *7 Union St., Nantucket* ☎ *508/228–9222* 🌐 *www.unioninn.com* ⏲ *Closed Nov.–late Apr., except for Christmas stroll weekend in early Dec.* 🛏 *12 rooms* 🍴 *Free breakfast.*

★ **White Elephant**

$$$$ | RESORT | One of the island's most elegant properties, the White Elephant has an unbeatable location, right on Nantucket Harbor, steps from some of the island's best beaches, shops and restaurants. **Pros:** excellent service; great central location; extras like beach toys and chairs are available. **Cons:** not all rooms have patios or decks; pricey rates; minimum stay might be required. $ *Rooms from: $700* ✉ *50 Easton St., Nantucket* ☎ *800/445–6574* 🌐 *www.whiteelephantnantucket.com* 🛏 *66 room* 🍴 *No meals.*

Nightlife

Chicken Box (*The Box*)

MUSIC CLUBS | Live music—including some big-name bands—plays six nights a week in season, and weekends year-round. ✉ *16 Dave St., Nantucket* ☎ *508/228–9717* 🌐 *www.thechickenbox.com.*

Muse

BARS/PUBS | This is a year-round venue hosting live bands, including the occasional big-name act. The crowd—the barnlike space can accommodate nearly 400—can get pretty wild. There's also an eatery serving great pizza, burgers, and other bar-type snacks. ✉ *44 Surfside Rd., Nantucket* ☎ *508/228–6873* 🌐 *www.themusenantucket.com.*

Performing Arts

Dreamland

CULTURAL FESTIVALS | Originally built in 1832 as a Quaker meetinghouse, this gem has been fully restored and is now home to year-round entertainment and enrichment. Current movies are shown here, as well as live theater, comedy, and other performing arts. Theater workshops are available for all ages. ✉ *17 S. Water St., Nantucket* ☎ *508/228–1784, 508/332–4822* 🌐 *www.nantucketdreamland.org.*

Activities

BIKING

The best way to tour Nantucket is by bicycle. Nearly 30 miles of paved bike paths wind through all types of terrain from one end of the island to the other: for details, consult the maps posted by Wheels, Heels, and Pedals (🌐 *www.wheelsheelsandpedals.com*), which supports alternative modes of transportation. It is possible to bike around the entire island in a day; should you tire, however, you and your bike are welcome aboard the in-season Nantucket Regional Transit Authority (NRTA) buses. The main bike routes start within ½ mile of town. ⚠ **That first stretch can be dauntingly congested.** All routes are well marked and lead—eventually—to popular beaches. The paths are also perfect for runners and bladers—but not mopeds, which must remain on the road (to the frustration of impatient drivers). Note that Nantucket requires bike riders 12 and under to wear a helmet. Several shorter spurs connecting popular routes have been continuously added in the island's quest to make Nantucket even more bike-friendly. ■ **TIP→ There are multiple bike rental outfits downtown, very close to the ferry terminal; most offer delivery to lodging per request.**

The easy 2.2-mile **Surfside Bike Path** leads to Surfside, the island's premier ocean beach. A drinking fountain and rest stop are placed at about the halfway point. The **Milestone Bike Path,** a straight shot linking Nantucket Town and 'Sconset, is probably the most monotonous of the paths but can still be quite pleasant. (It's about 6 miles; paired with the scenic Polpis Road Path, it becomes a 16-mile island loop.) The **Old South Road Bike Path** spurs off from the Milestone Rotary and ends about 1½ miles later close to the airport. At 1.2 miles, the **Cliff Road Path,** on the north shore, is one of the easiest bike paths, but it's still quite scenic, with gentle hills. It intersects with the Eel Point and Madaket paths.

The **Eel Point/Dionis Beach Path** starts at the junction of Eel Point Road and Madaket Road and links the Cliff Road and Madaket bike paths to Dionis Beach; it's less than a mile long. The 9-mile **Polpis Road Path** skirts scenic bays and bogs as it wends its way toward 'Sconset; it intersects with Milestone Path east of the rotary. The **Madaket Path** starts at the intersection of Quaker and Upper Main Streets and follows Madaket Road out to Madaket Beach on the island's west end, about 6 miles from the edge of Nantucket Town. About a third of the way along, you could turn off onto Cliff Road Path or the Eel Point/Dionis Beach Path.

BOATING
Nantucket Community Sailing
BOATING | FAMILY | Renting sailboats, sailboards, and kayaks at Jetties Beach, NCS also offers youth and adult sailing classes and water-sport clinics for disabled athletes. Its Outrigger Canoe Club—a Polynesian tradition—heads out several evenings a week in season. ⊠ *Jetties Beach, Bathing Beach Rd., Nantucket* ☎ *508/228–6600* ⊕ *www.nantucketcommunitysailing.org.*

🛍 Shopping

Much of the appeal of Nantucket is its concentrated downtown area, all of it easily walkable—just watch your step along the lumpy historic cobblestones. Shoppers will find many high-end stores here, offering up elegant housewares, art, jewelry, upscale women and men's clothing, and many things that Nantucket holds dear: whale belts, "Nantucket Reds," Nantucket baskets, and all things maritime and nautical. Despite being the slow season, the annual Christmas Stroll (⊕ *christmasstroll.com*) during the first weekend in December is still a popular time, when shops stay open late and offer refreshments, but it's more than just a holiday shopping event now. Hundreds of trees decorate downtown and carolers roam the streets in costume, belting out songs of cheer.

LIQUOR
Cisco Brewers
WINE/SPIRITS | The microconglomerate of Cisco Brewers, Nantucket Vineyard, and Triple Eight Distillery makes boutique beers, wine, and vodka on-site. Tours and tastings are available (fee) and there is regular live music starting in the late afternoon and sometimes food trucks. ⊠ *5 Bartlett Farm Rd., Nantucket* ☎ *508/325–5929* ⊕ *www.ciscobrewers.com.*

MARKETS
★ Bartlett's Farm
OUTDOOR/FLEA/GREEN MARKETS | Bartlett's Farm encompasses 100 acres overseen by eighth-generation Bartletts. Healthy, tasty prepared foods—within a minisupermarket—are added incentive to make the trek out. If you're not up it, however, a produce truck is parked on Main Street through the summer. ⊠ *33 Bartlett Farm Rd., Nantucket* ☎ *508/228–9403* ⊕ *www.bartlettsfarm.com.*

Siasconset

7 miles east of Nantucket Town.

First a fishing outpost and then an artists' colony—Broadway actors favored it in the late 19th century—Siasconset (or 'Sconset, in local vernacular) is a charming cluster of rose-covered cottages linked by driveways of crushed clamshells; at the edges of town, the former fishing shacks give way to magnificent sea-view mansions. The small town center consists of a market, post office, café, lunchroom, and a combination liquor store–lending library.

Sights

Altar Rock

VIEWPOINT | A dirt track leads to the island's highest point, Altar Rock (101 feet), and the view is spectacular. The hill overlooks approximately 4,000 acres of rare coastal heathland laced with paths leading in every direction. ✉ *Altar Rock Rd., 3 miles west of Milestone Rd. rotary on Polpis Rd., Siasconset.*

Beaches

Siasconset Beach

BEACH—SIGHT | Siasconset Beach is known for its wilder surf and for its dunes; this beautiful spot is repeatedly blasted by winter erosion. Restaurants and restrooms are in the nearby village. **Amenities**: lifeguards. **Best for**: surfing; swimming; walking. ✉ *Milestone Rd., at the end, Siasconset.*

Restaurants

Topper's

$$$$ | MODERN AMERICAN | The Wauwinet, a lavishly restored 19th-century inn on Nantucket's northeastern shore, is where islanders and visitors alike go to experience utmost luxury—and that includes the food. In the creamy-white dining room, awash in lush linens and glorious flowers, you can choose from prix-fixe menus or order à la carte, and more casual fare is on offer out on the deck. **Known for:** vast wine list; atmospheric experience; boat taxi from town to restaurant and back. [$] *Average main: $48* ✉ *The Wauwinet, 120 Wauwinet Rd., Wauwinet* ☎ *508/228–8768* 🌐 *www.wauwinet.com/dining* 🕒 *Closed Nov.–Apr. No dinner Sun.*

Coffee and Quick Bites

Handlebar Cafe

$ | CAFÉ | Opened by the founders of Nantucket Bike Tours, this cozy spot offers a welcome space to relax with a coffee or tea and check your email, or just read a book. If you need a snack, scones, muffins, and nuts can be ordered to go with your beverage of choice. **Known for:** espresso drinks; small snacks like muffins; open year-round. [$] *Average main: $3* ✉ *15 Washington St., Nantucket* ☎ *508/825–5929* 🌐 *handlebar-cafe.myshopify.com.*

Hotels

★ **The Wauwinet**

$$$$ | RESORT | This resplendently updated 1850 resort straddles a "haulover" poised between ocean and bay (think beaches on both sides); it features cushy country-chic guest rooms (lavish with Pratesi linens) and a splendid restaurant, Topper's. **Pros:** the staff-to-guest ratio exceeds one-to-one; dual beaches; peaceful setting. **Cons:** not for those with small children; distance from town; pricey rates. [$] *Rooms from: $825* ✉ *120 Wauwinet Rd., Wauwinet* ☎ *508/228–0145* 🌐 *www.wauwinet.com* 🕒 *Closed Nov.–Apr.* 🛏 *32 rooms, 4 cottages* 🍴 *Free breakfast.*

Activities

BIKING

'Sconset Bike Path

BICYCLING | This 6½-mile bike path starts at the rotary east of Nantucket Town and parallels Milestone Road, ending in 'Sconset. It is mostly level, with some gentle hills. Slightly longer (and dippier), the 9-mile **Polpis Road Path,** veering off to the northeast, is far more scenic and leads to the turnoff to Wauwinet. ✉ *Off Milestone Rd., Siasconset.*

Chapter 6

THE BERKSHIRES AND WESTERN MASSACHUSETTS

Updated by
Lindsey Hollenbaugh

◉ Sights	🍴 Restaurants	🛏 Hotels	⬤ Shopping	▼ Nightlife
★★★★☆	★★★★☆	★★★★☆	★★★☆☆	★★☆☆☆

WELCOME TO THE BERKSHIRES AND WESTERN MASSACHUSETTS

TOP REASONS TO GO

★ **The Countryside:** Rolling hills, dense stands of forest, open pastures, and scenic valleys greet your eye at every turn.

★ **The Food:** Experience farm-to-table cuisine where community-supported agriculture was first founded in the 1980s.

★ **Summer Festivals:** Watch renowned dance companies perform at Jacob's Pillow, or listen to the Boston Symphony Orchestra at Tanglewood in Lenox.

★ **Under-the-Radar Museums:** Western Massachusetts has an eclectic assortment of institutions, from the Eric Carle Museum of Picture Book Art to the Basketball Hall of Fame.

★ **Pioneer Valley College Towns:** Three academic centers—Amherst (University of Massachusetts, Amherst College, and Hampshire College), Northampton (Smith College), and South Hadley (Mount Holyoke College)—pulse with cultural activity and youthful energy.

1 North Adams. The ideal Berkshires getaway location is home to the Massachusetts Museum of Contemporary Arts.

2 Williamstown. Built around the prestigious Williams College, this town has two noteworthy art museums and the renowned Williamstown Theatre Festival.

3 Hancock. A great location for year-round outdoor enthusiasts, it's also the closest town to the ski and snowboard resort, Jiminy Peak.

4 Pittsfield. This busy little city is home to the Hancock Shaker Village, a living history museum with restored buildings, crafts, and activities.

5 Lenox. The famed Tanglewood music festival takes up residence every summer.

6 Otis. Plenty of outdoor activities are available here year-round, but the popular Jacob's Pillow Dance Festival, in nearby Becket, draws the attention in the summer months.

7 Stockbridge. A quintessential New England town that even Norman Rockwell called home.

8 Great Barrington. A great place for delicious food and antiques hunting.

9 Springfield. The city's home to the Naismith Memorial Basketball Hall of Fame and the Springfield Museums, which includes the Amazing World of Dr. Seuss.

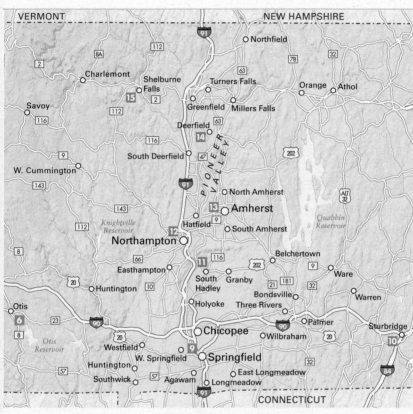

10 Sturbridge. A re-created early-19th-century village, Old Sturbridge Village is the area's premier attraction.

11 South Hadley. A quiet college town home to Mount Holyoke College.

12 Northampton. The cultural hub of Western Massachusetts is also home to Smith College.

13 Amherst. A mecca for world-renowned authors, poets, and artists, Amherst is also known for its trio of colleges: Amherst, Hampshire, and the University of Massachusetts.

14 Deerfield. The perfect New England village complete with a white-steepled church and perfectly maintained 18th-century homes.

15 Shelburne Falls. The community is filled with art galleries, shops, and farm stands.

The Bay State's most westerly portion consists of the Berkshires, a bucolic highland region filled with winding mountain roads, and the Pioneer Valley, home to the elite "Five College Consortium": Amherst, Hampshire, Mount Holyoke, Smith, and UMass Amherst. In addition to their natural advantages, the area supports dynamic cultural venues and risk-taking restaurants.

The burgeoning Berkshires arts community arose from the ruins of a manufacturing economy—aging mills having been converted into artist lofts and a former electric plant morphing into a contemporary art museum. Smaller museums can be found throughout the region, and you can view the creations of its myriad artists and craftspeople at their studios or in local galleries. Hikers, from the casual wanderer to the intrepid trailblazer, also have plenty to experience. In autumn, leaf peepers descend to explore this area renowned for fall foliage with vibrant oranges, yellows, and reds that typify the harvest season.

Though it might be presumptuous to proclaim a "renaissance," it can't be denied that the concentration of arts and culture in the Berkshires has reinvigorated the whole region. Along with this artistic explosion, a renewed focus on fresh, local food grown just up the road from many high-class restaurants helps turn this formerly depressed postindustrial area into a hot spot for farm-to-table cuisine with festivals celebrating everything from ice sculptures to the spoken word. The trend continues in the Pioneer Valley, especially in college towns like Northampton, propelled forward by the youthful energy of a large student population. The region is also beginning to embrace the state's newest industry: cannabis. Small recreational marijuana shops have begun popping up in most major towns and cities in the region, offering an educated, tasteful experience for those looking to partake. However, if it's not your thing, you won't even notice most of the shops that boast streamlined, discreet store fronts.

MAJOR REGIONS

Occupying the far western end of the state, **the Berkshires** are only about three hours by car from Boston or New York City, yet the region lives up to the storybook picture of rural New England: wooded hills, narrow winding roads, fall foliage, and quaint downtowns. Skiing is popular in winter—**Hancock** is the closest village to Jiminy Peak—and sugar-maple sap runs in the spring. Summer brings cultural events, like the renowned Tanglewood classical music festival in **Lenox,** the theater festival in **Williamstown,** and the Jacob's Pillow Dance Festival in Becket. Norman Rockwell called **Stockbridge** home, the Hancock Shaker Village is in **Pittsfield,** and **North Adams** has the Massachusetts Museum of Contemporary Arts. **Great Barrington** has great food, antiques shops, and the Mahaiwe Performing Arts Center.

Overshadowed somewhat by Boston to the east and the Berkshires to the west, **the Pioneer Valley** is home to historic settlements, unique museums, college towns, and natural treasures. **Sturbridge's** Old Sturbridge Village—a re-created early-19th-century village with restored buildings, reenactments, and activities—is the premier attraction here. The principal city here is **Springfield,** home to the Naismith Memorial Basketball Hall of Fame and the family-friendly Springfield Museums, but most of the area is quite rural—this is where the idyllic New England countryside of the imagination comes to life. College towns like **South Hadley, Northampton,** and **Amherst** serve as cultural hubs that have attracted former city dwellers who relish the ample natural scenery, sophisticated cultural venues, and lively dining and shopping. The picturesque towns of **Deerfield** and **Shelburne Falls** draw visitors for foliage and history tours.

Planning

Getting Here and Around

AIR
Most travelers arrive at Boston's Logan International Airport, the state's major airline hub. From Boston you can reach most parts of the Pioneer Valley in less than two hours by car, the Berkshires in about three.

Bradley International Airport in Windsor Locks, Connecticut, 18 miles south of Springfield, Massachusetts, on Interstate 91, serves the Pioneer Valley and the Berkshires. Another alternative—and actually closer to the area than Logan—is T. F. Green International Airport in Providence, Rhode Island.

CAR
Public transportation can be spotty in this region, with buses that don't run on Sunday or in the evening, so you'll almost certainly need a car. But you'll want one anyway so you can take leisurely drives to see the fall foliage. Be warned, though, that the winding mountain roads here are not for the fainthearted.

TRAIN
The Northeast Corridor and high-speed Acela services of Amtrak link Boston with the principal cities between it and Washington, D.C. Amtrak's *Lake Shore Limited,* which stops at Springfield and Pittsfield in the Berkshires, carries passengers from Chicago to Boston. For destinations north and west of Boston, trains depart from Boston's North Station.

Restaurants

On the menus at country inns, upscale restaurants, and even the coffee shop around the corner in the Berkshires and the Pioneer Valley, you will most likely learn what farm provided each ingredient, right down to the cheese platter or garnishes for cocktails. Chefs, restaurant owners, and local farmers have close, almost familial relationships in these parts, and the food is all the better for it.

Don't expect baked beans or slow-boiled meats of New England winters past when you visit. Instead, modern cafés and trendy restaurants now serve everything from fusion cuisine to pizza with inspired, seasonally appropriate toppings.

Hotels

The signature accommodation outside Boston is the country inn; in the Berkshires, where magnificent mansions have been converted into luxury lodgings, these inns have reached a very grand scale indeed. Less extravagant and less expensive are bed-and-breakfast establishments, many in private homes. Make reservations for inns well ahead during peak periods (summer through winter in the Berkshires).

Campers can pitch their tents amid acres of pine forest dotted with rivers and lakes or in the shadows of the rolling Berkshire Hills. The camping season in Massachusetts generally runs late May–mid-October. For more about camping, contact the Massachusetts Department of Conservation and Recreation (☎ 617/626–1250 ⊕ www.mass.gov/topics/parks-recreation). Hotel reviews have been shortened. For full information, visit Fodors.com.

WHAT IT COSTS in U.S. Dollars			
$	$$	$$$	$$$$
RESTAURANTS			
under $18	$18–$24	$25–$35	over $35
HOTELS			
under $200	$200–$299	$300–$399	over $399

Visitor Information

CONTACTS Berkshire Regional Transit Authority. ☎ 800/292–2782, 413/499–2782 ⊕ www.berkshirerta.com. **Massachusetts Department of Fish and Game.** ☎ 617/626–1500 ⊕ www.mass.gov/eea/agencies/dfg. **1Berkshire.** ☎ 413/499–1600 ⊕ www.berkshires.org.

When to Go

The dazzling foliage and cool temperatures make fall the best time to visit Western Massachusetts, but the Berkshires and the Pioneer Valley are evolving into a year-round destination. Visit in spring, and witness the burst of color that signals winter's end. Summer is a time of festivals, adventure sports, and outdoor concerts. Many towns save their best for winter, when inns open their doors to carolers and shops serve eggnog. Though usually considered the off-season, it's the perfect time to try cross-country skiing or to spend a night by the fireplace, tucked under a quilt while catching up on books by Nathaniel Hawthorne or Henry David Thoreau.

North Adams

130 miles northwest of Boston, 73 miles northwest of Springfield, 20 miles south of Bennington, Vermont.

If you're looking for a Berkshires getaway that combines culture with outdoor fun and a cool place to stay, put North Adams on your short list. In addition to the Massachusetts Museum of Contemporary Arts (Mass MoCA), North Adams has a number of smaller art galleries, as well as a few mills and factory buildings that have been converted into artist studios. This city with a "small town" feel is always hosting festivals, downtown parades, and on most weekends, a farmers' market where locals shop, visit, and grab up in-season produce from their favorite farms. The 11-mile Ashuwillticook Rail Trail is accessible in nearby Adams, as is Mt. Greylock State Reservation, if you venture there on foot via one of the local trailheads.

The Ins and Outs of Cannabis

Travelers looking for a little extra relaxation may be interested in stopping by one of the region's newest recreational marijuana shops open to those 21 or older. While these aren't your parents' pot shops with lingering smells and tie-dye wall hangings (these days, dispensaries—as they prefer to be called—go for a more clean, almost clinical look with modern fixtures that include elements of nature) you may still have to wait in a parking lot to get your fix. In order to meet state capacity guidelines, there's often a line snaking around parking lots filled with shoppers waiting to enter.

The Basics

How to pay: Due to federal marijuana laws, many national and state-chartered banks that are federally insured do not want to be involved with marijuana transactions. Therefore, many dispensaries ask for cash only, and a few may take debit cards. Your best bet? Always come prepared with cash.

Identification: You'll need a government-issued ID for age validation. Acceptable forms include a driver's license, passport, state ID card, or military ID. Make sure you check that

expiration date—if your ID is expired it will not be accepted. You don't have to live in the state to purchase marijuana, but remember, products purchased in the Bay State are only legal here. If you cross state lines, you're on your own.

What to buy: Recreational marijuana customers may legally purchase up to 1 ounce of marijuana flower or 5 grams of marijuana concentrate per day. Shops now offer a variety of options—from edibles such as gummies and chocolate bars, to vaping products and prerolled joints. Western Mass sellers have built a reputation for being friendly, helpful, and more than willing to offer advice on what to purchase and at what concentrate. Don't be afraid to ask for recommendations.

Now what? Once you leave the store, you can't have an open container of any form of marijuana in the passenger area of your car while on the road or at a place where the public has access. It must be stored in a closed container in your trunk or a locked glove compartment. It also cannot be used in public areas, only in private where owners are OK with it. Check with your lodging for specific rules and regulations.

GETTING HERE AND AROUND

Arrive at North Adams from Pittsfield in the south via Route 8, or from Williamstown in the west via Route 2. Once in town you can see everything on foot in good weather, with most of the action within a few blocks of Main Street. Natural Bridge State Park is the exception, but it's still a reasonable walk.

Sights

Down Street Art

ARTS VENUE | FAMILY | This public-arts project includes 31 galleries in downtown North Adams. From late June through September, DSA presents visual and performing arts events including exhibitions, video screenings, site-specific installations, and, on the last Thursday of the month, opening galas and performances. ✉ *51 Main St.* ☎ *413/662–5253.*

★ Massachusetts Museum of Contemporary Arts (*Mass MoCA*)

ARTS VENUE | FAMILY | Formerly the home of the Sprague Electrical Company, the nation's largest center for contemporary visual and performing arts is one of the finest such facilities in the world, a major draw for its art shows, large music festivals, dance presentations, and film screenings. Expansion in 2017 nearly doubled the amount of gallery space, bringing the total to a quarter million square feet, which includes the wall drawings of Sol LeWitt, an immersive light-based exhibit by James Turrell, sculptures from Louise Bourgeois, and a large room in the main gallery that allows for massive exhibits that wouldn't fit anywhere else. A Kidspace, studios, cafés, shops, and festivals and other special events round out the offerings. ✉ *87 Marshall St.* ☎ *413/662–2111* ⊕ *www. massmoca.org* 🎫 *$20 (2-day ticket).*

Natural Bridge State Park

NATIONAL/STATE PARK | The 30-foot span that gives this 48-acre park its name crosses Hudson Brook, yielding appealing views of rocky chasms. The marble arch at the park's center rises in what functioned as a marble quarry from the early 1880s to the mid-1900s. Natural Bridge has picnic sites, hiking trails, and well-maintained restrooms. In winter the area is popular for cross-country skiing. ✉ *McCauley Rd., off Rte. 8* ☎ *413/663–6392* ⊕ *www.mass.gov/locations/natural-bridge-state-park.*

Susan B. Anthony Birthplace Museum

MUSEUM | This museum celebrates the extraordinary life and legacy of Susan B. Anthony, who played a pivotal role in winning women the right to vote. In addition to viewing suffrage mementos, you can learn about the abolition and temperance movements, in which she also participated. Definitely worth a look is the collection of 19th-century postcards supporting these three campaigns. ✉ *67 East Rd., Adams* ☎ *413/743–7121* ⊕ *www.susanbanthonybirthplace.com* 🎫 *$6.*

Western Gateway Heritage State Park

LOCAL INTEREST | FAMILY | The old Boston & Maine Railroad yard is the site of this park whose free museum has exhibits that trace the construction of the Hoosac Tunnel and the impact of train travel on the region. A scale model of North Adams in the 1950s is on display, and there's a short film that documents the intense labor required to construct the nearby Hoosac Tunnel; the tunnel is best viewed from a pedestrian bridge one block from the park where you can see the tracks as they disappear into the tunnel. ✉ *9 Furnace St., Bldg. 4* ☎ *413/663–6312* ⊕ *www.mass.gov/locations/western-gateway-heritage-state-park* 🎫 *Free* ⏲ *Museum closed Tues. and Wed. Nov.–Apr.*

🍴 Restaurants

A-OK Berkshire Barbeque

$$ | BARBECUE | FAMILY | Tucked in the former Sprague Electric Guardhouse on the Mass MoCA campus, this barbecue joint has become a local favorite for its towering sandwiches on freshly baked rolls with killer sides like fresh slaw, tangy barbecue beans, and homemade kosher pickle slices. Grab your food to go and take it to A-OK's neighbor, Bright Ideas Brewing, to enjoy a pint with your hot brisket or shredded chicken sandwich. **Known for:** 14-hour slow-smoked brisket sandwiches; rolls, bread baked in-house; sandwich specials that sell out fast. 💲 *Average main: $18* ✉ *2601 Mass MoCA Way* ☎ *413/398–5079* ⊕ *www.aokbbq.com* ⏲ *Closed Tues.–Thurs.*

Brewhaha

$ | CAFÉ | After moving to the historic West End Market in 2018, Brewhaha is no longer as convenient to Main Street but remains an excellent option for brunch or breakfast at any hour. The spacious interior with its open kitchen welcomes guests with ubiquitous world music and shelves of books that keep children (and adults) entertained while enjoying a coffee or grilled panini sandwich. **Known for:** variety of grilled muffins; cider chai; lack of parking. [$] *Average main: $9* ✉ *437 W. Main St.* ☎ *413/664–2020* 🌐 *www.cafebrewhaha.com* 🕒 *Closed Wed. No dinner.*

Gramercy Bistro

$$ | **FRENCH FUSION** | Within the Mass MoCA complex, the Edison bulbs and large windows that overlook the patio lend a comfortable atmosphere to this upscale-casual eatery that serves everything from chicken-liver mousse to seafood paella. Chef-owner Alexander Smith relies on organic meats and locally grown produce when possible, adding serious zip with sauces made from wasabi and saffron. **Known for:** Sunday brunch; sweet breads; chocolate desserts. [$] *Average main: $24* ✉ *87 Marshall St.* ☎ *413/663–5300* 🌐 *www.gramercybistro.com* 🕒 *Closed Tues. No lunch Mon.*

Coffee and Quick Bites

Jack's Hot Dog Stand

$ | **HOT DOG** | Not much has changed at this hole-in-the-wall including its single lunch counter lined with a small row of stools and its cash-only policy. Locals head here for inexpensive wieners and hamburgers, plain or topped with chili, cheese, or both, but don't expect to find a seat during lunch hour. **Known for:** a family-owned institution since 1917; onion rings and fries; hot-dog-eating contests. [$] *Average main: $3* ✉ *12 Eagle St.* ☎ *413/664–9006* 🌐 *www.jackshotdogstand.com* 💳 *No credit cards* 🕒 *Closed Sun.*

Hotels

★ Porches Inn

$$ | **B&B/INN** | Around the corner from Mass MoCA and Main Street, these Victorian mill-workers' houses dating to the 1890s have been restored and are connected with one long porch and some interior hallways walled with exteriors of the old houses to become one of New England's quirkiest hotels. **Pros:** outdoor heated pool and hot tub; large guest rooms; packages that include museum admission. **Cons:** small breakfast room; no indoor pool; not much indoor public space. [$] *Rooms from: $289* ✉ *231 River St.* ☎ *413/664–0400* 🌐 *www.porches.com* 🛏 *47 rooms* 🍴 *Free breakfast.*

Topia Inn

$$ | **B&B/INN** | Innkeepers Nana Simopoulos and Caryn Heilman have transformed a derelict downtown building into an eco-friendly marvel, with solar panels and natural clay walls. **Pros:** artsy rooms; organic breakfasts; workshops on green cooking and cleaning. **Cons:** short on parking; next door to a bar; you can't bring your own nonorganic shampoos—it's a hotel rule. [$] *Rooms from: $275* ✉ *10 Pleasant St., Adams* ☎ *413/743–9600* 🌐 *www.topiainn.com* 🛏 *8 rooms* 🍴 *Free breakfast.*

★ TOURISTS

$$ | **HOTEL** | This minimalist hotel has many oak-covered surfaces, a large fireplace in the rustic lobby, amazing views of Mt. Greylock from the patio deck and courtyard, and walking trails that lead guests to a suspension bridge, sound sculpture, and a restaurant. **Pros:** outdoor showers in every room; trendy Airport Room eatery attached for late-night snacks; some rooms have private balconies. **Cons:** no tubs in bathrooms; no phone in room; location is traffic heavy. [$] *Rooms from: $290* ✉ *915 State Rd.* ☎ *413/346–4933* 🌐 *www.touristswelcome.com* 🛏 *48 rooms* 🍴 *No meals.*

Activities

KAYAKING

Berkshire Outfitters

KAYAKING | If you're itching to explore the Cheshire lakes by kayak, the Ashuwillticook Rail Trail by bike, or Mt. Greylock's summit on snowshoes, visit Berkshire Outfitters. Just 300 yards from the trail, this shop rents bicycles, kayaks, canoes, paddleboards, snowshoes, and cross-country skis. The knowledgeable staff are happy to dispense free trail maps and advice. ⊠ *169 Grove St., Adams* 🕾 *413/743–5900* ⊕ *www.berkshireoutfitters.com.*

Williamstown

5 miles west of North Adams.

Williamstown is largely built around the prestigious Williams College, a smallish but verdant campus bisected by Route 2. Williams is one of the "Little Ivies," and indeed there are ivy-covered buildings, a Gothic-style chapel, marble columns, and various other architectural features. Although "downtown" consists of just a few streets, two noteworthy art museums can be found near the town center, and there are enough upscale shops and restaurants offering international cuisine. In summertime, theatergoers replace college students for the **Williamstown Theatre Festival**; if you're lucky, you may catch a famous actor at a local bar.

GETTING HERE AND AROUND

Williamstown encompasses the surrounding farms and rolling hills, but the town proper straddles Route 2. On the Williams College campus you can walk to Spring Street and Water Street, and anything else you want to see is probably just a short drive off Route 2 (or you can a hop onto the BRTA bus).

👁 Sights

★ Clark Art Institute

MUSEUM | One of the nation's notable small art museums, the Clark has won numerous architectural awards for its 2014 redesign by Reed Hilderbrand and for the new Clark Center by Pritzker Prize–winning architect Tadao Ando. The polished concrete of the latter visually connects it to the landscape through glass windows and open spaces. The museum has a large collection of Impressionist

works, in particular many significant Renoir paintings. Other strengths include English silver, European and American photography 1840–1920, and 17th- and 18th-century Flemish and Dutch masterworks. ⊠ *225 South St.* 🕾 *413/458–2303* ⊕ *www.clarkart.edu* 🍴 *$20 (2-day ticket)* ☉ *Closed Mon. Sept.–June.*

Mt. Greylock State Reservation

MOUNTAIN—SIGHT | The centerpiece of this 10,327-acre reservation south of Williamstown is Mt. Greylock, the highest point in Massachusetts at 3,491 feet, and the fictional location of Pottermore's North American school of magic, Ilvermorny School of Witchcraft and Wizardry. The reservation has facilities for cycling, fishing, horseback riding, camping, and snowmobiling. Many treks—including a portion of the Appalachian Trail—start from the parking lot at the summit in Adams, an 8-mile drive from the mountain's base. ⊠ *Visitor center, 30 Rockwell Rd., Lanesborough* 🕾 *413/499–4262* ⊕ *www.mass.gov/locations/mount-greylock-state-reservation.*

★ Williams College Museum of Art

MUSEUM | **FAMILY** | The collection at this fine museum spans a range of eras and cultures, with American and 20th-century art two major focuses. The original octagonal structure facing Main Street was built as a library in 1846, and the painted wall above the stairs is by Sol LeWitt—actually the third mural to occupy the wall. Special events take place on the outdoor patio on Thursday night in summer. ⊠ *15 Lawrence Hall Dr.* 🕾 *413/597–2376* ⊕ *wcma.williams.edu* 🍴 *Free.*

🍴 Restaurants

Berkshire Palate

$ | **MODERN AMERICAN** | The unassuming interior of this small restaurant matches its signature "Little Buns" in size, but not bite. Known for specialty sliders that range in flavors from Korean barbecue to fried Buffalo chicken with crumbled

Winslow Homer's *West Point, Prout's Neck* is among the notable paintings at Williamstown's Clark Art Institute.

blue cheese, this quiet spot away from downtown is perfect for sharing dishes and catching up with friends. **Known for:** "Little Bun" flights of your choosing; salt and vinegar fries with garlic aioli; limited menu, changes seasonally. [$] *Average main: $14* ✉ *234 Main St.* ☎ *413/458–6304* 🌐 *berkshirepalate.com* 🕓 *Closed Mon. and Tues.*

★ Coyote Flaco

$ | MEXICAN | The best Mexican food in the Berkshires can be found at this unassuming spot where traditional cuisine meets local ingredients. The menu is small but every item is done well, and often served with side dishes in cute little tortilla cups. **Known for:** enchilada Oaxaca with mole sauce; delicious margaritas; nightly specials. [$] *Average main: $16* ✉ *505 Cold Spring Rd.* ☎ *413/458–4240* 🌐 *www.coyoteflacomass.com* 🕓 *Closed Mon.*

Mezze Bistro & Bar

$$$ | ECLECTIC | With a beautiful hilltop location and dishes inspired by local ingredients, the bistro can get crowded in summer, when Williamstown Theatre Festival ticket holders try to squeeze in dinner before the curtain goes up. With an emphasis on local and seasonal ingredients, the menu is always in a state of flux, but it's bound to contain steak, duck, and a great burger. **Known for:** excellent cocktail, wine list; Garganelli pasta with beef ragu; smallish portions. [$] *Average main: $27* ✉ *777 Cold Spring Rd.* ☎ *413/458–0123* 🌐 *www.mezzerestaurant.com* 🕓 *No lunch.*

☕ Coffee and Quick Bites

A-Frame Bakery

$ | BAKERY | The tiny A-frame at the intersection of U.S. 7 and Route 2 isn't much to look at, but the bakery within sells delectable goods that inspire loyalty in locals and visitors alike. The

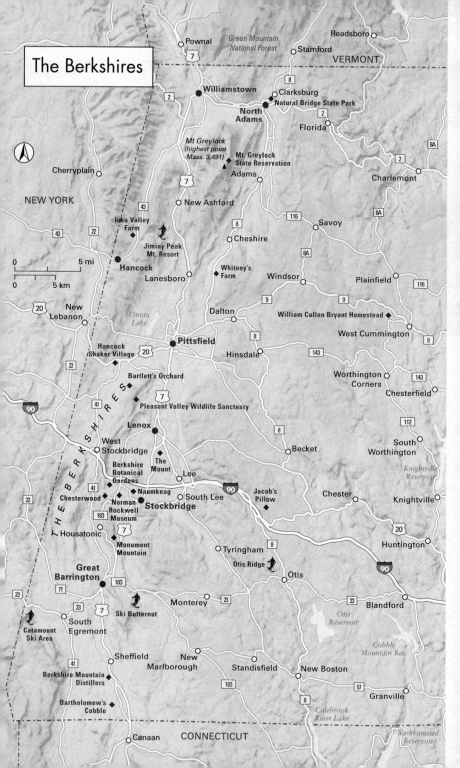

babka—especially the chocolate, though there's also a cinnamon edition—is second to none and must be ordered a day ahead. **Known for:** crumb cakes, scones, and muffins; many items need to be ordered a day in advance; buttercream frosting. [$] *Average main: $3* ✉ *1194 Cold Spring Rd.* ☎ *413/458–3600* ⏲ *Closed Mon. and Tues.* 💳 *No credit cards.*

Tunnel City Coffee

$ | **CAFÉ** | After doing some shopping along Spring Street, stop in for a pick-me-up of freshly brewed drip coffee, espresso, or tea and one of the many delicious baked goods made on-site. During the summer, you're sure to bump into famous actors in between rehearsals stopping by for specialty coffee reminiscent of what they'd get in Manhattan. **Known for:** bean blends that can be enjoyed at home; fresh blueberry muffins; cold brew coffee. [$] *Average main: $6* ✉ *100 Spring St.* ☎ *413/458–5010* 🌐 *www.tunnelcitycoffee.com.*

Hotels

Guest House at Field Farm

$ | **B&B/INN** | Built in 1948, this guesthouse contains a fine collection of art on loan from Williams College and the Whitney Museum, as well as lobby that wouldn't be out of place on a 1960s movie set. **Pros:** wonderful art collection; luxurious robes and towels; seasonal swimming pool. **Cons:** no TV in rooms; children under 12 not permitted; off the beaten path. [$] *Rooms from: $195* ✉ *554 Sloan Rd.* ☎ *413/458–3135* 🌐 *www.guesthouseatfieldfarm.org* ⏲ *Closed Jan.–Mar.* 🔑 *6 rooms* 🍴 *Free breakfast.*

Orchards Hotel

$$ | **HOTEL** | Although it's near Route 2 and surrounded by parking lots, this thoroughly proper hostelry compensates with a courtyard filled with fruit trees and a pond stocked with koi, which the inner guest rooms look out onto; outer rooms with fireplaces are more appealing in winter. **Pros:** elegant rooms; flat-screen TVs; chocolate chip cookies at turndown. **Cons:** no in-room coffeemakers; some service lapses; minor wear and tear visible. [$] *Rooms from: $279* ✉ *222 Adams Rd.* ☎ *413/458–9611, 800/225–1517* 🌐 *www.orchardshotel.com* 🔑 *49 rooms* 🍴 *No meals.*

★ **River Bend Farm**

$ | **B&B/INN** | Listed on the National Register of Historic Places, this 1770 Georgian Colonial is a rustic place to discover simpler times. **Pros:** free Wi-Fi; good breakfast; friendly innkeepers. **Cons:** uneven floors; shared bathrooms; no TVs; credit cards not accepted. [$] *Rooms from: $120* ✉ *643 Simonds Rd.* ☎ *413/458–3121* 🌐 *www.riverbendfarmbb.com* 💳 *No credit cards* ⏲ *Closed Nov.–Mar.* 🔑 *4 rooms* 🍴 *Free breakfast.*

Performing Arts

Images Cinema

FILM | The Berkshires' premier (and, admittedly, only) year-round nonprofit independent film house showcases art-house films, documentaries, and the latest from Sundance on two screens. There are outdoor shows during the summer. ✉ *50 Spring St.* ☎ *413/458–5612* 🌐 *www.imagescinema.org.*

★ **Williamstown Theatre Festival**

ARTS FESTIVALS | The festival, a past Tony Award winner for outstanding regional theater, is Williamstown's hottest summer ticket. From June through August, the long-running event presents well-known theatrical works featuring famous performers on the Main Stage and contemporary works on the Nikos Stage. ✉ *Williams College, '62 Center for Theatre and Dance, 1000 Main St.* ☎ *413/458–3253* 🌐 *www.wtfestival.org.*

Shopping

The Store at 5 Corners

FOOD/CANDY | This store's 239-year streak of continual operation ended in 2011, when it closed for the first time since the 1770s. In addition to being a gift shop and small market for fresh fruits and cheeses, its reincarnation doubles as a café, with a large wooden table and benches where you can have breakfast, fancy baked goods, or just coffee. ✉ *6 New Ashford Rd., U.S. 7 at Rte. 43* ☎ *413/458–6105* 🌐 *www.thestoreatfive-cornersma.com.*

★ **Where'd You Get That?**

TOYS | FAMILY | Jam-packed with toys, games, and more bizarre novelty items than you could possibly imagine, this store benefits from the enthusiasm of owners Ken and Michele Gietz. Grab an offbeat gift for a friend (and some of the interesting candies for yourself). ✉ *100 Spring St.* ☎ *413/458–2206* 🌐 *www.wygt.com.*

Hancock

15 miles south of Williamstown.

Tiny Hancock, the village closest to the Jiminy Peak ski resort, really comes into its own in winter, though it's also a great base for outdoors enthusiasts year-round, with biking, hiking, and other options in summer.

GETTING HERE AND AROUND

You can take Route 43 from Williamstown, U.S. 7 north from Pittsfield to Bailey Road west in Lanesborough, or the BRTA bus from Lanesborough, with plenty of mountain views and trees along the way.

Sights

Ioka Valley Farm

FARM/RANCH | FAMILY | Bring the kids to this 600-acre farm whose family-friendly activities include games and tractor rides. Seasonal offerings range from pick-your-own pumpkins (mid-September–October) to cut-your-own Christmas trees (late November–late December) and a petting farm from late June through August. For a real treat, catch a weekend brunch (late February–early April) with homemade maple syrup atop pancakes, waffles, and French toast. ✉ *3475 Rte. 43* ☎ *413/738–5915* 🌐 *www.iokavalleyfarm.com.*

Hotels

Country Inn at Jiminy Peak

$ | RESORT | FAMILY | Massive stone fireplaces in the lobby and lounge lend this hotel a ski-lodge atmosphere—suites in the building's rear overlook the slopes—and the condo-style suites (privately owned but put into a rental pool) can accommodate up to four people. **Pros:** lodging-and-skiing package deals; nice bathrooms; eat-in kitchenettes. **Cons:** remote location; outdoor pool is small; rooms have no character. [$] *Rooms from: $135* ✉ *37 Corey Rd.* ☎ *413/738–5500, 800/882–8859* 🌐 *www.jiminypeak.com* 🛏 *103 suites* 🍴 *No meals.*

Activities

SKIING

Jiminy Peak

SKIING/SNOWBOARDING | The only full-service ski and snowboard resort in the Berkshires, Jiminy Peak is also the largest in southern New England. This is mostly a cruising mountain. Trails are groomed daily, though some small moguls are left to build up along the slope sides. The steepest black-diamond runs are on the upper head walls; longer, outer runs make for good intermediate

Many of New England's back roads are lined with historic split-rail fences or stone walls.

terrain. There's night skiing daily, and snowmaking capacity can cover 93% of skiable terrain. Jiminy has three terrain parks, as well as a weekends-only mountain coaster: a two-person cart that shoots down the mountain at speeds of up to 25 mph. During the summer, the resort transforms into an adventure park. **Facilities:** 45 trails; 170 acres; 1,150-foot vertical drop; 9 lifts. ✉ *37 Corey Rd.* ☎ *413/738–5500, 888/454–6469* ⊕ *www. jiminypeak.com* ✉ *Lift ticket: $76.*

Pittsfield

21 miles south of Williamstown, 11 miles southeast of Hancock.

Pittsfield is a workaday city without the quaint, rural demeanor of the comparatively small Colonial towns that surround it. There's a positive buzz in Pittsfield these days, though, thanks to a resurgence of sorts: the beautifully restored Colonial Theatre hosts 250 performances every year, and a number of new shops and restaurants have appeared along North Street. City-sponsored art walks and a major renovation of the Berkshire Museum are additional evidence of Pittsfield's comeback.

GETTING HERE AND AROUND

U.S. 7 (1st Street, in town), U.S. 20 (South Street), and Route 9 (East Street) all converge on Pittsfield. Trains and buses stop at the Intermodal Transportation Center, one block from North Street, along which you can walk to museums, interesting stores, and all sorts of restaurants. Buses service the mall and Allendale, but to get elsewhere you'll need to drive.

◉ Sights

Arrowhead

HISTORIC SITE | Literary fans (and those particularly fond of *Moby-Dick*) will want to visit this historical 18th-century house where Herman Melville lived and wrote his most famous works. After viewing all the exhibits, take a walk around the meadow that boasts over 100 species of wildflowers, hike a trail, or just enjoy the majestic view of Mt. Greylock, the inspiration for Melville's white whale. ■ TIP→ **Tours on the hour.** ⊠ *780 Holmes Rd.* ☎ *413/442–1793* ⊕ *www.mobydick. org* ⊠ *$15 (guided tours included)* 🕙 *Closed Nov.–May.*

Bartlett's Orchard

FARM/RANCH | The smell of freshly baked cider doughnuts greets you upon entering this orchard's market, which also sells cider and maple syrup. Seasonally you'll find many apple varieties bagged for purchase, but it's more fun to head into the orchard and pick your own. ⊠ *575 Swamp Rd., Richmond* ☎ *413/698–2559* ⊕ *www.bartlettsorchard.com.*

Berkshire Museum

MUSEUM | **FAMILY** | Opened in 1903, this "universal" museum has a little bit of everything: paintings from the Hudson River School, local artifacts, and natural history specimens both animal and mineral. The Hall of Innovation showcases Berkshires innovators whose creations range from special effects for *Star Wars* to the paper used for U.S. currency. Don't miss the Egyptian mummy, or the aquarium with a touch tank in the basement. The museum's cinema screens American independent and foreign films. ⊠ *39 South St.* ☎ *413/443–7171* ⊕ *www. berkshiremuseum.org* ⊠ *$13.*

★ Hancock Shaker Village

HISTORIC SITE | America's third Shaker community, Hancock was founded in the 1790s. At its peak in the 1840s, the village had almost 300 inhabitants who made their living farming, selling seeds and herbs, making medicines, and producing crafts. The religious community officially closed in 1960, but visitors today can still see demonstrations of blacksmithing, woodworking, and more. Many examples of Shaker ingenuity are on display: the Round Stone Barn and the Laundry and Machine Shop are two of the most interesting buildings. The

Shaker focus on sustainability has been maintained in the form of water turbines, sustainable gardens, and a solar array. There's also a farm (with a wonderful barn), some period gardens, a museum shop with reproduction Shaker furniture, a picnic area, and a café. Visit in April to catch the baby animals at the farm, or in September for the country fair. Reserve early if you want a spot at the Shaker-inspired suppers in October. ⊠ *34 Lebanon Mountain Rd., off U.S. 20 at Rte. 41* ☎ *413/443–0188, 800/817–1137* ⊕ *www. hancockshakervillage.org* ⊠ *$20.*

Whitney's Farm

FARM/RANCH | **FAMILY** | In addition to offering pick-your-own blueberries, tomatoes, and pumpkins on a seasonal basis, Whitney's sells fresh produce, herbs, and dairy products. A deli and a bakery are also on-site, as well as an outdoor playground and greenhouse. ⊠ *1775 S. State Rd., Cheshire* ☎ *413/442–4749* ⊕ *www. whitneysfarm.com.*

🍴 Restaurants

★ District Kitchen & Bar

$$ | **MODERN AMERICAN** | Delicious food and good wine keep this small restaurant packed most nights. This gem can almost be missed just off busy North Street, but professionals and couples looking for an intimate date-night or after-work drinks have made it a hot spot. **Known for:** delicious burgers; house fries with aioli sauce you won't want to share; small rotating seasonal menu. Ⓢ *Average main: $24* ⊠ *40 West St.* ☎ *413/442–0303* ⊕ *district.kitchen.*

★ Elizabeth's

$$ | **ITALIAN** | You'd never guess this little white house was a restaurant, let alone one serving such superb Italian fare that emphasizes high-quality ingredients. Between the large portions of rich entrées and tableside visits from the owner-chef, an evening at Elizabeth's can feel like dinner at a dear friend's house.

Known for: accepting personal checks or even IOUs; giant salads of local ingredients; primarily vegetarian offerings, with daily meat specials. $ *Average main: $23* ⊠ *1264 East St., off Rte. 9* ☎ *413/448–8244* ▬ *No credit cards* ⊗ *No lunch. Closed Sun.–Tues.*

La Fogata

$ | **SOUTH AMERICAN** | The open kitchen looks almost like a lunch counter at this no-frills corner restaurant known for good, honest Colombian food, where it's hard to go wrong unless you're a vegetarian. Served with chimichurri and plantains, all the meats are delicious, from the thin, perfectly seasoned chicken to the pork rind that bacon aspires to be. **Known for:** Latin American soft drinks; South American food market in corner; "Picada La Fogata" giant meat platter. $ *Average main: $15* ⊠ *770 Tyler St.* ☎ *413/443–6969* ⊗ *Closed Mon.*

Mission Bar and Tapas

$$ | **MODERN AMERICAN** | The slightly rustic high wooden tables combine with the art triptychs on the wall to create a very upscale casual atmosphere, which is reflected in the food as well. Standard favorites like meatballs and tacos are spruced up with interesting twists (think peppercorn cream sauce or blue cheese mousse) and locally sourced ingredients. **Known for:** truffle fries; creative wine list; live music. $ *Average main: $19* ⊠ *438 North St.* ☎ *413/499–1736* ⊕ *www.missionberkshires.com* ⊗ *Closed Sun. No lunch.*

☕ Coffee and Quick Bites

Ayelada

$ | **AMERICAN** | **FAMILY** | FroYo lovers won't want to miss this locally crafted frozen yogurt made with ingredients from nearby farms, right down to the milk. Enjoy the tart, yet refreshing, Original flavor, or one of the rotating special flavors like Peach Pie or S'Mores. **Known for:** rotating flavors; friendly service; toppings bar

complete with fruit, candies, and cereals. $ *Average main: $7* ⊠ *505 East St.* ☎ *413/344–4126* ⊕ *www.ayelada.com.*

Dottie's Coffee Lounge

$ | **AMERICAN** | The raised seating area by the windows somehow adds a touch of class to this quintessential coffee shop where the art crowd hangs out. In addition to fine coffee, friendly baristas serve soups and sandwiches, as well as Sunday brunch alongside live music. **Known for:** tasty baked goods; peanut butter lattes; artsy events. $ *Average main: $8* ⊠ *444 North St.* ☎ *413/443–1792* ⊕ *www.dottiescoffeelounge.com* ⊗ *No food Sat.*

🛏 Hotels

★ Hotel on North

$ | **HOTEL** | This restored building in the center of town mixes original brickwork and hardwood with tasteful modern decor to provide spacious accommodations and common spaces, including a large horseshoe bar. **Pros:** on-site restaurant with oyster bar; spacious bathrooms; flat-screen TVs and Wi-Fi in rooms. **Cons:** creaky floors; exposed brick may not appeal to everyone; Central Pittsfield location is not picturesque. $ *Rooms from: $199* ⊠ *297 North St.* ☎ *413/358–4741* ⊕ *hotelonnorth.com* ⇥ *45 rooms* ⍾ *No meals.*

🎭 Performing Arts

★ Barrington Stage Company

THEATER | In the summer, this theater company keeps two stages bustling with creative activity. The Main Stage hosts major musical productions and big names, while a smaller black box theater showcases new works-in-progress. Cabaret nights and a winter 10-minute play festival round out the yearly offerings. ⊠ *Boyd-Quinson Mainstage, 30 Union St.* ☎ *413/236–8888* ⊕ *barringtonstageco.org.*

Colonial Theatre

MUSIC | Back in the day, stars such as Helen Hayes and Al Jolson appeared at this 780-seat 1903 theater; now restored, it hosts live music, theater and popular traveling shows. A second stage, the Garage, hosts $5 comedy nights and programs for children. ⊠ *111 South St.* ☎ *413/997–4444* ⊕ *www.berkshiretheatregroup.org.*

Activities

HIKING

Ashuwillticook Rail Trail

TRAIL | **FAMILY** | Passing through the Hoosac River Valley, the paved 12.7-mile Ashuwillticook (pronounced *Ash*-oo-will-ti-cook) trail links Adams with Lanesborough. The trail follows an old railroad, passing through rugged woodland and alongside Cheshire Reservoir. Walkers, joggers, cyclists, in-line skaters, and cross-country skiers all enjoy this route. ⊠ *3 Hoosac St., Adams* ☎ *413/442–8928* ⊕ *www.mass.gov/eea/agencies/dcr/massparks/region-west/ashuwillti-cook-rail-trail.html.*

SKIING

Bousquet Ski Area

SKIING/SNOWBOARDING | **FAMILY** | On the tamer side of Berkshire ski options, Bousquet has 23 trails if you count merging slopes separately. Experts will probably wish to go elsewhere: Bousquet has a few steeper pitches, but it's focused mainly on good beginner and intermediate runs. There are three double chairlifts, two carpet lifts, and a small terrain park. In summer, Bousquet offers waterslides, a large activity pool, a miniature golf course, a climbing wall, an adventure park, a bouncy castle, go-karts, and a zipline. **Facilities:** 23 trails; 200 acres; 750-foot vertical drop; 5 lifts. ⊠ *101 Dan Fox Dr., off U.S. 7* ☎ *413/442–8316, 413/442–2436 for snow conditions* ⊕ *bousquetmountain.com* ⌦ *Lift ticket: $45.*

Ramblewild

ZIP LINING | **FAMILY** | One of the Northeast's largest tree-to-tree adventure parks, Ramblewild has eight trails with over a hundred physical challenges that range in difficulty—including climbing, swinging, leaping, ziplining, and even a "skayak"—throughout 11 acres of forest. Privately guided hikes and climbing tours are also available on the 1,400-acre property. ⊠ *110 Brodie Mountain Rd., Lanesborough* ☎ *413/499–9914* ⊕ *www.ramblewild.com* ⌦ *$69.*

🛍 Shopping

Museum Facsimiles Outlet Store

GIFTS/SOUVENIRS | This store has the perfect mix of artsy home decor and interesting artwork that will check off anyone on your shopping list. Book lovers will love the signature book spine artwork and hand-stamped stationery. An added plus, all purchases come with free gift wrapping. ⊠ *31 South St.* ☎ *413/499–1818* ⊕ *museumfacsimiles.com.*

Lenox

10 miles south of Pittsfield, 130 miles west of Boston.

The famed Tanglewood music festival has been a fixture in upscale Lenox for decades, and it's one of the reasons the town remains fiercely popular in summer. Booking a room here or in any of the nearby communities can set you back dearly during musical or theatrical events. Many of the town's most impressive homes are downtown; others you can only see by setting off on the curving back roads that thread the region. In the center of the village, a few blocks of shabby-chic Colonial buildings contain shops and eateries. Five miles south of Lenox is **Lee,** famous for its harder-than-average marble, quarried in 19th century for use in the cottages of the

Vanderbilts and their ilk. Today the bustling downtown area has a mix of touristy and workaday shops and restaurants.

GETTING HERE AND AROUND
Just off Interstate 90, Lenox is south of Pittsfield. During the summer Tanglewood season, traffic in Lenox and environs often moves at a slow pace.

ESSENTIALS
VISITOR INFORMATION Lenox Chamber of Commerce. ☎ 413/637–3646 ⊕ www. lenox.org.

◉ Sights

Berkshire Scenic Railway Museum
MUSEUM | FAMILY | In a restored 1903 railroad station, the museum's collection includes antique rail equipment, vintage items, a children's area, and a large working model railway. Short rides aboard the Lenox Jitney train from one end of the grounds to the other are available, but if you want a longer ride, try the sister site, Hoosac Valley Service, in North Adams, where themed (fall foliage, Christmas) hour-long train rides make the 10-mile journey between Adams and North Adams in restored historic cars. ⊠ 10 Willow Creek Rd. ⊕ www.berkshiretrains. org ⊠ Museum free ⊙ Closed Sept.–May and Sun.–Fri., May–Sept.

Frelinghuysen Morris House & Studio
HOUSE | This modernist property on a 46-acre site exhibits the works of American abstract artists Suzy Frelinghuysen and George L. K. Morris, as well as those of their contemporaries, including Pablo Picasso, Georges Braque, and Juan Gris. In addition to the paintings, frescoes, and sculptures on display, a 57-minute documentary on Frelinghuysen and Morris plays on a continuous loop. Tours are offered on the hour—just be aware that it's a long walk to the house. Painting demonstrations and workshops occasionally take place. ⊠ 92 Hawthorne St. ☎ 413/637–0166 ⊕ www.frelinghuysen. org ⊠ $16.

★ Jacob's Pillow Dance Festival
ARTS VENUE | For 10 weeks every summer, the tiny town of Becket, 14 miles southeast of Lenox, becomes a hub of the dance world. The Jacob's Pillow Dance Festival showcases world-renowned performers of ballet, modern, and international dance. Before the main events, works in progress and even some of the final productions are staged outdoors, often free of charge. ⊠ 358 George Carter Rd., at U.S. 20, Becket ☎ 413/243–0745 ⊕ www.jacobspillow.org.

★ The Mount
HOUSE | This 1902 mansion with myriad classical influences was the summer home of novelist Edith Wharton. The 42-room house and 3 acres of formal gardens were designed by Wharton, who is considered by many to have set the standard for 20th-century interior decoration. In designing the Mount, she followed the principles set forth in her book *The Decoration of Houses* (1897), creating a calm and well-ordered home. To date, nearly $15 million has been spent on an ongoing restoration project. Summer is a fine time to enjoy the informal café and occasional free concerts on the terrace. Guided tours take place during regular hours, the private "ghost tour" after hours, and noteworthy authors make regular visits to discuss their latest books. ⊠ 2 Plunkett St. ☎ 413/551–5111, 888/637–1902 ⊕ www. edithwharton.org ⊠ $20.

Pleasant Valley Wildlife Sanctuary
FOREST | FAMILY | Beaver ponds, hardwood forests, and sun-dappled meadows abound at this preserve run by the Massachusetts Audubon Society. Recent wildlife sightings are noted on whiteboards at the entrance and the visitor center, so you'll know what to watch for on the 7 miles of trails. These include loops that range in difficulty from a half-hour stroll around a pond to a three-hour mountain hike. Trails are also open in winter for snowshoeing. At the visitor center

there's a nature play area for children. ✉ *472 W. Mountain Rd.* ☎ *413/637–0320* 🌐 *www.massaudubon.org* 🎫 *$5.*

★ Schantz Galleries

MUSEUM | Jim Schantz's gallery is small and tucked behind a bank, but it displays some of the finest glasswork in the world. With items from nearly five dozen contemporary artists—including Dale Chihuly and Lino Tagliapietra—the museum-quality collection is truly stunning. ✉ *3 Elm St., Stockbridge* ☎ *413/298–3044* 🌐 *www.schantzgalleries.com.*

Ventfort Hall Mansion and Gilded Age Museum

HOUSE | Built in 1893, Ventfort Hall was the summer "cottage" of Sarah Morgan, the sister of financier J. P. Morgan. Lively tours offer a peek into the lifestyles of Lenox's superrich "cottage class." The museum's temporary exhibits explore the role of Lenox and the Berkshires as the era's definitive mountain retreat. Victorian high tea served during guest lectures and workshops is among the highlights. ✉ *104 Walker St.* ☎ *413/637–3206* 🌐 *www.gildedage.org* 🎫 *$18* 🕒 *Closed Wed.*

★ The Wit Gallery

MUSEUM | If you walked past this gallery, you'd inevitably end up ducking in for a closer inspection of the stunning glassworks in the windows. The expertly curated selection inside has more to offer, however, including everything from wooden sculptures to cold-cast metal faces, almost every piece demanding attention. ✉ *27 Church St.* ☎ *413/637–8808* 🌐 *www.thewitgallery.com* 🎫 *Free.*

🍴 Restaurants

★ Alpamayo

$$ | PERUVIAN | Don't let the no-frills decor fool you; what this family-owned restaurant lacks in style it more than makes up for in bold flavors, especially at dinner. Enjoy a menu of fresh and flavorful Peruvian favorites ranging from ceviche to plantains, and don't forget to grab a caramel custard for dessert. **Known for:** chicha morada (incredible purple corn drink); lomo saltado (steak strips sauteed with tomatoes, onions, and fries); Peruvian corn on the cob. [$] *Average main: $19* ✉ *60 Main St., Lee* ☎ *413/243–6000* 🌐 *www.alpamayorestaurant.com* 🕒 *Closed Mon.*

Bistro Zinc

$$$ | FRENCH | Pastel-yellow walls, tall windows, a pressed-metal ceiling, and small-tile floors set an inviting tone at this stylishly modern French bistro with a long zinc-top bar from which it gets its name. The kitchen turns out expertly prepared and refreshingly simple classics, from steak frites to coq au vin. **Known for:** attentive service; duck confit rolls; trendy nightlife at the bar. [$] *Average main: $26* ✉ *56 Church St.* ☎ *413/637–8800* 🌐 *www.bistrozinc.com.*

Café Lucia

$$$ | ITALIAN | The menus change with the seasons at this northern Italian restaurant, so you might find anything from veal piccata with anchovies, lemons, and capers in summer to osso buco in winter. The spacious porch is one of the best places to take everything in during the summer; otherwise, you can enjoy the intimate elegance of the bar and tables inside this converted farmhouse. **Known for:** wild mushroom ravioli; linguine Bolognese; busy on weekends. [$] *Average main: $29* ✉ *80 Church St.* ☎ *413/637–2640* 🌐 *www.cafelucialenox.com* 🕒 *Closed Sun. and Mon. No lunch.*

★ Chez Nous Bistro

$$$ | FRENCH | This cozy spot for a romantic dinner was created by the marriage of a French chef and an American pastry chef. Chef Franck Tessier brings French cuisine to the region with his house-made pâté selection, duck two-ways and a classic boeuf bourguignonne, and you'll never want to skip dessert thanks to Rachel Portnoy's house-made pastries. **Known for:** excellent wine selection; use of fresh, local ingredients; desserts you won't want to skip, especially flourless chocolate cake. $ *Average main: $32* ✉ *150 Main St., Lee* ☎ *413/243–6397* ⊕ *cheznousbistro.com* ⊘ *Closed Mon.*

Firefly Gastropub and Catering Co.

$$$ | **MODERN AMERICAN** | This upscale pub with a few modern dining rooms and porch seating is the perfect place to grab dinner if you're looking for something casual. The menu isn't large, but offers reliably good pub standards. **Known for:** Pig on a Stick (pork belly); nightly discount specials; live music Friday and Saturday. $ *Average main: $25* ✉ *71 Church St.* ☎ *413/637–2700* ⊕ *www.fireflylenox.com* ⊘ *Closed Mon. and Tues. Sept.–June. No lunch.*

☕ Coffee and Quick Bites

★ Chocolate Springs Cafe

$ | **BAKERY** | Escape into chocolate bliss here, where even the aromas are intoxicating. This award-winning chocolatier offers wedges of decadent cakes, ice creams, and sorbets, and dazzling chocolates all made on-site. **Known for:** decadent hot chocolate; truffles, truffles, truffles; perfect, prepackaged gift boxes for any occasion. $ *Average main: $6* ✉ *Lenox Commons, 55 Pittsfield/Lenox Rd.* ☎ *413/637–9820* ⊕ *www.chocolatesprings.com.*

Starving Artist Creperie and Cafe

$ | **BISTRO** | **FAMILY** | If you can find a parking spot along the busy main road through Lee, you'll want to stop and grab a sweet or savory crepe from this casual breakfast and lunch spot. Menu choices include delicious flavor pairings like spicy Reuben crepe or lemon lavender crepe. **Known for:** flavorful, innovative crepes; coffees, smoothies, and a killer mango mimosa; busy on weekends, but service is quick. $ *Average main: $15* ✉ *40 Main St., Lee* ☎ *413/394–5046* ⊕ *starvingartistcreperie.com.*

🛏 Hotels

Applegate Inn

$$ | **B&B/INN** | Just across from a golf course, this 1925 Georgian Revival mansion sits at the end of a regal circular drive, overlooking 6 acres of lush lawns and apple trees. **Pros:** charming dining room; complimentary snacks always available; heated pool. **Cons:** some traffic noise; archaic bathrooms; could use some renovation. $ *Rooms from: $210* ✉ *279 W. Park St., Lee* ☎ *413/243–4451* ⊕ *www.applegateinn.com* ⊷ *11 rooms* ⦿ *Free breakfast.*

Blantyre

$$$$ | **B&B/INN** | Modeled after a castle in Scotland, this supremely elegant 1902 manor house sits amid nearly 117 acres of manicured lawns and woodlands where guests can enjoy the impressive surroundings and exceedingly attentive service. **Pros:** impressive lobby; high-end toiletries; exquisitely maintained property; sophisticated restaurant. **Cons:** some rooms have quirky configurations; very pricey; cottage rooms don't feel supremely elegant. $ *Rooms from: $795* ✉ *16 Blantyre Rd., off U.S. 20* ☎ *413/637–3556* ⊕ *www.blantyre.com* ⊷ *32 rooms, 4 cottages* ⦿ *Free breakfast* ⊷ *Adults only property.*

Brook Farm Inn

$$ | **B&B/INN** | Tucked away in a wooded glen a short distance from Tanglewood, this cozy 1880s inn often has classical music playing in the fireplace-lighted library; the breakfast room, overlooking the glen, serves afternoon tea with homemade scones on weekends. **Pros:** massage room; delicious breakfasts; close proximity to Tanglewood. **Cons:** books up fast; feels old-fashioned; surrounding area busy during Tanglewood season. $ *Rooms from: $200* ✉ *15 Hawthorne St.* ☎ *413/637–3013, 800/285–7638* ⊕ *www.brookfarm.com* ⊷ *15 rooms* ⦿ *Free breakfast.*

Chambery Inn

$ | B&B/INN | A converted 19th-century country schoolhouse houses these unique accommodations in downtown Lee where the cavernous guest rooms—some big enough for two queen beds—maintain their schoolhouse roots with blackboards still hanging on their walls. **Pros:** good value; spacious suites; restaurants within walking distance. **Cons:** limited choices for breakfast; walls are a bit thin; no common space. $ *Rooms from: $189* ⊠ *199 Main St., Lee* ☏ *413/243–2221, 800/537–4321* ⊕ *www.chamberyinn.com* ⤴ *9 rooms* ⫯◯⫯ *Free breakfast.*

★ Devonfield Inn

$$ | B&B/INN | Occupying a grand Federal house from 1800, the Devonfield sits atop a birch-shaded hillside overlooking 32 acres of rolling meadows, and offers elegant but not ostentatious guest rooms that deftly blend Colonial style (four-poster beds, working fireplaces, some Oriental rugs) and modern convenience (Wi-Fi, flat-screen TVs, and in some cases whirlpool tubs). **Pros:** heated pool; separate cottage available; beautiful lawns and tennis court. **Cons:** not ideal for children; only 11 rooms; breakfast menu is not very large. $ *Rooms from: $265* ⊠ *85 Stockbridge Rd., Lee* ☏ *413/243–3298, 800/664–0880* ⊕ *www.devonfield.com* ⤴ *11 rooms* ⫯◯⫯ *Free breakfast.*

★ Gateways Inn and Restaurant

$$$ | B&B/INN | Once the 1912 summer cottage of Harley Procter (as in, Procter & Gamble), this beautifully updated country inn has guest rooms and suites in various configurations and styles; most have working fireplaces, detailed moldings, and plush carpeting. **Pros:** well-appointed rooms; great location in the heart of Lenox; late-night nibbles in the piano bar. **Cons:** lots of stairs; weddings sometimes take over the lobby; in-house dining options lacking. $ *Rooms from: $300* ⊠ *51 Walker St.* ☏ *413/637–2532* ⊕ *www.gatewaysinn.com* ⤴ *11 rooms* ⫯◯⫯ *Free breakfast.*

Wyndhurst Manor & Club

$$ | RESORT | FAMILY | This 380-acre resort recently underwent a $130 million renovation and name change, transforming the former Cranwell Resort into a more polished, high-end Miraval property. **Pros:** golfing with a view; variety of packages that include local attractions; delicious, healthy dining options. **Cons:** extra cost for some amenities; ongoing construction; steep prices for packages. $ *Rooms from: $280* ⊠ *55 Lee Rd., Rte. 20* ☏ *413/637–1364, 800/232–3969* ⊕ *www.wyndhurstmanorandclub.com* ⤴ *146 rooms* ⫯◯⫯ *No meals.*

⦿ Performing Arts

Shakespeare and Company

THEATER | The works of William Shakespeare and other writers are performed between four theaters. The Tina Packer Playhouse and Elayne P. Bernstein Theatre are both indoors, so you can enjoy productions throughout much of the year. Outdoor theaters include the Roman Garden Theatre and the Rose Footprint Theatre, the latter of which reflects the dimensions of the Rose, Shakespeare's first performance space in London. ⊠ *70 Kemble St.* ☏ *413/637–3353* ⊕ *www.shakespeare.org.*

★ Tanglewood

CONCERTS | FAMILY | The 200-acre summer home of the Boston Symphony Orchestra, Tanglewood attracts thousands every summer to concerts by world-famous musicians. The 5,000-seat main shed hosts larger concerts; the more intimate Seiji Ozawa Hall seats around 1,200 and is used for chamber music and solo performances. The hall is named for the renowned conductor, for years the BSO's music director, a job now held by the Latvian-born Andris Nelsons. Among the most rewarding ways to experience Tanglewood is to purchase lawn tickets, arrive early with blankets or lawn chairs, and enjoy a picnic under the stars. Except for the occasional big-name concert, lawn tickets cost only $21–$23. Inside the shed, tickets vary in price, with most of the good seats costing $50–$120. You can hear the same music for much less by attending an open rehearsal. ⊠ *297 West St., off Rte. 183* ☎ *617/266–1492, 888/266–1492* ⊕ *www.bso.org.*

🏃 Activities

SPAS

Canyon Ranch

SPA/BEAUTY | Set in Bellefontaine Mansion, an 1897 replica of Le Petit Trianon in Versailles, the Berkshires' outpost of the Arizona resort couldn't be more elegantly old-fashioned. Looks can be deceiving, though: housed within is a state-of-the-art fitness center with the latest classes and the best equipment, a staff of chefs cooking up healthful cuisine, and, of course, a holistic spa. Treatments range from Eastern-inspired therapies like ayurvedic treatments to the Canyon Ranch's signature full-body massages—hot stones optional. If you're looking to get away from it all, this is the place to enjoy a spa day in between hiking and paddling through the Berkshire countryside. ⊠ *165 Kemble St.* ☎ *800/742–9000, 413/637–4400* ⊕ *www. canyonranch.com.*

🛍 Shopping

Hoadley Gallery

ART GALLERIES | One of New England's foremost crafts centers, the gallery shows and sells American arts and crafts, with a strong focus on pottery, jewelry, and textiles. ⊠ *21 Church St.* ☎ *413/637–2814* ⊕ *www.hoadleygallery.com.*

Purple Plume

CLOTHING | Carefully curated artsy tops, scarves, and jewelry fill this store bursting with color and fun fashion finds. The boutique also specializes in graphic prints and fabrics, flowing tops, and statement necklaces. It's the perfect stop before your next local gallery opening. ⊠ *35 Church St.* ☎ *413/637– 3442* ⊕ *www.thepurpleplume.com.*

Stockbridge

20 miles northwest of Otis, 7 miles south of Lenox.

The quintessence of small-town New England charm, Stockbridge is untainted by large-scale development. It is also the blueprint for small-town America as represented on the covers of the *Saturday Evening Post* by painter Norman Rockwell, the official state artist of Massachusetts. From 1953 until his death in 1978, Rockwell lived in Stockbridge and painted the simple charm of its buildings and residents. James Taylor sang about the town in his hit "Sweet Baby James," as did balladeer Arlo Guthrie in his famous Thanksgiving anthem "Alice's Restaurant," in which he tells what ensued when he tossed some garbage out the back of his Volkswagen bus down a Stockbridge hillside.

GETTING HERE AND AROUND

Stockbridge is accessible from West Stockbridge or Lee, both of which are exits off the Massachusetts Turnpike (Interstate 90). Once here, you can easily walk around the village and drive around the larger area.

ESSENTIALS

VISITOR INFORMATION Stockbridge Chamber of Commerce. ☎ *413/298–5200, 413/298–5200* ⊕ *www.stockbridgechamber.org.*

👁 Sights

★ Berkshire Botanical Gardens

GARDEN | FAMILY | The gardens' 15 acres contain extensive plantings of exotic and native flora—some 2,500 varieties in all—plus greenhouses, ponds, nature trails, and a small gallery. A guided tour, included with admission, leaves daily at 11 am, or grab a self-guided tour at your leisure.

Norman Rockwell: Illustrating America

I was showing the America I knew and observed to others who might not have noticed. My fundamental purpose is to interpret the typical American. I am a storyteller. —Norman Rockwell

If you've ever seen old copies of the *Saturday Evening Post*, no doubt you're familiar with American artist Norman Rockwell. He created 321 covers for the well-regarded magazine, and the *Post* always sold more copies when one of Rockwell's drawings was on the front page. The accomplished artist also illustrated Boy Scouts of America calendars, Christmas cards, children's books, and even a few stamps for the U.S. Postal Service—in 1994 a stamp bearing his image came out in his honor. His illustrations tended to fit the theme of Americana, family, or patriotism.

Born in New York City in 1894, the talented designer had a knack for art early on but strengthened his talent with instruction at the National Academy of Design and the Art Students League. He was only 22 when he sold his first cover to the *Post*. He married three times and had three sons by his second wife. He died in 1978 in Stockbridge, Massachusetts, where he had lived since 1953.

Famous Rockwell works include his *Triple Self-Portrait* and the *Four Freedoms*, illustrations done during World War II. The latter series of oil paintings represents freedom of speech, freedom of worship, freedom from want, and freedom from fear. In a poetic turn, in 1977, President Gerald R. Ford bestowed on Rockwell the Presidential Medal of Freedom, the highest civilian honor a U.S. citizen can be given. Ford praised Rockwell for his "vivid and affectionate portraits of our country."

October's Harvest Festival is by far the biggest of the facility's annual events. ⊠ *5 W. Stockbridge Rd.* ☎ *413/298–3926* ⊕ *www.berkshirebotanical.org* ⊠ *$15.*

Chesterwood

HISTORIC SITE | For 33 years, this was the summer home of the sculptor Daniel Chester French (1850–1931), who created *The Minute Man* in Concord and the Lincoln Memorial's famous seated statue of the president in Washington, D.C. Occasional tours are given of the house, which is maintained in the style of the 1920s, but the real prize is the studio, where you can view the casts and models French used to create the Lincoln Memorial. The beautifully landscaped 122-acre grounds make for an enchanting stroll or bucolic picnic. ⊠ *4 Williamsville Rd., off Rte. 183* ☎ *413/298–3579*

⊕ *www.chesterwood.org* ⊠ *From $10* ☺ *Closed Oct.–May.*

★ Naumkeag

HOUSE | The Berkshire cottage of Joseph Choate (1832–1917), an influential New York City lawyer and the ambassador to Great Britain during President William McKinley's administration, provides a glimpse into the Gilded Age lifestyle. The 44-room gabled mansion, designed by Stanford White and completed in 1887, sits atop Prospect Hill. Its many original furnishings and artworks span three centuries; the collection of Chinese porcelain is particularly noteworthy. The meticulously kept 8 acres of formal gardens, a three-decade project of Choate's daughter, Mabel, and landscape designer Fletcher Steele, alone make this site worth a visit. Creative use of the property now includes a Winter Lights display, with over 200,000 twinkling LED lights; a Halloween-inspired pumpkin trail and haunted house; live music nights with picnics; and a springtime Daffodil Festival. ✉ *5 Prospect Hill Rd.* ☎ *413/298–8138* 🌐 *www.thetrustees.org* 🎟 *$20* 🕒 *Closed Oct.–May.*

Norman Rockwell Museum

MUSEUM | FAMILY | This charming museum traces the career of one of America's most beloved illustrators, beginning with his first *Saturday Evening Post* cover in 1916. The crown jewel of the 570 Rockwell illustrations is the famed Four Freedoms gallery, although various works—including his *Post* covers and self-portraits—are equally charming. The museum also mounts exhibits of work by other artists. Rockwell's studio was moved to the museum grounds and is complete in every detail. Stroll the 36-acre site, picnic on the grounds, or relax at the outdoor café (late May–mid-October). There's a children's version of the audio tour and a scavenger hunt. ✉ *9 Rte. 183* ☎ *413/298–4100* 🌐 *www.nrm.org* 🎟 *$20.*

Restaurants

Once Upon a Table

$$$ | ECLECTIC | They picked a cute little name for a cute little restaurant in the mews off Stockbridge's Main Street. And the owners of this upscale eatery picked a menu to match: a small but appealing selection of Continental and contemporary American cuisine ranging from raspberry-sauced duck to rack of lamb. **Known for:** escargot potpie; seared crab cakes with capers; garlic mashed potatoes. [$] *Average main: $25* ✉ *36 Main St.* ☎ *413/298–3870* 🌐 *www.onceuponatablebistro.com.*

Rouge Restaurant and Bistro

$$$ | FRENCH | In West Stockbridge (5 miles northwest), this intimate French restaurant has been such a success that it has expanded to include a bar and a larger dining area. Chef William Merelle is from Provence, and his American wife and co-owner, Maggie, was formerly a wine merchant; together they provide a mix of French and new American cuisine, backed by a solid wine list. **Known for:** braised duck with shredded potato cake; upscale desserts; cooking classes. [$] *Average main: $30* ✉ *3 Center St., West Stockbridge* ☎ *413/232–4111* 🌐 *www.rougerestaurant.com* 🕒 *Closed Mon. and Tues. No lunch.*

Truc Orient Express

$$ | VIETNAMESE | Mixed in among shops filled with arts and crafts, this family-owned business has been serving up authentic Vietnamese food for more than 30 years. *Bánh xèo* (rice pancakes) figure prominently on the menu, among other classics, but there's some adventurous fare, too. **Known for:** *ca chien* (whole fried flounder in a pungent fish sauce); *bánh xèo*; Vietnamese crafts store in entryway. [$] *Average main: $21* ✉ *3 Harris St.* ☎ *413/232–4204* 🕒 *Closed Mon.–Thurs. No lunch.*

Coffee and Quick Bites

No. Six Depot Roastery & Cafe

$ | CAFÉ | This small-batch roastery and café also serves as an art gallery and community hangout. Stop in for expertly poured slow drip coffee or cold brew made with their own coffee bean blend soaked in cold water for 18 hours. **Known for:** rich, bold cold brew; expert Americano, latte and espresso pours; cool community vibe. [$] *Average main: $8* ✉ *6 Depot St., West Stockbridge* ☎ *413/232–0205* 🌐 *www.sixdepotcafe.com.*

Hotels

★ The Inn at Stockbridge

$$$ | B&B/INN | Antique furnishings accent the guest rooms of this comfortable 1906 Georgian Revival inn, where each of the spacious and airy rooms has a decorative theme, such as Kashmir, Provence, or the Berkshires. **Pros:** heated pool; some rooms have gas fireplaces or whirlpool tubs; lovely furniture. **Cons:** noise from highway (most noticeable in suites); not within walking distance of town; pool is outdoors. [$] *Rooms from: $320* ✉ *30 East St.* ☎ *413/298–3337* 🌐 *www.stockbridgeinn.com* 🛏 *16 rooms* 🍴 *Free breakfast.*

The Red Lion Inn

$$$ | **B&B/INN** | An inn since 1773, the Red Lion has hosted presidents, senators, and other celebrities, in the large and historic main building filled with antiques and small guest rooms. **Pros:** inviting lobby with fireplace; rocking chairs on porch; quaintly romantic. **Cons:** overpriced dining; minuscule fitness center; no mobile reception. [$] *Rooms from: $300* ✉ *30 Main St.* ☎ *413/298–5545, 413/298–1690* 🌐 *www.redlioninn.com* 🛏 *150 rooms* 🍴 *No meals.*

🎟 Performing Arts

Berkshire Theatre Group

THEATER | This theater company has presented plays since 1929. Those on the Main Stage tend to be better-known works with established actors. A smaller theater mounts more experimental works, and some festival productions, including family-friendly shows and the holiday staple "A Christmas Carol" take place at the Colonial Theatre in Pittsfield. ✉ *6 Main St.* ☎ *413/298–5576* 🌐 *www.berkshiretheatregroup.org.*

🛍 Shopping

Kripalu Center

SPA/BEAUTY | You'll see many people sitting peacefully on the grounds as you approach this health and yoga retreat proficient at helping patrons achieve a heightened state of grace. Meals always include gluten-free items in addition to more standard fare. A great spot to pick up new yoga gear, vegan cookbooks, or self-help books. ✉ *57 Interlaken Rd.* ☎ *866/200–5203, 800/741–7353* 🌐 *www.kripalu.org.*

Williams and Sons Country Store

CONVENIENCE/GENERAL STORES | **FAMILY** | Well-worn wooden floors and old-time music provide an authentic feel that pairs well with the country-store staples for sale here: toys, maple goodies, jams, and an abundance of candy. **■ TIP→ Don't confuse Williams and Sons with the sparse "general store" down the street.** ✉ *38 Main St.* ☎ *413/298–3016.*

Great Barrington

7 miles southwest of Stockbridge, 13 miles north of Canaan, Connecticut.

The largest town in South County became, in 1781, the first place in the United States to free a slave under due process of law and was also the birthplace, in 1868, of W. E. B. DuBois, the civil rights leader, author, and educator. The many ex–New Yorkers who live in Great Barrington expect great food and service, and the restaurants here accordingly deliver complex, delicious fare. The town is also a favorite of antiques hunters, as are the nearby villages of South Egremont and Sheffield. On U.S. 7 alone, dozens of antiques shops await your discerning eye.

GETTING HERE AND AROUND

The nearest international airports are Bradley International Airport in Windsor Locks, Connecticut, and Albany International Airport in Albany, New York, but you are better off driving in on U.S. 7 from either Stockbridge or Canaan, Connecticut. Great Barrington is also on the BRTA bus line from Stockbridge. There's plenty of parking in town, most of which is walkable as well.

ESSENTIALS

VISITOR INFORMATION Southern Berkshire Chamber of Commerce. ☎ *413/528–1510, 800/269–4825* 🌐 *southernberkshirechamber.com.*

Sights

Bartholomew's Cobble

TRAIL | FAMILY | This rock garden beside the Housatonic River (the Native American name means "river beyond the mountains") is a National Natural Landmark, with 5 miles of hiking trails passing through fields of wildflowers. The 277-acre site has a visitor center and a museum, as well as the state's largest cottonwood trees. ✉ *105 Weatogue Rd., Sheffield* ☎ *413/229–8600* 🌐 *www.thetrustees.org* 🎟 *$5.*

★ Berkshire Mountain Distillers

WINERY/DISTILLERY | The sweet scent of the country's premier craft gin permeates the Berkshires' first legal distillery since Prohibition. The retail store, open every afternoon, sells Greylock Gin, a multiple gold-medal winner, and Ethereal Gin, whose ingredients are reimagined every season, among other spirits. Hour-long distillery tours take place on Friday and Saturday. The head distiller, Jon, is friendly, knowledgeable, and happy to pour a taste of a gin, whiskey, or even maple syrup aged in a bourbon cask. ✉ *356 S. Main St., Sheffield* ☎ *413/229–0219* 🌐 *www.berkshiremountaindistillers.com* 🎟 *Tour $10.*

Monument Mountain

MOUNTAIN—SIGHT | FAMILY | For great views with minimal effort, hike Monument Mountain, famous as a spot for literary inspiration. Nathaniel Hawthorne and Herman Melville trekked it on August 5, 1850, seeking shelter in a cave during a thunderstorm. There they discussed ideas that would become part of a novel called *Moby-Dick*. While poet William Cullen Bryant stayed in the area, he penned a lyrical poem, "Monument Mountain," about a lovesick Mohican maiden who jumped to her death from the cliffs. Most hikers find the 2½-mile loop an easy stroll. ✉ *Trailhead at parking lot on west side of U.S. 7, 3 miles north of Rte. 183* ☎ *413/298–3239* 🌐 *www.thetrustees.org.*

Vault Gallery

BANK | Housed inside a former bank, this small art gallery based on French salon galleries includes the vault room with the original safe door intact. While the building itself is impressive, the gallery also features artwork by owner Marilyn Kalish in a variety of media, as well as some work by other artists and a small collection of antiques. ✉ *322 Main St.* ☎ *413/854–7744* 🌐 *vaultgallery.net.*

Restaurants

Aroma Bar and Grill

$ | INDIAN | Popular with college students for its reasonable prices, this restaurant serves up delicious food all day with especially good deals at lunch and the Sunday brunch buffets. The cooks do well with everything from tandoori chicken and other standards to the full Raja Thali dinner special, all served with a trio of flavorful chutneys. **Known for:** stuffed naan; moist minced-lamb seekh kebab; takeout available on Monday. [$] *Average main: $16* ✉ *485 Main St.* ☎ *413/528–3116* 🌐 *aromabarandgrill.com.*

Baba Louie's Sourdough Pizza Co

$ | PIZZA | Specialty pizzas at this trattoria go far beyond the usual toppings, from roasted sweet potatoes and fennel to pineapple and coconut: combinations are weird, but tasty. Baba Louie's fires up sourdough ground wheat, spelt-berry, and even gluten-free crusts in their often crowded, rustic interior. **Known for:** excellent thin-crust pizza; Hannah Jo special (mozz, ricotta, shrimp, pineapple, green chili sauce); smallish dining area and portions. [$] *Average main: $14* ✉ *286*

Main St. ☎ 413/528–8100 ⊕ www.baba-louiespizza.com.

Bizen

$$ | JAPANESE | Expect crowds—and, on busy nights, a wait—at this Railroad Street mainstay where dining room tables wrap around three sides of the large central sushi bar that offers an extensive menu of very fresh fish. Besides the sushi menu, dishes range from *robata* (charcoal grill) to katsu and tempura. **Known for:** harumaki (deep-fried lobster and fish in rice paper); una jyu (grilled river eel in a sweet sauce); tea ceremonies and 10-course tasting menus by reservation. $ *Average main: $22* ⊠ *17 Railroad St.* ☎ *413/528–4343* ⊕ *www.bizensushi.com.*

☕ Coffee and Quick Bites

★ The Bistro Box

$ | AMERICAN | FAMILY | Just a short drive from the busy downtown you'll find this seasonal road-side food shack that always has a line of locals waiting to order the famous Box Burger with hand-cut parmesan and truffle oil fries. Fresh lobster and crab rolls, fish tacos, and pulled pork sandwiches with rhubarb barbecue sauce are the last thing you'd expect to find at this eclectic spot along a busy road out of town. **Known for:** delicious burgers and hand-cut fries; freshly squeezed lemonade and fruit slushies; Spring Fries made with ramp pesto, wild mushrooms, goat cheese, and a balsamic reduction. $ *Average main: $15* ⊠ *937 Main St.* ☎ *413/717–5958* ⊕ *www.thebistrobox.rocks* ⊗ *Closed Wed. and Nov.–Apr.*

SoCo Creamery

$ | AMERICAN | FAMILY | Micro-batched and hand-crafted ice cream makes this small shop tucked in a side street a must stop for any ice-cream lover. Be adventurous and try one-of-a-kind flavors like Blueberry Honey Lavender or Mission Figs, made with figs hand-shucked by the makers. **Known for:** using local ingredients; Madagascar Vanilla, which is better than any vanilla ice cream you've ever tasted; new, surprise flavors every few months. $ *Average main: $6* ⊠ *5 Railroad St.* ☎ *413/528–8400* ⊕ *www.sococreamery.com.*

🛌 Hotels

The Barrington

$$ | B&B/INN | As a third-floor bed-and-breakfast above retail frontage, the Barrington may lack the exterior aesthetic appeal of its Berkshire peers, but it more than compensates for this by its central Main Street location and spacious, eclectically furnished guest rooms. **Pros:** flat-screens and Wi-Fi; conscientious innkeepers; handicapped-accessible suite with piano. **Cons:** no guest lobby; dismal exterior and hallway; pricey for the setting. $ *Rooms from: $275* ⊠ *281 Main St., 3rd fl.* ☎ *413/528–6159* ⊕ *www.thebarringtongb.com* ⇌ *6 rooms* ⦿ *Free breakfast.*

🆕 Performing Arts

Mahaiwe Performing Arts Center

ARTS CENTERS | Catch a performance by Arlo Guthrie or the Paul Taylor Dance Company at the center's stunning 1905 theater. The year-round schedule includes theater, music, dance, comedy, and film. ⊠ *14 Castle St.* ☎ *413/528–0100* ⊕ *www.mahaiwe.org.*

🏃 Activities

HIKING

A 90-mile swath of the Appalachian Trail cuts through the Berkshires. You'll also find hundreds of miles of trails elsewhere throughout the area's forests and parks.

Appalachian Trail

HIKING/WALKING | You can walk part of the Appalachian Trail on a moderately strenuous stretch that leads to Ice Gulch, a gorge so deep and cold that there is often ice in it, even in summer. Follow the Ice Gulch ridge to the shelter and a large, flat rock from which you can enjoy a panoramic view of the valley. The hike takes about 45 minutes one-way. ⊠ *Trail-head on Lake Buel Rd., about 100 feet northwest of Deerwood Park Dr.* ⊕ *www. appalachiantrail.org.*

SKIING
Catamount Ski Area
SKIING/SNOWBOARDING | FAMILY | Skiers seeking a family experience often end up here. Although it's not the biggest mountain in the area, Catamount can be less crowded than other options when it's not a holiday weekend, and the terrain is varied. The Sidewinder, an intermediate cruising trail, is more than 1 mile from top to bottom. Just watch out for ice on the tougher trails. There's also night skiing and snowboarding, plus three terrain parks for snowboarders and others. During the summer, the aerial adventure park has guests traveling between treetops. **Facilities:** 36 trails; 130 acres; 1,000-foot vertical drop; 7 lifts. ⊠ *3290 Rte. 23, South Egremont* ☎ *413/528–1262, 413/528–1262 for snow conditions* ⊕ *www.catamountski.com* ☒ *Lift ticket: $68.*

Ski Butternut
SKIING/SNOWBOARDING | With a variety of trails and slopes, including a 1½-mile run, Ski Butternut is good for skiers of all ability levels. There are a few beginner and advanced trails, and more than half the mountain is mellow intermediate terrain. For snowboarders there are top-to-bottom terrain parks and a beginner park, and eight lanes are available for snow tubing. Eleven lifts, including four carpet lifts and the longest quad in the Berkshires, keep traffic spread out. **Facilities:** 22 trails; 110 acres; 1,000-foot vertical drop; 11 lifts. ⊠ *380 State Rd.* ☎ *413/528–2000, 413/528–4433 for ski school, 800/438–7669 for snow conditions* ⊕ *www.skibut-ternut.com* ☒ *Lift ticket: $60.*

🛍 Shopping
ANTIQUES
The Great Barrington area, including the small towns of Sheffield and South Egremont, has the Berkshires' greatest concentration of antiques stores. Some shops are open sporadically, and many are closed on Tuesday.

Elise Abrams Antiques
ANTIQUES/COLLECTIBLES | The owner of this store selling dining-related antique porcelain, glassware, and tabletop accessories is an expert in the field. The prices match the high quality of her selections. ⊠ *11 Stockbridge Rd., near Rte. 183* ☎ *413/528–3201* ⊕ *www.eliseabramsan-tiques.com.*

Great Barrington Antiques Center
ANTIQUES/COLLECTIBLES | The feeling is "indoor flea market" in this space, where 30-plus dealers sell oriental rugs, vintage furniture, and smaller decorative pieces. ⊠ *964 S. Main St.* ☎ *413/644–8848* ⊕ *www.greatbarringto-nantiquescenter.com.*

CRAFTS
Sheffield Pottery
CERAMICS/GLASSWARE | Many of the roughly 100 local potters whose creative output can be found here use native Sheffield clay to fashion their vases, bird-baths, colorful dinner platters, and other ceramics. The resident shop cat adds to the down-home ambience. In addition to the diverse pottery, ceramics supplies are available for purchase. ⊠ *995 N. Main St., Sheffield* ☎ *888/774–2529* ⊕ *www. americanmadepottery.com.*

FOOD
Bizalion's Fine Food
FOOD/CANDY | This French specialty-food shop carries imported cheeses, cured meats, and the finest olive oils from carefully sourced producers, who also sell their wares to fancy restaurants in New York City and Martha's Vineyard. Bizalion doubles as an informal eatery;

on the small menu are some appealing sandwiches, including one with arugula, pine nuts, prosciutto, goat cheese, and olive oil on toasted bread. ✉ *684 Main St.* ☎ *413/644–9988* ⊕ *www.bizalions.com.*

Blueberry Hill Farm

FOOD/CANDY | Organic blueberries are ripe for the picking here on midsummer weekends starting in late July. Bring your own container; payment is by cash or check only. ✉ *100 East St., Mount Washington* ✛ *About 10 miles southwest of Great Barrington* ☎ *413/528–1479* ⊕ *www.austinfarm.com* ✆ *Free.*

Boardman's Farm Stand

FOOD/CANDY | Known for its sweet corn, Boardman's makes a fine quick stop to pick up fresh fruits and vegetables, from pumpkins and peppers to peaches and nectarines. ✉ *64 Hewins St., off Maple Ave., southeast from U.S. 7, Sheffield* ☎ *413/229–8554.*

Howden Farm

FOOD/CANDY | About 4 miles south of the town center, you can pick raspberries from Labor Day to mid-October and pumpkins late September–October. Locals have snatched up the farm's famous sweet corn for decades. ✉ *303 Rannapo Rd., off Rte. 7A, Sheffield* ☎ *413/229–8481* ⊕ *www.howdenfarm.com.*

Robin's Candy

FOOD/CANDY | **FAMILY** | You'll feel like a kid in a candy shop, no matter what your age, in this store packed with hard-to-find sweets that you haven't seen since childhood. Owner Robin Helfand searches out and buys up vintage candy and keeps a stock of jelly beans in just about every flavor imaginable. ✉ *288 Main St.* ☎ *413/528–8477* ⊕ *www.robinscandy.com.*

Taft Farms

FOOD/CANDY | **FAMILY** | Raspberries ripen here early July–August, and you can pick your own pumpkin September and October. Grab a roast turkey (or other) sandwich, served on freshly baked bread, for a fine homemade lunch. If you have time to linger, check out the small turtle pond in the plant nursery, and see the animal area replete with goats, chickens, llamas, and more. ✉ *119 Park St. N.* ☎ *413/528–1515* ⊕ *taftfarmsgb.com.*

HOME DECOR

★ Asia Barong

ANTIQUES/COLLECTIBLES | The eye-catching sculptures visible from the roadside only hint at the vast spectacle inside what bills itself as America's largest Asian art store—customers include the Smithsonian and the Hell's Angels Clubhouse. Carvings of every conceivable material (from wood to whalebone), size (from half an inch to 8 feet tall), and subject matter (albeit heavy on the gods and dragons) can be found here (or made to order and shipped). The sheer volume of art outstrips many museums, but you can still buy a traditional sarong or a gift from the $5 shelves. Humorous signs throughout the store add a touch of character. ✉ *199 Stockbridge Rd.* ☎ *413/528–5091* ⊕ *www.asiabarong.com.*

Springfield

90 miles west of Boston, 30 miles north of Hartford, Connecticut.

Springfield is the busy hub of the Pioneer Valley. Known as the birthplace of basketball—the game was devised here in 1891 as a gym instructor's last-ditch attempt to keep a group of unruly teenagers occupied in winter—the city also has a cluster of fine museums and family attractions.

GETTING HERE AND AROUND

Springfield is roughly the center of Massachusetts, accessible by bus, train, and Interstates 90 and 91. Parts of Springfield are walkable, but you're better off driving or using the local PVTA buses.

ESSENTIALS

VISITOR INFORMATION Greater Springfield Convention & Visitors Bureau. ☎ *413/787–1548, 800/723–1548* ⊕ *explorewesternmass.com.*

 Sights

The Amazing World of Dr. Seuss Museum

MUSEUM | FAMILY | Opened in 2017, this museum offers a look into the Springfield childhood of Theodor Geisel (aka Dr. Seuss) with a wide range of interactive exhibits and wall drawings, all among rooms so colorful that the museum is like walking into a Dr. Seuss book. Part art gallery, part hands-on children's museum, the second floor re-creates Geisel's studio and living room (with the furniture and art materials he actually used); you'll see never before publicly displayed artwork. ⊠ *21 Edwards St.* ☎ *413/425–9289* ⊕ *springfieldmuseums.org* 💲 *$25.*

George Walter Vincent Smith Art Museum

MUSEUM | The museum houses a fascinating private art collection that includes a salon gallery with 19th-century American paintings by Frederic Church and Albert Bierstadt, as well as a Japanese antiquities room filled with armor, textiles, porcelain, and carved jade. Lovers of architecture will appreciate the Italian palazzo-style building, built in 1896, with fully restored original Tiffany stained glass windows—the windows are rare examples of Tiffany work commissioned for a museum building. ⊠ *21 Edwards St.* ☎ *413/425–9289* ⊕ *springfieldmuseums. org/about/smith-art-museum* 💲 *$25.*

The Lyman and Merrie Wood Museum of Springfield History

MUSEUM | Learn about the town's manufacturing heritage, including bikes and memorabilia from the former Indian Motorcycle Company, which was headquartered in Springfield. The Firearms Collection includes more than 1,600 firearms, with the largest collection of Smith & Wesson guns in the world. Board game lovers will enjoy the Hasbro GameLand exhibit, which honors Milton Bradley, who after moving to Springfield in 1856, created "The Checkered Game of Life." ⊠ *21 Edwards St.* ☎ *413/425–9289* ⊕ *springfieldmuseums.org/about/ museum-of-springfield-history* 💲 *$25.*

The Michele and Donald D'Amour Museum of Fine Arts

MUSEUM | This small gem of a museum houses a comprehensive collection of American, Asian, and European paintings, prints, watercolors, and sculpture. The Currier & Ives (active 1834–1907) Collection is the largest holdings of lithographs in the nation. ⊠ *21 Edwards St.* ☎ *413/425–9289* ⊕ *springfieldmuseums. org/about/museum-of-fine-arts* 💲 *$25.*

★ Naismith Memorial Basketball Hall of Fame

MUSEUM | FAMILY | This 80,000-square-foot facility—named for Canadian phys-ed instructor Dr. James Naismith, who invented the game of basketball in 1891 during his five years at Springfield's YMCA Training Center—showcases plenty of jerseys, memorabilia, and video highlights. High-profile players such as Michael Jordan and Kareem Abdul-Jabbar of the NBA and Nancy Lieberman of the WNBA are among the nearly 300 enshrinees, but the hall celebrates the accomplishments of players, coaches, and others at all levels of the sport. In addition to displays chronicling basketball history, the hall has a soaring domed arena where you can practice jumpers, walls of inspirational quotes you can view, dozens of interactive exhibits, and video footage and interviews with former players. The hall is easy to find: look for the 15-story spire with an illuminated basketball on top. ⊠ *1000 Hall of Fame Ave* ☎ *413/781–6500, 877/446–6752* ⊕ *www.hoophall.com* 💲 *$28.*

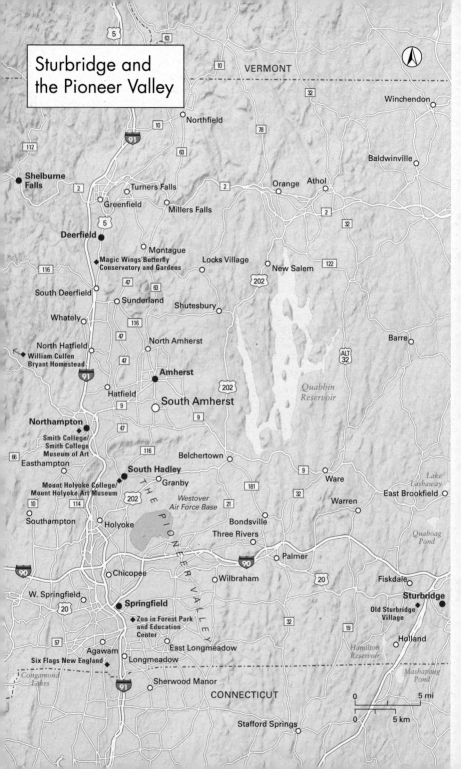

Sturbridge and the Pioneer Valley

VERMONT

Winchendon

Baldwinville

Northfield

Shelburne Falls

Turners Falls
Greenfield
Millers Falls

Orange Athol

Deerfield

Montague
Magic Wings Butterfly
Conservatory and Gardens

Locks Village

New Salem

South Deerfield

Sunderland
Shutesbury

Whately

North Amherst

Barre

North Hatfield
William Cullen
Bryant Homestead

Amherst

Quabbin Reservoir

Hatfield

South Amherst

Northampton

Smith College/
Smith College
Museum of Art

Easthampton

Belchertown

Ware
East Brookfield

Lake Lashaway

South Hadley
Granby

Mount Holyoke College/
Mount Holyoke Art Museum

Westover
Air Force Base

Warren

Quaboag Pond

Southampton

Holyoke

Bondsville
Three Rivers

Palmer

Chicopee

Wilbraham

Fiskdale

Sturbridge

W. Springfield

Springfield

Zoo in Forest Park
and Education
Center

Old Sturbridge
Village

Holland

Agawam

East Longmeadow

Six Flags New England

Longmeadow

Hamilton Reservoir

Congamond Lakes

Sherwood Manor

Mashapaug Pond

CONNECTICUT

Stafford Springs

0   5 mi

0   5 km

Six Flags New England

AMUSEMENT PARK/WATER PARK | FAMILY | With more than 160 rides and shows, this massive attraction is the region's largest theme and water park. You can visit Looney Tunes town and climb aboard DC Superhero rides such as Batman: The Dark Knight and Superman: The Ride, which is more than 20 stories tall and has a top speed of 77 mph. New rides are added frequently, like the Wicked Cyclone, a hybrid wooden structure with a steel track, and the Fireball, a seven-story loop coaster. Visit in autumn to catch Fright Fest haunted events and attractions. ✉ *1623 Main St., Agawam* ☎ *413/786–9300* 🌐 *www.sixflags.com/newengland* 🎫 *$70.*

The Springfield Science Museum

MUSEUM | FAMILY | Scientists young and old will enjoy taking in a show at the oldest operating planetarium in the United States. There are also dinosaur exhibits, an extensive collection of stuffed and mounted animals, and an African Hall through which you can take an interactive tour of that continent's flora and fauna. There's also a small aquarium, where you'll see fishes from tropical reefs around the world as well as frogs, turtles, snakes, and spiders from the rain forests. ✉ *21 Edwards St.* ☎ *413/425–9289* 🌐 *springfieldmuseums.org/about/springfield-science-museum* 🎫 *$25.*

Zoo in Forest Park and Education Center

CITY PARK | FAMILY | At this leafy, 735-acre retreat, hiking paths wind through the trees, paddleboats navigate Porter Lake, and hungry ducks float on a small pond. The zoo, where Theodor Geisel—better known as Dr. Seuss—found inspiration for his children's books, is home to nearly 200 animals, from camels and bobcats to lemurs and wallabies. It's manageable in size, and spotting animals in the exhibits is fairly easy, which makes this an especially good stop for families with small children. Another plus: you can purchase small cones of food from the gift shop to feed many of the animals. Leave time to explore the park after you finish the zoo. ✉ *293 Sumner Ave.* ☎ *413/733–2251* 🌐 *www.forestparkzoo.org* 🎫 *$10.*

🍴 Restaurants

Pho Saigon

$ | VIETNAMESE | A little out of the way, this understated eatery serves authentic Vietnamese cuisine at wallet-pleasing prices. Whether you enjoy the eponymous made-from-scratch soups, fried dishes with meat, or plentiful vegetarian options, the menu has you covered. **Known for:** variety of authentic homemade pho; bánh xèo; getting your car towed if you park in the lot across the street. [$] *Average main: $10* ✉ *400 Dickinson St.* ☎ *413/781–4488* 🌐 *www.phosaigonspringfield.com* ⏲ *Closed Wed.*

Red Rose

$$ | ITALIAN | FAMILY | Featuring massive chandeliers, an open kitchen, and a large dining area, this half-century-old family restaurant is a big, brassy eatery where everyone from canoodling couples to huge parties can feel right at home. The menu features the usual gamut of Italian favorites such as the exquisite eggplant dishes, as well as a variety of pizzas made from a half-century-old recipe. **Known for:** eggplant Parmigiana; primavera pizza; heaping platters of pasta. [$] *Average main: $19* ✉ *1060 Main St.* ☎ *413/739–8510* 🌐 *www.redrosepizzeria.com* ⏲ *Closed Mon.*

★ **Student Prince**

$$ | GERMAN | Impressive beer-stein and corkscrew collections at the bar and darkwood paneling lend this restaurant the feel of a convivial hunting lodge, which the antlers and stained-glass windows in the side dining room accentuate. The menu is decidedly meat-centric—beef, chicken, veal, lamb, pork, and delectable homemade sausages—focused on German dishes with some must-have sauerkraut. **Known for:** incredible homemade sauerkraut; various German sausages; impressive decor. [$] *Average main: $21*

✉ *8 Fort St.* ☎ *413/734–7475* ⊕ *www.studentprince.com.*

☕ Coffee and Quick Bites

Donut Dip
$ | **AMERICAN** | **FAMILY** | This family-run business has been making doughnuts since 1957. Doughnut purists go there for the Old Fashioned Sour Cream, Apple Cider, and Honey Dip, but if you're feeling more adventurous there's plenty to choose from in the jelly, frosting, and sprinkles department, including a decadent bacon-topped creation. **Known for:** Old Fashioned Sour Cream doughnuts; friendly service—if you don't see a doughnut you want, ask for it; freshly brewed coffee. $ *Average main: $5* ✉ *1305 Riverdale St.* ☎ *413/733–9604* ⊕ *donutdip.com.*

La Fiorentina Pastry Shop
$ | **BAKERY** | Springfield's South End is home to a lively Little Italy, including this full bakery that has doled out a wide variety of heavenly pastries (and coffee) since the 1940s. **Known for:** chocolate-covered cannoli; breakfast menu; attached deli. $ *Average main: $3* ✉ *883 Main St.* ☎ *413/732–3151* ⊕ *www.lafiorentinapastry.com.*

🛏 Hotels

★ Naomi's Inn
$ | **B&B/INN** | This elegantly restored house in a residential neighborhood is long on charm, due in no small part to the comfortable and character-filled suites, which are individually decorated—the Louis XIV suite has 19th-century armoires and a down-filled sofa, while the Global Fusion suite has a four-poster bed and a loveseat; a family suite offers a custom-made king-size bed and adjoining room with bunk beds. **Pros:** Bluetooth, bidets, and big-screen TVs with Netflix in rooms; luxe linens and other fabrics; warm and knowledgeable hosts. **Cons:**

near a hospital, so you may hear sirens; smallish kitchen; no pool. $ *Rooms from: $125* ✉ *20 Springfield St.* ☎ *413/433–6019, 888/762–6647* ⊕ *www.naomisinn.net* ⇨ *8 suites* ❙⊘❙ *Free breakfast.*

Sturbridge

35 miles east of Springfield.

Sturbridge is a bit farther toward the coast than the rest of the Pioneer Valley, and off the beaten path lies a rural area that exemplifies old New England. Nowhere is this more true than in Old Sturbridge Village, a re-created early-19th-century village with restored buildings and reenactments, which serves as the central attraction of the town. This is a large enough draw that many inns and hotels are available within walking distance of Old Sturbridge Village, but most of the more appealing dining options, such as The Duck, will require a drive.

GETTING HERE AND AROUND
From Springfield, take Interstate 90 East (or the slower Route 20 East if you're allergic to toll roads). Old Sturbridge Village is centrally located just off Route 20, as are most places you'll want to eat or stay (if they're not right on Route 20, known as Sturbridge's Main Street).

ESSENTIALS
VISITOR INFORMATION Sturbridge Area Tourist Association. ☎ *800/628–8379, 508/347–2761* ⊕ *www.sturbridgetownships.com.*

Sights

★ Old Sturbridge Village
MUSEUM VILLAGE | A re-creation of a New England village circa 1790–1840, this site contains more than 40 historic buildings moved here from other towns. There are several industrial buildings, including a

Costumed historians are part of the 19th-century Old Sturbridge Village.

working sawmill, and guides in period costumes demonstrate home-based crafts like spinning, weaving, and shoemaking. In season, take an informative stagecoach ride, or cruise the Quinebaug River while learning about river life in 19th-century New England and catching glimpses of ducks, geese, turtles, and other local wildlife. Other popular seasonal events include Christmas by Candlelight weekends in December, and the Redcoats and Rebels reenactment brigade during the first week of August. An associated inn is available for those looking to spend multiple days immersed. ✉ *1 Old Sturbridge Village Rd., Sturbridge* ☎ *508/347–3362, 800/733–1830* 🌐 *www.osv.org* 🎫 *$28* 🕑 *Closed Mon. and Tues.*

🍴 Restaurants

B.T.'s Smokehouse

$ | **BARBECUE** | Walk up to the counter and order perfectly cooked barbecued meat by the pint or tray at this no-frills barbecue joint. There aren't many tables: grab one while someone else in your group orders. **Known for:** friendly staff; pulled pork and beef brisket; constantly busy. [$] *Average main: $11* ✉ *392 Main St., Sturbridge* ☎ *508/347–3188* 🌐 *btsmokehouse.com* 🕑 *Closed Mon.*

The Duck

$$ | **MODERN AMERICAN** | In a Greek Revival–style building known as the Whistling Swan lie two restaurants; the more notable one is on the second floor in an unpretentious space resembling a barn hayloft. The Duck offers up generous portions of everything from salad to braised lamb as well as various dishes, which, naturally, incorporate duck. **Known for:** duck confit poutine; lobster deviled duck eggs; bar and sister Italian restaurant (Avellino) downstairs. [$] *Average main: $24* ✉ *502 Main St., 2nd fl., Sturbridge* ☎ *508/347–2321* 🌐 *www.theducksturbridge.com* 🕑 *Closed Mon.*

Coffee and Quick Bites

Whoopie-Doo & Cupcakes Too
$ | **BAKERY** | **FAMILY** | This small bakery is big on cupcake creativity. Beyond your basic vanilla or chocolate, this spot offers flavors like Root Beer Float, Strawberry Crunch and the occasional Unicorn Poop, which is a fun, colorful sprinkle concoction. **Known for:** creative cupcakes with towering buttercream toppings; delicious bagels; whoopie pies. [$] *Average main: $5* ✉ *179 Main St., Sturbridge* ☎ *774/241–3370* 🌐 *www.whoopie-doocupcakes.com/* 🕓 *Closed Sun.–Wed.*

Hotels

The Publick House
$ | **B&B/INN** | Step back in time at this rambling 1771 inn, whose 60-acre property sits on the town green encompassing five buildings including the neighboring Chamberlain House and the Country Motor Lodge. **Pros:** Colonial ambience and architecture; historical significance; flat-screen TVs. **Cons:** slanted hallway floor; thin walls, loud pipes; rooms outside main inn less appealing. [$] *Rooms from: $189* ✉ *277 Main St., Sturbridge* ☎ *508/347–3313, 800/782–5425* 🌐 *www.publickhouse.com* 🛏 *100 rooms* 🍴 *No meals.*

Sturbridge Host
$ | **HOTEL** | Across the street from Old Sturbridge Village and beside a pleasant lake that some room balconies overlook, this hotel has luxuriously appointed bedrooms in Colonial style, reproduction furnishings, and updated baths with granite tops. **Pros:** lakefront property with picnic tables and paddleboat rentals; quiet setting; indoor courtyard with pool and restaurants. **Cons:** often hosts conferences; smell of the pool's chlorine through whole building; inner courtyard can be noisy. [$] *Rooms from: $145* ✉ *366 Main St., Sturbridge* ☎ *508/347–7393, 800/582–3232* 🌐 *www.sturbridgehosthotel.com* 🛏 *233 rooms* 🍴 *No meals.*

South Hadley

12 miles north of Springfield.

A quiet college town with a cluster of Main Street cafés and stores, South Hadley is surrounded by rolling hills and farmland. It's best known for the Mount Holyoke College Art Museum, one of the region's finest cultural facilities.

GETTING HERE AND AROUND

With Bradley International Airport and the Springfield Amtrak station to the south, South Hadley is easy to access. By car, it's east of Interstate 91 and north of U.S. 202 at the intersection of Route 47 and Route 116. You can walk around the Mount Holyoke campus, but you'll need to drive to get most anywhere else.

Sights

Mount Holyoke College
COLLEGE | Founded in 1837, Mount Holyoke was the first women's college in the United States. Among its alumnae are poet Emily Dickinson and playwright Wendy Wasserstein. The handsome wooded campus, encompassing two lakes and lovely walking or riding trails, was landscaped by Frederick Law Olmsted, the co-designer of Manhattan's Central Park. ✉ *50 College St.* ☎ *413/538–2000* 🌐 *www.mtholyoke.edu.*

Mount Holyoke College Art Museum
MUSEUM | The 24,000 works in the college's collection include Asian, European, and American paintings, as well as sculpture and contemporary art from around the world. The coins and numismatics exhibit is definitely worth a look. On summer Wednesdays and Sundays, the Skinner Museum, a church packed full of the eclectic collection of a wealthy mill owner, is open. ✉ *Lower Lake Rd.* ✥ *3 blocks north of Morgan St.* ☎ *413/538–2245* 🌐 *www.mtholyoke.edu/artmuseum* 🎟 *Free* 🕓 *Closed Mon.*

🍴 Restaurants

Food 101 Bar & Bistro

$$$ | **ECLECTIC** | There's nothing basic about this popular restaurant across from the Mount Holyoke campus, and the atmosphere—from the fancy plating to the nice lighting—almost justifies the high prices, which is why this little spot is a magnet for foodies, yuppies, and college students on their parents' tabs. Dishes—everything from seafood to steak—are complicated but mostly successful. **Known for:** bread sticks with various dips; french fries with wasabi mayo; mushroom ravioli in veal shallot reduction. [$] *Average main: $26* ✉ *19 College St.* ☎ *413/535–3101* 🌐 *www.food101bistro.com* 🕓 *Closed Mon. No lunch.*

IYA Sushi and Noodle Kitchen

$ | **JAPANESE** | With puns on the menu and the staff's shirts, this sushi and noodle bar serves up fun in addition to ramen, bao, and a wide variety of sushi. The atmosphere is upscale casual and would be even more pleasant if it weren't always busy, but that's the price you pay for good food. **Known for:** amusing food puns located everywhere; big bowls of rich-brothed ramen; poke bowls. [$] *Average main: $13* ✉ *Village Commons, 15 College St.* ☎ *413/532–8000* 🌐 *iyasushi.com.*

☕ Coffee and Quick Bites

Flayvors of Cook Farm

$ | **AMERICAN** | **FAMILY** | The main advantage of stopping for the delicious homemade ice cream at this family farm is that you can see the dairy cows from the dining tables—and even pet them, if you're brave. Sandwiches and mac and cheese are available as well, if for some reason, you're not in the mood for ice cream. **Known for:** very locally sourced dairy; proximity to cows; asparagus ice cream. [$] *Average main: $5* ✉ *Cook Farm, 129 S. Maple St., Hadley* ☎ *413/584–2224* 🌐 *www.flayvors.com.*

🛍 Shopping

The Odyssey Bookshop

BOOKS/STATIONERY | In addition to stocking 50,000 new and used titles, Odyssey has readings and book signings by locally (and sometimes nationally) known authors. There's a special event more nights than not. ✉ *9 College St.* ☎ *413/534–7307* 🌐 *www.odysseybks.com.*

Northampton

10 miles northeast of South Hadley.

The cultural center of Western Massachusetts is without a doubt the city of Northampton (nicknamed "Noho"), whose vibrant downtown is packed with interesting restaurants, lively clubs, and offbeat boutiques. The city attracts artsy types, academics, activists, lesbians and gays, and just about anyone else seeking the culture and sophistication of a big metropolis but the conviviality and easy pace of a small town.

GETTING HERE AND AROUND

Amtrak's *Vermonter* train, which travels between Washington, D.C., and St. Albans, Vermont, stops in Northampton. The city is also served by buses from nearby Springfield's train station, although most people arrive by car on Interstate 91. Downtown is crossed by Routes 5, 9, and 10, and walking to most downtown locations is not only possible, but an excellent way to spend an afternoon. Local PVTA buses are also available. If you're arriving by car, your best bet is to park in the garage attached to Thorne's Marketplace, which is the center of this mostly walkable city.

ESSENTIALS

VISITOR INFORMATION Greater Northampton Chamber of Commerce. ☎ *413/584–1900* 🌐 *www.explorenorthampton.com.*

👁 Sights

⭐ R. Michelson Galleries

MUSEUM | FAMILY | In an unassuming former bank lies a large multifloor gallery filled with the works of many artists, but the collection's crown jewel is the room filled with the work from dozens of children's book illustrators. Originals by everyone from Maurice Sendak to Mo Willems are featured, as well as a Dr. Seuss area that includes a few sculptures along with his illustrations. ⊠ *132 Main St.* ☎ *413/586–3964* ⊕ *www.rmichelson.com.*

Smith College

COLLEGE | The nation's largest liberal arts college for women opened its doors in 1875, funded by a bequest from Sophia Smith, a local heiress. Renowned for its School of Social Work, Smith has a long list of distinguished alumnae, among them activist Gloria Steinem, chef Julia Child, and writer Margaret Mitchell. One of New England's most serene campuses, Smith is a leading center of political and cultural activity. The on-campus **Lyman Plant House** is worth a visit. The flourishing **Botanic Garden of Smith College** covers the entire 150-acre campus. ⊠ *College La.* ☎ *413/584–2700* ⊕ *www.smith.edu.*

Smith College Museum of Art

MUSEUM | A floor of galleries with natural light, an enclosed courtyard, and artist-designed restrooms and benches make up this museum, whose permanent collection's highlights include pivotal paintings by Mary Cassatt, Paul Cézanne, Edgar Degas, Georgia O'Keeffe, Auguste Rodin, and Georges Seurat. More recent acquisitions include African, Asian, and Islamic art. ⊠ *Brown Fine Arts Center, 20 Elm St., at Bedford Terr.* ☎ *413/585–2760* ⊕ *www. smith.edu/artmuseum* ≅ *$5 (free 2nd Fri. of month 4–8)* ⊗ *Closed Mon.*

William Cullen Bryant Homestead

HOUSE | About 20 miles northwest of Northampton, in the scenic hills west of the Pioneer Valley, is the country estate of the 19th-century poet and author William Cullen Bryant. The 195-acre grounds overlooking the Westfield River Valley are a great venue for bird-watching, cross-country skiing, and picnics. Take a guided tour of the house, offered on weekends, or experience one of the many literary-themed events held throughout the year on the property. ⊠ *207 Bryant Rd., Cummington* ☎ *413/200–7262* ⊕ *thetrustees.org/place/ william-cullen-bryant-homestead* ≅ *Free.*

🍽 Restaurants

Bombay Royale

$ | INDIAN | The deep-blue walls and spacious interior lend a calming vibe to this Indian restaurant, whose extensive menu ranges from South Indian to Indo-Chinese dishes. Whether you're in the mood for chicken, lamb, or something vegan, you'll have a dozen good options in your chosen category. **Known for:** lunch buffets; giant masala dosa; spotty service. $ *Average main: $16* ⊠ *1 Roundhouse Plaza, Suite 4* ☎ *413/341–3537* ⊗ *Closed Mon.*

Caminito Steakhouse

$$$ | ARGENTINE | Caminito's red-and-black interior offers casual elegance in spades. The menu is small, but the flavor is not, so you can count on excellent results whether you order your steak raw as tartare, baked into empanadas, or simply as a large individual cut. **Known for:** filet mignon; empanadas with rotating fillings; live Spanish guitar music at a reasonable volume. $ *Average main: $26* ⊠ *7 Old South St.* ☎ *413/387–6387* ⊕ *caminitosteakhouse.com* ⊗ *Closed Mon. No lunch.*

Northampton Brewery

$$ | AMERICAN | In a rambling building in Brewster Court, this noisy and often-packed pub has extensive outdoor seating on a deck. The kitchen turns out sandwiches and comfort food, including stuffed peppers and burgers with blue cheese and caramelized onions. **Known for:** flaky-light catfish bites; humanely sourced meat; beer-battered appetizers.

[$] *Average main: $18* ✉ *11 Brewster Ct., near Hampton Ave.* ☎ *413/584–9903* 🌐 *www.northamptonbrewery.com.*

Osaka

$$ | JAPANESE | The hillside enclosed porch overlooking the center of town makes Osaka the most recognizable restaurant in Northampton, as well as one of the best dining spots. Whether you're in the mood for sushi, a bento box lunch, or a full hibachi dinner, Osaka serves up traditional Japanese favorites in a welcoming atmosphere. **Known for:** kobe beef sushi; entertaining hibachi chefs; bento box lunches. [$] *Average main: $20* ✉ *7 Old South St.* ☎ *413/587–9548* 🌐 *www.osakarestaurantgroup.com.*

Coffee and Quick Bites

★ Herrell's Ice Cream

$ | CAFÉ | On the lower level of Thornes Marketplace, Herrell's is known for not only having some of the state's best ice cream, but also for being the first ice-cream shop to mix in brand-name candies with its ice cream. Flavors often rotate, but an up-to-the-minute list is available online. **Known for:** homemade small-batch hot fudge; malted vanilla and chocolate pudding flavors; dairy-free and sugar-free flavors. [$] *Average main: $5* ✉ *8 Old South St.* ☎ *413/586–9700* 🌐 *www.herrells.com* 💳 *No credit cards.*

The Roost

$ | CAFÉ | The Noho coffee scene is filled with small spots for college students to refuel and tourists to take a break, but none have the same vintage-meets-industrial charm of The Roost. Grab a house-drip coffee with a breakfast sandwich or one of their bakery items. **Known for:** industrial coffeehouse vibe with exposed brick and subway tiles; theme nights that include bingo, board game nights; inventive vegan options. [$] *Average main: $8* ✉ *1 Market St.* ☎ *413/587–2625* 🌐 *roostnorthampton.com* 🕑 *Closed Mon. and Tues.*

Hotels

Hotel Northampton

$$ | HOTEL | Commanding a huge presence in downtown Northampton with its formidable glass-paned front, this 1927 hotel is a magnet for visiting professors and parents, although location—shops and restaurants are right outside the door—is the main thing the historic property has going for it. **Pros:** on-site tavern and restaurant are favorite hangouts of visitors and locals; top location in town; flat-screen TVs. **Cons:** small rooms; drain pipes are loud; surge pricing. [$] *Rooms from: $200* ✉ *36 King St.* ☎ *413/584–3100, 800/547–3529* 🌐 *www.hotel-northampton.com* 🛏 *106 rooms* 🍴 *Free breakfast.*

Nightlife

Fitzwilly's

BARS/PUBS | A reliable bar for a night out, Fitzwilly's draws a friendly mix of locals and tourists for drinks and tasty pub fare. (Try the Gorgonzola garlic bread.) ✉ *23 Main St.* ☎ *413/584–8666* 🌐 *www.fitzwillys.com.*

Activities

Norwottuck Rail Trail

BICYCLING | FAMILY | Part of the Connecticut River Greenway State Park, this paved 11-mile path links Northampton with Belchertown by way of Amherst. Great for biking, rollerblading, jogging, and cross-country skiing, it runs along the old Boston & Maine Railroad route. Free trail maps are available on the Mass.gov website. ✉ *446 Damon Rd., at Rte. 9* ☎ *413/586–8706* 🌐 *www.mass.gov.*

Shopping

★ Thornes Marketplace

SHOPPING CENTERS/MALLS | A quintessential stop on any Northampton visit—and not just because the market's centrally located garage is your best bet for convenient parking—Thornes contains an eclectic lineup of shops ranging from **Glimpse of Tibet** for Tibetan handicrafts to **Herrell's Ice Cream** and **Captain Candy** for sweets and desserts. Also here are **Booklink Booksellers, Cedar Chest,** a yoga studio, a chair-massage parlor, and clothing and jewelry stores. ✉ *150 Main St.* ☎ *413/584–5582* ⊕ *www.thornesmarketplace.com.*

Williamsburg General Store
CONVENIENCE/GENERAL STORES | This Pioneer Valley landmark has an in-store bakery in addition to the usual candy, spices, jams, maple confections, kitchen items, and other gifts you might expect. Try a "Wrapple": a hand pie made with apples from local orchards. ✉ *12 Main St.* ☎ *413/268–3036* ⊕ *www.wgstore.com.*

Amherst

8 miles northeast of Northampton.

One of New England's most visited spots, Amherst is known for its scores of world-renowned authors, poets, and artists. The above-average intelligence quotient of its population is no accident, as Amherst is home to a trio of colleges: Amherst, Hampshire, and the University of Massachusetts. Art galleries, book and music stores, and several downtown cultural venues tickle the intellectual fancy of the college-age crowd, the locals, and the profs.

GETTING HERE AND AROUND
The closest airport is Bradley International in Connecticut. Amtrak's *Vermonter* train stops in nearby Northampton. From there you can take a PVTA bus into town, where the buses are also a good way to get around. If driving, reduce hassle by bringing change for the parking kiosks.

ESSENTIALS
VISITOR INFORMATION Amherst Area Chamber of Commerce. ☎ *413/253–0700* ⊕ *www.amherstarea.com.*

◉ Sights

Emily Dickinson Museum
HOUSE | The famed Amherst poet lived and wrote in this brick Federal-style home. Admission is by guided tour only, and to say that the tour guides are knowledgeable would be a massive understatement; the highlight of the tour is the sunlit bedroom where the poet wrote many of her works. Next door is **The Evergreens,** the imposing Italianate Victorian mansion in which Emily's brother Austin and his family resided for more than 50 years. ✉ *280 Main St.* ☎ *413/542–8161* ⊕ *www.emilydickinsonmuseum.org* 🎫 *$15* 🕐 *Closed Mon. and Tues. and Jan. and Feb.*

★ Eric Carle Museum of Picture Book Art
ARTS VENUE | FAMILY | If you have kids in tow—or if you just love children's book illustrations—"the Carle" is a must-see. This light-filled museum celebrates and preserves not only the works of renowned children's book author Eric Carle, who penned *The Very Hungry Caterpillar,* but also original picture-book art by Maurice Sendak, William Steig, Chris Van Allsburg, and many others. Puppet shows and storytelling events are among the museum's ongoing programs. Children are invited to create their own works of art in the studio or read classics or discover new authors in the library. ✉ *125 W. Bay Rd.* ☎ *413/559–6300* ⊕ *www.picturebookart.org* 🎫 *$9* 🕐 *Closed Mon. Sept.–June.*

Yiddish Book Center
LIBRARY | Founded in 1980, this nonprofit organization received a National Medal for Museum and Library Service for its role in preserving the Yiddish language and Jewish culture. The award recognized the center's rescue of more than a million Yiddish books that might otherwise have been lost. Housed in a cool, contemporary structure that mimics a traditional Eastern European shtetl, or village, the collection comprises more than 100,000 volumes. Special programs

take place throughout the year. The biggest is Yidstock, a mid-July festival celebrating klezmer and other Jewish music. ✉ *Hampshire College, 1021 West St.* ☎ *413/256–4900* 🌐 *www.yiddishbookcenter.org* 🎟 *$8* 🕒 *Closed Sat.*

Restaurants

Bub's Bar-B-Q

$ | **BARBECUE** | You can smell the sweet and tangy homemade barbecue sauce even before you enter this down-home rib joint where awards and positive newspaper reviews line the walls and a stuffed pig carries your order to the kitchen. Everything from fried gator to pulled pork is expertly done, and the dinners all come with a large and sumptuous buffet of sides. **Known for:** free jukebox; hot bar and cold bar; copious outdoor seating. [$] *Average main: $14* ✉ *676 Amherst Rd., Sunderland* ☎ *413/548–9630* 🌐 *www.bubsbbq.com* 🕒 *Closed Mon.–Wed.*

Mission Cantina

$ | **MEXICAN** | Diners pack this loud and colorful cantina daily to enjoy Mexican food at reasonable prices. What the small menu lacks in variety, it makes up for in reliability; everything from the crispy fish tacos to the carnitas enchiladas is worth trying. **Known for:** long waits during prime dinner hours; delicious (but not free) chips and salsa; offbeat margaritas with interesting fruits and flavors. [$] *Average main: $13* ✉ *485 West St.* ☎ *413/230–3580* 🌐 *www.themissioncantinaamherst.com* 🕒 *No lunch weekdays.*

Coffee and Quick Bites

Amherst Coffee + Bar

$ | **CAFÉ** | Grab a coffee or a cocktail before the movies at this hip café-by-morning, bar-by-night spot that shares an address with the Amherst Cinema building. **Known for:** great scotch menu; friendly service; impressive latte art. [$] *Average main: $7* ✉ *28 Amity St., Northampton* ☎ *413/256–8987* 🌐 *amherstcoffee.com.*

Hotels

Allen House Inn

$ | **B&B/INN** | Meticulous attention to detail distinguishes this late-19th-century inn, which has been gloriously restored to reflect Victorian aesthetics—colorful wall coverings, plentiful antiques, lace curtains, and hand-stenciled details—though the guest-room beds topped with goose-down comforters are the finest that modernity has to offer. **Pros:** charm and elegance; great linens; free parking. **Cons:** dark and cluttered with ornate furnishings; tiny baths; easy to drive past. [$] *Rooms from: $175* ✉ *599 Main St.* ☎ *413/253–5000* 🌐 *www.allenhouse.com* 🛏 *14 rooms* 🍴 *Free breakfast.*

Inn on Boltwood

$$ | **B&B/INN** | On the town common of downtown Amherst, this rambling 1926 inn owned by Amherst College is a favorite among visiting parents and professors for its variety of rooms, from smallish doubles to larger suites. **Pros:** great location on the town common; various weekend packages including a farmers' market special; spacious lobby and rooms. **Cons:** some baths are closet-size; many wedding, school, and graduation celebrations are held here. [$] *Rooms from: $285* ✉ *30 Boltwood Ave.* ☎ *413/253–2576* 🌐 *www.lordjeffery-inn.com* 🛏 *49 rooms* 🍴 *No meals.*

Shopping

Atkins Farms Country Market

OUTDOOR/FLEA/GREEN MARKETS | An institution in the Pioneer Valley, this market sells produce, baked goods, and specialty foods—try a cider doughnut to sample the best of all three. ✉ *1150 West St.* ☎ *413/253–9528* 🌐 *www.atkinsfarms.com.*

Historic Deerfield is one of many places in the region to experience America's past through living history.

Deerfield

10 miles northwest of Amherst.

In Deerfield a horse pulling a carriage clip-clops past perfectly maintained 18th-century homes, neighbors tip their hats to strangers, kids play ball in fields by the river, and the bell of the impossibly beautiful brick church peals from a white steeple. This is the perfect New England village, though not without a past darkened by tragedy. Its original Native American inhabitants, the Pocumtucks, were all but wiped out by deadly epidemics and a war with the Mohawks. English pioneers eagerly settled into this frontier outpost in the 1660s and '70s, but two bloody massacres at the hands of Native Americans and the French prompted them to abandon it until 1707, when construction began on the buildings that remain today.

GETTING HERE AND AROUND

You can take the train to Springfield, but the most direct public transportation to Deerfield is a Peter Pan bus. If you're driving, take Route 10 from the south or Route 2 from the west. Aside from walking around Historic Deerfield, however, you won't get far without a car.

◉ Sights

★ Historic Deerfield

HISTORIC SITE | With 52 buildings on 93 acres, Historic Deerfield provides a vivid glimpse into 18th- and 19th-century America. Along the tree-lined main street are 12 museum houses, built between 1720 and 1850, some with original doorways. Four are open to the public on self-guided tours, and the remainder can be seen on guided tours that begin on the hour. The **Frary House** displays arts and crafts from the 1900s; the attached Barnard Tavern was the main meeting place for Deerfield's villagers. Other houses depict 18th-century life, including everything from kitchens to adult cradles for those who had fallen victim to tuberculosis. Also of note is a one-room schoolhouse, an old burial ground, and the **Flynt Center of Early New England Life,** which contains needlework, textiles, and clothing dating back to the 1600s. The visitor center is located at Hall Tavern, 80 Old Main Street. Plan to spend at least one full day at Historic Deerfield. ✉ *Old Main St.* ☎ *413/775–7214* 🌐 *www.historic-deerfield.org* 🎟 *$18.*

Magic Wings Butterfly Conservatory and Gardens

GARDEN | FAMILY | This glass conservatory glitters with more than 4,000 butterflies. Kids love the butterfly nursery, where newborns first take flight. Outside is a three-season garden filled with plants that attract local species. There's also a snack bar and gift shop. ✉ *281 Greenfield Rd., South Deerfield* ☎ *413/665–2805* 🌐 *www.magicwings.com* 🎟 *$16.*

Coffee and Quick Bites

Richardson's Candy Kitchen

$ | CAFÉ | The name is no joke: the back half of this store is a kitchen where you can see delectable chocolates being made. A short drive from Historic Deerfield, Richardson's sells luscious cream-filled chocolates, truffles, and other handmade confections, not to mention ice cream. **Known for:** melt-in-your-mouth Almond Acorns; selection of sugar-free chocolates; chocolate-covered strawberries. [$] *Average main: $5* ✉ *500 Greenfield Rd.* ☎ *413/772–0443* 🌐 *www.richardsonscandy.com* 💳 *No credit cards.*

Shopping

★ **The Montague Bookmill**

SHOPPING CENTERS/MALLS | This old mill complex along the Saw Mill River—since converted into a quintet of businesses—exudes old New England. **The Bookmill** is a quirky secondhand bookshop whose comfortable chairs make it easy to curl up with a book. The good-humored staffers at the adjoining **Lady Killigrew** café serve beer, coffee, and bagels; there's free Wi-Fi, too. The fantastic waterfall views from the deck of **Alvah Stone,** which serves lunch and dinner, justify its slightly elevated prices. From Friday to Sunday, you can visit **Turn It Up** for music and movies, and Wednesday through Monday the **Sawmill River Arts** crafts gallery offers items by local artists. The complex is incredibly picturesque, if not entirely wheelchair accessible. ✉ *440 Greenfield Rd., Montague* ✣ *¼ mile past village green over small bridge* ☎ *413/367–9206* 🌐 *www.montaguebookmill.com.*

Shelburne Falls

18 miles northwest of Deerfield.

A tour of New England's fall foliage wouldn't be complete without a trek across the famed Mohawk Trail, a 63-mile section of Route 2 that runs past Shelburne Falls. The community, separated from neighboring Buckland by the Deerfield River, is filled with little art galleries and interesting shops on Bridge Street. The surrounding area is filled with orchards, farm stands, and sugar houses.

GETTING HERE AND AROUND

Shelburne Falls lies on Route 2, otherwise known as the Mohawk Trail, useful not only for driving through town, but for setting off to the Berkshires as well.

Sights

Bridge of Flowers

GARDEN | From April to October, an arched, 400-foot trolley bridge is transformed into this promenade bursting with color and a wide variety of flowers. ✉ *Water St.* ☎ *413/625–2544* 🌐 *www.bridgeofflowersmass.org.*

Shelburne Falls Trolley Museum

MUSEUM | Take a ride on an old-fashioned trolley from 1896 at this tribute to the old Colrain Street Railway Combine No. 10, which was the first car on the Shelburne line in the early 20th century. A car barn and rails host other trolleys being restored, including a PCC, the last trolley built in Massachusetts. ⊠ *14 Depot St.* ☎ *413/625–9443* ⊕ *www.sftm.org* ✉ *All-day trolley pass $4.*

Restaurants

Hearty Eats

$ | **VEGETARIAN** | You don't have to be vegetarian to appreciate the fresh, local, organic offerings at this tiny community-focused café. Sharing an entrance with an arts co-op, the café itself lacks ambience, but does offer up a tasty variety of healthy options that exclude any meat except fish. **Known for:** wide vegetarian selection; falafel and fried-fish bites; fresh juices. $ *Average main: $10* ⊠ *24 Bridge St.* ☎ *413/625–6460* ⊕ *heartyeats.org.*

West End Pub

$$ | **AMERICAN** | Overlooking the Bridge of Flowers and Deerfield River, this quaint upscale pub filled with plants and local artwork is a charming place to catch lunch. Tables on the enclosed porch offer a nice view while you enjoy a hearty burger or fancy salad. **Known for:** grass-fed Black Angus beef burgers from local farms; gluten-free rolls and pasta; tough to access bathroom. $ *Average main: $18* ⊠ *16 State St.* ☎ *413/625–6216* ⊕ *westendpubinfo.com* ⊙ *Closed Mon.*

☕ Coffee and Quick Bites

Mocha Maya's Coffee House

$ | **CAFÉ** | Locals come here for the cool vibe, live music, and great coffee. Local art, which is often for sale, decorates the rich red walls, completing the artsy vibe. **Known for:** live music; craft/micro-brewed beers; fun blended drinks like frozen hot chocolate. $ *Average main: $5* ⊠ *47 Bridge St.* ☎ *413/625–6292* ⊕ *www.mochamayas.com.*

🏃 Activities

RAFTING

Zoar Outdoor

WHITE-WATER RAFTING | White-water rafting, canoeing, and kayaking in the Class II–III rapids of the Deerfield River are popular summer activities. From April to October, Zoar Outdoor conducts kid-friendly rafting trips along 10 miles of challenging rapids, as well as floats along gentler sections of the river. Zipline tours and rock climbing are also offered in season. ⊠ *7 Main St., off Rte. 2, Charlemont* ☎ *800/532–7483* ⊕ *www.zoaroutdoor.com.*

🛍 Shopping

Salmon Falls Gallery

CERAMICS/GLASSWARE | The showroom features sculpture, pottery, and glass by more than 100 artisans, including hand-blown pieces by Josh Simpson. ⊠ *1 Ashfield St., Suite 9* ☎ *413/625–9833* ⊕ *www.salmonfallsgallery.com* ⊙ *Closed Tues.–Thurs. Jan.–Apr.*

Sidehill Farm

FOOD/CANDY | This farm sells yogurt, raw milk, and cheese, as well as beef, from grass-fed cows. Vegetables and fruits are generally available throughout the year. ⊠ *58 Forget Rd., Hawley* ☎ *413/339–0033* ⊕ *www.sidehillfarm.net.*

Chapter 7

CONNECTICUT

Updated by
Jane Zarem

◉ Sights	🍴 Restaurants	🛏 Hotels	🛍 Shopping	🍸 Nightlife
★★★★★	★★★★☆	★★★☆☆	★★★☆☆	★★☆☆☆

WELCOME TO CONNECTICUT

TOP REASONS TO GO

★ **Country Driving:** Meander along the winding roads of Litchfield County through charming towns and villages like Kent, Salisbury, Washington, and Litchfield itself.

★ **Maritime History:** New London, Groton, and Mystic are all packed with interesting nautical attractions related to Connecticut's rich seafaring history.

★ **Urban Exploring:** Anchored by Yale University, downtown New Haven buzzes with hip restaurants, smart boutiques, and acclaimed theaters.

★ **Literary Giants:** In one historic Hartford neighborhood, you can explore the homes—and legacies—of Mark Twain and Harriet Beecher Stowe; in New London, visit Eugene O'Neill's summer cottage.

★ **Antiques Hunting:** You'll find fine antiques shops, galleries, and auction houses in cities and towns all around the state, but Woodbury and Putnam are two towns that particularly stand out.

1 Greenwich. Huge estates and a picture-perfect downtown.

2 Stamford. Restaurants, nightlife, shopping, and Amtrak.

3 Norwalk. A center for shopping, dining, and culture.

4 Ridgefield. Pretty main street and great art museum.

5 Westport. A magnet for artists and musicians and Sherwood Island State Park.

6 Bridgeport. A handful of family-friendly attractions.

7 New Milford. Shops, galleries, and dining around the town green.

8 Kent. Numerous art galleries and Kent Falls State Park.

9 Cornwall. Great vistas and a covered bridge.

10 Norfolk. One of the Northeast's best-preserved villages.

11 Litchfield. A classic New England downtown with shops and restaurants.

12 Washington. One of Connecticut's best-preserved Colonial towns.

13 Woodbury. Numerous antiques shops for browsing.

14 Hartford. Capital city with arts and culture.

15 Wethersfield. A Hartford suburb with a great historic district.

16 Middletown. Home to Wesleyan University and Dinosaur State Park.

17 New Haven. Yale, the Peabody Museum, and New Haven pizza.

18 Madison. Ice-cream shops, boutiques, and

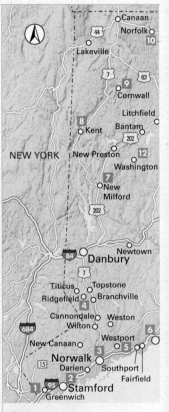

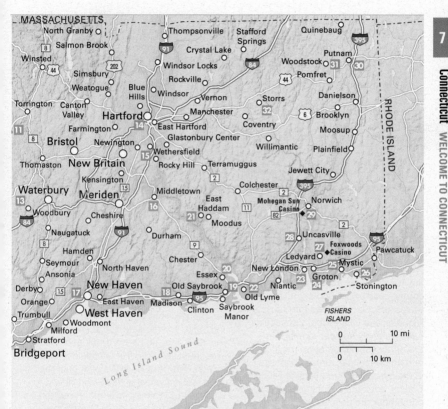

Hammonasset Beach State Park.

19 Old Saybrook. A picturesque small town.

20 Essex. A quaint river town and home to the Essex Steam Train.

21 East Haddam. Old-fashioned charm and a historic downtown.

22 Old Lyme. Lovely countryside and shoreline.

23 New London. Home to the U.S. Coast Guard, Connecticut College, and Ocean Beach Park.

24 Groton. Location of the U.S. Naval Submarine Base and submarine museum.

25 Mystic. Mystic Seaport and Mystic Aquarium.

26 Stonington. A pretty fishing village.

27 Ledyard. Foxwoods casino.

28 Uncasville. Mohegan Sun casino.

29 Norwich. Mill town with beautiful homes.

30 Putnam. Hub of the Quiet Corner's antiques trade.

31 Woodstock. A picturesque town.

32 Storrs. Home to UCONN's main campus.

You can travel from just about any point in Connecticut to any other in less than two hours; this small state is fewer than 60 miles top to bottom and only about 100 miles across. Yet, it would take weeks to ramble all of Connecticut's "back roads," visit all of its small towns and quaint villages, and enjoy all of its unique attractions.

Along Connecticut's 253 miles of shoreline, salty sea air wafts across beach communities like Madison, Old Lyme, New London, and Stonington, while a patchwork of forested hills and tiny towns fill the state's northwestern corner—and once-upon-a-time mill towns line rivers such as the Housatonic, Moodus, and Quinebaug. Connecticut has seemingly endless farmland in the northeast, where cows might just outnumber people; directly opposite, in the upscale communities of Fairfield County, boutique shopping bags probably outnumber the people.

Just as diverse as the landscape are the state's residents, who number more than 3½ million. Many "Connecticut Yankees" can trace their roots to the 1600s, when Connecticut was settled as one of the 13 original colonies; but the state motto is "He who transplanted still sustains." And so the face of the Nutmegger today is both the family from Naples making pizza in New Haven and the farmer in Norfolk whose land dates back five generations, the grandmother in New Britain who makes the state's best pierogi and the ladies who lunch in Westport, the celebrity nestled in the Litchfield Hills and the Bridgeport entrepreneur trying to close the gap between Connecticut's struggling cities and its affluent suburbs.

Qualities that all Connecticut Yankees seem to have in common, historically, is inventiveness, intellect, and the desire to have a little fun. For example: the nation's first public library opened in New Haven in 1656; its first state house, in Hartford in 1776. Tapping Reeve developed America's first law school in Litchfield in 1784, West Hartford's Noah Webster published the first dictionary in 1806, and New Haven's Eli Whitney invented the cotton gin. On the fun side, Lake Compounce in Bristol was the country's first amusement park; Bethel's P.T. Barnum staged the first three-ring circus; and the hamburger, the lollipop, the can opener, the Frisbee, the whiffle ball, FM radio, the portable typewriter, the.45 Colt revolver, even the lobster roll—and, of course, the nuclear submarine—were all invented in Connecticut.

Today, due to the state's rich history, cultural environment, and abundant natural beauty (including 92 state parks and 30 state forests), tourism has become one of Connecticut's leading industries.

MAJOR REGIONS

Southwestern Connecticut, otherwise known as Fairfield County, is a rich swirl of vintage New England and suburban New York—a region that consistently reports one of the highest costs of living and most expensive homes of any area in the country. Its commuter towns are home primarily to white-collar executives. Venture beyond the wealthy bedroom communities of **Greenwich** and **Westport,** and you'll discover cities struggling through various stages of urban renewal: **Stamford, Norwalk, Bridgeport,** and **Danbury.** These four have some of the region's best cultural and shopping opportunities, but the economic disparity between Connecticut's large cities and its upscale towns is perhaps most visible in Fairfield County.

Less touristy than the coast, the **Hartford** and the **Connecticut River Valley** is a swath of small towns and uncrowded state parks punctuated by a few small cities and one large one: the capital city of **Hartford.** South of Hartford, with the exception of industrial **Middletown,** genuinely quaint river towns and hamlets with names like **Essex, East Haddam,** and **Wethersfield** vie for attention with antiques shops, scenic drives, and romantic restaurants and country inns.

The Litchfield Hills present some of the most enchanting scenery in Connecticut. Two highways, Interstate 84 and Route 8, form the southern and eastern boundaries of the region; New York, to the west, and Massachusetts, to the north, complete the rectangle. Rolling farmlands abut thick forests, and trails—including a section of the Appalachian Trail—traverse state parks and forests. Two rivers, the Housatonic and the Farmington, and two large lakes, Bantam and Waramaug, attract anglers, canoers, hikers, and campers. Sweeping town greens and stately homes anchor **Litchfield** and **New Milford; Kent** and **Woodbury** draw avid antiquers; **Washington** and **Norfolk** provide

a glimpse of New England village life as it might have been two centuries ago; and **Cornwall** is known for its fantastic vistas and covered bridge.

As you drive northeast along Interstate 95 to culturally rich **New Haven,** and the **Southeastern Coast,** you can first wander through Yale's campus or visit the dinosaurs at the Peabody Museum of Natural History before dining at a classic New Haven pizzeria. Then continue east along the jagged coastline that stretches to the Rhode Island border, weaving your way through the quiet town of **Old Saybrook** and the relatively undisturbed beaches in **Madison.** Fans of antiques and boutiques will want to stop in Guilford and Clinton, as well. The cities of **New London** and **Groton** are on either side of the Thames River, and **Mystic,** home to the Mystic Seaport, as well as the small fishing village of **Stonington** are not far beyond. In **Uncasville,** north of New London, the Mohegan Tribe runs the Mohegan Sun casino; near the towns of **Ledyard** and North Stonington, the Mashantucket Pequot Reservation owns and operates the Foxwoods Casino and the Mashantucket Pequot Museum & Research Center. Along with gaming, those two properties have noteworthy hotels, marquee restaurants, and events galore.

Few visitors to Connecticut experience the old-fashioned ways of the **The Quiet Corner,** a vast patch of sparsely populated, mostly rural towns that seem a world away from the rest of the state. The cultural capital of this region is **Putnam,** a small mill town on the Quinebaug River; the formerly industrial town center has been transformed into a year-round antiques mart. In nearby **Woodstock,** authentic Colonial homesteads still abound. The scenic drive along 169 toward Woodstock has been named a National Scenic Byway. University of Connecticut's main campus occupies the majority of the tiny village of **Storrs.**

7

Connecticut

Planning

The Nutmeg State is a confluence of different worlds—where farm country meets country homes, and fans of the New York Yankees and Boston Red Sox can (quasi-) peacefully coexist. To get a true sense of Connecticut's variety, start in the scenic Litchfield Hills, where you can relax on historic town greens and at trendy cafés. Head south, if you have a bit more time, to explore the wealthy south-western corner of the state and then over to New Haven, with its cultural pleasures. If you have five days or a week, add the capital city of Hartford, the villages of the Connecticut River Valley, and the Southeastern Connecticut shoreline.

Getting Here and Around

AIR

People visiting Connecticut from afar can fly into New York City, Boston, or Providence—or directly into Hartford or smaller regional airports in New Haven or Westchester County (NY).

AIRPORT CONTACTS Bradley International Airport. ⊠ 11 Schoephoester Rd., Windsor Locks ☎ 860/292–2000 ⊕ www.bradleyairport.com. **Tweed New Haven Airport.** ⊠ 155 Burr St., New Haven ☎ 203/466–8833 ⊕ www.flytweed.com.

CAR

Interstates are the quickest routes to or between many points in Connecticut, but those highways can be quite congested. From New York City, Interstate 95 hugs the Connecticut shoreline into Rhode Island; for Hartford and the Litchfield Hills, head north on Interstate 684, then east on Interstate 84. From central New England, Interstate 91 intersects Interstate 84 in Hartford and, farther south, Interstate 95 in New Haven. From Boston, take Interstate 95 south through Providence or take the Massachusetts Turnpike west to Interstate 84. Interstate

395 runs north–south between south-eastern Connecticut and Massachusetts.

Often more pleasant because of no truck traffic, the historic Merritt Parkway (Route 15) winds its way between Greenwich and Stratford, then becomes the Wilbur Cross Parkway and continues on to Middletown where it meets up with Interstate 91; U.S. 7 and Route 8 extend between Interstate 95 and the Litchfield Hills; Route 9 heads south from Hartford through the Connecticut River Valley to Essex and Old Saybrook; and scenic Route 169 meanders through the Quiet Corner.

FERRY

Seasonal ferry service is available to passengers (and bicycles) between New London and Rhode Island's Block Island, while year-round ferries carry passengers and vehicles between New London and Orient Point, at the tip of New York's Long Island. Year-round ferries also transport passengers and vehicles between Bridgeport and Port Jefferson, Long Island.

FERRY CONTACTS Block Island Express. ⊠ 2 Ferry St., New London ☎ 860/444–4624 ⊕ www.goblockisland.com. **Bridgeport & Port Jefferson Steamboat Co..** ⊠ 1 Ferry Access Rd., Bridgeport ☎ 888/443–3779 ⊕ 88844ferry.com. **Chester–Hadlyme Ferry.** ⊠ Ferry Rd., Rte. 148, Chester ☎ 860/662–0701 ⊕ portal.ct.gov/DOT/Traveler/ferries/Chester-Hadlyme-Ferry. **Cross Sound Ferry.** ⊠ 2 Ferry St., New London ☎ 860/443–5281 ⊕ www.longislandferry.com.

TRAIN

Amtrak runs from New York to Boston, stopping in Stamford, Bridgeport, and New Haven, before heading either north through Hartford or east through New London. Metro-North runs along the coastline between New York and New Haven, stopping in several towns in Fairfield County (including Greenwich, Stamford, Darien, South Norwalk,

Westport, and Fairfield). Shore Line East is a commuter line that runs between New Haven and New London, stopping at towns in between.

TRAIN CONTACTS Amtrak. ☎ 800/872–7245 ⊕ www.amtrak.com. **Metro-North Railroad.** ☎ 877/690–5116 ⊕ www.mta. info. **Shore Line East.** ☎ 877/287–4337 ⊕ www.shorelineeast.com.

Restaurants

Southern New England is enjoying a gastronomic revolution. Preparation and ingredients reflect the culinary trends of nearby Manhattan and Boston; indeed, the quality and diversity of many Connecticut restaurants rival those of sophisticated metropolitan areas. Although traditional favorites remain—New England clam chowder, buttery lobster rolls, and fish-and-chips—you may also find that sliced duck is wrapped in phyllo, served with a ginger-plum sauce (the orange glaze decidedly absent) and that everything from lavender to fresh figs is used to season and complement dishes. Dining is also increasingly international: You'll find Indian, Vietnamese, Thai, Malaysian, South American, and Japanese restaurants—even Spanish tapas bars—in both cities and suburbs. The farm-to-table movement influences what appears on your plate in many establishments, with conscientious chefs partnering up with local producers to provide the best seasonal ingredients. The one drawback of this turn toward sophistication is that finding a dinner entrée for less than $10 is difficult. *Restaurant reviews have been shortened. For full information, visit Fodors.com.*

Hotels

Connecticut has plenty of the usual chain hotels and low-budget motels, along with the more unusual and atmospheric inns,

resorts, bed-and-breakfasts, and country hotels that are typical of New England. You'll pay dearly for rooms on the coast in summer, when the beaches beckon, and in the hills in autumn, when the changing leaves attract thousands of visitors. Rates are lowest in winter, but so are the temperatures; spring is lovely and also a good season for bargain seekers. *Hotel reviews have been shortened. For full information, visit Fodors.com.*

WHAT IT COSTS in U.S. Dollars			
$	$$	$$$	$$$$
RESTAURANTS			
under $18	$18–$24	$25–$35	over $35
HOTELS			
under $200	$200–$299	$300–$399	over $399

Tours

Connecticut Freedom Trail
DRIVING TOURS | FAMILY | The state's African American heritage is documented and celebrated on the trail, which includes more than 130 historic sights across 50 towns. ☎ 860/256–2800 ⊕ www.ctfreedomtrail.org.

Taste of New Haven
GUIDED TOURS | Colin Caplan and his guides take you on foodie adventures—walking, bike, and party bike tours—in and around New Haven, which boasts a burgeoning restaurant scene and, of course, the famous New Haven pizza! ☎ 888/975–8664 ⊕ tasteofnewhaven.com.

Visitor Information

VISITOR CONTACTS Connecticut Office of Tourism. ☎ 888/288–4748 ⊕ www.ctvisit. com.

When to Go

Connecticut is lovely year-round, but fall and spring are particularly appealing times to visit. An autumn drive along the state's back roads or the Merritt Parkway, a National Scenic Byway, is a memorable experience when spots of yellow, orange, and red leaves dot the landscape. The state blooms in springtime, too, when town greens are filled with daffodils and tulips and dogwoods and flowering fruit trees punctuate the rich green countryside. The prime time for attractions, however, is summer, when travelers have the most options but also plenty of company—especially at beaches along the shore.

Greenwich

35 miles northeast of New York City, 82 miles southwest of Hartford.

Leafy woodlands, rolling hills, elegant homes, beautiful views overlooking sparkling Long Island Sound, and a picture-perfect downtown area filled with chic boutiques and trendsetting restaurants: welcome to Greenwich. It's easy to see why this ritzy enclave has become a haven for the rich and famous. Soak up some history and culture at the Bruce Museum, then head to Greenwich Avenue for excellent (expensive) shopping and dining.

GETTING HERE AND AROUND

If you're traveling north from New York City, Greenwich will be the first town in Connecticut once you cross the state line. Greenwich is easily accessible from either Interstate 95 or the Merritt Parkway if you're coming by car; Metro-North commuter trains also service Greenwich.

◉ Sights

★ Bruce Museum of Arts and Science

MUSEUM | FAMILY | The owner of this 19th-century home, wealthy textile merchant Robert Moffat Bruce, bequeathed it to the town of Greenwich in 1908 with the stipulation that it be used "as a natural history, historical, and art museum." Today this diversity remains, reflected in the museum's changing exhibitions— more than a dozen new ones each year—highlighting fine and decorative arts, natural history, and anthropology. On permanent display is a spectacular mineral collection. Kids especially enjoy the touchable meteorite and glow-in-the-dark minerals, as well as the fossilized dinosaur tracks. ⊠ *1 Museum Dr.* ✛ *Off I-95, Exit 3* ☎ *203/869–0376* ⊕ *www. brucemuseum.org* ⊠ *$10 (free Tues.).*

Bush-Holley Historic Site

HISTORIC SITE | In the 1890s, visitors from New York's Art Students League journeyed to the Cos Cob section of Greenwich to take classes taught by American Impressionist John Henry Twachtman at a boarding house for artists and writers run by Josephine and Constant Holley. Thus, the Cos Cob Art Colony was born and flourished until 1920. Today, the circa-1730 house is the Bush-Holley Historic Site, which displays a wonderful collection of 19th- and 20th-century art by sculptor John Rogers, potter Leon Volkmar, and painters that include Childe Hassam, Elmer Livingston MacRae, and, of course, Twachtman. The collection also includes personal papers, photographs, and records that reflect the long history of Greenwich and its inhabitants, from farmers to Gilded Age barons, politicians, artists and writers, shopkeepers, and more. ⊠ *47 Strickland Rd.* ☎ *203/869– 6899* ⊕ *www.greenwichhistory.org* ⊠ *$10* ⊘ *Closed Mon. and Tues.*

Greenwich Audubon Center

NATURE PRESERVE | **FAMILY** | Opened in 1943 as the National Audubon Society's first educational nature center, the sanctuaries and trails are the best location in the area for bird-watching. During the Fall Festival and Hawk Watch each September, you can spot large numbers of hawks and other migrating raptors. Other events include early morning bird walks, summer and winter bird counts, birding classes, and field trips. The center is filled with interactive exhibits, galleries, classrooms, a wildlife observation room, and a deck with sweeping views of wildlife activity. Outside are 7 miles of hiking trails passing through 285 acres of woodland, wetland, and meadow. ✉ *613 Riversville Rd.* ☎ *203/869–5272* 🌐 *greenwich.audubon.org* 🎫 *$6.*

🍴 Restaurants

Boxcar Cantina

$$ | **SOUTHWESTERN** | **FAMILY** | If it's Southwestern food you're craving, Boxcar Cantina delivers the freshest and most authentic Tex-Mex dishes in the area. Diners rave about the margaritas, pairing them happily with fish tacos, quesadillas, enchiladas, and burritos. **Known for:** chefs take special care to source local organic ingredients; the restaurant has a stand at the nearby Westport Farmers' Market on Thursday; takeout is available. [$] *Average main: $19* ✉ *44 Old Field Point Rd.* ☎ *203/661–4774* 🌐 *www.boxcarcantina.com* 🕒 *No lunch weekends.*

Elm Street Oyster House

$$$ | **SEAFOOD** | Locals come here for outstanding oysters and the freshest fish in town; expect an especially lively crowd on weekends. Menu standouts include the varied selection of fresh oysters from all over the country, classic lobster rolls, and outstanding paella. **Known for:** seafood, seafood, seafood—and a cheeseburger or steak for landlubbers; colorful artwork adds cheer to the rather cramped dining room; friendly, efficient service—but you're never rushed. [$] *Average main: $34* ✉ *11 W. Elm St.* ☎ *203/629–5795* 🌐 *www.elmstreetoysterhouse.com.*

The Ginger Man

$$ | **AMERICAN** | **FAMILY** | Come for lunch when shopping along Greenwich Avenue, brunch on Sunday, dinner anytime, or just liquid refreshment, as The Ginger Man has a long, friendly bar and casual seating up front, a cozy dining room with a fireplace in back, and formal dining upstairs via a grand curved staircase. Whether you order a burger and fries or a NY strip with roasted fingerlings, you won't leave hungry—or thirsty. **Known for:** burgers famously served on an English muffin; relaxing, local atmosphere; more than 50 beers, half on tap. [$] *Average main: $24* ✉ *64 Greenwich Ave.* ☎ *203/861–6400* 🌐 *gingermanct.com.*

🛏 Hotels

★ Delamar Greenwich Harbor Hotel

$$$ | **HOTEL** | This luxury waterfront hotel just blocks from downtown Greenwich resembles a villa on the Italian Riviera. **Pros:** the champagne welcome sets a luxe tone; easy walk (or free Tesla shuttle) to downtown restaurants, shopping, and train; complimentary kayaks, bicycles, and (seasonal) harbor cruises. **Cons:** fairly pricey; "nontipping" hotel adds a fee to your bill to cover tips; dogs are welcome in first floor rooms—just so you know. [$] *Rooms from: $309* ✉ *500 Steamboat Rd.* ☎ *203/661–9800, 866/335–2627* 🌐 *www.delamar.com/greenwich-harbor* 🛏 *82 rooms* 🍴 *Free breakfast.*

Hyatt Regency Greenwich

$ | **HOTEL** | In a grand turreted building that once housed the Condé Nast publishing offices, the Hyatt greets guests in its vast but comfortable atrium containing a flourishing lawn and abundant flora. **Pros:** courtesy shuttle to downtown and the train; the heated indoor pool; buffet breakfast in the atrium. **Cons:** frequent

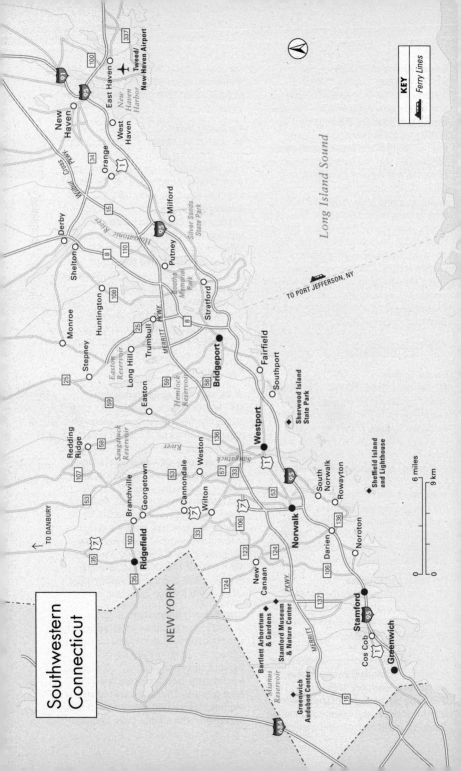

Southwestern Connecticut

KEY

🚢 Ferry Lines

Long Island Sound

TO PORT JEFFERSON, NY

New Haven
East Haven
Tweed/New Haven Airport
New Haven Harbor
West Haven
Orange
Milford
Silver Sands State Park
Derby
Putney
Shelton
Stratford
Monroe
Huntington
Booth Memorial Park
Stepney
Trumbull
Long Hill
Bridgeport
Fairfield
Southport
Sherwood Island State Park
Easton Reservoir
Easton
Hemlock Reservoir
Westport
Redding Ridge
Branchville
Georgetown
Saugatuck Reservoir
Cannondale
Weston
Saugatuck River
Norwalk
South Norwalk
Rowayton
Sheffield Island and Lighthouse
Wilton
Ridgefield
Darien
Noroton
Stamford
New Canaan
Bartlett Arboretum & Gardens
Stamford Museum & Nature Center
Cos Cob
Greenwich
Greenwich Audubon Center
Mianus Reservoir

NEW YORK

TO DANBURY

Wilbur Cross Pkwy
Housatonic River
Merritt Pkwy

100
337
34
1
15
110
8
108
25
59
58
136
57
33
53
107
102
35
7
106
123
124
137
15
136

6 miles
9 km

95
7
25
91
684

wedding, meeting, and event venue; pay to park; noise from halls or neighboring rooms. $ *Rooms from: $179* ✉ *1800 E. Putnam Ave., Old Greenwich* ☎ *203/637–1234* ⊕ *greenwich.hyatt.com* ⇆ *373 rooms* �‖ *No meals.*

Stamford

6 miles northeast of Greenwich, 40 miles southwest of New Haven.

While business is often what brings people to Stamford, what keeps them here are the quality restaurants, nightclubs, and shops along Atlantic and lower Summer Streets. Weekenders have plenty of options beyond the downtown canyons: beaches, boating on the sound, and hiking are only minutes away.

GETTING HERE AND AROUND
Stamford is easily accessible from Interstate 95 and the Merritt Parkway. It is also a major rail hub for Metro-North commuter trains and Amtrak; its high-speed Acela trains also stop here en route between Boston and Washington, D.C.

 Sights

Bartlett Arboretum & Gardens
GARDEN | FAMILY | This 93-acre natural sanctuary is home to more than 2,000 varieties of annuals, perennials, wildflowers, and trees. There's also a greenhouse, marked ecology trails (dogs are welcome), a pretty pond, and a boardwalk through a red maple swamp. Brilliant, bold colors make the wildflower garden stunning in spring. Sunday afternoon is the time to visit for a guided walk. ✉ *151 Brookdale Rd., off High Ridge Rd.* ☎ *203/322–6971* ⊕ *www.bartlettarboretum.org* ✍ *Free.*

Stamford Museum & Nature Center
MUSEUM VILLAGE | FAMILY | Oxen, sheep, pigs, and other animals roam this 118-acre New England farmstead. Once the estate of Henri Bendel, the property includes a Tudor Revival stone mansion

housing exhibits on natural history, art, and Americana. An observatory, open to the public on Friday evenings (except January and February), has a 22-inch research telescope—perfect for stargazing—and nature trails wind through 80 acres of woods. Maple sugaring is a special February experience, and there's cidering on fall weekends. ✉ *39 Scofieldtown Rd.* ☎ *203/977–6521* ⊕ *www.stamfordmuseum.org* ✍ *Grounds $12, observatory $5* ⊗ *Observatory closed Jan. and Feb.*

🍴 Restaurants

⭐ **The Capital Grille**
$$$$ | STEAKHOUSE | This swanky and splurge-worthy steak house serves up impeccable steaks and chops, along with a host of other well-crafted entrées, in the dimly lit dining room with an old-school gentleman's club feel. Though dry-aged, hand-carved steaks are the specialty, Capital Grille also excels at seafood: pan-seared scallops, Maine lobster, and sushi-grade seared sesame tuna are equally delicious choices. **Known for:** the steaks, of course, prepared exactly as you like; creamed spinach, truffle fries, lobster mac 'n' cheese—lots of sides to share; perfect for a special occasion (or when you're really hungry). $ *Average main: $43* ✉ *Stamford Town Center, 230 Tressor Blvd.* ☎ *203/967–0000* ⊕ *www.thecapitalgrille.com* ⊗ *No lunch weekends.*

The Stamford Diner
$$ | AMERICAN | FAMILY | The menu at this art deco–style diner, alive with bright colors and shiny chrome, runs the gamut from griddle cakes to smoked salmon Benedict at breakfast, classic sandwiches to Greek specialties at lunch, chicken in a basket to rib-eye steak at dinner—or anything you'd like at any time of day or night. If that's not enough, the diner hosts frequent musical, comedy, and kids' events. **Known for:** classic diner menu—v-e-r-y long and varied; early-morning breakfast and late-night dinner—every day; family-friendly

atmosphere. $ *Average main: $20* ✉ *135 Harvard Ave.* ☎ *203/348–7000* ⊕ *www.stamforddiner.com.*

🛏 Hotels

The Lloyd

$ | HOTEL | Named for John Lloyd, a prominent 18th-century shipping magnate and businessman from Stamford, The Lloyd is a luxury boutique hotel (opened in spring 2020) that offers personalized, "curated" service to travelers looking for a convenient, comfortable place to stay. **Pros:** walk to businesses, shopping, restaurants, theaters; 24-hour fitness center; free shuttle service (within 5 miles). **Cons:** no full restaurant, but breakfast and light "bar bites" are available; some rooms are quite small; slow elevator. $ *Rooms from: $195* ✉ *909 Washington Blvd.* ☎ *203/569–0500* ⊕ *thelloydstamford.com* ⟿ *94 rooms* ⊚ *No meals.*

Stamford Marriott Hotel & Spa

$$ | HOTEL | FAMILY | Business travelers in particular appreciate the 16-floor hotel's up-to-date facilities and convenience to trains and airport shuttles. **Pros:** an easy walk to downtown restaurants and Stamford Mall; complimentary shuttle to nearby train station; weekend travelers enjoy lower prices. **Cons:** rooms are ready for updating, which apparently is planned; hotel restaurants are good but pricey; parking garage is expensive. $ *Rooms from: $244* ✉ *243 Tresser Blvd.* ☎ *203/357–9555, 888/236–2427* ⊕ *www.marriott.com* ⟿ *506 rooms* ⊚ *No meals.*

Nightlife

BARS

Tigín Irish Pub

BARS/PUBS | Stop in for the perfect pint and "happy hour" snacks at this Irish pub with an authentic atmosphere. ✉ *175 Bedford St.* ☎ *203/353–8444* ⊕ *www.tiginirishpub.com.*

🎭 Performing Arts

MUSIC

★ Stamford Symphony

MUSIC | Performing at The Palace Theatre October–April, this orchestra always includes a popular holiday concert performed at a local church—and kids' tickets for that are free. ✉ *The Palace Theatre, 61 Atlantic St.* ☎ *203/325–1407, 203/325–4466 for tickets* ⊕ *www.stamfordsymphony.org.*

THEATER

The Palace Theatre

THEATER | FAMILY | Plays, comedy shows, musicals, and film festivals are presented at the 1,500-seat Palace, originally a vaudeville house, which is now owned and operated by the Stamford Center for the Arts. ✉ *61 Atlantic St.* ☎ *203/325–4466* ⊕ *www.palacestamford.org.*

Norwalk

10 miles northeast of Stamford, 45 miles northeast of New York City.

In the 19th century, Norwalk was a major New England port and manufacturing center that produced hats, pottery, clocks, watches, shingle nails, and paper. The city later fell into neglect and remained so for much of the 20th century. In the 1980s and '90s, however, Norwalk's coastal business district was the focus of major redevelopment. Much of South Norwalk has since turned into a hot spot for trendy shopping, culture, and dining—much of it along Washington Street. Known as SoNo, it's *the* place to be if you're young, single, and living it up in Fairfield County.

GETTING HERE AND AROUND

If you are traveling by car, Norwalk is most easily reached by Interstate 95 or the Merritt Parkway. Metro-North commuter trains also make two stops here. Exit at the South Norwalk station to put yourself within walking distance of SoNo shops, restaurants, and bars.

Sights

The Lockwood-Mathews Mansion Museum
HOUSE | This ornate tribute to Victorian decorating, built in 1864 as the summer home of LeGrand Lockwood, remains one the oldest (and finest) surviving Second Empire–style country homes in the United States. It's hard not to be impressed by its octagonal skylighted rotunda and more than 50 rooms of gilt, frescoes, marble, intricate woodwork, and etched glass. Movie buffs will be interested in knowing that the mansion was used as the location of the Stepford Men's Association in *The Stepford Wives*—the original (1975) film. ✉ *295 West Ave.* ☎ *203/838–9799* 🌐 *www.lockwoodmathewsmansion.com* 🎟 *From $10* 🕐 *Closed Mon., Tues., Feb., and Mar.*

★ **Maritime Aquarium at Norwalk**
ZOO | **FAMILY** | This 5-acre waterfront center, the cornerstone of the city's SoNo district, explores the marine life and maritime culture of Long Island Sound. The aquarium's more than 20 habitats include some 1,000 creatures indigenous to the sound, including sting rays, sea turtles, harbor seals, river otters, and dozens of jellyfish. You can see toothy bluefish and sand tiger sharks in the 110,000-gallon Ocean Beyond the Sound aquarium. The Maritime Aquarium also operates an Environmental Education Center, leads marine-mammal cruises aboard *R/V Spirit of the Sound,* and has the state's largest IMAX theater. ✉ *10 N. Water St.* ☎ *203/852–0700* 🌐 *www.maritimeaquarium.org* 🎟 *$27.*

Sheffield Island and Lighthouse
LIGHTHOUSE | **FAMILY** | This 3-acre island, part of the Stewart B. McKinney National Wildlife Refuge, is a prime spot for a picnic and some bird-watching. The 1868 lighthouse has 10 rooms on four levels that you can explore. Clambakes are held Thursday evenings June–September. To get here, take a ferry from the Sheffield Island Dock. ✉ *Sheffield Island Dock, 4 N. Water St. at Washington St.* ☎ *800/838–3006 for tickets, 203/838–2898 for dock* 🌐 *www.seaport.org* 🎟 *From $30* 🕐 *Closed Oct.–Apr.; closed weekdays, May, June, and Sept.*

Stepping Stones Museum for Children
MUSEUM | **FAMILY** | The ColorCoaster, a 27-foot-high kinetic structure in constant motion, is the centerpiece of this hands-on museum with exhibits organized by age. Visit the Energy Lab, where youngsters learn about wind, water, and solar power while splashing around the extensive water play area. The Light Gallery has colorful LED displays; and for babies and toddlers, Tot Town is a safe place where they can play with toys and puzzles, "cook" in a play kitchen, and learn about animals on Old MacDonald's Farm. ✉ *Mathews Park, 303 West Ave.* ☎ *203/899–0606* 🌐 *www.steppingstonesmuseum.org* 🎟 *$16* 🕐 *Closed Mon. Labor Day–Memorial Day.*

Restaurants

★ **Match**
$$$ | **MODERN AMERICAN** | A SoNo fixture since 1999, Match's high ceilings, exposed brick, and industrial fixtures provide a sleek, urban look. Indulge in one of the signature wood-fired pizzas straight out of the oven or savor the light-as-air gnocchi in tossed in brandy-truffle cream, blackened swordfish, or steak frites. **Known for:** something delicious at every price point; creative wood-oven pizzettes, including bacon-potato-egg and shrimp fra diablo; "New School" raw bar, featuring Norwalk oysters. [$] *Average main: $30* ✉ *98 Washington St.* ☎ *203/852–1088* 🌐 *www.matchsono.com.*

Hotels

Hotel Zero Degrees Norwalk
$ | **HOTEL** | **FAMILY** | This ultramodern boutique lodging is a great addition to a region choked with lackluster chain hotels. **Pros:** large bathrooms with a huge walk-in shower; tasty food at Mediterraneo, the

Norwalk's Maritime Aquarium is a great way to come eye-to-eye with animals endemic to Long Island Sound, like green sea turtles.

in-house restaurant; free shuttle service within 3 miles. **Cons:** noise from the nearby train tracks; weeknight prices can jump 30%–40%; complimentary breakfast choices are limited. [$] *Rooms from: $149* ✉ *353 Main Ave.* ☎ *203/750–9800* 🌐 *www.hotelzerodegrees.com/hotels/norwalk* 🛏 *96 rooms* 🍴 *Free breakfast.*

Nightlife

★ Barcelona Wine Bar
WINE BARS—NIGHTLIFE | Savor wines primarily from Spain—tinto, rosado, or blanco, with more than 40 available by the glass—while nibbling on charcuterie, cheese, or a selection of tapas. ✉ *515 West Ave.* ☎ *203/854–5600* 🌐 *www.barcelonawinebar.com.*

Local Kitchen and Beer Bar
BARS/PUBS | Exposed brick, rustic wooden booths, and metal accents give this pub in the heart of bustling SoNo an industrial feel. Pair one of the 30-plus craft beers on tap with the to-die-for burger. ✉ *68 Washington St.* ☎ *203/957–3352* 🌐 *www.sonolocal.com.*

Ridgefield

15 miles north of Norwalk, 43 miles west of New Haven.

In Ridgefield, you'll find an outstanding contemporary art museum nestled in a classic New England town within an hour of Manhattan. Main Street, a large leafy boulevard, has a number of small businesses; otherwise, "downtown" is largely a residential sweep of lawns and majestic homes. Ridgefield is snug against the Connecticut/New York border; to reach the state line, you drive along Peaceable Street—which pretty much sums up Ridgefield.

GETTING HERE AND AROUND

From Interstate 95 or the Merritt Parkway, head north on U.S. 7 to Route 33 to reach Ridgefield; Metro-North will take you to the Branchville station in Ridgefield, but you'll need a car from there.

Sights

★ The Aldrich Contemporary Art Museum

MUSEUM | Cutting-edge art is not necessarily what you'd expect to find in a stately, 18th-century structure that, by turns, served as a general store, a post office, and, for 35 years, a church. Nicknamed "Old Hundred," this historic building is just part of the vast facility, which includes a 17,000-square-foot exhibition space that puts its own twist on traditional New England architecture. The white-clapboard-and-granite structure houses 12 galleries, a screening room, a sound gallery, a 22-foot-high project space for large installations, a 100-seat performance space, and an education center. Outside is a 2-acre sculpture garden. **■ TIP→ Every third Saturday, admission is free.** ✉ *258 Main St.* ☎ *203/438–4519* 🌐 *thealdrich.org* 🎟 *$12* 🕒 *Closed Tues.*

Restaurants

Luc's Café

$$ | **BISTRO** | A cozy French bistro set inside a stone building with low ceilings and closely spaced tables, Luc's takes full advantage of its handy location in Ridgefield's iconic downtown. The place charms patrons with carefully prepared food—salade niçoise, croque monsieur, or the classic steak au poivre with a velvety Roquefort sauce and crispy frites—and low-key, friendly service. **Known for:** nonstop service from 11 am until closing; special plat du jour offered daily; all dishes prepared à la minute. [$] *Average main: $22* ✉ *3 Big Shop La.* ☎ *203/894–8522* 🌐 *www.lucscafe.com* 🕒 *Closed Sun.*

Coffee and Quick Bites

Heibeck's Stand

$ | **FAST FOOD** | Just south of the Ridgefield town line on U.S. 7, you'll see a huge ice cream cone on the roadside marking Heibeck's Stand, where you can choose a made-to-order burger or hot dog with a variety of toppings or a sandwich, Philly cheesesteak, lobster roll, taco, salad... even a house-marinated portobello mushroom "burger." Best of all is the ice cream, which is rich, creamy, and deee-licious—in midsummer, try the fresh peach ice cream. **Known for:** the ice cream; patio dining in the back; easy in, easy out, easy parking. [$] *Average main: $12* ✉ *951 Danbury Rd., U.S. 7, Wilton* ☎ *203/917–9313* 🌐 *www.heibecksstand.com* 🕒 *Closed early Oct.–mid-Apr. Closed Mon.*

Sycamore Drive-In

$ | **DINER** | **FAMILY** | Heading north from Fairfield County toward the Litchfield Hills along rural Route 53, definitely stop at the Sycamore Drive-In in Bethel for a burger, fries, milk shake, and authentic 1950s atmosphere. During the summer, Saturday "Cruise Nights" see classic cars and "hot rods" fill the parking lot (more parking across the street) and rock 'n' roll music (sometimes live) fill the air. **Known for:** the "Dogwood Burger" with everything on it; eat inside or in your car; Saturday "Cruise Night." [$] *Average main: $10* ✉ *282 Greenwood Ave., corner of Rte. 53, Bethel* ☎ *203/748–2716* 🌐 *www.sycamoredrivein.com.*

Performing Arts

★ The Ridgefield Playhouse

FILM | **FAMILY** | This historic, fully renovated, country playhouse presents national and local musicians, comedians, magicians, theatrical performances, classic and new films, and insightful lectures. Stars ranging from Stevie Wonder to Gordon Lightfoot, Dana Carvey to The Capitol Steps, and even Disney's *Beauty and the Beast* and the Bolshoi Ballet have been headliners over the years. ✉ *80 East Ridge* ☎ *203/438–5795* 🌐 *ridgefieldplayhouse.org.*

Westport

47 miles northeast of New York City.

Westport, an artists' community since the turn of the 20th century, continues to attract creative types despite an influx of commuters and corporations over the years.

GETTING HERE AND AROUND

You can reach Westport by car via Interstate 95 (Exit 17 will take you closer to the center of town and main shopping areas) or the Merritt Parkway. Metro-North also has two stops here: Westport (closer to town) and Greens Farms (farther east).

👁 Sights

★ Sherwood Island State Park

BEACH—SIGHT | FAMILY | Summer visitors congregate at this state park, Connecticut's first, which has a 1½-mile sweep of sandy beach, two picnic areas at the water's edge, sports fields, and several food stands (open seasonally). The on-site nature center offers various programs from bird-watching to nature walks. ⊠ *Sherwood Island Connector* ⊹ *Off I–95, Exit 18* ☎ *203/226–6983* ⊕ *www.ct.gov/deep/sherwoodisland* 🎫 *CT residents, free; nonresidents from $15, $7 parking* ⊗ *Nature Center: closed Mon. and Tues., Labor Day–Memorial Day.*

🍴 Restaurants

Spotted Horse Tavern

$$$ | MODERN AMERICAN | The theme in this neighborhood favorite is horse, of course; the atmosphere reflects the historic building (circa 1808), and the menu offers old-fashioned comfort foods with modern flourishes. The grilled pork chop has a whole-grain mustard glaze, chicken Milanese includes a side of lemon yogurt sauce, steak frites has Parmesan fries— and items on the Pony Menu will delight the kids. **Known for:** street-side alfresco dining in warm months; busy bar; convenient downtown location. $ *Average main: $25* ⊠ *26 Church La.* ☎ *203/557– 9393* ⊕ *spottedhorsect.com.*

Terrain Garden Café

$$$ | AMERICAN | Within the Terrain garden store, you'll find a bright, cheery café that offers exquisitely prepared dishes using locally sourced organic produce so fresh you'll want to become a gardener yourself. Entrées like line-caught Atlantic cod with squash risotto or the braised beef short ribs are served with a delicious (and frankly adorable) terra-cotta pot of baked bread. **Known for:** creatively presented dishes; artisanal cuisine (like the grilled avocado snack); browse the store and its eclectic home accessories, plants, and garden supplies while awaiting your table. $ *Average main: $26* ⊠ *561 Post Rd. E* ☎ *203/226–2750* ⊕ *www.shop-terrain.com/westport-restaurant* ⊗ *No dinner Mon. and Tues.*

Via Sforza Trattoria

$$$ | ITALIAN | Whether you come for the pasta (pappardelle, fettuccini, tagliolini, gnocchi...) or the *secondi* (scalloppine, scampi, pollo, vitello...), diners here enjoy authentic Italian cuisine in a setting where you can actually have a conversation. You can also opt for a brick-oven pizza—with usual or unusual toppings— too. **Known for:** reasonably priced wines; vegetarian or gluten-free options; popular Sunday brunch. $ *Average main: $28* ⊠ *243 Post Road W* ☎ *203/454–4444* ⊕ *viasforza.com.*

The Whelk

$$$ | SEAFOOD | This upscale seafood restaurant serves straight-from-the-sea clams, oysters, and fish inventively prepared and exquisitely presented. The clean lines of the dining room give the nearly always crowded restaurant a maritime feel that perfectly complements the food. **Known for:** extensive raw bar; seafood, of course, but also roast chicken or a burger; outdoor seating in nice

weather. $ *Average main: $35* ✉ *575 Riverside Ave.* ☎ *203/557–0902* ⊕ *www. thewhelkwestport.com* ⊘ *Closed Sun. and Mon.*

🎭 Performing Arts

The Levitt Pavilion for the Performing Arts
CONCERTS | FAMILY | Enjoy an excellent series of free outdoor summer concerts here that range from jazz to classical, folk to blues, and one night each week focused especially on children. Bring a blanket or beach chair—and a picnic, if you like, but snacks and drinks are also available. ✉ *40 Jesup Rd.* ☎ *203/221–2153 concert hotline, 203/226–7600 office* ⊕ *www.levittpavilion.com* 💲 *Free.*

Westport Country Playhouse
THEATER | Long associated with local benefactors Joanne Woodward and the late Paul Newman, the venerable and intimate Westport Country Playhouse presents high-quality performances from March through November and special family programs from December through March. ✉ *25 Powers Ct.* ☎ *203/227–4177* ⊕ *www.westportplayhouse.org.*

Bridgeport

12 miles east of Westport, 22 miles west of New Haven.

Bridgeport, Connecticut's most populous city is working hard to revitalize itself with improvements such as Webster Arena at Harbor Yard, a 10,000-seat indoor sports and entertainment space, and Harbor Yard Amphitheater ("The Amp"), a 5,500-seat outdoor entertainment venue hosting concerts and festivals from spring through fall. A handful of family-friendly attractions make Bridgeport a worthwhile stop for families with young kids.

👁 Sights

Connecticut's Beardsley Zoo
ZOO | FAMILY | The indoor, walk-through South American rain forest alone justifies a visit to this zoo. It comes alive with dozens of species, some rare and endangered, such as keel-billed toucans, broad-snouted caimans, and black-and-gold howler monkeys living in a lush environment of waterfalls, ponds, greenery, and bamboo. The zoo itself has 36 acres of exhibits featuring more than 300 animals: bison, tigers, timber wolves, sloths, a red panda, bald eagles—and proud peacocks that freely roam the property right along with you. There's also a colorful carousel and a New England farmyard. ✉ *1875 Noble Ave.* ☎ *203/394–6565* ⊕ *www.beardsleyzoo.org* 💲 *$15.*

Discovery Museum and Planetarium
MUSEUM | FAMILY | Visitors young and old learn about science and technology through hands-on STEM learning experiences and demonstrations that explore electricity, computers, sound, light, magnetism, and energy. Particular draws include the Space Galleries, where you can touch a real meteorite and Skylab artifacts, and the toddler-friendly Preschool Power, where little ones can explore soft, brightly colored structures while developing balance and motor skills. Don't miss the planetarium shows—some geared to young children and others to all age groups. ■ TIP➔ **Bring a picnic to enjoy in adjacent Adventure Park.** ✉ *4450 Park Ave.* ☎ *203/372–3521* ⊕ *www.discoverymuseum.org* 💲 *From $11* ⊘ *Museum closed Mon.*

New Milford

56 miles west of Hartford, 37 miles north of Norwalk.

If you're approaching the Litchfield Hills from the south, New Milford is a practical starting point to begin a visit. It was also a starting point for a young cobbler (and later a lawyer) named Roger Sherman, who opened the town's first shop in 1743 at the corner of Main and Church streets. A Declaration of Independence signatory, Sherman also helped draft the Articles of Confederation and the Constitution. You'll find shops, galleries, and eateries all within a short stroll of the New Milford town green.

GETTING HERE AND AROUND
New Milford is best visited by car. From Danbury and points south, take U.S. 7 to U.S. 202 to reach the town.

Sights

★ Elephant's Trunk Flea Market
MARKET | FAMILY | In the same spot since 1976, this outdoor flea market has grown from a dozen or so vendors to more than 500 on a typical Sunday, along with food trucks offering everything from a snack to full meals. You'll never know what usual and unusual treasures you'll find spread out on the field, as every Sunday brings out a different collection of vendors selling all manner of antiques, collectibles, housewares, and merchandise, along with, simply, "things." Serious buyers arrive by 4:45 am (and pay $20–$40 admission for the privilege); the rest of us are happy to browse from 7 am to 3:30 pm. ⊠ *490 Danbury Rd., U.S. 7/U.S. 202* ☎ *860/355–1448* ⊕ *www.etflea.com* 💲 *$3, free after 2 pm* ☉ *Closed Mon.– Sat. and mid-Dec.–late Mar.*

🍴 Restaurants

The Cookhouse
$$ | BARBECUE | Stop here for some of the best "slow-smoked" barbecue in Connecticut or for one of the comfort-food staples on the extensive menu. Try the chicken-fried steak, cookhouse meat loaf, or "BBQ Sundae," a mason jar layered with pulled pork, baked beans, coleslaw, BBQ sauce, and a pickle. **Known for:** barbecue baby back ribs and pulled pork; Thursday night's all-you-can-eat—and a free beer— for $21; good selection of draft beers. 💲 *Average main: $20* ⊠ *31 Danbury Rd.* ☎ *860/355–4111* ⊕ *thecookhouse.com.*

🛏 Hotels

★ The Homestead Inn
$ | B&B/INN | FAMILY | High on a hill overlooking New Milford's town green, this Victorian masterpiece opened as an inn in 1928. **Pros:** open year-round; close to shops and restaurants; substantial, delicious, homemade breakfasts. **Cons:** 2-night minimum on weekends; free breakfast only for main house guests; some bathrooms are tiny, with sinks in the bedroom. 💲 *Rooms from: $109* ⊠ *5 Elm St.* ☎ *860/354–4080* ⊕ *www.homesteadct.com* 🛏 *16 rooms* ⬥ *Free breakfast.*

Kent

14 miles northwest of New Milford.

Kent once had many ironworks; today, it boasts the area's greatest concentration of art galleries—some nationally renowned—as well as an eponymous prep school, the scenic and functional Bull's Covered Bridge (one of three in Connecticut), and the Schaghticoke Indian Reservation. During the Revolutionary War, 100 Schaghticokes helped defend the colonies by transmitting army intelligence, from the hilltops of Litchfield Hills to Long Island Sound, by way of shouts and drumbeats.

GETTING HERE AND AROUND

To reach Kent by car, travel 14 miles north from New Milford on U.S. 7.

Sights

Eric Sloane Museum & Kent Iron Furnace

MUSEUM | Hardware-store buffs and vintage-tool aficionados will feel right at home at this museum. Artist and author Eric Sloane (1905–85) was fascinated by Early American woodworking tools, and his collection showcases examples of American craftsmanship from the 17th to the 19th century. The museum contains a re-creation of Sloane's last studio and also encompasses the ruins of a 19th-century iron furnace. Sloane's books and prints, which celebrate vanishing aspects of Americana such as barns and covered bridges, are available for sale here. ✉ *31 Kent–Cornwall Rd. (U.S. 7), 1 mile north of Rte. 341 intersection* ☎ *860/927–3849* 🌐 *www.ericsloane.com/museum.htm* 🎫 *$8* 🕓 *Closed Labor Day–Memorial Day.*

Kent Falls State Park

NATIONAL/STATE PARK | Heading north from Kent toward Cornwall, you'll pass the entrance to 295-acre Kent Falls State Park, where you can hike a short way to one of the most impressive series of waterfalls in the state and picnic in the green meadows at the base of the falls. ✉ *462 Kent Cornwall Rd. (U.S. 7)* ☎ *860/927–3238* 🌐 *www.ct.gov/deep/kentfalls* 🎫 *Parking for nonresidents Memorial Day–Oct. weekends $15, free for Connecticut residents.*

Macedonia Brook State Park

NATIONAL/STATE PARK | Early-season trout fishing (license required) is superb at 2,300-acre Macedonia Brook State Park, where you can also hike and cross-country ski. The Blue Trail crosses several peaks, and you can see as far away as New York's Catskills and Taconics. The leaves are magnificent in the fall. ✉ *159 Macedonia Brook Rd., off Rte. 341* ☎ *860/927–3238* 🌐 *www.ct.gov/deep/macedoniabrook* 🎫 *Free.*

Hotels

Fife 'n Drum Inn

$ | B&B/INN | If you like to shop, eat, and rest your head in a cozy, simple place, you can do all three at this family-owned inn. **Pros:** quaint inn in quaint town; walk to local shops and galleries; adjacent to popular restaurant. **Cons:**"front desk" in the next-door restaurant; book early for fall foliage season; two-night minimum May–October weekends. [$] *Rooms from: $180* ✉ *53 Main St.* ☎ *860/927–3509* 🌐 *www.fifendrum.com* 🕓 *Restaurant closed Tues.* 🛏 *15 rooms* 🍴 *No meals.*

Activities

Appalachian Trail

HIKING/WALKING | The 2,190-mile Appalachian Trail, which stretches through 14 states from Georgia to Maine, is the longest hiking-only footpath in the world. About 51 miles of the trail pass through the northwestern tip of Connecticut. Just off Route 341, the nearly 5-mile-long, well-maintained River Walk from Kent to Cornwall Bridge meanders along the Housatonic River—one of the longest sections of the trail that, mile after mile, follows a river. ✉ *Kent* 🌐 *www.appalachiantrail.org.*

Cornwall

12 miles northeast of Kent.

Connecticut's Cornwalls can get confusing: there's Cornwall, Cornwall Bridge, West Cornwall, Cornwall Hollow, East Cornwall, and North Cornwall. This quiet part of the Litchfield Hills is known for its fantastic vistas of woods and mountains and for its covered bridge, which spans the Housatonic River.

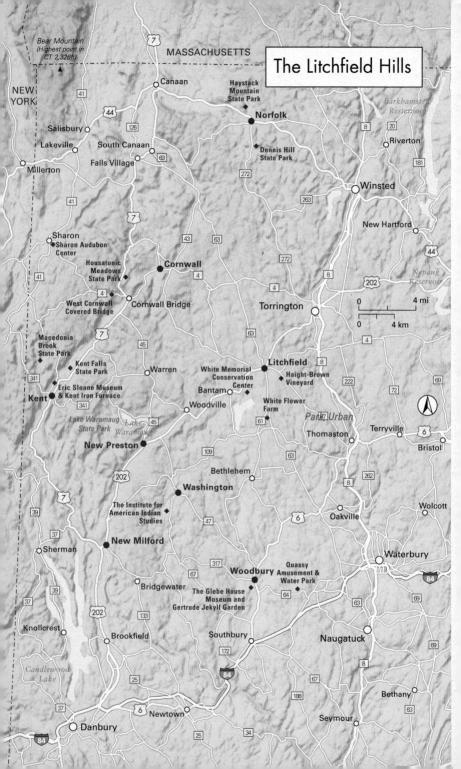

The Litchfield Hills

Bear Mountain
(Highest point in
CT. 2,326 ft)

MASSACHUSETTS

NEW YORK

Canaan

Haystack
Mountain
State Park

Norfolk

Barkhamsted
Reservoir

Salisbury

Lakeville

South Canaan

Millerton

Falls Village

Dennis Hill
State Park

Riverton

Winsted

New Hartford

Sharon
Sharon Audubon
Center

Housatonic
Meadows
State Park

Cornwall

West Cornwall
Covered Bridge

Cornwall Bridge

Torrington

Nepaug
Reservoir

Macedonia
Brook
State Park

Kent Falls
State Park

Eric Sloane Museum
& Kent Iron Furnace

Kent

Lake Waramaug
State Park

Warren

Woodville

New Preston

White Memorial
Conservation
Center

Bantam

Litchfield

Haight-Brown
Vineyard

White Flower
Farm

Paul Urban

Thomaston

Terryville

Bristol

Washington

The Institute for
American Indian
Studies

Bethlehem

Oakville

Wolcott

New Milford

Sherman

Bridgewater

Woodbury

The Glebe House
Museum and
Gertrude Jekyll Garden

Quassy
Amusement &
Water Park

Waterbury

Naugatuck

Knollcrest

Brookfield

Southbury

Bethany

Candlewood
Lake

Newtown

Seymour

Danbury

0   4 mi

0   4 km

GETTING HERE AND AROUND

Head north from Kent on U.S. 7 to reach the various Cornwalls.

 Sights

Cornwall Bridge Pottery

FACTORY | Visitors are welcome to watch potters as they work, producing a variety of items that are fired in an on-site, 35-foot-long, wood-fired tube kiln. A selection of items are available for purchase—including seconds. ⊠ *69 Kent Rd. S (U.S. 7), Cornwall Bridge* ☎ *860/946–9679* ⊕ *cbpots.com.*

Housatonic Meadows State Park

NATIONAL/STATE PARK | The park is marked by its tall pine trees near the Housatonic River and has terrific riverside campsites (seasonal). Fly-fishers consider this 2-mile stretch of the river among the best places in New England to test their skills against trout and bass (license required). ■TIP➔ **This is a family-friendly park: no alcohol allowed!** ⊠ *90 U.S. 7 N, Sharon* ☎ *860/927–3238* ⊕ *www.ct.gov/deep/housatonicmeadows* 🎫 *Free.*

Sharon Audubon Center

NATURE PRESERVE | **FAMILY** | With 11 miles of hiking trails, this 1,147-acre property—a mixture of forests, meadows, wetlands, ponds, and streams—provides myriad hiking opportunities. The visitor center shares its space with small hawks, an owl, and other animals in the live-animal display in the Natural History Exhibit Room; in the Children's Adventure Center, kids learn about the importance of water quality and watersheds, crawl through a tunnel to a beaver lodge, and look for various fish and other sea life in the large aquarium. ⊠ *325 Cornwall Bridge Rd., Sharon* ☎ *860/364–0520* ⊕ *sharon.audubon.org* 🎫 *Visitor center free, aviaries and trails $3* 🕐 *Visitor center closed Mon.*

West Cornwall Covered Bridge

BRIDGE/TUNNEL | A romantic reminder of the past, this single-lane bridge over the Housatonic River is on Route 128, just east of U.S. 7, in West Cornwall. The 172-feet-long and 15-feet-wide lattice truss bridge was built in 1841 and still carries vehicular traffic. The design incorporates strut techniques that were later copied by bridge builders around the country. ⊠ *Junction of U.S. 7 and Rte. 128, West Cornwall.*

 Hotels

Cornwall Inn

$ | **B&B/INN** | **FAMILY** | This 19th-century inn, with four bedrooms and a two-bedroom suite, combines country charm with contemporary elegance; eight rustic guest rooms in the adjacent lodge are slightly more private and have cedar-post beds. **Pros:** tranquil setting and lovely grounds; seasonal swimming pool and year-round hot tub; welcoming to kids and pets. **Cons:** a bit far from neighboring towns; allergy alert: pets are allowed in lodge rooms but not in the main inn; rooms are fairly small and bathrooms are quite small. 💲 *Rooms from: $169* ⊠ *270 Kent Rd. S* ☎ *860/672–6884* ⊕ *www.cornwall-inn.com* ⇆ *13 rooms* ⦿| *Free breakfast.*

🏃 Activities

BOATING AND RAFTING

Clarke Outdoors

CANOEING/ROWING/SKULLING | **FAMILY** | This outfitter rents canoes, kayaks, paddle-boards, and rafts—and operates 10-mile canoe or raft trips downstream from Falls Village to Housatonic Meadows State Park. The water is a mix of flat water and easy white water, suitable for novices. ⊠ *163 U.S. 7, West Cornwall* ✛ *1 mile south of covered bridge* ☎ *860/672–6365* ⊕ *www.clarkeoutdoors.com.*

FISHING

Housatonic Anglers

FISHING | Enjoy a half- or full-day guided fishing trip on the Housatonic River and its tributaries with this company. You can also take fly-fishing lessons. ⊠ *26 Bolton Hill Rd.* ☎ *860/672–4457* ⊕ *www.housatonicanglers.com.*

Housatonic River Outfitters

FISHING | This outfitter operates a full-service fly shop, leads guided fishing trips, conducts classes in fly-fishing, and offers a good selection of vintage and antique gear. ⊠ *24 Kent Rd., Cornwall Bridge* ☎ *860/672–1010* ⊕ *www.dryflies.com.*

SKIING

Mohawk Mountain

SKIING/SNOWBOARDING | **FAMILY** | The trails at Mohawk Mountain include plenty of intermediate terrain, a few trails for beginners, and a few steeper sections for more advanced skiers. A small area is devoted to snowboarders. Trails are serviced by five triple lifts and three magic carpets; 12 trails are lighted for night skiing. The base lodge has a cafeteria and a retail shop; halfway up the slope the Pine Lodge Restaurant offers full-service dining, a roaring fire in a natural stone fireplace, and an outdoor patio. **Facilities**: 25 trails; 112 acres; 650-foot vertical drop; 8 lifts; snowmaking on 99% of all terrain. ⊠ *46 Great Hollow Rd., off Rte. 4* ☎ *860/672–6100* ⊕ *www.mohawkmtn. com* ⊠ *Lift tickets from $32.*

Norfolk

23 miles northeast of Cornwall, 41 miles west of Hartford, 60 miles north of New Haven.

Thanks to having the coolest temperatures in Connecticut and a rather rocky terrain, Norfolk has resisted development and stands as one of the best-preserved villages in the Northeast. Notable industrialists have been summering here for two centuries, and many enormous homesteads still exist. The striking town green, at the junction of Route 272 and U.S. 44, has a fountain designed by Augustus Saint-Gaudens (executed in 1889 by Stanford White) at its southern corner. The fountain is a memorial to Joseph Battell, who turned Norfolk into a major trading center in the mid-19th century.

GETTING HERE AND AROUND

To reach Norfolk by car, use U.S. 7 or U.S. 8 and U.S. 44.

◉ Sights

Dennis Hill State Park

NATIONAL/STATE PARK | **FAMILY** | Dr. Frederick Shepard Dennis, the former owner of these 240 acres and a noted New York surgeon, lavishly entertained his guests—among them President William Howard Taft and several Connecticut governors—in the stone pavilion at the summit of the estate. From its 1,627-foot height, you have a panoramic view of Haystack Mountain and parts of New Hampshire to the north and, on a clear day, the New Haven harbor about 60 miles south. Picnic on the park's grounds or hike one of its many trails. ⊠ *Rte. 272* ☎ *860/482–1817* ⊕ *www.ct.gov/deep/ dennishill* ⊠ *Free.*

Haystack Mountain State Park

NATIONAL/STATE PARK | **FAMILY** | One of the most spectacular views in the state can be seen from the 34-foot high stone tower atop Haystack Mountain (1,716 feet). You can see the Berkshires in Connecticut and Massachusetts, as well as peaks in New York and the Green Mountains of Vermont. A winding road will get you halfway there; then you hike a rugged half-mile trail to the top. ⊠ *Rte. 272* ☎ *860/482–1817* ⊕ *portal.ct.gov/DEEP/State-Parks/Parks/ Haystack-Mountain-State-Park.*

Hotels

Blackberry River Inn

$ | B&B/INN | Set upon 27 acres in Connecticut's Berkshire Mountains, this historic (1763) home turned inn has two rooms and two suites in the Main House and a dozen simpler—but still lovely—rooms in the adjacent Carriage House, plus a full home-cooked breakfast is served in a sunny breakfast room every morning. **Pros:** swimming pool open in summer; wood-burning fireplaces in most Main House rooms; raised waffles (made with yeast) and real maple syrup at breakfast. **Cons:** two-night minimum on weekends; no room TV in Main House rooms; beware of wildlife (an occasional bear). [$] *Rooms from: $159* ✉ *538 Greenwoods Rd. W (U.S. 44 W)* ☎ *860/542–5100* 🌐 *www.blackberryriverinn.com* 🛏 *17 rooms* 🍴 *Free breakfast.*

Manor House Inn

$$ | B&B/INN | Among the remarkable appointments in this 1898 Bavarian Tudor-style building are its wood-beam ceilings, graceful arches, and antique beds—along with 20 stained-glass windows designed by Louis Comfort Tiffany. **Pros:** interesting building with lots of nooks and crannies and sumptuous decor; lavish breakfasts; peaceful atmosphere with lots to do nearby. **Cons:** no phone or TV in guest rooms (and mobile reception is iffy in these parts); rooms and bathrooms need updating; third-floor rooms are the least comfortable. [$] *Rooms from: $239* ✉ *69 Maple Ave.* ☎ *860/542–5690* 🌐 *www.manorhouse-norfolk.com* 🛏 *9 rooms* 🍴 *Free breakfast.*

Performing Arts

★ Infinity Music Hall & Bistro

CONCERTS | Built in 1883, this modernized 300-seat music hall with a world-class sound system hosts more than 200 shows a year by local performers as well as nationally known folk, soft rock, and jazz groups. The intimate setting puts you close to the stage. Have drinks, snacks, or a meal in the Bistro before the performance. ✉ *20 Greenwoods Rd. W (U.S. 44)* ☎ *860/542–5531* 🌐 *www.infinityhall.com.*

Norfolk Chamber Music Festival

FESTIVALS | Held at the Music Shed on the 70-acre Ellen Battell Stoeckel Estate, the Norfolk Chamber Music Festival presents world-renowned artists and ensembles on Friday and Saturday evenings in summer. Students from the Yale School of Music perform on Thursday evening and Saturday morning. Stroll the 70-acre grounds or visit the art gallery. ✉ *Ellen Battell Stoeckel Estate, 20 Litchfield Rd.* ☎ *860/542–3000* 🌐 *music.yale.edu/norfolk.*

Litchfield

60 miles northeast of Norwalk, 34 miles west of Hartford, 40 miles northwest of New Haven.

Everything in Litchfield, the most noteworthy town in the Litchfield Hills, seems to exist on a larger scale than in neighboring villages, especially the impressive Litchfield Green and the white Colonial and Greek Revival homes that line the broad, tree-lined streets. Harriet Beecher Stowe, author of *Uncle Tom's Cabin,* and her brother, abolitionist preacher Henry Ward Beecher, were born and raised in Litchfield, and many famous Americans earned their law degrees at the Litchfield Law School. Today, lovely but expensive boutiques and restaurants line the downtown area.

GETTING HERE AND AROUND

To reach Litchfield by car from points north or south, take U.S. 8 to Route 118 west.

Sights

Haight-Brown Vineyard

WINERY/DISTILLERY | A founding member of the Connecticut Wine Trail, the state's oldest winery opened its doors in 1975. You can stop in for tastings; winery tours are available on Saturday at 1 pm (advance reservations required). Seasonal events include barrel tastings in April and a harvest festival in September. ✉ *29 Chestnut Hill Rd., off Rte. 118* ☎ *860/567–4045* 🌐 *www.haightbrownwine.com* 🎟 *Tasting $12* 🕒 *Closed Tues. and Wed.*

Litchfield History Museum

MUSEUM | In this well-regarded museum, seven neatly organized galleries highlight family life and work during the 50 years following the American Revolution. The extensive reference library has information about the town's historic buildings, including the Sheldon Tavern where George Washington slept on several occasions and the Litchfield Female Academy where, in the late 1700s, Sarah Pierce taught girls not only sewing and deportment but also mathematics and history. ✉ *7 South St., at Rtes. 63, 118, and U.S. 202* ☎ *860/567–4501* 🌐 *www.litchfieldhistoricalsociety.org* 🎟 *Free* 🕒 *Closed Mon. and Dec.–mid-Apr.*

Tapping Reeve House and Litchfield Law School

HISTORIC SITE | In 1773, Judge Tapping Reeve enrolled his first student, Aaron Burr, in what became the first law school in the country. (Before Judge Reeve, students studied the law as apprentices, not in formal classes.) This school is dedicated to Reeve's achievement and to the notable students who passed through its halls, including three U.S. Supreme Court justices. There are multimedia exhibits, an excellent introductory film, and restored facilities. ✉ *82 South St.* ☎ *860/567–4501* 🌐 *www.litchfieldhistoricalsociety.org* 🎟 *Free* 🕒 *Closed Mon. and Dec.–mid-Apr.*

White Flower Farm

GARDEN | A stroll through these landscaped grounds is always a pleasure and will provide gardeners with myriad ideas. The nursery and garden center ships annuals, perennials, shrubs, vines, bulbs, and houseplants to gardeners throughout the United States. Visitors are welcome to stroll through and around the acres of trial and display gardens. There is also a retail store on-site. ✉ *167 Litchfield Rd., Rte. 63, Morris* ☎ *860/567–8789* 🌐 *www.whiteflowerfarm.com* 🕒 *Closed Dec.–Mar.*

★ White Memorial Conservation Center

MUSEUM | **FAMILY** | This 4,000-acre nature preserve houses top-notch natural-history exhibits. There are 30 bird-watching platforms, two self-guided nature trails, several boardwalks, boating facilities, and 35 miles of hiking, cross-country-skiing, and horseback-riding trails. The Nature Museum has displays depicting the natural diversity found throughout the preserve, dioramas, live animals, a beehive, a digital microscope, and other unique exhibits of interest to kids of all ages (especially the scavenger hunt). ✉ *80 Whitehall Rd., off U.S. 202* ☎ *860/567–0857* 🌐 *www.whitememorialcc.org* 🎟 *Grounds free, museum $6.*

Restaurants

The Village Restaurant

$$ | **AMERICAN** | Beloved among visitors and locals alike, this storefront eatery in a redbrick town house serves tasty, unfussy food—inexpensive pub grub in one room, updated contemporary American cuisine in the other. Whether you order a burger or horseradish-and-Parmesan-crusted salmon, you're bound to be pleased. **Known for:** really good food at reasonable prices; Mexican Monday, Tapas Tuesday, and Italian Wednesday; weekday happy hours. [$] *Average main: $23* ✉ *25 West St.* ☎ *860/567–8307* 🌐 *www.village-litchfield.com.*

West Street Grill

$$$ | **MODERN AMERICAN** | This sophisticated dining room on the town green is *the* place to see and be seen. Dinner selections might include free-range chicken with potato puree and mushrooms, braised short ribs over a Gorgonzola-polenta cake, or organic Irish salmon with fingerling potatoes. **Known for:** alfresco tables overlooking the town green; perfect for a casual lunch or formal dinner; house-made ice creams and sorbets. $ *Average main: $34* ✉ *43 West St.* ☎ *860/567–3885* 🌐 *www.weststreetgrill.com.*

Hotels

The Litchfield Inn

$ | **B&B/INN** | This Colonial-style inn offers 12 theme rooms, each uniquely decorated, as well as more standard-style guest rooms with modern decor. **Pros:** on-site restaurant and lounge; bridal suite with a fireplace; particularly comfy beds. **Cons:** not within walking distance of attractions and restaurants; uneven service; more like a small hotel than a country inn. $ *Rooms from: $179* ✉ *432 Bantam Rd.* ☎ *860/567–4503* 🌐 *www.litchfieldinnct.com* 🛏 *32 rooms* 🍴 *No meals.*

★ Winvian Farm

$$$$ | **RESORT** | This private, 113-acre hideaway a few miles south of Litchfield consists of 18 of the most imaginative and luxuriously outfitted cottages you'll ever lay eyes on, each with a distinctive, often amusing, theme—like the Helicopter Cottage, with a genuine, 17,000-pound U.S. Coast Guard helicopter (the fuselage has been fitted with a wet bar) in it. **Pros:** whimsical and superplush accommodations; outstanding cuisine; stunning setting. **Cons:** superpricey; size and amenities differ for each cottage; two-night stays required on weekends. $ *Rooms from: $599* ✉ *155 Alain White Rd., Morris* ☎ *860/567–9600* 🌐 *www.winvian.com* 🛏 *19 suites* 🍴 *Free breakfast.*

Activities

HIKING

Mt. Tom State Park

HIKING/WALKING | Hike the mile-long trail to the stone lookout tower atop Mt. Tom and enjoy expansive views—or take a swim in the pond below and picnic on the beach. ✉ *U.S. 202* ✢ *7 miles southwest of Litchfield* ☎ *860/868–2592 (Labor Day–Memorial Day), 860/567–8870 (Memorial Day–Labor Day)* 🌐 *www.ct.gov/deep/mounttom* 🎫 *Parking free for residents, $15 on weekends for nonresidents.*

HORSEBACK RIDING

Lee's Riding Stable

HORSEBACK RIDING | **FAMILY** | Ride a well-behaved steed through Litchfield's rolling hills and countryside. Adults and kids age seven and up are welcome to join a guided, hour-long trail ride. Youngsters enjoy a pony ride around the ring. Private or semiprivate lessons are also available. Or you can just enjoy a delightful afternoon at Windfield Morgan Farm, where Lee's Riding Stable is located. ✉ *57 E. Litchfield Rd.* ☎ *860/567–0785* 🌐 *www.windfieldmorganfarm.com* 🎫 *Trail rides, $50 per hr; pony rides, from $20.*

Washington

14 miles southwest of Litchfield.

The beautiful buildings of The Gunnery, a private prep school, mingle with stately homes and churches in Washington, one of Connecticut's best-preserved Colonial towns. The Mayflower Inn, south of The Gunnery on Route 47, attracts an exclusive clientele. The town was settled in 1734; in 1779, it became the country's first town to be named for the country's first president.

GETTING HERE AND AROUND

Washington is accessible only by car. Route 47 runs through the rural town, connecting it with New Preston to the north and Woodbury to the south.

Sights

The Institute for American Indian Studies

MUSEUM | FAMILY | The exhibits in this small but excellent and thoughtfully arranged collection detail the history and continuing presence of 10,000 years of Native American life in New England, specifically in "Quinnetukut." Highlights include nature trails, a simulated archaeological site, and an authentically constructed Algonkian Village with wigwams, a longhouse, a rock shelter, and more. A gift shop presents the work of some of the country's best Native American artists. ✉ *38 Curtis Rd., off Rte. 199* ☎ *860/868–0518* 🌐 *www.iaismuseum.org* 🎟 *$10* 🕒 *Closed Mon. and Tues.*

Restaurants

G. W. Tavern

$$ | AMERICAN | This cozy tavern, once an 1850s-era Colonial home overlooking the Shepaug River, is named for George Washington, who passed through the little village back in the day. The chef prepares traditional New England favorites like oven-roasted cod, chicken potpie, and meat loaf, as well as seasonal specialties like soft shell crabs in spring and game throughout the winter. **Known for:** "George's cherry pie" for dessert; relax by the floor-to-ceiling fireplace with a glass of wine or draught beer; outdoor riverside dining in summertime. [$] *Average main: $21* ✉ *20 Bee Brook Rd., Washington Depot* ☎ *860/868–6633* 🌐 *gwtavern.com* 🕒 *Closed Wed.*

Hotels

★ **Mayflower Inn & Spa**

$$$$ | RESORT | Running streams, rambling stone walls, and rare-specimen trees fill the country manor–style inn's 58 acres of rolling countryside. **Pros:** special activities for kids, some free and some for a fee; solicitous but relaxed service; hiking, biking, and nature walks at the back door. **Cons:** very pricey; $42.50 per day resort fee added to all rates; tired rooms undergoing well-needed refurbishment. [$] *Rooms from: $699* ✉ *118 Woodbury Rd.* ☎ *860/868–9466* 🌐 *aubergeresorts.com/mayflower* 🛏 *30 rooms* 🍴 *No meals.*

Woodbury

10 miles southeast of Washington.

There may be more antiques shops in Woodbury than in all other towns in the Litchfield Hills combined. Some of the best-preserved examples of Colonial architecture in New England can be found here, as well, including five magnificent churches and the Greek Revival King Solomon's Lodge No. 7 Masonic Temple (1838).

GETTING HERE AND AROUND

To reach Woodbury by car from Washington, take Route 47 south; from elsewhere, take Interstate 84 to U.S. 6 north.

Sights

The Glebe House Museum and Gertrude Jekyll Garden

GARDEN | This property in the center of town includes the large, antiques-filled, gambrel-roof Georgian Colonial home of Dr. Samuel Seabury—who, in 1783, was elected the first Episcopal bishop in the United States. The house, built in 1740, and its outstanding furniture collection, is one of the earliest and most authentic house museums in the region. The

garden was designed in the 1920s by renowned British horticulturist Gertrude Jekyll. Though small, it's a classic, old-fashioned, English-style garden and the only one of the three Jekyll-designed gardens in the United States that are still in existence. ✉ *49 Hollow Rd.* ☎ *203/263–2855* 🌐 *www.glebehousemuseum.org* 🎫 *$7* 🕒 *Museum closed Mon. and Tues. and mid-Oct.–Apr.*

Quassy Amusement & Water Park
AMUSEMENT PARK/WATER PARK | FAMILY | Families have been enjoying the rides here for more than a century. There are kiddie rides, family rides that mom and dad even enjoy, and thrill rides—more than two-dozen rides altogether—plus Splash Away Bay Water Park. The custom-designed Wooden Warrior roller coaster is rated one of the top 25 in the world. ✉ *Lake Quassapaug, 2132 Middlebury Rd. (Rte. 64)* ✣ *4 miles southeast of Woodbury via U.S. 6 and Rte. 64* ☎ *203/758–2913* 🌐 *www.quassy.com* 🎫 *$30* 🕒 *Closed Oct.–Apr.*

🍴 Restaurants

★ Good News Restaurant & Bar
$$ | AMERICAN | Since Carole Peck—a well-known name throughout New England (and beyond)—opened here in 1992, foodies have been flocking to Woodbury to sample her superb cuisine. The emphasis is on healthy, innovative, and surprisingly well-priced fare like wok-seared Gulf shrimp with new potatoes, grilled green beans, and a garlic aioli. **Known for:** "star" chef cooks up creative cuisine; farm-to-table dishes feature local, seasonal ingredients; decor includes original artwork by local artists. [$] *Average main: $24* ✉ *Sherman Village Plaza, 694 Main St. S* ☎ *203/266–4663* 🌐 *goodnewsrestaurantandbar.com* 🕒 *Closed Mon. and Tues.*

☕ Coffee and Quick Bites

★ Ferris Acres Creamery
$ | AMERICAN | FAMILY | This popular creamery, located on a massive family owned-and-operated dairy farm since 1864, creates its own made-on-the-farm frozen desserts (that's *ice cream*!) daily. Choose from more than 30 "regular" flavors, like coffee almond fudge and maple walnut, and as many "special" flavors, like Caramalt and Sunset on the Peach (with a raspberry swirl). **Known for:** fun flavor names like Ali-Oop, Bad Habit, Elvis Dream, and Route 302 Chocolate Moo; bucolic scene with 50 dairy cows roaming the adjacent pastures; about as close as you can get to homemade ice cream without making it yourself. [$] *Average main: $6* ✉ *144 Sugar St., Newtown* ✣ *About 15 miles and scenic ½-hr drive southwest of Woodbury* ☎ *203/426–8803.*

🛏 Hotels

Evergreen Inn Bed + Breakfast
$ | B&B/INN | A short drive from Woodbury's antiques shops and restaurants, this Federal Colonial house (circa 1818) offers a bounty of pleasing comforts—from high-quality antique furnishings and soft bedding with lots of pillows to floral gardens and a stone-and-granite pool surrounded by a private hedge. **Pros:** delicious, made-from-scratch full breakfast; beautifully kept grounds and garden; 24-hour self-serve snack bar with coffee/wine/beer. **Cons:** only five rooms, so reserve in advance; on a fairly busy road; you won't want to leave. [$] *Rooms from: $189* ✉ *782 Main St. N (Rte. 6), Southbury* ✣ *3 miles south of Woodbury* ☎ *203/586–1876* 🌐 *www.evergreeninnsouthbury.com* 🛏 *5 rooms* 🍴 *Free breakfast.*

🛍 Shopping

Mill House Antiques

ANTIQUES/COLLECTIBLES | The Mill House carries formal and country English and French furniture and decor. ⊠ *1068 Main St. N* ☎ *203/263–3446* ⊕ *www.millhouse-antiquesandgardens.com.*

Monique Shay Antiques & Designs

ANTIQUES/COLLECTIBLES | The six barns that make up Monique Shay's store are packed with French Canadian country antiques. ⊠ *920 Main St. S* ☎ *203/263–3186* ⊕ *www.moniqueshay.com.*

Hartford

39 miles north of New Haven, 52 miles northwest of New London, 78 miles northeast of Stamford.

Midway on the inland route between New York City and Boston, Hartford is Connecticut's capital city and the "Insurance Capital of the World." Founded in 1635 on the banks of the Connecticut River, Hartford was once home to authors Mark Twain and Harriet Beecher Stowe, inventors Samuel and Elizabeth Colt, landscape architect Frederick Law Olmsted, and Ella Grasso, the first woman to be elected a state governor. Today Hartford boasts a revitalized downtown core featuring a bustling convention center and a top-notch science museum, the Connecticut Science Center. The city is once again on the verge of discovery.

GETTING HERE AND AROUND

Hartford is located in the middle of the state, at the intersection of two main highways: Interstate 91, which runs north from New Haven, across central Massachusetts and along the entire length of Vermont to the Canadian border, and Interstate 84, which runs generally east–west from the small town of Union at Connecticut's northeast border with Massachusetts, through Hartford and Danbury to the New York border. Amtrak serves Hartford on the Northeast Regional line. Bradley International Airport in Windsor Locks, 15 minutes north of Hartford, offers nonstop flights to more than 30 destinations in the United States, Canada, Ireland, and the Caribbean.

👁 Sights

Bushnell Park

CITY PARK | FAMILY | Fanning out from the State Capitol building, this city park, created in 1850, was the first public space in the country with natural landscaping. The original designer, a Swiss-born landscape architect and botanist named Jacob Weidenmann, planted 157 varieties of trees and shrubs to create an urban arboretum. Kids love the Bushnell Park Carousel (open April–September), with its intricately hand-carved horses and booming Wurlitzer band organ, built in 1914 by the Artistic Carousel Company of Brooklyn, New York. A welcome oasis of green in a busy city, the park has a pond and about 750 trees, including a first-generation offspring of the state's historic Charter Oak (the state tree) and four enormous state champion trees. ⊠ *99 Trinity St.* ☎ *860/232–6710* ⊕ *www.bushnellpark.org* 🆓 *Free.*

Butler-McCook Homestead

GARDEN | Built in 1782, this was home to four generations of Butlers and McCooks until it became a museum in 1971. Today, it houses Hartford's oldest intact collection of art and antiques, including Connecticut-crafted furnishings, family possessions, and Victorian-era toys that show the evolution of American tastes over nearly 200 years. The beautifully restored Victorian garden was originally designed by Jacob Weidenmann. ⊠ *396 Main St.* ☎ *860/522–1806* ⊕ *www.ctland-marks.org* 💵 *$13* ⊙ *Closed Jan.–Apr.*

The Children's Museum

MUSEUM | FAMILY | A life-size walk-through replica of a 60-foot sperm whale greets patrons at this museum. Located in West Hartford, the museum also has a wildlife sanctuary and a planetarium with real-life images of outer space beamed in from NASA, as well as a hands-on puzzle exhibit that introduces kids to various scientific and mathematical concepts and optical illusions. ✉ *950 Trout Brook Dr., 5 miles west of downtown, West Hartford* ☎ *860/231–2824* ⊕ *www.thechildrensmuseumct.org* 💲 *$15* ⊙ *Closed Mon. Sept.–June.*

★ Connecticut Science Center

MUSEUM | FAMILY | This strikingly modern building, designed by world-renowned architect César Pelli, houses 40,000 square feet of exhibit space under a wavelike roof that appears to float over the structure. Among the more than 165 hands-on exhibits, youngsters, teens, and adults alike can dive into a black hole and examine the moon's craters in the Exploring Space exhibit, race mini-sailboats and magnetic trains at Forces in Motion, and discover hidden athletic talents in the Sports Lab. Kid Space is perfect for ages three to six, and everyone enjoys mingling with free-flying butterflies in the Butterfly Encounter. Complete your visit by taking in a movie in the 3-D digital theater. ✉ *250 Columbus Blvd.* ☎ *860/724–3623* ⊕ *www.ctscienceecenter.org* 💲 *From $25* ⊙ *Closed Mon. Labor Day–Memorial Day.*

Harriet Beecher Stowe Center

HOUSE | Abolitionist and author Harriet Beecher Stowe (1811–96) spent her final years at this 1871 Victorian Gothic cottage, now a popular stop on the Connecticut Freedom Trail. The center was built around the cottage in tribute to the author of the antislavery novel, *Uncle Tom's Cabin.* Stowe's personal writing table and effects are housed inside. ✉ *77 Forest St.* ☎ *860/522–9258* ⊕ *www. harrietbeecherstowecenter.org* 💲 *$16* ⊙ *Closed Tues. Jan.–Mar.*

★ Mark Twain House & Museum

HOUSE | Built in 1874, this building was the home of Samuel Langhorne Clemens (better known as Mark Twain) until 1891. In the time he and his family lived in this 25-room Victorian mansion, Twain published seven major novels, including *The Adventures of Tom Sawyer, The Adventures of Huckleberry Finn,* and *The Prince and the Pauper.* The home has one of only two Louis Comfort Tiffany–designed domestic interiors open to the public. A contemporary museum on the grounds presents an up-close look at the author and screens an outstanding documentary on his life introduced by Ken Burns. ✉ *351 Farmington Ave., at Woodland St.* ☎ *860/247–0998* ⊕ *marktwainhouse.org* 💲 *From $6* ⊙ *Closed Tues. Jan. and Feb.*

Noah Webster House

HOUSE | This 18th-century farmhouse is the birthplace and childhood home of Noah Webster (1758–1843), the famed teacher, lawyer, early abolitionist, and author of the first American dictionary. Inside you'll find Webster memorabilia, period furnishings, and a one-room schoolhouse theater. ✉ *227 S. Main St., West Hartford* ☎ *860/521–5362* ⊕ *www.noahwebsterhouse.org* 💲 *$8* ⊙ *Closed mornings.*

Old State House

HISTORIC SITE | This Federal-style house with an elaborate cupola and roof balustrade was designed in the early 1700s by Charles Bulfinch, architect of the U.S. Capitol. It served as Connecticut's state capitol until a new building opened in 1879, when it became Hartford's city hall until 1915. In the 1820 Senate Chamber, where everyone from John Adams and Abraham Lincoln to Jimmy Carter and George H. W. Bush has spoken, you can view a portrait of George Washington by Gilbert Stuart; and in the Courtroom, you can find out about the trial of the *Amistad* Africans in the very place it began. In summer, enjoy concerts and a farmers' market (which dates back to the 1600s); don't forget to stop by the Museum of Natural and Other Curiosities. ✉ *800 Main St.* ☎ *860/522–6766* ⊕ *www.cga. ct.gov/osh* 💲 *$8* ⊙ *Closed Sun. Also closed Mon. early July–early Oct., Sat. early Oct.–early July.*

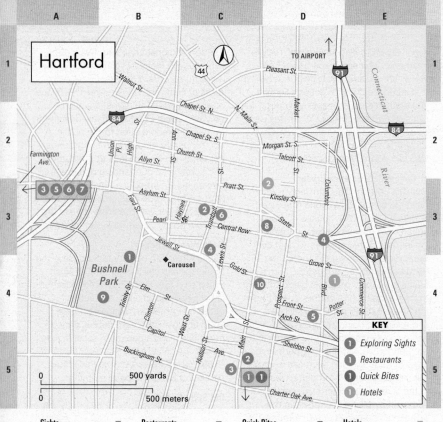

Hartford

Sights ▼

1 Bushnell Park **B4**
2 Butler-McCook
   Homestead **C5**
3 The Children's
   Museum **A3**
4 Connecticut
   Science Center **D3**
5 Harriet Beecher
   Stowe Center............ **A3**
6 Mark Twain House &
   Museum **A3**
7 Noah Webster
   House **A3**
8 Old State House......... **D3**
9 State Capitol............. **B4**
10 Wadsworth Atheneum
    Museum of Art **C4**

Restaurants ▼

1 First and Last Tavern **C5**
2 Max Downtown.......... **C3**
3 Peppercorn's Grill........ **C5**
4 Salute **C3**
5 Ted's Montana Grill...... **D4**
6 Trumbull Kitchen......... **C3**

Quick Bites ▼

1 Mozzicato De Pasquale's
  Bakery &
  Pastry Shop **C5**

Hotels ▼

1 Hartford Marriott
  Downtown............... **D4**
2 Residence Inn
  Hartford Downtown **D3**

Connecticut's Victorian Gothic state capitol rises from Hartford's Bushnell Park.

★ State Capitol

GOVERNMENT BUILDING | **FAMILY** | The gold-domed State Capitol building, built in 1878 overlooking Bushnell Park, houses the state's executive offices and legislative chamber, as well as historical memorabilia. On a tour, you walk past a statue Nathan Hale, the official state hero, to the Hall of Flags, which displays a number of historic battle flags carried by Connecticut troops in wars from the Civil War through the Korean Conflict, along with a camp bed used by Marquis de Lafayette when he came to Hartford to meet with George Washington during the Revolutionary War. When the General Assembly is in session (January–early June in odd-numbered years; February–early May in even-numbered years), visitors can observe the proceedings from the public galleries. ⊠ *210 Capitol Ave.* ☎ *860/240–0222* ⊕ *www.cga. ct.gov/capitoltours* 🖼 *Free* ☉ *Closed weekends.*

★ Wadsworth Atheneum Museum of Art

MUSEUM | The nation's oldest public art museum—and the first American museum to acquire works by Salvador Dalí and Italian Renaissance artist Caravaggio—houses more than 50,000 artworks and artifacts spanning 5,000 years, along with 7,000 items documenting African American history and culture in partnership with the Amistad Foundation. Particularly impressive are the museum's Baroque, Impressionist, and Hudson River School collections. ⊠ *600 Main St.* ☎ *860/278–2670* ⊕ *www.thewadsworth.org* 🖼 *$15* ☉ *Closed Mon. and Tues.*

🍽 Restaurants

First and Last Tavern

$$ | **ITALIAN** | What looks to be a simple neighborhood spot south of downtown is actually one of the state's most hallowed Italian restaurants and pizza parlors, serving superb thin-crust pies and much more since 1936. The old-fashioned wooden bar is jammed most evenings with suburbia-bound daily-grinders; the main dining room, which is just as noisy, has a brick wall covered with celebrity photos. **Known for:** brick-oven pizzas and great bread; sauce like Mom used to make (if she's Italian!); separate bakery/ deli across the street. $ *Average main: $20* ✉ *939 Maple Ave.* ☎ *860/956–6000* ⊕ *www.firstandlasttavern.com.*

★ **Max Downtown**
$$$$ | **AMERICAN** | With its contemporary design, extensive martini list, and sophisticated cuisine, this chop house is a favorite among the city's well-heeled, as well as a popular after-work spot. Creative entrées include spiced tuna with Korean bacon, aged shoyu, and puffed rice; seared sea scallops with heirloom grains and black trumpet mushrooms; and a wide range of perfectly prepared steaks with sauces like red wine rosemary jus or cognac peppercorn cream. **Known for:** whiskey bar with more than 200 selections from around the world; simply but exquisitely prepared fish; tavern menu with sandwiches and small plates. $ *Average main: $40* ✉ *185 Asylum St.* ☎ *860/522–2530* ⊕ *www.maxrestaurantgroup.com/downtown* ⊗ *No lunch weekends.*

Peppercorn's Grill
$$$ | **ITALIAN** | This mainstay of Hartford's restaurant scene presents contemporary Italian cuisine in a lively but cozy setting. Enjoy homemade potato gnocchi, slow-roasted osso buco, or a simply grilled veal chop—but save room for the warm chocolate bread pudding or warm Valrhona chocolate cake. **Known for:** homemade gelato and sorbet; mozzarella bar with your choice of toppings; first Thursday of the month happy hour with live music. $ *Average main: $26* ✉ *357 Main St.* ☎ *860/547–1714* ⊕ *www.peppercornsgrill.com* ⊗ *Closed Sun. No lunch Sat.*

Salute
$$$ | **ITALIAN** | Packed every night, Salute is *the* downtown spot for consistently delicious Italian fare and pleasant service. The kitchen serves up a lengthy list of pasta dishes—try the chicken gnocchi with pesto cream or the perfectly executed fettuccine with clams—and traditional Italian desserts like tiramisu and gelato. **Known for:** warm, comfortable, welcoming spot to enjoy good food; excellent selection of wine and draft beer; half-price garage parking next door—important in the city. $ *Average main: $26* ✉ *100 Trumbull St.* ☎ *860/899–1350* ⊕ *www.salutehartford.com* ⊗ *No lunch Sun.*

Ted's Montana Grill
$$$ | **STEAKHOUSE** | Venture into this busy, "Old West"-style steak house for a juicy burger (beef, bison, chicken, or veggie) with your choice of 15 toppings, a mouth-watering rack of BBQ ribs with meat that nearly falls off the bone, a grilled hand-cut steak (again, beef or bison), and more—plenty more. This is a perfect spot for dinner if you're heading to a concert at Infinity Hall, right across the street, or an event at the nearby XL Center. **Known for:** if you haven't had bison, this is the place to try it; "the best" onion rings; friendly servers. $ *Average main: $25* ✉ *35 Front St.* ☎ *860/692–1167* ⊕ *tedsmontanagrill.com.*

Trumbull Kitchen
$$$ | **ECLECTIC** | **FAMILY** | Upbeat, hip, and casual, Trumbull Kitchen is the place to see and be seen. A loft-style dining area with leather-clad walls overlooks the action below where an eclectic, global-theme menu features selections like Asian lettuce cups, Szechuan pork dumplings, seafood pad Thai, and prosciutto-crusted Atlantic haddock or a "stone pie" (pizza). **Known for:** the place to see and be seen; something for everyone, even the kids; convenient to the XL Center and nearby theaters. $ *Average*

main: $27 ⊠ 150 Trumbull St. ☎ 860/493–7412 ⊕ www.maxrestaurantgroup.com/trumbull ⊗ No lunch Sun.

☕ Coffee and Quick Bites

Mozzicato De Pasquale's Bakery & Pastry Shop

$ | BAKERY | FAMILY | Located on Franklin Avenue in Hartford's Little Italy neighborhood, this shop serves delectable Italian pastries in the bakery and espresso, cappuccino, and gelato in The Caffé. **Known for:** cookie platters to take home or gift; authentic Italian atmosphere; full liquor bar, too. $ *Average main: $10* ⊠ *329 Franklin Ave.* ☎ *860/296–0426* ⊕ *www.mozzicatobakery.com.*

🛏 Hotels

Hartford Marriott Downtown

$$$$ | HOTEL | FAMILY | This convenient, upscale hotel is connected to the Connecticut Convention Center and within walking distance of the Connecticut Science Center, Wadsworth Atheneum, Old State House, and other attractions. **Pros:** lots of restaurants nearby; Starbucks café in the lobby; accessible rooms available. **Cons:** convenient location comes at a price; pay for parking (nearby or valet); room service items are prepackaged and ready-to-eat—not cooked to order. $ *Rooms from: $469* ⊠ *200 Columbus Blvd.* ☎ *860/249–8000* ⊕ *www.marriott.com* ⊅ *409 rooms* ⦿ *No meals.*

Residence Inn Hartford Downtown

$ | HOTEL | FAMILY | The all-suites Residence Inn, in the historic Richardson Building, is convenient to the XL Center, theaters, and the Old State House. **Pros:** spacious suites are perfect for families or extended stays; on-site City Steam Brewery Café for drinks or a hearty meal; free shuttle service within 5 miles. **Cons:** rather dated room furnishings; walking around area at night isn't recommended; street noise can be an issue in some rooms. $ *Rooms from: $195* ⊠ *942 Main*

St. ☎ 860/524–5550 ⊕ www.marriott.com ⊅ 120 suites ⦿ Free breakfast.

🍸 Nightlife

BARS

Arch Street Tavern

BARS/PUBS | This bar—in a former carriage factory, firehouse, and body shop—hosts local rock bands. You can get a bite to eat, too. ⊠ *85 Arch St.* ☎ *860/246–7610* ⊕ *www.archstreettavern.com.*

Black-Eyed Sally's Southern Kitchen & Bar

BARS/PUBS | For barbecue and live blues, jazz, rock, and roots music, head to laid-back Black-Eyed Sally's. ⊠ *350 Asylum St.* ☎ *860/278–7427* ⊕ *www.blackeyedsallys.com.*

🎭 Performing Arts

MUSIC

★ Infinity Music Hall & Bistro

CABARET | This intimate, acoustically excellent, 500-seat music hall—a sister venue to Infinity Hall in Norfolk, Connecticut—presents live music (folk, jazz, rock, alternative) and comedy shows throughout the year. The mezzanine level features cabaret-style seating and beverage service. ⊠ *32 Front St.* ☎ *860/560–7757, 866/666–6306 box office* ⊕ *www.infinityhall.com.*

THEATER

The Bushnell

CONCERTS | In addition to national tours of major Broadway shows, concerts, comedy acts, and family theater, The Bushnell is home to the Hartford Symphony Orchestra. ⊠ *166 Capitol Ave.* ☎ *860/987–5900 box office* ⊕ *www.bushnell.org.*

Hartford Stage Company

THEATER | The Hartford Stage Company presents new and classic plays from around the world in an intimate (489-seat) setting. ⊠ *50 Church St.* ☎ *860/527–5151* ⊕ *www.hartfordstage.org.*

TheatreWorks

THEATER | This is the Hartford equivalent of Off-Broadway, where new and experimental dramas are presented. ✉ *233 Pearl St.* ☎ *860/527–7838* 🌐 *twhartford.org.*

Wethersfield

6 miles south of Hartford, 34 miles northeast of New Haven.

Wethersfield, a vast Hartford suburb, dates to 1634 and has the state's largest and, some say, the most picturesque historic district, with more than 100 pre-1849 buildings. Old Wethersfield has the oldest firehouse in the state, the oldest historic district in the state, and the oldest continuously operating seed company. Today, this "dated" community has new parks and new shops; but history is still its main draw.

GETTING HERE AND AROUND

Wethersfield is only a few miles south of Hartford, and most easily reached by car. From Hartford, take Interstate 91 south to Route 3 south.

Sights

★ New Britain Museum of American Art

MUSEUM | An important stop for art lovers, this 100-year-old museum's collection of more than 10,000 works from 1740 to the present focuses solely on American art. Among its treasures number paintings by John Singer Sargent, Winslow Homer, and Georgia O'Keeffe, as well as sculpture by Isamu Noguchi. Of particular note is the selection of Impressionist artists, including Mary Cassatt, William Merritt Chase, Childe Hassam, and John Henry Twachtman, as well as Thomas Hart Benton's five-panel mural *The Arts of Life in America.* The museum also has a café, a large shop, and a library of art books. ✉ *56 Lexington St., New Britain* ✣ *About 10 miles west of Wethersfield* ☎ *860/229–0257* 🌐 *www.nbmaa.org* 🎟 *$15 (free Sat. 10–noon)* ⏲ *Closed Mon.*

Webb-Deane-Stevens Museum

MUSEUM | For a true sample of Wethersfield's historic past, stop by the Joseph Webb House, the Silas Deane House, and the Isaac Stevens House—all adjacent to each other along Main Street and all built in the mid- to late 1700s. These well-preserved examples of Georgian architecture reflect their owners' lifestyles as, respectively, a merchant, a diplomat, and a tradesman. The Webb House, a registered National Historic Landmark, was the site of the strategy conference between George Washington and French general Jean-Baptiste Rochambeau, which led to the British defeat at Yorktown. ✉ *211 Main St., off I–91* ☎ *860/529–0612* 🌐 *webb-deane-stevens.org* 🎟 *$12* ⏲ *Closed Jan.–Mar., weekdays Apr. and Nov.*

Coffee and Quick Bites

Heirloom Market at Comstock Ferre

$ | **CAFÉ** | **FAMILY** | The post-and-beam buildings of Comstock Ferre & Co., the country's oldest continuously operating seed company (founded in 1820), is now home to a "seed-to-plate" natural foods café. Open all day for wraps, toasts, soup, salad, juices, coffee, tea, and smoothies. **Known for:** breakfast wrap served all day; fresh-baked pastries and breads; organic juices (red, green, or orange, depending on the ingredients). [$] *Average main: $12* ✉ *263 Main St.* ☎ *860/257–2790* 🌐 *heirloommkt.com* ⏲ *Closed Mon. No dinner.*

Middletown

16 miles south of Hartford, 27 miles northeast of New Haven.

With its Connecticut River setting, easy access to major highways, and historic architecture, Middletown is perhaps best known as the location of Wesleyan University. The town's High Street is an architecturally eclectic thoroughfare—Charles

Connecticut's Historic Gardens

These extraordinary Connecticut gardens form Connecticut's Historic Gardens, a "trail" of natural beauties across the state. For more information on each of the gardens, visit ⊕ *www.cthistoricgardens.org*.

Bellamy-Ferriday House & Garden, North Bethlehem. Highlights of this garden include an apple orchard and a circa-1915 formal parterre garden that blossoms with peonies, roses, and lilacs.

Butler-McCook House & Garden, Hartford. Landscape architect Jacob Weidenmann created a Victorian garden full of peonies, roses, and iris that serves as an amazing respite from downtown city life.

Florence Griswold Museum, Old Lyme. The gardens at the historic Florence Griswold Museum, once the home of a prominent Old Lyme family and later a haven for artists, have been restored to their 1910 appearance and feature masses of hollyhocks, iris, foxglove, day lilies, and heliotrope.

Glebe House Museum, Woodbury. Legendary British garden writer and designer Gertrude Jekyll designed only three gardens in the United States, and the one at the Glebe House Museum is the only one still in existence. It is a classic example of Jekyll's ideas about color harmony and plant combinations; a hedge of mixed shrubs encloses a mix of perennials.

Harriet Beecher Stowe Center, Hartford. The grounds at the Harriet Beecher Stowe Center feature Connecticut's largest magnolia tree, a pink dogwood that's more than 100 years old, and eight distinct gardens: an antique rose garden; a woodland garden; a wildflower meadow; a high-Victorian texture garden; a blue cottage garden; and formal color-coordinated gardens.

Hill-Stead Museum, Farmington. The centerpiece of the Hill-Stead Museum is a circa-1920 sunken garden enclosed in a yew hedge and surrounded by a wall of rough stone. At the center of the octagonal design is a summerhouse with 36 flowerbeds and brick walkways radiating outward.

Promisek at Three Rivers Farm, Bridgewater. The prolific Beatrix Farrand designed the original garden at Promisek; restored in recent years, it now overflows with beds of annuals and perennials that include hollyhocks, peonies, and always-dashing delphiniums.

Roseland Cottage, Woodstock. At Roseland Cottage, the boxwood parterre garden includes 21 flowerbeds surrounded by boxwood hedges.

Thankful Arnold House Museum, Haddam. Gravel paths divide granite-edged Colonial Revival-style gardens filled with more than 50 varieties of herbs that Thankful Arnold likely used in the early 1800s for cooking, medicine, dyeing, fragrance, and other household uses.

Webb-Deane-Stevens Museum, Wethersfield. This Colonial Revival garden is filled with fragrant, old-fashioned flowers such as peonies, pinks, phlox, hollyhocks, and larkspur, as well as a profusion of roses.

7

Connecticut MIDDLETOWN

Dickens once called it "the most beautiful street I have seen in America." Wesleyan students add a youthful vigor to the town when school is in session.

GETTING HERE AND AROUND

Middletown is best reached by car. From Hartford, follow Interstate 91 south to Route 9 south. From the coast, take Interstate 95 to Route 9 north.

Sights

Dinosaur State Park

ARCHAEOLOGICAL SITE | FAMILY | In this park in Rocky Hill, about 9 miles north of downtown Middletown (halfway to Hartford), see 500 tracks left by the dinosaurs that roamed the area some 200 million years ago. The tracks are preserved under a giant geodesic dome and 1,500 more are buried for preservation, making it one of the largest dinosaur-track sites in North America. You can even make plaster casts of tracks on a special area of the property; call ahead to learn what materials you need to bring. ✉ *400 West St., 1 mile east of I–91, Exit 23, Rocky Hill* ☎ *860/529–8423* 🌐 *www.dinosaurstatepark.org* 🎫 *$6* ⏲ *Closed Mon.*

★ Lyman Orchards

FARM/RANCH | FAMILY | Looking for a quintessential New England outing? These orchards just south of Middletown are not to be missed. Get lost in the sunflower maze, then pick your own seasonal fruits—berries, peaches, pears, apples, and even pumpkins—from June to October. Or stop by the Apple Barrel Market, open all year long, to shop for farm-fresh pies, fruit baskets, jams and preserves, and gifts. ✉ *32 Reeds Gap Rd., Junction of Rtes. 147 and 157, Middlefield* ☎ *860/349–6000* 🌐 *www.lymanorchards.com.*

Wesleyan University

COLLEGE | Founded in 1831, Wesleyan University is one of the oldest Methodist institutions of higher education in the country. The roughly 2,800 undergraduates give Middletown a contemporary, college-town feel. Note the massive, fluted Corinthian columns of the 1828 Greek Revival Russell House at the corner of Washington Street, across from the pink Mediterranean-style Davison Art Center, built 15 years later. Farther along you'll find gingerbreads, towering brownstones, Tudors, and Queen Annes. A few hundred yards up on Church Street, which intersects High Street, is the Olin Library. This 1928 structure was designed by Henry Bacon, architect of the Lincoln Memorial. ✉ *45 Wyllys Ave., off High St.* ☎ *860/685–2000* 🌐 *www.wesleyan.edu.*

Restaurants

O'Rourke's Diner

$ | AMERICAN | FAMILY | This glass-and-steel classic is the place to go for top-notch diner fare, including creative specialties like the omelet stuffed with roasted portobello mushrooms, Brie, and asparagus. Arrive early for lunch, as the lines often file out the door. **Known for:** steamed cheeseburgers—a favorite since 1941; Irish dishes, like bangers, colcannon, and Irish stew; breakfast served 6 am–3 pm. [$] *Average main: $13* ✉ *728 Main St.* ☎ *860/346–6101* 🌐 *www.orourkesmiddletown.com* ⏲ *No dinner. No lunch weekends.*

Hotels

Inn at Middletown

$$ | HOTEL | Centrally located in an 1800s-era National Guard Armory in the heart of downtown Middletown, rooms in the Inn mix Colonial-style furnishings with modern amenities; all have views of the Connecticut River. **Pros:** two blocks from Wesleyan campus; steps from downtown shopping; accessible rooms available with ADA-compliant amenities. **Cons:** no real grounds; rates rise when Wesleyan is in session; valet parking fee. [$] *Rooms from: $219* ✉ *70 Main St.*

Connecticut's Unusual Museums

American Clock & Watch Museum in Bristol is devoted entirely to clocks and watches—more than 5,500 timepieces are on display, including clocks dating back to 1680 and watches dating back to 1595. The best time to come? Noon, of course.

Also in Bristol, the **New England Carousel Museum** has one of the largest antique carousel collections in the country, both full-size pieces and miniatures. Oddly enough, it's also home to the **Museum of Fire History**, which displays vintage equipment and memorabilia.

The Company of Fifers & Drummers in Ivoryton, whose mission is to perpetuate America's heritage in fife and drum music, maintains **The Museum of Fife & Drum**, which has artifacts dating back to the 1700s. It's open on some weekends in summer.

At Windsor's **Vintage Radio & Communications Museum of Connecticut** exhibits explain how communications have changed over the years—from Morse code to satellites and everything in between. An offshoot of the museum, **Vintage Hi-Fi Museum** in West Hartford, displays mid-20th-century TVs, stereo sets, and other baby boomer artifacts.

If you're fascinated by locks, the **Lock Museum of America** in Terryville is for you. The collection includes thousands of antique door locks, padlocks, safe locks, handcuffs, keys, escutcheon plates, and more—including a 4,000-year-old lock from Egypt and a treasure chest from the Spanish Armada.

Many of the buttons for soldier uniforms in the Revolutionary War,

the War of 1812, both sides of the Civil War, and even recent wars were made in Connecticut. The **Waterbury Button Museum** has examples of military buttons and thousands of others on display.

At New Haven's **Eli Whitney Museum**, there are exhibits on the man, his cotton gin, and the dam built to power the historic building—plus exhibits on A. C. Gilbert, the inventor of the erector set and maker of educational toys.

The buildings and grounds at the **Connecticut Antique Machinery Association Museum** in Kent display old-fashioned steam engines, agricultural equipment, combustion engines, steam shovels, a narrow-gauge railroad with a steam locomotive, and mining artifacts. The Hall of Geology and Paleontology adds dinosaur tracks and fossils.

The whole family will get a chuckle out of the **Barker Character Comic & Cartoon Museum** in Cheshire, which has 80,000 toys and collectibles on display—from Betty Boop to Popeye, Shirley Temple dolls to the Simpsons, Halloween costumes, lunch boxes, and so much more.

The Glass House in New Canaan, built between 1949 and 1995 by architect Philip Johnson and now a National Trust Historic Site, has a permanent collection of 20th-century paintings and sculpture.

And for all things PEZ, head for the **PEZ Visitor Center** in Orange, which has the largest collection of PEZ memorabilia in the world, and, of course, a retail shop.

☎ 860/854–6300 ⊕ www.innatmiddle-town.com ⇆ 100 rooms ⦁❍⦁ No meals.

🎭 Performing Arts

THEATER
Wesleyan University Center for the Arts
ARTS CENTERS | See modern dance or a provocative new play, hear top play-wrights and actors discuss their craft, or take in an art exhibit or concert at this college arts center. ✉ 271 Washington Terr. ☎ 860/685–3355 ⊕ www. wesleyan.edu/cfa.

New Haven

46 miles northeast of Greenwich.

Though the city is best known as the home of Yale University, New Haven's historic district dates back to the 17th century—and the city's distinctive shops, prestigious museums, and highly respected theaters are major draws. In recent years, the restaurant scene has also garnered considerable acclaim, par-ticularly the city's unique "apizza" legacy.

GETTING HERE AND AROUND
By car, New Haven is accessible from both Interstate 95 and Interstate 91. By rail, Amtrak's Northeast Regional and high-speed Acela trains stop here; New Haven is also the end of the Metro-North commuter line from New York City. Shore Line East train service connects New Haven with Old Saybrook, Madison, and New London. Tweed New Haven Airport has limited regional service for both scheduled commercial and private planes.

ESSENTIALS
VISITOR INFORMATION Visit New Haven.
✉ 5 Science Park ☎ 203/777–8550, 800/332–7829 ⊕ www.visitnewhaven. com.

◉ Sights

Beinecke Rare Book and Manuscript Library
LIBRARY | The library's collection of literary papers, early manuscripts, and rare books include a Gutenberg Bible and original Audubon bird prints; the exhibition spaces on the ground floor and mezzanine are open to the public. The building that houses them is an attraction in its own right: the walls are made of marble cut so thin that the light shines through, making the interior a breath-taking sight on sunny days. Introductory tours for individuals are offered on Satur-day afternoons; group tours are Yale-led and require advance registration at the Yale Visitor Information Center ✉ 121 Wall St. ☎ 203/432–2977 ⊕ beinecke.library. yale.edu ⌦ Free.

★ IT Adventure Indoor Ropes Course
AMUSEMENT PARK/WATER PARK | FAMILY | Oddly enough, you'll find the world's larg-est indoor adventure ropes course within Jordan's Furniture Store. The 60-foot-high courses have more than 100 activities like walking across zigzag swinging beams, climbing walls, rope ladders, bridges, moving planks, a 50-foot free-fall jump, four 200-foot-long ziplines, and more. At Little IT, toddlers and little kids can zip along, too. ✉ Jordan's Furniture Store, 40 Sargent Dr., adjacent to I–95 ☎ 203/780–9199 ⊕ www.jordans.com/ attractions/it ⌦ $25.

New Haven Green
HISTORIC SITE | FAMILY | Bordered on its west side by the Yale campus, the New Haven Green is a fine example of early urban planning. Village elders set aside the 16-acre plot as a town common as early as 1638. Three early-19th-century churches—the Gothic Revival-style **Trinity Episcopal Church,** the Federal-style **Center Congregational Church,** and **United Church**—have contributed to its present appeal. For a year, from September 1839 to August 1840, survivors of the slave ship *Amistad* were incarcerated in a jail

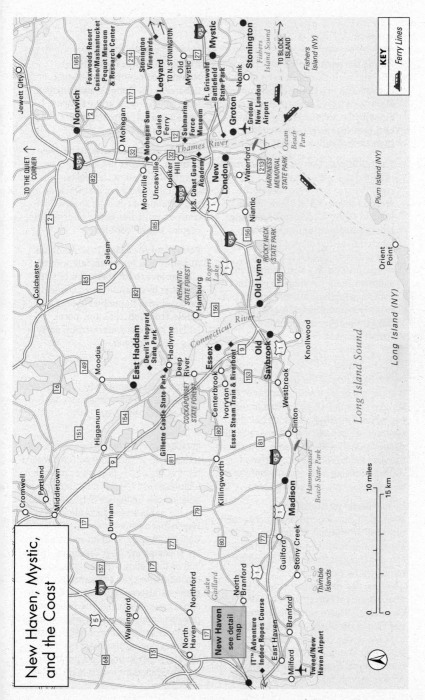

New Haven, Mystic, and the Coast

KEY
⛴ Ferry Lines

Connecticut Lobster Rolls

Behold the lobster roll: Sweet, succulent, and sinfully rich, it's the ultimate buttery icon of a Connecticut summer. Many New Englanders prefer to chill out with a cold lobster salad in their bun, but Nutmeggers generally like their lobster rolls served hot, hot, hot.

The traditional Connecticut lobster roll, said to have been invented in the early 1930s at Perry's, a now-defunct seafood shack on the Boston Post Road in Milford, consists of nothing more than plump chunks of hot lobster meat and melted butter served on a butter-toasted roll; in other words, heaven on a bun. From seafood shanties along the shore to gourmet getaways farther inland, Connecticut is fairly swimming in eateries that offer these revered rolls. Here are three favorites:

Abbott's Lobster in the Rough, Noank. A lobster roll at Abbott's Lobster in the Rough is best enjoyed from a picnic table at the edge of Noank Harbor, watching boats bobbing at anchor.

Captain Scott's Lobster Dock, New London. Whether hot and buttery or cold and creamy, the lobster rolls at Captain Scott's Lobster Dock, on a spit of land overlooking Shaw's Cove, come on grilled-in-butter buns—either regular size or "foot-long."

Lenny and Joe's Fish Tale, Madison. At Lenny and Joe's Fish Tale, kids of all ages love to eat their lobster rolls outdoors by a hand-carved Dentzel carousel with flying horses (and a whale, frog, lion, seal, and more), which the restaurant operates early May–early October.

on the east side of the green and were brought out of jail to exercise there. An *Amistad* memorial now resides at the site of the former jail. Besides being a pleasant urban park, the Green is also the venue for festivals and events throughout the year. ⊠ *250 Temple St., between Church, College, Elm, and Chapel Sts.* ⊕ *www.downtownnewhaven.com.*

★ Yale Center for British Art
MUSEUM | Featuring the largest collection of British art outside Britain, the center surveys the development of English art, life, and thought from the Elizabethan period to the present. The skylighted galleries, one of architect Louis I. Kahn's final works, contain artwork by John Constable, William Hogarth, Thomas Gainsborough, Joshua Reynolds, and J. M. W. Turner, to name but a few. You'll also find rare books and paintings documenting English history. Explore on your own or take a free, docent-led

tour. ⊠ *1080 Chapel St.* ☎ *203/432–2800, 203/432–2800* ⊕ *britishart.yale.edu* 🖾 *Free* 🕑 *Closed Mon.*

★ Yale University
COLLEGE | FAMILY | New Haven's manufacturing history dates to the 19th century, but the city owes its fame to merchant Elihu Yale. In 1718, his contributions enabled the Collegiate School, founded in 1701 at Saybrook, to settle in New Haven and change its name to Yale College. In 1887, all of its schools were consolidated into Yale University. This is one of the nation's great institutions of higher learning, and its campus holds some handsome neo-Gothic buildings and noteworthy museums. Student guides conduct hour-long walking tours that include Connecticut Hall in the Old Campus, one of the oldest buildings in the state, which housed a number of illustrious students—including Nathan

Hale, Noah Webster, and Eli Whitney. Tours start from the visitor center. ✉ *Yale Visitor Center, 149 Elm St.* ☎ *203/432–2300* 🌐 *visitorcenter.yale.edu* 🎫 *Free.*

★ Yale University Art Gallery
MUSEUM | Since its founding in 1832, this art gallery has amassed more than 200,000 works from around the world, dating from ancient Egypt to the present day. Highlights include works by Vincent van Gogh, Edouard Manet, Claude Monet, Pablo Picasso, Winslow Homer, and Thomas Eakins, as well as Etruscan and Greek vases, Chinese ceramics and bronzes, early Italian paintings, and a collection of American decorative arts that is considered one of the world's finest. The gallery's landmark main building is also of note: opened in 1953, it was renowned architect Louis I. Kahn's first major commission and the first modernist building on the neo-Gothic Yale campus. ✉ *1111 Chapel St., at York St.* ☎ *203/432–0600* 🌐 *artgallery.yale.edu* 🎫 *Free* 🕒 *Closed Mon.*

🍴 Restaurants

Barcelona
$$ | **SPANISH** | There's no need to take a transatlantic flight to Spain when you can feast on authentic Spanish cuisine right here in New Haven. There are entrées and salads on the menu, but the tapas are the best bet—rich, tasty, and full of flavor. **Known for:** more than a dozen tapas on the menu; charcuterie and cheese menu; 2,000-bottle wine cellar. [$] *Average main: $22* ✉ *Omni New Haven Hotel, 155 Temple St.* ☎ *203/848–3000* 🌐 *www.barcelonawinebar.com* 🕒 *No lunch Mon.–Sat.*

★ Frank Pepe's Pizzeria Napoletana
$$ | **PIZZA** | **FAMILY** | Pepe's may serve the best pizza in the world, as so many people claim. Try the justifiably famous white-clam pie (especially good topped with bacon), but just thinking about the original tomato pie (with mozzarella) makes your mouth water. **Known for:** long line for a table—often an hour or more—but takeout is quicker; thin-crust pizza baked in a coal-fired brick oven; pies cut in odd-shaped pieces—great for kids. [$] *Average main: $24* ✉ *157 Wooster St.* ☎ *203/865–5762* 🌐 *www.pepespizzeria.com* 💳 *No credit cards.*

Louis' Lunch
$ | **AMERICAN** | This all-American luncheonette, opened since 1895 and now on the National Register of Historic Places, is also recognized as the birthplace of the "hamburger sandwich." Its first-rate burgers are cooked to order in an old-fashioned cast-iron grill (that dates back to 1898) and served with a slice of tomato, onion, and cheese on two pieces of white toast. Add potato salad or chips and a slice of pie, and you're all set! **Known for:** no ketchup allowed; fourth-generation family-run restaurant; open until 2 am Thursday–Saturday. [$] *Average main: $10* ✉ *261 Crown St.* ☎ *203/562–5507* 🌐 *louislunch.com* 💳 *No credit cards* 🕒 *Closed Sun. and Mon.*

Modern Apizza
$ | **PIZZA** | **FAMILY** | It's not what Modern Apizza has that sets it apart from the rest but what its signature pie doesn't have: toppings. The pizzeria's "plain" pie is a thin crust with a layer of tomato sauce and just a sprinkling of Parmesan cheese. [$] *Average main: $15* ✉ *874 State St.* ☎ *203/776–5306* 🌐 *modernapizza.com* 🕒 *Closed Mon.*

Sally's Apizza
$$ | **PIZZA** | **FAMILY** | This place has been a rival of Frank Pepe's since 1938, when Salvatore Consiglio, Pepe's nephew, decided to break away from his relatives and open his own place. The result of this family feud is two competing pizzerias and a divided city: those who believe Frank Pepe's serves the best pizza and those who are devoted to Sally's. **Known for:** plan to wait—for a table and then for your pizza; hand-tossed pies baked in a coal-fired brick oven; Sal's family sold out

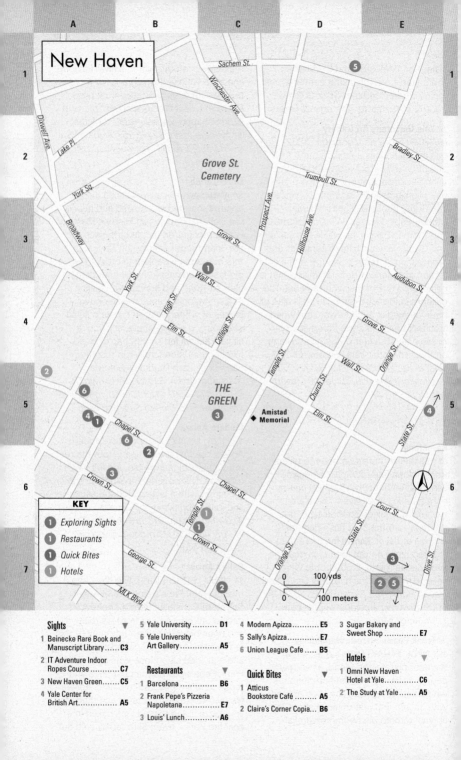

New Haven

Sights ▼

1 Beinecke Rare Book and
  Manuscript Library **C3**
2 IT Adventure Indoor
  Ropes Course **C7**
3 New Haven Green **C5**
4 Yale Center for
  British Art **A5**
5 Yale University **D1**
6 Yale University
  Art Gallery **A5**

Restaurants ▼

1 Barcelona **B6**
2 Frank Pepe's Pizzeria
  Napoletana **E7**
3 Louis' Lunch **A6**
4 Modern Apizza **E5**
5 Sally's Apizza **E7**
6 Union League Cafe **B5**

Quick Bites ▼

1 Atticus
  Bookstore Café **A5**
2 Claire's Corner Copia ... **B6**
3 Sugar Bakery and
  Sweet Shop **E7**

Hotels ▼

1 Omni New Haven
  Hotel at Yale **C6**
2 The Study at Yale **A5**

KEY

1 *Exploring Sights*
1 *Restaurants*
1 *Quick Bites*
1 *Hotels*

New Haven Pizza 101

New Haven has been on pizza lovers' radars for decades. The "apizza" (pronounced "ah-beetz" by locals) style, defined by its thin, chewy crust, is baked in a coal-fired brick oven, which makes for a unique—and, some would argue, superior—pizza experience. For everything from the original tomato pie to white clam and other specialty pies, check out these three authentic New Haven pizzerias *(see Restaurants for more details)*.

Frank Pepe Pizzeria Napoletana—known simply as Pepe's Pizza—is where it all began: In 1925, Frank Pepe opened his eponymous pizzeria and created what would become the iconic New Haven–style pizza. Eager customers line up for hours to get a taste of the famous thin-crust pies, in particular Frank Pepe's pièce de résistance—the white clam pizza. This masterful creation consists of olive oil, garlic, oregano, grated Parmesan cheese, and littleneck clams atop a thin crust.

Just two blocks from Pepe's on Wooster Street (New Haven's Little Italy), **Sally's Apizza** has been a rival of Frank Pepe's since 1938, when Pepe's nephew opened his own place. Now visitors to New Haven must pledge their allegiance to just one of these famed Wooster Street pizzerias, although no one will blame you if you decide to be a double agent.

If you don't want to get involved with that feud, there's always **Modern Apizza**, which differentiates itself by *not* being on Wooster Street. Serving its signature plain pies (with a layer of tomato sauce and a sprinkling of Parmesan cheese) since 1934, you can add mozzarella and other toppings if you want, including clams, bacon, hot cherry peppers, salami, and more.

in 2017, but new owners vow to continue the tradition. $ *Average main: $18* ✉ *237 Wooster St.* ☎ *203/624–5271* ⊕ *www. sallysapizza.com* ▭ *No credit cards.*

★ **Union League Cafe**

$$$$ | FRENCH | In a gorgeous Beaux Arts dining room, this lively brasserie wins high marks for its updated French cuisine. The knowledgeable staff are happy to recommend wine pairings to complement whatever dishes you select—perhaps walnut-crusted Arctic char with lemon and parsley, slow-roasted veal chop with creamy morel sauce, or entrecôte au poivre with cippolini onions. **Known for:** prices are steep but worth the splurge; elegant atmosphere and impeccable service; quite reasonable midafternoon Club Room menu. $ *Average main: $36* ✉ *1032 Chapel St.* ☎ *203/562–4299* ⊕ *www.unionleaguecafe. com* ☾ *Closed Sun. No lunch Sat.*

☕ Coffee and Quick Bites

Atticus Bookstore Café

$ | CAFÉ | Come to this independent bookstore, café, and bakery to buy a book, have lunch (or breakfast), or have breakfast (or lunch) *and* buy a book. "Nourishment for mind and body" is the approach here—in the style of a European neighborhood café. **Known for:** sandwiches, salads, soups, and a few "plates & bowls"; delicious homemade breads and pastries; congenial atmosphere all day long. $ *Average main: $10* ✉ *1082 Chapel St.* ☎ *203/776–4040* ⊕ *www.atticusbookstorecafe.com.*

Claire's Corner Copia

$ | VEGETARIAN | Claire's has been a New Haven institution since 1975, and it remains a popular destination for vegetarians and vegans. The large menu offers

Yale's leafy campus is home to many neo-Gothic buildings.

quesadillas, burritos, gluten-free dishes, kosher food, salads of every sort, and breakfast items served all day. **Known for:** organic, sustainable ingredients; no alcohol; try the signature Lithuanian coffee cake. $ *Average main: $12* ⊠ *1000 Chapel St.* ☏ *203/562–3888* ⊕ *www. clairescornercopia.com.*

Sugar Bakery and Sweet Shop

$ | BAKERY | FAMILY | Stop in to try one of 25 different kinds of cupcake rotated daily or one of the 16 special flavors each month—or you may see one of its "cupcake trucks" parked around town. With flavors like cannoli, cookie dough, and the Elvis (banana cupcake with peanut-butter-and-jelly buttercream frosting), you're bound to find one (or more) to fuel your perfect sugar high. **Known for:** past winner of Food Network's Cupcake Wars; full-size cakes, too; plus vegan and gluten-free cupcakes. $ *Average main: $4* ⊠ *424 Main St., East Haven* ☏ *203/469–0815* ⊕ *www.thesugarbakery. com* ⊙ *Closed Sun.*

🛏 Hotels

Omni New Haven Hotel at Yale

$$ | HOTEL | FAMILY | This comfortable hotel near the heart of New Haven is outfitted with all the modern amenities; some upper-floor guest rooms enjoy great views. **Pros:** inviting lobby with complimentary fruit-infused ice water or hot chocolate; nice gym and spa; walk to shops and restaurants. **Cons:** no pool; rooms could use upgrading; view of rooftops from most rooms. $ *Rooms from: $200* ⊠ *155 Temple St.* ☏ *203/772–6664* ⊕ *www.omnihotels.com/hotels/new-haven-yale* ⇄ *306 rooms* ⊠ *No meals.*

The Study at Yale

$$ | HOTEL | With a pair of spectacles emblazoned on all hotel signature items and overflowing bookshelves in the hotel's lobby, the Study is chic lodging for the scholarly set. **Pros:** valet parking; excellent restaurant; great location in the middle of everything. **Cons:** tiny bathrooms; room refrigerator available only upon request; street noise

can be an issue in front-facing rooms. $ *Rooms from: $200* ✉ *1157 Chapel St.* ☎ *203/503–3900* ⊕ *www.thestudyatyale. com* ↪ *124 rooms* ⦿ *No meals.*

 Nightlife

BARS
★ BAR
BREWPUBS/BEER GARDENS | This spot is a cross between a dance club, a brick-oven pizzeria, and a brewpub. Come for dancing and drinks Thursday–Saturday; pizza, anytime. ✉ *254 Crown St.* ☎ *203/495– 8924* ⊕ *www.barnightclub.com.*

Toad's Place of New Haven
MUSIC CLUBS | Alternative and traditional rock, hip-hop, blues, and other types of bands play at Toad's Place, which has attracted college students and other "cool" clubbers since the 1970s. ✉ *300 York St.* ☎ *203/624–8623* ⊕ *www.toad- splace.com.*

🎭 Performing Arts

THEATER
★ Long Wharf Theatre
THEATER | The well-regarded Long Wharf Theatre presents works by contemporary writers and revivals of neglected classics. The season runs October through May. ✉ *222 Sargent Dr.* ☎ *203/693–1486 box office* ⊕ *www.longwharf.org.*

Shubert Theatre
ARTS CENTERS | Broadway musicals, dance performances, comedy, music concerts, and more are on the bill at the Shubert, a 1,600-seat theater that originally opened in 1914. ✉ *247 College St.* ☎ *203/624– 1825 box office* ⊕ *www.shubert.com.*

Woolsey Hall
MUSIC | Built in 1901 to commemorate Yale's bicentennial, the 2,650-seat Woolsey Hall hosts performances by the New Haven Symphony Orchestra, Yale Symphony Orchestra, Yale Philharmonia, Yale Concert Band, and Yale Glee Club,

as well as occasional guest recitals on the Newberry Memorial Organ. ✉ *500 College St., at Grove St.* ☎ *203/432–4158 box office* ⊕ *woolsey.yale.edu.*

Yale Repertory Theatre
THEATER | This theater stages both premieres and fresh interpretations of classics from October through May. ✉ *1120 Chapel St.* ☎ *203/432–1234 box office* ⊕ *www.yalerep.org.*

Yale School of Music
MUSIC | Most of the 200-plus performances in the impressive roster of concerts by the Yale School of Music—featuring students, faculty, and guest artists—take place in Sprague Memorial Hall, and many are free. Other venues include Woolsey Hall, Sudler Recital Hall, and Marquand Chapel—all on the Yale campus. ✉ *Sprague Memorial Hall, 98 Wall St.* ☎ *203/432–4158 box office* ⊕ *music. yale.edu.*

Madison

21 miles east of New Haven, 65 miles northeast of Greenwich.

Coastal Madison has an understated charm. Ice-cream parlors and dozens of locally owned boutiques prosper along U.S. 1, the town's main street. Stately Colonial homes line the town green, site of summer concerts and a farmers' market, while iconic cedar-shingled beach homes line the waterfront. The Madison shoreline, particularly the long stretch of soft white sand at Hammonasset Beach State Park, draws visitors year-round, although they have to bundle up in the dead of winter.

GETTING HERE AND AROUND
Madison is accessible by both car and train. Drive north on Interstate 95 from New Haven or take the Shore Line East train to the Madison stop.

Beaches

★ **Hammonasset Beach State Park**
PARK—SPORTS-OUTDOORS | FAMILY | The largest of the state's public beach parks, Hammonasset Beach State Park has 2 miles of white-sand beach, a top-notch nature center, excellent birding, and a hugely popular campground with more than 550 open sites. **Amenities:** food and drink; lifeguards; parking (fee); showers; toilets. **Best for:** swimming; walking. ✉ *1288 Boston Post Rd. (U.S. 1), off I–95* ☎ *203/245–2785 for park, 203/245–1817 for campground* 🌐 *www.ct.gov/deep/hammonasset* 🎫 *CT residents free; nonresidents parking fee from $15.*

Restaurants

Lenny and Joe's Fish Tale
$$ | SEAFOOD | FAMILY | At Lenny and Joe's Fish Tale, kids of all ages love to eat their lobster rolls or fried seafood served indoors or outdoors by a hand-carved Dentzel carousel with flying horses (and a whale, frog, lion, seal, and more), which the restaurant runs from early May through early October and donates all proceeds to charity. Most of the menu involves fish of one kind or another, but Lenny and Joe's also serves burgers, franks, and chicken sandwiches or dinners. [$] *Average main: $19* ✉ *1301 Boston Post Rd. (U.S. 1)* ☎ *203/245–7289* 🌐 *www.ljfishtale.com.*

Coffee and Quick Bites

Ashley's Ice Cream
$ | AMERICAN | FAMILY | Right in the town center, a hop and a skip from popular Hammonasset State Park and Beach, Ashley's of Madison has flavors of homemade ice cream to tempt every tastebud. The business that began in New Haven in 1979 was named for the owner's champion Frisbee-catching dog, Ashley Whippet, who's favorite flavor was chocolate banana. **Known for:** more than 100 possible flavors and always adding more; ice-cream pies and cakes to go, too; more Ashley's are in New Haven, Hamden, Branford, and Guilford. [$] *Average main: $6* ✉ *724 Boston Post Rd (U.S. 1)* ☎ *203/245–1113* 🌐 *www.ashleysicecream.net/madison.*

Hotels

Scranton Seahorse Inn
$ | B&B/INN | In the heart of Madison, this historic (1833) inn run by pastry chef Michael Hafford offers a restful retreat within walking distance of the beach and shops. **Pros:** central location; gracious innkeeper; meticulous attention to detail. **Cons:** books up quickly; rooms need a little attention; rooms are small, but this is a historic home after all. [$] *Rooms from: $150* ✉ *818 Boston Post Rd. (U.S. 1)* ☎ *203/245–0550* 🌐 *www.scrantonseahorseinn.com* 🛏 *7 rooms* 🍴 *Free breakfast.*

Old Saybrook

19 miles west of New London, 32 miles east of New Haven.

Old Saybrook, at the mouth of the Connecticut River, was one of the three original settlements of the Connecticut Colony (called Saybrook at the time) and an important 17th-century trading port. Today, Old Saybrook is a picturesque small town with more than 100 historic homes, a downtown that's an especially pleasing place for a stroll, and a shoreline that attracts boaters and others lured by the salt air of summer.

GETTING HERE AND AROUND

Drive north on Interstate 95 to Route 154 south to reach Old Saybrook. The town is also served by Amtrak's Northeast Regional line and the Shore Line East commuter trains between New Haven and New London.

Sights

★ Katharine Hepburn Cultural Arts Center
ARTS VENUE | The Kate, as the Center is generally known, is an intimate, 250-seat theater in the historic Old Saybrook Town Hall building. The Kate presents a full calendar of concerts, dance, drama, opera, comedy, films (including some classic Hepburn films), and children's theater. (Some performances are broadcast on PBS TV in the national series, "The Kate.") In addition to the performances and presentations, a small museum displays memorabilia and reminiscences about Katharine Hepburn's life and career. She was a resident of Old Saybrook from 1912 (age five) until her death in 2003. *✉ 300 Main St. ☎ 860/510–0453 box office 🌐 www.katharinehepburntheater.org 🎟 Museum free ⏲ Museum closed Sat.–Mon.*

Restaurants

The Back Porch
$$ | AMERICAN | FAMILY | If you're going to be on the coast, you'll want to dine in an open-air restaurant on the waterfront—and The Back Porch is just that. Gaze at the river, watch the boats come and go, and dine on New England classics like fried clams, fish-and-chips, crumb-crusted scrod, sandwiches, burgers, salads, and plenty more. **Known for:** indoor and outdoor seating; kids' menu; live entertainment on summer weekends. *[$] Average main: $24 ✉ 142 Ferry Rd. ☎ 860/510–0282 🌐 www.backporchold-saybrook.com ⏲ Closed Mon. and Tues. Oct.–May.*

Café Routier
$$$ | FRENCH | Grilled hanger steak with cauliflower gratin and seared scallops with pancetta and butternut squash puree are among the favorites at this bistro, which specializes in regional favorites and seasonal dishes. Check out the Mood Lounge for excellent cocktails and smaller plates meant for sharing. *[$] Average main: $26 ✉ 1353 Boston Post Rd. (U.S. 1), 5 miles west of Old Saybrook, Westbrook ☎ 860/399–8700 🌐 www.caferoutier.com ⏲ No lunch.*

Hotels

Saybrook Point Resort & Marina
$$$ | HOTEL | Guest rooms at the cushy Saybrook Point Inn are done up in 18th-century style, with reproductions of British furnishings and Impressionist art; many have fireplaces, making them especially cozy on cool evenings. **Pros:** tasteful decor; great spa; marina provides a picturesque setting. **Cons:** comparatively pricey; you'll need a car to get to local attractions; the water view from "water view" rooms varies considerably. *[$] Rooms from: $300 ✉ 2 Bridge St. ☎ 860/395–2000 🌐 www.saybrook.com 🛏 100 rooms 🍴 No meals.*

Essex

29 miles east of New Haven.

Essex, hugging the west bank of the Connecticut River, is one of the most appealing small towns in the United States—and still looks much as it did at the height of its shipbuilding prosperity in the mid-19th century. Essex's boat manufacturing was so important to the early United States that the British burned 28 ships here during the War of 1812. Gone are the days of steady trade with the West Indies, when the aroma of imported rum, molasses, and spices hung in the air. Now, whitewashed houses—many the former roosts of sea captains—line Main Street, which has shops that sell clothing, antiques, paintings and prints, and sweets.

GETTING HERE AND AROUND

The best way to reach Essex is by car; take Interstate 95 to Route 9 north (Exit 69).

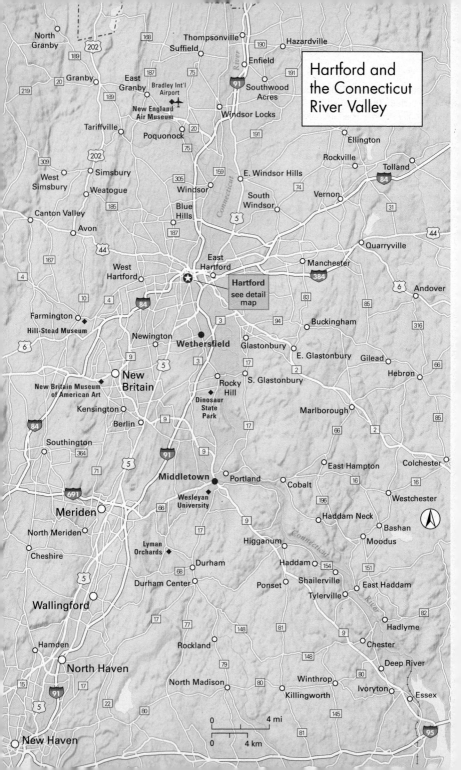

Hartford and the Connecticut River Valley

North Granby
202
189 Granby
20
219
189 East Granby
168 Suffield
Thompsonville
190 Enfield
Hazardville
191 Southwood Acres
187
75
91
Bradley Int'l Airport
New England Air Museum
Windsor Locks

Tariffville
Poquonock
20
75
191
309
202
Simsbury
305 E. Windsor Hills
Rockville
Tolland
84

West Simsbury
Weatogue
159
74 Vernon
31

185 Windsor
South Windsor
Canton Valley
Blue Hills
5
Quarryville
44

Avon
187
44
167
East Hartford
Manchester
384
4
West Hartford
Hartford see detail map
6 Andover

10
44
84
83
316
4
3
94 Buckingham
85
Farmington
Hill-Stead Museum
Newington
Wethersfield
Glastonbury
E. Glastonbury
Gilead
66

6
9
3
17
Hebron
S. Glastonbury
2

New Britain
New Britain Museum of American Art
Rocky Hill
Dinosaur State Park
17
85

84
Kensington
9
Marlborough
2

Southington
Berlin
66
364
9
East Hampton
Colchester

71
5
91
Middletown
Portland
Cobalt
16
16

691
Wesleyan University
196
Westchester
Meriden
66
Haddam Neck
Bashan

North Meriden
17
9
Moodus
Cheshire
Lyman Orchards
Higganum
5
154
151

68 Durham
Haddam
Shailerville
East Haddam
Wallingford
Durham Center
Ponset
Tylerville

82
Hamden
77
148
81
9
Hadlyme

North Haven
15
17
Rockland
79
148
Chester
Deep River

91
North Madison
80
Winthrop
80
Ivoryton
Essex

5
22
80
Killingworth
145
81
95

New Haven

0   4 mi

0   4 km

Sights

★ Connecticut River Museum

MUSEUM | FAMILY | Housed in an 1878 steamboat warehouse, this museum tells the story of the Connecticut River through maritime artifacts, interactive displays, and ship models. The riverfront museum even has a full-size working reproduction of the world's first submarine, the *American Turtle* (named for its appearance); the original was built by David Bushnell in 1775 as a "secret weapon" to win the Revolutionary War. ⊠ *Steamboat Dock, 67 Main St.* ☎ *860/767–8269* ⊕ *www.ctrivermuseum. org* 🖼 *$10* ☉ *Closed Mon. Columbus Day–Memorial Day.*

★ Essex Steam Train & Riverboat

TRANSPORTATION SITE (AIRPORT/BUS/FERRY/ TRAIN) | FAMILY | This excursion offers some of the best views of the Connect-icut River Valley from a vintage steam locomotive, pulled by 1920s-era coaches, and an old-fashioned riverboat. The train, traveling along the Connecticut River through the lower valley, makes a 12-mile round-trip from Essex to Deep River Landing. Before returning by train to Essex, you have the option of boarding the *Becky Thatcher* riverboat and cruising along the river past Gillette Castle, Goodspeed Opera House, and fascinating deep-water coves and inlets. (The open promenade deck on the boat's third level offers the best views.) The train also hosts themed excursions such as Tha'r Be Pirates on the Connecticut River, the seasonal North Pole Express (a nighttime trip to pick up Santa), Day Out With Thomas—(perfect for little ones who love the *Thomas & Friends* television show), and many more. ⊠ *Valley Railroad Company, 1 Railroad Ave.* ☎ *860/767–0103, 800/377–3987* ⊕ *essexsteamtrain.com* 🖼 *Steam train from $22* ☉ *Closed late Oct.–early May.*

🍴 Restaurants

The Essex

$$$ | MODERN AMERICAN | Applying French technique to "modern cuisine" and "old favorites," the chef prepares timeless entrées such as chicken fricasse with lentils, potato, peas, tarragon, and fennel topped with phyllo dough and braised halibut with garlic butter, toasted panko, and artichokes Barigoule (braised with vegetables in white wine). The "Our Changing Oceans" tasting menu ($95) features nine courses of various wild-caught and sustainably fished seafood—and a 10th course of sorbet. **Known for:** locally sourced ingredients from farm and sea; big stone fireplace for cozy winter dining; kid's menu, too. Ⓢ *Average main: $35* ⊠ *30 Main St.* ✛ *In Centerbrook, 1 mile west of downtown Essex* ☎ *860/237–4189* ⊕ *theessex.com* ☉ *Closed Mon. and Tues.*

🛏 Hotels

Copper Beech Inn

$ | B&B/INN | A magnificent copper beech tree shades this 1890 inn, set on 7 acres of Connecticut River Valley woodlands. **Pros:** perfect for a romantic weekend; excellent on-site dining in the Oak Room; Carriage House rooms are a good deal. **Cons:** some rooms and baths are ready for a face-lift; short drive from downtown Essex; rooms too near the bar-restaurant can be noisy. Ⓢ *Rooms from: $179* ⊠ *46 Main St., Ivoryton* ✛ *4 miles west of Essex* ☎ *860/767–0330* ⊕ *www.copper-beechinn.com* 🛏 *22 rooms* ⦿ *No meals.*

The Griswold Inn

$ | B&B/INN | Two-plus centuries of catering to changing tastes at what's billed as one of America's oldest continuously operating inns has resulted in a kaleidoscope of decor—some Colonial, a bit of Federal, a little Victorian—with just as many modern touches as necessary to meet present-day expectations. **Pros:** in the heart of historic downtown Essex;

Ride along the Connecticut River on a vintage Essex Steam Train.

rich history—since opening in 1776; fun pub with live music every night. **Cons:** dated furnishings, but that's being addressed; no room TVs—head for the common room if you must; some rooms are quite small. $ *Rooms from: $160* ⊠ *36 Main St.* ☎ *860/767–1776* ⊕ *griswoldinn.com* ↪ *33 rooms* ⦿ *Free breakfast.*

East Haddam

15 miles north of Essex, 28 miles southeast of Hartford.

Farms, tanneries, and blacksmiths were the chief enterprises of 17th-century East Haddam, on the east bank of the Connecticut River. By the 20th century, residents (including actor William Gillette) were drawn to the area for its rural nature and riverside location. Now, fully into the 21st century, this lovely community retains its old-fashioned charm, mostly centered around the historic downtown.

GETTING HERE AND AROUND

The best way to reach East Haddam is by car. From Interstate 95, take Route 156 north in Old Lyme to Route 82 west.

◉ Sights

Devil's Hopyard State Park

NATIONAL/STATE PARK | Chapman Falls, a 60-foot cascade, is the centerpiece of this 860-acre park, an idyllic spot for bird-watching, picnicking, trout fishing (you'll need a license), camping, hiking, or simply dipping your toes in a clear, cold stream. The campground is open from mid-April through Labor Day. ⊠ *366 Hopyard Rd.* ☎ *860/526–2336* ⊕ *www. ct.gov/deep/devilshopyard* ⛺ *Free.*

★ Gillette Castle State Park

CASTLE/PALACE | FAMILY | The outrageous, 24-room, oak-and-fieldstone hilltop castle—modeled after medieval castles of the Rhineland and built between 1914 and 1919 by the eccentric actor and playwright William Gillette—is the park's main attraction. You can tour the castle (and its secret passages) and hike trails near the remains of a 3-mile private railroad, which chugged about the property until the owner's death in 1937. Gillette, who was born in Hartford, wrote two famous plays about the Civil War and was especially beloved for his play *Sherlock Holmes* (in which he performed the title role). In his will, he demanded that the castle not fall into the hands of "some blithering saphead who has no conception of where he is or with what surrounded." ✉ *67 River Rd., off Rte. 82* ☎ *860/526–2336* 🌐 *www.ct.gov/deep/gillettecastle* 🎟 *Park free, castle $6.*

★ Goodspeed Opera House

ARTS VENUE | This magnificent 1876 Victorian-gingerbread "wedding cake" theater on the Connecticut River—so called for its turrets, mansard roof, and grand filigree—is widely recognized for its role in the preservation and development of American musical theater. More than 20 Goodspeed productions have gone on to Broadway, including *Annie* and *Man of La Mancha.* Performances take place from May through early December; one-hour Opera House tours are offered on Saturday from June through October. ✉ *6 Main St.* ☎ *860/873–8668* 🌐 *www.goodspeed.org* 🎟 *Tour $5.*

Hotels

The Boardman House

$$ | **B&B/INN** | Built around 1860 for wealthy silversmith Norman S. Boardman, this glamorous Second Empire–style mansion combines the charm of the gilded age with modern conveniences. **Pros:** style and sophistication in a sleepy riverside village; a short stroll to/from Goodspeed Opera House and riverside restaurants; perfect for a romantic getaway, anniversary, or honeymoon. **Cons:** two-night minimum stay; some traffic noise heard in front rooms; breakfast on the light side. [$] *Rooms from: $259* ✉ *8 Norwich Rd., Rte. 82* ☎ *860/873–9233* 🌐 *boardmanhouse.com* 🛏 *5 rooms* 🍴 *No meals.*

Old Lyme

34 miles east of New Haven, 15 miles west of New London.

Old Lyme, on the eastern shore at the mouth of the Connecticut River (opposite Old Saybrook), is renowned among art lovers for its past as the home of the Lyme Art Colony—the most famous gathering of Impressionist painters in the United States. Artists (and others) continue to be attracted to the area for its lovely countryside and shoreline, especially in the summer.

GETTING HERE AND AROUND

Old Lyme is best reached by car. Drive north on Interstate 95 and bear right over the bridge from Old Saybrook.

Sights

★ Florence Griswold Museum

MUSEUM | **FAMILY** | Central to Old Lyme's artistic reputation is this grand late-Georgian-style mansion, which served as a boardinghouse for members of the Lyme Art Colony in the first decades of the 20th century. When artists such as Willard Metcalf, Clark Voorhees, Childe Hassam, and Henry Ward Ranger flocked to the area to paint its varied landscape, Miss Florence Griswold offered both housing and artistic encouragement. The house has been restored to its 1910 appearance, when the colony was in full flower (clues to the house's layout and decor were gleaned from members' paintings). The museum's 10,000-square-foot Krieble Gallery, on the riverfront, hosts changing exhibitions of American art. Café Flo, on-site, serves lunch on the veranda or have a picnic on the lawn. ✉ *96 Lyme St.* ☎ *860/434–5542* 🌐 *www.florencegriswoldmuseum.org* 🎟 *$10* 🕒 *Closed Mon.*

Coffee and Quick Bites

Hallmark Drive-In

$ | **FAST FOOD** | **FAMILY** | En route to or from the beach—or to or from anywhere, for that matter—stop at this seasonal roadside stand for a bite to eat (burgers, hot dogs, sandwiches, grinders, fish-and-chips) or just a summertime treat. Arguably the best ice cream around, whether in a cup, on a cone, or in a milk shake, root beer float, or sundae. **Known for:** the ice cream, of course; picnic area with a view of Long Island Sound; occasional live music in the evening. [$] *Average main: $12* ✉ *113 Shore Rd. (Rte. 156)* ☎ *860/598–9680* 🌐 *hallmarkdrivein.com* 🕒 *Closed Oct.–late Apr.*

Hotels

★ Bee and Thistle Inn

$ | **B&B/INN** | Behind a weathered stone wall in the town's historic district sits this three-story 1756 Colonial house with 5½ acres of broad lawns, formal gardens, and herbaceous borders. **Pros:** a short walk from Griswold Museum; lovely old home; the on-site Chestnut Grille exudes romance, with fireplaces and candlelight, and innovative American cuisine. **Cons:** may hear traffic noise from Interstate 95; lacks some modern amenities. [$] *Rooms from: $150* ✉ *100 Lyme St.* ☎ *860/434–1667* 🌐 *www.beeandthistleinn.com* 🛏 *11 rooms* 🍴 *Free breakfast.*

New London

46 miles east of New Haven, 52 miles southeast of Hartford.

New London, on the western bank of the Thames River (pronounced *thaymes,* not *tems*), was founded in 1646 by John Winthrop Jr. The Pequot Indians called the area "Nameaug," and the Connecticut Colony's legislature wanted it renamed "Faire Harbour," but the colonists prevailed and named it after their hometown. In the mid-1800s, New London was the second-largest whaling port in the world. Today, the U.S. Coast Guard Academy uses its campus on the Thames to educate and train its cadets. The prestigious Connecticut College is across the avenue from the Academy; Ocean Beach Park, an old-fashioned playland with a broad sandy beach and long wooden boardwalk, is a perfect place for the whole family to spend a hot summer day.

GETTING HERE AND AROUND

New London is accessible by car off Interstate 95 and can also be reached via Amtrak's high-speed Acela and Northeast Regional trains, as well as Shore Line East commuter trains from New Haven and towns in between.

Sights

Fort Trumbull State Park

NATIONAL/STATE PARK | **FAMILY** | Formerly the location of the original U.S. Coast Guard Academy and U.S. Navy Underwater Sound Laboratory and originally built to protect New London Harbor from British attack, you'll now find a 19th-century stonework-and-masonry fort, an extensive visitor center focusing on military history, a top-rate fishing pier, a waterfront boardwalk with fantastic views, and a picnic area when you want to relax. ✉ *90 Walbach St.* ☎ *860/444–7591* 🌐 *portal.ct.gov/DEEP/State-Parks/Parks/Fort-Trumbull-State-Park* 🎟 *Grounds and parking free, visitor center $6.*

Lyman Allyn Art Museum

MUSEUM | Housed in a neoclassical granite building that overlooks the U.S. Coast Guard Academy and Long Island Sound, this museum was founded in 1932 with funds bequeathed by Harriet Upson Allyn in memory of her whaling merchant father, Captain Lyman Allyn (1797–1874). Inside is an impressive collection of more than 15,000 objects covering a span of 5,000 years. Works also include contemporary, modern, and Early American fine arts; American Impressionist paintings; Connecticut decorative arts; and European works from the 16th through 19th centuries. The 12 acres of surrounding grounds includes a sculpture trail. ✉ *625 Williams St.* ☎ *860/443–2545* 🌐 *www.lymanallyn.org* 🎫 *$12* 🕒 *Closed Mon.*

U.S. Coast Guard Academy
COLLEGE | The 100-acre cluster of redbrick buildings you see overlooking the Thames River makes up one of the four U.S. military academies. Visitors are welcome, and security is obviously tight, but being there when the Coast Guard training ship, the barque *Eagle,* is in port is a special treat. A small museum, located in Waesche Hall on the grounds, explores the Coast Guard's 200 years of maritime service and includes some 200 ship models, as well as figureheads, paintings, uniforms, life-saving equipment, and cannon. ✉ *31 Mohegan Ave.* ☎ *860/444–8270 for public affairs, 860/444–8511 for the museum* 🌐 *www.uscga.edu* 🎫 *Free* 🕒 *Museum closed weekends.*

Beaches

★ Ocean Beach Park
BEACH—SIGHT | **FAMILY** | Possibly the state's finest beach, the 50-acre park has a broad white-sand beach, an Olympic-size outdoor pool with a triple waterslide, an 18-hole miniature-golf course, an arcade, a half-mile-long boardwalk, kiddie rides, food concessions, a nature trail, and a picnic area. **Amenities:** food and drink; lifeguards; parking (fee); showers; toilets. **Best for:** partiers; swimming; walking. ✉ *98 Neptune Ave., at foot of Ocean Ave.* ☎ *860/447–3031* 🌐 *www.ocean-beach-park.com* 🎫 *Walk-in $8, parking and admission from $18.*

Restaurants

Captain Scott's Lobster Dock
$$ | **SEAFOOD** | **FAMILY** | Don't be put off by the long line waiting to order classic fare like lobster rolls (hot or cold, small or large), steamers, fried clams, homemade clam fritters, and "chowda." This outdoor restaurant on Shaw's Cove—where you eat at picnic tables (BYOB) alongside the marina—is a great place to eat and a great place to spend time on a hot summer day. **Known for:** picturesque waterfront spot; everything made on-site and to order; Ed's hot fudge sundae. [$] *Average main: $18* ✉ *80 Hamilton St., off Howard St.* ☎ *860/439–1741* 🌐 *www.captscottsnl.com* 🕒 *Closed mid-Oct.–mid-Apr.*

Coffee and Quick Bites

Michael's Dairy
$ | **AMERICAN** | **FAMILY** | The local go-to place for authentic, old-fashioned, New England-style ice cream, Michael's Dairy has been a fixture on the campus of Mitchell College since 1943. The 39 flavors (plus sherbet, sorbet, frozen yogurt) range from old favorites like butter crunch, orange pineapple, and black raspberry to more modern flavors like salted caramel chocolate pretzel, campfire s'mores, and birthday cake. **Known for:** a few tables and chairs inside and out; scoops, sundaes, milk shakes, floats—plus pints, quarts, and half-gallons; sugar-free and vegan offerings, too. [$] *Average main: $6* ✉ *629 Montauk Ave.* ☎ *860/443–2464* 🌐 *www.michaelsdairynl.com.*

Performing Arts

Garde Arts Center
ARTS CENTERS | National and international opera and dance performances, concerts, comedy, Broadway musicals, film festivals, and children's events are all on the bill at this arts center—a beautifully restored, 1,440-seat, art deco theater. ✉ *325 State St.* ☎ *860/444–7373* 🌐 *www.gardearts.org.*

Groton

10 miles south of Ledyard.

Across the river from New London, Groton is the location of Naval Submarine Base New London, the U.S. Navy's primary East Coast submarine base, and of the Electric Boat Division of General Dynamics, designer and manufacturer of nuclear submarines. Often referred to as the "Submarine Capital of the World," Groton is the birthplace of *Nautilus,* the nation's first nuclear submarine and a National Historic Landmark, which is now permanently berthed here at the Submarine Force Museum.

👁 Sights

Fort Griswold Battlefield State Park

MEMORIAL | FAMILY | It was here (legend has it), on the Groton side of the Thames River, that the infamous traitor Benedict Arnold stood watching the important port of New London burn in 1781 during the Revolutionary War. Whether Arnold actually stood there is open to question; but the American defenders of Ft. Griswold were massacred by Arnold's British troops during the Battle of Groton Heights—and New London did burn according to his orders. The 134-foot-high Groton Monument, which you can climb for a sweeping view of the river and New London, is a memorial to the fallen. The adjacent Monument House Museum has historic displays; the Ebenezer Avery House, on the grounds and recently restored, is where the wounded were sheltered in 1781. ⊠ *Park Ave. at Monument St.* ☎ *860/449–6877 seasonal, 860/444–7591 c/o Fort Trumbull State Park* ⊕ *portal. ct.gov/DEEP/State-Parks/Parks/Fort-Griswold-Battlefield-State-Park* 💲 *Free.*

★ Submarine Force Museum

MILITARY SITE | FAMILY | The world's first nuclear-powered submarine, USS *Nautilus (SSN-571)*—and the first submarine to complete a submerged transit of the North Pole (in 1958)—was launched and commissioned in Groton in 1954. The *Nautilus* spent 25 active years as a showpiece of U.S. technological know-how and is now permanently docked at the Submarine Force Museum, a couple of miles upriver from where it was built. Visitors are welcome to climb aboard and explore. The museum, just outside the entrance to the Naval Submarine Base New London, is a repository of artifacts, documents, and photographs detailing the history of the U.S. Submarine Force component of the U.S. Navy, along with educational and interactive exhibits. ⊠ *1 Crystal Lake Rd.* ☎ *800/343–0079* ⊕ *www.ussnautilus.org* 💲 *Free* ☾ *Closed Tues.*

Mystic

10 miles east of New London, 8 miles south of Ledyard.

Mystic, a village that lies half in the town of Groton and half in the town of Stonington, has devoted itself to recapturing the seafaring spirit of the 18th and 19th centuries. Some of the nation's fastest clipper ships were built here in the mid-19th century; today, the 37-acre Mystic Seaport is the state's most popular attraction. Downtown Mystic has an interesting collection of boutiques and galleries.

GETTING HERE AND AROUND
By car, take Interstate 95 to Route 27 south to reach Mystic. Amtrak's Northeast Regional train service also stops here.

👁 Sights

★ Mystic Aquarium

ZOO | FAMILY | The famous Arctic Coast exhibit—which holds 750,000 gallons of water, measures 165 feet at its longest point by 85 feet at its widest point, and ranges from just inches to 16½ feet deep—is just a small part of this revered establishment and home to several graceful beluga whales and a pair of

Mystic Seaport exhibits a number of vessels that you can board and tour, including the *Charles W. Morgan.*

rescued harbor seals. You can also see African penguins, fascinating sea horses, Pacific octopuses, and sand tiger sharks. Don't miss feeding time at the Ray Touch Pool, where rays suction sand eels right out of your hand. The animals here go through 1,000 pounds of herring, capelin, and squid each day—Juno, a male beluga whale, is responsible for consuming 85 pounds of that himself. ⊠ *55 Coogan Blvd.* ☎ *860/572–5955* ⊕ *www.mysticaquarium.org* ⊡ *$19.*

★ Mystic Seaport Museum

MUSEUM VILLAGE | FAMILY | The nation's leading maritime museum, Mystic Seaport encompasses 19 acres stretched along the Mystic River. The indoor and outdoor exhibits include a re-created New England coastal village, a working shipyard, and formal museum buildings with more than 1 million artifacts, including figureheads, paintings, models, tools, ship plans, scrimshaw, paintings, photos, and recordings. Along the narrow village streets and in some of the historic buildings, craftspeople demonstrate skills such as open-hearth cooking and weaving, interpreters bring the past to life, musicians sing sea chanteys, and special squads with maritime skills show how to properly set sails on a square-rigged ship. The museum's more than 500 vessels include the *Charles W. Morgan,* the last remaining wooden whaling ship afloat, and the 1882 training ship *Joseph Conrad;* you can climb aboard both for a look around or for sail-setting demonstrations and reenactments of whale hunts. ■ **TIP→ Children under three are admitted free.** ⊠ *75 Greenmanville Ave. (Rte. 27)* ✛ *1 mile south of I–95* ☎ *860/572–0711* ⊕ *www.mysticseaport.org* ⊡ *$30.*

🍴 Restaurants

★ Abbott's Lobster in the Rough

$$ | SEAFOOD | FAMILY | If you want some of the freshest lobsters, mussels, crabs, or clams on the half shell (there are also non-seafood options), head down to this unassuming seaside lobster shack in sleepy Noank, a few miles southwest of Mystic. Most seating is outdoors or on the dock, where the views of Noank Harbor are magnificent. **Known for:** fresh seafood by the seaside in the fresh air; lobster dinner, lobster roll, lobster bisque—all delish; perfect coastal atmosphere. $ *Average main: $22* ⊠ *117 Pearl St., Noank* ☎ *860/536–7719* ⊕ *abbottslobster.com* ☉ *Closed Columbus Day–Apr. and Mon.–Thurs. early May and Sept.*

☕ Coffee and Quick Bites

Mystic Drawbridge Ice Cream

$ | AMERICAN | FAMILY | Sit inside or outside at this classic ice cream parlor right next to the Mystic River Drawbridge and enjoy homemade ice cream and other soda fountain favorites—maybe a New York egg cream or an ice cream shake. This ice cream has half the air whipped into it compared to other "homemade" and mass-produced products, making it richer, creamier, and more flavorful. **Known for:** Drawbridge original flavors—Mystic Mud, Mystic Turtle, and Seaport Salty Swirl; espresso, pastries, and smoothies, too; close up view of the drawbridge opening and closing to allow boats to pass through. $ *Average main: $6* ⊠ *2 W. Main St.* ☎ *860/572–7978* ⊕ *www. mysticdrawbridgeicecream.com.*

🛏 Hotels

Mystic Marriott Hotel and Spa

$ | HOTEL | FAMILY | This six-story, Georgian-style hotel has modern rooms accented with old-world touches, such as rich fabrics, gleaming wood furnishings, and elegant detailing. **Pros:** convenient to Mystic attractions; Starbucks coffee bar in the lobby; swim winter or summer in the indoor pool. **Cons:** on a busy road; often busy with conference or wedding guests; you might prefer an outdoor pool. $ *Rooms from: $189* ⊠ *625 North Rd. (Rte. 117), Groton* ✛ *5 miles west of downtown Mystic* ☎ *860/446–2600* ⊕ *www.marriott.com* ⤶ *285 rooms* ⦿ *No meals.*

Setting Sail at Mystic Seaport 🏃

Kids can learn the ropes—literally—of what it takes to be a sailor during one of Mystic Seaport's many sailing classes and camps. Younger children and those who wish to stay ashore can sign up for courses on building boats (from construction to varnish), blacksmithing, wood carving, and open-hearth cooking. The Seaport's planetarium also offers instruction on navigating a ship by the stars. Prices for classes vary. Call Mystic Seaport (☎ 860/572–5331) or visit its website (⊕ www.mysticseaport.org) for details.

The Whaler's Inn

$$ | HOTEL | A perfect compromise between a chain motel and a country inn, this five-building complex with public rooms furnished with lovely antiques is one block from the Mystic River and downtown area. **Pros:** in-room Roku units; complimentary afternoon treats; charging station for electric vehicles. **Cons:** rooms in some buildings have less character; on the busy main street; pleasant hotel but not "luxurious." $ *Rooms from: $214* ⊠ *20 E. Main St.* ☎ *860/536–1506* ⊕ *www.whalersinnmystic.com* ⤶ *45 rooms* ⦿ *No meals.*

Stonington

7 miles southeast of Mystic, 57 miles east of New Haven.

Pretty Stonington Borough, the seaside "downtown" of the town of Stonington, pokes into Fishers Island Sound. A quiet fishing community clustered around white-spired churches, "the Borough," as it's called, is far less commercial than downtown Mystic. In the 19th century, though, it was a busy whaling, sealing, and transportation center. Historic buildings line the town green and border both sides of Water Street up to the imposing Old Lighthouse Museum.

GETTING HERE AND AROUND

Stonington is a rather large town, but "The Borough" is a seaside village (Connecticut's oldest) that serves as Stonington's town center. Take a leisurely stroll down Water Street, past boutiques and galleries, to the old stone lighthouse. From Mystic by car, take Route 1 north (you'll actually be heading eastward, but don't be concerned) to Route 1A.

👁 Sights

Stonington Vineyards
WINERY/DISTILLERY | At this small coastal winery, you can browse the works of local artists in the gallery or enjoy a picnic lunch on the grounds. Whichever you choose, the vineyard's Seaport White, a Vidal-Chardonnay blend, is a nice accompaniment. ✉ 523 Taugwonk Rd. 📞 860/535–1222 ⊕ www.stoningtonvineyards.com 🍷 Tasting $16, tour free.

🍽 Restaurants

Breakwater
$$$ | SEAFOOD | FAMILY | Enjoy fresh-caught New England seafood dockside at Breakwater, midway along Water Street in Stonington Borough. Dine inside or outside on the deck in warm weather; the roomy bar is a popular gathering place in winter months. **Known for:** takeout and boatside delivery; amazing sunsets; all-day dining. $ Average main: $28 ✉ 66 Water St. 📞 860/415–8123 ⊕ breakwaterstonington.com.

Dog Watch Café
$$ | SEAFOOD | FAMILY | Seafood is the draw at this harborside restaurant—clam chowder, oysters or clams on the half-shell," dogwiches," fish-and-chips,

bouillabaisse, roasted cod, Stonington scallops, and more. Alternatively, choose a grilled chicken sandwich, flat-iron steak, burger, or soup and salad. **Known for:** great food, of course; lawn games and live music in the "Dog Pound"; the ice cream tent. $ Average main: $22 ✉ 194 Water St. 📞 860/415–4510 ⊕ www.dogwatchcafe.com.

🛏 Hotels

★ The Inn at Stonington
$$ | B&B/INN | The views of Stonington Harbor and Fishers Island Sound are spectacular from this waterfront inn in the heart of Stonington Borough. **Pros:** seaside rooms face the harbor and Fishers Island Sound; walking distance to village shops and dining; intimate adult (and kids 14-plus) atmosphere. **Cons:** no on-site restaurant (but several nearby); minimum stay on summer weekend and holidays; strict seven-day notice for cancellations, no exceptions. $ Rooms from: $285 ✉ 60 Water St. 📞 860/535–2000 ⊕ innatstonington.com ⬅ 19 rooms ⎮⊖⎮ Free breakfast.

Ledyard

10 miles south of Norwich, 37 miles southeast of Hartford.

In the woods of southeastern Connecticut between Norwich and the coastline, rural Ledyard has become known in recent years as the location of the Mashantucket Pequot Tribal Nation's vast Foxwoods Resort Casino and its excellent Mashantucket Pequot Museum & Research Center, through which the tribe is educating the public about its history and that of other Northeast Woodland tribes.

GETTING HERE AND AROUND

Driving is probably the best way to get to Ledyard: take Interstate 95 to Route 2 west. If you are only planning to visit Foxwoods, many bus companies run direct charter trips.

Sights

Foxwoods Resort Casino
ARTS VENUE | FAMILY | Owned and operated by the Mashantucket Pequot Tribal Nation on reservation lands near Ledyard, Foxwoods is the largest resort casino in North America. The enormous compound, which opened in 1992, draws 40,000-plus visitors daily to its seven casinos with more than 3,500 slot machines, 250 gaming tables, and a 3,600-seat bingo parlor. This 9-million-square-foot complex includes four luxury hotels, a 5,500-square-foot pool "sanctuary," two full-service spas, a retail concourse, numerous dining options, several theaters and other venues that attract national performers, a video arcade, extreme sports facilities, a bowling alley, children's activities, an 18-hole championship golf course, and—as counterpoint to all that action—marked trails through the surrounding woods. ✉ *350 Trolley Line Blvd., Mashantucket* ☎ *800/369–9663* 🌐 *www.foxwoods.com.*

★ Mashantucket Pequot Museum & Research Center
MUSEUM | FAMILY | Housed in a large complex 1 mile from Foxwoods, this museum brings to life in exquisite detail the history and culture of the Northeastern Woodland tribes in general and the Mashantucket Pequots in particular. Highlights include views of an 18,000-year-old glacial crevasse, a caribou hunt from 11,000 years ago, and a 17th-century fort. Perhaps most remarkable is a sprawling "immersion environment": a 16th-century village with more than 50 life-size figures and real smells and sounds. Audio devices provide detailed information about the sights. A full-service restaurant offers both Native and traditional American cuisine. ✉ *110 Pequot Tr., Mashantucket* ☎ *800/411–9671* 🌐 *www.pequotmuseum.org* 🎟 *$15* 🕒 *Closed Thurs.–Sun. Dec.–Mar., and Sun.–Tues. Apr.–Nov.*

Hotels

Foxwoods Resort Casino
$ | HOTEL | FAMILY | Mere steps from the gaming floors, Foxwoods has several options for accommodations: the deluxe, 23-story Grand Pequot Tower with 808 rooms, suites, and villas; the modern, upbeat Fox Tower with 825 rooms; the woodsy (but still close to the action) Great Cedar Hotel with 317 rooms and suites; and the smaller, more tranquil, pet-friendly Two Trees Inn with 280 rooms and suites. **Pros:** a variety of hotel styles and sizes; free parking; nice views from upper floors. **Cons:** checking in is a hassle–front desk understaffed; rooms due for some TLC; don't expect Frette linens. [$] *Rooms from: $99* ✉ *350 Trolley Line Blvd., Mashantucket* ☎ *800/369–9663* 🌐 *www.foxwoods.com* 🛏 *2230 rooms* 🍴 *No meals.*

Stonecroft Country Inn
$$ | B&B/INN | The sunny, 19th-century Georgian Colonial–style house marks the center of Stonecroft: 6½ acres of green meadows, woodlands, and rambling stone walls. **Pros:** scenic and verdant grounds; cheerful service; near Mystic attractions. **Cons:** secluded location requires a car to get around; no room TVs in 1807 House rooms; dim lighting in rooms. [$] *Rooms from: $220* ✉ *515 Pumpkin Hill Rd.* ☎ *860/572–0771* 🌐 *stonecroft.com* 🛏 *10 rooms* 🍴 *No meals.*

Norwich

15 miles north of New London, 40 miles southeast of Hartford.

Handsome restored Georgian and Victorian houses surround the historic Norwich town green in the city of Norwich, founded in 1659 on land that a handful of settlers purchased from Mohegan Sachem Uncas; more historic buildings can be found downtown by the Thames River. The former mill town is hard at work on restoration and rehabilitation efforts.

GETTING HERE AND AROUND

To reach Norwich from the coast by car, take Interstate 95 to Interstate 395 north to Route 82 east.

Sights

Leffingwell House Museum

HISTORIC SITE | What began as a two-room home around 1675 evolved into a pre-Revolutionary War tavern and, by 1776, was the elegant home of a local patriot that has since been lovingly restored by the Society of the Founders of Norwich. The house is furnished with Early American artifacts, and interpreters explain the architecture of the house and the lifestyle of those who lived or frequented the home so many centuries ago. ✉ *348 Washington St.* ☎ *860/889–9440* 🌐 *www.leffingwellhousemuseum.org* 🎟 *$5* 🕒 *Closed Sun.–Fri. and Nov.–Mar.*

Mohegan Sun

ARTS VENUE | **FAMILY** | The Mohegan Tribe of Connecticut, known as the Wolf People, operates this casino just south of Norwich with has more than 300,000 square feet of gaming space in three casino areas, totaling 6,000 slot machines and more than 250 gaming tables. Also part of the complex: the Kids Quest/Cyber Quest family entertainment center, a shopping mall with 36 retail stores, 46 dining options, 17 bars and lounges, and two soaring, high-rise luxury hotels—each with a pool and a full-service spa. The 10,000-seat Mohegan Sun Arena, home to the WNBA's Connecticut Sun and the New England Black Wolves lacrosse team, draws major national acts; bands play in the 300-seat Wolf Den nearly every night; Comix Mohegan Sun presents comedy acts, as the name implies; and the 375,000-square-foot Earth Expo & Convention Center holds events. ✉ *1 Mohegan Sun Blvd., off I–395, Uncasville* ☎ *888/226–7711* 🌐 *mohegansun.com.*

Hotels

Mohegan Sun

$$ | **HOTEL** | Two luxury high-rise hotels—the huge, 34-story Sky Tower and the newer 13-story Earth Tower—are Mohegan Sun's on-site lodging choices. **Pros:** numerous restaurants just steps from the lobby; beautiful views from upper floors; excellent spas. **Cons:** casinos are the primary focus; kids are welcome, but it is a casino environment; 4 pm check-in (5 pm on Sunday). [$] *Rooms from: $219* ✉ *1 Mohegan Sun Blvd., off I–395, Uncasville* ☎ *888/777–7922* 🌐 *mohegansun.com* 🛏 *1563 rooms* 🍴 *No meals.*

The Spa at Norwich Inn

$$ | **HOTEL** | On 42 rolling acres right by the Thames River and a stone's throw from Mohegan Sun, this Georgian-style inn is best known for its spa, which offers the full range of skin-care regimens, body treatments, and fitness classes. **Pros:** excellent spa treatments; expansive grounds; Kensington's serves Connecticut-sourced, health-conscious fare (it has a chocolate truffle menu, too). **Cons:** focused mainly on spa guests (who are often wandering around in their robes); few activities beyond the spa; Villa rooms need attention—choose the Main Inn. [$] *Rooms from: $225* ✉ *607 W. Thames St. (Rte. 32)* ☎ *860/425–3500, 860/425–3500* 🌐 *www.thespaatnorwichinn.com* 🛏 *100 rooms* 🍴 *No meals.*

Putnam

50 miles east of Hartford, 34 miles north of Norwich.

Ambitious antiques dealers have reinvented Putnam, a mill town 30 miles west of Providence, Rhode Island, that was neglected after the Depression. Putnam's downtown Antiques Marketplace, a four-level emporium with space for 350 antiques and collectibles dealers, is the heart of the Quiet Corner's antiques trade.

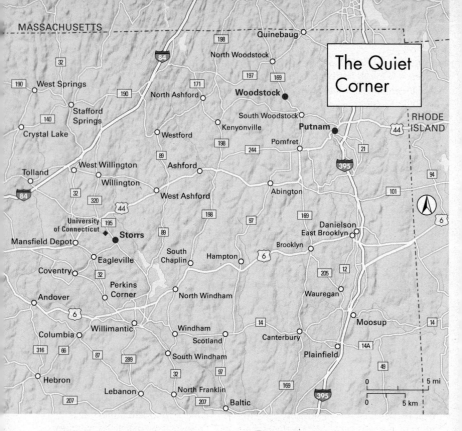

The Quiet Corner

GETTING HERE AND AROUND

By car from Hartford, take Interstate 384 and U.S. 44 east; from Norwich, follow Interstate 395 north to Route 12 north.

🍴 Restaurants

85 Main

$$$ | MODERN AMERICAN | FAMILY | This stylish bistro is *the* place to go for a break from antiquing. Typical lunchtime offerings include roasted corn and clam chowder, pesto chicken salad, and burgers with hand-cut fries; dinner could be maple-glazed sea scallops, steak frites, or veal Bolognese. **Known for:** seafood and steaks worthy of a big city; raw bar and full sushi menu; outdoor patio for warm-weather dining. $ *Average main: $27* ⊠ *85 Main St.* ☎ *860/928–1660* ⊕ *85main.com.*

🛍 Shopping

Antiques Marketplace

ANTIQUES/COLLECTIBLES | This four-level emporium features more than 350 dealers selling everything from fine furniture to tchotchkes. Come to buy or just have fun looking. ⊠ *109 Main St.* ☎ *860/928–0442.*

Woodstock

40 miles north of Norwich, 46 miles northeast of Hartford.

The landscape of this enchanting town that cozies up to the Massachusetts border is splendid in every season: the rolling hills seem to stretch for miles. Scenic roads lead past antiques shops, a country inn in the grand tradition, orchards, livestock grazing in grassy fields, and the fairgrounds of one of the state's oldest agricultural fairs, held each Labor Day weekend.

GETTING HERE AND AROUND
By car from Hartford, follow Interstate 384 east to U.S. 44 east and Route 169 north; from Norwich, follow Interstate 395 north to U.S. 44 west and Route 169 north.

Sights

Roseland Cottage
HOUSE | This pink board-and-batten Gothic Revival-style house was built in 1846 as a summer home for New York silk merchant, publisher, and abolitionist Henry C. Bowen. The house and outbuildings (including a carriage house with private bowling alley) hold a prominent place in history, having hosted four U.S. presidents: Ulysses S. Grant, Rutherford B. Hayes, William Henry Harrison, and William McKinley. The parterre garden features 21 flower beds surrounded by 600 yards of boxwood hedge. ⊠ *556 Rte. 169* ☎ *860/928–4074* ⊕ *www.historicne-wengland.org/property/roseland-cottage* ☞ *$15* ☉ *Closed Mon. and Tues. and Oct.–May.*

Coffee and Quick Bites

We-Li-Kit Ice Cream
$ | AMERICAN | FAMILY | When moseying around the Quiet Corner of Connecticut, stop by We-Li-Kit for a dish, cone, sundae, frappe, float, or banana split made with premium farmstead-fresh ice cream. Choose among dozens of flavors change with the seasons—then enjoy your treat, relax in the gardens, and visit the farm animals. **Known for:** hand-packed pints and quarts, ice-cream cakes, and custom flavors (in advance); New England clam chowder and clam cakes on Friday and weekends; maple syrup from the sugar house and farm-fresh USDA beef, too.

$ *Average main: $6* ⊠ *728 Hampton Rd. (Rte. 97), Pomfret Center* ⊹ *About 10 miles (15 min.) south of Woodstock via Rte. 169 and Rte. 97* ☎ *860/974–1095* ⊕ *www.welikit.com* ☉ *Closed Nov.–Mar.*

Hotels

The Inn at Woodstock Hill
$ | B&B/INN | Filled with antiques, this massive inn overlooking the countryside has guest rooms with four-poster beds, handsome fireplaces, pitched ceilings, and timber beams. **Pros:** beautiful grounds and gardens; pretty rooms; several pleasant sitting areas for afternoon tea. **Cons:** rooms are small; quite a hike up to third-floor rooms; expensive restaurant. $ *Rooms from: $190* ⊠ *94 Plaine Hill Rd.* ☎ *860/928–0528* ⊕ *www.woodstockhill.com* ➲ *21 rooms* ⦿ *Free breakfast.*

Storrs

25 miles southwest of Woodstock.

Storrs, an otherwise rural village in the town of Mansfield, is primarily occupied by the 4,100 acres (and some 19,000 students) of the main campus of the University of Connecticut. As a result, many cultural programs, sporting events, and other happenings take place here.

Sights

Mansfield Drive-In
FILM | FAMILY | Spring through fall, one of the state's few remaining drive-in theaters (family-run since 1954) shows films on its three big screens, and there's a huge flea market held on the grounds each Sunday. ■ TIP➜ **No pets, please!** ⊠ *228 Stafford Rd., Mansfield* ☎ *860/423–4441 movies, 860/456–2578 flea market* ⊕ *mansfielddrivein.com* ☞ *$9.*

University of Connecticut

COLLEGE | **FAMILY** | UConn's large, sprawling main campus offers lots for visitors to see and do. The William Benton Museum of Art's permanent collection includes centuries-old European and American paintings, drawings, prints, photographs, and sculptures, and the Jorgensen Center for the Performing Arts presents a series of 25–30 music, dance, and theater programs during the academic year. The Ballard Institute Museum of Puppetry has more than 2,500 puppets on display (UConn is one of two colleges in the country that offer a puppetry degree); and, depending on the season, you might catch a Connecticut Huskies football game or watch the amazing women's basketball team play at home. ✉ *Storrs Rd., Rte. 195* ☎ *860/486–2000* 🌐 *uconn.edu.*

☕ Coffee and Quick Bites

UConn Dairy Bar

$ | **AMERICAN** | **FAMILY** | Stop by the UConn Dairy Bar in the UConn Department of Animal Science Creamery for the most delicious ice cream you've ever tasted. Students produce the 24 regular, two seasonal, and occasional limited-edition flavors. **Known for:** ice cream as a learning experience; shakes, floats, parfaits, plus sandwiches, salads and soups; farm-fresh eggs and creamery-made heeses. [$] *Average main: $5* ✉ *George White Bldg., 17 Manter Rd.* ☎ *860/486–1021* 🌐 *dining.uconn.edu/uconn-dairy-bar.*

Chapter 8

RHODE ISLAND

Updated by
Kim Knox Beckius

👁 **Sights**
★★★★★

🍴 **Restaurants**
★★★★★

🛏 **Hotels**
★★★☆☆

🛍 **Shopping**
★★★★☆

🍸 **Nightlife**
★★☆☆☆

WELCOME TO RHODE ISLAND

TOP REASONS TO GO

★ **Mansions:** See how the social elite lived during Newport's Gilded Age on a tour of The Breakers, Cornelius Vanderbilt's opulent, 70-room "summer cottage."

★ **Historic Streets:** For a mile-long walk through history, follow Benefit Street on Providence's East Side and see ornate homes built by leading Colonial merchants.

★ **Nature:** Block Island is one of the most serene spots on the Eastern Seaboard—especially at Rodman's Hollow, where winding paths lead to the sea.

★ **Sand:** Take your pick of South County's numerous white-sand beaches—perhaps East Matunuck State Beach in South Kingstown.

★ **Food Enclave:** From food trucks to upscale dining, Providence has an exciting culinary scene fueled in large part by young chefs trained at Johnson & Wales University.

1 Providence. The capital of Rhode Island is also a vibrant college town with great food and a thriving arts community.

2 Pawtucket. This former mill town has found new life as a hub for arts and culture.

3 Woonsocket. South of Providence, this tiny mill town is home to the interactive Museum of Work and Culture.

4 Westerly. Galleries, shops, restaurants, and more than 15 buildings on the National Historic Register provide this seaside town with tons of charm.

5 Watch Hill. With perfect beaches and luxurious lodgings, this seaside village is the ideal spot for a chic vacation.

6 Misquamicut. This family-friendly destination has old-school amusements, movies on the beach, and evening concerts.

7 Charlestown. A sheltered coastline makes it a great spot for swimming, sailing, birdwatching, and beachcombing.

8 South Kingstown. Home to the 1,200 acre main campus of the University of Rhode Island.

9 Narragansett. Beautiful beaches and the Point Judith Lighthouse are highlights of this quiet beach town.

10 Jamestown. Also known as Conanicut Island, Jamestown has beautiful parks and a quaint downtown.

11 Newport. One of the world's great sailing cities also hosts world-class music festivals, Gilded Age mansions, and the International Tennis Hall of Fame.

12 Portsmouth. On Aquidneck Island with Newport, the community has polo matches and tastings at Greenvale Vineyards.

13 Bristol. Once a center for boatbuilding, Bristol is now known for its long running July 4 celebration.

14 Tiverton and Little Compton. East of Newport, this bucolic corner of the state is home to artists and farmers.

15 Block Island. This laidback resort island is about an hour's ferry ride from Point Judith.

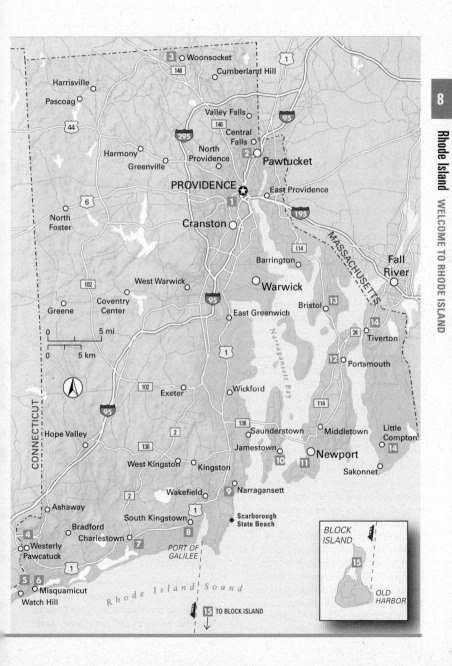

Consider the Ocean State's small size its biggest asset. You can drive across it in less than an hour—but take your time: Rhode Island has nearly 400 miles of shoreline to explore, more than 100 beaches, acres of open space with hiking and biking paths, and dozens of historic landmarks.

Rhode Island has a long history of forward thinking and a spirit of determination and innovation embodied in the bronze, 11-foot-tall Independent Man atop the marble-domed State House. The first of the 13 colonies to declare independence from Britain can also claim the first successful textile mill (Slater Mill in Pawtucket), America's oldest synagogue (Touro in Newport), and the first lunch wagon (by Walter Scott in Providence). A state founded on the principle of religious liberty drew Baptists, Jews, Quakers, and others throughout the 17th and 18th centuries, then flourished in the 19th and 20th centuries with the factories, silver foundries, and jewelry companies that brought workers from French Canada, Italy, Ireland, England, Portugal, and Eastern Europe.

Rhode Island remains an attractive, spirited place to live or visit. A public works project begun in the mid-1980s opened up the rivers in Downtown Providence; infrastructural improvements at Ft. Adams State Park in Newport allow it to host famed music festivals; extended commuter rail service makes it easy to travel between Providence and Green Airport; and bike-path expansions allow cyclists to traverse South County, East Bay, and the Blackstone Valley. Rhode Island's 39 cities and towns—none more than 50 miles apart—offer natural beauty, inspired culinary artistry, and many opportunities to relax and enjoy their scenic vistas.

MAJOR REGIONS

Visit **Providence** on an empty stomach, so you can fully enjoy its exciting culinary scene. Prestigious colleges and universities give Providence intellectual and cultural vitality, while restored Colonial and Victorian houses on the East Side preserve its history.

The Blackstone River powered the factories that led America's Industrial Revolution in the 19th century. Both **Pawtucket** and **Woonsocket** have fascinating museums that honor the laborers and labor movement. Bike miles of paved path along the river's edge, or see this resurgent valley aboard a tour boat.

Officially named Washington County, **South County** is home to beautiful beaches and charming locales like **Westerly, Watch Hill, Misquamicut, Charlestown, Narragansett, Wickford,** and **South Kingstown.**

Newport County, a longtime yachting enclave, consists of **Newport, Jamestown, Portsmouth,** and **Tiverton and Little Compton.** Between Newport and Providence, **East**

Bay's Bristol hosts one of the country's oldest July 4 celebrations.

Block Island has 17 miles of beaches—including Crescent Beach, one of New England's best—offering a classic seaside escape in summer, even when the population swells from the regular 1,050 to more than 15,000. Relax at one of the Victorian inns or bed-and-breakfasts, peruse the galleries and shops, and have a seafood lunch or farm-to-table dinner.

Planning

By car, it's an hour or less from any one place in Rhode Island to another. Although distances are short, Rhode Island is the second-most-densely populated state (after New Jersey), so allow extra time for traffic congestion in and around Providence.

Most sights in Providence can be seen in two or three days. The Blackstone Valley makes a good day trip from Providence. Newport, though not even 12 square miles, offers enough to fill two days—and the same can be said for South County, with its superb beaches. If you have a full week, you can visit all four regions of the state, as well as Block Island.

Getting Here and Around

AIR
Rhode Island's main airport, T. F. Green International Airport (PVD) in Warwick, just south of Providence, is served by most domestic air carriers. Smaller commercial airports, with limited carriers, are in Westerly and on Block Island, and Newport has a general aviation airport. Boston's Logan Airport is an hour's drive from Providence.

AIR CONTACT T. F. Green Airport. ✉ *2000 Post Rd., off I–95, Warwick* ☎ *401/691–2000* ⊕ *www.pvdairport.com.*

BUS
Rhode Island Public Transit Authority (RIPTA) offers low-cost bus service throughout the entire state—just $2 per ride or $6 per day within the city, to another town, or to the beach.

BUS CONTACT Rhode Island Public Transit Authority (RIPTA). ✉ *Kennedy Plaza Passenger Terminal, 1 Kennedy Plaza, Providence* ☎ *401/781–9400* ⊕ *www.ripta.com.*

CAR
New England's main highway, Interstate 95, cuts diagonally through Rhode Island, spanning 43 miles from Connecticut to Massachusetts.

Interstate 195 southeast from Providence leads to New Bedford, Massachusetts, and Cape Cod. Route 146 northwest from Providence passes through the Blackstone Valley en route to Worcester, Massachusetts, and Interstate 90 (Massachusetts Turnpike). U.S. 1 follows much of the Rhode Island coast heading east from Connecticut before turning north to Providence. Route 138 heads east from Interstate 95 or U.S. 1 to Jamestown, Newport, and Portsmouth in easternmost Rhode Island. Route 114 leads south from East Providence down through the East Bay community of Bristol and then to Newport.

Once you're here, a car is your best way to get around the state. Parking is easy to find outside cities, though challenging and sometimes expensive in Downtown Providence and Newport. Parts of Providence and Newport are easily walkable.

Activities

Department of Environmental Management's Division of Licenses
Contact the department for boating and fishing information, regulations, and licenses. A three-day nonresident freshwater fishing license costs $16; a nonresident saltwater fishing license costs

$10 and is good for a year. Licenses can be purchased online. ⊠ *235 Promenade St., Downtown* ☎ *401/222–6647 boating, 401/222–3576 licenses* ⊕ *www.dem. ri.gov/programs/managementservices.*

HIKING
Audubon Society of Rhode Island

The society manages nearly 9,500 acres in more than a dozen wildlife refuges across the state, plus one nearby in Massachusetts. All trails are open free to the public, and visitors are welcome to hike from sunrise to sunset (unless posted otherwise). ⊠ *12 Sanderson Rd., Smithfield* ☎ *401/949–5454* ⊕ *www.asri.org.*

Dining

The creative passion of award-winning chefs, many in their twenties and early thirties, fuels Rhode Island's vibrant restaurant scene. Abundant fresh seafood makes for outstanding variations on New England staples like fish-and-chips, clam chowder, and stuffed quahogs (hard clams)—all best savored at a beachside clam shack. Fresh-caught Block Island swordfish can't be beat. Then there's uniquely Rhode Island fare, such as the johnnycake (a thin corn pancake cooked on a griddle), coffee milk, Del's frozen lemonade, and Gray's Ice Cream. Authentic Italian-American restaurants can be found in Providence's Federal Hill neighborhood.

WHAT IT COSTS in U.S. Dollars			
$	$$	$$$	$$$$
RESTAURANTS			
under $18	$18–$24	$25–$35	over $35
HOTELS			
under $200	$200–$299	$300–$399	over $399

Lodging

Major chain hotels are certainly represented in Rhode Island, but boutique hotels, small bed-and-breakfasts, and historic inns provide a more intimate experience. Rates vary seasonally. In Newport, for example, a winter stay often costs less than half the summer price. Some inns in coastal towns are closed in winter. *Reviews have been shortened. For full information, visit Fodors.com.*

Tours

Blackstone Valley Explorer

TOUR—SIGHT | FAMILY | Narrated 50-minute Blackstone River tours aboard the 40-passenger riverboat *Blackstone Valley Explorer* take place seasonally and depart from locations in Central Falls, East Providence, Pawtucket, and Woonsocket. Topics covered on this pretty ride include area ecology and industrial history. ⊠ *Blackstone Valley Visitor Center, 175 Main St., Pawtucket* ☎ *401/724–2200* ⊕ *www.rivertourblackstone.com* ⌦ *$12* ⊗ *Closed late Oct.–late May.*

Visitor Information

CONTACTS Blackstone Valley Visitor Center. ☎ *401/724–2200* ⊕ *www. tourblackstone.com.* **Discover Newport.** ⊠ *23 America's Cup Ave., Newport* ☎ *401/849–8048* ⊕ *www.discovernewport.org.* **Providence Warwick Convention & Visitors Bureau.** ⊠ *10 Memorial Blvd., Providence* ☎ *401/456–0200* ⊕ *www. goprovidence.com.* **South County Tourism Council.** ☎ *401/789–4422, 800/548–4662* ⊕ *www.southcountyri.com.* **Visit Rhode Island.** ☎ *800/556–2484* ⊕ *www.visitrhodeisland.com.*

When to Go

With its arts and music festivals and gorgeous beach days, summer is high season in Rhode Island and a great time to visit, but there are fun and exciting things to do here year-round. Newport's Jazz and Folk Festivals heat up the town in late July and early August, just after the Newport Music Festival for classical music fans in July. This is also the time to take the ferry to low-key, beach-ringed Block Island for a day trip or overnight stay.

The shoulder seasons (April and May and September and October) bring pleasant weather and more affordable accommodations. In late summer, the return of student life to Providence colleges and universities gives the capital city energy and a youthful vibe. October is a good time to catch fall foliage in the Blackstone Valley, around the University of Rhode Island in Kingston, or in picturesque Tiverton and Little Compton.

Late fall, winter, and early spring each have their own charms—such as ice bumper cars at the Providence Rink and restaurant weeks in Newport and Narragansett, when eateries offer special multicourse prix-fixe menus.

Providence

Big-city sophistication with small-city charm: Providence has the best of both worlds. A thriving arts community, prestigious Brown University and Rhode Island School of Design (RISD), an impressive restaurant scene bolstered by the College of Culinary Arts at local Johnson & Wales University, countless festivals and events, a revitalized Downtown, and on-water recreation all help the city live up to its nickname: the Creative Capital. Providence is a worthy stop on any New England tour.

The Moshassuck and Woonasquatucket Rivers merge just southeast of the Rhode Island State House to form the Providence River. Scenic Waterplace Park hosts WaterFire, a crowd-pleasing series of summer and fall evening bonfires on the rivers. This relatively recent tradition beloved by locals and visitors alike began in the 1990s, but Providence gives equal weight to its long history, celebrating everything from its wealth of Colonial architecture to its literary tradition. After all, H. P. Lovecraft, author of fantasy and horror fiction, was a son of Providence, and Edgar Allan Poe courted poet Sarah Helen Whitman here.

GETTING ORIENTED

The narrow Providence River acts as a natural boundary between two major neighborhoods in the heart of the city. Downtown, the business district, lies west of the river; the East Side, on the opposite shore, is where the city's history began. (Don't confuse Providence's East Side with East Providence, a separate city.) Federal Hill, historically an Italian neighborhood, pushes west of Downtown along Atwells Avenue, Broadway, and Westminster Street. The white-marble dome of the Rhode Island State House is visible just north of Downtown. On the East Side, South Main and Benefit Streets run parallel to the Providence River. The Brown University campus is in the East Side neighborhood called College Hill, at the top of which Thayer Street runs north–south. Farther north and east are mainly residential neighborhoods.

GETTING HERE AND AROUND
AIR

T. F. Green International Airport, 10 miles south of Providence in Warwick, is served by Air Canada, Allegiant, American, Delta, Frontier, JetBlue, Southern Airways Express, Southwest, Sun Country, and United. By taxi, the ride between the airport and Downtown hotels takes about 20 minutes and costs around $32. An

Uber or LYFT ride will cost $15–$25, depending on your destination. The Massachusetts Bay Transportation Authority (MBTA) commuter rail service connects the airport and Downtown for $3.25.

BUS

At Kennedy Plaza, Downtown, you can board the local Rhode Island Public Transit Authority (RIPTA) buses. The Route 92 bus links Federal Hill to the East Side, and the Route 6 bus links Downtown to the Roger Williams Park Zoo. RIPTA fares are $2 per ride; an all-day pass is $6. Exact change is needed when boarding buses, or you'll get your change back in the form of a fare card. RIPTA buses also service T. F. Green International Airport from Providence via Route 20.

CAR

Overnight parking is not generally allowed on Providence streets. During the day it can be difficult to find curbside parking, especially Downtown and on Federal Hill and College Hill. There is a large parking garage at Providence Place mall.

TAXI

The basic taxi rate in Providence is $3.50 for the first mile, and $0.30 for each succeeding tenth of a mile.

TRAIN

Amtrak trains between New York and Boston stop at Westerly, West Kingston, and Providence. From Boston, you can also take an MBTA commuter train to Providence.

DINING

The hard part about dining in Providence is choosing among its many superb restaurants. If you're in the mood for Italian, take a stroll along Atwells Avenue on Federal Hill; Downtown is home to excellent fine-dining establishments; and the East Side has great neighborhood and upscale-casual restaurants, as well as an assortment of spots with a hip ambience and an international menu.

NIGHTLIFE

For events listings, consult the daily *Providence Journal* or the website ⊕ *www. golocalprov.com*. The monthly *Motif* or *Providence Monthly* are both available (free) in restaurants and shops.

SHOPPING

Providence has a handful of small but engaging shopping areas. In Fox Point, Wickenden Street has many antiques stores and several art galleries. Near Brown University, Thayer Street has a number of boutiques, though there has been an influx of chain stores. With its eclectic collection of specialty stores, Hope Street has branded itself as the East Side's "Main Street." Wayland Square, also on the East Side, is a historic neighborhood emerging as a destination for upscale homegoods and clothing. Downtown's Westminster Street has morphed into a strip of independently owned fashion boutiques and design stores.

TOURS

Gallery Night Providence

SPECIAL-INTEREST | During Gallery Night, held on the third Thursday of the month March–November, many galleries and museums hold open houses and mount special exhibitions. Two-hour Trolley Tours, some led by local celebrities, visit four or five galleries; tours depart at scheduled times, typically between 5:30 pm and 7 pm, from the Graduate Providence. ⊠ *Graduate Providence, 11 Dorrance St., Downtown* ☎ *401/484–0726* ⊕ *www. gallerynight.org.*

Providence Preservation Society

SELF-GUIDED | The society publishes a 10-page self-guided walking tour of the city's architecturally splendid Benefit Street. The booklet is available at the Society's headquarters during regular hours of business. ⊠ *24 Meeting St., at Benefit St., East Side* ☎ *401/831–7440* ⊕ *www.ppsri.org/tours* ⊜ *$3.*

Rhode Island Red Food Tours

SPECIAL-INTEREST | This Newport-based tour company offers food journeys (3–3½ hours) in Providence's Downcity Arts District, tasting and sipping your way through at least six eateries—from casual comfort food to fine-dining restaurants. Along the way you'll learn about the district's architecture and history. The tours are offered on Friday and Saturday, April through November, starting at noon. It's a walking tour, so wear comfortable shoes. ⊠ *270 Bellevue Ave., Newport* ☎ *866/736–6343* ⊕ *www.rhodeislandred-foodtours.com* ⊠ *From $69.*

ESSENTIALS

TRANSPORTATION CONTACTS Massachusetts Bay Transportation Authority. *(MBTA)* ☎ *617/222–3200* ⊕ *www.mbta.com.* **Rhode Island Public Transit Authority.** *(RIPTA)* ⊠ *Kennedy Plaza Passenger Terminal, 1 Kennedy Plaza, Downtown* ☎ *401/781–9400* ⊕ *www.ripta.com.*

VISITOR INFORMATION Providence Warwick Convention & Visitors Bureau. ⊠ *10 Memorial Blvd.* ☎ *401/456–0200* ⊕ *www. goprovidence.com.*

Downtown

Providence has 25 official neighborhoods and a handful of unofficial ones, each with its own identity. The Downtown neighborhood, sometimes referred to as Downcity, is the city's thriving artistic, financial, mercantile, transportation, and political core. Downtown comprises a very walkable area (it's flat!) roughly bordered by the Providence River on the east, Interstate 95 on the west, the Rhode Island State House to the north, and the Providence City Bridge in the south. You'll find theaters, hotels, shops, restaurants, and college buildings on Downtown's maze of streets, as well as the often-bustling Waterplace Park—a perfect place to watch the summer and autumn WaterFire displays.

◉ Sights

★ BankNewport City Center

LOCAL INTEREST | FAMILY | The 14,000-square-foot outdoor ice rink, right in the heart of downtown Providence, is twice the size of the one at New York City's Rockefeller Center. The facility is open for skating and ice bumper cars daily, late November–mid-March, and skate and helmet rentals are available. In summer, kids love driving the bumper cars, roller skating, and bubble soccer (trying to score while wearing a giant bubble). The center also hosts summer concerts, festivals, and other events. ⊠ *2 Kennedy Plaza, Downtown* ☎ *401/680–7390* ⊕ *www.theprovidencerink.com* ⊠ *From $7.*

★ Providence Children's Museum

MUSEUM | FAMILY | The vibrant, interactive, hands-on learning environments here are geared to children ages 1 to 11 and their families. Favorite exhibits and activities include Water Ways, ThinkSpace, Maker Studio, and Feeling Real or Really Feeling?, a sensory playground which the museum installed with creative input from two local artists. Littlewoods, for toddlers, has a tree house, bear cave, and a slide. Kids can also explore an outdoor climbing structure and imitate burrowing creatures in Underland. ⊠ *100 South St., Downtown* ☎ *401/273–5437* ⊕ *www.childrenmuseum.org* ⊠ *$12.*

Rhode Island State House

GOVERNMENT BUILDING | FAMILY | Designed by the noted architecture firm McKim, Mead & White and completed in 1904, Rhode Island's beautiful capitol building boasts the world's fourth-largest self-supported marble dome. The gilded Independent Man statue that tops the dome was struck by lightning at least 27 times before lightning rods were installed in 1975. Inside, visitors can see a full-length portrait of George Washington by Rhode Islander Gilbert Stuart, who also painted the portrait of Washington that

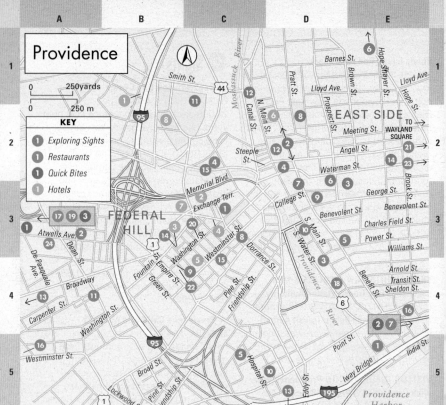

Providence

KEY
- Exploring Sights
- Restaurants
- Quick Bites
- Hotels

appears on the $1 bill. On display in the Governor's State Room are the military accoutrements of Nathanael Greene, a Quaker who served as George Washington's second-in-command during the Revolutionary War. The State Library, on the north side of the building, has moon rocks and the state flag carried on board Apollo 11's first lunar landing mission in 1969 among its displays. The centerpiece of the State House's Charter Museum is Rhode Island's original 1663 Colonial Charter granted by King Charles II—the first charter signed by a monarch that guaranteed religious liberty. Guided tours lasting 50 minutes are offered on weekdays, excluding holidays. You can also follow a self-guided tour. ✉ *82 Smith St., Downtown* ☎ *401/222–3983* 🌐 *www.sos.ri.gov/divisions/civics-and-education/ri-state-house* 🎫 *Free* 🕒 *Closed weekends.*

Roger Williams National Memorial

MEMORIAL | This 4½-acre park dedicated to Rhode Island's founder has a symbolic well to mark the site of the spring around which Roger Williams built Providence's original settlement in 1636. A visitor center has a five-minute film about the park's namesake. A demonstration garden shows how Native Americans cultivated corn, beans, and squash, and how English colonists grew herbs. The park has several picnic tables and 20 free parking spaces (a two-hour parking limit is strictly enforced). ✉ *282 N. Main St., Downtown* ☎ *401/521–7266* 🌐 *www.nps.gov/rowi* 🎫 *Free.*

★ Roger Williams Park Zoo & Carousel Village

NATIONAL/STATE PARK | **FAMILY** | Plan a full day to take in this regal 435-acre Victorian park where you can picnic, see diverse plantlife at the indoor-outdoor Botanical Center, rent a swan-shape paddleboat, and ride a Victorian-style carousel. The 40-acre zoo—one of the nation's oldest—has African elephants, Masai giraffes, zebras, red pandas, snow leopards, moon bears, gibbons, tree kangaroos, and harbor seals in natural settings. Howler monkeys, Chilean flamingos, giant river otters, a giant anteater, toucans, and more inhabit the Rainforest exhibit, opened in summer 2018. In October, more than 5,000 creatively carved pumpkins are illuminated for the well-attended Jack-O-Lantern Spectacular. In Carousel Village, a short walk from the zoo, kids love the classic horses and other creatures on the carousel, pony rides, and train excursions (all individually priced). ✉ *1000 Elmwood Ave., Elmwood* ☎ *401/785–9450 for museum, 401/785–3510 for zoo* 🌐 *www.rwpzoo.org* 🎫 *Zoo $18.*

Waterplace Park

ARTS VENUE | **FAMILY** | Venetian-style footbridges, cobblestone walkways, and an amphitheater encircling a tidal basin set the tone at this 4-acre tract along the Woonasquatucket River near where it joins the Moshassuck to form the Providence River. In summer and fall, it's the site of **WaterFire,** a multisensory installation featuring music, performances, and 80 wood-fired braziers permanently placed in the middle of the river and set afire between dusk and midnight on some nights. WaterFire attracts nearly 1 million visitors annually. ✉ *1 Finance Way, overlooking Woonasquatucket River, Downtown* ☎ *401/273–1155 for WaterFire information.*

🍴 Restaurants

CAV

$$$ | **ECLECTIC** | Chandeliers hang from the ceiling, and African and Asian artwork adorns the walls (everything is for sale) at this restaurant-antiques store. The menu is extensive, the food is rich in flavor, and the ambience is full of personality. **Known for:** imaginative presentation of menu favorites; bistro menu Monday–Wednesday; sit at a table or the 19th-century bar. [$] *Average main: $29* ✉ *14 Imperial Pl., Downtown* ☎ *401/751–9164* 🌐 *www.cavrestaurant.com.*

Providence's annual WaterFire festival has more than 80 bonfires set upon the river.

The Dorrance Kitchen & Cocktails

$$$ | **MODERN AMERICAN** | The opulent first floor of the former Union Trust Building is home to one of Providence's best-known purveyors of New England fare with international flair. Siena marble, ornate plaster detailing, and stained-glass windows lend the place a Newport-mansion vibe. **Known for:** creative cocktails at the long and luxurious bar; contemporary New England cuisine in a spectacular dining room; fresh, local oysters both raw and cooked. $ *Average main: $28* ⊠ *60 Dorrance St., Downtown* ☎ *401/521–6000* ⊕ *www.thedorrance.com* ☾ *No lunch.*

★ Gracie's

$$$$ | **MODERN AMERICAN** | The city's best spot for a romantic meal is Table 21 in a private alcove at Gracie's, across the street from the Trinity Rep theater. Owner Ellen Slattery mixes sophistication with whimsy in the main dining room, and executive chef Matthew Varga sources many of his ingredients from a local Rhode Island farmer. **Known for:** seasonally inspired menu; four-course prix-fixe and seven-course, wine-paired chef's tasting menus; personalized service. $ *Average main: $55* ⊠ *194 Washington St., Downtown* ☎ *401/272–7811* ⊕ *www.graciesprov.com* ☾ *Closed Sun.–Tues. No lunch.*

North

$ | **FUSION** | Thoughtful chef James Mark's nontraditional restaurant adjacent to the Dean Hotel serves a creative menu of small plates and larger dishes to share. Most menu items have an Asian flare—or try grilled local fish, Rhode Island-farmed lamb, or skewered chicken meatballs and shishitos. **Known for:** tiny country ham biscuits with mustards; vegan options; no phone, no reservations. $ *Average main: $15* ⊠ *Dean Hotel, 122 Fountain St., Downtown* ⊕ *www.foodbynorth.com* ☾ *No lunch.*

Oberlin

$ | **AMERICAN** | An open kitchen offers glimpses of one of Providence's most lauded chefs, Benjamin Sukle, and his team at work, deftly composing small plates that are uncomplicated yet wholly satisfying. Dishes take New England ingredients off on new adventures, always with a comforting hint of the familiar. **Known for:** whole roasted fish and other incomparably fresh seafood from local waters; handcrafted pastas; simple preparations, expertly executed. [$] *Average main: $16* ✉ *186 Union St., Downtown* ☎ *401/588–8755* 🌐 *www.oberlinrestaurant.com* 🕒 *Closed Tues. and Wed. No lunch.*

Red Fin Crudo + Kitchen
$$ | **TAPAS** | Television celebrity chefs Julio Lazzarini and Jenny Behm-Lazzarini—he's been on *Chopped,* and she's been on *Cutthroat Kitchen*—serve up tastes of New England, northern Spain, the Mediterranean, and the Caribbean at their popular tapas and cocktails restaurant. **Known for:** if you like ceviche, you'll love theirs; eat at the bar or at a cozy table; menu combines locally sourced ingredients and imported specialty items. [$] *Average main: $20* ✉ *71 Washington St., Downtown* ☎ *401/454–1335* 🕒 *Closed Sun. and Mon. No lunch Tues.–Fri.*

★ **Rosalina**
$$ | **ITALIAN** | You'll find some of the best southern Italian food you've ever tasted at this cozy, family-run Italian restaurant, although the chef also serves up delicious seared scallops, whole grilled branzino, NY strip steak, and more. Be sure to have the antipasto, fried dough with pomodoro sauce, or eggplant parm appetizers—all great for sharing. **Known for:** focus on locally sourced foods; imported olive oil from family-owned groves in Kalamata, Greece; portions are generous so prepare to share. [$] *Average main: $21* ✉ *50 Aborn St., Downtown* ☎ *401/270–7330* 🕒 *No lunch.*

Hotels

Christopher Dodge House
$ | **B&B/INN** | Rooms on the east side of this three-story 1858 Italianate brick town house have direct views of the State House, though Interstate 95 lies between. **Pros:** huge windows in most rooms; cooked-to-order breakfasts with locally roasted coffee; free parking and 24-hour complimentary drinks and snacks. **Cons:** I–95 may be too close for light sleepers; steep stairs to third-floor rooms; 30-minute walk to Federal Hill restaurants. [$] *Rooms from: $139* ✉ *11 W. Park St., Downtown* ☎ *401/351–6111* 🌐 *www.providence-hotel.com* 🛏 *14 rooms* 🍴 *Free breakfast.*

Courtyard by Marriott Providence Downtown
$$ | **HOTEL** | **FAMILY** | Located a short walk from the Rhode Island Convention Center and Waterplace Park and not far from Providence Place Mall and the State House, this is one of New England's larger links in the Courtyard by Marriott chain. **Pros:** central location; reasonable price; pet-friendly. **Cons:** limited baggage service; self-parking only; limited food and beverage in The Bistro. [$] *Rooms from: $229* ✉ *32 Exchange Terr., at Memorial Blvd., Downtown* ☎ *401/272–1191, 888/887–7955* 🌐 *www.marriott.com* 🛏 *219 rooms* 🍴 *No meals.*

The Dean
$ | **HOTEL** | A building that once housed a strip club is now a trendy boutique hotel with minimalist, masculine decor and a studious vibe. **Pros:** central location; setting looks adult, but the property welcomes guests with children and pets; trendy restaurant on-site. **Cons:** central location can be noisy; masculine vibe may not appeal to everyone; European-size (smallish) rooms. [$] *Rooms from: $139* ✉ *122 Fountain St., Downtown* ☎ *401/455–3326* 🌐 *www.thedeanhotel.com* 🛏 *52 rooms* 🍴 *No meals.*

Graduate Providence
$ | **HOTEL** | **FAMILY** | The city's beloved landmark since 1922, the former Providence Biltmore revels in nostalgia for its flapper heyday, but it has refreshed appeal for tourists thanks to a chic and studious makeover and rebranding by new owners. **Pros:** spacious suites with a literary vibe; great Downtown location;

complimentary bikes; Poindexter Coffee is off the lobby. **Cons:** some bathrooms are cramped; street noise, especially in lower-floor rooms; no on-site restaurant. [$] *Rooms from: $160* ✉ *11 Dorrance St., Downtown* ☎ *401/421–0700* 🌐 *www.graduatehotels.com/providence* 🛏 *294 rooms* 🍴 *No meals.*

Hotel Providence
$$ | **HOTEL** | In the heart of the city's Arts and Entertainment District, this intimate boutique hotel sets the standard for elegant decor and attentive service. **Pros:** convenient location for theatergoers; handicapped accessible rooms available; pet-friendly; restaurant, Backstage Kitchen + Bar, serves creative, well-prepared small plates, light meals, and full entrées. **Cons:** late risers may not appreciate the 8 am pealing of Grace Church's 16 bells; street noise also an issue; parking is $30 per night. [$] *Rooms from: $229* ✉ *139 Mathewson St., Downtown* ☎ *401/861–8000, 800/861–8990* 🌐 *www.hotelprovidence.com* 🛏 *80 rooms* 🍴 *No meals.*

★ Omni Providence
$ | **HOTEL** | **FAMILY** | Towering over Downtown, the Omni is steps from restaurants, the Rhode Island Convention Center, the Dunkin' Donuts Center, and Waterplace Park, home of WaterFire. **Pros:** indoor pool; beautiful views of the city from upper floors; child- and pet-friendly. **Cons:** rooms are rather ordinary; in-room Wi-Fi costs extra; breakfast is $10.95 and up; valet parking is $32. [$] *Rooms from: $161* ✉ *1 W. Exchange St., Downtown* ☎ *401/598–8000, 888/444–6664* 🌐 *www.omnihotels.com/hotels/providence* 🛏 *564 rooms* 🍴 *No meals.*

Renaissance Providence Downtown Hotel
$ | **HOTEL** | This luxury hotel occupies one of Providence's most mysterious addresses, a stately nine-story Neoclassical Revival building constructed as a Masonic temple between 1926 and 1928 but unoccupied for an inconceivable 79 years. **Pros:** convenient location next to Providence Place Mall; three meals per day served at on-site Public Kitchen & Bar; beautiful views of the Capitol. **Cons:** some rooms have small windows or no view; rooms on I–95 side can be noisy; valet parking is $32 per night. [$] *Rooms from: $183* ✉ *5 Ave. of the Arts, Downtown* ☎ *401/919–5000, 800/468–3571* 🌐 *www.marriott.com* 🛏 *272 rooms* 🍴 *No meals.*

Nightlife

BARS

The Eddy
BARS/PUBS | The Eddy specializes in classic cocktails like a Manhattan, gin and tonic, or Gibson; creative concoctions like the bourbon-based "grilled peach smash" or basil-vodka-based "green gardens"; draft and bottled beers; and a few interesting wines. Add charcuterie, cheese, sliders, seafood, and good bread, and you have a great night out. ✉ *95 Eddy St., Downtown* ☎ *401/831–3339* 🌐 *www.eddybar.com.*

Rooftop at the Providence G
BARS/PUBS | On the rooftop of the Providence G residential building, the lively bar is open evenings year-round (it has a retractable glass rooftop and fire pits) for drinks, snacks, dinner, music, and general conviviality. Valet parking is complimentary. ✉ *Providence G Hotel, 100 Dorrance St., Downtown* ☎ *401/632–4904* 🌐 *www.rooftopattheg.com.*

MUSIC CLUBS

The Boombox Karaoke
MUSIC CLUBS | At Downtown's first and only karaoke lounge, have a drink, belt out a tune from a searchable app of more than 30,000 songs (updated each month), or book a private room for yourself and your friends. ✉ *The Dean Hotel, 122 Fountain St., Downtown* ☎ *401/861–0040* 🌐 *singboombox.com.*

The Independent Man sculpture atop the State House symbolizes Rhode Island's free-thinking spirit.

Performing Arts

THEATERS

Providence Performing Arts Center

ARTS CENTERS | The 3,100-seat center, which opened in 1928 as a Loew's Movie Palace, hosts concerts, national tours of hit Broadway shows, and other large-scale performances and events. Major renovations to this building, which is listed on the National Register of Historic Places, restored the stage, lobby, and arcade to their original splendor. The mighty Wurlitzer organ is a particular source of pride. ⊠ *220 Weybosset St., Downtown* ☏ *401/421–2787* ⊕ *www.ppacri.org.*

Trinity Repertory Company

THEATER | A past Tony Award winner for outstanding regional theater company, this troupe presents classic plays, intimate musicals, and new works by young playwrights, as well as an annual version of *A Christmas Carol*—all in a renovated former vaudeville house. ⊠ *201 Washington St., Downtown* ☏ *401/351–4242* ⊕ *www.trinityrep.com.*

The Vets

CONCERTS | This 1,900-seat auditorium has a proscenium stage and an exquisite interior; it hosts concerts, operas, and comedy and dance performances. From September to May, the Vets is the home of the Rhode Island Philharmonic Orchestra. ⊠ *1 Ave. of the Arts, Downtown* ☏ *401/421–2787* ⊕ *www.thevetsri.com.*

Shopping

ANTIQUES AND HOME FURNISHINGS

Craftland

BOOKS/STATIONERY | Etsy fans will be delighted by the handmade wares at this colorful shop and gallery: jewelry, notecards, prints, silk-screened T-shirts, fashion accessories, bags, and other sparkly handmade objects by local artists are all for sale. You'll save money on every purchase, too, because there's no sales tax on art in Rhode Island. ⊠ *212 Westminster St., Downtown* ☏ *401/272–4285* ⊕ *www.craftlandshop.com.*

Roger Williams

It was an unthinkable idea: total separation of church and state. Break the tie between them, and where would the government get its authority? The answer threatened the Puritan way of life. And that's why in the winter of 1636 the Massachusetts Bay Colony banished a certain preacher with radical opinions. Roger Williams fled south into the wilderness, with the goal of establishing a new colony founded on religious tolerance and fair dealings with native tribes, and arranged to buy land from the Narragansett sachems Canonicus and Miantonomoh at the confluence of the Woonasquatucket and Moshassuck rivers. Word spread that this new settlement, which Williams named Providence, was a place where civil power rested in the hands of the people. Those persecuted for their beliefs flocked there, and it thereafter grew into a prosperous Colonial shipping port. What started out as a radical experiment became the basis of American democracy.

HomeStyle

HOUSEHOLD ITEMS/FURNITURE | Drop by HomeStyle along increasingly gentrified Westminster Street for eye-catching objets d'art, stylish housewares, and other innovative, extraordinary, or whimsical decorative items. ✉ *229 Westminster St., Downtown* ☎ *401/277–1159* ⊕ *www.homestyleri.com* ☞ *Validated parking at InTown Parking Lot on Weybosset St.*

CLOTHING
The Vault Collective

CLOTHING | This high-ceilinged, multidealer emporium is a standout in a city known for its vintage boutiques. Walk your wardrobe back in time with colorful finds, from designer dresses to throwback Patriots merch to rock concert tees. ✉ *235 Westminster St., Downtown* ☎ *401/250–2587* ⊕ *www.thevaultcollective.com.*

FOOD
★ Yoleni's

FOOD/CANDY | There's a deli to the left and café seating to the right, but straight back in this bright corner shop you'll find all kinds of amazing Greek specialty products all packaged up and ready to go: olives, olive oil, honey, nuts, sauces, spreads and dips, pastas, legumes, herbs and spices, cookies and candy. Buy some for yourself, pick out a ready-made gift, or both. ✉ *292 Westminster St., Downtown* ☎ *401/500–1127* ⊕ *www.yolenis.com.*

JEWELRY
Copacetic Rudely Elegant Jewelry

SPECIALTY STORES | Expect the unusual at this 35-year-old shop, which sells jewelry, gadgets, clocks, and gifts handcrafted by more than 100 artists. ✉ *17 Peck St., Downtown* ☎ *401/273–0470* ⊕ *www.copaceticjewelry.com.*

MALLS
The Arcade Providence

SHOPPING CENTERS/MALLS | Built in 1828, America's oldest indoor shopping mall has a handful of restaurants on its first floor and one signature shop, the **Lovecraft Arts & Sciences Council**, for quirky gifts and books on the supernatural by Providence's own H. P. Lovecraft and other authors. The Greek Revival building has entrances on both Westminster and Weybosset Streets. ✉ *65 Weybosset St., Downtown* ☎ *401/454–4568* ⊕ *www.arcadeprovidence.com.*

Providence Place

SHOPPING CENTERS/MALLS | Macy's, Boscov's, and an Apple Store are among the anchor tenants at this large mall with 13 restaurants include the Cheesecake Factory and P. F. Chang's. Also here are Dave & Buster's and a 16-screen cinema and IMAX theater. Parking in the garage is free for the first two hours. ⊠ *1 Providence Pl., at Francis and Hayes Sts., Downtown* ☎ *401/270–1000* ⊕ *www. providenceplace.com.*

East Side

Home to Brown University and the Rhode Island School of Design (RISD), the East Side is Providence's intellectual center and a beautiful residential neighborhood. The East Side neighborhood highlights include Benefit Street, dubbed the "mile of history" for its high concentration of Colonial architecture; RISD's top-quality art museum; and Thayer Street, a gentrified mix of shops, restaurants, and an art-house cinema.

Sights

★ Benefit Street

HISTORIC SITE | **FAMILY** | The city's wealthiest lived along this Colonial thoroughfare, dubbed "the mile of history," during the 18th and early 19th centuries—and most of the original wood-frame structures have been beautifully restored as homes for today's families. Benefit Street passes through the campuses of Brown University and the Rhode Island School of Design. From mid-June through October, the Rhode Island Historical Society conducts 50-minute street tours ($12) that depart from the John Brown House Museum (92 Power Street) on a regular schedule (book tickets online). ⊠ *Benefit St., Downtown* ☎ *401/331–8575 for tour information* ⊕ *www.rihs.org.*

Brown University

COLLEGE | Founded in 1764, this Ivy League institution is the nation's seventh-oldest college and offers degrees in 82 undergraduate concentrations, 33 master's programs, and 51 doctoral programs. On a stroll through the College Hill campus, you'll encounter Gothic and Beaux Arts structures, as well as the imposing Van Wickle Gate, which opens twice a year—in fall to welcome first-year students and spring to bid graduating seniors farewell. On the ground floor of Manning Hall, the Haffenreffer Museum of Anthropology exhibits artifacts from around the world. The David Winton Bell Gallery in the List Art Building hosts several major art exhibitions a year. The Humanity-Centered Robotics Initiative's Robot Block Party, held in April, celebrates robots and how they are being used to solve the world's problems. ⊠ *Stephen Robert '62 Campus Center, 75 Waterman St., East Side* ☎ *401/863–2378* ⊕ *www.brown.edu.*

First Baptist Church in America

HISTORIC SITE | This historic house of worship was built in 1775 for a congregation originally established in 1638 by Roger Williams and his fellow Puritan dissenters. The writer H. P. Lovecraft attended Sunday school here briefly as a child. Architecture and design buffs will appreciate the 185-foot, glistening white steeple, erected in just 3½ days, as well as the auditorium's large crystal chandelier from Ireland, installed in 1792. Guided tours of the Meeting House are available weekdays and Sundays at the conclusion of worship services. Self-guided tours are also an option, and booklets are available in multiple languages. ⊠ *75 N. Main St., East Side* ☎ *401/454–3418* ⊕ *firstbaptistchurchinamerica.org* ⊠ *Guided tour $2, self-guided tour free.*

John Brown House Museum

HISTORIC SITE | Rhode Island's most famous 18th-century home was the stately residence of John Brown, a wealthy businessman, slave trader, politician, and China trade merchant. John Quincy Adams called the home, designed in late-Georgian, early-Federal style and the first mansion built in Providence, "the most magnificent and elegant private mansion that I have ever seen on this continent." An ardent patriot, Brown was a noteworthy participant in the defiant burning of the British customs ship *Gaspee* in 1772—which, Rhode Islanders will remind you, took place 18 months before the Boston Tea Party. Tours are by reservation. ⊠ *52 Power St., East Side* ☎ *401/331–8575* ⊕ *www.rihs. org/locations/the-john-brown-house-museum* ⊠ *$10* ⊗ *Closed Sun.–Tues. and Thurs. and Fri.*

John Hay Library

LIBRARY | Built in 1910 and named for Abraham Lincoln's secretary, "the Hay" houses Brown University Library's collections of rare books and manuscripts. World-class collections of Lincoln-related items, H. P. Lovecraft letters, Napoléon's death mask, Walt Whitman's personal copy of *Leaves of Grass*, and 6,000 toy soldiers are of particular interest. The library is open to the public, but you need a photo ID to enter. ⊠ *20 Prospect St., East Side* ☎ *401/863–2146* ⊕ *library. brown.edu/hay* ⊠ *Free* ⊗ *Closed Sat.*

★ Museum of Art, Rhode Island School of Design

MUSEUM | This museum houses more than 100,000 objects ranging from ancient art to work by contemporary artists and designers from around the world. Highlights include impressionist paintings, costumes, textiles, decorative arts, Gorham silver, Newport furniture, an ancient Egyptian mummy, and a 12th-century Buddha—the largest historic Japanese wooden sculpture in the United States. Artists represented include major figures in the history of visual art and culture, including Cézanne, Chanel, Copley, Degas, Hirst, Homer, LeWitt, Matisse, Manet, Picasso, Rothko, Sargent, Turner, Twombly, van Gogh, and Warhol—to name a few. Particularly significant are the displays of current and past RISD faculty and students. Stop by the museum's Café Pearl for a bite to eat. ⊠ *20 N. Main St., East Side* ✛ *Additional entrance at 224 Benefit St.* ☎ *401/454–6500* ⊕ *www.risdmuseum.org* ⊠ *$15, free Thurs. 5–9 and Sun.*

Prospect Terrace

NEIGHBORHOOD | **FAMILY** | This pocket park in College Hill offers one of the most scenic views of Downtown, particularly in the fall when the surrounding foliage plays spectacularly off the urban backdrop. Prospect Terrace's centerpiece is a statue of Roger Williams, Rhode Island's forward-thinking founder—who here seems to be groovin' to the 1980s song "Walk Like an Egyptian." ⊠ *Between Congdon and Pratt Sts., at Cushing St., East Side.*

Providence Athenaeum

LIBRARY | Philadelphia architect William Strickland designed this 1838 Greek Revival library building in which Edgar Allan Poe courted the poet (and avid reader) Sarah Helen Whitman; the collection here includes a Poe-signed periodical containing "Ulalume," a poem he published anonymously. An 1870s Manet print that illustrated Poe's "The Raven" hangs in the rare book room, which also contains two medieval illuminated manuscripts. Raven signs are posted at eight points of interest on a self-guided library tour. Among them is a special cabinet modeled after an Egyptian temple, which houses the library's multivolume imperial edition of *Description de l'Egypte* (1809–22), commissioned by Napoléon. ⊠ *251 Benefit St., East Side* ☎ *401/421–6970* ⊕ *www.providenceathenaeum.org* ⊠ *Free.*

Providence in One Day

Begin at the **Rhode Island State House**, where the south portico looks over the city of Providence, the Providence River, and the head of Narragansett Bay. Cross the Moshassuck River to the East Side, drive up the hill a block, and stroll south along **Benefit Street** toward College Hill and Brown University. Touring possibilities in this neighborhood of abundant Colonial architecture are **Prospect Terrace**, a pocket park with a statue of Roger Williams and a gorgeous view of Downtown, the magnificent **John Brown House Museum** at the corner of Benefit and Power streets, the **Providence Athenaeum**, and the **Museum of Art, Rhode Island School of Design.** You'll find plenty of great lunch options, as well as some cool shops, along **Wickenden Street**, at Benefit Street's southern end.

Head back along Benefit, South Main, or South Water Street and cross over the Steeple Street bridge toward Downtown, strolling along **Waterplace Park and Riverwalk**, the centerpiece of the city's revitalization. As dinnertime approaches, make your way west into the famed Italian-American neighborhood of **Federal Hill**, where you'll find dozens of restaurants and cafés.

Thayer Street

NEIGHBORHOOD | Bustling Thayer Street bears a proud old New England name and is very much a part of campus life at Brown, RISD, and other local colleges. Gentrification has resulted in an influx of chain stores. In the blocks between Waterman and Bowen Streets, though, you'll still find fashion boutiques, shops selling funky gifts, the art deco–style Avon Cinema, and restaurants serving every kind of cuisine from Greek to Korean. ✉ *Thayer St., between Waterman and Bowen Sts., East Side* 🌐 *www.thayerstreetdistrict.com.*

Wickenden Street

NEIGHBORHOOD | Named for a Baptist minister who was one of Providence's first settlers, this main artery in the Fox Point district is home to antiques stores, art galleries, and trendy cafés. It also hosts the Coffee Exchange, one of the area's most popular gathering spots. Sidewalk sales are held in the spring and fall. Once home to mainly working-class Portuguese-Americans, the Wickenden Street area has seen waves of gentrification over the years; Our Lady of the Rosary Church on adjacent Traverse Street still conducts some weekend Masses in Portuguese. ✉ *Wickenden St., East Side.*

🍴 Restaurants

★ Al Forno

$$$ | **ITALIAN** | When it opened in 1980, Al Forno put Providence on the national dining map. Still consistently good, the restaurant retains a loyal following for its thin-crust pizzas, handmade pastas, and wood-grilled or roasted entrées. **Known for:** spicy roasted clams; fabulous desserts; upstairs tables, where the city's movers and shakers congregate. [$] *Average main: $28* ✉ *577 S. Water St., East Side* ☎ *401/273–9760* 🌐 *www.alforno.com* ⏲ *Closed Sun. and Mon. No lunch.*

Bácaro

$$$ | **ITALIAN** | The informal first floor of this two-level Italian restaurant has a deli case stocked with cured meats, cheeses, olives, and traditional Italian-style small plates; upstairs is a more traditional dining room with impressive views of the Providence River. Every table receives a separate checklist of the cured meats and other items the deli sells, and selections come on a beautifully arranged board. **Known for:** seasonal menu with farm-to-table focus; garden patio for alfresco dining; authentic Italian desserts. [$] *Average main: $30* ✉ *262 S. Water St., East Side* ☎ *401/751–3700* 🌐 *www.bacarorestaurant.net* 🕓 *Closed Sun. and Mon. No lunch.*

Chez Pascal

$$$ | **FRENCH** | You can tell that this French bistro will be welcoming and unpretentious from its logo: a trio of pigs in striped shirts and berets. In a quiet residential neighborhood, Chez Pascal's menu follows the French tradition but also includes homemade sausages and "pork of the day." **Known for:** house-butchered pork; escargot à la bourguignonne, of course; homemade sausages served to-go from the Wurst Kitchen window. [$] *Average main: $28* ✉ *960 Hope St., East Side* ☎ *401/421–4422* 🌐 *www.chezpron.com* 🕓 *Closed Sun. and Mon. No lunch.*

Chomp Kitchen & Drinks

$ | **AMERICAN** | A tiny Warren restaurant known for offbeat beers and a burger stacked 10 inches tall has blossomed into this second location with more expansive indoor-outdoor seating and an equally enticing menu of decidedly adult, made-from-scratch comfort grub. Pair zesty Mozambique chicken tenders that are definitely not your kids' chicken nuggets with frozen sangria on a summer's day. **Known for:** gourmet burgers including the piled-high Stack; rich, gooey mac and cheese you won't want to share; eclectic and revolving menu of rare, limited-edition craft beers. [$] *Average main: $15* ✉ *117 Ives St., Fox Point* ☎ *401/537–7556* 🌐 *www.chompri.com* 🕓 *Closed Mon. and Tues. No lunch Wed.–Fri.*

Hemenway's

$$$ | **SEAFOOD** | In a city where culinary newcomers tend to garner all the attention, Hemenway's continues to be one of the state's best seafood restaurants. The high-ceiling dining room's huge windows look out on Providence's World War II Memorial; in warm weather, dine outside on the front patio. **Known for:** raw bar platters; fresh-caught lobster stuffed with scallops, shrimp, and crab; extensive wine cellar and craft-beer list. [$] *Average main: $30* ✉ *121 S. Main St., East Side* ☎ *401/351–8570* 🌐 *www.hemenwaysrestaurant.com* 🕓 *No lunch.*

Mill's Tavern

$$$$ | **MODERN AMERICAN** | Handsome brick walls and vaulted casement ceilings lend a cozy New England vibe to this contemporary, French-influenced American restaurant. The menu includes selections from both land and sea, cooked in the open kitchen's fiery oven. **Known for:** menu changes to reflect the seasons; steaks, chops, and seafood always a good choice; three-course prix-fixe menu offered Sunday to Thursday. [$] *Average main: $36* ✉ *101 N. Main St., East Side* ☎ *401/272–3331* 🌐 *www.millstavernrestaurant.com* 🕓 *No lunch.*

Plant City

$ | **VEGETARIAN** | Even omnivores can get behind this chic vegan food hall, positioned near the waterfront and the city's new Providence River Pedestrian Bridge. On two floors and cascading outdoors, you'll find three restaurants, a bakery, a coffee bar, and a market offering familiar fare like tacos, pizza, lasagna... even burgers... all made exclusively from plants. **Known for:** world's first plant-based food hall; gorgeous patio dining; grab-and-go options. [$] *Average main: $17* ✉ *334 S. Water St., Fox Point* ☎ *401/429–2029* 🌐 *www.matthewkenneycuisine.com/plant-city-pvd.*

Red Stripe

$$ | **ECLECTIC** | A giant fork hangs outside this neighborhood brasserie in Wayland Square, and the chefs do things big here—from the everything-but-the-kitchen-sink chopped salad to supersize sangrias. The menu is eclectic, but you'll find plenty of Italian- and French-inspired bistro items, including French onion soup, steak frites, rigatoni Bolognese,

and mussels prepared six ways and served with hand-cut frites. **Known for:** large, varied menu with something to appeal to everyone; homemade bread is fabulous; lively atmosphere (i.e., noisy). $ *Average main: $18 ⊠ 465 Angell St., East Side ☎ 401/437–6950 ⊕ www. redstriperestaurants.com.*

The Salted Slate

$$$ | AMERICAN | Ben Lloyd, the chef-owner of this "agri-driven" American restaurant, is committed to honoring the origins of the food he prepares. He purchases humanely raised and harvested meat, poultry, and fish whole from local vendors, butchers them in-house, and uses every part from nose to tail—combined with eggs at breakfast, cheese and fries at lunch, and fresh vegetables at dinner. **Known for:** small-batch artisanal cheeses and house-cured charcuterie; innovative menus change frequently; best bacon you'll ever eat. $ *Average main: $25 ⊠ Wayland Sq., 186 Wayland Ave., East Side ☎ 401/270–3737 ⊕ www.salted-slate.com ⊗ Closed Mon.*

☕ Coffee and Quick Bites

PVDonuts

$ | BAKERY | FAMILY | Just as sneakerheads line up for hot releases, doughnutheads stake their places on the sidewalk outside this one-of-a-kind shop to try limited-edition flavors like S'mores or Chocolate Churro. There are filled and old-fashioned-style donuts to sample, but the stars of the monthly changing line-up are the light and fluffy, oversized brioche dough orbs. **Known for:** cereal-studded doughnuts and trademark creations like the Friendsgiving doughnut; vegan options; locally roasted coffee. $ *Average main: $5 ⊠ 79 Ives St. ⊕ www.pvdonuts. com ⊗ Closed Mon. and Tues.*

🛏 Hotels

The Old Court Bed and Breakfast

$ | B&B/INN | You'll understand why parents of Brown and RISD students book their stays in this three-story Italianate inn on historic Benefit Street a few years before graduation once you see the lovely antiques, richly colored wallpaper, and authentic period light fixtures. **Pros:** on a historic residential street; period decor and modern-day conveniences; free parking. **Cons:** small bathrooms; third-floor rooms require a trek upstairs; street traffic can be noisy at times. $ *Rooms from: $125 ⊠ 144 Benefit St., East Side ☎ 401/751–2002 ⊕ www.oldcourt.com ⇥ 10 rooms ⊚ Free breakfast.*

🍸 Nightlife

BARS

Fish Co.

BARS/PUBS | Marina and skyline views, live tunes, beer buckets, frozen concoctions, and the city's best clam cakes and chowder make this indoor-outdoor bar and grill on the Fox Point waterfront an ideal place to unwind. The name is a nod to a time when the docks below were the domain of fishermen, not pleasure boaters. ⊠ *15 Bridge St., Fox Point ☎ 401/588–5158 ⊕ www.fishcopvd.com.*

Hot Club

BARS/PUBS | You may recognize the Hot Club from the opening scenes of the movie *Something About Mary*. For more than 30 years, this place has been a favorite hangout for young professionals, university professors, and politicians. On summer afternoons until the wee hours of the morning, you'll find the hip set on the outdoor deck overlooking the Providence River. For cheap eats, try local favorites like the Saugy dog (hot dog) or the stuffed quahog (a Rhode Island seafood staple). ⊠ *25 Bridge St., East Side ☎ 401/861–9007 ⊕ www.hotclub-prov.com.*

🎫 Performing Arts

FILM

Avon Cinema

FILM | This independent movie theater on College Hill, near Brown University, screens primarily art-house, independent, and foreign films. The theater's art deco styling dates back to its opening in 1938. ✉ 260 Thayer St., East Side ☎ 401/421–0020 ⊕ www.avoncinema.com.

🏃 Activities

BIKING

East Bay Bike Path

BICYCLING | **FAMILY** | This mostly flat, 14½-mile bike path connects Providence's India Point Park with Independence Park in Bristol. Along the way, you pass six additional parks and enjoy views of coves and saltwater marshes. A half-mile detour on Crescent View Avenue in East Providence leads to the 1895 Charles Looff–designed Crescent Park Carousel. The route can be congested on fine-weather weekends. ■ TIP➔ **Check out the George Redman Linear Park on the Washington Bridge over the Seekonk River. It's accessible from India Point Park.** ✉ India Point Park, India St., Fox Point ☎ 401/667–6200 ⊕ www.dot.ri.gov/travel/bikeri/eastbay.php.

🛍 Shopping

ANTIQUES

The Stanley Weiss Collection

ANTIQUES/COLLECTIBLES | The country's largest collection of fine classical and Colonial furniture and antiques is available for viewing (and for sale) Saturday 11–5, or by appointment. ✉ 212 4th St., East Side ☎ 401/272–3200 ⊕ www.stanleyweiss.com.

ART GALLERIES

Bert Gallery

ART GALLERIES | This gallery showcases late 19th- and early-20th-century paintings by regional artists, by appointment only. ✉ 24 Bridge St., East Side ☎ 401/751–2628 ⊕ www.bertgallery.com.

HANDICRAFTS AND HOME FURNISHINGS

Frog + Toad

CLOTHING | Clothing, housewares, fair trade handicrafts, and locally designed goods can all be found at this small curiosity shop and gift boutique. ✉ 795 Hope St., East Side ☎ 401/831–3434 ⊕ www.frogandtoadstore.com.

Rhody Craft

BOOKS/STATIONERY | Whimsy and practicality converge at this shop devoted to goods lovingly conceived and handmade in little Rhody. Each item, whether something useful for your kitchen or baby or a decidedly frivolous indulgence, is curated to make you smile. ✉ 769 Hope St., East Side ☎ 401/626–1833 ⊕ www.rhodycraft.com.

RISD Store

BOOKS/STATIONERY | This shop associated with RISD's art museum has a selection of inspired toys, totes, gifts, and jewelry, plus accessories by Rhode Island School of Design alumni, including designer Andrea Valentini's sustainable-fabric bags. ✉ 30 N. Main St., East Side ☎ 401/454–6464 ⊕ www.risdstore.com.

Stock Culinary Goods

CERAMICS/GLASSWARE | Gourmet treats and useful, whimsical, and always well-designed utensils, stemware, dishes, and culinary gifts are the specialty of this foodie paradise with an industrial kitchen vibe. ✉ 756 Hope St., East Side ☎ 401/521–0101 ⊕ www.stockculinarygoods.com ⊘ Closed Mon. and Tues.

Federal Hill

Federal Hill has been home to generations of Italian-American families. While the neighborhood may no longer be predominantly Italian-American, it remains infused with Italian charm and hospitality. The stripe down Atwells Avenue, the main thoroughfare, is painted in red, white, and green; and a huge pine cone (*La Pigna*), an Italian symbol of abundance and quality, hangs on an arch soaring over the street. Grocers sell pasta, pastries, and hard-to-find Italian groceries. To get the full experience, have a seat near the fountain in DePasquale Square, especially during the Feast of St. Joseph in March, the Federal Hill Stroll in early in June, the Federal Hill Summer Festival in late June, or the three-day Columbus Day Weekend Festival and parade in October. Federal Hill lies to the west of Downtown, separated by Interstate 95, and is bounded by Westminster Street to the south and Route 6 to the west and north. For a look at what's on, check out 🌐 *www.federalhillprov.com.*

🍴 Restaurants

Angelo's Civita Farnese

$ | **ITALIAN** | **FAMILY** | Locals come to this third-generation, family-owned restaurant in the heart of Federal Hill for the chicken or eggplant Parmesan, veal with peppers, and braciola like (your Italian) grandma used to make. The prices are reasonable; the atmosphere, warm and casual. **Known for:** family-friendly; familiar southern Italian menu; a landmark since 1924. [$] *Average main: $16* ✉ *141 Atwells Ave., Federal Hill* ☎ *401/621–8171* 🌐 *www.angelosri.com.*

Broadway Bistro

$$ | **AMERICAN** | On the city's increasingly gentrified West Side (which fringes Federal Hill), this convivial bar and restaurant occupies a single-story redbrick storefront with a handful of sidewalk tables. A mix of students, artists, and neighborhood locals find their way here nightly for fair-priced, deftly prepared bistro chow. **Known for:** cozy comfort food; casual, come-as-you-are vibe; quirky cocktails and good wine and beer selection. [$] *Average main: $19* ✉ *205 Broadway, Federal Hill* ☎ *401/331–2450* 🌐 *www.broadwaybistrori.com* 🕒 *Closed Sun. and Mon. No lunch.*

Kitchen

$ | **AMERICAN** | The lone chef and solitary waiter at this five-table restaurant produce what some patrons describe as "breakfast nirvana." People wait in line for thick-cut bacon, Portuguese sweetbread French toast, and grilled blueberry muffins. **Known for:** best breakfast in the city; limited seating—plan to wait in line; order extra muffins to take home. [$] *Average main: $10* ✉ *94 Carpenter St., Federal Hill* ☎ *401/474–6740* 🕒 *Closed weekdays* 💳 *No credit cards.*

★ **Nick's on Broadway**

$$ | **MODERN AMERICAN** | Make reservations for brunch at this trendy West End restaurant, where chef Derek Wagner entices diners with peach pancakes, poached eggs on a buttermilk biscuit with hollandaise and basil pesto, and other well-prepared brunch fare. The restaurant also serves dinner, at which the chef's passionate embrace of farm-and-sea-to-table precepts—not to mention his attention to detail—are even more in evidence. **Known for:** satisfying seasonal risottos; homemade ice creams and sorbets; opt for patio seating for an escape from the pace of the city. [$] *Average main: $20* ✉ *500 Broadway, Federal Hill* ☎ *401/421–0286* 🌐 *www.nicksonbroadway.com* 🕒 *Closed Mon. and Tues. No dinner Sun.*

Ogie's Trailer Park

$ | **AMERICAN** | Fun and kitschy Ogie's bar and restaurant fuses trailer-park chic and colorful (maybe even garish) 1950s-style decor. The menu emphasizes "gourmet comfort food," which translates into the likes of tater tots with white truffle oil, grilled peanut butter and jelly, and mac 'n' cheese croquettes. **Known for:** Rhody fried chicken, encrusted with Doritos!; Outdoor dining on front and back patios; drinks at the outdoor tiki bar in warm weather. $ *Average main: $10* ✉ *1155 Westminster St., Federal Hill* ☎ *401/383–8200* ⊕ *www.ogiestrailerpark.com* ◷ *No lunch Mon.–Sat.*

Pane e Vino
$$$ | ITALIAN | Portions are big in the Rhode Island comfort-food tradition at this southern Italian *ristorante* on Federal Hill; count on fresh ingredients presented in a simple, straightforward way. Share a pasta if you dare, but keep in mind that the veal chop could probably topple Fred Flintstone's footmobile; gluten-free dishes are also available. **Known for:** all your favorites, Italian style; dozens of regional Italian wines; $24 prix-fixe menu at dinner (except Friday and Saturday). $ *Average main: $25* ✉ *365 Atwells Ave., Federal Hill* ☎ *401/223–2230* ⊕ *www. panevino.net* ◷ *No lunch.*

Providence Oyster Bar
$$$ | SEAFOOD | In a neighborhood where Italian food dominates, this spirited seafood restaurant offers a refreshing alternative. Oysters—and clams, lobster, and shrimp—are the main attraction, of course, but landlubbers will enjoy a steak or grilled chicken breast. **Known for:** oysters—mostly local—on the raw bar; sushi creations like the surf-and-turf roll; splurge-worthy hot buttered lobster rolls. $ *Average main: $28* ✉ *283 Atwells Ave., Federal Hill* ☎ *401/272–8866* ⊕ *www. providenceoysterbar.com* ◷ *No lunch Mon.–Thurs.*

Siena
$$ | NORTHERN ITALIAN | This place gener-ates well-deserved buzz for its wine-braised beef short rib and for its pasta with a rich Bolognese—as well as for the kitchen's willingness to satisfy off-menu cravings. It's best to split an appetizer, as portions here are huge. **Known for:**

Tuscan-style cuisine; excellent wine list; signature "tasting board" antipasti. $ *Average main: $23* ✉ *238 Atwells Ave., Federal Hill* ☎ *401/521–3311* ⊕ *www. sienari.com* ◷ *No lunch.*

☕ Coffee and Quick Bites

★ Costantino's Venda Ravioli
$$ | ITALIAN | FAMILY | The scents and fla-vors of Italy surround you at Costantino's as you peruse the amazing selection of homemade pastas and imported foods. The convivial banter between customers and employees adds to the atmosphere. $ *Average main: $21* ✉ *275 Atwells Ave., Federal Hill* ☎ *401/421–9105* ⊕ *www. vendaravioli.com* ⊟ *No credit cards.*

Tony's Colonial Food
$ | ITALIAN | This superb grocery offers a family-friendly atmosphere in which to peruse the finest of Italian meats and cheeses; imported vinegars and olive oils; and candies and pastries—all at reasonable prices. In addition, Tony's deli stocks freshly prepared foods to eat on the premises or take with you; try the Italian grinder, a Rhode Island lunchtime staple. $ *Average main: $12* ✉ *311 Atwells Ave., Federal Hill* ☎ *401/621–8675* ⊕ *www.tonyscolonial.com* ⊟ *No credit cards.*

🍸 Nightlife

BARS
Courtland Club
BARS/PUBS | In a dimly lit space born as a bakery in the 1920s and converted to a social club at the tail end of World War II, this speakeasy is also a pizza joint and ice creamery. Pair your favorite boozy concoction with the POW (Pizza of the Week) and small-batch sorbet and ice-cream flavors like mint chocolate chip made with real mint. ✉ *51 Courtland St., Federal Hill* ☎ *401/227–9300* ⊕ *www. courtlandclub.com.*

Old Slater Mill in Pawtucket is regarded as the country's first successful water-powered spinning mill.

Pawtucket

5 miles north of Providence.

Once a thriving mill town, Pawtucket went through tough times before artists discovered its old mills and low rents. The city remains the world headquarters of the toy manufacturer Hasbro, creator of Mr. Potato Head, and has a thriving arts and cultural scene. A visit to the engaging Old Slater Mill National Historic Landmark, America's first successful water-powered factory, provides a sense of Pawtucket's pivotal role in the American Industrial Revolution. Inside a converted mill, the Hope Artiste Village hints at the future with its mix of art studios, lofts, retail shops, light-industrial workshops, and the Met music venue.

◉ Sights

Hope Artiste Village

LOCAL SPECIALTIES | The surviving redbrick buildings of the former Hope Webbing Company's textile mill now hold artists' studios, galleries (including the always-interesting Giraffes and Robots), shops, the Met music venue, and the marvelously retro BreakTime Bowl and Bar duckpin bowling alley. ✉ *1005 Main St.* ☎ *401/312–3850* ⊕ *www.hopeartistevillage.com.*

★ Old Slater Mill National Historic Landmark

HISTORIC SITE | FAMILY | Concord and Lexington may legitimately lay claim to what Ralph Waldo Emerson called "the shot heard round the world" in 1775, but Pawtucket's Slater Mill provided the necessary economic shot in the arm in 1793. This National Historic Landmark, the first successful water-powered spinning mill in America, touched off an industrial revolution that helped secure America's sovereign independence in the early days of the republic. The museum complex explores this era with National Park Rangers and expert interpretive guides, who demonstrate fiber-to-yarn and yarn-to-fabric processes and hand-operated and-powered machinery and discuss how industrialization forever changed this nation. It's peaceful just to watch the water wheel turn and to contemplate how much we owe to "Slater the Traitor." ✉ *67 Roosevelt Ave.* ☎ *401/725–8638* 🌐 *www.nps.gov/blrv* 🎟 *$12* 🕒 *Closed Mon.–Wed.*

Slater Memorial Park

CAROUSEL | FAMILY | Within the stately grounds of this park along Ten Mile River are picnic tables, tennis courts, a playground, a dog park, and a disc golf course. The park's **Looff Carousel,** built by Charles I. D. Looff in 1895, has 44 horses, three dogs, a lion, a camel, a giraffe, and two chariots that are the earliest examples of the Danish immigrant's work—rides operate spring through fall and cost 50¢. The Pawtucket chapter of the Daughters of the American Revolution gives tours (by appointment) of the park's **Daggett House,** which dates to 1685. ✉ *401 Newport Ave.* ☎ *401/728–0500 park information* 🌐 *www.pawtucketri.com* 🎟 *Free.*

🍴 Restaurants

Modern Diner

$ | DINER | FAMILY | This 1941 Sterling Streamliner diner is a beauty to behold. In addition to the extensive breakfast and lunch menu, you'll often find 30 or more specials posted on the wall. **Known for:** breakfast served all day until closing; modern addition with retro counter seating; first diner to appear on National Register of Historic Places. [$] *Average main: $9* ✉ *364 East Ave.* ☎ *401/726–8390* 🌐 *www.moderndinerri.com* 💳 *No credit cards* 🕒 *No dinner.*

Rasoi

$ | INDIAN | Taking its name from the Hindi word for kitchen, this restaurant near the Providence city line serves cuisine from a staggering 27 regions of India. The menu includes numerous spicy, gluten-free, dairy-free, and vegan selections. **Known for:** lunch-size portions of all entrées; all dishes custom-spiced to your heat tolerance; colorful orange and blue decor. [$] *Average main: $17* ✉ *727 East Ave.* ☎ *401/728–5500* 🌐 *www.rasoirestaurant.com.*

Westerly

45 miles southwest of Providence, 95 miles southwest of Boston, 140 miles northeast of New York City.

The picturesque and thriving business district in this town of 23,000 people bordering Pawcatuck, Connecticut, has a lot going for it: art galleries, shops, and restaurants; a Victorian strolling park; and more than 15 structures on the National Register of Historic Places. Once a busy little railroad town in the late 19th century, Westerly is now a stop on the New York–Boston Amtrak corridor. The town was known in the past for its red granite, which was used in monuments around the country. It has since sprawled out along U.S. 1 and grown to encompass more than a dozen villages in a 30-square-mile area including Westerly itself (also called downtown Westerly), along with Watch Hill, Dunn's Corners, Misquamicut, Bradford, Shelter Harbor, and Weekapaug.

GETTING HERE AND AROUND

When traveling between New York City and Boston, Amtrak makes stops at Westerly, West Kingston, and Providence.

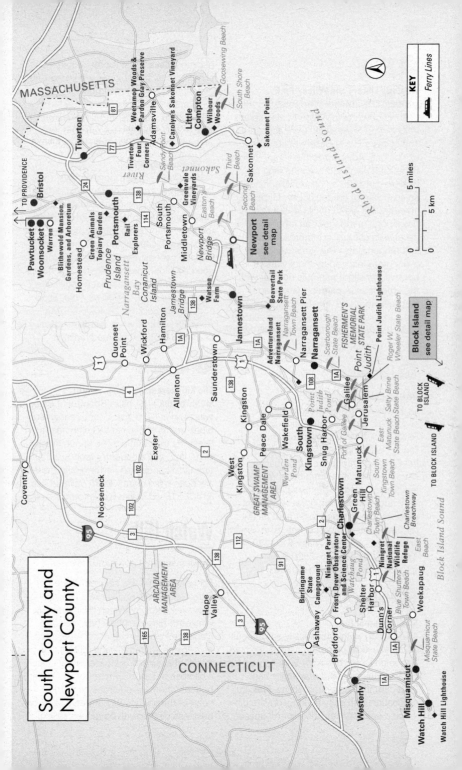

👁 Sights

Westerly Library and Wilcox Park

HISTORIC SITE | FAMILY | The library, in the heart of downtown Westerly, also serves neighboring Pawcatuck, Connecticut. The library's Hoxie Gallery holds art exhibitions. Adjacent to the library, Wilcox Park, a 14½-acre Victorian strolling park designed in 1898 by Warren Manning—an associate of Frederick Law Olmsted, co-creator of New York's Central Park—has a pond, a meadow, an arboretum, a perennials garden, sculptures, fountains, and monuments. *The Runaway Bunny*, a sculpture inspired by the children's book of the same name, is popular with the little ones. A garden market, arts festivals, concerts, and Shakespeare-in-the-park productions are held periodically. ✉ *44 Broad St.* ☎ *401/596–2877* ⊕ *www.westerlylibrary.org* 🔗 *Free.*

🍴 Restaurants

B&B Dockside

$ | AMERICAN | It's all about breakfast and burgers at this café overlooking the Pawcatuck River. Burgers rule the lunch menu, including the deliciously decadent Fat Elvis—with peanut butter, bacon, cheese, and caramelized bananas, it'll leave you saying, "Thank you, thankyou-verymuch." **Known for:** great waterfront view; mouthwatering roast beef hash—for breakfast; friendly service, even when crowded. $ *Average main: $10* ✉ *19 Margin St.* ☎ *401/315–2520* ⊕ *www.bnbdockside.com* ⊙ *Closed Tues.*

🛏 Hotels

Shelter Harbor Inn

$ | B&B/INN | With whimsically sumptuous decor styled by celebrity fashion designer Randolph Duke, this early-19th-century farmhouse inn and restaurant has 21st-century Instagrammability. **Pros:** quiet location with easy parking; on-site dining and spa services; ideal for off-season escapes. **Cons:** most rooms require a climb up stairs; nothing is within walking distance; two-night minimum on summer weekends. $ *Rooms from: $139* ✉ *10 Wagner Rd., off U.S. 1, Shelter Harbor* ☎ *401/322–8883* ⊕ *www.shelterharborinnri.com* 🔗 *23 rooms* ⦿ *No meals.*

★ Weekapaug Inn

$$$$ | RESORT | Guest rooms at this lovingly restored inn on Quonochontaug (Quonnie) Pond are furnished with luxury linens and the work of area artists. **Pros:** low-key luxury; guest pantry stocked with tasty treats; complimentary use of kayaks and canoes; meals made with locally sourced food. **Cons:** expensive; not directly oceanside; few off-season activities (after Labor Day). $ *Rooms from: $590* ✉ *25 Spray Rock Rd.* ☎ *401/637–7600, 855/679–2995* ⊕ *www.weekapauginn.com* 🔗 *31 rooms* ⦿ *Free breakfast.*

🍸 Nightlife

The Knickerbocker Music Center

MUSIC CLUBS | The band Roomful of Blues was born at "The Knick," and renowned blues artists still gig at this club near the Westerly train station. The venue hosts R&B, jazz, and alt-country touring acts, too; local bands also perform, and there are open-mike nights. ✉ *35 Railroad Ave.* ☎ *401/315–5070* ⊕ *www.knickmusic.org.*

Watch Hill

6 miles south of downtown Westerly.

For generations, this seaside village has attracted movers and shakers looking for a low-key getaway. Watch Hill has nearly 2 miles of gorgeous beaches, including Napatree Point Conservation Area, a great spot to see shorebirds and raptors and take in the sunset. Stargazers might catch a glimpse of Taylor Swift or Conan O'Brien, both of whom have homes here. The heart of the town is Bay Street, a seasonal business district with boutiques selling upscale beachwear, fashions, home goods, jewelry, and souvenirs. There are also cafés and a historic carousel.

Sights

Flying Horse Carousel

CAROUSEL | FAMILY | At the beach end of Bay Street twirls one of the oldest carousels in America, built by the Charles W. F. Dare Company of New York City and part of a traveling carnival that came to Watch Hill before 1883. The carved wooden horses with real horsehair manes and leather saddles are suspended from chains attached to the ceiling, creating the impression the horses are flying. Riders must be under 13. Grab the brass ring for a free ride. ⊠ *151 Bay St.* ☎ *401/348–6007* ⊕ *www.merrygoroundbeach.com* ⊠ *$1 inside horse, $2 outside horse* ⊗ *Closed mid-Sept.–mid-May.*

Watch Hill Lighthouse

MUSEUM | A tiny museum at this 1856 lighthouse contains the original Fresnel light, letters and journals from lighthouse keepers, documentation of famous local shipwrecks, and photographs of the hurricane of 1938 and 19th- and early-20th-century sailing vessels off Watch Hill. Parking is for the handicapped and senior citizens only; everyone else must walk down the peninsula along a private road off Larkin Road. ⊠ *Lighthouse Rd.* ☎ *401/596–7761* ⊕ *www.watchhilllighthousekeepers.org* ⊠ *Free* ⊗ *Museum closed mid-Sept.–June and Fri.–Mon.*

Restaurants

★ Olympia Tea Room

$$$ | AMERICAN | Overlooking the water since it first opened as an ice cream parlor in 1916, the Olympia's varnished wood booths and a long marble counter echo the restaurant's rich history. The kitchen focuses on local and artisanal ingredients served with simple elegance and abundant flavor, including spicy flaked haddock and Milanese-style crispy chicken. **Known for:** bistro-style menu; sidewalk tables outside and antique booths inside; a fine selection of wines available by the glass. $ *Average main: $25* ⊠ *74 Bay St.* ☎ *401/348–8211* ⊕ *www.olympiatearoom.com* ⊗ *Closed early Nov.–early Apr.*

Hotels

★ Ocean House

$$$$ | RESORT | High on bluffs overlooking Block Island Sound stands this extraordinary replica of the Victorian grande dame of the same name built here in 1868. **Pros:** exceptional service; beach with private cabanas; championship croquet lawn; spa with 25-meter lap pool. **Cons:** expensive during high season (and low season); three-night minimum on weekends; an uphill walk from Watch Hill's shopping and dining. $ *Rooms from: $1020* ⊠ *1 Bluff Ave.* ☎ *401/584–7000, 855/678–0364* ⊕ *www.oceanhouseri.com* ⊅ *67 rooms* ¶Ⓞ¶ *No meals.*

Misquamicut

2½ miles northeast of Watch Hill.

This family-oriented summer destination, stretching 7 miles from Watch Hill to Weekapaug, has an ocean-facing sandy beach the color of brown sugar. From hermit crab races to kiddie rides, the town's family-geared amusements provide countless diversions. You can also hop on a Jet Ski, pedal a hydrobike, or find a spot for sunbathing. Evenings bring concerts and movies on the beach, and there are shoreside festivals in the spring and fall.

The Native American name for this sandy strip of beachfront means "Red Fish," referring to the Atlantic salmon common to the Pawcatuck River; the entire Westerly area, settled in 1661, once bore this name.

Sights

Atlantic Beach Park

AMUSEMENT PARK/WATER PARK | FAMILY | The largest and busiest of the kid-oriented amusements along Misquamicut Beach, this century-old facility offers nostalgic fun for the entire family, including an antique (1915) carousel, bumper cars, a dragon roller coaster, a surf bar, and a large arcade with games that spout tickets you can redeem for prizes. ✉ *321 Atlantic Ave.* ☎ *401/322–0504* 🌐 *www.atlanticbeachpark.com* 🎟 *Free entry, $2 per ride; parking from $20* 🕒 *Closed late Oct.–Apr.*

Beaches

Misquamicut State Beach

BEACH—SIGHT | FAMILY | Part of the several-mile-long stretch of sandy beach that makes up Misquamicut, this ½-mile state-run portion is exceedingly popular. Expect the 2,100-space parking lot to fill up on sunny summer weekends. Bring your own chairs or blankets. **Amenities:** food and drink; lifeguards (seasonal); parking (fee); showers; toilets. **Best for:** sunset; swimming; family fun. ✉ *257 Atlantic Ave.* ☎ *401/322–8910* 🌐 *www.riparks.com* 🎟 *Parking: from $12 (nonresident).*

Restaurants

Maria's Seaside Cafe

$$$ | MEDITERRANEAN | This family-owned restaurant serves Italian cuisine at dinnertime. It's right across the street from the beach and a standout on a strip of ice-cream stands, take-out shacks, and motels that have seen better days. **Known for:** indoor-outdoor seating with heaters for cool summer nights; homemade pasta; lobster pizza. [$] *Average main: $27* ✉ *132 Atlantic Ave.* ☎ *401/596–6886* 🌐 *www.mariasseasidecafe.com* 🕒 *Closed early Sept.–May.*

Hotels

Breezeway Resort

$$ | HOTEL | A great choice for families, this well-maintained boutique motel is less than a quarter-mile from the ocean. **Pros:** access to private stretch of Misquamicut Beach; complimentary bicycles for adults; away from the late-night hubbub near the beach. **Cons:** rooms are a bit cramped; can be noisy with so many kids; hotel prices, motel accommodations. [$] *Rooms from: $282* ✉ *70 Winnapaug Rd.* ☎ *401/348–8953* 🌐 *www.breezewayresort.com* 🕒 *Closed late Oct.–early May* 🛏 *50 rooms* 🍴 *Free breakfast.*

Charlestown

10 miles northeast of Misquamicut.

Charlestown's secluded coastline makes it a great spot for swimming, sailing, surfing, beachcombing, bird-watching, and boating. Approximately 20% of Charlestown is conservation and recreation land, including Burlingame State Park, Ninigret Wildlife Refuge, Ninigret Park, and East Beach. The city regulates outdoor lighting to keep the night sky dark, so it's a fantastic place for stargazers of all ages. Charlestown is also home to the Narragansett Indian Tribe Reservation, which every August holds the oldest recorded annual powwow in North America.

Sights

Burlingame State Campground

NATIONAL/STATE PARK | This 3,100-acre state park attracts many campers to its 731 rustic campsites and shelters, nature trails, picnic and swimming areas, and boating and fishing opportunities on crystal clear Watchaug Pond. ✉ *1 Burlingame State Park Rd.* ☎ *401/322–8910* 🌐 *www.riparks.com/Locations/LocationBurlingameCampground.html.*

★ **Frosty Drew Observatory and Science Center**

OBSERVATORY | FAMILY | In Ninigret Park but independently operated by a non-profit, the observatory offers the state's best views of the night sky. Frosty Drew opens every Friday around sunset for stargazing and stays open until early Saturday morning if the skies are clear. It's also open on nights when meteor showers and other astronomical events are forecast. On cloudy nights, astronomers give presentations and offer tours. The place isn't heated, so dress for the season. ⊠ *Ninigret Park, 61 Park La., off Old Post Rd.* ☎ *401/859–1450* ⊕ *www. frostydrew.org/observatory* ☞ *Free.*

Ninigret National Wildlife Refuge

BODY OF WATER | FAMILY | Spring brings opportunities to view the male American woodcock's mating ritual at this 858-acre refuge, but bird-watchers flock here year-round to commune with nature among 9 miles of trails and diverse upland and wetland habitats, including grasslands, shrublands, wooded swamps, and freshwater ponds. There's an abandoned naval air station on Ninigret Pond, the state's largest coastal salt pond, and a fine place to watch the sunset. Wear blaze orange while hiking between November and January, when permitted hunters are allowed to cull white-tailed deer. Explore an impressive collection of wildlife and natural history displays at the Kettle Pond Visitor Center on the southbound side of U.S. 1 at 50 Bend Road. ⊠ *Ninigret Entrance Rd., off U.S. 1* ☎ *401/364–9124* ⊕ *www.fws.gov/refuge/ninigret* ☞ *Free.*

Ninigret Park

BEACH—SIGHT | FAMILY | This 227-acre park off Old Post Road, formerly a World War II–era naval air training base, now features picnic grounds, ball fields, a playground, a bike path, tennis and basketball courts, a criterium bicycle course, nature trails, a disc-golf course, and a 3-acre spring-fed swimming pond. The Charlestown Seafood Festival is held here in August. ⊠ *5 Park La., off U.S. 1* ☎ *401/364–1222* ⊕ *www.charlestownri.org* ☞ *Free.*

🏖 Beaches

Blue Shutters Town Beach

BEACH—SIGHT | With wonderful views of Block Island Sound, Blue Shutters is a popular escape for beachcombers and quietude seekers who don't mind paying a bit extra for soft sand, sea, and serenity. Beachgoers can see Block Island and Long Island from the shaded deck of the pavilion. Beach-accessible wheelchairs are available at no cost. **Amenities:** lifeguards; showers; toilets; parking (fee). **Best for:** walking; sunsets. ⊠ *469 E. Beach Rd.* ☎ *401/364–1222* ⊕ *www. charlestownri.org* ☞ *Nonresident parking from $20.*

East Beach

BEACH—SIGHT | This tranquil and unspoiled barrier beach spans 3 narrow miles of shoreline that fronts and separates Ninigret Pond from the ocean. East Beach stands in stark contrast to Narragansett's bustling Scarborough Beach. Parking is limited, and the lot fills up quickly. Be careful when swimming: the ocean side is known for riptides. **Amenities:** lifeguards; parking (fee); toilets. **Best for:** solitude; walking. ⊠ *East Beach Rd., off U.S. 1* ☎ *401/322–8910* ⊕ *www.riparks. com/Locations/LocationEastBeach.html* ⏱ *Nonresident parking from $12.*

🍴 Restaurants

The Charlestown Rathskeller

$$ | AMERICAN | The hand-cut fries at this former speakeasy hidden in the woods are revered across southern New England, and steaks and burgers are big and cooked to perfection. Lawn games like horseshoes, bocce, and corn hole; an enormous stone fire pit; and the "Down Back" outdoor music stage make the grounds feel like the backyard of your dreams. **Known for:** the coldest beer in

Rhode Island Treats

Clam Cakes. It's not summer for locals without a pilgrimage to a clam shack for these hunks of fried dough with briny, meaty clams inside. Pair them with the chowder of your choice.

Coffee Milk. The official state drink, coffee milk is like chocolate milk but made instead with coffee-flavored syrup, preferably Autocrat Coffee Syrup.

Del's Frozen Lemonade. You can get one of these refreshingly cold slushes from one of many Del's trucks making the rounds in the summer or at a Del's storefront.

NY System Wieners. Try a hot dog "done all the way": topped with meat sauce, mustard, onions, and celery salt. (They're said to be a great hangover cure.)

Rhode Island Johnnycakes. Essentially unleavened cornmeal pancakes typically served for breakfast in diners—or anywhere in South County—johnnycakes can be thick or thin and served with butter, maple syrup, honey, fruit, or powdered sugar.

Rhode Island-Style Calamari. This dish of lightly fried squid with hot cherry peppers and garlic is the official state appetizer for a good reason: the Port of Galilee in Narragansett lands tens of millions of pounds of squid annually.

Rhode Island; schnitzels, stroganoff, and pretzels; seafood selections, too. $ *Average main: $24* ⊠ *489A Old Coach Rd.* ☎ *401/792–1000* ⊕ *www.thecharlestownrathskeller.com.*

🏃 Activities

BOATING
Ocean House Marina
BOATING | This full-service marina on scenic Ninigret Pond offers luxury boat rentals, fishing supplies, fuel, and maintenance service. ⊠ *60 Town Dock Rd., off U.S. 1* ☎ *401/364–6040* ⊕ *oceanhousemarina.com.*

🛍 Shopping

Fantastic Umbrella Factory
GIFTS/SOUVENIRS | FAMILY | With a hippie vibe, the kid- and couple–friendly Fantastic Umbrella Factory contains a handful of rustic shops built around a wild garden and bamboo forest. Unusual flowers, succulents, and other plants are for sale, along with interesting clothing and jewelry, CBD products, soy candles, creative pottery, Native American handcrafts, quirky gifts, and incense. For $3 you can acquire a bag full of seeds to feed the fenced-in emus, guinea hens, and ducks. The Lunch Box food truck serves elevated comfort food. ⊠ *4820 Old Post Rd., off U.S. 1* ☎ *401/364–1060* ⊕ *www.fantasticumbrellafactory.com.*

South Kingstown

10 miles northeast of Charlestown.

People often discover South Kingstown through the University of Rhode Island but return for its historic charm, arts-oriented community, great surfing beaches, and outdoors lifestyle. Almost a third of South Kingstown's 57 square miles is protected open space, allowing the town to maintain a rural character even as the population has doubled. There are two beaches, three rivers, several salt ponds, a 7-mile bike path, and numerous hiking trails, making it a great place for outdoors enthusiasts. ■TIP→ Locals don't refer to it as South Kingstown. They use the names of its 14 distinct villages, including Wakefield, Peace Dale, Matunuck, Snug Harbor, West Kingston, and Kingston, home of the University of Rhode Island's main campus. Note that Kingston and West Kingston omit South Kingstown's "w."

Beaches

★ East Matunuck State Beach

BEACH—SIGHT | FAMILY | Its vigorous waves, white sands, and views of Block Island on crystal-clear days account for the popularity of this 144-acre beach. Crabs, mussels, and starfish populate the rock reef that extends to the right of the strand, inspiring visitors to channel their inner marine biologist. A wind turbine provides power for the Daniel L. O'Brien Pavilion, named for a police officer killed in the line of duty while rescuing people stranded in this area during Hurricane Carol in 1954. ⚠ Currents can be strong, so keep an eye on kids. Amenities: food and drink; lifeguards; parking (fee); showers; toilets. Best for: swimming; walking. ✉ 950 Succotash Rd. ☎ 401/789–8374 ⊕ www.riparks.com/Locations/LocationEastMatunuck.html ⚓ Nonresident parking: from $12.

South Kingstown Town Beach

BEACH—SIGHT | FAMILY | The ⅓-mile-long town beach—with a playground, a boardwalk, a volleyball court, and picnic tables—cannot be seen from the road and doesn't fill as quickly as the nearby state beaches. Amenities: lifeguards; parking (fee); toilets. Best for: sunset; swimming; walking. ✉ 719 Matunuck Beach Rd. ☎ 401/789–9331 ⊕ southkingstownri.com/Facilities/Facility/Details/Town-Beach-8 ⊙ Closed after Labor Day–late May.

Restaurants

★ Matunuck Oyster Bar

$$ | SEAFOOD | Shuckers are hard at work at the raw bar in this awesome waterside restaurant, an offshoot of the nearby Matunuck Oyster Farm. This year-round business committed to serving fresh, local produce, along with farm-raised and wild-caught seafood, draws a crowd—snag an outside table if you can. Known for: alfresco dining at sunset; mainly seafood menu but a handful of other choices; raw oysters raised right here are sweet, on the smaller side, and beginner-friendly. $ Average main: $22 ✉ 629 Succotash Rd. ☎ 401/783–4202 ⊕ www.rhodyoysters.com.

Mews Tavern

$ | AMERICAN | This cheery tavern always has three bars and 69 beers on tap, but hungry folks flock here for burgers and tasty pizzas—like the Pink Panther, which is topped with chicken, prosciutto, and pasta in a house-made pink vodka sauce. Also on the menu are Mexican dishes, mac and cheeses with local Whalers beer in the sauce, and other comfort foods. Known for: going strong since 1947; appetizers, snacks, full entrées, and more; rare, limited, and local beers with "no crap on tap". $ Average main: $15 ✉ 456 Main St., Wakefield ☎ 401/783–9370 ⊕ www.mewstavern.com.

Nightlife

For an extensive calendar of South County events pick up the free South County Life magazine or browse ⊕ www.independentri.com/calendar.

Ocean Mist

BARS/PUBS | The Ocean Mist has a beachfront deck where you can watch surfers on the point and catch some rays while enjoying a beer, a burger, or breakfast. Bands, including rock, throwback pop, and reggae acts, perform nightly in summer and on weekends the rest of the year. Considered one of Rhode Island's best hangouts, "the Mist," as it's called by locals, is that cool beach bar that every coastal area has—or wishes it had. ✉ *895 Matunuck Beach Rd., Matunuck* ☎ *401/782–3740* ⊕ *www.oceanmist.net.*

🎭 Performing Arts

★ Theatre By The Sea

THEATER | FAMILY | Directors, choreographers, and performers come from New York City to present a season of summer musicals, concerts, and events (including a children's festival) in an old 500-seat barn theater a quarter mile from the ocean. This is high-quality summer stock. Arrive early for dinner at the bistro on the property and to enjoy the stunning gardens. ✉ *364 Cards Pond Rd., Wakefield* ☎ *401/782–8587* ⊕ *www.theatrebythe-sea.com* 🎫 *Varied* ⊗ *Closed early Sept.– late May.*

🏃 Activities

BIKING
William C. O'Neill Bike Path

BICYCLING | FAMILY | This scenic 8-mile paved route, also known as South County Bike Path, begins at Kingston Train Station in West Kingston and travels through farmlands, the Great Swamp, and downtown Peace Dale and Wakefield, ending close enough to Narragansett Town Beach to reach the shore via local roads. Public art, including a sanctioned graffiti tunnel, decorates the path. Where it crosses Main Street in Wakefield, a comfort station with restrooms is open during daylight hours. ✉ *1 Railroad Ave.* ☎ *401/789–9301* ⊕ *www.southcounty-bikepath.org.*

Narragansett

6 miles east of South Kingstown, 30 miles south of Providence.

A summer resort destination during the Victorian era, Narragansett still has as its main landmark The Towers, the last remaining section of the 1886 Narragansett Pier Casino designed by McKim, Mead & White. The town is much quieter now, but it has beautiful beaches and remains home to a large commercial fishing fleet. Take a scenic drive down Ocean Road to see the churning Atlantic and grand old shingle-style homes. You'll eventually wind up at Point Judith Lighthouse, which has been in continuous operation since the 19th century.

Planning

TOURS
Frances Fleet

BOAT TOURS | FAMILY | With four boats and expert captains who know just where the fish are biting and the whales are spouting, this tour company offers myriad on-water adventures. In July and August, whale-watching excursions aboard the 105-foot *Lady Frances* take you through the impressive Block Island Wind Farm out to where you'll get a chance to spot finback whales and other species. Sightings are guaranteed, or you'll receive a voucher for a future sailing. The company also conducts a range of fishing trips, from beginner-friendly fluke chases to late night squid hunts. ✉ *Frances Fleet, 33 State St.* ☎ *401/783–4988, 800/662–2824* ⊕ *www.francesfleet.com* 🎫 *From $50.*

Seven B's V

BOAT TOURS | Year-round, this tour service takes both novices and experienced anglers on memorable voyages. Even if you don't reel in a hefty cod or a googly eyed fluke, you'll learn about the species that inhabit these waters and appreciate your next fish dinner all the more.

Point Judith Lighthouse is just one of 21 such beacons in the Ocean State.

The 80-foot *Seven B's V* holds up to 113 passengers and departs daily, conditions permitting. ✉ *Port of Galilee Dock RR, 30 State St.* ☎ *401/789–9250, 800/371–3474* ⊕ *www.sevenbs.com.*

👁 Sights

Adventureland Narragansett
AMUSEMENT PARK/WATER PARK | FAMILY | Kids love the bumper boats, nautical-theme miniature golf course, batting cages, carousel, go-kart track, and other carnival-like attractions, which all add up to great fun. ✉ *112 Point Judith Rd. (Rte. 108)* ☎ *401/789–0030* ⊕ *www.adventurelandri.com* 🎫 *From $2* 🕐 *Closed mid-Oct.–mid-Apr.*

Point Judith Lighthouse
LIGHTHOUSE | From the Port of Galilee, it's a short drive to this 1857 lighthouse and a beautiful ocean view. Because the lighthouse is an active Coast Guard Station, only the grounds are open to the public. At times when the grounds are closed, head back out Ocean Road and watch for a tiny white sign on the left for the Fisherman's Memorial. A dirt road drive leads to this elevated park, from which you'll have a spectacular view of the lighthouse, as well as to Camp Cronin, a secret beach and fishing area. ✉ *1460 Ocean Rd.* ☎ *401/789–0444* 🎫 *Free.*

Port of Galilee
BEACH—SIGHT | FAMILY | This little corner of Narragansett is a working fishing village, where you can eat lobster on a deck overlooking the wharf, go for a swim at one of two state beaches, or watch fishermen unload their catch and sometimes even buy from them right on the docks. This is also the location of the mainland terminal for the ferry service to Block Island. ✉ *Great Island Rd., off Galilee Escape Rd., west from Rte. 108* ☎ *401/789–1044* ⊕ *www.narragansettri.gov/383/port-of-galilee.*

South County Museum

MUSEUM | **FAMILY** | On part of Rhode Island's Civil War-era governor William Sprague's 19th-century estate, now a town park, this museum founded in 1933 holds 25,000 artifacts dating from pre-European settlement to the mid-20th century. Six exhibit buildings include a print shop, a blacksmith forge, a carpentry shop, and a horse-drawn carriage barn. A living-history farm has Romney sheep, Nubian goats, and a heritage flock of Rhode Island Red chickens, the state bird. ■TIP→ **Attending the annual chick hatching is an Independence Day tradition for local families.** ✉ *115 Strathmore St.* ☎ *401/783–5400* ⊕ *www.southcounty-museum.org* ☞ *$12* ⊘ *Closed Oct.–Apr., Sun.–Thurs.*

⊕ Beaches

Narragansett Town Beach

BEACH—SIGHT | **FAMILY** | This beloved and lively beach is perfect for surfing, sunbathing, people-watching, sandcastle making, crab hunting, and strolling its half-mile length. A sea wall (with free on-street parking) stretches along Ocean Road and attracts an eclectic crowd, including guitarists and motorcyclists. Covering approximately 19 acres, Narragansett Town Beach has a beautiful sandy beachfront, but it is the only beach in the state that charges fees for both admission (ages 12 and up) and parking. **Amenities:** food and drink; lifeguards; parking (fee); showers; toilets. **Best for:** surfing; swimming; nostalgic views. ■TIP→ **The beach has seven ADA surf chairs, offered on a first-come, first-served basis.** ✉ *39 Boston Neck Rd.* ☎ *401/783–6430* ⊕ *www.narragansettri.gov/323/Narragansett-Town-Beach* ☞ *Beach $10; parking from $10.*

Roger W. Wheeler State Beach

BEACH—SIGHT | **FAMILY** | This beach—which some locals still call Sand Hill Cove, even though the name changed decades ago—has calm, warm water and find white sand that slopes gently into the water. It's a perennial favorite for parents with young children. **Amenities:** food and drink; lifeguards; playground; parking (fee); showers; toilets. **Best for:** classic vibe; family time; swimming; walking. ✉ *100 Sand Hill Cove Rd.* ☎ *401/789–8374* ⊕ *www.riparks.com/Locations/LocationRogerWheeler.html* ☞ *Parking: from $12.*

Salty Brine State Beach

BEACH—SIGHT | Formerly known as Galilee State Beach, Salty Brine was renamed in 1990 for a Rhode Island radio legend. It's a small but popular destination, especially for foodies. Located near the state's largest commercial fishing port of Galilee, Salty Brine is permeated with the sights, sounds, and scents of Rhode Island's daily fishing culture. The beach, near bustling seafood restaurants, provides the best seat in the state for viewing the steady parade of ferries, fishing boats, and charters moving in and out of the channel while noshing on a lobster roll or fried clams. People flock to the beach for the annual Blessing of the Fleet parade of vessels on the last weekend in July. **Amenities:** food and drink; lifeguards; parking (fee); showers; toilets. **Best for:** saltwater fishing; sunset; swimming; walking. ✉ *254 Great Island Rd.* ☎ *401/789–8374* ⊕ *www.riparks.com/Locations/LocationSaltyBrine.html* ☞ *Parking: from $12.*

⊕ Restaurants

★ Aunt Carrie's

$$$ | **SEAFOOD** | **FAMILY** | Family owned and operated for four generations, this iconic Point Judith indoor-outdoor dining spot has been a must for Rhode Islanders every summer since it opened in 1920. Its peerless, waterside location and unpretentious atmosphere are the main draws, along with favorites like steamers, fish-and-chips, and namesake Carrie Cooper's own invention: clam cakes. **Known for:** complete shore dinners;

delicious pies based on Carrie Cooper's recipes; picnic tables and an ice-cream stand across the street. $ *Average main: $25* ⌂ *1240 Ocean Rd., Point Judith* ☎ *401/783–7930* ⊕ *www.auntcarriesri. com* ⊘ *Closed Oct.–Mar.*

★ Coast Guard House

$$$ | SEAFOOD | Built in 1888 as a U.S. Life-Saving Service Station, this restaurant has been nearly destroyed twice by storms—by Hurricane Bob in 1991 and Superstorm Sandy in 2012. **Known for:** raw bar and local seafood; alfresco drinks and dining on the deck; stunning view of Rhode Island Sound. $ *Average main: $27* ⌂ *40 Ocean Rd.* ☎ *401/789–0700* ⊕ *www.thecoastguardhouse.com.*

Crazy Burger Cafe & Juice Bar

$ | ECLECTIC | Vegetarians, vegans, and omnivores flock to this funky café not far from Narragansett Town Beach for smoothies, creative juice blends, and breakfast served until 4 pm daily. White Christmas lights and colorful lanterns are part of the indoor and covered patio decor, as is a red phone booth behind the counter that houses condiments (like the house-made ketchup). **Known for:** extensive menu; often a wait to be seated; BYOB, but there is a corkage fee. $ *Average main: $14* ⌂ *144 Boon St.* ☎ *401/783–1810* ⊕ *www.crazyburger. com.*

★ George's of Galilee

$$ | SEAFOOD | Owned by the same family since 1948, this local landmark near Salty Brine State Beach has its own private patch of sand and beach blanket service in the summertime. Try traditional Rhode Island favorites, including calamari, clam cakes, and "stuffies" (stuffed quahogs), as well as raw bar treats like oyster shooters. **Known for:** alfresco dining with spectacular waterfront views; summertime takeout clam shack and beach service; fish bowl cocktails. $ *Average main: $23* ⌂ *250 Sand Hill Cove Rd., Port of Galilee* ☎ *401/783–2306* ⊕ *www. georgesofgalilee.com.*

Spain of Narragansett

$$$ | SPANISH | This Spanish restaurant earns high marks for beautifully prepared and presented food and deft service. Arched architectural features and greenery help create a Mediterranean mood, and in summer you can dine on a patio anchored by a three-tier fountain and a massive brick fireplace. **Known for:** traditional seafood paella (for two); impressive wine list—plus sangria; well-run restaurant with upscale, professional service. $ *Average main:* ⌂ *1144 Ocean Rd.* ☎ *401/783–9770* ⊕ *www.spainri.com* ⊘ *Closed Mon. and Tues. No lunch.*

Trio

$$ | SEAFOOD | Close to Narragansett Town Beach, this welcoming place emphasizes seafood and classic comfort food favorites and artisanal pizzas. The festive patio is where you'll want to be on a bright day, sipping summer flavors like watermelon, cucumber, and peach mixed into refreshingly creative cocktails. **Known for:** easy, free parking; more than 20 wines by the glass; patio dining in summer. $ *Average main: $22* ⌂ *15 Kingstown Rd.* ☎ *401/792–4333* ⊕ *www. trio-ri.com* ⊘ *No lunch weekdays.*

🛏 Hotels

★ The Break

$$ | HOTEL | Narragansett's sole upscale boutique hotel has a laid-back boho surfer vibe—minus the feel of the cramped VW Vanagon—and on a clear day, you can see the Newport Bridge and Block Island from the rooftop bar. **Pros:** complimentary gourmet small-plates breakfast; Chair Five, the restaurant named after a gathering spot at the town beach, serves locally sourced seasonal cuisine; spa services available. **Cons:** a hike to the beach; small signs, you might miss it the first drive by; two-night minimum on summer weekends. $ *Rooms from: $279* ⌂ *1208 Ocean Rd.* ☎ *401/363–9800* ⊕ *www. thebreakhotel.com* ⤳ *16 rooms* ⊚ *Free breakfast.*

Activities

SURFING

Narragansett Surf and Skate Shop
SURFING | This shop rents surfboards, SUPs, and wet suits and offers individual and group surfing or standup paddleboard lessons. ⊠ *74 Narragansett Ave.* ☎ *401/789–7890* ⊕ *http://narragansettsurfandskate.com.*

Jamestown

31 miles south of Providence, 5 miles west of Newport.

Surrounded by Narragansett Bay's East and West passages, Conanicut Island comprises the town of Jamestown. About 9 miles long and 1 mile wide, the island is home to beautiful state parks, historic Beavertail Lighthouse, farmland, and a downtown village with a quaint mix of shops and restaurants.

Sights

Beavertail State Park
MUSEUM | **FAMILY** | Water conditions range from tranquil to harrowing at this park straddling the southern tip of Conanicut Island. On a clear, calm day, however, the park's craggy shoreline seems intended for sunning, hiking, and climbing. There are portable restrooms open daily, year-round. On several dates (May–October), the Beavertail Lighthouse Museum Association opens the 1856 **Beavertail Lighthouse,** the nation's third-oldest lighthouse, letting you climb the tower's 49 steps (and then a 7-foot ladder) to enjoy the magnificent panorama from the observation catwalk. A museum occupies the lighthouse keeper's former quarters; the lighthouse's last "beehive" Fresnel lens is on display. The old fog signal building has a saltwater aquarium with local species of fish. Both are open seasonally. ⊠ *Beavertail Rd.* ☎ *401/884–2010* ⊕ *www.riparks.com/Locations/LocationBeavertail.html* ⊠ *Free.*

Jamestown Fire Department Memorial Museum
MUSEUM | **FAMILY** | A working 1859 hand pumper and an 1894 horse-drawn steam pump are among the antique equipment at this informal firefighting equipment display in a garage that once housed the fire company. Inquire at the fire station next door if the place is locked. ⊠ *50 Narragansett Ave.* ☎ *401/423–0062* ⊕ *www.jamestownfd.com/museum.html* ⊠ *Free.*

Jamestown Windmill
WINDMILL | This English-designed smock windmill built in 1787 ground corn for more than 100 years. One of the most photographed sights on the island, the structure, named for its resemblance to farmers' smocks of yore, still works. In summer and early fall, you can enter the three-story, octagonal structure and see the 18th-century technology. ⊠ *North Rd., north of Weeden La.* ☎ *401/423–0784 summer, 401/423–7202 year-round* ⊕ *www.jamestownhistoricalsociety. org* ⊙ *Closed mid-Oct.–mid-June and Mon.–Thurs.*

Watson Farm
FARM/RANCH | **FAMILY** | This Historic New England–operated farm on Narragansett Bay, in existence since 1789, is still a working farm. The farmers use sustainable practices to raise heritage-breed cows and sheep and to produce wool blankets for local markets. They also host educational programs; for example, during the annual Sheep Shearing Day in May you can visit the baby lambs, see the flock being shorn by local shearers, and watch spinning and weaving demonstrations. You can also stroll more than 2 miles of trails and view seasonal farm activities. ⊠ *455 North Rd.* ☎ *401/423–0005* ⊕ *www.historicnewengland.org/ property/watson-farm* ⊠ *$10* ⊙ *Closed Sun.–Fri.*

🍴 Restaurants

★ Simpatico Jamestown
$$ | **AMERICAN** | With nine indoor-outdoor dining rooms and a menu of seasonal classic American cuisine prepared with flair, it's tough to have a bad evening at this casually elegant restaurant. Couples looking for romance should seek out the Beech Tree room, with its tree fort ambience and an incredible light show as the moon and stars sparkle through the tree leaves. **Known for:** competition for tables; shareable appetizers; photo-worthy decor and dishes. [$] *Average main: $23* ✉ *13 Narragansett Ave.* ☎ *401/423–2000* 🌐 *www.simpaticojamestown.com* 🕒 *Closed Mon.–Thurs. and New Year's Eve–mid-Mar. No lunch.*

🛏 Hotels

East Bay Bed & Breakfast
$$ | **B&B/INN** | This 1892 Victorian is peaceful day and night, even though it's only a block from Jamestown's two main streets and ferry wharf. **Pros:** quick, easy access to Newport; large rooms; fine, Massachusetts-made Matouk bedding. **Cons:** small showers; only three parking spaces; no kids under 13. [$] *Rooms from: $225* ✉ *14 Union St.* ☎ *401/423–0330, 800/243–1107* 🌐 *www.eastbaybnb.com* 🔑 *5 rooms* 🍽 *Free breakfast.*

Newport

34 miles south of Providence, 72 miles south of Boston.

The Gilded Age mansions on Bellevue Avenue are the go-to attraction for many Newport visitors. These ornate, late-19th-century "cottages," designed for very wealthy New Yorkers, are almost obscenely grand. Their owners—Vanderbilts, Astors, Belmonts, and other budding aristocrats who made Newport their summer playground for a mere six- to eight weeks each year—helped establish the best young American architects and precipitated the arrival of the New York Yacht Club, which turned Newport into the sailing capital of the world.

Newport's music festivals are another draw: Bob Dylan famously went electric at the Newport Folk Festival; in recent years, the outdoor festival has featured up-and-coming and internationally known indie and folk bands. In its earlier days, the Newport Jazz Festival hosted the likes of Miles Davis and Frank Sinatra; today it remains a showcase of traditional and avant-garde jazz. The Newport Music Festival brings classical music to the mansions, many of the artists and ensembles making their American debuts.

History buffs are enthralled by the large collection of Colonial-era architecture—Trinity Episcopal Church, Touro Synagogue, and the Colony House among them—reveling in these monuments to Newport's past as a haven for seekers of religious freedom.

Pedestrian-friendly Newport has so much else to offer in such a relatively small geographical area—beaches, seafood restaurants, galleries, shopping, and cultural life. Summer can be extremely busy, but fall and spring are almost as nice and far less crowded, and winter by the sea can be magical and soul-soothing.

GETTING HERE AND AROUND

You'll need to cross at least one of four major bridges to reach Newport. The largest is the Claiborne Pell Newport Bridge, spanning Narragansett Bay's East Passage via Route 138 and linking the island community of Jamestown with Newport. The toll is $4 both ways for motorists with or without an EZ-Pass transponder. Newport anchors Aquidneck Island, also home to the towns of Middletown and Portsmouth. From the north end of Portsmouth, Route 24 takes you across the Sakonnet River Bridge to Tiverton. Follow Route 77 south through Tiverton to reach quiet Little Compton. From the north-western end of Portsmouth, you cross the Mt. Hope Bridge to reach the charming town of Bristol in Bristol County, home to the oldest continuously held Independence Day celebration in the country. The Jamestown Verrazzano Bridge connects Jamestown to North Kingstown over Narragansett Bay's West Passage.

FERRY

Visitors headed to Newport from the west can save themselves the hassle of parking in Newport, as well as the Newport Bridge toll, by parking their cars for free (if they're lucky to find street parking) in Jamestown and boarding the Jamestown Newport Ferry. Conanicut Marine operates this open-air passenger ferry from 1 East Ferry Wharf in Jamestown and offers a free shuttle service from a large paid parking area at 260 Conanicus Avenue. The ferry runs daily, early June–mid-October. The ferry links the village of Jamestown to Rose Island, Ft. Adams State Park, Perrotti Park, and Ann Street Pier. A $26 round-trip rate is good for all day, but one-way passage rates and bicycle/stroller rates are available. In the summer, ferry service starts at 9 am in Jamestown, and the last run leaves Newport around 9:30 pm. The ferry operates on an abbreviated schedule in spring and fall.

Oldport Marine Services operates a harbor shuttle service Monday–Thursday noon–6 and on Friday and weekends 11–7 ($12 hop on/off all day). The shuttle lands at Perrotti Park, Bowen's Wharf, Ann Street Pier, the Sail Newport dock, Ft. Adams, and Goat Island.

Seastreak operates seasonal ferry service (Memorial Day–Columbus Day) between Providence (India Point) and Newport (Perrotti Park). The fare is $11 each way, and parking is free at the Providence Ferry Terminal; a complimentary shuttle bus makes several trips between the ferry terminal and the train station, convention center, and downtown.

TAXI

Orange Cab of Newport connects Aquidneck Island towns with the West Kingston train station and T. F. Green Airport in Warwick.

PARKING

In Newport several lots around town offer pay parking. The largest and most economical is the Gateway parking lot and garage at 23 America's Cup Avenue, where the rate is $2 for the first half-hour, $1.50 for each additional half-hour, from June–October. Parking is free November–April. Street parking can be difficult to find in summer.

FESTIVALS

★ Newport Folk Festival

CONCERTS | The Newport Folk Festival has been going strong since 1959, when it introduced musicians such as Joan Baez and the Kingston Trio. Held the last full weekend in July, the festival's acts now span folk, blues, country, bluegrass, folk rock, alt-country, indie folk, folk punk, even reggae. Lineups mix veteran performers like Sheryl Crow, Phil Lesh, and Grace Potter with younger stars like Hozier, Molly Tuttle, and Bonny Light Horseman. The festival is held rain or shine, and seating is general admission on a large, uncovered lawn. Purchase tickets early. ⊠ *Ft. Adams State Park, 90 Ft. Adams Dr.* ☎ *401/566–4125* ⊕ *www. newportfolk.org* ⌧ *From $90.*

Newport Jazz Festival

MUSIC | The grandfather of all jazz festivals, founded in 1954, takes place over three days at the end of July and/or beginning of August. The festival showcases both jazz veterans and up-and-coming artists, playing traditional and avant-garde styles. Performers in recent years have included Herbie Hancock, Wynton Marsalis, Dianne Reeves, Kendrick Scott, Dee Dee Bridgewater, and Diana Krall. The festival is held rain or shine, with open-air lawn seating. ⊠ *Ft. Adams State Park, 90 Ft. Adams Dr.* ☎ *401/848–5055* ⊕ *www.newportjazz.org* ⌧ *From $79.*

★ Newport Music Festival

CONCERTS | A great way to experience one of the Newport mansions is at one of the 30 or so classical music concerts presented every July during the Newport Music Festival. Performances by world-class artists are scheduled at the Elms, the Breakers, and other venues. Selected works are chosen from 19th-century chamber music, vocal repertoire, Romantic-era piano literature, and even Broadway and popular music. Every year features a tribute to a composer and a free family concert. ✉ *Newport* ☎ *401/849–0700* ⊕ *www.newportmusic.org.*

TOURS

More than a dozen companies run boat tours of Newport Harbor and Narragansett Bay. Outings usually run two hours and cost anywhere from $25 to $100 per person.

★ Classic Cruises of Newport

BOAT TOURS | FAMILY | You have your choice of two vessels at Classic Cruises of Newport: the 19th-century-style *Madeleine* is a 72-foot schooner that cruises around the harbor; the 1929 yacht *Rum Runner II,* built for two New Jersey mobsters to carry "hooch," evokes the days of smuggling along the coast. Choose from a variety of tours, including gorgeous sunset sails. ✉ *24 Bannister's Wharf* ☎ *401/847–0298* ⊕ *www.cruisenewport.com* 🚢 *From $28.*

Newport Historical Society

WALKING TOURS | Various guided walking tours focus on Newport's four centuries of American history. The 60-minute tours are available April–December, weather permitting, as well as during Winter Festival in February. ✉ *Newport Historical Society Museum & Shop, 127 Thames St.* ☎ *401/841–8770* ⊕ *www.newporthistorytours.org* 🚢 *From $15.*

Sightsailing of Newport

BOAT TOURS | From May through early November, the 80-foot schooner *Aquidneck,* 46-foot sloop *Sightsailer,* and 34-foot sailboat *Starlight* depart Bowen's Wharf on 105-minute or longer public or private tours of Newport Harbor and Narragansett Bay. ✉ *32 Bowen's Wharf* ☎ *401/849–3333* ⊕ *www.sightsailing.com* 🚢 *From $33.*

★ Viking Tours of Newport

BUS TOURS | Viking offers 90-minute narrated trolley tours of Newport daily, April–October, Friday and Saturday November–December, and on Tuesday, Friday, and Saturday, January–March. ✉ *23 America's Cup Ave.* ☎ *401/847–6921* ⊕ *www.vikingtoursnewport.com* 🚢 *$25.*

ESSENTIALS

TRANSPORTATION CONTACTS **Jamestown Newport Ferry.** ✉ *1 E. Ferry Wharf, Jamestown* ☎ *401/423–9900* ⊕ *www.jamestownnewportferry.com.* **Oldport Marine Services.** ✉ *1 Sayer's Wharf* ☎ *401/847–9109* ⊕ *www.oldportmarine.com.* **Seastreak New England.** ✉ *25 India St., Providence* ☎ *800/262–8743* ⊕ *www.seastreak.com.*

VISITOR INFORMATION **Discover Newport.** ✉ *23 America's Cup Ave.* ☎ *401/849–8048, 800/326–6030* ⊕ *www.discovernewport.org.*

Downtown Newport and Historic Hill

Downtown Newport and, just beyond, the city's Historic Hill neighborhood are the city's Colonial heart. More than 200 pre-Revolutionary buildings, mostly private residences, remain on the streets running uphill from Newport Harbor; but you'll also encounter 19th-century landmarks such as St. Mary's Church; at the corner of Spring Street and Memorial Boulevard West, where John Fitzgerald

Kennedy and Jacqueline Bouvier were married on September 12, 1953. The waterfront is beautiful, and there are many boutiques and restaurants on the very active wharfs that jut into the harbor. In summer, traffic is thick and narrow one-way streets can be frustrating to navigate; consider parking in a pay lot and exploring the area on foot.

Sights

Colony House

HISTORIC SITE | Completed in 1739, this National Historic Landmark on Washington Square was the center of political activity in Colonial Newport. The Declaration of Independence was read from its steps on July 20, 1776, and British troops later used this structure as a barracks during their occupation of Newport. In 1781, George Washington met here with the French general Rochambeau, cementing an alliance that led to the American victory at Yorktown. Colony House served as Rhode Island's primary statehouse until 1901, when the new statehouse opened in Providence. The Newport Historical Society manages the Colony House and offers guided tours. ⊠ *Washington Sq.* ☎ *401/841–8770* ⊕ *newporthistory.org* 🖾 *$15.*

Great Friends Meeting House

BUILDING | The oldest surviving house of worship in Rhode Island reflects the quiet reserve and steadfast faith of Colonial Quakers, who gathered here to discuss theology, peaceful alternatives to war, and the abolition of slavery. Built in 1699, the two-story structure has wide-plank floors, simple benches, a balcony, and a wood-beam ceiling. ⊠ *21 Farewell St.* ☎ *401/846–0813* ⊕ *newporthistory.org* 🖾 *Tour $15.*

Hunter House

HOUSE | The oldest house owned and maintained by the Preservation Society of Newport County, constructed between 1748 and 1754, Hunter House served as the Revolutionary War headquarters of French admiral Charles Louis d'Arsac de Ternay after the home's Loyalist owner fled the city. Featuring a balustraded gambrel roof and heavy stud construction, it is an excellent example of early Georgian Colonial architecture. The carved pineapple over the doorway was a symbol of welcome throughout Colonial America. A collection of Colonial furniture includes pieces crafted by Newport's famed 18th-century Townsend-Goddard family of cabinetmakers and paintings by Cosmo Alexander, Gilbert Stuart, and Samuel King. The house is named for William Hunter, a U.S. Senator and President Andrew Jackson's chargé d'affaires to Brazil. ⊠ *54 Washington St.* ☎ *401/847–1000* ⊕ *www.newportmansions.org* 🖾 *$35* ⊘ *Closed mid-Oct.–mid-May.*

Museum of Newport History at Brick Market

MUSEUM | **FAMILY** | The restored 1762 Brick Market building houses the Museum of Newport History that explores the city's social and economic influences. Antiques such as the printing press of James Franklin (Ben's brother) inspire the imagination. Designed by Peter Harrison, who was responsible as well for Touro Synagogue and the Redwood Library, the building also served as a theater and a town hall. Today, besides the museum exhibits, there's a very nice gift shop and the Newport Visitors' Information Center, which is a departure point for guided walking tours of Newport. ⊠ *127 Thames St.* ☎ *401/841–8770* ⊕ *www.newporthistory.org* 🖾 *$5 suggested donation.*

Newport Art Museum

MUSEUM | Founded in 1912, the museum today spans three buildings: the Cushing/Morris Gallery, the Coleman Center for Creative Studies, and the 1864 Griswold House, a National Historic Landmark designed by Richard Morris Hunt. In the museum's permanent collection are works by Fitz Henry Lane, George Inness, William Trost Richards, John La Farge, Nancy Elizabeth Prophet, Gilbert Stuart, and Helena Sturtevant, as well as contemporary artists like Dale Chihuly, Howard Ben Tré, and Joseph Norman. ⊠ *76 Bellevue Ave.* ☎ *401/848–8200* ⊕ *www.newportartmuseum.org* ⊠ *$15* ⊙ *Closed Mon.*

Redwood Library & Athenaeum

HISTORIC SITE | In 1747, Abraham Redwood gave 500 pounds sterling to found a library of arts and sciences; three years later, this Georgian Palladian–style building opened with 751 titles. More than half of the original collection vanished during the British occupation of Newport, though most of it has been recovered or replaced. Paintings on display include five portraits by Gilbert Stuart. Look for the portrait of the Colonial governor's wife, whose low neckline later led to the commissioning of Stuart's daughter, Jane, to paint a bouquet over her cleavage. Self-guided tour booklets are available. The library presents talks by authors, musicians, and historians. ⊠ *50 Bellevue Ave.* ☎ *401/847–0292* ⊕ *www. redwoodlibrary.org* ⊠ *$10.*

★ Touro Synagogue

HISTORIC SITE | In 1658, more than a dozen Jewish families whose ancestors had fled Spain and Portugal during the Inquisition founded a congregation in Newport. A century later, Peter Harrison designed this two-story Palladian house of worship for them. George Washington wrote a famous letter to the group in which he pledged the new American nation would give "to bigotry no sanction, to persecution no assistance." The oldest surviving synagogue in the country, Touro was dedicated in 1763 and its simple exterior and elegant interior remain virtually unchanged. A small trapdoor in the platform upon which the Torah is read symbolizes the days of persecution when Jews were forced to worship in secret. The John L. Loeb Visitors Center has two floors of state-of-the-art exhibits on early American Jewish life and Newport's history of religious freedom.

■**TIP**➔ **Tickets, available at the Loeb Visitors Center, are required for entry into the synagogue.** ⊠ *Loeb Visitors Center, 52 Spring St.* ☎ *401/847–4794* ⊕ *www. tourosynagogue.org* ⊠ *$12* ⌖ *Closed Sat. May–Oct., Closed Mon.–Sat. Nov.– Apr. No tours on Jewish holidays.*

Trinity Episcopal Church

CEMETERY | George Washington once sat in the distinguished visitor pew close to this church's distinctive three-tier wineglass pulpit. Completed in 1726, this structure is similar to Boston's Old North Church; both were inspired by the designs of Sir Christopher Wren. Trinity's 1733 London-made organ is believed to be the first big pipe organ in the 13 colonies. Among those buried in the churchyard's historic cemetery is French admiral d'Arsac de Ternay, commander of the allied French Navy in Newport, who was buried with special permission in 1780 as there were then no Roman Catholic cemeteries in New England. ⊠ *1 Queen Anne Sq.* ☎ *401/846–0660* ⊕ *www.trinitynewport.org* ⊠ *$5 donation* ⊙ *No tours during parish events and Mon.–Sat. in Nov.–late May.*

Wanton-Lyman-Hazard House

HISTORIC SITE | As Newport's oldest surviving house, built circa 1697, this residence provides a glimpse of the city's Colonial and Revolutionary history. The dark-red building was damaged during the city's Stamp Act riots of 1765. After the British Parliament levied a tax on most printed material, the Sons of Liberty stormed the house, which was then occupied by a prominent Loyalist. ⊠ *17 Broadway* ☎ *401/841–8770* ⊕ *newporthistory.org* ⊠ *Tour $15.*

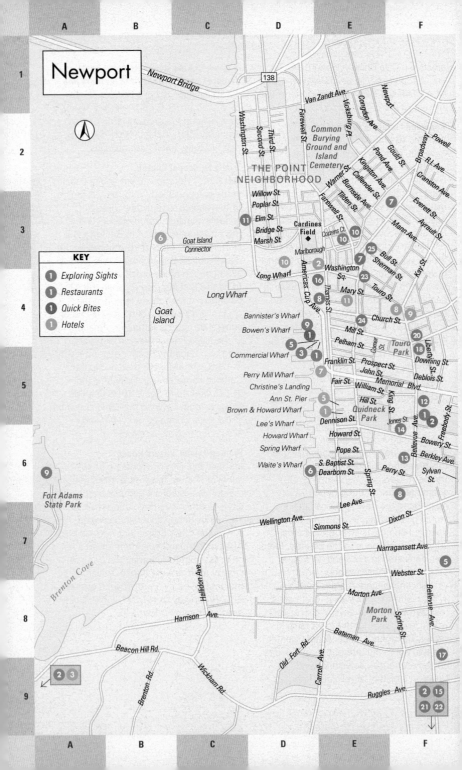

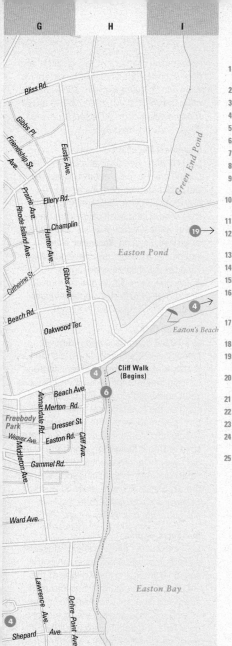

Sights ▼

1 Audrain Automobile Museum **F5**

2 Belcourt of Newport **F9**

3 The Breakers............. **H9**

4 Chateau-sur-Mer **G8**

5 Chepstow................. **F7**

6 Cliff Walk **H5**

7 Colony House **E3**

8 The Elms.................. **F6**

9 Fort Adams State Park **A6**

10 Great Friends Meeting House **E3**

11 Hunter House **C3**

12 International Tennis Hall of Fame............. **F5**

13 Isaac Bell House **F6**

14 Kingscote................. **F6**

15 Marble House........... **F9**

16 Museum of Newport History at Brick Market **E4**

17 National Museum of American Illustration ... **F8**

18 Newport Art Museum... **F5**

19 Norman Bird Sanctuary............ **I3**

20 Redwood Library & Athenaeum **F4**

21 Rosecliff **F9**

22 Rough Point Museum... **F9**

23 Touro Synagogue........ **E4**

24 Trinity Episcopal Church **E4**

25 Wanton-Lyman-Hazard House **E3**

Restaurants ▼

1 The Black Pearl.......... **E4**

2 Castle Hill Inn............ **A9**

3 Clarke Cooke House..... **E4**

4 Flo's Clam Shack.......... **I4**

5 Fluke Newport **E4**

6 Restaurant Bouchard **D6**

7 Salvation Café............ **F3**

8 Stoneacre Garden........ **E4**

9 22 Bowen's Wine Bar & Grille........ **D4**

10 The White Horse Tavern.................... **E3**

Quick Bites ▼

1 Coffee Grinder............ **D4**

2 CRU Cafe.................. **F5**

Hotels ▼

1 Admiral Fitzroy Inn........ **E5**

2 The Brenton **E3**

3 Castle Hill Inn............ **A9**

4 The Chanler at Cliff Walk **H5**

5 The Francis Malbone House **E5**

6 Gurney's Newport Resort & Marina **B3**

7 Hammetts Hotel........... **E5**

8 Hotel Viking............... **F4**

9 Hydrangea House Inn... **F4**

10 Newport Marriott....... **D3**

11 The Vanderbilt............ **E4**

🍴 Restaurants

The Black Pearl

$$$ | **SEAFOOD** | Choose your ambience at this mainstay on the Newport waterfront: the posh, plank-floored Commodore's Room (proper dress required and reservations essential) features country pâté, escargots, rack of lamb, stuffed lobster tails, and other classic offerings; for a more casual experience, with standard American fare like salads, burgers, and grilled meat or fish, visit the Tavern, where old nautical charts hang on the walls. **Known for:** popular dining spot for nearly a half century; raw bar and clam chowder at the year-round, heated outdoor patio; chowder to go—by the case. [$] *Average main: $32* ✉ *Bannister's Wharf* ☎ *401/846–5264* 🌐 *www.blackpearlnewport.com* 🕒 *Closed Jan. and Feb.* 👔 *Jacket required.*

★ Clarke Cooke House

$$$ | **AMERICAN** | Drinks at a bar favored by the sailing crowd, intimate dinners by the fire, and relaxing lunches overlooking Newport Harbor are a few of the experiences possible at this multilevel complex. The first-floor Candy Store serves casual fare and has a sushi bar; the second floor offers casual dining in the Bistro and cocktails in the Midway Bar; and the Summer Porch and 12 Metre Yacht Club Room on the third floor have elegant fine dining requiring proper dress. **Known for:** clam chowder—"best in the city"; "Snowball in Hell" ice-cream dessert; busy, busy, busy place. [$] *Average main: $30* ✉ *26 Bannister's Wharf* ☎ *401/849–2900* 🌐 *www.clarkecooke.com.*

Fluke Newport

$$$$ | **SEAFOOD** | Handcrafted cocktails made with freshly pressed juices, along with one or more appetizers, are the best way to start your meal at this hot spot. Entrées focus on local seafood—maybe George's Bank scallops, crispy oysters, black sea bass, and (of course) fluke. **Known for:** menu changes frequently to reflect local markets; steak, chicken, and pork schnitzel for landlubbers; extensive wine list. [$] *Average main: $36* ✉ *Bannister's Wharf* ☎ *401/849–7778* 🌐 *www.flukenewport.com* 🕒 *Closed Mon. and Tues. and Jan.–mid-Feb.*

Restaurant Bouchard

$$$ | **FRENCH** | Regional variations on French cuisine are the focus at this upscale yet laid-back establishment inside a gambrel-roof 1785 Colonial. Nightly specials are based on the fresh catch from Rhode Island waters, which may include scallops, swordfish, and cod. **Known for:** excellent dining, excellent service; extensive wine list; no children under age seven. [$] *Average main: $35* ✉ *505 Thames St.* ☎ *401/846–0123* 🌐 *www.bouchardnewport.com* 🕒 *Closed Tues. No lunch.*

Salvation Café

$$ | **CAFÉ** | Vegetarians and red-meat fanatics alike can easily find a dish to love at this funky lounge and eatery adored by local hipsters for its lighthearted vibe. You could build a meal around starters such as the roasted beet salad or pork belly flatbread, while the vegetarian pad Thai, bistro filet, and teriyaki salmon are solid entrées. **Known for:** worth the wander away from the touristy waterfront; "craft-on-draft" beers; alfresco seating at the tiki bar. [$] *Average main: $22* ✉ *140 Broadway* ☎ *401/847–2620* 🌐 *www.salvationcafe.com* 🕒 *No lunch.*

Stoneacre Garden

$$$ | **AMERICAN** | Share garlicky mussels, spiced-up bang bang lobster, and other seasonal small and large plates at this circus-theme restaurant. Enormous in size, with big-top-style, red-and-yellow-striped awnings and sprawling indoor-outdoor bars and seating, it's a quirky-fun meet-up spot that takes everything from buttermilk brunch biscuits to fruity cocktails and mocktails seriously. **Known for:** hot, new foodie spot; creative, five-hour weekend brunch menu; lush greenery, inspired by Frederick Law Olmsted's landscape design for the Stoneacre

Estate. $ *Average main: $28* ✉ *151 Swinburne Row* ☎ *401/619–8400* ⊕ *www.stoneacrebrasserie.com.*

★ 22 Bowen's Wine Bar & Grille

$$$$ | STEAKHOUSE | Excellent service, perfectly cooked steaks, and an extensive, award-winning wine list make dinner here a memorable experience. Although the restaurant is known for its steaks—and it's impossible to go wrong ordering one—you'll find plenty of choices if you're in the mood for something from the sea. **Known for:** steaks, chops, and fresh local seafood; choose one of eight sauces/butters to accompany your steak; abundant gluten-free options. $ *Average main: $40* ✉ *22 Bowen's Wharf* ☎ *401/841–8884* ⊕ *www.22bowens.com.*

The White Horse Tavern

$$$ | AMERICAN | The first tavern opened here in 1673—and ever since, the premises have served, in turn, as a tavern, boardinghouse, restaurant, and even a meetinghouse for Colonial Rhode Island's General Assembly. Today, the tavern provides an intimate fine-dining experience, the mood set by the low dark-beam ceilings, uneven plank floors, and four still-working fireplaces. **Known for:** oldest operating restaurant in the country; beef Wellington, fresh seafood, just-picked produce; extensive wine list. $ *Average main: $32* ✉ *26 Marlborough St.* ☎ *401/849–3600* ⊕ *www.whitehorsenewport.com.*

☕ Coffee and Quick Bites

Coffee Grinder

$ | CAFÉ | Occupying the prime real estate at the tip of Bannister's Wharf, this tiny espresso bar has an enormous view of Newport's vibrant harbor. Pair a flavored latte and a pastry on a fog-bound early morning, and you'll feel the essence of the city as it awakens around you. **Known for:** coffee drinks made-to-order with real Italian espresso; savory scones and turnovers; just a handful of seats on the deck, so it's worth going early or at off

times. $ *Average main: $8* ✉ *33 Bannister's Wharf* ☎ *401/847–9307* ⊕ *www.coffeegrindernewport.com.*

CRU Cafe

$ | CAFÉ | From Russell Morin, one of Newport's most exclusive caterers, comes this chalkboard-menu cafe where beautifully crafted light fare is served at surprisingly down-to-earth prices. Breakfast—try the egg- and tomato-topped avocado toast—is served all day, and creative salads and sandwiches are the makings of a perfect picnic to tote down the street and enjoy on an oceanview mansion lawn. **Known for:** hidden in a parking lot on tony Bellevue Avenue; elevated, farm-fresh cuisine; CRU at night entrees on Fri. and Sat. evenings during the summer season. $ *Average main: $9* ✉ *1 Casino Terr.* ☎ *401/314-0500* ⊕ *www.crucafenewport.com.*

🛏 Hotels

Admiral Fitzroy Inn

$$ | B&B/INN | The restful retreat in the heart of Newport's bustling waterfront district was once a convent in a different location—the tidy 1854 Victorian building was dismantled in 1986 and rebuilt to its original size and style in its current location. **Pros:** elevator service to first three floors; close to shops, restaurants, and bars; complimentary parking; continental breakfast included. **Cons:** some noise from Thames Street in summer; walk up from third floor to rooftop rooms and deck; rooms are fairly small but it is a historic property. $ *Rooms from: $239* ✉ *398 Thames St.* ☎ *401/848–8000, 866/848–8780* ⊕ *www.admiralfitzroy.com* ⇥ *18 rooms* ❍❑ *Free breakfast.*

★ The Brenton

$$$ | HOTEL | Inside and out, every detail of Newport's newest hotel is a thoughtful homage to its place on the waterfront and in the city's architectural progression. **Pros:** largest rooms in Newport; entirely pet-friendly; local inspiration and artisanship throughout the property. **Cons:** prime location comes at a price; pool and fitness center off-site at the adjacent Newport Marriott; parking is $40 per night. [$] *Rooms from: $350* ✉ *31 America's Cup Ave.* ☎ *401/849–3100* 🌐 *www.brentonhotel.com* 🛏 *57 rooms* 🍴 *No meals.*

The Francis Malbone House
$$$ | **B&B/INN** | The painted-brick main house overlooks a private courtyard with a fountain and, across the street, to the harbor. **Pros:** steps from many restaurants and shops; highly professional service; complimentary off-street parking; a sumptuous breakfast is served in a dome-ceiling dining room, and tea is served daily 3–6. **Cons:** Thames Street abounds with tourists in summer; two-night stay required on peak weekends; you'll want to structure sightseeing so as not to miss tea. [$] *Rooms from: $325* ✉ *392 Thames St.* ☎ *401/846–0392, 800/846–0392* 🌐 *www.malbone.com* 🛏 *20 rooms* 🍴 *Free breakfast.*

★ **Gurney's Newport Resort & Marina**
$$$ | **RESORT** | **FAMILY** | A former Navy base that's now connected by causeway to the downtown area, Goat Island is home to this resort that comes complete with a walking path around the island, a marina full of yachts, Seawater Spa, a fitness center, and a picturesque lighthouse. **Pros:** indoor and outdoor swimming pools; kids' club (seasonal); ADA accessible rooms available; numerous dining options. **Cons:** no shuttle service, and it's a 15-minute walk to downtown activities; $40 nightly resort fee; valet parking is an extra. [$] *Rooms from: $385* ✉ *1 Goat Island* ☎ *401/849–2600, 833/235–7500* 🌐 *www.gurneysresorts.com/newport* 🛏 *257 rooms* 🍴 *No meals.*

Hammetts Hotel
$$$ | **HOTEL** | Opened in the midst of challenging 2020, this anchor of the newly built Hammetts Wharf shopping, lodging, yachting, and dining complex instantly booked up on weekends. **Pros:** enormous windows with city or water views; chic outdoor deck reserved for guests; freestyle Italian cuisine (try the olive oil cake) at adjacent Giusto restaurant. **Cons:** rooms are somewhat bland and on the smaller side; only one elevator; tiny fitness room overlooks the city, not the water. [$] *Rooms from: $300* ✉ *4 Commercial Wharf* ☎ *401/324–7500* 🌐 *www.hammettshotel.com* 🛏 *84 rooms* 🍴 *No meals.*

Hotel Viking
$$ | **HOTEL** | At the north end of Bellevue Avenue, this elegant redbrick hotel dates back to 1926. **Pros:** Historic Hill location; Top of Newport rooftop bar has spectacular views; on-site SpaFjör; One Bellevue restaurant serves three meals and afternoon tea. **Cons:** comparatively expensive; relatively small rooms and tiny bathrooms; an uphill walk from the action at the waterfront. [$] *Rooms from: $229* ✉ *1 Bellevue Ave.* ☎ *401/847–3300* 🌐 *www.hotelviking.com* 🛏 *208 rooms* 🍴 *No meals.*

Hydrangea House Inn
$$ | **B&B/INN** | This mid-19th-century inn, with decadent suites and guest rooms, exudes romance. **Pros:** convenient central location; huge rooms and great bathrooms; highly personal service. **Cons:** slightly over-the-top decor; street-level rooms can be noisy at night; no kids 12 and under. [$] *Rooms from: $295* ✉ *16 Bellevue Ave.* ☎ *401/846–4435, 800/945–4667* 🌐 *www.hydrangeahouse.com* 🛏 *10 rooms* 🍴 *Free breakfast.*

Newport Marriott
$$$ | **HOTEL** | A light-filled atrium lobby with rope-draped seating areas and a front desk that looks like a boat set a contemporary nautical tone at this luxury hotel on the harbor at Long Wharf. **Pros:** convenient location; harbor views from many rooms; indoor swimming pool. **Cons:** pricey for a Marriott; rather typical hotel guest rooms; $25 daily on-site parking fee. [$] *Rooms from: $332* ✉ *25 America's Cup Ave.* ☎ *401/849–1000, 888/236–2427* 🌐 *www.newportmarriott.com* 🛏 *319 rooms* 🍴 *No meals.*

The Vanderbilt

$$$$ | HOTEL | Built in 1909 by Alfred Gwynne Vanderbilt for his mistress, Agnes O'Brien Ruiz, this Auberge Resorts property aims to impress—and does, with its exclusive mansion feel and enormous guest rooms. **Pros:** full-service spa; indoor and outdoor pools; boozy popsicles and cocktails served on the hidden Garden Terrace. **Cons:** on a narrow street that's busy in summer; somewhat sterile decor; minimum stay requirements may apply. $ *Rooms from: $650* ✉ *41 Mary St.* ☎ *401/846–6200, 833/242–8850* ⊕ *www.aubergeresorts. com/vanderbilt* ⟿ *33 rooms* ⊙ *No meals.*

Bellevue Avenue and Beyond

East of Newport Harbor and the historic part of town, you begin to discover stunning, opulent mansions along Bellevue Avenue and its ocean-leading side streets. These "summer cottages" were built by wealthy families in the late 1800s and early 1900s as seasonal residences.

🏖 Beaches

Easton's Beach (*First Beach*)

BEACH—SIGHT | FAMILY | A ¾-mile-long surfing beach, Easton's has a boardwalk, vintage carousel, aquarium, and playground. Public facilities include restrooms, indoor and outdoor showers, an elevator, and beach wheelchairs for people with disabilities. The snack bar's twin lobster rolls are very popular (and a great deal). **Amenities:** food and drink; lifeguards; parking (fee); showers; toilets. **Best for:** swimming; walking. ✉ *175 Memorial Blvd.* ☎ *401/845–5810* ⊕ *www. cityofnewport.com/visiting-newport/ eastons-beach.*

Sachuest Beach (*Second Beach*)

BEACH—SIGHT | The western end of this mile-long sandy beach attracts many surfers. Surfboard and standup paddleboard rentals are available. **Amenities:** food and drink; lifeguards; parking (fee); showers; toilets. **Best for:** surfing; swimming; walking; sunsets. ✉ *474 Sachuest Point Rd., Middletown* ☎ *401/849–2822* ⊕ *beach.middletownri.com.*

Third Beach

BEACH—SIGHT | Located near the mouth of the Sakonnet River, Third Beach is more peaceful than the nearby ocean beaches and a great spot for families. It has grills, picnic tables, and a shade structure near the boat ramp. Third Beach is a favorite of windsurfers. You'll find gear rentals near the south end. **Amenities:** parking (fee); lifeguards. **Best for:** swimming; walking; windsurfing. ✉ *3rd Beach Rd., Middletown* ☎ *401/849–2822* ⊕ *beach. middletownri.com.*

👁 Sights

Audrain Automobile Museum

MUSEUM | The museum showcases a revolving selection of impressive vehicles, curated from collections of more than 350 rare, fully restored automobiles dating from 1899 to the present day. You might see super cars, mini- and micro-cars, pre–World War II specimens, or touring cars. Auto enthusiasts will enjoy perusing past exhibitions on the museum's website. ✉ *222 Bellevue Ave.* ☎ *401/856–4420* ⊕ *www.audrainautomuseum.org* ➤ *$18.*

Belcourt of Newport

HOUSE | Richard Morris Hunt based his design for this 60-room mansion, built in 1894 for wealthy bachelor Oliver H. P. Belmont, on the hunting lodge of Louis XIII. Billionaire founder of Alex & Ani, Carolyn Rafaelian, a native Rhode Islander, purchased Belcourt in 2012 and

Continued on page 386

Above left, stair hall of Château-sur-Mer, the first of the Bellevue Avenue mansions.

Opposite, Romantic Rosecliff's terracotta tiles look magical at dusk.

Below left, Statues of cherubs watch over the exterior of the Elms.

Right, Go behind the entrance gate on a tour of the Breakers.

The Mansions of Newport

GILDED AGE GEMS

By Andrew Collins, Debbie Harmsen, and Janine Weisman

Would you call a home with 70 rooms a cottage? If not, you're obviously not Cornelius Vanderbilt II. The Breakers, the "summer cottage" of the 19th-century multimillionaire, is one of a dozen mansions in Newport that are now by far the city's top attractions. Many of the homes are open to the public for tours, giving you a peek into the lives of the privileged.

THE SOCIAL SCENE

The Breakers dining room, just one of the opulent mansion's 70 rooms.

To truly appreciate a visit to Newport's mansions, you need to understand the times and the players—those who built these opulent homes and summered here for six weeks a year.

Newport at the turn of the 20th century was where the socialites of Boston, New York, and Philadelphia came for the summer. They were among the richest people in America at the time—from railroad tycoons and coal barons to plantation owners.

The era during which they lived here, the late 1800s up through the 1920s, is often referred to as the Gilded Age, a term coined by Mark Twain and co-author Charles Dudley Warner in a book by the same name. It was a time when who you knew was everything.

Caroline Schermerhorn Astor was the queen of New York and Newport society; her list of the "Four Hundred" was the first social register. Three übersocialites were Alva Vanderbilt Belmont, Mary Ann (Mamie) Fish, and Tessie Oelrichs. These ladies who seriously lunched threw most of *the* parties in Newport.

While the women gossiped, planned soirees, and dressed and redressed thoughout the summer days, the men were usually off yachting.

In terms of the deepest pockets, the two heavyweight families during Newport's Gilded Age were the Vanderbilts and the Astors.

Madeleine Force was only 19 when she married John Jacob Astor IV at the Beechwood mansion in 1911; he was 47.

LEADING FAMILIES

Alva Vanderbilt Belmont

Beechwood will soon be reinvented as an art museum.

Cornelius Vanderbilt

THE VANDERBILTS Cornelius Vanderbilt I, called Commodore Cornelius Vanderbilt, built his empire on steamships and railroads. Cornelius had amassed almost $100 million before he died in 1877. He gave most of it to his son William Henry, who, also shrewd in the railroading business, nearly doubled the family fortune over the next decade. William Henry Vanderbilt willed $70 million to his son Cornelius Vanderbilt II, who became the chairman and president of New York Central Railroad; and $55 million to son William K. Vanderbilt, who also managed railroads for a while and saw his yacht, *The Defender*, win the America's Cup in 1895. One of Cornelius Vanderbilt II's sons, Alfred Gwynne Vanderbilt, died on the Lusitania, which sank three years after the *Titanic*. **Visit:** The Breakers, Marble House.

John Jacob Astor IV

THE ASTORS Meanwhile, in the Astor camp, John Jacob Astor IV, who perished on the *Titanic*, had the riches his great-granddad had made in the fur trade as well as his own millions earned from successful real estate ventures, including New York City hotels such as the St. Regis and the Astoria (later the Waldorf–Astoria). His mother was Caroline Astor. Her mansion, Beechwood, is now owned by Oracle CEO Larry Ellison.

John Jacob Astor

WHICH MANSION SHOULD I VISIT?

Even though the Newport "summer cottages" were inhabited for only six weeks each year, it would take you almost that long to explore all the grand rooms and manicured grounds. Each mansion has its own style and unique features. Here are the characteristics of each to help you choose those you'd like to visit:

★ **The Breakers:** The most opulent; enormous Italian Renaissance mansion built by Cornelius Vanderbilt II; tours are often big and very crowded; open most of the year.

Château-sur-Mer: The prettiest gardens and grounds; High Victorian–style mansion built in 1852; enlarged and modified in 1870s by Richard Morris Hunt.

Chepstow: Italianate villa with a fine collection of art; a bit less wow factor; summer hours only.

★ **The Elms:** A French chatea-style home with 10 acres of stunningly restored grounds; new guided servant quarters tour takes you into a hidden dormitory, roof, and basement; open most of the year.

Hunter House: Fantastic collection of Colonial furniture; downtown location, not on Bellevue Avenue; pricey admission; summer hours only.

Isaac Bell House: Currently undergoing restoration; less dramatic shingled Victorian displays an unusual mix of influences; less visited; summer hours only.

Kingscote: Gothic Revival–style home includes early Tiffany glass; one of the first summer cottages built in 1841; summer hours only.

★ **Marble House:** Outrageously opulent and sometimes crowded; former Vanderbilt home modeled on Petit Trianon in Versailles; tour at your own pace with digital audio tour; open most of the year.

Rosecliff: Romantic 1902 mansion; modeled after Grand Trianon in Versailles; somewhat crowded tours.

Portrait of Mrs. Cornelius Vanderbilt II circa 1880, The Breakers.

Rough Point: More contemporary perspective in 20th-century furniture; 1889 English manor–style home; tours are expensive and have limited availability.

MANSION TOURS

Preservation Society of Newport County. The Preservation Society maintains 11 historic properties and the Newport Mansions Store on Bannister's Wharf. Both guided tours and audio tours are available; you can purchase a combination ticket to see multiple properties for a substantial discount. The hours and days the houses are open in fall and winter vary. P401/847–1000 wwww.newportmansions. org. ✉ The Newport Mansions Experience (admission to any 5 properties excluding Hunter House) $32.99.

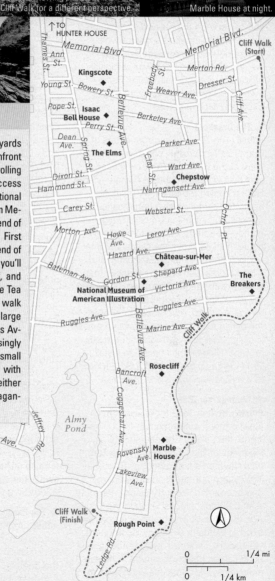

Consider viewing mansions from the Cliff Walk for a different perspective.

Marble House at night.

TOP EXPERIENCE

★ **Cliff Walk.** See the backyards of Newport's famous oceanfront Gilded Age mansions while strolling along this 3½-mile public access walkway. The designated National Recreation Trail stretches from Memorial Boulevard at the west end of Easton's Beach (also called First Beach) southerly to the east end of Bailey's Beach. Along the way you'll pass the Breakers, Rosecliff, and Marble House and its Chinese Tea House. The north half of the walk is paved but the trail turns to large flat boulders south of Ruggles Avenue. Be prepared for increasingly rough terrain not suitable for small children, strollers, or people with mobility problems. Park on either Memorial Boulevard or Narragansett Avenue.

has been working to restore the home to its former glory in an eco-conscious way, employing solar panels and thermal-heating-and-cooling systems. Jennifer Lawrence famously chose the estate as her 2019 wedding venue. On a restoration tour, which takes about 45 minutes followed by a 15-minute Q&A session, you can admire the stained glass, carved wood, and chandeliers—one of which has 20,000 pieces and another that weighs 460 pounds and was originally held up by a single nail. ⊠ *657 Bellevue Ave.* ⊕ *www.belcourt.com* ⊠ *$18* ⊙ *Closed Mon. and Tues.*

★ The Breakers

HOUSE | The 70-room summer estate of Cornelius Vanderbilt II, chairman and president of the New York Central Railroad, was built in 1895. Architect Richard Morris Hunt modeled the four-story residence after 16th-century Italian Renaissance palaces. This mansion is not only big, but grand—be sure to look for the sculpted figures tucked above the pillars. The interior includes rare marble, alabaster, and gilded rooms with open-air terraces that reveal magnificent ocean views. Noteworthy are a blue marble fireplace and walls in the billiard room, rose alabaster pillars in the dining room, and a porch with a mosaic ceiling that took six months for Italian artisans, lying on their backs, to install. ⊠ *44 Ochre Point Ave.* ☎ *401/847–1000* ⊕ *www.newportmansions.org* ⊠ *$26.*

★ Chateau-sur-Mer

HOUSE | Built in 1852 for William Shepard Wetmore, a merchant in the China Trade, the palatial Chateau-sur-Mer, a landmark of High Victorian architecture, was Newport's first grand residence. In 1857, Wetmore threw an extravagant, unprecedented "country picnic" for more than 2,000 people, ushering in the Gilded Age in Newport. The house is a treasure trove of Victorian architecture, furniture, wallpapers, ceramics, and stenciling; see hand-carved Italian woodwork, Chinese porcelains, and Japanese and Egyptian

Revival wallpapers. The grounds contain rare trees from as far away as Mongolia. ⊠ *474 Bellevue Ave.* ☎ *401/847–1000* ⊕ *www.newportmansions.org* ⊠ *$18* ⊙ *Closed early Nov.–late Mar.*

Chepstow

HOUSE | Though only slightly less grand than some of the other Newport mansions, this Italianate-style villa with a mansard roof houses a remarkable collection of art and furniture gathered by the Morris family of New York City. Its significant 19th-century American paintings include Hudson River School landscapes. Built in 1860, the home was designed by George Champlin Mason, a Newport architect, for Edmund Schermerhorn, a descendent of one of the first settlers of New Netherland and first cousin of Mrs. William Astor. ⊠ *120 Narragansett Ave.* ☎ *401/847–1000* ⊕ *www.newportmansions.org* ⊠ *$18* ⊙ *Closed mid-Oct.–mid-May.*

★ Cliff Walk

TRAIL | See the "backyards" of Newport's famous oceanfront Gilded Age mansions while strolling along this 3½-mile public walkway. The designated National Recreation Trail stretches from Memorial Boulevard at the western end of Easton's Beach (also called First Beach) south to the eastern end of Bailey's Beach. Along the way you'll pass Salve Regina University's Ochre Court, the Breakers, Forty Steps at Narragansett Avenue, Rosecliff, and Marble House and its Chinese Tea House. Park on either Memorial Boulevard or Narragansett Avenue. The trail is relatively flat and easily walkable, although some parts are unpaved and rocky. ■ **TIP→ Apply sunscreen, wear comfortable rubber-soled shoes, and bring your own water.** ⊠ *Memorial Blvd.* ☎ *401/845–5300* ⊕ *www.cliffwalk.com* ⊠ *Free.*

★ The Elms

HOUSE | Architect Horace Trumbauer modeled this imposing 48-room French neoclassical home and its grounds after the Château d'Asnières near Paris. The Elms was built in 1901 for Edward Julius

Berwind, a coal baron from Philadelphia and New York. It was one of the first Newport mansions to be fully electrified. At the foot of the 10-acre estate is a spectacular sunken garden, marble pavilions, and fountains. The Servant Life tour, which offers a glimpse into the lives of the Elms' staff members and the operation of facilities like the boiler room and kitchen, is one of the best of any of the mansion tours. ⊠ *367 Bellevue Ave.* ☎ *401/847–1000* ⊕ *www.newportmansions.org* 🖃 *$18* ⊘ *Closed Jan.–mid-Feb.*

Fort Adams State Park

BEACH—SIGHT | FAMILY | The largest coastal fortress in the United States can be found at this park, which hosts Newport's annual folk and jazz festivals and sailing events like the Ocean Race. The nonprofit Ft. Adams Trust offers a varied schedule of guided tours of the fort, where soldiers lived from 1841 to 1950. Tours take in the fort's overlooks and underground tunnels, as well as its impressive walls. The views of Newport Harbor and Narragansett Bay are exquisite. ⊠ *80 Ft. Adams Dr.* ☎ *401/841–0707* ⊕ *www.fortadams.org* 🖃 *Park free, guided tour $12, self-guided tour $6.*

★ International Tennis Hall of Fame

MUSEUM | FAMILY | Tennis fans and lovers of history, art, and architecture will enjoy visiting the birthplace of U.S. championship tennis. The museum contains interactive exhibits, a holographic theater that simulates being in a room with Roger Federer, displays of clothing worn by the sport's biggest stars, video highlights of great matches, and memorabilia that includes the 1874 patent from England's Queen Victoria for the game of lawn tennis. The 7-acre site is home to the Bill Talbert Stadium with its manicured grass courts, the historic shingle-style Newport Casino—which opened in 1880 and was designed by architects McKim, Mead & White—and the recently restored Casino Theatre. The 13 grass tennis courts, one clay court, and an indoor tennis facility are

Scenic Drive 👁

Ocean Drive. Also called Ten-Mile Drive, this is a stunningly scenic route from Bellevue Avenue at Memorial Boulevard south to Ocean Avenue and out to Castle Hill Avenue, Ridge Road, and Harrison Avenue. You'll pass by Ft. Adams State Park and President Eisenhower's "summer White House"; Hammersmith Farm, Jacqueline Bouvier Kennedy Onassis' family home and the site of her wedding reception when she married John F. Kennedy in 1953; and, about halfway along, the 89-acre Brenton Point State Park.

8

Rhode Island NEWPORT

open to the public for play. ⊠ *194 Bellevue Ave.* ☎ *401/849–3990* ⊕ *www.tennisfame.com* 🖃 *$16* ⊘ *Closed Mon.–Wed.*

Isaac Bell House

HOUSE | Revolutionary in design when it was completed in 1883, the shingle-style Isaac Bell House combines Old English and European architecture with Colonial American and exotic details, such as a sweeping open floor plan and bamboo-style porch columns. McKim, Mead & White of New York City designed the home for Isaac Bell, a wealthy cotton broker. ⊠ *70 Perry St., at Bellevue Ave.* ☎ *401/847–1000* ⊕ *www.newportmansions.org* 🖃 *$18* ⊘ *Closed mid-Oct.–mid-May.*

Kingscote

HOUSE | Among Newport's first summer cottages, this 1841 Gothic Revival mansion designed by Richard Upjohn was built for George Noble Jones, a Georgia plantation owner. The house is named for its second owners, the King family, one of whose members hired McKim, Mead & White to expand and redesign it. The dining room, one of the 1881 additions, contains a cork ceiling and one of the first installations of Tiffany glass windows. Furnishings reflect the King family's involvement in the China trade. ✉ *253 Bellevue Ave.* ☎ *401/847–1000* ⊕ *www.newportmansions.org* 🎫 *$18* ⊗ *Closed mid-Oct.–mid-May.*

★ Marble House

HOUSE | One of the most opulent of the Newport mansions, Marble House contains 500,000 cubic feet of marble (valued at $7 million when the house was built from 1888 to 1892). William K. Vanderbilt, grandson of Commodore Cornelus Vanderbilt, gave Marble House to his wife, Alva, as a gift for her 39th birthday. The house was designed by architect Richard Morris Hunt, who took inspiration from the Petit Trianon at Versailles. The Vanderbilts divorced three years later, in 1895. Alva married Oliver H. P. Belmont and moved down the street to Belcourt. After Belmont's death, she reopened Marble House and had the Chinese Tea House built on the back lawn, where she hosted "Votes for Women" rallies. ✉ *596 Bellevue Ave.* ☎ *401/847–1000* ⊕ *www. newportmansions.org* 🎫 *$18.*

National Museum of American Illustration

HOUSE | This museum exhibits original work by Norman Rockwell, J. C. Leyendecker, Maxfield Parrish, N. C. Wyeth, and more than 150 others spanning the "Golden Age of American Illustration" (1895–1945). All 323 of Rockwell's printed *Saturday Evening Post* covers are on display. The 1898 beaux-arts–style building, an adaptation of an 18th-century French château, was designed by the same architects responsible for the New York Public Library and other landmarks; Frederick Law Olmsted designed the grounds. ✉ *492 Bellevue Ave.* ☎ *401/851–8949* ⊕ *www.americanillustration.org* 🎫 *$20.*

Norman Bird Sanctuary

NATURE PRESERVE | FAMILY | Stroll through the woods or hike to the top of Hanging Rock for a spectacular view at this 325-acre sanctuary for diverse wildlife including more than 300 species of birds. The sanctuary has about 7 miles of trails traversing ridges, forests, thickets, fields, ponds, streams, salt marsh, and sandy beach. ■TIP➔ **The raucous dawn chorus of birdsong in the spring is one of the great wildlife experiences in Rhode Island.** ✉ *583 Third Beach Rd., Middletown* ☎ *401/846–2577* ⊕ *www.normanbirdsanctuary.org* 🎫 *$7.*

Rosecliff

HOUSE | Newport's most romantic mansion was commissioned by Tessie Fair Oelrichs, who inherited a Nevada silver fortune from her father. Stanford White modeled the 1902 palace after the Grand Trianon at Versailles. Rosecliff has a heart-shape staircase and Newport's largest private ballroom. Rosecliff stayed in the Oelrichs family until 1941, went through several ownership changes, and then was purchased by Mr. and Mrs. J. Edgar Monroe of New Orleans in 1947. The Monroes were known for throwing big parties. Scenes from the films *The Great Gatsby* (1974), *True Lies* (1994), and *Amistad* (1997) were shot here. ✉ *548 Bellevue Ave.* ☎ *401/847–1000* ⊕ *www.newportmansions.org* 🎫 *$18.*

★ Rough Point Museum

HOUSE | Tobacco heiress, philanthropist, and preservationist Doris Duke furnished her 39,000-square-foot English manorial–style house at the southern end of Bellevue Avenue with family treasures and fine art and antiques purchased on her world travels. Highlights include paintings by Renoir, Van Dyck, and Gainsborough, numerous Chinese porcelains, Turkish carpets and Belgian tapestries, and a suite of Louis XVI chairs. Duke's two camels, Baby and Princess (who came with an airplane she had purchased from a Middle Eastern businessman), once summered here on the expansive grounds designed by landscape architect Frederick Law Olmsted. Duke bequeathed the oceanfront house with all of its contents to the Newport Restoration Foundation to operate as a museum after her death. Each year, the foundation assembles an exhibit devoted to Duke's lifestyle and interests, which is included with a guided tour. ✉ *680 Bellevue Ave.* ☎ *401/847–8344* 🌐 *www.newportrestoration.org* 🎟 *$20* ⏱ *Closed mid-Nov.–early Apr.*

🍴 Restaurants

★ Castle Hill Inn

$$$$ | AMERICAN | No other restaurant in Newport can compete with the spectacular water views from the Sunset Room, one of four dining rooms inside the historic main inn. A perfect spot for a romantic dinner, Castle Hill Inn also serves lunch and dinner on The Lawn, allowing you to savor regional cuisine while watching sunlit clouds drift by. **Known for:** New England food done well; prix-fixe dinner menus; 800-bottle wine list. [$] *Average main: $85* ✉ *590 Ocean Dr.* ☎ *888/466–1355, 401/849–3800* 🌐 *www.castlehillinn.com.*

Flo's Clam Shack

$$ | SEAFOOD | FAMILY | With Bruce the shark out front and a weathered, kitschy vibe, this local institution across from Easton's Beach is as casual as they come. Lobster rolls, fried seafood, baked fish, clam cakes, cold beer, and a great raw bar make for long lines in summer. **Known for:** the best fried clams—ever; raw bar and other dishes served at the upstairs bar; outdoor seating is available. [$] *Average main: $19* ✉ *4 Wave Ave., Middletown* ☎ *401/847–8141* 🌐 *www.flosclamshacks.com* 💳 *No credit cards* ⏱ *Closed Mon.–Wed., and Dec.–early Mar.*

🛏 Hotels

★ Castle Hill Inn

$$$$ | HOTEL | Built as a summer house in 1874 for Alexander Agassiz, a scientist and explorer, this luxurious and romantic getaway on a 40-acre peninsula has its own private beach, Farmaesthetics spa, and trails to the Castle Hill Lighthouse, as well as Adirondack chairs on the lawn that beckon you to relax and watch the passing boats. **Pros:** stunning views; excellent restaurant with an elaborate Sunday brunch with live jazz music; variety of rooms; home to the Retreat at Castle Hill, a "wellness sanctuary" by Rhode Island's own Farmaesthetics. **Cons:** 3 miles from downtown Newport; very expensive; no children under 13 in mansion rooms. [$] *Rooms from: $745* ✉ *590 Ocean Dr.* ☎ *401/849–3800, 888/466–1355* 🌐 *www.castlehillinn.com* 🔑 *33 rooms* 🍽 *Free breakfast.*

★ The Chanler at Cliff Walk

$$$$ | HOTEL | The custom-designed rooms at this 19th-century mansion on the Cliff Walk, now a landmark boutique hotel, represent the most unique and luxurious accommodations in Newport. **Pros:** celebrity-level exclusivity and privacy; panoramic water views from many rooms; excellent fine-dining restaurant; complimentary car service. **Cons:** no elevator; some rooms have steps to access bathroom; off-the-charts expensive. [$] *Rooms from: $1025* ✉ *117 Memorial Blvd.* ☎ *401/847–1300, 866/793–5664* 🌐 *www.thechanler.com* 🔑 *20 rooms* 🍽 *No meals.*

🍸 Nightlife

To sample Newport's lively nightlife, you need only stroll down Thames Street or the southern end of Broadway after dark.

BARS AND CLUBS

Fastnet Pub

BARS/PUBS | Named for the Fastnet Lighthouse off the coast of Cork, Ireland, this pub hosts Irish jam sessions on Sunday evening, when guest musicians, singers, and dancers familiar with traditional Irish repertoire are invited to participate. ✉ *1 Broadway* ☎ *401/845–9311* 🌐 *www.thefastnetpub.com.*

The Fifth Element

BARS/PUBS | This chic lounge offers specialty cocktails and elevated bar fare. Outside, new addition Outer Element is a cute little beer garden where you can toss back a Gansett and ditch Newport's preppy side. ⊠ *111 Broadway* ☎ *401/619–2552* ⊕ *www.thefifthri.com.*

Newport Blues Café

MUSIC CLUBS | Housed in a former bank building built in 1892, this café hosts live music, including touring blues acts and tribute bands, plus improv comedy nights. ⊠ *286 Thames St.* ☎ *401/841–5510* ⊕ *www.newportblues.com.*

One Pelham East

MUSIC CLUBS | An all-ages crowd heads here for eats, drinks, and live music seven days a week including dueling pianos on Friday and Saturday night. ⊠ *270 Thames St.* ☎ *401/847–9460* ⊕ *www.thepelham.com.*

🛍 Shopping

Many of Newport's shops and art and crafts galleries are on Thames Street, Spring Street, and at Bowen's and Bannister's Wharfs. The Brick Market area—between Thames Street and America's Cup Avenue—has more than 25 shops. Bellevue Avenue, just south of Memorial Boulevard near the International Tennis Hall of Fame, contains a strip of high-end fashion, skin care, and jewelry shops.

ANTIQUES

Aardvark Antiques

ANTIQUES/COLLECTIBLES | This shop specializes in distinctive architectural salvage such as mantels, doors, stained glass, fountains, and garden statuary including items plucked from places like Belcourt Castle. ⊠ *9 J.T. Connell Hwy.* ☎ *401/849–7233, 800/446–1052* ⊕ *aardvarkantiques.com* ☉ *Closed Sun.*

ART AND CRAFTS GALLERIES

Mariner Gallery

ART GALLERIES | Serious collector or casual art lover, you'll be mesmerized by the luminous maritime paintings exhibited within the 1772 Stephen DuBois House. Works by contemporary masters are strongly represented. Don't leave without making a voyage downstairs to the Constellation Room, a gallery space paneled in solid oak and modeled after the *USS Constellation.* ⊠ *267 Spring St.* ☎ *401/236–2454* ⊕ *www.marinergallery.com* ☉ *Closed Mon.*

Spring Bull Gallery

ART GALLERIES | This Rhode Island artists' cooperative, a working studio gallery, changes its shows frequently. One wall is dedicated to its members, who are primarily painters. ⊠ *55 Bellevue Ave.* ☎ *401/849–9166* ⊕ *www.springbullgallery.com.*

★ Thames Glass

ART GALLERIES | Through a window in the gallery at Thames Glass, you can watch Matthew Buechner and his team making blown-glass gifts. Sign up for a lesson to make an ornament, paperweight, or vase out of molten glass. ⊠ *688 Thames St.* ☎ *401/846–0576* ⊕ *www.thamesglass.com.*

SPAS

The Retreat at Castle Hill by Farmaesthetics

SPA—SIGHT | Located at Castle Hill Inn, this "wellness sanctuary" operates in collaboration with Farmaesthetics, a Rhode Island-based line of 100% natural herbal skin-care products. Many of the ingredients are harvested from local seaside farms. Spa services include facials, therapeutic and acupressure massage, and pre- or posttreatment saltwater soaks. ⊠ *Castle Hill Inn, 590 Ocean Dr.* ☎ *401/849–3800* ⊕ *www.castlehillinn.com/boutique-spa.*

Newport's naturally protected harbor has made the city a sailing capital.

SpaFjör

SPA—SIGHT | The outstanding SpaFjör, located in Hotel Viking, offers custom-designed Balinese massage and body rituals and other globally inspired spa experiences—facials, bath rituals, and body wraps—that promote health and well-being but also provide a sense of complete relaxation. For a truly luxurious escape, pick a package: the three-hour Day of Bliss (massage, body wrap, and facial) or the 3½-hour Ultimate Escape (Balinese massage, facial, back and foot treatment, and bath ritual). ⊠ *Hotel Viking, 1 Bellevue Ave.* ☎ *401/847–3300* ⊕ *www.hotelviking.com/spa.*

⚡ Activities

BASEBALL

Cardines Field

BASEBALL/SOFTBALL | **FAMILY** | One of America's oldest ballparks, with a circa-1908 original backstop, is home to the Newport Gulls of the New England Collegiate Baseball League. Home games, June–early August, draw a family-friendly crowd. The field hosted barnstorming all-stars in the early 20th century, including the players of Negro League clubs. ⊠ *20 America's Cup Ave.* ⊕ *www.newport-gulls.com* ⊠ *$5.*

BIKING

The 10-mile swing down Bellevue Avenue to Ocean Drive and back offers amazing coastal views.

Ten Speed Spokes

BICYCLING | **FAMILY** | This shop rents hybrid bikes for $40 per day, road bikes for $45. You can also rent by the week. ⊠ *18 Elm St.* ☎ *401/847–5609* ⊕ *www.tenspeedspokes.com* 🚶 *Closed Sun. and Mon.*

BOATING

Sail Newport

BOATING | Enjoy a one-hour "Try Sailing!" experience, take private lessons, or rent a 22-foot sailboat at Sail Newport, New England's largest public sailing center. ⊠ *Ft. Adams State Park, 72 Ft. Adams Dr.* ☎ *401/846–1983* ⊕ *www.sailnewport.org* ☞ *Closed Nov.–Memorial Day weekend.*

Newport Off Season

Summer in Newport can be busy and pricey, but the more affordable off-season takes on a serene, romantic character. No crowds, lower lodging rates, easy and free parking, and midweek specials at restaurants all make the city an appealing destination. The twice-a-year Newport Restaurant Week, held in early November and late March or early April, offers two-course $20 lunches and three-course $35 dinners at 50 or more participating restaurants.

Fall visitors will enjoy end-of-season sales up and down Thames Street. Although there may be no need to pack a bikini, brisk walks on the beach and Cliff Walk get the blood flowing. In the wintertime, holiday lights glimmer in the early dusk, and bundled-up folks duck into restaurants to warm themselves by the fire and enjoy a drink and a bite to eat.

Newport's holiday season is lovely. A light snowfall can peel back the years, and it isn't difficult to imagine the city 200 years ago. Bowen's Wharf, decked out in white lights, provides Newport with its version of the Rockefeller Center tree. "Christmas in Newport," a program that began in 1971, hosts a number of activities—tree lightings, Nativity scenes, a lighted boat parade, dances, concerts, and visits by Santa—for nearly every day of the December calendar. The Breakers, the Elms, and Marble House are dressed up in full holiday regalia beginning in mid-November. The Breakers, filled with evergreens and thousands of poinsettias, hosts live holiday music on Saturday evenings, and Rosecliff is an exquisite setting for performances of *The Nutcracker*.

Fun options with the kids are ice skating at Gurney's outdoor rink and, during February school break, the annual Newport Winter Festival, with concerts, ice-carving demos, the Mac & Cheese Smackdown, and a chili cook-off.

FISHING
Sara Star Charters
FISHING | Capt. Joe Aiello and his first mate, daughter Coral Rose, will take you on a half- or full-day inshore or offshore fishing trip where you can try to catch your dinner and have a good time. All gear is provided—you just relax and reel. ✉ *142 Long Wharf* ☎ *401/623–1121* ⊕ *www.sarastarcharters.com.*

Performing Arts

Pick up the free *Newport This Week*, or visit ⊕ *www.newportri.com* or ⊕ *www.newportri.com* for entertainment listings and news about featured events.

FILM
newportFILM
FILM | FAMILY | Enjoy documentary films curated from film festivals around the world thanks to this nonprofit group that hosts outdoor screenings and minifestivals in various outdoor spaces around Newport, with programming for both adults and students throughout the year. ✉ *174 Bellevue Ave., Suite 314* ☎ *401/649–2784* ⊕ *www.newportfilm.com.*

Spend an afternoon wandering among living sculptures at the Green Animals Topiary Garden in Portsmouth.

Portsmouth

9 miles north of Newport.

Largely a bedroom community for Newport, Portsmouth attracts visitors for polo matches, its fanciful topiary garden, and the Greenvale winery. The town also has an interesting history. A religious dissident named Anne Hutchinson (for whom New York's Hutchinson River Parkway is named) led a group of settlers to the Portsmouth area in 1638 after being banished from the Massachusetts Bay Colony. The town was also the site of the Battle of Rhode Island on August 29, 1778, when American troops—including a locally recruited African-American regiment—withdrew, leaving Aquidneck Island under British control.

◉ Sights

Green Animals Topiary Garden

GARDEN | FAMILY | Fanciful animals, a sailing ship, and geometric shapes populate this large topiary garden on a Narragansett Bay-side Victorian estate that served as the summer residence of a Fall River, Massachusetts, textile mill owner. In addition to the whimsical topiaries, there are flower and herb gardens, orchards, winding pathways, and a white clapboard house with original family furnishings and an antique toy collection. ✉ *380 Cory's La., off Rte. 114* ☎ *401/847–1000* ⊕ *www.newportmansions.org* ✉ *$18.*

Greenvale Vineyards

WINERY/DISTILLERY | A restored stable on an eight-generations-old farm houses the tasting room of this small producer. All wines, including the semisweet Skipping Stone White with peach notes and the well-balanced Meritage red blend, are made from grapes grown and hand-harvested on the property. Tastings are offered daily most of the year, and outdoor tables overlooking neat rows of vines abound. On Saturday, May–early December, the winery hosts live jazz concerts. ⊠ *582 Wapping Rd.* ☎ *401/847-3777* ⊕ *www.greenvale.com* ⊠ *Tastings and tours from $15* ⊙ *Closed weekdays Jan.–mid-Feb.*

Rail Explorers

SCENIC DRIVE | FAMILY | The tracks were laid in the 1860s; the tandem and quad rail machines are newfangled contraptions that make it easy to glide six miles along Narragansett Bay as long as at least one member of your group is willing to pedal. Guide-led tours of either the Northern Ramble or Southern Circuit offer glimpses of shorebirds, coastal woodlands, and historic sites few travelers get the chance to see. ⊠ *1 Alexander Rd.* ☎ *877/833-8588* ⊕ *www.railexplorers. net* ⊙ *Closed Nov.–mid-May.*

🏃 Activities

POLO

Newport International Polo Series

PARK—SPORTS-OUTDOORS | FAMILY | Head to America's oldest polo club for an action-packed afternoon. Teams from across the nation and around the world compete in Saturday matches during the Newport International Polo Series, June to November, in Portsmouth. Spectators are invited to stomp divots at the half and mingle with players and pet the horses after the match. Dress spiffy and arrive early with your picnic lunch to get a choice tailgating spot. Food trucks and walk-up bars are also available, or have the Veuve Clicquot Cart deliver bubbly to your picnic spot. ⊠ *Glen Farm, 250 Linden La.* ☎ *401/846-0200* ⊕ *www.nptpolo.com* ⊠ *From $20.*

Bristol

15 miles north of Newport, 17 miles southeast of Providence.

The home of the longest-running July 4 celebration—it began in 1785—Bristol shows off its patriotism with a red-white-and-blue center stripe down Hope Street, its charming business district, and flags flying from many homes and businesses. Midway between Newport and Providence—each a 30-minute drive away—Bristol sits on a 10-square-mile peninsula between Narragansett Bay to the west and Mt. Hope Bay to the east. Bristol was once a boatbuilding center; the Herreshoff Manufacturing Company built five consecutive America's Cup defenders between 1893 and 1920. Independence Park marks the southern end of the 14½-mile East Bay Bike Path, which crosses the access road for Colt State Park, a great spot for picnicking and kite flying.

👁 Sights

Blithewold Mansion, Gardens, and Arboretum

GARDEN | FAMILY | Starting with a sea of daffodils in April, this 33-acre estate on Bristol Harbor blooms all the way to fall. Highlights include fragrant pink chestnut roses and one of the largest giant sequoia trees on the East Coast. The gardens are open year-round. The 45-room English-style manor house, opened seasonally, is filled with original antiques and artworks. ⊠ *101 Ferry Rd. (Rte. 114)* ☎ *401/253-2707* ⊕ *www. blithewold.org* ⊠ *$15* ⊙ *Closed Mon. and mansion closed mid-Oct.–early Apr. except for Dec. holiday programming.*

Herreshoff Marine Museum/America's Cup Hall Of Fame

MUSEUM | This maritime museum, devoted to the sport of yachting, honors the Herreshoff Manufacturing Company, maker of yachts for five consecutive America's Cup defenses. The museum's several dozen boats range from an

8½-foot dinghy to the *Defiant*, a 75-foot successful America's Cup defender. Halsey Herreshoff, a four-time cup defender and the grandson of yacht designer and company co-founder Nathanael Greene Herreshoff, established the hall of fame in 1992 as an arm of the museum, which hosts talks on yacht design and restoration and operates a sailing school for both kids and adults. ✉ *1 Burnside St.* ☎ *401/253–5000* 🌐 *www.herreshoff.org* 🎟 *$15.*

Warren

TOWN | North of Bristol, Warren has the distinction of being the smallest town in the smallest county in the smallest state in the United States. The East Bay Bike Path travels through Warren's commercial district, so stop for a Del's frozen lemonade. ✉ *Warren* 🌐 *www.discoverwarren.com.*

🍴 Restaurants

Beehive Café

$ | AMERICAN | This aptly named two-story café is abuzz with college students and foodies who appreciate the freshly baked bread, especially when it's used to make inventive sandwiches like roasted butternut squash with caramelized onions, Vermont cheddar, and tangy-sweet pesto. The extensive breakfast menu (served 12 hours a day) includes thick-cut French toast, cornbread hash, and gluten-free granola made on-site. **Known for:** downtown location; cozy seating; patio and balcony dining in warm weather. [$] *Average main: $14* ✉ *10 Franklin St.* ☎ *401/396–9994* 🌐 *www.thebeehivecafe.com* 🕒 *Closed Tues. and Wed.*

DeWolf Tavern

$$ | ECLECTIC | An 1818 rum distillery houses this distinctive waterfront restaurant—look for the timber ceilings, African granite from slave ship ballast in the walls, and framed sections of early-19th-century graffiti-covered plaster. Chef Sai Viswanath reinvents traditional New England fare by combining it with Indian preparations to create dishes like lobster roasted in a 900°F tandoor oven and seafood stew simmered in a coconut, coriander, and Thai-chili broth. **Known for:** buck-a-shuck oysters on Monday; alfresco dining on the back deck in summer; cozy dining upstairs by the fireplace in winter; breakfast on weekends. [$] *Average main: $24* ✉ *259 Thames St.* ☎ *401/254–2005* 🌐 *www.dewolftavern.com.*

The Lobster Pot

$$$ | SEAFOOD | Folks have been coming here since 1929 for lobster: salad roll, on pizza, or whole—but wait, there's also grilled swordfish, roasted cod, broiled scallops, bouillabaise, and steak or chicken, too. At lunch or dinner, start with a craft brew or cocktail, then build your own plate from the raw bar: jumbo shrimp, oysters, littleneck and cherrystone clams, or cold lobster cocktail. **Known for:** classic New England seafood; harborside location; patio dining in summer, cozy fireplace in winter. [$] *Average main: $32* ✉ *119 Hope St.* ☎ *401/253–9100* 🌐 *www.lobsterpotri.com* 🕒 *Closed Mon. in off-season.*

Roberto's

$$$ | ITALIAN | The East Bay's best Italian restaurant can compete with any establishment on Federal Hill with its house-made arancini, nine classic veal and chicken preparations, and owner Robert Vanderhoof's thoughtful wine list. One wall of the elegant dining room is paneled with wine crates. **Known for:** cell-phone-free zone; reservations essential on summer weekends; alfresco dining in summer. [$] *Average main: $25* ✉ *450 Hope St.* ☎ *401/254–9732* 🕒 *No lunch.*

🛏 Hotels

Bristol Harbor Inn

$ | HOTEL | Ideally situated adjacent to DeWolf Tavern and just steps from the East Bay Bike Path, this waterfront boutique hotel has fresh, nautical styling and sunny guest rooms. **Pros:** reasonably priced for a waterfront hotel;

Fishing boats rest off the coast of Rhode Island.

convenient location; spa on-site; free parking. **Cons:** other than shops, restaurants, and marina, there are no exterior grounds; no breakfast or coffee available free to guests (although Empire Tea & Coffee is on-site); no room service. $ *Rooms from: $169* ✉ *Thames Landing, 259 Thames St.* ☎ *401/254–1444, 866/254–1444* ⊕ *www.bristolharborinn.com* ⤶ *52 rooms* ⦿ *No meals.*

🏃 Activities

BIKING
East Bay Bike Path
BICYCLING | FAMILY | Affording majestic views of Narragansett Bay, the flat, paved, 14½-mile East Bay Bike Path connects Providence and Bristol's historic downtown. ✉ *Thames St.* ☎ *401/253–7482* ⊕ *www.riparks.com/Locations/LocationEastBay.html.*

Tiverton and Little Compton

Tiverton, 8 miles south of Bristol; Little Compton, 12 miles south of Tiverton.

This southernmost corner of Rhode Island, home to artists and working farms, is a pleasant afternoon drive from Newport or Bristol. Consider a hike in Tiverton's Weetamoo Woods or Little Compton's Wilbour Woods—or wander Tiverton Four Corners and check out the village's artist studios and arts center.

GETTING HERE AND AROUND
From Route 24 at the Sakonnet River Bridge, take Route 77 south for about 5¾ miles to reach historic Tiverton Four Corners. Continuing south to Little Compton you'll pass rolling estates, lovely homes, farmland, woods, and a gentle shoreline.

◉ Sights

Carolyn's Sakonnet Vineyard

WINERY/DISTILLERY | White, rosé, red, and dessert wines are all in the portfolio of this winery founded in 1975 and reinvigorated since 2012 by second owner Carolyn Rafaelian. If you've ever wondered what a Rhode Island Red (not the chicken!) might taste like, here's your chance to find out. Several of the wines are award winners. In the winery's tasting room you can sample seven of them and keep the glass. ⊠ *162 W. Main Rd., Little Compton* ☎ *401/635–8486* ⊕ *www.sakonnetwine.com* ✉ *Tasting $14* ⟳ *Closed Tues. and Wed.*

Little Compton Commons

PLAZA | This archetypal rural New England town square is actually Rhode Island's only town common. More of a long triangle than a square, the common is anchored by the Georgian-style United Congregational Church. Among the headstones in the nearby cemetery, you'll find one for Elizabeth Pabodie, the eldest daughter of *Mayflower* Pilgrims John and Priscilla Alden. Surrounding the green are a rock wall and all the elements of a small community: town hall, community center, schools, library, general store, and restaurant. ⊠ *1 Commons, Little Compton* ⊕ *www.littlecomptonri.org.*

Sakonnet Point

NATURE SITE | A scenic drive down Route 77 ends at this quiet southeastern tip of Rhode Island. People like to fish off the Army Corps of Engineers breakwater, or walk along it to enjoy views of the harbor. The 1884 Sakonnet Lighthouse on Little Cormorant Rock is picturesque, offshore, and not open to the public. Parking is limited in the area. ⊠ *Sakonnet Point, 19 Bluff Head Ave., Little Compton.*

Tiverton Four Corners

ARTS VENUE | Historic Tiverton Four Corners has been a part of Tiverton's history since 1629 when Governor Bradford of the Plymouth Colony purchased the area (then called Pocasset) from the native inhabitants. The "four corners" intersection follows the original trails. Today, the Four Corners Arts Center, in the circa 1800 Soule-Seabury House, hosts an annual antiques show, as well as art festivals and exhibits, concerts and movement classes, and other special events. ⊠ *Rte. 179, at Rte. 77, Tiverton* ⊕ *www.tivertonfourcorners.com.*

Weetamoo Woods & Pardon Gray Preserve

FOREST | **FAMILY** | Weetamoo Woods takes its name from a formidable female sachem of the Pocasset Wampanoag tribe. There are more than 10 miles of walking trails within this 650-acre town-owned parcel and the adjacent 230-acre Tiverton Land Trust nature preserve, which encompass a coastal oak-holly forest, an Atlantic white cedar swamp, two grassland meadows, early-American cellar holes, and the remains of a mid-19th-century village sawmill. The main entrance to Weetamoo Woods, ¼-mile east of Tiverton Four Corners, has a parking area and a kiosk with maps. ⊠ *East Rd., Tiverton* ☎ *401/625–1300* ⊕ *www.tivertonlandtrust.org.*

Wilbour Woods

FOREST | **FAMILY** | This 85-acre hollow with picnic tables and a waterfall is a good place for a casual hike along a marked 1.6-mile loop trail that winds along and over Dundery Brook. The trail passes a boulder dedicated to Queen Awashonks, who ruled the local Saugkonnates tribe during the early Colonial period. ⊠ *111 Swamp Rd., Little Compton.*

◉ Coffee and Quick Bites

★ Gray's Ice Cream

$ | **AMERICAN** | A summertime pilgrimage destination for people from every corner of the state, this ice-cream stop that's been around since 1923 sells more than 30 flavors of ice cream, all made on the premises. Coffee is the go-to flavor for most Rhode Islanders, but specialties such as Indian pudding and apple caramel spice have their adherents. **Known for:** cones, cups, cabinets (milk shakes without ice cream), and frappes (milk shakes with ice cream), frozen yogurt, sherbet, and sugar-free flavors, too; open 365 days year-round. [$] *Average main:* ✉ *16 East Rd., Tiverton* ☎ *401/624–4500* 🌐 *www.graysicecream.com.*

Block Island

Block Island, with its 1,050 year-round residents, is a laid-back community about 12 miles off Rhode Island's southern coast. The island has 17 miles of beaches that are all open to everyone. Despite the influx of summer visitors and thanks to the efforts of local conservationists, Block Island's beauty remains intact. More than 43% of the land is preserved, and the relatively small island's 365 freshwater ponds support some 150 bird species that migrate seasonally along the Atlantic Flyway.

Also known by its sole town's name, New Shoreham, Block Island is not all beaches and birds. Nightlife abounds in the summer at bars and restaurants, and it's casual—you can go anywhere in shorts and a T-shirt. The busiest season, when the population explodes to 15,000 to 20,000 per day, is May–mid-October. If you plan to stay overnight in the summer, make reservations well in advance: for weekends in July and August, booking in March is not too early. In the off-season, most restaurants, inns, stores, and visitor services close down, though some visitors brave the elements on Groundhog Day to join island residents who gather at a local pub for an informal census.

Cell service and Internet can be spotty here, especially when it is raining and the entire island seems to be trying to stream content simultaneously. GPS isn't terribly useful, because street addresses aren't commonly used.

GETTING HERE AND AROUND

AIR

New England Airlines operates frequent scheduled flights year-round between Westerly and Block Island State Airport.

FERRY

There's year-round car-and-passenger ferry service to Block Island from the Port of Galilee, in the town of Narragansett in Rhode Island's South County. Seasonal passenger-only ferry service is available from Newport; New London, Connecticut; Fall River, Massachusetts; and Montauk, New York. Most ferry companies permit bicycles; the charge for bicycles runs $3.50–$10 each way.

The most heavily trafficked route is Block Island Ferry's car-passenger service and high-speed passenger service between Point Judith Terminal in Galilee, on the mainland, and Block Island's Old Harbor. By traditional ferry, the 55-minute trip costs about $12 one-way for passengers (rates fluctuate with oil prices) and $40 one-way for automobiles. Ferries run from one to three times per day in winter to eight or nine times per day in summer. Make car reservations well ahead by telephone. Arrive 45 minutes ahead in high season to allow time to find parking in the pay lots ($5–$15 per day) that surround the docks. From early June to mid-October daily (and Friday through Sunday until late November, plus daily Thanksgiving week), the high-speed service makes two to six 30-minute trips ($20 one-way) along the same route. There is no auto service on the high-speed ferry, but you can bring a bicycle ($4); passenger reservations are recommended.

Block Island Ferry also operates seasonal high-speed service from Newport's Perrotti Park to Old Harbor. The passengers-only ferry makes two trips a day, each way, from late June through Labor Day. One-way rates are about $25.50; online reservations are recommended. Approximate sailing time is 60 minutes.

From late May through Labor Day, passenger-only ferries operated by Block Island Express run between New London, Connecticut, and Old Harbor. The ferries depart from New London several times a day and take about 80 minutes. Tickets are about $26 one-way; bikes cost $10. Reservations are recommended.

Viking Fleet runs high-speed passenger service from Montauk, Long Island, to New Harbor on Block Island from Memorial Day through Columbus Day. The boat departs from Montauk at 10 am and leaves Block Island at 2 pm, plus an additional trip on Sundays in July and August that departs from Block Island at noon and Montauk at 5 pm. The fare is $40 one-way; bicycles are allowed. Travel time is one hour and 15 minutes.

GETTING AROUND

Block Island has two harbors, Old Harbor and New Harbor. Approaching the island by sea from New London, Newport, or Point Judith, you'll see Old Harbor, the island's only village, and its group of Victorian hotels. Most of the smaller inns, shops, and restaurants are also here. It's a short walk from the ferry landing to beaches, interesting sights, and many accommodations.

A car isn't necessary but can be helpful if you're staying far from Old Harbor or visiting for a long time. You can rent one at Block Island Bike and Car Rental.

ESSENTIALS

AIR TRAVEL CONTACTS Block Island State Airport. ✉ *4 Center Rd., New Shoreham* ☎ *401/466–5511* ⊕ *www.pvdairport.com/ corporate/general-aviation/block-island-bid.* **New England Airlines.** ✉ *Westerly State Airport, 56 Airport Rd., Westerly* ☎ *401/596–2460, 800/243–2460* ⊕ *www. blockislandsairline.com.* **Westerly State Airport.** ✉ *56 Airport Rd., Westerly* ☎ *401/596–2357* ⊕ *www.pvdairport.com/ corporate/general-aviation/westerly-wst.*

BIKE AND CAR RENTAL CONTACT Block Island Bike and Car Rental. ✉ *834 Ocean Ave., New Shoreham* ☎ *401/466–2297* ⊕ *www.blockislandbikeandcarrental.com.*

BOAT AND FERRY CONTACTS Block Island Express. ✉ *2 Ferry St., New London* ☎ *401/466–2212, 860/444–4624* ⊕ *www. goblockisland.com.* **Block Island Ferry.** ✉ *304 Great Island Rd., Narragansett* ☎ *401/783–7996, 866/783–7996* ⊕ *www. blockislandferry.com.* **Viking Fleet.** ✉ *462 W. Lake Dr., Montauk* ☎ *631/668–5700* ⊕ *www.vikingfleet.com.*

VISITOR INFORMATION Block Island Chamber of Commerce. ☎ *401/466–2982* ⊕ *www.blockislandchamber.com.* **Block Island Tourism Council.** ☎ *401/466–5200, 800/383–2474* ⊕ *www.blockislandinfo.com.*

◉ Sights

★ Mohegan Bluffs

BEACH—SIGHT | FAMILY | The dramatic 200-foot clay cliffs along Mohegan Trail, one of the island's top sights, offer a craggy beauty not found anywhere else in New England. On a clear day you can see all the way to Montauk Point on Long Island. The bluffs can be enjoyed from street level, but to access the beach below requires descending a steep set of more than 140 stairs that lead to the bottom. The cove to the west has a narrow strip of secluded sandy beach, with wave action that attracts surfers. ■ **TIP→ Wear walking shoes, and don't attempt the descent unless you're in reasonably good shape, as you may have to scramble over rocks at the base of the stairs.** Remember, you'll also have to climb back up! ✉ *Mohegan Bluffs Trailhead, 289 Spring St., New Shoreham.*

New Harbor

COMMERCIAL CENTER | The Great Salt Pond has a culture all its own, centered on the three marinas, several inns and a resort hotel, and four restaurants clustered along its southern shore that make up this commercial area about a 30-minute walk from Old Harbor. Up to 2,000 boats create

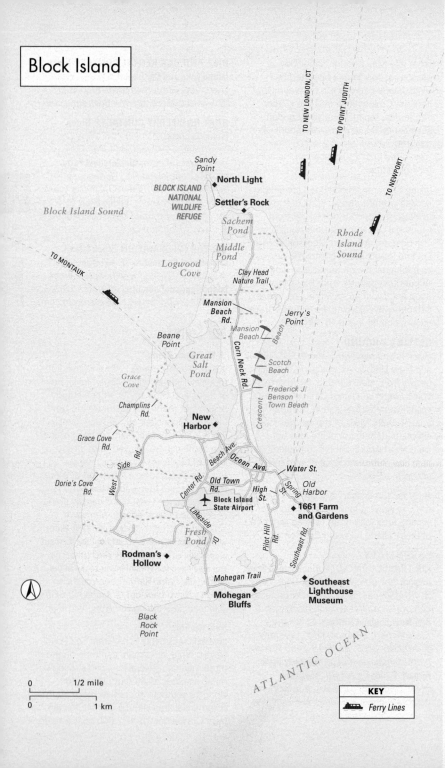

a forest of masts on summer weekends, drawn by sail races and fishing tournaments. Over on the quiet north and east shores, clammers and windsurfers claim the tidal flats. The Montauk ferry docks at Champlin's, the largest of the marinas. ⌧ *Great Salt Pond, New Shoreham.*

North Light

HISTORIC SITE | FAMILY | An 1867 granite lighthouse on the northern tip of the Block Island National Wildlife Refuge (the fourth lighthouse on this site), North Light also serves as a maritime museum. The refuge is home to American oystercatchers, piping plovers, and other rare migrating birds. From a parking lot at the end of Corn Neck Road, it's a ½-mile hike over sand to the lighthouse. Seals sun themselves on nearby Sandy Point in winter, and some even summer here. ⌧ *Block Island National Wildlife Refuge, Corn Neck Rd., New Shoreham* ☎ *401/364–9124* ⊕ *www.fws.gov/refuge/ block_island* ⌧ *Suggested donation.*

★ Rodman's Hollow

NATURE PRESERVE | FAMILY | This easy-to-find nature preserve is many people's first point of contact with the island's Greenway Trails system. The main trail runs south about 1 mile to clay bluffs with great ocean views, from which a winding path descends to the rocky beach below. Side trails cross the 230-acre tract, offering longer hikes and the allure of getting mildly lost. The striking, if muted, natural beauty makes it easy to understand why, 40 years ago, this was the property that first awoke the local land conservation movement, now close to achieving its goal of preserving half the island. Geology buffs will appreciate this fine example of a glacial outwash basin. Nature lovers may enjoy looking for the Block Island meadow vole (field mouse), the northern harrier (a threatened raptor species), and the American burying beetle (the equally imperiled state insect). A small parking lot sits just south of Cooneymus Road near a stone marker. ⌧ *Cooneymus Rd., New Shoreham* ⊕ *www.nature.org.*

1661 Farm and Gardens

FARM/RANCH | FAMILY | Animals you know and love and some you never knew existed—like the zedonk, a cross between a zebra and a donkey—are on display at this farm. Camels, llamas, a yak, kangaroos, and even fainting goats (whose legs stiffen when they get excited, causing them to keel over) will all gladly munch pellets out of your hand. Black swans stroll about, and lemurs leap around their own enclosure. A herd of gentle alpacas provides fibers for the adjacent North Light Fibers textile mill and shop. ⌧ *Off Spring St., New Shoreham* ☎ *401/466–2421, 800/626–4773* ⊕ *www.blockislandresorts. com/exotic-farm-and-gardens* ⌧ *Free.*

Southeast Lighthouse Museum

MUSEUM | The small museum is housed inside an 1875 redbrick lighthouse with striking architectural details. The lighthouse, which was moved back 300 feet from the eroded clay cliffs of Mohegan Bluffs, is a National Historic Landmark. Tower tours are sometimes offered during the summer. ⌧ *122 Mohegan Tr., New Shoreham* ☎ *401/466–5009* ⌧ *Tours $10* ⊙ *Closed Columbus Day–Memorial Day.*

🏖 Beaches

Block Island is ringed by 17 miles of ocean beaches, all open free to the public. Beaches on the eastern side of the island, in particular, have calm, warm waters that are ideal for swimming June–September.

★ Crescent Beach

BEACH—SIGHT | This 3-mile beach runs north from Old Harbor, and its white sands become wider and the crowds thinner the farther away from town you go. It is divided into smaller beaches with access points off Corn Neck Road. Farthest north is Mansion Beach: look for the sign, then follow the dirt road to the right. From the parking area, it's a short hike to reach what is easily one of New England's most beautiful beaches. In the morning, you might spot deer on the dunes; to the north, surfers can often be seen dotting Jerry's Point. Closer to Old Harbor, Scotch Beach, with its small parking lot directly off Corn Neck Road, attracts a lively crowd of young adults. Fred Benson Town Beach, in the middle, is where you'll find facilities. **Amenities:** food and drink; lifeguards; parking (no fee); showers; toilets. **Best for:** sunrise; sunset; swimming; walking. ⊠ *Corn Neck Rd., New Shoreham.*

 Restaurants

The Beachead

$$ | SEAFOOD | FAMILY | The food—especially the sriracha-sauced mussels—is consistently great, the price is right, and you won't feel like a tourist at this local favorite. Catch ocean breezes on the patio, or in stormy weather sit at the bar and watch breakers roll in 30 feet away. **Known for:** Block Island-caught lobster cooked five ways; children's menu; alfresco dining on the patio or porch. $ *Average main: $22* ⊠ *598 Corn Neck Rd., New Harbor, New Shoreham* ☎ *401/466–2249* ⊕ *www.beacheadbi.com* ⊙ *Closed mid-Oct.–Apr.*

Eli's

$$$ | AMERICAN | Creative cuisine emerges from the kitchen of this intimate bistro. The fare changes seasonally but may include pan-seared sea scallops, brined chicken, and the mouthwatering Eli's burger with seasoned fries. **Known for:** Rhode Island–caught tuna; vegetarian menu; popular with locals. $ *Average main: $30* ⊠ *456 Chapel St., Old Harbor, New Shoreham* ☎ *401/466–5230* ⊕ *www.elisblockisland.com* ⊙ *Closed Jan.–mid-Mar. No lunch.*

Finn's

$$ | SEAFOOD | A Block Island institution, Finn's serves fresh, reliable fried and broiled seafood, and a wonderful smoked bluefish dip. The island's best bet for simple steamed lobster, this is also the spot for an unfussy lunch or fried chicken with your choice of sauces and sides. **Known for:** deck seating; takeout

window and raw bar; on-site fish market. $ *Average main: $24* ⊠ *212 Water St., at ferry landing, Old Harbor, New Shoreham* ☎ *401/466–2473* ⊕ *www.finnsseafood.com* ⊙ *Closed mid-Sept.–late May.*

★ Manisses Restaurant

$$$ | AMERICAN | The chef at the island's romantic spot for elegant American cuisine relies heavily on locally caught seafood and herbs and vegetables from local farms. The many small plates make this a place to splurge without breaking the bank, and the garden seating around a fountain is tranquil. **Known for:** prix-fixe tasting menu on Tuesday and Wednesday; island-inspired cocktails; weekend brunch. $ *Average main: $30* ⊠ *Hotel Manisses, 251 Spring St., Old Harbor, New Shoreham* ☎ *401/466–9898* ⊕ *www.hotelmanisses.com/dine* ⊙ *Closed Oct.–late May.*

Restaurant 1879

$$$ | AMERICAN | At the Atlantic Inn, the food and beverage experience is as elevated as the hilltop location. The menu includes both small and large plates with abundant enticements for vegetarians as well as dishes that feature local fish and game. **Known for:** extensive tapas menu; house-made charcuterie platter; impressive wine list. $ *Average main: $32* ⊠ *The Atlantic Inn, 359 High St., Old Harbor, New Shoreham* ☎ *401/466–5883, 800/224–7422* ⊕ *www.atlanticinn.com/dining* ⊙ *Closed Mon. and Tues. and mid-Oct.–early May.*

☕ Coffee and Quick Bites

Payne's Donuts

$ | AMERICAN | In a state that takes its doughnuts seriously, the best doughy orbs require an island jaunt. Now served from a humble food truck, Payne's "killer" doughnuts have been a summer morning tradition for generations. **Known for:** an inexpensive treat; worth the mile-long walk or bike ride from the ferry dock; limited beverages and other menu items. $ *Average main: $2* ⊠ *1 Ocean Ave., New Shoreham* ⊙ *Closed Columbus Day–late June.*

Hotels

It's advisable to book accommodations well in advance, especially for weekends in July and August when many hotels require a two-night minimum. The Block Island Chamber of Commerce tracks last-minute availability at member properties. Many visitors rent homes for stays of a week or more, and there are many direct rentals not listed on the best-known booking sites.

★ The Atlantic Inn

$$ | **HOTEL** | Perched on a hill amid floral gardens and undulating lawns, away from the hubbub of the Old Harbor area, this classic Victorian (1879) resort dazzles guests with its big windows, high ceilings, sweeping staircase, and mesmerizing views. **Pros:** spectacular hilltop location; beautiful veranda for whiling away the afternoon; grand decor; excellent Restaurant 1879 serves small and large plates. **Cons:** an uphill trek from the ferry dock; no handicap-accessible rooms; no TV in most rooms and slow Internet in the lobby only. [$] *Rooms from: $250* ✉ *359 High St., Old Harbor, New Shoreham* ☎ *401/466–5883, 800/224–7422* 🌐 *www.atlanticinn.com* 🕒 *Closed mid-Oct.–early May* 🛏 *21 rooms* 🍴 *Free breakfast.*

The Barrington Inn

$$ | **B&B/INN** | **FAMILY** | This 19th-century Victorian farmhouse, high on a hill overlooking Great Salt Pond, is now a quiet, refreshed, and bright B&B inn with water views from most rooms. **Pros:** commanding views; reasonably priced; close to beaches. **Cons:** three-night minimum on July and August weekends; extra nightly fee for children ages six and up; breakfast not included for weekly guests. [$] *Rooms from: $200* ✉ *584 Beach Ave., New Harbor, New Shoreham* ☎ *401/466–5510* 🌐 *www.barringtoninnbi.com* 🕒 *Closed Dec.–Apr.* 🛏 *7 rooms* 🍴 *Free breakfast.*

Blue Dory Inn

$$ | **B&B/INN** | This Old Harbor district inn, with a main building and three suites in an adjacent cottage, has been a guesthouse since its construction in 1898. **Pros:** great in-town location—walk to the ferry; Block Island Barnacle cookies are a treat; pets allowed in some rooms with notice. **Cons:** some units are small; two-night minimum required May–mid-October; extra charge for pets. [$] *Rooms from: $250* ✉ *61 Dodge St., Old Harbor, New Shoreham* ☎ *401/466–5891* 🌐 *www.blockislandinns.com/blue-dory* 🛏 *11 rooms, 3 suites* 🍴 *Free breakfast.*

★ Payne's Harbor View Inn

$$ | **B&B/INN** | This 2002 inn, designed to blend with the island's historic architecture, occupies a breezy hillside overlooking the Great Salt Pond and is just minutes from Crescent Beach. **Pros:** free parking; kayak and paddleboard rentals; handicap ramp and accessible shower in Room 1. **Cons:** books up fast; no children under 12; about a mile from "town." [$] *Rooms from: $235* ✉ *111 Beach Ave., corner of Ocean Ave., New Shoreham* ✥ *New Harbor* ☎ *401/466–5758* 🌐 *www.paynesharborviewinn.com* 🕒 *Closed mid-Oct.–late May* 🛏 *10 rooms* 🍴 *Free breakfast.*

Rose Farm Inn

$ | **B&B/INN** | With simple accommodations in a late-19th-century farmhouse and more luxurious units in a more modern structure across a country lane, this property is set on a 20-acre pastoral farmstead. **Pros:** choose an ocean or countryside view; informal hospitality; quiet setting yet easy, 10-minute walk to town. **Cons:** full payment due at time of booking; no kids under age 12; "light" continental breakfast. [$] *Rooms from: $149* ✉ *1005 High St., Old Harbor, New Shoreham* ☎ *401/466–2034* 🌐 *www.rosefarminn.com* 🕒 *Closed mid-Oct.–early May* 🛏 *19 rooms* 🍴 *Free breakfast.*

★ Spring House Hotel

$$ | **HOTEL** | **FAMILY** | The rooms in this charming old (1852) seaside inn—the island's oldest, largest, and most famous hotel—suit today's expectations. **Pros:** welcoming atmosphere; stunning views from the breezy front porch; happily accommodates infants and children; farm-to-table, indoor-outdoor dining on-site from June–September. **Cons:** dining areas sometimes closed for private events; no elevator; about a 15-minute walk to the activity at Old Harbor. [$] *Rooms from: $295* ✉ *52 Spring St., Old Harbor, New Shoreham* ☎ *401/466–5844* 🌐 *www.springhouseblockisland.com* 🕒 *Closed Nov.–Apr.* 🛏 *33 rooms (Main House)* 🍴 *No meals.*

Nightlife

Nightlife, at least in season, is one of Block Island's highlights—and you have your pick of some two dozen places to grab a drink. Check the Block Island Chamber's online calendar for music and entertainment listings.

Ballard's Beach Resort

BARS/PUBS | On its own private beach, Ballard's has oceanfront tiki bars, VIP cabana rentals, and a barnlike restaurant with a dance floor and live music. It's party time all the time here. ✉ *42 Water St., Old Harbor, New Shoreham* ☎ *401/466–2231, 844/405–3275* 🌐 *www.ballardsbi.com* 🎫 *No cover charge.*

Captain Nick's Rock n' Roll Bar

BARS/PUBS | This place sets itself apart from the others by hosting June's Block Island Music Festival, a free roundup of soon-to-be-discovered bands from around the country. It has live music inside and out, a dog-friendly area, frozen cocktails, and a suntanned crowd. Disco Monday has been an island tradition for more than two decades. ✉ *34 Ocean Ave., New Shoreham* ☎ *401/466–5670* 🌐 *www.captainnicksbi.com.*

Club Soda

BARS/PUBS | One of the few spots open year-round, Club Soda is a lively hangout with a 12x8-foot outdoor TV. Shoot pool or tuck into some tasty pub grub. Live music

One of the few spots open year-round, Club Soda is a lively hangout with a 12x8-foot outdoor TV. Shoot pool or tuck into some tasty pub grub. Live music ✉ *35 Connecticut Ave., New Shoreham* ☎ *401/466–5397.*

Mahogany Shoals

BARS/PUBS | A tiny shack built over the water at Payne's Dock, Mahogany Shoals has a laid-back vibe and live music every night. The place has expanded, gracefully, with an outdoor bar and an upper-level deck. It remains the best spot on the island to enjoy a quiet drink, peer at beautiful yachts, and catch a breeze on even the hottest of nights. ✉ *Payne's Dock, 133 Ocean Ave., New Harbor, New Shoreham* ☎ *401/466–5572* 🌐 *paynes-dock.com.*

Yellow Kittens Tavern

BARS/PUBS | Patrons here amuse themselves with darts, pinball, table tennis, and pool, to the sound of live bands or DJs on many summer nights. By day, order drinks and a big plate of nachos on Los Gatitos Deck overlooking the dunes at the southern end of Crescent Beach. ✉ *214 Corn Neck Rd., New Harbor, New Shoreham* ☎ *401/466–5855* 🌐 *www.yellowkittens.com.*

Activities

BIKING

The best way to explore Block Island is by bicycle ($20–$30 a day to rent) or moped (from $35 per hour, from $95 per day). Most rental places are open spring–fall and offer baby seats and tag-alongs for bikes and free helmets (required for those under 16). All rent bicycles in various styles and sizes, including mountain bikes, comfort cruisers, tandems, and children's bikes.

Island Moped and Bike Rentals

BICYCLING | FAMILY | This shop has bikes of all kinds and scooters for hourly, daily, multiday, and weekly rentals. Pickup is free from anywhere on the island; discounts are available for groups of three or more. ⊠ *41 Water St., Old Harbor* ☎ *401/466–2700* ⊕ *www.bimopeds.com.*

Old Harbor Bike Shop

BICYCLING | FAMILY | Descend from the Block Island Ferry and hop right on a bike at this shop, which rents cruisers, tandems, and baby seats, tag-alongs, and trailers, as well as mopeds. ⊠ *1 Water St., south of ferry dock, New Shoreham* ☎ *401/466–2029* ⊕ *blockislandmoped.com.*

BOATING

Fort Island Kayaks & SUPs

KAYAKING | FAMILY | Kayaks and standup paddleboards (including pedalboards) are available for all ages and abilities and may be rented by the hour, half- or full-day, or week. ⊠ *Block Island Fishworks, 40 Ocean Ave., New Harbor, New Shoreham* ☎ *401/466–5392* ⊕ *www.sandypointco. com* ⌣ *Closed Nov.–Apr.*

★ Pond and Beyond

BOATING | FAMILY | Guided paddling eco-tours around the Great Salt Pond are a specialty here, as are family and full moon kayak tours. Located on the Block Island Maritime Institute property, this outfitter also rents single and double kayaks and provides a brief introduction for those who want to explore for an hour or more on their own. ⊠ *216 Ocean Ave., corner West Side Rd., New Harbor, New Shoreham* ☎ *401/578–2773* ⊕ *www. pondandbeyondkayak.com* ⊙ *Closed mid-Oct.–late May.*

FISHING

Most of Rhode Island's record-setting fish have been caught on Block Island—in fact, it's held the striped bass record (currently a 77.4-pound whopper caught in 2011) since 1984. From almost any beach, skilled anglers can land tautog and bass. The Coast Guard channel is a good spot to hook porgy. Shellfishing licenses ($11 for 14 days) may be obtained online or at the harbormaster's building at the Boat Basin in New Harbor.

Block Island Fishworks

FISHING | A tiny shop in New Harbor, Block Island Fishworks sells bait and tackle and rents rods and reels. It also offers guide services and charter fishing trips targeting stripers, blues, sea bass, bonito, albies, and the occasional tuna. ⊠ *40 Ocean Ave., New Shoreham* ☎ *401/742–3992, 401/466–5392* ⊕ *www. sandypointco.com.*

Twin Maples

FISHING | For more than 60 years this family-run shop has sold bait, handmade lures, sophisticated fishing tackle, and coveted "Eat Fish" T-shirts from its Great Salt Pond location. ⊠ *63 Beach Ave., New Harbor, New Shoreham* ☎ *401/466–5547* ⊕ *jswienton.squarespace.com.*

HIKING

★ Clay Head Nature Trail

HIKING/WALKING | FAMILY | The outstanding Clay Head Nature Trail meanders past Clay Head Swamp and along 150-foot clay bluffs. Songbirds chirp and flowers bloom along the paths; stick close to the ocean for a stunning hike that ends at Sachem Pond or venture into the interior's intertwining paths for hours of wandering and blackberrying in an area called The Maze. The trailhead is recognizable by a simple white post marker on the east side of Corn Neck Road, about 2 miles north of Old Harbor. ⊠ *Clay Head Trail, New Shoreham.*

WATER SPORTS

Diamondblue Surf Shop

WATER SPORTS | This shop stocks surf gear and offers wet suit, boogie board, surfboard, and standup paddleboard rentals. Their instructors will get you up riding waves. ⊠ *442 Dodge St., corner Corn Neck Rd., New Harbor, New Shoreham* ☎ *401/466–3145* ⊕ *www.diamondbluebi.com.*

🛍 Shopping

ART GALLERIES

Jessie Edwards Studio

ART GALLERIES | This gallery specializes in the work of local and regional artists: photographs, sculptures, ceramics, and contemporary American paintings, often with coastal themes. ⊠ *Post Office Bldg., 32 Water St., 2nd fl., New Shoreham* ✛ *Old Harbor* ☎ *401/466–5314* ⊕ *www. jessieedwardsgallery.com.*

Malcolm Greenaway Gallery

ART GALLERIES | Malcolm Greenaway has taken magnificent photographs of Block Island places and scenes since moving here in 1974. In his Water Street gallery, he sells prints in various sizes—print only, matted, or matted and framed. ⊠ *Water St., Old Harbor, New Shoreham* ☎ *401/466–5331, 800/840–5331* ⊕ *www. malcolmgreenaway.com.*

Spring Street Gallery

ART GALLERIES | The gallery, located in an old (renovated) horse barn for nearly 40 years, exhibits paintings, photographs, pottery, and jewelry by island artists and artisans. ⊠ *105 Spring St., Old Harbor, New Shoreham* ☎ *401/466–5374* ⊕ *www. springstreetgallery.org.*

JEWELRY

Golddiggers

JEWELRY/ACCESSORIES | You can pick up handmade pendants, rings, earrings, and bracelets with maritime (and Block Island) themes at this jewelry store. ⊠ *90 Chapel St., Old Harbor, New Shoreham* ☎ *401/466–2611* ⊕ *www.blockislandgold-diggers.com.*

TEXTILES

★ North Light Fibers

CLOTHING | The adjoining 1661 Farm supplies wool from its alpacas, llamas, yaks, and sheep to make beautiful yarns, clothing, and blankets. Classes are offered in knitting, crochet, and felting—and you can tour the Micro Yarn Mill where the yarns are made. ⊠ *1661 Farm, Spring St., Old Harbor, New Shoreham* ☎ *401/466–2050* ⊕ *www.northlightfibers.com.*

Chapter 9

VERMONT

Updated by
Julia Clancy

◉ Sights	🍴 Restaurants	🛏 Hotels	💼 Shopping	🍸 Nightlife
★★★★★	★★★★☆	★★★★☆	★★★☆☆	★★☆☆☆

WELCOME TO VERMONT

TOP REASONS TO GO

★ **Small-Town Charm:** Vermont rolls out a seemingly never-ending supply of tiny towns replete with white-steepled churches, town greens, red barns, general stores, and bed-and-breakfasts.

★ **Ski Resorts:** The East's best skiing can be found in well-managed, modern facilities with great views and lots and lots of powdery, fresh snow.

★ **Fall Foliage:** Perhaps the most vivid colors in North America wave from the trees in September and October.

★ **Gorgeous Landscapes:** This sparsely populated, heavily forested state is an ideal place to find peace and quiet amid the mountains, valleys, and lakes.

★ **Vibrant Local Eats:** The rich soil and an emphasis on the state's maker-artisan culture has led to great dairies, orchards, vineyards, specialty stores, and farm-to-table restaurants. Even the world-famous beer scene is known to highlight state-grown hops and locally made malt.

1 Brattleboro. A hippie enclave with an artistic and activist disposition.

2 Wilmington. The hub of Mt. Snow Valley.

3 Bennington. The economic center of southwest Vermont.

4 Arlington. Once the home of painter Norman Rockwell.

5 Manchester. Sophisticated with upscale shopping.

6 Dorset. Home to two of the state's best and oldest general stores.

7 Stratton. It's all about Stratton Mountain Resort.

8 Weston. Home to the Vermont Country Store.

9 Ludlow. Okemo Mountain Resort's home.

10 Grafton. Both a town and a museum.

11 Norwich. One of the most picturesque towns.

12 Quechee. Restaurants and shops in old mills.

13 Woodstock. Upscale shops and the venerable Woodstock Inn.

14 Killington. East Coast's largest ski resort.

15 Rutland. Slowly gaining traction as a foodie town.

16 Brandon. Artists Guild and the Basin Bluegrass Festival.

17 Middlebury. Restaurants, shops, and Middlebury College.

18 Waitsfield and Warren. The ski meccas of Mad River Glen and Sugarbush.

19 Montpelier. The state's capital.

20 Stowe. Quintessential eastern ski town.

21 Jeffersonville. The four-season Smugglers' Notch Resort.

22 Burlington. Vermont's most populous city with a lively food scene.

23 Shelburne. Shelburne Farms and Shelburne Museum.

24 Lake Champlain Islands. Numerous islands including Isle La Motte, North Hero, Grand Isle, and South Hero.

25 Montgomery and Jay. Small village near the Jay Peak ski resort and the Canadian border.

26 Lake Willoughby. Home to the world-renowned Bread and Puppet Theater museum.

27 Greensboro. Home to one of the world's best breweries.

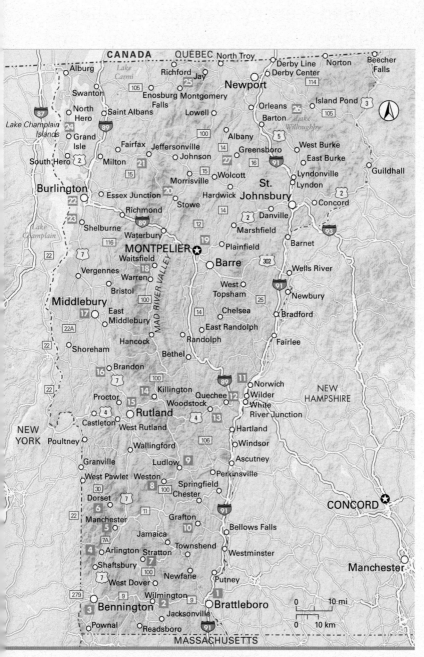

Vermont's a land of hidden treasures and unspoiled scenery. Wander anywhere in the state—nearly 80% is forest—and you'll find pristine countryside dotted with farms and framed by mountains. Tiny towns with picturesque church steeples, village greens, and covered bridges are perfect for exploring.

Sprawl has no place here. Highways are devoid of billboards by law, and on some roads cows still stop traffic twice a day en route to and from pasture. In spring, sap boils in sugarhouses, some built generations ago, while up the road a chef trained at the New England Culinary Institute in Montpelier might use the syrup to glaze a pork tenderloin.

It's the landscape, for the most part, that attracts people to Vermont. Rolling hills belie rugged terrain underneath the green canopy of forest growth. In summer, clear lakes and streams provide ample opportunities for swimming, boating, and fishing; hills attract hikers and mountain bikers. The more than 14,000 miles of roads, many of them only intermittently traveled by cars, are great for biking. In fall the leaves have their last hurrah, painting the mountainsides in vibrant yellow, gold, red, and orange. Vermont has the best ski resorts in the eastern United States, centered on the spine of the Green Mountains running north to south; and the traditional heart of skiing here is the town of Stowe. Almost anywhere you go, no matter what time of year, the Vermont countryside will make you reach for your camera.

Although Vermont may seem locked in time, technological sophistication appears where you least expect it: wireless Internet access in a 19th-century farmhouse-turned-inn and cell phone coverage from the state's highest peaks. Like an old farmhouse under renovation, though, the state's historic exterior is still the main attraction.

MAJOR REGIONS
Vermont can be divided into three regions: **Southern Vermont, Central Vermont,** and **Northern Vermont.**

Most people's introduction to the state is **Southern Vermont,** a relatively short drive from New York and Boston. As elsewhere across the state, you'll find unspoiled towns, romantic bed-and-breakfasts, lush farms, and pristine forests. The area is flanked by **Bennington** on the west and **Brattleboro** on the east. There are charming towns like **Wilmington, Arlington, Manchester, Dorset, Weston, Grafton,** and **Townshend,** as well as ski destinations like **Stratton** and **Ludlow** (home to Okemo Resort).

Central Vermont is characterized by the rugged Green Mountains, which run north–south through the center of the state, and the gently rolling dairy lands east of Lake Champlain. It's home to the state's capital, **Montpelier,** the former mill towns of **Quechee** and **Middlebury,** artist enclaves like **Brandon,** and beautiful towns like **Norwich** and **Woodstock,** and plucky **Rutland.** Ski buffs flock to **Killington** and **Waitsfield** and **Warren** (for Mad River Glen and Sugarbush).

Northern Vermont is a place of contrasts. It's where you'll find the area known as the Northeast Kingdom, a refuge for nature lovers and those who love getting away from it all, as well as the state's largest city, **Burlington,** which has dramatic views of Lake Champlain and the Adirondacks, and it's neighboring **Winooski.** There's plenty of skiing in **Stowe, Jeffersonville** (Smugglers' Notch Resort), and **Jay** (Jay Peak) as well as outdoor adventures in **Lake Willoughby** and **East Burke.** And postcard perfect scenery oozes in **Shelburne, Charlotte, Montgomery,** and the **Lake Champlain Islands.**

Planning

There are many ways to take advantage of Vermont's beauty: skiing or hiking its mountains, biking or driving its back roads, fishing or sailing its waters, shopping for local products, visiting museums and sights, or simply finding the perfect inn and never leaving the front porch.

Getting Here and Around

Distances are relatively short, yet the mountains and back roads will slow a traveler's pace. You can see a representative north–south cross section of Vermont in a few days; if you have up to a week, you can really hit the highlights.

AIR

American, Delta, JetBlue, Porter, and United fly into Burlington International Airport. Rutland State Airport has daily service to and from Boston on Cape Air.

BOAT
Lake Champlain Ferries

This company operates ferries on three routes between Vermont and New York: from Grand Isle to Plattsburgh, New York; Burlington to Port Kent; and Charlotte to Essex. ☎ *802/864–9804* ⊕ *www.ferries. com* ⊗ *No Burlington–Port Kent service late Sept.–mid-June.*

CAR

Vermont is divided by a mountainous north–south middle, with a main highway on either side: scenic U.S. 7 on the western side and Interstate 91 (which begins in New Haven, Connecticut, and runs through Hartford, central Massachusetts, and along the Connecticut River in Vermont to the Canadian border) on the east. Interstate 89 runs from New Hampshire across central Vermont from White River Junction to Burlington and up to the Canadian border. For current road conditions, check ⊕ *www.511vt.com* or call ☎ *511* in Vermont and ☎ *800/429–7623* from other states.

TRAIN
Amtrak

Amtrak has daytime service on the *Vermonter,* linking Washington, D.C., and New York City with Brattleboro, Bellows Falls, Windsor, White River Junction, Randolph, Montpelier, Waterbury, Essex Junction, and St. Albans. Amtrak's *Ethan Allen Express* connects New York City with Castleton and Rutland. ☎ *800/872–7245* ⊕ *www.amtrak.com.*

Hotels

Vermont's relatively rare large chain hotels are mostly found in Burlington, Manchester, and Rutland; elsewhere it's primarily inns, bed-and-breakfasts, and small motels. The inns and B&Bs, some of them quite luxurious, provide what many visitors consider the quintessential Vermont lodging experience. Most areas have traditional ski-base condos; at these you sacrifice charm for ski-and-stay deals and proximity to the lifts. Lodging rates are highest during foliage season, late September–mid-October, and lowest in late spring and November, although many properties close during these times. Winter is high season at ski resorts. *Hotel reviews have been shortened. For full reviews visit Fodors.com.*

Restaurants

Everything that makes Vermont good and wholesome is distilled in its restaurants. Many of them belong to the **Vermont Fresh Network** (⊕ *www.vermontfresh. net*), a partnership that encourages chefs to create menus emphasizing Vermont's wonderful bounty; especially in summer and early fall, the produce and meats are impeccable.

Great chefs come to Vermont for the quality of life, and the Montpelier-based New England Culinary Institute is a recruiting ground for new talent. Seasonal menus use local fresh herbs and vegetables along with native game. Look for imaginative approaches to New England foods like maple syrup (Vermont is the largest U.S. producer); dairy products (cheese in particular); native fruits and berries; heritage apples (explore the ever-growing cider scene); and regional game like venison, quail, and pheasant. Small-batch goods, from salsa to caramels, are made with Vermont ingredients. Beer has become yet another claim to fame in Vermont, thanks to more breweries per capita than any other state and recognition far and wide. Indeed, craft brewers as far away as Poland are now producing "Vermont-style" IPAs, and Hill Farmstead in Greensboro has been dubbed the best brewery in the world seven times by RateBeer, a brew-review website, since opening doors in 2010.

Your chances of finding a table for dinner vary with the season: lengthy waits are common in tourist centers at peak times—a reservation is always advisable.

Creemee vs. Soft-Serve

A creemee is Vermont's answer to soft-serve ice cream. It often has a higher fat content than typical soft-serve—thanks in part to state specialties like local dairy and maple syrup—making it especially rich, silky and, well, creamy. (Hence the name.)

WHAT IT COSTS in U.S. Dollars

	$	$$	$$$	$$$$
RESTAURANTS				
	under $18	$18–$24	$25–$35	over $35
HOTELS				
	under $200	$200–$299	$300–$399	over $399

Tours

Inn to Inn

TOUR—SPORTS | This company arranges guided and self-guided hiking, skiing, snowshoeing, and biking trips from inn to inn in Vermont. ⊠ *52 Park St., Brandon* ☎ *802/247–3300, 800/838–3301* ⊕ *www. inntoinn.com* ✉ *From $645.*

P.O.M.G. Bike Tours of Vermont

TOUR—SPORTS | The initials in this outfitter's name are short for "Peace Of Mind Guaranteed." The company leads weekend and multiday bike tours around the state. ☎ *802/434–2270, 888/635–2453* ⊕ *www.pomgbike.com* ✉ *From $1795.*

VBT Bicycling and Walking Vacations

TOUR—SPORTS | This guide company leads bike tours across the state. ☎ *802/951–6100, 800/245–3868* ⊕ *www.vbt.com* ✉ *From $1945.*

Visitor Information

CONTACTS Ski Vermont/Vermont Ski Areas Association. ☎ 802/223–2439 ⊕ www. skivermont.com. **Vermont Department of Tourism and Marketing.** ☎ 802/828–3237, 800/837–6668 ⊕ www.vermontvacation. com. **Vermont Foliage Hotline.** ☎ 802/828–3239 for foliage information. **Vermont's Northeast Kingdom.** ☎ 802/626–8511 ⊕ getnekedvt.com.

When to Go

In summer Vermont is lush and green, and in winter the hills and towns are blanketed white with snow, inspiring skiers to challenge the peaks at Stowe and elsewhere. Fall, however, is always the most amazing time to come. If you have never seen the state's kaleidoscope of autumn colors, it's well worth braving the slow-moving traffic and shelling out a few extra bucks for lodging. The only time things really slow down is during "stick season" in November, when the leaves have fallen but there's no snow yet, and "mud season" in late spring, when even innkeepers counsel guests to come another time. Activities in the Champlain Islands essentially come to a halt in the winter, except for ice fishing and snowmobiling, and two of the biggest attractions, Shelburne Farms and the Shelburne Museum, are closed mid-October–April. Otherwise, Vermont is open for business year-round.

Brattleboro

60 miles south of White River Junction.

Brattleboro has drawn political activists and earnest counterculturists since the 1960s. The arts-oriented town and environs (population 12,000) remains politically and culturally active; after Burlington, this is Vermont's most offbeat locale.

GETTING HERE AND AROUND

Brattleboro is near the intersection of Route 9, the principal east–west highway also known as the Molly Stark Byway, and Interstate 91. For downtown, take Exit 2 from Interstate 91.

ESSENTIALS

VISITOR INFORMATION Brattleboro Area Chamber of Commerce. ☎ 802/254–4565, 877/254–4565 ⊕ www.brattleborochamber.org.

⊙ Sights

Brattleboro Museum and Art Center
MUSEUM | Downtown is the hub of Brattleboro's art scene, at the forefront of which is this museum in historic Union Station. It presents changing exhibitions of works by local, national, and international artists, and hosts lectures, readings, and musical performances. ✉ 10 Vernon St. ☎ 802/257–0124 ⊕ www. brattleboromuseum.org ⚐ $8 ☉ Closed Tues.

Putney
TOWN | Nine miles upriver, this town of fewer than 3,000 residents—the country cousin of bustling Brattleboro—is a haven for writers and fine-craft artists. There are many pottery studios to visit, the requisite general store, and a few orchards. Each November during the Putney Craft Tour, dozens of artisans open their studios and homes for live demonstrations and plenty of fun. ✉ Putney ⊕ www. discoverputney.com.

ⓧ Restaurants

Cai's Dim Sum Catering
$ | CHINESE | The sourcing and gathering of local ingredients at the heart of chef-owner Cai Xi Silver's cooking is inspired by the food memories of her childhood in Chongqin, China. Her family's Sichuan and Shanghai influences come to life in a to-go menu that includes delicate steamed buns, perfect

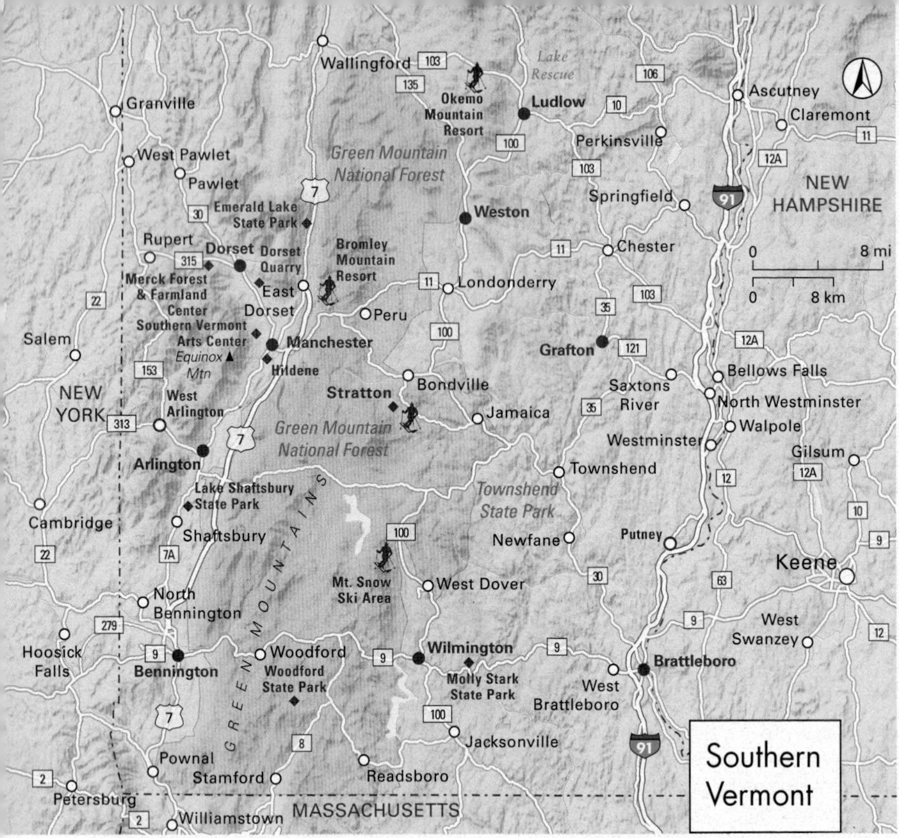

dumplings, and abundance boxes highlighting regional home cooking backed by Vermont ingredients. **Known for:** steamed buns; assorted seasonal dumplings; abundance boxes with local vegetables, rice, chicken, or tofu. [$] *Average main: $15* ✉ *814 Western Ave.* ☎ *802/257–7898* 🌐 *dimsumvt.com* 🕒 *Closed for in-room dining; catering, private dinners and take-out/delivery only.*

★ Peter Havens

$$$ | **AMERICAN** | A longtime Brattleboro favorite helmed since 2012 by chef Zachary Corbin, this chic little bistro is known for impeccably presented cuisine that draws heavily on local sources. One room is painted a warm red, another in sage, and a changing lineup of contemporary paintings adorns the walls of both rooms. **Known for:** pan-roasted duck breast; cocktail and wine list; vanilla bean crème brûlée. [$] *Average main: $30* ✉ *32 Elliot St.* ☎ *802/257–3333* 🌐 *www.peterhavens.com* 🕒 *Closed Mon. and Tues. No lunch Sun., Wed., and Thurs. Nov.–May.*

Three Stones Mexican Mayan Cocina

$ | **MEXICAN** | **FAMILY** | This cozy, family-owned restaurant is inspired by centuries of passed-down recipes from the ancient Maya, where three stones were traditionally laid to build the hearth. Dishes are infused with the culture of the Mexican state Yucutàn, and fresh tortillas are made daily alongside tamales, empanadas, and vibrant platters of rice, beans, and vegetables. **Known for:** tamales wrapped in banana leaves with achiote sauce and chicken; daily-made fresh tortillas in three authentic preparations; pumpkin seed specialty/Onzicil (toasted ground pumpkin seeds served with salad, rice and beans). [$] *Average* main: $15 ✉ 105 Canal St. ☎ 802/246–1035 ⊕ threestonesrestaurant.com ⊘ Closed Sun.–Tues.

Top of the Hill Grill
$ | BARBECUE | FAMILY | Don't let the diminutive size of this roadside smokehouse deceive you. The place produces big flavors locals line up for: hickory-smoked ribs, apple-smoked turkey, beef brisket, and pulled pork, to name a few. **Known for:** "burnt ends" (brisket burnt ends); excellent view of West River; outdoor deck. $ *Average main: $15* ✉ 632 Putney Rd. ☎ 802/258–9178 ⊕ www.topofthehill-grill.com ⊘ Closed Nov.–Mar.

Whetstone Station Restaurant and Brewery
$ | INTERNATIONAL | One of Brattleboro's most happening hangouts is this nano-brewery and restaurant perched over the Connecticut River. The beer and classic American comfort food are good, but it's the view of the river and its forested banks that drops jaws. **Known for:** rooftop beer garden; "Big 'Stoner" imperial IPA; poutine and steak tips. $ *Average main: $16* ✉ 36 Bridge St. ☎ 802/490–2354 ⊕ www.whetstonestation.com.

☕ Coffee and Quick Bites

★ Chelsea Royal Diner
$ | DINER | FAMILY | Built into a vintage 1938 Worcester diner, one of the few remaining in the country, the Chelsea Royal Diner serves all-day breakfast and Blue Plate specials from produce (eggs included) sourced from their backyard farm. Save room for homemade ice cream made with local milk and cream from the St. Albans Co-op Creamery—flavors range from VT Maple Cream to Blueberry, Pumpkin, and Mocha Malted Milk Ball. **Known for:** homemade ice cream and soft serve; all-Day Breakfast; Blue Plate Specials, like Friday Fish Fry and Sunday Yankee Pot Roast. $ *Average main: $13* ✉ 487 Marlboro Rd. ☎ 802/254–8399 ⊕ www.chelsearoyaldiner.com.

Mocha Joe's Cafe
$ | CAFÉ | The team at this spot for coffee and conversation takes great pride in sourcing direct-trade beans from places like Kenya, Ethiopia, and Guatemala, and pairs them with an assortment of cookies, cakes, and muffins. This is ground zero for Brattleboro's bohemian contingent and fellow travelers. **Known for:** socially conscious coffee; maple latte; trendy clientele. $ *Average main: $5* ✉ 82 Main St., at Elliot St. ☎ 802/257–7794 ⊕ www.mochajoes.com.

🛏 Hotels

Hickory Ridge House
$$ | B&B/INN | The historic redbrick 1808 Federal-style mansion strikes a sturdy pose on a wide meadow of a former sheep farmhouse. **Pros:** surrounded by hundreds of acres of preserved land; historic property; great for hiking and cross-country skiing. **Cons:** not within walking distance of town; lots of flowered upholstery, rugs, and curtains; two-night minimum during peak periods. $ *Rooms from: $255* ✉ 53 Hickory Ridge Rd., Putney ⊹ 11 miles north of Brattleboro ☎ 802/387–5709, 800/380–9218 ⊕ www.hickoryridgehouse.com ⤴ 8 rooms ⓞ Free breakfast.

★ The Inn on Putney Road
$$ | B&B/INN | Thoughtful and comforting details abound in this 1931 French-style manse such as the mini-refrigerator and basket stocked with complimentary soda, water, granola bars, and snacks, as well as gas fireplaces in several guest rooms. **Pros:** lovely breakfast room; nice blend of traditional and modern design; pottery by artist Steven Procter scattered throughout. **Cons:** tight parking; outside downtown; rooms in front sometimes suffer traffic noise. $ *Rooms from: $239* ✉ 192 Putney Rd. ☎ 802/536–4780 ⊕ www.vermontbandbinn.com ⤴ 6 rooms ⓞ Free breakfast.

Latchis Hotel

$ | **HOTEL** | Though not lavish, the guest rooms in this 1938 art deco building have the original sinks and tiling in the bathrooms, and many overlook Main Street, with New Hampshire's mountains in the background. **Pros:** heart-of-town location; lots of personality; reasonable rates. **Cons:** limited breakfast; sound-masking machines sometimes required; few parking spots. $ *Rooms from: $130* ✉ *50 Main St.* ☎ *802/254–6300; 800/798–6301* ⊕ *www.latchishotel.com* ⬎ *33 rooms* ⦿ *Free breakfast.*

🎭 Performing Arts

Latchis Theatre

THEMED ENTERTAINMENT | This movie theater's architecture represents a singular blending of art deco and Greek Revival style, complete with statues, columns, and 1938 murals by Louis Jambor (1884–1955), a noted artist and children's book illustrator. The Latchis hosts art exhibits, streams live events, and has four screening rooms. For a sense of the theater's original grandeur, buy a ticket for whatever is showing on the big screen. Though the space may not be a state-of-the-art cinema, watching a film here is far more memorable than at any multiplex. ✉ *50 Main St.* ☎ *802/254–6300, 800/798–6301* ⊕ *www.latchis.com.*

🏃 Activities

BIKING

Brattleboro Bicycle Shop

BICYCLING | This shop rents hybrid bikes (call ahead to reserve one), does repair work, and sells maps and equipment. ✉ *165 Main St.* ☎ *802/254–8644, 800/272–8245* ⊕ *www.bratbike.com.*

CANOEING AND KAYAKING

Vermont Canoe Touring Center

CANOEING/ROWING/SKULLING | Canoes and kayaks are available for rent here. Payment is by cash or check only. ✉ *451 Putney Rd.* ☎ *802/257–5008* ⊕ *www. vermontcanoetouringcenter.com.*

HIKING

Fort Dummer State Park

PARK—SPORTS-OUTDOORS | You can hike and camp within the 217 acres of forest at this state park, the location of the first permanent European settlement in Vermont. That site is now submerged beneath the Connecticut River, but it is viewable from the northernmost scenic vista on Sunrise Trail. ✉ *517 Old Guilford Rd.* ☎ *802/254–2610* ⊕ *www. vtstateparks.com/fortdummer.html* ✉ *$4* ⊙ *Facilities closed early Sept.–late May.*

MULTISPORT OUTFITTERS

Burrows Specialized Sports

BICYCLING | This full-service sporting goods store rents and sells bicycles, snowboards, skis, and snowshoes, and has a repair shop. ✉ *105 Main St.* ☎ *802/254–9430* ⊕ *www.burrowssports. com.*

Sam's Outdoor Outfitters

LOCAL SPORTS | At this labyrinthine two-story sports emporium you can find outerwear, shoes, and gear for all seasons and activities. Grab a bag of free popcorn while you're shopping. ✉ *74 Main St.* ☎ *802/254–2933* ⊕ *www. samsoutfitters.com.*

Wilmington

18 miles west of Brattleboro.

The village of Wilmington, with its classic Main Street lined with 18th- and 19th-century buildings, anchors the Mt. Snow Valley. Most of the valley's lodging and dining establishments, however, can be found along Route 100, which travels 5 miles north to West Dover and Mt. Snow, where skiers flock on winter weekends. The area abounds with cultural activity from concerts to art exhibits year-round.

GETTING HERE AND AROUND

Wilmington is at the junction of Route 9 and Route 100. West Dover and Mt. Snow are a few miles to the north along Route 100.

ESSENTIALS

VISITOR INFORMATION Southern Vermont Deerfield Valley Chamber of Commerce. ☎ *802/464–8092, 877/887–6884* 🌐 *www.visitvermont.com.*

Sights

Molly Stark State Park

The park is known for it's great camping (there are two loops) and popular snowshoe trails, and there's a picnic pavilion. The Molly Stark Heritage Trail runs through this area, known as a scenic bypass. There is a 1.7-mile loop hike to the fire tower atop Mt. Olga that culminates in a 360-degree view of southern Vermont and northern Massachusetts. ✉ *705 Rte. 9 E* ☎ *802/464–5460* 🌐 *www.vtstateparks.com/mollystark.html.*

Who Was Molly Stark?

In the heart of Wilmington beside the Crafts Inn stands a sculpture in honor of Molly Stark, the wife of the Revolutionary War general John Stark. The general was said to have roused his troops in the Battle of Bennington, vowing victory over the British: "They are ours, or this night Molly Stark sleeps a widow!" He lived, and hence the victory path across Vermont (now Route 9) is called the Molly Stark Trail (or Byway).

Coffee and Quick Bites

Butter Mountain Bakery

$ | **BAKERY** | Chewy homemade bagels, craggy loaves of sourdough, and brown butter maple cookies are just a handful of the offerings waiting at this tucked away hidden gem. Keep an eye out for seasonal specials like fresh fruit galettes and walnut-studded chocolate brownies—the menu is always changing. **Known for:** crusty loaves of sourdough; seasonal galettes, like strawberry-basil; snickerdoodle cookies. [$] *Average main: $5* ✉ *1 School St.* ☎ *802/780–0232.*

Hotels

Deerhill Inn

$ | **B&B/INN** | The restaurant at this quintessential New England inn is among the best in town. **Pros:** complimentary house-baked cookies; some rooms have whirlpool tubs; toiletries by L'Occitane. **Cons:** must drive to Mt. Snow and town; traditional flowered wallpaper and upholstery in spots; two-night minimum required for weekends. [$] *Rooms from: $165* ✉ *14 Valley View Rd., West Dover* ☎ *802/464–3100, 800/993–3379* 🌐 *www.deerhillinn.com* 🛏 *13 rooms* 🍴 *Free breakfast.*

Grand Summit Hotel

$$$ | **RESORT** | **FAMILY** | Mt. **Pros:** easy ski access; lots of children's activities; fitness center. **Cons:** somewhat bland decor; can be busy and crowded; resort fee. [$] *Rooms from: $380* ✉ *39 Mt. Snow Rd., West Dover* ☎ *800/451–4211* 🌐 *www.mountsnow.com* 🛏 *196 rooms* 🍴 *No meals.*

Activities

Molly Stark State Park is home to some of the state's most popular snowshoe trails. Mount Olga Trail is a relatively easy 1.7-mile loop culminating in a 360-degree view of southern Vermont and northern Massachusetts.

SKIING
Mount Snow

SKIING/SNOWBOARDING | The closest major ski area to all of the Northeast's big cities, Mt. Snow prides itself on its hundreds of snowmaking fan guns—more than any other resort in North America. There are four major downhill areas. The main mountain comprises mostly intermediate runs, while the north face has the majority of expert runs. The south face, Sunbrook, has wide, sunny trails. It connects to Carinthia, which is dedicated to terrain parks and glade skiing. In summer, the 600-acre resort has an 18-hole golf course, 11.3 miles of lift-serviced mountain-bike trails, and an extensive network of hiking trails. In 2018, the resort debuted a brand-new, $22 million, 42,000-square-foot Carinthia Base Lodge, five times the size of the previous lodge. **Facilities:** 86 trails; 600 acres; 1,700-foot vertical drop; 20 lifts. ⊠ *39 Mt. Snow Rd., West Dover* ☎ *802/464–3333, 802/464–2151 for snow conditions, 800/245–7669* ⊕ *www.mountsnow.com* ✉ *Lift ticket: $110.*

Timber Creek

SKIING/SNOWBOARDING | North of Mt. Snow, this appealingly small cross-country skiing and snowshoeing center has 4½ miles of groomed loops. You can rent equipment and take lessons here. ⊠ *13 Tanglewood Rd., at Rte. 100, West Dover* ☎ *802/464–0999* ⊕ *www.timbercreekxc.com* ✉ *$20.*

Bennington

21 miles west of Wilmington.

Bennington is the commercial focus of Vermont's southwest corner and home to Bennington College. It's really three towns in one: Downtown Bennington, Old Bennington, and North Bennington. Downtown has retained much of the industrial character it developed in the 19th century, when paper mills, gristmills, and potteries formed the city's economic base. The outskirts of town are commercial and not worth a stop, so make your way right into Downtown and Old Bennington to appreciate the area's true charm.

GETTING HERE AND AROUND

The heart of modern Bennington is the intersection of U.S. 7 and Route 9. Old Bennington is a couple of miles west on Route 9, at Monument Avenue. North Bennington is a few miles north on Route 67A.

ESSENTIALS

VISITOR INFORMATION Bennington Area Chamber of Commerce. ☎ *802/447–3311* ⊕ *www.bennington.com.*

◉ Sights

Bennington Battle Monument

MEMORIAL | FAMILY | This 306-foot stone obelisk with an elevator to the top commemorates General John Stark's Revolutionary War victory over the British, who attempted to capture Bennington's stockpile of supplies. Inside the monument you can learn all about the battle, which took place near Walloomsac Heights in New York State on August 16, 1777, and helped bring about the surrender of British commander "Gentleman Johnny" Burgoyne two months later. The top of the tower affords commanding views of the Massachusetts Berkshires, the New York Adirondacks, and the Vermont Green Mountains. ⊠ *15 Monument Circle, Old Bennington* ☎ *802/447–0550* ⊕ *www.benningtonbattlemonument.com* ✉ *$5* ⊘ *Closed Nov.–Apr.*

Bennington College

COLLEGE | Contemporary stone sculpture and white-frame neo-Colonial dorms surrounded by acres of cornfields punctuate the green meadows of the placid campus of Bennington College. ⊠ *1 College Dr., off U.S. 7, North Bennington* ☎ *802/442–5401* ⊕ *www.bennington.edu.*

The poet Robert Frost is buried in Bennington at the Old First Church.

★ Bennington Museum

MUSEUM | The rich collections here feature military artifacts, early tools, dolls, and the Bennington Flag, one of the oldest of the Stars and Stripes in existence. Other areas of interest include early Bennington pottery, the Gilded Age in Vermont, mid-20th-century modernist painters who worked in or near Bennington, glass and metalwork by Lewis Comfort Tiffany, and photography, watercolors, and other works on paper. The highlight for many visitors, though, is the largest public collection of works by Grandma Moses (1860–1961), the popular self-taught artist who lived and painted in the area. ⊠ *75 Main St., Old Bennington* ☎ *802/447–1571* ⊕ *www.benningtonmuseum.org* ⊠ *$10* ⊘ *Closed Jan.; Wed. Feb.–May.*

Lake Shaftsbury State Park

NATIONAL/STATE PARK | **FAMILY** | You'll find a swimming beach, nature trails, boat and canoe rentals, and a snack bar at this pretty park. ⊠ *262 Shaftsbury State Park Rd., 10½ miles north of Bennington* ☎ *802/375–9978* ⊕ *www.vtstateparks. com/shaftsbury.html* ⊘ *Facilities closed early Sept.–mid-May.*

Old Bennington

HISTORIC SITE | West of downtown, this National Register Historic District is well endowed with stately Colonial and Victorian mansions. The site of the Catamount Tavern, where Ethan Allen organized the Green Mountain Boys to capture Ft. Ticonderoga in 1775, is marked by a bronze statue of Vermont's indigenous mountain lion, now extinct. ⊠ *Monument Ave., Old Bennington.*

The Old First Church

CEMETERY | In the graveyard of this church, the tombstone of the poet Robert Frost proclaims, "I had a lover's quarrel with the world." ⊠ *1 Monument Circle, at Monument Ave., Old Bennington* ☎ *802/447–1223* ⊕ *www.oldfirstchurch-benn.org* ⊠ *Free.*

Park-McCullough House

HOUSE | The architecturally significant Park-McCullough House is a 35-room classic French Empire–style mansion, built in 1865 and furnished with period pieces. Several restored flower gardens grace the landscaped grounds, and a barn holds some antique carriages. Guided tours happen on the hour while the house is open. The grounds are open daily year-round. ✉ *1 Park St., at West St., North Bennington* ☎ *802/442–5441* 🌐 *www.parkmccullough.org* 🎟 *$15* 🕓 *Closed Oct.–May; Mon.–Thurs. June–Sept.*

Robert Frost Stone House Museum

HOUSE | Robert Frost came to Shaftsbury in 1920, he wrote, "to plant a new Garden of Eden with a thousand apple trees of some unforbidden variety." The museum, now part of Bennington College, tells the story of the poet's life and highlights the nine years (1920–29) he spent living in the house with his wife and four children. It was here that he penned "Stopping by Woods on a Snowy Evening" and published two books of poetry. You can wander 7 of the Frost family's original 80 acres. Among the apple boughs you just might find inspiration of your own. ✉ *121 Historic Rte. 7A, Shaftsbury* ☎ *802/447–6200* 🌐 *www.bennington.edu* 🎟 *$10* 🕓 *Closed Mon., Tues., and Nov.–Apr. also Sun. in May.*

Woodford State Park

PARK—SPORTS-OUTDOORS | **FAMILY** | At 2,400 feet, this has the highest state campground in Vermont. Adams Reservoir is the dominant feature and focus of activities, with swimming, fishing, and boating, including canoes, kayaks, and paddleboards for rent. A nature trail also circles the reservoir. ✉ *142 State Park Rd.* ✣ *10 miles east of Bennington* ☎ *802/447–7169* 🌐 *www.vtstateparks.com/woodford.html* 🕓 *Facilities closed mid-Oct.–mid-May.*

🍴 Restaurants

Harvest Brewing

$ | **MEXICAN FUSION** | This nanobrewery in the heart of downtown Bennington is a haven of rich IPAs glowing with New England-style haze and inventive brews like chai-spiced stout. All of these beers become the perfect palate cleansers for good pub fare like loaded nachos and stuffed enchiladas. **Known for:** hazy IPAs; hearty Mexican-inspired pub fare; seasonal brews from smooth stouts to crisp lagers. [$] *Average main: $8* ✉ *201 South St.* ☎ *802/430–9915.*

Madison Brewing Company

$$ | **BURGER** | Since opening in the 1990s as the area's first brewpub, this enclave of exposed brick and bubbling brewing tanks has become a watering hole for fresh IPAs and stacked burgers. A full bar and myriad pub fare offer plenty of reasons to elbow up to the wraparound bar. **Known for:** craft beer on draft; classic New England–style pub fare; gourmet burgers. [$] *Average main: $21* ✉ *428 Main St.* ☎ *802/442–7397.*

Pangaea/Lounge

$$$ | **AMERICAN** | This rustic-chic restaurant comes with two faces: the classy, casual "Lounge" on one side that turns out tuned-up, locally sourced versions of bistro classics; and a full-blown, fine-dining experience on the "Pangaea" side. The latter is the more memorable, with gussied-up and coiffed waiters guiding you through a three-course meal of French-influenced American cuisine. **Known for:** extensive wine list; roasted Long Island duck; Vermont boar and Brie Wellington. [$] *Average main: $31* ✉ *1 Prospect St., 3 miles north of Bennington, North Bennington* ☎ *802/442–7171* 🌐 *www.vermontfinedining.com* 🕓 *No lunch.*

☕ Coffee and Quick Bites

Bakkerij Krijnen

$ | **DUTCH** | Some of the flakiest and most delectable pastries in Vermont can be ordered at this Dutch bakery helmed by husband-and-wife team Hans and Jennifer Krijne. Everything is made from scratch and uses local, organic, and all-natural ingredients—and tastes that way. **Known for:** artisanal breads; Douwe Egberts Dutch coffee; homemade stroopwafels. Ⓢ *Average main: $10* ⊠ *1001 Main St.* ☎ *802/ 442–1001.*

🛏 Hotels

The Eddington House Inn

$ | **B&B/INN** | In the heart of North Bennington, just around the corner from three covered bridges and Bennington College, this impeccably maintained, 18th-century three-bedroom house is a great value. **Pros:** budget prices for a great bed-and-breakfast; "endless desserts" in dining room 24 hours a day; summer guest passes to Lake Paran. **Cons:** slightly off usual tourist track; only three rooms so it fills up fast; no front desk or after-hours reception. Ⓢ *Rooms from: $159* ⊠ *21 Main St., North Bennington* ☎ *802/442–1511* ⊕ *www.eddingtonhouseinn.com* ⇱ *3 suites* ⎮⊙⎮ *Free breakfast.*

★ Four Chimneys Inn

$ | **B&B/INN** | This exquisite, three-story, neo-Georgian (circa 1915) looks out over a substantial lawn and a wonderful old stone wall. **Pros:** walking distance to several Bennington sights; a complimentary full country breakfast; extremely well kept. **Cons:** dinner only offered for special events; no coffee or tea in rooms; a bit stuffy. Ⓢ *Rooms from: $189* ⊠ *21 West Rd., Old Bennington* ☎ *802/447–3500* ⊕ *www.fourchimneys.com* ⇱ *11 rooms* ⎮⊙⎮ *Free breakfast.*

Billboardless Vermont 👁

Did you know that there are no billboards in Vermont? The state banned them in 1967 (similar laws exist in Maine, Alaska, and Hawaii), and the last one came down in 1975, so when you look out your window, you see trees and other scenery—not advertisements.

The Hardwood Hill

$ | **HOTEL** | Built in 1937, this fully renovated roadside motel has been given a distinct artsy, boutique upgrade by a foursome of new owners, three of whom are working artists, which translates into a sculpture garden out front, regular workshops by a resident artist, and performances on the red stage on the vast, hammock-dappled back lawn. **Pros:** excellent restaurant right next door; good value for cost; "arts package" includes tickets and discounts at local sights. **Cons:** must drive to town; rooms somewhat small; no restaurant or dining area. Ⓢ *Rooms from: $99* ⊠ *864 Harwood Hill Rd.* ☎ *802/442–6278* ⊕ *www.harwoodhillmotel.com* ⇱ *17 rooms* ⎮⊙⎮ *Free breakfast.*

🎭 Performing Arts

Basement Music Series

MUSIC | The Vermont Arts Exchange sponsors this fun and funky contemporary music series at the downtown Masonic Lodge. Some performances sell out, so it's wise to purchase tickets in advance. ⊠ *504 Main St.* ☎ *800/838–3006 for ticket hotline* ⊕ *www.vtartxchange.org/music.*

Vermont Maple Syrup

Vermont is the country's largest producer of maple syrup. A visit to a maple farm is a great way to learn all about sugaring, the process of extracting maple tree sap and making syrup. Sap is stored in a sugar maple tree's roots in the winter, and in the spring when conditions are just right, the sap runs up and can be tapped. Sugaring season runs March to April, which is when all maple syrup in the state is produced.

One of the best parts of visiting a maple farm is getting to taste and compare the four grades of syrup. As the sugaring season goes on and days become warmer, the sap becomes progressively darker and stronger in flavor. Grades are defined by color, clarity, density, and flavor. Is one grade better than another? Nope, it's just a question of taste. Sap drawn early in the season produces the lightest color, and has the most delicate flavor: this is called golden. Amber has a mellow flavor. Dark is much more robust, and Very Dark is the most flavorful, making it often the favorite of first-time tasters.

When visiting a maple farm, make sure they make their own syrup, as opposed to just bottling or selling someone else's. You'll learn more about the entire process that way. **Vermont Maple Syrup** (☎ 802/858–9444 ⊕ www.vermontmaple.org), a great resource, has a map of maple farms that host tours, a directory of producers open year-round, and a list of places from which you can order maple syrup by mail. You can also get the lowdown on events such as the annual Maple Open House Weekend, when sugarhouses throughout the state open their doors to visitors.

Oldcastle Theatre Company
MUSIC | This fine regional theater company focuses on American classics and crowd-pleasing musicals. The group's venue also hosts occasional concerts. ✉ 331 Main St. ☎ 802/447–0564 ⊕ www.oldcastletheatre.org ☉ Closed Dec.–Mar.

⚡ Activities

HIKING
Long Trail
HIKING/WALKING | Four miles east of Bennington, the Long Trail crosses Route 9 and runs south to the top of Harmon Hill. Allot two or three hours for this steep hike. ✉ Bennington.

Arlington

15 miles north of Bennington.

Smaller than Bennington and more down-to-earth than upper-crust Manchester to the north, Arlington exudes a certain Rockwellian folksiness, and it should: the illustrator Norman Rockwell lived here from 1939 to 1953, and many neighbors served as models for his portraits of small-town life.

GETTING HERE AND AROUND
Arlington is at the intersection of Route 313 and Route 7A. Take Route 313 West to reach West Arlington.

Sights

West Arlington

TOWN | Norman Rockwell once lived in this place with a quaint town green. If you follow Route 313 west from Arlington, you'll pass by the Wayside Country Store, a slightly rickety charmer where you can pick up sandwiches and chat with locals. The store carries everything from ammo and sporting goods to toys, teas, and maple syrup. Continue on, and cross West Arlington's red covered bridge, which leads to the town green. To loop back to Route 7A, take River Road along the south side of the Battenkill River, a scenic drive. ✉ *West Arlington.*

Coffee and Quick Bites

Arlington Dairy Bar

$ | **AMERICAN** | **FAMILY** | The big red barn with a sprawling lawn and walk-up ice cream window is a quintessential summer snack shack. It's where paper boats holding cheeseburgers, loaded hot dogs, and lobster rolls make way for soft serve sundaes, stacked ice cream cones, and root beer floats. **Known for:** nostalgic snack bar atmosphere; ice-cream cones and sundaes; cheeseburgers and hot dogs. [$] *Average main: $5* ✉ *3158 VT Rte 7A* ☎ *802/375–2546.*

Wayside Country Store

$ | **AMERICAN** | **FAMILY** | The motto of Arlington's one-stop-shop says it all: "If we don't have it, you don't need it!" This charming country store is known for carrying anything from toilet paper to boxed cocoa mix and boasts a popular deli complete with build-your-own sandwiches, prepared foods, and house-made specials like freshly baked biscuits. **Known for:** locally made goods; deli wraps and sandwiches; specialty prepared foods, from stuffed peppers to roasted chicken legs. [$] *Average main: $7* ✉ *3307 VT Rte. 313 W* ☎ *802/375–2792.*

Hotels

The Arlington Inn

$ | **B&B/INN** | The Greek Revival columns of this 1847 home lend it an imposing presence in the middle of town, but the atmosphere within is friendly and old-fashioned. **Pros:** heart-of-town location; friendly atmosphere; rigorously eco-friendly. **Cons:** expensive dining; elegant but old-fashioned decor; no tea or coffee in rooms. [$] *Rooms from: $199* ✉ *3904 Rte. 7A* ☎ *802/375–6532* 🌐 *www.arlingtoninn.com* 🛏 *17 rooms* 🍴 *Free breakfast.*

★ Hill Farm Inn

$$ | **B&B/INN** | **FAMILY** | Few hotels or inns in Vermont can match the sumptuous views of Mt. Equinox and surrounding hillscape of this former dairy farm built in 1830, whether seen from the large wraparound porch, the fire pit (where you can roast s'mores), or the outdoor hot tub. **Pros:** outdoor pool and hot tub; perfect Vermont wedding setting; Vermont Castings stoves in many rooms. **Cons:** books up on weekends with weddings; bringing alcohol not allowed; can be buggy in summer, like all Vermont. [$] *Rooms from: $235* ✉ *458 Hill Farm Rd., off Rte. 7A, Sunderland* ☎ *802/375–2269* 🌐 *www.hillfarminn.com* 🛏 *12 rooms* 🍴 *Free breakfast.*

West Mountain Inn

$$ | **B&B/INN** | **FAMILY** | This 1810 farmhouse sits on 150 mountainside acres with hiking trails and easy access to the Battenkill River, where you can canoe or go tubing; in winter, guests can sled down a former ski slope or borrow snowshoes or cross-country skis. **Pros:** atmospheric Colonial dining room; lots of activities; wood-panel dining room with fireplace. **Cons:** dining room not ideal for kids; dirt road to property uneven and pitted; tiny bathrooms in some rooms. [$] *Rooms from: $205* ✉ *144 W. Mountain Inn Rd., at Rte. 313* ☎ *802/375–6516* 🌐 *www.westmountaininn.com* 🛏 *20 rooms* 🍴 *Free breakfast.*

The formal gardens and mansion at Robert Todd Lincoln's Hildene are a far cry from his father's log cabin.

🛍 Shopping

Village Peddler

GIFTS/SOUVENIRS | FAMILY | This shop has a "chocolatorium," where you can learn all about cocoa. It sells fudge and other candies and stocks a large collection of teddy bears, one of whom is giant and made of chocolate. ✉ *261 Old Mill Rd., East Arlington* ☎ *802/375–6037* ⊕ *www.villagepeddlervt.com.*

Manchester

9 miles northeast of Arlington.

Well-to-do Manchester has been a popular summer retreat since the mid-19th century, when city dwellers traveled north to take in the cool, clean air at the base of 3,840-foot Mt. Equinox. Manchester Village's tree-shaded marble sidewalks and stately old homes—Main Street here could hardly be more picture-perfect—reflect the luxurious resort lifestyle of more than a century ago. A mile north on Route 7A,

Manchester Center is the commercial twin to Colonial Manchester Village; it's also where you'll find the town's famed upscale factory outlets doing business in attractive faux-Colonial shops.

Manchester Village houses the world headquarters of Orvis, the outdoor-goods brand that was founded here in the 19th century and has greatly influenced the town ever since. The complex includes a fly-fishing school featuring lessons given in its casting ponds and the Battenkill River.

GETTING HERE AND AROUND

Manchester is the main town for the ski resorts of Stratton (a half-hour drive on Route 30) and Bromley (15 minutes to the northeast on Route 11). It's 15 minutes north of Arlington along scenic Route 7A.

ESSENTIALS

VISITOR INFORMATION **Green Mountain National Forest Visitor Center.** ✉ *2538 Depot St.* ☎ *802/362–2307* ⊕ *www. fs.usda.gov/main/gmfl.* **Manchester Visitor Center.** ✉ *4826 Main St.* ☎ ⊕ *www.man-chestervermont.com.*

Sights

American Museum of Fly Fishing

MUSEUM | This museum houses the world's largest collection of angling art and angling-related objects—more than 1,500 rods, 800 reels, 30,000 flies, including the tackle of Winslow Homer, Babe Ruth, Jimmy Carter, and other notables. Every August, vendors sell antique equipment at the museum's fly-fishing festival. You can also practice your casting out back. ⊠ *4070 Main St.* ☎ *802/362–3300* ⊕ *www.amff.org* ⌧ *$5* ☽ *Closed Mon.; also Sun. Nov.–May.*

★ Hildene

GARDEN | **FAMILY** | A twofold treat, the summer home of Abraham Lincoln's son Robert provides insight into the lives of the Lincoln family, as well as an introduction to the lavish Manchester life of the early 1900s. In 1905, Robert built a 24-room Georgian Revival mansion where he and his descendants lived until 1975. It's the centerpiece of a beautifully preserved 412-acre estate and holds many of the family's prized possessions, including one of three surviving stovepipe hats owned by Abraham and a Lincoln Bible. When the 1,000-pipe Aeolian organ is played, the music reverberates as though from the mansion's very bones.

Rising from a 10-acre meadow, Hildene Farm is magnificent. The agriculture center is built in a traditional style—post-and-beam construction of timber felled and milled on the estate, and you can watch goat cheese being made.

The highlight, though, may be the elaborate formal gardens, where a thousand peonies bloom every June. There is also a teaching greenhouse, restored 1903 Pullman car, a 600-foot floating boardwalk across the Battenkill wetlands, and more than 12 miles of walking trails. When conditions permit, you can cross-country ski and snowshoe on the property. ⊠ *1005 Hildene Rd., at Rte. 7A* ☎ *802/362–1788, 800/578–1788* ⊕ *www.hildene.org* ⌧ *$23.*

★ Southern Vermont Arts Center

ARTS VENUE | At the end of a long, winding driveway, this center has a permanent collection of more than 800 19th- and 20th-century American artworks and presents temporary exhibitions. The original building, a Georgian mansion set on 100 acres, contains 12 galleries with works by more than 600 artists, many from Vermont. The center also hosts concerts, performances, and film screenings. In summer and fall, the views from the café at lunchtime are magnificent. ⊠ *930 SVAC Dr., West Rd.* ☎ *802/362–1405* ⊕ *www.svac.org* ⌧ *Free* ☽ *Closed Mon. Nov.–May.*

🍴 Restaurants

Chantecleer

$$$$ | **EUROPEAN** | There is something wonderful about eating by candlelight in an old barn; and with the rooster art above their rough-hewn wooden beams, Chantecleer's dining rooms are especially romantic. The international menu runs the gamut from veal schnitzel to New York strip to Dover sole. **Known for:** great fieldstone fireplace; duck Grand Marnier; Thursday burger night at the bar. $ *Average main: $38* ⊠ *8 Reed Farm La., 3½ miles north of Manchester, East Dorset* ☎ *802/362–1616* ⊕ *www.chantecleer-restaurant.com* ☽ *Closed Mon., Tues., mid-Nov., and mid-Apr. No lunch.*

Chop House

$$$$ | **STEAKHOUSE** | Walk to the very back room of the Equinox's Marsh Tavern to enter this special, very expensive, and very delicious steak house, with aged corn- or grass-fed beef broiled at 1,400°F and finished with marrow butter. The marble above the fireplace is chiseled "L.L. **Known for:** New York strip; craft cocktails; tuna tartare. $ *Average main: $47* ⊠ *3567 Main St.* ☎ *802/362–4700* ⊕ *www.equinoxresort.com* ☽ *No lunch.*

The Crooked Ram

$ | **WINE BAR** | Originally a tiny bottle shop when it opened doors in 2017, the Crooked Ram has since transformed into a cozy beer-and-wine bar with an expertly sourced market. It's now a destination for hyperlocal drafts, seasonal small plates, and brimming Vermont cheese boards, plus a thoughtful stock of unique ciders and natural wines to-go. **Known for:** drafts of local craft beer in stemmed beer glasses; award-winning Vermont cheeses and charcuterie; seasonal patio seating. $ *Average main: $15* ⊠ *4026 Main St.* ☎ *802/231–1315* ⊕ *thecrookedramvt.com* ⊘ *Closed Mon. and Tues.*

Mistral's at Toll Gate

$$$$ | **FRENCH** | This classic French restaurant is tucked in a grotto on the climb to Bromley Mountain. The two dining rooms are perched over the Bromley Brook, and at night a small waterfall is magically illuminated—ask for a window table. **Known for:** chateaubriand béarnaise; crispy sweetbreads Dijonnaise; wine list. $ *Average main: $36* ⊠ *10 Toll Gate Rd., off Rte. 11/30* ☎ *802/362–1779* ⊕ *www.mistralsattollgate.com* ⊘ *Closed Tues. and Wed. No lunch.*

★ Moonwink

$ | **BURMESE** | May and Wes Stannard opened this counter-service spot in 2018, spotlighting May's native Burmese cooking in Wes's childhood hometown. In one of the best stops for Burmese fare on the East Coast, you'll find vibrant noodle bowls like *Nan Gyi Thoke* (thick round rice noodles with chicken curry), fermented tea leaf salad, and "Burma Bowls" with sprouted peas and chicken curry. **Known for:** oh no kuo swel (creamy coconut broth with vegetables or chicken served over egg noodles); la phat thok (Moonwink's take on the Burmese fermented tea leaf salad); mo hinga (a special fish stew with noodles served on Friday and Saturday only). $ *Average main: $13* ⊠ *4479 Main St.* ☎ *802/768–8671* ⊘ *Closed Mon. and Tues.*

★ Mystic Cafe & Wine Bar

$$ | **ECLECTIC** | This spacious, brand-new, Euro-chic restaurant is earning plenty of local praise for its gussied-up takes on international cuisines with a Vermont-farmhouse accent. That means plenty of kale, butternut squash, sweet potato, and cheddar in the salads, sandwiches, and tapas-style shared plates. **Known for:** paella with Israeli couscous; French toast; wine list. $ *Average main: $20* ⊠ *4928 Main St., Manchester Center* ☎ *802/768–8086* ⊕ *www.mysticcafeandwinebar.com* ⊘ *Closed Mon. and Tues.*

Ponce Bistro

$$$ | **INTERNATIONAL** | The Spanish influence adds much to the charm of this small, atmospheric restaurant, as does a fireplace in the front room. No alcohol is served, but glasses are happily provided for any who bring their own beer and wine, and no corkage fee, to boot. **Known for:** Spanish meat loaf; sweet and savory crepes; homemade salad dressings. $ *Average main: $28* ⊠ *4659 Main St., Mendon* ☎ *802/768–8095* ⊕ *www.poncebistro.com* ⊘ *No dinner Sun.–Wed.*

The Reluctant Panther Inn & Restaurant

$$$$ | **AMERICAN** | The dining room at this luxurious inn is a large, modern space where rich woods and high ceilings meld into a kind of "nouveau Vermont" aesthetic. The contemporary American cuisine emphasizes farm-to-table ingredients and has earned the restaurant "Gold Barn" honors from the Vermont Fresh Network. **Known for:** wine list; chef of the year award by the Vermont Chamber of Commerce; lobster-and-Brie fondue. $ *Average main: $37* ⊠ *39 West Rd.* ☎ *800/822–2331, 802/362–2568* ⊕ *www.reluctantpanther.com* ⊘ *Closed Sun. No lunch.*

★ The Silver Fork at the Old Library

$$$ | **ECLECTIC** | This intimate, elegant bistro is owned by husband-and-wife team Mark and Melody French, who spent years in Puerto Rico absorbing the flavors of the island that are reflected in the eclectic international menu. After

nine years in their original space on Main Street, in 2020 the couple moved their restaurant into the newly renovated, 123-year-old Skinner Library, fashioning a bartop from the 1897 wooden shelving. **Known for:** shrimp mofongo (with mashed plantains); wine and cocktail list; special occasions. $ *Average main: $30* ✉ *48 West Rd.* ☎ *802/768–8444* ⊕ *www.thesilverforkvt.com* ◷ *Closed Sun. No lunch.*

Ye Olde Tavern

$$$ | **AMERICAN** | This circa-1790 Colonial inn dishes up Yankee favorites along with plenty of New England charm, made all the more intimate by the candlelight. To learn more about the colorful history of the building, simply ask the manager, who makes a regular appearance at tables. **Known for:** cheddar-and-ale onion soup; traditional pot roast; 1790 Taproom Ale (custom brew by Long Trail). $ *Average main: $26* ✉ *5183 Main St.* ☎ *802/362–0611* ⊕ *www.yeoldetavern.net.*

☕ Coffee and Quick Bites

★ Mrs. Murphy's Donuts

$ | **BAKERY** | **FAMILY** | This locally beloved doughnut shop turns out fresh doughnuts daily from their small, white-clapboard storefront. Old-fashioned doughnuts come hot from the fryer in the wee hours of the morning, so arrive early for the best selection of flavors like cinnamon, maple cream, and cakey cider doughnuts loaded with warming spices. **Known for:** cinnamon raised; cider cake; sugar-dusted crullers. $ *Average main: $3* ✉ *374 Depot St.* ☎ *802/362–1874.*

🛏 Hotels

Equinox

$$$ | **RESORT** | In Manchester Village, nearly all life revolves around the historic Equinox Inn, whose fame and service have carved it into the Mt. Rushmore of accommodation in Vermont. **Pros:** fitness center and pool; excellent steak house on-site; extensive network of walking trails. **Cons:** somewhat corporate feel; lines at reception can make checking in and out take long; lots of weddings can sometimes overcrowd. $ *Rooms from: $391* ✉ *3567 Main St.* ☎ *802/362–4700, 866/837–4219* ⊕ *www.equinoxresort.com* ⇄ *147 rooms* ⎰ *No meals.*

Taconic Hotel

$$$ | **HOTEL** | Vermont's only Kimpton, which opened in 2015, attempts to walk the fine line between its corporate boutique design and a Vermont flavor—the latter of which is distilled, quite literally, in The Copper Grouse, the hotel's on-site enclave of seasonal plates and craft cocktails. **Pros:** locally handmade walking sticks from Manchester Woodcraft in rooms; no additional fee for pets; the house restaurant, the Copper Grouse, does a good turn on American bistro cuisine, cocktails included. **Cons:** not very Vermonty experience; only chain's rewards members get free high-speed Internet/Wi-Fi; tiny pool. $ *Rooms from: $339* ✉ *3835 Main St.* ☎ *802/362–0147* ⊕ *www.taconichotel.com* ⇄ *87 rooms* ⎰ *No meals.*

★ Wilburton Inn

$$ | **B&B/INN** | Stepping into this hilltop 1902 Tudor-style mansion, you might think you've stumbled on a lavish film set: there's a palpably cinematic quality to the richly paneled guest rooms and the common rooms, which make an ideal setting for "murder-mystery weekends," "Innkeeper's Daughter Cabaret," and more quirky events. **Pros:** unique activities and adornments; easy access to Manchester; views of surrounding landscape. **Cons:** limited indoor facilities; lots of floral wallpaper and traditional frills; two-night minimum stay is required on most weekends. $ *Rooms from: $205* ✉ *257 Wilburton Dr.* ☎ *802/362–2500* ⊕ *www.wilburtoninn.com* ⇄ *40 rooms* ⎰ *Free breakfast.*

Nightlife

Falcon Bar

MUSIC CLUBS | This sophisticated bar has live music on weekends. In summer, don't miss the wonderful outdoor deck. In winter, the place to be is around the giant Vermont slate firepit. ⊠ *Equinox Resort, 3567 Main St.* ☎ *800/362–4747* ⊕ *www.equinoxresort.com.*

Union Underground

BARS/PUBS | One of Manchester's newest hot spots, this part underground, part aboveground pub and restaurant offers lots of space, a sleek green-marble bar, craft beer, a pool table, and tasty classics with all the fixings. ⊠ *4928 Main St., Manchester Center* ☎ *802/367–3951.*

Activities

BIKING

Battenkill Bicycles

BICYCLING | This shop rents, sells, and repairs bikes and provides maps and route suggestions. ⊠ *99 Bonnet St.* ☎ *802/362–2734* ⊕ *battenkillbicycles.com.*

FISHING

Battenkill Anglers

FISHING | Teaching the art and science of fly-fishing, Battenkill Anglers offers both private and group lessons. ⊠ *6204 Main St.* ☎ *802/379–1444* ⊕ *www.battenkill-angler.com.*

HIKING

There are bountiful hiking trails in the Green Mountain National Forest. Shorter hikes begin at the Equinox Resort, which owns about 1,000 acres of forest and has a great trail system open to the public.

Equinox Preserve

HIKING/WALKING | A multitude of well-groomed walking trails for all abilities thread the 914 acres on the slopes of Mt. Equinox, including a trail to the summit. ⊠ *Multiple trailheads, End of West Union St.* ☎ *802/366–1400 Equinox Preservation Trust* ⊕ *www.equinoxpreservationtrust.org.*

Long Trail

HIKING/WALKING | One of the most popular segments of Vermont's Long Trail leads to the top of Bromley Mountain. The strenuous 5.4-mile round-trip takes about four hours. ⊠ *Rte. 11/30* ⊕ *www.greenmountainclub.org.*

Lye Brook Falls

HIKING/WALKING | This 4.6-mile hike starts off Glen Road and ends at Vermont's most impressive cataract, Lye Brook Falls. The moderately strenuous journey takes four hours. ⊠ *Off Glen Rd., south from E. Manchester Rd. just east of U.S. 7* ⊕ *www.greenmountainclub.org.*

Mountain Goat

HIKING/WALKING | Stop here for hiking, cross-country-skiing, and snowshoeing equipment (some of which is available to rent), as well as a good selection of warm clothing. ⊠ *4886 Main St.* ☎ *802/362–5159* ⊕ *www.mountaingoat.com.*

SPAS

★ Spa at Equinox

SPA/BEAUTY | Some of Vermont's best spa treatments are found behind the mahogany doors and beadboard wainscoting of the Equinox Spa and are well worth the splurge. At one end are an indoor pool and outdoor hot tub; at the other end are the treatment rooms. The signature 100-minute Spirit of Vermont combines Reiki, reflexology, and massage, and will leave you feeling like a whole, complete person. The locker rooms feature steam rooms and saunas. Day passes are available for all ages. ⊠ *Equinox Resort, 3567 Rte. 7A* ☎ *802/362–4700, 800/362–4747* ⊕ *www.equinoxresort.com.*

Shopping

ART AND ANTIQUES

Long Ago & Far Away

ANTIQUES/COLLECTIBLES | This store specializes in fine indigenous artwork, including Inuit stone sculpture. ⊠ *Green Mountain Village Shops, 4963 Main St.* ☎ *802/362–3435* ⊕ *www.longagoandfaraway.com.*

Manchester Woodcraft
CRAFTS | The millions of trees in the Green Mountains make Vermont a wood-carver's dreamscape. The saws, planes, and scrapers of the woodshop here turn out a range of handsome household goods, plus a wide selection of pieces and parts for DIY fans. ⊠ *175 Depot St., Manchester Center* ☎ *802/362–5770* ⊕ *www. manchesterwoodcraft.com.*

Tilting at Windmills Gallery
ANTIQUES/COLLECTIBLES | This large gallery displays the paintings and sculptures of nationally known artists. ⊠ *24 Highland Ave., Manchester Center* ☎ *802/362–3022* ⊕ *www.tilting.com.*

BOOKS
Northshire Bookstore
BOOKS/STATIONERY | FAMILY | The heart of Manchester Center, this bookstore is adored by visitors and residents alike for its ambience, selection, and service. Up the iron staircase is a second floor dedicated to children's books, toys, and clothes. ⊠ *4869 Main St.* ☎ *802/362–2200, 800/437–3700* ⊕ *www.northshire.com.*

CLOTHING
Manchester Designer Outlets
CLOTHING | This is the most upscale collection of stores in northern New England—and every store is a discount outlet. The architecture reflects the surrounding homes, so the place looks a bit like a Colonial village. The long list of famous-brand clothiers here includes Kate Spade, Yves Delorme, Michael Kors, Ann Taylor, Tumi, BCBG, Armani, Coach, Polo Ralph Lauren, Brooks Brothers, and Theory. ⊠ *97 Depot St.* ☎ *802/362–3736, 800/955–7467* ⊕ *www.manchesterdesigneroutlets.com.*

Orvis Flagship Store
CLOTHING | The lodgelike Orvis store carries the company's latest clothing, fly-fishing gear, and pet supplies—there's even a trout pond. At this required shopping destination for many visitors—the Orvis name is pure Manchester—there are demonstrations of how fly rods are constructed and tested. You can attend fly-fishing school across the street. ⊠ *4180 Main St.* ☎ *802/362–3750* ⊕ *www.orvis.com.*

Dorset

7 miles north of Manchester.

Lying at the foot of many mountains and with a village green surrounded by white clapboard homes and inns, Dorset has a solid claim to the title of Vermont's most picture-perfect town. Dorset has just 2,000 residents, but two of the state's best and oldest general stores.

The country's first commercial marble quarry opened here in 1785. Dozens more opened, providing the marble for the main research branch of the New York Public Library and many 5th Avenue mansions, among other notable landmarks, as well as the sidewalks here and in Manchester. A remarkable private home made entirely of marble can be seen on Dorset West Road, a beautiful residential road west of the town green. The marble Dorset Church on the green has two Tiffany stained-glass windows.

◉ Sights

★ Dorset Quarry
BODY OF WATER | FAMILY | On hot summer days the sight of dozens of families jumping, swimming, and basking in the sun around this massive 60-foot-deep swimming hole makes it one of the most wholesome and picturesque recreational spots in the region. First mined in 1785, the stone from the country's oldest commercial marble quarry was used to build the main branch of the New York Public Library and the Montreal Museum of Fine Arts. ⊠ *Rte. 30* 🎫 *Free.*

Emerald Lake State Park

PARK—SPORTS-OUTDOORS | This park has a well-marked nature trail, a small beach, boat rentals, and a snack bar. ✉ *65 Emerald Lake La., East Dorset* ☎ *802/362–1655* 🌐 *www.vtstateparks.com/emerald.html* 🎟 *$4* ⏲ *Facilities closed mid-Oct.–mid-May.*

Merck Forest & Farmland Center

FARM/RANCH | **FAMILY** | This 3,162-acre educational center has 30 miles of nature trails for hiking, cross-country skiing, snowshoeing, horseback riding, and rustic camping. You can visit the 62-acre farm, which grows organic fruit and vegetables (sold at the visitor center), and check out the horses, sheep, pigs, and chickens while you're there—you're even welcome to help out with the chores. ✉ *3270 Rte. 315, Rupert* ☎ *802/394–7836* 🌐 *www.merckforest.org* 🎟 *Free.*

🍴 Restaurants

The Dorset Inn

$$$ | **AMERICAN** | Built in 1796, this inn has been continuously operating ever since, and the comfortable tavern and formal dining room serve a Colonial-influenced bistro menu. A member of the Vermont Fresh Network, the restaurant benefits greatly from its strong connections with local farmers. **Known for:** wine list; brunch in sunny garden room; whiskey and bourbon menu. [$] *Average main: $27* ✉ *Dorset Green, 8 Church St.* ☎ *802/867–5500* 🌐 *www.dorsetinn.com* ⏲ *No lunch.*

Inn at West View Farm

$$$ | **ECLECTIC** | Chef-owner Raymond Chen was the lead line cook at New York City's Mercer Kitchen before opening this restaurant inside a traditional inn. Chen skillfully applies French techniques to Asian dishes crafted from fresh Vermont ingredients for a nice break from the usual regional cuisine. **Known for:** big picture windows with view; dim sum; roasted and confit duck. [$] *Average main: $30* ✉ *2928 Rte. 30* ☎ *802/867–5715, 800/769–4903* 🌐 *www.innatwestviewfarm.com* ⏲ *Closed Tues. and Wed. No lunch.*

🛏 Hotels

Barrows House

$$ | **HOTEL** | This renovated 19th-century manse, once the residence of the town's pastor, incorporates a modern boutique aesthetic into the traditional-style inn, especially in the attached gastropub, which features a long, polished metal bar and backlighted marble. **Pros:** good bar and restaurant; chintz-free decor; large gardens. **Cons:** rooms can become drafty in cold weather; robes only in luxury suites; no coffee or tea in rooms. [$] *Rooms from: $275* ✉ *3156 Rte. 30* ☎ *802/867–4455* 🌐 *www.barrowshouse.com* 🔑 *27 rooms* 🍽 *Free breakfast.*

Squire House Bed & Breakfast

$$ | **B&B/INN** | On a wonderfully quiet road, this inn, built in 1918, has guest rooms that combine modern comforts and antique fixtures. **Pros:** big estate feels like your own; wood-burning fireplace in two rooms; crème brûlée French toast at breakfast. **Cons:** basic bathrooms; two-night minimum required for peak periods; one-night reservation costs additional $60 fee in some periods. [$] *Rooms from: $210* ✉ *3395 Dorset West Rd.* ☎ *802/867–0281* 🌐 *www.squirehouse.com* 🔑 *4 rooms* 🍽 *Free breakfast.*

🎟 Performing Arts

Dorset Players

THEATER | The prestigious summer theater troupe presents the annual Dorset Theater Festival. Plays are staged in a wonderful converted pre-Revolutionary War barn. ✉ *Dorset Playhouse, 104 Cheney Rd.* ☎ *802/867–5570* 🌐 *www.dorsetplayers.org.*

Shopping

Dorset Union Store

CONVENIENCE/GENERAL STORES | Dating to 1816, this 200-year-old general store is the oldest continuously operating country store in Vermont. Under the reigns of co-owners Cindy Laudenslager and Gretchen Schmidt, it has great prepared dinners, a full deli, delicious homemade baked goods, and a big wine selection. It also sells interesting gifts, and houses its own soft-serve ice cream machine. ✉ *Dorset Green, 31 Church St.* ☎ *802/867–4400* 🌐 *www.dorsetunionstore.com.*

Stratton

26 miles southeast of Dorset.

Stratton is really Stratton Mountain Resort, a mountaintop ski resort with a self-contained "town center" of shops, restaurants, and lodgings clustered at the base of the slopes. When the snow melts, golf, tennis, and a host of other summer activities are big attractions, but the ski village remains quiet.

GETTING HERE AND AROUND

From Manchester or U.S. 7, follow Route 11/30 east until they split. Route 11 continues past Bromley ski mountain, and Route 30 turns south 10 minutes toward Bondville, the town at the base of the mountain. At the junction of Routes 30 and 100 is the village of Jamaica, with its own cluster of inns and restaurants on the eastern side of the mountain.

Restaurants

J.J. Hapgood General Store and Eatery

$ | **AMERICAN** | **FAMILY** | You won't find a better meal at any other general store in the state. This is really more of a classic American restaurant, serving farm-to-table breakfast, lunch, and dinner, than a place to pick up the essentials, but like any good general store, it's a friendly and relaxed gathering spot for locals. **Known for:** buttermilk biscuits; outdoor patio; wood-fired pizzas. [$] *Average main: $12* ✉ *305 Main St., Peru* ☎ *802/824–4800* 🌐 *www.jjhapgood.com* ⏲ *No dinner Mon. and Tues.*

The Red Fox Inn

$$$ | **AMERICAN** | This converted bi-level barn has the best nightlife in town, including Grammy-award-winning acts, and a fun dining room. The restaurant, serving elk chops, shepherd's pie, coq au vin, and the like is on the upper level, where you'll see wagon wheels and a carriage suspended from the A-frame ceiling. **Known for:** apple pie was served at the inauguration of President Obama; huge fireplace; Irish music with half-price Guinness, and fish-and-chips on Wednesday. [$] *Average main: $26* ✉ *103 Winhall Hollow Rd., Bondville* ☎ *802/297–2488* 🌐 *www.redfoxinn.com* ⏲ *Closed mid-Apr.–mid-May; Sun. and Mon. late May–July. No lunch.*

Coffee and Quick Bites

Coyote Coffee Cafe

$ | **CAFÉ** | This espresso and dessert bar offers maple lattes, baked goods, and myriad local products from the Stratton area. Another bonus: it's a close walk from the bottom of the Stratton Mountain ski trails. **Known for:** maple lattes; homemade baked goods; local grocery products, from eggs and bread to coffee and CBD. [$] *Average main: $5* ✉ *8c Stratton Village Way* ☎ *802/999–4245* 🌐 *www.stratton.com/things-to-do/dining/coyote.*

Hotels

Long Trail House

$$ | **RENTAL** | Directly across the street from the ski village, this condo complex is one of the closest to the slopes. **Pros:** across the street from ski lift; views of the mountain; outdoor heated pool and hot tub. **Cons:** 4:30 check-in later than most in Vermont; two-night stay required on weekends; busy tourist

center in season. $ *Rooms from: $230* ✉ *759–787 Stratton Mountain Access Rd.* ☎ *802/297–4000, 800/787–2886* ⊕ *www. stratton.com* ⤴ *145 rooms* ❍❙ *No meals.*

★ **Three Mountain Inn**

$$ | **B&B/INN** | A 1780s tavern, this romantic inn in downtown Jamaica feels authentically Colonial, from the wide-plank paneling to the low ceilings. **Pros:** romantic setting; well-kept rooms; enchanting dinners alongside wood-burning fireplaces. **Cons:** 15-minute drive to skiing; two-night reservations requested for weekends and peak foliage; deposit equal to 50% of the reserved stay required. $ *Rooms from: $234* ✉ *30 Depot St., Jamaica* ✛ *10 miles northeast of Stratton* ☎ *802/874–4140* ⊕ *www. threemountaininn.com* ⤴ *10 rooms* ❍❙ *Free breakfast.*

▼ Nightlife

Mulligans

BARS/PUBS | Popular Mulligans hosts bands and DJs in the downstairs Green Door Pub on weekends. Upstairs, cozy up beside the fireplace with ribs, steak, and traditional fish-and-chips, or opt for tempura plates and sushi bowls from Mulligans' newest in-house offshoot, Snowfish Sushi. ✉ *Village Sq., Stratton Mountain* ☎ *802/297–9293* ⊕ *www. mulligansstratton.com.*

⚡ Activities

SKIING

Bromley Mountain Resort

SKIING/SNOWBOARDING | FAMILY | About 20 minutes from Stratton, Bromley is a favorite with families thanks to a child-care center for kids ages six weeks–six years and programs for ages 2½–17. The trails are evenly split among beginner, intermediate, and advanced, with nothing too challenging. Beginning skiers and snowboarders have expanded access to terrain-based training in the dedicated Learning Zone, and everyone can unwind in the base lodge

and "village." An added bonus: trails face south, making for glorious spring skiing and warm winter days. **Facilities:** 47 trails; 300 acres; 1,334-foot vertical drop; 9 lifts. ✉ *3984 Rte. 11, Peru* ☎ *802/824–5522, 866/856–2201 for snow conditions* ⊕ *www.bromley.com* ⛷ *Lift ticket: $80.*

Stratton Mountain

SKIING/SNOWBOARDING | About 25 minutes from Manchester, and featuring an entire faux Swiss village at its base, Stratton Mountain draws families and young professionals. Beginners will find more than 40% of the mountain accessible to them, but that doesn't mean there aren't some great steeps for the experts. The resort prides itself on its immaculate grooming and excellent cruising on all trails. An on-site day-care center takes children ages six weeks–five years for indoor activities and outdoor excursions. Children also love careening down one of four groomed lift-serviced lanes at the resort's Coca Cola Tube Park. Stratton has 11 miles of cross-country skiing, and in summer there are 15 outdoor clay tennis courts, 27 holes of golf, and hiking trails accessed by a gondola. The sports complex (open year-round) has a 75-foot indoor saltwater pool, sauna, indoor tennis courts, and a fitness center. **Facilities:** 97 trails; 670 acres; 2,003-foot vertical drop; 11 lifts. ✉ *5 Village Lodge Rd., Bondville* ☎ *802/297–4211 for snow conditions, 800/787–2886* ⊕ *www.stratton.com* ⛷ *Lift ticket: $115.*

Weston

17 miles north of Stratton.

Best known as the home of the Vermont Country Store, Weston was one of the first Vermont towns to discover its own intrinsic loveliness—and marketability. With its summer theater, classic town green with Victorian bandstand, and an assortment of shops, the little village really lives up to its vaunted image.

Hotels

The Inn at Weston

$$ | B&B/INN | A short walk from the town green and a stone's throw from four ski areas, this 1848 inn is run by Bob and Linda Aldrich, whose love of plants is evident from their immaculate gardens. **Pros:** afternoon refreshments in library; terrific town location; outdoor and gazebo dining. **Cons:** high-end rooms are expensive; lots of flower wallpaper, upholstery, and bedding; on busy main road. $ *Rooms from: $239* ⊠ *630 Main St.* ☎ *802/824–6789* ⊕ *www.innweston. com* ⇨ *13 rooms* ⊙ *Free breakfast.*

Performing Arts

Weston Playhouse

THEATER | The oldest professional theater in Vermont produces plays, musicals, and other works. The season runs mid-June–late October. ⊠ *703 Main St., off Rte. 100* ☎ *802/824–5288* ⊕ *www.westonplayhouse.org.*

Shopping

The Vermont Country Store

CONVENIENCE/GENERAL STORES | This store opened in 1946 and is still run by the Orton family, though it has become something of an empire, with a large catalog and online business. One room is set aside for Vermont Common Crackers and bins of fudge and copious candy. In others you'll find nearly forgotten items such as Lilac Vegetol aftershave, as well as practical items like sturdy outdoor clothing. Nostalgia-evoking implements dangle from the rafters. The associated Bryant House restaurant next door serves three country meals a day and, if you can't get enough, there's a second store on Route 103 in Rockingham. ⊠ *657 Main St.* ☎ *802/824–3184* ⊕ *www. vermontcountrystore.com.*

Ludlow

9 miles northeast of Weston.

Ludlow, once a largely nondescript industrial town, is a budding hub of inns, restaurants, and cafés beside Okemo, one of Vermont's largest and most popular ski resorts.

GETTING HERE AND AROUND
Routes 100 and 103 join in northern Ludlow, separating about 2 miles south in the small downtown, where Route 103 becomes Main Street.

Restaurants

★ The Downtown Grocery

$$$ | BISTRO | There's a cozy romance to this oasis of seasonal and local cooking, with its corner seats, tea lights, intimate bar, and chalkboard menu. It was the area's first farm-to-table restaurant when co-owners Abby and Rogan Lechthaler opened doors in 2010, and it has continued to be a mainstay thanks to excellent hospitality, warm-spirited creativity, and nightly-changing specials. **Known for:** seasonal cocktails; small-producer-focused wine list; nightly changing chalkboard specials. $ *Average main: $30* ⊠ *41 Depot St.* ☎ *802/228–7566* ⊕ *thedowntowngrocery.com* ⊙ *Closed Tues. and Wed.*

Goodman's American Pie

$ | PIZZA | FAMILY | This place has the best wood-fired pizza in town. It also has character to spare: sit in chairs from old ski lifts and step up to the counter fashioned from a vintage VW bus to design your pie from 29 ingredients. **Known for:** arcade games and pool table in the back; pizza by the slice; outdoor deck. $ *Average main: $17* ⊠ *5 Lamere Sq.* ☎ *802/228–4271* ⊕ *www.goodmansamericanpie. com* ⊙ *Closed Mon. and Tues.*

Vermont Artisanal Cheese 🍴

Vermont is the artisanal cheese capital of the country, with several dozen creameries open to the public churning out hundreds of different cheeses. Many creameries are "farmstead" operations, meaning that the animals whose milk is made into cheese are kept on-site. If you eat enough cheese during your time in the state, you may be able to differentiate between the many types of milk (cow, goat, sheep, or even water buffalo) and make associations between the geography and climate of where you are and the taste of the local cheeses.

This is one of the reasons that taking a walk around a dairy is a great idea: you can see the process in action, from grazing to aging to eating. The **Vermont Cheese Trail map**, which you can view or download on the website of the Vermont Cheese Council (☎ *866/261–8595* 🌐 *www.vtcheese.com*), has a comprehensive list of dairies, many of which you can visit. Though hours are given for some, it's generally recommended that you still call ahead.

At the **Vermont Cheesemakers Festival** (☎ *802/261–8595* 🌐 *www.vtcheesefest.com*), which takes place in July or August in Shelburne, cheese makers gather to sell their various cheeses. Beer and wine are served to wash it all down.

★ The Hidden Kitchen at The Inn at Weathersfield

$$$ | **FRENCH FUSION** | So many Vermont restaurants claim the farm-to-table, local-sourcing, organic approach to cooking, but the chef at the Inn at Weathersfield is more passionate and rigorous than most, with more than 75% of ingredients coming from within a 25-mile radius in season. Enjoy the exquisite French-influenced regional dishes inside the inn itself, on its back patio, or in the separate "Hidden Kitchen" at the back of the property, where monthly cooking workshops and tastings take place. **Known for:** wine list; charcuterie and cheese boards; atmospheric inside and out. [$] *Average main: $28* ✉ *1342 Rte. 106, Perkinsville* ✣ *15 miles east of Ludlow* ☎ *802/263–9217* 🌐 *www.weathersfieldinn.com* 🕒 *Closed Mon., Tues., and mid-Apr. and early Nov. No lunch.*

Mojo Cafe

$ | **FUSION** | In 2014, Jodi and John Seward opened this funky, casual watering hole fusing Mexican and Cajun cooking. Tacos, burritos, bowls, and po' boys frequently feature Vermont meats and produce, while craft beers and specialty cocktails continue to highlight the state's bounty in local beer and spirits. **Known for:** blackened redfish taco with pineapple pico; alligator and andouille gumbo; funky burritos like the "Betty," with tequila-citrus tofu and avocado sauce. [$] *Average main: $10* ✉ *106 Main St.* ☎ *802/228–6656.*

☕ Coffee and Quick Bites

★ Green Mountain Sugar House

$ | **BAKERY** | **FAMILY** | This red-roofed sugarhouse on the edge of Lake Rescue has one of the best maple creemees in the state of Vermont. Locals Ann and Doug Rose have owned the sugaring house since 1985, and almost four decades later continue to uphold their destination-worthy reputation for award-winning maple syrup. **Known for:** Vermont maple creemees; award-winning maple brittle and fudge. Ⓢ *Average main: $5* ✉ *820 Rte. 100 N* ☎ *800/643–9338* ⊕ *www.gmsh.com.*

Hotels

Homestyle Hostel

$ | HOTEL | Vermont natives Eliza Greene and Justin Hyjek opened their updated inn and restaurant in 2014, renovating a 19th-century home on Main Street to offer the kind of food and housing they grew to love while working on a hostel-meets-farmstead in the hills of Colombia. **Pros:** farm-fresh restaurant on-site; memory-foam mattresses and Egyptian cotton sheets; central location and wraparound porch. **Cons:** the restaurant and bar have limited seating; only some rooms have en suite bathrooms; the rest are private, though down the hall; 8 rooms are limited, though offer a variety of options. Ⓢ *Rooms from: $140* ✉ *119 Main St.* ☎ *802/975–0030* ⊕ *homestylehotel. com* ⇋ *8 rooms* ⦿ *No meals.*

Inn at Water's Edge

$ | B&B/INN | Former Long Islanders Bruce and Tina Verdrager converted their old ski house and barns into this comfortably refined haven, perfect for those who want to ski but not stay in town. **Pros:** bucolic setting on a lakefront, with swimming access; two canoes for guest use; golf and spa packages are available. **Cons:** ordinary rooms; lots of flowered wallpaper and upholstery; no sights within walking distance. Ⓢ *Rooms from: $175* ✉ *45 Kingdom Rd.* ✛ *5 miles north of Ludlow* ☎ *802/228–8143, 888/706–9736* ⊕ *www.innatwatersedge.com* ⇋ *11 rooms* ⦿ *Free breakfast.*

★ Inn at Weathersfield

$$ | B&B/INN | Set far back from the road, this 1792 home built by a Revolutionary War veteran is a world unto itself, and an Eden-esque one at that, with flowering gardens, croaking frog pond, and extensive forest on its 21 acres. **Pros:** dynamite restaurant and tavern; ideal for weddings; monthly cooking classes. **Cons:** 15-mile drive from the Okemo slopes; no sights within walking distance; no coffee or tea in rooms. Ⓢ *Rooms from: $219* ✉ *1342 Rte. 106, Perkinsville* ☎ *802/263–9217* ⊕ *www.weathersfieldinn.com* ☾ *Closed 1st 2 wks in Nov.* ⇋ *12 rooms* ⦿ *Free breakfast.*

🏃 Activities

SKI AREAS
Okemo Mountain Resort

SKIING/SNOWBOARDING | FAMILY | Family fun is the focus of southern Vermont's highest vertical ski resort, which has dozens of beginner trails, some wide intermediate runs, terrain parks throughout, a tubing facility, a nursery, an ice rink, indoor basketball and tennis courts, and a children's pool with slides. There's even a Kids' Night Out child-care program on Saturday evening during the regular season, so parents can have date nights. The Okemo Valley Nordic Center has miles of cross-country and snowshoeing trails. Summer diversions include golfing, mountain biking, and activities and rides in the Adventure Zone. The newer Jackson Gore base features the latest (and fanciest) venues the resort has to offer. **Facilities:** 121 trails; 667 acres; 2,200-foot vertical drop; 20 lifts. ✉ *77 Okemo Ridge Rd.* ☎ *802/228–1600 resort services, 802/228–5222 for snow conditions, 800/786–5366* ⊕ *www.okemo.com* 🎫 *Lift ticket: $92.*

Grafton

20 miles south of Ludlow.

Out-of-the-way Grafton is as much a historical museum as a town. During its heyday, citizens grazed 10,000 sheep and spun their wool into sturdy yarn for locally woven fabric. As the wool market declined, so did Grafton. In 1963 the Windham Foundation—Vermont's second-largest private foundation—commenced the town's rehabilitation. The Old Tavern (now called the Grafton Inn) was preserved, along with many other commercial and residential structures.

GETTING HERE AND AROUND
Routes 11, 35, and 103 intersect in Grafton.

Sights

Historical Society Museum

MUSEUM | This endearingly cluttered museum documents the town's history with photographs, soapstone displays, quilts, musical instruments, furniture, tools, and other artifacts. ⊠ *147 Main St.* ☎ *802/843–2584* ⊕ *www.graftonhistoricalsociety.com* ⊠ *$5* ⊙ *Closed Tues. and Wed. Memorial Day–Columbus Day, and Tues., Wed., and weekends Columbus Day–Memorial Day.*

🍴 Restaurants

Phelps Barn Pub at The Grafton Village Inn

$$ | BURGER | This wood-clad restaurant with a second-floor loft, hanging tea lights, and Vermont-inspired pub fare was originally a carriage house for the guests' horses at The Grafton Village Inn. Today, it's a beautiful and rustic spot for eating local, from crispy skinned local duck breast to seasonal vegetable risotto to a Vermont beef burger capped with Grafton cheddar cheese. **Known for:** rustic interiors with a sense of history; the Phelps burger with local beef and Grafton cheddar; local ingredients as a member of the Vermont Fresh Network. ⓢ *Average main: $24* ⊠ *92 Main St.* ☎ *802/843–2248* ⊕ *www.graftoninnvermont.com* ⊙ *Closed Sun. and Mon.*

☕ Coffee and Quick Bites

MKT: Grafton

$ | CAFÉ | FAMILY | When the 19th-century Grafton Village Store shuttered 174 years after opening, locals June Lupiani and Alexandra Hartman decided to revive the abandoned building and give it new life. Their modern, newly renovated general store opened doors in 2015, and quickly became a meeting spot for locals and travelers seeking groceries, deli sandwiches, prepared foods, and home-made pastries. **Known for:** scratch-made pastries; local groceries; deli sandwiches and salads. ⓢ *Average main: $10* ⊠ *162 Main St.* ☎ *802/843–2255.*

🛏 Hotels

The Grafton Inn

$ | B&B/INN | This 1801 classic encourages you to linger on its wraparound porches, in its authentically Colonial common rooms, or with a book by the fire in its old-fashioned library, but those who want to get outside can access the nearby Grafton Ponds Outdoor Center and its 2,000 acres of trails, forests, and fields. **Pros:** handsome historic building; seasonal swim pond; game room with pool table and Ping-Pong; two dining options—the Old Tavern and Phelps Barn Pub—serve American fare. **Cons:** lots of flowered upholstery and wallpaper; resort fee; no tea or coffee in rooms. ⓢ *Rooms from: $189* ⊠ *92 Main St.* ☎ *802/234–8718, 800/843–1801* ⊕ *www.graftoninnvermont.com* ⊅ *45 rooms* ⍾ *Free breakfast.*

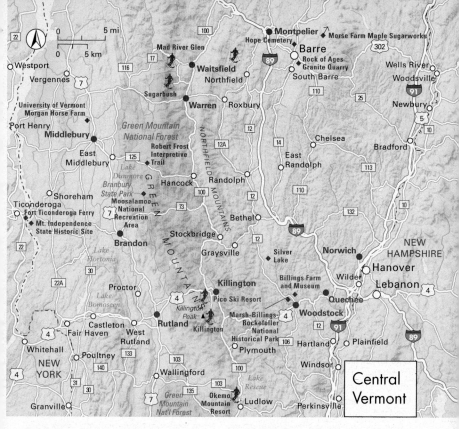

Norwich

6 miles north of White River Junction.

On the bank of the Connecticut River, Norwich is graced with beautifully maintained 18th- and 19th-century homes set about a handsome green. Norwich is the Vermont sister town to sophisticated Hanover, New Hampshire (home of Dartmouth College), across the river.

GETTING HERE AND AROUND

Most attractions are off Interstate 91; the town sits a mile to the west.

◉ Sights

★ Montshire Museum of Science

MUSEUM | FAMILY | Numerous hands-on exhibits at this 100-acre science museum explore nature and technology. Kids can make giant bubbles, watch marine life swim in aquariums, construct working hot air balloons, and explore a maze of outdoor trails by the river. Adults will happily join the fun. An ideal destination for a rainy day, this is one of the finest museums in New England. ✉ *1 Montshire Rd.* ☎ *802/649–2200* ⊕ *www.montshire.org* ✏ *$17 mid-June– early Sept., $15 early Sept.–mid-June.*

☕ Coffee and Quick Bites

Blue Sparrow Cafe

$ | CAFÉ | FAMILY | Locally sourced food and big smiles are touted at this small, neighborly café on Main Street. Stop in early for organic muesli and a local egg sandwich with house-made salsa, or peruse the lengthy sandwich menu come lunchtime. **Known for:** breakfast sandwiches and burritos; coffee and pastries; creative deli sandwiches.

$ *Average main: $8* ⊠ *289 Main St.* ☎ *802/649–7003* ⊕ *bluesparrowkitchen. com* ☾ *Closed Sun.*

King Arthur Flour Baker's Store

$ | **BAKERY** | The café at King Arthur Flour is a fine spot for both the pit-stop sandwich and the leisurely pastry and latte. The adjacent shop and market area is a must-see for those who love bread; the shelves are stocked with all the ingredients and tools in the company's Baker's Catalogue, including flours, mixes, and local jams, and syrups. **Known for:** croissants, cookies, and brownies; freshly baked loaves of bread; goods to-go, such as local butter, housemade granola, and cheesy crackers. $ *Average main: $12* ⊠ *105 U.S. 5 S* ☎ *802/649–3361* ⊕ *www. kingarthurflour.com.*

🏃 Activities

Lake Morey Ice Skating Trail

ICE SKATING | For the most fun you can have on skates, head to America's longest ice-skating trail. From January to March, the frozen lake is groomed for ice-skating, providing a magical 4½-mile route amid forested hillsides. Bring your own skates or rent them at the Lake Morey Resort, which maintains the trail. ⊠ *1 Clubhouse Rd., Fairlee* ☎ *800/423–1211* ⊕ *www.lakemoreyresort.com.*

Quechee

11 miles southwest of Norwich, 6 miles west of White River Junction.

A historic mill town, Quechee sits just upriver from its namesake gorge, an impressive 165-foot-deep canyon cut by the Ottauquechee River. Most people view the gorge from U.S. 4. To escape the crowds, hike along the gorge or scramble down one of several trails to the river.

👁 Sights

★ Simon Pearce

ARTS VENUE | **FAMILY** | A restored woolen mill by a waterfall holds Quechee's main attraction: this marvelous glassblowing factory, store, and restaurant. Water power still drives the factory's furnace. Take a free self-guided tour of the downstairs factory floor, and see the amazing glassblowers at work. The store sells beautifully crafted contemporary glass and ceramic tableware. An excellent, sophisticated restaurant with outstanding views of the falls uses Simon Pearce glassware and is justifiably popular. ⊠ *The Mill, 1760 Quechee Main St.* ☎ *802/295–2711* ⊕ *www. simonpearce.com.*

Vermont Institute of Natural Science Nature Center

COLLEGE | **FAMILY** | Next to Quechee Gorge, this science center has 17 raptor exhibits, including bald eagles, peregrine falcons, and owls. All caged birds were found injured and are unable to survive in the wild. In summer, experience "Raptors Up Close," a 30-minute live bird program that happens three times a day. ⊠ *149 Natures Way* ☎ *802/359–5000* ⊕ *www.vinsweb.org* ▤ *$16.*

🍴 Restaurants

★ The Mill at Simon Pearce

$$$ | **AMERICAN** | Sparkling glassware from the studio downstairs, exposed brick, flickering candles, and large windows overlooking the falls of the roaring Ottauquechee River create an ideal setting for contemporary American cuisine—the food alone is worth the pilgrimage. The wine cellar holds several hundred labels. **Known for:** romantic atmosphere; Simon Pearce glassware and pottery; complimentary housemade potato chips. $ *Average main: $28* ⊠ *1760 Main St.* ☎ *802/295–1470* ⊕ *www.simonpearce.com.*

Hotels

Quechee Inn at Marshland Farm

$$ | B&B/INN | Each room in this handsomely restored 1793 country home has Queen Anne–style furnishings and period antiques and guests have privileges at the Quechee Club—a private golf, tennis, and ski club—and Wilderness Trails operates from the property. **Pros:** home of Colonel Joseph Marsh, Vermont's first lieutenant governor; spacious grounds; fresh baked cookies every afternoon. **Cons:** some bathrooms are dated; fills up with weddings; lots of flowered upholstery and wallpaper. $ *Rooms from: $287* ⊠ *1119 Main St.* ☎ *802/295–3133, 800/235–3133* ⊕ *www.quecheeinn.com* ⊐ *25 rooms* ⊙ *Free breakfast.*

Activities

Wilderness Trails and Vermont Fly Fishing School

FISHING | In summer, Wilderness Trails leads fly-fishing workshops; rents bikes, canoes, kayaks, and paddleboards; and arranges guided canoe, kayaking, and hiking trips. In winter, the company conducts cross-country skiing and snow-shoeing treks. ⊠ *1119 Quechee Main St.* ☎ *802/295–7620.*

Woodstock

4 miles west of Quechee.

Woodstock is a Currier & Ives print come to life. Well-maintained Federal-style houses surround the tree-lined village green, across the street from a covered bridge. The town owes much of its pristine appearance to the Rockefeller family's interest in historic preservation and land conservation and to native George Perkins Marsh, a congressman, diplomat, and conservationist who wrote the pioneering book *Man and Nature* (1864) about humanity's use and abuse of the land. Only busy U.S. 4 mars the tableau.

ESSENTIALS

VISITOR INFORMATION Woodstock Vermont Area Chamber of Commerce. ☎ *802/457–3555, 888/496–6378* ⊕ *www. woodstockvt.com.*

Sights

Billings Farm and Museum

FARM/RANCH | FAMILY | Founded by Frederick H. Billings in 1871, this is one of the oldest operating dairy farms in the country. In addition to watching the herds of Jersey cows, horses, and other farm animals at work and play, you can tour the restored 1890 farmhouse, and in the adjacent barns learn about 19th-century farming and domestic life. The biggest takeaway, however, is a renewed belief in sustainable agriculture and stewardship of the land. Pick up some raw-milk cheddar while you're here. ⊠ *69 Old River Rd.* ⊕ *½ mile north of Woodstock* ☎ *802/457–2355* ⊕ *www.billingsfarm.org* ⊠ *$16* ⊙ *Closed Mar. and Apr.; weekdays Nov.–Feb.*

Marsh-Billings-Rockefeller National Historical Park

HOUSE | Vermont's only national park is the nation's first to focus on conserving natural resources. The pristine 555-acre spread includes the mansion, gardens, and carriage roads of Frederick H. Billings (1823–90), a financier and the president of the Northern Pacific Railway. The entire property was the gift of Laurance S. Rockefeller (1910–2004), who lived here with his wife, Mary (Billings's granddaughter). You can learn more at the visitor center, tour the residential complex with a guide every hour on the hour, and explore the 20 miles of trails and old carriage roads that climb Mt. Tom. ⊠ *54 Elm St.* ☎ *802/457–3368* ⊕ *www.nps.gov/mabi* ⊠ *Tour $8.*

Silver Lake

NATIONAL/STATE PARK | Vermont lakes don't get more picturesque than this gem across the street from the Barnard General Store. Plus, it's open for swimming, boating, fishing, and camping. ⊠ *20 State*

Simon Pearce is a glassblowing factory, store, and restaurant; the factory's furnace is still powered by hydroelectricity from Quechee Falls.

Park Beach Rd., Barnard ☎ *802/234–9451* ⊕ *www.vtstateparks.com/silver.html.*

🍴 Restaurants

Angkor Wat Restaurant

$$ | **CAMBODIAN** | Chef Chy Tuckerman was raised in Cambodia, Thailand, Oregon, and New Hampshire until moving to Woodstock in 1997 to continue learning the art of baking at local Mountain Creamery. A decade later, he opened his sunny, BYOB restaurant just off Route 4, where he fuses the Cambodian and Thai cooking of his heritage into mouthwatering dishes like ginger chicken stir fry, Khmer curry soup, and traditional luk lok made with beef from nearby Cloudland Farm. **Known for:** cozy atmosphere and BYOB dining; house-made desserts; dishes fusing traditional Khmer and Thai cooking. ⓢ *Average main: $18* ⊠ *61 Pleasant St.* ☎ *802/457–9029* ⊕ *www. angkorwatvt.com* ⊘ *Closed Mon.*

Barnard Inn Restaurant and Max's Tavern

$$$$ | **AMERICAN** | The dining room in this 1796 brick farmhouse exudes 18th-century charm, but the food is decidedly 21st century. Former San Francisco restaurant chef-owner Will Dodson creates inventive three- and four-course prix-fixe menus with international flavors, or more casual versions at Max's Tavern, also on-site. **Known for:** device-free restaurant; popular for weddings; pond and perennial gardens. ⓢ *Average main: $60* ⊠ *5518 Rte. 12, 8 miles north of Woodstock, Barnard* ☎ *802/234–9961* ⊕ *www.barnardinn.com* ⊘ *Closed Sun. and Mon. No lunch.*

Cloudland Farm

$$$$ | **AMERICAN** | With the table literally on the farm, this restaurant delivers a unique farm-to-table experience that makes it worth the short drive from Woodstock. All ingredients for the seasonal prix-fixe menus come fresh from the farm or local growers, especially Cloudland's own pork, beef, chicken, and turkey. **Known for:** large fireplace in dining room; homemade carrot cake with red

wine caramel and carrot jam; bring your own wine or beer. $ *Average main: $45* ⊠ *1101 Cloudland Rd., North Pomfret* ☎ *802/457–2599* ⊕ *www.cloudlandfarm. com* ⊗ *No lunch. Closed Sun.–Wed.*

★ Mountain Creamery

$ | AMERICAN | FAMILY | This locally beloved diner in the town center sources most of its ingredients from their own farm in Killington. "Mile High Apple Pie," ice cream made with local dairy, and daily blue plate specials are only a handful of reasons Mountain Creamery is a Woodstock mainstay. **Known for:** homemade ice cream made with local dairy; farm-sourced diner fare; blue plate specials. $ *Average main: $12* ⊠ *33 Central St.* ☎ *802/457–1715* ⊕ *www.mountain-creameryvt.com.*

The Prince and the Pauper

$$ | FRENCH | Modern French and American fare with a Vermont accent is the focus of this candlelit Colonial restaurant off the town green. Three-course prix-fixe meals cost $53, but a less expensive bistro menu is available in the lounge. **Known for:** artwork for sale; complimentary cinema tickets; wine list. $ *Average main: $24* ⊠ *24 Elm St.* ☎ *802/457–1818* ⊕ *www.princeandpauper.com* ⊗ *No lunch.*

Ransom Tavern

$$$ | ITALIAN | Arrive early for a seat at the wraparound bar and a perfectly made negroni. The wood-fired, Neopolitan-style pizzas are excellent, as is the inventive cocktail list and the plentiful supply of local beers on draft. **Known for:** wood-fired pizza; craft cocktail and local drafts; farm-fresh ingredients. $ *Average main: $30* ⊠ *4778 South Rd., South Woodstock* ☎ *802/457–1473* ⊕ *www.kedronvalleyinn. com* ⊗ *No lunch. Closed Mon.–Wed.*

★ Worthy Kitchen

$ | AMERICAN | FAMILY | One of Woodstock's liveliest and most popular places to eat, this upscale pub and bistro remains buzzing through most evenings. The chalkboard on the wall lists the hearty menu of American comfort classics given farm-to-table twists, and the craft beer selection is excellent. **Known for:** beer list; social hot spot; burgers with Wagyu beef patties. $ *Average main: $14* ⊠ *442 Woodstock Rd.* ☎ *802/457–7281* ⊕ *www.worthyvermont.com* ⊗ *No lunch weekdays.*

☕ Coffee and Quick Bites

Mont Vert Cafe

$ | CAFÉ | This charming two-story café in the center of Woodstock sources most of its ingredients in state. It's the perfect stop for a Vermont maple latte with local dairy, produce-laden salads, and wraps or egg sandwiches worthy of a long line. **Known for:** espresso drinks; breakfast sandwiches; seasonal specials. $ *Average main: $12* ⊠ *28 Central St.* ☎ *802/457–7143* ⊕ *www.monvertcafe. com* ⊗ *Closed Thurs.*

🛏 Hotels

★ The Fan House Bed and Breakfast

$$ | B&B/INN | This charming inn dating to 1840 is as authentic as it gets in Vermont. **Pros:** 300-plus-thread-count linens and down comforters; walking distance to Silver Lake and general store; library nook. **Cons:** no major sights in walking distance; on busy main road; set back and difficult to see from road. $ *Rooms from: $200* ⊠ *6297 Rte. 12 N* ☎ *802/234–6704* ⊕ *www.thefanhouse.com* ▤ *No credit cards* ⊗ *Closed Apr.* 🛏 *3 rooms* ⦿ *Free breakfast.*

506 On the River

$ | HOTEL | FAMILY | Behind a somewhat bland prefab exterior lies an eclectic boutique experience, thanks in large part to the virtual curiosity cabinet of exotic (or faux exotic) knickknacks stuffed throughout the premises, brought by the Africa-based owners. **Pros:** impressive cocktail menu in bar; patio dining with view of river; lots of activities and

The upscale Woodstock area is known as Vermont's horse country.

space for families. **Cons:** 5 miles west of Woodstock; child-friendly means lots of children; a bit buggy. $ *Rooms from: $199* ✉ *1653 W. Woodstock Rd., Burlington* ☎ *802/457–5000* ⊕ *www. ontheriverwoodstock.com* ⤳ *45 rooms* ❑ *Free breakfast.*

Kedron Valley Inn

$ | **B&B/INN** | You're likely to fall in love at first sight with the main 1828 three-story brick building here, the centerpiece of this 15-acre retreat, but wait until you see the spring-fed pond, which has a white sand beach with toys for kids. **Pros:** on-site restaurant with a great wine list; historic facade with modern interiors and amenities; next door to South Woodstock Country Store. **Cons:** 5 miles south of Woodstock; limited cell service; no sights within walking distance. $ *Rooms from: $199* ✉ *4778 South Rd., South Woodstock* ☎ *802/457–1473, 800/836–1193* ⊕ *www.kedronvalleyinn.com* ☾ *Closed Apr.* ⤳ *16 rooms* ❑ *Free breakfast.*

The Shire Riverview Motel

$ | **HOTEL** | Many rooms in this immaculate motel have decks, and most have fabulous views of Ottauquechee River, which runs right along the building. **Pros:** within walking distance of Woodstock's green and shops; sweeping river views; discounted access to Woodstock Recreation Center pool and fitness center. **Cons:** basic rooms; unexciting exterior; not all rooms have river views. $ *Rooms from: $198* ✉ *46 Pleasant St.* ☎ *802/457–2211* ⊕ *shirewoodstock. com* ⤳ *42 rooms* ❑ *No meals.*

★ Twin Farms

$$$$ | **RESORT** | Let's just get it out there: Twin Farms is the best lodging in Vermont, and the most expensive, but it's worth it. **Pros:** luxury fit for A-list Hollywood stars, including Oprah Winfrey and Tom Cruise; Japanese furo in woods; on-site spa. **Cons:** steep prices; no children allowed; minimum stays during peak periods and many weekends. $ *Rooms from: $1900* ✉ *452 Royalton Tpke., Barnard* ☎ *802/234–9999* ⊕ *www.twinfarms.com* ⤳ *20 rooms* ❑ *All-inclusive.*

★ The Woodstock Inn and Resort
$$$ | RESORT | FAMILY | A night at the Woodstock Inn, one of Vermont's premier accommodations, is an experience in itself, with a location on Woodstock's gorgeous green that's hard to beat. **Pros:** historic property; perfect central location; one of the best spas in Vermont. **Cons:** posh ambience not for everyone; slightly slick and corporate; very expensive for Vermont. [$] *Rooms from: $339* ✉ *14 The Green* ☎ *802/332–6853, 888/338–2745* 🌐 *www.woodstockinn.com* 🛏 *142 rooms* 🍴 *No meals.*

Activities

GOLF

Woodstock Inn and Resort Golf Club
GOLF | Robert Trent Jones Sr. designed the resort's challenging course. ✉ *76 South St.* ☎ *802/457–6674, 888/338–2745* 🌐 *www.woodstockinn.com/golf-club* 🎟 *$75 for 9 holes, $95 for 18 holes, weekdays; $95 for 9 holes, $135 for 18 holes, weekends* ⛳ *18 holes, 6001 yards, par 70.*

SKIING

Tubbs Snowshoes & Fischer Nordic Adventure Center
SKIING/SNOWBOARDING | The Woodstock Inn's Nordic complex has nearly 25 miles of picturesque groomed cross-country ski trails around Mt. Tom and Mt. Peg. Equipment and lessons are available. ✉ *76 South St.* ☎ *802/457–6674* 🌐 *www.woodstockinn.com* 🎟 *Trail pass: $25.*

SPAS

The Bridge House Spa at Twin Farms
SPA/BEAUTY | A visit to Twin Farms is a trip to another world, and a spa treatment here completes the getaway. The spa at the luxury lodging expounds a philosophy of wellness that goes beyond the realm of massages and skin treatments. Employing an organic product line by Vermont-based Tata Harper and Lunaroma, the spa offers facials, polishes, aromatherapy, massages, and mud wraps that administer a heavenly reboot to your skin and muscles. ✉ *Twin Farms, 452 Royalton Tpke., Barnard* ☎ *802/234–9999* 🌐 *www.twinfarms.com.*

Spa at the Woodstock Inn and Resort
SPA/BEAUTY | A mesmerizing, 10,000-square-foot, nature-inspired facility, this LEED-certified spa is a world unto itself, with 10 treatment rooms, ultratranquil relaxation area, eucalyptus steam room, and a sophisticated shop stocked with designer bath products. Elegant, minimalist design accentuates the beautiful setting: natural light pours into sparkling dressing rooms and the firelit Great Room, and an outdoor meditation courtyard has a hot tub and a Scandinavian-style sauna. The mood is serene, the treatments varied: start with the 80-minute Himalayan Salt Stone Massage. ✉ *Woodstock Inn and Resort, 14 The Green* ☎ *802/457–6697, 888/338–2745* 🌐 *www.woodstockinn.com/spa.*

Killington

20 miles northwest of Woodstock.

With only a gas station, a post office, a motel, and a few shops at the intersection of U.S. 4 and Route 100, it doesn't quite feel like the East's largest ski resort is nearby. The village of Killington has suffered from unfortunate strip development along the access road to the ski resort, but the 360-degree views atop Killington Peak, accessible via the resort's gondola, make it worth the drive.

Coffee and Quick Bites

Liquid Art Coffeehouse & Eatery
$ | CAFÉ | This cerulean blue A-frame is a mountainside gem for morning baked goods, award-winning chilli, and specialty drinks like the Mounds latte (espresso, steamed milk, coconut, and chocolate syrup). It also doubles as a local art gallery, so you can peruse Vermont artists

over a pick-me-up. **Known for:** specialty lattes; cozy corner tables and free Wi-Fi; award-winning vegetarian chilli. [$] *Average main: $6* ✉ *37 Miller Brook Rd.* ☎ *802/422–2787* 🌐 *www.liquidartvt.com* ⏲ *Closed Wed. and Thurs.*

Hotels

Birch Ridge Inn

$ | **B&B/INN** | A slate-covered carriageway about a mile from the Killington ski resort leads to this popular off-mountain stay, a former executive retreat in two renovated A-frames. **Pros:** variety of quirky designs; five-minute drive to the slopes; near Killington nightlife. **Cons:** restaurant closed Sunday and Monday; outdated and tired style; no coffee or tea in rooms. [$] *Rooms from: $139* ✉ *37 Butler Rd.* ☎ *802/422–4293, 800/435–8566* 🌐 *www.birchridge.com* ⏲ *Closed May* 🛏 *10 rooms* 🍴 *Free breakfast.*

The Mountain Top Inn & Resort

$$$ | **RESORT** | **FAMILY** | This four-season resort hosts everything from cross-country skiing and snowshoeing on 37 miles of trails in the winter to horseback riding, tennis, and swimming and boating in the 740-acre lake throughout the rest of the year. **Pros:** family-friendly vibe; three suites have fireplaces; views of mountains and lake from some rooms. **Cons:** fees for activities can add up; tea/coffeemakers only in suites; limited to no cell service. [$] *Rooms from: $325* ✉ *195 Mountain Top Rd., Chittenden* ☎ *802/483–2311* 🌐 *www.mountaintopinn.com* 🛏 *59 rooms* 🍴 *No meals.*

Nightlife

McGrath's Irish Pub

BARS/PUBS | On Friday and Saturday, listen to live Irish music and sip Guinness draft at the Inn at Long Trail's pub. ✉ *709 U.S. 4* ☎ *802/755–7181* 🌐 *www.innatlongtrail.com.*

Pickle Barrel Night Club

DANCE CLUBS | During ski season, this club has live music on Friday and Saturday. After 8, the crowd moves downstairs for dancing, sometimes to big-name bands. ✉ *1741 Killington Rd.* ☎ *802/422–3035* 🌐 *www.picklebarrelnightclub.com.*

Activities

BIKING

True Wheels Bike Shop

BICYCLING | Part of the Basin Sports complex, this shop rents bicycles and has information about local routes. ✉ *2886 Killington Rd.* ☎ *802/422–3234, 877/487–9972* 🌐 *www.basinski.com/true-wheels-bike-shop.*

CROSS-COUNTRY SKIING

FISHING

Gifford Woods State Park

FISHING | This state park's Kent Pond is a terrific fishing spot. ✉ *34 Gifford Woods Rd., ½ mile north of U.S. 4* ☎ *802/775–5354* 🌐 *www.vtstateparks.com/gifford.html* ⏲ *Facilities closed late Oct.–mid-May.*

GOLF

Killington Golf Course

GOLF | At its namesake resort, the course has a challenging layout. ✉ *4763 Killington Rd.* ☎ *802/422–6700* 🌐 *www.killington.com/summer/golf_course* 🎟 *$30 for 9 holes and $50 for 18 holes, weekdays; $45 for 9 holes and $65 for 18 holes, weekends* ⛳ *18 holes, 6186 yards, par 72* ⏲ *Closed mid-Oct.–mid-May.*

HIKING

Deer Leap Trail

HIKING/WALKING | This 3-mile round-trip hike begins near the Inn at Long Trail and leads to a great view overlooking Sherburne Gap and Pico Peak. ✉ *Trailhead off U.S. 4, just east of Inn at Long Trail, Rutland.*

SKIING
★ Killington

SKIING/SNOWBOARDING | FAMILY | "Mega-mountain" aptly describes Killington. Thanks to its extensive snowmaking capacity, the resort typically opens in early November, and the lifts often run into late April or early May. Skiing includes everything from Outer Limits, the East's steepest and longest mogul trail, to the 6½-mile Great Eastern. The 18-foot Superpipe is one of the best rated in the East. There are also acres of glades. Après-ski activities are plentiful, and Killington ticket holders can also ski Pico Mountain—a shuttle connects the two areas. Summer activities at Killington–Pico include mountain biking, hiking, and golf. **Facilities:** 155 trails; 1,509 acres; 3,050-foot vertical drop; 21 lifts. ■ **TIP→ Park at the base of the Skyeship Gondola to avoid the more crowded access road.** ✉ 4763 Killington Rd. ☎ 802/422–3261 for snow conditions, 800/734–9435 ⊕ www.killington.com 🎟 Lift ticket: $115.

Pico

SKIING/SNOWBOARDING | When weekend hordes descend upon Killington, locals head to Pico. One of Killington's "seven peaks," Pico is physically separated from its parent resort. Trails range from elevator-shaft steep to challenging intermediate runs near the summit. Easier terrain can be found near the bottom of the mountain's nearly 2,000-foot vertical drop, and the learning slope is separated from the upper mountain, so hotshots won't bomb through it. The lower express quad can get crowded, but the upper one rarely has a line. **Facilities:** 57 trails; 468 acres; 1,967-foot vertical drop; 7 lifts. ✉ 73 Alpine Dr., Mendon ☎ 802/422–1330, 802/422–1200 for snow conditions ⊕ www.picomountain.com 🎟 Lift ticket: $79.

SNOWMOBILE TOURS
Snowmobile Vermont

SNOW SPORTS | Blazing down forest trails on a snowmobile is one way Vermonters embrace the winter landscapes. Rentals are available through Snowmobile Vermont at several locations, including Killington and Okemo. Both have hour-long guided tours across groomed ski trails ($99). If you're feeling more adventurous, take the two-hour backcountry tour through 25 miles of Calvin Coolidge State Forest ($159). ✉ 170 Rte. 100, Bridgewater Corners ☎ 802/422–2121 ⊕ www.snowmobilevermont.com.

Rutland

15 miles southwest of Killington, 32 miles south of Middlebury.

The strip malls and seemingly endless row of traffic lights on and around U.S. 7 in Rutland are very un-Vermont. Two blocks west, however, stand the mansions of marble magnates. In Rutland you can grab a bite and see some interesting marble, and Depot Park hosts the county farmers' market Saturday 9–2. This isn't a place to spend too much time sightseeing, though.

ESSENTIALS
VISITOR INFORMATION Rutland Region Chamber of Commerce. ☎ 802/773–2747, 800/756–8880 ⊕ www.rutlandvermont.com.

🍴 Restaurants

Little Harry's

$$ | ECLECTIC | Laminated photos of regular customers adorn the tabletops of this restaurant, which locals have packed since 1997, when chef-owners Trip Pearce and Jack Mangan brought Vermont-cheddar ravioli and lamb lo mein to downtown Rutland. The place is "little" compared to the bigger Harry's, near Ludlow. **Known for:** pad Thai; a wide variety of customers; entire menu can be packed to go. $ Average main: $22 ✉ 121 West St. ☎ 802/747–4848 ⊕ www.littleharrys.com ⊙ No lunch.

Roots

$$ | MODERN AMERICAN | Since opening in 2011, chef-owner Donald Billings has created a locavore restaurant driven by ingredients made within miles of the dining room. Humanely raised livestock and Vermont-grown produce is the inspiration behind menu favorites like laden cheeseboards, braised pork belly, and homemade Parker House rolls served warm with Vermont butter. **Known for:** Vermont beers and spirits; frequently changing locavore menu; special Prime Rib Thursday. $ *Average main: $24* ✉ *55 Washington St.* ☎ *802/747–7414* ⊕ *www. rootsrutland.com* ⊗ *Closed Sun. and Mon.*

☕ Coffee and Quick Bites

★ Jones' Donuts

$ | BAKERY | Since 1923, Jones' has been a destination for doughnuts and baked goods made fresh each day in the earliest hours of the morning. Fill a box with cinnamon rolls, pie squares, apple turnovers, and some of the best doughnuts in the state. **Known for:** maple glazed doughnuts; crullers; sticky buns. $ *Average main: $2* ✉ *23 West St.* ☎ *802/773–7810* ⊗ *Closed Mon. and Tues.*

Brandon

15 miles northwest of Rutland.

Thanks to an active group of artists, tiny Brandon is making a name for itself. In 2003 the Brandon Artists Guild, led by American folk artist Warren Kimble, auctioned off 40 life-size fiberglass pigs painted by local artists. The "Really Really Pig Show" raised money for the guild, and has since brought small-town fame to this community through its annual shows. Brandon is also home to the Basin Bluegrass Festival, held in July.

ESSENTIALS

VISITOR INFORMATION Brandon Visitor Center. ✉ *4 Grove St.* ☎ *802/247–6401* ⊕ *www.brandon.org.*

◉ Sights

Brandon Artists Guild

MUSEUM | The guild exhibits and sells affordable paintings, sculpture, and pottery by more than 30 local member artists. ✉ *7 Center St.* ☎ *802/247–4956* ⊕ *brandonartistsguild.org* ◪ *Free* ⊗ *Closed Mon. Dec.–Apr.*

Brandon Museum at the Stephen A. Douglas Birthplace

MUSEUM | The famous statesman was born in this house in 1813. He left 20 years later to establish himself as a lawyer, becoming a three-time U.S. senator and arguing more cases before the U.S. Supreme Court than anyone else. This museum recounts the early Douglas years, early town history, and the antislavery movement in Vermont, the first state to abolish slavery. ✉ *4 Grove St., at U.S. 7* ☎ *802/247–6401* ⊕ *www. brandon.org* ◪ *Free* ⊗ *Closed Sun. and mid-Oct.–mid-May.*

Foley Brothers Brewery

WINERY/DISTILLERY | Though this is a bare bones tasting room—no food, no tours, just glass pours and growlers—we argue that it has great charm, unique Vermont personality, and some of the best beer in the state. There is space to sit outside in the summer months in a nearby field with beautiful views, and the brewery's golden retriever is locally beloved. ✉ *79 Stone Mill Dam Rd.* ☎ *802/465–8413* ⊕ *foleybrothersbrewing.com* ⊗ *Closed Mon. and Tues., and Sun. Jan.–May.*

Moosalamoo National Recreation Area

NATIONAL/STATE PARK | Covering nearly 16,000 acres of the Green Mountain National Forest, this area northeast of Brandon attracts hikers, mountain bikers, and cross-country skiers who enjoy the

70-plus miles of trails through wondrous terrain. If there is anywhere to stop and smell the flowers in Vermont, this is it. ✉ *Off Rtes. 53 and 73* 🌐 *www.moosalamoo.org.*

Mt. Independence State Historic Site

ARCHAEOLOGICAL SITE | Mt. Independence is one of the nation's most revered Revolutionary War sites, documenting the efforts to defend New York, New England, and the battle for American liberty. This key defensive position gained its name between 1776 and 1777, when the barely dried ink of the Declaration of Independence was read to United States soldiers assembled on the rugged peninsula east of Lake Champlain. Annual events include guided nature and history hikes on the site's 6 miles of hiking trails; historical lectures; archaeological investigations; a "Soldiers Atop the Mount" living history weekend; and a yearly reading of the Declaration of Independence. ✉ *497 Mt. Independence Rd., Orwell* ☎ *802/948–2000* 🌐 *historicsites.vermont.gov/mount-independence.*

Red Clover Ale

WINERY/DISTILLERY | Red Clover Ale opened in Brandon's tiny town center under the reigns of two brothers and a brother-and-law. The family trio focuses on creative ales alongside skilled representations of the classics, like their pitch-perfect pilsners and stouts. Their ongoing IPA series is as special as the birds they're named after, like American Redstart and Yellow Warbler. Excellent pop-up food vendors are occasionally found on-site—otherwise, a corkboard near the entrance is covered in local takeout menus for perusing to one's liking. ✉ *43 Center St.* ☎ *802/465–8412* 🌐 *www.redcloverale.com* 🕒 *Closed Mon.–Wed.*

🍴 Restaurants

Café Provence

$$ | **CAFÉ** | Robert Barral, the former executive chef of the New England Culinary Institute, graces Brandon with this informal eatery one story above the main street. Flowered seat cushions, dried-flower window valences, and other hints of Barral's Provençal birthplace abound, as do his eclectic, farm-fresh dishes. **Known for:** Sunday brunch; thin tomato pie; seafood stew. [$] *Average main: $23* ✉ *11 Center St.* ☎ *802/247–9997* 🌐 *www.cafeprovencevt.com* 🕒 *Closed Mon. in winter.*

☕ Coffee and Quick Bites

Gourmet Provence Bakery

$ | **BAKERY** | Next door to Café Provence, this French bakery offers coffee, pastries (yes, there are croissants and eclairs), prepared food, and specialty goods during the day. There's also a modest wine shop featuring plenty of old-world bottles. **Known for:** coffee and espresso drinks; homemade pastries; wine shop and artisanal goods. [$] *Average main: $8* ✉ *37 Center St.* ☎ *802/247–3002* 🌐 *cafeprovencevt.com* 🕒 *Closed Mon.*

🛏 Hotels

★ Blueberry Hill Inn

$$ | **B&B/INN** | In the Green Mountain National Forest, 5½ miles off a mountain pass on a dirt road, you'll find this secluded inn with lush gardens and a pond with a wood-fired sauna on its bank; there's lots to do if you're into nature: biking, hiking, and cross-country skiing on 43 miles of trails. **Pros:** skis and snowshoes to rent in winter; the restaurant prepares a Vermont-infused, four-course prix-fixe menu most nights; homemade cookies. **Cons:** fills up with wedding parties; no cell phone service; no coffee or tea in rooms. [$] *Rooms*

from: $269 ⊠ 1245 Goshen–Ripton Rd., Goshen ☎ 802/247–6735 ⊕ www.blue-berryhillinn.com ⇆ 12 rooms ⎮ Free breakfast.

The Lilac Inn

$ | **B&B/INN** | The best bed-and-breakfast in town has cheery, comfortable guest rooms in a central setting half a block from the heart of Brandon. **Pros:** many rooms have king beds; within walking distance of town; garden gazebo for relaxation. **Cons:** busy in summer with weddings; quaint but tepid tradition-al design; no coffee or tea in rooms. $ Rooms from: $169 ⊠ 53 Park St. ☎ 802/247–5463, 800/221–0720 ⊕ www.lilacinn.com ⇆ 9 rooms ⎮ Free breakfast.

🏃 Activities

GOLF
Neshobe Golf Club

GOLF | This bent-grass course has terrific views of the Green Mountains. Several local inns offer golfing packages. ⊠ 224 Town Farm Rd. ☎ 802/247–3611 ⊕ ne-shobe.com ⎘ $22 for 9 holes, $42 for 18 holes ⚑ 18 holes, 6341 yards, par 72.

HIKING
Branbury State Park

HIKING/WALKING | A large turnout on Route 53 marks the trailhead for a moderate hike to the Falls of Lana, a highlight of this park on the shores of Lake Dunmore near the Moosalamoo National Recre-ation Area. ⊠ 3570 Lake Dunmore Rd. ⊕ www.vtstateparks.com/branbury.html ⎘ $4 ⊙ Facilities closed late Oct.–late May.

Mt. Horrid

HIKING/WALKING | For great views from a vertigo-inducing cliff, hike up the Long Trail to Mt. Horrid. The steep, hour-long hike starts at the top of Brandon Gap. ⊠ Trailhead at Brandon Gap Rte. 73 park-ing lot, about 8 miles east of Brandon ⊕ www.fs.usda.gov/main/gmfl.

Middlebury Tasting Trail ⚲

Among Vermont's craft beer, cider, spirits, and wine explosion, the Middlebury area stands out, with a large cluster of producers with welcoming tasting rooms. Seven, all within a 10-mile radius of the city, have banded together to create to Middlebury Tasting Trail. Find full details at ⊕ www.middtastingtrail. com.

Trails at Mt. Independence State Historic Site

HIKING/WALKING | West of Brandon, four trails—two short ones of less than a mile each and two longer ones—lead to some abandoned Revolutionary War fortifica-tions. ⊠ 497 Mt. Independence Rd., just west of Orwell, Orwell ⊹ Parking lot is at top of hill ☎ 802/948–2000 ⊕ historic-sites.vermont.gov/mount-independence ⎘ $5 ⊙ Closed mid-Oct.–late May.

Middlebury

17 miles north of Brandon, 34 miles south of Burlington.

In the late 1800s Middlebury was the largest Vermont community west of the Green Mountains, an industrial center of river-powered wool and grain mills. This is Robert Frost country: Vermont's late poet laureate spent 23 summers at a farm east of Middlebury. Still a cultural and economic hub amid the Champlain Valley's serene pastoral patchwork—and the home of top-notch Middlebury Col-lege—the town and rolling countryside invite a day of exploration.

◉ Sights

Edgewater Gallery

MUSEUM | This gallery sits alongside picturesque Otter Creek, and the paintings, jewelry, ceramics, and pieces of furniture inside are just as arresting. Exhibitions in the bright, airy space change regularly, demonstrating the owner's ambition to be more gallery than shop, though all pieces are for sale. A second gallery is across the creek in the Battell Building. ⊠ 1 Mill St. ☎ 802/458–0098 ⊕ edgewatergallery.co ☜ Free.

Fort Ticonderoga Ferry

TRANSPORTATION SITE (AIRPORT/BUS/FERRY/ TRAIN) | Established in 1759, the Fort Ti cable ferry crosses Lake Champlain between Shoreham and Fort Ticonderoga, New York, at one of the oldest ferry crossings in North America. The trip takes seven minutes. ⊠ 4831 Rte. 74 W, Shoreham ☎ 802/897–7999 ⊕ www. forttiferry.com ☜ Cars $12, bicycles $2, pedestrians $1 ⊙ Closed Nov.–Apr.

Lincoln Peak Vineyard

WINERY/DISTILLERY | Named "Winery of the Year" at the International Cold Climate Wine Competition in 2016, this vineyard is enjoying the fruits of its labor, with an increase in traffic to its tasting room and shop. Enjoy the Frontenac, La Crescent, and Marquette varieties on the postcard-pretty porch overlooking a small pond. ⊠ 142 River Rd. ☎ 802/388–7368 ⊕ www.lincolnpeakvineyard.com ⊙ Closed Mon. and Tues. late Oct.–Dec.; Mon.–Thurs. Jan.–late May.

Middlebury College

COLLEGE | Founded in 1800, this college was conceived as a more godly alternative to the worldly University of Vermont, though it has no religious affiliation today. The postmodern architecture of the **Mahaney Center for the Arts,** which offers music, theater, and dance performances throughout the year, stands in provocative contrast to the early-19th-century stone buildings in the middle of town.

⊠ 131 College St. ☎ 802/443–5000 ⊕ www.middlebury.edu.

Otter Creek Brewery

WINERY/DISTILLERY | One of Vermont's oldest breweries still knows how to compete with the new generation of start-ups, adopting a fun, summery, colorful tone that invites beer fans to "hop on the bus!" (get it?) at its spacious and chic tasting room. Next to the outdoor patio is a space for lawn games, and a concert series brings live music in the warm weather. ⊠ 793 Exchange St. ☎ 802/388–0727 ⊕ www.ottercreekbrewing.com.

Robert Frost Interpretive Trail

TRAIL | Plaques along this easy 1.2-mile wooded trail bear quotations from Frost's poems. A picnic area is across the road from the trailhead. ⊠ Trailhead on Rte. 125, 10 miles east of downtown ⊕ www. fs.usda.gov/main/gmfl.

University of Vermont Morgan Horse Farm

FARM/RANCH | FAMILY | The Morgan horse, Vermont's official state animal, has an even temper, high stamina, and slightly truncated legs in proportion to its body. This farm, about 2½ miles west of Middlebury, is a breeding and training center where in summer you can tour the stables and paddocks. ⊠ 74 Battell Dr., off Morgan Horse Farm Rd., Weybridge ☎ 802/388–2011 ⊕ www.uvm.edu/morgan ☜ $5 ⊙ Closed late Oct.–Apr.

Vermont Folklife Center

MUSEUM | The redbrick center's exhibits include photography, antiques, folk paintings, manuscripts, and other artifacts and contemporary works that examine various facets of Vermont life. ⊠ 88 Main St. ☎ 802/388–4964 ⊕ www.vermontfolklifecenter.org ☜ Donations accepted ⊙ Closed Sun. and Mon.

Woodchuck Cider House

WINERY/DISTILLERY | This cidery has come a long way since its beginnings in a two-car garage in Proctorsville in 1991, transforming into this $34 million complex that divides its space between a pub, gift shop, and factory. A self-guided tour, with informational signs, includes a look through large windows onto the production floor. ✉ *1321 Exchange St.* ☎ *802/385–3656* 🌐 *www.woodchuck.com* 🕑 *Closed Mon. and Tues.*

🍴 Restaurants

American Flatbread Middlebury Hearth
$$ | **PIZZA** | If you love pizza, you're in for a treat. Wood-fired clay domes create masterful thin crusts for innovative, delicious pizzas with a distinct Vermont attitude and an array of locally sourced ingredients. **Known for:** former marble works; fireside dining with earthen oven; local beer and wine. [$] *Average main: $18* ✉ *137 Maple St.* ☎ *802/388–3300* 🌐 *www.americanflatbread.com* 🕑 *Closed Sun. and Mon. No lunch.*

★ The Arcadian
$$$ | **ITALIAN** | Chef-owner Matt Corrente cut his teeth at awarded restaurants in Boston and New York City before opening his own place on the quiet banks of Otter Creek. Corrente's knowledge of handmade pasta and regional Italian cuisine comes to life with hyperlocal ingredients; dishes like spicy squid ink orrechiette, chewy bucatini all'Amatriciana, and a nightly special of wine-braised pork cheeks are both transporting and entirely of the Green Mountain State. **Known for:** drink menu with expert cocktails and small-producer winemakers; regional handmade pasta; mini Parmesan Haymakers, a nod to the restaurant's daytime bakery. [$] *Average main: $26* ✉ *7 Bakery La.* ☎ *802/989–7026* 🌐 *www.thearcadianvt.com* 🕑 *Closed Sun. and Mon.*

★ Mary's at Baldwin Creek
$$ | **AMERICAN** | People drive from the far reaches of Vermont to dine at this family-owned, farm-to-table restaurant just beyond Bristol, 13 miles northeast of Middlebury. Allow a little extra time to visit the sprawling gardens around the beautiful property; they represent the slow approach to cooking that earned this restaurant its stellar reputation. **Known for:** cream of garlic soup; hand-churned, small-batch ice cream; cooking classes. [$] *Average main: $23* ✉ *1868 N. Rte. 116, Bristol* ☎ *802/453–2432* 🌐 *www.innatbaldwincreek.com* 🕑 *Closed Mon. and Tues.*

☕ Coffee and Quick Bites

★ Haymaker Bun Co
$ | **BAKERY** | This sunlit café and bakery overlooking Otter Creek houses some of the best coffee and pastries in the state thanks to chef-owner Caroline Corrente, who honed her skills at pastry school in France before zeroing in on a love for brioche dough. Corrente's specialty sweet and savory buns change daily based on what is available locally—many ingredients are found within a few miles of Haymaker's doors. **Known for:** sweet and savory brioche buns; locally roasted Brio coffee and espresso; patio seating and riverside views. [$] *Average main: $6* ✉ *7 Bakery La.* ☎ *802/989–7026* 🌐 *www.haymakerbuns.com* 🕑 *Closed Sun. and Mon.*

Royal Oak Coffee
$ | **CAFÉ** | After a decade of fine-tuning their skills and tastebuds in the coffee industry, Royal Oak co-owners Alessandra and Matthew Delia-Lobo opened their own café on Seymour Street, an easy pit-stop along the Middlebury Tasting Trail. The menu, featuring Vermont-based beans from Vivid Coffee Roasters, is known for shaken ice maple lattes in the summer and frothy cardamom-vanilla lattes in the winter (a seasonal special that, say the Delia-Lobos, now never leaves the menu due to popularity). **Known for:** specialty lattes using scratch-made syrups; cold brew; Gibralters, hot and iced. [$] *Average main: $5* ✉ *30 Seymour St.* ☎ *802/349–1609* 🌐 *www.royaloakcoffee.com.*

Stone Leaf Teahouse

$ | **CAFÉ** | Partially hidden in Middlebury's historic Marble Works district, this oasis of tea is known for made-to-order spiced chai, house-roasted oolong, and loose leaf teas imported from small farmers in China, India, Nepal, Japan, and Taiwan. **Known for:** specialty teaware sold on-site; oolong roasted in-house; seasonal herbal tea blends. [$] *Average main: $5* ✉ *Marble Works, 111 Maple St.* ☎ *802/458–0460* 🌐 *www.stoneleaftea.com.*

Hotels

Inn on the Green

$ | **B&B/INN** | Listed on the National Register of Historic Places, this 1803 inn and its carriage house sit in the center of bucolic Middlebury near the college campus; the inn offers a delicious breakfast, bicycles you are free to use, and Adirondack chairs that are perfect for enjoying the grounds and views. **Pros:** ideal, central location; complimentary continental "breakfast-in-bed"; Aveda hair and skin-care products. **Cons:** some rooms small and close together; typical country-inn design; no coffee or tea in rooms. [$] *Rooms from: $169* ✉ *71 S. Pleasant St.* ☎ *802/388–7512, 888/244–7512* 🌐 *www.innonthegreen.com* 🛏 *11 rooms* 🍴 *Free breakfast.*

★ **Swift House Inn**

$ | **B&B/INN** | The 1814 Georgian mansion channels a classic New England style into three buildings on 4 acres of lawns and gardens. **Pros:** attractive, spacious, well-kept rooms; complimentary day pass to Middlebury Fitness Club; some rooms have private decks; on-site restaurant, Jessica's, is one of the best fine-dining options in town. **Cons:** not quite in the heart of town; weak Wi-Fi in some areas; somewhat typical country-inn design. [$] *Rooms from: $165* ✉ *25 Stewart La.* ☎ *866/388–9925* 🌐 *www.swifthouseinn.com* 🛏 *20 rooms* 🍴 *Free breakfast.*

Nightlife

Two Brothers Tavern

$ | **BARS/PUBS** | Head to this watering hole for pub food a cut above the usual, plus local microbrews on tap in the sports-friendly bar. Look closely at the dollar bills pasted to the ceiling. There's even a marriage proposal up there, along with the answer. Food is served until at least midnight. ✉ *86 Main St.* ☎ *802/388–0002* 🌐 *www.twobrotherstavern.com.*

Waitsfield and Warren

32 miles northeast (Waitsfield) and 25 miles east (Warren) of Middlebury.

Skiers first discovered the high peaks overlooking the pastoral Mad River Valley in the 1940s. Today, this valley and its two towns, Waitsfield and Warren, attract the hip, the adventurous, and the low-key. Warren in particular is tiny and adorable, with a general store popular with tour buses. The gently carved ridges cradling the valley and the swell of pastures and fields lining the river seem to keep notions of ski-resort sprawl at bay. With a map from the Sugarbush Chamber of Commerce you can investigate back roads off Route 100 that have exhilarating valley views.

ESSENTIALS

VISITOR INFORMATION Visitor Information Center. ✉ *44 Bridge St., Waitsfield* ☎ *802/496–3409* 🌐 *www.madrivervalley.com.*

Restaurants

★ **American Flatbread Waitsfield**

$$ | **PIZZA** | The organically grown flour and vegetables—and the wood-fired clay ovens that unite them—take the pizza here to another level. In summer, you can dine outside around fire pits in the beautiful valley. **Known for:** maple–fennel sausage pie; homemade fruit crisp

with Mountain Creamery ice cream; Big Red Barn art gallery on-site. $ *Average main: $18* ✉ *46 Lareau Rd., off Rte. 100, Waitsfield* ☎ *802/496–8856* ⊕ *www. americanflatbread.com* ⊘ *Closed Mon.– Wed. No lunch.*

The Mad Taco

$ | MEXICAN | Mexican cuisine rooted in Vermont ingredients makes this a go-to stop for locals and travelers alike— particularly those who just ascended the rugged incline of nearby Camel's Hump, one of the state's highest peaks. Chef-owner Joey Nagy and Georgia Von Trapp, his partner, source much of their local haul from their own Marble Hill Farm, fueling delicious cooking from carnitas and al pastor to fresh house- made salsa and slow-roasted yams in the outside smoker. **Known for:** tacos with local All Souls tortillas; Cubano sandwich with smoked Vermont meat; house-made margaritas and local craft beer. $ *Average main: $12* ✉ *5101 Main St., Waitsfield* ☎ *802/496–3832* ⊕ *www. themadtaco.com.*

★ Peasant

$$$ | EUROPEAN | The menu may be short in this small, rustic-chic space serving French- and Italian-influenced country fare, but the tastiness is immense, with some of the best pasta dishes in the state. Additional warmth is added by its "peasant family" operation, too, with dad in the kitchen, mom decorat- ing the scene, and daughter running the front of house. **Known for:** unique "Peasant's Prunes" dessert; Vermont pork Bolognese with penne and Asiago; craft cocktail and wine list. $ *Average main: $26* ✉ *40 Bridge St., Waitsfield* ☎ *802/496–6856* ⊕ *www.peasantvt.com* ⊘ *Closed Tues. and Wed. No lunch.*

Pitcher Inn Dining Room and Tracks

$$$ | AMERICAN | Claiming two aesthetics and one menu, this dining experience offers a posh and pretty upstairs dining room with classic white tablecloths or a stony, subterranean "Tracks," with billiards and shuffleboard on the side. Dishes cover upscale versions of regional classics, with a few international flavors, too. **Known for:** cocktail list with Vermont spirits; duck breast; artisanal cheese board with onion chutney. $ *Average main: $30* ✉ *275 Main St., Warren* ☎ *802/496–6350* ⊕ *www.pitcherinn.com* ⊘ *Closed Mon. and Tues.*

☕ Coffee and Quick Bites

Canteen Creemee Company

$ | AMERICAN | FAMILY | Stop by the takeout window of this new-wave snack shack for fried chicken, griddled burgers, and kimchi-stuffed grilled cheese. Stay for the homemade creemees, Vermont's answer to soft-serve ice cream; state classics like maple are always on offer, as are seasonal specials like ginger, cinnamon, lemon, and fresh blueberry. **Known for:** creemees and sundaes; fried chicken; griddled burgers and hot dogs. $ *Aver- age main: $8* ✉ *5123 Main St., Waitsfield* ☎ *802/496–6003* ⊕ *www.canteen- creemee.com* ⊘ *Closed Mon.–Thurs.*

🛏 Hotels

★ The Inn at Round Barn Farm

$$ | B&B/INN | A Shaker-style round barn—one of only five in Vermont—is the centerpiece of this eminently charming bed-and-breakfast set among the hills of the Mad River Valley with resident ducks, squirrels, chipmunks, and songbirds that make it feel like a Disney movie. **Pros:** miles of walking and snowshoe trails; game room with billiard table and board games; gorgeous gardens with lily ponds. **Cons:** no a/c in common areas; fills up for wedding parties; no sights within walking distance. $ *Rooms from: $219* ✉ *1661 E. Warren Rd., Waitsfield* ☎ *802/496–2276* ⊕ *www.theroundbarn. com* ⇌ *12 rooms* ⦿ *Free breakfast.*

Mad River Barn

$ | **B&B/INN** | This supposed former bunk house for the Civilian Conservation Corps in the 1930s is now one of the Mad River Valley's chicest accommodations, thanks to extensive renovations in 2013 that transformed it into a rustic farmhouse with an edge of industrial. **Pros:** multiple sized rooms, sleeping up to six people; game room includes shuffleboard, air hockey, foosball, and more; several family suites, with bunkbeds. **Cons:** first-floor rooms can suffer noise; lots of weddings in summer can keep it busy and booked; no TVs in rooms. [$] *Rooms from: $145* ✉ *2849 Mill Brook Rd., Waitsfield* ☎ *802/496–3310, 800/631–0466* 🌐 *www.madriverbarn.com* 🛏 *18 rooms* 🍴 *Free breakfast.*

★ The Pitcher Inn

$$$$ | **B&B/INN** | One of Vermont's three Relais & Châteaux properties, the unique Pitcher Inn has it all including a supremely romantic restaurant and bubbling brook running alongside. **Pros:** exceptional and fun design; across from Warren General Store; complimentary hybrid bikes and access to the Sugarbush Health and Racquet Club. **Cons:** two-night minimum stay on many weekends in peak period; limited to no cell phone service; restaurant closed on Tuesday. [$] *Rooms from: $500* ✉ *275 Main St., Warren* ☎ *802/496–6350* 🌐 *www.pitcherinn.com* 🛏 *11 rooms* 🍴 *Free breakfast.*

Activities

GOLF

Sugarbush Resort Golf Club

GOLF | Great views and challenging play are the hallmarks of this mountain course designed by Robert Trent Jones Sr. ✉ *Sugarbush, 1840 Sugarbush Access Rd., Warren* ☎ *802/583–6725* 🌐 *www.sugarbush.com* 🎫 *$105 for 18 holes, weekdays; $120 for 18 holes, weekends* ⛳ *18 holes, 6464 yards, par 70.*

MULTISPORT OUTFITTER

Clearwater Sports

TOUR—SPORTS | **FAMILY** | This outfitter rents canoes and kayaks, and leads guided river trips in warmer months. When the weather turns cold, it offers snowshoeing and backcountry skiing tours. ✉ *4147 Main St., Waitsfield* ☎ *802/496–2708* 🌐 *www.clearwatersports.com.*

SKIING

Blueberry Lake Cross Country and Snowshoeing Center

SKIING/SNOWBOARDING | This ski area has 18 miles of trails through thickly wooded glades. ✉ *424 Plunkton Rd., East Warren* ☎ *802/496–6687* 🌐 *www.blueberrylakeskivt.com* 🎫 *Trail pass: $14.*

Mad River Glen

SKIING/SNOWBOARDING | A pristine alpine experience, Mad River attracts rugged individualists looking for less polished terrain. The area was developed in the late 1940s and has changed relatively little since then. It remains one of only three resorts in the country that ban snowboarding, and it's one of only two in North America that still has a single-chair lift. Mad River is steep, with slopes that follow the mountain's fall lines. The terrain changes constantly on the interconnected trails of mostly natural snow (expert trails are never groomed). Telemark skiing and snowshoeing are also popular. **Facilities:** 53 trails; 115 acres; 2,037-foot vertical drop; 5 lifts. ✉ *62 Mad River Resort Rd., off Rte. 17, Waitsfield* ☎ *802/496–3551* 🌐 *www.madriverglen.com* 🎫 *Lift ticket: $89.*

Sugarbush

SKIING/SNOWBOARDING | **FAMILY** | A true skier's mountain, Sugarbush has plenty of steep, natural snow glades and fall-line drops. Not as rough around the edges as Mad River Glen, the resort has an extensive computer-controlled system for snowmaking and many groomed trails between its two mountain complexes. This a great choice for intermediate skiers, who will find top-to-bottom

runs all over the resort; there are fewer options for beginners. Programs for kids include the enjoyable Sugarbear Forest, a terrain garden full of fun bumps and jumps. At the base of the mountain are condominiums, restaurants, shops, bars, and a health-and-racquet club. **Facilities:** 111 trails; 484 acres; 2,600-foot vertical drop; 16 lifts. ⊠ *102 Forest Dr., Warren* ⊹ *From Rte. 17, take German Flats Rd. south; from Rte. 100, take Sugarbush Access Rd. west* ☎ *802/583–6300, 800/537–8427* ⊕ *www.sugarbush.com* ⊠ *Lift ticket: $119.*

⬤ Shopping

All Things Bright and Beautiful
ANTIQUES/COLLECTIBLES | This eccentric Victorian house is filled to the rafters with stuffed animals of all shapes, sizes, and colors, as well as folk art, European glass, and Christmas ornaments. ⊠ *27 Bridge St., Waitsfield* ☎ *802/496–3997.*

The Warren Store
FOOD/CANDY | This general store has everything you'd hope to find in tiny but sophisticated Vermont: a nice selection of local beer and wine, cheeses, baked goods, strong coffee, and delicious sandwiches and prepared foods. In summer, grab a quick lunch on the small deck by the water; in winter, warm up at the wood stove. Warm, woolly clothing and accessories can be found upstairs. ⊠ *284 Main St., Warren* ☎ *802/496–3864* ⊕ *www.warrenstore.com.*

Montpelier

38 miles southeast of Burlington, 115 miles north of Brattleboro.

With only about 8,000 residents, little Montpelier is the country's smallest capital city, but it has a youthful energy and a quirky spirit that's earned it the local nickname "Montpeculiar." The quaint, historic downtown area bustles by day

with thousands of state and city workers walking to meetings and business lunches. The nightlife can't match Burlington's, but several bars, theaters, and cinemas provide ample entertainment. The city is also a springboard for exploring the great outdoors of Central Vermont.

Vermont's capital city is easily accessible from Interstate 89, taking about 45 minutes from Burlington by car through the heart of the Green Mountains. It's also on the main Boston–Montreal bus route. Downtown is flat and easily walkable, but exploring the surrounding hills requires a modest level of fitness as well as a solid pair of shoes or boots, especially during the winter.

⬤ Sights

★ Hope Cemetery
CEMETERY | Montpelier's regional rival, Barre, the "Granite Capital of the World," may lack the polish and pedigree of the state capital, but it's home to this gorgeous cemetery filled with superbly crafted tombstones by master stonecutters. A few embrace the avant-garde, while others take defined shapes like a race car, a biplane, and a soccer ball. ⊠ *201 Maple Ave., Barre* ☎ *802/476–6245.*

Hubbard Park
HIKING/WALKING | Rising behind the Vermont State House and stretching 196 acres, this heavily forested park offers locals (and their happy, leash-free dogs) miles of pretty trails and wildlife to enjoy. On its highest peak is a romantic stone tower that looks out to 360-degree views of the surrounding mountains. ⊠ *400 Parkway St.* ☎ *802/ 223–7335 Montpelier Parks department* ⊕ *www.montpelier-vt. org* ⊠ *Free.*

★ Morse Farm Maple Sugarworks
FACTORY | FAMILY | With eight generations of sugaring, the Morses may be the oldest maple family in existence, so you're sure to find an authentic experience at their farm. Burr Morse—a local

legend—heads up the operation now, along with his son Tom. More than 5,000 trees produce the sap used for syrup (you can sample all the grades), candy, cream, and sugar—all sold in the gift shop. Grab a maple creemee (soft-serve ice cream), take a seat on a swing, and stay awhile. Surrounding trails offer pleasant strolls in summer and prime cross-country skiing in winter. ⊠ 1168 County Rd. ☎ 800/242–2740 ⊕ www.morsefarm.com ⊠ Free.

Rock of Ages Granite Quarry

NATURE SITE | Attractions here range from the awe-inspiring (the quarry resembles the Grand Canyon in miniature) to the mildly ghoulish (you can consult a directory of tombstone dealers throughout the country) to the whimsical (an outdoor granite bowling alley). At the crafts center, skilled artisans sculpt monuments and blast stone, while at the quarries themselves, workers who clearly earn their pay cut 25-ton blocks of stone from the sheer 475-foot walls. (You may recognize these walls from a chase scene in the 2009 Star Trek movie.) ⊠ 558 Graniteville Rd., off I–89, Graniteville ☎ 802/476–3119, 866/748–6877 ⊕ www.rockofages.com ⊠ Guided tours $5 ⊙ Closed Sun. and mid-Oct.–mid-May.

Vermont History Museum

MUSEUM | The collection here, begun in 1838, focuses on all things Vermont—from a catamount (the now-extinct local cougar) to Ethan Allen's shoe buckles. The museum store stocks fine books, prints, and gifts. A second location in Barre, the Vermont History Center, has rotating exhibits with notable photographs and artifacts. ⊠ 109 State St. ☎ 802/828–2291 ⊕ www.vermonthistory.org ⊠ $7 ⊙ Closed Sun. and Mon.

Vermont State House

GOVERNMENT BUILDING | The regal capitol building surrounded by forest is emblematic of this proudly rural state. With a gleaming dome and columns of Barre granite measuring 6 feet in diameter, the State House is home to the country's oldest legislative chambers still in their original condition. Interior paintings and exhibits depict much of Vermont's sterling Civil War record. A self-guided tour, available year-round, takes you through the governor's office and the house and senate chambers. Free guided tours run from late June to October. ⊠ 115 State St. ☎ 802/828–2228 ⊕ statehouse.vermont.gov ⊠ Donations accepted ⊙ Closed Sun.; also Sat. Nov.–June.

🍴 Restaurants

Kismet

$$$ | ECLECTIC | One of Montpelier's more upscale restaurants, Kismet embraces the farm-to-table philosophy and gives it a shiny gloss and an international flavor. Tranquilly humming in the evening, particularly after State House employees get off work, Kismet buzzes most during its popular weekend brunches. **Known for:** multiple eggs Benedict versions; wine and cocktail list; expensive for Vermont. $ Average main: $34 ⊠ 52 State St. ☎ 802/223–8646 ⊕ www.kismetkitchens.com ⊙ Closed Mon. and Tues. No dinner Sun. No lunch.

Sarducci's

$$ | ITALIAN | FAMILY | Montpelier's most popular restaurant draws its crowd less for the classic American Italian dishes than the conviviality, charm, and sizeable portions, not to mention the picturesque Winooski River flowing directly alongside the windows. The pizza comes fresh from wood-fired ovens, while the rest of the menu features your favorite pennes, alfredos, and raviolis, with pleasing tweaks on the old formulas. **Known for:** date night; large gluten-free menu; local favorite. $ Average main: $18 ⊠ 3 Main St. ☎ 802/223–0229 ⊕ www.sarduccis.com ⊙ No lunch Sun.

The Skinny Pancake

$ | CAFÉ | This dine-in creperie makes a great stop for breakfast, lunch, or an easy dinner. The signature crepes go sweet and savory and are filled with fruit, vegetables, and meat from more than a dozen Vermont farms. **Known for:** inventive hot chocolate recipes; Localvore's Dream crepe with chicken, cran-apple chutney, spinach, and blue cheese; Pooh Bear crepe with cinnamon sugar and local honey. [$] *Average main: $9* ✉ *89 Main St.* ☎ *802/262–2253* 🌐 *www.skinnypancake.com.*

★ Three Penny Taproom

$ | **ECLECTIC** | This celebrated taproom remains one of the state's best, thanks in large part to its ability to acquire beers few others in the region can. The vibe feels straight out of an artsy neighborhood in Brussels, but with the earthiness of Vermont. **Known for:** darn good burger; top happy-hour hangout in town; premier Vermont and hard-to-get brews. [$] *Average main: $15* ✉ *108 Main St.* ☎ *802/223–8277* 🌐 *www.threepennytaproom.com.*

★ Wilaiwan's Kitchen

$ | **THAI** | In 2012, co-owners Wilaiwan Phonjan-Azarian and Timothy Azarian traded their locally adored street cart for a brick-and-mortar location offering some of the best Thai food in the state, if not on the East Coast. Most of the menu reflects the Laotian influence of Phonjan-Azarian's upbringing in northeast Thailand, and Vermont ingredients from eggs to chiles inspire dishes that change weekly. **Known for:** weekly changing menus featuring local ingredients; noodle specials, like khao soy and gwit diow, with homemade chili pastes; sunny interiors covered with artwork. [$] *Average main: $10* ✉ *34 State St.* ☎ *802/613–3587* 🌐 *wilaiwanskitchen.com* ⏲ *Closed Sun.*

☕ Coffee and Quick Bites

Bohemian Bakery

$ | **BAKERY** | The original Bohemian Bakery began in 2010 as a Sunday-only pop-up in the home of co-owners Annie Bakst and Robert Hunt; it quickly became a weekly haunt for expertly made French pastries. The couple opened a small storefront six years later, where they now roast coffee beans in small batches and fill daily orders of rotating favorites, like buttery kougin-amman and croissants, custard-filled Danishes, and tall slices of cornmeal cake. **Known for:** seasonal tarts with fresh fruit and pastry cream; croissants of all kinds; coffee roasted in-house. [$] *Average main: $8* ✉ *78 Barre St.* ☎ *802/461–8119* 🌐 *www.bohemianbakeryvt.com* ⏲ *Closed Mon. and Tues.*

★ Red Hen Baking Co.

$ | **CAFÉ** | If you're a devotee of artisanal bakeries, it'd be a mistake not to trek the 7-plus miles from Montpelier (15 from Stowe) to have lunch, pick up freshly baked bread, or sample a sweet treat at what many consider Vermont's best bakery. Red Hen supplies bread to some of the state's premier restaurants, including Hen of the Wood, and has varied offerings every day. **Known for:** breads and pastries; local hangout; soups and sandwiches. [$] *Average main: $8* ✉ *961 U.S. 2, Suite B, Middlesex* ☎ *802/223–5200* 🌐 *www.redhenbaking.com* ⏲ *No dinner.*

🛏 Hotels

Capitol Plaza Hotel

$ | **HOTEL** | Montpelier's only major hotel benefits much from the State House across the street, hosting many of its visiting politicians, lobbyists, and business makers, not to mention tourists seeking a certain quality of accommodation. **Pros:** easy walking distance to all local sights, including bike path; small fitness center; the resident steak house, J. Morgans, serves probably the best cuts in town. **Cons:** somewhat bland design; slight corporate feel; street-facing room may suffer street and bell-tower noise. [$] *Rooms from: $192* ✉ *100 State St.* ☎ *802/223–5252, 800/274–5252* 🌐 *www.capitolplaza.com* 🔑 *65 rooms* 🍴 *No meals.*

Inn at Montpelier

$$ | **B&B/INN** | The capital's most charming lodging option, this lovingly tended inn dating to 1830 has rooms filled with antique four-poster beds and Windsor chairs—all have private (if small) baths. **Pros:** beautiful home; relaxed central setting means you can walk everywhere in town; amazing porch. **Cons:** some rooms are small; somewhat bland, traditional design; no tea or coffee in rooms. $ *Rooms from: $200* ⊠ *147 Main St.* ☎ *802/223–2727* ⊕ *www.innatmontpelier.com* ⤳ *19 rooms* ⦿❘ *Free breakfast.*

🛍 Shopping

Vermont Creamery

FOOD/CANDY | A leader in the artisanal cheese movement, this creamery invites aficionados to visit its 4,000-square-foot production facility, where goat cheeses such as Bonne Bouche—a perfectly balanced, cloudlike cheese—are made on weekdays. The creamery is in Websterville, southwest of Montpelier. ⊠ *20 Pitman Rd., Websterville* ☎ *802/479–9371, 800/884–6287* ⊕ *www.vermontcreamery.com.*

Stowe

22 miles northwest of Montpelier, 36 miles east of Burlington.

Long before skiing came to Stowe in the 1930s, the rolling hills and valleys beneath Vermont's highest peak, 4,395-foot Mt. Mansfield, attracted summer tourists looking for a reprieve from city heat. Most stayed at one of two inns in the village of Stowe. When skiing made the town a winter destination, visitors outnumbered hotel beds, so locals took them in. This spirit of hospitality continues, and many of these homes are now country inns. The village itself is tiny—just a few blocks of shops and restaurants clustered around a picture-perfect white church with a lofty steeple—but it serves as the anchor for Mountain Road, which leads north past restaurants, lodges, and shops on its way to Stowe's fabled slopes. The road to Stowe also passes through Waterbury, which is rapidly regenerating thanks to a thriving arts and dining scene.

ESSENTIALS

VISITOR INFORMATION Stowe Area Association. ☎ *802/253–7321, 877/467–8693* ⊕ *www.gostowe.com.*

◉ Sights

★ Ben & Jerry's Factory

LOCAL INTEREST | **FAMILY** | The closest thing you'll get to a Willy Wonka experience in Vermont, the 30-minute tours at the famous brand's factory are unabashedly corny and only skim the surface of the behind-the-scenes goings-on, but this flaw is almost forgiven when the samples are dished out. To see the machines at work, visit on a weekday (but call ahead to confirm if they will indeed be in operation). Another highlight is the "Flavor Graveyard," where flavors of yore are given tribute with tombstones inscribed with humorous poetry. Free, family-friendly outdoor movies also play through summer on Friday. ⊠ *1281 Waterbury-Stowe Rd., Waterbury* ☎ *802/882–2047* ⊕ *www.benjerry.com* ⬛ *Tours $4.*

Vermont Ski and Snowboard Museum

MUSEUM | The state's skiing and snowboarding history is documented here. Exhibits cover subjects such as the 10th Mountain Division of World War II, the national ski patrol, Winter Olympians, and the evolution of equipment. An early World Cup trophy is on loan, and one of the most memorable mobiles you'll ever see, made from a gondola and ski-lift chairs, hangs from the ceiling. One recent exhibit, Slope Style, focused on ski fashion from 1930 to 2014. ⊠ *1 S. Main St.* ☎ *802/253–9911* ⊕ *www.vtssm.com* ⬛ *$5* ⦿ *Closed Sun.–Thurs.*

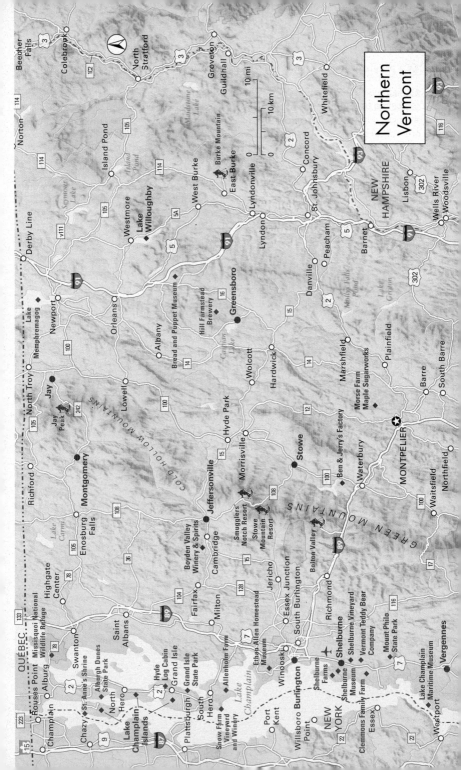

Northern Vermont

🍽 Restaurants

Bierhall

$$ | **AUSTRIAN** | In 2016, the Von Trapp family finally realized its long-held dream of opening a brewery making Austrian-style lagers on the grounds, and what a brewery it is. Built of thick, massive Vermont wood beams, the cavernous chalet-style space houses a rustic-chic restaurant and bar alongside the beer-making facilities serving Germanic classics, with plenty of beer to wash it down. **Known for:** Bavarian pretzels with beer-cheese dip; chicken schnitzel; Sachertorte and apple strudel. ⓢ *Average main: $20* ✉ *1333 Luce Hill Rd.* ☎ *802/253–5750* ⊕ *www.vontrapp-pbrewing.com.*

Cork

$$ | **INTERNATIONAL** | Pursuing a mission that "the best wines are grown, not made," this natural wine bar meticulously curates an inventory of organic, biodynamic, no-additive, unfiltered, and wild-fermented vintages, either for sale in the small retail section in the front, or complementing upscale bistro dishes and boards in the classy dining room. **Known for:** mostly old-world wines, with some local labels; lots of charcuterie and shareable appetizers; in the heart of Stowe village. ⓢ *Average main: $23* ✉ *35 School St.* ☎ *802/760–6143* ⊕ *www.corkvt.com* ⊘ *Closed Tues.*

Doc Ponds

$$ | **AMERICAN** | A gastropub from the folks behind the Hen of the Wood restaurant, this place has one of the best beer lists in the state. The food is excellent and the ski-lodge vibe is perfect for lunch or dinner, families or romantic two-top or solo bar seats. **Known for:** lengthy local beer list; pub fare with Vermont ingredients; log cabin atmosphere with apres-ski coziness. ⓢ *Average main: $22* ✉ *294 Mountain Rd.* ☎ *802/760–6066* ⊕ *www.docponds.com.*

Harrison's Restaurant

$$ | **AMERICAN** | A lively locals' scene, booths by the fireplace, and creative American cuisine paired with well-chosen wines and regional brews make this place perfect for couples and families alike. The inviting bar is a good spot to dine alone or to chat with a regular. **Known for:** peanut-butter pie; wine and cocktail list; wood fireplace. ⓢ *Average main: $23* ✉ *25 Main St.* ☎ *802/253–7773* ⊕ *www.harrisonsstowe.com* ⊘ *No lunch.*

★ Hen of the Wood

$$$ | **ECLECTIC** | Ask Vermont's great chefs where they go for a tremendous meal, and Hen of the Wood inevitably tops the list, thanks to its sophisticated, almost artful, dishes that showcase an abundance of local produce, meat, and cheese. The utterly romantic candlelit setting is riveting: a converted 1835 gristmill beside a waterfall. **Known for:** special occasions and dates; outstanding cooking; wine and cocktail list. ⓢ *Average main: $28* ✉ *92 Stowe St., Waterbury* ☎ *802/244–7300* ⊕ *www.henofthewood.com* ⊘ *Closed Sun. and Mon. No lunch.*

Idletyme Brewing Company

$$$ | **AMERICAN** | In prime position on the mountain road and the Stowe Recreation Path, this brewpub benefits from the culinary chops of owner Michael Kloeti, of Michael's on the Hill. Add to that a range of Bavarian-style lagers and Vermont IPAs brewed on-site, a large outdoor patio, vegetable garden, and a rich, rustic, chic design, and it's easy to understand what makes it so popular. **Known for:** "brew-ski" beer flights; ample space for large groups; outdoor Biergarten. ⓢ *Average main: $26* ✉ *1859 Mountain Rd.* ☎ *802/253–4765* ⊕ *www.idletyme-brewing.com.*

Continued on page 468

LET IT SNOW

WINTER ACTIVITIES IN VERMONT

by Elise Coroneos

SKIING AND SNOWBOARDING IN VERMONT

Less than 5 miles from the Canadian border, Jay Peak is Vermont's northernmost ski resort.

Ever since America's first ski tow opened in a farmer's pasture near Woodstock in January 1934, skiers have headed en masse to Vermont in winter. Today, 19 alpine and 30 nordic ski areas range in size and are spread across the state, from Mount Snow in the south to Jay Peak near the Canadian border. The snow-making equipment has also become more comprehensive over the years, with more than 80% of the trails in the state using man-made snow. Here are some of the best ski areas by various categories:

GREAT FOR KIDS **Smugglers' Notch, Okemo,** and **Bromley Mountain** all offer terrific kids' programs, with classes organized by age categories and by skill level. Kids as young as 3 (4 at some ski areas) can start learning. Child care, with activities like stories, singing, and arts and crafts, are available for those too young to ski; some ski areas, like Smuggler's Notch, offer babysitting with no minimum age daytime and evening.

BEST FOR BEGINNERS Beginner terrain makes up nearly half of the mountain at **Stratton,** where options include private and group lessons for first-timers. Also good are small but family-friendly **Bolton Valley** and **Bromley Mountains,** which both designate a third of their slopes for beginners.

EXPERT TERRAIN The slopes at **Jay Peak** and massive **Killington** are most notable for their steepness and pockets of glades. About 40% of the runs at these two resorts are advanced or expert. Due to its far north location, Jay Peak tends to get the most snow, making it ideal for powder days. Another favorite with advanced skiers is Central Vermont's **Mad River Glen,** where many slopes are ungroomed (natural) and the motto is "Ski it if you can." In addition, **Sugarbush, Stowe,** and **Smugglers' Notch** are all revered for their challenging untamed side country.

Mount Mansfield is better known as Stowe.   Stratton Mountain clocktower

NIGHT SKIING Come late afternoon, **Bolton Valley** is hopping. That's because it's the only location in Vermont for night skiing. Ski and ride under the lights from 4 until 8 Wednesday through Saturday, followed by a later après-ski scene.

APRÈS-SKI The social scenes at **Killington, Sugarbush,** and **Stowe** are the most noteworthy (and crowded). Book a seat on the Snowcat that takes intrepid partiers to the Motor Room Bar in Killington, or stop by the always popular Wobbly Barn. For live music, try Castlerock Pub in Sugarbush or the Matterhorn Bar in Stowe.

SNOWBOARDING Boarders (and some skiers) will love the latest features for freestyle tricks in Vermont. **Stratton** has four terrain parks for all abilities, one of which features a boarder cross course. **Mount Snow's** Carinthia Peak is an all-terrain park–dedicated mountain, the only of its kind in New England. Head to **Killington** for Burton Stash, another beautiful all-natural features terrain park. **Okemo** has a superpipe and eight terrain parks and a gladed park with all-natural features. Note that snowboarding is not allowed at skiing cooperative **Mad River Glen.**

CROSS-COUNTRY To experience the best of cross-country skiing in the state, simply follow the Catamount Trail, a 300-mile nordic route from southern Vermont to Canada. **The Trapp Family Lodge** in Stowe has 37 miles of groomed cross-country trails and 62 miles of back-country trails. Another top option is **The Mountain Top Inn & Resort,** just outside of Killington. Its Nordic Ski and Snowshoe Center provides instruction for newcomers, along with hot drinks and lunches when it is time to take a break and warm up.

TELEMARK Ungroomed snow and tree skiing are a natural fit with free-heel skiing at **Mad River Glen. Bromley** and **Jay Peak** also have telemark rentals and instruction.

MOUNTAIN-RESORT TRIP PLANNER

TIMING

Snow Season. Winter sports time is typically from Thanksgiving through April, weather permitting. Holidays are the most crowded.

March Madness. Most of the season's snow tends to come in March, so that's the time to go if you want to ski on fresh, nature-made powder. To increase your odds, choose a ski area in the northern part of the state.

Summer Scene. During summertime, many ski resorts reinvent themselves as prime destinations for golfers, zipline and canopy tours, mountain bikers, and weddings. Other summer visitors come to the mountains to enjoy hiking trails, climbing walls, aquatic centers, chairlift and horseback rides, or a variety of festivals.

Avoid Long Lift Lines. Try to hit the slopes early—many lifts start at 8 or 9 am, with ticket windows opening a half-hour earlier. Then take a mid-morning break as lines start to get longer and head out again when others come in for lunch.

SAVINGS TIPS

Choose a Condo. Especially if you're planning to stay for a week, save money on food by opting for a condominum unit with a kitchen. You can shop at the supermarket and cook breakfast and dinner.

Rent Smart. Consider ski rental options in the villages rather than those at the mountain. Renting right at the ski area may be more convenient, but it may also cost more.

Discount Lift Tickets. Online tickets are often the least expensive; multi-day discounts and and ski-and-stay packages will also lower your costs. Good for those who can plan ahead, early-bird tickets often go on sale before the ski season even starts.

Hit the Peaks Off-peak. In order to secure the best deals at the most competitive rates, avoid booking during school holidays. President's Week in February is the busiest, because that's when Northeastern schools have their spring break.

Top left, Killington's six mountains make up the largest ski area in Vermont. Top right, Stratton has a Snowboard-cross course.

THINK WARM THOUGHTS

It can get cold on the slopes, so be prepared. Consider proper face warmth and smart layering, plus ski-specific socks, or purchase a pair each of inexpensive hand and feet warmers that fit easily in your gloves and boots. Helmets, which can also be rented, provide not only added safety but warmth.

VERMONT SKI AREAS BY THE NUMBERS

Okemo's wide slopes attract snowbirds to Ludlow in Central Vermont.

Numbers are a helpful way to compare mountains, but remember that each resort has a distinct personality. This list is composed of ski areas in Vermont with at least 100 skiable acres. For more information, see individual resort listings.

SKI AREA	Vertical Drop	Skiable Acres	# of Trails & Lifts	Terrain Type ●	■	◆/◆◆	Snowboarding Options
Bolton Valley	1704	300	70/6	36%	37%	27%	Terrain Park
Bromley Mountain	1334	178	47/9	30%	36%	34%	Terrain Park
Burke Mountain	2011	270	50/6	10%	44%	46%	Terrain Park
Jay Peak Resort	2153	385	78/22	22%	39%	41%	Terrain Park
Killington Resort	3050	1509	155/21	17%	40%	43%	Terrain Park, Halfpipe
Mad River Glen	2037	115	52/5	30%	30%	40%	Snowboarding Not Allowed
Magic Mountain	1500	205	50/6	26%	30%	44%	Terrain Park
Mount Snow Resort	1700	588	80/20	14%	73%	13%	Terrain Park, Halfpipe
Okemo	2200	655	120/19	31%	38%	31%	Terrain Park, Superpipe, TerrainCross Park
Pico Mountain	1967	468	58/7	18%	46%	36%	Triple Slope, Terrain Park
Smugglers' Notch Resort	2610	311	78/8	19%	50%	31%	Terrain Park
Stowe Mountain Resort	2160	485	116/13	16%	59%	25%	Terrain Park
Stratton Mountain Resort	2003	670	99/11	40%	30%	25%	Terrain Park, Halfpipe, SnowboardCross Course
Sugarbush Resort	2600	578	111/16	20%	45%	30%	Terrain Park
Suicide Six	650	100	24/3	30%	40%	30%	Terrain Park

CONTACT THE EXPERTS

Ski Vermont (☎ 802/223-2439 ⊕ www. skivermont.com), a non-profit association in Montpelier, Vermont, and **Vermont Department of Tourism** (⊕ www.vermontvacation. com) are great resources for travelers planning a wintertime trip to Vermont.

KNOW YOUR SIGNS

On trail maps and the mountains, trails are rated and marked:

● Beginner ◆ Advanced

■ Intermediate ◆◆ Expert

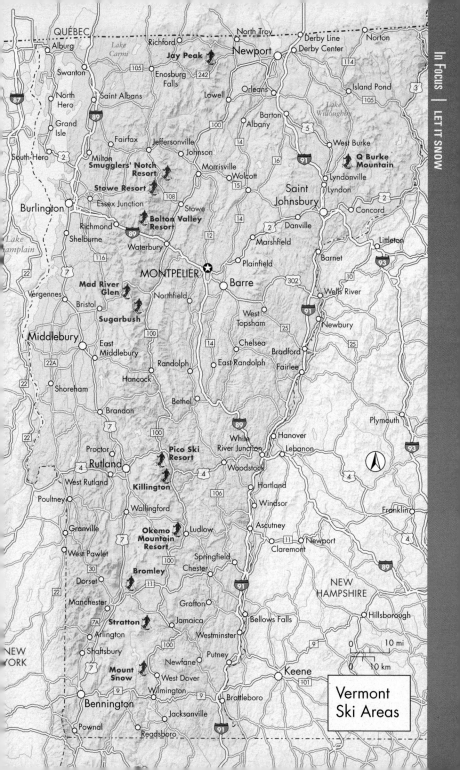

QUÉBEC

Lake Carmi

Alburg

Richford

North Troy

Derby Line
Derby Center

Norton

Swanton

Jay Peak

Newport

105

Enosburg Falls

242

114

Saint Albans

87

North Hero

100

Lowell

Orleans

Island Pond

105

Grand Isle

Fairfax

Jeffersonville

Barton
Albany

5

91

West Burke

3

South Hero

2

Milton

89

Johnson

Morrisville

16

Q Burke Mountain

Smugglers' Notch Resort

108

Wolcott

Lyndonville

Lyndon

2

Burlington

Stowe Resort

Essex Junction

15

Stowe

Saint Johnsbury

Concord

Lake Champlain

Richmond

89

Bolton Valley Resort

14

Danville

Littleton

Shelburne

116

Waterbury

12

Marshfield

Barnet

93

22

7

MONTPELIER

Plainfield

Wells River

10

Vergennes

Mad River Glen

Barre

302

91

Bristol

Northfield

West Topsham

Newbury

Middlebury

Sugarbush

25

East Middlebury

100

14

Chelsea

Bradford

25

22A

Randolph

East Randolph

Fairlee

22

Shoreham

Hancock

Bethel

Plymouth

Brandon

7

89

White River Junction

Hanover

93

100

Lebanon

Proctor

Pico Ski Resort

4

Woodstock

4

4

Rutland

West Rutland

Killington

106

Hartland

Franklin

Poultney

Wallingford

Windsor

4

Granville

Okemo Mountain Resort

Ludlow

Ascutney

11

Newport

89

West Pawlet

7

Springfield

Claremont

30

100

Chester

Bromley

Dorset

11

91

NEW HAMPSHIRE

Manchester

Grafton

Hillsborough

22

7A

Stratton

Jamaica

Bellows Falls

NEW YORK

Arlington

Westminster

9

Shaftsbury

100

Putney

0   10 mi

7

Mount Snow

Newfane

Keene

0   10 km

Bennington

9

West Dover

Wilmington

9

Brattleboro

101

Pownal

Jacksonville

Readsboro

91

Vermont Ski Areas

Michael's on the Hill

$$$ | EUROPEAN | Swiss-born chef Michael Kloeti trained in Europe and New York City before opening this establishment in a 19th-century farmhouse outside Stowe. The seasonal three-course prix-fixe menus ($45 and $67) blend European cuisine with farm-to-table earthiness, exemplified by dishes such as spice-roasted duck breast and venison *navarin* (ragout). **Known for:** homemade potato gnocchi; wine list; views of Green Mountains and sunsets. $ *Average main: $34* ⊠ *4182 Stowe-Waterbury Rd., 6 miles south of Stowe, Waterbury Center* ☎ *802/244–7476* ⊕ *www.michaelsonthehill.com* ☉ *Closed Tues. No lunch.*

★ Prohibition Pig

$ | AMERICAN | This restaurant and brewery in downtown Waterbury is always packed for a reason: fabulous craft beers, sandwiches, salads, and North Carolina–style barbecue served in an airy and friendly bar and dining room. If you just want a quick bite and a draft, belly up to the tasting-room bar at the brewery in the back, or pop across the street to the Craft Beer Cellar, one of the state's best beer stores. **Known for:** duck-fat fries; "craft" mac and cheese; one of the state's best draft lists. $ *Average main: $15* ⊠ *23 S. Main St., Waterbury* ☎ *802/244–4120* ⊕ *www.prohibitionpig.com* ☉ *No lunch Tues.–Thurs.*

Zen Barn

$$ | ECLECTIC | What's more Vermont than the name "Zen Barn," especially when it includes its own yoga studio in a former hayloft? Add to that an expansive, rustic-chic interior with local art and a stage for live music, an outdoor patio looking out on green fields and mountains, and a menu of eclectic, farm-to-table fare, and the local experience is complete. **Known for:** CBD cocktails; ramen soup; live performances. $ *Average main: $18* ⊠ *179 Guptil Rd., Waterbury* ☎ *802/244–8134* ⊕ *www.zenbarnvt.com* ☉ *Closed Sun. and Mon.*

☕ Coffee and Quick Bites

PK Coffee

$ | CAFÉ | The inviting atmosphere of this neighborhood joint, with locations in Stowe and Waterbury, is increased by the beans they use—North Carolina–based roasters Counter Culture Coffee, known for its coffee education and sustainable sourcing. Milk comes from Sweet Rowen Farmstead, and rotating breakfast sandwiches and baked goods, like buttermilk banana bread, are made in house. **Known for:** maple lattes; expertly made espresso and drip coffee; baked goods and breakfast sandwiches. $ *Average main: $5* ⊠ *1880 Mountain Rd.* ☎ *802/760–6151* ⊕ *pkcoffee.com.*

🛏 Hotels

Field Guide

$ | HOTEL | This boutique enterprise just north of Stowe village is a whimsically stylish alternative to the town's staid resorts and cadre of inns stuck in ski-chalet mold. **Pros:** waffle kimono robes; seasonal heated pool and hot tub; Trail Suite, with a loft bedroom and view of Stowe's iconic white church. **Cons:** unique style not for everyone; no elevator; no coffee/tea in rooms. $ *Rooms from: $110* ⊠ *433 Mountain Rd.* ☎ *802/253–8088* ⊕ *www.fieldguidestowe.com* ⤴ *30 rooms* ⦿ *Free breakfast.*

Green Mountain Inn

$ | B&B/INN | Smack-dab in the center of Stowe Village, this classic redbrick inn has been welcoming guests since 1833; rooms in the main building and the annex feel like a country inn, while the newer buildings refine with added luxury and space. **Pros:** easy walking distance to entire village and main sights; luxury rooms include large Jacuzzis; 300-thread-count Egyptian cotton bedding and Frette bathrobes. **Cons:** farther from skiing than other area hotels; road noise in front of building; no tea in rooms. $ *Rooms from: $169* ⊠ *18 Main St.* ☎ *802/253–7301, 800/253–7302* ⊕ *www.greenmountaininn.com* ⤴ *104 rooms* ⦿ *No meals.*

Stone Hill Inn

$$$ | B&B/INN | A contemporary, romance-inducing bed-and-breakfast where classical music plays in the hallways, Stone Hill has guest rooms with two-sink vanities and two-person whirlpools in front of double-sided fireplaces. **Pros:** perennial gardens with stream; complimentary toboggan and snowshoes; Gilchrist & Soames bathroom amenities. **Cons:** possibly depressing for single people; two-night minimum on weekends and in peak period; no children allowed. $ *Rooms from: $309* ✉ *89 Houston Farm Rd.* ☎ *802/253–6282* ⊕ *www. stonehillinn.com* 🛏 *9 rooms* ⦿ *Free breakfast.*

Stowe Motel & Snowdrift

$ | HOTEL | FAMILY | The accommodations at this family-owned motel on 14 acres range from studios with small kitchenettes and modern two-bedroom suites warmed by their own fireplaces to rental houses that can sleep 10 or more people. **Pros:** good value for cost; complimentary bikes; 16 acres of landscaped grounds next to river. **Cons:** basic motel-style accommodations; design and furnishings could use an update; occasional road noise. $ *Rooms from: $149* ✉ *2043 Mountain Rd.* ☎ *802/253–7629, 800/829–7629* ⊕ *www.stowemotel.com* 🛏 *62 rooms* ⦿ *Free breakfast.*

★ Spruce Peak

$$ | RESORT | At the base of the ski slopes, this lodge would be king of the hill for its location alone, but a stay here also affords many perks including the rustic-meets-contemporary accommodations that run the gamut from studio to three-bedroom units, many with outdoor terraces. **Pros:** mountain views; lots of children's activities; many shops supply all needs. **Cons:** somewhat sterile feel; no separate kids' pool; expensive breakfast. $ *Rooms from: $269* ✉ *7412 Mountain Rd.* ☎ *802/253–3560, 888/478–6938 reservations* ⊕ *www.sprucepeak.com* 🛏 *300 rooms* ⦿ *No meals.*

Stoweflake Mountain Resort and Spa

$ | RESORT | With one of the largest spas in the area, Stoweflake lets you enjoy an herb-and-flower labyrinth, a fitness center reached via a covered bridge, and a hydrotherapy waterfall that cascades into a hot tub. **Pros:** walking distances to many restaurants; wide range of rooms; across the street from the recreation path. **Cons:** mazelike layout can make rooms a bit hard to find; uninspired room design; no tea in rooms. $ *Rooms from: $198* ✉ *1746 Mountain Rd.* ☎ *800/253– 2232* ⊕ *www.stoweflake.com* 🛏 *180 rooms* ⦿ *No meals.*

Sun & Ski Inn and Suites

$ | HOTEL | Not many hotels can boast having a bowling alley, but this part-new, part-renovated inn can top even that, adding an 18-hole minigolf course, an indoor pool, and small fitness center. **Pros:** close to the slopes; the family-friendly restaurant is open daily for lunch and dinner; tea/coffeemakers in rooms. **Cons:** not very Vermonty; family friendly can mean lots of children; often two-night minimum stay. $ *Rooms from: $189* ✉ *1613 Mountain Rd.* ☎ *802/253–7159, 800/448–5223* ⊕ *www.sunandskiinn.com* 🛏 *39 rooms* ⦿ *Free breakfast.*

★ Topnotch Resort

$$$ | RESORT | FAMILY | On 120 acres overlooking Mt. Mansfield, this posh property has a contemporary look, excellent dining options, and one of the best spas in Vermont, which combine to create a world unto itself. **Pros:** ski shuttle will take you directly to the slopes; complimentary tea and cookies every afternoon; American bistro cuisine at the intimate Flannel or tuned-up bar bites at the Roost, the lively lobby bar. **Cons:** boutique style may not be for everyone; no tea in rooms; room rates fluctuate wildly. $ *Rooms from: $350* ✉ *4000 Mountain Rd.* ☎ *800/451– 8686, 802/253–8585* ⊕ *www.topnotchresort.com* 🛏 *91 rooms* ⦿ *No meals.*

★ Trapp Family Lodge

$$ | **RESORT** | **FAMILY** | Built by the Von Trapp family (of *The Sound of Music* fame), this Tyrolean lodge is surrounded by some of the best mountain views in Vermont and abundant romantic ambience, making it a favorite for weddings. **Pros:** alive with the sound of music; excellent beer brewed on-site; concert series and festivals in warm weather. **Cons:** some sections appear tired and in need of updating; overrun by tourists, especially on weekends; if not an active person, you'll miss half the amenities. [$] *Rooms from: $225* ✉ *700 Trapp Hill Rd.* ☎ *802/253–8511, 800/826–7000* 🌐 *www.trappfamily.com* 🛏 *214 rooms* 🍴 *No meals.*

Performing Arts

Helen Day Art Center

ART GALLERIES—ARTS | Above the local library, Stowe's premier art center hosts impressive rotating exhibitions of contemporary and local art throughout the year, as well as film screenings. It also provides art education to adults and children alike through workshops, lectures, events, and courses. ✉ *90 Pond St.* ☎ *802/253–8358* 🌐 *www.helenday.com.*

Spruce Peak Performing Arts Center

CONCERTS | Part of the Spruce Peak complex, this state-of-the-art space hosts theater, music, and dance performances. ✉ *122 Hourglass Dr.* ☎ *802/760–4634* 🌐 *www.sprucepeakarts.org.*

Activities

CANOEING AND KAYAKING

Umiak Outdoor Outfitters

CANOEING/ROWING/SKULLING | This full-service outfitter rents canoes and kayaks, organizes tours, and sells equipment. It has seasonal outposts at the Waterbury Reservoir and at North Beach in Burlington. ✉ *849 S. Main St.* ☎ *802/253–2317* 🌐 *www.umiak.com.*

FISHING

The Fly Rod Shop

FISHING | This shop provides a guide service, offers introductory classes, and rents tackle and other equipment. ✉ *2703 Waterbury Rd., 1½ miles south of Stowe* ☎ *802/253–7346* 🌐 *www.flyrodshop.com.*

HIKING

Moss Glen Falls

HIKING/WALKING | Four miles outside of town, this short hike leads to a stupendous 125-foot waterfall that makes a great way to cool down in summer. ✉ *615 Moss Glen Falls Rd.* ☎ *888/409–7579 Vermont State Parks* 🌐 *www.vtstateparks.com.*

Mt. Mansfield

HIKING/WALKING | Ascending Mt. Mansfield, Vermont's highest mountain, makes for a challenging day hike. Trails lead from Mountain Road to the summit, where they meet the north–south Long Trail. Views encompass New Hampshire's White Mountains, New York's Adirondacks, and southern Québec. The Green Mountain Club publishes a trail guide. ✉ *Trailheads along Mountain Rd.* ☎ *802/244–7037* 🌐 *www.greenmountainclub.org.*

★ Stowe Recreation Path

HIKING/WALKING | An immaculately maintained, paved recreation path begins behind the Community Church in town and meanders about 5 miles along the river valley, with many entry points along the way. Whether you're on foot, skis, bike, or in-line skates, it's a tranquil spot to enjoy the outdoors. In autumn, there's a corn maze, and at least four shops along the path rent bikes. ✉ *Stowe* 🌐 *www.stowerec.org.*

SKIING

Stowe Mountain Resort

SKIING/SNOWBOARDING | The name of the village is Stowe, and the name of the mountain is Mt. Mansfield—but to generations of skiers, it's all just plain "Stowe." The area's mystique attracts as many serious skiers as social ones. Stowe is a giant among Eastern ski mountains with intimidating expert runs, but its symmetrical shape allows skiers of all abilities to enjoy long, satisfying runs from the summit. Improved snowmaking capacity, new lifts, and free shuttle buses that gather skiers along Mountain Road have made it all much more convenient. Yet the traditions remain, like the Winter Carnival in January and the Sugar Slalom in April, to name two. Spruce Peak, where you'll find the Adventure Center and the Mountain Lodge, is separate from the main mountain; the peak has a teaching hill and offers a pleasant experience for intermediates and beginners. In the summer, there's a TreeTop Adventure course and an awe-inspiring zipline that extends from the top of the gondola to the bottom in three breathtaking runs. **Facilities:** 116 trails; 485 acres; 2,160-foot vertical drop; 13 lifts. ⊠ *5781 Mountain Rd.* ☎ *802/253–3000, 802/253–3600 for snow conditions* ⊕ *www.stowe.com* ⌑ *Lift ticket: $99.*

SLEDDING

Peace Pups Dog Sledding
LOCAL SPORTS | **FAMILY** | This one-man (and multiple-dog) company offers two-hour tours with a team of eight Siberian huskies. You can ride inside a padded toboggan or learn how to mush and drive on your own. If you prefer to walk the trails yourself, snowshoe rentals are also available. In summer, the trails are open to hiking. Lake Elmore is a roughly 20-minute drive from Stowe. ⊠ *239 Cross Rd., Lake Elmore* ☎ *802/888–7733* ⊕ *www.peacepupsdogsledding.com* ⌑ *$318 for dog sledding tours.*

SPAS

Spa and Wellness Center at Spruce Peak
SPA/BEAUTY | This 21,000-square-foot facility has 18 private treatment rooms, a fitness center, and a year-round outdoor pool and hot tub. In addition to the usual array of facials, scrubs, and massages for adults, the spa offers a separate program for kids. ⊠ *Spruce Peak, 7412 Mountain Rd.* ☎ *802/760–4782* ⊕ *www.sprucepeak.com.*

Spa at Stoweflake
SPA/BEAUTY | One of the largest spas in New England, the Spa at Stoweflake features a massaging hydrotherapeutic waterfall, a Hungarian mineral pool, 30 treatment rooms, and more than 150 treatments like the Bingham Falls Renewal, named after a local waterfall. This treatment begins with a body scrub and a Vichy shower, followed by an aromatherapy oil massage. The spacious men's and women's sanctuaries have saunas, steam rooms, and whirlpool tubs. ⊠ *Stoweflake Mountain Resort and Spa, 1746 Mountain Rd.* ☎ *802/760–1083* ⊕ *www.stoweflake.com.*

Spa at Topnotch
SPA/BEAUTY | Calm pervades the Spa at Topnotch, with its birchwood doors, natural light, and cool colors. Signature treatments include the Mt. Mansfield Saucha, a three-stage herbal body treatment, and the Little River Stone Massage, which uses the resort's own wood-spice oil. There's even Rover Reiki (really) for your canine friend. Locker areas are spacious, with saunas, steam rooms, and whirlpool tubs. The indoor pool has lots of natural light. Daily classes in tai chi, yoga, and Pilates are offered in the nearby fitness center. ⊠ *Topnotch Resort and Spa, 4000 Mountain Rd.* ☎ *802/253–6463* ⊕ *www.topnotchresort.com.*

👜 Shopping

CRAFTS

Jeremy Ayers Pottery
CERAMICS/GLASSWARE | One of Vermont's most skilled and distinctive potters welcomes visitors to his shop and studio in downtown Waterbury. Keep an eye out for his Waterbury Breakfast Club, which adds food trucks and artists every other Sunday, June–September. A few apartments are also available to rent in the guesthouse; the on-site venue space, 18 Elm, is open for dinner parties and special occasion events. ⊠ *18 Elm St., Waterbury* ☎ *802/363–3592* ⊕ *www.jeremyayerspottery.com.*

FOOD AND DRINK

★ Alchemist Brewery and Visitors Center
FOOD/CANDY | The brewery that launched a beer revolution in Vermont with its "Heady Topper" now welcomes guests to its brand-new shop and tasting room. Intense demand still keeps stocks of beer for sale limited. ✉ *100 Cottage Club Rd.* ☎ *802/882–8165* 🌐 *www.alchemist-beer.com.*

Cabot Cheese Annex Store
FOOD/CANDY | In addition to shelves of Vermont-made jams, mustards, crackers, and maple products, the store features a long central table with samples of a dozen Cabot cheeses. ✉ *2657 Waterbury–Stowe Rd., 2½ miles north of I–89* ☎ *802/244–6334* 🌐 *www.cabotcheese.coop.*

★ Cold Hollow Cider Mill
FOOD/CANDY | **FAMILY** | You can watch apples pressed into possibly the world's best cider at this working mill and sample it right from the tank. Its store sells all the apple butter, jams and jellies, and Vermont-made handicrafts you could want, plus the legendary 75¢ cider doughnuts. Kids love watching the "doughnut robot" in action. ✉ *3600 Waterbury–Stowe Rd., Waterbury Center* ✥ *3 miles north of I–89* ☎ *800/327–7537* 🌐 *www.coldhollow.com.*

Jeffersonville

18 miles north of Stowe.

Jeffersonville is just over Smugglers' Notch from Stowe but miles away in feeling and attitude. In summer, you can drive over the notch road as it curves precipitously around boulders that have fallen from the cliffs above, then pass open meadows and old farmhouses and sugar shacks on the way down to town. Below the notch, Smugglers' Notch Ski Resort is the hub of activity year-round. Downtown Jeffersonville, once home to an artists' colony, is quiet but has excellent dining and nice art galleries.

Like most places in Vermont, a car is essential to exploring this area. From Burlington, it's about a 45-minute drive along Route 15. Or you can cruise north on Route 108 from Stowe for 30 minutes; however, the road is closed for much of the winter.

Sights

Boyden Valley Winery & Spirits
WINERY/DISTILLERY | On a beautiful stretch of farmland west of Jeffersonville, this winery conducts tours and tastings and showcases an excellent selection of Vermont specialty products and local handicrafts. The winery's Big Barn Red is full-bodied, but the real fun may be in the ice wines, maple crème liqueur, and hard ice cider. ✉ *64 Rte. 104, Cambridge* ☎ *802/644–8151* 🌐 *www.boydenvalley.com* 🎟 *Tasting $10.*

Restaurants

158 Main Restaurant and Bakery
$ | **AMERICAN** | One of the most popular restaurants in Jeffersonville easily earns its accolades with big portions and small prices. The menu features all the classic egg, pancake, and corn-beef-hash dishes a person could wish for at breakfast, and a surprisingly wide-ranging international menu for dinner. **Known for:** $5 Two Egg Basic; Sunday brunch; homemade bread. [$] *Average main: $13* ✉ *158 Main St.* ☎ *802/644–8100* 🌐 *www.158Main.com* 🕒 *Closed Mon. No dinner Sun.*

Coffee and Quick Bites

Burger Barn
$ | **AMERICAN** | **FAMILY** | Local grassfed burgers and handcut fries are the name of the game at this bright-green food truck. Try one of Burger Barn's more inventive offshoots, like the Nutty Goat: goat cheese, maple crushed walnuts, caramelized onions, bacon and mayo. **Known for:** grassfed burgers; food truck

atmosphere and outside dining; cash only. $ *Average main: $8* ✉ *4968 VT-15* ☎ *802/730–3441* ▭ *No credit cards.*

🛏 Hotels

★ Smugglers' Notch Resort

$$$ | RESORT | FAMILY | With five giant water parks for summer fun and just about every winter activity imaginable, including the new 26,000-square-foot indoor "FunZone 2.0," this resort is ideal for families; nightly rates include lift tickets, lessons, and all resort amenities. **Pros:** great place for families to learn to ski; views of several mountains; shuttles to the slopes. **Cons:** not a romantic getaway for couples; extra cost for daily cleaning; very busy during peak season. $ *Rooms from: $322* ✉ *4323 Rte. 108 S* ☎ *802/332–6841, 800/419–4615* ⊕ *www. smuggs.com* ⊷ *600 condominiums* ⦿ *No meals.*

🏃 Activities

KAYAKING

Vermont Canoe and Kayak

KAYAKING | This outfitter rents canoes and kayaks for use on the Lamoille River, and leads guided canoe trips to Boyden Valley Winery. ✉ *4805 Rte. 15, behind the Family Table* ☎ *802/644–8336* ⊕ *vtcanoe- andkayak.com* ⊗ *Closed mid-Sept.–late May.*

LLAMA RIDES

Northern Vermont Llama Co.

LOCAL SPORTS | These llamas carry everything, including snacks and lunches, for half-day treks along the trails of Smugglers' Notch. Reservations are essential. ✉ *766 Lapland Rd., Waterville* ☎ *802/644–2257* ⊕ *www.northernver- montllamaco.com* ✉ *$60* ⊗ *Closed early Sept.–late May.*

Smugglers' Notch

SKIING/SNOWBOARDING | FAMILY | The "granddaddy of all family resorts," Smugglers' Notch (or "Smuggs") receives consistent praise for its family programs. Its children's ski school is one of the best in the country—possibly *the* best—and there are challenges for skiers of all levels, spread over three separate areas. There's ice-skating, tubing, seven terrain parks, Nordic skiing, snowshoe trails, and a snowboarding area for kids ages 2½–6. Summer brings waterslides, treetop courses, ziplines, and crafts workshops— in other words, something for everyone. **Facilities:** 78 trails; 300 acres; 2,610-foot vertical drop; 8 lifts. ✉ *4323 Rte. 108 S* ☎ *802/332–6854, 800/419–4615* ⊕ *www. smuggs.com* ✉ *Lift ticket: $79.*

🛍 Shopping

ANTIQUES

Route 15 between Jeffersonville and Johnson is dubbed the "antiques highway."

Buggy Man

ANTIQUES/COLLECTIBLES | This store sells all sorts of collectibles, including horse-drawn vehicles. ✉ *853 Rte. 15, 7 miles east of Jeffersonville, Johnson* ☎ *802/635–2110.*

CLOTHING

★ Johnson Woolen Mills

CLOTHING | This factory store has great deals on woolen blankets, household goods, and the famous Johnson outerwear. ✉ *51 Lower Main St. E, 9 miles east of Jeffersonville, Johnson* ☎ *802/635–2271* ⊕ *www.johnsonwoolen- mills.com.*

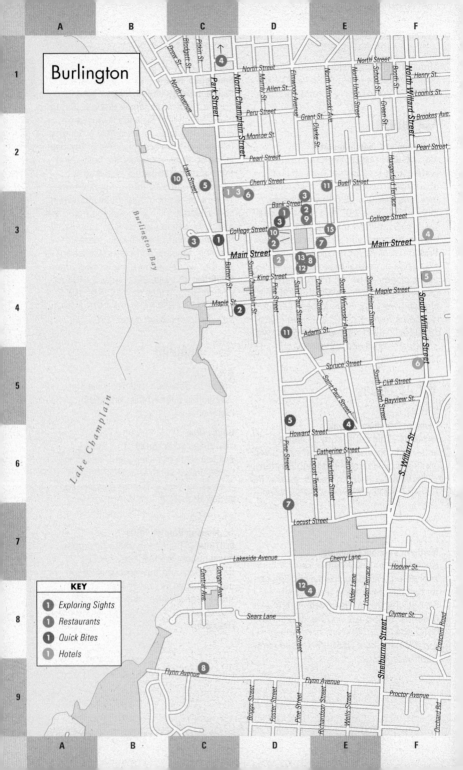

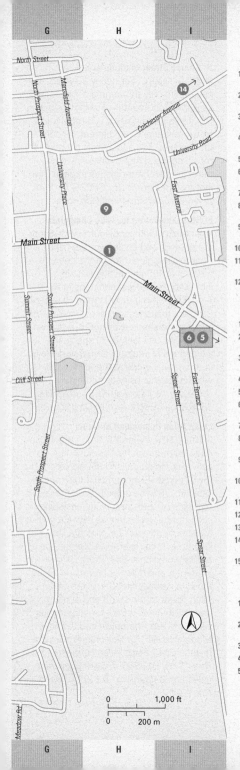

Sights ▼

1 Burlington
Farmers' Market **H3**

2 Church Street
Marketplace **D3**

3 ECHO Leahy Center for
Lake Champlain **C3**

4 Ethan Allen Homestead
Museum **C1**

5 Foam Brewers **C2**

6 Green Mountain Audubon
Nature Center **I4**

7 Pine Street **D7**

8 Switchback
Brewing Co. **C9**

9 University of
Vermont **H3**

10 Waterfront Park **C2**

11 ZAFA Wines and
CO Cellars **D4**

12 Zero Gravity
Brewery **D8**

Restaurants ▼

1 A Single Pebble **D3**

2 American Flatbread
Burlington **D3**

3 Farmhouse
Tap and Grill **D3**

4 The Great Northern **D8**

5 Guild Tavern **I4**

6 Hen of the Wood
Burlington **D3**

7 Honey Road **E3**

8 Istanbul
Kebab House **E3**

9 Leunig's Bistro
and Cafe **D3**

10 Monarch & the
Milkweed **D3**

11 Penny Cluse Cafe **E2**

12 Pizzeria Verita **D3**

13 Trattoria Delia **D3**

14 Waterworks
Food + Drink **I1**

15 Zabby and Elf's
Stone Soup **E3**

Quick Bites ▼

1 Burlington Bay
Market & Cafe **C3**

2 Kestrel Coffee
Roasters **C4**

3 Onyx Tonics **D3**

4 Shy Guy Gelato **E6**

5 Speeder & Earl's
Coffee **D5**

Hotels ▼

1 Courtyard
Burlington Harbor **C2**

2 Hilton Garden Inn **D3**

3 Hotel Vermont **C2**

4 The Lang House on
Main Street **F3**

5 Made INN Vermont **F4**

6 Willard Street Inn **F5**

Burlington

31 miles southwest of Jeffersonville, 76 miles south of Montréal, 349 miles north of New York City, 223 miles northwest of Boston.

As you drive along Main Street toward downtown Burlington, it's easy to see why this three-college city is often called one of the most livable small cities in the United States. Downtown Burlington is filled with hip restaurants and bars, art galleries, and vinyl-record shops. At the heart is the Church Street Marketplace, a bustling pedestrian mall with trendy shops, crafts vendors, street performers, and sidewalk cafés. To the west, Lake Champlain shimmers beneath the towering Adirondacks on the New York shore and provides the best sunsets in the state. The revitalized Burlington waterfront teems with outdoors enthusiasts who bike or stroll along its recreation path, picnic on the grass, and ply the waters in sailboats and motor craft in summer.

To the north, the eclectic enclave of Winooski, a newly refurbished ex New England mill town, houses its own cadre of interesting bars, cafés, shops, and eateries.

◉ Sights

★ Burlington Farmers' Market

MARKET | Burlington's Saturday farmers' market is an absolute must-see when visiting in summer or fall. Set up in City Hall Park and spilling onto an adjacent street, the market is jam-packed with local farmers selling a colorful array of organic produce, flowers, baked goods, maple syrup, meats, cheeses, and prepared foods. Local artisans also sell their wares, and there's live music on the green. From November to April, the market is held every other Saturday at the University of Vermont's Dudley H. Davis Center. ✉ *City Hall Park, College and St. Paul Sts.* ☎ *802/310–5172* ⊕ *www.burlingtonfarmersmarket.org* ✆ *Free.*

★ Church Street Marketplace

MARKET | FAMILY | For nearly 40 years, this pedestrian-only thoroughfare has served as Burlington's center of commerce, dining, and entertainment, with boutiques, cafés, restaurants, and street vendors the focus by day, and a lively bar and music scene at night. On sunny days, there are few better places to be in Burlington. ✉ *2 Church St.* ☎ *802/863–1648* ⊕ *www.churchstmarketplace.com.*

ECHO Leahy Center for Lake Champlain

ZOO | FAMILY | Kids and adults can explore the geology and ecology of the Lake Champlain region through the center's more than 100 interactive exhibits, including the newest additions at the Action Lab. The lab's 3D Water Projection Sandbox manages to make learning about watersheds exciting. You can also get an up-close look at 70 species of indigenous animals, or immerse digitally in the natural world at the 3D theater, which presents science and nature films every day. ✉ *1 College St.* ☎ *802/864–1848* ⊕ *www.echovermont.org* ✆ *$15.*

Ethan Allen Homestead Museum

HISTORIC SITE | When Vermont hero Ethan Allen retired from his Revolutionary activities, he purchased 350 acres along the Winooski River and built this modest cabin in 1787. The original structure is a real slice of 18th-century life, including such frontier hallmarks as saw-cut boards and an open hearth for cooking. The kitchen garden resembles the one the Allens would have had. There's also a visitor center and miles of biking and hiking trails. In warmer months, climb Ethan Allen Tower at the south end of neighboring Ethan Allen Park for stupendous views of Lake Champlain and the Green Mountains. ■ TIP➔ **Don't forget mosquito repellent.** ✉ *1 Ethan Allen Homestead, off Rte. 127* ☎ *802/865–4556* ⊕ *www.ethanallenhomestead.org* ✆ *$10* ⊙ *Closed Nov.–Apr.*

★ Foam Brewers

WINERY/DISTILLERY | Co-founder and acclaimed brewer Todd Haire spent 13 years at Magic Hat Brewing and another two years at Switchback before opening his own Burlington operation alongside fellow co-founders Bobby Grim, Sam Keane, Jon Farmer, and Dani Casey in 2016. Since then, Foam has gained international praise, including a spot as one of the world's 10 best new breweries—bestowed by BeerAdvocate—the year they opened. Snack boards and food truck pit-stops compliment their sought-after drafts, and an outdoor patio faces the stunning views of the Lake Champlain Waterfront. ✉ *112 Lake St.* ☎ *802/399–2511* ⊕ *www.foambrewers. com.*

Green Mountain Audubon Nature Center

NATURE PRESERVE | FAMILY | This is a wonderful place to discover Vermont's outdoor wonders. The center's 255 acres of diverse habitats are a sanctuary for all things wild, and the 5 miles of trails provide an opportunity to explore the workings of differing natural communities. Events include bird-monitoring walks, wildflower rambles, nature workshops, and educational activities for children and adults. ✉ *255 Sherman Hollow Rd., 18 miles southeast of Burlington, Huntington* ☎ *802/434–3068* ⊕ *vt.audubon.org* ⊠ *Donations accepted.*

Pine Street

NEIGHBORHOOD | A once-abandoned relic of the Industrial Revolution, Pine Street is the heartbeat of Burlington's recently revamped South End Arts District, an enclave of bars, restaurants, breweries, art galleries, and eateries. Start at the intersection of Pine and Maple Street and begin walking south to find a treasure trove of all things art, music, food, and drink. Dedalus Wine Market & Bar has one of the most expansive selections of natural wine on the East Coast. Myers Bagels has been turning out wood-fired, Montréal-style bagels for over twenty years. The S.P.A.C.E Gallery and Conant Metal & Light attract artists from within state borders and far beyond, and the popular restaurant and performance venue ArtsRiot hosts weekly food truck celebrations in the warmer months. Make sure to stop by The Soda Plant, a small business incubator with over thirty local artisans, artists and makers inside a newly refurbished 19th century industrial soda factory. Brio Coffee, ZAFA Wines, CO Cellars, and Shacksbury Cider are a few of the nationally acclaimed businesses inside. ✉ *Pine St., between Maple and Flynn.*

Switchback Brewing Co.

WINERY/DISTILLERY | Switchback may not get as much press as other more famous craft Vermont beers, but it's a solid, respected brew that's well worth exploring at the brewery and taproom in Burlington's buzzing South End. In addition to superfresh beer right from the tap and a short but savory menu of bar bites, the space hosts regular events and live music throughout the year. ✉ *160 Flynn Ave.* ☎ *802/651–4114* ⊕ *www. switchbackvt.com.*

University of Vermont

COLLEGE | Crowning the hilltop above Burlington is the University of Vermont, known as UVM for the abbreviation of its Latin name, Universitas Viridis Montis, meaning the University of the Green Mountains. With nearly 12,000 students, this is the state's principal institution of higher learning. The most architecturally impressive buildings face the main campus green and have gorgeous lake views, as does the statue of founder Ira Allen, Ethan's brother. ✉ *85 S. Prospect St.* ☎ *802/656–3131* ⊕ *www.uvm.edu.*

★ Waterfront Park

CITY PARK | This formerly derelict industrial district and railroad depot underwent a remarkable transformation in the late '80s and early '90s into a gorgeous stretch of green, with a boardwalk lapped by the lake. It's also a linchpin for a number of sights and facilities, with the Echo Center on the south end, a bodacious skate park on the north, and the Burlington Bike Path running through it all. Sunsets are particularly popular. ✉ *10 College St.* ☎ *802/864–0123 City of Burlington Parks, Recreation & Waterfront* 🌐 *www.enjoyburlington.com* 🎟 *Free.*

ZAFA Wines and CO Cellars

WINERY/DISTILLERY | Winemaker and farmer Krista Scruggs has gained national praise for her nuanced, idiosyncratic natural wines made without chemical intervention from grape-growing to fermentation that are available through a limited release annually (subscribe to the newsletter to stay in the loop). ZAFA Wines also has CO Cellars, a collaboration with local cidermakers Shacksbury Cider that can be found inside The Soda Plant on Pine Street. As a working winery for ZAFA and a innovation incubator for Shacksbury, the tasting room at CO is an exciting stop for genre-bending wines, co-ferments, and more. Electric Mayhem, for instance, merges grapes from ZAFA's Vermont vineyards with foraged wild apples for a citrusy, floral, and effervescent wine-cider hybrid that has been barrel aged for 18 months with wild yeast strains. Better yet, it's extraordinarily delicious. ✉ *The Soda Plant, 266 Pine St., Suite 122* 🌐 *zafawines.com* 🕒 *Closed Sun.–Thurs.*

Zero Gravity Brewery

WINERY/DISTILLERY | What started as a single bar tap in a pizza restaurant has turned into one of Burlington's most successful and hippest beers, thanks to frothy gems like Conehead and Green State Lager. Its shiny new brewery in the South End Arts District is always buzzing. Tasty complements include bratwurst, Italian sausage, and crispy cheddar curds. ✉ *716 Pine St.* ☎ *802/497–0054* 🌐 *www.zerogravitybeer.com.*

Beaches

North Beach

BEACH—SIGHT | **FAMILY** | Along Burlington's "new" North End a long line of beaches stretches to the Winooski River delta, beginning with North Beach, which has a grassy picnic area, a snack bar, and boat rentals. Neighboring Leddy Park offers a more secluded beach. **Amenities:** food and drink; lifeguards; parking (fee); showers; toilets. **Best for:** partiers; swimming; walking; windsurfing. ✉ *North Beach Park, 52 Institute Rd., off North Ave.* ☎ *802/865–7247* 🌐 *www.enjoyburlington.com/venue/north-beach* 🎟 *Parking $8 (May–Oct.).*

Restaurants

American Flatbread Burlington

$$ | **PIZZA** | Seating is first-come, first-served at this popular pizza spot, and the wood-fired clay dome ovens pump out delicious and amusingly named pies like "Dancing Heart" (garlic oil, Italian grana padano cheese, toasted sesame seeds) and "Power to the People" (chicken, buffalo sauce, carrots, mozzarella, and blue cheese dressing) in full view of the tables. Fresh salads topped with locally made cheese are also popular. **Known for:** bar run by Zero Gravity Brewery; spacious outdoor seating area; many ingredients sourced from farm 2 miles away. [$] *Average main: $18* ✉ *115 St. Paul St.* ☎ *802/861–2999* 🌐 *www.americanflatbread.com.*

A Single Pebble

$$ | **CHINESE** | "Gather, discover, and connect" is the slogan and theme at this intimate Chinese restaurant on the first floor of a residential row house. Traditional Cantonese- and Sichuan-style dishes are served family style, and the "mock eel" was given two chopsticks up on the Food Network's *The Best Thing I Ever Ate.* **Known for:** many vegetarian options; fire-blistered green beans wok-tossed with flecks of pork;

dim sum on Sunday. $ *Average main: $22* ⊠ *133 Bank St.* ☎ *802/865–5200* ⊕ *www.asinglepebble.com.*

Farmhouse Tap and Grill

$$ | AMERICAN | The line out the door on a typical weekend night should tell you a lot about the local esteem for this farm-to-table restaurant. Serving only local beef, cheese, and produce in a classy but laid-back style, Farmhouse Tap and Grill provides one of the finest meals in the area. **Known for:** local cheese and char-cuterie plates; downstairs taproom or the outdoor beer garden; raw bar. $ *Average main: $20* ⊠ *160 Bank St.* ☎ *802/859–0888* ⊕ *www.farmhousetg.com.*

The Great Northern

$$ | MODERN AMERICAN | This woody, indus-trial space benefits not only from being neighbors to Zero Gravity Brewery, but also its location at the heart of Burling-ton's hippest district, the South End. The menu follows the neighborhood zeitgeist, with foodie-friendly bistro bites for lunch and dinner, a raw bar, and a superpopular brunch on weekends. **Known for:** trendy interior design; artisanal cocktail list; hangout of the young and hip. $ *Average main: $20* ⊠ *716 Pine St.* ☎ *802/489–5102* ⊕ *www.thegreatnorthernvt.com* ⊗ *No dinner Sun.*

Guild Tavern

$$$ | STEAKHOUSE | Some of Vermont's best steak—all meat is sourced from local farms, dry-aged a minimum of 21 days, and cooked to absolute per-fection—can be found roasting over hardwood coals in this tavern's open kitchens. The space itself is also a treat, with antique chicken feeders serving as light fixtures and a soapstone-topped bar in the center. **Known for:** steak for two combo; poutine with hand-cut fries; extensive cocktail list. $ *Aver-age main: $25* ⊠ *1633 Williston Rd.* ☎ *802/497–1207* ⊕ *www.guildtavern. com* ⊗ *No lunch.*

★ Hen of the Wood Burlington

$$$ | MODERN AMERICAN | The Burlington branch of Hen of the Wood offers a slicker, more urban vibe than its original Waterbury location but serves the same inventive yet down-to-earth cuisine that sets diners' hearts aflutter and tongues wagging. Indeed, many consider this the best restaurant in Vermont, so drop your finger anywhere on the menu and you won't go wrong. **Known for:** mushroom toast; dollar oysters every night 4–5 pm; perfect date night spot. $ *Average main: $30* ⊠ *55 Cherry St.* ☎ *802/540–0534* ⊕ *www.henofthewood.com* ⊗ *No lunch.*

★ Honey Road

$$$$ | MEDITERRANEAN | This Church Street restaurant has garnered multiple James Beard Foundation nominations, launching it into a golden age under the helm of co-owners Allison Gibson and chef Cara Chigazola-Tobin. Serving arguably the best dinner in Burlington, high expec-tations are satisfied thanks to creative takes on eastern Mediterranean cuisine, including a selection of sensational mez-es. **Known for:** daily Honey Time happy hour with $1 chicken wings; muham-mara (hot pepper) dip with house-made pita; the cutting edge of local cuisine. $ *Average main: $45* ⊠ *156 Church St.* ☎ *802/497–2145* ⊕ *www.honeyroadres-taurant.com* ⊗ *No lunch.*

Istanbul Kebab House

$$ | TURKISH | FAMILY | The classics of Turkish cuisine are served with surprising authenticity and maximum deliciousness thanks to the culinary talents of its Istan-bul-raised owners, plus locally sourced produce and meats. The open terrace upstairs offers the only rooftop dining in Burlington. **Known for:** Turkish casseroles (güveç) baked in earthenware bowls; best kebabs in Burlington, if not Vermont; lavash bread made to order. $ *Average main: $19* ⊠ *175 Church St.* ☎ *802/857–5091* ⊕ *www.istanbulkebabhousevt.com* ⊗ *Closed Sun.*

Leunig's Bistro and Cafe

$$$ | **CAFÉ** | This popular café delivers alfresco bistro cuisine with a distinct French flavor, plus a friendly European-style bar and live jazz. Favorite entrées include salade niçoise, *soupe au pistou* (vegetable and white bean soup with Asiago and pesto), and beef bourguignonne. **Known for:** crème brûlée; Sunday brunch; outdoor seating on Church Street. [$] *Average main: $28* ✉ *115 Church St.* ☎ *802/863–3759* 🌐 *www.leunigsbistro.com.*

Monarch & the Milkweed

$ | **AMERICAN** | A trendy vibe mixes with exquisite pastries at this café and cocktail bar on the west side of City Hall Park. Buzzing nearly all day, the petite space serves elegant breakfasts by morning, "creative" coffee by day, and artisanal cocktails well into the night, particularly on weekends. **Known for:** CBD sweets; grilled-cheese sandwich; biscuits and gravy. [$] *Average main: $13* ✉ *111 St. Paul St.* ☎ *802/310–7828* 🌐 *www.monarchandthemilkweed.com* ⏲ *No dinner Sun.*

Penny Cluse Cafe

$ | **AMERICAN** | **FAMILY** | The lines can be long on weekends to enter this popular breakfast and brunch spot, but it's for a reason. The bright, warm ambience makes a perfect setting for breakfast, brunch, or lunch, with inventive versions of the classic dishes, like fritatta-stuffed breakfast burritos layered with local cheddar and avocado crema; slabs of griddled homemade banana bread with maple-walnut cream cheese; and hearty rice bowls with escabeche-style vegetables. **Known for:** gingerbread-blueberry pancakes; "zydeco" breakfast with andouille sausage and corn muffins; photo ops for local and visiting politicians. [$] *Average main: $13* ✉ *169 Cherry St.* ☎ *802/651–8834* 🌐 *www.pennycluse.com* ⏲ *No dinner.*

Pizzeria Verita

$$$ | **ITALIAN** | "The truth is in the dough" is the long-standing motto of Burlington's destination for expert Neopolitan pies. The bubbled, chewy crusts are flame-kissed by live fire, and Italian-inspired ingredients are sourced mostly from local farmers like the house-made mozzarella that graces classic pies like the beautifully simple Margherita. **Known for:** excellent cocktails, especially the house negroni; wood-fired Neopolitan pizza; farm-sourced ingredients. [$] *Average main: $30* ✉ *156 St. Paul St.* ☎ *802/489–5644* 🌐 *www.pizzeriaverita.com.*

Trattoria Delia

$$$ | **ITALIAN** | If you didn't make that trip to Umbria this year, the next best thing is this Italian country eatery around the corner from City Hall Park. The secret to the ambience goes well beyond the high-quality, handmade pasta dishes to the supercozy woody interior, a transplanted sugarhouse from New Hampshire. **Known for:** excellent wine list; wood-grilled prosciutto wrapped Vermont rabbit; primo Italian desserts. [$] *Average main: $27* ✉ *152 St. Paul St.* ☎ *802/864–5253* 🌐 *www.trattoriadelia.com* ⏲ *No lunch.*

Waterworks Food + Drink

$$$ | **AMERICAN** | In an old textile mill on the banks of the Winooski River, this restaurant comes with great views from nearly every table thanks to a glass wall. The expansive bar and dining room adds to the scene with lofty wood-beam ceilings, exposed brick, and a range of American bistro-style dishes. **Known for:** window seats overlooking river; cocktails; classy, upscale ambience. [$] *Average main: $25* ✉ *20 Winooski Falls Way, Winooski* ☎ *802/497–3525* 🌐 *www.waterworksvt.com.*

Zabby and Elf's Stone Soup

$ | **AMERICAN** | The open front, woody interior, and community spirit make Stone Soup a downtown favorite for lunch, especially on warm days. The small but robust salad bar is the centerpiece, with excellent hot and cold dishes—a perfect complement to the wonderful soups and fresh sandwiches. **Known for:** vegetarian dishes; gluten-free baked goods; New York Jewish-style cooking. $ *Average main: $13* ✉ *211 College St.* ☎ *802/862–7616* ⊕ *www.stonesoupvt.com* ⊘ *Closed Sun.*

🌑 Coffee and Quick Bites

Burlington Bay Market & Cafe
$ | **AMERICAN** | This may be a local hub for grabbing a quick sandwich or a case of beer, but its true fame stands with its seasonal creemee window. During the warmer months, lines snake around the corner for the café's beloved soft serve, particularly the house specialty: twisted black raspberry and maple ice cream in a cone, extra sprinkles. **Known for:** maple and black raspberry creemees; grocery staples and necessities; sandwiches, burgers, and hot dogs. $ *Average main: $5* ✉ *125 Battery St.* ☎ *802/864–0110* ⊕ *www.burlingtonbaycafe.com.*

Kestrel Coffee Roasters
$ | **CAFÉ** | Two alumni of Blue Hill at Stone Barns, one of the country's most lauded restaurants, moved to Burlington in 2017 to realize their dreams of opening a coffee shop together. The duo focus on meticulously sourced beans roasted fresh in-house, scratch-made baked goods, and a frequently changing menu of farm-sourced sandwiches. **Known for:** small-batch roasted coffee beans; homemade baked goods; maple lattes. $ *Average main: $5* ✉ *47 Maple St.* ☎ *802/391–0081* ⊕ *www.kestrelcoffees. com* ⊘ *Closed Mon.*

Onyx Tonics
$ | **CAFÉ** | This coffee-tasting bar would satisfy the staunchest coffee aficionado, with its rotating menu of specialty drinks designed to highlight the texture and flavor profile of distinct beans and roasters; so it's not surprising that co-founder

Jason Gonzales won a top 10 spot in the 2013 World Cup Tasting Championship (the coffee Olympics). If a coffee education is what you want with your morning cup, Onyx Tonics offers it—thankfully with a friendly and inviting atmosphere—as baristas have been known to warn against adding milk to a certain drip coffee, because it would raise the acidity of the brew and alter its delicate flavor. **Known for:** coffee-tasting bar; the VT Big Easy, coffee and chicory mixed with milk and maple syrup; featured espresso and drip coffee beans. $ *Average main: $6* ✉ *126 College St.* ☎ *802/777–2583* ⊕ *onyxtonics.com.*

Shy Guy Gelato
$ | **ITALIAN** | Some of the best gelato outside of Italy is found on a quiet corner of St. Paul Street. Co-owner Paul Sansone was inspired by his Italian heritage to work abroad as an apprentice to some of Southern Italy's most notable gelato masters; he returned to Vermont years later to open his own scoop shop alongside one of Burlington's longtime farm-to-table restaurant owners, Tim Elliot. **Known for:** small-batch gelato and sorbet made with local ingredients; fior di latte (fresh mozzarella) gelato; vegan-friendly sorbets. $ *Average main: $5* ✉ *457 St. Paul St.* ☎ *802/355–2320* ⊕ *shyguygelato.com* ⊘ *Closed Mon.–Wed.*

Speeder & Earl's Coffee
$ | **CAFÉ** | This family-owned coffee roaster has been turning out small-batch beans and blends since 1993, making it a well-loved local watering-hole for almost three decades. This quirky, funky café is a prime old-school spot to pick up a bag of beans or mull over the morning paper with a cup of Maple French Roast. **Known for:** small-batch coffee blends; house-roasted beans; quirky vibes in a sunny café space. $ *Average main: $4* ✉ *412 Pine St.* ☎ *802/658–6016* ⊕ *speederandearls.com.*

Burlington's Church Street is an open-air mall with restaurants, shops, festivals, and street performers.

🛏 Hotels

Courtyard Burlington Harbor

$$$ | HOTEL | A block from the lake and a five-minute walk from the heart of town, this attractive chain hotel has a pretty bar and lobby area with couches around a fireplace. **Pros:** right in downtown; some of the best lake views in town; across the street from park and lake. **Cons:** lacks local charm; a bit corporate in ambience; fee for self-parking. $ Rooms from: $329 ⊠ 25 Cherry St. ☎ 802/864–4700 ⊕ www.marriott.com ⇱ 161 rooms ⦿ No meals.

Hilton Garden Inn

$$$ | HOTEL | One of Burlington's newest hotels, this more playful edition of the Hilton family sits on an ideal location halfway between downtown and the lakefront, putting both in easy walking reach. **Pros:** some rooms have views of the lake; Vermont Comedy Club in the same building; well above average restaurant. **Cons:** uninspired design in rooms; surrounded by busy streets with traffic; small pool. $ Rooms from: $309 ⊠ 101 Main St. ☎ 802/951–0099 ⊕ www.hiltongardeninn3.hilton.com ⇱ 139 rooms ⦿ No meals.

★ Hotel Vermont

$$$ | HOTEL | Since opening in 2013, the Hotel Vermont has held the hospitality crown for style and cool, which is showcased in the almost magically spacious lobby, with its crackling wood fire, walls of smoky black Vermont granite, reclaimed oak floors, and local artwork. **Pros:** Juniper restaurant serves excellent cocktails; gorgeous rooms; unbelievable service. **Cons:** luxury doesn't come cheap; view of the lake often blocked by other buildings; additional fee for breakfast and self-parking. $ Rooms from: $309 ⊠ 41 Cherry St. ☎ 802/651–0080 ⊕ www.hotelvt.com ⇱ 125 rooms ⦿ No meals.

The Lang House on Main Street

$$ | B&B/INN | Within walking distance of downtown in the historic hill section of town, this grand 1881 Victorian home charms completely with its period furnishings, fine woodwork, plaster detailing,

stained-glass windows, and sunlit dining area. **Pros:** family-friendly vibe; interesting location; fantastic breakfast. **Cons:** no elevator; on a busy street; old-fashioned design not for everyone. Ⓢ *Rooms from: $219* ✉ *360 Main St.* ☎ *802/652–2500, 877/919–9799* ⊕ *www.langhouse.com* ⇨ *11 rooms* ⦿❘ *Free breakfast.*

★ Made INN Vermont
$$ | B&B/INN | Few accommodations in Vermont find a dynamic balance between the traditional inn and trendy boutique spirit, but this eminently charming and quirky 1881 house topped with a cute cupola has done it. **Pros:** excellent location between the University of Vermont and Champlain College; vivacious and involved innkeeper; hot tub out back. **Cons:** bathrooms are private, but not en suite; rooms are modest in size; higher cost than most other inns in town. Ⓢ *Rooms from: $259* ✉ *204 S. Willard St.* ☎ *802/399–2788* ⊕ *www.madeinnvermont.com* ⇨ *4 rooms* ⦿❘ *Free breakfast.*

Willard Street Inn
$ | B&B/INN | High in the historic hill section of Burlington, this ivy-covered house with an exterior marble staircase and English gardens incorporates elements of Queen Anne and Georgian Revival styles including the stately foyer, with cherry paneling, and the flower-decked solarium that overlooks the back garden. **Pros:** innkeepers passionate about their job; lots of friendly attention; complimentary chef-plated breakfast. **Cons:** a tad old-fashioned; walk to downtown can be a drag in winter; no elevator. Ⓢ *Rooms from: $175* ✉ *349 S. Willard St.* ☎ *802/651–8710, 800/577–8712* ⊕ *www.willardstreetinn.com* ⇨ *14 rooms* ⦿❘ *Free breakfast.*

Nightlife

ArtsRiot
MUSIC CLUBS | This unofficial headquarters of the South End Arts District has grown in recent years to include a full-service restaurant serving bistro bites and a concert stage that hosts local and national acts. Every Friday evening in summer, food trucks set up shop in the back parking lot. ✉ *400 Pine St.* ☎ *802/540–0406* ⊕ *www.artsriot.com.*

Citizen Cider
BARS/PUBS | The tiny parking lot out front gets jammed after 5 pm, as the spacious "tasting room" of this hard-cider maker fills with exuberant young, hip professionals and students. Sample cider straight or in a dozen or so cocktails. There's a full bistro menu, too. ✉ *316 Pine St., Suite 114* ☎ *802/497–1987* ⊕ *www.citizencider.com.*

Higher Ground
MUSIC CLUBS | When you feel like shaking it up to live music, come to Higher Ground—it gets the lion's share of local and national musicians. ✉ *1214 Williston Rd., South Burlington* ☎ *802/652–0777* ⊕ *www.highergroundmusic.com.*

Mule Bar
BARS/PUBS | This Winooski watering hole pours some of the best craft brews from around the state and is a must for aficionados. Outdoor seating and above-average bar bites seal the deal for its young and hip clientele. ✉ *38 Main St., Winooski* ☎ *802/399–2020* ⊕ *www.mulebarvt.com.*

Nectar's
BARS/PUBS | Jam band Phish got its start at Nectar's, which is always jumping to the sounds of local bands, stand-up comics, and live-band karaoke and never charges a cover. Don't leave without a helping of the bar's famous fries and gravy. ✉ *188 Main St.* ☎ *802/658–4771* ⊕ *www.liveatnectars.com.*

Radio Bean
BARS/PUBS | For some true local flavor, head to this funky place for nightly live music, an artsy vibe, and a cocktail. Performances happen every day, but Tuesday night is arguably the most fun, as the Honkey Tonk band blazes through covers of Gram Parsons, Wilco, and the like. ✉ *8 N. Winooski Ave.* ☎ *802/660–9346* ⊕ *www.radiobean.com.*

🎭 Performing Arts

★ Flynn Center for the Performing Arts

CONCERTS | It's a pleasure to see any show inside this grandiose art deco gem. In addition to being home to Vermont's largest musical theater company, it hosts the Vermont Symphony Orchestra, as well as big-name acts like Neko Case and Elvis Costello. The adjacent Flynn Space is a coveted spot for more offbeat, experimental performances. ⊠ 153 Main St. ☎ 802/863–5966 ⊕ www.flynncenter.org.

🏃 Activities

BIKING

★ Burlington Bike Path

BICYCLING | FAMILY | Anyone who's put the rubber to the road on the 7½-mile Burlington Bike Path and its almost equally long northern extension on the Island Line Trail sings its praises. Along the way there are endless postcard views of Lake Champlain and the Adirondack Mountains. The northern end of the trail is slightly more rugged and windswept, so dress accordingly. ⊠ Burlington ☎ 802/864–0123 ⊕ enjoyburlington.com/place/burlington-greenway.

North Star Sports

BICYCLING | In addition to stocking an extensive supply of sports apparel and accessories, this family-owned shop rents bikes and provides cycling maps. ⊠ 100 Main St. ☎ 802/863–3832 ⊕ www.northstarsportsvt.com.

Ski Rack

BICYCLING | Burlington's one-stop shop for winter sports equipment, the Ski Rack also rents bikes and sells running gear throughout the year. ⊠ 85 Main St. ☎ 802/658–3313, 800/882–4450 ⊕ www.skirack.com.

BOATING

Burlington Community Boathouse

BOATING | This boathouse administers the city's marina as well as a summertime watering hole called Splash, one of the best places to watch the sun set over the lake. ⊠ Burlington Harbor, College St. ☎ 802/865–3377 ⊕ enjoyburlington.com.

Community Sailing Center

BOATING | FAMILY | Burlington's shiny new 22,000-square-foot Community Sailing Center has 150 watercraft to rent including kayaks, sailboats, and standup paddleboards for as little as $15 an hour. Private instruction and family lessons are available, as are floating yoga classes. ⊠ 505 Lake St. ☎ 802/864–2499 ⊕ www.communitysailingcenter.org ⊘ Closed mid-Oct.–mid-May.

Lake Champlain Shoreline Cruises

BOATING | FAMILY | The trilevel *Spirit of Ethan Allen III*, a 363-passenger vessel, offers narrated cruises, theme dinners, and sunset sails with breathtaking Adirondacks and Green Mountains views. The standard 1½-hour cruise runs four times a day; sunset cruises leave at 6:30 pm on Friday and Saturday. ⊠ Burlington Boat House, 1 College St. ☎ 802/862–8300 ⊕ www.soea.com 🛥 From $23.

True North Kayak Tours

CANOEING/ROWING/SKULLING | This company conducts two- and five-hour guided kayak tours of Lake Champlain that include talks about the region's natural history and customized lessons. ⊠ 25 Nash Pl. ☎ 802/238–7695 ⊕ www.vermontkayak.com.

SKIING

Bolton Valley Resort

SKIING/SNOWBOARDING | FAMILY | The closest ski resort to Burlington, about 25 miles away, Bolton Valley is a family favorite. In addition to downhill trails—more than half rated for intermediate and beginner skiers—Bolton offers 62 miles of cross-country and snowshoe trails, night skiing, and a sports center. **Facilities:** 71 trails; 300 acres; 1,704-foot vertical drop; 5 lifts. ⊠ 4302 Bolton Valley Access Rd., north off U.S. 2, Bolton ☎ 802/434–3444, 877/926–5866 ⊕ www.boltonvalley.com 🛥 Lift ticket: $74.

🛍 Shopping

With each passing year, Burlington's industrial South End attracts ever greater numbers of artists and craftspeople, who set up studios, shops, and galleries in former factories and warehouses along Pine Street. The district's annual "Art Hop" in September is the city's largest arts celebration—and a roaring good time.

CLOTHING

April Cornell

CLOTHING | The Vermont designer's flagship store stocks her distinctive floral-print dresses and linens. ✉ 131 Battery St. ☎ 802/863–0060 ⊕ www. aprilcornell.com.

CRAFTS

Bennington Potters North

CERAMICS/GLASSWARE | Along with the popular pottery line, this store stocks interesting kitchen items. ✉ 127 College St. ☎ 802/863–2221 ⊕ www.bennington-potters.com.

★ Frog Hollow

CERAMICS/GLASSWARE | This nonprofit collective and gallery sells contemporary and traditional crafts, paintings, and photographs by more than 200 Vermont artists and artisans. ✉ 85 Church St. ☎ 802/863–6458 ⊕ www.froghollow. org.

FOOD

Lake Champlain Chocolates

FOOD/CANDY | This chocolatier makes sensational truffles, caramels, candies, fudge, and hot chocolate. The chocolates are all-natural, made in Vermont, and make a great edible souvenir. Factory tours are available. A retail branch is also on Church Street. ✉ 750 Pine St. ☎ 802/864–1807 Pine St., 802/862–5185 Church St., 800/465–5909 ⊕ www.lakechamplainchocolates.com.

NU Chocolat

FOOD/CANDY | This European-style chocolate boutique combines Swiss-trained chocolatier, premier Belgian equipment, a minimalist's eye for detail, and a family-owned mentality. Owners Laura and Kevin Toohey and their children, co-founders Rowan and Virginia Toohey, spotlight their chocolate craftsmanship with delights like cocoa-dusted almonds, chocolate-covered candied orange peel, and uniquely beautiful seasonal truffles. ✉ 180 Battery St. ☎ 802/540–8378 ⊕ www.nuchocolat.com.

SPORTING GOODS

Burton

SPORTING GOODS | The folks who helped start snowboarding—a quintessential Vermont company—sell equipment and clothing at their flagship store. A second retail branch is in downtown Burlington, on 162 College Street. ✉ 80 Industrial Pkwy. ☎ 802/660–3200, 802/333–0400 College St. ⊕ www.burton.com.

Shelburne

5 miles south of Burlington.

A few miles south of Burlington, the Champlain Valley gives way to fertile farmland, affording views of the rugged Adirondacks across the lake. In the middle of this farmland is the village of Shelburne, chartered in the mid-18th century and partly a bedroom community for Burlington. Shelburne Farms and the Shelburne Museum are worth at least a few hours of exploring, as are Shelburne Orchards in fall, when you can pick your own apples and drink fresh cider while admiring breathtaking views of the lake and mountains beyond.

Just south of Shelburne is beautiful, rural town of Charlotte. Expect to find open farmstands, rolling pastures and grazing cows along these serpentine roads, many of which offer hidden gems like u-pick berries and seasonal barbecues on the farm.

Vermont's African American Heritage Trail 👁

The Vermont African American Heritage Trail (👁 *vtafricanameri-canheritage.net*) helps share the link between Vermont, the first state constitution to outlaw slavery, and African American residents who have lived here since the Revolutionary War. There are 22 sights throughout the state, including seven museums: Ferrisburgh's **Rokeby Museum & the Underground Railroad**; Middlebury's **Vermont Folklife Center**; the **Brandon Museum**; Manchester's **Hildene, The Lincoln Family Home**;

the **Grafton History Museum**; Windsor's **Old Constitution House State Historic Site**; and Browningon's **Old Stone House Museum and Brownington Village.** The 148-acre **Clemmons Family Farm** in Charlotte, another stop along the heritage trail, celebrates the history, culture, arts and sciences of the African American diaspora via programs like on-site artist residencies, theater performances, literary events, and guided tours through the verdant property and its six historic buildings.

GETTING HERE AND AROUND

Shelburne is south of Burlington after the town of South Burlington, which is notable for its very un-Vermont traffic congestion and a commercial and fast food–laden stretch of U.S. 7. It's easy to confuse Shelburne Farms (2 miles west of town on the lake) with Shelburne Museum, which is right on U.S. 7 just south of town, but you'll want to make time for both.

👁 Sights

★ Clemmons Family Farm

ARTS VENUE | Founded in 1962 by Jackson and Lydia Clemmons, this 148-acre farm is one of a handful of Black-owned arts and culture nonprofit organizations in the state, and one of the 22 landmarks on Vermont's African-American Heritage Trail. Along with acres of lush farmland, forest, meadows and ponds, six historic buildings offer space for artist residencies, art exhibits, creative studios, retreats, small performances, and community events celebrating the African diaspora. The Storytelling Room in the Barn House is a community hub for arts, sciences and culture programs, including featured exhibits and speakers' series. ✉ *2213–2122 Greenbush Rd., Charlotte* ☎ *765/560–5445* ⊕ *www.clemmonsfamilyfarm.org.*

Fiddlehead Brewing Company

WINERY/DISTILLERY | There isn't much to the tasting room here, but there doesn't need to be: Fiddlehead only occasionally cans its celebrated beer, making this the best place outside of a restaurant to sample it on tap (and for free). Decide which one you like best and buy a growler to go—or, better yet, take it to Folino's Pizza next door, where the pies are mighty fine. ✉ *6305 Shelburne Rd.* ☎ *802/399–2994* ⊕ *www.fiddleheadbrewing.com* 🍽 *Free.*

Mount Philo State Park

NATIONAL/STATE PARK | **FAMILY** | For many Vermont kids, this is their first hike, thanks to the relatively easy, gently rising, paved road that snakes around the sides to the top, where fabulous views of the lake and landscape await. If less inclined to walk, feel free to drive. ✉ *5425 Mt. Philo Rd., Charlotte* ☎ *802/425–2390* ⊕ *www.vtstateparks.com/philo.html* 🍽 *$4.*

★ Shelburne Farms
COLLEGE | **FAMILY** | Founded in the 1880s as a private estate for two very rich New Yorkers, this 1,400-acre farm is much more than an exquisite landscape: it's an educational and cultural resource center with a working dairy farm, an award-winning cheese producer, an organic market garden, and a bakery whose aroma of fresh bread and pastries is an olfactory treat. It's a brilliant place for parents to expose their kids to the dignity of farmwork and the joys of compassionate animal husbandry—indeed, children and adults alike will get a kick out of hunting for eggs in the oversize coop, milking a cow, and watching the chicken parade. There are several activities and tours daily, and a lunch cart serves up fresh-from-the-farm soups, salads, and sandwiches. Frederick Law Olmsted, the co-creator of New York City's Central Park, designed the magnificent grounds overlooking Lake Champlain; walk to Lone Tree Hill for a splendid view. If you fall in love with the scenery, arrange a romantic dinner at the lakefront mansion, or spend the night. ✉ *1611 Harbor Rd., west of U.S. 7* ☎ *802/985–8686* 🌐 *www.shelburnefarms.org* 🎟 *$8.*

★ Shelburne Museum
MUSEUM | **FAMILY** | You can trace much of New England's history simply by wandering through the 45 acres and 39 buildings of this museum. Some 25 buildings were relocated here, including an old-fashioned jail, an 1871 lighthouse, and a 220-foot steamboat, the *Ticonderoga*. The outstanding 150,000-object collection of art, design, and Americana consists of antique furniture, fine and folk art, quilts, trade signs, and weather vanes; there are also more than 200 carriages and sleighs. The Pizzagalli Center for Art and Education is open year-round with changing exhibitions and programs for kids and adults. ✉ *6000 Shelburne Rd.* ☎ *802/985–3346* 🌐 *www.shelburnemuseum.org* 🎟 *$25* 🕒 *Call for hrs, which vary by season and museum.*

Shelburne Vineyard
WINERY/DISTILLERY | From U.S. 7, you'll see rows and rows of organically grown vines. Visit the attractive tasting room and learn how wine is made. Also available on-site is a Shelburne Vineyard collaboration called Iaepetus, a natural wine label from notable biodynamic winemaker Ethan Joseph. ✉ *6308 Shelburne Rd.* ☎ *802/985–8222* 🌐 *www.shelburnevineyard.com* 🎟 *Tasting $7, tour free.*

Vermont Teddy Bear Company
FACTORY | **FAMILY** | On the 30-minute tour of this fun-filled factory you'll hear more puns than you ever thought possible, while learning how a few homemade bears sold from a cart on Church Street turned into a multimillion-dollar business. Patrons and children can relax, eat, and play under a large canvas tent in summer, or wander the beautiful 57-acre property. ✉ *6655 Shelburne Rd.* ☎ *802/985–3001* 🌐 *www.vermontteddybear.com* 🎟 *Tour $4.*

🍴 Restaurants

The Bearded Frog
$$ | **ECLECTIC** | This restaurant is perfect for a casual dinner at the bar or a more sophisticated experience in the attractive dining room. At the bar, try the soups, burgers, and terrific cocktails; the dining room serves fresh salads, seared seafood, roasted poultry, grilled steaks, and decadent desserts. **Known for:** $1 pints of Fiddlehead on Friday; entire menu available to go; many gluten-free, vegetarian, and vegan choices. [$] *Average main: $23* ✉ *5247 Shelburne Rd.* ☎ *802/985–9877* 🌐 *www.thebeardedfrog.com* 🕒 *No lunch.*

★ The Dining Room at the Inn at Shelburne Farms
$$$ | **AMERICAN** | Dinner here will make you dream of F. Scott Fitzgerald, as piano music wafts in from the library of this 1880s mansion on the shores of Lake Champlain. **Known for:** possibly best Sunday brunch in area; beautiful gardens; farmhouse cheddar. [$] *Average main: $33*

At the Shelburne Museum, the restored 220-foot Ticonderoga steamboat is the last existing walking beam side-wheel passenger steamer.

✉ *Inn at Shelburne Farms, 1611 Harbor Rd.* ☎ *802/985–8498* ⊕ *www.shelburne-farms.org* ⏱ *Closed mid-Oct.–mid-May.*

Rustic Roots

$$ | AMERICAN | Scuffed wood floors and chunky country tables bring the "rustic" at this converted farmhouse—but not too much. An intimate bar and maroon walls adorned with woodcrafts and art add a touch of elegance, and the French-inspired food is carefully prepared. **Known for:** coffee-maple sausage; pastrami on rye; Bloody Marys. 💲 *Average main: $21* ✉ *195 Falls Rd.* ☎ *802/985–9511* ⊕ *www.rusticrootsvt.com* ⏱ *Closed Mon. and Tues. No dinner Wed., Thurs., and Sun.*

☕ Coffee and Quick Bites

Philo Ridge Farm & Market

$ | AMERICAN | This 400-acre diversified farm is a leader in regenerative agriculture, and its on-site market and café show the depth of the land's bounty. Two hundred of those acres are dedicated to organic vegetable, flower, herb, and fruit production, which is then channeled into the sandwiches, salads, prepared foods, and pantry goods in the on-site market. **Known for:** locally roasted coffee with Vermont milk and cream; housemade pastries; sandwiches, salads, and lunch specials made with farm ingredients. 💲 *Average main: $14* ✉ *2766 Mt. Philo Rd., Charlotte* ☎ *802/539–2912* ⊕ *philoridgefarm.com.*

Vermont Cookie Love

$ | BAKERY | The "Love Shack" on the side of VT Route 7 is known to have one of the best maple creemees in the state due to its use of Vermont maple syrup and high-butterfat dairy from Kingdom Creamery of Vermont. There are also coffee, vanilla, and chocolate creemees on offer, along with local Wilcox hard ice cream and house-made cookies made daily on-site. **Known for:** homemade cookies; maple and coffee soft serve; crushed cookie crumbles for topping cones and sundaes. 💲 *Average main: $4* ✉ *6915 Rte. 7, Ferrisburgh* ☎ *802/425–8181* ⊕ *www.vermontcookielove.com* ⏱ *Creemee window closed Nov.–Mar.*

Hotels

Heart of the Village Inn
$ | **B&B/INN** | Each of the elegantly furnished rooms at this bed-and-breakfast in an 1886 Queen Anne Victorian provides coziness and tastefully integrated modern conveniences. **Pros:** easy walk to shops and restaurants; elegant historical building; hypoallergenic bedding and memory foam mattresses. **Cons:** near to but not within Shelburne Farms; no room service; no children under 12. [$] *Rooms from: $189* ✉ *5347 Shelburne Rd.* ☎ *802/985–9060* 🌐 *www.heartofthevillage.com* 🛏 *9 rooms* 🍴 *Free breakfast.*

★ **The Inn at Shelburne Farms**
$ | **B&B/INN** | It's hard not to feel like an aristocrat at this exquisite turn-of-the-20th-century Tudor-style inn, perched at the edge of Lake Champlain—even Teddy Roosevelt stayed here. **Pros:** stately lakefront setting in a historic mansion; endless activities; proposal-worthy restaurant. **Cons:** lowest-priced rooms have shared baths; closed in winter; no air-conditioning. [$] *Rooms from: $170* ✉ *1611 Harbor Rd.* ☎ *802/985–8498* 🌐 *www.shelburnefarms.org* 🕒 *Closed mid-Oct.–mid-May* 🛏 *28 rooms* 🍴 *No meals.*

★ **Mt. Philo Inn**
$$$ | **B&B/INN** | Practically on the slopes of Mt. Philo State Park in Charlotte, the 1896 inn offers gorgeous views of Lake Champlain from its outdoor porches and an ideal blend of historical and contemporary boutique decor. **Pros:** walking trail goes directly to Mt. Philo State Park; lots of local stonework incorporated; complimentary breakfast basket includes all the fixings. **Cons:** not walking distance to any sights; rooms too big for just one guest; you cook breakfast yourself. [$] *Rooms from: $320* ✉ *27 Inn Rd., Charlotte* ☎ *802/425–3335* 🌐 *www.mtphiloinn.com* 🛏 *4 suites* 🍴 *No meals.*

Lake Champlain Islands

Lake Champlain stretches more than 100 miles south from the Canadian border and forms the northern part of the boundary between New York and Vermont. Within it is an elongated archipelago comprising several islands—Isle La Motte, North Hero, Grand Isle, and South Hero—and the Alburg Peninsula. Enjoying a temperate climate, the islands hold several apple orchards and are a center of water recreation in summer and ice fishing in winter. A scenic drive through the islands on U.S. 2 begins at Interstate 89 and travels north to Alburg Center; Route 78 takes you back to the mainland.

ESSENTIALS

VISITOR INFORMATION Lake Champlain Islands Chamber of Commerce. ☎ *802/372–8400, 800/262–5226* 🌐 *www.champlainislands.com.* **Lake Champlain Regional Chamber of Commerce.** ☎ *802/863–3489, 877/686–5253* 🌐 *www.vermont.org.*

Sights

Alburgh Dunes State Park
PARK—SPORTS-OUTDOORS | This park has one of the longest sandy beaches on Lake Champlain and some fine examples of rare flora and fauna along the hiking trails. The wetlands are also an important area for wildlife refuge, providing a safe habitat for breeding, feeding, and nesting for surrounding animals like deer and wild turkey. ✉ *151 Coon Point Rd., off U.S. 2, Alburg* ☎ *802/796–4170* 🌐 *www.vtstateparks.com/alburgh.html* 🎟 *$4.*

★ **Allenholm Farm**
FARM/RANCH | The pick-your-own apples at this farm are amazingly tasty—if you're here at harvest time, don't miss out. The farm also has a petting area with donkeys, miniature horses, sheep, goats, and other animals. At the store, you can buy cheeses, dried fruit, homemade pies, and maple creemees. ✉ *111*

South St., South Hero ☎ *802/372–5566* 🌐 *www.allenholm.com* 🎫 *Free.*

Grand Isle State Park

PARK—SPORTS-OUTDOORS | You'll find hiking trails, boat rentals, and shore fishing at Grand Isle. ✉ *36 E. Shore S, off U.S. 2, Grand Isle* ☎ *802/372–4300* 🌐 *www.vtstateparks.com/grandisle.html* 🎫 *$4.*

Hyde Log Cabin

BUILDING | Built in 1783, this log cabin on South Hero is often cited as the country's oldest surviving specimen. It's now home to the Grand Isle Historical Society. ✉ *228 U.S. 2, Grand Isle* ☎ *802/828–3051* 🎫 *$3* 🕓 *Closed weekdays mid-Oct.–May.*

Missisquoi National Wildlife Refuge

HIKING/WALKING | On the mainland east of the Alburg Peninsula, the refuge consists of 6,729 acres of federally protected wetlands, meadows, and woods. It's a beautiful area for bird-watching, canoeing, and walking nature trails. ✉ *29 Tabor Rd., 36 miles north of Burlington, Swanton* ☎ *802/868–4781* 🌐 *www.fws.gov/refuge/missisquoi.*

Snow Farm Vineyard and Winery

WINERY/DISTILLERY | Vermont's first vineyard was started here in 1996; today, the winery specializes in nontraditional botanical hybrid grapes designed to take advantage of the island's microclimate, similar to that of Burgundy, France. Take a self-guided tour and sip some samples in the tasting room—dessert wines are the strong suit. On Thursday evening, late May–September, you can picnic and enjoy the free concerts on the lawn. ✉ *190 W. Shore Rd., South Hero* ☎ *802/372–9463* 🌐 *www.snowfarm.com* 🎫 *Free* 🕓 *Closed late Dec.–Apr.*

St. Anne's Shrine

RELIGIOUS SITE | This spot marks the site where, in 1665, French soldiers and Jesuits put ashore and built a fort, creating Vermont's first European settlement. Vermont's first Roman Catholic Mass was celebrated here on July 26, 1666. ✉ *92 St. Anne's Rd., Isle La Motte* ☎ *802/928–3362* 🌐 *www.saintannesshrine.org* 🎫 *Free.*

🍴 Restaurants

Blue Paddle Bistro

$$ | **AMERICAN** | This cozy, white clapboard house with an indicative blue awning has been a community staple for 15 years. Co-owner Mandy Hotchkiss and chef-owner Pheobe R. **Known for:** farm-to-table nightly specials; local beef burgers; plenty of Vermont-grown vegetables. [$] *Average main: $24* ✉ *316 U.S. Rte. 2, South Hero* ☎ *802/372–4814* 🌐 *www.bluepaddlebistro.com.*

🛏 Hotels

North Hero House Inn and Restaurant

$ | **B&B/INN** | **FAMILY** | This inn has four buildings right on Lake Champlain, among them the 1891 Colonial Revival main house with a restaurant, pub, and library. **Pros:** resort really gets away from it all; superb lakefront setting; many rooms have screened-in porches. **Cons:** much less to do in winter; two-night minimum on weekends and holidays; relatively bland design. [$] *Rooms from: $140* ✉ *3643 U.S. 2, North Hero* ☎ *802/372–4732, 888/525–3644* 🌐 *www.northherohouse.com* 🕓 *Closed mid-Oct.–Dec.* 🔑 *26 rooms* 🍽 *Free breakfast.*

Ruthcliffe Lodge & Restaurant

$ | **HOTEL** | If you're looking for an inexpensive summer destination—to take in the scenery, canoe the lake, or go biking—this will do quite nicely as the lodge is on the rarely visited Isle La Motte. **Pros:** inexpensive rates; high-quality restaurant; laid-back vibe. **Cons:** two-night minimum stays on weekends and holiday periods; quite remote; simple, bland design. [$] *Rooms from: $142* ✉ *1002 Quarry Rd., Isle La Motte* ☎ *802/928–3200* 🌐 *www.ruthcliffe.com* 🕓 *Closed mid-Oct.–mid-May* 🔑 *7 rooms* 🍽 *Free breakfast.*

Did You Know?

Long and skinny Lake Champlain is sometimes called the sixth Great Lake. Several small and scenic islands, like Grand Isle, are popular seasonal getaways in warm weather.

⚡ Activities

Apple Island Resort

BOATING | The resort's marina rents pontoon boats, rowboats, canoes, kayaks, and pedal boats. ✉ *71 U.S. 2, South Hero* ☎ *802/372–3922* ⊕ *www.appleislandresort.com.*

Hero's Welcome

BOATING | This general store rents bikes, canoes, kayaks, and paddleboards; come winter, they switch to ice skates, cross-country skis, and snowshoes. ✉ *3537 U.S. 2, North Hero* ☎ *802/372–4161* ⊕ *www.heroswelcome.com.*

North Hero State Park

PARK—SPORTS-OUTDOORS | The 399-acre North Hero has a swimming beach and nature trails. It's open to rowboats, kayaks, and canoes. ✉ *3803 Lakeview Dr., North Hero* ☎ *802/372–8727* ⊕ *www.vtstateparks.com/northhero.html* 🎟 *$4.*

Sand Bar State Park

BEACHES | One of Vermont's best swimming beaches is at Sand Bar State Park, along with a snack bar, a changing room, and boat rentals. ✉ *1215 U.S. 2, South Hero* ☎ *802/893–2825* ⊕ *vtstateparks.com/sandbar.html* 🎟 *$4.*

Montgomery and Jay

51 miles northeast of Burlington.

Montgomery is a small village near the Jay Peak ski resort and the Canadian border. Amid the surrounding countryside are seven covered bridges.

GETTING HERE AND AROUND

Montgomery lies at the junction of Routes 58, 118, and 242. From Burlington, take Interstate 89 north to Routes 105 and 118 east. Route 242 connects Montgomery and, to the northeast, the Jay Peak Resort.

👁 Sights

Lake Memphremagog

BODY OF WATER | Vermont's second-largest body of water, Lake Memphremagog extends 33 miles north from Newport into Canada. Prouty Beach in Newport has tennis courts, boat rentals, and a 9-hole disc-golf course. Watch the sunset from the deck of the East Side Restaurant, which serves excellent burgers and prime rib. ✉ *242 Prouty Beach Rd., Newport* ☎ *802/334–6345* ⊕ *www.newportrecreation.org.*

☕ Coffee and Quick Bites

Miso Hungry

$ | **JAPANESE** | At the base of mammoth Jay Peak sits a wood-shingled food truck cooking arguably the best ramen in the state. Owners Momoko and Jordan Antonucci met as rafting guides in Japan, and spent three winters in Hokkaido gravitating towards the steaming bowls of noodles made at après-ski ramen trucks parked mountainside. **Known for:** spicy miso ramen; seasonal onigiri; authentic Japanese cooking made with Vermont-sourced ingredients. 💲 *Average main: $13* ✉ *830 Jay Peak Rd., Jay* ☎ *518/605–4474* ⊕ *www.misohungryramen.com.*

🛏 Hotels

★ The INN

$ | **B&B/INN** | This smart chalet-style lodge comes with tons of character. **Pros:** Trout River views from back rooms; within walking distance of shops and supplies; smart, individually designed rooms. **Cons:** noise from bar can seep into nearby rooms; two-night minimum stay; outside food and alcohol not allowed. 💲 *Rooms from: $169* ✉ *241 Main St.* ☎ *802/326–4391* ⊕ *www.theinn.us* 🛏 *11 rooms* 🍽 *Free breakfast.*

Jay Peak Resort
$$ | **HOTEL** | **FAMILY** | Accommodations at Jay Peak include standard hotel rooms, suites, condominiums, town houses, and cottage and clubhouse suites. **Pros:** slopes never far away; 60,000-square-foot indoor water park; kids 14 and under stay and eat free and complimentary child care is provided. **Cons:** can get noisy; not very intimate; service can be lackluster. *[$] Rooms from: $239 ✉ 830 Jay Peak Rd. ☎ 802/988–2611 🌐 www.jaypeakresort.com 🛏 515 units 🍴 Free breakfast.*

Phineas Swann Bed & Breakfast Inn
$ | **B&B/INN** | The top-hatted bulldog on the sign of this 1880 farmhouse isn't just a mascot: it reflects the hotel's welcoming attitude to pet owners. **Pros:** walking distance from shops and supplies; lots of dogs; each room has different design. **Cons:** decor is a tad old-fashioned; dog theme (and actual dogs) not for everyone; no outside alcohol allowed. *[$] Rooms from: $199 ✉ 195 Main St. ☎ 802/326–4306 🌐 www.phineasswann.com 🛏 9 rooms 🍴 Free breakfast.*

Activities

ICE-SKATING

Ice Haus Arena
HOCKEY | **FAMILY** | The sprawling arena contains a professional-size hockey rink and seating for 400 spectators. You can practice your stick handling, and the rink is open to the public for skating several times a week. There are tournaments throughout the year. *✉ 830 Jay Peak Rd., Jay ☎ 802/988–2727 🌐 www.jaypeakresort.com 🎟 $6.*

SKIING

Hazen's Notch Association
SKIING/SNOWBOARDING | Delightfully remote at any time of the year, this center has 40 miles of marked and groomed trails and rents equipment and snowshoes. *✉ 1423 Hazen's Notch Rd. ☎ 802/326–4799 🌐 www.hazensnotch.org 🎟 Trail pass: $12.*

Jay Peak
SKIING/SNOWBOARDING | Sticking up out of the flat farmland, Jay Peak averages 349 inches of snow per year—more than any other Vermont ski area—and it's renowned for its glade skiing and powder. There are two interconnected mountains, the highest reaching nearly 4,000 feet. The smaller mountain has straight-fall-line, expert terrain that eases mid-mountain into an intermediate pitch. Beginners should stay near the bottom on trails off the Metro quad lift. There are also five terrain parks, snowshoeing, telemark skiing, and a state-of-the art ice arena for hockey, figure skating, and curling. The Pump House, an indoor water park with pools and slides, is open year-round. **Facilities:** 78 trails; 385 acres; 2,153-foot vertical drop; 9 lifts. *✉ 830 Jay Peak Rd., Jay ☎ 802/988–2611 🌐 www.jaypeakresort.com 🎟 Lift ticket: $84.*

Lake Willoughby

30 miles southeast of Montgomery (summer route; 50 miles by winter route), 28 miles north of St. Johnsbury.

The jewel of the Northeast Kingdom is clear, deep, and chilly Lake Willoughby, edged by sheer cliffs and surrounded by state forest. The only town on its shores is tiny Westmore, which has a beach and a few shops that cater to campers and seasonal residents.

Sights

Bread and Puppet Museum
MUSEUM | **FAMILY** | This ramshackle barn houses a surrealistic collection of props used by the world-renowned Bread and Puppet Theater. The troupe has been performing social and political commentary with the towering (they're supported by people on stilts) and eerily expressive puppets for more than 50 years. In July and August, there are performances on Saturday night and Sunday afternoon,

with museum tours before Sunday shows. ⊠ *753 Heights Rd., 1 mile east of Rte. 16, Glover* ☎ *802/525–3031* ⊕ *www. breadandpuppet.org* ✉ *Donations accepted* ⊗ *Closed Nov.–May.*

Lake Willoughby

BODY OF WATER | The cliffs of Mt. Pisgah and Mt. Hor drop to the edge of Lake Willoughby on opposite shores, giving this beautiful, deep, glacially carved lake a striking resemblance to a Norwegian fjord. The trails to the top of Mt. Pisgah reward hikers with glorious views. Take note: the beach on the southern end is Vermont's most famous nude beach. ⊠ *Westmore.*

Greensboro

30 miles northwest of St. Johnsbury.

Tucked along the southern shore of Caspian Lake, Greensboro has been a summer resort for literati, academics, and old-money types for more than a century. Yet it exudes an unpretentious, genteel character—most of the people running about on errands seem to know each other. The town beach is right off the main street.

◉ Sights

★ Hill Farmstead Brewery

WINERY/DISTILLERY | It is difficult to quantify owner and master brewer Shaun Hill's contribution to the international explosion of craft beer. Hill Farmstead has won Best Brewery in the World six times in the past decade, and it's a key player in Vermont tourism, where beer contributes as much to the state economy as skiing and hiking. Since opening in 2010, Hill's

eighth generation family farmstead off a rural mountain pass, miles from cell service, has drawn millions of local and international travelers pilgrimaging for a coveted pint and a growler to-go. A beautiful bar is surrounded by acres of woods and lawnspace, and a small lake sits at the bottom of a sloping field—a nice spot for pondering over a pint. ⊠ *403 Hill Rd.* ☎ *802/533–7450* ⊕ *hillfarmstead.com.*

⬤ Shopping

The Willey's Store

CONVENIENCE/GENERAL STORES | This is a classic general store of the "if-we-don't-have-it-you-don't-need-it" kind. It's also the spot where locals in the know can snag hard-to-find Vermont gems like Jasper Hill Farm cheeses and bottles of Hill Farmstead beer. ⊠ *7 Breezy Ave.* ☎ *802/533–2621.*

Chapter 10

NEW HAMPSHIRE

Updated by
Andrew Collins

👁 **Sights**
★★★★★

🍴 **Restaurants**
★★★☆☆

🛏 **Hotels**
★★★★☆

🛍 **Shopping**
★★★★☆

🍸 **Nightlife**
★★★☆☆

WELCOME TO NEW HAMPSHIRE

TOP REASONS TO GO

★ **The White Mountains:** Offering spectacular hiking and skiing, these dramatic peaks and notches are unforgettable.

★ **Lake Winnipesaukee:** Beaches, arcades, boat cruises, and classic summer camps fuel a whole season of family fun.

★ **Fall Foliage:** Head to the Kancamagus Highway in autumn for one of America's best drives, or seek out a less-trafficked route that's equally stunning.

★ **Portsmouth:** Less than an hour's drive from Boston, this small, upbeat American city abounds with colorful Colonial architecture, cosmopolitan dining, and easy access to New Hampshire's only stretch of the Atlantic coastline.

★ **Pristine Towns:** Peterborough, Walpole, Tamworth, Center Sandwich, Bethlehem, and Jackson are among the most charming tiny villages in New England.

1 Portsmouth. Colonial homes meet hip dining.

2 Rye. Sweeping beaches and lavish oceanfront homes.

3 Exeter. Café culture and a famous prep school.

4 Durham. Home of the University of NH.

5 Wolfeboro. The U.S.'s oldest summer resort.

6 Laconia and Weirs Beach. Lake Winnipesaukee's hub of family fun.

7 Meredith. A bustling marina and mills converted to hotels.

8 Plymouth. A lively college town and gateway to the White Mountains.

9 Holderness. Base camp for Squam and Little Squam Lakes.

10 Center Sandwich. Lake Winnipesaukee's quiet, scenic side.

11 Tamworth. Tranquility and Mt. Chocorua views.

12 North Conway. Outlet shops and family-friendly amusements.

13 Jackson. A storybook White Mountains town.

14 Mt. Washington. Highest peak in the northeastern United States.

15 Bartlett. A scenic ski and hiking hub.

16 Bretton Woods. The cog railway and a grande dame resort.

17 Bethlehem. An artsy alpine hamlet.

18 Littleton. A scenic river town with a lively Main Street.

19 Franconia. One of the White Mountains' favorite recreation hubs.

20 Lincoln and North Woodstock. Ski resorts and kitschy family spots.

21 Waterville Valley. A four-season resort and recreation village.

22 New London. Charming gateway to Lake Sunapee.

23 Newbury. Skiing, boating, and the nation's oldest crafts fair.

24 Hanover. Home to Dartmouth College.

25 Cornish. Covered bridges and the Saint-Gaudens estate.

26 Walpole. A pretty village green and Connecticut River views.

27 Keene. A classic Main Street and views of Mt. Monadnock.

28 Peterborough. The inspiration for Thornton Wilder's *Our Town*.

29 Manchester. The Granite State's largest city.

30 Concord. The small but lively state capital.

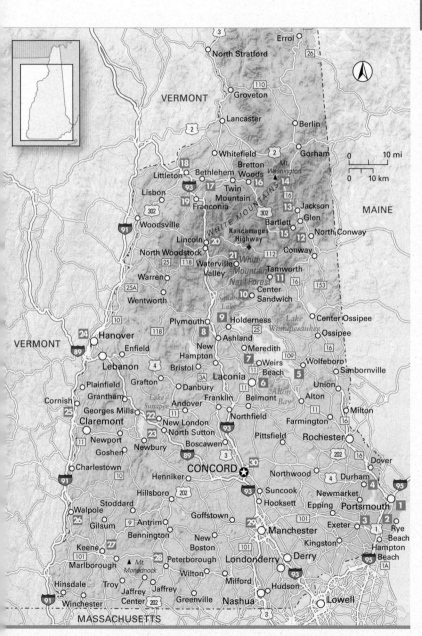

VERMONT

Errol

North Stratford

Groveton

Lancaster

Berlin

VERMONT

Whitefield

Gorham

Littleton
Bethlehem
Bretton
Woods
Mt.
Washington

MAINE

Lisbon

Twin
Mountain

Jackson

Franconia

Glen

Woodsville

Bartlett

North Conway

Lincoln

Kancamagus
Highway

Conway

North Woodstock

WHITE MOUNTAINS

Warren

Waterville
Valley

White
Mountain
Nat'l Forest

Tamworth

Wentworth

Center
Sandwich

Square
Lake

Plymouth

Holderness

Center Ossipee

Hanover

Enfield

New
Hampton

Ashland

Lake
Winnipesaukee

Ossipee

VERMONT

Lebanon

Bristol

Meredith

Weirs
Beach

Wolfeboro

Sanbornville

Plainfield

Grafton

Danbury

Laconia

Union

Grantham

Belmont

Alton

Milton

Cornish

Georges Mills

Andover

Franklin

Alton
Bay

Claremont

New London

Northfield

Farmington

Newport

North Sutton

Pittsfield

Rochester

Goshen

Newbury

Boscawen

Dover

Charlestown

Henniker

CONCORD

Northwood

Durham

Walpole

Stoddard

Hillsboro

Suncook

Newmarket

Portsmouth

Gilsum

Antrim

Goffstown

Hooksett

Epping

Exeter

Bennington

Keene

New
Boston

Manchester

Kingston

Rye
Beach

Marlborough

Mt.
Monadnock

Peterborough

Londonderry

Derry

Hampton
Beach

Hinsdale

Troy

Wilton

Milford

Hudson

Jaffrey
Center

Jaffrey

Greenville

Nashua

Lowell

Winchester

MASSACHUSETTS

10 mi
10 km

New Hampshire's precipitous terrain, clear air, and sparkling lakes attract trailblazers, artists, and countless tourists. A varied geography and myriad outdoor activities are part of the draw, but visitors also appreciate this place of beauty, history, and hospitality. Whether you're seeking adventure or just want to laze on the porch swing of a century-old inn, you'll find ample ways to engage with this rugged, diverse state that stretches from the sea to the Northeast's highest mountain peaks.

Ralph Waldo Emerson, Henry David Thoreau, Nathaniel Hawthorne, and Louisa May Alcott all visited and wrote about the state, sparking a fervent literary tradition. It also has a strong political history: this was the first colony to declare independence from Great Britain, the first to adopt a state constitution, and the first to require its constitution be referred to the people for approval. Politically, it remains a fiercely independent swing state that holds some of the earliest election primaries in the country and that's known for both its libertarian and progressive tendencies.

The state's varied terrain makes it popular with everyone from hard-core climbers and skiers to young families looking for easy access to nature. You can hike, ski, snowboard, snowshoe, and fish, as well as explore on snowmobiles, sailboats, kayaks, and mountain bikes. New Hampshirites have no objection to others enjoying the beauty here as long as they leave a few dollars behind: it's the only state in the union with neither sales nor income taxes, so tourism brings in much-needed revenue (and tourists can enjoy tax-free shopping).

With a few communities consistently rated among the most livable in the nation, New Hampshire has grown a bit faster than most other northeastern states since 1990. The state is gradually developing two distinct personalities: one characterized by rapid urbanization in the southeast and the other by quiet village life in the west and north. Although newcomers have brought change, the free-spirited sensibility of the Granite State remains intact, as does its natural splendor.

MAJOR REGIONS

The **Seacoast,** New Hampshire's 18-mile stretch of coastline, packs in plenty of gorgeous scenery and lively diversions. The northern portion of the shoreline, from the charmingly historic regional hub, **Portsmouth,** south through the affluent town of **Rye,** is especially pristine and free from the honky-tonk excess of the southern section (around Hampton Beach and Seabrook). From Rye, you can branch inland to the prep-school town of **Exeter,** and then cut north through **Durham** (home to the University of New Hampshire). From here it's a short drive to the Lakes Region.

Throughout central New Hampshire, you'll encounter lakes and more lakes in the aptly named **Lakes Region.** The largest, Lake Winnipesaukee, has 180 miles of coastline and attracts all sorts of water-sports enthusiasts to the towns of **Wolfeboro, Laconia (with its bustling Weirs Beach section),** and **Meredith.** You'll find smaller and more secluded lakes with enchanting B&Bs in **Holderness,** which adjoins famously scenic Squam Lake. **Plymouth, Center Sandwich,** and **Tamworth** are great bases to explore the surrounding lakes and as well as the southern reaches of the White Mountains.

Skiing, snowshoeing, and snowboarding in the winter; hiking, biking, and riding scenic railways in the summer: the Whites, as locals call **The White Mountains,** have plenty of natural wonders. **Mt. Washington,** the tallest mountain in the Northeast, can be conquered by trail, train, or car; other towns with strong railroad ties include up-and-coming **Littleton** and touristy **North Conway. Lincoln and North Woodstock** and **Waterville Valley** are lively resort areas, and **Bethlehem, Jackson,** and **Franconia** are stunning alpine jewels. **Bretton Woods** and **Bartlett** are great ski towns.

Quiet villages proliferate in the **Lake Sunapee** region; the lake itself is a wonderful place to swim, fish, or enjoy a cruise. **Hanover,** home to Dartmouth College (founded 1769), retains that true New England college-town feel, with ivy-draped buildings and cobblestone walkways. **New London** is one of the area's main hubs, while **Newbury,** on the edge of Mt. Sunapee State Park, is one of the region's outdoor recreation centers. **Cornish,** once the haunt of J. D. Salinger, is where you'll find Cornish-Windsor Bridge, the country's second-longest covered bridge

New and old coexist in **the Monadnocks and Merrimack Valley,** the state's southwestern and south-central regions, respectively. Here high-tech firms have helped reshape the cities of **Manchester** and **Concord** while small towns in the hills surrounding Mt. Monadnock, southern New Hampshire's largest peak, like **Keene** and **Peterborough,** celebrate tradition and history. **Walpole** has one of the state's loveliest town greens.

Planning

Getting Here and Around

Some people come to New Hampshire to hike or ski the mountains, fish and sail the lakes, or cycle along backcountry roads. Others prefer to drive through scenic towns, stopping at museums and general stores or crafts shops along the way. Although New Hampshire is a small state, roads curve around lakes and mountains, making distances sometimes much longer than they appear on a map. You can get a taste of the coast, lake, and mountain areas in three to five days; eight days will give you time to make a more complete loop.

AIR

Manchester-Boston Regional Airport, the state's largest, has nonstop service from more than a dozen U.S. cities. The drive from Boston's Logan Airport to most places in New Hampshire takes one to three hours; the same is true for Bradley International Airport, near Hartford, Connecticut.

CAR

New Hampshire is an easy drive north from Boston. Many key destinations are near major highways, and local public transit is very limited, so getting around by car is the best way to explore. Interstate 93 stretches from Boston to Littleton and on into neighboring Vermont. Interstate 89 will get you from Concord to Hanover and eventually to Burlington, Vermont. To the east, Interstate 95 (a toll road) passes through southern New Hampshire's coastal area between Massachusetts and Maine. Throughout the state, quiet backcountry lanes and winding roads can take a little longer but often reward travelers with gorgeous scenery.

The speed limit on interstate and limited-access highways is usually 65 to 70 mph. On state and U.S. routes, speed limits vary considerably, from 25 mph to 55 mph, so watch signs carefully. The website of the **New Hampshire Department of Transportation** (⊕ hb.511nh.com) has up-to-the-minute information about traffic and road conditions.

TRAIN

Amtrak's *Downeaster* passenger train operates between Boston and Portland, Maine, with New Hampshire stops in Exeter, Durham, and Dover.

Hotels

In the mid-19th century, wealthy Bostonians retreated to imposing New Hampshire country homes in the summer. Grand hotels were built across the state, especially in the White Mountains, which at that time competed with Saratoga Springs, Newport, and Bar Harbor to draw the nation's elite vacationers. A handful of these hotel-resorts survive. And many of those country houses have since been converted into inns. The smallest have only a few rooms and are typically done in period style; the largest contain 30 or more rooms and suites and often have in-room fireplaces and even hot tubs. You'll also find a great many well-kept motor lodges and cottage compounds, particularly in the White Mountains and Lakes regions. In ski areas, expect the usual ski condos and lodges, but most slopes are also within a short drive of a country inn or two. In the Merrimack River valley, as well as along major highways, chain hotels and motels predominate. The state is rife with campgrounds, especially in the White Mountains. *Hotel reviews have been shortened. For full information, visit Fodors.com.*

Restaurants

New Hampshire prides itself on its seafood: not only lobster, but also breaded haddock, steamed mussels, fried clams, and fish-and-chips. Across the state you'll find country taverns with both old-school and increasingly diverse modern American menus, many of them emphasizing regional ingredients—in smaller hamlets, the best restaurant in town is often inside the historic inn. As in the rest of New England, the state has no shortage of greasy-spoon diners, pizzerias, and pubs that serve hearty comfort fare, but a growing number of contemporary, locavore-driven bistros, third-wave coffee roasters, mixology-minded cocktail bars, and artisanal craft breweries have cropped up in recent years—along with a growing selection of Asian and other ethnic restaurants—especially in Portsmouth, Manchester, and Concord, but also in some surprisingly little towns, such as Keene, Walpole, Bethlehem, and Walpole. No matter where you go, reservations are seldom required, and dress is casual. *Restaurant reviews have been shortened. For full information, visit Fodors.com.*

WHAT IT COSTS in U.S. Dollars

$	$$	$$$	$$$$
RESTAURANTS			
under $18	$18–$24	$25–$35	over $35
HOTELS			
under $150	$150–$225	$226–$300	over $300

Visitor Information

CONTACTS Lakes Region Tourism Association. ☎ 603/286–8008 ⊕ www.lakesregion.org. **Lake Sunapee Region Chamber of Commerce.** ☎ 603/526–6575 ⊕ www.lakesunapeeregionchamber.com. **Ski New Hampshire.** ☎ 603/745–9396 ⊕ www.skinh.com. **Visit New Hampshire.** ☎ 603/271–2665, 800/386–4664 ⊕ www.visitnh.gov. **White Mountains Visitors Center.** ☎ 603/745–8720 ⊕ www.visit-whitemountains.com.

When to Go

Summer and fall are the best, but also the most popular and expensive, times to visit most of New Hampshire. Winter is a great time to travel to the White Mountains, but most other tourist sights in the state, including museums in Portsmouth and many attractions in the Lakes Region, close from late fall until May or June. In summer people flock to beaches, mountain trails, and lakeside boat launches; in the cities, festivals showcase food and beer, music, theater, and crafts. Fall brings leaf peepers, especially to the White Mountains and the Monadnocks. Skiers and snowboarders take to the slopes in winter, when Christmas lights and carnivals brighten the long, dark nights. Spring's unpredictable weather—along with April's mud and late May's black flies—tends to deter visitors. Still, the season has its joys, not

the least of which is the appearance, mid-May–early June, of the state flower, the purple lilac, soon followed by the blooming of colorful rhododendrons and fields of lupine.

Portsmouth

47 miles east of Concord, 50 miles south of Portland, Maine, 56 miles north of Boston.

A small but lively Colonial port across the river from Kittery, Maine, upscale Portsmouth buzzes with trendy restaurants, swank cocktails bars, contemporary art galleries and boutiques, and acclaimed cultural venues that host nationally recognized speakers and performers—the action is focused largely around downtown's Market Square. Settled in 1623 as Strawbery Banke, Portsmouth grew into a prosperous port before the Revolutionary War, during which it harbored many Tory sympathizers. These days, this city of 22,000 has many grand residences from the 18th to the early 20th century, some of them preserved within or—such as the Wentworth-Coolidge Mansion and Governor John Langdon House—on the blocks near the fascinating Strawbery Banke Museum, and others are close by, such as the Wentworth-Gardner House. For a scenic drive or bike ride, follow Rte. 1B east from downtown across the Piscataqua River, following it around leafy New Castle Island—where you'll pass Fort Constitution and the grand, historic Wentworth by the Sea Hotel.

GETTING HERE AND AROUND
Both Interstate 95 and U.S. 1 connect Portsmouth with the rest of coastal New England, while U.S. 4 and Route 101 are the easiest ways to get here from inland New Hampshire. Downtown Portsmouth is walkable, though you'll need a car for attractions farther afield.

BOAT TOURS
Gundalow Company

BOAT TOURS | FAMILY | Sail the Piscataqua River in a flat-bottom gundalow (a type of barge) built at Strawbery Banke. Help the crew set sail, steer the vessel, and trawl for plankton while learning about the region's history from an onboard educator. Passengers are welcome to bring food and beverages. ⊠ *60 Marcy St.* ☎ *603/433–9505* ⊕ *www.gundalow. org* ✉ *From $30* ⊙ *Closed early Oct.– late May.*

Portsmouth Harbor Cruises

BOAT TOURS | Tours of Portsmouth Harbor and the Isles of Shoals, inland-river foliage trips, and sunset and wine cruises are all in this company's repertoire. ⊠ *64 Ceres St.* ☎ *603/436–8084, 800/776– 0915* ⊕ *www.portsmouthharbor.com* ✉ *From $18* ⊙ *Closed Nov.–early May.*

WALKING TOURS
★ Discover Portsmouth

WALKING TOURS | FAMILY | The Portsmouth Historical Society operates this combination visitor center–museum, where you can pick up maps, get the scoop on what's happening while you're in town, and view cultural and historical exhibits. Here you can also learn about self-guided historical tours and to sign up for guided ones. ⊠ *10 Middle St.* ☎ *603/436–8433* ⊕ *www.portsmouthhistory.org* ✉ *Tours from $15.*

★ Portsmouth Black Heritage Trail

WALKING TOURS | FAMILY | Important local sites in African American history can be seen on the 75-minute guided Sankofa Tour. Included are the African Burying Ground and historic homes of local slave traders and abolitionists. Tours, which begin at the Old Meeting House, are conducted on Saturday afternoon throughout the summer. ⊠ *280 Marcy St.* ☎ *603/570–8469* ⊕ *www.blackheritagetrailnh.org* ✉ *$20.*

VISITOR INFORMATION
The Portsmouth tourism office (Chamber Collaborative of Greater Portsmouth) is the official government source of visitor info for the entire Seacoast region.

Chamber Collaborative of Greater Portsmouth

⊠ *Portsmouth* ☎ *603/610–5510* ⊕ *www. portsmouthchamber.org.*

Sights

Albacore Park

MILITARY SITE | Built in Portsmouth in 1953, the USS *Albacore* is the centerpiece of Albacore Park. You can board this prototype submarine, which served as a floating laboratory to test an innovative hull design, dive brakes, and sonar systems for the Navy. The visitor center exhibits *Albacore* artifacts, and the nearby Memorial Garden is dedicated to those who have lost their lives in submarine service. ⊠ *600 Market St.* ☎ *603/436–3680* ⊕ *www.ussalbacore.org* ✉ *$9* ⊙ *Closed Mon. and Tues.*

Great Bay Estuarine National Research Reserve

INFO CENTER | FAMILY | Just inland from Portsmouth is one of southeastern New Hampshire's most precious assets. In this 10,235 acres of open and tidal waters, you can spot blue herons, ospreys, and snowy egrets, particularly during the spring and fall migrations. The Great Bay Discovery Center has indoor and outdoor exhibits, a library and bookshop, and a 1,700-foot boardwalk, as well as other trails, which wind through mudflats and upland forest. ⊠ *89 Depot Rd., Greenland* ☎ *603/778– 0015* ⊕ *www.greatbay.org* ✉ *Free* ⊙ *Discovery Center closed Mon. and Tues., weekdays in Oct., and Nov.–Apr.*

Isles of Shoals

ISLAND | FAMILY | Four of the nine small, rocky Isles of Shoals belong to New Hampshire (the other five belong to Maine), many of them still known by the earthy names—Hog and Smuttynose, to cite but two—17th-century fishermen bestowed on them. A history of piracy, murder, and ghosts suffuses the archipelago, long populated by an independent lot who, according to one writer, hadn't the sense to winter on the mainland. Celia Thaxter, a native islander, romanticized these islands with her poetry in *Among the Isles of Shoals* (1873). In the late 19th century, **Appledore Island** became an offshore retreat for Thaxter's coterie of writers, musicians, and artists. **Star Island** contains a small museum, the Rutledge Marine Lab, with interactive family exhibits. From May to late October you can take a narrated history cruise of the Isles of Shoals and walking tours of Star Island with Isles of Shoals Steamship Company. ⊠ *Barker Wharf, 315 Market St.* ☎ *800/441–4620, 603/431–5500* ⊕ *www.islesofshoals.com* ☞ *Cruises from $28.*

John Paul Jones House

BUILDING | FAMILY | Revolutionary War hero John Paul Jones lived at this boardinghouse while he supervised construction of the USS *America* for the Continental Navy. The 1758 hip-roof building displays furniture, costumes, glass, guns, portraits, and documents from the late 18th century. The collection's specialty is textiles, among them some extraordinary early-19th-century embroidery samplers. ⊠ *43 Middle St.* ☎ *603/436–8420* ⊕ *www.portsmouthhistory.org* ☞ *$7* ⊗ *Closed mid-Oct.–late May.*

★ Moffatt-Ladd House and Garden

GARDEN | The period interior of this striking 1763 mansion tells the story of Portsmouth's merchant class through portraits, letters, and furnishings. The Colonial Revival garden includes a horse chestnut tree planted by General William Whipple when he returned home after signing the Declaration of Independence in 1776. ⊠ *154 Market St.* ☎ *603/436–8221* ⊕ *www.moffattladd.org* ☞ *$8; garden only $5* ⊗ *Closed mid-Oct.–May.*

Prescott Park

ARTS VENUE | FAMILY | Picnicking is popular at this 3½-acre waterfront park near Strawbery Banke, whose large formal garden with fountains is perfect for whiling away an afternoon. The park contains Point of Graves, Portsmouth's oldest burial ground, and two 17th-century warehouses. The summerlong Prescott Park Arts Festival features concerts, outdoor movies, and food-related events. ⊠ *105 Marcy St.* ☎ *603/436–2848* ⊕ *www.prescottpark.org.*

★ Strawbery Banke Museum

GARDEN | FAMILY | The first English settlers named what's now Portsmouth for the wild strawberries along the shores of the Piscataqua River. The name survives in this 10-acre outdoor history museum, which comprises 37 homes and other structures dating from 1695 to 1820, some restored and furnished to a particular period, others with historical exhibits. Half of the interior of the Shapley-Drisco House depicts its use as a Colonial dry-goods store, but its living room and kitchen are decorated as they were in the 1950s, showing how buildings were adapted over time. The Shapiro House has been restored to reflect the life of the Russian-Jewish immigrant family who lived there in the early 1900s. Done in decadent Victorian style, the 1860 Goodwin Mansion is one of the more opulent buildings. Although the houses are closed in winter, the grounds are open year-round, and an outdoor skating rink operates December–February. ⊠ *14 Hancock St.* ☎ *603/433–1100* ⊕ *www.strawberybanke.org* ☞ *$20* ⊗ *Homes closed Nov.–Apr. except for guided tours on Nov. weekends.*

Warner House

HOUSE | The highlight of this circa 1716 gem is the curious folk-art murals lining the hall staircase, which may be the oldest-known murals in the United States still gracing their original structure. The house, a notable example of brick Georgian architecture, contains original art, furnishings, and extraordinary examples

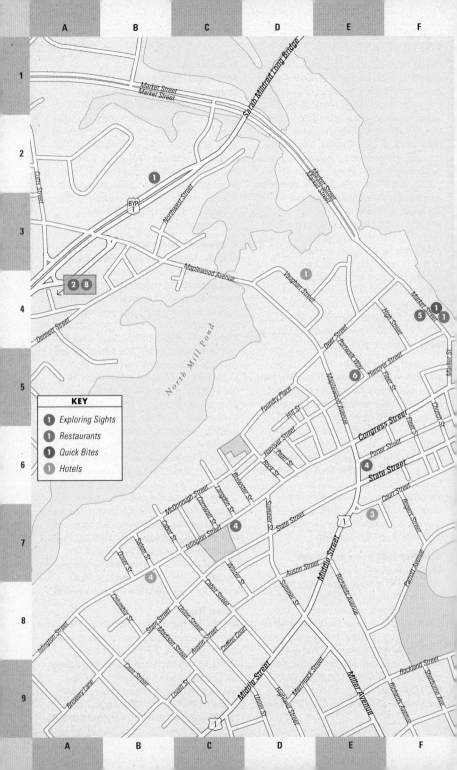

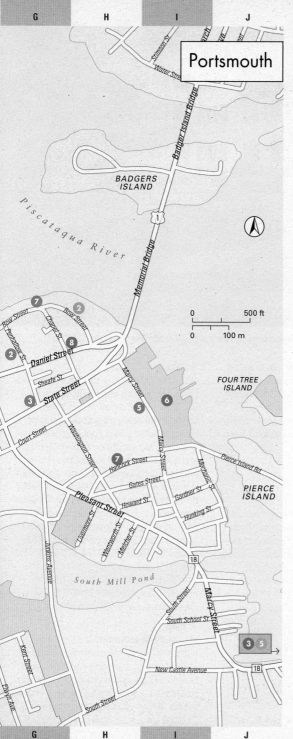

Portsmouth

Sights ▼

1 Albacore Park..................... **B2**
2 Great Bay Estuarine National
   Research Reserve................. **A4**
3 Isles of Shoals **J9**
4 John Paul Jones House............ **E6**
5 Moffatt-Ladd
   House and Garden................. **F4**
6 Prescott Park....................... **I5**
7 Strawbery Banke Museum....... **H6**
8 Warner House **H5**

Restaurants ▼

1 Black Trumpet Bistro.............. **F4**
2 Cava................................ **G5**
3 Cure **G5**
4 Lexie's Joint **C7**
5 Mombo............................. **I5**
6 Row 34 .... **E5**
7 Surf Restaurant **G4**
8 Vida Cantina....................... **A4**

Quick Bites ▼

1 Annabelle's Natural
   Ice Cream.......................... **F4**

Hotels ▼

1 AC Hotel Portsmouth.............. **D4**
2 Ale House Inn **H4**
3 Hotel Portsmouth **E7**
4 Martin Hill Inn **B7**
5 Wentworth by the Sea **J9**

Strawbery Banke Museum includes period gardens and 37 homes and other structures.

of area craftsmanship. The west-wall lightning rod is believed to have been installed in 1762 under the supervision of Benjamin Franklin. ✉ *150 Daniel St.* ☎ *603/436–5909* ⊕ *www.warnerhouse. org* 🎫 *$8* ⏱ *Closed Nov.–May and Tues.*

🍴 Restaurants

Black Trumpet Bistro

$$$ | **CONTEMPORARY** | This romantic harbor-view restaurant brings the bold flavors of Latin America and the Mediterranean to bear on such eclectic fare as smoked corn–and–brandade–crusted halibut, lobster and grits, and roast chicken with couscous, olive harissa, and preserved lemon. The chef belongs to the Heirloom Harvest Project and brings unusual vegetables—sometimes in surprising colors—to the table. **Known for:** creative vegetarian options; a lively upstairs wine bar; flourless dark-chocolate torte. 💲 *Average main: $28* ✉ *29 Ceres St.* ☎ *603/431–0887* ⊕ *www. blacktrumpetbistro.com* ⏱ *No lunch.*

★ Cava

$$$ | **TAPAS** | Having a meal at this sophisticated little wine and tapas bar down a tiny alley near the downtown riverfront can feel like going on a secret mission, or being ushered into a special dinner party. It has a small exhibition kitchen and bar, and just a handful of tables and chairs, where guests can enjoy stellar food that includes an extensive selection of bocadillos, tapas, and pintxos—from Medjool dates with Serrano and manchego to char-grilled baby octopus—plus a few larger plates, such as paella. **Known for:** a superb, interesting wine list; authentic Spanish tapas; churros with hot chocolate. 💲 *Average main: $26* ✉ *10 Commercial Alley* ☎ *603/319–1575* ⊕ *www. cavatapasandwinebar.com* ⏱ *No lunch.*

★ Cure

$$$ | **MODERN AMERICAN** | As its name hints, this buzzy neighborhood bistro in a lively dining room with redbrick walls, beam ceilings, and hardwood floors specializes in cured, brined, and slow-cooked meats, which you can sample through

beautifully presented charcuterie boards, smoked ribs, and slow-roasted Moroccan lamb shank. But take heart if you're less disposed toward red meat—you'll find plenty of creative seafood and veggie dishes on the menu, including gooey lobster mac and cheese. **Known for:** locally sourced ingredients; well-chosen wine list; lively but romantic dining room. [$] *Average main: $26* ✉ *189 State St.* ☎ *603/427–8258* 🌐 *www.curerestaurant-portsmouth.com* 🕓 *No lunch.*

Lexie's Joint

$ | **BURGER** | **FAMILY** | What began as a humble downtown burger joint has blossomed into a regional mini empire, thanks to the high-quality ingredients, upbeat service, and groovy "peace, love, and burgers"–themed decor. The burgers are reasonably priced and topped with all sorts of goodies, but there are also hot dogs and a few sandwiches, plus plenty of addictive sides. **Known for:** milk shakes with Shain's of Maine homemade ice cream; fried pickles with chipotle aioli; more great locations in Dover, Exeter, and Newburyport. [$] *Average main: $7* ✉ *212 Islington St.* ☎ *603/815–4181* 🌐 *www.peaceloveburgers.com.*

Mombo

$$$ | **INTERNATIONAL** | A short stroll from Strawbery Banke Museum and the pretty gardens of Prescott Park, this romantic restaurant is set in a Colonial red saltbox house with high timber-beam ceilings and wrought-iron chandeliers. In contrast to the historic setting, the food is artfully contemporary and worldly—specialties include jerk-spiced slow-braised oxtail, and pad Thai with sesame-crusted yellowfin tuna and spicy peanuts. **Known for:** elaborate cheese-and-charcuterie plate; international flair; peaceful setting in historic neighborhood. [$] *Average main: $28* ✉ *66 Marcy St.* ☎ *603/433–2340* 🌐 *www.momborestaurant.com* 🕓 *Closed Mon. No lunch.*

Row 34

$$$ | **SEAFOOD** | Set in a gleaming, industrial-chic dining room with tall windows, exposed air ducts, and metal tables and chairs, this contemporary and slightly fancy take on a classic seafood house is the sort of place that's equally appropriate for special celebrations and casual beer-and-oysters happy hours with friends. From tuna tartare to scallop ceviche, you can't go wrong with anything from the raw bar, but also check out the extensive variety of steamed and grilled fare, such as roasted monkfish and grilled salmon collar. **Known for:** fantastic beer selection; $1 raw oysters at happy hour; Sunday brunch. [$] *Average main: $27* ✉ *5 Portwalk Pl.* ☎ *603/319–5011* 🌐 *www.row34nh.com.*

Surf Restaurant

$$$ | **SEAFOOD** | Whether you eat inside the conversation-filled, high-ceilinged dining room or out on the breezy deck, you'll be treated to expansive views of Old Harbour and the Piscataqua River—an apt setting for consistently fresh and tasty seafood. The menu branches into several directions, including lobster rolls, shrimp-pork ramen, sushi, and Tuscan-style spaghetti with seafood, but manages everything well, and there's a well-curated wine and cocktail selection to complement your choice. **Known for:** raw-bar specialties; water views; creative sushi rolls. [$] *Average main: $27* ✉ *99 Bow St.* ☎ *603/334–9855* 🌐 *www.surf-seafood.com* 🕓 *Closed Mon. No lunch Tues. and Wed.*

Vida Cantina

$ | **MODERN MEXICAN** | In a state sorely lacking notable Latin restaurants, this airy contemporary space south of downtown stands out for the ambitious modern Mexican cuisine of chef-owner and James Beard award–nominated chef David Vargas. Several kinds of street-food-style tacos are offered, including barbacoa and pork belly, along with a tangy goat cheese version of queso fundido and sous vide short rib with charred-rhubarb salsa. **Known for:** confit pig's head carnitas platter (not for the faint of heart); interesting sides, like blue cornbread and shishito peppers; boozy weekend brunches. [$] *Average main: $17* ✉ *2456 Lafayette Rd.* ☎ *603/501–0648* 🌐 *www.vidacantinanh.com.*

Coffee and Quick Bites

Annabelle's Natural Ice Cream

$ | **CAFÉ** | **FAMILY** | On sunny days, a stroll around historic downtown Portsmouth isn't complete without a dish or cone of the thick and luscious ice cream doled out at this long-running parlor. Try a dish of maple-walnut, cinnamon spice, or rich French vanilla—the latter is made with golden egg yolks. **Known for:** seasonal flavors like pumpkin pie and peachy peach; fruit sorbets; all-natural ingredients. [$] *Average main: $6* ✉ *49 Ceres St.* ☎ *603/436–3400* 🌐 *www.annabellesicecream.com.*

Hotels

AC Hotel Portsmouth

$$ | **HOTEL** | One of a few hotels that have opened recently in downtown Portsmouth's fast-growing, formerly industrial North End, this sleek midrise boutique hotel offers contemporary rooms with plenty of techy gadgets and creature comforts, plus a spacious lobby-bar with a fireplace, a popular rooftop restaurant, and a well-outfitted gym. **Pros:** smartly designed rooms; hip rooftop bar and restaurant; steps from dining and museums. **Cons:** lacking good views; some may find the modern, urban aesthetic a bit cold; expensive parking. [$] *Rooms from: $195* ✉ *299 Vaughan St.* ☎ *603/427–0152* 🌐 *www.marriott.com* 🛏 *156 rooms* 🍴 *No meals.*

Ale House Inn

$$$ | **HOTEL** | Each of the stylish rooms in this urbane inn occupying a converted Victorian redbrick brewery on the historic riverfront has plenty of fun amenities, such as iPads filled with local information, iPod docks, and plush robes, and the modern bathrooms have handsome Italian tilework. **Pros:** welcome beers from local breweries upon arrival; free parking; bicycles for local jaunts. **Cons:** no breakfast; several steps to enter hotel; rooms are a bit compact. [$] *Rooms from: $235* ✉ *121 Bow St.* ☎ *603/431–7760* 🌐 *www.alehouseinn.com* 🛏 *10 rooms* 🍴 *No meals.*

Hotel Portsmouth

$$$ | **HOTEL** | This downtown Victorian mansion built in 1881 by a sea captain is now a 32-room boutique hotel with elegantly updated furnishings, plush bed linens, and such modern conveniences as iPads preloaded with local information and flat-screen TVs. **Pros:** close to Market Square; free parking; lounge serving wine, beer, and small bites. **Cons:** thin walls result in occasional noise; some rooms have bland views; two-night minimum during busy times. [$] *Rooms from: $235* ✉ *40 Court St.* ☎ *603/433–1200* 🌐 *www.thehotelportsmouth.com* 🛏 *32 rooms* 🍴 *Free breakfast.*

Martin Hill Inn

$$ | **B&B/INN** | The quiet rooms in this yellow 1815 house surrounded by flower-filled gardens are furnished with antiques and decorated with fine period antiques; a generous full breakfast is served each morning, featuring lemon-ricotta pancakes and other delectable treats. **Pros:** refrigerators in rooms; excellent breakfast; off-street parking. **Cons:** a little outside the downtown core on busy street; breakfast is served at a communal table; no children under 12. [$] *Rooms from: $210* ✉ *404 Islington St.* ☎ *603/436–2287* 🌐 *www.martinhillinn.com* 🛏 *7 rooms* 🍴 *Free breakfast.*

★ Wentworth by the Sea

$$$$ | **RESORT** | Nearly demolished in the 1980s, one of coastal New England's most elegant Victorian grand resorts—where the likes of Harry Truman and Gloria Swanson once vacationed—has been meticulously restored and now ranks among the cushiest golf, boating, and

Four of the nine rocky Isles of Shoals belong to New Hampshire; the other five belong to Maine.

spa getaways in New Hampshire. **Pros:** amenities include an expansive full-service spa, heated indoor pool, and an outstanding golf course; marina with charters for harbor cruises and deep-sea fishing; excellent food in main restaurant and casual waterfront bistro. **Cons:** 10- to 15-minute drive from downtown Portsmouth; steep rates in summer; large property lacks intimacy. $ *Rooms from: $389* ⊠ *588 Wentworth Rd., New Castle* ☎ *603/422–7322, 866/384–0709* ⊕ *www.wentworth. com* ⤳ *161 rooms* ⏇ *No meals.*

Nightlife

BARS AND BREWPUBS

★ Earth Eagle Brewings
BREWPUBS/BEER GARDENS | This bustling gastropub produces unusual, boldly flavorful ales in the Belgian style, some using distinctive botanicals—lemongrass, ginger root—rather than hops. The food is terrific, there's an airy outdoor beer garden, and musicians perform many evenings. ⊠ *175 High St.* ☎ *603/502–2244* ⊕ *www.eartheaglebrewings.com.*

Portsmouth Book & Bar
BARS/PUBS | Combine an old-school indie bookstore with a funky café–cocktail bar, set it inside a restored 1817 customhouse, and you've got this endearing hangout that's popular with everyone from college students to artists to tourists. Live music and readings are offered, too. ⊠ *40 Pleasant St.* ☎ *603/427–9197* ⊕ *www.bookandbar.com.*

Performing Arts

ARTS VENUES

★ Music Hall
CONCERTS | Beloved for its acoustics, the 895-seat hall built in 1878 presents top-drawer music concerts, from pop to classical, along with dance and theater. The more intimate Music Hall Loft, around the corner, screens art films and hosts lectures. ⊠ *28 Chestnut St.* ☎ *603/436–2400* ⊕ *www.themusichall. org.*

Seacoast Repertory Theatre

THEATER | Here you'll find a year-round schedule of musicals, classic dramas, and works by up-and-coming playwrights, as well as everything from a youth theater to drag cabaret nights. ⊠ *125 Bow St.* ☎ *603/433–4472* ⊕ *www.seacoastrep. org.*

🛍 Shopping

The historic city center, especially around Market Square, abounds with gift and clothing boutiques, book and gourmet food shops, and crafts stores and art galleries.

Byrne & Carlson

FOOD/CANDY | Watch elegant cream truffles and luscious chocolates being made in the European tradition at this small artisanal shop. ⊠ *121 State St.* ☎ *207/439–0096* ⊕ *www.byrneandcarlson.com.*

Nahcotta

ART GALLERIES | This contemporary design boutique specializes in the stylish ceramics, jewelry, glassware, and art of dozens of regional talents. ⊠ *110 Congress St.* ☎ *603/433–1705* ⊕ *www.nahcotta.com.*

Off Piste

GIFTS/SOUVENIRS | Look to this quirky emporium for offbeat gifts and household goods—everything from painted buoy birdhouses to irreverent books, games, and mugs. ⊠ *37 Congress St.* ☎ *603/319–6910.*

Piscataqua Fine Arts

ART GALLERIES | This gallery mainly shows works by master woodcutter Don Gorvett, who creates spellbinding scenes of New England's coast, particularly the Portsmouth area. There are also works by some of New England's finest printmakers, including Sidney Hurwitz, Alex deConstant, and Sean Hurley. ⊠ *123 Market St.* ☎ *603/436–7278* ⊕ *www. dongorvettgallery.com.*

Portsmouth Farmers' Market

MARKET | FAMILY | One of the best and longest-running farmers' markets in the state showcases seasonal produce along with regional treats such as maple syrup and artisanal cheeses. There's live music, too. It's held Saturday morning, May–early November. ⊠ *Little Harbour School, 50 Clough Dr.* ⊕ *www.seacoastgrowers.org.*

Rye

8 miles south of Portsmouth.

In 1623 the English established a settlement at Odiorne Point in what is now the largely undeveloped and picturesque town of Rye, making it the birthplace of New Hampshire. Today, the area's main draws include a lovely state park, beaches, and the views from Route 1A, which is prettiest if you follow it south, passing the group of late-19th- and early-20th-century mansions known as **Millionaires' Row.** Strict town laws prohibit commercial development in Rye, creating a dramatic contrast with its frenetic neighbor, Hampton Beach.

GETTING HERE AND AROUND

Interstate 95 and U.S. 1, both west of town, provide easy access, but Rye shows its best face from coastal Route 1A.

👁 Sights

★ Fuller Gardens

GARDEN | Arthur Shurtleff, a noted landscape architect from Boston, designed this late-1920s estate garden in the Colonial Revival style. In a gracious seaside residential neighborhood a couple of miles south of Jenness Beach, this peaceful little botanical gem encompasses 1,700 rosebushes, hosta and Japanese gardens, and a tropical conservatory. ⊠ *10 Willow Ave., North Hampton* ☎ *603/964–5414* ⊕ *www.fullergardens. org* 🎫 *$9* ⊗ *Closed Nov.–mid-May.*

★ Odiorne Point State Park
NATURE PRESERVE | FAMILY | These 135 acres of protected seaside land are where David Thompson established New Hampshire's first permanent English settlement. Several signed nature trails provide vistas of the nearby Isles of Shoals and interpret the park's military history. The rocky shore's tidal pools shelter crabs, periwinkles, and sea anemones. The park's **Seacoast Science Center** hosts exhibits on the area's natural history. Its tidal-pool touch tank and 1,000-gallon Gulf of Maine deepwater aquarium are popular with kids. ✉ *570 Ocean Blvd.* ☎ *603/436–8043* 🌐 *www.seacoastsciencecenter.org* 🎟 *Park $4, Science Center $10.*

Beaches

Jenness State Beach
BEACH—SIGHT | FAMILY | Good for swimming and sunbathing, this long, sandy beach is a favorite among locals who enjoy its light crowds and nice waves for bodysurfing. Wide and shallow, Jenness Beach is a great place for kids to run and build sand castles. **Amenities:** lifeguards; parking (fee); showers; toilets. **Best for:** surfing; swimming; walking. ✉ *2280 Ocean Blvd.* ☎ *603/227–8722* 🌐 *www.nhstateparks.org* 🎟 *Parking $2/hr May–Sept., $1/hr Apr. and Oct.*

★ Wallis Sands State Beach
BEACH—SIGHT | FAMILY | This family-friendly swimmers' beach has bright white sand, a picnic area, a store, and beautiful views of the Isles of Shoals. **Amenities:** food and drink; lifeguards; parking (fee); showers; toilets. **Best for:** swimming; walking. ✉ *1050 Ocean Blvd.* ☎ *603/436–9404* 🌐 *www.nhstateparks.org* 🎟 *$15 per car (late May–early Sept.).*

Restaurants

The Carriage House
$$$ | SEAFOOD | Across from Jenness Beach, this elegant cottage serves innovative dishes with an emphasis on local seafood, from raw bar specialties like scallop crudo and littleneck clams on the half shell to roasted cod and tarragon lobster salad. A first-rate hanger steak and lamb stew with eggplant and fry bread round out the menu. **Known for:** classic daily blue-plate specials; breezy, refreshing cocktails; cozy upstairs tavern with ocean views. [$] *Average main: $28* ✉ *2263 Ocean Blvd.* ☎ *603/964–8251* 🌐 *www.carriagehouserye.com* 🕒 *No lunch.*

Hotels

Atlantic Breeze Suites
$$ | HOTEL | FAMILY | The spacious rooms in this contemporary all-suites boutique hotel look either south over the ocean and down along the Hampton Beach shoreline or north over pristine Hampton Salt Marsh Conservation Area, and all have good-size balconies from which to soak up the views. **Pros:** free off-street parking; across the street from the beach; private balconies. **Cons:** books up way in advance in high season; on the north end of the beachfront, a bit of a walk from many restaurants; 15-minute drive from the quieter Rye beaches. [$] *Rooms from: $220* ✉ *429 Ocean Blvd., Hampton Beach* ☎ *603/967–4781* 🌐 *www.atlanticbreezesuites.com* 🛏 *11 rooms* 🍴 *No meals.*

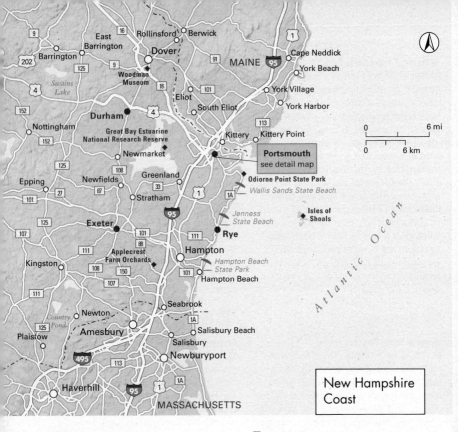

🏃 Activities

WHALE-WATCHING

Granite State Whale Watch

WHALE-WATCHING | FAMILY | This respected outfitter conducts naturalist-led whale-watching tours aboard the 100-passenger *Granite State*, along with excursions around the Isles of Shoals and to Star Island. ✉ *Rye Harbor State Marina, 1870 Ocean Blvd.* ☎ *603/964–5545, 800/964–5545* ⊕ *www.granites-tatewhalewatch.com* ✎ *$40* ⊘ *Closed mid-Oct.–mid-May.*

Exeter

11 miles west of Rye.

During the Revolutionary War, Exeter was the state capital, and it was here amid intense patriotic fervor that the first state constitution and the first Colonial Declaration of Independence from Great Britain were put to paper. These days Exeter shares more in appearance and personality with Boston's blue-blooded satellite communities than the rest of New Hampshire. Cheerful cafés, coffeehouses, and shops with artisanal wares fill the bustling town center.

GETTING HERE AND AROUND

Amtrak's *Downeaster* stops here between Boston and Portland, Maine. By car, Route 101 provides access from the east or west to this walkable river town.

ESSENTIALS

VISITOR INFORMATION Exeter Area Chamber of Commerce. ☎ *603/772–2411* 🌐 *www.exeterarea.org.*

Sights

American Independence Museum

HISTORIC SITE | Guided tours of this museum that celebrates the nation's birth focus on the family who lived here during the Revolutionary War. Among 3,000 artifacts, see drafts of the U.S. Constitution and the first Purple Heart, as well as letters and documents written by George Washington and the household furnishings of John Taylor Gilman, one of New Hampshire's early governors. In July, the museum hosts the two-week American Independence Festival, and occasional architectural tours are offered, too. ✉ *Ladd-Gilman House, 1 Governor's La.* ☎ *603/772–2622* 🌐 *www.independencemuseum.org* 🎫 *$8* 🕒 *Closed Sun. and Mon. and Dec.–Apr.*

Applecrest Farm Orchards

FARM/RANCH | **FAMILY** | At this 250-acre farm, pick apples and berries or buy freshly baked fruit pies and cookies and outstanding homemade ice cream. A bistro serves quite good farm-to-table fare. Fall brings cider pressing, hayrides, pumpkins, and music on weekends. Author John Irving's experiences working here as a teen inspired *The Cider House Rules.* ✉ *133 Exeter Rd., Hampton Falls* ☎ *603/926–3721* 🌐 *www.applecrest.com.*

Phillips Exeter Academy

BUILDING | The grounds of this elite 1,100-student prep school, open to the public, resemble an Ivy League university campus. The school's library is one of the masterworks of modernist architect Louis I. Kahn. The Lamont Gallery, in the Frederick R. Mayer Art Center, mounts free contemporary art exhibitions. ✉ *20 Main St.* ☎ *603/772–4311* 🌐 *www.exeter.edu.*

Restaurants

Blue Moon Evolution

$ | **MODERN AMERICAN** | In this barnlike building on the edge of downtown, the menu shifts according to whatever the locavore-minded kitchen wizards have procured—maybe fresh summer peaches (grilled with feta, blueberries, and basil pesto) or sea scallops (pan-seared with sweet-and-sour kale, corn, and cherry tomatoes). Shareable apps, artisan-bread sandwiches, and creative seafood and veggies plates round out the menu. **Known for:** sustainable ingredients; cocktails infused with local berries and herbs; organic blueberry-lemon cashew tarts. [$] *Average main: $16* ✉ *8 Clifford St.* ☎ *603/778–6850* 🌐 *www.bluemoonevolution.com* 🕒 *Closed Sun.–Tues.*

★ Otis

$$ | **MODERN AMERICAN** | Given the caliber of cuisine and the exceptional beverage program of this romantic, urbane restaurant set inside the early-19th-century Inn by the Bandstand, it's remarkable that most main dishes cost under $25—it's a terrific value. The farm-to-table menu here changes often to reflect what's in season, but has featured roasted duck breast with wild mushrooms and a signature dessert of sticky-toffee pudding, with everything always plated beautifully. **Known for:** emphasis on market-fresh, seasonal ingredients; views of charming village center; well-executed craft cocktails. [$] *Average main: $24* ✉ *Inn by the Bandstand, 4 Front St.* ☎ *603/580–1705* 🌐 *www.otisrestaurant.com* 🕒 *Closed Sun. and Mon. No lunch.*

☕ Coffee and Quick Bites

Laney & Lu

$ | **CAFÉ** | **FAMILY** | This snug counter service café is a handy option for organic coffees, blended tea elixirs, and creative smoothies and bowls—the blueberry-basil with banana, avocado, spinach, and almond milk is a standout. Or tuck into a salad of locally sourced fruit, veggies, and greens, or try one of the hearty but healthy salads made on locally baked sourdough. **Known for:** artisan toasts with different toppings; fresh smoothies; a great kids' menu. $ *Average main: $9* ✉ *26 Water St., #6* ☎ *603/580–4952* ⊕ *www.laneyandlu.com* ⊗ *No dinner.*

🛏 Hotels

★ Inn by the Bandstand

$$$ | **B&B/INN** | This gorgeously appointed, luxury B&B in the heart of downtown Exeter exudes character and comfort, with individually themed rooms furnished with fine antiques, oriental rugs, and cushy bedding. **Pros:** attractive downtown location; exceptional dining in Otis restaurant; fabulous breakfasts. **Cons:** minimum stay on busy weekends; in a busy part of downtown; rates are a bit steep. $ *Rooms from: $259* ✉ *6 Front St.* ☎ *603/772–6352* ⊕ *www.innbytheband-stand.com* ⇆ *8 rooms* ⦿⦿ *Free breakfast.*

🛍 Shopping

★ Exeter Fine Crafts

CRAFTS | This acclaimed nonprofit cooperative formed in 1966 features creations by more than 300 of Northern New England's top pottery, painting, jewelry, textile, glassware, and other artisans. ✉ *61 Water St.* ☎ *603/778–8282* ⊕ *www.exeterfinecrafts.com.*

Durham

12 miles north of Exeter, 11 miles west of Portsmouth.

A lively college town settled in 1635, and later the home of Revolutionary War hero and three-time New Hampshire governor John Sullivan, Durham became a maritime hub in the 19th century thanks to its easy access to Great Bay via the Oyster River. With the University of New Hampshire anchoring its town center, it's a good hub for exploring two other nearby riverfront communities with thriving historic downtowns, Dover and Newmarket.

GETTING HERE AND AROUND
You can reach Durham on Route 108 from the north or south and on U.S. 4 from Portsmouth or Concord. The *Downeaster* Amtrak train stops here.

👁 Sights

★ Woodman Museum

HOUSE | **FAMILY** | This campus of four impressive, historic museums consists of the 1675 Damm Garrison House, the 1813 Hale House (home to abolitionist Senator John P. Hale from 1840 to 1873), the 1818 Woodman House, and the 1825 Keefe House, which contains the excellent Thom Hindle Gallery. Exhibits focus on Early American cooking utensils, clothing, furniture, and Indian artifacts, as well as natural history and New Hampshire's involvement in the Civil War. ✉ *182 Central Ave., Dover* ☎ *603/742–1038* ⊕ *www.woodmanmuseum.org* 🎟 *$13* ⊗ *Closed Mon. and Tues. and mid-Dec.–Mar.*

🍴 Restaurants

Hop + Grind

$ | **BURGER** | Students and faculty from UNH, whose campus is just a few blocks away, congregate over mammoth burgers with flavorful, original sides (kimchi, fries topped with cilantro-pickled peppers or black-garlic-truffle aioli) and other creative takes on gastropub fare. This is a hot spot for craft-beer aficionados, who appreciate the long list of options, including a rotating cache of rare and seasonal selections. **Known for:** impressive local beer selection; fun and lively student crowd; malted milk shakes in unusual flavors. $ *Average main: $10* ✉ *Madbury Commons, 17 Madbury Rd.* ☎ *603/397–5564* ⊕ *www.hopandgrind.com.*

★ Stages at One Washington

$$$$ | **MODERN AMERICAN** | Offering stunning, reservation-only prix-fixe dinners featuring 8 to 10 small courses, this intimate open-kitchen space occupies the third floor of a converted redbrick mill building in Dover. The daily menu is based on what the talented culinary team here has sourced from farms and fishing boats—perhaps grilled lamb with apples, truffles, and miso, or lobster mushrooms with coffee, razor clams, and hazelnuts. **Known for:** artfully presented food; lavish multicourse dinners; optional wine pairings. $ *Average main: $120* ✉ *1 Washington St., Dover* ☎ *603/842–4077* ⊕ *www.stages-dining.com* ⊗ *Closed Sun.–Tues. No lunch.*

🛏️ Hotels

Three Chimneys Inn

$ | **B&B/INN** | Since 1649, this stately yellow house has graced a hill overlooking the Oyster River; it now offers attractive rooms filled with period antiques and reproductions in the main house and a 1795 barn. **Pros:** charming, historic ambience; delicious breakfast included; very reasonable rates. **Cons:** a long walk (or short drive) into town; restaurant is uneven in quality; books up on fall and spring weekends. $ *Rooms from: $144* ✉ *17 Newmarket Rd.* ☎ *603/868–7800, 888/399–9777* ⊕ *www.threechimneysinn. com* ⤴ *23 rooms* ⭐ *Free breakfast.*

🎭 Nightlife

★ Stone Church

MUSIC CLUBS | This cool music club and pub in beautifully restored 1835 former Methodist church on a hilly bluff in historic Newmarket presents first-rate rock, reggae, folk, jazz, and blues. ✉ *5 Granite St., Newmarket* ☎ *603/659–7700* ⊕ *www.stonechurchrocks.com.*

🏃 Activities

Wagon Hill Farm

HIKING/WALKING | **FAMILY** | At this 139-acre property across from Emery Farm, you can stroll along scenic trails from the farmhouse to the old farm wagon and through the woods to the picnic area overlooking the Oyster River. There's sledding and cross-country skiing in winter. ✉ *U.S. 4* ⊕ *www.ci.durham.nh.us.*

🛍️ Shopping

★ Emery Farm

FOOD/CANDY | **FAMILY** | In the same family since the 1660s, Emery Farm sells berries and produce in summer, pumpkins in fall, and Christmas trees in winter. The farm shop carries breads, pies, and local crafts, and a café serves sandwiches, ice cream, cider doughnuts, and other light fare. Enjoy pumpkin-patch hayrides in autumn and visit the petting barn May–October. ✉ *147 Piscataqua Rd.* ☎ *603/742–8495* ⊕ *www.emeryfarm.com.*

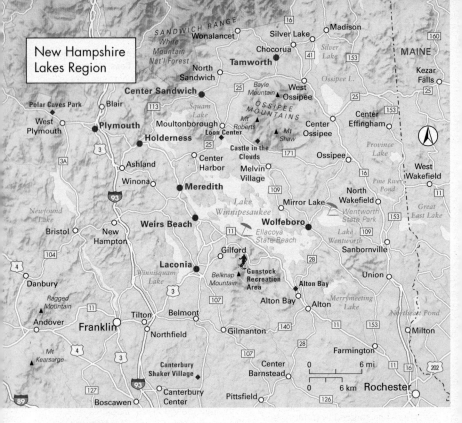

New Hampshire Lakes Region

Wolfeboro

40 miles northwest of Durham, 40 miles northeast of Concord.

Quietly upscale and decidedly preppy Wolfeboro has been a vacation getaway since Royal Governor John Wentworth built a home on the shore of Lake Winnipesaukee in 1768—hence its reputation as the country's oldest summer resort. Its waterfront downtown bursts with tony boutiques and eateries, while smaller Lake Wentworth—a few miles east—offers a quieter vibe. The century-old, white clapboard buildings of Brewster Academy prep school bracket the town's southern end.

GETTING HERE AND AROUND
Route 28 connects Wolfeboro with the rest of Lake Winnipesaukee. Be prepared for lots of traffic in the summer.

ESSENTIALS
VISITOR INFORMATION Wolfeboro Area Chamber of Commerce. ☎ 603/569–2200 ⊕ www.wolfeborochamber.com.

👁 Sights

Alton Bay
BODY OF WATER | FAMILY | Two mountain ridges frame picturesque Alton Bay, which is the name of both a narrow 4-mile inlet and village at the southern tip of Lake Winnipesaukee, near Wolfeboro. Cruise boats dock here, and small float planes buzz just over the bay, sometimes flying in formation. There's a boardwalk,

mini golf, a public beach, and a Victorian-style bandstand, and a few basic but fun short-order eateries near the waterfront, such as Pop's Clam Shell and Stillwells Ice Cream. ✉ *Rte. 11 at Rte. 28A, Alton Bay.*

★ New Hampshire Boat Museum

MUSEUM | FAMILY | Set in a 1950s quonset hut–style former dance hall near Lake Wentworth, this small but fascinating museum and boat-building center celebrates New Hampshire's maritime legacy with displays of vintage wooden boats, models, antique engines, racing photography, trophies, and vintage marina signs. You can also attend workshops on boat building and restoration, take sailing lessons, and go on 45-minute narrated rides on Lake Winnipesaukee in a reproduction 1928 triple-cockpit HackerCraft. ✉ *399 Center St.* ☎ *603/569–4554* 🌐 *www.nhbm.org* 🎟 *$9, boat tours $25* 🕒 *Closed mid-Oct.–late May.*

Wright Museum

MILITARY SITE | Uniforms, vehicles, and other artifacts at this museum illustrate the contributions of those on the home front to the U.S. World War II effort. ✉ *77 Center St.* ☎ *603/569–1212* 🌐 *www.wrightmuseum.org* 🎟 *$12* 🕒 *Closed Nov.–Apr.*

Beaches

Wentworth State Park

BEACH—SIGHT | FAMILY | Away from the hustle and bustle of Wolfeboro on pretty little Lake Wentworth, this simple park features a quiet beach with good fishing, picnic tables and grills, and ballfields. **Amenities:** parking (no fee); showers; toilets. **Best for:** swimming; walking. ✉ *297 Governor Wentworth Hwy.* ☎ *603/569–3699* 🌐 *www.nhstateparks.org* 🎟 *$4.*

Restaurants

East of Suez

$$ | MODERN ASIAN | In a countrified lodge on the south side of town, this friendly restaurant serves creative Asian cuisine, with an emphasis on Philippine fare, such as *lumpia* (pork-and-shrimp spring rolls with a sweet-and-sour fruit sauce) and *pancit canton* (panfried egg noodles with sautéed shrimp and pork and Asian vegetables with a sweet oyster sauce). You can also sample Thai red curries, Japanese tempura, and Korean-style flank steak. **Known for:** BYOB policy; banana tempura with coconut ice cream; plenty of vegan options. [$] *Average main: $22* ✉ *775 S. Main St.* ☎ *603/569–1648* 🌐 *www.eastofsuez.com* 🕒 *Closed Mon. and early Sept.–late May. No lunch.*

Pavilion

$$$ | MODERN AMERICAN | Customers at the Pickering House hotel had become so enamored of the inn's occasional dinners and other food events that the owners decided in 2020 to open a full-time restaurant in the Victorian house next door. Serving creative American fare sourced locally and seasonally as much as possible, the kitchen serves an oft-changing menu that might feature herb-roasted pork tenderloin with garden pepper vinaigrette, followed by sheep's milk yogurt panna cotta with preserved Italian prune plums and brown-butter almond crumble. **Known for:** elegant early 19th-century building; exceptional wine list; creative seasonal fruit desserts. [$] *Average main: $29* ✉ *126 S. Main St.* ☎ *603/569–6948* 🌐 *www.pavilionwolfeboro.com* 🕒 *No lunch.*

With 240 miles of shoreline, Lake Winnipesaukee has something for everyone.

Hotels

Lake Wentworth Inn

$ | **HOTEL** | New owners completely renovated this old motorlodge a five-minute walk from Lake Wentworth and Albee Beach, brightening up the pet-friendly rooms with an inviting midcentury cottage look and adding such family-friendly features as a game room and guest library. **Pros:** pool, game rooms, and library; short walk to beach; clean and very affordable. **Cons:** no breakfast; not directly on the water; a short drive from downtown. [$] *Rooms from: $144* ✉ *427 Center St.* ☎ *603/569–1700* 🌐 *www.lakewentworthinn.com* 🛏 *43 rooms* 🍴 *No meals.*

★ Pickering House

$$$$ | **B&B/INN** | Following an extensive two-year renovation by amiable innkeepers Peter and Patty Cook, this striking yellow 1813 Federal mansion now ranks among New Hampshire's most luxurious small inns. **Pros:** ultracushy rooms; the adjacent restaurant, Pavilion, is superb; in-town location. **Cons:** on busy street; among the highest rates in the region; not suitable for children. [$] *Rooms from: $430* ✉ *116 S. Main St.* ☎ *603/569–6948* 🌐 *www.pickeringhousewolfeboro.com* 🛏 *10 rooms* 🍴 *Free breakfast.*

Nightlife

Lone Wolfe Brewing

BREWPUBS/BEER GARDENS | Sample raspberry sours and the heady Dipp'ah Double IPA in the cheerful taproom of this downtown brewhouse that also serves tasty pub fare and presents live music many weekends inside or in the outdoor beer garden. ✉ *36 Mill St.* ☎ *603/515–1099* 🌐 *www.thelonewolfe.com.*

Activities

HIKING

Abenaki Tower

HIKING/WALKING | **FAMILY** | A quarter-mile hike to this 100-foot post-and-beam tower north of town, followed by a climb to the top, rewards you with views of Lake Winnipesaukee and the Ossipee mountain range. It's particularly photogenic at sunset. ⊠ *Rte. 109, Tuftonboro.*

Blue Job Mountain
HIKING/WALKING | A wildflower-strewn 3.3-mile loop trail reaches the summit of Blue Job Mountain, 25 miles south of Wolfeboro, where a 1913 fire tower provides a panoramic view of the Atlantic Ocean, White Mountains, and even Boston on a clear day. ⊠ *First Crown Point Rd., Strafford.*

★ Mt. Major
HIKING/WALKING | About 5 miles north of Alton Bay, a rugged 3-mile trail up a series of granite cliffs leads to this dramatic summit. At the top you'll find a four-sided stone shelter built in 1925, but the real reward is the spectacular view of Lake Winnipesaukee. ⊠ *Rte. 11, Alton Bay.*

WATER SPORTS
Dive Winnipesaukee Corp
WATER SPORTS | This operation runs charters out to wrecks—including the *The Lady,* a 125-foot-long cruise ship that sank in 30 feet of water in 1895—and also rents boats and gear. ⊠ *Wolfeboro Bay, 4 N. Main St.* ☎ *603/569–8080* ⊕ *www.divewinnipesaukee.com.*

🛍 Shopping

Black's Paper Store
GIFTS/SOUVENIRS | Browse regionally made soaps, chocolates, maple products, pottery, candles, lotions, potions, yarns, toys, and gifts at this vast old-fashioned emporium that dates back to the 1860s. ⊠ *8 S. Main St.* ☎ *603/569–4444* ⊕ *www.blacksgiftsnh.com.*

The Country Bookseller
BOOKS/STATIONERY | FAMILY | You'll find an excellent regional-history section and plenty of children's titles at this independent bookstore, where you can do a little reading in the small café. ⊠ *23A N. Main St.* ☎ *603/569–6030* ⊕ *www.thecountrybookseller.com.*

Yum Yum Shop
FOOD/CANDY | Picking up freshly baked breads, pastries, cookies, ice cream, and other sweets here has been a tradition since 1948. ⊠ *16 N. Main St.* ☎ *603/569–1919* ⊕ *www.myyumyumshop.com.*

Laconia and Weirs Beach

25 miles west of Wolfeboro, 27 miles north of Concord.

The arrival of the railroad in 1848 turned the sleepy hamlet of Laconia into the Lakes Region's chief manufacturing hub—downtown's 1823 Belknap Mill still stands as a monument to this legacy. At the north end of town, Weirs Beach is a hub of summertime arcade activity, with souvenir shops, fireworks, the Bank of NH outdoor concert pavilion, and hordes of kids. Cruise boats also depart from here, and the refurbished Winnipesaukee Pier has family-oriented restaurants and other amusements. In June, bikers from around the world arrive for Laconia Motorcycle Week.

GETTING HERE AND AROUND
Laconia offers easy access from Interstate 93 in Tilton, where you'll find a clutch of outlet shops, to both Winnisquam and Winnipesaukee lakes, via U.S. 3 or Route 11.

👁 Sights

★ Canterbury Shaker Village
FARM/RANCH | FAMILY | Established in 1792, this village 15 miles south of Laconia flourished in the 1800s and practiced equality of the sexes and races, common ownership, celibacy, and pacifism. The last member of the religious community passed away in 1992. Shakers invented such household items as the clothespin and the flat broom and were known for the simplicity and integrity of their designs. Engaging guided tours—you can also explore on your own—pass through some of the 694-acre property's more than 25 restored buildings, many of them

View simple yet functional furniture, architecture, and crafts at Canterbury Shaker Village.

with original furnishings. Crafts demonstrations take place daily. The café offers light lunch fare and sells seasonal vegetables and maple syrup. An excellent shop sells handcrafted wares. ✉ *288 Shaker Rd., Canterbury* ☎ *603/783–9511* ⊕ *www.shakers.org* 💲 *$20* ◷ *Closed weekdays in Nov. and in early Dec.–early May.*

Funspot
AMUSEMENT PARK/WATER PARK | FAMILY |
The mothership of Lake Winnipesaukee's family-oriented amusement parks, Funspot's more than 500 video games make it the world's largest arcade—there's even an arcade museum. You can also work your way through an indoor minigolf course and 20 lanes of bowling. Rates vary depending on the activity. ✉ *579 Endicott St. N, Weirs Beach* ☎ *603/366–4377* ⊕ *www.funspotnh.com.*

★ M/S *Mount Washington*
BODY OF WATER | FAMILY | The 230-foot M/S *Mount Washington* offers 2½-hour scenic cruises of Lake Winnipesaukee, departing Weirs Beach with stops at Wolfeboro, Alton Bay, Center Harbor, and

Meredith depending on the day. Sunset cruises include live music and a buffet dinner. The same company operates the *Sophie C.* ($32), which has been the area's floating post office for more than a century. The boat departs from Weirs Beach with mail and passengers, passing through parts of the lake not accessible to larger ships. The M/V *Doris E.* ($22) has one-hour scenic cruises into Meredith Bay and nearby islands throughout the summer. ✉ *211 Lakeside Ave., Weirs Beach* ☎ *603/366–5531* ⊕ *www.cruisenh.com* 💲 *From $35* ◷ *Closed mid-Oct.–mid-May.*

Winnipesaukee Scenic Railroad
LOCAL INTEREST | FAMILY | You can board this scenic railroad's restored cars at Weirs Beach or Meredith for one- or two-hour rides along the shoreline. Special excursions include fall foliage and the Santa train. ✉ *211 Lakeside Ave., Weirs Beach* ☎ *603/745–2135* ⊕ *www.hoborr.com* 💲 *From $20.*

Beaches

Ellacoya State Park

BEACH—SIGHT | FAMILY | Families enjoy this secluded 600-foot sandy beach and park on the southwestern shore of Lake Winnipesaukee. Ellacoya, with views of the Sandwich and Ossipee mountains, has a shallow beach that's safe for small children, sheltered picnic tables, and a small campground. **Amenities:** parking (fee); toilets. **Best for:** solitude; swimming. ✉ *266 Scenic Rd., Gilford* ☎ *603/293–7821* 🌐 *www.nhstateparks.org* 🎫 *$5 weekends late May–early Sept.*

Restaurants

Local Eatery

$$$ | **MODERN AMERICAN** | Proof that impressive dining in the Lakes Region isn't always near the water, this elegant restaurant is set beneath the soaring ceiling of downtown Laconia's historic train depot. Favoring local ingredients, the kitchen turns out inventive renditions of classic American dishes, like scallops and grits with a sweet corn butter sauce, and coffee-rubbed pork tenderloin. **Known for:** Maryland-style crab cakes with remoulade; attractive patio; warm and "gooey" chocolate cobbler. [$] *Average main: $27* ✉ *21 Veterans Sq.* ☎ *603/527–8007* 🌐 *www.laconialocaleatery.com* 🕒 *Closed Mon. No lunch.*

Hotels

★ Lake House at Ferry Point

$$$ | **B&B/INN** | This gracious red Victorian farmhouse, built as a summer getaway for the Pillsbury family of baking fame, has a peaceful setting on Lake Winnisquam. **Pros:** hearty full breakfast included; free use of kayaks; private dock and a small beach. **Cons:** not within walking distance of dining or shopping; may be a little quiet for some families; two-night minimum many weekends. [$] *Rooms from: $210* ✉ *100 Lower Bay Rd., Sanbornton* ☎ *603/637–1758* 🌐 *new-hampshire-inn.com* 🛏 *9 rooms* 🍴 *Free breakfast.*

Lake Opechee Inn & Spa

$$$ | **HOTEL** | Slightly removed from, but within a short drive of, the crowds of Weirs Beach, this boutique spa hotel set in a converted mill is a great place to chill out, enjoy a shiatsu massage or cranberry facial, and savor dinner and cocktails on a patio overlooking the lake. **Pros:** views of Lake Opechee; appealing spa and restaurant; many rooms have balconies, gas fireplaces, and jetted tubs. **Cons:** indoor pool is small; in a busy part of Laconia; 10-minute drive to Winnipesaukee. [$] *Rooms from: $205* ✉ *62 Doris Day Ct.* ☎ *603/524–0111* 🌐 *www.opecheeinn.com* 🛏 *34 rooms* 🍴 *Free breakfast.*

Activities

SKIING

Gunstock Mountain Resort

BICYCLING | FAMILY | This ski resort with a 2,267-foot summit and ample snowmaking capacity offers plenty of beginner terrain along with snow-tubing and a 22-acre terrain park. Nearly half of the trails offer night skiing, and you'll find 13 miles of cross-country and snowshoeing runs. In summer the Adventure Park offers a fantastic zipline system—the longest run at 3,981 feet—an aerial obstacle course, a 4,100-foot mountainside roller coaster (also open in winter), and scenic chairlift rides that access great hiking (the Ridge Trail is especially scenic). There's also mountain biking, a wetlands boardwalk, e-bike tours, kayak rentals, and a stocked fishing pond. **Facilities:** 53 trails; 227 acres; 1,340-foot vertical drop; 6 lifts. ✉ *719 Cherry Valley Rd., Gilford* ☎ *603/293–4341* 🌐 *www.gunstock.com* 🎫 *Lift ticket: $96.*

What's your vessel of choice for exploring New Hampshire's Lakes Region: kayak, canoe, powerboat, or sailboat?

Meredith

11 miles north of Laconia.

For many years a workaday mill town with relatively little tourism appeal, Meredith has become a popular summer getaway thanks largely to the transformation in recent years of several historic downtown buildings into Mill Falls, now a cluster of hotels, restaurants, and shops overlooking Lake Winnipesaukee. Take a stroll down Main Street, which is dotted with intimate cafés, boutiques, and antiques stores, and along the lakefront, where you'll find a bustling marina, sculpture walk, and some lively dockside restaurants.

GETTING HERE AND AROUND

You can reach Meredith from Interstate 93 via Route 104, or from points south on U.S. 3 (beware the heavy weekend traffic). In town, it's easy to get around on foot.

ESSENTIALS

VISITOR INFORMATION Meredith Area Chamber of Commerce. ☎ *877/279–6121, 603/279–6121* ⊕ *www.mereditharea-chamber.com.*

Sights

Hermit Woods Winery

WINERY/DISTILLERY | Stop by this contemporary downtown winery to sample the light and fruity wines and hard ciders, made with local blueberries, apples, cranberries, and honeys as well as imported grapes. Tours, which include a barrel tasting, are available, and you can order cheese, charcuterie, and other treats from the deli to enjoy while sipping outside on the deck. ⊠ *72 Main St.* ☎ *603/253–7968* ⊕ *www.hermitwoods.com.*

Meredith Sculpture Walk

PUBLIC ART | FAMILY | Throughout town, especially in parks beside the lake and at the gardens at Mill Falls Marketplace, you'll see colorful contemporary artworks. They're part of the Annual

Meredith Sculpture walk, a year-round juried event featuring 32 distinctive pieces by renowned sculptors. Each June, a new collection of sculptures is installed. For a detailed look, take a free guided tour, offered at 10 am on Wednesday and Saturday, July and August. ✉ *Meredith* 🌐 *www.meredithsculpturewalk.org.*

🍴 Restaurants

Canoe
$$ | MODERN AMERICAN | Just up the road in Center Harbor, this boathouse-inspired bistro sits high above Lake Winnipesaukee and has seating in both a quieter dining room and a convivial bar with an open kitchen. It's known for seafood, including wood-fired, bacon-wrapped scallops and a creamy, entrée-size haddock chowder topped with herbs and crushed Ritz Crackers. **Known for:** fun people-watching at the bar; great wine and beer selection; salted-caramel brownie sundaes. [$] *Average main: $24* ✉ *232 Whittier Hwy., Center Harbor* ☎ *603/253–4762* 🌐 *www.magicfoodsrestaurantgroup.com* ⏲ *No lunch Mon.–Thurs.*

Lakehouse Grille
$$$ | AMERICAN | With big windows overlooking the lake and timber posts and ceiling beams, this popular restaurant inside the Church Landing at Mill Falls hotel captures the rustic ambience of an old-fashioned camp dining room. Feast on classic American favorites with interesting twists, such as eggs Benedict topped with Maine lobster in the morning, and char-grilled steaks, chops, and seafood in the evening. **Known for:** blueberry pie with lemon ice cream; water views; Sunday jazz brunch. [$] *Average main: $27* ✉ *Church Landing, 281 Daniel Webster Hwy.* ☎ *603/279–5221* 🌐 *www.thecman.com.*

🛏 Hotels

Mill Falls at the Lake
$$$ | HOTEL | Choose from four lodgings at this rambling resort: relaxing Church Landing and Bay Point are both on the shore of Lake Winnipesaukee; convivial Mill Falls—with a pool—and Chase House are across the street, next to a 19th-century mill that houses shops and restaurants. **Pros:** activity center with boat rentals and lake cruises; many dining options; spa with heated indoor-outdoor pool. **Cons:** rooms with water views are expensive; some properties aren't directly on the lake; somewhat impersonal, corporate feel. [$] *Rooms from: $234* ✉ *312 Daniel Webster Hwy.* ☎ *603/279–7006, 844/745–2931* 🌐 *www.millfalls.com* 🛏 *188 rooms* 🍴 *No meals.*

🍸 Nightlife

Twin Barns Brewing
BREWPUBS/BEER GARDENS | Serving a roster of well-crafted ales along with tasty comfort food (flatbread pizzas, wings), this beer-centric compound occupies a handsome 1850s restored barn with a large tented beer garden. ✉ *194 Daniel Webster Hwy.* ☎ *603/279–0876* 🌐 *www.twinbarnsbrewing.com.*

🎟 Performing Arts

Interlakes Summer Theatre
THEATER | During its 10-week season of summer stock, this striking 420-seat theater presents classic Broadway musicals like *42nd Street, Evita,* and *West Side Story.* ✉ *1 Laker La.* ☎ *603/707–6035* 🌐 *www.interlakestheatre.com.*

★ **Winnipesaukee Playhouse**
THEATER | Since this critically lauded theater opened in a rustic yet state-of-the-art red-barn-style venue in 2013, it's become one of the top performing arts centers in the region, presenting well-known Broadway shows and original dramas and

comedies year-round. ✉ *33 Footlight Circle* ☎ *603/279–0333* ⊕ *www.winnipesaukeeplayhouse.org.*

Activities

BOATING

Home to a popular marina, Meredith is also near the quaint village of Center Harbor, another boating hub that's in the middle of three bays at the north end of Lake Winnipesaukee.

★ EKAL

BOATING | At the lakefront activity center at Mill Falls, you can rent standup paddleboards, kayaks, canoes, aqua cycles, and bicycles, and book excursions on a restored 1931 Chris Craft runabout. ✉ *281 Daniel Webster Hwy. (U.S. 3)* ☎ *603/677–8646* ⊕ *www.ekalactivitycenter.com.*

GOLF

Waukewan Golf Club

GOLF | This beautiful, well-groomed course with undulating fairways and several challenging blind shots has been a local favorite since the late '50s. ✉ *166 Waukewan Rd., Center Harbor* ☎ *603/279–6661* ⊕ *www.waukewangolfclub.com* ✎ *$30* ⚑ *18 holes, 5828 yards, par 71.*

🛍 Shopping

Annalee Dolls

TOYS | **FAMILY** | Everyone from young kids to ardent collectors makes the pilgrimage to the showroom of this internationally renowned shop that's been hand-crafting whimsical dolls since 1934. Annalee's expressive mice are a top draw, but holiday figurines are also highly popular. ✉ *339 Daniel Webster Hwy.* ☎ *800/433–6557* ⊕ *www.annalee.com.*

Home Comfort

HOUSEHOLD ITEMS/FURNITURE | This huge showroom is filled with designer furnishings, antiques, and accessories with lake-house flair. ✉ *38 Plymouth St., Center Harbor* ☎ *603/253–6660* ⊕ *www.homecomfortnh.com.*

★ League of New Hampshire Craftsmen

CRAFTS | This eclectic gallery offers wares by more than 250 artisans working in everything from stained glass and ceramics to wrought iron and mixed media. Prices are surprisingly reasonable for many items, and there are additional branches in Center Sandwich, Concord, Littleton, North Conway, and few other towns. ✉ *279 Daniel Webster Hwy.* ☎ *603/279–7920* ⊕ *www.meredith.nhcrafts.org.*

Plymouth

7 miles northwest of Holderness, 22 miles south of North Woodstock.

Home to Plymouth State College, whose small but attractive campus clings to a steep hill looming over an attractive, bustling downtown, Plymouth acts as a bridge between White Mountains and the Lakes Region; it's especially convenient for visiting 4,000-acre Newfound Lake, one of the state's deepest and purest bodies of water, as well as Squam Lake. From town you can also reach some great hiking to the west, including 3,121-foot Mt. Cardigan, in nearby Alexandria, and Big and Little Sugarloaf peaks, the trailhead for which is reached along West Shore Road, near the entrance to Wellington State Park.

GETTING HERE AND AROUND

Plymouth is just off Interstate 93.

👁 Sights

Polar Caves Park

CAVE | **FAMILY** | From the attractive log cabin–style main lodge, an easy trail leads to nine granite caves that formed some 50,000 years ago, during the last ice age. This family-friendly attraction begun in 1922 also contains a small petting zoo with a herd of adorable fallow deer. ✉ *705 Rte. 25, Rumney* ☎ *603/536–1888* ⊕ *www.polarcaves.com* ✎ *$25* ⏱ *Closed mid-Oct.–mid-May.*

Restaurants

★ Benton's Sugar Shack

$ | AMERICAN | FAMILY | A legit contender in New Hampshire's fierce battle for the best pancake house, this rustic timber-frame roadhouse between Plymouth and North Woodstock is run by a family who've been producing maple syrup for five generations. Open only on weekends, Benton's serves stacks of pancakes in several flavors, including strawberry shortcake, Mounds Bar, and Grandma's apple cinnamon. **Known for:** sides of maple kielbasa and baked beans; "design your own" pancakes with custom fillings; raspberry-stuffed French toast. $ *Average main: $9* ⊠ *2010 Rte. 175, Thornton* ☎ *603/726–3867* ⊕ *www.bentonssugarshack.com* ⊘ *Closed weekdays. No dinner.*

★ Little Red Schoolhouse

$$ | AMERICAN | FAMILY | Lobster roll aficionados flock to this funky converted schoolhouse with screened-in and outdoor seating high on a bluff above the Pemigewasset River. Start with a cup of lobster bisque or clam chowder before digging into a traditional (lightly dressed, with mayo) or hot-buttered lobster roll—both come on a warm, buttered brioche roll, best enjoyed with a side of garlic fries. **Known for:** pretty river and forest views; good craft beer selection; homemade ice-cream sandwiches. $ *Average main: $18* ⊠ *1994 Daniel Webster Hwy., Campton* ☎ *603/726–6142* ⊕ *www.littleredschoolhousenh.com* ⊘ *Closed mid-Oct.–mid-May.*

Six Burner Bistro

$$ | MODERN AMERICAN | In this charming red Victorian house on Plymouth's bustling Main Street, with some seats on the front veranda and others set in a warren of cozy rooms with art on the walls, this casually elegant spot offers tasty American and international fare. Consider panfried pork dumplings with sesame-ginger sauce, and the blackened grilled chicken with honeydew-melon salsa and tzatziki sauce.

Known for: sourcing from local farms; well-selected wine and beer list; creative salad options with myriad protein add-ons. $ *Average main: $23* ⊠ *13 S. Main St.* ☎ *603/536–9099* ⊕ *www.sixburnerbistro.com* ⊘ *Closed Sun. and Mon.*

Hotels

Common Man Inn & Spa

$ | HOTEL | This contemporary hotel with country lodge–inspired furnishings, just off I–93 a little north of downtown, contains warmly appointed rooms in a variety of configurations; some have whirlpool tubs and fireplaces, and a few have cozy sleeping lofts. **Pros:** pets are welcome; relaxing spa; convenient to White Mountains and Lakes Region. **Cons:** often booked up with weddings; small pool; 15-minute walk from downtown. $ *Rooms from: $139* ⊠ *231 Main St.* ☎ *603/536–2200, 866/843–2626* ⊕ *www.thecmaninnplymouth.com* ⌁ *38 rooms* ¦◎¦ *Free breakfast.*

Henry Whipple House

$ | B&B/INN | About 2 miles south of Newfound Lake in the quiet mill town of Bristol, this magnificent turreted Queen Anne house with such original details as bronze fireplaces, chandeliers, and stained-glass windows has five antiques-filled rooms, two with wood-burning fireplaces. **Pros:** elegantly furnished; great value; great breakfasts. **Cons:** books up quickly; two-night minimum in peak periods; not within walking distance of lake. $ *Rooms from: $145* ⊠ *75 Summer St., Bristol* ☎ *603/744–6157* ⊕ *www.thewhipplehouse.com* ⌁ *8 rooms* ¦◎¦ *Free breakfast.*

Performing Arts

★ Flying Monkey

CONCERTS | Set in downtown Plymouth's brightly restored 1920s movie house, this cinema and performing arts center presents dinner theater and other live comedy and music shows, plus retro movies. A balcony bar serves wine and beer. ✉ *39 Main St.* ☎ *603/536–2551* ⊕ *www.flying-monkeynh.com.*

🏃 Activities

★ Effortless Adventure

CAMPING—SPORTS-OUTDOORS | This trusty outfitter is a one-stop for planning camping or backpacking adventures in the White Mountains—they provide everything you need, including full one- to six-person tent and gear rental packages, and all the instruction you need, even if you're a novice camper, along with guidance on hikes, fly-fishing, yoga, and other activities. The staff can even book your campsite. ✉ *231 Main St.* ☎ *603/726–1702* ⊕ *www.effortlessadventure.com.*

★ Wellington State Park

BEACHES | **FAMILY** | At this picturesque 204-acre park on the west shore of glorious Newfound Lake, about 12 miles from Plymouth, you'll find the largest freshwater beach in the state park system. Enjoy the picnic and fishing areas, numerous hiking trails, and boat launch. **Amenities:** food and drink; parking (fee); toilets. **Best for:** swimming; walking. ✉ *617 W. Shore Rd., Bristol* ☎ *603/744–2197* ⊕ *www.nhstateparks.org* 🎫 *$5 mid-May–mid-Sept.*

Holderness

8 miles northwest of Meredith.

This peaceful village straddles two of the state's most scenic lakes, Squam and Little Squam, both of which have been spared from excessive development but do offer some memorable inns that are perfect for a tranquil getaway. *On Golden Pond,* starring Katharine Hepburn and Henry Fonda, was filmed on Squam, whose beauty attracts nature lovers.

GETTING HERE AND AROUND

Holderness is easy to reach from Interstate 93 and U.S. 3.

⊙ Sights

★ Squam Lakes Natural Science Center

BODY OF WATER | **FAMILY** | This 230-acre property includes a ¾-mile nature trail that passes by trailside exhibits of black bears, bobcats, otters, fishers, mountain lions, red foxes, and raptors. A pontoon boat cruise offers the best way to tour the waterfront—naturalists talk about native fauna, from bald eagles to loons; dinner and sunset options are available. Kids' programs teach about insects and wilderness survival skills. The center also operates nearby 1-acre Kirkwood Gardens and maintains three short hiking trails, all of which you can access for free. ✉ *23 Science Center Rd.* ☎ *603/968–7194* ⊕ *www.nhnature.org* 🎫 *Trail $15, lake cruise $27* ⊙ *Live-animal exhibits closed Nov.–Apr.*

🍴 Restaurants

Walter's Basin

$$ | **AMERICAN** | A former bowling alley in the heart of Holderness makes an unlikely but charming setting for meals overlooking Little Squam Lake—local boaters dock right beneath the dining room. Among the specialties on the seafood-intensive menu are shellfish paella, and sea scallops with a creamy bacon-corn-poblano succotash, while sandwiches and salads are among the lighter options. **Known for:** dockside setting; live music some summer evenings; fried whole-belly clams. ⓢ *Average main: $22* ✉ *859 U.S. 3* ☎ *603/968–4412* ⊕ *www.waltersbasin.com.*

🛏 Hotels

Cottage Place on Squam

$ | **RENTAL** | This sweet, old-fashioned compound of cottages and suites on Little Squam Lake is a terrific find—and value—for families, as nearly all units have partial or full kitchens, and many can comfortably sleep up to five guests (there's also a six-bedroom lodge that groups can rent entirely). **Pros:** reasonably priced;

lots of on-site activities, from kayaking to shuffleboard; well-curated shop has fun one-of-a-kind gifts. **Cons:** the retro ambience isn't at all fancy; family popularity might be a turnoff if seeking peace and quiet; no restaurant. [$] *Rooms from: $139* ✉ *1132 U.S. 3* ☎ *603/968–7116* 🌐 *www.cottageplaceonsquam.com* 🛏 *15 rooms* 🍴 *No meals.*

Glynn House

$ | **B&B/INN** | Squam Lake is just a short drive from this romantic inn that comprises a beautifully restored 1890s Queen Anne–style Victorian and, next door, a handsome 1920s carriage house. **Pros:** posh decor and room amenities; complimentary afternoon hors d'oeuvres; impressive multicourse breakfasts. **Cons:** not on the water; two-night minimum during some weekends; in a small, sleepy town. [$] *Rooms from: $159* ✉ *59 Highland St., Ashland* ☎ *603/968–3775* 🌐 *www.glynnhouse.com* 🛏 *12 rooms* 🍴 *Free Breakfast.*

★ Inn on Golden Pond

$$$ | **B&B/INN** | The hospitable innkeepers at this comfortable and informal bed-and-breakfast a short distance from Squam Lake make every possible effort to accommodate their guests—many of whom are repeat clients—from providing them with hiking trail maps to using rhubarb grown on property to make the jam served during the delicious country breakfasts. **Pros:** 50-acre property with woodland and lake views; comfortable indoor and outdoor common spaces; generous full breakfast. **Cons:** not directly on the lake; not especially fancy; can't accommodate pets. [$] *Rooms from: $235* ✉ *1080 U.S. 3* ☎ *603/968–7269* 🌐 *www.innongoldenpond.com* 🛏 *8 rooms* 🍴 *Free breakfast.*

Manor on Golden Pond

$$$ | **B&B/INN** | A name like this is a lot to live up to, but the Manor generally succeeds: it's one of the region's most atmospheric inns, situated on a slight rise overlooking Squam Lake, with 15 acres of lawns, towering pines, and hardwood trees, and a grand restaurant serving lavish modern European fare, and a small but well-outfitted spa. **Pros:** fireplaces and Jacuzzis in many rooms; gracious common spaces; afternoon high tea is served in the library. **Cons:** the top-tier suites are quite expensive; furnishings could stand a little refreshing; not suitable for younger kids. [$] *Rooms from: $234* ✉ *31 Manor Rd., off Shepard Hill Rd.* ☎ *603/968–3348, 800/545–2141* 🌐 *www.manorongoldenpond.com* 🛏 *24 suites* 🍴 *Free breakfast.*

Squam Lake Inn

$$$ | **B&B/INN** | Graceful Victorian furnishings fill this peaceful farmhouse inn a short stroll from Squam Lake, each of its 10 rooms richly outfitted with comfortable beds, organic toiletries, and soft bathrobes. **Pros:** secluded and serene; superb restaurant; sumptuous gourmet breakfasts. **Cons:** short walk from lake; open only seasonally; minimum-night stays during busy times. [$] *Rooms from: $249* ✉ *28 Shepard Hill Rd.* ☎ *603/968–4417, 800/839–6205* 🌐 *www.squamlakeinn.com* ⏲ *Closed late Oct.–May* 🛏 *10 rooms* 🍴 *Free breakfast.*

Activities

★ Squam Lakes Association

BOATING | **FAMILY** | You can rent kayaks, canoes, and standup paddleboards, reserve campsites, enroll kids in education programs, and learn about local wildlife watching, fishing, and hiking opportunities at this nonprofit organization that's been focused on lake conservation since it formed in 1904. ✉ *534 U.S. 3* ☎ *603/968–7336* 🌐 *www.squamlakes.org.*

West Rattlesnake Mountain

HIKING/WALKING | The nearly 500-foot elevation gain of this moderately strenuous but fairly short 2.3-mile loop trail to the top of West Rattlesnake Mountain will get your heart pounding, but the panoramic views over Squam Lake are a satisfying reward. ✉ *Rte. 113.*

Center Sandwich

19 miles northeast of Plymouth, by way of Holderness.

With Squam Lake to the west, Lake Winnipesaukee to the south, and the Sandwich Mountains to the north, Center Sandwich offers one of the prettiest settings in the Lakes Region. So appealing are the town and its views that John Greenleaf Whittier used the Bearcamp River as the inspiration for his poem "Sunset on the Bearcamp." The town attracts artisans—crafts shops abound among its clutch of charming 18th- and 19th-century buildings.

GETTING HERE AND AROUND

You reach this rural town from Holderness via Route 113 and Meredith—by way of Center Harbor and Moultonborough—by Routes 25 and 109.

Sights

★ Castle in the Clouds

CASTLE/PALACE | Looking like a fairy-tale castle, this grand 1914 mountaintop estate is anchored by an elaborate mansion with 16 rooms, 8 bathrooms, and doors made of lead. Owner Thomas Gustave Plant spent $7 million—the bulk of his fortune—on this project and died penniless in 1941. Tours include the mansion and the Castle Springs water facility on this high Ossipee Mountain Range property overlooking Lake Winnipesaukee. Hiking (and cross-country skiing in winter) and pony and horse rides are also offered, along with lakeview terrace jazz dinners many summer evenings at the Carriage House restaurant, which is also open for lunch when mansion tours are offered. ✉ *455 Old Mountain Rd., Moultonborough* ☎ *603/476–5900* 🌐 *www.castleintheclouds.org* 🎟 *$18* 🕒 *Closed late Oct.–mid-May.*

Loon Center

BODY OF WATER | FAMILY | Recognizable for its eerie calls and striking black-and-white coloring, the loon resides on many New Hampshire lakes but is threatened by the gradual loss of its habitat. Two trails wind through the 200-acre Loon Center, which has made great progress in helping to restore the state's loon population; vantage points on the Loon Nest Trail overlook the spot resident loons sometimes occupy in late spring and summer. ✉ *183 Lee's Mills Rd., Moultonborough* ☎ *603/476–5666* 🌐 *www.loon.org* 🎟 *Free* 🕒 *Closed Sun.–Wed. in winter.*

Restaurants

Corner House Inn

$$ | AMERICAN | In a converted barn adorned with paintings by local artists, this rustic tavern in an 1840s building in charming Center Sandwich village dishes up classic American fare. Salads made with local greens and a maple vinaigrette are a house specialty, but don't overlook the mac-and-cheese with house-made sauce and steak tips–and–lobster surf and turf. **Known for:** inviting art-filled dining room; tender steaks and prime rib; good list of reasonably priced wines. [$] *Average main: $22* ✉ *22 Main St.* ☎ *603/476–3060* 🌐 *www.cornerhouserestaurantandbar.com* 🕒 *Closed Tues. No lunch.*

Coffee and Quick Bites

Sandwich Creamery

$ | CAFÉ | FAMILY | Part of the fun of visiting this rural artisan dairy in the foothills of the White Mountains, with a self-serve shop that dispenses farmstead-made cheddar cheese and ice cream, is the scenic drive up from Center Sandwich or Tamworth. You'll find ice cream and ice-cream sandwiches in about two-dozen flavors, many using local berries and produce, plus goods from other nearby purveyors, such as delicious breads from Sunnyfield Brick Oven Bakery. **Known for:** PB&J ice cream sandwiches; artisan cheddar cheeses; serene picnic area with views of the farm. $ *Average main: $4* ⊠ *130 Hannah Rd.* ☎ *603/284–6675.*

🛍 Shopping

Old Country Store and Museum

LOCAL SPECIALTIES | A quirky spot to pick up maple syrup, aged cheeses, jams, molasses, penny candy, and other treats, this rambling shop dates to 1781 and also contains antique farm and forging equipment and other artifacts. ⊠ *1011 Whittier Hwy., Moultonborough* ☎ *603/476–5750* ⊕ *www.nhcountrystore.com.*

🏃 Activities

BOATING
Wild Meadow Canoes & Kayaks

BOATING | Canoes and kayaks at this shop at the north tip of Lake Winnipesaukee, near the Center Harbor town line. ⊠ *6 Whittier Hwy., Moultonborough* ☎ *603/253–7536* ⊕ *www.wildmeadowcanoes.com.*

HIKING
Red Hill

HIKING/WALKING | **FAMILY** | This 2,030-foot mountain really does turn red in autumn. At the top of the moderately steep 1.7-mile Fire Tower Trail, you can climb a fire tower for 360-degree views of Lake Winnipesaukee and Squam Lake, as well as the White Mountains beyond. To make a loop, return via the Cabin Trail. At the parking area, a small snack bar (open mostly on weekends) dispenses organic coffee, ice cream, and other treats. ⊠ *Red Hill Rd., 2 miles west of Rte. 25, Moultonborough.*

Tamworth

13 miles east of Center Sandwich.

President Grover Cleveland summered in what remains a place of almost unreal quaintness: Tamworth is equally photogenic in verdant summer, during the fall foliage season, or under a blanket of winter snow. Cleveland's son, Francis, returned and founded the acclaimed Barnstormers Theatre in 1931. One of America's first summer theaters, it continues to this day. Tamworth has a clutch of villages within its borders, and six historic churches. In the hamlet of Chocorua, the view through the birches of Chocorua Lake has been so often photographed that you may experience déjà vu. Rising above the lake is Mt. Chocorua (3,490 feet), which has many good hiking trails.

GETTING HERE AND AROUND

Tamworth's main village, at the junction of Routes 113 and 113A, is tiny and can be strolled.

👁 Sights

Remick Country Doctor Museum and Farm

FARM/RANCH | **FAMILY** | For 99 years (1894–1993) Dr. Edwin Crafts Remick and his father provided medical services to the Tamworth area and operated a family farm. These two houses now comprise a farm museum, with the second floor of the house kept as it was when Remick passed away, providing a glimpse into the life of a country doctor. The still-working farm features special activities, such as maple-syrup making, and has hiking trails and picnicking areas. ⊠ *58 Cleveland Hill Rd.* ☎ *603/323–7591* ⊕ *www.remickmuseum.org* 🖭 *Pay as you wish* ⊗ *Closed Sun. and early Dec.–early May.*

★ Tamworth Distilling & Mercantile

WINERY/DISTILLERY | Using a 250-gallon copper still constructed in Kentucky, this artisanal distillery set in a stately barn just a short stroll from famed Barnstormers

Theatre produces exceptional craft spirits, including Chocorua Straight Rye, Von Humboldt's Turmeric Cordial, Tamworth Garden Spruce Gin, and several flavorful cordials. If you're lucky, your stop will include a chance to sample Eau de Musc, a limited-release whiskey infused with an oil extracted from the castor glands of beavers. ⊠ *15 Cleveland Hill Rd.* ☎ *603/323–7196* ⊕ *www.tamworth-distilling.com* ⊘ *Closed Mon.–Wed.*

🍴 Restaurants

★ Art in the Age Cafe

$ | CAFÉ | With its timber-beam ceiling and hardwood floors, this folksy-looking 1826 mercantile–cum–café run by nearby Tamworth Distilling stocks carefully curated artisanal foods, craft beers, and hip gifts and accessories. The menu offers delicious quinoa bowls, cage-free-egg-and–cheddar breakfast croissants, and roast pork loin sandwiches with sesame kraut and white miso mayo. **Known for:** gourmet specialty foods; a convivial mix of locals and tourists; impressive beer, wine, coffee, and tea selection. $ *Average main: $9* ⊠ *85 Main St.* ☎ *603/323–5120* ⊕ *www.tamworthlyceum.com* ⊘ *No dinner.*

Jake's Seafood and Grill

$$ | SEAFOOD | Oars and other nautical trappings adorn the wood-panel walls at this classic New England seafood restaurant about 8 miles southeast of Tamworth. The kitchen serves fresh fish and shellfish, notably lobster pie, fried clams, and seafood casserole, but you'll also find steak, ribs, and chicken dishes. **Known for:** Thursday-night fish fries; nostalgic, old-school decor; lobster bakes to go. $ *Average main: $19* ⊠ *2055 White Mountain Hwy., West Ossipee* ☎ *603/539–2805* ⊕ *www.jakesseafood-co.com.*

🎭 Performing Arts

★ Barnstormers Theatre

THEATER | Founded in 1931, this highly respected theater company presents dramas and comedies June–August. ⊠ *104 Main St.* ☎ *603/323–8500* ⊕ *www. barnstormerstheatre.org.*

🏃 Activities

White Lake State Park

PARK—SPORTS-OUTDOORS | The 72-acre stand of native pitch pine here is a National Natural Landmark. The park has a picnic area and a sandy beach, trails you can hike, trout you can fish for, and canoes you can rent. ⊠ *94 State Park Rd.* ☎ *603/323–7350* ⊕ *www.nhstateparks. org* ⊠ *$5 mid-May–early Sept.*

North Conway

20 miles north of Tamworth, 42 miles east North Woodstock, 62 miles northwest of Portland, Maine.

Before the arrival of the popular Settlers Green outlet stores, this town drew visitors for its inspiring scenery, ski resorts, and access to White Mountain National Forest. Today, however, the feeling of natural splendor is gone. Shopping is the big sport, and businesses line Route 16 for several miles. You'll get a close look at them as traffic often slows to a crawl. It's a bit of a food desert, too, with plenty of options but few of them notable.

GETTING HERE AND AROUND

Route 16 bisects town but can be clogged with traffic. Take the scenic West Side Road from Conway to Intervale, or even on Bartlett is you're headed farther north, to circumvent the traffic and take in splendid views.

ESSENTIALS

VISITOR INFORMATION Mt. Washington Valley Chamber of Commerce. ☎ *603/356–5701* ⊕ *www.mtwashingtonvalley.org.*

Sights

Conway Scenic Railroad

SCENIC DRIVE | FAMILY | Departing from historic North Conway Station, the railroad operates various trips aboard vintage trains. The Notch Train to Crawford Depot or to Fabyan Station travels through rugged territory yielding wonderful views. Seating options include lunch or a seat in the Upper Dome car, which affords the most spectacular views. The Valley Train overlooks Mt. Washington during a 55-minute round-trip journey to Conway or a 1¾-hour excursion to Bartlett. The 1874 station displays lanterns, old tickets and timetables, and other artifacts. Reserve early during foliage season. ✉ *38 Norcross Cir.* ☎ *603/356–5251, 800/232–5251* 🌐 *www.conwayscenic.com* 🎫 *From $19* 🕒 *Closed Dec.–Mar.*

Echo Lake State Park

NATIONAL/STATE PARK | FAMILY | You don't have to be a rock climber to enjoy the views from the 700-foot White Horse and Cathedral ledges, which you can reach via a 1.7-mile road. From the top, you'll see the entire valley, including Echo Lake, which offers fishing, swimming, boating, and, on quiet days, an excellent opportunity to shout for echoes. ✉ *68 Echo Lake Rd., Conway* ☎ *603/356–2672* 🌐 *www.nhstateparks.org* 🎫 *$4 mid-May–mid-Oct.*

Weather Discovery Center

INFO CENTER | FAMILY | Ever wonder what it's like to be in a cabin at the summit of Mt. Washington while 200 mph winds shake the rafters? Find out at this fun, interactive museum, where you can experience simulations of different weather conditions and learn about how weather affects our lives. There's a twice-daily video link (one late morning and one early afternoon) with scientists atop Mt. Washington Observatory. ✉ *2779 Main St.* ☎ *603/356–2137* 🌐 *www.mountwashington.org* 🎫 *$2.*

Restaurants

Muddy Moose

$ | AMERICAN | FAMILY | This playfully themed lodge-style restaurant buzzes with the sound of happy kids, but everyone seems to enjoy the rustic trappings, which include a huge stone fireplace, moose-antler chandeliers, and mounted animals. The comfort food here is reliably good, from barbecue rack of ribs to peppercorn-mushroom burgers, and there's a good selection of local beers. **Known for:** half-pound burgers with plenty of toppings; extensive kids offerings; Paradise four-layer chocolate cake. [$] *Average main: $17* ✉ *2344 White Mountain Hwy.* ☎ *603/356–7696* 🌐 *www.muddymoose.com.*

Table + Tonic Farm Bistro

$$ | MODERN AMERICAN | The green-thumb-savvy proprietors of the popular and adjacent Local Grocer natural foods market and café operate this hip farm-to-table bistro and bar. It features seasonal fare produced with organic produce and baked goods and boldly flavored cocktails fashioned from house-made shrubs, bitters, syrups, and cordials. **Known for:** healthy breakfast and lunch items in adjacent café and market; creative craft cocktails; attractive side patio overlooking a leafy garden. [$] *Average main: $22* ✉ *3358 White Mountain Hwy.* ☎ *603/356–6068* 🌐 *www.tableandtonic.com* 🕒 *Closed Tues. and Wed. No lunch.*

Hotels

The Buttonwood Inn

$$ | B&B/INN | A tranquil oasis in a busy resort area, the Buttonwood sits on Mt. Surprise, 2 miles northeast of North Conway village—close enough to access area dining and shopping, but far away from noise and crowds of downtown. **Pros:** comfy bedding; year-round outdoor hot tub and fire pit; 6 acres of peaceful grounds. **Cons:** too secluded for some; swimming pool is seasonal;

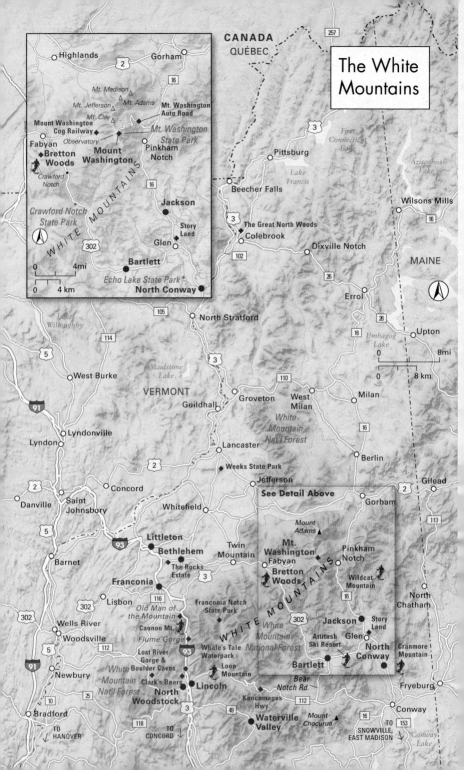

The White Mountains

CANADA
QUÉBEC

MAINE

VERMONT

See Detail Above

WHITE MOUNTAINS

Detail map labels
Highlands
Gorham
Mt. Madison
Mt. Jefferson
Mt. Adams
Mt. Clay
Mt. Washington Auto Road
Mount Washington Cog Railway
Observatory
Fabyan
Bretton Woods
Mount Washington
Mt. Washington State Park
Pinkham Notch
Crawford Notch
Crawford Notch State Park
Jackson
Story Land
Glen
Bartlett
Echo Lake State Park
North Conway

0 4mi
0 4 km

Main map labels
Pittsburg
Lake Francis
First Connecticut Lake
Aziscohos Lake
Beecher Falls
Wilsons Mills
The Great North Woods
Colebrook
Dixville Notch
Errol
Upton
Umbagog Lake
North Stratford
West Milan
Milan
Groveton
Guildhall
West Burke
Maidstone Lake
Lake Willoughby
Lyndonville
Lyndon
Lancaster
Weeks State Park
Jefferson
Berlin
Whitefield
Gorham
Concord
Danville
Saint Johnsbury
Gilead
Littleton
Bethlehem
Twin Mountain
Mount Adams
Mt. Washington
Fabyan
Bretton Woods
Pinkham Notch
Wildcat Mountain
The Rocks Estate
Franconia
Barnet
Lisbon
Old Man of the Mountain
Franconia Notch State Park
White Mountain National Forest
Jackson
Story Land
Glen
North Chatham
Wells River
Woodsville
Cannon Mt.
Flume Gorge
Whale's Tale Waterpark
Attitash Ski Resort
Bartlett
North Conway
Cranmore Mountain
Lost River Gorge & Boulder Caves
Loon Mountain
Clark's Bears
White Mountain Nat'l Forest
Newbury
North Woodstock
Lincoln
Bear Notch Rd.
Fryeburg
Bradford
Kancamagus Hwy.
Waterville Valley
Mount Chocorua
Conway
Conway Lake
TO HANOVER
TO CONCORD
TO SNOWVILLE EAST MADISON

0 8mi
0 8 km

some rooms have private baths down the hall. $ *Rooms from: $199* ✉ *64 Mt. Surprise Rd.* ☎ *603/356–2625* ⊕ *www.buttonwoodinn.com* ⇨ *10 rooms* ⦿ *Free breakfast.*

Darby Field Inn
$$ | B&B/INN | Most rooms in this unpretentious 1826 farmhouse near the boundary of White Mountain National Forest—just off the eastern end of the famously picturesque Kancamagus Highway—have stunning views, and several also have fireplaces. **Pros:** romantic setting; away-from-it-all feel; memorable full country breakfast included. **Cons:** not suitable for kids; a drive to the nearest town; sometimes booked with weddings. $ *Rooms from: $165* ✉ *185 Chase Hill, Albany* ☎ *603/447–2181* ⊕ *www.darbyfield.com* ⇨ *13 rooms* ⦿ *Free breakfast.*

Inn at Crystal Lake
$$ | B&B/INN | In the quaint village of Eaton Center, about 10 miles south of North Conway, this stately 1884 Greek Revival inn contains finely appointed rooms with dramatic themes, each filled with a mix of curious and whimsical art and collectibles from the innkeepers' travels. **Pros:** short walk to the lake; convivial pub with good food; good base for White Mountains, Lakes Region, and Maine's Stone Mountain Arts Center. **Cons:** secluded area; few dining options nearby; old-fashioned decor may not suit all tastes. $ *Rooms from: $169* ✉ *2356 Eaton Rd., Eaton Center* ☎ *603/447–2120* ⊕ *www.innatcrystallake.com* ⇨ *11 rooms* ⦿ *Free breakfast.*

★ Snowvillage Inn
$$ | B&B/INN | The finest room in this pastoral inn's main gambrel-roof house (built in 1916) has 12 windows that look out over the Presidential Range, and many guest rooms—some in a carriage house and a new outbuilding—have fireplaces. **Pros:** spectacular views; use of snowshoes and 10 acres of trails; delicious full breakfasts. **Cons:** off the beaten path; no TVs in rooms; not many

dining options nearby. $ *Rooms from: $199* ✉ *136 Stewart Rd., Eaton Center* ☎ *603/447–2818* ⊕ *www.snowvillageinn.com* ⇨ *17 rooms* ⦿ *Free Breakfast.*

▼ Nightlife

Delaney's Hole in the Wall
BARS/PUBS | This legendary après-ski tavern has a real fondness for ski history, displaying early photos of local ski areas, old signs and placards, and odd bits of lift equipment. Guests enjoy

This legendary après-ski tavern has a real fondness for ski history, displaying early photos of local ski areas, old signs and placards, and odd bits of lift equipment. Guests enjoy ✉ *2966 White Mountain Hwy.* ☎ *603/356–7776* ⊕ *www.delaneys.com.*

★ Tuckerman Brewing Co.
BREWPUBS/BEER GARDENS | Offering live music on weekends, seating inside as well as—during the warmer months—in a huge tented beer garden, light snacks, and some of the freshest and tastiest beer in the state, this venerable craft brewery on the edge of downtown Conway is a fun place to relax after a hike or mingle with friends. ✉ *66 Hobbs St., Conway* ☎ *603/447–5400* ⊕ *www.tuckermanbrewing.com.*

🏃 Activities

FISHING
North Country Angler
FISHING | One of the best tackle shops in the state, North Country offers casting clinics and guided fly-fishing trips throughout the region. ✉ *2988 White Mountain Hwy.* ☎ *603/356–6000* ⊕ *www.northcountryangler.com.*

SKIING
Cranmore Mountain Resort
SKIING/SNOWBOARDING | FAMILY | This fun-to-ski area has been a favorite with families since it opened in 1938. Most runs are naturally formed intermediates that weave

in and out of glades. Beginners have several slopes and routes from the summit; experts must be content with a few short, steep pitches. Snowboarders can explore five different terrain parks. A mountain coaster, a tubing park, a giant swing, and a zipline provide additional entertainment. Night skiing is offered on Saturday and holidays. **Facilities:** 56 trails; 170 acres; 1,200-foot vertical drop; 9 lifts. ⊠ *1 Skimobile Rd.* ☏ *800/786–6754* ⊕ *www.cranmore.com* ⊠ *Lift ticket: $89.*

Mt. Washington Valley Ski Touring and Snowshoe Foundation

SKIING/SNOWBOARDING | Nearly 30 miles of groomed cross-country trails weave through the North Conway countryside, maintained by this foundation. Membership to the Mt. Washington Valley Ski Touring Club, available by the day or year, is required. Equipment rentals are available. ⊠ *279 Rte. 16/U.S. 302, Intervale* ☏ *603/356–9920* ⊕ *www. mwvskitouring.org.*

🛍 Shopping

CRAFTS
Handcrafters Barn
CRAFTS | The work of 150 area artists and artisans are sold in this attractive red-clapboard building. ⊠ *2473 White Mountain Hwy.* ☏ *603/356–8996* ⊕ *www. handcraftersbarn.com.*

Jackson

9 miles north of North Conway.

Just off Route 16 via a red covered bridge, photogenic Jackson retains its storybook New England character. Art and antiques shopping, tennis, golf, fishing, and hiking to waterfalls are among the draws, as well as a high concentration of upscale country inns. When the snow falls, Jackson becomes the state's cross-country skiing capital, and there are also four downhill ski areas nearby—hotels and inns provide ski shuttles.

ESSENTIALS
GETTING HERE AND AROUND
Jackson is on Route 16, just north of the junction with U.S. 302.

VISITOR INFORMATION Jackson Area Chamber of Commerce. ☏ *603/383–9356* ⊕ *www.jacksonnh.com.*

👁 Sights

Story Land
AMUSEMENT PARK/WATER PARK | FAMILY | This theme park with life-size storybook and nursery-rhyme characters is geared to kids (ages 2–12). The 23 rides include a flumer, a river raft, and the Roar-O-Saurus and Polar Coaster roller coasters. Play areas and magic shows provide additional entertainment. The Living Shores Aquarium was added to the complex in 2020, offering 32,000-square-feet of mostly interactive, touch-friendly pools and exhibits. ⊠ *850 Rte. 16, Glen* ☏ *603/383–4186* ⊕ *www.storylandnh. com* ⊠ *$33, aquarium $25.*

🍴 Restaurants

★ **Thompson House Eatery**
$$$ | MODERN AMERICAN | The domain of celebrated chef-owner Jeff Fournier, whose cooked at some of Boston's most celebrated restaurants, this exceptional eatery is set inside a chicly restored farmhouse in the village of Jackson. Ethereal highlights from the oft-changing menu include braised beef ragu shell-shaped lumache pasta and a Merlot broth, and a superb cheese board with blueberry and yuzu jams, nuts, and local honey. **Known for:** elegant and historic farmhouse setting; on-site shop with gourmet goods to go; seasonally flavored house-made ice creams. $ *Average main: $28* ⊠ *193 Main St.* ☏ *603/383–9341* ⊕ *www.thethompsonhouseeatery. com* ☾ *Closed Mon. and Tues. No lunch.*

Hotels

Inn at Ellis River

$$ | **B&B/INN** | Most of the rooms—which are all outfitted with armchairs and ottomans and floral-print duvet covers and featherbeds—in this unabashedly romantic 1893 inn on the Ellis River have fireplaces, and some also have balconies with Adirondack chairs and whirlpool tubs. **Pros:** pretty riverside location; abundantly charming; multicourse breakfasts and afternoon refreshments included. **Cons:** some rooms up steep stairs; not suitable for kids under 12; the least expensive rooms are a bit compact. [$] *Rooms from: $179* ✉ *17 Harriman Rd.* ☎ *603/383–9339, 800/233–8309* 🌐 *www.innatellisriver.com* 🛏 *21 rooms* 🍴 *Free breakfast.*

Inn at Jackson

$ | **B&B/INN** | This homey yet distinctive B&B—designed in 1902 by famed architect Stanford White for the Baldwin family of piano fame—is reasonably priced, charmingly furnished, and in the heart of the village. **Pros:** great value considering its many charms; peaceful setting; wonderful breakfasts. **Cons:** top-floor rooms lack fireplaces; bathrooms need updating; a bit frilly for some tastes. [$] *Rooms from: $139* ✉ *Thorn Hill Rd. and Main St.* ☎ *603/383–4321, 800/289–8600* 🌐 *www.innatjackson.com* 🛏 *14 rooms* 🍴 *Free breakfast.*

★ The Inn at Thorn Hill & Spa

$$ | **B&B/INN** | With a large reception room and sweeping staircase, a deck overlooking the rolling hills around the village, and a common area with a wet bar and a cozy fireplace, this lovely inn—modeled after an 1891 Victorian designed by Stanford White—is breathtaking throughout. **Pros:** superb restaurant; soothing full spa; exceptional full breakfasts. **Cons:** rigid peak-season cancellation policy; not suitable for kids; carriage house and cottages are less sumptuous. [$] *Rooms from: $229* ✉ *42 Thorn Hill Rd.* ☎ *603/383–4242* 🌐 *www.innatthornhill.com* 🛏 *22 rooms* 🍴 *No meals.*

Wentworth

$$ | **B&B/INN** | **FAMILY** | Thoughtful renovations have given new life and elegance to the guest rooms at this baronial 1869 Victorian, whose amenities include a full spa, a first-rate restaurant, and access to a terrific golf course and cross-country ski trails. **Pros:** discounts at neighboring Wentworth Golf Club; interesting architecture; very good farm-to-table restaurant. **Cons:** some rooms up steep stairs; two-night minimum many weekends; at a somewhat busy intersection. [$] *Rooms from: $189* ✉ *1 Carter Notch Rd.* ☎ *603/383–9700, 800/637–0013* 🌐 *www.thewentworth.com* 🛏 *61 rooms* 🍴 *Free breakfast.*

Activities

CROSS-COUNTRY SKIING

★ Jackson Ski Touring Foundation

SKIING/SNOWBOARDING | **FAMILY** | This acclaimed cross-country ski operation has an attentive staff and 80 miles of groomed trails for skiing, skate skiing, and snowshoeing. The varied terrain offers something for all abilities—lessons and rentals are offered, too. Trails wind through covered bridges and into the picturesque village of Jackson, where you can warm up in cozy trailside restaurants. ✉ *153 Main St.* ☎ *603/383–9355* 🌐 *www.jacksonxc.org.*

ICE-SKATING

Nestlenook Farm

ICE SKATING | **FAMILY** | This picturesque farm maintains an outdoor ice-skating rink with rentals, music, and a bonfire as well as offering snowshoeing and sleigh rides. ✉ *66 Dinsmore Rd.* ☎ *603/383–7101* 🌐 *www.nestlenookfarmsleighrides.com.*

Mt. Washington

12 miles north of Jackson, 39 miles east of Bretton Woods.

At 6,288 feet, Mt. Washington is the tallest peak in the northeastern United States. The world's highest winds, 231 mph, were recorded here in 1934. You can take a guided van tour, a drive, or a hike to the summit. A number of trails circle the mountain and access the other peaks in the Presidential Range, but all of them are fairly strenuous and best attempted only if you're somewhat experienced and quite fit. It gets cold up here: even in the summer, you'll want a jacket.

GETTING HERE AND AROUND

Mt. Washington Auto Road heads west from Route 16, about 2 miles north of Wildcat Mountain ski resort and 8 miles south of Gorham.

Sights

★ Mt. Washington Auto Road

MOUNTAIN—SIGHT | FAMILY | The drive to the top of this imposing summit is truly memorable. Your route: the narrow, curving Mt. Washington Auto Road, which climbs 4,600 feet in about 7 miles. Drivers can download an app with a narrated tour and receive a bumper sticker that reads, "This car climbed Mt. Washington." The narration is fascinating, and the views are breathtaking. Once at the top, check out **Extreme Mount Washington,** an interactive museum dedicated to science and weather. If you're nervous about heights or the condition of your car, book a guided van tour or a ride up the cog railway in Bretton Woods. ✉ *1 Mt. Washington Auto Rd., Gorham* ☎ *603/466–3988* 🌐 *www.mt-washington.com* 🎟 *Car and driver $35; guided bus tour $39; museum $2 (free with auto tour)* ⏲ *Closed late Oct.–early May.*

Restaurants

Nonna's Kitchen

$$ | ITALIAN | FAMILY | Set in a vintage barber shop in downtown Gorham—8 miles north of the Mt. Washington Auto Road—and looking very old-school, this homey restaurant was opened in 2017 as a tribute to the owners' Italian grandmothers. Indeed, the menu reads like a roll call of favorites from the best restaurants in Boston's or New Haven's Little Italy neighborhoods—classic antipasto, feathery gnocchi with pesto, eggplant parmigiana, veal piccata, and linguine with clams and red sauce. **Known for:** friendly service; cod puttanesca; fresh handmade pastas, cooked to order. [$] *Average main: $19* ✉ *19 Exchange St., Gorham* ☎ *603/915–9203* 🌐 *www.nonnasgorham.com* ⏲ *Closed Mon. and Tues. No lunch.*

Hotels

★ Glen House Hotel

$$ | HOTEL | The latest of four Glen House hotels that have stood on this site at the base of the Mt. Washington Auto Road since 1852, this upscale three-story retreat opened in 2018 in a Shaker-inspired building whose soaring windows, a yellow clapboard exterior, and simple lines hark back to its predecessors. **Pros:** easy access to Mt. Washington activities; beautifully designed; excellent on-site restaurant. **Cons:** remote area; may be a bit shiny and new for some tastes; limited dining options in the area. [$] *Rooms from: $169* ✉ *979 Rte. 16, Gorham* ☎ *603/466–3420* 🌐 *www.theglenhouse.com* 🔑 *68 rooms* 🍴 *Free breakfast.*

Activities

All trails to Mt. Washington's peak are demanding and require a considerable investment of time and effort. Perhaps the most famous is the **Tuckerman Ravine Trail,** the path used by extreme skiers who risk life and limb to fly down the

The highest peak in New England, Mt. Washington rewards those who drive or hike to the top with spectacular views.

face of the steep ravine. The hike to the top can easily take six–nine hours round-trip. However you get to the top, because the weather here is so erratic, it's critical to check weather conditions, to be prepared, and to keep in mind that Mt. Washington's summit is much colder than its base.

CROSS-COUNTRY SKIING

★ Great Glen Trails Outdoor Center

SKIING/SNOWBOARDING | FAMILY | Featuring a dramatic 28-mile network of both mild and wild cross-country ski and mountain-biking trails at the foot of Mt. Washington, Great Glen provides access to more than 1,100 acres of backcountry. You can also book to the summit via SnowCoach, a nine-passenger van refitted with triangular snowmobile-like treads. You have the option of skiing or snowshoeing down or just enjoying the magnificent winter view. There's also a huge ski and sports shop, a food court, and a climbing wall. In summer you can also rent kayaks and book excellent paddling, rafting, and float trips along the Androscoggin River. ⊠ 1 Mt. Washington Auto Rd., at Rte. 16, Gorham ☎ 603/466–3988 ⊕ www.greatglentrails. com ☜ SnowCoach tours $55.

HIKING

Pinkham Notch

HIKING/WALKING | On Mt. Washington's eastern slopes, scenic Pinkham Notch encompasses several ravines, including famous Tuckerman. The Appalachian Mountain Club operates a visitor center that provides trail information. Guided hikes leave from here, and outdoor skills workshops are offered. On-site are an outdoors shop, a lodge with basic overnight accommodations, and a dining hall. Not all the trails ascend Mt. Washington or are necessarily strenuous. Good bets for shorter, moderate hikes include Glen Ellis Falls and Crystal Cascade, which both lead to scenic waterfalls. ⊠ AMC Pinkham Notch Visitor Center, 361 Rte. 16, Gorham ☎ 603/466–2721 ⊕ www. outdoors.org.

SKIING
Wildcat Mountain

SKIING/SNOWBOARDING | Glade skiers love Wildcat's 80 acres of tree skiing. Runs include some stunning double–black diamond trails; experts can really zip down the Lynx. Beginners, as long as they can hold a wedge, should check out the 2½-mile-long Polecat, which offers excellent views of the Presidential Range. The trails are classic New England—narrow and winding—and the vistas are stunning. For an adrenaline rush, there's a terrain park. In summer you can dart to the top on the four-passenger gondola, hike the many trails, and fish in the crystal clear streams. **Facilities:** 48 trails; 225 acres; 2,112-foot vertical drop; 5 lifts. ⊠ *Rte. 16, Gorham* ☎ *603/466–3326, 888/754–9453 for snow conditions* ⊕ *www.skiwildcat.com* ⊐ *$92.*

Bartlett

19 miles south of Mt. Washington, 9 miles northwest of North Conway.

With Bear Mountain to its south, Mt. Parker to its north, Mt. Cardigan to its west, and the Saco River to its east, Bartlett—incorporated in 1790—has an unforgettable setting. Lovely Bear Notch Road (closed in winter) has the only midpoint access to the Kancamagus Highway. There isn't much town to speak of: the dining options listed are actually nearby in Glen. It's best known for the Attitash Ski Resort.

GETTING HERE AND AROUND
U.S. 302 passes through Bartlett from Bretton Woods and west from Glen.

🍴 Restaurants

White Mountain Cider Co.
$$$ | MODERN AMERICAN | Set in a historic cider mill near the Saco River, this rustic yet elegant bistro and adjacent gourmet market and deli presses fresh cider in the fall—it's served with traditional homemade cider doughnuts. But it's also a terrific farm-to-table restaurant, featuring a seasonal menu of eclectic, contemporary dishes. **Known for:** flavorful sandwiches and soups in the adjacent market; creative cocktails; friendly, knowledgeable service. $ *Average main: $25* ⊠ *207 U.S. 302, Glen* ☎ *603/383–9061* ⊕ *www.ciderconh.com* ⊗ *Closed Tues. No lunch in restaurant.*

🛏 Hotels

★ Bernerhof Inn
$$ | B&B/INN | Skiers, hikers, and adventurers who favor a luxurious, intimate lodging over a bustling condo resort adore this grand Victorian inn operated with eco-friendly practices and furnished with a mix of fine antiques and period reproductions. **Pros:** excellent on-site cooking school; exudes old-world charm; small but wonderfully relaxing spa. **Cons:** no on-site restaurant; some rooms receive little road noise; not good for kids. $ *Rooms from: $189* ⊠ *342 U.S. 302, Glen* ☎ *603/383–4200, 877/389–4852* ⊕ *www.bernerhof-inn.com* ⇌ *12 rooms* �‖ *Free breakfast.*

Grand Summit Hotel at Attitash
$ | HOTEL | FAMILY | All of the pleasantly furnished rooms at this ski-in, ski-out condo-style resort at the base of Bear Peak have kitchenettes, and many have private balconies with splendid views. **Pros:** appealing slope-side setting; ski-package deals; kitchenettes in rooms. **Cons:** generally bland decor; could use some sprucing up; restaurants are a bit meh. $ *Rooms from: $129* ⊠ *104 Grand Summit Rd.* ☎ *603/374–1900* ⊕ *www.grandsummitattitash.com* ⇌ *143 rooms* �‖ *No meals.*

🍸 Nightlife

Red Parka Pub
BARS/PUBS | This homey pub decorated with license plates and ski memorabilia has been an institution, especially during winter ski season, since the early 1970s, providing a fun and festive venue for après-ski or-hike socializing.

Beer is served in Mason jars, the kitchen serves up juicy steaks and comfort fare, and there's live music many evenings. ⊠ *3 Station St., Glen* ☎ *603/383–4344* ⊕ *www.redparkapub.com.*

🏃 Activities

SKIING

Attitash Ski Resort

SKIING/SNOWBOARDING | FAMILY | With one of New Hampshire's higher vertical drops, Attitash Mountain has dozens of trails to explore, and there are more on the adjacent Attitash Bear Peak. You'll find traditional New England ski runs and challenging terrain alongside wide-open cruisers that suit all skill levels. There are acres of glades, plus a progressive free-style terrain park. The Attitash Adventure Center offers rentals, lessons, and children's programs. **Facilities:** 68 trails; 311 acres; 1,750-foot vertical drop; 10 lifts. ⊠ *775 U.S. 302* ☎ *800/223–7669* ⊕ *www. attitash.com* ✉ *Lift ticket: $92.*

Bretton Woods

21 miles northwest of Bartlett.

In the early 1900s private railcars brought the elite from New York and Philadelphia to the Mount Washington Hotel, the jewel of the White Mountains. A visit to this property, which was the site of the 1944 United Nations conference that created the International Monetary Fund and the International Bank for Reconstruction and Development (and the birth of many conspiracy theories), is not to be missed. The area is also known for its cog railway to the summit of Mt. Washington, Bretton Woods ski resort, and unparalleled hiking.

GETTING HERE AND AROUND

Bretton Woods is in the heart of the White Mountains on U.S. 302. A free shuttle makes it easy to get around the resort's various facilities.

👁 Sights

★ Crawford Notch State Park

BODY OF WATER | FAMILY | Scenic U.S. 302 winds southeast of Bretton Woods through the steep, wooded mountains on either side of spectacular Crawford Notch. Now a state park, you can picnic and hike to Arethusa Falls, the longest drop in New England, or to the Silver and Flume cascades—they're among more than a dozen outstanding trails. The 5,775-acre park has a number of roadside photo ops, plus an Adirondack-style visitor center, gift shop, snack bar, and fishing pond. ⊠ *1464 U.S. 302, Hart's Location* ☎ *603/374–2272* ⊕ *www.nhstateparks.org.*

★ Mount Washington Cog Railway

MOUNTAIN—SIGHT | FAMILY | In 1858, Sylvester Marsh petitioned the state legislature for permission to build a steam railway up Mt. Washington. One politico retorted that Marsh would have better luck building a railroad to the moon, but 11 years later the Mount Washington Cog Railway chugged its way up to the summit along a 3-mile track on the mountain's west side. Today it's a beloved attraction—a thrill in either direction. A small museum has exhibits about the cog rail, and a casual restaurant offers great views of the trains beginning their ascent. The full trip takes three hours including an hour at the summit. ⊠ *3168 Base Station Rd.* ☎ *603/278–5404, 800/922–8825* ⊕ *www.thecog.com* ✉ *From $72* ⊗ *Closed Dec.–Apr.*

🛏 Hotels

★ The Notchland Inn

$$$ | B&B/INN | Built in 1862 by Sam Bemis, America's grandfather of landscape photography, the gracious granite manor house exudes mountain charm and is popular with Crawford Notch hikers who favor luxury. **Pros:** set amid soaring mountains; marvelous house and common rooms; outstanding breakfasts and dinners. **Cons:** very isolated;

fills up well in advance on summer and fall weekends; not ideal for young kids. $ *Rooms from: $275* ✉ *2 Morey Rd., Hart's Location* ☎ *603/374–6131, 800/866–6131* ⊕ *www.notchland.com* ⇨ *15 rooms* ❑ *Free breakfast.*

★ Omni Mount Washington Hotel

$$$ | **RESORT** | **FAMILY** | The two most memorable sights in the White Mountains might just be Mt. Washington and this dramatic 1902 resort with a 900-foot veranda, glimmering public rooms, astonishing views of the Presidential Range, and dozens of recreational activities like tubing, sleigh rides, horseback riding, and fly-fishing. **Pros:** incomparable setting and ambience; loads of amenities and dining options; free shuttle to skiing and activities. **Cons:** lots of kids running around the hotel; a drive from nearest decent-size town; rates soar on summer–fall weekends. $ *Rooms from: $279* ✉ *310 Mt. Washington Hotel Rd., off U.S. 302* ☎ *603/278–1000, 888/444–6664* ⊕ *www.mountwashingtonresort.com* ⇨ *200 rooms* ❑ *No meals.*

🏃 Activities

SKIING

★ Bretton Woods

SKIING/SNOWBOARDING | **FAMILY** | New Hampshire's largest ski area is also one of the country's best family ski resorts. The views of Mt. Washington alone are worth the visit, and the scenery is especially beautiful from the two-story restaurant atop 3,000-foot-elevation Mt. Rosebrook, reached via an all-glass eight-passenger Skyway Gondola that opened in 2019.

The resort has something for everyone, from extensive kids' programs and lessons to some seriously steep pitches near the top of the 1,500-foot vertical. And the 35 glades will keep experts busy, while snowboarders enjoy the three terrain parks. The Nordic trail system has 62 miles of cross-country ski trails. Both night skiing and snowboarding are available on weekends and holidays.

There's also the year-round Canopy Tour, with nine ziplines, two sky bridges, and three rappelling stations. **Facilities:** 102 trails; 464 acres, 1,500-foot vertical drop; 10 lifts. ✉ *99 Ski Area Rd.* ☎ *603/278–3320, 603/278–1000 for conditions* ⊕ *www.brettonwoods.com* 🎟 *Lift ticket: $104.*

Bethlehem

14 miles west of Bretton Woods.

In the days before antihistamines, hay-fever sufferers came by the trainload to this enchanting village whose crisp air has a blissfully low pollen count. Today this progressive, artsy hamlet with fewer than 1,000 residents is notable for its art deco Colonial Theatre (which presents indie films and concerts), distinctive galleries and cafés, and stately Victorian and Colonial homes, many of which line the village's immensely picturesque Main Street, a highly enjoyable locale for a stroll.

GETTING HERE AND AROUND

U.S. 302 and Route 142 intersect in the heart of this small village center that's easy to explore on foot.

👁 Sights

The Rocks Estate

FARM/RANCH | **FAMILY** | The estate of John Jacob Glessner (1843–1936), one of the founders of International Harvester, now serves as a 1,400-acre conservation and education center. The property is named for the many surface boulders on the estate when Glessner bought it—some were used to erect the rambling rock walls that flanks the estate's striking shingle-style restored buildings. The

Rocks presents natural-history programs and has self-guided tours and hiking trails with excellent views of the Presidential Range. Come winter, cross-country ski trails and a select-your-own-Christmas-tree farm open up. In early spring, you can watch how maple syrup is made. ✉ *4 Christmas La., Bethlehem* ☎ *603/444-6228* 🌐 *www.therocks.org.*

Restaurants

★ Cold Mountain Cafe

$$ | ECLECTIC | Adjacent to the Marketplace at WREN, this homey art-filled storefront eatery and wine bar is one of the area's social focal points, with a welcoming staff a thoughtful, international menu. Pork tacos, Indian lamb stew, and heirloom tomato caprese salads are a few of the best dishes, but save room for the flourless chocolate torte with strawberry-balsamic coulis. **Known for:** friendly, upbeat crowd and staff; bounteous salads; intriguing cocktail list. [$] *Average main: $22* ✉ *2015 Main St., Bethlehem* ☎ *603/869-2500* 🌐 *www.coldmountaincafe.com* 🕒 *Closed Sun.*

Coffee and Quick Bites

Maia Papaya

$ | CAFÉ | Pause during your stroll through inviting Bethlehem for breakfast, lunch, smoothies, lattes, or homemade chai tea at this quirky organic café that specializes in vegetarian fare and made-from-scratch baked goods (try not to pass up one of the justly renowned scones). On cool mornings, warm up with the rich and delicious bread pudding French toast; terrific lunchtime options include the artichoke melt panini or the bountiful green salad. **Known for:** plenty of gluten-free and vegetarian options; fruit-filled oat bars; organic oatmeal with local maple syrup. [$] *Average main: $7* ✉ *2161 Main St., Bethlehem* ☎ *603/869-9900* 🌐 *www.themaiapapaya.com* 🕒 *No dinner.*

Hotels

★ Adair Country Inn and Restaurant

$$$ | B&B/INN | An air of yesteryear refinement suffuses Adair, a three-story Georgian Revival home that attorney Frank Hogan built as a wedding present for his daughter in 1927—her hats adorn the place, as do books and old photos from the era. **Pros:** a superb, romantic restaurant; rates include a memorable breakfast and afternoon tea; cross-country skiing and hiking trails. **Cons:** not within walking distance of town; sometimes books up with weddings; closed for a month each fall and spring. [$] *Rooms from: $279* ✉ *80 Guider La., Bethlehem* ☎ *603/444-2600, 888/444-2600* 🌐 *www.adairinn.com* 🕒 *Closed mid-Nov. and Apr.* 🛏 *11 rooms* 🍴 *Free breakfast.*

★ Bear Mountain Lodge

$$$ | B&B/INN | This striking log cabin–style inn on 26 secluded acres with arresting views of the Presidential Range looks like something you'd expect to find out West, and indeed, its owners based the design on lodges they visited in Alaska. **Pros:** gorgeous decor and architecture; utterly tranquil setting; exquisite full breakfasts. **Cons:** Western log cabin style isn't to everyone's taste; not within walking distance of town; minimum-night stays during busy times. [$] *Rooms from: $245* ✉ *3249 Main St., Bethlehem* ☎ *603/869-2189* 🌐 *www.bearmountainlodge.net* 🛏 *10 rooms* 🍴 *Free Breakfast.*

Nightlife

★ Rek-Lis Brewing Company

BREWPUBS/BEER GARDENS | After a day of hiking or skiing, grab a seat inside this cozy tavern or out on one of the expansive decks and savor the outstanding house-made beers along with guest taps from other notable breweries. There's great pub food, too, and a popular Sunday brunch. ✉ *2085 Main St., Bethlehem* ☎ *603/991-2357* 🌐 *www.reklisbrewing.com.*

Shopping

★ Marketplace at WREN

ART GALLERIES | WREN (the Women's Rural Entrepreneurial Network) has been a vital force in little Bethlehem's steady growth into a center of artists, craftspersons, and other business owners. At WREN's headquarters, there's an outstanding gallery that presents monthly juried exhibits and a retail gift boutique, Local Works, featuring crafts, foods, and other products. ✉ *2011 Main St., Bethlehem* ☎ *603/869–9736* ⊕ *www.wrenworks.org.*

Littleton

5 miles west of Bethlehem.

One of northern New Hampshire's largest towns (this isn't saying much, mind you) sits on a granite shelf along the Ammonoosuc River, whose swift current and drop of 235 feet enabled the community to flourish as a mill center in its early days. The railroad came through later, and Littleton grew into the region's commercial hub. Long merely a place to stock up than a real destination, it's reinvented itself in recent decades, and its lively Main Street now abounds with intriguing shops and eateries set inside tidy 19th- and early-20th-century buildings you might expect to see in an old Jimmy Stewart movie.

GETTING HERE AND AROUND

Littleton sits just off Interstate 93, and it's downtown is easily explored on foot.

ESSENTIALS

VISITOR INFORMATION Littleton Area Chamber of Commerce. ☎ *603/444–6561* ⊕ *www.littletonareachamber.com.*

Sights

The Great North Woods

INFO CENTER | The collective name for New Hampshire's northern panhandle, which is reached from Littleton via Route 116 to U.S. 3, the Great North Woods covers about 1,800 square miles, an area slightly larger than Rhode Island. Sparsely populated and with few roads, this expanse of dense woodland and mountains is hugely popular with fishing, hunting, hiking, and other backcountry recreation enthusiasts, but it's also appealing for a picturesque country drive, especially for moose viewing (drive carefully) and admiring fall foliage from mid-September through early October. The Canadian border is about 85 miles from Whitefield and takes two hours each way without stops, but passes through interesting little towns—like Lancaster, Colebrook, and Pittsburg—and snakes along the shores of the upper Connecticut River and the three pristine Connecticut Lakes. From Colebrook, you can also detour east along a dramatic stretch of Route 26 to Dixville Notch, site of the famous but currently closed Balsams Grand Resort Hotel and one of the first election districts in the nation to vote in presidential general elections. The area has a handful of popular businesses, like Le Rendez Vous pastry shop in Colebrook, Rainbow Grille in Pittsburg, and the Cabins at Lopstick and Glen at Bear Tree lodgings, both in Pittsburg. ✉ *North County Chamber of Commerce, Colebrook* ☎ *603/237–8939* ⊕ *www. chamberofthenorthcountry.com.*

Weeks State Park

HOUSE | A few miles north of Whitefield's famous Mountain View Grand Resort, this 446-acre park occupies the early 20th-century estate of conservationist and U.S. Senator John W. Weeks, whose 1911 Weeks Act enabled the acquisition of some 19 million acres of wilderness, including White Mountain National

Forest. An auto road winds to the 2,037-foot summit of Prospect Mountain, where a stone tower offers astounding views of Vermont and New Hampshire. One-hour tours of the Weeks mansion are available, and a 3.4-mile loop hiking trail traverses the property. ✉ *200 Week's State Park Rd., Lancaster* ☎ *603/788–4004* 🌐 *www.nhstateparks.org* 🎟 *$4.*

🍴 Restaurants

★ Schilling Beer Taproom

$ | **AMERICAN** | With a storybook setting in a converted 18th-century mill on the Ammonoosuc River, this craft brewpub offers tasty wood-fired pizzas, bratwurst sandwiches, house-baked soft pretzels, and other fare that pairs well with its distinctive European ales. The pie topped with prosciutto, pears, chèvre, mozzarella, and beer-caramelized onions is a favorite, best enjoyed with a farmhouse-style saison. **Known for:** seating overlooking the river; beer tastings; great pizzas. [$] *Average main: $14* ✉ *18 Mill St.* ☎ *603/444–4800* 🌐 *www.schillingbeer.com.*

★ Tim-Bir Alley

$$$ | **MODERN AMERICAN** | In this terrific contemporary downtown restaurant, you can sample some of the tastiest farm-to-table fare in the White Mountains. The menu changes frequently and uses regional American ingredients in creative ways—try country pâté with venison and pistachio, followed by skin-on salmon with olive oil–poached tomatoes and a black-olive vinaigrette. **Known for:** stylish yet unpretentious; local artisan cheese plates; beautifully plated desserts. [$] *Average main: $28* ✉ *7 Main St.* ☎ *603/444–6142* 🌐 *www.timbiralleyrestaurant.com* 💳 *No credit cards* ⏲ *Closed Mon. and Tues. No lunch.*

☕ Coffee and Quick Bites

The Inkwell

$ | **CAFÉ** | Drop by this funky old yellow house with indoor and outdoor seating overlooking the Ammonoosuc River for a light bite, to relax with a book, or sip one of the well-crafted fair-trade coffee or organic loose-leaf tea drinks. Several kinds of toast with tasty toppings (ricotta and lemon honey; cheddar, ham, and egg) are available at breakfast, along with myriad scones, cookies, and gluten-free pastries. **Known for:** toasts with creative toppings; endearing riverfront setting; iced and hot coffees with local maple syrup. [$] *Average main: $7* ✉ *42 Mill St.* ☎ *603/324–0942* 🌐 *www.inkwellnh.com* ⏲ *Closed Sun. No dinner.*

🛏 Hotels

Mountain View Grand Resort & Spa

$$ | **RESORT** | **FAMILY** | Casual elegance and stunning views of the White Mountains define this stately yellow wedding cake of a hotel that dates to 1865 and sprawls over 1,700 acres that include a working farm and a well-maintained golf course. **Pros:** full-service spa; dozens of activities; babysitting service and summer camp. **Cons:** breakfast not included in rates; not too many dining options nearby; sometimes fills up with corporate meetings and retreats. [$] *Rooms from: $189* ✉ *101 Mountain View Rd., Whitefield* ☎ *855/837–2100* 🌐 *www.mountainviewgrand.com* 🔑 *144 rooms* 🍽 *No meals.*

Thayers Inn

$ | **HOTEL** | This former grande dame with a distinguished roster of past guests—including Ulysses S. Grant, Henry Ford, and P.T. **Pros:** some rooms have kitchenettes; fascinating building filled with memorabilia and exhibits; on lively and festival Main Street. **Cons:** no elevator; basic decor; tiny bathrooms. [$] *Rooms from: $119* ✉ *111 Main St.* ☎ *603/444–6469* 🌐 *www.thayersinn.com* 🔑 *34 rooms* 🍽 *Free Breakfast.*

🎭 Performing Arts

ARTS VENUES

Weathervane Theatre

THEATER | This beloved 250-seat theater near the Mountainview Grand Resort presents seven musicals each summer. ✉ *389 Lancaster Rd. (U.S. 3), White-field* ☎ *603/837–9322* ⊕ *www.weathervanenh.org.*

🛍 Shopping

Chutters

FOOD/CANDY | **FAMILY** | Boasting the world's longest candy counter, at 112 feet, this kid- and adult-approved century-plus-old candy shop with satellite locations in Lincoln, Loon Mountain Resort, and Bretton Woods carries just about every variety of sweet treat you could imagine. ✉ *43 Main St* ☎ *603/444–5787* ⊕ *www.chutters.com.*

★ Crumb Bum

FOOD/CANDY | Stop by this cute cake shop to stock up on creative, and utterly delectable, baked goods, such as grapefruit-rosemary-cardamom short bread cookies, maple cinnamon rolls, and macarons in a variety of flavors, and egg-bacon-cheese breakfast sandwiches constructed on ethereal duck-fat biscuits. Fine coffees are available, too. ✉ *97 Main St.* ☎ *603/575–5590* ⊕ *www.crumbbumbakery.com.*

★ Just L Modern Antiques

ANTIQUES/COLLECTIBLES | Fans of midcentury furnishings, from low-slung modern sofas and sleek Danish coffee tables to both fashionable and kitschy housewares, vintage paintings, and kitchen items flock to this enormous two-floor emporium set along Littleton's increasingly hip Main Street. ✉ *35 Main St.* ☎ *603/259–3125.*

Little Village Toy and Book Stop

BOOKS/STATIONERY | **FAMILY** | Maps, history books, unusual children's toys and many adult fiction and nonfiction titles fill this cheerful shop, the lower level of which contains a branch of the venerable League of New Hampshire Craftsmen's gallery. ✉ *81B Main St.* ☎ *603/444–4869* ⊕ *www.littlevillagetoy.com.*

Pentimento

GIFTS/SOUVENIRS | This eclectic shop, packed into a Victorian house a few steps from the historic Opera House, is great place to find unusual jewelry, candles, fashion eyewear, and handmade cards. ✉ *34 Union St.* ☎ *603/444–7797.*

Franconia

7 miles south of Littleton.

Travelers have long passed through spectacular Franconia Notch, and in the late 18th century this town evolved just to the north. It and the region's jagged rock formations and heavy coat of evergreens stirred the imaginations of Washington Irving, Henry Wadsworth Longfellow, and Nathaniel Hawthorne, who penned a short story about the iconic—though now crumbled—cliff known as the Old Man of the Mountain. There's barely a downtown, just a handful of businesses and the remains of the interesting old 1840s Besaw Iron Furnace. Drive west 4 miles to visit Sugar Hill, a village of about 500 people that's famous for its spectacular sunsets and views of Franconia Ridge, best seen from Sunset Hill, where a row of grand hotels and mansions once stood.

GETTING HERE AND AROUND

Franconia has few services but is right off Interstate 93, making it a good base for visiting many nearby ski areas and mountain villages.

ESSENTIALS

VISITOR INFORMATION Franconia Notch Chamber of Commerce. ☎ *603/823–5661* ⊕ *www.franconianotch.org.*

Sights

★ Franconia Notch State Park

BEACH—SIGHT | FAMILY | Traversed by the Appalachian Trail and a stretch of Interstate 93 that narrows for 8 miles to become Franconia Notch Parkway, this stunning 6,692-acre state park feels as awesome as a national park and offers dozens of diversions, including myriad hiking trails, summer swimming at **Echo Lake Beach,** and winter downhill skiing at **Cannon Mountain,** whose 4,080-foot summit observation deck you can explore on the **Aerial Tramway,** an 80-passenger cable car. One of the top park draws, the dramatic, narrow 800-foot-long **Flume Gorge** is reached from a modern visitor center via a picturesque 2-mile loop hike along wooden boardwalks and stairways. The park was long famous as the site of the **Old Man of the Mountain,** an iconic profile high on a granite cliff that crumbled unexpectedly in 2003. Overlooking Profile Lake, at the small Old Man of the Mountain Park, you can walk the short but pretty paved trail to view the mountain face through steel rods that seem literally to put the beloved visage back on the mountain. You can see related photographs and memorabilia in a small museum, and also visit the **New England Ski Museum** to learn how skiing was popularized as a sport in New England, through artifacts, clothing, and equipment, as well as Bode Miller's five Olympic medals. ✉ *260 Tramway Dr.* ☎ *603/823–8800* 🌐 *www.nhstateparks.org* 🎫 *Aerial Tramway $19, Echo Lake parking $4, Flume Gorge $16, museums free.*

The Frost Place Museum

HOUSE | Robert Frost's year-round home from 1915 to 1920, this modest homestead on a peaceful unpaved road is surrounded by well-tended gardens and offers stunning mountain views. The place is imbued with the spirit of his work—two rooms contain memorabilia and signed editions of his books. Out back, you can follow short trails marked with lines from his poetry. Poetry readings are scheduled some summer evenings. ✉ *158 Ridge Rd.* ☎ *603/823–5510* 🌐 *www.frostplace.org* 🎫 *$5* ⏲ *Closed mid-Oct.–Apr.*

Restaurants

★ Polly's Pancake Parlor

$ | AMERICAN | FAMILY | In the Dexter family for generations, Polly's has been serving up pancakes and waffles (from its own original recipe, with several batter options available, including cornmeal and gingerbread) since the 1930s—the current space dates to 2015 but retains the original country charm. Try the smoked bacon and ham, eggs Benedict, sandwiches on homemade bread, delicious baked beans, and such tempting desserts as raspberry pie. **Known for:** gift shop with maple products; gingerbread pancakes with blueberries and walnuts; pretty hilltop setting. 💲 *Average main: $11* ✉ *672 Rte. 117* ☎ *603/823–5575* 🌐 *www.pollyspancakeparlor.com* ⏲ *Closed Wed. No dinner.*

Hotels

Franconia Inn

$ | RESORT | FAMILY | At this 107-acre family-friendly resort anchored by an affordable three-story inn with unfussy country furnishings, you can play tennis on four clay courts, soak in the outdoor heated pool or hot tub, hop on a mountain bike, or soar in a glider, and cross-country ski on 40 miles of groomed trails. **Pros:** tons of family-oriented activities; outdoor heated pool; peaceful setting with mountain views. **Cons:** a bit remote; historic hotel with some quirks; popularity with families can make it a little noisy. 💲 *Rooms from: $136* ✉ *1172 Easton Rd.* ☎ *603/823–5542, 800/473–5299* 🌐 *www.franconiainn.com* ⏲ *Closed Apr.–mid-May* 🔑 *34 rooms* 🍽 *No meals.*

Sunset Hill House

$ | HOTEL | It's all about the view at this striking Victorian inn set high on a ridge in tiny Sugar Hill, its 70 acres holding lovely gardens, a seasonal outdoor pool, and a great little golf course. **Pros:** mesmerizing views; excellent 9-hole golf course; unusually good restaurant with outdoor dining. **Cons:** slightly remote setting; not a great option for kids; some bathrooms are shower-only. $ *Rooms from: $155* ⊠ *231 Sunset Hill Rd., Sugar Hill* ☎ *603/823–7244* ⊕ *www.thesunsethillhouse.com* ⇴ *28 rooms* ⊙*| Free breakfast.*

★ Sugar Hill Inn

$$$ | **B&B/INN** | Although this upscale inn surrounded by neatly manicured gardens dates to 1789, it has a decidedly current vibe, from its sumptuous rooms with such modern perks as whirlpool tubs, gas fireplaces, and Bose sound systems, to the superb prix-fixe restaurant serving sublime contemporary American fare. **Pros:** many rooms have private decks; dining packages available; gorgeous countryside setting. **Cons:** somewhat remote; books up well ahead on weekends; not a good fit for families. $ *Rooms from: $278* ⊠ *116 Sugar Hill Rd. (Rte. 117), Sugar Hill* ☎ *603/869–7543* ⊕ *www.sugarhillinn.com* ⇴ *15 rooms* ⊙*| Free breakfast.*

🏃 Activities

SKIING

Cannon Mountain

SKIING/SNOWBOARDING | **FAMILY** | Serviced by the first aerial tramway in North America, which was built in 1938, this classic New England ski resort inside Franconia Notch State Park offers terrain that runs the gamut from steep pitches off the peak to gentle blue cruisers. Beginners may want to head over to the separate Tuckerbrook family area, which offers 13 trails and four lifts. Adventurous types will want to try out the Mittersill area, which has 86 acres of lift-accessed "side country" trails and glades where the snow is au naturel. **Facilities:** 97 trails; 285 acres; 2,180-foot vertical drop; 11 lifts. ⊠ *260 Tramway Dr.* ☎ *603/823–8800, 603/823–7771 snow conditions* ⊕ *www.cannonmt.com* 🎟 *Lift ticket: $88.*

🛍 Shopping

★ Harman's Cheese & Country Store

FOOD/CANDY | It's worth a slight but pretty detour over the hill from Franconia to visit this rambling old village store and dairy that turns out legendarily rich, sharp aged cheddar, which is also available smoked and in port-and-cognac spreads. The venerable red-clapboard shop carries plenty of other foodie-pleasing products, and on summer Fridays, they hold farm-to-fire pizza nights. ⊠ *1400 Rte. 117, Sugar Hill* ☎ *603/823–8000* ⊕ *www.harmans-cheese.com.*

Lincoln and North Woodstock

17 miles south of Franconia, 42 miles west of North Conway, 64 miles north of Concord.

These neighboring towns at the White Mountains' southwestern corner are the western gateway to the famed Kancamagus Highway. They form a lively resort base camp, especially for metro Boston families who can make an easy two-hour drive straight up Interstate 93. Although the town itself isn't much of an attraction, myriad festivals and activities keep Lincoln swarming with visitors year-round.

Tiny North Woodstock maintains a more inviting village feel and is close to some easy, scenic, family-friendly hikes, such as Georgiana Falls and the slightly more ambitious Indian Head Trail.

GETTING HERE AND AROUND

Accessed from Interstate 93, Lincoln and North Woodstock are connected by Route 112—it's a short 1-mile drive between the two.

ESSENTIALS

VISITOR INFORMATION Western White Mountains Chamber of Commerce.
☎ 603/745–6621 ⊕ www.western-whitemtns.com.

TOURS

Pemi Valley Moose Tours

TOUR—SPORTS | FAMILY | If you're eager to see a mighty moose, embark on a moose-watching bus tour into the northernmost White Mountains. The three-hour trips depart at 8:30 pm late April to mid-October for the best wildlife-sighting opportunities. ⊠ 136 Main St., Lincoln ☎ 603/745–2744 ⊕ www.moosetoursnh.com ⊠ $35.

 Sights

Clark's Bears

AMUSEMENT PARK/WATER PARK | FAMILY | Chock-full of hokum, this kids-oriented old-time amusement park is famous for its performing live-bear shows. There are also short train trips over a 1904 covered bridge, segway rides, a museum of Americana inside an 1880s firehouse, a restored gas station with antique cars, an Old Man of the Mountain rock-climbing tower, and a huge, kitschy gift shop with penny-candy. ⊠ 110 Daniel Webster Hwy., Lincoln ☎ 603/745–8913 ⊕ www.clarksbears.com ⊠ $24 ⊗ Closed mid-Oct.–mid-May.

Hobo Railroad

LOCAL INTEREST | FAMILY | Restored vintage train cars take you on 80-minute excursions along the scenic banks of the Pemigewassett River. A Santa Express runs late November–late December. ⊠ 64 Railroad St., Lincoln ☎ 603/745–2135 ⊕ www.hoborr.com ⊠ $19 ⊗ Closed Jan.–Apr.

★ Kancamagus Highway

NATIONAL/STATE PARK | FAMILY | In 1937, two old local roads were connected from Lincoln to Conway to create this remarkable 34.5-mile national designated scenic byway through a breathtaking swath of the White Mountains. This section of Route 112 known as the Kancamagus—often called simply "the Kanc"—contains no businesses or billboards and is punctuated by overlooks, picnic areas, and memorable hiking trailheads. These include **Lincoln Woods,** an easy 6-mile round-trip trek along a railroad bed that departs from the Lincoln Woods Visitor Center, crosses a dramatic suspension bridge over the Pemigewasset River, and ends at a swimming hole formed by dramatic Franconia Falls. There's also **Sabbaday Falls,** a short ½-mile stroll to a multilevel cascade that plunges through two potholes and a flume. For a slightly harder but less crowded trek, take the 3.5-mile **Boulder Loop Trail,** which rises precipitously some 1,000 feet from the banks of the Swift River to a granite-crowned summit with mountain views. The road's highest point, at 2,855 feet, crosses the flank of Mt. Kancamagus, near Lincoln—a great place to view the fiery displays of foliage each autumn. On-site in lots and overlooks costs $5. ☎ 603/536–6100 ⊕ www.fs.usda.gov/whitemountain.

★ Lost River Gorge & Boulder Caves

NATURE SITE | FAMILY | Parents can enjoy the looks of wonder on their kids' faces as they negotiate wooden boardwalks and stairs leading through a granite gorge formed by the roaring waters of the Lost River. One of the 10 caves they can explore is called the Lemon Squeezer (and it's a tight fit). Visitors can also pan for gems and search for fossils and walk through a fascinating giant man-made birdhouse, venture across a suspension bridge, and climb up into a big tree house. The park offers lantern tours on weekend evenings. ⊠ 1712 Lost River Rd., North Woodstock ☎ 603/745–8720 ⊕ www.lostrivergorge.com ⊠ $20 ⊗ Closed Nov.–Apr.

Seven Birches Winery

WINERY/DISTILLERY | With a tasting room at Lincoln's RiverWalk resort and steps away in a bright and modern wine bar with a big patio, this respected winery offers its classic European-varietal dry wines and sweeter fruit wines by the glass or flight, along with a selection of snacks. ✉ *22 S. Mountain Dr., Lincoln* ☎ *603/745–7550* 🌐 *www.sevenbirches.com.*

Whale's Tale Waterpark

AMUSEMENT PARK/WATER PARK | FAMILY | You can float on an inner tube along a gentle river, plunge down one of five waterslides, hang five on the Akua surf simulator, or bodysurf in the large wave pool at Whale's Tale. There's plenty here for toddlers and small children, too. ✉ *491 Daniel Webster Hwy. (U.S. 3), Lincoln* ☎ *603/745–8810* 🌐 *www.whalestalewaterpark.net* 🎟 *From $39* ⏲ *Closed early Oct.–Apr.*

🍴 Restaurants

Woodstock Inn Brewery

$$ | AMERICAN | This big and festive brewpub inside a late-1800s train station is decorated with old maps, historic photographs, and other fun curiosities. The kitchen turns out reliably good pub fare—pizza, burgers, steaks, seafood—and filling breakfasts, and the brewery produces nearly 20 different varieties of exceptionally good beers. **Known for:** game room and kids' menu; brewery tours; inviting indoor and outdoor seating. [$] *Average main: $18* ✉ *135 Main St., North Woodstock* ☎ *603/745–3951* 🌐 *www.woodstockinnnh.com.*

☕ Coffee and Quick Bites

The Moon Bakery & Cafe

$ | CAFÉ | A must for delicious sustenance and potent lattes before hitting the slopes or hiking along the Kancamagus Highway, this homey café offers ample seating indoor in exposed-brick-wall nook or outside on the sidewalk. Popular items include ham and cheddar sandwiches with maple mustard, avocado-egg breakfast sandwiches, and matcha green tea smoothies. **Known for:** fresh smoothies; hefty sandwiches on house-baked bread; trailmix cookies. [$] *Average main: $7* ✉ *28 S. Mountain Dr., Lincoln* ☎ *603/745–5013* 🌐 *www.themoonnh.com* ⏲ *No dinner.*

🛏 Hotels

Indian Head Resort

$ | RESORT | FAMILY | This early-20th-century resort identified by its 100-foot-tall observation tower and its lovely setting overlooking Shadow Lake, offers inexpensive and spacious rooms, making it a good choice for families on a budget. **Pros:** near kid-friendly attractions; fun, old-school personality; a free ski shuttle to Cannon or Loon Mountain. **Cons:** some rooms overlook parking lot; on busy road 5 miles north of Woodstock; shows wear in places. [$] *Rooms from: $131* ✉ *664 U.S. 3, Lincoln* ☎ *603/745–8000, 800/343–8000* 🌐 *www.indianheadresort.com* 🔑 *148 rooms* 🍽 *Free breakfast.*

Mountain Club on Loon

$$ | RESORT | FAMILY | With a diverse range of accommodations, including large family suites, and many units with full kitchens, this functional if pretty standard condo-style lodge provides convenient ski-in, ski-out accommodations on Loon Mountain. **Pros:** within walking distance of the lifts; full-service spa; easy proximity to hiking in national forest. **Cons:** very busy on winter weekends; decor is a bit dated; not within walking distance of town. [$] *Rooms from: $189* ✉ *90 Loon Mountain Rd., Lincoln* ☎ *603/745–2244, 800/229–7829* 🌐 *www.mtnclub.com* 🔑 *235 rooms* 🍽 *No meals.*

🏃 Activities

HIKING

Mt. Moosilauke

HIKING/WALKING | One of the most rewarding, though heavily trafficked, summits in the White Mountains, 4,802-foot Mt. Moosilauke soars high to the west of the Pemigewasset Valley and can be

Continued on page 558

HIKING THE APPALACHIAN TRAIL

Tucked inside the nation's most densely populated corridor, a simple footpath in the wilderness stretches more than 2,100 miles, from Georgia to Maine. The Appalachian Trail passes through some of New England's most spectacular regions, and daytrippers can experience the area's beauty on a multitude of accessible, rewarding hikes. By Melissa Kim

Running along the spine of the Appalachian Mountains, the trail was fully blazed in 1937 and designed to connect anyone and everyone with nature. Within a day's drive of two-thirds of the U.S. population, it draws an estimated two to three million people every year. Through-hikers complete the whole trail in one daunting six-month season, but all ages and abilities can find renewal and perspective here in just a few hours. One-third of the AT passes through New England, and it's safe to say that the farther north you go, the harder the trail gets. New Hampshire and Maine challenge experienced hikers with windy, cold, and isolated peaks.

Top, hiking in New Hampshire's White Mountains. Above, autumn view of Profile Lake, Pemigewasset, NH.

ON THE TRAIL

New England's prime hiking season is in late summer and early fall, when the blaze of foliage viewed from a high peak is unparalleled. Popular trails see high crowds; if you seek solitude, try hiking at sunrise, a peaceful time that's good for wildlife viewing. You'll have to curb your enthusiasm in spring and early summer to avoid mud season in late April and black flies in May and June.

With the right gear, attitude, and preparation, winter can also offer fine opportunities for hiking, snowshoeing, and cross-country skiing.

FOLLOW THE TRAIL

Most hiking trails are marked with blazes, blocks of colored paint on a tree or rock. The AT, and only the AT, is marked by vertical, rectangular 2- by 6-inch white blazes. Two blazes mark route changes; turn in the direction of the top blaze. At higher elevations, you might also see cairns, small piles of rocks carefully placed by trail rangers to show the way when a blaze might be obscured by snow or fog.

Scenic U.S. 302—and the AT—pass through Crawford Notch, a spectacular valley in New Hampshire's White Mountains.

Hikers gather outside Lakes of the Clouds Hut, near the peak of Mount Washington.

TRIP TIPS

WHAT TO WEAR: For clothes, layer with a breathable fabric like polypropylene, starting with a shirt, a fleece, and a wind- or water-resistant shell. Bring gloves, a hat, and a change of socks.

WHAT TO BRING: Carry plenty of water and lightweight high-energy food. Don't forget sunscreen and insect repellent. Bring a map and compass. Just in case: a basic first-aid kit, a flashlight or headlamp, whistle, multi-tool, and matches.

PLAN AHEAD: In your car, leave a change of clothing, especially dry socks and shoes, as well as extra water and food.

PLAY IT SAFE: Tell someone your hiking plan and take a hiking partner. Carry a rescue card with emergency contact information and allergy details.

BE PREPARED: Plan your route and check the weather forecast in advance.

REMEMBER YOUR BEGINNINGS: Look back at the trail especially at the trailhead and at tricky junctions. If you've got a digital camera, photograph trail maps posted at the trailhead or natural landmarks to help you find your way.

WHERE TO STAY

Day hikers looking to extend the adventure can also make the experience as hard or as soft as they choose. Through-hikers combine camping with overnight stays in primitive shelters, mountain huts, comfortable lodges, and resorts just off the trail.

Rustic cabins and lean-tos provide basic shelter in Maine's Baxter State Park. In Maine and New Hampshire, the Appalachian Mountain Club runs four-season lodges as well as a network of mountain huts for backcountry hikers. A hiker code of camaraderie and conviviality prevails in these huts. Experience a night and you might just find yourself dreaming of a through-hike.

FOR MORE INFORMATION

Appalachian Trail Conservancy
(⊕ www.appalachiantrail.org)

Appalachian National Scenic Trail
(⊕ www.nps.gov/appa)

Appalachian Mountain Club
(⊕ www.outdoors.org)

ANIMALS ALONG THE TRAIL

❶ Black bear

Black bears are the most common—and smallest—bear in North America. Clever and adaptable, these adroit mammals will eat whatever they can (though they are primarily vegetarian, favoring berries, grasses, roots, blossoms, and nuts). Not naturally aggressive, black bears usually make themselves scarce when they hear hikers. The largest New England populations are in New Hampshire and Maine.

❷ Moose

Spotting a moose in the wild is unforgettable: their massive size and serene gaze are truly humbling. Treasure the moment, then slowly back away. At more than six feet tall, weighing 750 to 1,000 pounds, a moose is not to be trifled with, particularly during rutting and calving seasons (fall and spring, respectively). Dusk and dawn are the best times to spot the iconic animal; you're most likely to see one in Maine, especially in and around ponds.

⚠ Black flies

Especially fierce in May and June, these pesky flies can upset the tranquility of a hike in the woods as they swarm your face and bite your neck. To ward them off, cover any exposed skin and wear light colors. You'll get some relief on a mountain peak; cold weather and high winds also keep them at bay.

❸ Bald eagles

Countless bird species can be seen and heard along the AT, but what could be more exciting than to catch a glimpse of our national bird as it bounces back from near extinction? Now it's not uncommon to see the majestic bald eagle with its tremendous wing span, white head feathers, and curved yellow beak. The white head and tail distinguish the bald from the golden eagle, a bit less rare but just as thrilling to see. Most of New England's bald eagles are in Maine, but they are now present—albeit in small numbers—in all six states.

WILDFLOWERS ALONG THE TRAIL

❹ Mountain laurel

The clusters of pink and white blooms of the mountain laurel look like bursts of fireworks. Up close, each one has the delicate detail of a lady's parasol. Blooms vary in color, from pure white to darker pink, and have different amounts of red markings. Connecticut's state flower, mountain laurel flourishes in rocky woods, blooming in May and June. Look for the shrub in southern New England; it's rare along the Appalachian trail in Vermont and Maine.

❺ Mountain avens

A member of the rose family, these showy yellow flowers abound in New Hampshire's White Mountains. You can't miss the large buttercup-like blooms on long green stems when they are in bloom from June through August. So common here, yet extremely rare: the only other place in the whole world where you can find mountain avens is on an island off the coast of Nova Scotia.

❻ Painted trillium

You might smell a trillium before you see it; these flowers have an unpleasant odor that may attract the flies that pollinate it. To identify this impressive flower, look for sets of three: three large pointed blue-green leaves, three sepals (small leaves beneath the petals), and three white petals with a brilliant magenta center. It can take four or five years for a trillium to produce one flower, which blooms in May and June in wet woodlands.

❼ Pink lady slippers

These delicate orchids can grow from 6 to 15 inches high and favor specific wet wooded areas in dappled sunlight. The slender stalk rises from a pair of green leaves, then bends a graceful neck to suspend the paper-thin pale pink closed flower. The slow-growing plant needs help from fungus and bees to survive and can live to be 20 years old. New Hampshire's state wildflower, the pink lady slipper blooms in June throughout New England.

● = Somewhat Common ● = Rare

CHOOSE YOUR DAY HIKE

MAINE

GULF HAGAS, Greenville

Difficult, 8-plus miles round-trip, 6–7 hours

This National Natural Landmark in the North Maine Woods is a spectacular sight for the adventurous day hiker. It involves a long drive on logging roads east from Greenville (see Inland Maine section) to a remote spot and a slippery, sometimes treacherous 8-mile hike around the rim of what's been dubbed Maine's Grand Canyon. Swimming in one of the sparkling pools under a 30-foot-high waterfall and admiring the views of cliffs, cascades, gorges, and chasms in this slate canyon, otherwise unthinkable in New England, will take your breath away.

TABLE ROCK, Bethel

Medium, 2.4 miles round-trip, 2 hours

Maine's Mahoosuc Range is thought to be one of the most difficult stretches of the entire AT, but north of Bethel at Grafton Notch State Park, day hikes range from easy walks in to cascading waterfalls to strenuous climbs up Old Speck's craggy peak. The Table Rock trail offers interesting sights—great views of the notch from the immense slab of granite that gives this trail its name, as well as one of the state's largest system of slab caves—narrow with tall openings unlike underground caves.

NEW HAMPSHIRE

ZEALAND TRAIL, Berlin

Easy, 5.6 miles round-trip, 3.5–4 hours

New Hampshire's Presidential range gets so much attention and traffic that sometimes the equally spectacular Pemigewasset Wilderness, just to its west, gets overlooked. Follow State Route 302 to the trailhead on Zealand Rd. near Bretton Woods. For an easy day hike to one of the Appalachian Mountain Club's excellent overnight huts, take the mostly flat Zealand Trail over bridges and past a beaver swamp to Zealand Pond. The last tenth of a mile is a steep ascent to the mountain retreat, where you might spot an AT through-hiker taking a well-deserved rest. (Most north-bound through-hikers reach this section around July or August.) In winter, you can get here by a lovely cross-country ski trip.

TRAIL NAMES

For through-hikers, doing the AT can be a life-altering experience. One of the trail's most respected traditions is taking an alter ego: a trail name. Lightning Bolt: fast hiker. Pine Knot: tough as one. Bluebearee: because a bear got all her food on her very first night on the trail.

VERMONT

HARMON HILL, Bennington

Medium to difficult, 3.6 miles round-trip, 3–4 hours

This rugged hike in the Green Mountains goes south along the AT where it coincides with the Long Trail, Vermont's century-old "footpath in the wilderness." From the trailhead on Route 9 just east of Bennington, the first half mile or so is strenuous, with some rock and log staircases and hairpins. The payback is the sweeping view from the top; you'll see Mount Anthony, Bennington and its iconic war monument, and the rolling green hills of the Taconics to the west.

STRATTON MOUNTAIN, Stratton

Difficult, 6.6 miles round-trip, 5–6 hours

A steep and steady climb from the trailhead on Kelly Stand Rd. (between West Wardsboro and Arlington) up the 3,936-foot-high Stratton Mountain follows the AT and Long Trail through mixed forests. It's said that this peak is where Benton MacKaye conceived of the idea for the Appalachian Trail in 1921. An observation tower at the summit gives you a great 360-degree view of the Green Mountains. From July to October, you can park at Stratton resort and ride the gondola up (or down) and follow the .75-mile Fire Tower Trail to the southern true peak.

MASSACHUSETTS

MOUNT GREYLOCK, North Adams

Easy to difficult, 2 miles round-trip, less than 1 hour

There are many ways to experience Massachusetts's highest peak. From North Adams, follow Route 2 to the Notch Rd. trailheads. For a warm-up, try the Rounds Rock trail (Easy, 0.7 mi) for some spectacular views. Or drive up the 8-mile-long summit road and hike down the Robinson's Point trail (Difficult, 0.8 miles) for the best view of the Hopper, a glacial cirque that's home to an old-growth red spruce forest. At the summit, the impressive **Bascom Lodge**, built in the 1930s by the Civilian Conservation Corps, provides delicious meals and overnight stays (wwww. bascomlodge.net).

CONNECTICUT

LION'S HEAD, Salisbury

Medium, 4.6 miles round-trip, 3.5–4 hours

The AT's 52 miles in Connecticut take hikers up some modest mountains, including Lion's Head in Salisbury. From the trailhead on State Route 41, follow the white blazes of the AT for two easy miles, then take the blue-blazed Lion's Head Trail for a short, steep push over open ledges to the 1,738-foot summit with its commanding views of pastoral southern New England. Try this in summer when the mountain laurels—Connecticut's state flower—are in bloom.

EXPERIENCE MOUNT WASHINGTON

Looking at Mt. Washington from Mt. Bond in the Pemigewasset Wilderness Area, New Hampshire.

Mount Washington is the Northeast's peak of superlatives: worst weather in the world, highest spot in the northeast, windiest place on Earth. It snows in the summer, there are avalanches in winter, and it's foggy 60 percent of the time. Strong 35-mile-per-hour winds are the average, and extreme winds of 100 miles per hour with higher gusts blow year-round. Here, you can literally get blown away.

Explorers, scientists, artists, and botanists have been coming to the mountain for hundreds of years, drawn by its unique geologic features, unusual plants, and exceptional climate.

WHY SO WINDY? The 6,288-foot-high treeless peak is the highest point for miles around, so nothing dampens the force of the wind. Also, the sharp vertical rise causes wind to accelerate. Dramatic changes in air pressure also cause strong, high winds. Add to that the fact that three major storm tracks converge here, and you've got a mountain that has claimed more than 135 lives in the past 150 years.

GOING UP THE MOUNTAIN

An ascent up Mount Washington is for experienced hikers who are prepared for severe, unpredictable weather. Even in summer, cold, wet, foggy, windy conditions prevail. The most popular route to the top is on the eastern face up the Tuckerman Ravine Trail. But countless trails offer plenty of moderate day hikes, like the Alpine Garden Trail, as an alternative to a summit attempt. Start at the Pinkham Notch Visitor Center on Route 16 to review your options.

BACKPACKING ON THE MOUNTAIN

Lakes of the Clouds Hut perches 5,050 feet up the southern shoulder, providing bunkrooms and meals in summer; reservations are required. On the eastern face, the **Hermit Lake Shelter Area** has shelters and tent platforms; to camp here you'll need a first-come, first-served permit from the Visitors Center. Both are operated by the **AMC** (☎ 603/466-2727; ⊕ www.outdoors.org).

NON-HIKING ALTERNATIVES

In the summer, the **Auto Road** (☎ 603/466-3988 ⊕ mtwashingtonautoroad. com) and the **Cog Railway** (☎ 800/922-8825 ⊕ www. thecog.com) present alternate ways up the mountain; both give you a real sense of the mountain's grandeur. In winter, a **SnowCoach** (☎ 603/466-2333 ⊕ www.greatglentrails. com) hauls visitors 4.5 miles up the Auto Road with an option to cross-country ski, telemark, snowshoe, or ride the coach back down.

approached a few routes, including the Appalachian Trail and from Route 112 near Lost River Gorge. The most enjoyable trek is via the 7-mile South Peak Loop. It begins near Route 118 at the 1930s Moosilauke Ravine Lodge, which is operated by Dartmouth College and offers basic overnight accommodations. However you ascend to the treeless peak, you'll enjoy sweeping views of the Presidential Range, Lake Winnipesaukee, and even the Adirondacks. ⊠ *Ravine Rd., North Woodstock*.

SKIING
Loon Mountain
SKIING/SNOWBOARDING | FAMILY | Wide, straight, and consistent intermediate ski trails prevail at this modern resort on the Pemigewasset River. The most advanced runs are grouped on the North Peak, with beginner trails set apart. There's snow tubing on the lower slopes, and eight terrain parks suitable for all ability levels. A base lodge contains offers dining and lounges. You'll also find 13 miles of cross-country trails, an outdoor ice-skating rink, snowshoeing and snowshoeing tours, ziplining, and a rock-climbing wall. **Facilities:** 61 trails; 370 acres; 2,100-foot vertical drop; 11 lifts. ⊠ *90 Loon Mountain Rd., Lincoln* ☎ *603/745–8111* ⊕ *www.loonmtn.com* ⌨ *Lift ticket: $102*.

🛍 Shopping

Fadden's General Store
FOOD/CANDY | The Fadden family, who have been making maple syrup since the early 19th century, operates this inviting general store, sugarhouse, and maple museum that dates to 1896. Come in to buy syrup, souvenirs, and gourmet treats, or for a self-guided tour of the operations. ⊠ *109 Main St., North Woodstock* ☎ *603/745–8371* ⊕ *www.nhmaplesyrup.com*.

Waterville Valley

25 miles southeast of North Lincoln.

Although visitors have been exploring this dramatic southern White Mountains valley since 1835, and the first ski trails were installed on 3,997-foot Mt. Tecumseh in the 1930s, Watervalley Valley didn't become a major destination until a group of developers led by Olympic skier Tom Corcoran built a full-service ski area here in 1966. That led to a planned resort with several hotels and condominiums, a town square with shops and restaurants, a golf course, and other amenities. Today it's a terrific family-friendly winter-sports destination, but there's also plenty to do in warmer months, including great hiking and mountain-biking. Rates at the resort hotels come with passes that include cross-country ski and bike rentals, access to the well-equipped White Mountain Athletic Club, and other perks—it's a remarkable value.

GETTING HERE AND AROUND
You get here from Interstate 93 in Campton, via Route 49, which runs alongside the Mad River and dead-ends at the Town Square. Free shuttle buses whisk guests from hotels to the ski area. In summer, you travel here by way of unpaved Tripoli Road, a bumpy but beautiful route through White Mountain National Forest that accesses some amazing campgrounds and hikes, such as Mt. Osceola and Mt. Tecumseh. It leads out to Interstate 93 in Woodstock.

🍴 Restaurants

Coyote Grill
$$ | AMERICAN | FAMILY | On the second floor of the White Mountain Athletic Club, Waterville Valley's best restaurant is a rambling space with big windows offering up grand views of the White Mountains. The food is hearty and well-prepared, just what you need after a day of hiking or skiing. **Known for:** mountain

views; lighter fare served downstairs by the pool; Oreo-crusted white-chocolate cheesecake. $ *Average main: $21* ✉ *98 Valley Rd.* ☎ *603/236–4919* ⊕ *www. wildcoyotegrill.com* ⊙ *Closed Mon. and Tues. No lunch.*

🏨 Hotels

Golden Eagle Lodge

$$ | HOTEL | FAMILY | Waterville Valley's premier condominium resort, its steep roof punctuated by dozens of gabled dormers, recalls the grand hotels of an earlier era. **Pros:** steps from Town Square; units all have kitchens and lots of elbow room; sweeping mountain views. **Cons:** decor is a little dated; no a/c in many units; lots of kids and families create a sometimes hectic pace. $ *Rooms from: $179* ✉ *28 Packard's Rd.* ☎ *888/703–2453, 603/236– 4600* ⊕ *www.goldeneaglelodge.com* ⇲ *139 condos* ⦿ *No meals.*

Valley Inn

$ | HOTEL | FAMILY | One of the town's less expensive options, the Valley Inn offers few frills, but when you factor in the free activities pass and the quiet but convenient location, it's a solid option. **Pros:** good value; largest units have kitchens and can sleep six; peaceful setting. **Cons:** a few minutes' walk to Town Square; cookie-cutter decor; very basic breakfast. $ *Rooms from: $149* ✉ *17 Tecumseh Rd.* ☎ *603/236–8425* ⊕ *www.valleyinn.com* ⇲ *42 rooms* ⦿ *Free Breakfast.*

Activities

BIKING

Adventure Center

BICYCLING | Waterville Valley's one-stop for mountain-bike and cross-country-ski rentals, maps, and trail passes, this well-equipped shop has a helpful staff ready to dispense advice on where to explore. They also offer lessons and clinics. ✉ *6 Village Rd.* ☎ *603/236–4666* ⊕ *www. waterville.com.*

HIKING

★ Welch-Dickey Trail

HIKING/WALKING | This at times steep but gorgeous 4½-mile loop hike ascends a wooded hillside before climbing above the sheer granite faces of 2,605-foot Welch and 2,734-foot Dickey mountains. There are higher climbs in the White Mountains, but this trail offers incredible views in every direction. Parking costs $5. ✉ *Orris Rd.*

SKIING

Waterville Valley Resort

SKIING/SNOWBOARDING | FAMILY | This family-friendly ski area has hosted many World Cup races, so advanced skiers can look forward to a challenge. About two-thirds of the 50 trails are intermediate: straight down the fall line, wide, and agreeably long. About 20 acres of tree-skiing and six terrain parks add heart-pounding stimulus, and full snow-making coverage ensures good skiing even when nature doesn't cooperate. The resort also offers 46 miles of groomed cross-country trails. **Facilities:** 50 trails; 220 acres; 2,020-foot vertical drop; 11 lifts. ✉ *1 Ski Area Rd.* ☎ *603/236–8311, 800/468–2553* ⊕ *www.waterville.com* 🎫 *Lift ticket: $98.*

New London

60 miles southwest of Waterville Valley, 33 miles west of Laconia, 40 miles northwest of Concord.

New London, the home of Colby-Sawyer College (1837), is a good base for exploring the Lake Sunapee region. A campus of stately Colonial-style buildings abuts the picturesque downtown, where you'll find several cafés and boutiques.

GETTING HERE AND AROUND

New London is just off Interstate 89.

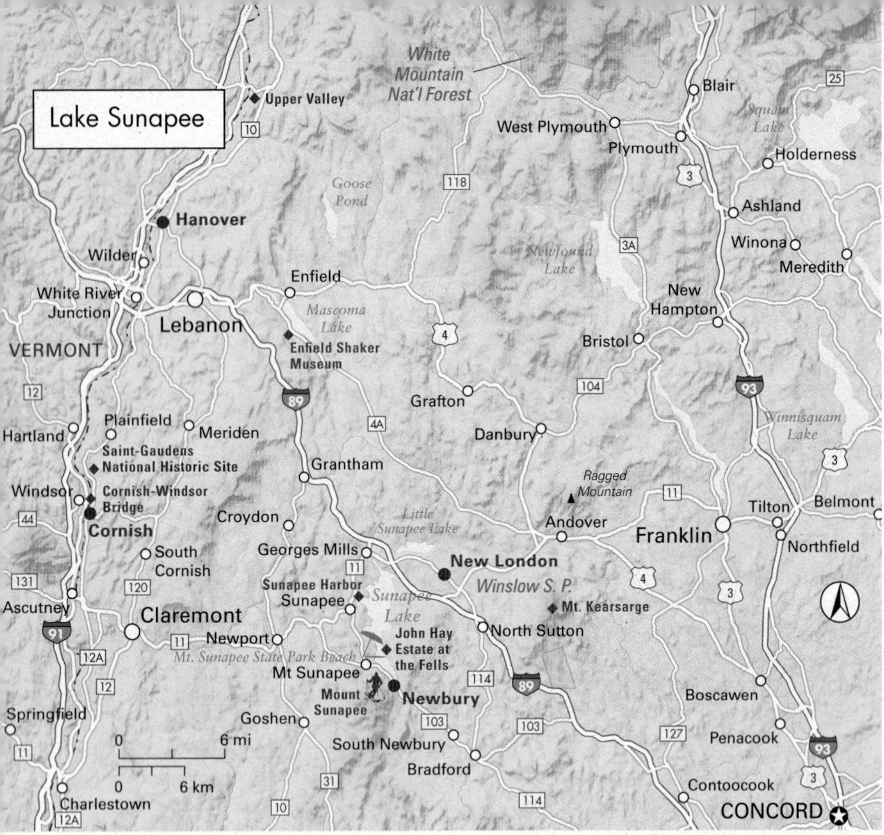

Sights

Mt. Kearsarge

NATIONAL/STATE PARK | There are two main ways to access this dramatic 2,937-foot granite peak east of Lake Sunapee. Approach it through **Winslow State Park,** which is closer to New London, by driving to the picnic area and hiking a 1.8-mile loop trail to the top. Or, more popularly, drive the 3½-mile scenic auto route through **Rollins State Park,** which snakes up the mountain's southern slope and leads to a ½-mile summit trail. However you get there, the views from the top are astounding. Rollins State Park is accessed from the cute colonial village of Warner, which is worth a quick stroll through. ✉ *Rollins State Park, 1066 Kearsarge Mountain Rd., Warner* ☎ *603/456–3808* 🌐 *www.nhstateparks.org* 🎟 *$4.*

Restaurants

★ Oak & Grain

$$$ | **MODERN AMERICAN** | The refined yet relaxed restaurant in the historic Inn at Pleasant Lake makes a splendid destination for a special occasion dinner, or simply to savor a delicious brunch in the window-lined dining room or out on the patio—both areas have views of the lake in the near distance. The kitchen here turns out artfully plated contemporary fare, such as kebabs of grilled shrimp, pork belly, and veggies with a spicy garlic-chili-lime aioli, and filet mignon with a foie gras–port wine sauce. **Known for:** pretty lake views; knowledgeable, friendly service; locally sourced meats and seafood. [$] *Average main: $31* ✉ *853 Pleasant St.* ☎ *603/873–4833* 🌐 *innatpleasantlake.com* 🕒 *Closed Mon. and Tues. No lunch.*

Peter Christian's Tavern

$$ | MODERN AMERICAN | Exposed beams, wooden tables, a smattering of antiques, and half shutters on the windows make the amiable Peter Christian's a cool summer oasis and a warm winter haven. From shepherd's pie to seafood and grits with lobster butter, the flavorful comfort fare relies heavily on seasonal ingredients. **Known for:** outstanding clam chowder; well-curated craft-beer and wine selection; dog-friendly patio. $ *Average main: $20* ✉ *195 N. Main St.* ☎ *603/526–2964* ⊕ *www.peterchristiansnh.com.*

Coffee and Quick Bites

Blue Loon Bakery

$ | BAKERY | Have a seat in this cheerful bakery's sunny seating nooks or out on the back patio, while you savor an egg-cheddar sandwich, house-made granola, a brie-fig-apple baguette, or one of the delectable pastries or cakes. Favorite treats include maple-pumpkin pie, seasonal fruit tarts, raspberry scones, and praline sticky buns. **Known for:** savory artisan breads; fresh-baked pies; picnic supplies for nearby hiking and beach adventures. $ *Average main: $7* ✉ *12 Lovering La.* ☎ *603/526–2892* ⊕ *www.blueloonbakery.com* ⊗ *No dinner.*

🛏 Hotels

Follansbee Inn

$ | B&B/INN | Built in 1840, this rambling country inn on the shore of Kezar Lake is the kind of place that almost automatically turns strangers into fast friends. **Pros:** relaxed lakefront setting with 3-mile walking trail; free use of canoes, kayaks, sailboats, rowboats, and bicycles; excellent breakfast. **Cons:** not all rooms have lake views; Wi-Fi can be spotty in places; no restaurants within walking distance. $ *Rooms from: $135* ✉ *2 Keyser St., North Sutton* ☎ *603/927–4221* ⊕ *www.follansbeeinn.com* ⇥ *17 rooms* ⦿ *Free breakfast.*

★ Inn at Pleasant Lake

$$ | B&B/INN | Overlooking the shore of Pleasant Lake, and offering views of majestic Mt. Kearsarge in the distance, and just a short drive from downtown New London, this beautifully appointed 1790s inn has spacious, bright rooms filled with fine country antiques and high-end bedding. **Pros:** adjacent to lakefront and a small beach; tennis courts; rates includes an outstanding full breakfast and afternoon tea. **Cons:** not within walking distance of town; not a good fit for kids; minimum stay at busy times. $ *Rooms from: $219* ✉ *853 Pleasant St.* ☎ *603/526–6271, 800/626–4907* ⊕ *innatpleasantlake.com* ⇥ *10 rooms* ⦿ *Free breakfast.*

🍸 Nightlife

Flying Goose Brew Pub

BREWPUBS/BEER GARDENS | Offering a regular menu of about a dozen handcrafted beers, including a much lauded black IPA and a heady barleywine as well as a few seasonal varieties—made with hops grown on-site—this pub, and solar-powered brewery is a hit with beer connoisseurs. The kitchen serves juicy ribs, paper-thin onion rings, excellent burgers, and other tasty victuals. ✉ *40 Andover Rd.* ☎ *603/526–6899* ⊕ *www.flyinggoose.com.*

🎭 Performing Arts

New London Barn Playhouse

THEATER | FAMILY | Broadway-style musicals and children's plays are presented here every summer in New Hampshire's oldest continuously operating theater. ✉ *84 Main St.* ☎ *603/526–6710* ⊕ *www.nlbarn.org.*

🛍 Shopping

Artisan's

CRAFTS | This downtown boutique gallery carries jewelry, beads, gourmet foods, clothing, and local crafts. ✉ *11 Pleasant St.* ☎ *603/526–4227* ⊕ *www.artisans-newlondon.com.*

Newbury

8 miles southwest of New London.

Newbury lies at the southern edge of 6-square-mile Lake Sunapee, one of the highest—and one of the cleanest—in the state, and a fine destination for boating, swimming, and fishing. Mt. Sunapee State Park has a picturesque beach on the lake as well as a mountain section that rises to an elevation of nearly 3,000 feet and offers some of the best skiing in southern New Hampshire. The popular League of New Hampshire Craftsmen's Fair, the oldest crafts fair in the nation, is held here in early August.

GETTING HERE AND AROUND
From Interstate 89, Route 103A leads here via the eastern shore of Lake Sunapee.

◉ Sights

★ John Hay Estate at the Fells
FOREST | The former home of the statesman who served as private secretary to Abraham Lincoln and U.S. Secretary of State to Presidents William McKinley and Theodore Roosevelt, built the 22-room Fells on Lake Sunapee as a summer home in 1890. House tours offer a glimpse of late Victorian life on a New Hampshire estate. The grounds, a gardener's delight, include a 100-foot-long perennial garden and a rock garden with a brook flowing through it. Miles of hiking trails can also be accessed on this 83½-acre estate. ⊠ *456 Rte. 103A* ☎ *603/763–4789* ⊕ *www.thefells.org* ⊠ *$10 when house open, $8 when house closed* ⊗ *House closed Mon. and Tues. and mid-Oct.–late May.*

★ Sunapee Harbor
BODY OF WATER | On the west side of Lake Sunapee, this old-fashioned summer resort community has a large marina, a few restaurants and shops on the water, a tidy village green with a gazebo, and a small museum. ⊠ *Main St. at Lake Ave., Sunapee.*

◉ Beaches

Mt. Sunapee State Park Beach
BEACH—SIGHT | FAMILY | A great family spot, this beach adjoining an 4,085-acre mountain park has picnic areas, fishing, and a bathhouse, plus access to great hiking trails. You can also rent canoes and kayaks, and there's a campground. **Amenities:** lifeguards; parking (fee); showers; toilets. **Best for:** swimming; walking. ⊠ *86 Beach Access Rd.* ☎ *603/763–5561* ⊕ *www.nhstateparks.org* ⊠ *$5 mid-May–mid-Oct.*

◉ Restaurants

Suna
$$ | MODERN AMERICAN | On a wooded country road just up the hill from Lake Sunapee, this lively little bar and bistro is great for a romantic meal or a relaxed bite after a day on the water or the mountain. The eclectic menu features a mix of classic American and Continental dishes with creative touches. **Known for:** excellent craft cocktails; lively après-ski scene; sublime desserts. $ *Average main: $22* ⊠ *6 Brook Rd., Sunapee* ☎ *603/843–8998* ⊕ *www.magicfoodsrestaurantgroup.com* ⊗ *Closed Mon.*

Wildwood Smokehouse
$ | BARBECUE | The hulking metal smoker outside this Old West–inspired tavern with high pressed-tin ceilings, chandeliers, and red Victorian wallpaper hints at the delicious barbecue served inside. Plates heaped with ribs, beef brisket, pulled chicken, and smoked bratwurst reveal the considerable skill of Wildwood's pit master, and plenty of tasty sides are offered, too, from mac and cheese to dirty rice. **Known for:** pecan pie; "hog wings" (pork shanks in barbecue sauce); popular early evening happy hour. $ *Average main: $17* ⊠ *45 Main St., Sunapee* ☎ *603/763–1178* ⊕ *www.wildwoodsmokehousesunapee.com* ⊗ *Closed Sun. and Mon. No lunch.*

🛏 Hotels

Sunapee Harbor Cottages

$$ | RENTAL | This cozy compound of six charming, eco-friendly cottages—each sleeping five–eight people and with small but well-equipped kitchens—is a stone's throw from Sunapee Harbor and an easy drive from winter skiing at nearby Mt. Sunapee. **Pros:** ideal for families or friends traveling together; free beach passes; pet-friendly. **Cons:** no maid service; limited clothes storage; cottage porches overlook one another. $ *Rooms from: $225* ✉ *4 Lake Ave., Sunapee Harbor* ☎ *603/763–5052* ⊕ *www.sunapee-harborcottages.com* ↩ *6 cottages* ❍ *No meals.*

🏃 Activities

BOAT TOURS

Sunapee Cruises

TOUR—SPORTS | This company operates narrated afternoon and dinner cruises of Lake Sunapee from June to mid-October. Ninety-minute afternoon cruises on the M/V *Mt. Sunapee* focus on Lake Sunapee's history and the mountain scenery. A buffet dinner is included on the two-hour sunset cruises aboard the M/V *Kearsarge*, a vintage-style steamship. ✉ *Town Dock, 81 Main St., Sunapee Harbor* ☎ *603/938–6465* ⊕ *www.sunapeecruises.com* ☞ *From $22.*

HIKING

Monadnock-Sunapee Greenway Trail

HIKING/WALKING | This 50-mile trail starts in Newbury at Mt. Sunapee and snakes through verdant forests and the handsome village greens of Washington and Nelson and over jagged granite peaks south to Mt. Monadnock. One of the most enjoyable ways to access this trail is to hike the 2.3-mile (one-way) Andrew Brook Trail up to the granite ledges above Lake Solitude, where you'll cross with it. ✉ *Andrew Brook Trailhead, Mountain Rd.* ⊕ *www.msgtc.org.*

SKIING

Mt. Sunapee

SKIING/SNOWBOARDING | FAMILY | This family-friendly resort is one of New England's best-kept secrets. The owners have spent millions upgrading their snow machines and grooming equipment and turning this into a four-season resort. Mt. Sunapee offers 66 trails and slopes for all abilities. There are four terrain parks and nine glade trails. In summer, the adventure park features a canopy zipline tour, an aerial challenge course, an 18-hole disc-golf course, miniature golf, and numerous hiking trails. **Facilities:** 67 trails; 233 acres; 1,510-foot vertical drop; 9 lifts. ✉ *1398 Rte. 103* ☎ *603/763–3500* ⊕ *www.mountsunapee.com* ☞ *Lift ticket: $94.*

🛍 Shopping

Gibson Pewter

CERAMICS/GLASSWARE | Jon Gibson crafts and sells museum-quality pewter mugs, oil lamps, vases, pitchers, and other stunning works in a barn and workshop overlooking one of the state's prettiest colonial town greens, in the rural hilltop village of Washington—about 15 miles south of Lake Sunapee. ✉ *26 N. Main St., Washington* ☎ *603/495–1776* ⊕ *www.gibsonpewter.com.*

Wild Goose Country Store

GIFTS/SOUVENIRS | FAMILY | On the harbor in Sunapee, this old-fashioned general store carries teddy bears, penny candy, pottery, and other engaging odds and ends. ✉ *77 Main St., Sunapee* ☎ *603/763–5516.*

Hanover

30 miles northwest of New London, 60 miles southwest of Littleton, 20 miles east of Woodstock, Vermont.

Eleazar Wheelock founded Hanover's Dartmouth College in 1769 to educate the Abenaki "and other youth." When he arrived, the town consisted of about 20 families. Over time the college and the town grew symbiotically, with Dartmouth eventually becoming the northernmost Ivy League school. Hanover is still synonymous with Dartmouth, but it's also a respected medical and cultural center. Shops, mostly of the independent variety, fill the town's commercial district, which blends almost imperceptibly with Dartmouth's campus. Hanover and West Lebanon, with Woodstock, Quechee, Norwich, and White River Junction across the Connecticut River in Vermont, form an appealing two-state vacation destination.

GETTING HERE AND AROUND

Lebanon Municipal Airport is served by Cape Air from Boston and White Plains, New York. By car, Interstates 91 and 89 are both nearby.

ESSENTIALS

AIRPORT Lebanon Municipal Airport. ✉ *5 Airpark Rd., West Lebanon* ☎ *603/298–8878* ⊕ *www.flyleb.com.*

VISITOR INFORMATION Upper Valley Business Alliance. ☎ *603/448–1203* ⊕ *www. uppervalleybusinessalliance.com.*

 Sights

Dartmouth College

COLLEGE | The poet Robert Frost spent part of a brooding freshman semester at this Ivy League school before giving up college altogether, but the school counts politician Nelson Rockefeller, actor Mindy Kaling, TV producer Shonda Rhimes, and author Theodor ("Dr.") Seuss Geisel among its many illustrious grads. The buildings clustered around the picturesque green, which is lovely for strolling, include the **Baker Memorial Library,** which houses such literary treasures as 17th-century editions of William Shakespeare's works. The library is also well-known for Mexican artist José Clemente Orozco's 3,000-square-foot murals that depict the story of civilization in the Americas. Free campus tours are available. ✉ *N. Main and Wentworth Sts.* ☎ *603/646–1110* ⊕ *www.dartmouth.edu.*

Enfield Shaker Museum

MUSEUM VILLAGE | In 1782, two Shaker brothers from Mt. Lebanon, New York, arrived on Lake Mascoma's northeastern side, about 12 miles southeast of Hanover. Eventually, they formed Enfield, the ninth of 18 Shaker communities in the United States, and moved it to the lake's southern shore, where they erected more than 200 buildings. The Enfield Shaker Museum preserves the legacy of the Shakers, who numbered 330 members at the village's peak. By 1923, interest in the society had waned, and the last 10 members joined the Canterbury community, south of Laconia. A self-guided walking tour takes you through 13 of the remaining buildings, among them an 1849 stone mill. Demonstrations of Shaker crafts techniques also take place, and overnight accommodations are available in the community's stately six-story Great Stone Dwelling. ✉ *447 Rte. 4A, Enfield* ☎ *603/632–4346* ⊕ *www. shakermuseum.org* ⊠ *$12.*

★ Hood Museum of Art

MUSEUM | Dartmouth's excellent art museum owns Picasso's *Guitar on a Table,* silver by Paul Revere, a set of Assyrian reliefs from the 9th century BC, along with other noteworthy examples of African, Peruvian, Oceanic, Asian, European, and American art. The range of contemporary works—including pieces by John Sloan, William Glackens, Mark Rothko, Fernand Léger, and Joan Miró—is particularly notable. Rivaling the collection is the museum's architecture: a series of austere, copper-roof, redbrick buildings arranged around a courtyard. The museum galleries received an ambitious renovation and expansion in 2019 that added five new galleries and a striking new entrance designed by the husband-and-wife architectural team of Tod Williams and Billie Tsien (known for the Barnes Foundation in Philadelphia and New York's downtown Whitney Museum). ✉ *Wheelock St.* ☎ *603/646–2808* ⊕ *hoodmuseum.dartmouth.edu* ⊘ *Closed Mon. and Tues.*

Hopkins Center for the Arts

ARTS VENUE | If the towering arcade at the entrance to the center appears familiar, it's probably because it resembles the project that architect Wallace K. Harrison completed just after designing it: New York City's Metropolitan Opera House at Lincoln Center. The complex includes a 900-seat theater for concerts and film screenings, a 480-seat theater for plays, and a black-box theater for new plays. This is the home of the Dartmouth Symphony Orchestra and several other performance groups. ✉ *2 E. Wheelock St.* ☎ *603/646–2422* 🌐 *hop.dartmouth.edu.*

★ Upper Valley

BODY OF WATER | From Hanover, make the beautiful 60-mile drive up Route 10 to Littleton for a stunningly scenic tour of the upper Connecticut River and lower Ammonoosuc river valleys. You'll have views of Vermont's Green Mountains from many points. The road passes through groves of evergreens, over leafy ridges, and through delightful hamlets abundant with fine Georgian- and Federal-style mansions. Grab gourmet picnic provisions at the historic general stores in Lyme or Bath, view several covered bridges on nearby side roads, and, stop by pastoral family farms, like Hatchland Farms Dairy Delites, for ice cream and Collins Farm for its corn maze. There are numerous spots for a picnic, including little-visited Bedell Bridge State Park in Haverhill, which overlooks the Connecticut River. ✉ *Hanover.*

🍴 Restaurants

★ Ariana's

$$$ | MODERN AMERICAN | With its stone fireplace, cathedral ceiling, and rustic-elegant barnlike interior, this inviting restaurant in the venerable Lyme Inn turns out farm-fresh modern American fare with international influences. Try the blackened scallops with an orange-chili-butter sauce or sliced-duck salad with shaved fennel and a ginger dressing, before moving on to herb-crusted swordfish with a saffron-sherry butter sauce. **Known for:** five-course prix-fixe chef dinners; a well-curated wine list; peaceful setting in a historic hamlet. [$] *Average main: $26* ✉ *1 Market St., Lyme* ☎ *603/353-4405* 🌐 *www.arianasrestaurant.com* 🕒 *Closed Mon. and Tues.*

Base Camp

$$ | NEPALESE | This inviting restaurant in the lower level of a downtown retail-dining complex serves authentic, prepared-to-order Nepalese cuisine. Start with an order of momos (steamed dumplings) bursting with buffalo, paneer-and-spinach, wild boar, or several other fillings, and then try one of the easily shared tarkari (tomato-based) curries or chilies, offered with an extensive variety of meats and vegetables, from goat and duck to sweet potato and mushroom. **Known for:** everything can be prepared from mild to very spicy; plenty of meatless options; helpful, friendly staff. [$] *Average main: $20* ✉ *3 Lebanon St.* ☎ *603/643–2007* 🌐 *www.basecampcafenh.com.*

Latham House Tavern

$$ | AMERICAN | This convivial, easy-going gastropub in historic Lyme's rambling Dowd's Country Inn—which also has pleasant guest accommodations—features an impressive list of New England craft beers as well as an enticing selection of reasonably priced comfort fare. Favorites include the half-pound house burger topped with bacon and a beer–smoked gouda fondue, and the pulled-pork poutine with a chipotle-cider barbecue sauce. **Known for:** elevated pub fare; interesting list of beers on tap; warmly lighted dining room with beam ceiling. [$] *Average main: $18* ✉ *9 Main St., Lyme* ☎ *603/795–9995* 🌐 *www.lathamhousetavern.com* 🕒 *Closed Tues.*

Lou's Restaurant

$ | AMERICAN | FAMILY | A Hanover tradition since 1948, this diner-cum-café-cum-bakery serves possibly the best breakfast in the valley, with favorites that include blueberry-cranberry buttermilk pancakes, and sausage-gravy biscuits with two

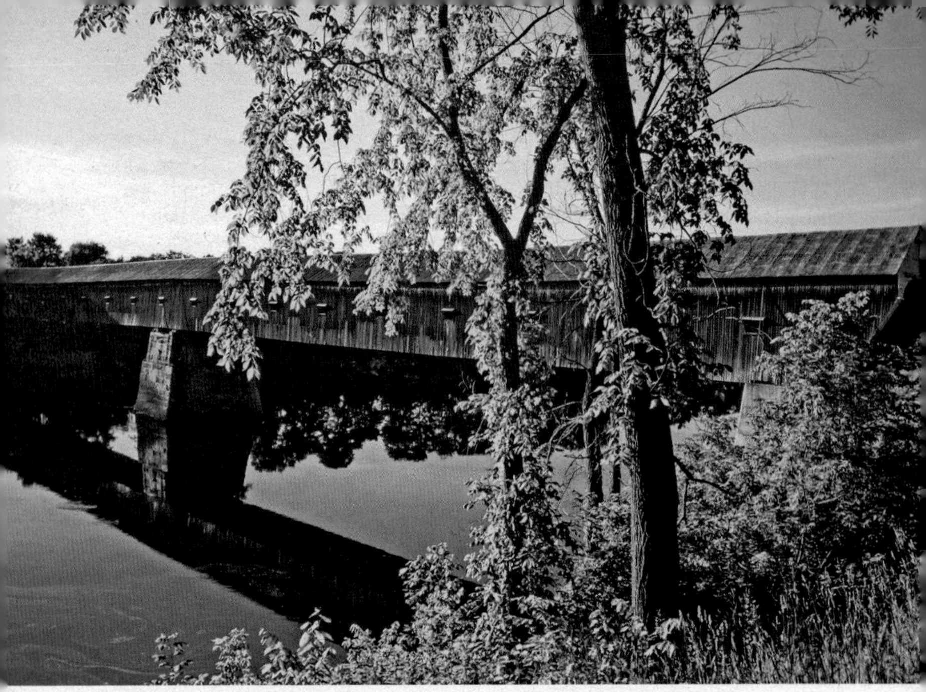

The Cornish–Windsor Bridge is the second-longest covered bridge in the United States.

eggs any style. Or just grab a seat at the old-fashioned soda fountain for a juicy burger and an ice-cream sundae. **Known for:** colorful mix of locals and Dartmouth folks; fresh-baked pastries and brownies; breakfast served all day. [$] *Average main: $11* ✉ *30 S. Main St.* ☎ *603/643–3321* 🌐 *lousrestaurant.com* 🕒 *No dinner.*

Murphy's on the Green

$$ | MODERN AMERICAN | Students, visiting alums, and locals regularly descend on this wildly popular pub, which has walls lined with shelves of old books. The varied menu features burgers and salads as well as meat loaf, lobster mac and cheese, and vegetarian dishes like crispy-tofu pad Thai and house-smoked tofu street tacos. **Known for:** sourcing ingredients from local farms; dinner menu available until late; extensive beer list. [$] *Average main: $18* ✉ *5 Main St.* ☎ *603/643–7777* 🌐 *www.murphysonthegreen.com.*

Hotels

Hanover Inn

$$$ | HOTEL | A sprawling Georgian-style brick structure rising six white-trimmed stories above Hanover's main square contains this chichi boutique hotel and is also home to the acclaimed farm-to-table restaurant, Pine. **Pros:** overlooks campus green in center of town; excellent restaurant and bar; well-equipped fitness center. **Cons:** expensive parking; pricey during busy times; books up way in advance many weekends. [$] *Rooms from: $271* ✉ *2 E. Wheelock St.* ☎ *603/643–4300, 800/443–7024* 🌐 *www.hanoverinn.com* 🛏 *108 rooms* 🍴 *No meals.*

★ Lyme Inn

$$ | B&B/INN | With an enchanted setting on the elliptical village common in colonial Lyme, this four-story inn that began life as a stagecoach stop in the early 1800s offers an elegant, tranquil respite from the crowds of Hanover and offers meals in an esteemed restaurant. **Pros:** quiet setting; rates include a tasty but light breakfast; good base for exploring Hanover as well as Norwich and Woodstock, Vermont. **Cons:** no elevator; a 15-minute drive to Hanover; minimum-night stays during busy times. $ *Rooms from: $229* ⊠ *1 Market St., Lyme* ☎ *603/795-4824* ⊕ *www.thelymeinn.com* ⥋ *14 rooms* ⦿ *Free Breakfast.*

Six South St Hotel

$$ | **HOTEL** | With its bold black and red color scheme and angular light fixtures and furnishings, this redbrick boutique hotel just off Hanover's bustling Main Street is a perfect roost for visiting Dartmouth and its museums. **Pros:** hip, contemporary design; great little bistro and bar; downtown location steps from campus. **Cons:** expensive parking; breakfast buffet costs extra; busy in-town setting. $ *Rooms from: $209* ⊠ *6 South St.* ☎ *603/643–0600* ⊕ *www.sixsouth. com* ⥋ *63 rooms* ⦿ *No meals.*

🏃 Activities

Ledyard Canoe Club

BOATING | On the banks of the Connecticut River, this outfitter rents canoes, kayaks, and standup paddleboards by the hour, as well as rustic cabins. ⊠ *9 Boathouse Rd.* ☎ *603/643–6709* ⊕ *www. ledyardcanoeclub.org.*

Cornish

22 miles south of Hanover.

Today Cornish is best known for its covered bridges and for having been the home of the late reclusive author J. D. Salinger, but at the turn of the 20th century the village was acclaimed as the home of the country's then-most-popular novelist, Winston Churchill (no relation to the British prime minister). His novel *Richard Carvel* sold more than a million

copies. Churchill was such a celebrity that he hosted President Theodore Roosevelt in 1902. At that time Cornish was an artistic enclave: painter Maxfield Parrish lived and worked here, and sculptor Augustus Saint-Gaudens set up his studio here, where he created the heroic bronzes for which he is known.

GETTING HERE AND AROUND

About 5 miles west of town off Route 12A, the Cornish–Windsor Bridge crosses the Connecticut River, leading to Interstate 91 in Vermont.

👁 Sights

Cornish-Windsor Bridge

BODY OF WATER | This 460-foot bridge, 1½ miles south of the Saint-Gaudens National Historic Site, connects New Hampshire to Vermont across the Connecticut River. Erected in 1866, it is the longest covered wooden bridge in the United States. The notice on the bridge reads, "Walk your horses or pay two dollar fine." ⊠ *Bridge St.*

★ Saint-Gaudens National Historic Site

GARDEN | On a bluff in rural Cornish with views of Vermont's stately Mt. Ascutney, this pastoral property celebrates the life and artistry of Augustus Saint-Gaudens, a leading 19th-century sculptor with renowned works on Boston Common, Manhattan's Central Park, and Chicago's Lincoln Park. In summer you can tour his house (with original furnishings), studio, and galleries, and year-round it's a pleasure to explore the 150 gorgeous acres of lawns, gardens, and woodlands dotted with casts of his works and laced with 2½ miles of hiking trails. Concerts are held Sunday from late June through August. ⊠ *139 Saint-Gaudens Rd., off Rte. 12A* ☎ *603/675–2175* ⊕ *www.nps.gov/saga* 🎟 *$10* ⊙ *Buildings closed Nov.–late May.*

Hotels

Common Man Inn

$ | **HOTEL** | New Hampshire's distinctive Common Man hotel and restaurant group runs this quirky boutique hotel fashioned out of a striking 19th-century redbrick mill on downtown Claremont's Sugar River; the on-site restaurant serves good pub fare and has great water views. **Pros:** distinct, historic architecture; deck and hot tub overlooking river; good location for exploring both sides of Connecticut River. **Cons:** 12 miles from Cornish; in a slightly downcast but historic small city; not many good dining options in area. $ *Rooms from: $109* ✉ *21 Water St., Claremont* ☎ *603/542–6171* ⊕ *www. thecmaninnclaremont.com* ⇝ *30 rooms* ⊚ *Free Breakfast.*

Walpole

33 miles south of Cornish.

Walpole possesses one of the state's prettiest town greens. Bordered by Elm and Washington streets, it's surrounded by homes dating to the 1790s, when the townsfolk constructed a canal around the Great Falls of the Connecticut River, bringing commerce and wealth to the area. This upscale little town now has 3,900 inhabitants. Walpole is also home to Florentine Films, documentarian Ken Burns's production company.

■ **TIP→ Charlestown, which boasts one of the state's largest historic districts, with about 60 homes—all handsome examples of Federal, Greek Revival, and Gothic Revival architecture (and 10 built before 1800), is just down the road from Walpole.**

GETTING HERE AND AROUND

Walpole is a short jaunt off Route 12, north of Keene.

Sights

Fort at No. 4

HISTORIC SITE | FAMILY | In 1747, this timber fort overlooking the Connecticut River, 15 miles north of Walpole, served as an outpost on the periphery of Colonial civilization. That year fewer than 50 militiamen at the fort withstood an attack by 400 French soldiers, ensuring that northern New England remained under British rule. Today, costumed interpreters at this living-history museum cook dinner over an open hearth and demonstrate weaving, gardening, and candle making. The museum also holds reenactments of militia musters and the battles of the French and Indian War. ✉ *267 Springfield Rd. (Rte. 11), Charlestown* ☎ *603/826–5700* ⊕ *www.fortat4.com* ✐ *$10* ⊘ *Closed Mon. and Tues. and Nov.–Apr.*

Restaurants

★ Hungry Diner

$ | **MODERN AMERICAN** | A departure from the old-school greasy-spoon diners that proliferate in New England, this contemporary space with a white-tile and light-wood interior and a big, inviting outdoor seating area serves delicious, eclectic comfort fare that relies heavily on seasonal, local ingredients, including pasture-raised meats. Think Korean barbecue tacos with house-made kimchi and pickled carrots, or the buttermilk-fried chicken sandwich with a tangy secret sauce and dill pickles. **Known for:** superb craft beer, wine, and cocktail program; mac-and-cheese with bacon; milk shakes and soft-serve ice cream. $ *Average main: $15* ✉ *9 Edwards La.* ☎ *603/756– 3444* ⊕ *www.hungrydinerwalpole.com* ⊘ *Closed Tues.*

★ The Restaurant at Burdick's

$$ | **FRENCH FUSION** | Famous artisanal chocolatier and Walpole resident Larry Burdick, who sells his hand-filled, hand-cut chocolates to top restaurants around the country, operates this acclaimed

restaurant next door to his shop in Walpole's charming little downtown. With the easygoing sophistication of a Parisian café and incredibly rich desserts, the restaurant features a French-inspired international menu that utilizes fresh, often local, ingredients and changes daily. **Known for:** noteworthy wine list; adjacent gourmet grocery with delicious picnic supplies; decadent desserts featuring house-made chocolates and pastries. $ *Average main: $22* ✉ *47 Main St.* ☎ *603/756–9058* ⊕ *www.47mainwalpole. com* ◷ *No dinner Sun. and Mon.*

☕ Coffee and Quick Bites

★ Walpole Creamery

$ | CAFÉ | FAMILY | Arguably the state's best purveyor of artisanal, small-batch ice-cream, this modest parlor in Walpole always features a long list of both regular and seasonal flavors, such as Fijan ginger, fresh peach, wild blueberry, and mint dark-chocolate-chip. Thick, rich, and using only all-natural ingredients, this luscious ice cream is also sold in many of the region's restaurants, farmstands, and groceries. **Known for:** using many local, seasonal ingredients; maple cream and maple walnut ice cream; brownie sundaes. $ *Average main: $5* ✉ *532 Main St.* ☎ *603/445–5700* ⊕ *www.walpolecreamery.com.*

Keene

17 miles southeast of Walpole, 20 miles northeast of Brattleboro, Vermont.

Keene, the largest city in southwestern New Hampshire (population 24,000), has one of the prettiest and widest main streets in the state, with several engaging boutiques and cafés—you can spend a fun few hours strolling along it. Home to Keene State College, the city's atmosphere is youthful and lively, with its funky crafts stores and eclectic entertainment, like the Monadnock International Film Festival, held in April.

GETTING HERE AND AROUND

Routes 9 and 101 pass through Keene, connecting it with Brattleboro, Vermont and Peterborough.

ESSENTIALS

VISITOR INFORMATION Greater Keene Chamber of Commerce. ☎ *603/352–1303* ⊕ *www.keenechamber.com.*

◉ Sights

Keene State College

ARTS VENUE | The hub of the local arts community is this bustling college. The permanent collection of the Thorne-Sagendorph Art Gallery includes works by Richard Sumner Meryman, Abbott Handerson Thayer, and Robert Mapplethorpe. ✉ *Thorne-Sagendorph Art Gallery, 229 Main St.* ☎ *603/358–2720* ⊕ *www.keene.edu* ◷ *Gallery closed June–Aug.*

Madame Sherri Forest

ARCHAEOLOGICAL SITE | FAMILY | The focal point of this rugged 513-acre tract of deciduous forest in West Chesterfield are the stone chimney, grand staircase, and foundation of a chateau-style summer house owned by Parisian-born socialite and theatrical costume designer Madama Antoinette Sherri (the house burned down in 1963, and she died shortly after). A short woodland path from the parking area accesses the fascinating ruins, while two fairly easy but hilly trails offer longer hikes through the surrounding forest, including the 3-mile round-trip trek up Wantastiquet Mountain, which offers clear views up and down the Connecticut River and across to Vermont. Trails also lead into the adjacent Wantastiquet State Forest, and there's more great hiking nearby in Pisgah State Park. ✉ *Gulf and Egypt Rds., West Chesterfield* ☎ *603/224–9945* ⊕ *www. forestsociety.org.*

Stonewall Farm

FARM/RANCH | FAMILY | At this picturesque nonprofit early 1800s farm and educational center, you can stop by to pick up produce and goods raised on-site (including delicious Frisky Cow Gelato) and procured from other artisanal producers in the area. But be sure to leave time to explore the grounds, dairy and small-animal barns, gardens, and chicken coops—a wide range of education tours are offered, plus seasonal hay and sleigh rides. There's also a maple sugaring house and small farm tool museum, and the property is traversed by hiking trails and accesses the 20-mile Cheshire Rail Trail, which stretches from Walpole through Keene and down to the Massachusetts border. ✉ *242 Chesterfield Rd.* ☎ *603/357–7278* 🌐 *www.stonewallfarm.org.*

🍴 Restaurants

★ Luca's Mediterranean Café

$$ | MEDITERRANEAN | A deceptively simple storefront bistro with sidewalk tables overlooking Keene's graceful town square, Luca's dazzles with epicurean creations influenced by Italy, France, Greece, Spain, and North Africa. There's always an extensive selection of small plates, such as almond-crusted fried mozzarella and roasted Brussels sprouts with bacon and pomegranate-infused honey, plus handmade pastas and complexly flavored grills and stews. **Known for:** fresh, creative pastas; affable but knowledgeable service; great wine list. [$] *Average main: $22* ✉ *10 Central Sq.* ☎ *603/358–3335* 🌐 *www.lucascafe.com* 🕒 *Closed Sun.*

Machina Kitchen & Art Bar

$$ | ECLECTIC | This farm-to-table restaurant in downtown Keene is a vital force in the community, offering not only stellar, sustainably sourced food and craft cocktails but also an art gallery with rotating exhibits and occasional live music performances. The menu changes often but always features a mix of classics and unexpected adventures like the salt cod croquettes with preserved-lemon remoulade, fried frog legs with mango-habanero salsa, or Korean-spiced-brisket bulgogi bowls with fresh pears and sesame. **Known for:** interesting cocktails and mocktails; friendly, creative-spirited crowd; occasional prix-fixe dinners with cocktail pairings. [$] *Average main: $18* ✉ *9 Court St.* ☎ *603/903–0011* 🌐 *www.machinaarts.org* 🕒 *Closed Sun. No lunch weekdays.*

🛏 Hotels

★ Chesterfield Inn

$$ | B&B/INN | Fine antiques and Colonial-style fabrics adorn the spacious guest quarters in this opulent yet unpretentious country inn nestled on a 10-acre farmstead a couple of miles from the Connecticut River. **Pros:** beautifully tended gardens; kids and pets are welcome; excellent full breakfast included. **Cons:** restaurant closed on Sunday; two-night minimum at busy times; remote town that's a 20-minute drive from Keene. [$] *Rooms from: $183* ✉ *20 Cross Rd., off Rte. 9, West Chesterfield* ☎ *603/256–3211* 🌐 *www.chesterfieldinn.com* 🛏 *15 rooms* 🍴 *Free breakfast.*

Fairfield Inn and Suites Keene Downtown

$ | HOTEL | It's unusual to find a midrange chain property set in a historic building on a picturesque downtown Main Street, but this property—inside the restored early 1900s Goodnow department store—is a rarity with its reasonably priced rooms, exposed-brick walls, 12-foot ceilings, and sleek modern furnishings. **Pros:** the bilevel loft suites have two bathrooms; good fitness room; steps from great dining and shopping. **Cons:** bustling downtown center can be a little noisy; complimentary breakfast is pretty basic; historic building with quirky layout. [$] *Rooms from: $161* ✉ *30 Main St.* ☎ *603/357–7070* 🌐 *www.fairfieldinnkeene.com* 🛏 *40 rooms* 🍴 *Free breakfast.*

The Inn at East Hill Farm

$$$ | **RESORT** | **FAMILY** | For those with kids who like animals, East Hill Farm is heaven: a family resort with daylong children's programs on a 160-acre farm overlooking Mt. Monadnock that include milking cows; collecting eggs; feeding the sheep, donkeys, cows, rabbits, horses, chickens, goats, and ducks; horseback and pony rides; hiking and hay rides in summer; and sledding and sleigh rides in winter. **Pros:** family-friendly; farm fun and activities galore; beautiful setting. **Cons:** very remote location; noisy dining room; not an ideal choice for adults seeking a romantic retreat. [$] *Rooms from: $310* ✉ *460 Monadnock St., Troy* ☎ *603/242–6495, 800/242–6495* 🌐 *www.east-hill-farm.com* 🛏 *65 rooms* 🍴 *All-inclusive.*

Riverside Hotel

$ | **HOTEL** | With a boat dock and dazzling views of the Connecticut River, this simple but nicely kept three-story hotel is perfect for price-conscious travelers exploring the southwestern Monadnocks as well as nearby Brattleboro, Vermont. **Pros:** stunning river views; just a hop across river from Brattleboro, Vermont; reasonable rates. **Cons:** decor is pleasant but not especially distinctive; noise travels between rooms; pretty basic breakfast. [$] *Rooms from: $159* ✉ *20 Riverside Dr., West Chesterfield* ☎ *603/256–4200* 🌐 *www.riversidehotelnh.com* 🛏 *34 rooms* 🍴 *Free Breakfast.*

Nightlife

Branch and Blade Brewing

BREWPUBS/BEER GARDENS | Don't be put off by the location inside a small industrial park—this convivial taproom offers a seating at picnic tables with wooden-keg tables, a big outdoor seating area with a food truck, and, most importantly, great beer, including a tart Gose and potent triple IPA. ✉ *17 Bradco St.* ☎ *603/354–3478* 🌐 *www.babbrewing.com.*

Performing Arts

ARTS VENUES

Colonial Theatre

CONCERTS | This renovated 1924 vaudeville theater shows art-house movies on the largest screen in town, and also hosts comedy, music, and dance performances. ✉ *95 Main St.* ☎ *603/352–2033* 🌐 *www.thecolonial.org.*

Shopping

Hannah Grimes Marketplace

GIFTS/SOUVENIRS | The pottery, kitchenware, soaps, greeting cards, toys, and specialty foods of more than 250 artisans are on display in this colorful downtown gallery. ✉ *42 Main St.* ☎ *603/352–6862* 🌐 *www.hannahgrimesmarketplace.com.*

Peterborough

20 miles east of Keene.

Thornton Wilder's play *Our Town* was based on Peterborough. The nation's first free public library opened here in 1833, and the town is home to the country's oldest continuously operating basket manufacturer—it's been making baskets since 1854. The town, which was the first in the region to be incorporated (1760), is still a commercial and cultural hub, drawing big crowds for its theater and concerts in summer. Downtown's charming Depot Square district abounds with distinctive boutiques, galleries, and restaurants. At Putnam Park on Grove Street, stand on the bridge and watch the roiling waters of the Nubanusit River.

GETTING HERE AND AROUND

It's easy to find street parking downtown, which is easy to reach via Route 101 and U.S. 202.

ESSENTIALS

VISITOR INFORMATION Monadnock Travel Council. 🌐 *www.monadnocktravel.com.*

Charming Peterborough was the inspiration for the fictional Grover's Corners in Thornton Wilder's *Our Town*.

⊙ Sights

Cathedral of the Pines

MUSEUM | This 236-acre outdoor memorial pays tribute to Americans who have sacrificed their lives in service to their country. There's an inspiring view of Mt. Monadnock and Mt. Kearsarge from the Altar of the Nation, which is composed of rock from every U.S. state and territory. All faiths are welcome, and you can hear organ music some afternoons. The Memorial Bell Tower, built in 1967 with a carillon of bells from around the world, is built of native stone. Norman Rockwell designed the bronze tablets over the four arches. Flower gardens, an indoor chapel, and a museum of military memorabilia share the hilltop, and several trails lace the property, leading to tranquil peaceful areas. ⊠ *10 Hale Hill Rd., Rindge* ☎ *603/899–3300* ⊕ *www.cathedralofthepines.org.*

Mariposa Museum

MUSEUM | FAMILY | You can play instruments or try on costumes from around the world and indulge your cultural curiosity at this nonprofit museum dedicated to hands-on exploration of international folk art. The three-floor museum is housed inside a historic Baptist church, across from the Universalist church in the heart of town. The museum hosts workshops and presentations on dance and arts and crafts. ⊠ *26 Main St.* ☎ *603/924–4555* ⊕ *www.mariposamuseum.org* 🎟 *$8* ⊘ *Closed Mon.*

Monadnock State Park

NATIONAL/STATE PARK | Said to be America's most-climbed mountain—more than 400 people sometimes crowd its bald peak—Monadnock rises to 3,165 feet, and on clear days you can see the Boston skyline. When the parking lots are full, rangers close the park, so it's prudent to get an early morning start, especially during fall foliage. Five trailheads branch out into more than two dozen trails of varying difficulty (though all rigorous) that wend their way to the top. Allow three–five hours for any round-trip hike. The visitor center has free maps as well as exhibits documenting the mountain's history. In winter, you can cross-country ski along roughly 12 miles of groomed trails on the lower elevations. Pets are not permitted in the park. ✉ *116 Poole Rd., off Rte. 124, Jaffrey* ☎ *603/532–8862* 🌐 *www.nhstateparks.org* 🎫 *$15 parking.*

🍴 Restaurants

Cooper's Hill Public House

$ | **IRISH** | Choose a sidewalk table overlooking bustling Depot Square or a table inside the conversation-filled dining room at this lively gastropub adjacent to Peterborough's popular independent cinema and steps from Mariposa Museum. The specialty here is rare whiskies, and there's also a nice selection of wines, craft beers, and other drinks, but don't overlook the consistently excellent Irish-influenced pub fare, including Guinness stew, mushroom-and-kale flatbread, bangers and mash, and terrific burgers. **Known for:** superb whiskey selection; ingredients sourced from New England farms; pecan bread pudding. [$] *Average main: $14* ✉ *6 School St.* ☎ *603/371–9036* 🌐 *www.coopershillpublichouse.com* 🕒 *No lunch.*

Pearl Restaurant & Oyster Bar

$$ | **ASIAN FUSION** | Despite its prosaic setting in a shopping center a little south of Petersborough's historic downtown, this sleek, contemporary Asian bistro and oyster bar is quite welcoming once inside. Several types of fresh oysters are always available, along with such diverse offerings as ahi tuna poke, Hanoi-style pork spring rolls, Korean barbecue pork, and coconut-veggie rice bowls. **Known for:** creative fusion fare; superb wine list; oysters on the half shell. [$] *Average main: $22* ✉ *1 Jaffrey Rd.* ☎ *603/924–5225* 🌐 *www.pearl-peterborough.com* 🕒 *Closed Sun. No lunch.*

🛏 Hotels

Benjamin Prescott Inn

$ | **B&B/INN** | Thanks to the dairy farm surrounding this 1853 Colonial house—with its stenciling and wide pine floors—you'll feel as though you're miles out in the country rather than just 10 minutes from Peterborough and even closer to the cute downtown of Jaffrey. **Pros:** reasonably priced; relaxing, scenic grounds; delicious breakfast included. **Cons:** minimum-night stays at busy times; not within walking distance of town; not suitable for young children. [$] *Rooms from: $129* ✉ *433 Turnpike Rd., Jaffrey Center* ☎ *603/532–6637* 🌐 *www.benjaminprescottinn.com* 🛏 *10 rooms* 🍽 *Free breakfast.*

Birchwood Inn

$ | **B&B/INN** | Overlooking the village green of tiny, quiet Temple, this affordable and friendly B&B built in 1775 once hosted Henry David Thoreau. **Pros:** friendly, old-fashioned tavern; quite affordable; good base for exploring Peterborough and Milford areas. **Cons:** secluded small town; quirky place with just three rooms; not suited for kids. [$] *Rooms from: $109* ✉ *340 Rte. 45, Temple* ☎ *603/878–3285* 🌐 *www.thebirchwoodinn.com* 🛏 *3 rooms* 🍽 *Free breakfast.*

★ Hancock Inn

$$ | **B&B/INN** | This Federal-style 1789 inn in the heart of quaint Hancock, close to the village green, is the real deal—the oldest in the state and the pride of this idyllic town 8 miles north of Peterborough. **Pros:** quintessential Colonial inn and New England village; many rooms have Jacuzzi tubs and gas fireplaces; excellent restaurant. **Cons:** quiet, off-the-beaten-path setting; some rooms have twin beds; a little old-fashioned for some. [$] *Rooms from: $179* ✉ *33 Main St., Hancock* ☎ *603/525–3318, 800/525–1789* 🌐 *www.hancockinn.com* 🛏 *13 rooms* 🍽 *Free breakfast.*

Jack Daniels Motor Inn

$ | HOTEL | FAMILY | This clean, bright, and handsomely decorated 17-room motor inn just a half-mile north of downtown Peterborough is a terrific find with large, affordable rooms furnished with attractive reproduction antiques. **Pros:** great value; one of the only lodgings in Peterborough; continental breakfast included. **Cons:** unfancy motel-style rooms; some street noise; a 10-minute walk from downtown. $ *Rooms from: $129* ⊠ *80 Concord St. (U.S. 202)* ☎ *603/924–7548* ⊕ *www.jackdanielsmotorinn.com* ⇆ *17 rooms* ❍ *Free breakfast*.

Nightlife

Post & Beam Brewing

BREWPUBS/BEER GARDENS | Serving boldly flavored saisons, grisettes, and other fine, mostly old-world-style ales and lagers as well as soft pretzels with hummus, chili, and other tasty edibles, this terrific brewery in downtown Peterborough has a beautiful setting inside the stately 1837 G.A.R. (Grand Army of the Republic) meeting hall. ⊠ *40 Grove St.* ☎ *603/784–5361* ⊕ *www.postandbeam-brewery.com*.

Performing Arts

Monadnock Music

CONCERTS | From early July to late August, Monadnock Music sponsors a series of solo recitals, chamber music concerts, and orchestra and opera performances by renowned musicians. Events take place throughout the area, and some of the offerings are free. ⊠ *Peterborough* ☎ *603/852–4345* ⊕ *www.monadnockmusic.org*.

Peterborough Folk Music Society

CONCERTS | The Music Society presents folk concerts by artists such as John Gorka, Red Molly, and Cheryl Wheeler at the Peterborough Players Theatre and Bass Hall at Monadnock Center. ⊠ *Peterborough* ☎ *603/827–2905* ⊕ *www.pfmsconcerts.org*.

★ Peterborough Players

THEATER | FAMILY | This first-rate summer (mid-June–mid-September) theater troupe has been performing since 1933, these days presenting seven main-stage productions in a converted 18th-century barn throughout the summer. The Players also present children's shows in July and August. ⊠ *55 Hadley Rd.* ☎ *603/924–7585* ⊕ *www.peterboroughplayers.org* ⊘ *Closed mid-Sept.–late June*.

Activities

GOLF

Crotched Mountain Golf Club

GOLF | Donald Ross, one of the earliest stars of golf-course architecture, designed this club's hilly, rolling, 18-hole layout. The course has a nice view of the Monadnocks. In winter you can rent cross-country skis and snowshoes from the on-site Nordic center. ⊠ *740 Francestown Rd., Francestown* ☎ *603/588–2923* ⊕ *www.crotchedmtngolf.com* ⛳ *From $27* ⚐. *18 holes, 6111 yards, par 71*.

Shopping

★ Harrisville Designs

CRAFTS | Hand-spun and hand-dyed yarn, as well as looms, felt, knitting yarn, and instruction books, are sold at this famous shop that occupies a striking redbrick, water-powered mill in the heart of a Monadnock village that's been famous for textiles since 1794. The shop also conducts classes in knitting, spinning, and weaving. ■**TIP→ Across the street, the inviting Harrisville General Store—open since 1838—serves tasty salads and sandwiches using locally sourced ingredients.** ⊠ *4 Mills Alley, 10 miles northwest of Peterborough, Harrisville* ☎ *800/338–9415* ⊕ *www.harrisville.com*.

★ Mayfair Farm

FOOD/CANDY | FAMILY | From Peterborough, it's a scenic 20-minute drive by way of the historic villages of Dublin and Harrisville to reach this sustainable farm set amid rolling fields and hardwood forest. Pick your own berries, apples, and pears in season, and buy humanely raised pork and lamb products as well as gourmet prepared foods from the farm store. If you're wanting to spend a bit more time strolling the farm fields and mingling with the livestock, book a stay in the stylishly furnished guest cottage. ☒ *31 Clymers Dr., Harrisville* ☎ *603/827–3925* ⊕ *www. mayfairfarmnh.com.*

Peterborough Basket Company

HOUSEHOLD ITEMS/FURNITURE | At this retail shop of the oldest continuously operating basket manufacturer in the country, a fixture in Peterborough since 1854, you'll find sturdy and handsome woven-hardwood baskets, perfect for stowing everything from picnic victuals to laundry. You'll also find lazy Susans, planters, pet beds, and other smart storage solutions. ☒ *130 Grove St.* ☎ *603/924–3861* ⊕ *www.peterborobasket.com.*

Manchester

45 miles west of Portsmouth, 53 miles north of Boston.

With 113,000 residents, New Hampshire's largest city grew up around the Amoskeag Falls on the Merrimack River, which drove small textile mills through the 1700s. By 1828 Boston investors had bought the rights to the Merrimack's water power and built the Amoskeag Mills, which became a testament to New England's manufacturing capabilities. In 1906 the mills employed 17,000 people and churned out more than 4 million yards of cloth weekly. This vast enterprise served as Manchester's entire economic base; when it closed in 1936, the town was devastated. Today Manchester is mainly a banking and business center, but many of the old mill buildings have been converted into condos, restaurants, museums, and office space, and both the dining and arts scenes have flourished in recent years.

GETTING HERE AND AROUND

The state's largest airport, Manchester-Boston Regional Airport, is a modern, cost-effective, and hassle-free alternative to Boston's Logan Airport, with nonstop service from about a dozen cities. Public transit is impractical for visitors—a car is your best way to get around.

ESSENTIALS

AIRPORT Manchester-Boston Regional Airport. ☒ *1 Airport Rd.* ☎ *603/624–6539* ⊕ *www.flymanchester.com.*

VISITOR INFORMATION Greater Manchester Chamber of Commerce. ☎ *603/792–4100* ⊕ *www.manchester-chamber.org.*

◉ Sights

★ Currier Museum of Art

BUILDING | The Currier maintains an astounding permanent collection of works by European and American masters, among them Claude Monet, Edward Hopper, Winslow Homer, John Marin, Andrew Wyeth, and Childe Hassam, and it presents changing exhibits of contemporary art. The museum also arranges guided tours of the nearby Zimmerman House. Completed in 1950, it's New England's only Frank Lloyd Wright–designed residence open to the public. Wright called this sparse, utterly functional living space "Usonian," a term he used to describe several dozen similar homes based on his vision of distinctly American architecture. ☒ *150 Ash St.* ☎ *603/669–6144* ⊕ *www.currier.org* ◱ *$15; $35 for Zimmerman House.*

Millyard Museum

LIBRARY | **FAMILY** | In one of the most architecturally striking Amoskeag Mills buildings, state-of-the-art exhibits depict the region's history from when Native Americans lived here and fished the Merrimack River to when the machines of Amoskeag Mills wove cloth. The museum also offers lectures and walking tours, and has a child-oriented Discovery Gallery. There's a very good book and gift

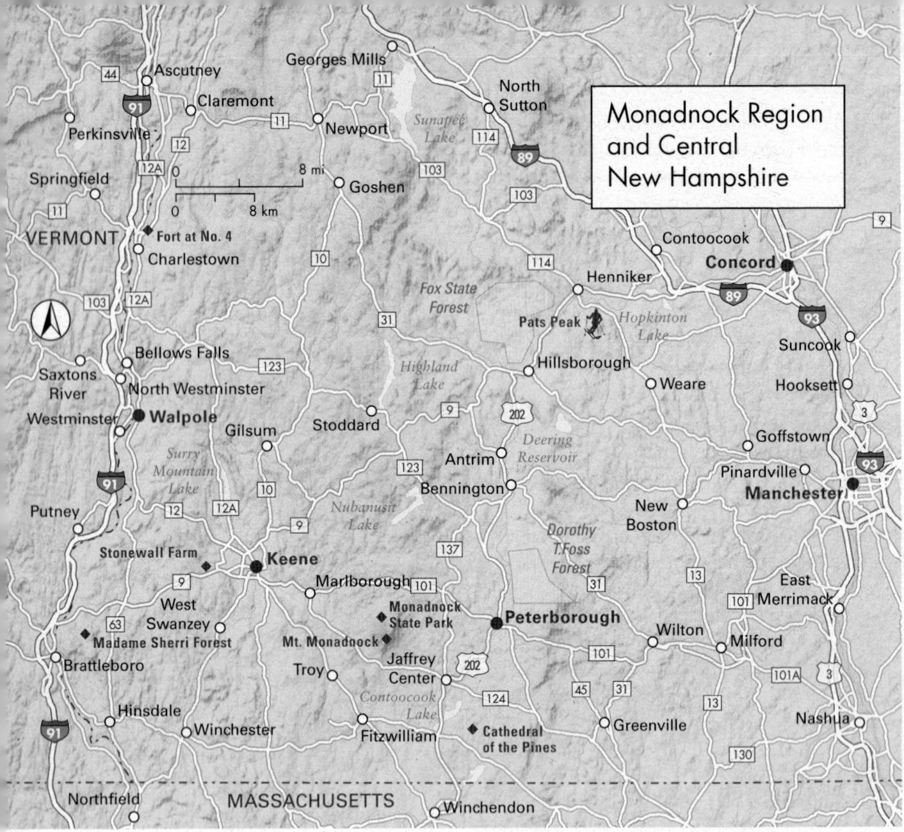

Monadnock Region and Central New Hampshire
VERMONT
MASSACHUSETTS
0 8 mi
0 8 km
Ascutney
Georges Mills
Claremont
North Sutton
Perkinsville
Newport
Sunapee Lake
Springfield
Goshen
Fort at No. 4
Charlestown
Contoocook
Concord
Henniker
Fox State Forest
Pats Peak
Hopkinton Lake
Suncook
Bellows Falls
Saxtons River
North Westminster
Hillsborough
Weare
Hooksett
Highland Lake
Westminster
Walpole
Gilsum
Stoddard
Goffstown
Deering Reservoir
Surry Mountain Lake
Antrim
Pinardville
Manchester
Bennington
Putney
Nubanusit Lake
New Boston
Dorothy T.Foss Forest
Stonewall Farm
Keene
Marlborough
East Merrimack
West Swanzey
Monadnock State Park
Peterborough
Madame Sherri Forest
Mt. Monadnock
Wilton
Milford
Brattleboro
Troy
Jaffrey Center
Contoocook Lake
Hinsdale
Winchester
Fitzwilliam
Cathedral of the Pines
Greenville
Nashua
Northfield
Winchendon

shop, too. ✉ *200 Bedford St.* ☎ *603/622–7531* 🌐 *www.manchesterhistoric.org* 🎫 *$8* ⏰ *Closed Sun. and Mon.*

SEE Science Center

LOCAL INTEREST | **FAMILY** | The world's largest permanent LEGO installation at minifigure scale, depicting Amoskeag Millyard and Manchester as they looked a century ago, is the star attraction at this hands-on science lab and children's museum. The mind-blowing exhibit, covering 2,000 square feet, is made up of about 3 million LEGO bricks. It conveys the massive size and importance of the mills, which ran a mile on each side of the Merrimack. The museum also contains touch-friendly interactive exhibits and offers daily science demonstrations. ✉ *Amoskeag Millyard, 200 Bedford St.* ☎ *603/669–0400* 🌐 *www.see-sciencecenter.org* 🎫 *$9.*

🍴 Restaurants

Cotton

$$ | **MODERN AMERICAN** | Mod lighting and furnishings lend this restaurant inside an old Amoskeag Mills building a swanky atmosphere, although on warm days you may want to have a seat on the patio, set in an arbor. The farm-to-table-inspired comfort food changes regularly but has featured pan-seared crab cakes, tuna tataki with wasabi aioli, and Delmonico steak with a choice of sauces. **Known for:** entrée-size salads; creative mixed drinks; handsome converted-warehouse setting. $ *Average main: $23* ✉ *75 Arms St.* ☎ *603/622–5488* 🌐 *www.cottonfood.com* ⏰ *No lunch weekends.*

Red Arrow Diner
$ | **AMERICAN** | One of New England's most celebrated diners, this bustling downtown greasy spoon has been catering to students, artists, and most famously U.S. Presidential candidates since 1922. **Known for:** filling breakfasts; colorful people-watching; house-brewed root beer and cream soda. [$] *Average main: $11* ✉ *61 Lowell St.* ☎ *603/626–1118* 🌐 *www.redarrowdiner.com.*

★ Republic Cafe
$$ | **MEDITERRANEAN** | A key player in downtown Manchester's steady ascendance into a bona fide dining and nightlife hub, this all-day bistro serves artfully prepared Mediterranean fare, with most ingredients sourced within a 50-mile radius. You can make a meal of several small plates—red-lentil cakes, lamb kefta, fig-and-goat cheese flatbreads—or tuck into one of the larger portions, perhaps steak frites or chickpea ragù. **Known for:** first-rate espresso drinks and desserts; creative Mediterranean small plates; outstanding Italian fare in adjacent Campo Enoteca. [$] *Average main: $21* ✉ *1069 Elm St.* ☎ *603/666–3723* 🌐 *www.republiccafe.com* 🕒 *Closed Sun. and Mon.*

Coffee and Quick Bites

Restoration Cafe
$ | **CAFÉ** | Set on the ground floor of a vintage redbrick apartment building on the east side of downtown, this hip café and gathering spot excels both with drinks—everything from nitro cold brews to creative smoothies—and healthy, well-crafted food. At breakfast, consider the egg-cheddar-chive brioche sandwich, while tandoori bowls and rare-seared tuna sandwiches, along with craft cocktails and beers, are popular late in the day. **Known for:** healthy smoothies; sleek industrial vibe; cheerful outdoor patio. [$] *Average main: $9* ✉ *235 Hanover St.* ☎ *603/518–7260* 🕒 *Closed Mon. No dinner.*

Hotels

★ Ash Street Inn
$$ | **B&B/INN** | Each of the five rooms in this striking sage-green 1885 B&B near the Currier Museum of Art and a few blocks from Elm Street dining is painted a different color, and all have soft bathrobes, flat-screen satellite TVs, and beds topped with Egyptian cotton linens. **Pros:** stylishly decorated rooms; excellent full breakfast included; free off-street parking. **Cons:** pricey for Manchester; not a great choice for children; in busy city neighborhood. [$] *Rooms from: $229* ✉ *118 Ash St.* ☎ *603/668–9908* 🌐 *www.ashstreetinn.com* 🛏 *5 rooms* 🍴 *Free breakfast.*

★ Bedford Village Inn
$$$ | **RESORT** | A few miles southwest of Manchester, this upscale complex consisting of an 1810 Federal inn and a bigger and new boutique hotel is all about luxury and pampering, with Italian marble bathrooms, whirlpool tubs, sumptuous linens, four-poster beds, and Molton Brown bath products in the rooms. **Pros:** ultraposh accommodations and amenities; gorgeous gardens and grounds; outstanding food and beverage. **Cons:** in a suburb outside Manchester; breakfast not included in rates; often booked with weddings on weekends. [$] *Rooms from: $259* ✉ *2 Olde Bedford Way, Bedford* ☎ *603/472–2001, 800/852–1166* 🌐 *www.bedfordvillageinn.com* 🛏 *64 rooms* 🍴 *No meals.*

Doubletree Manchester Downtown
$ | **HOTEL** | Of Manchester's many chain hotels, this 12-story tower with smartly appointed rooms and great views has the most central location: a short walk from Amoskeag Mills and the growing cluster of dining and nightlife options along Elm Street. **Pros:** steps from lots of great eateries and bars; free airport shuttle; indoor pool and fitness center. **Cons:** fee for parking; unattractive building; tends to draw a lot of meetings and conferences. [$] *Rooms from: $151* ✉ *700 Elm St.* ☎ *603/625–1000*

⊕ www.manchesterdowntownhotel.com
🛏 252 rooms ⦿ No meals.

☢ Nightlife

BARS

Crown Tavern

BARS/PUBS | Set in a stunningly restored downtown theater with a huge adjacent outdoor patio, the Crown is a splendid venue for dining, but it's the natty bar—with noteworthy craft-cocktail list, exposed-brick walls, and tile floor—that's especially alluring. If you are hungry, try the thick-cut truffle fries or Nashville hot chicken sandwich. ✉ 99 Hanover St. ☎ 603/218–3132 ⊕ www.thecrownonhanover.com.

815

BARS/PUBS | A scene-y crowd mixes and mingles at this dimly lighted Prohibition Era–inspired, speakeasy-style cocktail bar with plush arm chairs and sofas and Oriental rugs, and an impressive list of both innovative and classic cocktails, plus unusual local and international beers. ✉ 825 Elm St. ☎ 603/782–8086 ⊕ www.815nh.com.

☢ Performing Arts

The Palace Theatre

CONCERTS | This 1914 former vaudeville house presents musicals and plays, comedy, and concerts throughout the year. ✉ 80 Hanover St. ☎ 603/668–5588 ⊕ www.palacetheatre.org.

Concord

20 miles north of Manchester, 47 miles west of Portsmouth.

New Hampshire's capital (population 44,000) is a small and somewhat quiet city that tends to state business and little else. With that said, downtown has lately experienced an influx of restaurants and bars. Stop in town to get a glimpse of New Hampshire's State House, which is crowned by a gleaming, eagle-topped gold dome.

GETTING HERE AND AROUND

Interstate 93 bisects Concord north–south and is intersected by Interstate 89 and U.S. 202, which becomes Interstate 393 near the city line. Main Street near the State House is walkable, but a car is the best way to explore farther afield.

ESSENTIALS

VISITOR INFORMATION Greater Concord Chamber of Commerce. ☎ 603/224–2508 ⊕ www.concordnhchamber.com.

☢ Sights

McAuliffe-Shepard Discovery Center

MUSEUM | FAMILY | New England's only air-and-space center offers a full day of activities focused mostly on the heavens. See yourself in infrared light, learn about lunar spacecraft, examine a replica of the Mercury-Redstone rocket, or experience what it's like to travel in space—you can even try your hand at being a television weather announcer. There's also a café. ✉ 2 Institute Dr. ☎ 603/271–7827 ⊕ www.starhop.com 🎟 $12.

New Hampshire Historical Society

LIBRARY | Steps from the state capitol, this museum is a great place to learn about the Concord coach, a popular mode of transportation before railroads. The Discovering New Hampshire exhibit delves into a number of facets of the state's heritage, from politics to commerce. Rotating shows might include locally made quilts or historical portraits of residents. ✉ 30 Park St. ☎ 603/228–6688 ⊕ www.nhhistory.org 🎟 $7 ⊘ Closed Sun. and Mon.

Pierce Manse

HOUSE | Franklin Pierce lived in this Greek Revival home, which overlooks a scenic bend in the Merrimack River at the north edge of downtown. He moved to Washington to become the 14th U.S. president—although in the eyes of many historians, one of the least effective and admired. A guided tour covers his life in mid-19th-century historical context. ■ **TIP→ Fans of presidential history might want to make the half-hour drive west to Hillsborough's Franklin Pierce Homestead. Tours of his stately 1804 childhood home are offered late May–mid-October.** ✉ *14 Horseshoe Pond La.* ☎ *603/225–4555* 🌐 *www.piercemanse.org* 🎫 *$8* 🕒 *Closed Sun. and early Oct.–mid-June.*

★ State House

GOVERNMENT BUILDING | The gilded-dome state house, built in 1819, is the nation's oldest capitol building in which the legislature still uses the original chambers. From January through June, you can watch the two branches in action. The Senate has 24 members, and the House house has 400—a ratio of 1 representative per 3,500 residents (a world record). The visitor center coordinates guided and self-guided tours, bookable online or on-site, and displays history exhibits and paraphernalia from presidential primaries. ✉ *Visitor center, 107 N. Main St.* ☎ *603/271–2154* 🌐 *www.gencourt.state.nh.us* 🎫 *Free.*

🍴 Restaurants

★ The Grazing Room

$$$ | **CONTEMPORARY** | Floor-to-ceiling windows add a touch of elegance to this superb—if a bit spendy—farm-to-table restaurant in the colonial Colby Hill Inn, which also offers well-appointed accommodations. Fresh produce takes center stage on the diverse, contemporary menu, which might offer a watermelon-tomato-feta salad or goat cheese–blueberry pierogies to start. **Known for:** outdoor seating beside a barn with friendly goats; pierogies with seasonal fillings; fresh fruit tarts and galettes. [$] *Average main: $33* ✉ *33 The Oaks, Henniker* ☎ *603/428–3281* 🌐 *www.colbyhillinn.com* 🕒 *Closed Mon. and Tues. No lunch.*

★ Revival

$$ | **MODERN AMERICAN** | In this handsome, high-ceilinged redbrick building on a downtown side street, foodies and revelers congregate for some of the most creative and accomplished regional American cuisine in the Merrimack Valley. Highlights, in addition to an impressive selection of whiskies and cognacs, might include an artful platter of charcuterie and New England artisanal cheeses, hearty rabbit stew, and seared salmon with pancetta and olive tapenade, but the menu changes regularly. **Known for:** ingredients sourced from local farms; see-and-be-seen vibe; decadent desserts. [$] *Average main: $23* ✉ *11 Depot St.* ☎ *603/715–5723* 🌐 *www.revivalkitchennh.com* 🕒 *Closed Sun. and Mon. No lunch.*

☕ Coffee and Quick Bites

Granite State Candy Shoppe

$ | **CAFÉ** | **FAMILY** | Since 1927, this festive sweet shop and ice cream parlor with a second location in Manchester has been doling out old-fashioned candies, fudge, and other confections. **Known for:** homemade peanut butter–chocolate fudge; root beer floats; Maple Saurus Sundaes (with maple pecan ice cream and maple syrup). [$] *Average main: $4* ✉ *13 Warren St.* ☎ *603/225–2591* 🌐 *www.granitestatecandyshoppe.com* 💳 *No credit cards.*

🛏 Hotels

The Centennial

$$ | **HOTEL** | Concord's most distinctive and romantic hotel occupies an imposing brick-and-stone building constructed in 1892 for widows of Civil War veterans, but the interior has been given a head-to-toe makeover: boutique furnishings and contemporary art immediately set the tone in the lobby; pillow-top beds sport luxurious linens and down pillows; and bathrooms have stone floors, granite countertops, and stand-alone showers. **Pros:** sleek redesign of historic structure;

attractive residential setting; great bar and restaurant. **Cons:** not within walking distance of downtown dining; rooms facing road can get a little road noise; breakfast costs extra. $ *Rooms from: $179* ⊠ *96 Pleasant St.* ☎ *603/227–9000* ⊕ *www.thecentennialhotel.com* ⇨ *32 rooms* ⃝ *No meals.*

★ Hotel Concord

$$ | **HOTEL** | This sleekly stunning contemporary boutique hotel opened in 2018 within a short stroll of the city's top arts venues and eateries; the airy and light-filled rooms, many with balconies, have hardwood floors, distinctive artwork, big windows, and are outfitted with Amazon Echo devices, huge HD TVs, and spacious marble baths. **Pros:** reasonable rates for this level of luxury; hip, cosmopolitan design; lots to see and do within walking distance. **Cons:** on a busy street; some may find the in-room high-tech gadgets a little challenging; books up when statehouse is in session. $ *Rooms from: $179* ⊠ *11 S. Main St.* ☎ *603/504–3500* ⊕ *www.hotelconcordnh.com* ⇨ *38 rooms* ⃝ *Free Breakfast.*

🎟 Performing Arts

★ Capitol Center for the Arts

ARTS CENTERS | The Egyptian-motif artwork, part of the original 1927 decor, has been restored in this historic 1,304-seat venue that now hosts touring Broadway shows, dance companies, and musical acts. In 2019, the organization took over a disused movie house a few doors away (at 16 S. Main Street) and after an extensive renovation turned it into the **Bank of NH Stage.** This smaller space presents music, comedy, and other notable shows. ⊠ *44 S. Main St.* ☎ *603/225–1111* ⊕ *www.ccanh.com.*

🍸 Nightlife

Henniker Brewing

BREWPUBS/BEER GARDENS | It's worth the drive 15 miles west of Concord if you're a fan of craft beer to sample the hoppy IPAs, refreshing Kolsch-style ales, and refreshing sour red ales at this laid-back tap room in the woods of Henniker. Grab a seat on the patio in nice weather. ⊠ *129 Centervale Rd., Henniker* ☎ *603/428–3579* ⊕ *www.hennikerbrewing.com.*

🏃 Activities

Scenic RailRiders

TOUR—SPORTS | This family-owned outfitter offers scenic two-hour tours on custom-made "rail-bikes" on a picturesque stretch of disused rail tracks that extends for several miles north of town alongside the Merrimack River. The rail-bikes are easy to pedal and seat two to four participants. ⊠ *188 Sewalls Falls Rd.* ☎ *603/931–1700* ⊕ *www.scenicrailriders.com.*

Chapter 11

INLAND MAINE

Updated by
Mary Ruoff

⊙ Sights	🍴 Restaurants	🛏 Hotels	🛍 Shopping	🍸 Nightlife
★★★☆☆	★★★☆☆	★★★☆☆	★★☆☆☆	★★☆☆☆

WELCOME TO INLAND MAINE

TOP REASONS TO GO

★ **Baxter State Park:** Mt. Katahdin, the state's highest peak, stands sentry over Baxter's forestland in its "natural wild state."

★ **Moosehead Lake:** Surrounded by mountains, Maine's largest lake—dotted with islands and chiseled with inlets and coves—retains the rugged beauty that so captivated author Henry David Thoreau in the mid-1800s.

★ **Water Sports:** It's easy to get out on the water on scheduled cruises on large inland lakes; guided or self-guided boating, canoeing, and kayaking trips; and white-water rafting excursions on several rivers.

★ **Winter Pastimes:** Downhill skiing, snowmobiling, snowshoeing, cross-country skiing, fat-tire biking, and ice fishing are all popular winter sports. You can even go dogsledding!

★ **Foliage Drives:** Maine's best fall foliage is inland, where hardwoods outnumber spruce, fir, and pine trees in many areas.

Though Maine is well known for its miles of craggy coastline, the inland part of the state is surprisingly vast and far less populated. Not one hour's drive from the bays and ocean, huge swaths of forestland are punctuated by lakes (sometimes called ponds, despite their size). Summer camps, ski areas, and small villages populate the mountainous western part of the state, which stretches north along the New Hampshire border to Québec. In the remote North Woods, wilderness areas beckon outdoors lovers. You can take a drive (go slow!) down a "moose alley" in both regions.

1 Sebago Lake Area. Less than 20 miles northwest of Portland, the Sebago Lake area bustles with activity in summer.

2 Bridgton. Bridgton is a classic New England town with many nearby lakes to explore.

3 Bethel. In the valley of the Androscoggin River, Bethel is home to Sunday River, one of Maine's major ski resorts.

4 Rangeley. Rangeley, along its namesake lake, anchors a lake-dotted region with long stretches of pine, beech, spruce, and sky.

5 Kingfield. Just north of Kingfield is Sugarloaf Mountain Resort, Maine's other big ski resort, which has plenty to offer year-round.

6 Greenville. The woodsy town, on Moosehead Lake, Maine's largest, is a great base for day trips.

7 Millinocket. The gateway to the premier wilderness destinations of Baxter State Park and the Allagash Wilderness Waterway.

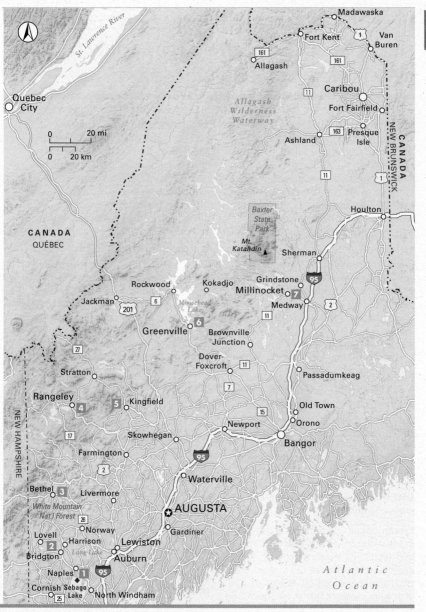

Unlike the state's higher-profile coastline, inland Maine is a four-season destination. Natural beauty is abundant here, in the form of mountains, lakes, rivers, and there's an ample supply of classic New England villages.

Sebago and Long lakes, north of Portland and the gateway to the Western Lakes and Mountains region, hum with boaters and watercraft in the summer. Mt. Katahdin, Maine's highest peak and the terminus of the Appalachian Trail, rises in 210,000-acre Baxter State Park, outside Millinocket in the North Woods.

Come winter, ski resorts—including Maine's largest, Sugarloaf and Sunday River, both in the state's western section—wait for large snowfalls (and make it themselves in between). Maine often receives snow when the rest of New England doesn't and vice versa, so track the weather if you're coming for winter sports or to bask in the serenity of a good snowfall.

Rangeley, in western Maine, has been a haven for anglers since the 19th century, but these days this lakes-strewn area is also known for hiking and winter sports. Remote forestland lines most of Moosehead Lake, New England's largest lake within a single state. Greenville, at its southern end, is the hub. Visitors come to enjoy the lake, explore nearby wilderness locales, and downhill and cross-country ski.

Wealthy urban "rusticators" began flocking to inland Maine on vacation in the mid-1800s. The legacy of the rusticators and the locals who catered to them lives on at sporting camps still found—albeit in smaller numbers than in days past—on

remote lakes and rivers, in displays at small but impressive regional museums, and through Maine's unique system of licensed outdoor guides. Known as Registered Maine Guides, these well-qualified practitioners lead excursions that might involve kayaking, white-water rafting, hiking, fishing, hunting, canoeing, and moose spotting.

MAJOR REGIONS
The sparsely populated **Western Lakes and Mountains** region stretches north and west, bordered by New Hampshire and Québec. Each season offers different outdoor highlights: you can choose from snow sports, hiking, mountain biking, leaf peeping, fishing, swimming, and paddling. **The Sebago Lake area** bustles with activity in summer. **Bridgton** is a classic New England town, as is **Bethel,** in the valley of the Androscoggin River. Sunday River, a major ski resort nearby, also offers summer activities. The more remote **Rangeley Lakes** region contains long stretches of pine, beech, spruce, and sky, and classic inns. Just north of **Kingfield** is Sugarloaf Mountain Resort, Maine's other big ski resort, which has plenty to offer year-round.

Much of **The North Woods** is best experienced by canoeing or kayaking, fishing, hiking, snowshoeing, cross-country skiing, or snowmobiling. **Millinocket** is the gateway to Baxter State Park, Allagash Wilderness Waterway, and Katahdin

Woods and Waters National Monument, all premier wilderness destinations open for public recreation. The woodsy town of **Greenville,** on Moosehead Lake, is a great base for day trips, including excursions into Maine's 100 Mile Wilderness.

Planning

Visitors to inland Maine often spend their entire vacation in the region. That's certainly true of those who come to ski at a resort, fish at a remote sporting camp, or just relax at a lakeside cabin. Resort towns offer scenic cruises, intriguing small museums, and nearby hiking but are also hubs for exploring further afield. Visitors may head out early for a white-water rafting or renowned outdoor recreation area an hour or two away, or day trip among the lake towns closer to Portland. The farther inland you go, the farther between destinations. Lodgings and rentals often have minimum stays during peak times.

Getting Here and Around

AIR

Two primary airports serve Maine: Portland International (PWM) and Bangor International (BGR). Portland is closer to the Western Lakes and Mountains area; Bangor is more convenient to the North Woods. Regional flying services, operating from regional and municipal airports, provide access to remote lakes and wilderness areas and offer scenic flights.

CAR

Because Maine is large and rural, a car is essential. U.S. 2 is the major east–west thoroughfare in Western Maine, winding from Bangor to New Hampshire. Interstate 95 is a departure point for many visitors to inland Maine, especially the North Woods. The highway heads inland at Brunswick and becomes a toll road (the Maine Turnpike) from the New

Hampshire border to Augusta. Because of the hilly terrain and abundant lakes and rivers, inland Maine can get curvy. Traffic rarely gets heavy, though highways often pass right through instead of around the larger towns, which can slow your trip a bit.

There are few public roads in Maine's North Woods, but private logging roads there are often open to the public (sometimes by permit and fee). When driving these roads, always give lumber-company trucks the right-of-way; loggers must drive in the middle of the road and often can't move over or slow down for cars. Be sure to have a full tank of gas before heading onto private roads in the region.

Activities

People visit inland Maine year-round, coming to hike, bike, camp, fish, canoe, kayak, white-water raft, downhill and cross-country ski, snowshoe, and snowmobile.

BIKING

Bicycle Coalition of Maine

BICYCLING | The coalition provides information about biking in the state. ☎ *207/623–4511* ⊕ *www.bikemaine.org.*

FISHING

Maine Department of Inland Fisheries and Wildlife

FISHING | You can get information about and purchase fishing and hunting licenses by phone and online through this state agency. ☎ *207/287–8000* ⊕ *www.maine. gov/ifw.*

GUIDE SERVICES

Maine Professional Guides Association

TOUR—SPORTS | The association can help you find a state-licensed guide to lead a fishing, hunting, hiking, kayaking, canoeing, white-water rafting, snowshoeing, birding, or wildlife-watching trip. ⊕ *www. maineguides.org.*

HIKING

Maine Appalachian Trail Club

HIKING/WALKING | The club publishes seven Appalachian Trail maps ($8), all of which are bound together in its Maine trail guide ($30; $15 without maps). Its interactive online map has information on everything from side trails to communities along the AT in Maine. ⊕ *www.matc. org.*

Maine Trail Finder

HIKING/WALKING | The website has trail descriptions, photos, user comments, directions, and interactive maps for trails to hike, walk, mountain bike, paddle, snowshoe, and cross-county ski. ⊕ *www. mainetrailfinder.com.*

SKIING

Ski Maine Association

SURFING | For alpine and cross-country skiing information. ☎ *207/773–7669* ⊕ *www.skimaine.com.*

SNOWMOBILING

Maine Snowmobile Association

SNOW SPORTS | The website has contacts and links for about 10,000 miles of local and regional trails, and an excellent statewide map of about 4,000 miles of interconnected trails. ☎ *207/622–6983* ⊕ *www.mesnow.com.*

WHITE-WATER RAFTING

Raft Maine Association

WHITE-WATER RAFTING | An association of four white-water rafting outfitters, the website has information on the companies and Maine's three major white-water rafting rivers—the Kennebec, the Dead, and the West Branch of the Penobscot, which together make Maine New England's premier destination for white-water rafting. The Kennebec and Dead rivers converge at The Forks in Western Maine, while the West Branch of the Penobscot flows near Millinocket in the North Woods. ■TIP→ **Family-friendly rafting trips are available.** ⊕ *www.raftmaine.com.*

Hotels

Well-run inns, bed-and-breakfasts, and motels can be found throughout inland Maine, including some more sophisticated lodgings. At places near ski resorts, peak-season rates may apply in winter and summer. Both hotel rooms and condo units are among the options at the two largest ski resorts, Sunday River and Sugarloaf. Greenville has the largest selection of lodgings in the North Woods region, with elaborate and homey accommodations alike. Lakeside sporting camps, from the primitive to the upscale, are popular around Rangeley and the North Woods; many have cozy cabins heated with wood stoves and serve three hearty meals a day. Conservation organizations also operate wilderness retreats. In Maine's mountains, as on its coast, many small inns don't have air-conditioning. *Hotel reviews have been shortened. For full reviews visit Fodors.com.*

Maine Campground Owners Association

The association's helpful membership directory is available by mail and on its website, which also has an interactive campground map. Many campgrounds have RV spaces and cabin rentals. ☎ *207/782–5874* ⊕ *www.campmaine.com.*

Maine Sporting Camp Association

Representing 45 camps, the association's goal is to "preserve the sporting camp's uniqueness" in Maine. Visit the website to search for camps by activity, meal plan, season of operation, and even the fish in local waters. ☎ *207/888–3931* ⊕ *www.mainesportingcamps.com.*

Maine State Parks Campground Reservations Service

You can get information about and make reservations for 12 state park campgrounds through this service. Note: reservations for Baxter State Park, which is administered separately, are not handled by the service. ☎ *207/624–9950, 800/332–1501 in Maine* ⊕ *www.campwithme.com.*

WHAT IT COSTS in U.S. Dollars

	$	$$	$$$	$$$$
RESTAURANTS				
	under $18	$18–$24	$25–$35	over $35
HOTELS				
	under $200	$200–$299	$300–$399	over $399

Restaurants

Fear not, lobster lovers: this succulent, emblematic Maine food is on the menu at many inland restaurants, from fancier establishments to roadside places. Dishes containing lobster are more common than boiled lobster dinners, but look for daily specials. Shrimp, scallops, and other seafood are also menu mainstays, and you may find bison burgers or steaks from a nearby farm. Organic growers and natural foods producers are found throughout the state and often sell their products to nearby restaurants. Pumpkins, blackberries, strawberries, and other seasonal foods make their way into homemade desserts, as do Maine's famed blueberries. Many lakeside resorts and sporting camps have a reputation for good food—some of the latter will even cook the fish you catch.

Visitor Information

The more than 2 million acres overseen by the Maine Bureau of Parks and Lands encompass 33 state parks, 15 historic sites, three scenic waterways, and more than 20,000 miles of ATV, snowmobile, and multiuse trails. Its public lands—nearly 600,000 acres—are wilderness areas managed for recreation, wildlife preservation, and timbering. Most areas are free to visit, but camping is primitive. Many lands are in remote areas accessible only by logging roads; others are relatively close to town centers and have trailheads, outhouses, and other facilities.

CONTACTS Maine Office of Tourism. ☎ *888/624–6345* ⊕ *www.visitmaine. com.* **Maine Tourism Association.** ⊕ *www. mainetourism.com.* **Maine Bureau of Parks and Lands.** ☎ *207/287–3821* ⊕ *www. parksandlands.com.*

When to Go

As a rule, inland Maine's most popular hiking trails and lakeside beaches get busier when the weather gets warmer, but if splendid isolation is what you crave, you can still find it. Summertime is when lodging rates peak and traffic picks up—though rarely jams, outside of a few spots—but the weather makes it a beautiful time of year to visit. Inland Maine gets hotter than the coast in July and August; lakes and higher elevations are naturally cooler. September is a good bet: the weather is more moderate, and the crowds thinner.

Western Maine is the state's premier destination for leaf peepers—hardwoods are more abundant here than on the coast. Peak foliage season runs late September–mid-October.

Maine's largest ski areas can make their own snow—at least one of them opens its doors in mid-November and remains open until May. Inland Maine typically has snow cover by Christmas, so cross-country skiing, snowshoeing, and snowmobiling are in full swing by the end of the year.

Early spring snowmelt ushers in mud season, which leads to black fly season mid-May–mid-June. The flies are especially pesky in the woods but less bothersome in town. Spring is prime time for canoeing and fishing.

Sebago Lake Area

20 miles northwest of Portland.

Seasonal and year-round dwellings, from simple camps to sprawling showplaces, line the shores of sprawling Sebago Lake and fingerlike Long Lake. Both are popular with water-sports enthusiasts, as is Brandy Pond and many other bodies of water in the area. Several rivers flow into Sebago Lake—Maine's second largest—linking nearby lakes and ponds to form a 43-mile waterway. Naples, on the causeway separating Long Lake from Brandy Pond, pulses with activity in the summer, when the area swells with seasonal residents and weekend visitors. Open-air cafés overflow with patrons, boats buzz along the water, and families parade along the sidewalk edging Long Lake. On clear days the view includes snowcapped Mt. Washington. The nonextant Cumberland and Oxford Canal was part of a water route from Long Lake to Portland in the mid-1800s. At Sebago Lake State Park, the one remaining canal lock operates on the Songo River, which connects Brandy Pond and Sebago Lake.

GETTING HERE AND AROUND

Sebago Lake, gateway to Maine's Western Lakes and Mountains, is less than 20 miles from Portland on U.S. 302.

VACATION RENTALS

CONTACTS Krainin Real Estate. ⊠ *1539 Roosevelt Tr., Raymond* 🕾 *207/655–3811* ⊕ *www.krainin.com.*

VISITOR INFORMATION

CONTACTS Sebago Lakes Region Chamber of Commerce. ⊠ *909 Roosevelt Tr., Suite A, Windham* 🕾 *207/892–8265* ⊕ *www. sebagolakeschamber.com.*

◉ Sights

Sabbathday Lake Shaker Village

MUSEUM VILLAGE | FAMILY | Established in the late 18th century, this is the last active Shaker community in the world. Several buildings with Shaker furniture, folk art, tools, farm implements, and crafts from the 18th to the early 20th century are open for guided hour-long tours. The structures include the 1794 Meetinghouse, the 1839 Ministry's Shop, where the elders and eldresses lived until the early 1900s, and the 1821 Sister's Shop, where household goods and candies were made. The 1850 Boys' Shop has a free exhibit about Shaker childhood. An exhibit in the 1816 Granary is included with the tour, but tickets are also sold separately. The Shaker Store sells community-produced foods and goods as well as handicrafts by area artisans. If you're visiting the village in late August, don't miss the popular and free Maine Native American Summer Market and Demonstration. ⊠ *707 Shaker Rd., New Gloucester* 🕾 *207/926–4597* ⊕ *www.maineshakers.com* 🎟 *From $7* ☾ *Closed mid-Oct.–late May and Sun. late May–mid-Oct.*

Sebago Lake State Park

BODY OF WATER | FAMILY | This 1,400-acre expanse on the north shore of Sebago Lake is a great spot for swimming, boating, and fishing for both salmon and togue (lake trout). Its 250-site campground is the largest at any Maine state park. Bicycling along the park's roads is a popular pastime in warm weather, as is hiking. Come winter, the park offers 4 miles of groomed cross-country trails and 6 miles of ungroomed trails, also used for snowshoeing. On the park's edge, Songo Lock State Historic Site, an operational lock along the twisting, narrow Songo River and a remnant of a 19th century canal system, is a pleasant—and free—picnic area. You can also fish off the handicapped-accessible pier and launch a kayak or canoe. ⊠ *11*

Park Access Rd., Casco ☎ *207/693–6231* ⊕ *www.maine.gov/sebagolake* ✉ *Nonresident $8, Maine resident $6.*

 Restaurants

Black Bear Cafe

$$ | **IRISH** | **FAMILY** | Owned by an Irishman and his wife, this pub offers Emerald Isle brews on tap and stocks nine Irish whiskeys. If you're hungry, the fare includes bangers and mash and fish-and-chips, or an entrée of petite beef tenderloin or seafood. **Known for:** seasonal shepherd's pie; beer balls appetizer; rock album covers on the bathroom walls. $ *Average main: $24* ✉ *215 Roosevelt Tr. (Rte 302), Naples* ☎ *207/693–4770* ⊕ *www. theblackbearcafe.com.*

 Hotels

Lakeview Inn

$ | **B&B/INN** | Built in 1906 as a hotel annex, the four-story inn has 16 rooms and suites—all on the upper floors—and a wide, inviting front porch that overlooks gardens and offers an angled view of Long Lake beyond the town's main thoroughfare. **Pros:** owner will carry up your bags; convenience center has kitchenette (no stove top) with courtesy beverages (nonalcoholic); several deluxe larger rooms and family-friendly suites. **Cons:** no elevator; stairs a bit steep; "comfy" rooms are smallish. $ *Rooms from: $169* ✉ *15 Lake House Rd., Naples* ☎ *207/693–9099* ⊕ *www.lakeviewinn-maine.com* ⊗ *Closed Nov.–Apr.* ⊲ *16 rooms* ⫮❍⫯ *Free breakfast.*

Activities

Sebago and Long lakes are popular areas for sailing, fishing, and motorboating. As U.S. 302 cuts through the center of Naples, at the Naples causeway you'll find rental craft for fishing or cruising.

TOURS

Songo River Queen II

TOUR—SPORTS | **FAMILY** | Departing from the Naples causeway, the *Songo River Queen II*, a 93-foot stern-wheeler, takes passengers on one- and two-hour cruises on Long Lake. The narration is awash in local history and fun facts about noteworthy dwellings along the shore. ✉ *841 Roosevelt Tr., Naples* ☎ *207/693–6861* ⊕ *www. songoriverqueen.net* ✉ *From $18.*

WATER SPORTS

Dingley's Wharf

WATER SPORTS | **FAMILY** | Smack in the middle of the Naples causeway on Long Lake, Dingley's offers lots of choices for getting out on the water. Wakeboarding, waterskiing, wake surfing, knee boarding, and tube riding excursions with a certified instructor include lessons. If you have your own boat, you can rent equipment for these activities. Dingley's also rents jet skis, aqua tikes, kayaks, canoes, standup paddleboards, runabouts, and pontoon boats. ✉ *851 Roosevelt Tr., Naples* ⊕ *On Naples causeway* ☎ *207/693–5253* ⊕ *www.dingleyswharf. com* ✉ *Rentals from $35.*

Bridgton

8 miles north of Naples, 30 miles south of Bethel.

Picturesque, lakeside Bridgton anchors a region whose many lakes and large ponds are popular for boating, fishing, and swimming. Downtown is a great place to spend the day, with its restaurants, movie theater, a museum, and a great mix of unique shops. Steps from the action, a covered pedestrian bridge leads to 66-acre Pondicherry Park, a nature preserve with a unique covered bridge, wooded trails, and two streams. Highland Beach (one of three town beaches) is just off the north end of Main Street, across from an inviting small park along the thoroughfare. On hot summer

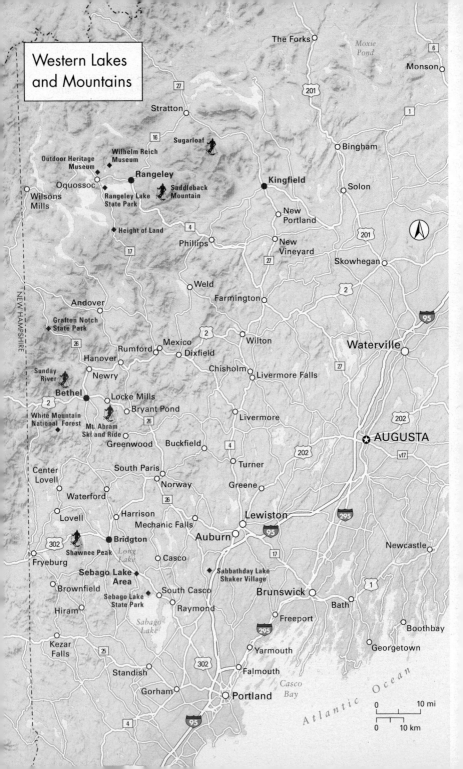

Western Lakes and Mountains

The Forks

Moxie Pond

Monson

6

27

Stratton

1

16

Sugarloaf

Bingham

Outdoor Heritage Museum

Wilhelm Reich Museum

Rangeley

Saddleback Mountain

Kingfield

Solon

201

Oquossoc

Rangeley Lake State Park

New Portland

201

Wilsons Mills

Height of Land

4

Phillips

New Vineyard

27

Skowhegan

17

Weld

Farmington

2

Andover

Grafton Notch State Park

26

Rumford

Mexico

Dixfield

Wilton

Waterville

95

Hanover

Newry

Chisholm

Livermore Falls

27

Sunday River

Bethel

2

Locke Mills

Bryant Pond

26

Livermore

202

White Mountain National Forest

Mt. Abram Ski and Ride

Greenwood

Buckfield

4

AUGUSTA

v17

Center Lovell

South Paris

Norway

Turner

202

Greene

NEW HAMPSHIRE

Waterford

26

Lovell

Harrison

Mechanic Falls

Lewiston

295

Shawnee Peak

302

Bridgton

Long Lake

Casco

Auburn

95

Fryeburg

Sabbathday Lake Shaker Village

17

Newcastle

Brownfield

Sebago Lake Area

South Casco

Brunswick

1

Hiram

Sebago Lake State Park

Raymond

Bath

Boothbay

Kezar Falls

25

Sabago Lake

Freeport

295

Georgetown

Standish

Yarmouth

Gorham

302

Falmouth

Casco Bay

Portland

95

Atlantic Ocean

0   10 mi

0   10 km

4

days, kids dive off the dock as mountains lounge on the horizon. Come winter, visitors hit the slopes at Shawnee Peak and cross-country ski at the ridgetop golf course. The surrounding countryside is a good choice for leaf peepers and outdoors lovers. A few miles north, Harrison anchors the northern end of Long Lake. In fall, Fryeburg is home to the Fryeburg Fair (🌐 *www.fryeburgfair.org*), the region's largest agricultural fair. North of here, Center Lovell draws boaters to Kezar Lake (author and Mainer Stephen King summers here) and hikers to Mount Sabbatus.

GETTING HERE AND AROUND

From Portland, U.S. 302 runs northwest to Bridgton along the east side of Sebago Lake and the west side of Long Lake. From there it continues west 15 miles to Fryeburg, where Route 5 continues north to Center Lovell.

VISITOR INFORMATION

CONTACTS Greater Bridgton Lakes Region Chamber of Commerce. ✉ *101 Portland Rd.* ☎ *207/647–3472* 🌐 *www.mainelakeschamber.com.*

👁 Sights

Rufus Porter Museum of Art and Ingenuity
MUSEUM | Local youth Rufus Porter became a leading folk artist in the early 1800s, painting landscape and harbor murals on the walls of New England homes, like this museum's barn red Cape Cod–style house, which bears unsigned murals by Porter (or one of his apprentices). In 2016, the late-18th-century structure was moved to the museum's downtown setting, where a circa-1830s dwelling has exhibits about Porter, also an "ahead of his time" inventor, writer, and founder of *Scientific American* magazine. Early issues are on display, as are models of some of his inventions and his miniature portraits. There's a video about Porter, an excellent gift shop with books about the author, and a large lawn with picnic tables. ✉ *121 Main St.* ☎ *207/647–2828* 🌐 *www.rufusportermuseum.org* 🎫 *$8* 🕒 *Closed mid-Oct.–mid-June and Sun.–Tues. mid-June–mid-Oct.*

🍴 Restaurants

Standard Gastropub
$ | **AMERICAN** | **FAMILY** | Like the facade, a cooler wall—stocked with hundreds of beers from around Maine and the world—attests to Gastropub's gas station past (it even served gas initially). Craft brews, many hard to find, accompany snazzy, farm-to-table takes on American classic and foreign-inspired comfort foods. **Known for:** smash burgers (local grass-fed beef) topped with house sauce and served with twice-fried fries; chili mayo-smothered smoked street corn (seasonal); loads of daily specials. [$] *Average main: $15* ✉ *233 Main St.* ☎ *207/647–4100* 🌐 *www.standardgastropub.com.*

🛏 Hotels

★ Noble House Inn
$ | **B&B/INN** | On a quiet road, this 1903 estate above Highland Lake offers a convenient location, plenty of creature comforts, and a relaxing atmosphere. **Pros:** homemade cookies daily; skiing and golfing packages; distinctive suites. **Cons:** limited lake views; only suites have TVs; foldable twin beds only fit in some rooms. [$] *Rooms from: $170* ✉ *81 Highland Rd.* ☎ *207/647–3733, 888/237–4880* 🌐 *www.noblehouseinn.com* 🔑 *8 rooms* 🍽 *Free breakfast.*

🏃 Activities

Shawnee Peak
SKIING/SNOWBOARDING | **FAMILY** | Just a few miles from Bridgton, Shawnee Peak appeals to families and to those who enjoy nighttime skiing—trails are lighted except most Sundays. Three terrain parks and seven glade areas offer alternatives to trails and downhill runs. The main base

lodge has a restaurant with an expansive deck; the smaller East Lodge has a second-floor bunkhouse. Lodging choices also include Shawnee Peak House and a mountaintop yurt and cabin. Summer visitors can hike and pick blueberries. **Facilities:** 43 trails; 249 acres; 1,300-foot vertical drop; 6 lifts. ⊠ *119 Mountain Rd., off U.S. 302* ☎ *207/647–8444* ⊕ *www. shawneepeak.com* ⛷ *Lift ticket: $77.*

🛍 Shopping

Whether you are a browser or a shopper, downtown Bridgton beckons. Main Street often looks and feels like a Normal Rockwell painting, and it's here that you'll find mostly year-round shops selling books, antiques, gifts, art, handcrafts, chocolates, souvenirs, T-shirts, and clothing, anchored by a branch of Renys (⊕ *www.fryeburgfair.org*), the state's friendly, spic-and-span outlet department store chain, aka "A Maine Adventure."

Firefly Boutique

CLOTHING | Picture windows line the walls of this corner boutique that sells unique women's attire from the "USA and beyond," including flower prints leggings, "cashmere feel" art print shawls, and chic rollneck alpaca sweaters. The lively dress selection has options for evenings out as well as running about. In business since 2009, Firefly is also known for fashion jewelry—including three Maine-made lines, one featuring recycled guitar string pieces—handbags, and gifts. Don't miss Sassy & Blue's adorable girlswear, also Maine-made, in the rear corner, and store sale items in the backroom. ⊠ *103 Main St.* ☎ *207/647–3672* ⊕ *www.fireflyshop-maine.com.*

Gallery 302

ART GALLERIES | Creative shop windows showcase an individual artist on a rotating biweekly basis, inviting passers-by into Bridgton Art Guild's wide-open tin-ceilinged gallery in a former hardware store. Eclectic and fun—definitely not stuffy—the gallery opened in 2003 and represents about 50 local and regional artists working in various media. Artists' displays have their bio and often their photograph. Don't miss the back-corner gift shop with cards, small prints, and the like. Along with hosting wine and cheese receptions and community events, the guild holds classes and workshops—many for a day or half day, so consider signing up. ⊠ *112 Main St.* ☎ *207/647–2787* ⊕ *www.gallery302.com.*

Bethel

27 miles north of Bridgton, 65 miles north of Portland, 66 miles south of Rangeley.

Bethel is pure New England: a town with white clapboard houses, a large green, white-steeple churches, and a mountain vista at the end of every street. Gould Academy, a college prep school founded in 1836, anchors the east side of downtown. On Main Street, the new Maine Mineral & Gem Museum honors the region's storied mining history—and has a moon rock collection that rocks. In winter, Bethel is ski country. Sunday River, one of Maine's big ski resorts, is only a few miles north in Newry, while family-friendly Mt. Abram is east of town. On the third weekend in July, Bethel Area Summerfest includes a parade, fireworks, live music, and a frog-jumping contest. Whatever the season folks hit the trails at Bethel Village Trails on the edge of the village and 978-acre Bethel Community Forest a few miles from the town center. Under the tutelage of nonprofit **Mahoosuc Pathways** (⊕ *www. mahoosucpathways.org*), both locales welcome hikers, mountain bikers, snowshoers, and cross-country skiers.

GETTING HERE AND AROUND

From the south, both Routes 35 and 5 lead to Bethel, overlapping several miles south of town. Route 5 from Bethel to

Fryeburg is especially pretty come fall, with long stretches of overhanging trees and glimpses of Kezar Lake as the road passes through tiny Center Lovell. If you're coming to Bethel from the west on U.S. 2, you'll pass White Mountain National Forest.

VACATION RENTALS

CONTACTS Four Seasons Realty & Rentals. ⊠ *32 Parkway Pl., Suite 1* ☎ *207/824–3776* ⊕ *www.fourseasonsrealtymaine.com.*

VISITOR INFORMATION

CONTACTS Bethel Area Chamber of Commerce. ⊠ *8 Station Pl., off Cross St.* ☎ *207/824–2282, 800/442–5826* ⊕ *www.bethelmaine.com.*

 # Sights

Artist's Bridge

BRIDGE/TUNNEL | The most painted and photographed of Maine's nine covered bridges can be found on a detour from Newry. Head south on U.S. 2 and then northwest on Sunday River Road (stay to the right at "Y" intersections). Trails flow alongside Sunday River from the pedestrian-only bridge, which is a popular swimming spot. ⊠ *Sunday River Rd., 4 miles northwest of U.S. 2, Newry.*

Grafton Notch State Park

NATIONAL/STATE PARK | **FAMILY** | Grafton Notch Scenic Byway along Route 26 runs through Grafton Notch, a favorite destination for viewing fall foliage that stretches along the Bear River Valley 14 miles north of Bethel. It's an easy walk from roadside parking areas to the distinctive Screw Auger Falls, which drops through a gorge, creating pools; Mother Walker Falls; and Moose Cave. Trailhead parking and the nicely shaded Spruce Meadow picnic area are also right along the road. Table Rock Loop Trail (2.4 miles round-trip) rewards hikers with views of the mountainous terrain. More challenging is the 7.6-mile round-trip trek along the Appalachian Trail to the viewing platform atop 4,180-foot Old Speck Mountain, one of the state's highest peaks. The Appalachian Trail also traverses the 31,764-acre Mahoosuc Public Land—its two tracts sandwich the park—whose trails offer stunning, if strenuous, backcountry hiking (there are backcountry campsites). In winter, a popular snowmobile trail follows the river through the park. ⊠ *1941 Bear River Rd., Newry* ☎ *207/824–2912 mid-May–mid-Oct. only, 207/624–6080* ⊕ *www.maine.gov/graftonnotch* ☑ *Nonresidents $4, Maine residents $3.*

★ Maine Mineral & Gem Museum

MUSEUM | **FAMILY** | Moon rocks, Maine mineralogy, and western Maine's legacy of mining minerals and gems—its pink and "watermelon" tourmaline are renowned—converge at this interactive 15,000-square-foot museum. Opened downtown in 2019 and founded by philanthropists, there's a garden out front with placarded large rocks, some resembling modern sculpture. The museum links two Main Street buildings, and its ticket area doubles as a gift store specializing in fine jewelry featuring Maine gems, as well as educational toys, books, and so on. A brightly lit gallery beside the shop showcases the state's geologic history and finds from around the world. Throughout the museum, touch screens invite you to dig into an item's provenance and makeup, and you can watch video interviews with those preserving the region's mining legacy. Exhibits about Bethel and environs spotlight gem discoveries and mica and feldspar mining—kids love the simulated blast. Don't miss the mica Christmas "snow" made before mining minerals for industrial purposes declined here. There are prized specimens displayed in a replica of a shuttered Maine mineral store and tourist hotspot. "Hall of Gems" bedazzles: the tourmaline necklace worn by Maine's First Ladies and first female governor is here. "Space Rocks," the large final gallery," has displays that include three of the world's ten largest lunar meteorites—five more are in the collection, as are 6,000 meteorites, 40,000 gems, and 15,000 Maine specimens. A 3D film beams about after the room darkens, launching a meteorite shower that blows up the walls, revealing Bethel. ✉ *99 Main St.* ☎ *207/824–3036* 🌐 *www.mainemineral-museum.org* 🎟 *$15* 🕒 *Closed Tues.*

Museums of the Bethel Historical Society
MUSEUM | Start your stroll in Bethel here, across from the Village Common. The center's campus comprises two buildings: the 1821 O'Neil Robinson House and the 1813 Dr. Moses Mason House, both listed on the National Register of Historic Places. The O'Neil Robinson House has changing and permanent exhibits pertaining to the region's history and a Maine Ski and Snowmobile Museum display. One parlor room serves as a gift shop with a nice book selection. The Moses Mason House has nine period rooms, and the front hall and stairway are decorated with Rufus Porter School folk art murals. The barn gallery has changing and traveling exhibits. ■ **TIP→** Head out back to check out the Sunday River snow roller, pulled by a team of horses back in the day. ✉ *10 Broad St.* ☎ *207/824–2908, 800/824–2910* 🌐 *www.bethelhistorical.org* 🎟 *O'Neil Robinson free, Moses Mason $5* 🕒 *O'Neil Robinson closed late Oct.–late May, Sun. and Mon. July and Aug., and Sat.–Mon. June and Sept.; Moses Mason closed Sept.–June and Sun.–Wed. July and Aug.*

White Mountain National Forest
FOREST | **FAMILY** | This forest straddles New Hampshire and Maine, with the highest peaks on the New Hampshire side. The Maine section, though smaller, has magnificent rugged terrain. Hikers can enjoy everything from hour-long nature loops to a day hike up Speckled Mountain. The mountain is part of the 14,000-acre Caribou-Speckled Mountain Wilderness Area, one of several in the forest, but the only one entirely contained within Maine. The most popular Maine access to the national forest is via Route 113, which runs south from its terminus at U.S. 2 in Gilead, 10 miles from downtown Bethel. Most of the highway is the Pequawket Trail Maine Scenic Byway, and the section through the forest is spectacular come fall. This stretch is closed in winter but is used by snowmobilers and cross-country skiers. Two of the forest's campgrounds are in Maine; backcountry camping is allowed. ✉ *Rte. 113, off U.S. 2, Gilead* ☎ *603/466–2713* 🌐 *www.fs.usda.gov/whitemountain* 🎟 *From $5 per car.*

☕ Coffee and Quick Bites

Good Food Store
$ | **AMERICAN** | **FAMILY** | A cheery red door welcomes customers to this hip, cozy grocery, opened in 1994 and selling specialty, organic, and Maine-produced foods and goods, from sodas to local poultry. Friendly staff suggest items from the specials-friendly, freshly prepared takeout menu, or for picnics or dinner at your cabin. **Known for:** pumpkin whoopie pies; "heat and eat" soups and meals; beer and wine selection. [$] *Average main: $8* ✉ *212 Mayville Rd.* ☎ *207/824–3754* 🌐 *www.goodfoodbethel.com* 🕒 *Smokin' Good BBQ closed mid-Apr.–mid-May and mid-Oct.–mid-Nov.*

🛏 Hotels

Holidae House Bed & Breakfast
$ | **B&B/INN** | Welcoming hospitality keeps guests returning year after year to this charming, affordable downtown bed-and-breakfast, where innkeepers are at the ready with day-trip tips and eight guest rooms occupy two floors of the antiques-filled home. **Pros:** courtesy cordials in parlor; fresh-baked treats in afternoon; blow-up mattresses available. **Cons:** no lawn; no mountain views; no king beds. [$] *Rooms from: $159* ✉ *85 Main St.* ☎ *207/824–3400* 🌐 *www.holidaehouse.com* 🔑 *8 rooms* 🍴 *Free breakfast.*

One of the Rangeley Lakes, Mooselookmeguntic is said to mean "portage to the moose feeding place" in the Abenaki language.

☄ Activities

CANOEING AND KAYAKING

Bethel Outdoor Adventure and Campground

CANOEING/ROWING/SKULLING | FAMILY | On the Androscoggin River, this outfitter rents canoes, kayaks, tubes, standup paddleboards, and a drift boat; runs river shuttles; sells state fishing licenses; leads guided kayak and canoe trips; and has a campground. There's also an open-air facility where you can sluice for precious and semiprecious gems and minerals (the Bethel region has a long history of mining for them). All Bethel Outdoor Adventure activities get customers a free trek on the Burma Bridge, which leads to a walking trail on the company's private, wild river island. For others it's just a buck. ✉ *121 Mayville Rd.* ☎ *207/824–4224* ⊕ *www.betheloutdoor-adventure.com.*

DOGSLEDDING

Mahoosuc Guide Service

LOCAL SPORTS | This acclaimed guide company leads day and multiday dog-sledding and canoeing expeditions in the Umbagog National Wildlife Refuge on the Maine–New Hampshire border. The outfitter also offers overnight excursions elsewhere in Maine and in Canada. One of the multiday canoe trips is an immersion in the ways of the Penobscot Nation, a Maine Native American tribe. Mahoosuc also runs fishing trips and has lodging for customers and groups. ✉ *1513 Bear River Rd., Newry* ☎ *207/824–2073* ⊕ *www.mahoosuc.com* ✉ *From $175.*

SKIING

Carter's Cross-Country Ski Center

SKIING/SNOWBOARDING | FAMILY | Mountain views await at this acclaimed cross-country ski center, which offers 34 miles of trails for all levels of skiers. Skis, snowshoes, and sleds to pull children are all available for rental, as are fat-tire bikes. The place also rents lodge rooms and

Whoopie Pies

When a bill aiming to make the whoopie pie Maine's official dessert was debated in state legislature, some lawmakers countered that the blueberry pie (made with Maine wild blueberries, of course) should have the honor. The blueberry pie won out, but what might have erupted into civil war instead ended civilly, with whoopie pies designated the official state "treat." Spend a few days anywhere in Maine and you'll notice just how popular it really is.

The name is misleading: it's a "pie" only in the sense of a having a filling between two "crusts"—namely, a thick layer of sugary frosting sandwiched between two saucers of rich cake, usually chocolate. It may have acquired its distinctive moniker from the jubilant "yelp" farmers emitted after discovering it in their lunchboxes. The whoopie pie is said to have Pennsylvania Dutch roots, but many Mainers insist that it originated here. Typically, the filling is made with butter or shortening; some recipes add Marshmallow Fluff. Many bakers have indulged the temptation to experiment with flavors and ingredients, particularly in the filling but also in the cake, offering pumpkin, raspberry, oatmeal cream, red velvet, peanut butter, and more.

ski-in cabins, available year-round. ⊠ *786 Intervale Rd.* ☏ *207/824–3880 Bethel location* ⊕ *www.cartersxcski.com* ⊠ *$18*.

Mt. Abram Ski and Ride

SKIING/SNOWBOARDING | FAMILY | Family-friendly and affordable, Mt. Abram is open Thursday–Sunday during ski season. It allows off-trail "boundary-to-boundary" skiing, has two terrain parks, and welcomes uphill snowshoers and skiers ($15 day pass). Westside, the popular lift-served beginner area, has its own base lodge. The main lodge is home to Loose Boots Lounge, which occasionally features live music. Mountain biking is big here during the warm months: Mt. Abram offers rentals and lessons and trails are lift-served—aside from one for the hearty. **Facilities:** 51 trails; 250 acres; 1,150-foot vertical drop; 4 lifts. ⊠ *308 Howe Hill Rd., off Rte. 26, Greenwood* ☏ *207/875–5000* ⊕ *www.mtabram.com* ⊠ *Lift ticket: $49*.

★ Sunday River

SKIING/SNOWBOARDING | FAMILY | Once-sleepy Sunday River has evolved into a sprawling resort that attracts skiers from around the world. Stretching for 3 miles, it encompasses eight trail-connected peaks and five terrain parks. Off-trail "boundary-to-boundary" skiing is allowed, and there is night skiing on Friday and Saturday. On some weekends and during holiday weeks, fireworks light the skies at the main South Ridge base lodge, one of three at the resort. Sunday River has several lodging choices, including condos and two slope-side hotels: the family-friendly Grand Summit, at one of the mountain bases, and the more upscale Jordan Grand, near a summit at the resort's western end. (It's really up there, several miles by vehicle from the base areas, but during ski season there's a shuttle, or you can ski over for lunch.) ■ TIP→ **At both slope-side hotels, the outdoor heated pool and hot tub are open year-round.** From the less costly Snow Cap Inn, it's a short walk to the slopes. Come summer, the resort offers archery, kayaking, and standup paddleboarding lessons and guided kayak tours, and the main South Ridge Base Lodge hosts a bungee trampoline, climbing wall, and chairlift rides to North Peak. Many visitors opt to hike down or hit a trail up top before riding down. You can hike or ride up to play disc golf—or head over to Sunday River Golf Club, acclaimed for its wide-open mountain and valley views and challenging elevation changes. ■ TIP→ **Don't golf? Grab a drink or a bite at the clubhouse and hit those views—there's a building-length deck and a soaring Palladian window framed by polished wood walls. Facilities:** 135 trails (includes glades); 870 acres; 2,340-foot vertical drop; 18 lifts. ⊠ *15 S. Ridge Rd., Newry* ☎ *207/824–3000, 207/824–5200 for snow conditions, 800/543–2754 for reservations* ⊕ *www.sundayriver.com* ✉ *Lift ticket: $119.*

Rangeley

66 miles north of Bethel.

With 100-plus lakes and ponds linked by rivers and streams, the vastly forested Rangeley region has a rough, wilderness feel and has long attracted winter-sports enthusiasts, hikers, and anglers—it's been hailed for centuries as a "fly-fishing mecca." The four-season resort town of Rangeley stretches along the north side of its namesake lake. Right behind Main Street, Lakeside Park ("Town Park" to locals) has a large swimming area, a playground, picnic shelters, and a boat launch. Come winter, Saddleback Mountain (set to reopen in 2020) lures downhill skiers, many of them families. Other winter activities in these parts include cross-country skiing, snowshoeing, fat-tire biking, snowmobiling, and pond skating. In late January, the Rangeley Snowmobile Snodeo offers thrilling snowmobile acrobatics, fireworks, a parade, and a cook-off for which area restaurants enter their chilies and chowders. Seven miles west on Route 4, tucked at the east end of Rangeley Lake near Mooselookmeguntic Lake, tiny Oquossoc is another hub for outdoor activities and dining. At the main crossroads, the Outdoor Heritage Museum beckons visitors; nearby Bald Mountain is a family-friendly day hike. South of the hamlet on Route

17 is the western gateway to the region, Height of Land—a must-see overlook with distant views stretching to mountains on the New Hampshire border.

GETTING HERE AND AROUND

To reach Rangeley on a scenic drive through Western Maine, take Route 17 north from U.S. 2 in Mexico past Height of Land to Route 4 in Oquossoc, then head east into town. Much of the drive is the **Rangeley Lakes National Scenic Byway** (⊕ *www.exploremaine.org/byways*) From Rangeley, Route 16 continues east to Sugarloaf ski resort and Kingfield.

VACATION RENTALS

CONTACTS Morton & Furbish Vacation Rentals. ⊠ *2478 Main St.* ☎ *207/864–9065, 888/218–4882* ⊕ *www.rangeleyrentals.com.*

VISITOR INFORMATION

CONTACTS Rangeley Lakes Chamber of Commerce. ⊠ *6 Park Rd.* ☎ *207/864–5364, 800/685–2537* ⊕ *www.rangeleymaine.com.*

 ## Sights

Height of Land

SCENIC DRIVE | Height of Land is the highlight of Rangeley Lakes National Scenic Byway, with unforgettable views of mountains and lakes. One of Maine's best overlooks, it hugs Route 17 atop Spruce Mountain several miles south of Rangeley's Oquossoc village. On a clear day, you can look west to mountains on the New Hampshire border. There's off-road parking, interpretive panels, stone seating, and a short path to the Appalachian Trail. Rangeley Lake unfolds at a nearby overlook on the opposite side of the road. ⊠ *Rte. 17.*

★ Moose Alley

LOCAL INTEREST | FAMILY | Bowling is just one reason families, couples, locals, and visitors head to this happening spot for a night out or a rainy (or sunny!) day in, one of the most popular spots in Rangeley. Open 365 days a year, the moose theme amps up but doesn't overwhelm the chic, fun modern decor. Don't miss the fish, moose, loon, and Rangeley Lake images on the dance floor—there's live music on weekends and sometimes weeknights. Antler chandeliers light the pool tables and walls with geometric patterns frame the 10 bowling lanes. There's also foosball, air hockey, and near the entrance, a video/game arcade. In the restaurant/bar area, settle onto a curved couch or at the warmly lit curved bar—like the pillars, faced to resemble river stones. Roomy armchairs circle the firepit: like the sign says, it's OK to put your feet on the surround, but not your food! That's ordered at a counter and delivered to your table, bar seat, lane, or game spot. The pub fare is delish (try the chipotle sweet potato fries) and the brunch menu available all day—food is served from 11 am until close. ⊠ *2809 Main St.* ☎ *207/864–9955* ⊕ *www.moosealley.me.*

★ Outdoor Heritage Museum

MUSEUM | FAMILY | Spruce railings and siding on the museum's facade replicate a local taxidermy shop from about 1900. Inside, there's an authentic log sporting camp from the same period, when grand hotels and full-service sporting lodges drew well-to-do rusticators on long stays. One of the big draws is the exhibit on local flytier Carrie Stevens, whose famed streamer flies increased the region's fly-fishing fame in the 1920s. The many diverse exhibits include displays on U.S. presidents Dwight D. Eisenhower and Herbert Hoover fishing in Rangeley; vintage watercraft; Native American birch-bark canoes and artifacts; art of the region; and gleaming fish mounts of world-record-size brook trout. With free exhibits out front, this a popular stop even when closed—don't miss the 12,000-year-old Native American meat cache. ⊠ *8 Rumford Rd., Oquossoc* ☎ *207/864–3091* ⊕ *www.rangeleyhistoricalsociety.org* ⊠ *$7* ⊙ *Closed Nov.–Apr. and Mon. and Tues. May, June, Sept., and Oct.*

Rangeley Lake State Park

NATIONAL/STATE PARK | FAMILY | On the south shore of Rangeley Lake, this 869-acre park has superb lakeside scenery, swimming, picnic tables, a playground, a boat ramp, a few short trails, and a campground. ⊠ *1 State Park Rd.* ⊹ *Turn on S. Shore Rd. from Rte. 17 or Rte. 4* ☎ *207/864–3858 May–mid-Oct. only, 207/624–6080 for regional state parks office* ⊕ *www.maine.gov/rangeleylake* ⊠ *Nonresident $6, Maine resident $4.*

Wilhelm Reich Museum

MEMORIAL | FAMILY | The museum showcases the life and work of Austrian physician, scientist, and writer Wilhelm Reich (1897–1957), who believed that all living matter and the atmosphere contain a force called orgone energy. The hilltop Orgone Energy Observatory exhibits biographical materials, inventions, and equipment used in his experiments, whose results were disputed by the Food and Drug Administration and other government agencies. Stone faces the exterior of the boxy 1949 structure, which is listed on the National Register of Historic Places. A midcentury gem inside and out, Reich's second-floor study, library, and laboratory look as they did in his day, with original sleek modern furniture. The observatory deck has magnificent countryside views. In July and August, the museum presents engaging nature programs; trails lace the largely forested 175-acre property, which has a vacation rental cottage. Reich's tomb sits next to one of his inventions, a cloud accumulator. ⊠ *19 Orgonon Cir., off Rte. 4* ☎ *207/864–3443* ⊕ *wilhelmreichmuseum.org* ⊠ *Museum $8, grounds free* ⊙ *Museum closed Oct.–June, Sun.–Tues. in July and Aug. and Sun.–Fri. in Sept. Private tours May–Oct. by appt.*

🍴 Restaurants

Gingerbread House Restaurant

$ | **AMERICAN** | **FAMILY** | With a fieldstone fireplace in the main dining room, tables about the garden-side deck, and an antique marble soda fountain, there are lots of reasons to stop at what really does look like a giant gingerbread house at the edge of the woods. The restaurant serves both breakfast and lunch, with expansive menus for each (but no dinner). **Known for:** baguette French toast and lobster eggs Benedict; crab cakes and pesto linguine lunch entrées; proximity to overlooks, hiking. [$] *Average main: $12* ✉ *55 Carry Rd., Oquossoc* ☎ *207/864–3602* 🌐 *www.gingerbreadhouserestaurant.net* 🕒 *Closed Apr. and Nov.; closed Mon. and Tues. Dec.–Mar. and May, June, Sept., and Oct. No lunch Sun. except in July and Aug. No dinner.*

☕ Coffee and Quick Bites

Pine Tree Frosty

$ | **FAST FOOD** | **FAMILY** | A summertime visit to Rangeley isn't complete without a stop at this cash-only snack bar—in business since 1964—for ice cream and simple meals like burgers and fries. Both hard and soft ice cream are served, as are sundaes, milk shakes, flurries, and banana splits. **Known for:** Maine-made Gifford's hard ice cream; lobster rolls; waterside Adirondack chairs and picnic tables. [$] *Average main: $6* ✉ *2459 Main St.* 🌐 *facebook.com/pinetreefrosty* 💳 *No credit cards.*

🛏 Hotels

The Rangeley Inn

$ | **HOTEL** | **FAMILY** | Painted eggshell blue, this historic downtown hotel was built around 1900 for wealthy urbanites on vacation—from the covered front porch, you step into a grand lobby with polished pine wainscoting and a brick fireplace; the "lodge" is a motel-style building out back on Hayley Pond. **Pros:** tavern with fireplace and elegant original dining room; nice variety of suites (largest sleeps six); courtesy canoes and kayaks for Hayley Pond, guided kayak photography trips (fee). **Cons:** no elevator; not on Rangeley Lake; a couple minutes walk from lodge to hotel. [$] *Rooms from: $175* ✉ *2443 Main St.* ☎ *207/864–3341* 🌐 *www.therangeleyinn.com* 🛏 *42 rooms* 🍴 *No meals.*

🏃 Activities

Rangeley and Mooselookmeguntic lakes are good for canoeing, kayaking, sailing, fishing, and motorboating. Lake fishing for landlocked salmon and the region's famed brook trout is at its best in May, June, and September. The area's rivers and streams are especially popular with fly-fishers, who enjoy the sport May–October. Ice fishing shacks dot Rangeley Lake come winter.

BIKING

Mountain bikers head to Rangeley Lakes Trails Center on Saddleback Mountain, where trails are groomed in winter for cross-country skiing, snowshoeing, and fat-tire biking. **■ TIP→ Fat-tire bikes, which you can rent in town, are increasingly popular for summer recreation in Rangeley and elsewhere in Maine because of the rough terrain and many rural backroads.**

AJ's Fat Bikes

BICYCLING | **FAMILY** | Half- and full-day and weekly fat-tire bike rentals are available during the warm months and after the snow flies at this friendly shop, which is at the ready with riding tips and routes (many of which aren't easy to find if you aren't in the know). It also sells and repairs bikes (various kinds) and gear. Rentals start at $35. ✉ *2745 Main St.* ☎ *207/864–2850.*

BOATING

★ River's Edge Sports

BOATING | FAMILY | Hugging Route 4 in Oquossoc and resembling a sporting lodge, this is a convenient stop for gear galore and great ways to get out on the water. Paddle at your own pace on the popular, shuttle-served canoe and kayak river trips, or rent a kayak, canoe, or stan-dup paddleboard—you can put in at the dock out back on Rangeley Lake, near the outflow into Rangeley River. River's Edge sells Maine fishing licenses, and owner Gerry White, a Registered Maine Guide, leads fishing trips on Rangeley and Mooselookmeguntic lakes. Along with camping, fishing, hunting, and hiking gear, the 8,000-some-item store stocks souvenirs, apparel—from jackets to Rangeley and Oqussoc hoodies and tees—and gifts, many Maine-made. Don't miss the bins of colorful flies for fishing and the mounted wildlife: the "indoor zoo" has salmon, bobcats, bears, moose, and more. River's Edge's helpful website has information about the area; Gerry and his wife, Sally, happily share tips in person, too. The store is closed from January through mid-April. ⊠ *38 Carry Rd. (Rte. 4), Oquossoc* ☎ *207/864–5582* ⊕ *www.riversedgesports.com* ▧ *Rentals from $25, trips from $45.*

GOLF

Mingo Springs Golf Course

GOLF | This popular course is known for its mountain and water views. The course is short but challenging, with very angled drives. The front nine holes are the hilliest; the back nine holes the longest. You can also take in the views and spot wildlife on the Mingo Springs Trail & Bird Walk, an easy 3-mile loop trail through the woods along the course. ⊠ *43 Country Club Rd.* ☎ *207/864–5021* ⊕ *www.mingosprings.com* ▧ *$32 for 9 holes, $44 for 18 holes* ⌇ *18 holes, 6024 yards, par 71.*

HIKING

Hiking options in the Rangeley Lakes region include 35 miles of trails and access roads on Rangeley Lakes Heritage Trust's 14,000 acres of conserved lands, which also welcome many other types of outdoor recreation. Trail maps and information are available at the organization's website (⊕ *www.fryeburgfair.org*) and its downtown Rangeley office (2424 Main Street).

ICE SKATING

Rangeley Skating Club (⊕ *www.fryeburg-fair.org*) clears a section of Haley Pond for ice skating, usually by Christmastime. The lake-size pond is behind Main Street at the east end of downtown. Skates, hockey sticks, and pucks are available at pondside Ecopelagicon, just off Main Street. There is rink-side warming hut, and the ice is lit until 10 nightly.

MULTISPORT OUTFITTERS

Ecopelagicon

KAYAKING | FAMILY | Off Main Street on Hayley Pond, this outfitter and retailer has an easy, affordable way to get you on the water: rent a kayak, canoe, or stan-dup paddleboard by the hour. Or rent one for a half-, full-, or multi days and paddle where you please; shuttle service, guided tours, and lessons are also offered. Come winter, you can rent snowshoes or grab courtesy skates to use on the pond rink. In business since 1993, this welcoming "nature store" sells outdoor recreation gear galore; Maine- and Rangeley-theme books, guides, and maps; a slew of New England-made gifts; and lots of games and arts-and-crafts for adults and kids. Shoppers linger at the back window to gaze at Saddleback Mountain and ducks and loons on the pond. Rentals start at $10. The store closes late October through mid-November and in April. ⊠ *7 Pond St.* ☎ *207/864–2771* ⊕ *www.ecopelagicon.com.*

SEAPLANES

★ Acadian Seaplanes

TOUR—SPORTS | In addition to 15-, 30- and 75-minute scenic flights high above the mountains by seaplane, this operator offers enticing "fly-in" excursions. You can travel by seaplane to wilderness locales to dine at a sporting camp, spot moose in their natural habitat, fish, or go white-water rafting on the remote Rapid River. Acadian also provides charter service, including between the Rangeley area and Boston, New York, Portland, Bangor, and other places within Maine. ⊠ *2640 Main St.* ☎ *207/864–5307* ⊕ *www.acadianseaplanes.com* ✈ *From $85.*

SKIING

Rangeley Lakes Trails Center

LOCAL SPORTS | A largely wooded, 34-mile trail network stretches along lower Saddleback Mountain and leads to Saddleback Lake. In winter, trails are groomed (double- and single-track) for cross-country skiing, snowshoeing, and fat-tire biking. A yurt lodge has ski, snowshoe, and fat-tire rentals and a snack bar known for tasty soups. Call ahead for ski, snowshoe, and fat-tire tours and cross-country lessons. In warmer weather, the trails are popular with mountain bikers, hikers, and runners. ⊠ *524 Saddleback Mountain Rd., Dallas* ☎ *207/864–4309 winter only* ⊕ *www.rangeleylakestrailscenter.org* ✈ *From $10.*

Saddleback Mountain

SKIING/SNOWBOARDING | FAMILY | Shuttered in 2015 and sold in January 2020, new owners installed what the previous ones had pined for—a high-speed quad lift. The beginner ski area is one of New England's best, partly because it is *below* the base lodge. At the other end of the spectrum, it's black diamonds all the way down at Kennebago Steeps!, touted as the East's largest steep-skiing area. Saddleback also has extensive glade areas, three terrain parks, and lots of natural snow. A fieldstone fireplace keeps things warm in the post-and-beam base lodge, which has a second-story pub. Recent renovations greatly expanded capacity and views. On-mountain lodging choices include ski-in, ski-out homes and trailside condos. The resort plans to ramp up summertime with activities such as mountain biking, kayaking, maple syruping, and guided hikes. **Facilities:** 66 trails; 220 acres; 2,000-foot vertical drop; 5 lifts. ⊠ *976 Saddleback Mountain Rd., Dallas* ☎ *207/864–5671, 866/918–2225* ⊕ *www.saddlebackmaine.com.*

Kingfield

38 miles east of Rangeley.

In the shadows of Mt. Abraham ("Mt. Abram" to locals) and Sugarloaf Mountain, home to the eponymous ski resort, Kingfield is "real" New England, dotted with white clapboard churches. The pretty Carrabassett River slices the village and flows over a dam downtown, creating a great swimming spot below the Route 16 bridge. Small pullouts mark swimming holes along Route 27 as it flows north along the rock-strewn river through Carrabassett Valley (also the name of the neighboring town) to the resort. On the other side of the waterway, the 6.6.-mile Narrow Gauge Pathway rail-trail wends through the narrow, steep-walled valley. The path was first cleared in the late 1800s for a narrower-than-standard railway that transported timber and tourists. Today it's part of an extensive and growing mountain biking network and one of many activities along the 47-mile State Route 27 Maine Scenic Byway (⊕ *www.exploremaine. org/byways*) from Kingfield to the remote Canadian border crossing at Coburn Gorge. Fantastic backcountry recreation awaits in the northern half of the drive around Eustis and Stratton. Near these small recreation hubs, the state's 36,000-acre **Bigelow Preserve** (⊕ *www.maine. gov/bigelowpreserve*) takes in the entire Bigelow Range and borders 20,000-acre Flagstaff Lake.

GETTING HERE AND AROUND

From Kingfield it is 37 miles to Rangeley, via Route 142 to Phillips, and from there, Route 4 north. Or head to Rangeley following the Route 27 Maine Scenic Byway from Kingfield to Stratton and take Route 16 from there to Rangeley—it's just 5 miles longer. You can link these routes for a scenic loop or fall foliage drive.

VISITOR INFORMATION

CONTACTS Franklin County Chamber of Commerce. ⊠ *615 Wilton Rd., Farmington* ☎ *207/778–4215* ⊕ *www.franklincounty-maine.org.*

Sights

Stanley Museum

MUSEUM | Original Stanley Steamer cars built by twin brothers Francis and Freelan Stanley—Kingfield's most famous natives—are the main draw at this museum inside a 1903 Georgian-style former school. Also well worth the stop here are exhibits about the glass-negative photography business the identical twins sold to Eastman Kodak, and the well-composed photographs, taken by their sister, Chansonetta Stanley Emmons, of everyday country life at the turn of the 20th century. ⊠ *40 School St.* ☎ *207/265–2729* ⊕ *www.stanleymuseum.org* ☕ *$8* ⊘ *Closed Jan. and Feb., Sat.–Mon. Mar.–May, and Mon. June–Oct.*

☕ Coffee and Quick Bites

Orange Cat Cafe

$ | AMERICAN | FAMILY | Just past downtown en route to Sugarloaf, this café serves breakfast burritos and wraps, flavor-filled lunch fare (wraps, sandwiches, soup, salads, quiche) and scrumptious baked goods. Local and organic ingredients are kitchen staples, and the coffee is great. **Known for:** turmeric-flavored coconut Golden Milk; Vegetarians Revenge wrap with hummus; huge chocolate chip cookies. $ *Average main: $9* ⊠ *329 Main St.* ☎ *207/265–2860* ⊕ *www.orangecatcafe.com.*

🏃 Activities

BIKING

Carrabassett Valley and environs has emerged as a prime mountain biking destination, with 80-plus miles of trails for all abilities. Several trailheads with kiosks are along or near Route 27 north of Kingfield. Come winter, some of these trails are used for cross-country skiing and fat-tire biking. The network links with the 6.6-mile Narrow Gauge Pathway (nonmotorized) along Carrabassett River through the valley and extends north to the remote Flagstaff Lake area. Maps, trail conditions and closures, and suggested loops are available at the website for the **Carrabassett Region of the New England Mountain Bike Association** (⊕ *www.carrabassettnemba.org*); area businesses distribute the group's large printed maps. You can rent mountain bikes in-season and get maps and trail advice at a couple of spots in Carrabassett Valley.

Allspeed Cyclery

BICYCLING | FAMILY | Portland-based Allspeed Cyclery rents mountain bikes from late May through mid-October at its satellite operation at Sugarloaf's Outdoor Center, where there is a trailhead. Adult rentals are $89 per day, and there are less expensive options for kids. The cost per day drops if you rent for multiple days. ⊠ *3001 Outdoor Center Rd., Carrabassett Valley* ☎ *207/779–3951* ⊕ *www.allspeed.com.*

Carrabassett Valley Bike

BICYCLING | A local mountain biking enthusiast runs this rental, repair, and sales outfit from late spring through early fall at Happy Tunes! Ski Service Center, where he works come winter. Rentals are $50 for a full day and $35 half day. ⊠ *1106 Valley Crossing, Carrabassett Valley* ✛ *Just off Rte. 27 next to Tufulio's Restaurant* ☎ *207/235–6019* ⊕ *www.carrabassettvalleybike.com.*

SKIING
Sugarloaf

SKIING/SNOWBOARDING | **FAMILY** | An eye-catching setting, abundant natural snow, and the only above-the-tree-line lift-service skiing in the East have made Sugarloaf one of Maine's best-known ski resorts. Glade areas, five terrain parks, and a border-cross track amp up the skiing options, as does ungroomed Side-country on Burnt Mountain and Brackett Basin. Snowshoers and uphill skiers can attack this terrain as well as "the Loaf" ($10 uphill ticket). Along with hundreds of slope-side condos and rental homes with ski-in, ski-out access, the resort has two slope-side hotels: Sugarloaf Mountain Hotel is in the ski village, as are shops and restaurants; smaller, more affordable Sugarloaf Inn is a bit down the mountain. Just off Route 27 below the mountain, the Outdoor Center has an NHL-size ice rink; is the gateway to a 56-mile network of groomed trails for cross-country skiing, snowshoeing, and fat-tire biking; and rents equipment for all these activities. ■**TIP**➜ After skiing or other winter fun, unwind on-mountain at the Sports & Fitness Center (fee), which includes a pool, sauna, hot tubs, steam rooms, and by-appointment massages (fee). Once at Sugarloaf, you'll find a car unnecessary—a shuttle connects all operations during the November–May ski season. In summer you can mountain bike, hike, or zipline; take a scenic lift ride or off-road Segway tour; rent a kayak or standup paddleboard; or play golf, either disc golf or a round on what many consider Maine's best golf course. **Facilities:** 162 trails (includes glades); 1,240 acres; 2,820-foot vertical drop; 13 lifts. ✉ *5092 Sugarloaf Access Rd., Carrabassett Valley* ☎ *207/237–2000, 800/843–5623 for reservations* ⊕ *www.sugarloaf.com* 🎿 *Lift ticket: $119.*

Greenville

155 miles northeast of Portland, 70 miles northwest of Bangor.

Greenville, tucked at the southern end of island-dotted, mostly forest-lined Moose-head Lake—at 75,000 acres, Maine's largest and the largest entirely within New England—is an outdoors lover's paradise. In the mid-1800s, Henry David Thoreau departed from here on two of his three famous trips into Maine's wilderness, led by Penobscot guides Chief Joseph Attean and Joseph Polis. In summer, boating, fishing, kayaking, canoeing, and hiking are popular in Moosehead Lake. Come winter, folks head here for ice fishing, snowmo-biling, snowshoeing, and cross-country and downhill skiing—you can enjoy both at Big Squaw Mountain ski area just north of town. Greenville has the best selection of shops, restaurants, and inns in the North Woods region. Restaurants and lodgings are also clustered 20 miles north in Rockwood, where the Moose River flows through the village and—across from Mt. Kineo's majestic cliff face—into the lake. There's also a hip cluster in hiking hub Monson, 14 miles south of Greenville. Maine's 100 Mile Wilderness, home to the most difficult and most northerly stretch of the Appalachian Trial, stretches from here to Mt. Katahdin.

GETTING HERE AND AROUND

To reach Greenville from Interstate 95, get off at Exit 157 in Newport and head north, successively, on Routes 7, 23, and 15.

VACATION RENTALS

VACATION RENTALS Vacasa (Moosehead Lake Cabin Rentals). ☎ *207/695–4300, 855/861–5757* ⊕ *www.vacasa.com/usa/Moosehead-Lake.*

VISITOR INFORMATION

CONTACTS Destination Moosehead Lake. ✉ *480 Moosehead Lake Rd.* ☎ *207/695–2702* ⊕ *www.destinationmoosehedlake.com.*

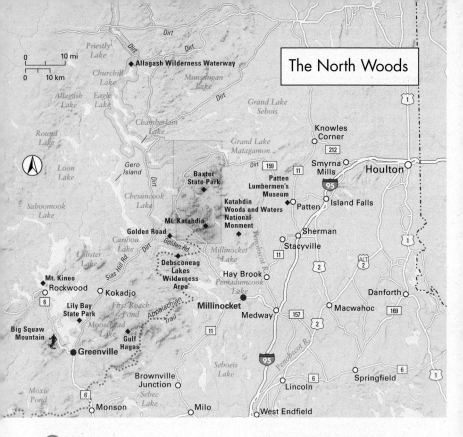

Sights

★ Center for Moosehead History and Moosehead Lake Aviation Museum

MUSEUM | FAMILY | Overlooking East Cove, a former church is home to the Moosehead Historical Society museums. The center has a fine exhibit of Native American artifacts and items from the Moosehead Lake region, dating from 9,000 BC to the present. Displays about Native American families spotlight Henry Perley, a Maliseet guide and author who gained fame as a performer in Wild West shows and silent movies. An interactive exhibit explores life in this logging town in the 1800s. The aviation museum focuses on the impact of aviation—from early bush pilots to Greenville's annual International Seaplane Fly-In on the weekend after Labor Day—in this remote region, in particular the Air Force B-52 crash north of town in January 1963; most of the plane's remnants remain scattered on Elephant Mountain, where seven of nine passengers and crew died.

■ TIP➜ The museum has handouts if you want to take the popular short hike to the debris-littered site, which is also a memorial. The historical society's Greenville walking tour booklet—available to purchase at the museum gift shop—has photos of sights past and present. Don't miss the garden with sculptures honoring Henry David Thoreau and his Native American guides, who departed from East Cove for Maine's wilds. ✉ 6 Lakeview St. ☎ 207/695–2909 Moosehead Historical Society office ⊕ www. mooseheadhistory.org ✉ $3 (includes both museums) ⊘ Closed mid-Oct.–mid-June and Sun.–Wed. mid-June–mid-Oct.

Gulf Hagas

BODY OF WATER | Called the "Grand Canyon of the East" and part of the Appalachian Trail Corridor, this National Natural Landmark has chasms, cliffs, four major waterfalls, pools, exotic flora, and intriguing rock formations. The West Branch of the Pleasant River flows through the 3-mile, slate-walled gorge east of Greenville in a remote, privately owned commercial forest, KI Jo-Mary, which allows access via gravel logging roads (always yield to trucks). A fee (cash or check only) is charged from late spring to late fall at forest checkpoints, where you can get trail maps and hiking information.

From either parking area you can hike to one of the showcase falls and mostly avoid the difficult rim trail. A good choice for families with young children: start at Head of Gulf parking area for a 3½-mile round-trip hike to Stair Falls on the gorge's western end. From the Gulf Hagas parking area, it's a 3-mile round-trip hike to spectacular Screw Auger Falls on the gulf's eastern end. Gulf hikers who start from this parking area must ford the Pleasant River—usually easily done in summer, but dangerous in high water—and pass through the Hermitage, a stand of old pines and hemlock. A loop route that follows the rim and the less difficult Pleasant River Tote Trail is an 8- to 9-mile trek; there are shorter loops as well. Slippery rocks and rugged terrain make for challenging progress along the rim trail. ⊠ *Greenville* ⊹ *From Greenville, travel 11 miles east via Pleasant St., which becomes Katahdin Iron Works Rd., to Hedgehog checkpoint. Follow signs to parking areas: Head of Gulf, 2½ miles; Gulf Hagas, 6½ miles* ⊕ *www.northmainewoods.org.*

Lily Bay State Park

NATIONAL/STATE PARK | FAMILY | Nine miles northeast of Greenville on Moosehead Lake, this 925-acre park has good lakefront swimming, a 2-mile walking trail with water views, two boat-launching ramps, a playground, and two campgrounds with a total of 90 sites. In winter, the entrance road is plowed to access the groomed cross-country ski trails and the lake for ice fishing and snowmobiling. ⊠ *13 Myrle's Way* ⊹ *Turn onto State Park Rd. from Lily Bay Rd.* ☎ *207/695–2700* ⊕ *www.maine. gov/lilybay* ⊠ *Nonresident $6, Maine resident $4.*

★ Moosehead Historical Society & Museums

MUSEUM | FAMILY | Guides in period attire lead tours of the Eveleth-Crafts-Sheridan Historical House, a late 19th-century Victorian mansion filled with antiques, most of them original to the home. There's a changing exhibit each year, and cooks will savor the impressive collection of utensils and appliances in the 1880s kitchen. You can even check out the attic. In the lower level of the carriage house, the Moosehead Lumbermen's Museum has exhibits about the region's logging history, anchored by a 30-foot bateau used on log drives until the 1960s. Tools abound, and there are models of steamboats that hauled logs and transported tourists and supplies on Moosehead Lake. Upstairs there's a small gift shop and a popular display about hotels on Mt. Kineo, where wealthy Americans flocked to vacation in the rusticator era. In the barn next door, the Moosehead Outdoor Heritage Museum's wide-ranging displays cover subjects like Maine Warden Service flight rescues; local wildlife (there are bobcat, moose, and caribou mounts); the tradition of Maine Registered Guides; and the region's vast commercial forests. You can enjoy lunch and the architecture of these meticulously maintained buildings from the art-accented sunken garden. ⊠ *444 Pritham Ave., Greenville Junction* ☎ *207/695–2909* ⊕ *www.mooseheadhistory.org* ⊠ *Main campus museums including Eveleth-Crafts-Sheridan Historical House $8* ⊙ *Closed mid-Oct.–mid-June, except for Lumbermen's Museum (closed Sat.–Mon. off-season); historic home closed Sun.– Wed. mid-June–mid-Oct., other museums closed Sun. and Mon. in-season.*

Mt. Kineo

NATIONAL/STATE PARK | FAMILY | Accessible primarily by steamship, Mt. Kineo House was a thriving upscale summer resort that sits below its namesake's 700-foot cliff on an islandlike, 1,200-acre peninsula jutting into Moosehead Lake. The last of three successive hotels with this name was built in 1884 and became America's largest inland waterfront hotel. It was torn down in 1938, but Kineo remains an outstanding day trip. Trails to the summit of the spectacular landmark, now part of Mt. Kineo State Park, lead to a fire tower that rewards with a 360-degree sweep of Maine's largest lake and rugged mountains. Hikers scramble on the challenging Indian Trail, but it also has amazing views. All hikes begin on the Carriage Trail, a flat, shore-hugging remnant of the halcyon hotel days. You can play a round on Mt. Kineo Golf Course, one of New England's oldest. There is no road access, but you can take a 15-minute boat trip from Rockwood on the golf course's seasonal shuttle. Historic summer "cottages" line the greens near the small club house, which has a snack bar and welcomes hikers. ⊠ *Kineo Dock, Village Rd., Rockwood* ☎ *207/534–9012 for golf course and shuttle, 207/941–4014 for park regional office* ⊕ *www.maine.gov/mountkineo* 🎫 *Nonresident $3, Maine resident $2.*

🍵 Coffee and Quick Bites

Harris Drug Store and Dairy Bar

$ | AMERICAN | FAMILY | Inside this tidy, well-stocked downtown drug store you can twist on a red stool at the well-kept 1960s-era soda fountain while enjoying a sundae or scoop of ice cream. Hot and cold drinks are also served. **Known for:** soda fountain milk shakes served in traditional glasses; owned by the Harris family since 1896 (not the original locale); soft and hard serve at the Dairy Bar. $ *Average main: $5* ⊠ *10 Pritham Ave.* ☎ *207/695–2921* ⊕ *facebook.com/harrisdrugstore* ⊘ *Dairy Bar closed mid-Sept.–mid-May.*

🛏 Hotels

★ Appalachian Mountain Club Maine Wilderness Lodges

$$$ | RESORT | FAMILY | In Maine's 100-Mile Wilderness, the Appalachian Mountain Club's 75,000 acres includes three historic sporting-camp retreats. **Pros:** courtesy canoes (some on outlying ponds), kayaks, and standup paddleboards (no boards at Little Lyford); Little Lyford and Gorman Chairback are near Gulf Hagas; Medawisla a good choice for beginner cross-country skiers. **Cons:** winter access only by cross-country skis, snowshoes, foot, or snowmobile transport (fee) at Little Lyford and Gorman Chairback; no waterfront cabins at Little Lyford; not many courtesy mountain bikes, none at Little Lyford. $ *Rooms from: $399* ⊠ *North Woods outside Greenville* ☎ *207/695–3085 AMC Greenville office, 207/358–5187 reservations* ⊕ *www.outdoors.org/lodging/mainelodges* ⊘ *Closed Apr., Nov., Dec. until after Christmas, and part of Mar. (Little Lyford and Gorman Chairback close early and Medawisla late in month).* 🛏 *Gorman Chairback: 12 cabins, 1 bunkhouse (sleeps 10); Little Lyford: 9 cabins, 1 bunkhouse (sleeps 14); Medawisla, 9 cabins, 2 bunkhouses (each sleeps 16)* 🍽 *Free Breakfast.*

★ Blair Hill Inn & Restaurant

$$$$ | B&B/INN | Beautiful gardens, high stone walls, and a hilltop location with marvelous views over the lake distinguish this 1891 country estate as one of New England's top inns; enjoy cocktails—and that view—from the veranda or the swank cocktail lounge. **Pros:** free concierge plans outdoor excursions, provides courtesy beach towels, etc.; reservation but no fee to use spa's cozy outdoor hot tub, sauna, and deck; helicopter, Tesla, and electric-car friendly. **Cons:** pricey; no direct lake access; three guestrooms on the third floor. $ *Rooms from: $499* ⊠ *351 Lily Bay Rd.* ☎ *207/695–0224* ⊕ *www.blairhill.com* ⊘ *Closed Nov.–mid-May* 🛏 *10 rooms* 🍽 *Free breakfast.*

Activities

BOATING

Capt. Rogers Pontoon Rental

BOATING | Operated by a captain with decades of experience on local waters, the business rents swim ladder-equipped pontoon boats for full- and half-day excursions (same-day only reservations for the latter) and overnight trips on 40-mile-long Moosehead Lake. In Rockwood on the Moose River a mile from the lake, boaters have plenty of time to head for nearby Mt. Kineo, Moosehead's famed landmark. ⊠ *9 Maynard Rd., Rockwood* ⌖ *At Moose River Bridge* ☎ *207/233–3820* ⊕ *www.captrogerspontoonrental. com.*

MULTISPORT OUTFITTERS

Northwoods Outfitters

TOUR—SPORTS | You can rent canoes, kayaks, standup paddleboards, camping and fishing equipment, UTVs and ATVs, comfort and mountain bikes, snowmobiles, snowshoes, cross-country skis, and winter clothing here. Northwoods also guides a host of outdoor trips (some multiday), including open-water and ice fishing, waterfall hikes, photography, snowmobiling, and moose-watching (by land or water); operates a shuttle to remote areas; and offers recreation packages with area lodging establishments. At the base in downtown Greenville, you can pick up sporting goods, souvenirs, and clothing; get trail advice; and kick back in the Hard Drive Café. ⊠ *5 Lily Bay Rd.* ☎ *207/695–3288, 866/223–1380* ⊕ *www.maineoutfitter.com.*

SEAPLANES

Currier's Flying Service

ZIP LINING | You can take sightseeing flights in vintage seaplanes over the Moosehead Lake region from ice-out until mid-October. ⊠ *447 Pritham Ave., Greenville Junction* ☎ *207/695–2778* ⊕ *www.curriersflyingservice.com* ⌨ *From $45.*

SKIING

Big Squaw Mountain

SKIING/SNOWBOARDING | FAMILY | A local nonprofit was formed in 2013 to reopen the lower portion of Big Moose Mountain (the resort uses the old name) after it closed for a few years, and the ski area now operates Thursday through Sunday, on holidays, and during school-vacation weeks. The summit chairlift, unused since 2004, and the shuttered hotel loom trailside like something out of a Stephen King novel (he's a Mainer, no less), but the mostly intermediate trails on the lower mountain are plenty high enough to wow skiers with views up and down Moosehead Lake, Maine's largest. On a clear day, Mt. Katahdin, the state's highest peak, accents the mountainous horizon. The terrain, cheap prices, a surface lift for beginners, and the spacious, retro-fun chalet lodge draw families. The resort also has free trails for cross-country skiing, snowshoeing, and fat-tire biking. **Facilities:** 28 trails; 58 acres; 660-foot vertical drop; 2 lifts. ⊠ *447 Ski Resort Rd., Greenville Junction* ☎ *207/695–2400* ⊕ *www.skibigsquaw. com* ⌨ *Lift ticket: $30.*

TOURS

Katahdin Cruises & Moosehead Marine Museum

TOUR—SPORTS | The Moosehead Marine Museum runs 3- and 5-hour afternoon trips on Moosehead Lake aboard the *Katahdin,* a 115-foot 1914 steamship converted to diesel. Cruisers learn about the rich logging and tourism history of Maine's largest lake and environs on the narrated excursions. (The longer one skirts Mt. Kineo's cliffs.) Also called the *Kate,* this ship carried resort guests to Mt. Kineo until 1938; the logging industry then used it until 1975. The boat and the free shoreside museum have displays about the steamships that transported people and cargo on Moosehead Lake for a century starting in the 1830s. ⊠ *12 Lily Bay Rd.* ☎ *207/695–2716* ⊕ *www. katahdincruises.com* ⌨ *From $40.*

Millinocket

67 miles north of Bangor, 88 miles north-west of Greenville.

Millinocket, a former paper-mill town with a population of about 4,000, is the gateway to "forever wild" Baxter State Park and a jumping off point for Maine's North Woods. The town is the place to stock up on supplies, fill your gas tank, and grab a hot meal or shower before heading into the wilderness. On the east side of Baxter, President Obama created the Katahdin Woods and Waters National Monument in 2016. Numerous rafting and canoeing outfitters and guides are based in the region. **Katahdin Woods & Waters Scenic Byway** (⊕ *www.katahdin-woodsandwaters.com*), much of which flows along Route 11, links the region's conserved lands and scattered towns.

GETTING HERE AND AROUND

From Interstate 95, take Route 157 (Exit 244) west to Millinocket. From here follow signs to Baxter State Park (Millinocket Lake Road becomes Baxter Park State Road), 18 miles from town.

VISITOR INFORMATION

CONTACTS Katahdin Chamber of Commerce. ⊠ *1029 Central St.* ☎ *207/723–4443* ⊕ *www.katahdinmaine.com.*

◉ Sights

Allagash Wilderness Waterway

BODY OF WATER | A spectacular 92-mile corridor of lakes, ponds, streams, and rivers, the waterway park cuts through vast commercial forests, beginning near the northwestern corner of Baxter State Park and running north to the town of Allagash, 10 miles from the Canadian border. From May to mid-October, the Allagash is prime canoeing and camping country. The Maine Bureau of Parks and Lands has campsites along the waterway, most not accessible by vehicle. The complete 92-mile course, part of the 740-mile Northern Forest Canoe Trail, which runs from New York to Maine, requires 7–10 days to canoe. Novices may want to hire a guide, as there are many areas with strong rapids. A good outfitter can help plan your route and provide equipment and transportation. ⊠ *Millinocket* ☎ *207/941–4014 for regional parks bureau office* ⊕ *www.maine.gov/allagash.*

★ Baxter State Park

NATIONAL/STATE PARK | **FAMILY** | A gift from Governor Percival Baxter, this is the jewel in the crown of northern Maine: a 210,000-acre wilderness area that surrounds **Mt. Katahdin,** Maine's highest mountain and the terminus of the Appalachian Trail. Every year, the 5,267-foot Katahdin draws thousands of hikers to make the daylong summit, rewarding them with stunning views of forests, mountains, and lakes. There are three parking-lot trailheads for Katahdin. Depart from the Roaring Brook trailhead for a route that includes the hair-raising Knife Edge Trail. ■ TIP➜ **Reserve a day-use parking space at the trailheads June 1–October 15.**

The crowds climbing Katahdin can be formidable on clear summer days and fall weekends, so if it's solitude you crave, tackle one of the park's many other mountains. Most are accessible from the extensive trail network, including 11 peaks exceeding an elevation of 3,000 feet. The Brothers and Doubletop Mountain are challenging daylong hikes; the Owl takes about six hours; and South Turner can be climbed in a morning—its summit has a great view across the valley. A trek around Daicey Pond, or from the pond to Big and Little Niagara Falls, are good options for families with young kids. Another option if you only have a couple of hours is renting a canoe at Daicey or Togue Pond (bring cash for this honor system). Park roads are unpaved, narrow, winding, and not plowed in winter; there are no pay phones, gas

There are amazing views from the top of the 5,267-foot-tall Mt. Katahdin.

stations, stores; and cell phone service is unreliable. Camping is primitive and reservations are required; there are 10 campgrounds plus backcountry sites. ■ TIP→ **The park has a visitor center at its southern entrance, but you can get information, make parking and camping reservations, and watch a video at park headquarters in Millinocket (64 Balsam Drive).** ✉ *Baxter State Park Rd.* ✚ *Togue Pond Gate (southern entrance) is 18 miles northwest of Millinocket; follow signs from Rte. 157. Matagamon Gate (northern entrance) is 27 miles west of Patten; follow signs from Rte. 159.* ☏ *207/723–5140* ⊕ *www.baxterstateparkauthority. com* ✏ *$15 per vehicle; Maine residents free* ☉ *Mt. Katahdin trails are closed and park access is limited in Nov. and Apr.–mid-May.*

Debsconeag Lakes Wilderness Area
NATURE PRESERVE | Bordering the south side of the Golden Road below Baxter State Park, the Nature Conservancy's 46,271-acre Debsconeag Lakes Wilderness Area is renowned for its rare

ice cave, old forests, abundant pristine ponds, and views of Mt. Katahdin— there are mesmerizing views along the 5-mile Rainbow Loop. The access road for the Ice Cave Trail (2 miles round-trip) and Hurd Pond is 17 miles northwest of Millinocket, just west of the Golden Road's Abol Bridge. The kiosk at this entrance has information about the preserve, including a large map. Nearby the Appalachian Trail exits the conservancy land, crossing the bridge en route to Baxter. Hugging the curving, scenic West Branch of the Penobscot River and revealing Katahdin, the first few miles of the 5-mile dirt access road deserve a drive even if you aren't stopping to recreate. Before hiking, paddling, fishing, or camping in the remote preserve (no fees or reservations required), visit the conservancy's website for directions, maps, and other information. ✉ *Golden Rd.* ⊕ *www. nature.org/maine.*

Golden Road

SCENIC DRIVE | For a scenic North Woods drive, set off on the roughly 21-mile stretch of this private east–west logging road near Baxter State Park northwest of Millinocket. Have patience with ruts and bumps, and yield to logging trucks (keep right!). From Millinocket follow the signs for Baxter State Park from Route 157. This scenic drive begins 8 miles from the railroad overpass as you exit town, at the crossover from Millinocket Lake Road to the Golden Road, the latter reportedly named for the huge sum a paper company paid to build it.

North Woods Trading Post is at this junction, across from Ambajejus Lake. Stop in not just for takeout, coffee, gas, or North Woods-theme gifts but to pick up a free handout noting stops along the Golden Road, with mileage—a godsend along this remote stretch, where ponds for moose spotting aren't signed and hiking spots that are signed can still be easy to miss. River Pond Nature Trail offers several treks; the access road is on the left about six miles from the trading post. Continuing along the Golden Road, you'll pass the aforementioned ponds (watch for spots to pull over and park); it's 4 miles to one-lane Abol Bridge over the West Branch of the Penobscot River. There are turnouts for parking, or stop before the bridge at Abol Bridge Campground, with a restaurant and store. ■ TIP→ **Take photos of Baxter's Mt. Katahdin from the footbridge alongside Abol Bridge: this view is famous.** Just beyond the bridge is an access road and kiosk for Debsconeag Lakes Wilderness Area. The 2-mile round-trip Ice Cave trailhead is 5 miles in on a river-hugging dirt road with more Katahdin views. Continuing from Abol Bridge, the Golden Road also flows alongside the waterway.

At the western end of the drive, the river drops 70-plus feet per mile through Ripogenus Gorge, giving white-water rafters a thrilling ride during scheduled releases from Ripogenus Dam. The Crib Works Rapid (Class V) overlook is off the Golden Road about 9 miles from Abol Bridge. (Turn right on Telos Road; parking is on the right after the bridge.) For the best gorge views, return to the Golden Road, and continue west about a mile and turn right into McKay Station, where many rafters put in. Be cautious on the downhill paths and atop the steep cliffs. To drive across the dam on Ripogenus Lake and view the gorge, get back on the Golden Road and head west three-quarters of a mile to Rip Dam Road, which veers right. Returning to the crossover at the North Woods Trading Post, turn left for Baxter or right for Millinocket. ✉ *Golden Rd.*

Katahdin Woods and Waters National Monument

NATIONAL/STATE PARK | Two rivers flow and streams and ponds abound at this 87,500-acre North Woods preserve, created east of Baxter State Park in 2016 and home to moose, bald eagles, salmon, and bobcats. Currently there are occasional visitor programs but no visitor center; you can get information at staffed welcome centers in Millinocket (200 Penobscot Avenue; only open Thursday afternoon in winter) and Patten (at Patten Lumbermen's Museum, 61 Shin Pond Road, seasonal). Access and park roads are gravel; sanitary facilities are limited; and there is no water, food, fuel, or reliable cell service. In the monument's southern portion, 16-mile Katahdin Loop Road has scenic views of Baxter's Mt. Katahdin and trailheads to short hikes and Barnard Mountain, a 4-mile round-trip that links with the International Appalachian Trail. There are mountain biking options as a few bike-designated routes link with the loop road (biking is allowed on park roads). In the northern section, visitors hike, mountain bike, cross-country ski (some groomed trails) and snowshoe along and near the waterfall-dotted East Branch of the Penobscot River. Folks paddle and fish on the river and other monument waters. ✉ *Patten* ⚓ *Southern entrance: From Rte. 11 in Stacyville, head west on gravel Swift Brook Rd. (use caution when turning; it's about 12 miles to Katahdin Loop Dr.). Northern entrance: from Pattern turn on Rte. 159 (becomes Grand Lake Rd.); it's about 30 miles to entrance (take 2nd left after crossing the East Branch of the Penobscot River)* ☎ *207/456–6001* ⊕ *www.nps.gov/kaww.*

Patten Lumbermen's Museum

MUSEUM | FAMILY | Two reproduction 1800s logging camps are among the 10 buildings filled with exhibits depicting the history of logging in Maine. They include sawmill and towboat models, dioramas of logging scenes, horse-drawn sleds, and a steam-powered log hauler. Exhibits also highlight local artists and history as well as logging-related topics. The museum is a welcome center for nearby Katahdin Woods and Waters National Monument. ✉ *61 Shin Pond Rd., Patten* ☎ *207/528–2650* ⊕ *www.lumbermensmuseum.org* 🎫 *$10* ⏱ *Closed mid-Oct.–mid-May and Mon. (except holidays in season); also closed Tues.–Thurs. late May–June.*

Penobscot River Trails

TRAIL | FAMILY | A New York philanthropist was so taken with the Mt. Katahdin region he spurred creation of 15.5 miles of free public recreation trails along the East Branch of the Penobscot River, conveniently off Route 11. Opened in 2019, the "crusher dust" paths are akin to the famed carriage trails at coastal Maine's Acadia National Park. The river trails are used for mountain biking and walking and, after the snow flies, groomed for cross-country skiing and fat-tire biking. There are also 9 miles of snowshoe trails. You can chill after a workout or eat your lunch in the woodsy chic visitor center. Come winter, wood stoves heat up two warming huts—one offers an outstanding view of Mt. Katahdin—along the trails. Courtesy bikes, snowshoes, cross-country skis, and reservation-only kayaks are available, or, of course, bring your own. ✉ *2540 Grindstone Rd., Stacyville* ☎ *207/746–5807* ⊕ *www. penobscotrivertrails.org.*

🍴 Restaurants

River Driver's Restaurant

$$$ | AMERICAN | FAMILY | At the deservedly popular restaurant—usually open daily for breakfast, lunch, and dinner—wood for the trim, wainscoting, bar, and floors was milled from old logs salvaged from local waters. Diners enjoy views of Katahdin from behind rows of windows or from the patio, and your dish may feature farm-to-table fare. **Known for:** great view of Katahdin; daily specials; seasonal, local, and fresh ingredients. 💲 *Average main: $25* ✉ *30 Twin Pines Rd.* ☎ *207/723–8475* ⊕ *www.neoc.com.*

☕ Coffee and Quick Bites

North Woods Trading Post

$ | AMERICAN | FAMILY | Yummy to-go fare includes breakfast and regular sandwiches, pizza, and baked goods, at this cabin-style "last stop" for gear, supplies, and gas before Baxter State Park. Quality Maine-made gifts and souvenirs; Baxter and Mt. Katahdin art and attire; and Maine- and park-theme books are tastefully arrayed. **Known for:** provides area information, as do placards at rest area next door; co-owned by a former Baxter ranger; across from Ambajejus Lake. 💲 *Average main: $10* ✉ *1605 Baxter State Park Rd.* ☎ *207/723–4326* ⊕ *www.northwoodstradingpostme. com* ⏱ *Closed late Oct.–early May.*

🏃 Activities

MULTISPORT OUTFITTERS

Katahdin Outfitters

BOATING | This company provides gear and shuttles for overnight canoe and kayak expeditions on the Allagash Wilderness Waterway, the West Branch of the Penobscot River, and the St. John River.

You can also rent canoes and kayaks from its location just outside Millinocket on the way to Baxter State Park. ✉ *360 Bates St.* ☎ *207/723–5700* ⊕ *www.katah-dinoutfitters.com* ✎ *Call for prices.*

★ **New England Outdoor Center** (*NEOC*)
TOUR—SPORTS | **FAMILY** | With Baxter State Park's Mt. Katahdin rising above the shore opposite both its locations, this business helps visitors enjoy the North Woods. Its year-round home base, NEOC/Twin Pines on Millinocket Lake, 8 miles from the park's southern entrance, has rental cabins and a restaurant (River Driver's Restaurant) and conducts many guided trips, some within the park. Older renovated log cabins (and a few newer ones) sit beneath tall pines on a grassy nub of land that juts into Millinocket Lake; upscale "green" units (spacious lodges and cozy cabins) are tucked among trees on a cove. Amenities include kayaks and canoes for use on the lake and a recreation center with a sauna.

NEOC offers a full slate of guided excursions: whitewater rafting, fishing, canoeing, kayaking, hiking, photography, moose- and wildlife-spotting, snow-mobiling, and ice fishing. It also rents canoes, kayaks, standup paddleboards, snowmobiles (attire, too), fat-tire bikes, cross-country skis, and snowshoes and offers cross-country skiing and paddling lessons. Trails for cross-country skiing (15-plus miles, groomed), snowshoeing, and mountain and fat-tire biking are right on the 1,400-acre property and link with adjoining trail networks for longer excursions. About 2 miles from Baxter, the seasonal Penobscot Outdoor Center on Pockwockamus Pond is the base for white-water rafting trips on the West Branch of the Penobscot River and home to a wooded campground. Some sites are near the water, looking toward Katahdin. There are tent sites as well as canvas tents and simple wood-frame cabins with cots or bunks. A circular fireplace anchors the open-plan base lodge with pool tables and, on rafting days, a beer bar. A towering window wall reveals glimpses of water through trees. Outdoors there's a communal fire pit and a sand volleyball court. ■**TIP**➔ **Nonguests can use showers for $2 after hiking or camping at Baxter.** ✉ *30 Twin Pines Rd.* ⟐ *From Baxter State Park Rd., take Black Cat Rd. east 1 mile* ☎ *207/723–5438, 800/766–7238* ⊕ *www.neoc.com.*

SEAPLANES
Katahdin Air Service
TOUR—SPORTS | In addition to operating ½- and 1-hour scenic flights over the Katah-din area, this seaplane operator offers fly-in excursions to backcountry locales to picnic at a pond beach, dine at a sporting camp, or moose-watch and bask in nature. It also provides charter service from points throughout Maine to the region's smaller towns and remote areas. ✉ *1888 Golden Rd.* ☎ *207/723–8378* ⊕ *www.katahdinair.com* ✎ *From $125.*

WHITE-WATER RAFTING
North Country Rivers
WHITE-WATER RAFTING | North Country Rivers's base for white-water rafting trips on the West Branch of the Penob-scot River is at Big Moose Inn, Cabins & Campground, on Millinocket Lake south of Baxter State Park. The busi-nesses team up on lodging packages. (In Western Maine, the outfitter runs white-water rafting trips on the Dead and Kennebec rivers in The Forks and has a resort south of there in Bing-ham.) ✉ *102A Baxter State Park Rd.* ☎ *800/348–8871* ⊕ *www.northcoun-tryrivers.com.*

Chapter 12

THE MAINE COAST

Updated by
John Blodgett

Sights   Restaurants   Hotels   Shopping   Nightlife
★★★★☆   ★★★★☆   ★★★★★   ★★★☆☆   ★★★☆☆

WELCOME TO THE MAINE COAST

TOP REASONS TO GO

★ **Lobster and Wild Maine Blueberries:** It's not a Maine vacation unless you don a bib and dig into a steamed lobster with drawn butter, and finish with a wild blueberry pie for dessert.

★ **Boating:** The coastline of Maine was made for boaters: whether it's your own boat, a friend's, or a charter, make sure you get out on the water.

★ **Hiking the Bold Coast:** Miles of unspoiled coastal and forest paths Down East make for a hiker's (and a birdwatcher's) dream.

★ **Cadillac Mountain:** Drive a winding 3½ miles to the 1,530-foot summit in Acadia National Park for the sunrise.

★ **Dining in Portland:** With more than 250 restaurants and counting, Forest City is a foodie haven with one of the highest per capita restaurant densities in the United States.

1 **Kittery.**

2 **The Yorks.**

3 **Ogunquit.**

4 **Wells.**

5 **Kennebunk and Kennebunkport.**

6 **Cape Elizabeth and Prout's Neck.**

7 **Portland.**

8 **Casco Bay Islands.**

9 **Freeport.**

10 **Brunswick.**

11 **Bath.**

12 **Wiscasset.**

13 **Boothbay.**

14 **Damariscotta.**

15 **Pemaquid Point.**

16 **Port Clyde.**

17 **Monhegan Island.**

18 **Rockland.**

19 **Rockport.**

20 **Camden.**

21 **Belfast.**

22 **Bucksport.**

23 **Blue Hill.**

24 **Deer Isle.**

25 **Bar Harbor.**

26 **Acadia National Park.**

27 **Bass Harbor.**

28 **Schoodic Peninsula.**

29 **Lubec.**

30 **Campobello Island, Canada.**

31 **Eastport.**

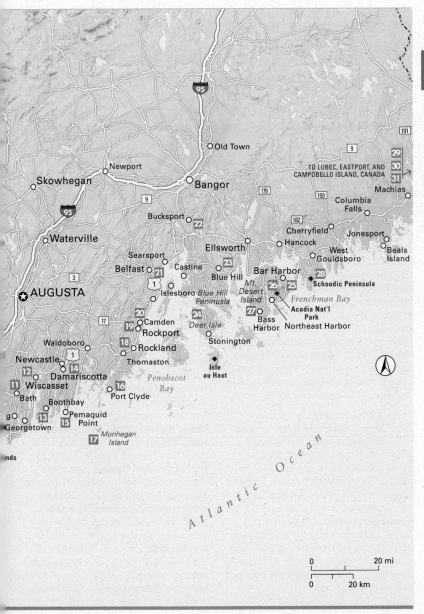

As you drive across the border into Maine, a sign reads, "The way life should be." It's a slogan that's hard to argue with once you've spent some time in the Pine Tree State. Here, time stays in step with you, and Mainers take their play just as seriously as their work.

Romantics thrill at the wind and salt spray in their faces on a historic windjammer. Birders fill their notebooks to the brim with new field notes. Families love the unspoiled beaches and sheltered inlets dotting the shoreline—not to mention the numerous homemade-ice-cream stands. Foodies revel in greater Portland's booming restaurant scene, while artists and art lovers find inspiration both on and off the canvas amid art galleries and museums or along the craggy seaboard. Adventure-seekers find many opportunities to kayak and cycle at the Bold Coast and Acadia National Park, whose trails invigorate hikers with their natural beauty. At night, the sky is dark enough to spot rare constellations and experience the magic of auroras.

The Maine Coast is several places in one. Classic New England townscapes with picturesque downtowns mingle with rocky shorelines punctuated by sandy beaches and secluded coves with sweeping views of lighthouses, forested islands, and the wide-open sea. So, no matter what strikes your fancy—a spontaneous picnic on the beach or a sunset cruise with a bottle of local wine, an afternoon exploring hidden tide pools or a dose of culture followed by shopping and dining in town—there's something to suit every disposition.

Counting all its nooks, crannies, and crags, Maine's coast would stretch thousands of miles if you could pull it straight, which means there's always some new, undiscovered territory awaiting you. Stretching north from Kittery to just outside Portland, the Southern Coast is the most popular area, with many top-notch restaurants, museums, and wineries. Don't let that stop you from heading farther Down East (Maine-speak for "way up the coast"), where you'll be rewarded with the majestic mountains and rugged coastline of Acadia National Park, as well as the unspoiled, dramatic scenery of the Bold Coast.

MAJOR REGIONS

Stretching north from Kittery to just outside Portland, **the Southern Coast** is Maine's most visited region; miles of sandy expanses and shore towns cater to summer visitors. **Kittery, the Yorks, Wells,** and the **Kennebunks** offer low-key getaways, all a stone's throw from **Portland,** Maine's largest city and foodie haven. **Ogunquit** is an artists' colony that's giving Provincetown a run for its money; the very popular Cliff House resort is nearby. The **Casco Bay Islands** lie just off the coast in various sizes, some are easier to access than others. Beautiful **Cape Elizabeth** is home to Portland Head Light; Winslow Homer's Studio is located in nearby Scarborough. About 17 miles north of Portland, **Freeport** is home to the headquarters of L.L. Bean and a lovely harbor.

North of Portland, from Brunswick to Monhegan Island, **the Mid-Coast Region** has a craggy coastline that winds its way around pastoral peninsulas. Its villages boast maritime museums, innovative restaurants, antiques shops, and beautiful architecture. **Brunswick,** while a bigger, more commercial city, has rows of historic brick and clapboard homes and is home to Bowdoin College. **Bath** is known for its maritime heritage. **Wiscasset** has arguably the best antiques shopping in the state. On its waterfront you can choose from a variety of seafood shacks competing for the best lobster rolls. **Damariscotta,** too, is worth a stop for its good seafood restaurants, and you'd be hard-pressed to find better-tasting oysters than those from the Damariscotta River. **Boothbay Harbor** is one of the quaintest towns in the Mid-Coast—and a busy tourist destinations come summer, with lots of little stores that are perfect for window-shopping. It's also one of three towns from which you can take a ferry to **Monhegan Island,** which seems to be inhabited exclusively by painters at their easels, intent on capturing the windswept cliffs and weathered homes with colorful gardens. **Pemaquid Point** sits at the tip of the Pemaquid Peninsula, while the sleepy town of **Port Clyde** sits at the end of the St. George Peninsula.

Penobscot Bay covers an estimated 1,070 square miles and is home to more than 1,800 islands. It's dramatic natural scenery highlights its picture-perfect coastal towns, which include **Belfast, Rockport,** and **Camden. Rockland** gets lots of attention thanks to a trio of attractions: the renowned Farnsworth Art Museum, the popular summer Lobster Festival, and the lively North Atlantic Blues Festival. **Bucksport** has the stunning Penobscot Narrows Bridge and the Fort Knox historic site.

The large **Blue Hill Peninsula** juts south into Penobscot Bay. Painters, photographers, sculptors, and other artists are drawn to the peninsula; you can find more than 20 galleries on Deer Isle and at least half as many on the mainland. Not far from the mainland are the islands of Little Deer Isle and **Deer Isle. Blue Hill** and **Castine** are the area's primary business hubs. **Isle Au Haut** is only accessible by mail boat, but worth the effort.

Millions come to enjoy **Acadia National Park and Mount Desert Island's** stunning peaks and vistas. **Bar Harbor** is fun to explore, with its many gift shops and restaurants, while **Bass Harbor** offers quieter retreats.

The "real Maine," as some call the region known as **Down East,** unfurls in thousands of acres of wild blueberry barrens, congestion-free coastlines, vast wilderness preserves, and a tangible sense of rugged endurance. The landscape of **Schoodic Peninsula's** craggy coastline, towering evergreens, and views over Frenchman Bay are breathtaking year-round. Towns on the peninsula include Grindstone Neck, Winter Harbor, and Gouldsboro; the peninsula's southern tip is home to the Schoodic section of Acadia National Park. **Lubec** is a popular destination for outdoor enthusiasts; a popular excursion is New Brunswick's **Campobello Island,** which has the Roosevelt Campobello International Park. **Eastport** is connected to the mainland by a granite causeway; it was once one of the nation's busiest seaports.

Planning

You could easily spend a lifetime's worth of vacations along the Maine Coast and never truly see it all. But if you are determined to travel the coast end-to-end, allot at least two weeks at a comfortable pace. Count on longer transit time getting from place to place in summer, as traffic along U.S. 1 can be agonizing in high season, especially in the areas around Wiscasset and Acadia National Park.

Getting Here and Around

AIR

Maine has two major international airports, Portland International Jetport and Bangor International Airport, to get you to or close to your coastal destination. Manchester–Boston Regional Airport. in New Hampshire is about 45 minutes away from the southern end of the Maine coastline. Boston's Logan Airport is the only truly international airport in the region; it's about 90 minutes south of the Maine border.

BUS

The Shoreline Explorer links seasonal trolleys in southern Maine beach towns from the Yorks to the Kennebunks, allowing you to travel between towns without a car. Concord Coach Lines has express service between Portland and Boston's Logan Airport and South Station. Concord operates out of the Portland Transportation Center (⊠ *100 Thompson's Point Rd.*).

Shoreline Explorer. ☎ *207/459–2932* ⊕ *www.shorelineexplorer.com.*

CAR

Once you are here the best way to experience the winding back roads of the craggy Maine Coast is in a car. There are miles and miles of roads far from the larger towns that have no bus service, and you won't want to miss the chance to discover your own favorite ocean vista while on a scenic drive.

TRAIN

Amtrak offers regional service from Boston to Portland via its Downeaster line, which originates at Boston's North Station and makes six stops in Maine: Wells, Saco, Old Orchard Beach (seasonal), Portland, Freeport, and Brunswick.

Driving in Coastal Maine

	Miles	Time
Boston–Portland	112	2 hours
Kittery–Portland	50	50 minutes
Portland–Freeport	18	20 minutes
Portland–Camden	80	2 hours
Portland–Bar Harbor	175	3 hours 20 minutes

When to Go

Maine's dramatic coastline and pure natural beauty welcome visitors year-round, but note that many smaller museums and attractions are open only in high season (Memorial Day–mid-October), as are many waterside attractions and eateries.

Summer begins in earnest on July 4, and you'll find that many smaller inns, B&Bs, and hotels from Kittery on up to Bar Harbor are booked a month or two in advance for dates through August. That's also the case come fall, when the fiery foliage draws leaf peepers. After Halloween, hotel rates drop significantly until ski season begins around Thanksgiving. Bed-and-breakfasts that stay open year-round but are not near ski slopes will often rent rooms at far lower prices than in summer.

In spring, the fourth Sunday in March is designated as Maine Maple Sunday, and farms throughout the state open their doors to visitors not only to watch sap turn into golden syrup but to sample the sweet results.

Activities

No visit to the Maine Coast is complete without some outdoor activity—on two wheels, two feet, holding two paddles, or pulling a bag full of clubs.

If your adventures find you swimming in the ocean or floating close to its surface on a kayak, be on the lookout for sharks. Their populations have rebounded in recent years following conservation and regulatory efforts. In the summer of 2020, off Bailey Island, a swimming woman was killed by a great white shark in Maine's first recorded shark fatality; authorities surmised her wetsuit caused her to appear to be a seal, a favored prey of sharks.

BIKING

Both the Bicycle Coalition of Maine and Explore Maine by Bike are excellent resources for trail maps and other riding information.

Bicycle Coalition of Maine. ⊠ 34 Diamond St., Portland ☎ 207/623–4511 ⊕ www. bikemaine.org. **Explore Maine by Bike.** ☎ 207/624–3300 ⊕ www.exploremaine. org/bike.

HIKING

Exploring the Maine Coast on foot is a quick way to acclimate yourself to the relaxed pace of life here—and sometimes the only way to access some of the best coastal spots. Many privately owned lands are accessible to hikers, especially Down East. Inquire at a local establishment about hikes that may not appear on a map.

KAYAKING

Nothing gets you literally off the beaten path like plying the salt waters in a graceful sea kayak.

Maine Association of Sea Kayak Guides and Instructors. ⊕ maskgi.org. **Maine Island Trail Association.** ⊠ 100 Kensington St., 2nd fl., Portland ☎ 207/761–8225 ⊕ www.mita.org.

Restaurants

Many breakfast spots along the coast open as early as 6 am to serve the working crowd, and as early as 4 am for fishermen. Lunch generally runs 11–2:30; dinner is usually served 5–9. Only in larger cities will you find full dinners offered much later than 9, although in larger towns you can usually find a bar or bistro with a limited menu available late into the evening.

Many restaurants in Maine are closed Monday. Resort areas make an exception to this in high season, but these eateries often shut down altogether in the off-season. *Unless otherwise noted in reviews, restaurants are open daily for lunch and dinner.*

Credit cards are generally accepted at restaurants throughout Maine, even in more modest establishments, but it's still a good idea to have cash on hand wherever you go, just in case.

The one signature meal on the Maine Coast is, of course, the lobster dinner. It typically includes a whole steamed lobster with drawn butter for dipping, a clam or seafood chowder, corn on the cob, coleslaw, and a bib. Lobster prices vary from day to day, but generally a full lobster dinner should cost around $25–$30, or about $18–$20 without all the extras.

Hotels

Beachfront and roadside motels, historic-home B&Bs and inns, as well as a handful of newer boutique hotels, make up the majority of lodging along the Maine Coast. There are a few larger luxury resorts, such as the Samoset Resort in Rockport or the Bar Harbor Inn in Bar Harbor, but most accommodations are simple, comfortable, and relatively inexpensive. You will find some chain hotels in larger cities and towns, including major tourist destinations like Portland, Freeport, and Bar

Harbor. Many properties close during the off-season (mid-October–mid-May); those that stay open year-round often drop their rates dramatically after high season. (It is often possible to negotiate a nightly rate with smaller establishments during low season.) There is a 9% state hospitality tax on all room rates. *Hotel reviews have been shortened. For full reviews visit Fodors.com.*

WHAT IT COSTS in U.S. Dollars

	$	$$	$$$	$$$$
RESTAURANTS				
	under $18	$18–$24	$25–$35	over $35
HOTELS				
	under $200	$200–$299	$300–$399	over $399

Visitor Information

CONTACTS Blue Hill Peninsula Chamber of Commerce. ☎ *207/374–3242* 🌐 *www.bluehillpeninsula.org.* **DownEast and Acadia Regional Tourism.** ✉ *7 Ames Way, Machias* ☎ *207/255–0983, 888/665–3278* 🌐 *www.downeastacadia.com.* **Maine Lobster Marketing Collaborative.** ✉ *2 Union St., Suite 204, Portland* ☎ *207/541–9310* 🌐 *www.lobsterfrommaine.com.* **Southern Midcoast Maine Chamber.** ☎ *207/725–8797* 🌐 *www.midcoastmaine.com.* **State of Maine Visitor Information Center.** ☎ *800/767–8709* 🌐 *www.mainetourism.com.*

Kittery

65 miles north of Boston, 3 miles north of Portsmouth, New Hampshire.

Known as the "Gateway to Maine," Kittery has become primarily a major shopping destination thanks to its massive complex of factory outlets. Flanking both sides of U.S. 1 are more than 120 stores, which attract serious shoppers year-round. But Kittery has more to offer than just retail therapy: head east on Route 103 to the area around **Kittery Point** to experience the great outdoors. Here you'll find hiking and biking trails, as well as fantastic views of Portsmouth, New Hampshire, Whaleback Ledge Lighthouse, and the nearby Isles of Shoals. The isles and the light, along with two others, can be seen from two forts near this winding stretch of Route 103: Fort McClary State Historic Site and Fort Foster, a town park (both closed to vehicles off-season).

GETTING HERE AND AROUND

Three bridges—on U.S. 1, U.S. 1 Bypass, and Interstate 95—cross the Piscataqua River from Portsmouth, New Hampshire, to Kittery. Interstate 95 has three Kittery exits. Route 103 is a scenic coastal drive through Kittery Point to York.

ESSENTIALS

VISITOR INFORMATION

Kittery Visitor Information Center
✉ *Kittery* ☎ *207/439–1319* 🌐 *www.mainetourism.com.*

🍴 Restaurants

Anju Noodle Bar
$ | ASIAN FUSION | With a cozy, open-plan dining area and a laid-back atmosphere, Anju Noodle Bar serves up reimagined versions of traditional dishes such as house-made slow-roasted pork shoulder buns, spicy miso ramen, and inspired local seafood dishes. This is one of the few places in the Pine Tree State outside Portland where you'll find fresh and innovative Asian-inspired cuisine done really well. **Known for:** sake heaven; free-style dishes; house-made kimchi. [$] *Average main: $15* ✉ *7 Wallingford Sq., Unit 102* ☎ *207/703–4298* 🌐 *www.anjunoodlebar.com* 🕓 *Closed Mon.*

Chauncey Creek Lobster Pier
$$$ | SEAFOOD | FAMILY | From the road you can barely see the red roof hovering below the trees, but chances are you can see the line of cars parked at this popular

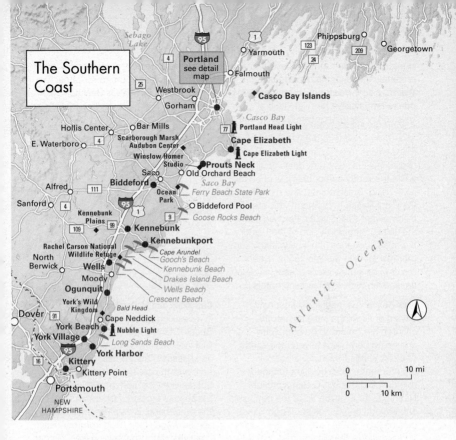

The Southern Coast

Sebago Lake

95

1

Phippsburg

Georgetown

Portland
see detail
map

123

209

4

Yarmouth

24

Falmouth

25

Westbrook

Casco Bay Islands

Gorham

Casco Bay

Hollis Center

Bar Mills

77

Portland Head Light

E. Waterboro

4

Scarborough Marsh
Audubon Center

Cape Elizabeth

Winslow Homer
Studio

Cape Elizabeth Light

Prouts Neck

Saco

Old Orchard Beach

Alfred

111

Biddeford

Saco Bay

Sanford

4

Ocean
Park

Ferry Beach State Park

95

1

Biddeford Pool

Kennebunk
Plains

9

Goose Rocks Beach

109

99

Kennebunk

Rachel Carson National
Wildlife Refuge

Kennebunkport

North
Berwick

Wells

Cape Arundel
Gooch's Beach
Kennebunk Beach
Drakes Island Beach

Moody

Atlantic Ocean

Ogunquit

Wells Beach

York's Wild
Kingdom

Crescent Beach

Dover

91

Bald Head

Cape Neddick

York Beach

Nubble Light

York Village

95

Long Sands Beach

16

York Harbor

Kittery

Kittery Point

Portsmouth

NEW
HAMPSHIRE

0   10 mi

0   10 km

outdoor restaurant that has been serving up fresh lobster for more than 70 years. Brightly colored picnic tables fill the deck and enclosed eating areas sit atop the high banks of the tidal river, beside a working pier, which delivers fresh seafood straight to your plate. **Known for:** classic lobster dinners; BYOB; ocean-to-plate. $ *Average main: $25* ⊠ *16 Chauncey Creek Rd.* ☎ *207/439–1030* ⊕ *www.chaunceycreek.com* ☉ *Closed Columbus Day–mid-May; closed Mon. post–Labor Day–Columbus Day.*

🏃 Activities

HIKING AND WALKING
Cutts Island Trail
HIKING/WALKING | For a peek into the Rachel Carson National Wildlife Refuge, this scenic 1.8-mile upland trail leads into the 800-acre Brave Boat Harbor Division

and is a prime bird-watching area. There's a restroom and an information kiosk at the trailhead. The trail is open dawn–dusk year-round; dogs are not allowed. ⊠ *Seapoint Rd.* ☎ *207/646–9226* ⊕ *www.fws. gov/refuge/rachel_carson.*

The Yorks

8 miles north of Kittery via I–95, U.S. 1, and U.S. 1A.

Spending an afternoon in York Village is like going back in time—and you really only need a couple of hours here to roam the historic streets of this pint-size but worthwhile town. One of the first permanent settlements in Maine, the village museums detail its rich history. York is also home to the flagship store of Stonewall Kitchen, one of Maine's signature gourmet-food purveyors; the store has a café and a cooking school. There's also a cluster of vibrant contemporary-art galleries.

A short distance from the village proper, York Harbor opens to the water and offers many places to linger and explore. The harbor itself is busy with boats of all kinds, while the sandy harbor beach is good for swimming. Much quieter and more formal than York Beach to the north, this area has a somewhat exclusive air. Perched along the cliffs on the north side of the harbor are huge "cottages" built by wealthy summer residents in the late 1800s, when the area became a premier seaside resort destination with several grand hotels.

York Beach is a real family destination, devoid of all things staid and stuffy— children are meant to be both seen and heard here. Just beyond the sands of Short Sands Beach are a host of amusements, from bowling to indoor minigolf and the Fun-O-Rama arcade. Nubble Light is at the tip of the peninsula separating Long Sands and Short Sands beaches. The latter is mostly lined with unpretentious seasonal homes, with motels and restaurants mixed in.

GETTING HERE AND AROUND

York is Exit 7 off Interstate 95; follow signs to U.S. 1, the modern commercial strip. From here, U.S. 1A will take you to the village center and on to York Harbor and York Beach before looping back up to U.S. 1 in Cape Neddick.

After passing through York Village to York Harbor (originally called Lower Town), U.S. 1A winds around and heads north to York Beach's village center, a 4-mile trip.

It's a scenic 6 miles to York Beach via the loop road, U.S. 1A, from its southern intersection with U.S. 1. Although 2 miles longer, it's generally faster to continue north on U.S. 1A to Cape Neddick and then U.S 1A south to the village center, home to Short Sands Beach. Here U.S. 1A is known as Ocean Avenue as it heads north from York Harbor along Long Sands Beach en route to York Beach village and Short Sands Beach.

A trolley along U.S. 1 links the beaches in summer. You can also get from beach to beach on a series of residential streets that wind around Nubble Point between these beaches.

ESSENTIALS
VISITOR INFORMATION

Greater York Region Chamber of Commerce. ☎ 207/363–4422 ⊕ www.gatewayto-maine.org. **York Trolley Co.** ☎ 207/363–9600 ⊕ www.yorktrolley.com.

◉ Sights

Cliff Walk and Fisherman's Walk

Two walking trails begin near Harbor Beach. Starting in a small nearby park, the Cliff Walk ascends its granite namesake and passes the summer "cottages" at the harbor entrance. There are some steps, but, as signs caution, tread carefully because of erosion. Fisherman's Walk, on the other hand, is an easy stroll. Starting across Stage Neck Road from the beach, it passes waterfront businesses, historic homes, and rocky harbor beaches on the way to York's beloved Wiggly Bridge. This pedestrian suspension bridge alongside Route 103 (there is minimal parking here) leads to Steedman Woods, a public preserve with a shaded loop trail along the York River estuary's ambling waters. You can also enter the preserve near the George Marshall Store in York Village. ⊠ Stage Neck Rd., off U.S. 1A, York.

George Marshall Store Gallery

ARTS VENUE | The storefront windows and beadboard trim at the George Marshall Store Gallery (built in 1867) pay homage to its past as a general store, but the focus here is on the present. Changing exhibits, installations, and educational programs focus on prominent and up-and-coming regional artists. ⊠ 140 Lindsay Rd. ☎ 207/351–1083 ⊕ www.georgemarshallstoregallery.com.

Museums of Old York

HISTORIC SITE | FAMILY | Nine historic 18th- and 19th-century buildings, clustered on York Street and along Lindsay Road and the York River, highlight York's rich history, which dates back to early Colonial times. The Old York Gaol (1719) was once the King's Prison for the Province of Maine; inside are dungeons, cells, and the jailer's quarters. The many period rooms in the Emerson-Wilcox House, the main part of which was built in 1742, display items from daily life here in centuries past, including furniture from the 1600s and an impressive ceramic dishware collection. The 1731 Elizabeth Perkins House reflects the Victorian style of its last occupants, the prominent Perkins family. Start your visit at the museum's visitor center, located at 3 Lindsay Road in the Remick Barn at the corner of U.S. 1A and Lindsay Road in York. ⊠ *Visitor center, 3 Lindsay Rd.* ☎ *207/363–1756* ⊕ *www.oldyork.org* ⊠ *From $8.*

★ Nubble Light

HISTORIC SITE | On a small island just off the tip of the cape in York Beach jutting dramatically into the Atlantic Ocean between Long Sands Beach and Short Sands Beach, Nubble Light is one of the most photographed lighthouses on the globe. Direct access is prohibited, but the small Sohier Park right across from the light has parking, historical placards, benches, and a seasonal information center that shares the 1879 light's history. ⊠ *End of Nubble Rd., off U.S. 1A, York Beach* ☎ *207/363–1040 (Memorial Day weekend–Labor Day)* ⊕ *www. nubblelight.org.*

Sayward-Wheeler House

HISTORIC SITE | Built in 1718, the waterfront home was remodeled in the 1760s by Jonathan Sayward, a local merchant who had prospered in the West Indies trade. By 1860 his descendants had opened the house to the public to share the story of their Colonial ancestors. Accessible only by guided tour (second and fourth Saturdays June–October 15, 11–4), the house reveals the decor of a prosperous New England family at the outset of the Revolutionary War. The parlor—considered one of the country's best-preserved Colonial interiors, with a tall clock and mahogany Chippendale-style chairs—looks pretty much as it did when Sayward lived here. ⊠ *9 Barrell La. Ext., York Harbor* ☎ *207/384–2454* ⊕ *www.historicnewengland.org* ⊠ *$10* ☽ *Closed mid-Oct.–May.*

Stonewall Kitchen

STORE/MALL | You've probably seen the kitchen's smartly labeled jars of gourmet chutneys, jams, jellies, salsas, and sauces in specialty stores back home. This complex houses the expansive flagship company store, which has a viewing area of the bottling process and stunning gardens. Sample all the mustards, salsas, and dressings you can stand, or have lunch at the café and take-out restaurant. The campus also houses a cooking school where you can join in evening or daytime courses. Reservations are required; most classes are shorter than two hours and cost $55–$80. ⊠ *2 Stonewall La., off U.S. 1* ☎ *207/351–2712* ⊕ *www.stonewallkitchen.com/yorkstore.html.*

York's Wild Kingdom

AMUSEMENT PARK/WATER PARK | FAMILY | Surrounded by forest, this popular zoo has more than 50 species of exotic animals, including lions, kangaroos, ring-tail lemurs, zebras, and numerous monkeys. There's a nostalgic charm to the amusement park, which includes bumper cars, food, and games, and a Ferris wheel with an ocean view, and offers discounts for kids under 10. ⊠ *1 Animal Park Rd., off U.S. 1, York Beach* ☎ *207/363–4911* ⊕ *www.yorkswildkingdom.com* ⊠ *From $12.*

🍴 Restaurants

Dockside Restaurant

$$$ | **SEAFOOD** | On an islandlike peninsula overlooking York Harbor, this restaurant has plenty of seafood on the menu. Floor-to-ceiling windows in the stepped modern dining space transport diners to the water beyond—every seat has a water view. **Known for:** "drunken" lobster (sautéed lobster, scallops, shallots, and herbs in an Irish-whiskey cream); beef tenderloin; lively, dockside vibe with spectacular views. [$] *Average main: $25* ✉ *22 Harris Island Rd., off Rte. 103, York Harbor* ☎ *207/363–2722* 🌐 *www.dockside-restaurant.com* 🕒 *Closed Tues. in summer and late Oct.–mid-May.*

Foster's Downeast Clambake

$$$ | **SEAFOOD** | **FAMILY** | Save your appetite for this one. Specializing in the traditional Maine clambake—a feast consisting of rich clam chowder, a pile of mussels and steamers, Maine lobster with drawn butter for dipping, corn on the cob, roasted potatoes and onions, and Maine blueberry crumb cake (phew!)—this massive complex provides musical entertainment to go with its belly-busting meals. **Known for:** finger-licking barbecue; classic Maine fare; gatherings for groups of families and friends. [$] *Average main: $28* ✉ *5 Axholme Rd., at U.S. 1A, York Harbor* ☎ *207/363–3255, 800/552–0242* 🌐 *www.fostersclambake.com* 🕒 *Closed early Sept.–late May, and weekdays late May–mid-June.*

The Goldenrod

$ | **AMERICAN** | **FAMILY** | People line the windows to watch Goldenrod Kisses being made the same way they have since 1896—and thousands of pounds are made every year at this restaurant that is Maine's oldest. Aside from the famous taffy (there's penny candy, too), this eatery is family oriented, very reasonably priced, and a great place to get homemade ice cream from the old-fashioned soda fountain. **Known for:** laid-back, kid-friendly atmosphere; breakfast served all day; classic American fare, like burgers, hot dogs, and baked dinners. [$] *Average main: $10* ✉ *2 Railroad Ave., York Beach* ☎ *207/363–2621* 🌐 *www.thegoldenrod.com* 🕒 *Closed mid-Oct.–mid-May.*

🛏 Hotels

Atlantic House Inn

$ | **B&B/INN** | **FAMILY** | In a nicely renovated 1888 beauty, this inn's standard guest rooms feel fresh with designer fabrics, gas fireplaces, and large tubs for a relaxing soak. **Pros:** lots of amenities; walk to beach, shops; suites are a good choice for weekly stay; some ocean views. **Cons:** not on beach; lacks public spaces; some rooms have a two-night minimum. [$] *Rooms from: $170* ✉ *2 Beach St., York Beach* ☎ *207/361–6677* 🌐 *www.atlantichouseinn.com* 🕒 *Closed Nov.–Apr.* 🔑 *16 rooms* 🍽 *No meals.*

★ Cliff House

$$$$ | **HOTEL** | **FAMILY** | This already luxurious hotel overlooking the Atlantic Ocean—you can watch the white crests smash the craggy bluffs below while nestled in your hooded flannel robe on your balcony—refreshed its rooms in a recent renovation. **Pros:** the view, the views, the views; rooms have private terraces; plenty of activities to keep everyone busy. **Cons:** communal coffee station on each floor only (but this is to help reduce waste); meals not included; central location means a drive to the nearest town centers. [$] *Rooms from: $600* ✉ *591 Shore Rd., Cape Neddick* ☎ *207/361–1000* 🌐 *www.cliffhouse-maine.com* 🔑 *226 rooms* 🍽 *No meals.*

Inn at Tanglewood Hall

$$ | **B&B/INN** | This 1880s shingle-style "cottage" is a haven of antiques, art, and eclectic decor and comfort—artfully painted floors, lush wallpaper, and meticulous attention to detail are the fruits of a former designation as a designers'

showcase home. **Pros:** authentic historic lodging; short walk to beaches; fireplaces in all rooms. **Cons:** no water views; dated decor consistent with historic property; no pets or children under 12. ⓢ *Rooms from: $175 ⊠ 611 York St., York Harbor ☎ 207/351–1075 ⊕ www.tanglewoodhall. com ⌁ 6 rooms ⍿ Free breakfast.*

★ Stage Neck Inn

$$$ | **RESORT** | **FAMILY** | A family-run operation that is now in the competent hands of the second generation, this resort hotel takes full advantage of its gorgeous harborside location, with Adirondack chairs, chaise longues and a fire pit on the surrounding lawns, water views from most guest rooms, and floor-to-ceiling windows in the common spaces. **Pros:** elaborate full-breakfast buffet with scrumptious baked goods; poolside service and snack bar in season; rooms have balconies or deck areas and most have water views. **Cons:** spa is on the smaller side; some rooms have only partial water views; rooms with two beds have doubles rather than queens. ⓢ *Rooms from: $300 ⊠ 8 Stage Neck Rd., off U.S. 1A, York Harbor ☎ 800/340–1130, 207/363–3850 ⊕ www.stageneck.com ⊘ Closed 1st 2 wks in Jan. ⌁ 60 rooms ⍿ Free breakfast.*

York Harbor Inn

$$ | **B&B/INN** | A mid-17th-century fishing cabin with dark timbers and a fieldstone fireplace forms the heart of this historic inn, which now includes several neighboring buildings. **Pros:** many rooms have harbor views; close to beaches; scenic walking trails; kid-friendly. **Cons:** rooms vary greatly in style, size, and appeal; no ocean views at the Chapman House; some rooms are not pet friendly. ⓢ *Rooms from: $200 ⊠ 480 York St., York Harbor ☎ 207/363–5119 ⊕ www. yorkharborinn.com ⌁ 65 rooms ⍿ Free breakfast.*

🛍 Shopping

Gateway Farmers' Market

OUTDOOR/FLEA/GREEN MARKETS | Bring your own bag for morning shopping at the Gateway Farmers' Market, held in the back lot at the Greater York Region Chamber of Commerce in summer (Saturday June–October, 9 am–1 pm), and inside the building in winter (designated Saturdays November–March, 9 am–1 pm). You'll find fresh local produce, lots of baked goods and artisanal breads, local seafood and meat, fresh flowers, and handcrafted items like soaps and candles. It's a good place to gather the makings for a beach picnic or to stock up on holiday gifts. ⊠ *1 Stonewall La., off U.S. 1, York ☎ 207/363–4422 ⊕ gateway-tomaine.org.*

Ocean Fire Pottery

CRAFTS | This artist-owned and-operated studio and gallery features unique wheel-thrown stoneware. Live demonstrations are available daily; call ahead to make sure the studio is open during the off-season. ⊠ *23 Woodbridge Rd. ☎ 207/361–3131 ⊕ www.oceanfirepottery.com.*

🏃 Activities

BIKING

Berger's Bike Shop

BICYCLING | This former auto garage and full-service bike shop rents hybrid bikes for local excursions and sells bikes of all kinds. ⊠ *241 York St., York ☎ 207/363–4070 ⊕ www.bergersbikeshop.com.*

FISHING

For a list of fishing charters, check the directory on the Maine Fishing Guides website (⊕ *www.maineguides.com/activity/fishing-guides*).

Ogunquit's Perkins Cove is a pleasant place to admire the boats (and wonder at the origin of their names).

Ogunquit

8 miles north of the Yorks via U.S. 1.

A resort village since the late 19th century, Ogunquit made a name for itself as an artists' colony. Today it has become a mini Provincetown, with a gay population that swells in summer, and many inns and small clubs cater to a primarily gay and lesbian clientele. The nightlife in Ogunquit revolves around the precincts of Ogunquit Square and Perkins Cove, where people stroll, often enjoying an after-dinner ice cream cone or espresso. For a scenic drive, take Shore Road from downtown to the 175-foot Bald Head Cliff; you'll be treated to views up and down the coast. On a stormy day the surf can be quite wild here.

GETTING HERE AND AROUND

Parking in the village and at the beach is costly and limited, so leave your car at the hotel or in a public parking space and hop the trolley. It costs $2 per trip and runs Memorial Day weekend–Columbus Day, with weekend-only service during the first few weeks. From Perkins Cove, the trolley runs through town along Shore Road and then down to Ogunquit Beach; it also stops along U.S. 1.

ESSENTIALS

TRANSPORTATION INFORMATION Shoreline Explorer. ☎ *800/965–5762* ⊕ *www.shorelineexplorer.com.*

VISITOR INFORMATION Ogunquit Chamber of Commerce. ☎ *207/646–1279* ⊕ *www.ogunquit.org.*

◉ Sights

Marginal Way

PROMENADE | This mile-long, paved footpath hugs the shore of a rocky promontory known as Israels Head. Thirty-nine benches along the easygoing path allow you to appreciate the open sea vistas. Expect heavy foot, even in the off-season—which is the only time of the year that dogs are allowed. ✉ *Perkins Cove Rd.* ⊕ *www.marginalwayfund.org.*

Perkins Cove

HISTORIC SITE | FAMILY | This neck of land off Shore Road in the lower part of Ogunquit village has a jumble of sea-weathered fish houses and buildings that were part of an art school. These have largely been transformed by the tide of tourism into shops and restaurants. When you've had your fill of browsing, stroll out along the mile-long Marginal Way. ⌧ *Perkins Cove Rd., off Shore Rd.*

 Restaurants

Amore Breakfast

$ | **AMERICAN** | You could hardly find a more satisfying, heartier breakfast than at this smart and busy joint just shy of the entrance to Perkins Cove where a lighthearted mix of retro advertising signs adorn the walls of the bright, open, and bustling dining room. The corned-beef hash is made with tender pulled brisket with spices and just a bit of diced potatoes and onions—try it topped with hollandaise in the Irish Benedict. **Known for:** innovative, rotating breakfast menus; bustling, laid-back atmosphere; chock-full of locals; community involvement. $ *Average main: $10* ⌧ *87 Main St.* ⌖ *At blinking light* ☎ *207/646–6667* ⊕ *www.amorebreakfast.com* ⊙ *Closed mid-Dec.–early Apr. No dinner.*

★ Northern Union

$$$ | **CONTEMPORARY** | From the moment you walk into Northern Union you know you're going to be very good hands. A genuine, welcoming staff and laid-back yet elegant design scheme put you in the mood for a slow, very memorable dinner consisting of seasonally inspired small plates like braised pork belly or duck confit and rotating entrées like seared scallops and lobster fettuccine with spot-on wine pairings that you won't find anywhere else in the area. **Known for:** almost everything is made in-house; dishes that can easily be shared; a terrific selection of cured meats and cheese boards with a local, seasonal bent. $ *Average main: $27* ⌧ *261 Shore Rd.* ☎ *207/216–9639* ⊕ *www.northern-union.me* ⊙ *No lunch.*

☕ Coffee and Quick Bites

Backyard Coffeehouse and Eatery

$ | **AMERICAN** | This eager-to-please coffeeshop is centrally located and a good stop for hot or iced coffee accompanied by a scone or bagel. For something more substantial, choose from a selection of breakfast or lunch sandwiches. **Known for:** locally sourced coffee, tea, and bagels; close to Marginal Way walking path; the North Country bacon, egg, and cheese breakfast sandwich. $ *Average main: $5* ⌧ *178 Main St.* ☎ *207/251–4554* ⊕ *www.backyardogunquit.com* ⊙ *Closed mid-Oct.–Apr.*

Wells

5 miles north of Ogunquit via U.S. 1.

Lacking any kind of discernible village center, Wells could be easily overlooked as nothing more than a commercial stretch of U.S. 1 between Ogunquit and the Kennebunks. But look more closely: this is a place where people come to enjoy some of the best beaches on the coast. Until 1980 the town of Wells incorporated Ogunquit, and today this family-oriented beach community has 7 miles of densely populated shoreline, along with nature preserves, where you can explore salt marshes and tidal pools.

GETTING HERE AND AROUND

Just $2 per trip, the seasonal Shoreline Trolley serves Wells Beach and Crescent Beach and has many stops along U.S. 1 at motels, campgrounds, restaurants, and so on. You can also catch it at the Wells Transportation Center when Amtrak's *Downeaster* pulls in.

ESSENTIALS

The Shoreline Trolley is part of the Shoreline Explorer network, which links seasonal trolleys in southern Maine beach towns from York to the Kennebunks, including the Wells area.

VISITOR INFORMATION Wells Chamber of Commerce. ☎ *207/646–2451* ⊕ *www. wellschamber.org.*

 ## Sights

Rachel Carson National Wildlife Refuge

NATURE PRESERVE | FAMILY | At the headquarters of the Rachel Carson National Wildlife Refuge, which has 11 divisions from Kittery to Cape Elizabeth, is the Carson Trail, a 1-mile loop. The trail traverses a salt marsh and a white-pine forest where migrating birds and waterfowl of many varieties are regularly spotted, and it borders Branch Brook and the Merriland River. ⊠ *321 Port Rd.* ☎ *207/646–9226* ⊕ *www.fws.gov/refuge/rachel_carson.*

Beaches

With its thousands of acres of marsh and preserved land, Wells is a great place to spend time outdoors. Nearly 7 miles of sand stretch along the boundaries of Wells, making beachgoing a prime occupation. Tidal pools sheltered by rocks are filled with all manner of creatures awaiting discovery. During the summer season a pay-and-display parking system (no quarters, receipt goes on dashboard) is in place at the public beaches.

A summer trolley serves **Crescent Beach,** along Webhannet Drive, and **Wells Beach,** at the end of Mile Road off U.S. 1. There is another parking lot, but no trolley stop, at the north end of Atlantic Avenue, which runs north along the shore from the end of Mile Road. Stretching north from the jetty at Wells Harbor is **Drakes Island Beach** (end of Drakes Island Road off U.S. 1). Lifeguards are on hand at all beaches, and all have public restrooms.

Crescent Beach

BEACH—SIGHT | FAMILY | Lined with summer homes, this sandy strand is busy in the summer, but the beach and the water are surprisingly clean, considering all the traffic. The swimming's good, and beachgoers can also explore tidal pools and look for seals on the sea rocks nearby. **Amenities:** food and drink; lifeguards; parking (fee); toilets. **Best for:** swimming. ⊠ *Webhannet Dr., south of Mile Rd.* ☎ *207/646–5113.*

Drakes Island Beach

BEACH—SIGHT | FAMILY | Smaller and quieter than the other two beaches in Wells, Drakes Island Beach is also a little more natural, with rolling sand dunes and access to salt-marsh walking trails at an adjacent estuary. The ice-cream truck swings by regularly in the summer. **Amenities:** lifeguards; parking (fee); toilets. **Best for:** walking. ⊠ *Island Beach Rd., 1 mile southwest of U.S. 1* ☎ *207/646–5113.*

Wells Beach

BEACH—SIGHT | FAMILY | The northern end of a 2-mile stretch of golden sand, Wells Beach is popular with families and surfers, who line up in the swells and preen on the boardwalk near the arcade and snack shop. The beach's northern tip is a bit quieter, with a long rock jetty perfect for strolling. **Amenities:** food and drink; lifeguards; parking (fee); toilets. **Best for:** surfing; walking. ⊠ *Atlantic Ave., north of Mile Rd.* ☎ *207/646–5113.*

Wheels and Waves

STORE/MALL | Rent bikes, surfboards, wet suits, boogie boards, kayaks, and all sorts of outdoor gear at Wheels and Waves. ⊠ *365 Post Rd., U.S. 1* ☎ *207/646–5774* ⊕ *www.wheelsnwaves.com.*

Restaurants

Billy's Chowder House

$ | SEAFOOD | FAMILY | Locals and vacationers head to this roadside seafood restaurant in the midst of a salt marsh en route to Wells Beach. The menu features classic seafood dishes like lobster rolls and chowders, but there are plenty of nonseafood choices, too. **Known for:** views of the Rachel Carson National Wildlife Refuge; generous lobster rolls; one of the oldest waterfront restaurants in Wells. [$] *Average main: $19* ✉ *216 Mile Rd.* ☎ *207/646–7558* 🌐 *www.billyschowderhouse.com* ⏲ *Closed mid-Dec.–mid-Jan.*

★ Bitter End

$$ | SEAFOOD | Pete and Kate Morency, the duo originally behind the ever-popular Pier 77 and the Ramp Bar and Grill in Kennebunkport, are also the masterminds behind this fabulous seafood spot that serves up brilliant, contemporary twists to American and Mediterranean classics, adding spins on staples such as fish-and-chips (think tempura batter with turmeric breading and tidewater coleslaw). The fabulous decor consists of an unlikely marriage of old-school American sports memorabilia and something that might be described as shabby ballroom chic—crystal chandeliers hang above old leather boxing gloves, and black-and-white photos of sports icons and an array of shiny trophies (including a 1961 Miss Universe cup) line the bar. **Known for:** cuisine fusion and a rotating menu; outdoor seating area with firepit; superbly curated bevy of liquors. [$] *Average main: $18* ✉ *2118 Post Rd.* ☎ *207/360–0904* 🌐 *www.bitterend.me* ⏲ *Closed Tues.*

Maine Diner

$ | DINER | One look at the 1953 exterior and you'll start craving diner food, but be prepared to get a little more than you bargained for: after all, how many greasy spoons make an award-winning lobster pie? There's plenty of fried seafood in addition to the usual diner fare, and breakfast is served all day. **Known for:** classic Maine diner fare; wild Maine blueberry pie; diner has a vegetable garden, which it uses as much as possible in the creation of its dishes. [$] *Average main: $15* ✉ *2265 Post Rd.* ☎ *207/646–4441* 🌐 *www.mainediner.com* ⏲ *Closed at least 1 wk in Jan.*

Spinnakers

$$ | SEAFOOD | FAMILY | Plenty of seafood shacks dot U.S. 1, but this roadside joint is really worth the stop, even if it's just to grab an ice-cream cone to escape the steady flow of summer traffic. Simple but pleasing contemporary design makes for a cheerful space to enjoy loaded lobster rolls, burgers and sandwiches, and a decidedly unholy lobster poutine consisting of hand-cut fries covered in a delicious mess of local cheese curds and topped with lobster gravy. **Known for:** pick-and-choose seafood basket combos; quick bites that pack a punch and scream Maine; eat in or grab something to go from the take-out window. [$] *Average main: $18* ✉ *139 Post Rd.* ☎ *207/216–9291* 🌐 *spinnakersmaine.com* ⏲ *Closed Mon. and Tues.*

Coffee and Quick Bites

Congdon's Doughnuts

$ | AMERICAN | FAMILY | These superior doughnuts have been made by the same family since 1945 and at the same location since 1955. Congdon's has about 40 different varieties, some seasonal, though the plain variety really gives you an idea of just how good these doughnuts are: it's the biggest seller, along with the honey dipped and black raspberry jelly. [$] *Average main: $3* ✉ *1090 Post Rd.* ☎ *207/646–4219* 🌐 *www.congdons.com* ⏲ *Closed Mon.–Wed. No dinner.*

Hotels

Haven by the Sea

$$ | B&B/INN | Once the summer mission of St. Martha's Church in Kennebunkport, this exquisite inn has retained many original details from its former life as a seaside church, including cathedral ceilings and stained-glass windows. **Pros:** unusual structure with elegant appointments; beach towels and beach chairs available; rotating breakfasts that cater to dietary restrictions without compromising taste; nightly happy hour with complimentary appetizers and courtesy sherry, port, and brandy in the main parlor. **Cons:** not an in-town location; distant ocean views; $50 cancellation fee no matter how far in advance. $ *Rooms from: $260* ✉ *59 Church St.* ☎ *207/646–4194* ⊕ *www.havenbythesea.com* �págin *9 rooms* ❍ *Free breakfast.*

Kennebunk and Kennebunkport

5 miles north of Wells via U.S. 1.

The town centers of Kennebunk and Kennebunkport are separated by 5 miles and two rivers, but united by a common history and a laid-back seaside vibe. Perhaps best described as the Hamptons of the Pine Tree State, Kennebunkport has been a resort area since the 19th century. Its most recent residents have made it even more famous: the dynastic Bush family is often in residence on its immense estate here, which sits dramatically out on Walker's Point on Cape Arundel. Newer homes have sprung up alongside the old, and a great way to take them all in is with a slow drive out Ocean Avenue along the cape.

Sometimes bypassed on the way to its sister town, Kennebunk has its own appeal. Once a major shipbuilding center, Kennebunk today retains the feel of a classic New England small town, with an inviting shopping district, steepled churches, and fine examples of 18th- and 19th-century brick and clapboard homes. There are also plenty of natural spaces for walking, swimming, birding, and biking, and the Kennebunks' major beaches are here.

GETTING HERE AND AROUND
Kennebunk's main village sits along U.S. 1, extending west from the Mousam River. The Lower Village is along Routes 9 and 35, 4 miles down Route 35 from the main village, and the drive between the

two keeps visitors agog with the splendor of the area's mansions, spread out on both sides of Route 35. To get to the grand and gentle beaches of Kennebunk, continue straight (the road becomes Beach Avenue) at the intersection with Route 9. If you turn left instead, Route 9 will take you across the Kennebunk River, into Kennebunkport's touristy downtown, called Dock Square (or sometimes just "the Port"), a commercial area with restaurants, shops, boat cruises, and galleries. Here you'll find the most activity (and crowds) in the Kennebunks.

Take the Intown Trolley for narrated 45-minute jaunts that run daily from Memorial Day weekend through Columbus Day. The $18 fare is valid for the day, so you can hop on and off—or start your journey—at any of the stops. The route includes Kennebunk's beaches and Lower Village as well as neighboring Kennebunkport's scenery and sights. The main stop is at 21 Ocean Avenue in Kennebunkport, around the corner from Dock Square.

ESSENTIALS
VISITOR INFORMATION Intown Trolley.
☎ *207/967–3686* ⊕ *www.intowntrolley. com.* **Kennebunk-Kennebunkport Chamber of Commerce.** ☎ *207/967–0857* ⊕ *www. gokennebunks.com.*

WALKING TOURS
To take a little walking tour of Kennebunk's most notable structures, begin at the Federal-style Brick Store Museum at 117 Main Street. Head south on Main Street (turn left out of the museum) to see several extraordinary 18th- and early-19th-century homes, including the **Lexington Elms** at No. 99 (1799), the **Horace Porter House** at No. 92 (1848), and the **Benjamin Brown House** at No. 85 (1788).

When you've had your fill of historic homes, head back up toward the museum, pass the 1773 **First Parish Unitarian Church** (its Asher Benjamin–style steeple contains an original Paul Revere bell), and turn right onto **Summer Street.** This street is an architectural showcase, revealing an array of styles from Colonial to Federal. Walking past these grand beauties will give you a real sense of the economic prowess and glamour of the long-gone shipbuilding industry.

For a guided 90-minute architectural walking tour of Summer Street, contact the museum at ☎ *207/985–4802.* Tours are offered Saturday, May through November, and other days by calling ahead. You can also purchase a $4.95 map that marks historic buildings or a $15.95 guidebook, *Windows on the Past.*

For a dramatic walk along Kennebunkport's rocky coastline and beneath the views of Ocean Avenue's grand mansions, head out on the **Parson's Way Shore Walk,** a paved 4.8-mile round-trip. Begin at Dock Square and follow Ocean Avenue along the river, passing the Colony Hotel and St. Ann's Church, all the way to Walker's Point. Simply turn back from here.

◉ Sights

Brick Store Museum
MUSEUM | FAMILY | The cornerstone of this block-long preservation of early-19th-century commercial and residential buildings is William Lord's Brick Store. Built as a dry-goods store in 1825 in the Federal style, the building has an openwork balustrade across the roofline, granite lintels over the windows, and paired chimneys. Exhibits chronicle the Kennebunk area's history and Early American decorative and fine arts. Museum staff lead architectural walking tours of Kennebunk's National Historic District by appointment late May–September. ✉ *117 Main St., Kennebunk* ☎ *207/985–4802* ⊕ *www.brickstoremuseum.org* ✉ *$7* ⊙ *Closed Mon.*

Dock Square
PLAZA | Clothing boutiques, T-shirt shops, art galleries, and restaurants line this bustling square, spreading out along the nearby streets and alleys. Walk onto the drawbridge to admire the tidal Kennebunk River; cross to the other side and you are in the Lower Village of neighboring Kennebunk. ✉ *Dock Sq., Kennebunkport.*

First Families Kennebunkport Museum
HOUSE | FAMILY | Also known as White Columns, the imposing Greek Revival mansion with Doric columns is furnished with the belongings of four generations of the Perkins-Nott family. From mid-July through mid-October, the 1853 house is open for guided tours and also serves as a gathering place for village walking tours. It is owned by the Kennebunkport Historical Society, which has several other historical buildings a mile away at 125–135 North Street, including an old jail and schoolhouse. ✉ *8 Maine St., Kennebunkport* ☎ *207/967–2751* ⊕ *www.kporths.com* ✉ *$10.*

First Parish of Kennebunk Unitarian Universalist Church
RELIGIOUS SITE | FAMILY | Built in 1773, just before the American Revolution, this stunning church is a marvel. The 1804 Asher Benjamin–style steeple stands proudly atop the village, and the sounds of the original Paul Revere bell can be heard for miles. The church holds Sunday service at 9:30 am in the summer (at 10:30 the rest of the year). ✉ *114 Main St., Kennebunk* ☎ *207/985–3700* ⊕ *www.uukennebunk.org.*

Kennebunk Plains
NATURE PRESERVE | FAMILY | For an unusual experience, visit this 135-acre grasslands habitat that is home to several rare and endangered species. Locals call it Blueberry Plains, and a good portion of the area is abloom with the hues of ripening wild blueberries in late July; after August 1, you are welcome to pick and eat all the berries you can find. The area is maintained by the Nature Conservancy. ✉ *Webber Hill Rd., Kennebunk* ✛ *4½ miles northwest of town* ☎ *207/729–5181* ⊕ *www.nature.org.*

Seashore Trolley Museum

MUSEUM | **FAMILY** | Streetcars were built here from 1872 to 1972, including trolleys for major metropolitan areas—from Boston to Budapest, New York to Nagasaki, and San Francisco to Sydney. Many of them are beautifully restored and displayed. Best of all, you can take a nearly 4-mile ride on the tracks of the former Atlantic Shoreline trolley line, with a stop along the way at the museum restoration shop, where trolleys are transformed from junk into gems. The outdoor museum is self-guided. ✉ *195 Log Cabin Rd., Kennebunkport* ☎ *207/967–2800* 🌐 *www.trolleymuseum.org* 🎫 *$12* 🕓 *Closed Nov.–Apr. except 1st 2 weekends in Dec.*

Beaches

Gooch's Beach

BEACH—SIGHT | **FAMILY** | Kennebunk has three beaches, one after another, along Beach Avenue, which is lined with cottages and old Victorians. The most northerly, and the closest to downtown Kennebunkport, is Gooch's Beach, the main swimming beach. Next is stony Kennebunk Beach, followed by Mother's Beach, which is popular with families. There's a small playground and tidal puddles for splashing; rock outcroppings lessen the waves. **Amenities:** lifeguards; parking (fee); toilets. **Best for:** walking; swimming. ✉ *Beach Ave., south of Rte. 9, Kennebunk.*

Goose Rocks Beach

BEACH—SIGHT | Three-mile-long Goose Rocks, a 10-minute drive north of town, has a good long stretch of smooth sand and plenty of shallow pools for exploring. It's a favorite of families with small children. Pick up a $15 daily parking permit at the Kennebunkport Town Office on Elm Street; the Goose Rocks General Store at 3 Dyke Road; or the Police Department at 101 Main Street. Dogs are allowed (on a leash during the high season), but only before 8 am and after 6 pm. No facilities are available at the beach. **Amenities:** parking (fee). **Best for:** walking. ✉ *Dyke Rd., off Rte. 9, Kennebunkport* 🌐 *www.visitmaine.com.*

Restaurants

The Kennebunks are chock-full of restaurants and cafés vying for attention. Service and food can be hit-or-miss in this area; often the best meals are those that you pack yourself into a picnic basket to enjoy on one of the area's many sandy beaches.

The Boathouse Restaurant

$$$ | **SEAFOOD** | You can't get more up-close and personal with Kennebunkport's harbor than at this stunning waterside restaurant and bar that serves dressed-up, contemporary takes on classic Maine fare, alongside top-notch cocktails and staples such as perfectly shucked local oysters, lobster tacos, and hearty clam and corn chowder. The inside spaces are warm and welcoming, with a maritime theme that's not too over-the-top; the outdoor wraparound deck is one of the best spots in town to grab a cocktail and watch the sun set over the Kennebunk River. **Known for:** amazing waterside location; cocktails on the outdoor wraparound deck; great seafood. [$] *Average main: $30* ✉ *21 Ocean Ave., Kennebunkport* ☎ *877/266–1304* 🌐 *boathouseme.com.*

The Burleigh at the Kennebunkport Inn

$$$ | **SEAFOOD** | Nautical accents give this trendy restaurant a laid-back vibe that is the perfect transition from a day out on the water (or at the beach) to a relaxed end-of-the-day meal. While fresh seafood plays a central role at the Burleigh, you can't go wrong with one of the excellent burgers or pork chops paired with one of the many rotating local craft-beer choices. **Known for:** the Burleigh burger (prime beef patty, cheddar cheese, smoked bacon, lettuce, tomato, onion, pickles, hand-cut fries); craft cocktails that will knock you off of your feet; excellent happy hour in the inn's Garden Social Club. $ *Average main: $30* ⊠ *1 Dock Sq., Kennebunkport* ☎ *207/967–2621* ⊕ *kennebunkportinn.com/dining.*

Duffy's Tavern and Grill

$ | AMERICAN | Every small town needs its own lively and friendly tavern, and this bustling spot is Kennebunk's favorite, housed in a former shoe factory, with exposed brick, soaring ceilings, and hardwood floors; right outside are the tumbling waters of the Mousam River as it flows from the dam. You'll find lots of comfortable standards, like burgers and pizza; the popular fish-and-chips and the tasty onion rings are hand-dipped. **Known for:** lively vibe that brings locals and visitors together; classic pub fare, such as fried calamari and hearty New England clam chowder; handcrafted pizzas. $ *Average main: $16* ⊠ *4 Main St., Kennebunk* ☎ *207/985–0050* ⊕ *www. duffyskennebunk.com.*

★ Earth at Hidden Pond

$$$$ | FUSION | This splurge-worthy place offers thoughtful attention to flavor and texture, using the freshest locally sourced ingredients—each and every dining experience at Hidden Pond feels like a special occasion. The seasonally inspired menu is always in flux, but you can be sure that even hard-core foodies will be delighted with this culinary experience. **Known for:** wood-fire surf-and-turf dishes; ingredients culled from its own garden; private dining sheds and cabanas for special occasions and groups. $ *Average main: $38* ⊠ *354 Goose Rocks Rd., Kennebunkport* ☎ *207/967–9050* ⊕ *hiddenpondmaine.com/earth.*

Mabel's Lobster Claw

$$$ | SEAFOOD | FAMILY | Since the 1950s, Mabel's has been serving lobsters (baked and in rolls), homemade pies, clam chowder, and lots of seafood for lunch and dinner in this tiny dwelling out on Ocean Avenue. The decor includes paneled walls, wooden booths, and autographed photos of various TV stars (and members of the Bush family), and there's outside seating. **Known for:** blueberry pie; Lobster Savannah: split and filled with scallops and shrimp, and baked in a Newburg sauce; take-out window where you can order ice cream and food. $ *Average main: $25* ⊠ *124 Ocean Ave., Kennebunkport* ☎ *207/967–2562* ⊕ *www.mabelslobster.com* ⊗ *Closed Nov.–early Apr.*

★ Ocean Restaurant

$$$$ | SEAFOOD | One of the best seats in town to watch the sun set (or rise) over the Atlantic, the large picture windows at Ocean Restaurant envelope an intimate dining space that features a touch of seaside elegance coupled with captivating, original local art. The menu showcases Maine seafood and other local ingredients and is chock-full of sheer ambrosial delights, with contemporary takes on classic dishes, such as lobster thermidor, foie gras, swordfish, and seafood velouté. **Known for:** equally perfect for a romantic evening or a gathering of friends; gracious, old-world service; ridiculously indulgent desserts that you may want to eat first. $ *Average main: $40* ⊠ *208 Ocean Ave., Kennebunkport* ☎ *855/346–5700* ⊕ *capearundelinn.com.*

Pearl Kennebunk Beach and Spat Oyster Cellar

$$ | SEAFOOD | At this classy but cozy seafood-centric restaurant you'll be treated to stellar seasonal fare using ingredients harvested from the Maine coast. Start with craft cocktails at the large, elegant bar and then move to a table close to the massive stone hearth that is particularly inviting on cooler evenings. **Known for:** excellent daily drink specials from 5–6; rotating selection of specials; crispy panfried chicken dishes. $ *Average main: $22* ⊠ *27 Western Ave., Kennebunk* ☎ *207/204–0860* ⊕ *www.pearlkennebunk.com* ⊗ *Closed Mon.–Wed.*

★ Pier 77 Restaurant

$$$ | AMERICAN | The phenomenal seaside view at this restaurant and bar shares center stage with the mouthwatering menu that features sophisticated fare with an emphasis on seafood. Located on the ground level, the restaurant's large windows overlook the harbor, ensuring that every seat has a nice view of the water; the tiny but oh-so-funky-and-fun Ramp Bar & Grill pays homage to a really good burger, fried seafood, and other pub-style classics. **Known for:** live music in summer; great spot for cocktails on the water while watching boats and sea life pass by; a packed house almost every meal in the summer (reservations highly recommended). $ *Average main: $25 ⊠ 77 Pier Rd., Kennebunkport ☎ 207/967–8500 ⊕ www.pier77restaurant.com.*

★ The Tides Beach Club Restaurant

$$$ | SEAFOOD | This unfussy, beachside dining spot is decorated in soft maritime accents and a crisp color palette, perfect for a relaxing post-beach meal. The menu features lighter seafood fare and salads alongside heartier options, such as lobster rangoons, crispy fried chicken sandwich, and burgers, which are complemented by a list of delicious craft cocktails. **Known for:** no dress code—think beach-hair-don't-care chic; perfect for a prebeach bite or postbeach sit-down dining experience; exceptional service that isn't cloying. $ *Average main: $26 ⊠ 254 Kings Hwy., Kennebunkport ☎ 207/967–3757 ⊕ tidesbeachclubmaine.com/food.*

☕ Coffee and Quick Bites

Dock Square Coffee House

$ | AMERICAN | European-style coffee drinks, tea, pastries, smoothies, and other snacks are on the menu at this bright and cheerful shop in the midst of Dock Square. The coffee is sourced from Portland-based and nationally recognized Coffee By Design, one of the state's best. **Known for:** locally sourced coffee, pastries and breakfast sandwiches; avocado toast; central location. $ *Average main: $5 ⊠ 18 Dock Sq., Kennebunkport ☎ 207/967–4422 ⊕ www.docksquarecoffeehouse.biz ⊗ Closed Jan.–Mar.*

🛏 Hotels

★ Cape Arundel Inn and Resort

$$$ | B&B/INN | This shingle-style 19th-century mansion, originally one of the area's many summer "cottages," commands a magnificent ocean view that takes in the Bush estate at Walker's Point; it's location is just far enough from the bustle of town to truly feel like you've gotten away from it all. **Pros:** exceptional staff that are gracious and discreet; luxurious beds and linens that will make you feel like a spring chicken upon waking; champagne welcome. **Cons:** not for the budget-minded; club-house amenities are ½ mile away from main house; some rooms without ocean views. $ *Rooms from: $309 ⊠ 208 Ocean Ave., Kennebunkport ☎ 855/346–5700 ⊕ www.capearundelinn.com ⊗ Closed Jan. ➚ 29 rooms ⊗ Free breakfast.*

★ Hidden Pond

$$$$ | RESORT | This unique resort hideaway, tucked away in a wooded, 60-acre enclave near Goose Rocks Beach, includes hiking trails, two pools, a spa, a phenomenal restaurant, and a working farm. **Pros:** use of beach facilities at the nearby Tides Beach Club, its sister property; complimentary beach shuttle and beach cruiser bikes; guests can cut fresh flowers and harvest vegetables from the property's many gardens; plenty of activities on-site including watercolor painting, children's activities, and fitness classes. **Cons:** steep prices; away from the center of town; no dogs allowed. $ *Rooms from: $549 ⊠ 354 Goose Rocks Rd., Kennebunkport ☎ 207/967–9050 ⊕ hiddenpondmaine.com ⊗ Closed Nov.–Apr. ➚ 46 units ⊗ No meals.*

Maine's rocky coastline stretches for about 3,400 miles including Kennebunkport.

★ The Inn at English Meadows

$$$ | **B&B/INN** | A stone's throw from the bustle of Kennebunkport and just a mile from the beach, this charming boutique B&B is housed in a gorgeously restored, historic 1860s farmhouse. **Pros:** luxurious bathroom amenities including rain showers and toiletries by Malin + Goetz; gas fireplaces in many rooms; home-baked goods available every afternoon. **Cons:** no pool; no water view; not wheelchair accessible. [$] *Rooms from: $339* ✉ *141 Port Rd., Kennebunk* ☎ *207/967–5766* 🌐 *englishmeadowsinn.com* 🛏 *11 rooms* 🍴 *Free breakfast.*

★ Sandy Pines Campground

$$ | **RENTAL** | The luxe "glamping" (glamorous camping) tents, camp cottages, and A-frame hideaway huts on wheels at Sandy Pines Campground deliver every bit as much comfort and luxury as a fine hotel (with a few caveats, including communal bathing areas), but give you a chance to get up close and personal with nature. **Pros:** the glamping areas of Sandy Pines are quiet zones; nightly bonfires under the stars without roughing it; all tents equipped with generous sitting areas that extend outside the tents. **Cons:** expect all that comes with being in nature; glamping tents are not pet-friendly; three-night minimum stay (seasonal). [$] *Rooms from: $266* ✉ *277 Mills Rd., Kennebunkport* ☎ *207/967–2483* 🌐 *sandypinescamping.com* 🕒 *Closed mid-Oct.–mid-May* 🛏 *60 units* 🍴 *No meals.*

The Tides Beach Club

$$$ | **B&B/INN** | The stately building that now houses the Tides Beach Club is a charming grande dame from the heyday of seaside "cure" retreats during the Gilded Age. Just steps from a long, sandy beach—like its sister property, Hidden Pond—this lively inn is the epitome of laid-back, seaside-chic design, which extends into each of the spacious, bungalowlike rooms that are decorated in rich, feel-good ocean blue and coral hues. **Pros:** use of the common spaces (pools, spa, garden) at the very exclusive Hidden Pond; beach service for a relaxed lunch or dinner on the sand;

most of the rooms have ocean views and balconies. **Cons:** definitely will lighten your purse; a lot of activity in and around the inn; not pet-friendly. [$] *Rooms from: $329* ✉ *254 Kings Hwy., Kennebunkport* ☎ *207/967–3757* 🌐 *tidesbeachclubmaine.com* 🕒 *Closed Nov.–Apr.* 🛏 *21 rooms* 🍴 *Free breakfast.*

★ The Yachtsman Hotel and Marina Club
$$$ | HOTEL | These chic new bungalows located smack-dab on the water are a long-overdue addition to Kennebunkport, with their hip beach-vibe design, private lawns that blur the distinction between indoors and outdoors, and harbor views. **Pros:** all rooms have fabulous harbor views; pull-out sofas offer more space in the deluxe harborfront bungalows; large marble showers and luxe toiletries from Malin + Goetz; free shuttle service around town. **Cons:** not on the beach; private lawns aren't exactly private with all the boats passing by; not family-friendly. [$] *Rooms from: $309* ✉ *59 Ocean Ave., Kennebunkport* ☎ *207/967–2511* 🌐 *yachtsmanlodge.com* 🕒 *Closed Nov.–Apr.* 🛏 *30 bungalows* 🍴 *Free breakfast.*

Activities

FISHING

Cast-Away Fishing Charters
BOATING | FAMILY | Half- and fill-day charters are available, as is a two-hour children's charter trip where kids can play lobsterman (or woman) for the day and haul in the traps. ✉ *Performance Marine, 4 Western Ave., Kennebunk* ☎ *207/284–1740* 🌐 *www.castawayfishingcharters.com.*

Rugosa
BOATING | FAMILY | Lobster-trap hauling trips aboard the *Rugosa* in the scenic waters off the Kennebunks run daily, Memorial Day–Columbus Day. ✉ *Nonantum Resort, 95 Ocean Ave., Kennebunkport* ☎ *207/468–4095* 🌐 *www.rugosalobstertours.com.*

WHALE-WATCHING

First Chance
TOUR—SPORTS | FAMILY | This company leads whale-watching cruises on 87-foot *Nick's Chance.* Scenic lobster cruises are also offered aboard 65-foot *Kylie's Chance.* Trips run daily in summer and on weekends in the shoulder season. ✉ *Performance Marine, 4 Western Ave., Kennebunk* ☎ *207/967–5507* 🌐 *www.firstchancewhalewatch.com.*

★ The Pineapple Ketch
SAILING | FAMILY | Here's a terrific way to get out on the water and see some marine life, aboard a classic 38-foot Down Easter ketch. The captain and crew are knowledgeable and let the passengers guide the direction of both the boat and the tour. Bring your own snacks and beverages, especially for the sunset cruises. ✉ *95 Ocean Ave., Kennebunkport* ☎ *207/468–7262* 🌐 *pineappleketch.com.*

Shopping

Abacus
GIFTS/SOUVENIRS | This shop sells eclectic crafts, jewelry, and furniture. It's a good place to pick up gifts. ✉ *2 Ocean Ave., at Dock Sq., Kennebunkport* ☎ *207/967–0111* 🌐 *www.abacusgallery.com.*

★ Daytrip Society
GIFTS/SOUVENIRS | The impossibly hip and well-selected array of goods that this modern-design shop stocks makes it an excellent place for both window-shopping and finding gifts for just about anyone on your list (including yourself). A refreshing departure from the rest of the somewhat stodgy gift shops in the village, this boutique is chock-full of eye candy, most of which is also functional. There are many locally sourced and decidedly contemporary products, from hats and jewelry to novelty books, home decor, and scents. Check out Daytrip Jr., its equally hip children's store around the corner. ✉ *4 Dock Sq., Kennebunkport* ☎ *207/967–4440* 🌐 *www.daytripsociety.com.*

★ **Farm + Table**

SPECIALTY STORES | This delightful shop is housed in a bright-red Maine barn filled with kitchen items both useful and pleasing to the eye. ⊠ *8 Langsford Rd., Cape Porpoise* ☎ *207/604–8029* ⊕ *www.farmtablekennebunkport.com.*

Maine Art

ART GALLERIES | Showcasing works by artists from Maine and New England, Maine Art has a two-story gallery with a sculpture garden. ⊠ *14 Western Ave., Kennebunk* ☎ *207/967–2803* ⊕ *www.maine-art.com.*

Cape Elizabeth and Prout's Neck

Prout's Neck: 7 miles south of Cape Elizabeth; Cape Elizabeth: 5 miles south of Portland.

Follow Route 77 through South Portland (sometimes called "SoPo") to reach the affluent bedroom community of Cape Elizabeth, where a detour along the two-lane Shore Road shows off the famed Portland Head Light and quite a few stunning oceanfront homes. A few minutes farther south is Cape Elizabeth Light, the subject of a well-known Edward Hopper painting.

Speaking of famous artists, Winslow Homer painted many of his famous oceanscapes from a tiny studio on the rocky peninsula known as Prout's Neck, a now exclusive gated community 7 miles south of Cape Elizabeth. The studio is open to tours only through the Portland Museum of Art; otherwise the public can access Prouts Neck only by parking outside the gates and walking along a popular cliff trail.

◉ Sights

★ **Cape Elizabeth Light**

LIGHTHOUSE | FAMILY | This was the first twin lighthouses erected on the Maine coast in 1828—and locals still call it Two Lights—but one of the lighthouses was dismantled in 1924 and converted into a private residence. The other half still operates, and you can get a great photo of it from the end of Two Lights Road. The lighthouse itself is closed to the public, but you can explore the tidal pools at its base for small, edible snails known as periwinkles, or just "wrinkles," as they're sometimes referred to in Maine. Picnic tables are also available. ⊠ *7 Tower Dr.* ⊹ *Off Rte. 77 in Cape Elizabeth. Take Rte. 77 to Two Lights Rd.* ☎ *207/799–5871.*

★ **Portland Head Light**

LIGHTHOUSE | FAMILY | Familiar to many from photographs and the Edward Hopper painting *Portland Head-Light* (1927), this lighthouse was commissioned by George Washington in 1790. The towering, white-stone structure stands over the keeper's quarters, a white home with a blazing red roof, today the Museum at Portland Head Light. The lighthouse is in 90-acre Fort Williams Park, a sprawling green space with walking paths, picnic facilities, a beach and—you guessed it—a cool old fort. ⊠ *Museum, 1000 Shore Rd.* ☎ *207/799–2661* ⊕ *www.portlandheadlight.com.*

Scarborough Marsh Audubon Center

NATURE PRESERVE | FAMILY | You can explore this Maine Audubon Society–run nature center by foot or canoe, on your own or by signing up for a guided walk or paddle. Canoes and kayaks are available to rent and come with a life jacket and map. The salt marsh is Maine's largest and is an excellent place for bird-watching and peaceful paddling along its winding ways. The center has a discovery room for kids, programs for all ages ranging from basket making to astronomy, and a good gift shop. Tours include birding walks. ✉ 92 Pine Point Rd., Scarborough ☎ 207/883–5100 🌐 www.maineaudubon.org 🎟 Free 🕐 Closed early Oct.–Apr.

★ Winslow Homer Studio

HOUSE | **FAMILY** | The great American landscape painter created many of his best-known works in this seaside home between 1883 until his death in 1910. It's easy to see how this rocky, jagged peninsula might have been inspiring. The only way to get a look is on a tour with the Portland Museum of Art, which leads 2½-hour strolls through the historic property. ✉ *5 Winslow Homer Rd., Scarborough* ☎ *207/775–6148* 🌐 *www.portlandmuseum.org* 🎟 *$65* 🕐 *Closed Nov.–Apr.*

🍴 Restaurants

★ Bite Into Maine

$$ | **SEAFOOD** | **FAMILY** | Hands down Maine's best lobster roll is found at this food truck that overlooks the idyllic Portland Head Light in Cape Elizabeth. Traditional lobster rolls smothered in ungodly amounts of drawn butter are delicious, but you've also got the option to get out of the lobster comfort zone with rolls featuring flavors like wasabi, curry, and chipotle, as well as a toothsome lobster BLT. **Known for:** quick bite; dining with a view over the ocean; always fresh lobster. [$] *Average main: $18* ✉ *1000 Shore Rd.* ☎ *207/289–6142* 🌐 *www.biteintomaine.com* 🕐 *Closed mid-Oct.–mid-Apr.*

The Lobster Shack at Two Lights

$$ | **SEAFOOD** | **FAMILY** | A classic spot since the 1920s, you can't beat the location—right on the water, below the lighthouse pair that gives Two Lights State Park its name—and the food's not bad either. Enjoy fresh lobster whole or piled into a hot-dog bun with a dollop of mayo, or opt for the delicious chowder, fried clams, or fish-and-chips. **Known for:** seafood boats; family-friendly environment; mini-homemade blueberry pies. [$] *Average main: $18* ✉ *225 Two Lights Rd.* ☎ *207/799–1677* 🌐 *www.lobstershacktwolights.com* 🕐 *Closed late Oct.–late Mar.*

★ Shade Eatery at Higgins Beach

$$ | **SEAFOOD** | **FAMILY** | This charming neighborhood restaurant and bar just steps from the beach serves up generous, deeply satisfying dishes filled with locally sourced ingredients. Seafood plays a big role in the menu, with unholy lobster rolls brimming with fresh meat; fish tacos stuffed with cilantro, lime crema, and coleslaw; a Portuguese seafood stew; and crispy calamari. **Known for:** family-friendly environment; three-season-porch dining; $1 freshly shucked oysters during happy hour. [$] *Average main: $20* ✉ *Higgins Beach Inn, 36 Ocean Ave., Scarborough* ☎ *207/883–6684* 🌐 *www.higginsbeachinn.com/shade.*

🛏 Hotels

Black Point Inn

$$$$ | **RESORT** | **FAMILY** | Toward the tip of the peninsula that juts into the ocean at Prout's Neck stands this stylish, tastefully updated 1878 resort inn with spectacular views up and down the coast. **Pros:** dramatic setting; geothermally heated pool; discounts in shoulder seasons. **Cons:** non-Atlantic view a little underwhelming with buildings on the horizon; rooms have an older, more stately feel to them; children are asked to only eat in pub area. [$] *Rooms from: $490* ✉ *510 Black Point Rd., Scarborough* ☎ *207/883–2500* 🌐 *www.blackpointinn.com* 🕐 *Closed late Oct.–early May* 🛏 *25 rooms* 🍽 *Free breakfast.*

★ Higgins Beach Inn

$ | **B&B/INN** | Decidedly "new Maine," this lovingly renovated inn with a laid-back, beach-hair-don't care kind of nonchalance is just steps from the surfer's paradise that is Higgins Beach. **Pros:** newly renovated; exceptionally efficient and warm service; small touches that make a difference, such as beach towels and a sparkling water dispenser. **Cons:** no pets allowed; a short walk to the beach; limited common areas. $ *Rooms from: $199* ✉ *34 Ocean Ave., Scarborough* ☎ *207/883–6684* ⊕ *www.higginsbeach-inn.com* ⊗ *Closed Oct.–Apr.* ⤳ *23 rooms* ⊚ *Free breakfast.*

★ **Inn by the Sea**

$$$$ | **B&B/INN** | With some of the highest-quality, gracious service in the state and a top-notch restaurant that delights at every meal, you'll never want to leave the aptly named Inn by the Sea, which is set on Cape Elizabeth's stunning Crescent Beach. **Pros:** your wish is their command; hands down the most dog-friendly accommodations in Maine; direct access to Crescent Beach with chic beach chairs, towels, and umbrellas at hand; native plants garden; gourmet menu for dogs. **Cons:** a short distance from Portland's food scene; not for the budget-minded; minimum stays in the high season. $ *Rooms from: $580* ✉ *40 Bowery Beach Rd.* ☎ *207/799–3134* ⊕ *www.innbythesea.com* ⤳ *61 rooms* ⊚ *No meals.*

Portland

28 miles from Kennebunk via I–95 and I–295.

Maine's largest city may be considered small by national standards—its population is just 66,000—but its character, spirit, and appeal make it feel much larger. It's well worth at least a day or two of exploration, even if all you do is spend the entire time eating and drinking at the many phenomenal restaurants, bakeries and specialty dessert shops, craft cocktail bars, and microbreweries scattered across the city. Work up your appetite roaming the working waterfront and strolling the Eastern Promenade, shopping in the boutiques along the brick streets of the Old Port, or sauntering through the galleries of its top-notch art museum.

A city of many names throughout its history, including Casco and Falmouth, Portland has survived many dramatic transformations, the most recent of which is the massive influx of hipsters and foodies who have opened up artisanal bars and quirky boutiques that are rapidly changing the city's character. Sheltered by the nearby Casco Bay Islands and blessed with a deep port, Portland was a significant settlement right from its start in the early 17th century. Settlers thrived on fishing and lumbering, repeatedly building up the area while the British, French, and Native Americans continually sacked it. Many considered the region a somewhat dangerous frontier, but its potential for prosperity was so apparent that settlers came anyway to tap its rich natural resources.

In 1632 Portland's first home was built on the Portland Peninsula in the area now known as Munjoy Hill. The British burned the city in 1775, when residents refused to surrender arms, but it was rebuilt and became a major trading center. Much of Portland was destroyed again in the Great Fire on July 4, 1866, when a flicked ash or perhaps a celebratory firecracker started a fire in a boatyard that grew into conflagration; 1,500 buildings burned to the ground.

GETTING HERE AND AROUND

From Interstate 95, take Interstate 295 to get to the Portland Peninsula and downtown. Commercial Street runs along the harbor, Fore Street is one block up in the heart of the Old Port, and the Arts District stretches along diagonal Congress Street. Munjoy Hill is on the eastern end of the peninsula and the West End on the opposite side.

ESSENTIALS
RESTAURANTS

America's "Foodiest Small Town" is how one magazine described Portland, which is practically bursting at the seams with fabulous restaurants to rival those of a major metropolis. It's worth it to

Portland's busy harbor is full of working boats, pleasure craft, and ferries headed to the Casco Bay Islands.

splurge and try as many as possible while visiting. Fresh seafood, including the famous Maine lobster, is still popular and prevalent, but it is being served up in unexpected ways that are a far cry from the usual bib and butter. There is a broad spectrum of cuisines to be enjoyed, and many chefs are pushing the envelope in their reinventions of traditional culinary idioms. More and more restaurants are using local meats, seafood, and organic produce as much as possible; changing menus reflect what is available in the region at the moment. Even the many excellent food trucks that have popped up across the city—several of which remain open in the off-season—reflect this trend. As sophisticated as many of these establishments have become in the way of food and service, the atmosphere is generally laid-back; with a few exceptions, you can leave your jacket and tie at home—just not your appetite.
■ TIP→ Smoking is banned in all restaurants, taverns, and bars in Maine.

HOTELS

As Portland's popularity as a vacation destination has increased, so have its options for overnight visitors. Though several large hotels—geared toward high-tech, amenity-obsessed guests—have been built in the Old Port, they have in no way diminished the success of smaller, more intimate lodgings. Inns and B&Bs have taken up residence throughout the West End, often giving new life to the grand mansions of Portland's wealthy 19th-century merchants. For the least expensive accommodations, you'll find chain hotels near the interstate and the airport.

Expect to pay at least $150 or so per night for a pleasant room (often with complimentary breakfast) within walking distance of the Old Port during high season, and more than $400 for the most luxurious of suites. At the height of summer, many places are booked; make reservations well in advance, and ask about off-season specials.

Cannabis in Vacationland

Though Maine voters approved legalizing the recreational use and sales of marijuana in November 2016, various delays prevented retail shops from opening until October 2020. Many of the initial license applications were from retailers in the Greater Portland area, but availability is expected to expand statewide (note that individual communities can decide whether to allow sales). Check in with the Maine Office of Marijuana Policy (☎ 207/287–3282 ⊕ www.maine.gov/dafs/omp) for information on availability and rules and regulations.

NIGHTLIFE

Portland's nightlife scene is largely centered on the bustling Old Port and a few smaller, artsy spots on Congress Street. There's a great emphasis on live music from local bands and pubs serving award-winning local microbrews. Several hip bars have cropped up, serving appetizers along with a full array of specialty wines and serious craft cocktails. Portland is a fairly sleepy city after midnight, but you can usually find a couple of bars and restaurants open, even after the clock strikes 12.

PERFORMING ARTS

Art galleries and studios have spread throughout the city, infusing many beautiful, old abandoned buildings and shops with new life. Many are concentrated along the Congress Street downtown corridor; others are hidden amid the boutiques and restaurants of the Old Port and the East End. A great way to get acquainted with the city's artists is to participate in the First Friday Art Walk, a free self-guided tour of galleries, museums, and alternative-art venues that happens—you guessed it—on the first Friday of each month.

SHOPPING

Exchange Street is great for arts and crafts and boutique browsing, while Commercial Street caters to the souvenir hound—gift shops are packed with nautical items, and lobster and moose emblems are emblazoned on everything from T-shirts to shot glasses.

ACTIVITIES

When the weather's good, everyone in Portland heads outside, whether for boating on the water, lounging on a beach, or walking and biking the promenades. There are also many green spaces nearby Portland, including Crescent Beach State Park, Two Lights State Park, and Fort Williams Park, home to Portland Head Light. All are on the coast south of the city in suburban Cape Elizabeth and offer walking trails, picnic facilities, and water access.

Various Portland-based skippers offer whale-, dolphin-, and seal-watching cruises; excursions to lighthouses and islands; and fishing and lobstering trips. Board the ferry to see nearby islands. Self-navigators can rent kayaks or canoes.

TOURS
BUS TOURS
Portland Discovery Land and Sea Tours
BUS TOURS | FAMILY | The informative trolley tours of Portland Discovery detail the city's historical and architectural highlights, Memorial Day–October. Options include combining a city tour with a bay or lighthouse cruise. ⊠ Long Wharf, 170 Commercial St. ☎ 207/774–0808 ⊕ www.portlanddiscovery.com ⌨ From $23.

WALKING TOURS
Greater Portland Landmarks
WALKING TOURS | **FAMILY** | Take 1½-hour walking tours of Portland's historic West End June–October, with Greater Portland Landmarks. Tours past the neighborhood's Greek Revival mansions and grand Federal-style homes begin at the group's headquarters and cost $10. You can also pick up maps for self-guided tours of the Old Port or the Western Promenade. ⌧ *93 High St.* ☎ *207/774–5561* ⊕ *www.portlandlandmarks.org* 🎫 *From $10.*

Maine Foodie Tours
SPECIAL-INTEREST | Learn about Portland's culinary history and sample local delights like lobster hors d'oeuvres, organic cheese, and the famous Maine whoopie pie. The culinary walking tours include stops at fishmongers, bakeries, and cheese shops that provide products to Portland's famed restaurants. From summer into early fall, you can also take a chocolate tour, a bike-and-brewery tour, or a trolley tour with a stop at a microbrewery. Tours begin at various locales in the Old Port. ⌧ *Portland* ☎ *207/233–7485* ⊕ *www.mainefoodietours.com* 🎫 *From $29.*

Portland Freedom Trail
SELF-GUIDED | **FAMILY** | The Portland Freedom Trail offers a self-guided tour of sites associated with the Underground Railroad and the antislavery movement. ⌧ *Portland* ⊕ *www.mainehistory.org/ PDF/walkingtourmap.pdf* 🎫 *Free.*

VISITOR INFORMATION
CONTACTS Downtown Portland. ☎ *207/772–6828* ⊕ *www.portlandmaine. com.* **Greater Portland Convention and Visitors Bureau.** ☎ *207/772–4994* ⊕ *www. visitportland.com.*

The Old Port and the Waterfront

A major international port and a working harbor since the early 17th century, Portland's Old Port and the Waterfront bridge the gap between the city's historic commercial activities and those of today. It is home to fishing boats docked alongside whale-watching charters, luxury yachts, cruise ships, and oil tankers from around the globe. Commercial Street parallels the water and is lined with brick buildings and warehouses that were built following the Great Fire of 1866. In the 19th century, candle makers and sail stitchers plied their trades here; today specialty shops, art galleries, and restaurants have taken up residence.

As with much of the city, it's best to park your car and explore the Old Port on foot. You can park at the city garage on Fore Street (between Exchange and Union streets) or opposite the U.S. Custom House at the corner of Fore and Pearl Streets. A helpful hint: look for the "Park & Shop" sign on garages and parking lots, and get one hour of free parking for each stamp collected at participating shops. Allow a couple of hours to wander at leisure on Market, Exchange, Middle, and Fore streets. The city is very pedestrian-friendly. Maine state law requires vehicles to stop for pedestrians in crosswalks.

◉ Sights

Harbor Fish Market
STORE/MALL | A Portland favorite since 1968, this freshest-of-the-fresh seafood market ships lobsters and other Maine delectables almost anywhere in the country. A bright-red facade on a working wharf opens into a bustling space with bubbling lobster tanks and fish, clams, and other shellfish on ice; employees are as skilled with a fillet knife as sushi

chefs. There is also a small retail store. ⊠ *9 Custom House Wharf, The Old Port and the Waterfront* ☎ *207/775–0251* ⊕ *www.harborfish.com* ⊠ *Free.*

Portland Fish Exchange

FISH HATCHERY | You may want to hold your nose as you take a dip into the Old Port's active fish business at the 20,000-square-foot Portland Fish Exchange. Peek inside coolers teeming with cod, flounder, and monkfish, and watch fishermen repairing nets outside. ⊠ *6 Portland Fish Pier, The Old Port and the Waterfront* ☎ *207/773–0017* ⊕ *www. pfex.org* ⊠ *Free.*

 Restaurants

Becky's Diner

$ | **DINER** | **FAMILY** | You won't find a more local or unfussy place—or one more abuzz with conversation at 4 am—than this waterfront institution way down on the end of Commercial Street. The food is cheap, generous in proportion, and has that satisfying, old-time-diner quality. **Known for:** classic Maine diner food featuring many seafood dishes; very lively atmosphere comingling locals and visitors; parking is easy—a rarity in Portland. $ *Average main: $14* ⊠ *390 Commercial St., The Old Port and the Waterfront* ☎ *207/773–7070* ⊕ *www. beckysdiner.com.*

★ Blyth & Burrows

$ | **CONTEMPORARY** | There are craft cocktails and there is Blyth and Burrows, where the alchemy of spirits is taken to the next level with creative concoctions that include the unholy integration of gorgeous (albeit unusual) ingredients such as absinthe foam, house-made black-lime cordial, blackstrap maple-chipotle syrup, and uncommon liqueurs and spirits. Delicious small plates, like lobster rolls, oysters on the half shell, tenderloin and chimichurri, and local meat and cheese boards keep you from falling

under the table. **Known for:** knock-you-under-the-table cocktails; nautical-theme atmosphere filled with antique ships and mermaid figureheads; food that goes well with cocktails. $ *Average main: $12* ⊠ *26 Exchange St., The Old Port and the Waterfront* ☎ *207/613–9070* ⊕ *www. blythandburrows.com.*

★ Fore Street

$$$ | **MODERN AMERICAN** | One of Maine's best chefs, Sam Hayward, opened this restaurant in a renovated warehouse on the edge of the Old Port in 1996; today every copper-top table in the main dining room has a view of the enormous brick oven and soapstone hearth that anchor the open kitchen. The menu changes daily to reflect the freshest ingredients from Maine's farms and waters, as well as the tremendous creativity of the staff. **Known for:** Turnspit roasted meats; handmade charcuterie; last-minute planners take heart: a third of the tables are reserved for walk-ins. $ *Average main: $30* ⊠ *288 Fore St., The Old Port and the Waterfront* ☎ *207/775–2717* ⊕ *www.forestreet.biz* ⊙ *No lunch.*

Gilbert's Chowder House

$$ | **SEAFOOD** | **FAMILY** | This is the real deal, as quintessential as old-school Maine dining can be. Clam rakes and nautical charts hang from the walls of this unpretentious waterfront diner, and the flavors come from the depths of the North Atlantic, prepared and presented simply: fried scallops, haddock, clams and extraordinary clam cakes, and fish, clam, and seafood chowders (corn, too). **Known for:** family-friendly environment; classic lobster rolls, served on toasted hot-dog buns bursting with claw and tail meat; an ice-cream parlor to round out your meal; chalkboard daily specials. $ *Average main: $19* ⊠ *92 Commercial St., The Old Port and the Waterfront* ☎ *207/871–5636* ⊕ *www.gilbertschowderhouse.com.*

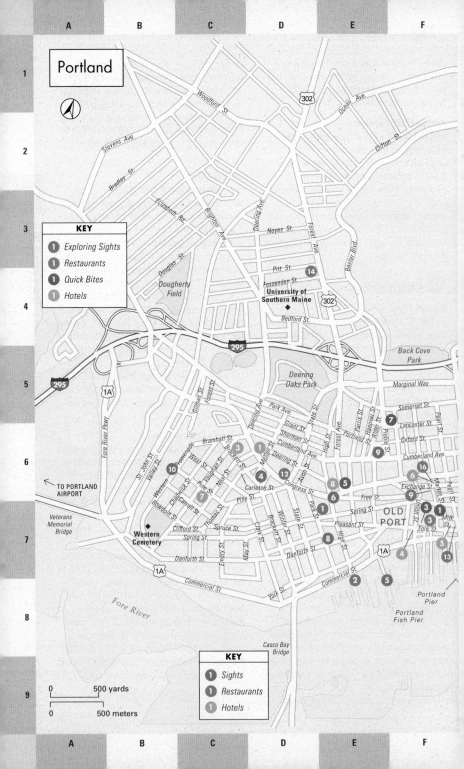

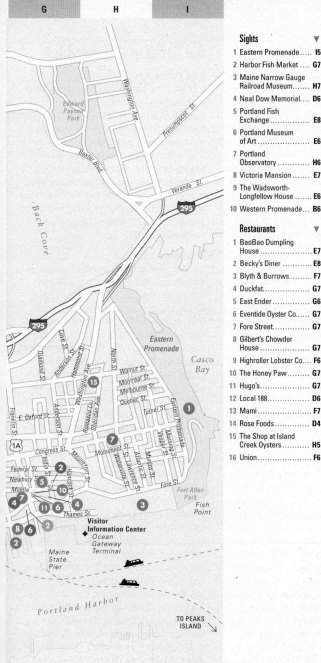

Sights ▼

1 Eastern Promenade I5
2 Harbor Fish Market G7
3 Maine Narrow Gauge Railroad Museum H7
4 Neal Dow Memorial D6
5 Portland Fish Exchange E8
6 Portland Museum of Art E6
7 Portland Observatory H6
8 Victoria Mansion E7
9 The Wadsworth-Longfellow House E6
10 Western Promenade ... B6

Restaurants ▼

1 BaoBao Dumpling House E7
2 Becky's Diner E8
3 Blyth & Burrows F7
4 Duckfat. G7
5 East Ender G6
6 Eventide Oyster Co. G7
7 Fore Street G7
8 Gilbert's Chowder House G7
9 Highroller Lobster Co. ... F6
10 The Honey Paw G7
11 Hugo's G7
12 Local 188 .... D6
13 Mami F7
14 Rose Foods D4
15 The Shop at Island Creek Oysters H5
16 Union F6

Quick Bites ▼

1 Bard Coffee. F7
2 Coffee by Design. G6
3 Gelato Fiasco. F7
4 The Holy Donut G7
5 Speckled Ax Wood Roasted Coffee E6
6 Standard Baking G7
7 Two Fat Cats Bakery F5

Hotels ▼

1 The Francis D6
2 Hilton Garden Inn Portland Downtown Waterfront G7
3 Morrill Mansion C6
4 Portland Harbor Hotel ... F7
5 The Portland Regency Hotel and Spa F7
6 The Press Hotel F6
7 West End Inn C6
8 The Westin Portland Harborview E6

Highroller Lobster Co.

$ | SEAFOOD | Opened in early 2018, this high-energy spot serves lobster numerous ways—in a roll, on a stick, on a burger, over a salad, or even with your Bloody Mary. If you're feeling adventurous, try one of the sauces (lime mayo, lobster ghee) on your roll, and wash it all down with a beer from the ever-changing menu, which depends on availability from local breweries. **Known for:** origins as a food cart; the lobby pop (a lobster tail on a stick); Highroller whoopie pies baked by the owner's mom. $ *Average main: $15* ✉ *104 Exchange St., The Old Port and the Waterfront* ☎ *207/536–1623* ⊕ *highrollerlobster.com.*

★ Mami

$ | JAPANESE | Japanese street food takes center stage at this cozy locale. The menu rotates regularly, but you're likely to find uncommon takes on burgers and soba noodles as well as some form of *okonomiyaki*—a savory pancake filled with crazy-delicious flavor and texture combinations. **Known for:** ramen; steamed buns; grilled rice balls. $ *Average main: $15* ✉ *339 Fore St., The Old Port and the Waterfront* ☎ *207/536–4702* ⊕ *mamiportland.com* ⊘ *Closed Sun. and Mon.*

★ Union

$$$ | AMERICAN | FAMILY | In the Press Hotel, Union Restaurant has a sophisticated but not stuffy air that is reflected in its menu, which focuses on local ingredients, many of which are foraged and fished, or gathered from its basement greenhouse. Most dishes are modern comfort food; breakfast and brunch are a treat: you'll find maple *pain perdu* served alongside smoked-salmon tartines and classic dishes like eggs Benedict. **Known for:** sustainable ingredients; decadent "chef's table," a multicourse meal with wine pairings and the chef's choice; signature truffle beef pot roast. $ *Average main: $30* ✉ *Press Hotel, 390 Congress St., The Old Port and the Waterfront* ☎ *207/808–8700* ⊕ *www.unionportland.com.*

☕ Coffee and Quick Bites

Bard Coffee

$ | CAFÉ | The beans sourcing this shop's delicious brew are bought from a handful of small growers—you can read their bios on the website—and roasted in-house. Enjoy your brew hot, cold, or iced with a locally made baked good. **Known for:** close relationships with sources; passionate, knowledgeable baristas; bulk coffee and tea. $ *Average main: $5* ✉ *185 Middle St., The Old Port and the Waterfront* ☎ *207/899–4788* ⊕ *www.bardcoffee.com.*

★ Gelato Fiasco

$ | CAFÉ | FAMILY | Proper Italian gelato and *sorbetto* here come in traditional flavors as well as more offbeat varieties like torched marshmallow s'more, mascarpone pistachio caramel, and mint brownie cookie. There are new flavors every day, along with espresso and other hot drinks. **Known for:** you can try every single flavor before deciding on what you'll get; long lines out the door in the summer; multigenerational bonding spot. $ *Average main: $5* ✉ *425 Fore St., The Old Port and the Waterfront* ☎ *207/699–4314* ⊕ *www.gelatofiasco.com.*

The Holy Donut

$ | CAFÉ | FAMILY | Don't pass up a chance to try these sweet and savory, all-natural, Maine potato-based doughnuts glazed in flavors such as dark chocolate-sea salt, maple, pomegranate, triple berry, and chai, or stuffed with delicious fillings like bacon and cheddar, or ricotta. There are always new inventions, too, such as salted chocolate caramel and key lime pie. **Known for:** long lines, but worth the wait; shop closes for the day once all the doughnuts are sold; vegan and gluten-free options are available. $ *Average main: $5* ✉ *7 Exchange St., The Old Port and the Waterfront* ☎ *207/775–7776* ⊕ *www.theholydonut.com.*

★ Standard Baking

$ | **BAKERY** | **FAMILY** | You'd be hard-pressed to find a more pitch-perfect bakery in the Pine Tree State, but you'll have to pop by early (or put in an order in advance) to get your mitts on these delectable baked goods. The perfectly airy croissants, crusty baguettes, beguiling tarts, dainty madeleines, and creative breads incorporate locally sourced grains and are nothing short of revelations. **Known for:** good selection of locally roasted coffees; amazing galettes and brioches; creative scones. $ *Average main: $3* ⊠ *75 Commercial St., The Old Port and the Waterfront* ☎ *207/772–5519* ⊕ *www. standardbakingco.com.*

🛏 Hotels

Hilton Garden Inn Portland Downtown Waterfront

$$$ | **HOTEL** | This bright, clean, and modern hotel is a perfect base for exploring on foot the adjacent Old Port and nearby East End, and it's only a walk across the street to catch a ferry to the Casco Bay islands. **Pros:** heated salt water lap pool; central location for exploring; some rooms with harbor view. **Cons:** no pets; no self-parking; some rooms face neighboring businesses. $ *Rooms from: $379* ⊠ *65 Commercial St., The Old Port and the Waterfront* ☎ *207/780–0780* ⊕ *www. hilton.com/en/hilton-garden-inn* ⤴ *120 rooms* ❘❍❘ *No meals.*

Portland Harbor Hotel

$$ | **HOTEL** | Extensively renovated in 2017, this nautically-themed hotel is in walking distance of both the waterfront and the Old Port. **Pros:** amid the action of the Old Port; pet-friendly ($50 per pet fee); courtesy car covers 4-mile radius. **Cons:** no pool; rooms facing Union Street pick up lively street noise; no water view. $ *Rooms from: $299* ⊠ *468 Fore St., The Old Port and the Waterfront* ☎ *207/775–9090, 888/798–9090* ⊕ *www.portlandharborhotel.com* ⤴ *101 rooms* ❘❍❘ *No meals.*

The Portland Regency Hotel and Spa

$$$ | **HOTEL** | Not part of a chain despite the "Regency" name, this brick building in the center of the Old Port served as Portland's armory in the late 19th century. **Pros:** easy walk to sites; pet-friendly ($75 nonrefundable cleaning fee); full-service spa with lounges, saunas, steam rooms, hot tub, and an array of luxurious treatments. **Cons:** no pool; busy downtown location; not all rooms have noteworthy views. $ *Rooms from: $300* ⊠ *20 Milk St., The Old Port and the Waterfront* ☎ *207/774–4200, 800/727–3436* ⊕ *www.theregency.com* ⤴ *95 rooms* ❘❍❘ *No meals.*

★ The Press Hotel

$$$ | **HOTEL** | **FAMILY** | In a former newspaper building, this boutique hotel is part of Marriott's Autograph Collection; the hotel feels both broadly cosmopolitan and distinctly Maine. **Pros:** Frette bed linens and Maine-made Cuddledown comforters and bed throws; sparkling-clean rooms with a modern-design feel; art gallery and excellent public spaces with tasteful furnishings. **Cons:** right next to the fire department; valet parking can be expensive; some rooms have underwhelming views. $ *Rooms from: $375* ⊠ *119 Exchange St., The Old Port and the Waterfront* ☎ *877/890–5641* ⊕ *www.thepresshotel. com* ⤴ *110 rooms* ❘❍❘ *No meals.*

🍸 Nightlife

Bull Feeney's

BARS/PUBS | For nightly specials, plenty of Guinness, and live entertainment, head to Bull Feeney's, a lively two-story Irish pub and restaurant. ⊠ *375 Fore St., The Old Port and the Waterfront* ☎ *207/773–7210* ⊕ *bullfeeneys.com.*

Gritty McDuff's Portland Brew Pub

BARS/PUBS | Maine's original brewpub serves fine ales, British pub fare, and seafood dishes. There are between six and eight rotating ales on tap, and there's always a seasonal offering. ⊠ *396 Fore*

St., The Old Port and the Waterfront ☎ 207/772–2739 ⊕ www.grittys.com.

★ Novare Res Bier Café

BARS/PUBS | At tucked-away Novare Res Bier Café, choose from some three dozen rotating drafts and about 500 bottled brews. Relax on an expansive deck, munch on antipasti, or share a meat-and-cheese plate. Maine craft beers occupy at least eight of the taps at any given time, and the rest span the globe, with an emphasis on Belgian and Trappist ales. ⊠ 4 Canal Plaza, off Exchange St., The Old Port and the Waterfront ☎ 207/761–2437 ⊕ www.novareresbiercafe.com.

★ Portland Hunt and Alpine Club

BARS/PUBS | Scandinavian-inspired dishes and serious craft cocktails drive this hip locale that includes excellent charcuterie and seafood boards in an intimate alpine-style hut. Go for the excellent happy hour, weekdays 1–6. ⊠ 75 Market St., The Old Port and the Waterfront ☎ 207/747–4754 ⊕ www.huntandalpineclub.com.

Vena's Fizz House

BARS/PUBS | The old-fashioned soda fountain gets a modern update at Vena's Fizz House, where flavors like cucumber mint, chocolate-cherry cordial, and frothy blood orange go into delicious, fizzy "mocktails," while the cocktails feature artisanal ingredients such as Maine pine bitters, saffron syrup, and ghost pepper extract. ⊠ 345 Fore St., The Old Port and the Waterfront ☎ 207/747–4901 ⊕ www.venasfizzhouse.com.

🛍 Shopping

ACCESSORIES
★ Sea Bags

SPECIALTY STORES | At Sea Bags, totes made from recycled sailcloth and decorated with bright, graphic patterns are sewn right in the store. ⊠ 25 Custom House Wharf, The Old Port and the Waterfront ☎ 207/780–0744 ⊕ www.seabags.com.

ART AND ANTIQUES
Abacus Gallery

ANTIQUES/COLLECTIBLES | This appealing crafts gallery has gift items in glass, wood, and textiles, as well as fine modern jewelry. ⊠ 44 Exchange St., The Old Port and the Waterfront ☎ 207/772–4880 ⊕ www.abacusgallery.com.

Greenhut Galleries

ANTIQUES/COLLECTIBLES | The contemporary art at this gallery changes with the seasons. Artists represented include David Driskell, an artist and leading art scholar. ⊠ 146 Middle St., The Old Port and the Waterfront ☎ 207/772–2693 ⊕ www.greenhutgalleries.com.

BOOKS
Longfellow Books

BOOKS/STATIONERY | This shop is known for its good service, author readings, and excellent selection of new and used books and magazines. Even if you go in looking for something specific, you'll almost certainly stumble on something even better you didn't know about before. ⊠ 1 Monument Way, The Old Port and the Waterfront ☎ 207/772–4045 ⊕ www.longfellowbooks.com.

★ Sherman's Maine Coast Book Shops

BOOKS/STATIONERY | Open since 1886, Sherman's is Maine's oldest bookstore chain. The Portland store has an impressive stock of well-selected books interspersed with excellent gift choices, such as stationery, candles, and holiday decor, as well as a fun array of toys. It's a good place to spend a cold or rainy day perusing the selection. ⊠ 49 Exchange St., The Old Port and the Waterfront ☎ 207/773–4100 ⊕ www.shermans.com.

CLOTHING
★ Aristelle

CLOTHING | For the fanciest knickers in downtown Portland and one of the best bra fittings around head to Aristelle, purveyors of elegant undergarments and lingerie, as well as naughty little numbers that would make Bettie Page blush. ✉ *92 Exchange St., The Old Port and the Waterfront* ☎ *207/842–6000* ⊕ *www.aristelle.com.*

Bliss

CLOTHING | Hip boutique Bliss stocks clothing and accessories by cutting-edge designers, plus jeans by big names like J Brand and Mother. There's also a great selection of Frye boots. ✉ *58 Exchange St., The Old Port and the Waterfront* ☎ *207/879–7125* ⊕ *www.blissboutiques. com.*

Joseph's

CLOTHING | A smart menswear boutique (and mainstay of the Old Port) that will have you looking suave in no time. ✉ *410 Fore St., The Old Port and the Waterfront* ☎ *207/773–1274* ⊕ *www.josephsofport-land.com.*

★ Judith

CLOTHING | Owned and operated by a former fashion designer, this stunning, well-curated concept boutique features women's apparel, shoes, accessories, and contemporary housewares. ✉ *131 Middle St., The Old Port and the Water-front* ☎ *207/747–4778* ⊕ *www.shopju-dith.com.*

HOME AND GIFTS

Asia West

HOUSEHOLD ITEMS/FURNITURE | For repro-duction and antique furnishings with a Far East feel, head to this stylish show-room on the waterfront. ✉ *128 Cassidy Point Dr., The Old Port and the Waterfront* ☎ *207/775–0066* ⊕ *www.asiawest.net.*

Lisa Marie's Made in Maine

GIFTS/SOUVENIRS | Here you'll find an excellent selection of locally sourced items from soaps and candles to dish towels, pottery, and jewelry, all made in the great state of Maine. ✉ *35 Exchange St., The Old Port and the Waterfront* ☎ *207/828–1515* ⊕ *www.lisamariesma-deinmaine.com.*

TOYS

★ Treehouse Toys

TOYS | FAMILY | An instant mood-lifter, this shop is chock-full of offbeat toys and novelty items that are certain to delight children of all ages. ✉ *47 Exchange St., The Old Port and the Waterfront* ☎ *207/775–6133* ⊕ *www.treehousetoys. us.*

🏃 Activities

BIKING

Portland Trails

BICYCLING | FAMILY | For local biking and hiking information, contact Portland Trails. The staff can tell you about designated paved and unpaved routes that wind along the water, through parks, and beyond. ✉ *305 Commercial St., The Old Port and the Waterfront* ☎ *207/775–2411* ⊕ *www.trails.org.*

BOATING

Casco Bay Lines

BOATING | FAMILY | Casco Bay Lines operates ferry service to the seven bay islands with year-round populations. Summer offerings include music cruises, lighthouse excursions, and a trip to Bailey Island with a stopover for lunch. ✉ *Maine State Pier, 56 Commercial St., The Old Port and the Waterfront* ☎ *207/774–7871* ⊕ *www.cascobaylines.com.*

Lucky Catch Cruises

BOATING | FAMILY | Set sail in a real lobster boat: this company gives you the genuine experience, which includes hauling traps and the chance to purchase the catch. ✉ *Long Wharf, 170 Commercial St., The Old Port and the Waterfront* ☎ *207/761–0941* ⊕ *www.luckycatch.com.*

Odyssey Whale Watch

BOATING | FAMILY | From mid-May to mid-October, Odyssey Whale Watch leads whale-watching and deep-sea-fishing excursions. ✉ *Long Wharf, 170 Commercial St., The Old Port and the Waterfront* ☎ *207/775–0727* ⊕ *www. odysseywhalewatch.com.*

Portland Discovery Land & Sea Tours

TOUR—SPORTS | FAMILY | For tours of the harbor and Casco Bay in a boat or on a trolley, including an up-close look at several lighthouses, try Portland Discovery Land & Sea Tours. ⊠ *Long Wharf, 170 Commercial St., The Old Port and the Waterfront* ☎ 207/774–0808 ⊕ *www. portlanddiscovery.com.*

★ Portland Schooner Co.

TOUR—SPORTS | FAMILY | May through October this company offers daily two-hour windjammer cruises aboard the vintage schooners *Bagheera, Timberwind,* and *Wendameen.* You can also arrange private charters. ⊠ *Maine State Pier, 56 Commercial St., The Old Port and the Waterfront* ☎ 207/766–2500 ⊕ *www. portlandschooner.com.*

The Arts District

This district starts at the top of Exchange Street, near the upper end of the Old Port, and extends west past the Portland Museum of Art. The district's central artery is Congress Street, which is lined with art galleries, specialty stores, and a score of restaurants and cafés. Parking is tricky; two-hour meters dot the sidewalks, but there are several garages nearby.

◉ Sights

Neal Dow Memorial

HOUSE | The mansion, once a stop on the Underground Railroad, was the home of Civil War general Neal Dow, who became known as the "Father of Prohibition." He was responsible for Maine's adoption of the anti-alcohol bill in 1851, which spurred a nationwide temperance movement. Now a museum, this majestic 1829 Federal-style home is open for guided tours that start on the hour. ⊠ *714 Congress St., Arts District* ☎ 207/773–7773 ⊕ *www.nealdowmemorial.org* ⊠ *$10.*

★ Portland Museum of Art

MUSEUM | Maine's largest public art institution's collection includes fine seascapes and landscapes by Winslow Homer, John Marin, Andrew Wyeth, Edward Hopper, Marsden Hartley, and other American painters. Homer's *Weatherbeaten,* a quintessential Maine Coast image, is here, and the museum owns and displays, on a rotating basis, 16 more of his paintings, plus more than 400 of his illustrations (and it offers tours of the Winslow Homer Studio in nearby Prouts Neck). The museum has works by Monet and Picasso, as well as Degas, Renoir, and Chagall. I. M. Pei's colleague Henry Cobb designed the strikingly modern Charles Shipman Payson building. ⊠ *7 Congress Sq., Arts District* ☎ 207/775–6148 ⊕ *www.portlandmuseum.org* ⊠ *$18 (free Fri. 10–8).*

Victoria Mansion

HOUSE | Built between 1858 and 1860, this Italianate mansion is widely regarded as the most sumptuously ornamented dwelling of its period remaining in the country. Architect Henry Austin designed the house for hotelier Ruggles Morse and his wife, Olive. The interior design—everything from the plasterwork to the furniture (much of it original)—is the only surviving commission of New York designer Gustave Herter. Behind the elegant brownstone exterior of this National Historic Landmark are colorful frescoed walls and ceilings, ornate marble mantelpieces, gilded gas chandeliers, a magnificent 6-foot-by-25-foot stained-glass ceiling window, and a freestanding mahogany staircase. A guided tour runs about 45 minutes and covers all the architectural highlights. Victorian era–themed gifts and art are sold in the museum shop, and the museum often has special theme events. ⊠ *109 Danforth St., Arts District* ☎ 207/772–4841 ⊕ *www.victoriamansion.org* ⊠ *$18* ☉ *Closed mid-Jan.–Apr.*

The Wadsworth–Longfellow House

HOUSE | The boyhood home of the famous American poet was the first brick house in Portland and the oldest building on the peninsula. It's particularly interesting, because most of the furnishings, including the young Longfellow's writing desk, are original. Wallpaper, window coverings, and a vibrant painted carpet are period reproductions. Built in 1785, the large dwelling (a third floor was added in 1815) sits back from the street and has a small portico over its entrance and four chimneys surmounting the roof. It's part of the Maine Historical Society, which includes an adjacent research library and a museum with exhibits about Maine life. After your guided tour, stay for a picnic in the Longfellow Garden; it's open to the public during museum hours. ✉ *489 Congress St., Arts District* ☎ *207/774–1822* 🌐 *www.mainehistory.org* 🎟 *House and museum $15, gardens free* 🕒 *Closed Nov.–Apr.*

🍴 Restaurants

Local 188

$$$ | **SPANISH** | There's an infectious vibe at this eclectic, Spanish-inspired Arts District hot spot that's accentuated by its 2,000-square-foot space, lofty tin ceilings, worn maple floors, and mismatched chandeliers. Regulars chat with servers about which just-caught seafood will decorate the paella or which organic veggies will star in the tortillas, one of several tapas choices. **Known for:** large bar area; some 150 different wines, mostly from Europe; a lively crowd and warm environment. [$] *Average main: $25* ✉ *685 Congress St., Arts District* ☎ *207/761–7909* 🌐 *www.local188.com* 🕒 *No lunch.*

☕ Coffee and Quick Bites

★ Speckled Ax Wood Roasted Coffee

$ | **CAFÉ** | The Speckled Ax serves up a seriously delicious coffee, whether cold brewed or piping hot with frothy milk. The secret to the richness of the beans is the painstaking roasting process, using a vintage Italian Petroncini roaster fired with local hardwood—ask to take a peek at that contraption while you wait for your drink. **Known for:** pastries and other baked goods; local gathering space; a hip vibe. [$] *Average main: $4* ✉ *567 Congress St., Arts District* ☎ *207/660–3333* 🌐 *www.speckledax.com.*

🛏 Hotels

The Westin Portland Harborview

$$ | **HOTEL** | This imposing structure was New England's largest hotel, the Eastland, when built in 1927 and is a well-known part of the Portland skyline. **Pros:** the views from the rooftop bar and lounge; pet friendly; on-site laundry. **Cons:** rooms with city views cost more; not all rooms have harbor views; often bustling with event attendees. [$] *Rooms from: $254* ✉ *157 High St., Arts District* ☎ *207/775–5411* 🌐 *www.marriott.com* 🛏 *289 rooms* 🍽 *No meals.*

🎭 Performing Arts

Merrill Auditorium

CONCERTS | **FAMILY** | This soaring concert hall hosts numerous theatrical and musical events, including performances by the Portland Symphony Orchestra and the Portland Opera Repertory Theatre. Ask about organ recitals on the auditorium's huge 1912 Kotzschmar Memorial Organ. ✉ *20 Myrtle St., Arts District* ☎ *207/842–0800* 🌐 *portlandmaine.gov/574/Merrill-Auditorium.*

Portland Stage

THEATER | **FAMILY** | This company mounts theatrical productions on its two stages September–May. ✉ *25-A Forest Ave., Arts District* ☎ *207/774–0465* 🌐 *www.portlandstage.org.*

Space Gallery
ART GALLERIES—ARTS | FAMILY | Space Gallery sparkles as a contemporary art gallery and alternative arts venue, opening its doors to everything from poetry readings and art fairs to live music to documentary films. The gallery is open Wednesday–Saturday. ⊠ *538 Congress St., Arts District* ☏ *207/828–5600* ⊕ *www.space538.org.*

🛍 Shopping

ART AND ANTIQUES
Portland Flea-for-All
ANTIQUES/COLLECTIBLES | FAMILY | Friday through Sunday, head to the city's Bayside neighborhood for the Portland Flea-for-All, where you'll find all sorts of vintage eye candy from an ever-rotating array of antiques and artisan vendors—a fun excursion, whether or not you actually buy anything. ⊠ *585 Congress St., Arts District* ☏ *207/370–7570* ⊕ *www.portlandfleaforall.com.*

Black Dinah Chocolatiers
FOOD/CANDY | Started on the tiny Isle au Haut, artful high-end chocolates and has a small café. ⊠ *The Westin Portland Harborview, 157 High St., Arts District.*

🏃 Activities

BIKING
Bicycle Coalition of Maine
BICYCLING | FAMILY | For state bike trail maps, club and tour listings, or hints on safety, contact the Bicycle Coalition of Maine. ⊠ *38 Diamond St., Arts District* ☏ *207/623–4511* ⊕ *www.bikemaine.org.*

Gorham Bike and Ski
BICYCLING | FAMILY | You can rent several types of bikes, including hybrid and electric models, starting at $35 per day. ⊠ *693 Congress St., Arts District* ☏ *207/773–1700* ⊕ *www.gorhambike.com.*

The East End

This neighborhood encompasses Munjoy Hill, the Eastern Promenade, East End Beach, and the Portland Observatory. It's an easy walk to the Old Port, and a great place to watch the harbor goings on, and see the July 4 fireworks.

👁 Sights

Eastern Promenade
HISTORIC SITE | FAMILY | Between the city's two promenades, this one, often overlooked by tourists, has by far the best view. Gracious Victorian homes, many now converted to condos and apartments, border one side of the street. On the other is 68 acres of hillside parkland that includes Ft. Allen Park and, at the base of the hill, the Eastern Prom Trail and tiny East End Beach and boat launch. On a sunny day the Eastern Prom is a lovely spot for picnicking and people-watching. ⊠ *Washington Ave. to Fore St., East End.*

Maine Narrow Gauge Railroad Museum
MUSEUM | FAMILY | Whether you're crazy about old trains or just want to see the sights from a different perspective, the railroad museum has an extensive collection of locomotives and rail coaches, and offers scenic tours on narrow-gauge railcars. The 3-mile jaunts run on the hour and take you along Casco Bay, at the foot of the Eastern Promenade. The operating season caps off with a fall harvest ride (complete with cider), and during the Christmas season there are special Polar Express rides, based on the popular children's book. ⊠ *58 Fore St., East End* ☏ *207/828–0814* ⊕ *www.mainenarrowgauge.org* 🎟 *Museum $5, train rides $12* ☉ *Closed Nov.–Apr.*

Portland Observatory
OBSERVATORY | FAMILY | This octagonal observatory on Munjoy Hill was built in 1807 by Captain Lemuel Moody, a retired sea captain, as a maritime signal tower.

Moody used a telescope to identify incoming ships, and flags to signal to merchants where to unload their cargo. Held in place by 122 tons of ballast, it's the last remaining historic maritime signal station in the country. The guided tour leads all the way to the dome, where you can step out on the deck and take in views of Portland, the islands, and inland toward the White Mountains. ✉ *138 Congress St., East End* ☎ *207/774–5561* 🌐 *www.portlandlandmarks.org* 🎟 *$10* 🕑 *Closed mid-Oct.–late May.*

🍴 Restaurants

Duckfat

$ | **MODERN AMERICAN** | Even in midafternoon, this small, hip panini-and-more shop in the Old Port is packed. The focus here is everyday farm-to-table fare: the signature Belgian fries are made with Maine potatoes cooked, yes, in duck fat and served in paper cones, and standards include meat loaf and the BGT (bacon, goat cheese, tomato). **Known for:** decadent poutine with duck-fat gravy; hopping atmosphere—waits for a table can be long; thick milk shakes prepared with local gelato by Gelato Fiasco. [$] *Average main: $12* ✉ *43 Middle St., East End* ☎ *207/774–8080* 🌐 *www.duckfat.com.*

★ East Ender

$$ | **AMERICAN** | **FAMILY** | The emphasis at this cozy neighborhood restaurant is on the superb food rather than the atmosphere, which isn't surprising, given that the owners formerly served their tasty, no-fuss fare from a truck. Lunch and dinner feature locally sourced, sustainable ingredients in dishes that reflect the seasons. **Known for:** mouthwatering house-smoked bacon; crispy, thrice-cooked fries; brunch cocktails that incorporate ingredients from local distilleries and house-made cordials. [$] *Average main: $24* ✉ *47 Middle St., East End* ☎ *207/879–7669* 🌐 *www.eastenderportland.com.*

★ Eventide Oyster Co

$ | **SEAFOOD** | Not only does Eventide have fresh, tasty oysters from all over Maine and New England, artfully prepared with novel accoutrements like kimchi, ginger ices, and cucumber-champagne mignonette, it also serves delicious crudos and ceviches with unique ingredients like blood orange and chili miso. The menu constantly changes, depending on what's in season, so it's best to order a handful of small plates, a glass of bubbly or one of the signature tiki-style cocktails, and, of course, a dozen oysters. **Known for:** brown-butter lobster rolls; a decent selection of alternatives for nonseafood lovers; teaming up with other local restaurants for special cook-offs and menus. [$] *Average main: $15* ✉ *86 Middle St., East End* ☎ *207/774–8538* 🌐 *www.eventideoysterco.com.*

The Honey Paw

$ | **ASIAN FUSION** | Come for the salty wontons, piping-hot broths, and wok-fried noodles; stay for the turntable music, the well-stocked cocktail bar, and the soft-serve ice cream that comes in flavors like orange curd, moxie, and charred corn. If you order one thing here, make it the lobster toast, topped with a scallop and lobster mousse, radish, lime, and an amazing tarragon emulsion. **Known for:** sister restaurant to Eventide Oyster Co.; house-made noodles; rotating wines on tap and an excellent selection of sake. [$] *Average main: $15* ✉ *7 Middle St., East End* ☎ *207/774–8538* 🌐 *www.thehoneypaw.com* 🕑 *Closed Tues.*

Hugo's

$$$ | **ECLECTIC** | Serving the freshest local, organic foods is a priority at Hugo's, and your server is sure to know everything about the various purveyors featured on the menu, which is updated daily and features smartly prepared, seasonally inspired dishes like crispy-skin pork belly and crepe-wrapped arctic char. You can choose five courses with a blind tasting menu for $90 or go à la carte—which could

be dangerous, as you may want to try everything on the creative menu. **Known for:** blind tasting menu; an open kitchen; dangerously delicious craft cocktails. $ *Average main: $28* ⊠ *88 Middle St., East End* ☎ *207/774–8538* ⊕ *www.hugos.net* ⊙ *Closed Sun. and Mon. No lunch.*

The Shop at Island Creek Oysters
$ | SEAFOOD | This no-fuss counter-service spot, opened by longtime wholesale purveyors of Island Creek Oysters (from Duxbury, MA), serves seriously fresh shellfish and excellent Maine microbrews (and wine) on tap. A clutch of imported, tinned fish and house-made pickled items that pair very well with oysters are also available. **Known for:** laid-back, family-friendly environment; impeccably scrubbed and shucked oysters; house-made mignonettes. $ *Average main: $10* ⊠ *123 Washington Ave., East End* ☎ *207/699–4466* ⊕ *portland.islandcreekoysters.com* ⊙ *Closed Mon.*

☕ Coffee and Quick Bites

Coffee By Design
$ | CAFÉ | Stop in this hip shop located in a former bakery building for quirky baked goods like vegan poptarts and sturdy coffee brewed from beans that have become a staple in many locals' home kitchens. **Known for:** among Portland's original artisanal coffee roasters; community commitment; three locations citywide. $ *Average main: $6* ⊠ *67 India St., East End* ☎ *207/780–6767* ⊕ *www.coffeebydesign.com.*

🎭 Performing Arts

Mayo Street Arts
ARTS CENTERS | FAMILY | An alternative-arts venue for the innovative and up-and-coming, Mayo Street Arts often features intimate concerts, contemporary exhibitions, and offbeat puppet shows in a repurposed church. ⊠ *10 Mayo St., East End* ☎ *207/879–4629* ⊕ *www.mayostreetarts.org.*

🏃 Activities

BIKING
Cycle Mania
BICYCLING | FAMILY | Rent hybrid bikes downtown at Cycle Mania. The $30 per day rate includes a helmet and lock. ⊠ *65 Cove St., East End* ☎ *207/774–2933* ⊕ *www.cyclemania1.com.*

BOATING
Portland Paddle
KAYAKING | FAMILY | Run by a pair of Registered Maine Guides, Portland Paddle leads introductory sea-kayaking clinics along with guided trips between the Casco Bay islands June through September. Two-hour sunset paddles ($40) are a fave, as are the full-moon standup paddleboard tours ($45). Kayak and SUP rentals are available. ⊠ *Eastern Promenade, East End Beach, off Cutter St., East End* ☎ *207/370–9730* ⊕ *www.portlandpaddle.net* ⊙ *Closed Nov.–May.*

The West End

A leisurely walk through Portland's West End, beginning at the top of the Arts District, offers a real treat to historic-architecture buffs. The quiet and stately neighborhood, on the National Register of Historic Places, presents an extraordinary display of architectural splendor, from High Victorian Gothic to lush Italianate, Queen Anne, and Colonial Revival.

👁 Sights

Western Promenade
PROMENADE | A good place to start is at the head of the Western Promenade, which has benches and a nice view. From the Old Port, take Danforth Street all the way up to Vaughn Street; take a right on Vaughn and then an immediate left onto Western Promenade. Pass by the Western Cemetery, Portland's second official burial ground, laid out in 1829—inside is the ancestral plot of

poet Henry Wadsworth Longfellow—and look for street parking. ⌧ *Danforth St. to Bramhall St., West End.*

🍴 Restaurants

BaoBao Dumpling House

$ | **ASIAN** | **FAMILY** | In a historic town house with traditional Asian decor (a 30-foot copper dragon watches over diners) in Portland's quaint West End, this dumpling house serves deeply satisfying Asian-inspired comfort food in an intimate setting. Start with the house made Asian slaw, then move to dumplings filled with tried-and-trues such as pork and cabbage or something less traditional, like beef bulgogi or shrimp and bacon. **Known for:** dishes integrating local, seasonal ingredients; tap takeovers by local brewmasters; dishes other than the namesake dumplings. $ *Average main: $12* ⌧ *133 Spring St., at Park St., West End* ☎ *207/772–8400* ⊕ *www. baobaodumplinghouse.com* ⊗ *Closed Mon. and Tues.*

Hotels

★ The Francis

$$$ | **HOTEL** | In the beautifully restored Mellen E. Bolster House, this charming boutique hotel has a midcentury-modern vibe that seamlessly compliments the building's immaculately preserved historical design elements. **Pros:** bars in rooms; smart spa on second floor; guest rooms feature custom-built furniture. **Cons:** only 15 rooms; some rooms not accessible by elevator; no bathtubs. $ *Rooms from: $300* ⌧ *747 Congress St., West End* ☎ *207/772–7485* ⊕ *www.thefrancis-maine.com* ⊃ *15 rooms* ⦿ *No meals.*

Morrill Mansion

$ | **B&B/INN** | **FAMILY** | This 19th-century town house has tastefully appointed rooms with well-executed color schemes—blue is a favorite hue here—and abundant thoughtful touches like well-stocked snack areas with fresh whoopie

pies baked by the innkeeper. **Pros:** close to Arts District; parlors on each floor for relaxing; tea, coffee, and baked treats available throughout the day. **Cons:** not on a grand block; no children under 14; no elevator. $ *Rooms from: $189* ⌧ *249 Vaughan St., West End* ☎ *207/774–6900, 888/566–7745* ⊕ *www.morrillmansion. com* ⊃ *8 rooms* ⦿ *Free breakfast.*

West End Inn

$$ | **B&B/INN** | Set among the glorious homes of the Western Promenade, this 1871 Georgian displays much of the era's grandeur, with high pressed-tin ceilings, intricate moldings, and ceiling medallions. **Pros:** fireplace library is a cozy place to relax; neighborhood is a historical walking tour; generous breakfast featuring local ingredients. **Cons:** 15- to 20-minute walk downtown; mostly street parking; some rooms without bathtubs. $ *Rooms from: $279* ⌧ *146 Pine St., West End* ☎ *207/772–1374* ⊕ *www.west-endbb.com* ⊃ *6 rooms* ⦿ *Free breakfast.*

Back Cove and Bayside

The Back Cove neighborhood is on the north side of 295 near the city's Back Cove basin—you'll hear some locals refer to it colloquially as Back Bay—which has a lovely 3½ mile trail around it. Its borders are Forest Avenue to Washington Avenue, and Canco Road to the Cove.

Bordered by Forest Avenue, Marginal Way, Cumberland Avenue, and Franklin Street, Bayside is home to Whole Foods, Trader Joe's, and the Bayside Trail.

🍴 Restaurants

★ Rose Foods

$ | **DELI** | **FAMILY** | The co-owner of the fabulous and consistently tasty Palace Diner in Biddeford has filled a long-neglected gap in Portland's food scene with this pitch-perfect bagel shop. Here you'll find spot-on New York-style bagels with both expected and unusual add-ons, including pastrami nova, chopped liver, and whitefish salad. **Known for:** family-friendly, neighborhood environment; house-cured gravlax; general-store-style shop items including books, games, and specialty food items. $ *Average main: $11* ✉ *428 Forest Ave., Back Cove and Bayside* ☎ *207/835–0991* ⊕ *www.rosefoods.me.*

☕ Coffee and Quick Bites

Two Fat Cats Bakery

STORE/MALL | This bakery's whoopie pies rely on light and fluffy, hand-scooped chocolate cake batter and a filling that's based on whipped vanilla buttercream, not the more typical marshmallow. The signature pie is made with wild Maine blueberries sourced from Maine-based and family-owned Wyman's. A second shop is located at 740 Broadway in South Portland. ✉ *195 Lancaster St., West End* ☎ *207/347–5144* ⊕ *www.twofatcatsbakery.com.*

🍸 Nightlife

★ Bayside Bowl

BOWLING | FAMILY | This 12-lane bowling alley sprang out of a survival technique among a group of friends for getting through Maine's harrowing winters. A community-minded locale that often puts on concerts and other events, Bayside Bowl also serves up some seriously delicious cocktails and local craft beers and snacks like fries and smoked chicken wings; the rooftop, which has a food truck that serves killer tacos, has one of the best views of the city (and the sunset) in town. ✉ *58 Alder St., West End* ☎ *207/791–2695* ⊕ *www.baysidebowl.com.*

Casco Bay Islands

The islands of Casco Bay are also known as the Calendar Islands, because an early explorer mistakenly thought there was one for each day of the year (in reality there are only 140 or so). These islands range from ledges visible only at low tide to populous Peaks Island, a suburb of Portland. Some are uninhabited; others support year-round communities, as well as stores and restaurants. Ft. Gorges commands Hog Island Ledge, and Eagle Island is the site of Arctic explorer Admiral Robert Peary's home. The brightly painted ferries of Casco Bay Lines are the islands' lifeline. There is frequent service to the most populated ones, including Peaks, Long, Little Diamond, and Great Diamond.

There is little in the way of overnight lodging on the islands—the population swells during the warmer months due to summer residents—and there are few restaurants or organized attractions other than the natural beauty of the islands themselves. Meandering about by bike or on foot is a good way to explore on a day trip.

GETTING HERE AND AROUND

Casco Bay Lines provides ferry service from Portland to the islands of Casco Bay.

ESSENTIALS

TRANSPORTATION INFORMATION Casco Bay Lines. ✉ *56 Commercial St., Portland* ☎ *207/774–7871* ⊕ *www.cascobaylines.com.*

Freeport

17 miles north of Portland via I–295.

Those who flock straight to L.L. Bean and see nothing else of Freeport are missing out. The town's charming backstreets are lined with historic buildings and old clapboard houses, and there's

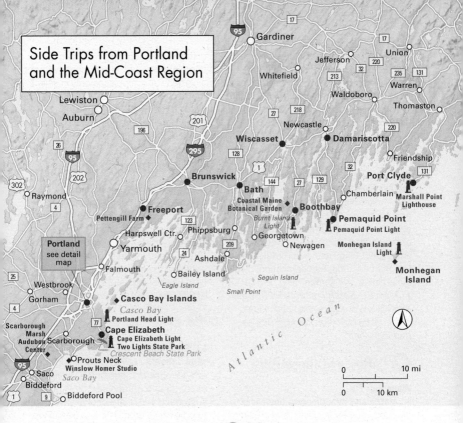

a pretty little harbor on the south side of the Harraseeket River. It's true that many who come to the area do so simply to shop: L.L. Bean is the store that put Freeport on the map, and plenty of outlets and some specialty stores have settled here. Still, if you choose, you can stay awhile and experience more than fabulous bargains; beyond the shops are bucolic nature preserves with miles of walking trails and plenty of places for leisurely ambling that don't require the overuse of your credit cards.

GETTING HERE AND AROUND
Interstate 295 has three Freeport exits and passes by on the edge of the downtown area. U.S. 1 is Main Street here.

◉ Sights

Freeport Historical Society
INFO CENTER | FAMILY | Pick up a village walking map and check out the historical exhibits at the Freeport Historical Society, located in Harrington House, a hybrid Federal- and Greek Revival–style home built in the 1830s. Always call ahead when planning a visit. ⊠ *45 Main St.* ☎ *207/865–3170* ⊕ *www.freeporthistoricalsociety.org.*

Pettengill Farm
FARM/RANCH | FAMILY | The grounds of the Freeport Historical Society's saltwater Pettengill Farm—140 beautifully tended acres along an estuary of the Harraseeket River—are open to the public. It's about a 15-minute walk from the parking area down a farm road to the circa-1800 saltbox farmhouse, which is open by appointment.

Little has changed since it was built, and it has rare etchings (called sgraffitti) of ships and sea monsters on three bedroom walls. ✉ *31 Pettengill Rd.* ☎ *207/865–3170* 🌐 *www.freeporthistoricalsociety.org* 🎟 *Free (donations appreciated).*

🍴 Restaurants

Harraseeket Lunch and Lobster Co

$$ | **SEAFOOD** | **FAMILY** | Seafood baskets and lobster dinners are the focus at this popular, bare-bones place beside the town landing in South Freeport. Order at the counter, find a seat inside or out, and expect long lines in summer. **Known for:** great seafood; harbor location; picnic table dining. [$] *Average main: $18* ✉ *36 S. Main St., South Freeport* ☎ *207/865–4888* 🌐 *www.harraseeketlunchandlobster.com* 💳 *No credit cards* 🕓 *Closed mid-Oct.–Apr.*

☕ Coffee and Quick Bites

When Pigs Fly

$ | **AMERICAN** | In addition to upward of two dozen types of classic and artisan breads, this bakery sells cookies and muffin-size cakes to grab and enjoy while walking among nearby outlet stores. Its low-carb option, a whole wheat loaf, is high on flavor and texture. **Known for:** all-natural ingredients with no preservatives; artisan breads like mango, pineapple, and raisin with toasted sesame and ginger; items baked daily. [$] *Average main: $4* ✉ *21 Main St.* ☎ *207/865–6006* 🌐 *sendbread.com.*

🛏 Hotels

Harraseeket Inn

$ | **HOTEL** | **FAMILY** | Despite some modern appointments, this large hotel has a country-inn ambience throughout—guest rooms have print fabrics and reproductions of Federal-style quarter-canopy beds. **Pros:** full breakfast; elevators and other modern touches; walk to shopping district. **Cons:** additions have diminished some authenticity; some rooms without a garden view; fireplaces only in select rooms. [$] *Rooms from: $179* ✉ *162 Main St.* ☎ *207/865–9377, 800/342–6423* 🌐 *www.harraseeketinn.com* 🛏 *84 rooms* 🍽 *Free breakfast.*

🎟 Performing Arts

L.L. Bean Summer Concert Series

CONCERTS | **FAMILY** | Throughout the summer, L.L. Bean hosts free activities, including concerts, at the L.L. Bean Discovery Park. It's set back from Main Street, along a side street the runs between the company's flagship and home furnishings stores. ✉ *18 Morse St.* ☎ *877/755–2326* 🌐 *www.llbean.com.*

🏃 Activities

L.L. Bean Outdoor Discovery Schools

TOUR—SPORTS | **FAMILY** | It shouldn't come as a surprise that one of the world's largest outdoor outfitters also provides its customers with instructional adventures to go with its products. L.L. Bean's year-round Outdoor Discovery Schools offer courses in canoeing, biking, kayaking, fly-fishing, snowshoeing, cross-country skiing, and other outdoor sports. ✉ *11 Desert Rd.* ☎ *888/552–3261* 🌐 *www.llbean.com/ods.*

🛍 Shopping

The *Freeport Visitors Guide* lists the more than 200 stores on Main Street, Bow Street, and elsewhere, including Coach, Brooks Brothers, Banana Republic, J.Crew, and Cole Haan. You can pick it up around town.

★ L.L. Bean

CLOTHING | **FAMILY** | Founded in 1912 as a mail-order merchandiser after its namesake invented a hunting boot, L.L. Bean's giant flagship store attracts more than 3 million shoppers annually and is open 365 days a year in the heart of Freeport's outlet shopping district. You can still find the original hunting boots, along with cotton and wool sweaters; outerwear of all kinds; casual clothing, boots, and shoes for men, women, and kids; and camping equipment. Nearby are the company's home furnishings store; bike, boat, and ski store; and outlet. ⊠ *95 Main St.* ☎ *877/755–2326* ⊕ *www.llbean.com.*

R. D. Allen Freeport Jewelers

JEWELRY/ACCESSORIES | This shop specializes in brightly colored tourmaline and other gemstones mined in Maine. Most of the pieces are the work of Maine artisans. Watermelon tourmaline is a specialty. ⊠ *13 Middle St.* ✛ *2 blocks from L.L. Bean* ☎ *207/865–1818* ⊕ *www. rdallen.com.*

★ Thos. Moser Cabinetmakers

HOUSEHOLD ITEMS/FURNITURE | Famed local furniture company Thos. Moser Cabinetmakers sells artful, handmade wood pieces with clean, classic lines. The store has information on tours at the workshop 30 minutes away in Auburn (by appointment only). ⊠ *149 Main St.* ☎ *207/865–4519* ⊕ *www.thosmoser.com.*

Brunswick

10 miles north of Freeport via U.S. 1.

Lovely brick and clapboard buildings are the highlight of Brunswick's Federal Street Historic District, which includes Federal Street and Park Row and the stately campus of Bowdoin College. From the intersection of Pleasant and Maine streets, in the center of town, you can walk in any direction and discover an impressive array of restaurants, as well as bookstores, gift shops, boutiques, and jewelers.

Below Brunswick are Harpswell Neck and the more than 40 islands that make up the town of Harpswell, known collectively as the Harpswells. Route 123 runs down Harpswell Neck, where small coves shelter lobster boats, and summer cottages are tucked away among birch and spruce trees. On your way down from Cook's Corner to Land's End at the end of Route 24, you cross Sebascodegan Island. Heading east here leads to East Harpswell and Cundy's Harbor. Continuing straight south down Route 24 leads to Orr's Island. Stop at Mackerel Cove to see a real fishing harbor; there are a few parking spaces, where you can stop to picnic and look for beach glass or put in your kayaks. Inhale the salt breeze as you cross the world's only cribstone bridge (designed so that water flows freely through gaps between the granite blocks) on your way to Bailey Island, home to a lobster pound made famous thanks in part to a Visa commercial.

GETTING HERE AND AROUND

From Interstate 295 take the Coastal Connector to U.S. 1 in Brunswick. From here Route 24 runs to Bailey Island and Route 123 down Harpswell Neck.

◉ Sights

★ Bowdoin College Museum of Art

ARTS CENTERS | FAMILY | This small museum housed in a stately building on Bowdoin's main quad features one of the oldest permanent collections of art in the United States, comprising paintings, sculpture, decorative arts, and works on paper. The museum often mounts well-curated, rotating exhibitions and has stellar programs for getting children excited about art. ⊠ *245 Maine St.* ☎ *207/725–3275* ⊕ *www.bowdoin.edu/art-museum* ⊠ *Free.*

🍴 Restaurants

★ Cook's Lobster and Ale House

$$$ | SEAFOOD | FAMILY | What began as a lobster shack on Bailey's Island in 1955 has grown into a huge, internationally famous family-style restaurant with a small gift shop. The restaurant still catches its own seafood, so you can count on the lobster roll and the haddock

sandwich to be delectable. **Known for:** traditional Maine seafood fare prepared simply; terrific selection of local craft beer and spirits; live music and festive atmosphere in the summer. $ *Average main: $26* ✉ *68 Garrison Cove Rd., Bailey Island* ☎ *207/833–2818* 🌐 *www.cookslobster.com* 🕒 *Closed early Jan.–mid-Feb.*

★ Frontier

$ | **MEDITERRANEAN** | There's nothing typical about Frontier, where indie films roll daily, artists and musicians from all over the world share their art, and a globally inspired menu features locally sourced ingredients in recipes culled from diverse cultures. Come for the inspiring events, stay for the delicious food and dangerously terrific cocktails. **Known for:** poblano and fish tacos and other seafood, as well as Mediterranean and Middle Eastern dishes; acting locally and thinking globally; menu staples such as curried mussels and vegan nachos. $ *Average main: $15* ✉ *14 Maine St., Mill 3 Fort Andross* ☎ *207/725–5222* 🌐 *www.explorefrontier.com* 🕒 *Closed Mon.*

☕ Coffee and Quick Bites

Little Dog Coffee Shop

$ | **AMERICAN** | Tide yourself over until lunch or dinner with coffee or chai and a muffin at this popular spot. There are also bagel sandwiches and wraps if you're hungrier. **Known for:** exhibiting local art; sidewalk seating; locally sourced goods. $ *Average main: $4* ✉ *87 Maine St., Freeport* ☎ *207/721–9500* 🌐 *www.littledogcoffeeshop.com.*

🏃 Activities

H2Outfitters

KAYAKING | The coast near Brunswick is full of hidden nooks and crannies waiting to be explored by kayak. H2Outfitters, at the southern end of Orr's Island just before the cribstone bridge, is the place in Harpswell to get on the water. It provides top-notch kayaking instruction and also offers half-day, full-day, bed-and-breakfast, and camping trips in the waters off its home base and elsewhere in Maine. ✉ *1894 Harpswell Island Rd., Orrs Island* ☎ *207/833–5257, 800/205–2925* 🌐 *www.h2outfitters.com.*

Bath

11 miles north of Brunswick via U.S. 1.

Bath has been a shipbuilding center since 1607. The result of its prosperity can be seen in its handsome mix of Federal, Greek Revival, and Italianate homes along Front, Centre, and Washington streets. In the heart of Bath's historic district are some charming 19th-century homes, including the 1820 Federal-style home at 360 Front Street; the 1810 Greek Revival mansion at 969 Washington Street, covered with gleaming white clapboards; and the Victorian gem at 1009 Washington Street, painted a distinctive shade of raspberry. All three operate as inns. One easily overlooked site is the town's City Hall; the bell in its tower was cast by Paul Revere in 1805.

The venerable Bath Iron Works completed its first passenger ship in 1890. During World War II, BIW (as it's locally known) launched a new ship every 17 days. Not only is it still in production today, BIW is one of the state's largest employers, with about 6,800 workers, who turn out destroyers for the U.S. Navy. (It's a good idea to avoid U.S. 1 on weekdays 3:15–4:30 pm, when a major shift change takes place.) You can tour BIW through the Maine Maritime Museum.

GETTING HERE AND AROUND

U.S. 1 passes through downtown and across the Kennebec River at Bath. Downtown is on the north side of the highway along the river.

Sights

★ Maine Maritime Museum

MUSEUM | **FAMILY** | No trip to Bath is complete without a visit to this cluster of buildings that once made up the historic Percy & Small Shipyard. Plan to spend at least half a day here. In fact, admission tickets are good for two days; there's just that much to see at this museum, which examines the world of shipbuilding and which is the only way to tour Bath Iron Works (June–mid-October). From late May through late October, daily nature and lighthouse boat tours cruise the scenic Kennebec River—one takes in 10 lights. The museum's flagship, the 1906 schooner Mary E, offers sails and dockside tours during the same period. Hour-long tours of the shipyard show how these massive wooden ships were built. In the boat shop, you can watch boatbuilders wield their tools, and see blacksmiths at work in the museum's forge. Inside the main museum building, exhibits use ship models, paintings, photographs, and historic artifacts to tell the maritime history of the region. A separate historic building houses a fascinating 6,000-square-foot lobstering exhibit. A gift shop and bookstore are on the premises, and you can grab a bite to eat in the café or bring a picnic to eat on the grounds. **■ TIP→ Kids ages six and younger get in free.** ✉ *243 Washington St.* ☎ *207/443–1316* 🌐 *www.mainemaritimemuseum.org* 🎫 *$18, good for 2 days within 7-day period.*

Restaurants

Beale Street Barbecue

$ | **BARBECUE** | Ribs are the thing at one of Maine's oldest barbecue joints, opened in 1996. Hearty eaters should ask for one of the platters piled high with pulled pork, pulled chicken, or shredded beef. **Known for:** three-cheese mac and cheese (American, cheddar, and Pecorino romano); Maine microbrews; key lime pie. [$] *Average main: $13* ✉ *215 Water St.* ☎ *207/442–9514* 🌐 *www.mainebbq.com.*

Coffee and Quick Bites

Café Crème

$ | **BAKERY** | Located in the heart of downtown, visitors and locals alike flock to this coffee shop for delicious coffee paired with baked-that-day goods and served with a smile. The cinnamon roll with maple bacon is a savory Maine take on the classic sweet treat. **Known for:** sweet and savory stuffed croissants; on-site bakery; friendly staff. [$] *Average main: $7* ✉ *56 Front St., at Centre St.* ☎ *207/443–6454.*

Hotels

★ Kennebec Inn Bed and Breakfast

$ | **B&B/INN** | Four immaculate, well-appointed rooms tastefully decorated with maritime touches, luxe bedding and towels, and welcoming common spaces await you at this hidden gem in a historic captain's home—you'll feel like you're at an exclusive retreat. **Pros:** calm and quiet atmosphere make for pure relaxation; delicious, multicourse breakfast you can take at your leisure; knowledgeable, warm innkeeper. **Cons:** only four rooms; a short walk into center of town; no pets. [$] *Rooms from: $180* ✉ *696 High St.* ☎ *207/443–5324* 🌐 *www.kennebecinn.com* 🛏 *4 rooms* 🍴 *Free breakfast.*

Sebasco Harbor Resort

$$ | **RESORT** | **FAMILY** | A family-friendly resort spread over 450 acres on the water near the foot of the Phippsburg Peninsula, this place has a golf course, spa, tennis courts, and a saltwater pool, among a host of other amenities. **Pros:** good choice for families; perfect location; children's activities; wonderful array of lawn games. **Cons:** no sand beach; heavy traffic and large number of rooms can diminish quality and service; golf fee not included in stay. [$] *Rooms from: $249* ✉ *29 Kenyon Rd., off Sebasco Rd., Phippsburg* ☎ *800/225–3819* 🌐 *www.sebasco.com* 🕒 *Closed late Oct.–mid-May* 🛏 *110 rooms* 🍴 *No meals.*

Continued on page 669

MAINE'S LIGHTHOUSES
GUARDIANS OF THE COAST
By John Blodgett

Perched high on rocky ledges, on the tips of wayward islands, and sometimes seemingly on the ocean itself are the more than five dozen lighthouses standing watch along Maine's craggy and ship-busting coastline.

LIGHTING THE WAY: A BIT OF HISTORY

Portland Head Light

Most lighthouses were built in the first half of the 19th century to protect vessels from running aground at night or when the shoreline was shrouded in fog. Along with the mournful siren of the foghorn and maritime lore, these practical structures have come to symbolize Maine throughout the world.

SHIPWRECKS AND SAFETY

These alluring sentinels of the eastern seaboard today have more form than function, but that certainly was not always the case. Safety was a strong motivating factor in the erection of the lighthouses. Commerce also played a critical role. For example, in 1791 Portland Head light was completed, partially as a response to local merchants' concerns about the rocky entrance to Portland Harbor and the varying depths of the shipping channel, but approval wasn't given until a terrible accident in 1787 in which a 90-ton sloop wrecked. In 1789, the federal government created the U.S. Lighthouse Establishment (later the U.S. Lighthouse Service) to manage them. In 1939 the U.S. Coast Guard took on the job.

Some lighthouses in Maine were built in a much-needed venue, but the points and islands upon which they sat were prone to storm damage. Along with poor construction, this meant that over the years many lighthouses had to be rebuilt or replaced.

LIGHTHOUSES TODAY

In modern times, many of the structures still serve a purpose. Technological advances, such as GPS and radar, are mainly used to navigate through the choppy waters, but a lighthouse or its foghorns are helpful secondary aids, and sometimes the only ones used by recreational boaters. The numerous channel-marking buoys still in existence also are testament to the old tried-and-true methods.

Of the 66 lighthouses along this far northeastern state, 55 are still working, alerting ships (and even small aircraft) of the shoreline's rocky edge. Government agencies, historic preservation organizations, and mostly private individuals own the decommissioned lights.

KEEPERS OF THE LIGHT

Some keepers also used bells and sirens, like this Fog Signal Station on Manana Island in 1898.

Pemaquid Point's fourth-order Fresnel lens

LIFE OF A LIGHTKEEPER

One thing that has changed with the modern era is the disappearance of the lighthouse keeper. In the early 20th century, lighthouses began the conversion from oil-based lighting to electricity. A few decades later, the U.S. Coast Guard switched to automation, phasing out the need for an on-site keeper.

While the keepers of tradition were no longer needed, the traditions of these stalwart, 24/7 employees live on through museum exhibits and retellings of Maine's maritime history, legends, and lore. The tales of a lighthouse keeper's life are the stuff romance novels are made of: adventure, rugged but lonely men, and a beautiful setting along an unpredictable coastline.

The lighthouse keepers of yesterday probably didn't see their own lives so romantically. Their daily narrative was one of hard work and, in some cases, exceptional solitude. A keeper's primary job was to ensure that the lamp was illuminated all day, every day. This meant that oil (whale or coal oil and later kerosene) had to be carried about and wicks trimmed on a regular basis. When fog shrouded the coast, they sounded the solemn horn to pierce through the damp darkness that hid their light. Their quarters were generally small and often attached to the light tower itself. The remote locations of the lights added to the isolation a keeper felt, especially before the advent of radio and telephone, let alone the Internet. Though some brought families with them, the keepers tended to be men who lived alone.

THE LIGHTS 101

Over the years, Fresnel (fray-NELL) lenses were developed in different shapes and sizes so that ship captains could distinguish one lighthouse from another. Invented by Frenchman Augustin Fresnel in the early 19th century, the lens design allows for a greater transmission of light perfectly suited for lighthouse use. Knowing which lighthouse they were near helped captains know which danger was present, such as a submerged ledge or shallow channel. Some lights, such as those at Seguin Island Light, are fixed and don't flash. Other lights are colored red.

DID YOU KNOW?

A lighthouse's personality shines through its flash pattern. For example, Bass Harbor Light (pictured) blinks red every four seconds. Some lights, such as Seguin Island Light, are fixed and don't flash.

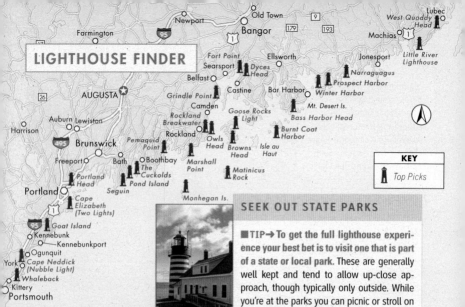

LIGHTHOUSE FINDER

Lubec
West Quoddy Head
Machias
Little River Lighthouse
Old Town
Newport
Bangor
9
179
193
Jonesport
Farmington
Fort Point
Searsport
Ellsworth
Narraguagus
Prospect Harbor
Dyces Head
Belfast
Castine
Bar Harbor
Winter Harbor
AUGUSTA
Grindle Point
Camden
Goose Rocks Light
Mt. Desert Is.
Bass Harbor Head
Auburn Lewiston
Rockland Breakwater
Burnt Coat Harbor
Harrison
Rockland
Brunswick
Pemaquid Point
Owls Head
Browns Head
Isle au Haut
Freeport
Bath
Boothbay
Marshall Point
Matinicus Rock
Portland Head
The Cuckolds
Pond Island
Seguin
Portland
Monhegan Is.
Cape Elizabeth (Two Lights)
Goat Island
Kennebunk
Kennebunkport
Ogunquit
York
Cape Neddick (Nubble Light)
Whaleback
Kittery
Portsmouth

26

KEY
Top Picks

West Quoddy Head

SEEK OUT STATE PARKS

■ TIP → **To get the full lighthouse experience your best bet is to visit one that is part of a state or local park.** These are generally well kept and tend to allow up-close approach, though typically only outside. While you're at the parks you can picnic or stroll on the trails. Wildlife is often abundant in and near the water; you might spot sea birds and even whales in certain locations (try West Quoddy Head, Portland Head, or Two Lights).

VISITING MAINE'S LIGHTHOUSES

As you travel along the Maine Coast, you won't see lighthouses by watching your odometer—there were no rules about the spacing of lighthouses. The decision as to where to place a lighthouse was a balance between a region's geography and its commercial prosperity and maritime traffic.

Lighthouses dot the shore from as far south as York to the country's easternmost tip at Lubec. Accessibility varies according to location and other factors. A handful are so remote as to be outright impossible to reach (except perhaps by kayaking and rock climbing). Some don't allow visitors according to Coast Guard policies, though you can enjoy them through the zoom lens of a camera. Others you can walk right up to and, occasionally, even climb to the top. Lighthouse enthusiasts and preservation groups restore and maintain many of them. All told, approximately 30 lighthouses allow some sort of public access.

MUSEUMS, TOURS, AND MORE

Most keeper's quarters are closed to the public, but some of the homes have been converted to museums, full of intriguing exhibits on lighthouses, the famous Fresnel lenses used in them, and artifacts of Maine maritime life in general. Talk to the librarians at the **Maine Maritime Museum** in Bath (⊕ www.mainemaritimemuseum. org) or sign up for one of the museum's daily lighthouse cruises to pass by no fewer than ten on the Lighthouse Lovers Cruise. In Rockland, the **Maine Lighthouse Museum** (⊕ www.mainelighthousemuseum.org) has the country's largest display of Fresnel lenses. The museum also displays keepers' memorabilia, foghorns, brassware, and more. Maine Open Lighthouse Day is the second Saturday after Labor Day; you can tour and even climb lights usually closed to the public.

For more information, check out the lighthouse page at Maine's official tourism site: ⊕ visitmaine.com.

SLEEPING LIGHT: STAYING OVERNIGHT

Goose Rocks, where you can play lighthouse keeper for a week.

Want to stay overnight in a lighthouse? There are several options to do so. ■ TIP→ **Book lighthouse lodgings as far in advance as possible, up to one year ahead.**

Our top pick is **Pemaquid Point Light** (*Newcastle Square Vacation Rentals* ☎ *207/563–6500* ⊕ *www.mainecoast-cottages.com*) because it has one of the most dramatic settings on the Maine coast. Two miles south of **New Harbor**, the second floor of the lighthouse keeper's house is rented out on a weekly basis early May through mid-November to support upkeep of the grounds. When you aren't enjoying the interior, head outdoors: the covered front porch has a rocking-chair view of the ocean. The one-bedroom, one-bath rental sleeps up to a family of four.

Situated smack dab in the middle of a major maritime thoroughfare between two Penobscot Bay islands, **Goose Rocks Light** (☎ *203/400–9565* ⊕ *www.beacon-preservation.org*) offers lodging for the adventuresome—the 51-foot "spark plug" lighthouse is completely surrounded by water. Getting there requires a ferry ride from Rockland to nearby **North Haven**, a 5- to 10-minute ride by motorboat, and then a climb up an iron-rung ladder from the pitching boat—all based on high tide and winds, of course. There's room for up to eight people. It's a bit more cushy experience than it was for the original keepers: there's a flat-screen TV with DVD player and a selection of music and videos for entertainment. In addition, a hammock hangs on the small deck that encircles the operational light; it's a great place from which to watch the majestic wind-jammers and the fishing fleet pass by.

Little River Lighthouse (☎ *877/276–4682* ⊕ *www.littleriverlight.org*), along the far northeastern reaches of the coast in **Cutler**, has three rooms available for rent in July and August. You're responsible for food and beverages, linens, towels, and other personal items (don't forget the bug spray), but kitchen and other basics are provided. The lighthouse operators will provide a boat ride to the island upon which the lighthouse sits.

TOP LIGHTHOUSES TO VISIT

BASS HARBOR LIGHT
Familiar to many as the subject of countless photographs is Bass Harbor Light, at the southern end of **Mount Desert Island.** It is within Acadia National Park and 17 miles from the town of Bar Harbor. The station grounds are open year-round.

CAPE ELIZABETH LIGHT
Two Lights State Park is so-named because it's next to two lighthouses. Both of these **Cape Elizabeth** structures were built in 1828. The western light was converted into a private residence in 1924; the eastern light, Cape Elizabeth Light, still projects its automated cylinder of light. The grounds surrounding the building and the lighthouse itself are closed to the public, but the structure is easily viewed and photographed from nearby at the end of Two Lights Road.

CAPE NEDDICK LIGHT
More commonly known as Nubble Light for the smallish offshore expanse of rock it rests upon, Cape Neddick Light sits a few hundred feet off a rock point in **York Beach.** With such a precarious location, its grounds are inaccessible to visitors, but close enough to be exceptionally photogenic, especially during the Christmas season.

MONHEGAN ISLAND LIGHT
Only the adventuresome and the artistic see this light, because **Monhegan Island** is accessible by an approximately one-hour ferry ride. To reach the lighthouse, you have an additional half-mile walk uphill from the ferry dock. The former keeper's quarters is home to the Monhegan Museum, which has exhibits about the island. The tower itself is closed to the public.

PORTLAND HEAD LIGHT
One of Maine's most photographed lighthouses (and its oldest), the famous Portland Head Light was completed in January 1791. At the edge of Fort Williams Park, in **Cape Elizabeth**, the towering white stone lighthouse stands 101 feet above the sea. The Coast Guard operates it and it is not open for tours. However the adjacent keeper's dwelling is now a museum.

WEST QUODDY HEAD LIGHT
Originally built in 1808 by mandate of President Thomas Jefferson, West Quoddy Head Light sits in **Lubec** on the easternmost tip of land in the mainland United States. The 49-foot-high lighthouse with distinctive red and white stripes, is part of Quoddy Head State Park.

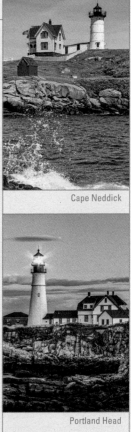
Cape Neddick

Portland Head

West Quoddy Head

Wiscasset

10 miles north of Bath via U.S. 1.

Settled in 1663, Wiscasset sits on the banks of the Sheepscot River. It bills itself "Maine's Prettiest Village," and it's easy to see why: it has graceful churches, old cemeteries, and elegant sea captains' homes (many converted into antiques shops or galleries).

There's also a good wine and specialty foods shop called Treats (stock up here if you're heading north). Pack a picnic and take it down to the dock on Water Street, where you can watch the fishing boats, or grab a lobster roll from Red's Eats or the lobster shack nearby. Wiscasset has expanded its wharf, and this is a great place to catch a breeze on a hot day.

GETTING HERE AND AROUND

U.S. 1 becomes Main Street, and traffic often slows to a crawl come summer. You'll likely have success parking on Water Street rather than Main. It's a good idea to do your driving around Wiscasset very early in the morning and after 7 in the evening when traffic eases a bit. The best way to get around here is on foot.

Restaurants

Red's Eats

$$ | **SEAFOOD** | **FAMILY** | It's hard to miss the long line of hungry customers outside this little red shack on the Wiscasset side of the bridge. Red's is a local landmark famous for its hamburgers, hot dogs, lobster and crab rolls, and crispy onion rings and clams fried in house-made batters. **Known for:** more than a whole lobster goes into each lobster roll; the unholy "Puff Dog," a hot dog loaded with bacon and cheese and deep-fried; long lines in summer. $ *Average main: $20* ⊠ *41 Water St.* ☎ *207/882–6128* ⊕ *www.redseatsmaine.com* ▭ *No credit cards* ☉ *Closed mid-Oct.–mid-Apr.*

Coffee and Quick Bites

Treats

$ | **AMERICAN** | What started as a candy shop over 30 years ago has grown into a Wiscasset staple featuring coffee, baked goods, wine, beer, and cheese and more. Order a gourmet picnic basket to go, or stick around and relax with a coffee and scone. **Known for:** scones made from owner's nana's recipe; "bronuts" filled with pastry cream; locally sourced ingredients. $ *Average main: $5* ⊠ *80 Main St.* ☎ *207/882–6192* ⊕ *www.treatsofmaine.com.*

Shopping

Edgecomb Potters

CERAMICS/GLASSWARE | Edgecomb Potters is not to be missed: they make vibrantly colored, exquisitely glazed porcelain known all around the country. The store also carries jewelry, glassware, and glass sculptures. ⊠ *727 Boothbay Rd., Edgecomb* ☎ *207/882–9493* ⊕ *www.edgecombpotters.com.*

In the Clover

CLOTHING | There's something charmingly old-school about this pretty boutique with its warm and friendly service and fine displays of women's clothing, accessories, and beauty products. Geared toward elegant but no-fuss women of every age, the shop stocks clothing items such as fine cashmere shawls; pretty but not froufrou lingerie; and sophisticated loungewear as well as a good selection of natural beauty products and fragrances, unique jewelry, and inspiring books. ⊠ *85 A. Main St.* ☎ *207/882–9435* ⊕ *inthecloverbeauty.com.*

★ Rock Paper Scissors

GIFTS/SOUVENIRS | Not your run-of-the-mill gift shop, this well-curated boutique stocks offbeat cards and letterpress stationery, local hand-crafted goods such as blankets, purses, and ceramics, and beautiful, one-of-a-kind objects for the home and kitchen. Stocked to the brim with charming goodies for anyone on your list (including yourself), this shop is decidedly contemporary, with a Scandinavian bent, and is well worth a stop, if only to peruse the gorgeously arranged array of products on display. ✉ *68 Main St.* ☎ *207/882–9930.*

Sheepscot River Pottery

CERAMICS/GLASSWARE | This shop boasts beautifully glazed kitchen tiles, as well as kitchenware and home accessories, including sinks. Jewelry and other items by local artisans are also on sale. ✉ *34 U.S. 1, Edgecomb* ☎ *207/882–9410* 🌐 *www.sheepscot.com.*

Boothbay

11 miles south of Wiscasset via Rte. 27.

The shoreline of the Boothbay Peninsula is a craggy stretch of inlets, where pleasure craft anchor alongside trawlers and lobster boats. The town of Boothbay comprises the village center, Boothbay Harbor, and East Boothbay. The harbor is like a smaller version of Bar Harbor—touristy, but friendly and fun—with pretty, winding streets and lots to explore. Commercial Street, Wharf Street, Townsend Avenue, and the By-Way are lined with shops and ice-cream parlors. One of the biggest draws here is the stunning Coastal Maine Botanical Gardens, with its beautiful café and gift shop, as well as its famous children's garden.

GETTING HERE AND AROUND

In season, boat trips to Monhegan Island leave from the piers off Commercial Street. Drive out to Ocean Point in East Boothbay for some incredible scenery. Boothbay is 11 miles south of Wiscasset via U.S. 1 and Route 27.

Sights

★ Coastal Maine Botanical Garden

GARDEN | **FAMILY** | Set aside a couple of hours to stroll among the roses, lupines, and rhododendrons at the 250-acre Coastal Maine Botanical Garden. In the summer, free docent-led tours leave from the visitor center at 11 every day May–October. The "children's garden" is a wonderland of stone sculptures, rope bridges, small teahouselike structures with grass roofs, and even a hedge maze. Children and adults alike adore the separate woodland fairy area. The on-site restaurant and café, as well as the bookshop and resource library, are also delightful. It's easy to spend an entire day here and not see everything—be sure to wear comfortable walking shoes. For those less inclined to go by foot, the gardens offer free shuttle service to most spots on the property. ✉ *132 Botanical Gardens Dr., off Rte. 27* ☎ *207/633–8000* 🌐 *www.mainegardens.org* 🎟 *$20.*

Restaurants

Boathouse Bistro Tapas Bar and Restaurant

$$ | **TAPAS** | The multitier rooftop terrace (complete with an outdoor bar) stays crowded all summer at the Boat House Bistro. Austrian-born chef Karin Guerin dishes up tapas-style small plates ranging from mojito ginger wings to Madagascar beef skewers. **Known for:** fried oysters with truffle pearls; Spanish-inspired dishes featuring locally caught seafood; a sizeable array of flatbread grillers featuring different toppings. [$] *Average main: $22* ✉ *12 The By-Way, Boothbay Harbor* ☎ *207/633–0400* 🌐 *www.theboathouse-bistro.com* 🕒 *Closed mid-Oct.–mid-Apr. and Wed. and Thurs.*

Coffee and Quick Bites

Red Cup Coffeehouse
$ | **AMERICAN** | Stop by while walking downtown Boothbay Harbor for a hot or iced espresso drink or cold fruit smoothie. There is also a selection of freshly baked goods to choose from. **Known for:** beans from Portland-based Coffee By Design; cold brew on nitro tap; breakfast sandwiches on fresh bread. [$] *Average main: $5* ✉ *29 Commercial St., Boothbay Harbor* ☎ *207/350–4228* 🌐 *www.redcupcoffeehouse.com* 🕒 *Closed Tues. in off-season.*

Hotels

Spruce Point Inn
$$ | **RESORT** | **FAMILY** | A great base for exploring Boothbay, this lovely seaside inn acts like a resort, while feeling more like you're visiting an old friend's house or a summer home. **Pros:** some pet-friendly lodging; family game room; laundry on-site; shuttle by boat to the town center; private boat launch. **Cons:** some private residences close to premises; no indoor pool; golfing access off-site. [$] *Rooms from: $250* ✉ *88 Grandview Ave., Boothbay Harbor* ☎ *207/633–4152* 🌐 *www.sprucepointinn.com* 🕒 *Closed mid-Oct.–mid-May* 🛏 *63 rooms* 🍴 *No meals.*

Topside Inn
$$ | **B&B/INN** | The Adirondack chairs on the immense lawn of this historic hilltop B&B have what is probably the best bay view in town. **Pros:** knockout views; plenty of green space for croquet; easy walk downtown. **Cons:** two person maximum per room; reservations fill quickly in summer; pets only allowed in the cottages. [$] *Rooms from: $299* ✉ *60 McKown St., Boothbay Harbor* ☎ *207/633–5404* 🌐 *www.topsideinn.com* 🕒 *Closed Nov.–Apr.* 🛏 *23 rooms* 🍴 *Free breakfast.*

Damariscotta

8 miles north of Wiscasset via U.S. 1.

The Damariscotta region comprises several communities along the rocky coast. The town itself sits on the water, a lively place filled with attractive shops and restaurants, as well as some of the best oysters around.

Just across the bridge over the Damariscotta River is the town of Newcastle, between the Sheepscot and Damariscotta rivers. Newcastle was settled in the early 1600s. The earliest inhabitants planted apple trees, but the town later became an industrial center, home to several shipyards and a couple of mills. The oldest Catholic church in New England, St. Patrick's, is here, and it still rings its original Paul Revere bell.

Bremen, which encompasses more than a dozen islands and countless rocky outcrops, has many seasonal homes along the water, and the main industries in the small community are fishing and clamming. Nobleboro, a bit north of here on U.S. 1, was settled in the 1720s by Colonel David Dunbar, sent by the British to rebuild the fort at Pemaquid. Neighboring Waldoboro is situated on the Medomak River and was settled largely by Germans in the mid-1700s. You can still visit the old German Meeting House, built in 1772. The Pemaquid Peninsula stretches south from Damariscotta to include Bristol, South Bristol, Round Pond, New Harbor, and Pemaquid.

GETTING HERE AND AROUND

In Newcastle, U.S. 1B runs from U.S. 1 across the Damariscotta River to Damariscotta. From this road take Route 129 south to South Bristol and Route 130 south to Bristol and New Harbor. From here you can return to U.S. 1 heading north on Route 32 through Round Pond and Bremen. In Waldoboro, turn off U.S. 1 on Jefferson Street to see the historic village center.

Maine is the largest lobster-producing state in the United States.

ESSENTIALS

VISITOR INFORMATION Damariscotta Region Chamber of Commerce. ☎ *207/563–8340* 🌐 *www.damariscottaregion.com.*

🍴 Restaurants

King Eider's Pub and Restaurant

$$$ | **AMERICAN** | **FAMILY** | This cozy, classic pub right downtown bills itself as having the finest crab cakes in New England. Start with the fresh local oysters that the Damariscotta region is known for, then move on to entrées like steak-and-ale pie, sea-scallop Florentine, or sautéed haddock with chips. **Known for:** live music; special gatherings; extensive whiskey collection. [$] *Average main: $29* ✉ *2 Elm St.* ☎ *207/563–6008* 🌐 *www.kingeiders-pub.com.*

★ Newcastle Publick House

$$ | **AMERICAN** | **FAMILY** | In a handsomely renovated historic building, Newcastle Publick House serves delicious comfort food, including fresh oysters, house-made pastrami, and local craft beers, as well as one of the best French onion soups around. There is often live music, making it a great place for a night out on a date or with the entire family. **Known for:** stacked burgers; cozy, old-school atmosphere; desserts and breads made by nearby Oysterhead Pizza Co. [$] *Average main: $20* ✉ *52 Main St., Newcastle* ☎ *207/563–3434* 🌐 *www.newcastlepublickhouse.com* 🕒 *Closed Mon.*

☕ Coffee and Quick Bites

Cupacity

$ | **AMERICAN** | Opened in the heart of downtown in 2019, this bright and friendly women-owned shop offers coffee, tea, wine, hard cider, beer, and small bites like falafel sliders and organic summer salads. **Known for:** locally sourced food and drinks; the "Krunk": part nitro cold brew, part lemonade; outdoor patio seating to watch the world go by. [$] *Average main: $10* ✉ *133 Main St.* ☎ *207/563–6127* 🌐 *www.cupacitycoffee.com* 🕒 *Closed Sun.–Wed.*

Hotels

Newcastle Inn

$$ | **B&B/INN** | **FAMILY** | A riverside location, tasteful decor, and lots of common areas (inside and out) make this a relaxing country inn. **Pros:** guests can order beer or wine; suites have sitting areas; water views in many rooms. **Cons:** short walk into the village; not all rooms have water views; some rooms without ample sitting areas. [$] *Rooms from: $200* ✉ *60 River Rd., Newcastle* ☎ *207/563–5685* 🌐 *www.newcastleinn.com* 🛏 *14 rooms* 🍴 *Free breakfast.*

Pemaquid Point

10 miles south of Damariscotta via U.S. 1, U.S. 1B, and Rte. 130.

Pemaquid Point is the tip of the Pemaquid Peninsula, bordered by Muscongus and Johns bays. It's home to the famous lighthouse of the same name and its attendant fog bell and tiny museum. Also at the bottom of the peninsula, along the Muscongus Bay, is the Nature Conservancy's Rachel Carson Salt Pond Preserve.

GETTING HERE AND AROUND

From U.S. 1, take U.S. 1B into Damariscotta and head south on Route 130 to Pemaquid Point.

Sights

★ **Pemaquid Point Light**

LIGHTHOUSE | **FAMILY** | At the end of Route 130, this lighthouse at the tip of the Pemaquid Peninsula looks as though it sprouted from the ragged, tilted chunk of granite it commands. Most days in the summer you can climb the tower to the light. The former keeper's cottage is now the Fishermen's Museum, which displays historic photographs, scale models, and artifacts that explore commercial fishing in Maine. Also here are the original fog bell and bell house. There are restrooms and picnic tables. ✉ *3115 Bristol Rd., New Harbor* ☎ *207/677–2492* 🌐 *www.bristolmaine.org* 🎟 *$3.*

Restaurants

★ **Muscongus Bay Lobster Co.**

$$ | **SEAFOOD** | **FAMILY** | The food here is practically guaranteed to be fresh: lobsters come in off the boat at one end of the pier, and the restaurant is at the other. Grab a picnic table and be careful not to hit your head on the colorful, dangling wooden buoys. **Known for:** laid-back, BYOB atmosphere; kid-friendly; repeat visitors meet and greet here. [$] *Average main: $18* ✉ *28 Landing Rd., Round Pond* ☎ *207/529–5528* 🌐 *www.mainefreshlobster.com* ⏲ *Closed mid-Oct.–mid-May.*

Round Pond Lobster

$$ | **SEAFOOD** | Sheltered Muscongus Bay is where you'll find this down-home lobster shack, right on the pier with pleasant views of the water. Competition with the neighboring Muscongus Bay Lobster Co. keeps the prices low for fresh-off-the-boat lobster and steamers. **Known for:** BYO drinks and sides; family-friendly; dog-friendly. [$] *Average main: $20* ✉ *25 Town Landing Rd., Round Pond* ☎ *207/529–5725* ⏲ *Closed Labor Day–mid-May.*

Activities

Hardy Boat Cruises

BOATING | **FAMILY** | Mid-May through mid-October, you can take a cruise to Monhegan with Hardy Boat Cruises. The company also offers seal- and puffin-watching trips and lighthouse and fall coastal cruises. Dogs are welcome on the boat for $5. ✉ *Shaw's Wharf, 132 Rte. 32, New Harbor* ☎ *207/677–2026* 🌐 *www.hardyboat.com.*

Maine State Prison Showroom

If you're traveling through Thomaston on Route 1, consider popping into the Maine State Prison Showroom for a uniquely locally made souvenir or gift. Since 1824, inmates participating in one of the state's skills-building industries programs have been handcrafting goods that are sold to the public.

Open year-round, the store contains hundreds of wood items; some are nautical-theme, such as ship models, while many are practical, including cutting boards, bookcases, and coffee and end tables. ⊠ *358 Hwy. 1, Thomaston* ☏ *207/354–9237* ⊕ *www.facebook. com/MSPShowroom*

Port Clyde

5 miles south of Tenants Harbor via Rte. 131.

At the end of the St. George Peninsula, the sleepy fishing village of Port Clyde is a haven for artists, with a number of galleries and a sweeping vista of the ocean that can't be beat. It's also a good spot to spend time nursing a beer or a coffee while waiting for your boat out to Monhegan. Like many places in Maine, lobster fishing is an economic mainstay here. Marshall Point Lighthouse, right in the harbor, has a small museum.

◉ Sights

★ Marshall Point Lighthouse

LOCAL INTEREST | FAMILY | This 31-foot lighthouse, which has been in operation since it was erected in 1858, is perhaps best known as the spot where Forrest Gump concluded his very long cross-country run in the 1994 film adaptation of the book by the same name. Be prepared for sweeping views of the ocean and a resounding "Run, Forrest, run!" coming from visitors taking full advantage of an exceptional photo op. The site also has a small museum and a gift shop, housed in the old lightkeepers' house. ⊠ *Marshall Point Rd.* ☏ *207/372–6450* ⊕ *www. marshallpoint.org.*

Monhegan Island

East of Pemaquid Peninsula, 10 miles south of Port Clyde.

If you love rocky cliffs, this is your place. And if you happen to be an artist, you might never leave: there are studios and galleries all over the island. The village bustles with activity in summer, when many artists open their studios. Several shops are open for browsing. You can escape the crowds on the island's 17 miles of hiking trails, which lead to the lighthouse and to the cliffs—bring your camera.

GETTING HERE AND AROUND

Three excursion boats dock here. The boat trip out to Monhegan is almost as exhilarating as exploring the island itself. You'll likely pass by the Marshall Point Lighthouse; be on the lookout for porpoises, seals, puffins, and small whales en route to the island.

Monhegan Boat Line

TRANSPORTATION SITE (AIRPORT/BUS/FERRY/ TRAIN) | FAMILY | The Port Clyde boat landing is home to the *Elizabeth Ann* and the *Laura B,* the mail boats that serve Monhegan Island, about 10 miles offshore. There are three round-trips daily mid-June–mid-Oct.; one daily in late fall and early spring; and three weekly in the winter. ⊠ *880 Port Clyde Rd., Port Clyde* ☏ *207/372–8848* ⊕ *www.monheganboat.com.*

Sights

Monhegan Island Light

LIGHTHOUSE | FAMILY | Getting a look at this squat stone lighthouse—from land, anyway—requires a slightly steep half-mile walk uphill from the island's ferry dock. The lighthouse was automated in 1959, and the former keeper's quarters became the Monhegan Museum shortly thereafter. Exhibits at the museum have as much to do with life on the island as they do with the lighthouse itself. The tower is open sporadically throughout the summer for short tours. ✉ *Lighthouse Hill Rd., ½ mile east of dock, Monhegan* ☎ *207/596–7003* 🌐 *monheganmuseum.org.*

Hotels

The Island Inn

$$ | B&B/INN | Local works of art are displayed throughout this three-story hotel, which dates to 1907; the property has a commanding presence on Monhegan Island's harbor. **Pros:** great food; great view; laid-back atmosphere. **Cons:** a little on the pricey side, but it's on an island after all; no a/c. $ *Rooms from: $200* ✉ *1 Ocean Ave., Monhegan* ☎ *207/596–0371* 🌐 *www.islandinnmonhegan.com* ⏲ *Closed Columbus Day–Memorial Day* 🛏 *32 rooms* 🍴 *Free breakfast* 💳 *No credit cards.*

Rockland

25 miles north of Damariscotta via U.S. 1.

This town is considered the gateway to Penobscot Bay and is the first stop on U.S. 1 offering a glimpse of the often-sparkling and island-dotted blue bay. Though once merely a place to pass through on the way to tonier ports like Camden, Rockland now gets attention on its own, thanks to a trio of attractions: the renowned Farnsworth Art Museum, the increasingly popular summer Lobster Festival, and the lively North Atlantic Blues Festival. Specialty shops and galleries line the main street, yet the town is still a large fishing port and the commercial hub of this coastal area.

Rockland Harbor bests Camden (by one) as home to the largest fleet of Maine windjammers. The best place in Rockland to view these handsome vessels as they sail in and out of the harbor is the mile-long granite breakwater, which bisects the outer portion of Rockland Harbor. To get there, from U.S. 1, head east on Waldo Avenue and then right on Samoset Road; follow this short road to its end.

GETTING HERE AND AROUND

U.S. 1 runs along Main Street here, while U.S. 1A curves through the residential neighborhood west of the business district, offering a faster route if you are passing through.

FESTIVALS

Maine Lobster Festival

FESTIVALS | FAMILY | Rockland's annual Maine Lobster Festival, held in early August, is the region's largest annual event. About 10 tons of lobsters are steamed in a huge lobster cooker—you have to see it to believe it. The festival, held in Harbor Park, includes a parade, live entertainment, food booths, and, of course, the crowning of the Maine Sea Goddess. ✉ *Harbor Park, Main St., south of U.S. 1* ☎ *800/576–7512* 🌐 *www.mainelobsterfestival.com.*

North Atlantic Blues Festival

FESTIVALS | FAMILY | About a dozen well-known musicians gather for the North Atlantic Blues Festival, a two-day affair held the first or second full weekend after July 4. The show officially takes place at the public landing on Rockland Harbor Park, but it also includes a "club crawl" through downtown Rockland on Saturday night. Admission to the festival is $45 at the gate, $75 for a weekend pass. ✉ *Public Landing, 275 Main St.* ☎ *207/596–6055* 🌐 *www.northatlantic-bluesfestival.com.*

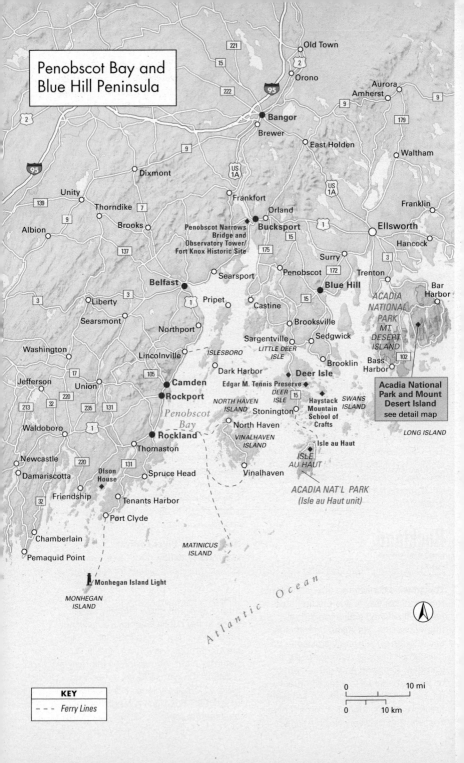

Penobscot Bay and Blue Hill Peninsula

Old Town
221
15
2
Orono
95
222
9
Aurora
Amherst
179
Bangor
Brewer
East Holden
Waltham
9
Dixmont
US 1A
Frankfort
Franklin
Unity
Thorndike
7
Orland
Ellsworth
139
Brooks
Penobscot Narrows Bridge and Observatory Tower/ Fort Knox Historic Site
Bucksport
1
Hancock
Albion
175
Surry
3
137
15
Penobscot
172
Trenton
Searsport
Blue Hill
Bar Harbor
Belfast
Searsport
Castine
15
ACADIA NATIONAL PARK
Liberty
Pripet
Brooksville
MT. DESERT ISLAND
3
1
Sargentville
Sedgwick
Searsmont
Northport
LITTLE DEER ISLE
Brooklin
Bass Harbor
Washington
Lincolnville
ISLESBORO
102
17
105
Dark Harbor
Deer Isle
Jefferson
Camden
Edgar M. Tennis Preserve
Acadia National Park and Mount Desert Island
see detail map
Union
Rockport
DEER ISLE
213
220
235
131
NORTH HAVEN ISLAND
Haystack Mountain School of Crafts
SWANS ISLAND
Waldoboro
1
Penobscot Bay
Stonington
LONG ISLAND
32
Rockland
North Haven
Newcastle
220
Thomaston
VINALHAVEN ISLAND
Isle au Haut
Damariscotta
Olson House
Spruce Head
ISLE AU HAUT
32
Friendship
Vinalhaven
ACADIA NAT'L PARK (Isle au Haut unit)
Tenants Harbor
Chamberlain
Port Clyde
Pemaquid Point
MATINICUS ISLAND
Monhegan Island Light
MONHEGAN ISLAND

Atlantic Ocean

KEY

– – – *Ferry Lines*

0   10 mi
0   10 km

VISITOR INFORMATION Penobscot Bay Area Chamber of Commerce. ☎ *207/596–0376, 800/562–2529* 🌐 *www.camden-rockland.com.*

Sights

★ Center for Maine Contemporary Art
MUSEUM | The newly minted Center for Maine Contemporary Art is a refreshing departure from the many galleries and museums in the state because it features works exclusively on nautical themes. Expect envelope-pushing exhibitions and impressive public programs. ✉ *21 Winter St.* ☎ *207/701–5005* 🌐 *cmcanow.org* 🎟 *$8.*

★ Farnsworth Art Museum
MUSEUM | **FAMILY** | One of the most important small museums in the country, much of the Farnsworth's collection is devoted to Maine-related works of the famous Wyeth family: N. C. Wyeth, an accomplished illustrator whose works were featured in many turn-of-the-20th-century books; his late son Andrew, one of the country's best-known painters; and Andrew's son James, also an accomplished painter, who like his elders before him summers nearby. Galleries in the main building always display some of Andrew Wyeth's works, such as *The Patriot, Witchcraft,* and *Turkey Pond.* The **Wyeth Center,** a former church, shows art by his father and son. The museum's collection also includes works by Fitz Henry Lane, George Bellows, Winslow Homer, Edward Hopper, Louise Nevelson, and Rockwell Kent. Changing exhibits are shown in the **Jamien Morehouse Wing.** The **Farnsworth Homestead,** a handsome circa-1850 Greek Revival dwelling that's part of the museum, retains its original lavish Victorian furnishings and is open late June–mid-October.

In Cushing, a tiny town about 10 miles south of Thomaston on the St. George River, the museum operates the **Olson House,** which is depicted in Andrew Wyeth's famous painting *Christina's World,* as well as in other works by the artist. It's accessible by guided tour only. ✉ *16 Museum St.* ☎ *207/596–6457* 🌐 *www.farnsworthmuseum.org* 🎟 *$15* 🕒 *Closed Mon. Nov.–May (except Memorial Day); also closed Tues. Jan.–Mar.*

Maine Lighthouse Museum
MUSEUM | **FAMILY** | The lighthouse museum has more than 25 Fresnel lighthouse lenses, as well as a collection of lighthouse artifacts and Coast Guard memorabilia. Permanent exhibits spotlight topics like lighthouse heroines—women who manned the lights when the keepers couldn't—and lightships. ✉ *1 Park Dr.* ☎ *207/594–3301* 🌐 *www.mainelighthousemuseum.org* 🎟 *$8.*

Restaurants

★ In Good Company
$$$ | **MODERN AMERICAN** | As the name suggests, this is an excellent spot to slow down and catch up with good friends over a bottle of wine, while savoring seasonally inspired, locally sourced dishes. The creative blend of textures and flavors that come out of the kitchen will charm your senses, a welcome surprise in this intimate space that was formerly a bank. **Known for:** outside dining in summer; excellent wine pairings; pared-down aesthetic with a focus on the food. [$] *Average main: $30* ✉ *415 Maine St.* ☎ *207/593–9110* 🌐 *www.ingoodcompanymaine.com.*

Coffee and Quick Bites

Atlantic Baking Company
$ | **AMERICAN** | Classic French and American breads and pastries, made with local and natural ingredients, emanate alongside wonderful smells daily from this bakery's ovens. There's a lunch sandwich menu for those wanting more than a snack. **Known for:** French macarons; classic sourdough; apricot pistachio oat cookies. [$] *Average main: $5* ✉ *351 Main St.* ☎ *207/596–0505* 🌐 *atlanticbakingco.com* 🕒 *Closed Sun. in mid-Sept.–May.*

Windjammer Excursions

Nothing defines the Maine coastal experience better than a sailing trip on a windjammer. These vessels were built all along the East Coast in the 19th and early 20th centuries. Designed primarily to carry cargo, these beauties (most are wood hulled) have a rich past: the schooner *Ladona* served in World War II, while others plied the waters in the lumbering, granite, fishing, and oystering trades or served as pilot boats. They vary in size but can be as small as 46 feet, holding six passengers (plus a couple of crew members), or more than 130 feet, holding 40 passengers and 10 crew members. During a windjammer excursion, passengers are usually able to participate in the navigation, be it hoisting a sail or playing captain at the wheel.

During the Camden Windjammer Festival, held Labor Day weekend, crowds gather to watch the region's fleet sail into the harbor, and most boats are open for tours. The schooner-crew talent show later in the weekend is a bit more irreverent than the majestic arrival ceremony.

A windjammer cruise gives you a chance to admire Maine's dramatic coast from the water. They can run anywhere from one to eight days, and day trips usually involve a tour of the harbor and some lighthouse sightseeing. Prices depend on length of trip and include all meals. Trips leave from Camden, Rockland, and Rockport. You can get information on the fleets by contacting one of two windjammer organizations:

Maine Windjammer Association. ☎ *800/807–9463* 🌐 *www.sailmainecoast.com.*

Maine Windjammer Cruises. Five handsome vessels offer a variety of cruises. ☎ *207/236–2938, 800/736–7981* 🌐 *www.mainewindjammercruises.com.*

Hotels

Berry Manor Inn
$$ | **B&B/INN** | Originally the residence of Rockland merchant Charles H. Berry, this 1898 shingle-style B&B sits in Rockland's National Historic District. **Pros:** a guest pantry is stocked with drinks, sweets, and treats—there's always pie; within walking distance of downtown and the harbor; some rooms can be combined to create two-room suites. **Cons:** view limited to the gardens; old-school design consistent with historic property; not pet-friendly. [$] *Rooms from: $200* ✉ *81 Talbot Ave.* ☎ *207/596–7696, 800/774–5692* 🌐 *www.berrymanorinn.com* 🛏 *12 rooms* 🍴 *Free breakfast.*

LimeRock Inn
$ | **B&B/INN** | Built in 1892 as a private home, the LimeRock is perfectly located in Rockland's National Historic District in the center of town. **Pros:** all rooms have TVs and DVD players; large in-town lot with gazebo; within easy walking distance of the Farnsworth Museum and many restaurants. **Cons:** not on the water; sometimes booked for weddings; not pet-friendly. [$] *Rooms from: $180* ✉ *96 Limerock St.* ☎ *207/594–2257, 800/546–3762* 🌐 *www.limerockinn.com* 🛏 *8 rooms* 🍴 *Free breakfast.*

★ Samoset Resort
$$$ | **RESORT** | **FAMILY** | Occupying 230 waterfront acres on the Rockland–Rockport town line, this all-encompassing resort was completely renovated in 2019.

Pros: full-service spa; children's programs; activities from basketball to croquet; the 18-hole course has been ranked among the best in the region. **Cons:** no beach; pool can be overcrowded in summer; high turnover, so service can be spotty. $ *Rooms from: $350* ⊠ *220 Warrenton St., Rockport* ☎ *207/594–2511, 800/341–1650* ⊕ *www.samosetresort.com* ⇨ *254 rooms* ❍ *Free breakfast.*

★ 250 Main Hotel

$$$ | HOTEL | With gorgeously designed guest rooms that have an inspired, mid-century-modern vibe, 250 Main has brought a forward-thinking lodging choice to Rockland. **Pros:** immaculately maintained; pet-friendly; complimentary wine-and-cheese hour in the evening. **Cons:** no pool; some traffic noise from the harbor in the morning; only guests are allowed on the roof garden. $ *Rooms from: $319* ⊠ *250 Main St.* ☎ *207/594–5994* ⊕ *250mainhotel.com* ⇨ *26 rooms* ❍ *Free Breakfast.*

🏃 Activities

Schooner *Heritage*

SAILING | FAMILY | This striking windjammer offers three- to six-day cruises and caters to individual wishes. Captain Doug Lee is a storyteller and author of nautical histories. ⊠ *North End Shipyard, 11 Front St.* ☎ *207/594–8007, 800/648–4544* ⊕ *www.schoonerheritage.com.*

★ Schooner J. & E. Riggin

SAILING | FAMILY | The family-run schooner *J. & E. Riggin* offers real-deal overnight sailing cruises that thoroughly immerse passengers in life on the water. The experience is distinguished from other local cruises by the culinary delights chef Annie concocts using locally sourced ingredients, including vegetables, eggs, and herbs freshly gathered from her own organic garden. Four-day sleeper cruises, with three freshly prepared, organic

meals and snacks each day start at $1,052; it's worth every penny. ⊠ *3 Captain Spear Dr.* ☎ *207/594–1875* ⊕ *www.mainewindjammer.com.*

Schooner *Ladona*

SAILING | A handsome racing yacht built in 1922 (and rebuilt in 1971), recently restored from nose to tail, the schooner *Ladona* leads chartered trips lasting from three to seven nights. All trips include breakfast, lunch and dinner, as well as a selection of wines and beers every evening. ⊠ *Rockland* ☎ *800/999–7352, 207/594–4723* ⊕ *www.schoonerladona.com.*

Rockport

4 miles north of Rockland via U.S. 1.

Heading north on U.S. 1, you come to Rockport before you reach the tourist mecca of Camden. The most interesting part of Rockport—the harbor—is not right on U.S. 1. Originally called Goose River, the town was part of Camden until 1891. The cutting and burning of limestone was once a major industry in this area. The stone was cut in nearby quarries and then burned in hot kilns, and the resulting lime powder was used to create mortar. Some of the massive kilns are still here.

One of the most famous sights in Rockport is the **Rockport Arch,** which crosses Union Street at the town line and says "Camden" on the other side. It was constructed of wood and mortar in 1926, demolished in 1984, then rebuilt by popular demand in 1985. The arch has been displayed in a number of movies, including *Peyton Place* and *In the Bedroom.*

GETTING HERE AND AROUND

Rockport is off U.S. 1 between Rockland and Camden. Turn on Pascal Avenue to get to the village center.

Walk From Rockport to Camden 👁

For a stunning walk or drive, take the two-lane paved road that winds up and down on its way out of Rockport, with occasional views of the ocean and the village, en route to Camden. Begin at the intersection of U.S. 1 and Pascal Avenue in Rockport. Take a right off U.S. 1 toward Rockport Harbor, then cross the bridge and go up the hill to Central Street. One block later, bear right on Russell Avenue, which becomes Chestnut Street at the Camden town line; take this all the way to downtown Camden.

Lining the way are some of the most beautiful homes in Maine, surrounded by an abundance of flora and fauna. Keep an eye out for views of the sparkling ocean, as well as for Aldermere Farm and its Belted Galloway cows. (These rare cows get their name from the foot-wide white "belt" around their middles.) The walk or drive is beautiful at any time of the year, but in fall it's breathtaking. Like the rest of New England, the coast of Maine gets a large number of fall-foliage "leaf peepers," and the reds and golds of the chestnut, birch, and elm trees along this winding route are especially beautiful.

🍴 Restaurants

★ 18 Central Oyster Bar and Grill

$$$ | SEAFOOD | The beautiful seaside village of Rockport has come alive with the opening of 18 Central Oyster Bar and Grill, which produces some of the best meals in the Mid-Coast in a cozy spot high above the working harbor. Seasonally inspired, locally harvested seafood with of hint of Southern comfort cooking is the backbone of most of the creative dishes—think fried green tomatoes with crab, chili oil, and microgreens or the crispy fried chicken accompanied by collard greens and heirloom grits. **Known for:** evenly paced, well-balanced dinners transition gracefully from one course to the next; lively atmosphere encouraged by botanically infused cocktails; packed as soon as the door opens for dinner. $ *Average main: $25* ✉ *18 Central St.* ☎ *207/466–9055* ⊕ *www.18central.com* ☉ *Closed Tues. and Wed.*

Nina June

$$$ | MEDITERRANEAN | FAMILY | Serving fresh takes on Mediterranean dishes using seafood harvested from Maine's rocky coast, this lovely trattoria gets just about everything right, from the cheery seaside setting to the family-style meals featuring a constantly changing menu where locally sourced ingredients shine. Everything from the noodles to the pickled veggies are made in-house and the presentation of each dish makes for sheer eye candy. **Known for:** family-style dinners; craft cocktails; harbor views; chef-lead cooking classes. $ *Average main: $26* ✉ *24 Central St.* ☎ *207/236–8880* ⊕ *www.ninajunerestaurant.com* ☉ *Closed Sun. and Mon.*

Camden

8 miles north of Rockland.

More than any other town along Penobscot Bay, Camden is the perfect picture-postcard of a Maine coastal village. It is one of the most popular destinations on the Maine Coast, and June–September the town is crowded with visitors—but don't let that scare you away: Camden is worth it. Just come prepared for busy traffic on the town's Main Street, and make reservations for lodging and restaurants well in advance.

Camden is famous not only for its geography, but also for its large fleet of windjammers—relics and replicas from the age of sailing—with their romantic histories and great billowing sails. At just about any hour during warm months you're likely to see at least one windjammer tied up in the harbor. Excursions, whether for an afternoon or a week, are best June–September.

The town's compact size makes it perfect for exploring on foot: shops, restaurants, and galleries line Main Street, as well as the side streets and alleys around the harbor. But be sure to include Camden's residential area on your walking tour. It is quite charming and filled with many fascinating old period houses from the time when Federal, Greek Revival, and Victorian architectural styles were the rage among the wealthy; many of them are now B&Bs. The Chamber of Commerce, at the Public Landing, can provide you with a walking map. Humped on the north side of town are the Camden Hills; drive or hike to the summit at the state park to enjoy mesmerizing views of the town, harbor, and island-dotted bay.

GETTING HERE AND AROUND

U.S. 1 becomes Camden's Main Street. Take Route 90 west from U.S. 1 and rejoin it in Warren to bypass Rockland—this is the quickest route south.

ESSENTIALS

VISITOR INFORMATION Penobscot Bay Regional Chamber of Commerce. ☎ *207/236–4404, 800/562–2529* 🌐 *www.camdenrockland.com.*

FESTIVALS

★ Windjammer Weekend

FESTIVAL | FAMILY | One of the biggest and most colorful events of the year is the Camden Windjammer Festival, which takes place over Labor Day weekend. The harbor is packed with historic vessels, there are lots of good eats, and visitors can tour the magnificent ships. ✉ *Camden* ☎ *800/807–9463* 🌐 *www.sailmainecoast.com.*

🍴 Restaurants

★ Long Grain

$ | ASIAN FUSION | This stylish Asian-fusion eatery places an emphasis on Thai curries and house-made noodles. A very popular restaurant with locals and visitors alike, reservations are essential, though you might be able to squeeze in at the tiny bar without one if you're dining solo and don't mind a little chaos; don't miss the Asian general store in the front of the restaurant, which is stocked with yummy and fun imported items. **Known for:** chef Ravin Nakjaroen is a James Beard nominated chef; consistently excellent delivery; great take-out options. [$] *Average main: $17* ✉ *20 Washington St.* ☎ *207/236–9001* 🌐 *www.longgraincamden.com* 🕒 *Closed Sun. and Mon.*

★ Natalie's Restaurant

$$$$ | MODERN AMERICAN | Located in the cozy and elegant Camden Harbour Inn, the restaurant is fine dining with a distinctly Maine flair, and seasonal ingredients—including vegetables and herbs from the property's garden—set the tone. One of the most sought-after dining spots in Camden, Natalie's is the creation of Dutch owners Raymond Brunyanszki and Oscar Verest, who brought in creative chefs to create splurge-worthy dishes in this intimate setting. **Known for:** phenomenal service with true attention to detail; signature five-course lobster tasting menu; an excellent view overlooking the harbor. [$] *Average main: $82* ✉ *Camden Harbour Inn, 83 Bay View St.* ☎ *866/658–1542, 207/236–7008* 🌐 *www.nataliesrestaurant.com* 🕒 *Closed Sun. Nov.–May. No lunch.*

☕ Coffee and Quick Bites

★ Owl and Turtle Bookshop and Cafe

BOOKS/STATIONERY | FAMILY | This pint-size but well-stocked independent bookstore with a cozy café has been serving Camden for more than 50 years. The full menu of coffee drinks is based on locally roasted beans and includes a selection of homemade baked goods. It's closed Sunday and Monday. ✉ *33 Bay View St.* ☎ *207/230–7335* 🌐 *www.owlandturtle.com.*

Hotels

Camden Hartstone Inn

$ | **B&B/INN** | This 1835 mansard-roofed Victorian home has been turned into a plush, sophisticated retreat and a fine culinary destination. **Pros:** pet-friendly; extravagant breakfasts; some private entrances. **Cons:** not on water; no wheelchair access; not all rooms have fireplaces. [$] *Rooms from: $159* ✉ *41 Elm St.* ☎ *207/236–4259* 🌐 *www.hartstoneinn.com* 🛏 *21 rooms* 🍴 *Free breakfast.*

Lord Camden Inn

$$ | **B&B/INN** | **FAMILY** | If you want to be in the center of town and near the harbor, look for this handsome brick building with the bright blue-and-white awnings. **Pros:** large continental breakfast; all rooms have balconies; mini-refrigerators in rooms. **Cons:** traffic noise in front rooms; no on-site restaurant; no on-site parking. [$] *Rooms from: $209* ✉ *24 Main St.* ☎ *207/236–4325, 800/336–4325* 🌐 *www.lordcamdeninn.com* 🛏 *36 rooms* 🍴 *Free breakfast.*

★ Norumbega Inn

$$$ | **B&B/INN** | This welcoming B&B is one of the most photographed pieces of real estate in Maine, and once you get a look at its castlelike facade, you'll understand why. **Pros:** eye-popping architecture; beautiful views of both the ocean and the gorgeously maintained; sloping lawn; champagne welcome toast, baked treats and infused waters throughout the day, and after-dinner port and cheese beside a roaring fire; firepit and lawn games in summer; secret beach within walking distance; ask the innkeepers. **Cons:** stairs to climb; a short distance from the center of town; no pets. [$] *Rooms from: $309* ✉ *63 High St.* ☎ *207/236–4646, 877/363–4646* 🌐 *www.norumbegainn.com* 🛏 *11 rooms* 🍴 *Free breakfast.*

★ Whitehall

$ | **B&B/INN** | **FAMILY** | Although the oldest part of the Whitehall is an 1834 white-clapboard sea captain's home, the bright and cheery design is decidedly contemporary with nostalgic touches here and there; the Millay Room pays homage to the poet Edna St. Vincent Millay, who grew up in the area and read her poetry at the Whitehall, where her career was launched. **Pros:** short walk to downtown and harbor; small-plates breakfast choices; beautifully renovated with a design focus. **Cons:** no good water views; walls can be a bit thin; no on-site restaurant. [$] *Rooms from: $119* ✉ *52 High St.* ☎ *207/236–3391, 800/789–6565* 🌐 *www.whitehallmaine.com* 🕒 *Closed mid-Oct.–mid-May* 🛏 *36 rooms* 🍴 *Free breakfast.*

Activities

BOATING

Heron

SAILING | **FAMILY** | This schooner, which had a cameo in the movie *The Rum Diary*, offers lunchtime sails, wildlife-watching trips, and sunset cruises. ✉ *Rockport Marine Park, Pascal Ave., Rockport* ☎ *207/236–8605, 800/599–8605* 🌐 *www.sailheron.com.*

★ *Mary Day*

SAILING | **FAMILY** | Sailing for more than 50 years, the *Mary Day* is the first schooner in Maine built specifically for vacation excursions. Meals are cooked on an antique wood-fired stove. ✉ *Camden Harbor, Atlantic Ave.* ☎ *800/992–2218* 🌐 *www.schoonermaryday.com.*

Olad

SAILING | Captain Aaron Lincoln runs two-hour trips on both the *Olad* and a smaller sailing vessel, spotting lighthouses, coastal mansions, the occasional seal, and the red-footed puffin cousins known as guillemots. Either boat can also be chartered for longer trips. ✉ *Camden Harbor, Bay View St.* ☎ *207/236–2323* 🌐 *www.maineschooners.com.*

Windjammer *Angelique*

SAILING | FAMILY | Captain Mike and Lynne McHenry have more than three decades' experience on the high seas. Three- to six-day cruise options aboard the *Angelique* include photography workshops and meteor-watching trips, as well as yoga and wellness excursions. ⊠ *Camden Harbor* ☎ *800/282–9989* ⊕ *www.sailangelique.com.*

🛍 Shopping

Camden's downtown area makes for excellent window-shopping, with lots of adorable and sophisticated boutiques stocking a curated assortment of local products. Most shops and galleries are along Camden's main drag. From the harbor, turn right on Bay View, and walk to Main/High Street. U.S. 1 has lots of names as it runs through Maine. Three are within Camden's town limits—it starts as Elm Street, changes to Main Street, then becomes High Street.

Lily, Lupine and Fern

FLOWERS | This full-service florist offers a wonderful array of gourmet foods, chocolates, wines, imported beers, high-quality olive oils, and cheeses. There's a small deck where you can enjoy harbor views and a cup of coffee. ⊠ *11 Main St.* ☎ *207/236–9600* ⊕ *www.lilylupine.com.*

★ Swans Island

HOUSEHOLD ITEMS/FURNITURE | For gorgeous, handmade blankets, throws, and pillows, as well as wraps and scarves, look no further. All products are made in Maine using natural, heirloom-quality yarns—the expert craftsmanship explains the hefty price tag. ⊠ *2 Bayview St.* ☎ *207/706–7926* ⊕ *swansislandcompany.com.*

Belfast

13 miles north of Lincolnville via U.S. 1.

Lots of Maine coastal towns like to think of themselves as the prettiest little town in the state, and any judge would be spoiled for choice. Charming Belfast (originally to be named Londonderry) is a strong contender, with a beautiful waterfront; an old and interesting main street rising from the harbor; a delightful array of B&Bs, restaurants, and shops; and friendly townsfolk. The downtown even has old-fashioned street lamps, which set the streets aglow at night.

GETTING HERE AND AROUND

U.S. 1 runs through Belfast as it travels up the coast. From Interstate 95, take U.S. 3 in Augusta to get here. The highways meet in Belfast, heading north. The information center has a large array of magazines, guidebooks, maps, and brochures that cover the entire Mid-Coast. It also can provide you with a free walking-tour brochure that describes the various historic buildings.

ESSENTIALS

VISITOR INFORMATION Belfast Area Chamber of Commerce. ☎ *207/338–5900* ⊕ *www.belfastmaine.org.*

👁 Sights

Belfast is a funky coastal town, where the streets are lined with eclectic boutiques, and a decidedly laissez-faire attitude presides. There is still evidence of the wealth of the mid-1800s, when Belfast was home to a number of business magnates, shipbuilders, ship captains, and so on. Their mansions still stand along High Street and in the residential area above it, offering excellent examples of Greek Revival and

Federal-style architecture. In fact, the town has one of the best showcases of Greek Revival homes in the state. Don't miss the "White House," where High and Church streets merge several blocks south of downtown.

🍴 Restaurants

Darby's Restaurant and Pub
$$ | AMERICAN | FAMILY | With pressed-tin ceilings, this charming, old-fashioned restaurant and bar—it's been such since 1865—is very popular with locals. Pad Thai and chicken with chili and cashews are signature dishes, but the menu also has hearty homemade soups and sandwiches and classic fish-and-chips. **Known for:** excellent happy hour; gluten-free menu choices; Buddha bowls. $ *Average main: $18* ✉ *155 High St.* ☎ *207/338–2339* ⊕ *www.darbysrestaurant.com.*

★ Young's Lobster Pound
$$$ | SEAFOOD | FAMILY | Right on the water's edge, across the harbor from downtown Belfast, this corrugated-steel building looks more like a fish cannery than a restaurant, but it's one of the best places for an authentic Maine lobster dinner. You'll see numerous tanks of live lobsters of varying size when you first walk in. **Known for:** "shore dinner": clam chowder or lobster stew, steamed clams or mussels, a 1½-pound boiled lobster, corn on the cob, and chips; family-friendly environment; BYOB. $ *Average main: $25* ✉ *2 Fairview St., off U.S. 1* ☎ *207/338–1160* ⊕ *www.youngslobsters. com* ⊗ *Takeout only Jan.–Mar.*

☕ Coffee and Quick Bites

The Only Doughnut
$ | AMERICAN | You can get anything here as long as it's a doughnut (accompanied by hot or iced coffee, if you wish). Made in the traditional cake style, what doughnuts they are; flavors might include salted caramel, buttermilk, and "full-tilt" blueberry with a glorious blueberry glaze. **Known for:**

the "citrus" (orange zest in the dough, lemon juice in the glaze); the "sea smoke" (chocolate doughnut, maple glaze, smokey salt); the "chocolate toasted coconut" (chocolate doughnut, coconut milk glaze, toasted coconut). $ *Average main: $3* ✉ *225 Northport Ave.* ☎ *207/218–1231* ⊕ *theonlydoughnut.com.*

Bucksport

9 miles north of Searsport via U.S. 1.

The stunning Penobscot Narrows Bridge, spanning the Penobscot River, makes Bucksport, a town founded in 1763, well worth a visit, even if you only stop while passing through to points north. Fort Knox, Maine's largest historic fort, overlooks the town from across the river. There are magnificent views of the imposing granite structure from the pleasant riverfront walkway downtown.

GETTING HERE AND AROUND
After you pass over the spectacular Penobscot Narrows Bridge onto Verona Island driving north on U.S. 1, you cross another bridge into Bucksport; turn left for downtown and right to continue on the highway.

👁 Sights

★ Penobscot Narrows Bridge and Observatory Tower/Fort Knox Historic Site
HISTORIC SITE | FAMILY | An "engineering marvel" is how experts describe the 2,120-foot-long Penobscot Narrows Bridge, which opened in 2006 and which is taller than the Statue of Liberty. From the surrounding countryside it pops up on the horizon like the towers of a fairy-tale castle. The bridge's 437-foot observation tower is the tallest in the world; an elevator shoots you to the top. Don't miss it—the panoramic views, which take in the hilly countryside and the river as it widens into Penobscot Bay, are

breathtaking. In summer, the observatory often offers moonrise viewings.

Also here is Fort Knox, the largest historic fort in Maine. It was built between 1844 and 1869, when, despite a treaty with Britain settling boundary disputes, invasion was still a concern—after all, the British controlled this region during both the Revolutionary War and the War of 1812. The fort never saw any real action, but it was used for troop training and as a garrison during the Civil War and the Spanish-American War. Visitors are welcome to explore the many rooms and passageways. Guided tours are given daily during the summer and several days a week in the shoulder seasons. ✉ *711 Ft. Knox Rd., off U.S. 1, Prospect* ☎ *207/469–6553* 🌐 *www.fortknoxmaine.com* 🎟 *Fort from $7* 🕘 *Closed Nov.–Apr.*

Blue Hill

20 miles east of Castine via Rtes. 166, 175, and 176.

Nestled snugly between 943-foot Blue Hill Mountain and Blue Hill Bay, the village of Blue Hill sits right beside its harbor. About 30 miles from Acadia National Park, Blue Hill makes for a more laid-back base for exploring the Mount Desert Island area, but bear in mind that 30 miles can take at least twice as long to travel with heavy traffic in summertime. Originally known for its granite quarries, copper mines, and shipbuilding, today the town is known for its pottery and the galleries, bookstores, antiques shops, and studios that line its streets. The Blue Hill Fair (🌐 *www.bluehillfair.com*), held Labor Day weekend, is a tradition in these parts, with agricultural exhibits, food, rides, and entertainment. A charming little park with a great playground is tucked away near the harbor downtown.

GETTING HERE AND AROUND

From U.S. 1 in Orland, Route 15 heads south to Blue Hill. To continue north on the highway, take Route 172 north to Ellsworth.

🍴 Restaurants

Arborvine

$$$ | MODERN AMERICAN | Glowing gas fireplaces, period antiques, exposed beams, and hardwood floors covered with oriental rugs distinguish the four candlelit dining areas in this renovated Cape Cod–style house. The seasonal menu features dishes made with organic ingredients that match well with its own beer, like crispy duck with rhubarb and lime glaze, or roasted rack of lamb with a basil-and-pine-nut crust—fresh fish dishes are also superb. **Known for:** fresh seafood dishes; classic New England fare; its adjacent nautical-themed DeepWater Brew Pub serves dishes made with organic ingredients to go with its own beer. [$] *Average main: $31* ✉ *33 Tenney Hill* ☎ *207/374–2119* 🌐 *www.arborvine.com* 🕘 *Closed Mon. No lunch.*

🛏 Hotels

Blue Hill Inn

$ | B&B/INN | One side of this Federal-style inn was built as a home in 1835, but it soon became lodging, adding a wing with a matching facade in the 1850s. **Pros:** plenty of charm; modern suites with kitchens in separate building; 30 miles from Acadia National Park; complimentary appetizers each evening if you order wine or spirits; only some rooms have fireplaces. **Cons:** some narrow stairs and thin walls consistent with historic property. [$] *Rooms from: $195* ✉ *40 Union St.* ☎ *207/374–2844* 🌐 *www.bluehillinn.com* 🕘 *Closed Nov.–mid-May, except for Cape House Suite and Studio* 🛏 *13 rooms* 🍴 *Free breakfast.*

🛍 Shopping

ART GALLERIES

Blue Hill Bay Gallery

ART GALLERIES | This gallery sells oil and watercolor landscapes and seascapes of Maine and New England from the 19th through the 21st century. It also carries the proprietor's own photography. Call ahead in the off-season. ⊠ 11 Tenney Hill ☎ 207/374–5773 ⊕ www.bluehillbaygallery.com.

POTTERY

Rackliffe Pottery

CERAMICS/GLASSWARE | A four-generation family business, this shop sells colorful pottery made with lead-free glazes. You can choose between water pitchers, serving platters, tea-and-coffee sets, and sets of canisters, among other lovely items. ⊠ 132 Ellsworth Rd. ☎ 888/631–3321 ⊕ www.rackliffepottery.com.

WINE

Blue Hill Wine Shop

WINE/SPIRITS | In a restored barn and cape, one of Blue Hill's earliest houses, the Blue Hill Wine Shop carries more than 3,000 carefully selected wines, cheeses, groceries, local and imported beer and ciders, coffee and teas. ⊠ 138 Main St. ☎ 207/374–2161 ⊕ www.bluehillwineshop.com.

Deer Isle

16 miles south of Blue Hill via Rtes. 176 and 15.

Reachable by a bridge, Deer Isle's thick woods give way to tidal coves. Stacks of lobster traps populate the backyards of shingled houses, and dirt roads lead to secluded summer cottages. This region is prized by artists, and studios and galleries are plentiful.

At the southern end of the island, Stonington is a charming seaside town with a lovely Main Street. It's also the gateway to Isle au Haut, which contains a remote section of Acadia National Park.

GETTING HERE AND AROUND

From Sedgwick, Route 15 crosses a 1930s suspension bridge onto Little Deer Isle and continues on to the larger Deer Isle.

Isle au Haut Boat Services provides a daily mail-boat ferry service out of Stonington to Isle au Haut. During the summer season, trips increase from two to five Monday–Saturday and from one to two on Sunday. From mid-June until late September, the boat also stops at Duck Harbor, in the island section of Acadia National Park (it will not unload bicycles, kayaks, or canoes at the Park Landing, but will at the Town Landing). Ferry service is scaled back in the fall, then returns to the regular or "winter" schedule.

VISITOR INFORMATION

CONTACTS Deer Isle–Stonington Chamber of Commerce. ☎ 207/348–6124 ⊕ www.deerisle.com. Isle au Haut Boat Services. ⊠ 37 Seabreeze Ave., Stonington ☎ 207/367–5193 ⊕ isleauhaut.com.

👁 Sights

Edgar M. Tennis Preserve

NATURE PRESERVE | Enjoy several miles of woodland and shore trails at the Edgar M. Tennis Preserve. Look for hawks, eagles, and ospreys and wander among old apple trees, fields of wildflowers, and ocean-polished rocks. ⊠ Tennis Rd., Deer Isle ☎ 207/348–2455 ⊕ www.islandheritagetrust.org 🆓 Free.

Haystack Mountain School of Crafts

COLLEGE | Want to learn a new craft? This school 6 miles from Deer Isle Village offers one- and two-week courses for people of all skill levels in crafts such as blacksmithing, basketry, printmaking, and weaving. Artisans from around the world present free evening lectures throughout summer. Tours of the school and studios are available on Wednesday.

✉ *89 Haystack School Dr., off Rte. 15, Deer Isle* ☎ *207/348–2306* ⊕ *www.haystack-mtn.org* ⌧ *Tours $5.*

Isle au Haut

ISLAND | French explorer Samuel D. Champlain discovered Isle au Haut—or "High Island"—in 1604, but heaps of shells suggest that native populations lived on or visited the island prior to his arrival. The island is accessible only by mail boat, but the 45-minute journey is well worth the effort. Acadia National Park extends to cover part of the island, with miles of trails, and the boat will drop visitors off there in peak season. The island has some seasonal rentals but no inns and only three stores. ✉ *Isle Au Haut* ⊕ *www.isleauhautmaine.us.*

🎩 Shopping

Nervous Nellie's Jams and Jellies

FOOD/CANDY | Jams and jellies are made right on the property at Nervous Nellie's. There is a tearoom with homemade goodies, and also a fanciful sculpture garden with everything from knights to witches to a lobster and a flamingo. They are the works of sculptor Peter Beerits, who operates Nervous Nellie's with his wife. ✉ *598 Sunshine Rd., off Rte. 15, Deer Isle* ☎ *207/348–6182* ⊕ *www.nervousnellies.com.*

Bar Harbor

34 miles from Blue Hill via Rte. 172 and U.S. 1.

A resort town since the 19th century, Bar Harbor is the artistic, culinary, and social center of Mount Desert Island, and it serves visitors to Acadia National Park with inns, motels, and restaurants. Around the turn of the last century the island was known as a summer haven for the very rich because of its cool breezes. The wealthy built lavish mansions throughout the island, many of which were destroyed in a huge fire that devastated the island in 1947—a good number of those that survived have been converted into businesses. In Bar Harbor, shops are clustered along Main, Mount Desert, and Cottage streets; take a stroll down West Street, a National Historic District, where you can see some fine old houses.

The island and the surrounding Gulf of Maine are home to a great variety of wildlife: whales, seals, eagles, falcons, ospreys, and puffins (though not right offshore here), and forest dwellers such as deer, foxes, coyotes, and beavers.

GETTING HERE AND AROUND

In Ellsworth, Route 3 leaves U.S. 1 and heads to Bar Harbor. In season, free Island Explorer buses (☎ *207/667–5796* ⊕ *www.exploreacadia.com*) take visitors to Acadia National Park and other island towns. There is also a passenger ferry to Winter Harbor across Frenchman Bay.

ESSENTIALS

VISITOR INFORMATION Bar Harbor Chamber of Commerce. ☎ *207/288–5103* ⊕ *www.visitbarharbor.com.*

👁 Sights

★ Abbe Museum

MUSEUM | **FAMILY** | This important museum dedicated to Maine's indigenous tribes—collectively known as the Wabanaki—is the state's only Smithsonian-affiliated facility and one of the few places in Maine to experience Native culture as interpreted by Native peoples themselves. The year-round archaeology exhibit displays spear points, bone tools, and other artifacts found around Mount Desert Island and exhibits often feature contemporary Native American art, and there are frequent demonstrations of everything from boatbuilding to basket weaving. Call on rainy days for impromptu children's activities. A second location, inside the park at Sieur de Monts Spring, open only during the summer, features artifacts from the earliest digs around the island. ✉ *26 Mount Desert St.* ☎ *207/288–3519* 🌐 *www.abbemuseum.org* 🎟 *$10.*

🍴 Restaurants

★ Burning Tree

$$$ | **SEAFOOD** | One of the top restaurants in Maine, this easy-to-miss gem with a festive dining room is on Route 3 five miles from Bar Harbor in the village of Otter Creek. The seasonal menu emphasizes freshly caught seafood, and seven species of fish are offered virtually every day—all from the Gulf of Maine. **Known for:** farm to table cuisine; Southeast Asian-inspired flavors; regionally sourced ingredients. [$] *Average main: $30* ✉ *69 Otter Creek Dr., Otter Creek* ✣ *5 miles from Bar Harbor, 7 miles from Northeast Harbor* ☎ *207/288–9331* ⏲ *Closed mid-Oct.–mid-June. No lunch.*

★ Havana

$$$ | **CUBAN** | A lively yet intimate spot, Havana serves Latin-inspired dishes paired with robust wines right in the middle of downtown Bar Harbor. In the summer, have a bite on "the Parrilla" (the informal, no-reservations patio); during winter months, dine in a pleasant indoor space with a modern aesthetic, featuring clean lines and cheery colors. **Known for:** Spanish tortillas; a lively atmosphere fueled by craft cocktails; after-dinner affogato made with MDI ice cream. [$] *Average main: $34* ✉ *318 Main St.* ☎ *207/288–2822* 🌐 *www.havanamaine.com* ⏲ *No lunch.*

☕ Coffee and Quick Bites

Lompoc Cafe and Books

$ | **AMERICAN** | This shop is nestled aside a shaded patio just a quick walk from the downtown Bar Harbor bustle. Stop in for a quiet respite for relaxing with a coffee or beer while noshing on a bagel or artisanal pizza and perusing a book. **Known for:** banh mi sandwich in breakfast and lunch versions; eclectic selection of books; located next to public parking lot. [$] *Average main: $11* ✉ *36 Rodick St.* ☎ *207/901–0004* 🌐 *www.lompoccafe.com* ⏲ *Closed Mon.*

🛏 Hotels

Bar Harbor Grand Hotel

$$ | **HOTEL** | Taking one of the well-appointed, modern rooms in this renovated historic building puts you right in the middle of Bar Harbor, just a stone's throw from lively restaurants, cafés, and gift shops. **Pros:** excellent center-of-town location; breakfast included; good value. **Cons:** street noise; decor could use updates; service can be hit or miss. [$] *Rooms from: $245* ✉ *269 Main St.* ☎ *207/288–5226* 🌐 *www.barharborgrand.com* ⏲ *Closed mid-Nov.–Mar.* 🛏 *71 rooms* 🍴 *Free breakfast.*

Bar Harbor Inn and Spa

$$$ | **HOTEL** | Originally established in the late 1800s as a men's social club, this waterfront inn has rooms spread among three buildings on well-landscaped grounds. **Pros:** bay and ocean views; proximity to downtown and Acadia National Park; shore path along the waterfront from the hotel. **Cons:** spotty cell phone service; views often include cruise ships in port; dining reservations recommended. [$] *Rooms from: $350* ✉ *1 Newport Dr.* ☎ *207/288–3351, 800/248–3351* 🌐 *www.barharborinn.com* ⏲ *Closed late Nov.–mid-Mar.* 🛏 *153 rooms* 🍴 *Free breakfast.*

Island Place

$ | **HOTEL** | **FAMILY** | This motel's clean rooms and central location make it a good base for exploring the Bar Harbor area. **Pros:** centrally located; microwave and refrigerator available for guests in lobby; free parking. **Cons:** two-night minimum in high season; basic rooms; renovated motel-style lodgings are not for everyone. [$] *Rooms from: $188* ✉ *51 Holland Ave.* ☎ *207/288–3771* 🌐 *www.islandplacebh.com* 🛏 *10 rooms* 🍴 *No meals.*

★ **West Street Hotel**

$$$$ | **RESORT** | Maine has some pretty phenomenal resort destinations in the Kennebunks and on the Mid-Coast, but to enjoy the state's premiere resort experience you'll do best to make the trek Down East to Bar Harbor to stay at the West Street Hotel, where resort culture truly shines. **Pros:** all the expected luxuries of a resort and then some; each floor is equipped with guest pantries filled with snacks and goodies; one of the most tastefully decorated resorts in Maine. **Cons:** it's a trek to get Down East; $25 daily resort fee; dogs allowed, but for an additional $75 per dog per night (two-dog limit). $ *Rooms from: $479* ✉ *50 West St.* ☎ *207/288–0825* ⊕ *www. theweststreethotel.com* ⇌ *85 rooms* ⎮◎⎮ *Free breakfast.*

⚡ Activities

AIR TOURS

★ **Acadia Air Tours**

FLYING/SKYDIVING/SOARING | This outfit runs sightseeing flights over Bar Harbor and Acadia National Park. Most tours run 15 minutes to an hour and range $75–$375 per person. The romantic sunset tour is $50 extra. ✉ *1 West St.* ☎ *207/288–0703* ⊕ *www.acadiaairtours.com.*

BIKING

Acadia Bike

BICYCLING | **FAMILY** | Rent mountain bikes and hybrids at Acadia Bike, both good models for negotiating the carriage roads in Acadia National Park. ✉ *48 Cottage St.* ☎ *207/288–9605, 800/526–8615* ⊕ *www. acadiabike.com.*

Bar Harbor Bicycle Shop

BICYCLING | Rent bikes for anywhere from four hours to a full week at the Bar Harbor Bicycle Shop. ✉ *141 Cottage St.* ☎ *207/288–3886* ⊕ *www.barharborbike. com.*

BOATING

Coastal Kayaking Tours

KAYAKING | **FAMILY** | This outfitter has been leading trips in the scenic waters off Mount Desert Island since 1982. Trips are limited to no more than 12 people. The season is mid-May–mid-October. ✉ *48 Cottage St.* ☎ *207/288–9605* ⊕ *www. acadiafun.com.*

Downeast Sailing Adventures

BOATING | **FAMILY** | Take two-hour sailing trips and sunset cruises for $50 per person with six passengers, or hire a private charter starting at $125 per hour. Boats depart the Upper Town Dock in Southwest Harbor and several other locations. ✉ *Eagle Lake Rd.* ☎ *207/288–2216* ⊕ *www.downeastsail.com.*

Margaret Todd

BOATING | **FAMILY** | The 151-foot four-masted schooner *Margaret Todd* operates 1½- to 2-hour trips three times daily among the islands of Frenchman Bay. The sunset sail has live folk music, and the 2 pm trip is sometimes narrated by an Acadia National Park ranger. Trips are $42–$48 and depart mid-May–mid-October. ✉ *Bar Harbor Inn pier, 7 Newport Dr.* ☎ *207/288–4585* ⊕ *www.downeastwindjammer.com.*

WHALE-WATCHING

Bar Harbor Whale Watch Co.

WHALE-WATCHING | **FAMILY** | This company has six boats, one of them a 130-foot jet-propelled double-hulled catamaran with spacious decks. The company offers lighthouse, lobstering, sunset, and seal-, puffin- and whale-watching cruises, as well as a trip to Acadia National Park's Baker Island. Most tours run $32–$63 per person; consider spending $199 for a nine-hour tour that passes 18 lighthouses, including seven in Canada. ✉ *1 West St.* ☎ *207/288–2386, 800/942–5374* ⊕ *www.barharborwhales.com.*

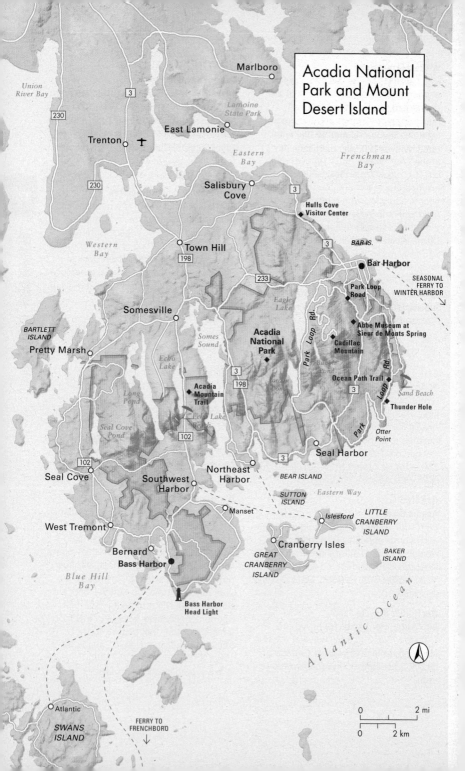

Acadia National Park and Mount Desert Island

Marlboro

Union River Bay

230

3

Lamoine State Park

East Lamonie

Trenton

230

Eastern Bay

Frenchman Bay

Salisbury Cove

3

Hulls Cove Visitor Center

BAR IS.

Town Hill

198

3

Bar Harbor

SEASONAL FERRY TO WINTER HARBOR

233

Park Loop Road

Somesville

Eagle Lake

Park Loop Rd.

Abbe Museum at Sieur de Monts Spring

BARTLETT ISLAND

Somes Sound

Acadia National Park

Cadillac Mountain

Pretty Marsh

Echo Lake

Ocean Path Trail

Loop Rd.

3

Western Bay

3

198

Acadia Mountain Trail

Sand Beach

Thunder Hole

Long Pond

Echo Lake Beach

Park

Otter Point

Seal Cove Pond

102

Seal Cove

102

Southwest Harbor

Northeast Harbor

3

Seal Harbor

BEAR ISLAND

Eastern Way

West Tremont

Manset

SUTTON ISLAND

Islesford

LITTLE CRANBERRY ISLAND

Bernard

Bass Harbor

Cranberry Isles

GREAT CRANBERRY ISLAND

BAKER ISLAND

Blue Hill Bay

Bass Harbor Head Light

Atlantic Ocean

Atlantic

SWANS ISLAND

FERRY TO FRENCHBORD

N

0   2 mi

0   2 km

🛍 Shopping

ART

Island Artisans

ART GALLERIES | This shop sells basketry, pottery, fiber work, and jewelry created by over 100 Maine artisans. It's open May–December. ⊠ *99 Main St.* ☎ *207/288–4214* ⊕ *www.islandartisans. com.*

Native Arts Gallery

ART GALLERIES | Silver and gold Southwest Indian jewelry is a specialty at Native Arts Gallery, open May–October. ⊠ *99 Main St.* ☎ *207/288–4474* ⊕ *www.nativearts-gallery.com.*

★ The Rock and Art Shop

BOOKS/STATIONERY | As advertised, there are both "rocks" and "art" for sale at this eclectic family-owned store. There are also taxidermied animals, fossils, home decor and plants, interesting jewelry, and bath products. They're open May–November. ⊠ *23 Cottage St.* ☎ *207/288–4800* ⊕ *www.therockandartshop.com.*

SPORTING GOODS

Cadillac Mountain Sports

SPORTING GOODS | One of the best sporting-goods stores in the state, Cadillac Mountain Sports has developed a following of locals and visitors alike. Here you'll find top-quality climbing, hiking, boating, paddling, and camping equipment, and in winter you can rent cross-country skis, ice skates, and snowshoes. ⊠ *26 Cottage St.* ☎ *207/288–4532* ⊕ *www. cadillacsports.com.*

Acadia National Park

3 miles from Bar Harbor via U.S. 3.

With about 49,000 acres of protected forests, beaches, mountains, and rocky coastline, Acadia National Park is one of the most visited national parks in America. According to the National Park Service, more than 2 million people visit Acadia each year, and the number is steadily rising. The park holds some of the most spectacular scenery on the Eastern Seaboard: a rugged coastline of surf-pounded granite and an interior graced by sculpted mountains, quiet ponds, and lush, deciduous forests. Cadillac Mountain (named after a Frenchman who explored here in the late 1600s and who later founded Detroit)—the highest point of land on the East Coast—dominates the park. Although rugged, the park also has graceful stone bridges, miles of carriage roads (popular with walkers, runners, and bikers as well as horse-drawn carriages), and the Jordan Pond House restaurant (famous for its popovers).

The 27-mile Park Loop Road provides an excellent overview, but to truly appreciate the park you must get off the main road and experience it by walking, hiking, biking, sea kayaking, or taking a carriage ride. Get off the beaten path, and you can find places you'll have practically all to yourself. Mount Desert Island was once a preserve of summer homes for the very rich (and still is for some), and, partly because of this, Acadia is the first national park in the United States largely created by donations of private land. There are two smaller parts of the park: on Isle au Haut, 15 miles away out in the ocean, and on the Schoodic Peninsula, on the mainland across Frenchman Bay from Mount Desert.

Acadia National Park Essentials

GETTING HERE AND AROUND

Island Explorer buses, which serve the park and island villages June 23–Columbus Day, offer transportation to and around the park. In addition to regularly scheduled stops, they also pick up and drop off passengers anywhere in the park it is safe to stop.

Long ramps on Maine's many docks make it easier to access boats at either high or low tide.

Route 3 leads to the island and Bar Harbor from Ellsworth and circles the eastern part of the island. Route 102 is the major road on the west side.

CONTACTS Island Explorer. ☎ *207/667–5796* ⊕ *www.exploreacadia.com.*

ESSENTIALS

A user fee is required May–October. The per-vehicle fee is $30 ($25 for motorcycles) for a seven-consecutive-day pass; you can walk or bike in on a $15 individual pass (also good for seven days); or you can use your National Park America the Beautiful Pass, which allows entrance to any national park in the United States. There are also a few fee-free days throughout the year.

The park is open 24 hours a day, year-round, but roads are closed December–mid-April, except for the Ocean Drive section of Park Loop Road and a small part of the road with access to Jordan Pond.

Acadia National Park
✉ *Acadia National Park* ☎ *207/288–3338* ⊕ *www.nps.gov/acad.*

Mount Desert Chamber of Commerce
✉ *Northeast Harbor* ☎ *207/276–5040* ⊕ *mtdesertchamber.org.*

Mount Desert Island Information Center at Thompson Island
✉ *Bar Harbor* ☎ *207/288–3338* ⊕ *www. nps.gov/acad/planyourvisit/hours.htm.*

◉ Sights

TRAILS

★ Acadia Mountain Trail

HIKING/WALKING | If you're up for a challenge, this is one of the area's best trails. The 2.5-mile round-trip climb up Acadia Mountain is a steep and strenuous 700-foot climb, but the payoff views of Somes Sound are grand. If you want a guided trip, look into ranger-led hikes for this trail. ✉ *Rte. 102* ☎ *207/288–3338* ⊕ *www.nps.gov/acad.*

★ Ocean Path Trail

HIKING/WALKING | This easily accessible 4.4-mile round-trip trail runs parallel to the Ocean Drive section of the Park Loop Road from Sand Beach to Otter Point. It has some of the best scenery in Maine: cliffs and boulders of pink granite at the ocean's edge, twisted branches of dwarf jack pines, and ocean views that stretch to the horizon. Be sure to save time to stop at **Thunder Hole,** named for the sound the waves make as they thrash through a narrow opening in the granite cliffs, into a sea cave, and whoosh up and out. Approximately halfway between Sand Beach and Otter Cliff, steps lead down to the water, where you can watch the wave action close up. Use caution as you descend (access may be limited due to storms), and also if you venture onto the outer cliffs along this walk. ✉ *Ocean Dr. section of Park Loop Rd.*

SCENIC DRIVES

★ Park Loop Road

SCENIC DRIVE | FAMILY | This 27-mile road provides a perfect introduction to the park. You can drive it in an hour, but allow at least half a day, so that you can explore the many sites along the way. The route is also served by the free Island Explorer buses, which also pick up and drop off passengers anywhere it is safe to stop along the route. Traveling south on Park Loop Road toward Sand Beach, you'll reach a small ticket booth, where, if you haven't already, you will need to pay the park entrance fee (May–October). Traffic is one-way from the Route 233 entrance to the Stanley Brook Road entrance south of the Jordan Pond House. The section known as Ocean Drive is open year-round, as is a small section that provides access to Jordan Pond from Seal Harbor. ✉ *Acadia National Park.*

SCENIC STOPS

★ Cadillac Mountain

MOUNTAIN—SIGHT | FAMILY | At 1,530 feet, this is one of the first places in the United States to see the sun's rays at daybreak. It is the highest mountain on the Eastern Seaboard north of Brazil. Hundreds of visitors make the trek to see the sunrise or—for those less inclined to get up so early—sunset. From the smooth summit you have a stunning 360-degree view of the jagged coastline that runs around the island. The road up the mountain is closed December–mid-May. ✉ *Cadillac Summit Rd.* ⊕ *www.nps. gov/acad.*

VISITOR CENTER

Hulls Cove Visitor Center

INFO CENTER | FAMILY | This is a great spot to get your bearings. A large 3D relief map of Mount Desert Island gives you the lay of the land, and a free 15-minute video about everything the park has to offer plays every half hour. You can pick up guidebooks, maps of hiking trails and carriage roads, and recordings for drive-it-yourself tours—don't forget to grab a schedule of ranger-led programs, which includes guided hikes and other interpretive events. Junior-ranger programs for kids, nature hikes, photography walks, tide-pool explorations, and evening talks are all popular. The Acadia National Park Headquarters, off Route 233 near the north end of Eagle Lake, serves as the park's visitor center during the off-season. ✉ *25 Visitor Center Rd., Bar Harbor* ☎ *207/288–3338* ⊕ *www.nps.gov/acad.*

Book a Carriage Ride

Riding down one of the park's scenic carriage roads in a horse-drawn carriage is a truly unique way to experience Acadia. You can book a reservation for a ride, late May–mid-October, with Wildwood Stables, located next to Park Loop Road (☎ *877/276–3622*). One of the carriages can accommodate wheelchairs.

All About Mount Desert Island

With some of the most dramatic and varied scenery on the Maine Coast—and home to Maine's only national park—Mount Desert Island (pronounced "dessert" by locals) is Maine's most popular tourist destination, attracting well over 2 million visitors a year. Much of the approximately 12-by-15-mile island belongs to Acadia National Park. You can take a scenic drive along the island's rocky coastline, whose stark cliffs rise from the ocean. A network of old carriage roads lets you explore Acadia's wooded interior, filled with birds and other wildlife, and trails for hikers of all skill levels lead to rounded mountaintops, providing views of Frenchman and Blue Hill bays and beyond. Ponds and lakes beckon you to swim, fish, or boat, and ferries and charter boats provide a different perspective on the island and a chance to explore the outer islands.

Mount Desert Island has four different towns, each with its own personality. The town of Bar Harbor is on the northeastern corner of the island and includes the little villages of Hulls Cove, Salisbury Cove, and Town Hill. Aside from Acadia, Bar Harbor is the major tourist destination here, with plenty of lodging, dining, and shopping. The town of Mount Desert, in the middle of the island, has four main villages: Somesville, Seal Harbor, Otter Creek, and Northeast Harbor, a summer haven for the very wealthy. Southwest Harbor includes the smaller village of Manset south of the village center. Tremont is at the southernmost tip of the island and stretches up the western shore. It includes the villages of Bass Harbor, Bernard, and Seal Cove. Yes, Mount Desert Island is a place with three personalities: the hustling, bustling tourist mecca of Bar Harbor; the "quiet side" on the western half; and the vast natural expanse of Acadia National Park.

Beaches

The park has two swimming beaches, Sand Beach and Echo Lake Beach. Sand Beach, along Park Loop Road, has changing rooms, restrooms, and a lifeguard on duty Memorial Day–Labor Day. Echo Lake Beach, on the western side of the island just north of Southwest Harbor, has much warmer water, as well as changing rooms, restrooms, and a lifeguard on duty throughout the summer. This beach is particularly well suited for small children, as the water remains relatively shallow fairly far out.

Echo Lake Beach
A quiet lake surrounded by woods in the shadow of Beech Mountain, Echo Lake draws swimmers to its sandy southern shore. The lake bottom is a bit muckier than the ocean beaches nearby, but the water is considerably warmer. The surrounding trail network skirts the lake and ascends the mountain. The beach is 2 miles north of Southwest Harbor. **Amenities:** lifeguards; toilets. **Best for:** swimming. ⊠ *Echo Lake Beach Rd., off Rte. 102.*

Sand Beach
This pocket beach is hugged by two picturesque rocky outcroppings, and the combination of the crashing waves and the chilly water (peaking at around 55°F) keeps most people on the beach. You'll find some swimmers at the height of summer, but the rest of the year this is a place for strolling and snapping photos. In the shoulder season, you'll have the

place to yourself. **Amenities:** lifeguards; parking; toilets. **Best for:** solitude; sunrise; walking. ⊠ *Ocean Dr. section of Park Loop Rd., 3 miles south of Rte. 3.*

🏃 Activities

The best way to see Acadia National Park is to get out of your vehicle and explore on foot or by bicycle or boat. There are more than 45 miles of carriage roads that are perfect for walking and biking in the warmer months and for cross-country skiing and snowshoeing in winter. There are 125 miles of trails for hiking, numerous ponds and lakes for canoeing or kayaking, two beaches for swimming, and steep cliffs for rock climbing.

CAMPING

Acadia National Park's two main campgrounds, Seawall and Blackwoods, don't have water views, but the price is right and the ocean is just a 10-minute walk from each. The park added a third campground on the Schoodic Peninsula in 2015.

Blackwoods Campground. Located only 5 miles from Bar Harbor, this is Acadia's most popular campground. It is open year-round and well served by the Island Explorer bus system. ⊠ *Rte. 3, 5 miles south of Bar Harbor* ☎ *877/444–6777 for reservations* ⊕ *www.recreation.gov.*

Schoodic Woods Campground. Opened in September 2015, this campground is in the Schoodic Peninsula section of Acadia, meaning you have to take the ferry from Winter Harbor to cross over to Mount Desert Island (or drive). It is open May–Columbus Day. ⊠ *Schoodic Loop Rd., 1 mile south of Rte. 186, Winter Harbor.*

Seawall Campground. On the quiet western side of the island, Seawall is open late May–September. ⊠ *Rte. 102A, 4 miles south of Southwest Harbor* ☎ *877/444–6777 for reservations* ⊕ *www.recreation.gov.*

The Early Bird 👁 Gets the Sun

During your visit to Mount Desert, pick a day when you are willing to get up very early, around 4:30 or 5 am. Drive with a friend, or a camera with a timer, to the top of Cadillac Mountain in Acadia National Park, and stand on the highest rock you can find and wait for the sun to come up. When it does, have your friend, or your camera, take a photo of you looking at it and label the photo something like, "The first person in the country to see the sun come up today."

HIKING

Acadia National Park maintains more than 125 miles of hiking trails, from easy strolls around lakes and ponds to rigorous treks with climbs up rock faces and scrambles along cliffs. Although hiking trails are concentrated on the east side of the island, the west side also has some scenic trails. For those wishing for a longer trek, try the trails leading up Cadillac Mountain or Dorr Mountain; you may also try Parkman, Sargeant, and Penobscot mountains. Most hiking is done mid-May–mid-November; snow falls early in Maine, so from as early as late November to the end of March, cross-country skiing and snowshoeing replace hiking. Volunteers groom most of the carriage roads if there's been 4 inches of snow or more. ■**TIP→ You can park at one end of any trail and use the free shuttle bus to get back to your starting point.**

Distances for trails are given for round-trips.

Bass Harbor

10 miles south of Somesville via Rtes. 102 and 102A.

Bass Harbor is a tiny lobstering village with a relaxed atmosphere and a few accommodations and restaurants. If you're looking to get away from the crowds, consider using this hardworking community as your base. Although Bass Harbor does not draw as many tourists as other villages, the Bass Harbor Head Light in Acadia National Park is one of the region's most popular attractions and is undoubtedly one of the most photographed lighthouses in Maine. From Bass Harbor, you can hike the Ship Harbor Nature Trail or take a ferry to Frenchboro or Swans Island.

GETTING HERE AND AROUND

From Bass Harbor, the Maine State Ferry Service operates the *Captain Henry Lee*, carrying both passengers and vehicles to Swans Island (40 minutes; $17.50 per adult round-trip, $38.50 per car with driver) and Frenchboro (50 minutes; $17.50 per adult round-trip, $38.50 per car with driver). Round-trip fare for passengers 6–17 is $11.25; children five and under ride free. Round-trip service to Frenchboro on the car ferry is available only on the first and third Wednesday; a round-trip passenger-only service to Frenchboro on a smaller boat is offered Friday April–November with trips departing Bass Harbor at 8 am and 5:15 pm with returns at 9 am and 6 pm.

ESSENTIALS

TRANSPORTATION INFORMATION Maine State Ferry Service. ✉ *45 Granville Rd.* ☎ *207/244–3254* 🌐 *www.maine.gov/mdot/ferry.*

Caution

Every few years, someone falls off one of the park's trails or cliffs and is swept out to sea. There is a lot of loose, rocky gravel along the shoreline, and sea rocks can often be slippery—so watch your step.

Sights

★ Bass Harbor Head Light

LIGHTHOUSE | Built in 1858, this lighthouse is one of the most photographed lights in Maine. Now automated, it marks the entrance to Bass Harbor and Blue Hill Bay. You can't actually go inside—the grounds and residence are Coast Guard property—but two trails around the facility have excellent views. It's within Acadia National Park, and there is parking. **■ TIP→ The best place to take a picture is from the rocks below—but watch your step, as they can be slippery.** ✉ *Lighthouse Rd., off Rte. 102A* ☎ *207/244–9753* 🎫 *Free.*

Restaurants

Thurston's Lobster Pound

$$ | **SEAFOOD** | Right on Bass Harbor, looking across to the village, Thurston's is easy to spot because of its bright yellow awning. You can order everything from a grilled-cheese crab sandwich, haddock chowder, or hamburger to a boiled lobster served with clams or mussels and dine at covered outdoor tables, or you can buy fresh lobsters to go. **Known for:** family-friendly environment; lobster fresh off the boat; good place to watch sunsets. [$] *Average main: $20* ✉ *Steamboat Wharf, 9 Thurston Rd., Bernard* ☎ *207/244–7600* 🌐 *www.thurstonforlobster.com* 🕒 *Closed mid-Oct.–Memorial Day.*

Schoodic Peninsula

25 miles east of Ellsworth via U.S. 1 and Rte. 186.

The landscape of Schoodic Peninsula's craggy coastline, towering evergreens, and views over Frenchman Bay are breathtaking year-round. A drive through the well-to-do summer community of Grindstone Neck shows what Bar Harbor might have been like before so many of its mansions were destroyed in the Great Fire of 1947. Artists and artisans have opened galleries in and around Winter Harbor. Anchored at the foot of the peninsula, Winter Harbor was once part of Gouldsboro, which wraps around it. The southern tip of the peninsula is home to the Schoodic section of Acadia National Park.

GETTING HERE AND AROUND

From U.S. 1, Route 186 loops around the peninsula. Route 195 runs from U.S. 1 to Prospect Harbor and on to its end in Corea.

Island Explorer

The Island Explorer operates on the Schoodic Peninsula, with bus service from Prospect Harbor, Birch Harbor, and Winter Harbor to anywhere in the Schoodic Peninsula section of the park that's safe to stop. The bus also connects with the Winter Harbor ferry terminal, where you can take a ferry back to Bar Harbor. ⊠ *Winter Harbor* ☎ *207/667–5796* ⊕ *www.exploreacadia.com.*

ESSENTIALS

VISITOR INFORMATION Schoodic Chamber of Commerce. ⊕ *schoodicchamber. com.*

◉ Sights

Within Gouldsboro on the Schoodic Peninsula are several small coastal villages. You drive through Wonsqueak and Birch Harbor after leaving the Schoodic section of Acadia National Park. Near Birch Harbor you can find Prospect Harbor, a small fishing village nearly untouched by tourism. In Corea, there's little to do besides watch fishermen at work, wander along stone beaches, or gaze out at the sea.

★ Acadia National Park

NATIONAL/STATE PARK | The only section of Maine's national park that sits on the mainland is at the southern end of the Schoodic Peninsula in the town of Winter Harbor. The park has a scenic 6-mile loop that edges along the coast, yielding views of Grindstone Neck, Winter Harbor, Winter Harbor Lighthouse, and, across the water, Cadillac Mountain. At the tip of the point, huge slabs of pink granite lie jumbled along the shore, thrashed unmercifully by the crashing surf, and jack pines cling to life amid the rocks. Fraser Point, at the beginning of the loop, is an ideal place for a picnic. Work off lunch with a hike up Schoodic Head for the panoramic views up and down the coast. During the summer season you can take a passenger ferry ($14 one-way, $28 round-trip) to Winter Harbor from Bar Harbor. In Winter Harbor catch the free Island Explorer bus, which stops throughout the park, but you'll need to take the ferry to get back to Bar Harbor. ⊠ *End of Moore Rd., off Rte. 186, Winter Harbor* ☎ *207/288–3338* ⊕ *www.nps.gov/acad.*

Schoodic Education and Research Center

COLLEGE | In the Schoodic Peninsula section of Acadia National Park, this center offers lectures, workshops, and kid-friendly events about nature. It's worth a drive-by just to see the Rockefeller Building, a massive 1935 French Eclectic and Renaissance-style structure with a stone-and-half-timber facade that served as naval offices and housing. The building now acts as a visitor center after an extensive renovation. ⊠ *9 Atterbury Circle, Winter Harbor* ☎ *207/288–1310* ⊕ *www.schoodicinstitute.org.*

🍴 Restaurants

Chase's Restaurant

$ | **SEAFOOD** | **FAMILY** | This family restaurant has a reputation for serving good, basic fare—and in this region that means a whole lot of fresh fish. There are large and small fried seafood dinners, as well as several more expensive seafood platters. **Known for:** family-friendly dining; classic Maine fare; no-frills atmosphere. Ⓢ *Average main: $14* ⊠ *193 Main St., Winter Harbor* ☎ *207/963–7171.*

🛏 Hotels

Acadia's Oceanside Meadows Inn

$ | **B&B/INN** | **FAMILY** | A must for nature lovers, this lodging sits on a 200-acre preserve dotted with woods, streams, salt marshes, and ponds; it's home to the Oceanside Meadows Innstitute for the Arts and Sciences, which holds lectures, musical performances, art exhibits, and other events in the restored barn. **Pros:** one of the region's few sand beaches; staff share info about the area over tea; most rooms have water views. **Cons:** need to cross road to beach; decor a bit dated. Ⓢ *Rooms from: $185* ⊠ *Rte. 195 Prospect Harbor Rd., Prospect Harbor* ☎ *207/963–5557* ⊕ *www.oceaninn.com* ☾ *Closed mid-Oct.–late May* ⌑ *15 rooms* ⍭⃝ *Free breakfast.*

🛍 Shopping

ANTIQUES

U.S. Bells

ANTIQUES/COLLECTIBLES | Hand-cast bronze doorbells and wind chimes are among the items sold at U.S. Bells. You can also buy finely crafted quilts and wood-fired pottery made by the owner's family. Ask for a tour of the foundry. ⊠ *56 W. Bay Rd., Prospect Harbor* ☎ *207/963–7184* ⊕ *www.usbells.com* ☾ *Closed Nov.–Mar.*

ART GALLERIES

Lee Fusion Art Glass

ART GALLERIES | Window glass is fused in a kiln to create unusual glass dishware. Colorful enamel accents depict birds, lighthouses, flowers, and designs made from doilies. The store is open June–October. ⊠ *679 S. Gouldsboro Rd., Rte. 186, Gouldsboro* ☎ *207/712–2148* ⊕ *www.leefusionartglass.com.*

Lubec

122 miles northeast of Belfast via U.S. 1 and Rte. 189.

Lubec is one of the first places in the United States to see the sunrise. A popular destination for outdoors enthusiasts, it offers plenty of opportunities for hiking and biking, and the birding is renowned. It's a good base for day trips to New Brunswick's Campobello Island, reached by a bridge—the only one to the island—from downtown Lubec, so don't forget to bring your passport. One of the main attractions there, Roosevelt Campobello International Park, operates a visitor center on the U.S. side of the border, which provides information about the region, generally; it's in a Whiting general store and gas station at the corner of U.S. 1 and Route 189. The village itself is perched at the end of a narrow strip of land at the end of Route 189, so you often see water in three directions in this laid-back, off-the-beaten-path place.

GETTING HERE AND AROUND

From U.S. 1 in Whiting, Route 189 leads to Lubec; it's about 13 miles to the village. You can stock up on groceries in nearby Machias, just before you hit Whiting, en route to Lubec. In summer you can take a water taxi from here to Eastport—about a mile by boat, but 40 miles by the circuitous northerly land route.

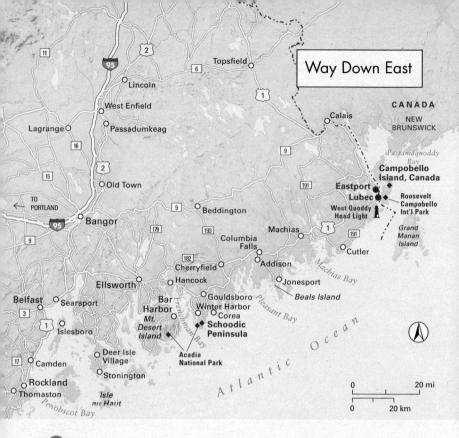

👁 Sights

★ West Quoddy Head Light

LIGHTHOUSE | FAMILY | The easternmost point of land in the United States is marked by candy-stripe West Quoddy Head Light, authorized in 1806 by President Thomas Jefferson. You can't climb the tower, but the former light-keeper's house has a visitor center with a video with shots of the interior, as well as displays on Lubec's maritime past; a gallery displays works by local artists. The mystical 4-mile round-trip path along the cliffs at Quoddy Head State Park (one of four trails) yields magnificent views of Canada's cliff-clad Grand Manan Island. Whales and seals—as well as the ubiquitous bald eagles—can often be sighted offshore. The 541-acre park has a picnic area with grills, but sometimes the best place to take lunch is perched on a rock overlooking the sea. Don't miss the easy, 1-mile round-trip bog trail that includes a fascinating array of subarctic vegetation, including carnivorous pitcher plants. ⊠ 973 S. Lubec Rd., off Rte. 189 ☎ 207/733–2180 ⊕ www.westquoddy. com ⊡ $4.

🍴 Restaurants

Water Street Tavern and Inn

$$$ | SEAFOOD | FAMILY | Perched right on the water in downtown Lubec, this favorite local restaurant serves some of the sweetest scallops you'll ever eat, Moqueca (a Brazilian seafood stew), and filet mignon for those so inclined. It's also a great place to grab a glass of wine or a cup of coffee while looking out at the water from the deck or through the picture windows. **Known for:** laid-back atmosphere; there's often live music by

local performers on Thursday; there are also two cozy suites and three guest rooms, most with good views of the water. $ *Average main: $25* ✉ *12 Water St.* ☎ *207/733–0122* ⊕ *www.watersttavernandinn.com* ⊗ *Closed late-Oct.–Mar.*

🛏 Hotels

★ Peacock House
$ | B&B/INN | Five generations of the Peacock family lived in this 1860 sea captain's home before it was converted to an inn in 1989. **Pros:** piano and fireplace in living room; lovely garden off deck; think-of-everything innkeepers direct guests to area's tucked-away spots. **Cons:** not on the water; nestled in the heart of sleepy Lubec; a short drive to Quoddy Head State Park. $ *Rooms from: $135* ✉ *27 Summer St.* ☎ *207/733–2403, 888/305–0036* ⊕ *www.peacockhouse.com* ↩ *7 rooms* ⦿ *Free breakfast.*

🛍 Shopping

Monica's Chocolates
$ | FOOD/CANDY | Taking in all the appetizing scents in this shop is almost enough, but sinking your teeth into one of Monica's truffles, bonbons, crèmes, or caramels is pure heaven. ✉ *100 County Rd.* ☎ *866/952–4500* ⊕ *www.monicaschocolates.com.*

Campobello Island, Canada

4 miles northeast of Lubec.

A popular excursion from Lubec, New Brunswick's Campobello Island has two fishing villages, Welshpool and Wilson's Beach. The only land route is the bridge from Lubec, but in summer a car ferry shuttles passengers from Campobello Island to Deer Island, where you can continue on to the Canadian mainland.

GETTING HERE AND AROUND
After coming across the bridge from Lubec, Route 774 runs from one end of the island to the other, taking you through the two villages and to Roosevelt Campobello International Park.

👁 Sights

★ Roosevelt Campobello International Park
HOUSE | FAMILY | President Franklin Roosevelt and his family spent summers at this estate, which is now an international park with neatly manicured lawns that stretch out to the beach. You can take a self-guided tour of the 34-room Roosevelt Cottage that was presented to Eleanor and Franklin as a wedding gift. The wicker-filled structure looks essentially as it did when the family was in residence. A visitor center has displays about the Roosevelts and Canadian-American relations. Eleanor Roosevelt Teas are held at 11 and 3 daily in the neighboring Wells-Shober Cottage. A joint project of the American and the Canadian governments, this park is crisscrossed with interesting hiking trails. Groomed dirt roads attract bikers. Eagle Hill Bog has a wooden walkway and signs identifying rare plants. ■ TIP→ Note that the Islands are on Atlantic Time, which is an hour later than Eastern Standard Time. ✉ *459 Rte. 774, Welshpool* ☎ *506/752–2922, 877/851–6663* ⊕ *www. fdr.net* ✉ *Free.*

Eastport

39 miles northeast of Lubec via Rte. 189, U.S. 1, and Rte. 190; 109 miles north of Ellsworth via U.S. 1 and Rte. 190.

Connected by a granite causeway to the mainland at Pleasant Point Reservation, Eastport has wonderful views of the nearby islands, and because the harbor is so deep, you can sometimes spot whales from the waterfront. Known for its diverse architecture, the island city was one of the nation's busiest seaports in the early 1800s.

If you find yourself in town mid- to late summer, you might catch one of a few notable events. For starters, Maine's largest July 4 parade takes place in Eastport—be sure to get downtown early to secure a viewing spot. Then, on the weekend of the second Sunday in August, locals celebrate Sipayik Indian Days at the Pleasant Point Reservation; this festival of Passamaquoddy culture includes canoe races, dancing, drumming, children's games, fireworks, and traditional dancing. And on the weekend after Labor Day, the Eastport Pirate Festival brings folks out in pirate attire for a ship race, a parade, fireworks, cutlass "battles" by reenactors, and other events, including a children's breakfast and a schooner ride with pirates.

GETTING HERE AND AROUND

From U.S. 1, Route 190 leads to the Island City. Continue on Washington Street to the water. In the summer, you can also take a water taxi from here to Lubec—a mile or so by boat, but about 40 miles by land.

ESSENTIALS

VISITOR INFORMATION Eastport Area Chamber of Commerce. ☎ *207/853–4644* 🌐 *www.eastport.net.*

🍴 Restaurants

Dastardly Dick's Wicked Good Coffee

$ | CAFÉ | FAMILY | The coffee isn't the only thing that's wicked good at this local café; homemade pastries, rich soups, and tasty sandwiches are all prepared daily, and the hot chocolate and chai are worth writing home about. **Known for:** local gathering spot; daily soup specials; wicked good baked goods. [$] *Average main: $6* ✉ *62 Water St.* ☎ *207/853–2090* 🕒 *Closed Mon.*

Index

Photo Credits

Notes